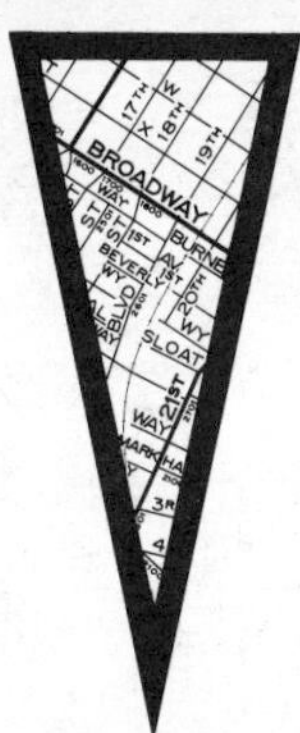

GOLDEN GATE

1991 Thomas Guide®

CONTENTS

Copyright, © 1991 by THOMAS BROS. MAPS.
Design, maps, index and text of this publication are copyrighted. It is unlawful to copy or reproduce any part thereof for personal use or resale.

Corporate Office & Showroom
17731 Cowan, Irvine, CA 92714 (714) 863-1984; toll-free, 1-800-899-MAPS
Retail Stores
603 W. 7th St., Los Angeles, CA 90017 (213) 627-4018
550 Jackson St., San Francisco, CA 94133 (415) 981-7520

GOLDEN GATE COMBINATION ***$33.95***

S0-DVC-394

MARIN CO.
SAN FRANCISCO CO.
SAN MATEO CO.
SANTA CLARA CO.
SONOMA CO.
MARIN CO
SOLANO CO.
CONTRA COSTA CO
ALAMEDA CO
SAN JOAQUIN CO
STANISLAUS CO
SANTA CRUZ CO
SAN FRANCISCO
OAKLAND
BERKELEY
SAN JOSE
FREMONT
HAYWARD
CONCORD
MARTINEZ
SAN RAFAEL
NOVATO
VALLEJO
BENICIA
PITTSBURG
ANTIOCH
WALNUT CREEK
LIVERMORE
PLEASANTON
DUBLIN
SAN LEANDRO
DALY CITY
SAN MATEO
REDWOOD CITY
PALO ALTO
MOUNTAIN VIEW
SUNNYVALE
SANTA CLARA
CUPERTINO
CAMPBELL
SARATOGA
LOS GATOS
MILPITAS
MORGAN HILL
HALF MOON BAY
PACIFICA
SAUSALITO
This Guide includes four Golden Gate Counties (Marin, San Francisco, San Mateo, Santa Clara) and is divided into four sections (one section per county). Use this key map for both long distance travel and for determining the correct county when looking for full detail. Each county section begins with a detail key map.
GOLDEN GATE
FREEWAY MAP
MILES
KILOMETERS
N
S
E
W
Thomas Bros Maps
COPYRIGHT © 1991 BY Thomas Bros Maps

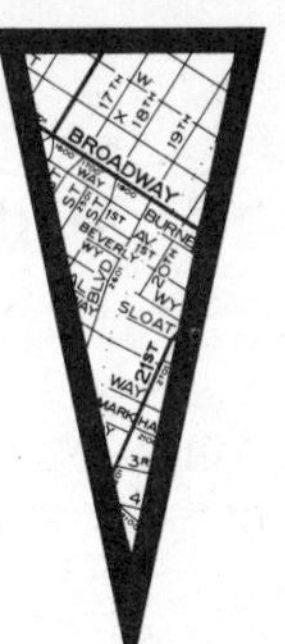

MARIN COUNTY
1991 *Thomas Guide*®

TABLE OF CONTENTS

Copyright, © 1991 by THOMAS BROS. MAPS.
Design, maps, index and text of this publication are copyrighted. It is unlawful to copy or reproduce any part thereof for personal use or resale.

Corporate Office & Showroom
17731 Cowan, Irvine, CA 92714 (714) 863-1984; toll-free, 1-800-899-MAPS
Retail Stores
603 W. 7th St., Los Angeles, CA 90017 (213) 627-4018
550 Jackson St., San Francisco, CA 94133 (415) 981-7520

GOLDEN GATE COMBINATION	TBM 4025	*$33.95*
SONOMA-MARIN COMBINATION	TBM 4020	*$19.95*
MARIN	TBM 3025	*$12.95*

HOW TO USE THE THOMAS GUIDE PAGE AND GRID SYSTEM

Finding Your Destination

- Use the Street Index to find the page number and grid location of a street name.
- Use the Cities and Communities or Points of Interest Index to find the page number and grid of a specific destination.

Planning Your Route

- Use the Key Maps or the Foldout Map to go from city to city, or to find what page your destination is on.
- Follow a street page to page by using the "See Map" page number in the border of each page.

COMO USAR EL SISTEMA DE PAGINA Y CUADRADO DEL THOMAS GUIDE

Encontrando Su Destinación

- Se puede usar el Indice de Calle para encontrar el número de página y locación del cuadrado del nombre de la calle.
- Se puede usar los Indices de las Ciudades y las Comunidades, o de Puntos de Interés para encontrar el número de página y el cuadrado de la destinación específica.

Planeando Su Ruta

- Se puede usar el Mapa Clave o el Mapa Doblado para viajar de ciudad a ciudad, o para encontrar la página de su destinación.
- Se puede usar el número de página con las palabras "See Map" se encuentran al borde de cada página para seguir una calle de página a página.

COPYRIGHT, © 1991 BY Thomas Bros Maps

LIST OF ABBREVIATIONS

AL	ALLEY
AR	ARROYO
ARR	ARROYO
AV	AVENUE
AVD	AVENIDA
AVD D LS	AVENIDA DE LOS
BCH	BEACH
BL	BOULEVARD
BLVD	BOULEVARD
CEM	CEMETERY
CIR	CIRCLE
CK	CREEK
CL	CALLE
CL DL	CALLE DEL
CL D LS	CALLE DE LAS CALLE DE LOS
CL EL	CALLE EL
CLJ	CALLEJON
CL LA	CALLE LA
CL LS	CALLE LAS CALLE LOS
CM	CAMINO
CM D	CAMINO DE
CM D LA	CAMINO DE LA
CM D LS	CAMINO DE LAS CAMINO DE LOS
CMTO	CAMINITO
CN	CANAL
COM	COMMON
CR	CRESCENT
CRES	CRESCENT
CSWY	CAUSEWAY
CT	COURT
CTE	CORTE
CTO	CUT OFF
CTR	CENTER
CV	COVE
CY	CANYON
CYN	CANYON
D	DE
DL	DEL
DR	DRIVE
DS	DOS
E	EAST
EST	ESTATE
EXPWY	EXPRESSWAY
EXT	EXTENSION
FRWY	FREEWAY
FRW	FREEWAY
FY	FREEWAY
GN	GLEN
GRDS	GROUNDS
GRN	GREEN
GRV	GROVE
HTS	HEIGHTS
HWY	HIGHWAY
HY	HIGHWAY
JCT	JUNCTION
KPN	KEY PENINSULA NORTH
KPS	KEY PENINSULA SOUTH
L	LA
LN	LANE
LP	LOOP
LS	LAS, LOS
MDW	MEADOW
MHP	MOBILE HOME PARK
MNR	MANOR
MT	MOUNT
MTN	MOUNTAIN
MTWY	MOTORWAY
MTY	MOTORWAY
N	NORTH
PAS	PASEO
PAS DE	PASEO DE
PAS DL	PASEO DEL
PAS D LS	PASEO DE LAS PASEO DE LOS
PGD	PLAYGROUND
PK	PARK
PK	PEAK
PKWY	PARKWAY
PL	PLACE
PT	POINT
PY	PARKWAY
PZ	PLAZA
RCH	RANCH
RCHO	RANCHO
RD	ROAD
RDG	RIDGE
RES	RESERVOIR
RIV	RIVER
RV	RIVER
RO	RANCHO
S	SOUTH
SN	SAN
SPG	SPRING
SPGS	SPRINGS
SQ	SQUARE
SRA	SIERRA
ST	SAINT
ST	STREET
STA	SANTA
STA	STATION
TER	TERRACE
THTR	THEATER
TK TR	TRUCK TRAIL
TR	TRAIL
VIA D	VIA DE
VIA D LS	VIA DE LAS VIA DE LOS
VIA DL	VIA DEL
VIS	VISTA
VLG	VILLAGE
VLY	VALLEY
VW	VIEW
W	WEST
WK	WALK
WY	WAY

LEGEND

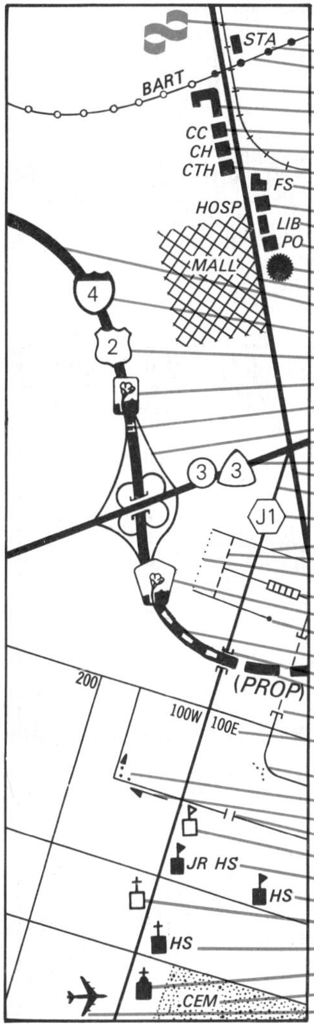

COPYRIGHT, © 1991 BY Thomas Bros Maps

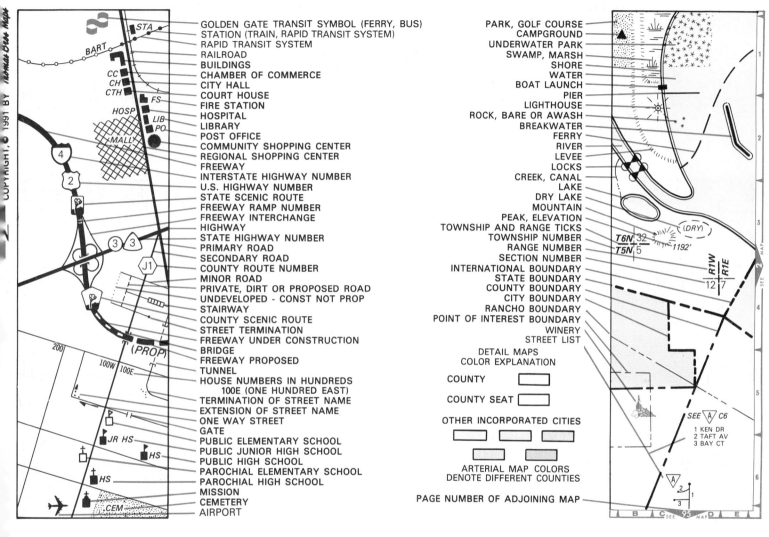

GOLDEN GATE TRANSIT SYMBOL (FERRY, BUS)
STATION (TRAIN, RAPID TRANSIT SYSTEM)
RAPID TRANSIT SYSTEM
RAILROAD
BUILDINGS
CHAMBER OF COMMERCE
CITY HALL
COURT HOUSE
FIRE STATION
HOSPITAL
LIBRARY
POST OFFICE
COMMUNITY SHOPPING CENTER
REGIONAL SHOPPING CENTER
FREEWAY
INTERSTATE HIGHWAY NUMBER
U.S. HIGHWAY NUMBER
STATE SCENIC ROUTE
FREEWAY RAMP NUMBER
FREEWAY INTERCHANGE
HIGHWAY
STATE HIGHWAY NUMBER
PRIMARY ROAD
SECONDARY ROAD
COUNTY ROUTE NUMBER
MINOR ROAD
PRIVATE, DIRT OR PROPOSED ROAD
UNDEVELOPED - CONST NOT PROP
STAIRWAY
COUNTY SCENIC ROUTE
STREET TERMINATION
FREEWAY UNDER CONSTRUCTION
BRIDGE
FREEWAY PROPOSED
TUNNEL
HOUSE NUMBERS IN HUNDREDS
100E (ONE HUNDRED EAST)
TERMINATION OF STREET NAME
EXTENSION OF STREET NAME
ONE WAY STREET
GATE
PUBLIC ELEMENTARY SCHOOL
PUBLIC JUNIOR HIGH SCHOOL
PUBLIC HIGH SCHOOL
PAROCHIAL ELEMENTARY SCHOOL
PAROCHIAL HIGH SCHOOL
MISSION
CEMETERY
AIRPORT

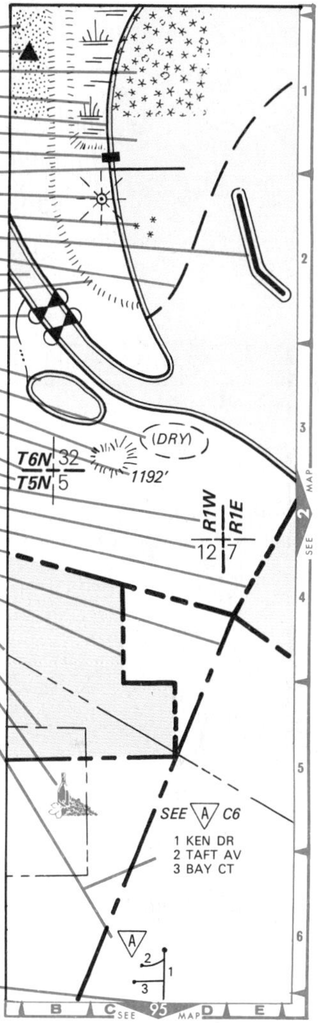

PARK, GOLF COURSE
CAMPGROUND
UNDERWATER PARK
SWAMP, MARSH
SHORE
WATER
BOAT LAUNCH
PIER
LIGHTHOUSE
ROCK, BARE OR AWASH
BREAKWATER
FERRY
RIVER
LEVEE
LOCKS
CREEK, CANAL
LAKE
DRY LAKE
MOUNTAIN
PEAK, ELEVATION
TOWNSHIP AND RANGE TICKS
TOWNSHIP NUMBER
RANGE NUMBER
SECTION NUMBER
INTERNATIONAL BOUNDARY
STATE BOUNDARY
COUNTY BOUNDARY
CITY BOUNDARY
RANCHO BOUNDARY
POINT OF INTEREST BOUNDARY
WINERY
STREET LIST

DETAIL MAPS
COLOR EXPLANATION

COUNTY

COUNTY SEAT

OTHER INCORPORATED CITIES

ARTERIAL MAP COLORS
DENOTE DIFFERENT COUNTIES

PAGE NUMBER OF ADJOINING MAP

SCALE OF MAP PAGES
1, 1A, 2, 3, 4, 8, 8A, 13, 14, 31
1 INCH TO ½ MILE

SCALE OF MAP PAGES
6A-6D, 7A-7D, 9A-9D, 10A-10D,
11A-11D, 12A-12D, 29, 30
1 INCH TO ¼ MILE

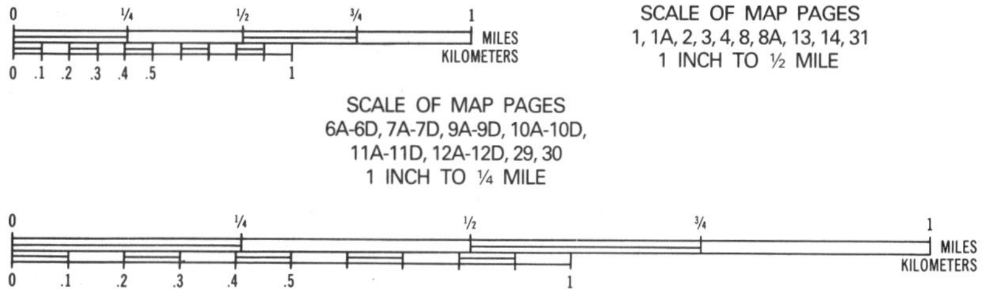

MAJOR DEPARTMENT STORES

EC	EMPORIUM CAPWELL
MA	MACYS
ME	MERVYNS
N	NORDSTROM
P	JC PENNEY
S	SEARS

1991 MARIN COUNTY CITIES AND COMMUNITIES INDEX

ESTIMATED POPULATION INCORPORATED CITIES	170,075
ESTIMATED POPULATION UNINCORPORATED AREAS	66,925
ESTIMATED TOTAL POPULATION	237,000

COMMUNITY NAME	ABBR.	ZIP CODE	AREA SQ. MI.	ESTIMATED POPULATION	PAGE
ALMONTE		94941			12C
ALTO		94941			12D
ANGEL ISLAND		94920			14
BEL AIRE		94920			12D
BEL MARIN KEYS		94949			2
* BELVEDERE	BVDR	94920	2.20	2,360	14
BELVEDERE GARDENS		94920			11D
BLACK POINT		94945			2
BOLINAS		94924			28
BURDELL		94945			1A
* CORTE MADERA	CM	94925	4.00	8,775	12A
DILLON BEACH		94929			15
DRAKES BEACH		94956			25
* FAIRFAX	F	94930	2.20	7,450	6C
FALLON		94952			15
FOREST KNOLLS		94933			5A
GALLINAS		94903			7A
GLENWOOD		94901			8
GREENBRAE		94904			10D
GREEN POINT		94945			2
HARBOR POINT		94941			12D
HILL HAVEN		94920			14
HOMESTEAD VALLEY		94941			12C
IGNACIO		94949			4
INVERNESS		94937			21
INVERNESS PARK		94937			22
KENTFIELD		94904			10A
LAGUNITAS		94938			5A
* LARKSPUR	L	94939	3.22	11,400	10C
LITTLE REEDS HEIGHTS		94920			11D
LOS RANCHITOS		94903			7C
MANZANITA		94941			13
MARIN BAY		94965			8
MARIN CITY		94965			13
- -MARIN COUNTY	MCO			237,000	
MARIN VILLAGE		94947			1
MARINWOOD		94903			4
MARSHALL		94940			18
* MILL VALLEY	MV	94941	4.70	13,450	12A
MUIR BEACH		94965			31
NICASIO		94946			23
NICASIO REDWOODS		94946			5A
* NOVATO	N	94949	23.00	48,750	1
OLEMA		94950			5
PARADISE CAY		94920			11C
PEACOCK GAP		94901			8
POINT REYES STATION		94956			22
REED		94920			12D
* ROSS	R	94957	2.50	2,740	9B
* SAN ANSELMO	SA	94960	2.67	12,150	6D
SAN GERONIMO		94963			5A
SAN MARIN		94945			1
SAN QUENTIN		94964			10D
* SAN RAFAEL	SR	94901	22.00	46,350	10A
SANTA VENETIA		94903			7B
* SAUSALITO	SLTO	94965	2.14	7,575	13
SLEEPY HOLLOW		94960			6B
STINSON BEACH		94970			28
STRAWBERRY MANOR		94941			12D
TAMALPAIS VALLEY		94941			13
TERRA LINDA		94903			7A
* TIBURON	TIB	94920	5.90	8,375	11D
TOCALOMA		94950			5
TOMALES		94971			15
WOODACRE		94973			5A

*INDICATES INCORPORATED CITY

COPYRIGHT, © 1991 BY Thomas Bros Maps

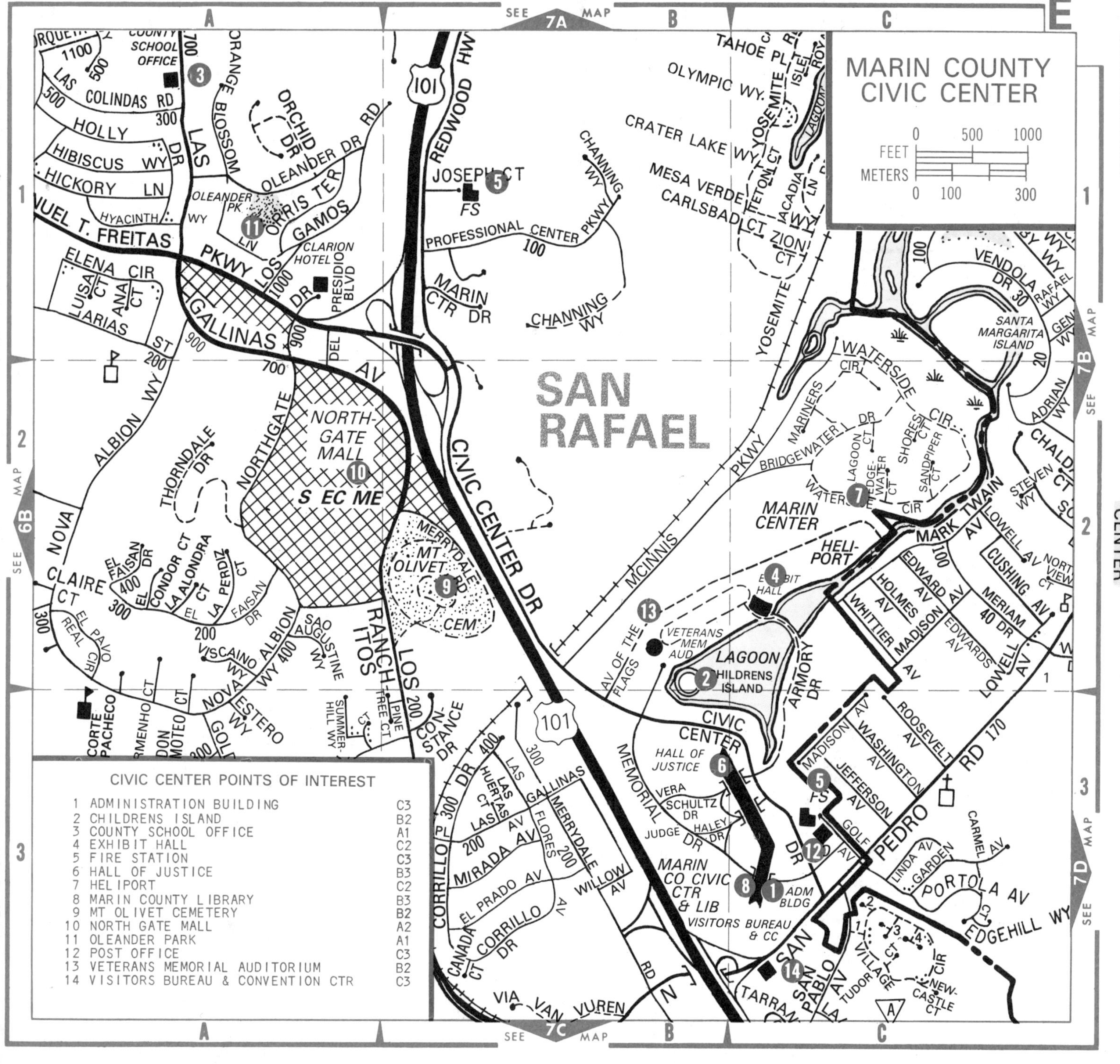

MARIN COUNTY CIVIC CENTER
0 500 1000
FEET
METERS
0 100 300
SEE 7A MAP
SEE 7B MAP
SEE 7C MAP
SEE 7D MAP
SEE 6B MAP
E
A
B
C
1
2
3
MARIN CO
CIVIC CENTER
SAN RAFAEL
CIVIC CENTER POINTS OF INTEREST
1 ADMINISTRATION BUILDING C3
2 CHILDRENS ISLAND B2
3 COUNTY SCHOOL OFFICE A1
4 EXHIBIT HALL C2
5 FIRE STATION C3
6 HALL OF JUSTICE B3
7 HELIPORT C2
8 MARIN COUNTY LIBRARY B3
9 MT OLIVET CEMETERY B2
10 NORTH GATE MALL A2
11 OLEANDER PARK A1
12 POST OFFICE C3
13 VETERANS MEMORIAL AUDITORIUM B2
14 VISITORS BUREAU & CONVENTION CTR C3
COUNTY SCHOOL OFFICE
LAS COLINDAS RD
HOLLY
HIBISCUS WY
HICKORY LN
HYACINTH WY
LAS GALLINAS
ORANGE BLOSSOM
ORCHID DR
OLEANDER DR
OLEANDER PK
ORRIS TER
LOS GAMOS
CLARION HOTEL
PRESIDIO BLVD
REDWOOD HWY
101
JOSEPH CT
FS
PROFESSIONAL CENTER PKWY
MARIN CTR DR
CHANNING WY
TAHOE PL
OLYMPIC WY.
CRATER LAKE WY
MESA VERDE
CARLSBAD CT
YOSEMITE
TETON CT
ACADIA WY
ZION CT
LAGOON
VENDOLA DR
SANTA MARGARITA ISLAND
RAFAEL WY
ADRIAN WY
ELENA CIR
LUISA CT
ANA CT
LARIAS
GALLINAS AV
DEL
NORTHGATE
NORTH-GATE MALL
SEE MAP
THORNDALE DR
ALBION WY
NOVA
CLAIRE CT
EL FAISAN DR
CONDOR CT
LA ALONDRA CT
LA PERDIZ CT
EL REAL
EL PAVO REAL CIR
VISCAINO WY
NOVA ALBION WY
SAO AUGUSTINE WY
RANCHITOS
LOS RANCHITOS
ESTERO WY
CORTE PACHECO
ARMENHO CT
DON MOTEO CT
SUMMER-HILL WY
PINE TREE CT
CON-STANCE DR
MERRYDALE RD
MT OLIVET CEM
CIVIC CENTER DR
MCINNIS PKWY
WATERSIDE CIR
MARINERS
BRIDGEWATER DR
LAGOON CT
EDGE-WATER CT
SHORES CT
SANDPIPER CT
WATERSIDE CIR
MARIN CENTER
HELI-PORT
EXHIBIT HALL
VETERANS MEM AUD
AV OF THE FLAGS
LAGOON
CHILDRENS ISLAND
ARMORY DR
MARK TWAIN AV
STEVEN WY
LOWELL AV
NORTH VIEW CT
CUSHING AV
MERIAM DR
EDWARD AV
HOLMES AV
WHITTIER AV
MADISON AV
EDWARDS AV
LOWELL AV
ROOSEVELT AV
WASHINGTON AV
JEFFERSON AV
MADISON AV
GOLF AV
SAN PEDRO RD
CARMEL AV
LINDA AV
GARDEN
PORTOLA AV
EDGEHILL WY
HALL OF JUSTICE
CIVIC CENTER
MEMORIAL DR
VERA SCHULTZ DR
HALEY DR
JUDGE DR
MARIN CO CIVIC CTR & LIB
ADM BLDG
VISITORS BUREAU & CC
SAN PABLO AV
TARRANT
TUDOR
VILLAGE CIR
NEW-CASTLE CT
LAS HUERTAS CT
LAS GALLINAS AV
MERRYDALE
FLORES
CORRILLO DR
MIRADA AV
EL PRADO AV
WILLOW AV
CANADA CT
VIA VAN VUREN

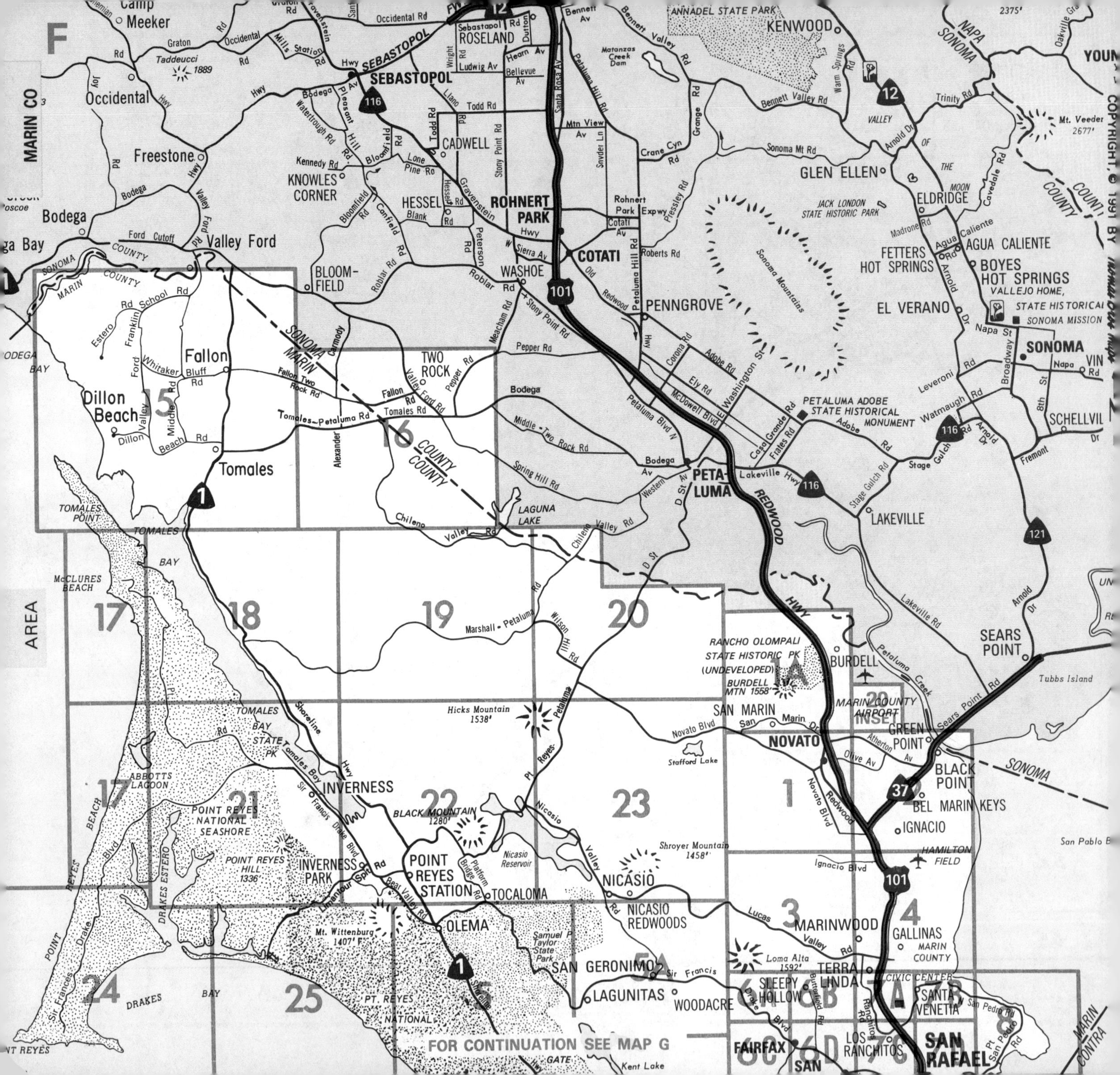
F
MARIN CO
AREA
Camp Meeker
Occidental
Freestone
Bodega
Valley Ford
SEBASTOPOL
ROSELAND
CADWELL
KNOWLES CORNER
HESSEL
ROHNERT PARK
COTATI
WASHOE
BLOOM-FIELD
PENNGROVE
KENWOOD
GLEN ELLEN
ELDRIDGE
AGUA CALIENTE
FETTERS HOT SPRINGS
BOYES HOT SPRINGS
EL VERANO
SONOMA
SCHELLVIL
ANNADEL STATE PARK
JACK LONDON STATE HISTORIC PARK
VALLEJO HOME, STATE HISTORICAL
SONOMA MISSION
Sonoma Mountains
VALLEY OF THE MOON
Mt. Veeder 2677'
Fallon
Dillon Beach
Tomales
TWO ROCK
PETALUMA
PETALUMA ADOBE STATE HISTORICAL MONUMENT
LAKEVILLE
LAGUNA LAKE
SEARS POINT
Tubbs Island
RANCHO OLOMPALI STATE HISTORIC PK (UNDEVELOPED)
BURDELL
BURDELL MTN 1558'
MARIN COUNTY AIRPORT
SAN MARIN
NOVATO
GREEN POINT
BLACK POINT
BEL MARIN KEYS
IGNACIO
HAMILTON FIELD
Stafford Lake
Hicks Mountain 1538'
TOMALES BAY STATE PK
INVERNESS
ABBOTTS LAGOON
POINT REYES NATIONAL SEASHORE
POINT REYES HILL 1336'
INVERNESS PARK
BLACK MOUNTAIN 1280'
POINT REYES STATION
TOCALOMA
Nicasio Reservoir
NICASIO
Shroyer Mountain 1458'
NICASIO REDWOODS
MARINWOOD
GALLINAS
MARIN COUNTY CIVIC CENTER
OLEMA
Mt. Wittenburg 1407'
Samuel P. Taylor State Park
SAN GERONIMO
LAGUNITAS
WOODACRE
Loma Alta 1592'
TERRA LINDA
SLEEPY HOLLOW
SANTA VENETIA
FAIRFAX
LOS RANCHITOS
SAN RAFAEL
Kent Lake
TOMALES POINT
McCLURES BEACH
DRAKES BAY
PT. REYES NATIONAL
FOR CONTINUATION SEE MAP G
COPYRIGHT © 1991 BY Thomas Bros. Maps

G
FOR CONTINUATION SEE MAP F
KEY TO ATLAS PAGES
NUMBERS WITHIN RECTANGLES INDICATE THE PAGE NUMBER AND AREA COVERED BY EACH DETAIL PAGE IN THIS ATLAS.
INCORPORATED CITY
COMMUNITY
FOR OVERVIEW SEE FOLD-OUT MAP
23
1
2
3
4
5A
6A
6B
6C
6D
7A
7B
7C
7D
8
8A
9A
9B
9C
9D
10A
10B
10C
10D
11A
11B
11C
11D
12A
12B
12C
12D
13
14
27
28
29
30
31
NOVATO
BLACK POINT
BEL MARIN KEYS
IGNACIO
HAMILTON FIELD
NICASIO
NICASIO REDWOODS
MARINWOOD
GALLINAS
SAN GERONIMO
LAGUNITAS
WOODACRE
TERRA LINDA
SLEEPY HOLLOW
SANTA VENETIA
FAIRFAX
LOS RANCHITOS
SAN RAFAEL
SAN ANSELMO
ROSS
KENTFIELD
GREENBRAE
LARKSPUR
CORTE MADERA
SAN QUENTIN
MILL VALLEY
BEL AIRE
BELVEDERE GARDENS
STINSON BEACH
BOLINAS
TAMALPAIS VALLEY
MARIN CITY
HILL HAVEN
TIBURON
BELVEDERE
SAUSALITO
MUIR BEACH
ANGEL ISLAND STATE PARK
FORT CRONKHITE
FORT BAKER
FORT BARRY
SAN FRANCISCO
PRESIDIO
FORT MILEY
GOLDEN GATE PARK
Seal Rocks
Thornton Beach
DALY CITY
COLMA
BAYSHORE
BRISBANE
CANDLESTICK PARK
SAN MATEO COUNTY
Hunters Point
Treasure Island
Yerba Buena Island
Alcatraz Island
San Pablo Bay
San Francisco Bay
VALLEJO
MARE ISLAND NAVAL RESERVATION
CROCKETT
BENICIA
PORT COSTA
MARTINEZ
RODEO
HERCULES
PINOLE
NORTH RICHMOND
SAN PABLO
EL SOBRANTE
RICHMOND
EL CERRITO
KENSINGTON
ALBANY
BERKELEY
ORINDA VILLAGE
ORINDA
LAFAY
EMERYVILLE
PIEDMONT
MONTCLAIR
CANYON
OAKLAND
ALAMEDA NAVAL AIR STATION
ALAMEDA
SOUTH SHORE
BAY FARM ISLAND
ALAMEDA COUNTY COLISEUM COMPLEX
SAN LEANDRO
OAKLAND INTERNATIONAL AIRPORT
MULFORD GARDENS
SAN LORENZO
HAYWARD
MARIN CONTRA COSTA COUNTY
SAN FRANCISCO COUNTY
SONOMA COUNTY
SAN RAFAEL - RICHMOND BRIDGE
JOHN KNOX FRWY
EASTSHORE FRWY
WARREN FRWY
MACARTHUR FRWY
NIMITZ FRWY
GOLDEN GATE FRWY
GOLDEN GATE BRIDGE
SAN FRANCISCO OAKLAND BAY BRIDGE
CARQUINEZ BRIDGE
UNITED STATES NAVAL STATION
Shroyer Mountain 1458'
Stafford Lake
Kent Lake
Alpine Lake
Bon Tempe Lake
Lagunitas Lake
Mt. Tamalpais 2567'
MT. TAMALPAIS STATE PARK
Bolinas Lagoon
Bolinas Bay
Gulf of the Farallones
Lake Merced
SAN BRUNO MT 1315'
Round Top 1763
San Pablo Reservoir
Briones Reservoir
GOLDEN GATE NATIONAL RECREATION AREA
101
1
37
580
80
780
4
24
13
123
980
880
480
280
35
61
77
185
112
131
COPYRIGHT, © 1991 BY Thomas Bros maps

1991 MARIN COUNTY
ZIP CODE POSTAL ZONES

POSTAL ZONE	ZIP CODE
BELVEDERE	94920
CORTE MADERA	94925
FAIRFAX	94930
GLENWOOD	94901
KENTFIELD	94904
LARKSPUR	94939
MARIN CITY	94965
MILL VALLEY	94941
MILL VALLEY P.O. BOXES	94942
NOVATO	94947
NOVATO (IGNACIO)	94949
NOVATO P.O. BOXES	94948
NOVATO (SAN MARIN)	94945
ROSS	94957
SAN ANSELMO	94960
SAN QUENTIN	94964
SAN QUENTIN P.O. BOXES	94974
SAN RAFAEL	94901
	94903
	94904
SAN RAFAEL P. O. BOXES	94912
SAN RAFAEL P. O. BOXES	94913
SAN RAFAEL P. O. BOXES	94914
SAN RAFAEL P. O. BOXES	94915
SANTA VENETIA	94903
SAUSALITO	94965
SAUSALITO P.O. BOXES	94966
TIBURON	94920

FOR ADDITIONAL INFORMATION REFER TO CITIES AND COMMUNITIES INDEX OR SEE OUR NORTHERN CALIFORNIA MINI WALL MAP TBM 7272.

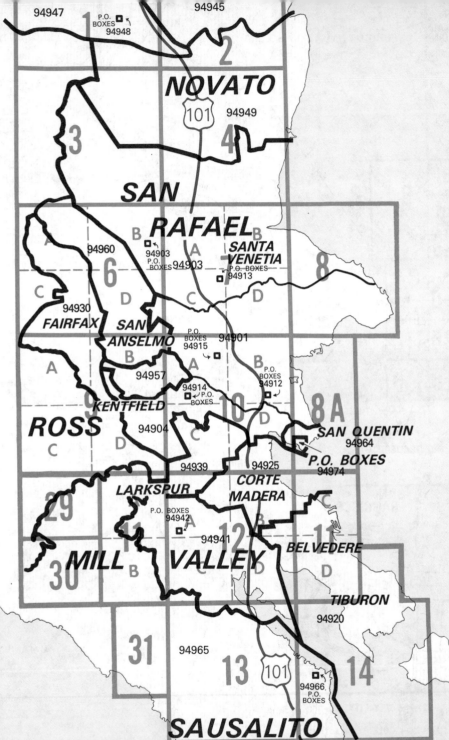

COPYRIGHT, © 1991 BY Thomas Bros Maps

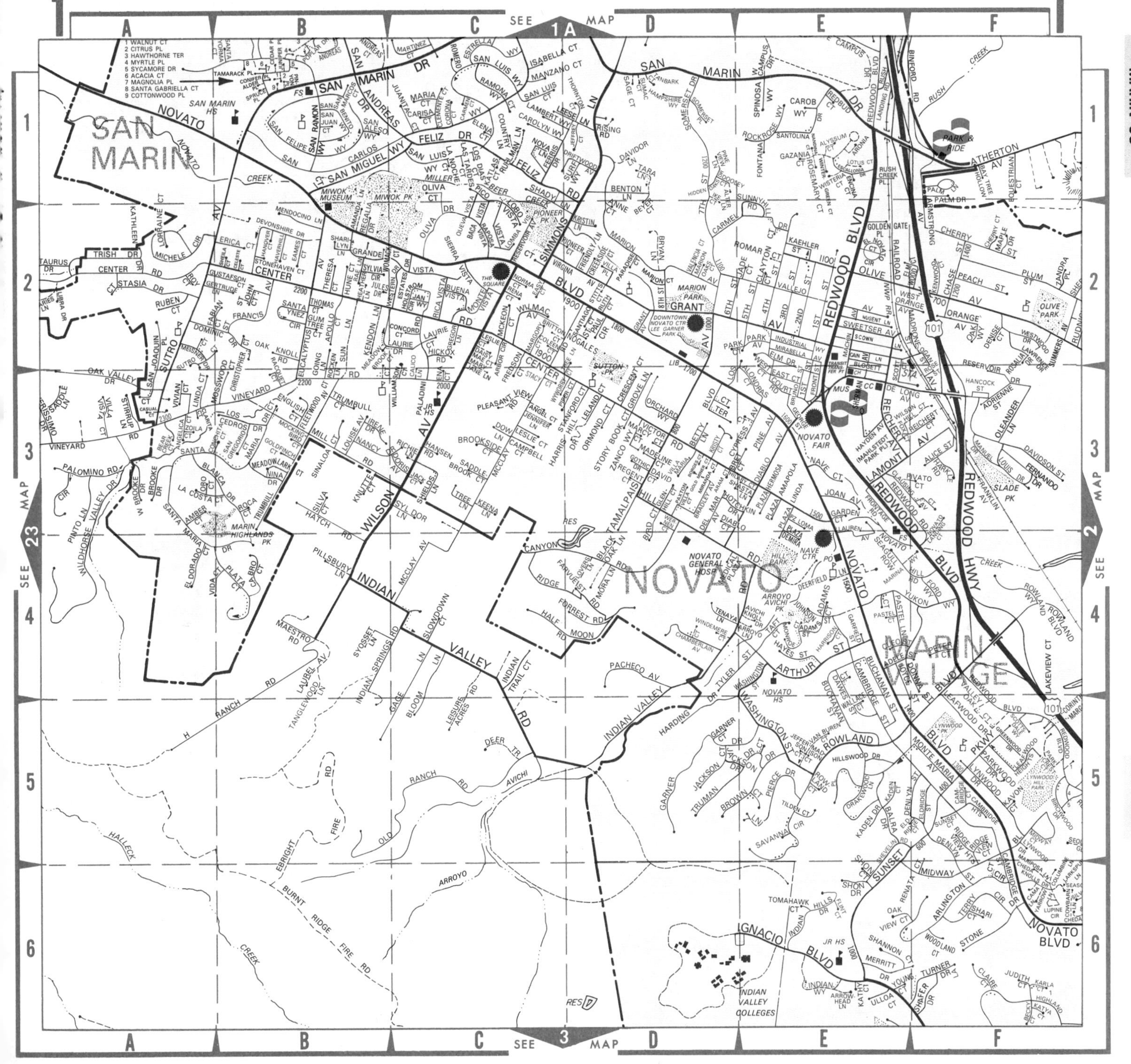

SEE 1A MAP
SEE 3 MAP
SEE 23 MAP
SEE 2 MAP
A
B
C
D
E
F
1
2
3
4
5
6
1 WALNUT CT
2 CITRUS PL
3 HAWTHORNE TER
4 MYRTLE PL
5 SYCAMORE DR
6 ACACIA CT
7 MAGNOLIA PL
8 SANTA GABRIELLA CT
9 COTTONWOOD PL
SAN MARIN
NOVATO
MARIN VILLAGE
SAN MARIN HS
MIWOK MUSEUM
MIWOK PK
PIONEER PK
MARION PARK
DOWNTOWN NOVATO CTR LEE GARNER PARK
SUTTON PK
NOVATO FAIR
NAVE CTR
NOVATO GENERAL HOSP
HILL PARK
MARIN HIGHLANDS PK
SLADE PK
OLIVE PARK
LYNWOOD PK
LYNWOOD HILL PARK
NOVATO HS
INDIAN VALLEY COLLEGES
PARK & RIDE
JR HS
SAN MARIN DR
NOVATO BLVD
REDWOOD BLVD
REDWOOD HWY
GRANT AV
SIMMONS LN
WILSON AV
INDIAN VALLEY RD
IGNACIO BLVD
ROWLAND BLVD
DIABLO AV
SUNSET PKWY
ATHERTON AV
VINEYARD
CENTER RD
HILL RD
ARTHUR ST
BURNT RIDGE FIRE RD
H RANCH RD
LAUREL AV
ARROYO
RES
101

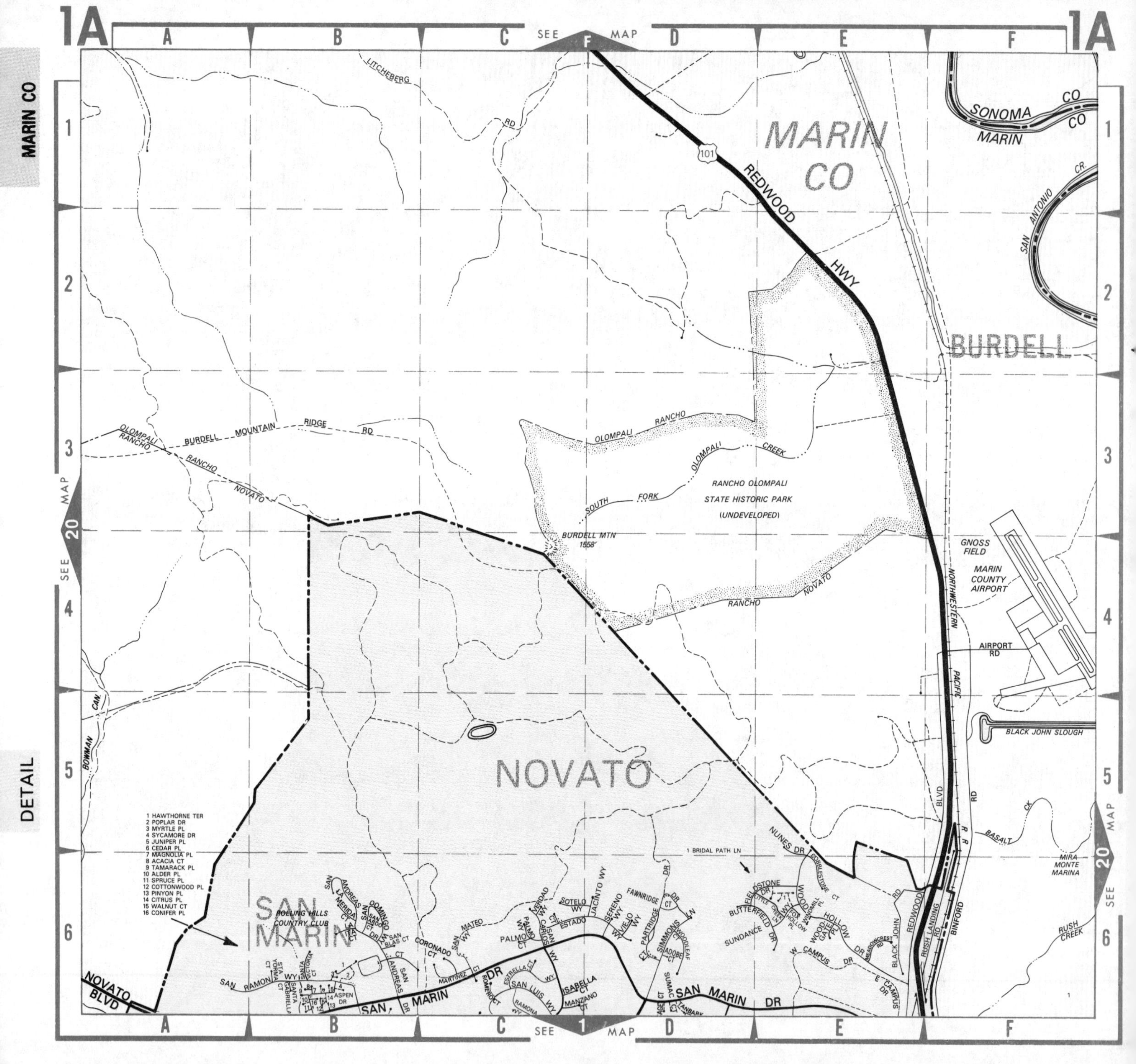
1A
SEE F MAP
SEE 1 MAP
SEE 20 MAP
MARIN CO
DETAIL
MARIN CO
SONOMA CO
MARIN CO
SAN ANTONIO CR.
BURDELL
LITCHEBERG RD
REDWOOD HWY
101
OLOMPALI RANCHO
BURDELL MOUNTAIN RIDGE RD
RANCHO NOVATO
OLOMPALI RANCHO
OLOMPALI CREEK
SOUTH FORK
RANCHO OLOMPALI STATE HISTORIC PARK (UNDEVELOPED)
BURDELL MTN 1558'
RANCHO NOVATO
GNOSS FIELD
MARIN COUNTY AIRPORT
NORTHWESTERN PACIFIC RR
AIRPORT RD
BLACK JOHN SLOUGH
BOWMAN CAN.
NOVATO
BASALT CK
MIRA MONTE MARINA
RUSH CREEK
1 HAWTHORNE TER
2 POPLAR DR
3 MYRTLE PL
4 SYCAMORE DR
5 JUNIPER PL
6 CEDAR PL
7 MAGNOLIA PL
8 ACACIA CT
9 TAMARACK PL
10 ALDER PL
11 SPRUCE PL
12 COTTONWOOD PL
13 PINYON PL
14 CITRUS PL
15 WALNUT CT
16 CONIFER PL
1 BRIDAL PATH LN
NUNES DR
COBBLESTONE CT
SAN MARIN
ROLLING HILLS COUNTRY CLUB
NOVATO BLVD
SAN RAMON WY
SAN MARIN DR
SAN ANDREAS DR
SAN DOMINGO
CORONADO CT
SAN MATEO
MARTINEZ CT
PALMO WY
ESTADO
SOTELO WY
JACINTO WY
SERENO WY
VIEJO WY
FAWNRIDGE DR
PARTRIDGE CT
SIMMONS LN
BUTTERFIELD DR
SUNDANCE
FIELDSTONE DR
WOOD HOLLOW DR
WINDMILL PL
W CAMPUS DR
E CAMPUS DR
BLACK JOHN RD
REDWOOD BLVD
RUSH LANDING RD
BINFORD RD
SAN LUIS WY
ISABELLA CT
MANZANO CT
ESTRELLA CT
RAMONA
ROMERO CT
SUMAC CT
TANBARK
ASPEN DR
MEADOWCREST RD

SEE 20 MAP

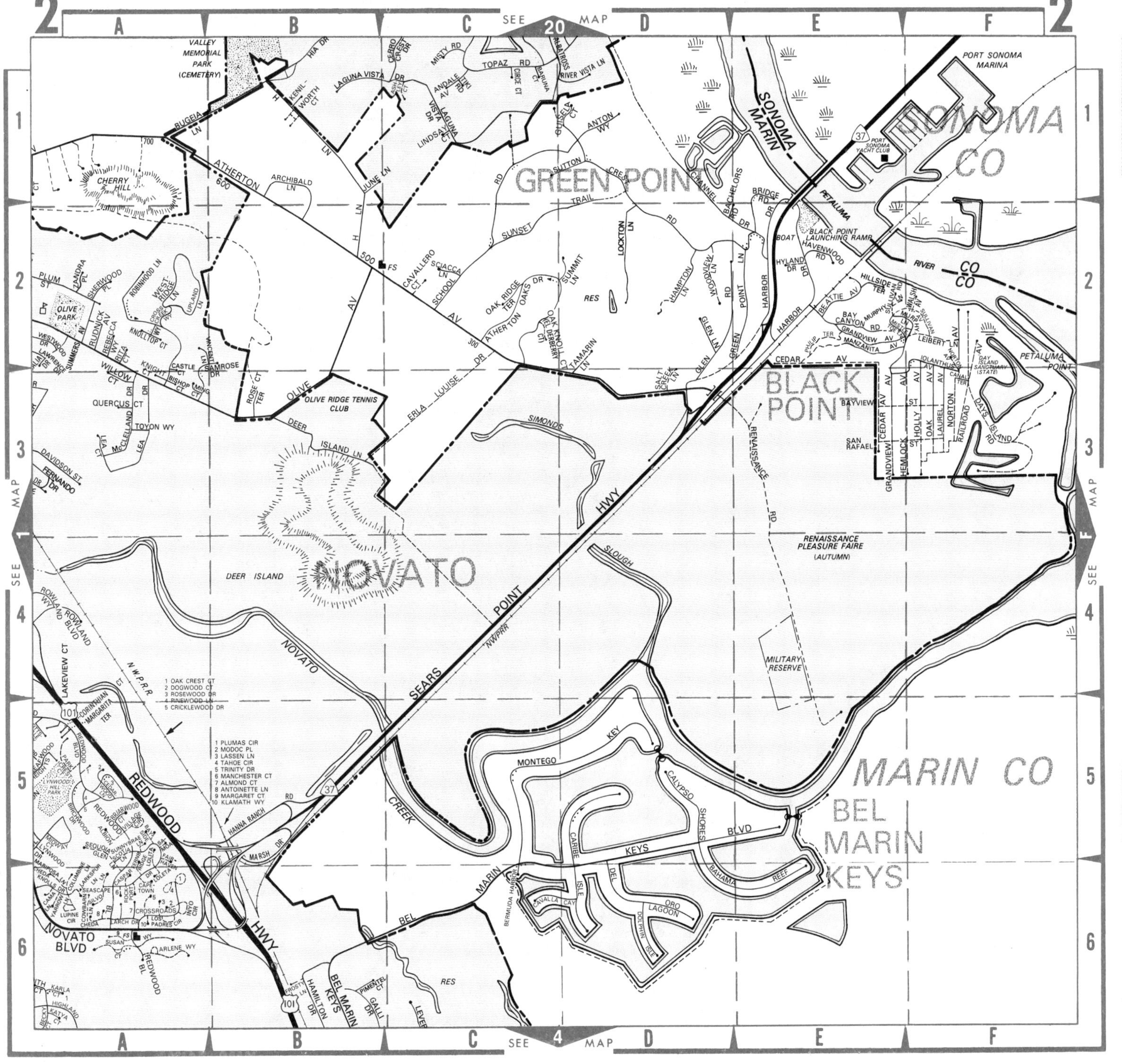

SEE 1 MAP
SEE F MAP
SEE 4 MAP

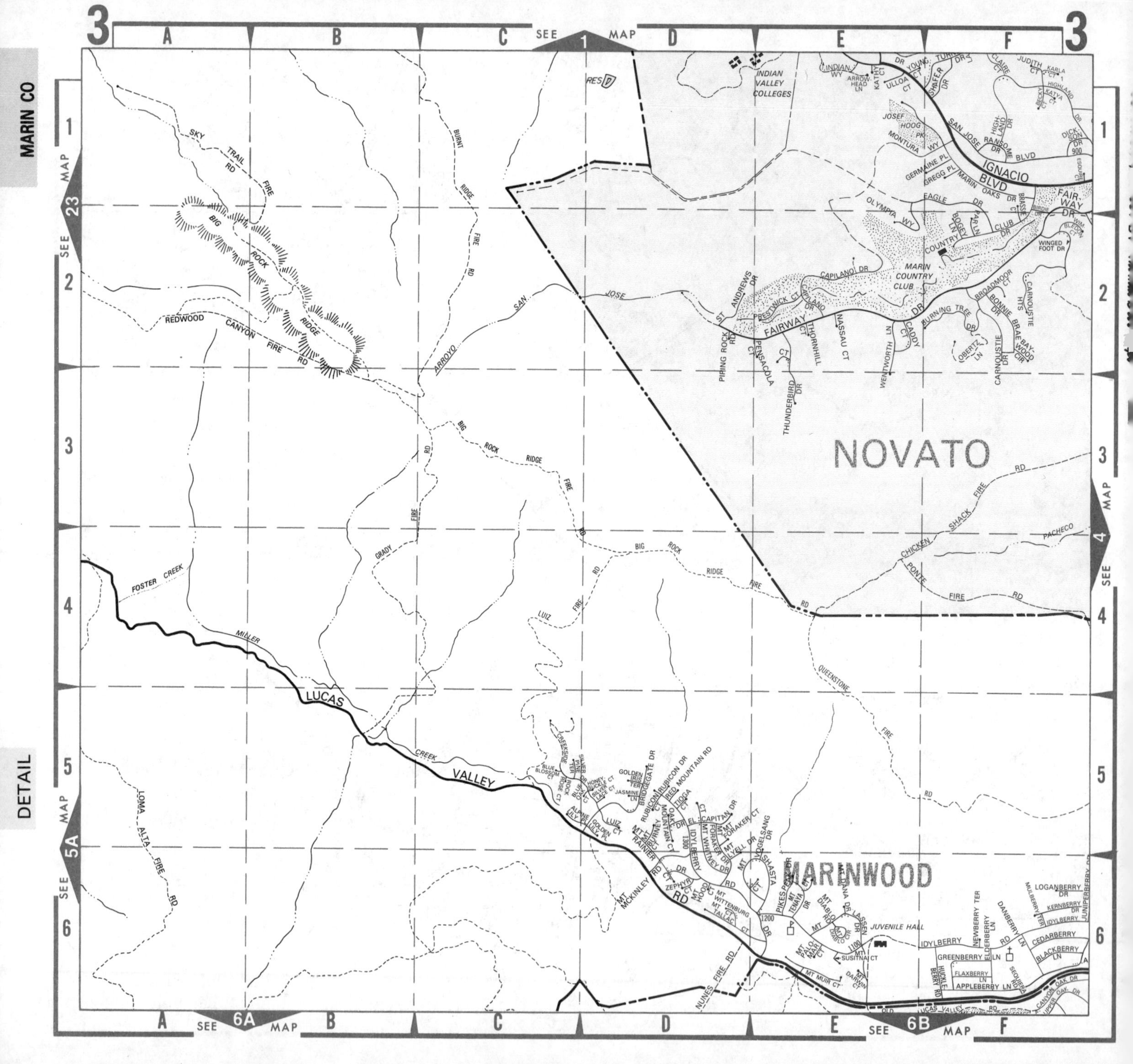

3
SEE 1 MAP
MARIN CO
SEE 23 MAP
SEE 4 MAP
DETAIL
SEE 5A MAP
SEE 6A MAP
SEE 6B MAP
NOVATO
MARINWOOD
INDIAN VALLEY COLLEGES
MARIN COUNTRY CLUB
IGNACIO BLVD
LUCAS VALLEY RD
BIG ROCK RIDGE FIRE RD
REDWOOD CANYON FIRE RD
SKY TRAIL FIRE RD
BURNT RIDGE FIRE RD
ARROYO SAN JOSE
FAIRWAY DR
GRADY FIRE RD
LUIZ FIRE RD
FOSTER CREEK
MILLER CREEK
LOMA ALTA FIRE RD
QUEENSTONE FIRE RD
CHICKEN SHACK FIRE RD
PONTE FIRE RD
NUNES FIRE RD
JUVENILE HALL

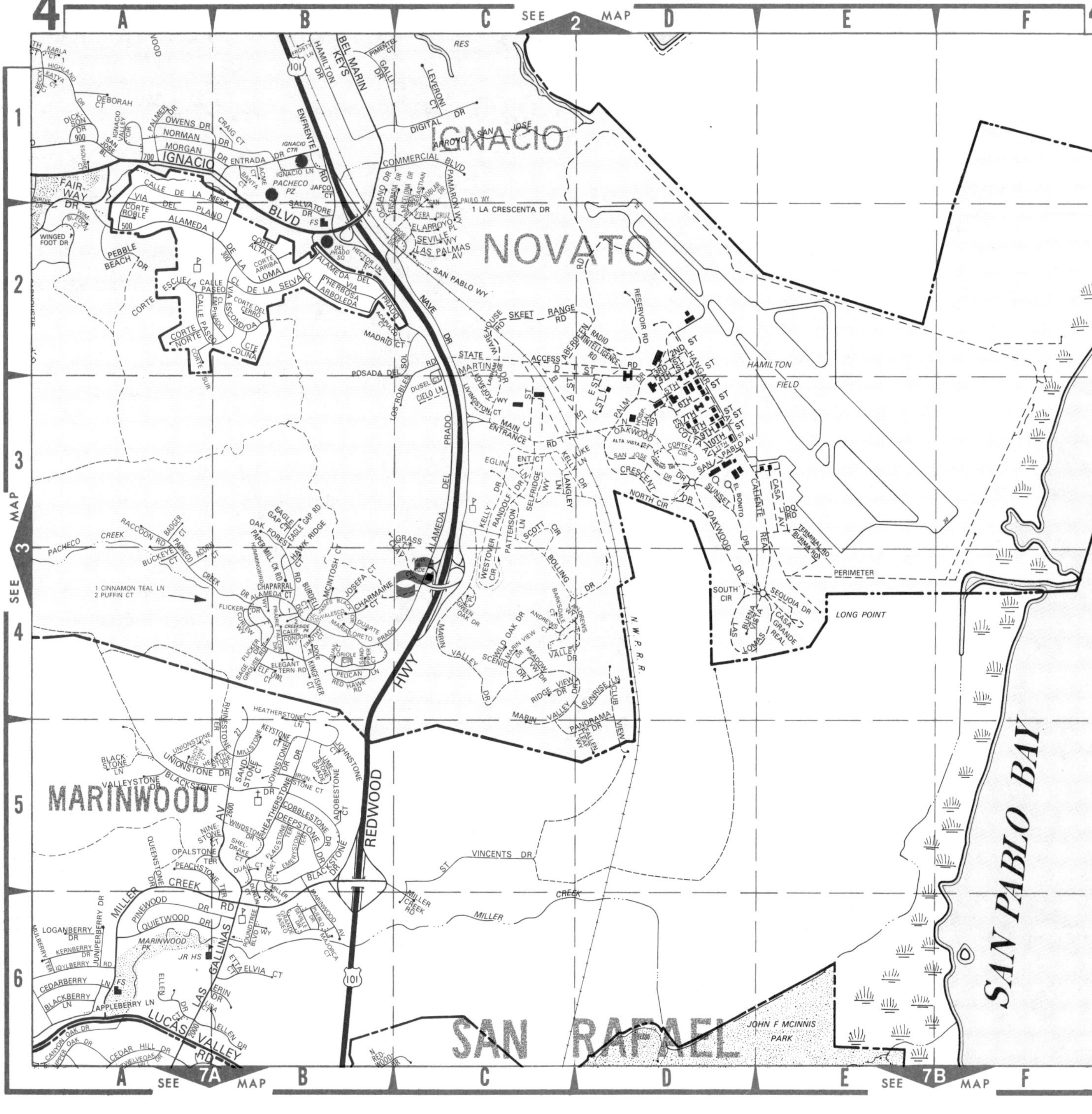

MARIN CO

DETAIL

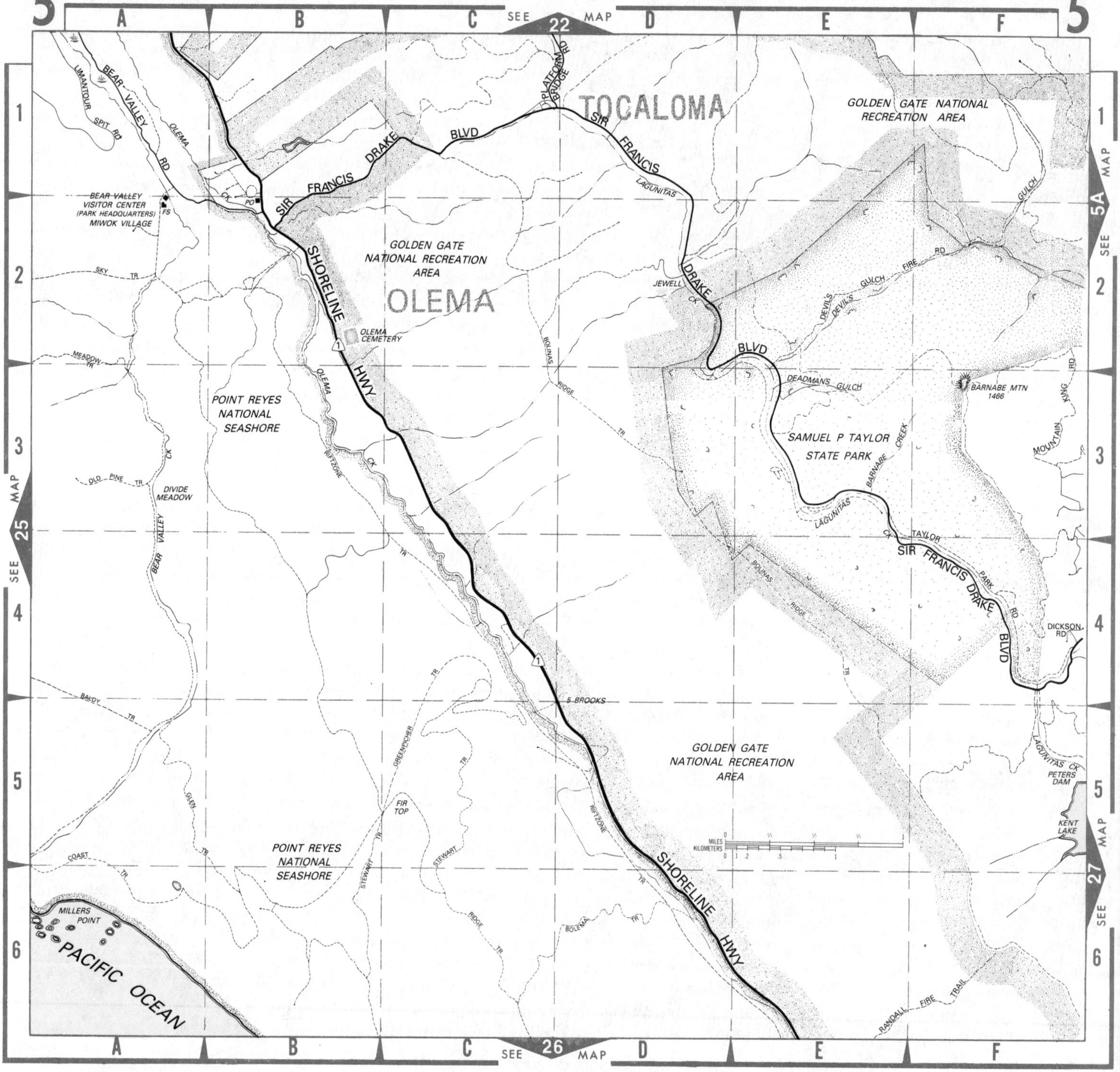

MARIN CO
DETAIL
A B C D E F
SEE MAP 22
SEE MAP 5A
SEE MAP 25
SEE MAP 27
SEE MAP 26
TOCALOMA
OLEMA
GOLDEN GATE NATIONAL RECREATION AREA
GOLDEN GATE NATIONAL RECREATION AREA
GOLDEN GATE NATIONAL RECREATION AREA
POINT REYES NATIONAL SEASHORE
POINT REYES NATIONAL SEASHORE
SAMUEL P TAYLOR STATE PARK
BEAR VALLEY VISITOR CENTER (PARK HEADQUARTERS) MIWOK VILLAGE
OLEMA CEMETERY
SIR FRANCIS DRAKE BLVD
SHORELINE HWY
PLATFORM BRIDGE RD
BEAR VALLEY RD
LIMANTOUR SPIT RD
OLEMA CK
LAGUNITAS CK
JEWELL CK
DEVILS GULCH
DEVILS GULCH FIRE RD
DEADMANS GULCH
BARNABE CREEK
BARNABE MTN 1466
KING MOUNTAIN RD
TAYLOR PARK RD
BOLINAS RIDGE TR
DICKSON RD
SKY TR
MEADOW TR
OLD PINE TR
DIVIDE MEADOW
BEAR VALLEY CK
RIFTZONE TR
BALDY TR
GLEN TR
GREENPICKER TR
FIR TOP
STEWART TR
COAST TR
5 BROOKS
PETERS DAM
KENT LAKE
RANDALL FIRE TRAIL
MILLERS POINT
PACIFIC OCEAN
MILES 0 ¼ ½ ¾ 1
KILOMETERS 0 .1 .2 .5 1

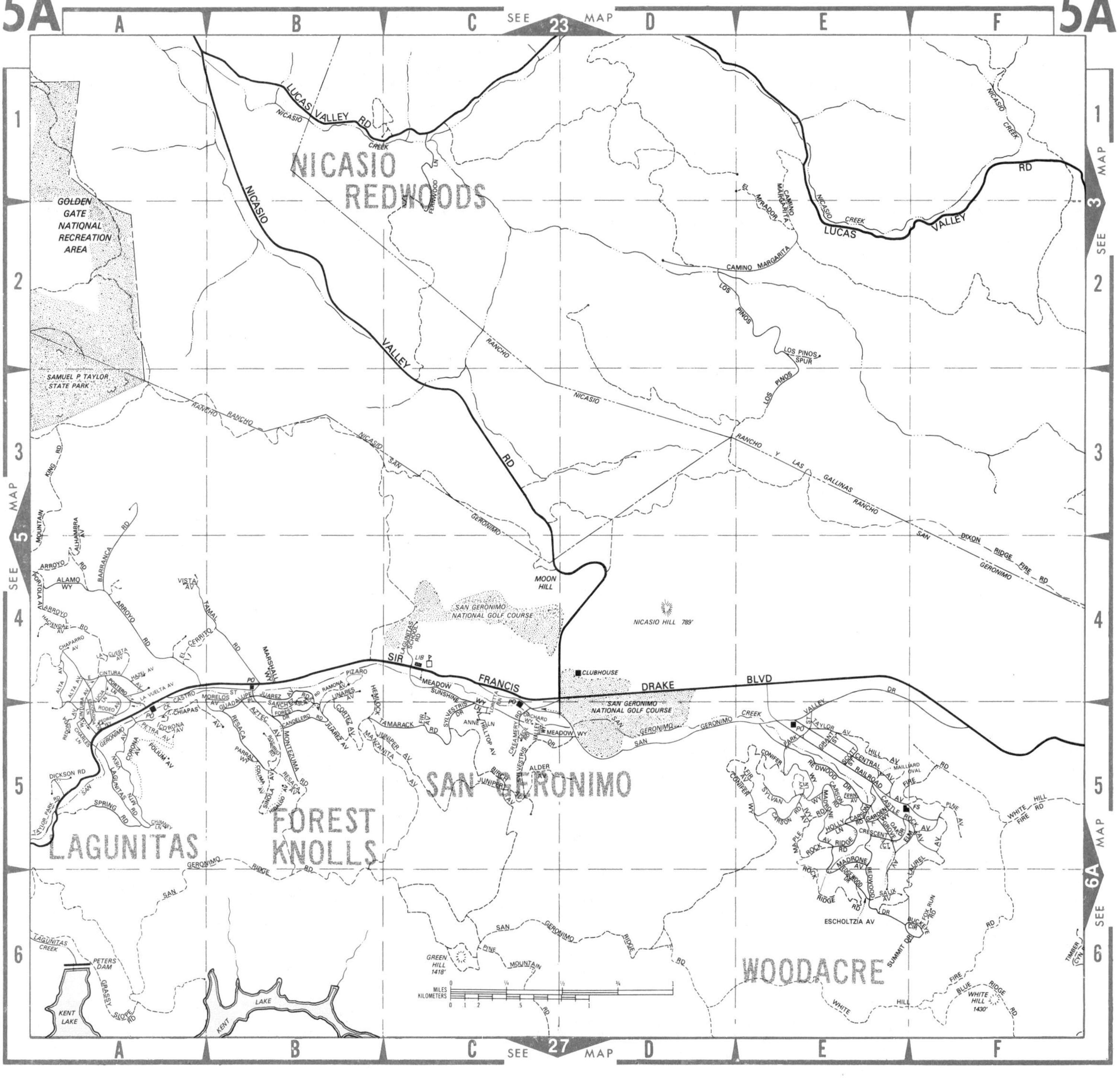

SEE MAP 23

MARIN CO

NICASIO REDWOODS

GOLDEN GATE NATIONAL RECREATION AREA

SAMUEL P TAYLOR STATE PARK

LUCAS VALLEY RD

NICASIO VALLEY RD

NICASIO CREEK

CAMINO MARGARITA

LOS PINOS

LOS PINOS SPUR

RANCHO NICASIO

RANCHO SAN GERONIMO

RANCHO Y LAS GALLINAS RANCHO

SAN GERONIMO RIDGE FIRE RD

DIXON RIDGE FIRE RD

MOON HILL

NICASIO HILL 789'

SAN GERONIMO NATIONAL GOLF COURSE

CLUBHOUSE

SIR FRANCIS DRAKE BLVD

SAN GERONIMO

LAGUNITAS

FOREST KNOLLS

WOODACRE

WHITE HILL FIRE RD

BLUE RIDGE FIRE RD

WHITE HILL 1430'

GREEN HILL 1418'

PINE MOUNTAIN RD

SAN GERONIMO RIDGE RD

LAGUNITAS CREEK

PETERS DAM

KENT LAKE

GRASSY SLOPE RD

TIMBER CYN

ESCHOLTZIA AV

MILES / KILOMETERS

SEE MAP 5

SEE MAP 3

DETAIL

SEE MAP 6A

SEE MAP 27

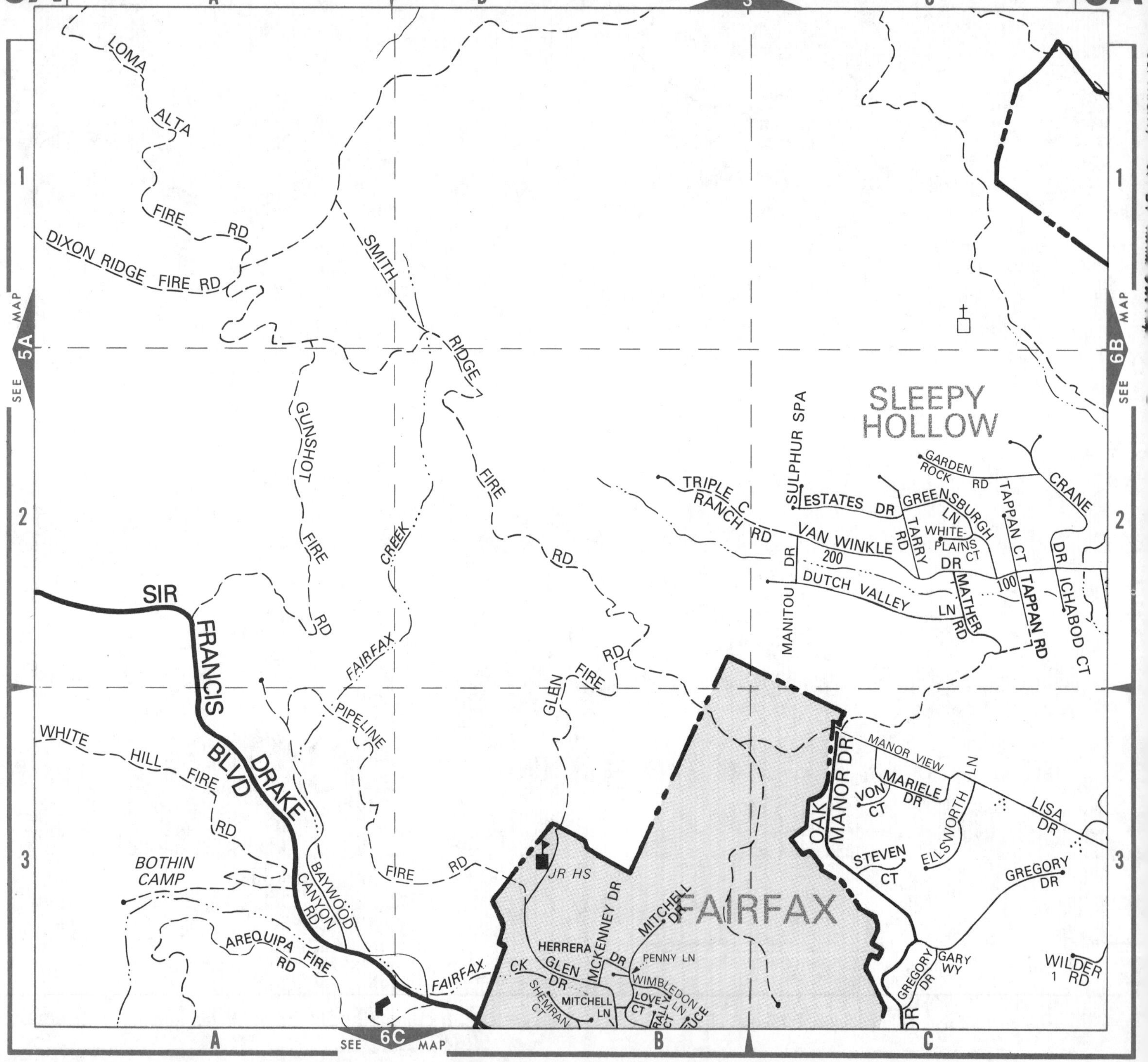

A B C

SEE MAP 3

6A

1

LOMA ALTA FIRE RD

DIXON RIDGE FIRE RD

SMITH RIDGE

SEE MAP 5A

SEE MAP 6B

GUNSHOT FIRE RD

CREEK

FIRE RD

SLEEPY HOLLOW

SULPHUR SPA

TRIPLE C RANCH RD

ESTATES DR

GREENSBURGH LN

GARDEN ROCK RD

CRANE

TARRY RD

WHITE-PLAINS CT

TAPPAN CT

2

VAN WINKLE DR

200

DUTCH VALLEY LN

MANITOU DR

MATHER RD

100

TAPPAN RD

ICHABOD CT

DR

SIR FRANCIS BLVD DRAKE

FAIRFAX PIPELINE

GLEN FIRE RD

WHITE HILL FIRE RD

MANOR VIEW

LN

MARIELE DR

VON CT

OAK MANOR DR

LISA DR

ELLSWORTH

STEVEN CT

GREGORY DR

3

BOTHIN CAMP

BAYWOOD CANYON RD

FIRE RD

JR HS

FAIRFAX

MCKENNEY DR

MITCHELL DR

AREQUIPA FIRE RD

HERRERA

GLEN DR

PENNY LN

FAIRFAX CK

SHEMIRAN CT

MITCHELL LN

WIMBLEDON LN

LOVE CT

RALLY CT

DUCE

GREGORY DR

GARY WY

WILDER RD

1

DR

A B C

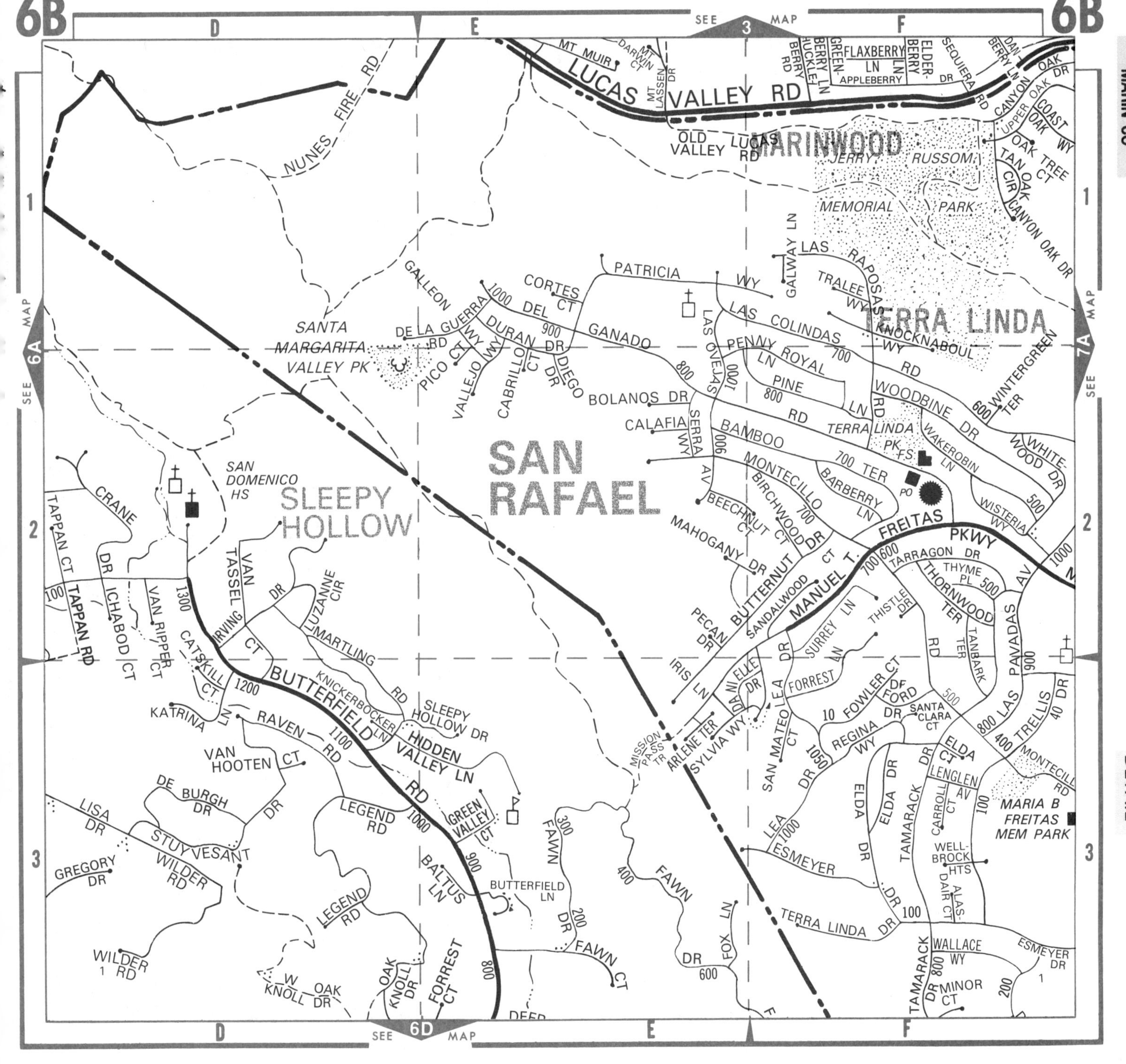
6B
6B
D
E
F
SEE 3 MAP
SEE 6A MAP
SEE 7A MAP
SEE 6D MAP
MARIN CO
DETAIL
1
2
3
LUCAS VALLEY RD
MARINWOOD
TERRA LINDA
SAN RAFAEL
SLEEPY HOLLOW
JERRY RUSSOM MEMORIAL PARK
SANTA MARGARITA VALLEY PK
SAN DOMENICO HS
MARIA B FREITAS MEM PARK
NUNES FIRE RD
MT MUIR CT
DARWIN CT
MT LASSEN DR
OLD VALLEY LUCAS RD
FLAXBERRY LN
APPLEBERRY
ELDERBERRY LN
SEQUEIRA DR
CANYON OAK DR
UPPER OAK
COAST OAK WY
OAK TREE CT
TAN OAK CIR
GALWAY LN
LAS RAPOSAS
TRALEE WY
PATRICIA WY
CORTES CT
DEL GANADO RD
GALLEON WY
DE LA GUERRA RD
DURAN DR
PICO CT
VALLEJO WY
CABRILLO CT
DIEGO DR
LAS COLINDAS
KNOCKNABOUL WY
PENNY ROYAL LN
PINE LN
LAS OVEJAS AV
WOODBINE DR
WINTERGREEN TER
BOLANOS DR
CALAFIA
SERRA WY
BAMBOO TER
TERRA LINDA PK
WAKEROBIN LN
WHITEWOOD DR
MONTECILLO RD
BARBERRY LN
BIRCHWOOD DR
BEECHNUT CT
MAHOGANY DR
WISTERIA WY
FREITAS PKWY
TARRAGON DR
THYME PL
THORNWOOD TER
MANUEL T. FREITAS PKWY
BUTTERNUT
SANDALWOOD CT
PECAN DR
THISTLE DR
SURREY LN
TANBARK TER
LAS PAVADAS AV
IRIS LN
DANIELLE DR
LEA DR
FORREST
FOWLER CT
DE FORD DR
SANTA CLARA CT
TRELLIS DR
MONTECILLO RD
ARLENE TER
SYLVIA WY
MISSION PASS TR
SAN MATEO CT
REGINA WY
ELDA CT
LENGLEN AV
ELDA DR
TAMARACK DR
CARROLL CT
WELLBROCK HTS
ESMEYER DR
ALAS-DAIR CT
TERRA LINDA DR
WALLACE WY
MINOR CT
CRANE DR
TAPPAN CT
TAPPAN RD
ICHABOD CT
VAN RIPPER CT
VAN TASSEL CT
IRVING DR
LUZANNE CIR
MARTLING RD
CATSKILL CT
KATRINA LN
RAVEN RD
BUTTERFIELD RD
KNICKERBOCKER LN
SLEEPY HOLLOW DR
HIDDEN VALLEY LN
VAN HOOTEN CT
DE BURGH DR
LEGEND RD
GREEN VALLEY CT
LISA DR
STUYVESANT DR
GREGORY DR
WILDER RD
BALTUS LN
BUTTERFIELD LN
FAWN DR
FAWN CT
FOX LN
OAK KNOLL DR
W KNOLL
OAK DR
FORREST CT
DEER
PO
FS

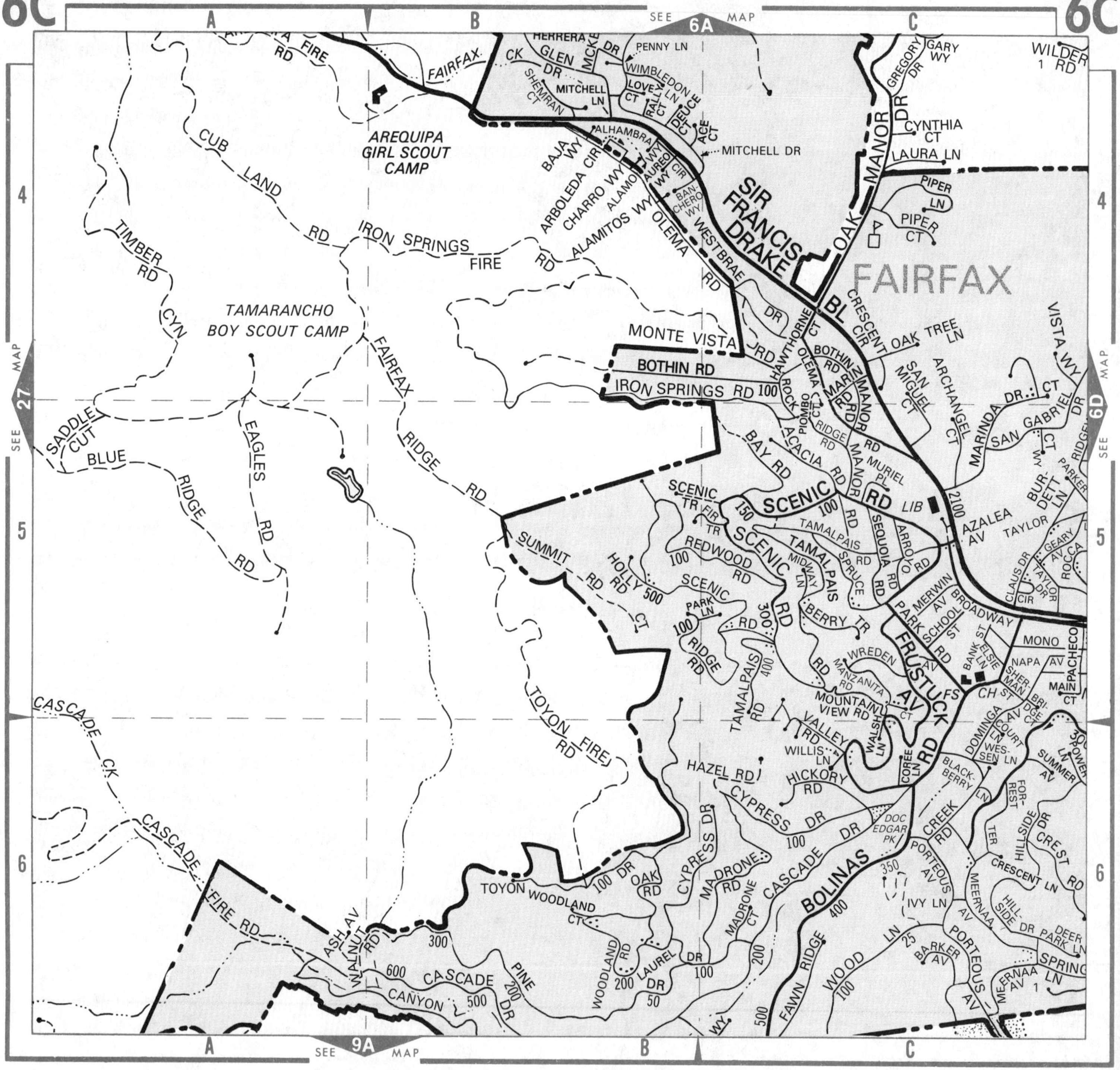

A B C

SEE 6A MAP

4
5
6

ARROYO FIRE RD
FAIRFAX
AREQUIPA GIRL SCOUT CAMP
CUB LAND RD
IRON SPRINGS FIRE RD
TIMBER RD
CYN
TAMARANCHO BOY SCOUT CAMP
FAIRFAX RIDGE RD
SADDLE CUT
BLUE RIDGE RD
EAGLES RD
MONTE VISTA
BOTHIN RD
IRON SPRINGS RD 100
SUMMIT RD
HOLLY RD
TOYON FIRE RD
CASCADE CK
CASCADE FIRE RD
ASH AV
WALNUT RD
CASCADE CANYON 600 500
PINE 200 DR
300
TOYON
WOODLAND CT
100 DR
OAK RD
CYPRESS DR
MADRONE RD
MADRONE CT
WOODLAND RD
200 LAUREL DR 50
DR 100
200
WY
CASCADE DR
500
FAWN RIDGE
BOLINAS 400
WOOD 100 LN 25
BARKER AV
PORTEOUS AV
MEERNAA AV 1
SPRING LN
DEER PARK LN
HILLSIDE DR
IVY LN
350
PORTEOUS AV
MEERNAA AV
CRESCENT LN
CREST RD
FOREST TER
HILLSIDE DR
SUMMER AV
POWER
300
CREEK RD
DOC EDGAR PK
CYPRESS DR 100
HAZEL RD
HICKORY RD
WILLIS LN
VALLEY RD
MOUNTAIN VIEW RD
WALSH LN
WREDEN
MANZANITA RD
CT
AV
FRUSTUCK RD
COREE LN
FS
CH
BLACKBERRY LN
DOMINGA AV
COURT LN
WESSEN LN
BRIDGE CT
SHERMAN ST
NAPA AV
MAIN CT
PACHECO
MONO
BANK ST
ELSIE LN
BROADWAY
SCHOOL ST
MERWIN AV
PARK RD
TAMALPAIS RD 300 400
RIDGE RD
100
PARK LN
SCENIC RD
HOLLY 500
REDWOOD RD 100
SCENIC RD
TAMALPAIS
MIDWAY LN
BERRY TR
SPRUCE
TAMALPAIS RD
SEQUOIA RD
ARROYO RD
SCENIC TR
FIR TR
150
SCENIC 100 RD
LIB
2100
AZALEA AV
TAYLOR
GEARY AV
TAYLOR DR
CLAUS DR
CIR
ROCCA
BURDETT LN
PARKER
RIDGEWAY
SAN GABRIEL DR
CT WY
MARINDA DR CT
ARCHANGEL CT
SAN MIGUEL CT
VISTA WY
OAK TREE LN
CRESCENT CIR
HAWTHORNE CT
DR
BOTHIN RD
MARIN RD
MANOR RD
OLEMA CT
ROCK
PIOMBO CT
RIDGE RD
ACACIA RD
BAY RD
MANOR RD
MURIEL PL
RD
FAIRFAX
SIR FRANCIS DRAKE BL
WESTBRAE RD
OLEMA
ALAMITOS WY
BANCHERO WY
CHARRO WY
ARBOLEDA CIR
ALAMO
AUREO WY
CIR
BAJA WY
ALHAMBRA
MITCHELL DR
OAK MANOR DR
CYNTHIA CT
LAURA LN
PIPER LN
PIPER CT
GREGORY DR
GARY WY
WILDER RD 1
HERRERA DR
MCKE
PENNY LN
GLEN DR
CK
SHEMRAN CT
MITCHELL LN
WIMBLEDON LN
LOVE CT
RALLY CT
DEUCE CT
ACE CT

SEE 27 MAP
SEE 6D MAP
SEE 9A MAP

6D

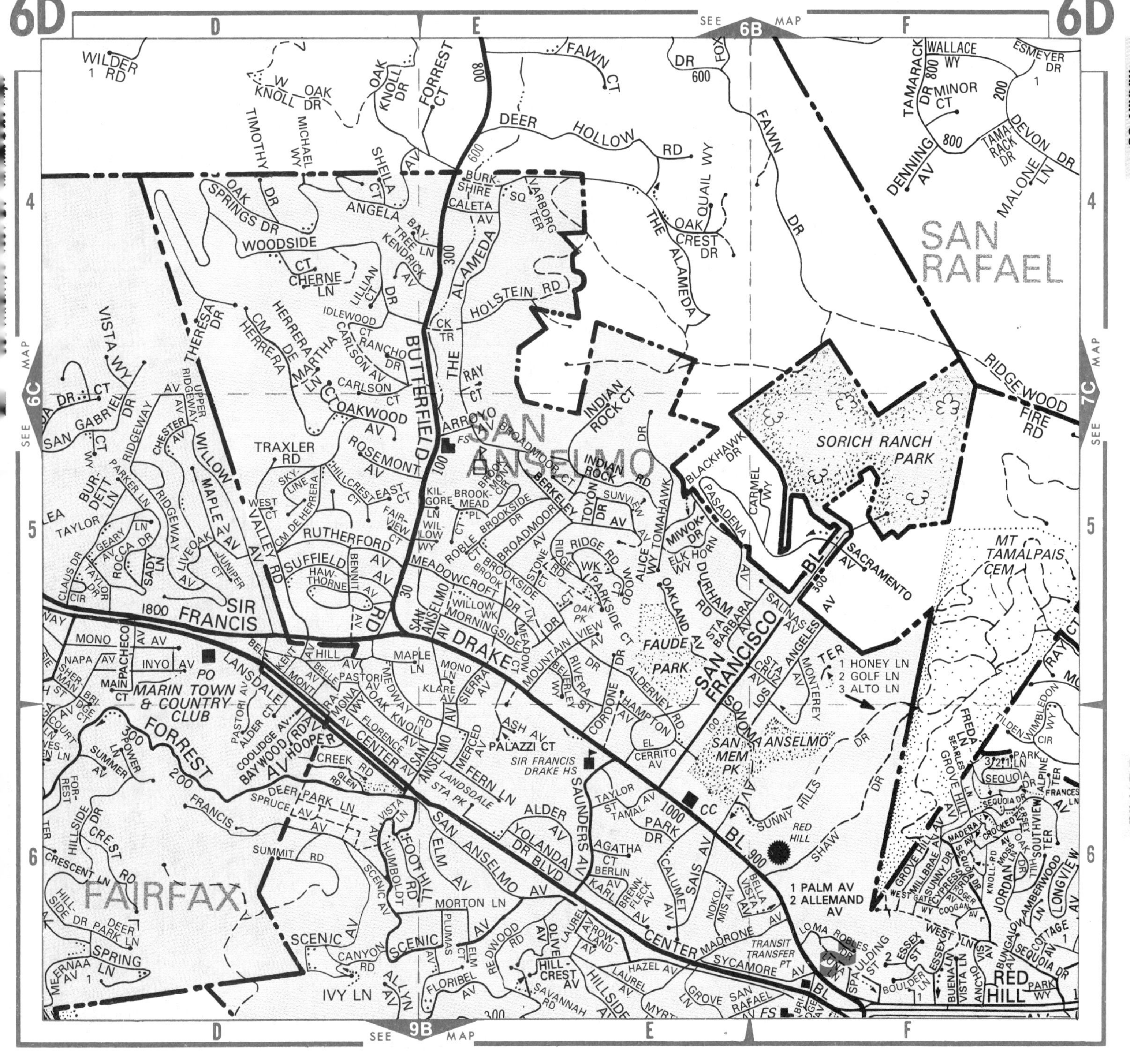
D
E
F
SEE 6B MAP
SEE 6C MAP
SEE 7C MAP
SEE 9B MAP
4
5
6
SAN RAFAEL
SAN ANSELMO
FAIRFAX
SORICH RANCH PARK
MT TAMALPAIS CEM
FAUDE PARK
SAN ANSELMO MEM PK
MARIN TOWN & COUNTRY CLUB
SIR FRANCIS DRAKE HS
PALAZZI CT
RED HILL
1 HONEY LN
2 GOLF LN
3 ALTO LN
1 PALM AV
2 ALLEMAND AV
TRANSIT TRANSFER PT
SIR FRANCIS DRAKE BLVD
BUTTERFIELD RD
SAN FRANCISCO BL
CENTER BLVD
RED HILL AV
SAN ANSELMO AV
THE ALAMEDA
DEER HOLLOW RD
FAWN DR
FAWN CT
RIDGEWOOD FIRE RD
SHAW DR
SUNNY HILLS DR
SACRAMENTO AV
FORREST AV
WILDER RD
WOODSIDE CT
OAK SPRINGS DR
ANGELA AV
HOLSTEIN RD
RUTHERFORD AV
OAKWOOD AV
ROSEMONT AV
TRAXLER RD
VALLEY RD
WILLOW AV
MAPLE AV
BROADMOOR AV
BROOKSIDE DR
MEADOWCROFT DR
MORNINGSIDE DR
INDIAN ROCK RD
TOMAHAWK DR
PASADENA AV
DURHAM RD
OAKLAND AV
SONOMA AV
LOS ANGELES AV
MONTEREY AV
ALDER AV
YOLANDA DR
SAUNDERS AV
PARK DR
CALUMET AV
SAIS AV
MADRONE AV
SYCAMORE AV
ESSEX ST
SPAULDING ST
LOMA ROBLES DR
BOULDER LN
BUENA VISTA LN
CRESCENT LN
SPRING LN
SCENIC AV
CANYON RD
IVY LN
MORTON LN
HUMBOLDT AV
DEER PARK LN
SPRUCE AV
SUMMIT RD
LANSDALE AV
HOOPER
PO
CC
FS

SEE 4 MAP

7A

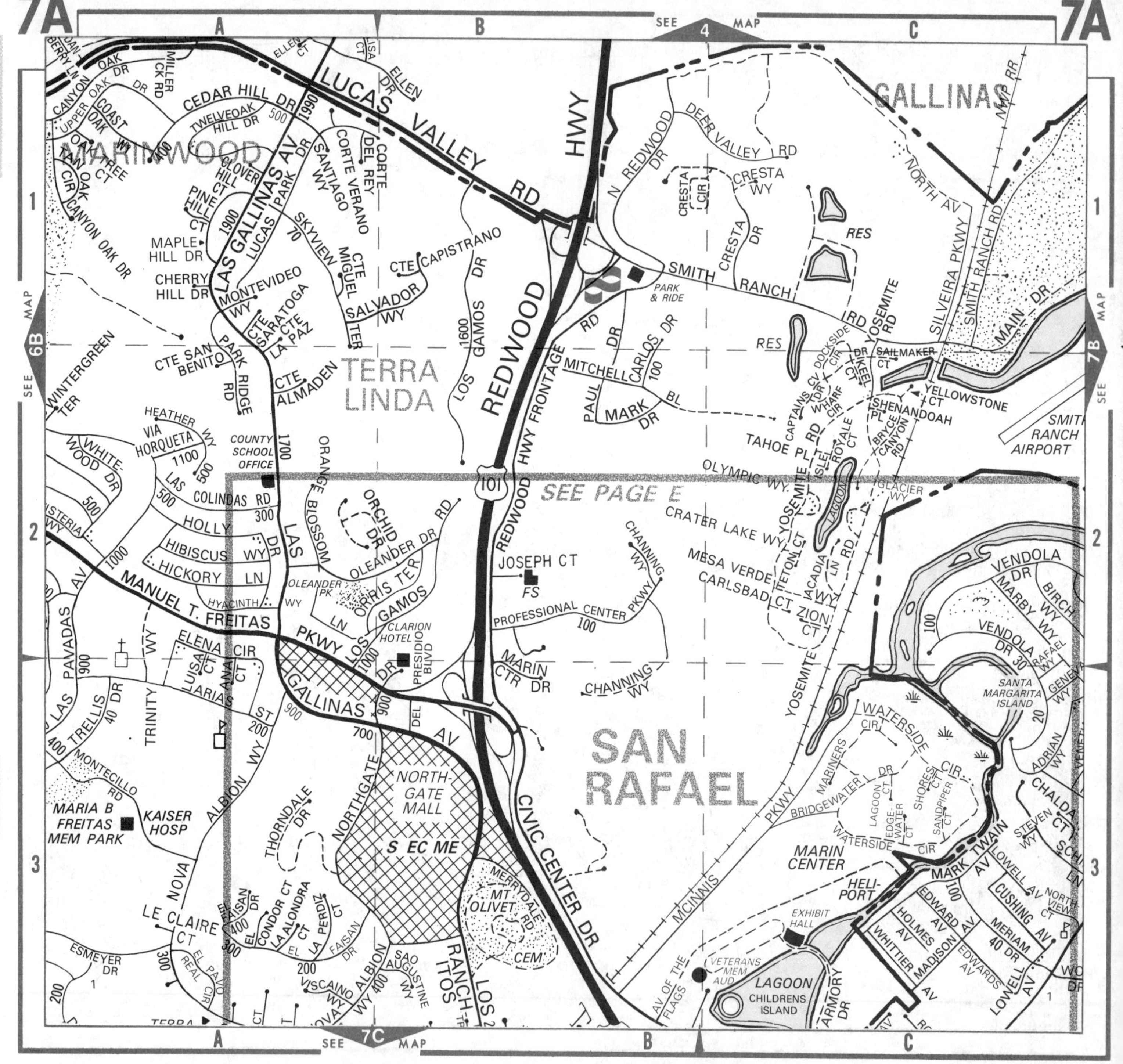

SEE 6B MAP

SEE 7B MAP

SEE 7C MAP

MARIN CO

DETAIL

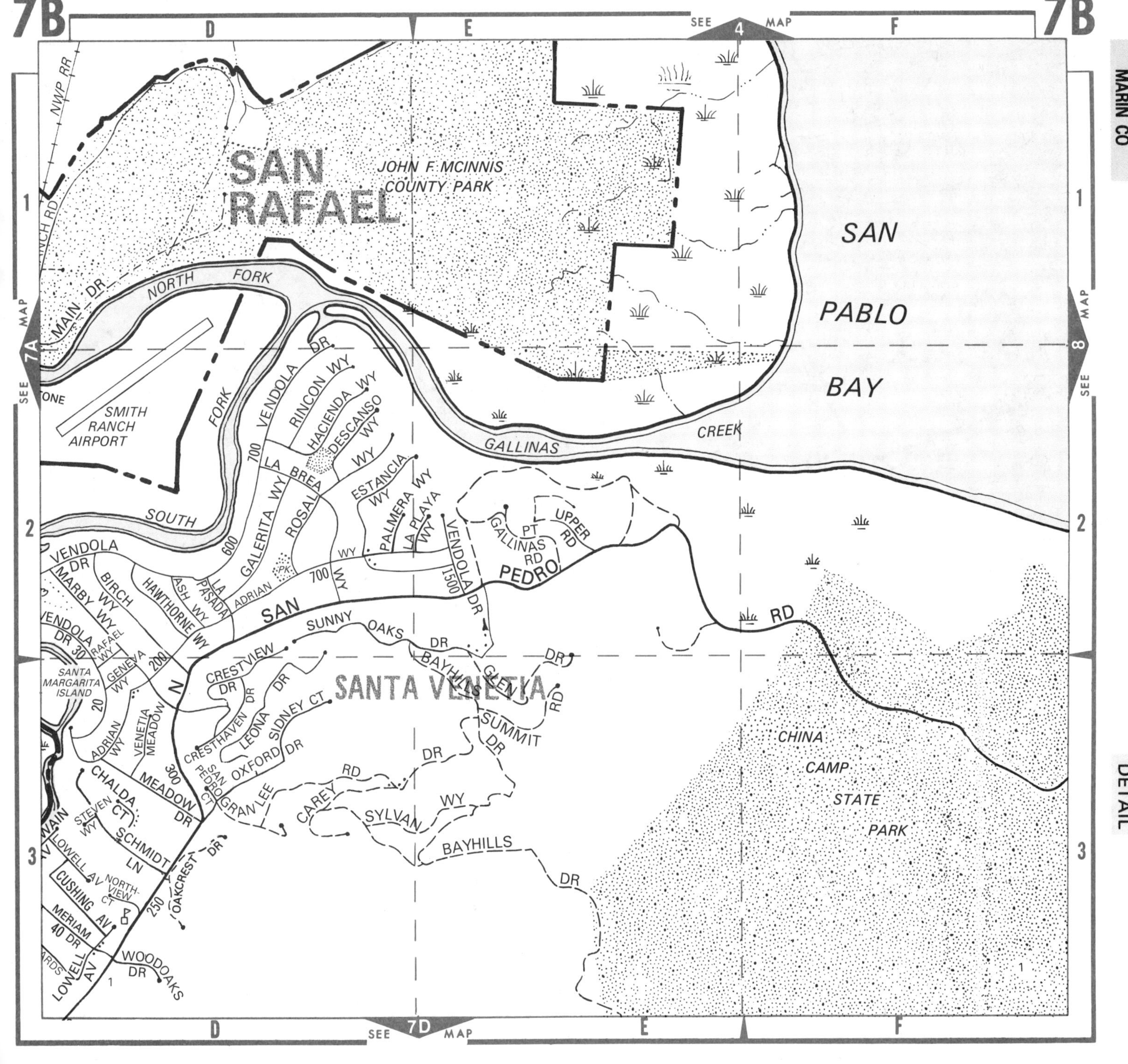
SEE MAP 4
SEE MAP 7A
SEE MAP 8
SEE MAP 7D
D
E
F
1
2
3
SAN RAFAEL
JOHN F. MCINNIS COUNTY PARK
SAN PABLO BAY
NWP RR
MAIN DR
NORTH FORK
SOUTH FORK
SMITH RANCH AIRPORT
GALLINAS CREEK
VENDOLA DR
RINCON WY
HACIENDA WY
DESCANSO WY
LA BREA
ESTANCIA WY
PALMERA WY
LA PLAYA WY
GALERITA WY
ROSAL WY
UPPER RD
GALLINAS PT RD
SAN PEDRO RD
ADRIAN WY
LA PASADA
ASH WY
HAWTHORNE WY
BIRCH WY
MARBY WY
RAFAEL WY
GENEVA WY
SANTA MARGARITA ISLAND
SUNNY OAKS DR
BAYHILLS DR
GLEN RD
CRESTVIEW DR
SANTA VENETIA
CRESTHAVEN DR
LEONA DR
SIDNEY CT
OXFORD DR
SUMMIT DR
CAREY RD
SYLVAN WY
GRAN LEE
SAN PEDRO CT
VENETIA MEADOW
MEADOW DR
ADRIAN WY
CHALDA CT
STEVEN WY
SCHMIDT LN
LOWELL AV
CUSHING AV
NORTHVIEW CT
MERIAM DR
OAKCREST DR
WOODOAKS DR
LOWELL AV
CHINA CAMP STATE PARK
PK
700
600
1500
200
30
20
300
250
40
1

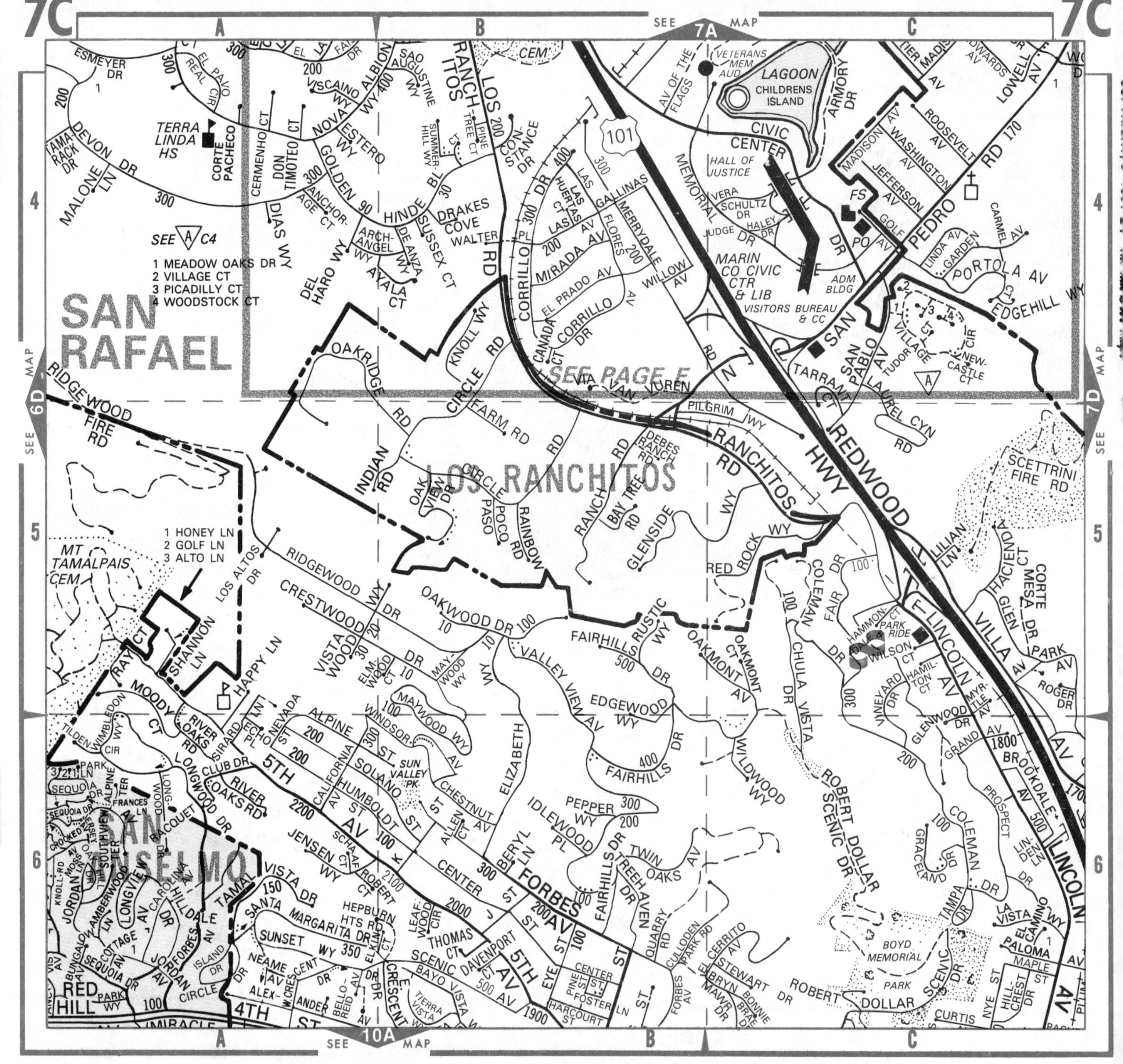

7C
MARIN CO
DETAIL
SEE 7A MAP
SEE 6D MAP
SEE 7D MAP
SEE 10A MAP
A
B
C
4
5
6
SAN RAFAEL
LOS RANCHITOS
SAN ANSELMO
SEE PAGE E
SEE A C4
1 MEADOW OAKS DR
2 VILLAGE CT
3 PICADILLY CT
4 WOODSTOCK CT
1 HONEY LN
2 GOLF LN
3 ALTO LN
TERRA LINDA HS
LAGOON
CHILDRENS ISLAND
VETERANS MEM AUD
CIVIC CENTER
HALL OF JUSTICE
MARIN CO CIVIC CTR & LIB
VISITORS BUREAU & CC
ADM BLDG
FS
PO
CEM
MT TAMALPAIS CEM
SUN VALLEY PK
BOYD MEMORIAL PARK
PARK & RIDE
101
REDWOOD HWY
LOS RANCHITOS RD
NOVA ALBION WY
DEVON DR
MALONE LN
ESMEYER DR
GOLDEN HINDE BL
DRAKES COVE
CORRILLO DR
LAS GALLINAS AV
MERRYDALE RD
MIRADA AV
EL PRADO AV
WILLOW AV
MEMORIAL DR
CIVIC CENTER DR
SAN PEDRO RD
PORTOLA AV
EDGEHILL WY
OAKRIDGE RD
CIRCLE RD
INDIAN RD
VITA VAN VUREN
PILGRIM WY
LAUREL CYN RD
SCETTRINI FIRE RD
RIDGEWOOD FIRE RD
RIDGEWOOD DR
CRESTWOOD DR
OAKWOOD DR
FAIRHILLS DR
VALLEY VIEW AV
EDGEWOOD WY
GLENSIDE WY
RED ROCK WY
COLEMAN DR
CHULA VISTA DR
ROBERT DOLLAR SCENIC DR
LINCOLN AV
VILLA AV
GLENWOOD DR
GRAND AV
BROOKDALE AV
5TH AV
FORBES AV
CENTER ST
ALPINE ST
SOLANO ST
CALIFORNIA AV
HUMBOLDT ST
CHESTNUT AV
ELIZABETH
IDLEWOOD PL
TWIN OAKS AV
MOODY CT
RIVER OAKS RD
LONGWOOD DR
HAPPY LN
SHANNON LN
RAY CT
SANTA MARGARITA DR
SUNSET WY
SCENIC AV
BAYO VISTA
CRESCENT DR
4TH ST
RED HILL

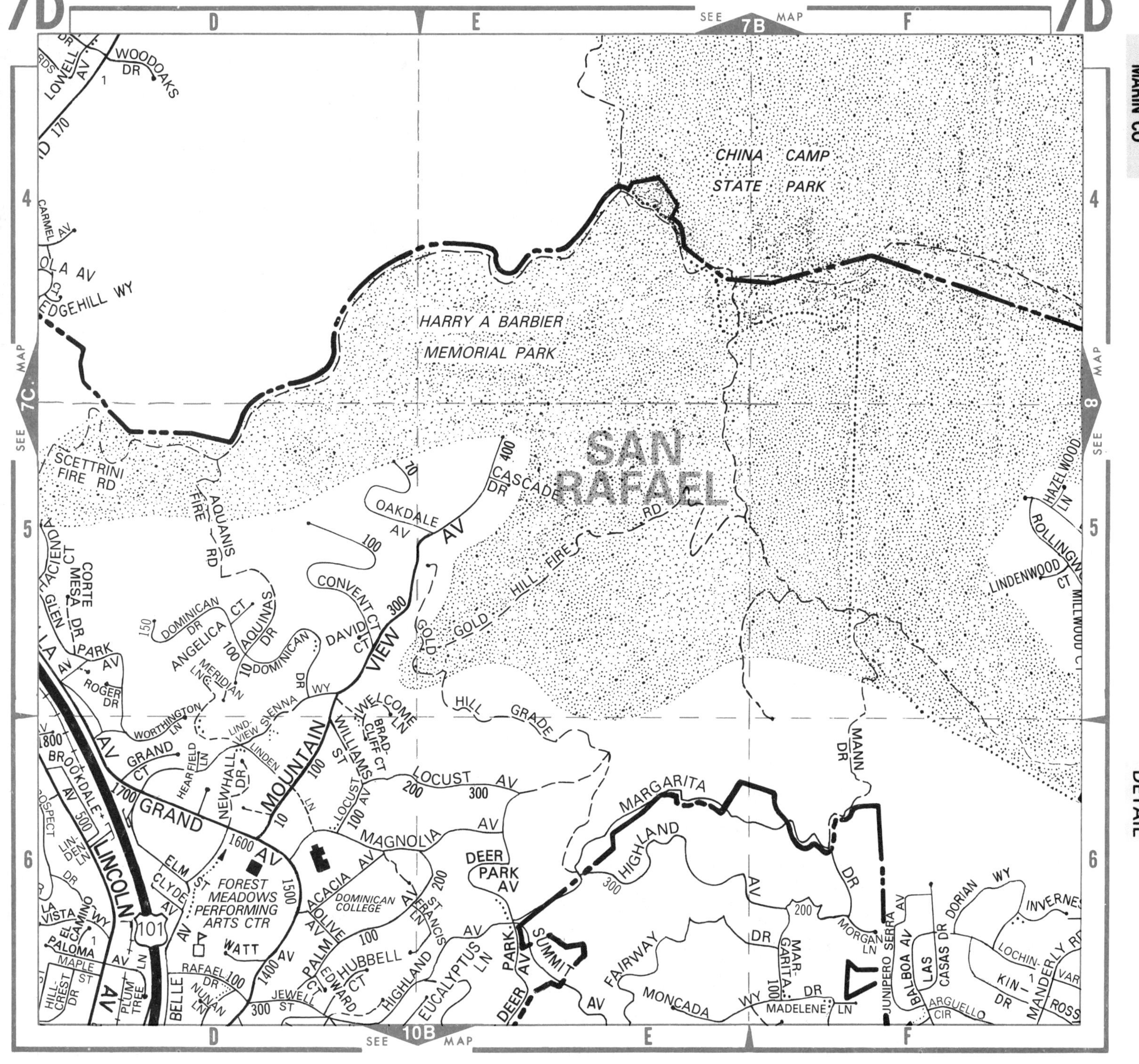

SEE 7B MAP
SEE 7C MAP
SEE 8 MAP
SEE 10B MAP

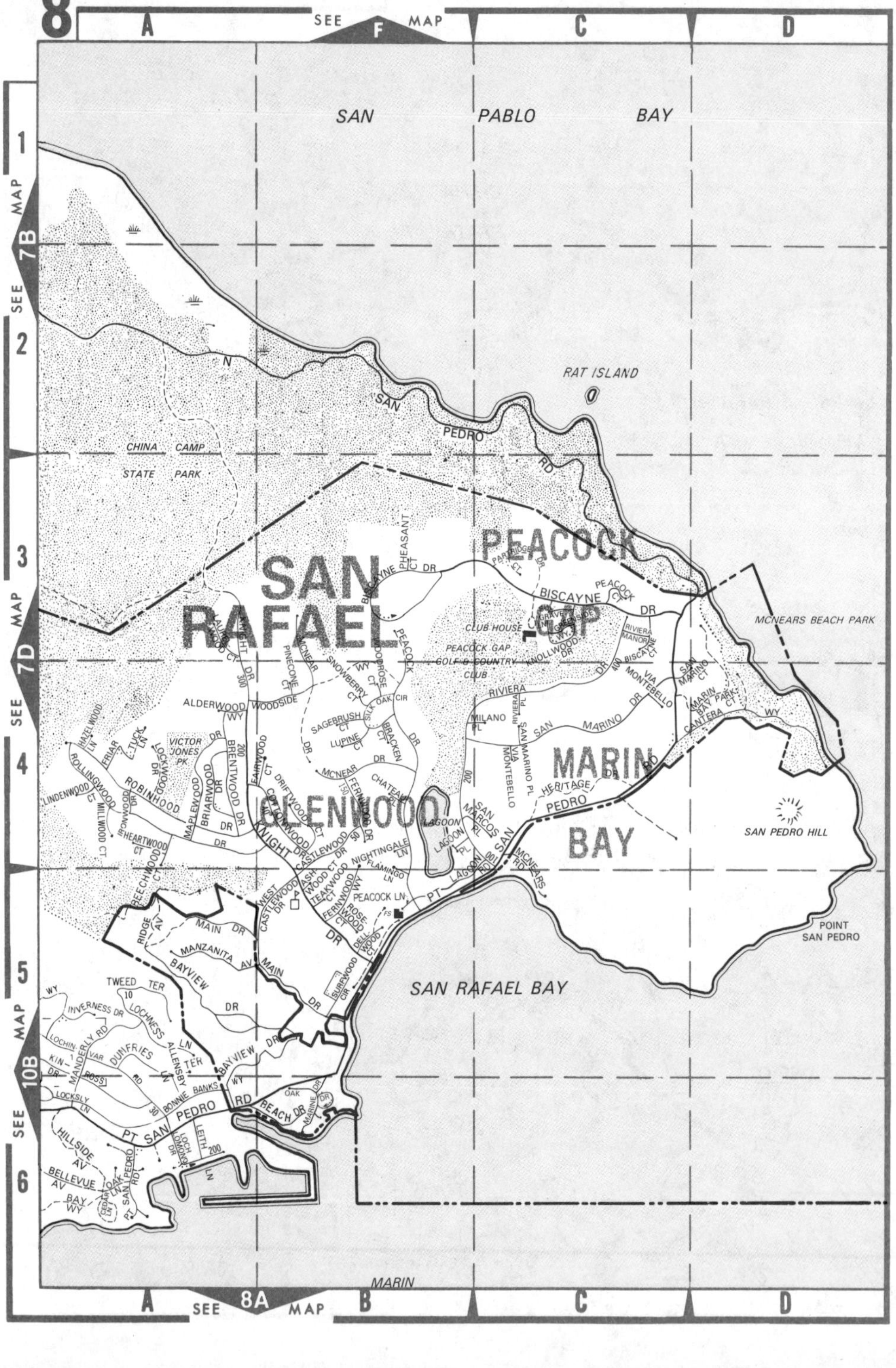

SEE F MAP
SEE 8 MAP
SEE 7B MAP
SEE 7D MAP
SEE 10B MAP
SEE 10D MAP
SEE G MAP
SEE 8A MAP
SEE 11C MAP

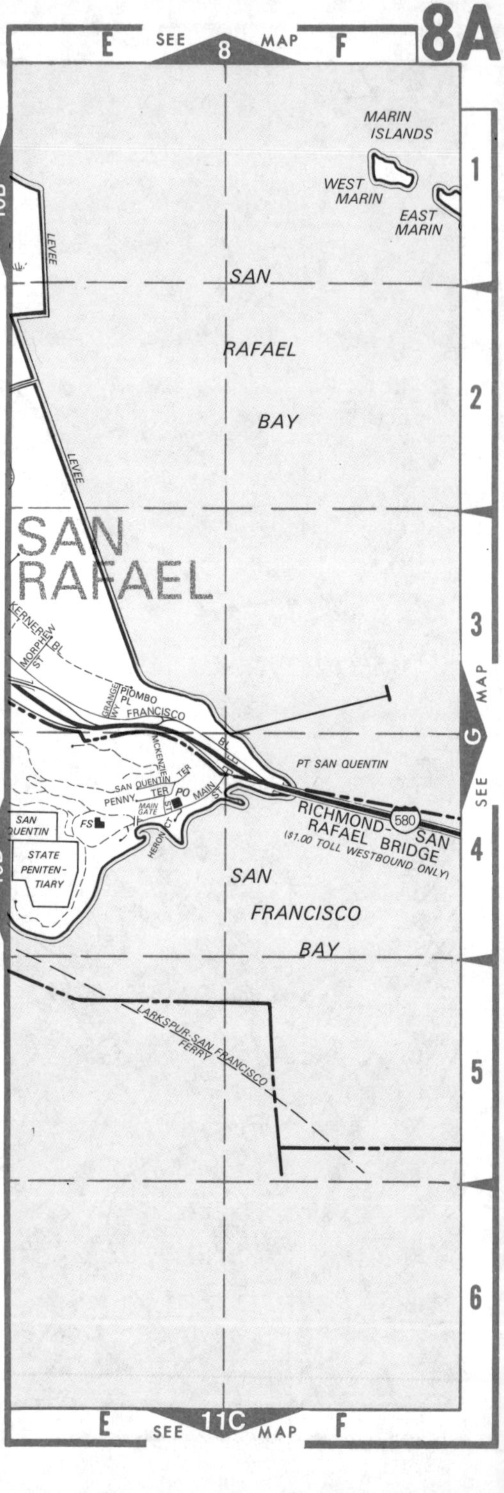

MARIN CO

DETAIL

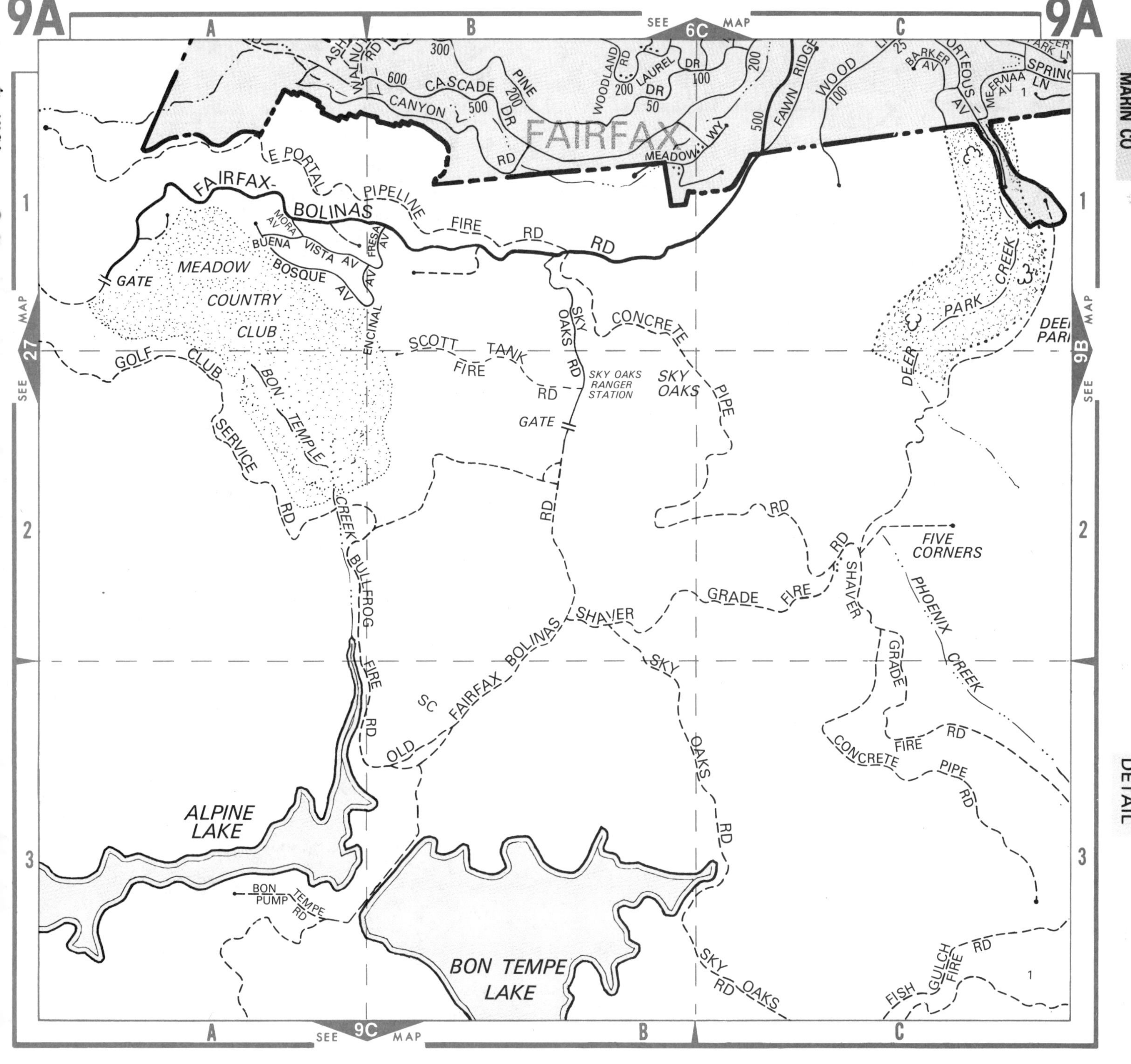

SEE 6C MAP
FAIRFAX
CASCADE
CANYON
PINE
DR
WOODLAND RD
LAUREL DR
MEADOW WY
FAWN RIDGE
WOOD LN
BARKER AV
PORTEOUS AV
SPRING LN
FAIRFAX-BOLINAS RD
E PORTAL
PIPELINE FIRE RD
MEADOW COUNTRY CLUB
GATE
BUENA VISTA AV
BOSQUE AV
MORA AV
FRESA AV
ENCINAL
GOLF CLUB SERVICE RD
BON TEMPLE
SCOTT TANK FIRE RD
SKY OAKS RD
SKY OAKS RANGER STATION
SKY OAKS
CONCRETE PIPE
DEER PARK CREEK
DEER PARK
CREEK
BULLFROG FIRE RD
FIVE CORNERS
PHOENIX CREEK
SHAVER GRADE FIRE RD
SHAVER GRADE
OLD FAIRFAX BOLINAS
SC
SKY OAKS RD
CONCRETE PIPE RD
FIRE RD
ALPINE LAKE
BON TEMPE LAKE
BON PUMP
TEMPE RD
FISH GULCH FIRE RD
SEE 27 MAP
SEE 9B MAP
SEE 9C MAP
MARIN CO
DETAIL

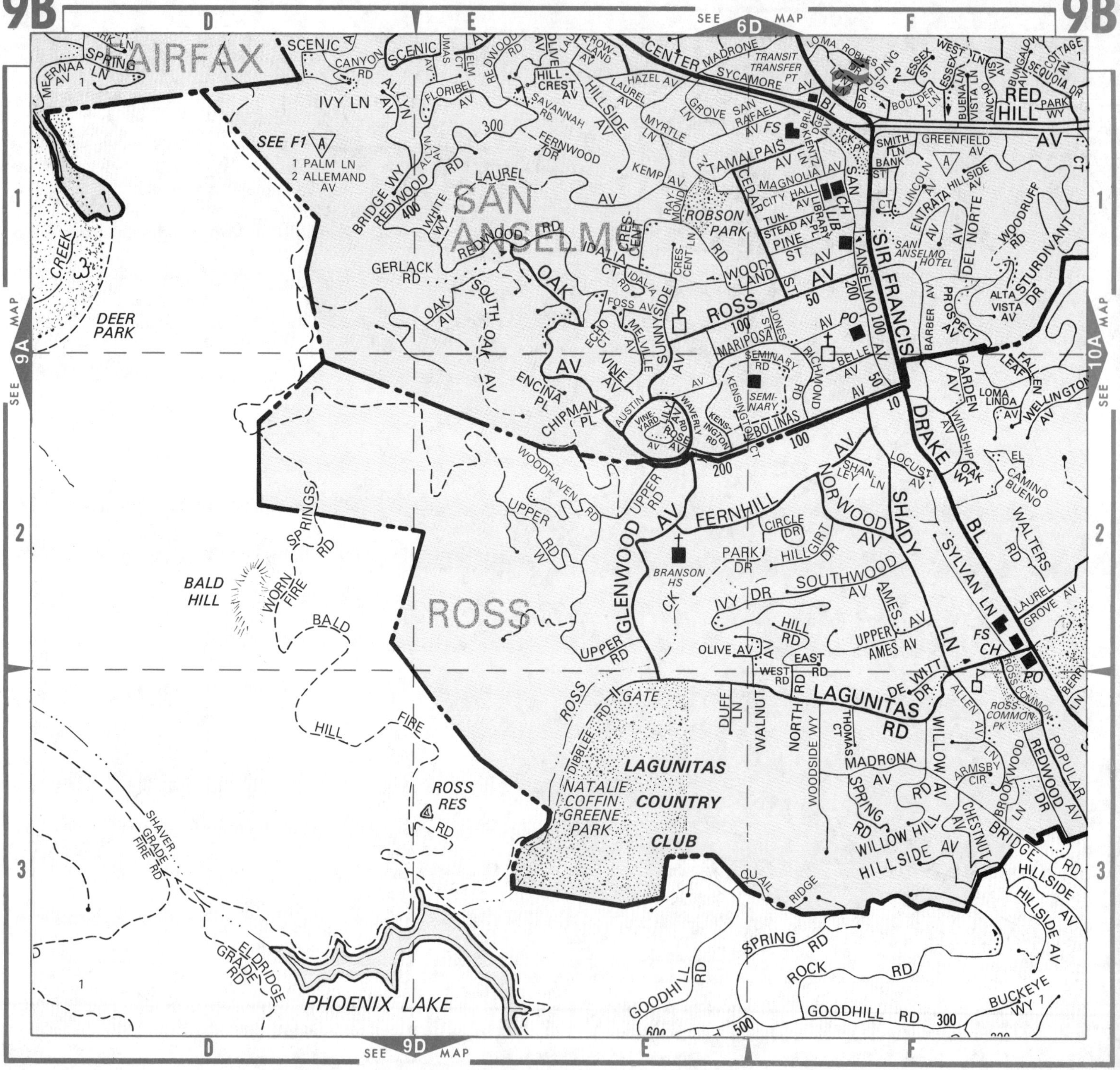

MARIN CO
DETAIL
FAIRFAX
SAN ANSELMO
ROSS
SEE 6D MAP
SEE 9A MAP
SEE 10A MAP
SEE 9D MAP
SEE F1 A
1 PALM LN
2 ALLEMAND AV
DEER PARK
BALD HILL
ROSS RES
PHOENIX LAKE
ROBSON PARK
LAGUNITAS COUNTRY CLUB
NATALIE COFFIN GREENE PARK
ROSS COMMON PK
BRANSON HS
SEMINARY
SAN ANSELMO HOTEL
TRANSIT TRANSFER PT
RED HILL
SIR FRANCIS DRAKE BL
CENTER BL
LAGUNITAS RD
GLENWOOD AV
SHADY LN
SHAVER GRADE FIRE RD
ELDRIDGE GRADE RD
WORN SPRINGS RD
BALD HILL FIRE RD
GOODHILL RD
SPRING RD
ROCK RD
BUCKEYE WY

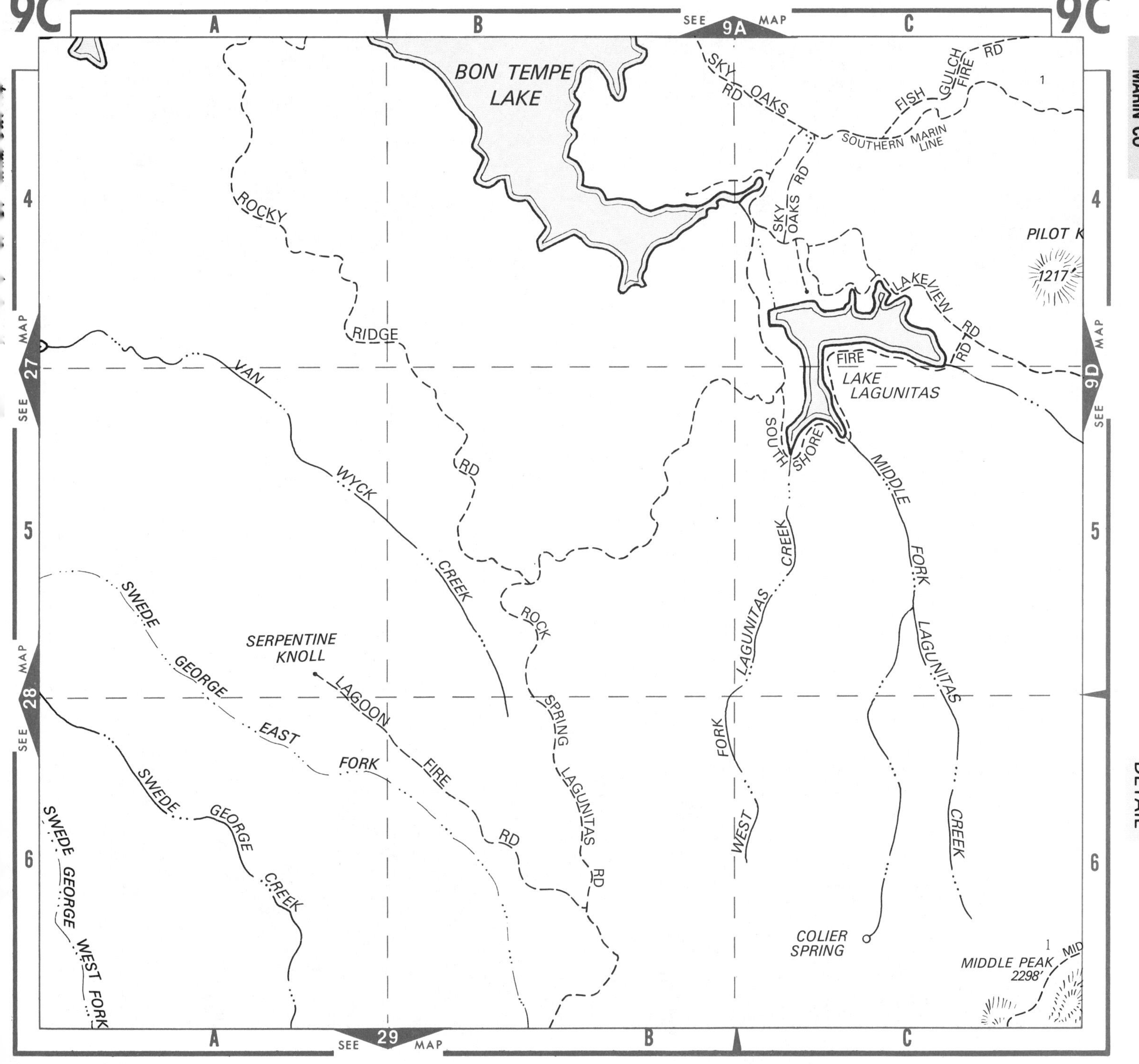
A
B
SEE 9A MAP
C
BON TEMPE LAKE
SKY OAKS RD
FISH GULCH FIRE RD
SOUTHERN MARIN LINE
SKY OAKS RD
ROCKY RIDGE RD
PILOT K
1217'
LAKEVIEW RD
FIRE RD
LAKE LAGUNITAS
SEE 27 MAP
SEE 9D MAP
VAN WYCK CREEK
SOUTH SHORE
MIDDLE FORK LAGUNITAS CREEK
LAGUNITAS CREEK
SWEDE GEORGE EAST FORK
SERPENTINE KNOLL
LAGOON FIRE RD
ROCK SPRING LAGUNITAS RD
WEST FORK LAGUNITAS CREEK
SEE 28 MAP
SWEDE GEORGE CREEK
SWEDE GEORGE WEST FORK
COLIER SPRING
MIDDLE PEAK 2298'
MID
4
5
6
SEE 29 MAP
MARIN CO
DETAIL

9C

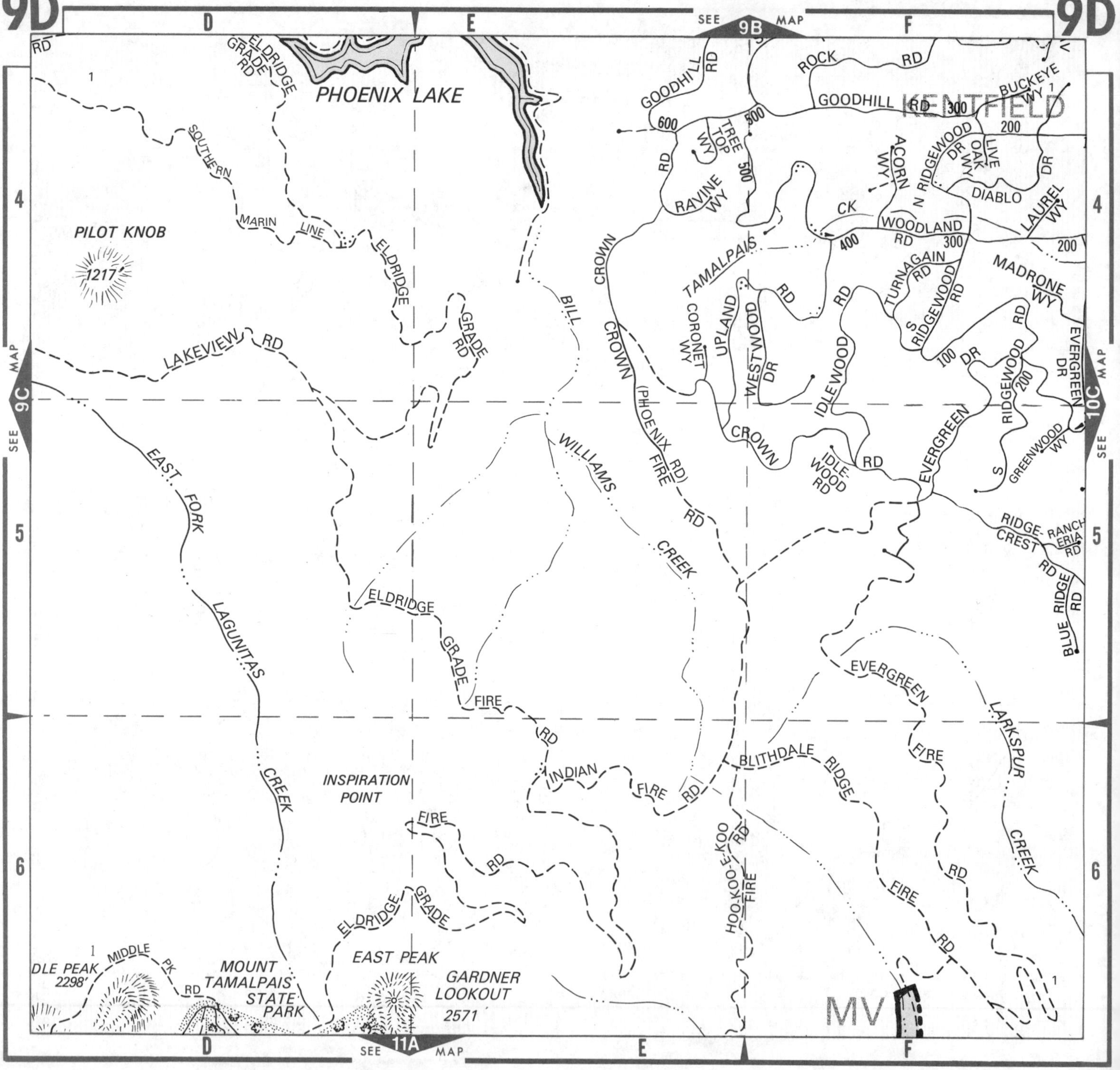

9D
SEE 9B MAP
SEE 9C MAP
SEE 10C MAP
SEE 11A MAP

MARIN CO

DETAIL

D E F

4 5 6

PHOENIX LAKE

KENTFIELD

PILOT KNOB
1217

ELDRIDGE GRADE RD
SOUTHERN MARIN LINE
ELDRIDGE GRADE RD
LAKEVIEW RD
BILL WILLIAMS CREEK
EAST FORK LAGUNITAS CREEK
ELDRIDGE GRADE FIRE RD
INDIAN FIRE RD
CROWN RD
CROWN (PHOENIX FIRE RD) RD
GOODHILL RD
ROCK RD
GOODHILL RD
BUCKEYE WY
TREE TOP WY
RAVINE WY
TAMALPAIS RD
CORONET WY
UPLAND
WESTWOOD DR
IDLEWOOD RD
IDLE WOOD RD
ACORN WY
N RIDGEWOOD DR
LIVE OAK WY
DIABLO
DR
LAUREL WY
WOODLAND RD
CK
TURNAGAIN RD
S RIDGEWOOD RD
MADRONE WY
EVERGREEN DR
RIDGEWOOD DR
S GREENWOOD WY
EVERGREEN
RIDGECREST RD
RANCHERIA RD
BLUE RIDGE RD
EVERGREEN FIRE RD
LARKSPUR CREEK
BLITHDALE RIDGE FIRE RD
HOO-KOO-E-KOO FIRE RD
INSPIRATION POINT
FIRE RD
ELDRIDGE GRADE
EAST PEAK
GARDNER LOOKOUT
2571
MOUNT TAMALPAIS STATE PARK
MIDDLE PK RD
DLE PEAK
2298'
MV

600 500 500 400 300 300 200 200 200 100 200 1 1 1 1

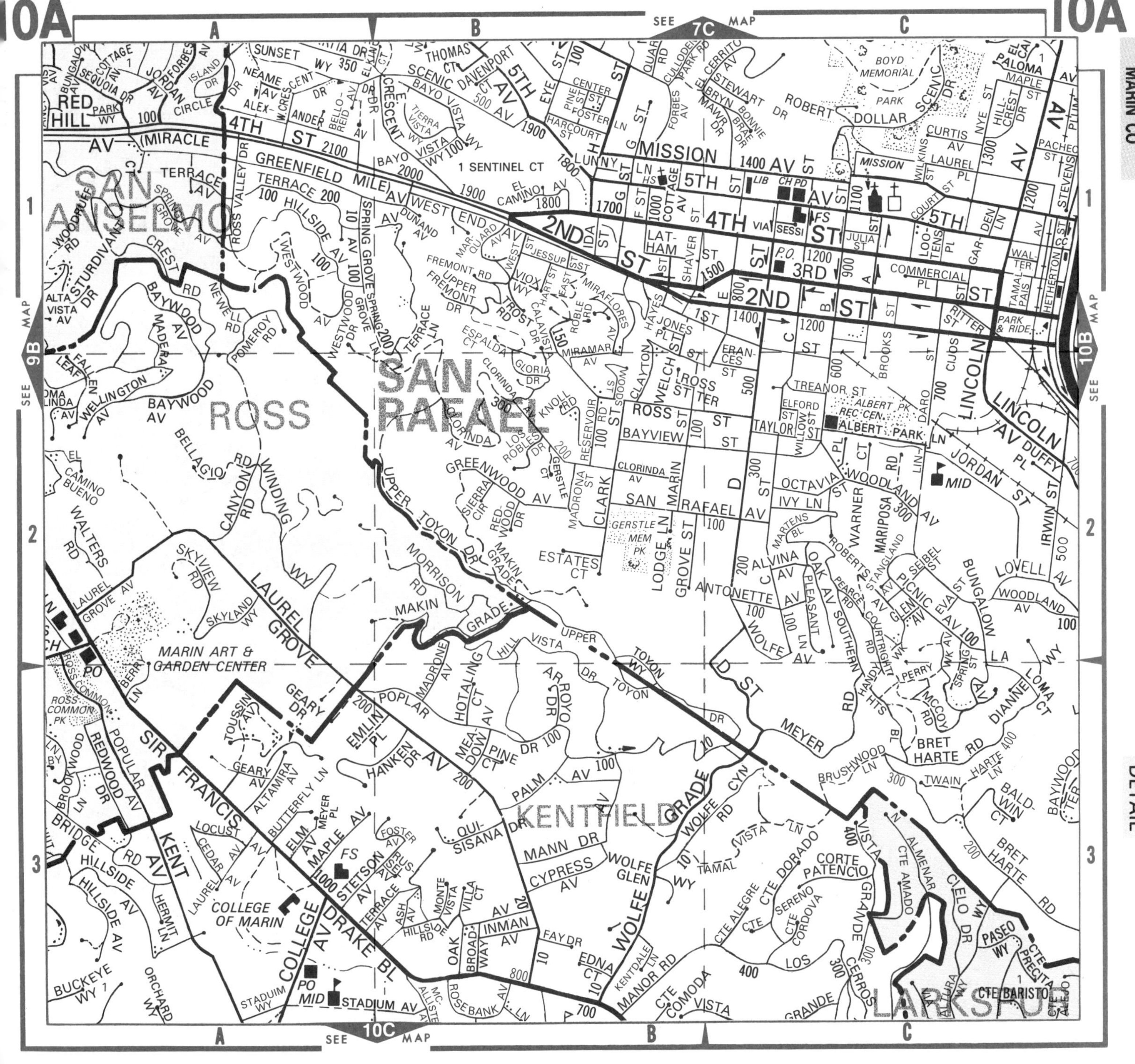

10A
SEE MAP 7C
SEE MAP 9B
SEE MAP 10B
SEE MAP 10C
A
B
C
1
2
3
MARIN CO
DETAIL
SAN ANSELMO
SAN RAFAEL
ROSS
KENTFIELD
LARKSPUR
RED HILL
MIRACLE MILE
4TH ST
GREENFIELD AV
MISSION AV
5TH AV
2ND ST
3RD ST
1ST ST
LINCOLN AV
SIR FRANCIS DRAKE BL
COLLEGE AV
KENT AV
BOYD MEMORIAL PARK
ROBERT DOLLAR SCENIC DR
ALBERT PARK
GERSTLE MEM PK
MARIN ART & GARDEN CENTER
ROSS COMMON PK
COLLEGE OF MARIN
STADIUM AV
MAGNOLIA AV
LAUREL GROVE AV
MAKIN GRADE
UPPER TOYON DR
WOLFE GRADE
D ST
SAN RAFAEL AV
BRET HARTE RD
CROSS TERR
WOODLAND AV
WEST END AV
SPRING GROVE AV
TERRACE AV
HILLSIDE AV
BAYWOOD AV
WINDING WY
CANYON RD
POPLAR AV
PALM AV
MANN DR
CYPRESS AV
INMAN AV
FAY DR
EDNA CT
MANOR RD
VISTA GRANDE
CTE DORADO
CORTE PATENCIO
CIELO DR
PASEO WY
CTE BARISTO
MERIDIAN
PARK & RIDE
LIB
CH
PD
FS
PO
HS
MID

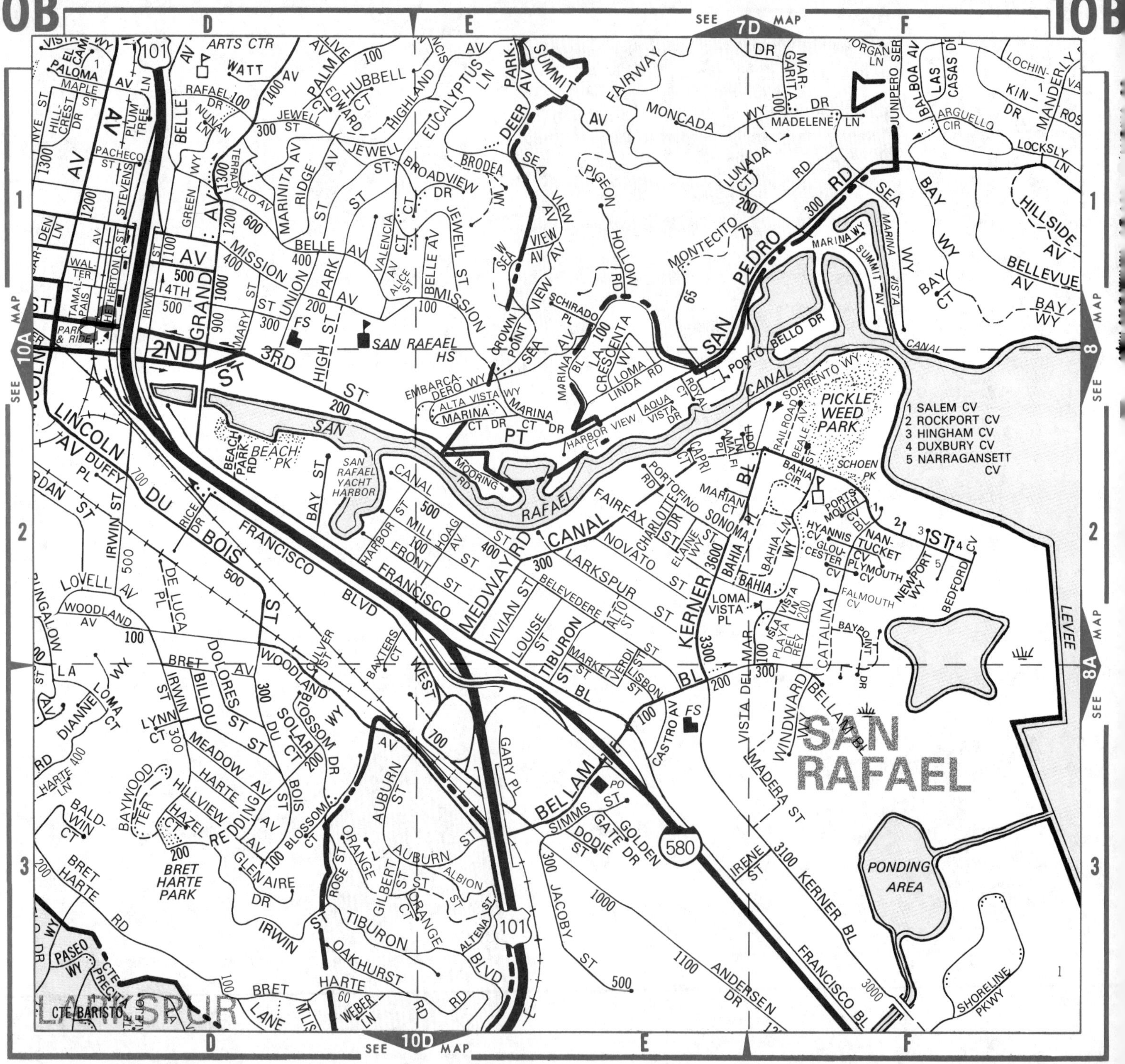

SEE 7D MAP

SEE 10A MAP

SEE 8 MAP

SEE 8A MAP

SEE 10D MAP

MARIN CO

DETAIL

SAN RAFAEL

LARKSPUR

1 SALEM CV
2 ROCKPORT CV
3 HINGHAM CV
4 DUXBURY CV
5 NARRAGANSETT CV

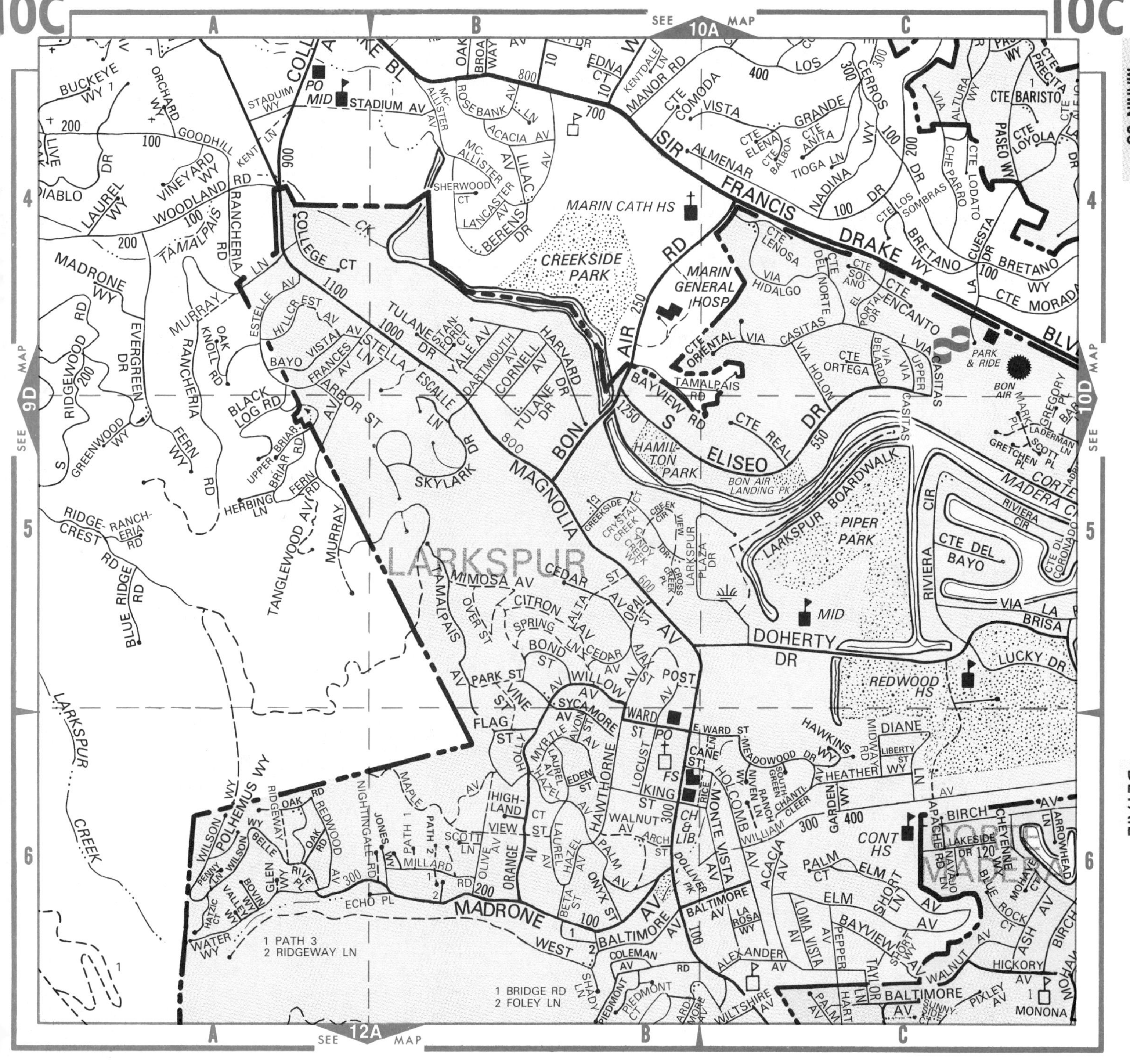
SEE 10A MAP
SEE 9D MAP
SEE 10D MAP
SEE 12A MAP
A
B
C
4
5
6
LARKSPUR
CORTE MADERA
SIR FRANCIS DRAKE BLVD
MARIN CATH HS
CREEKSIDE PARK
MARIN GENERAL HOSP
HAMILTON PARK
BON AIR LANDING PK
PIPER PARK
LARKSPUR BOARDWALK
REDWOOD HS
CONT HS
MID
PO
FS
CH & LIB
PARK & RIDE
BON AIR RD
MAGNOLIA AV
DOHERTY DR
S ELISEO DR
TAMALPAIS DR
MADRONE AV
BALTIMORE AV
WARD ST
E WARD ST
KING ST
HOLCOMB AV
MONTE VISTA AV
WILLIAM AV
HEATHER WY
MEADOWOOD DR
HAWKINS WY
DIANE LN
LIBERTY ST
BIRCH AV
LAKESIDE DR
CHEYENNE
ARROWHEAD
APACHE RD
NAVAJO LN
MOHAVE CT
BLUE ROCK CT
ASH AV
ELM AV
PALM CT
SHORT LN
BAYVIEW AV
WALNUT AV
HICKORY AV
PIXLEY AV
SUNNYSIDE
MONONA
TAYLOR
HART LN
PEPPER AV
LOMA VISTA AV
ALEXANDER AV
LA ROSA WY
ACACIA AV
WILTSHIRE AV
ARDMORE AV
PIEDMONT RD
PIEDMONT CT
SHADY LN
COLEMAN AV
WEST
HAWTHORNE AV
LOCUST AV
CANE ST
RICE LN
WALNUT AV
ARCH ST
PALM AV
ONYX ST
HAZEL AV
LAUREL AV
EDEN ST
MYRTLE AV
AVON ST
HOLLY AV
SYCAMORE AV
FLAG ST
VINE ST
PARK ST
WILLOW AV
POST ST
AJAX ST
CEDAR AV
SPRING LN
BOND ST
CITRON AV
ALTA AV
OPAL AV
MIMOSA AV
OVER ST
TAMALPAIS AV
HIGHLAND AV
VIEW ST
ORANGE AV
OLIVE AV
SCOTT LN
MAPLE AV
NIGHTINGALE RD
JONES WY
PATH 1
PATH 2
MILLARD RD
ECHO PL
RIDGEWAY
OAK RD
REDWOOD AV
POLHEMUS WY
WILSON WY
BELLE AV
GLEN WY
RIVE PL
BOVIN
VALLEY WY
PENNY LN
HATZIC CT
WATER WY
1 PATH 3
2 RIDGEWAY LN
1 BRIDGE RD
2 FOLEY LN
LARKSPUR CREEK
COLLEGE AV
COLLEGE CT
TULANE DR
STANFORD CT
YALE AV
DARTMOUTH AV
CORNELL AV
HARVARD DR
ESCALLE LN
STELLA LN
FRANCES AV
BAYO VISTA AV
HILLCREST AV
ESTELLE AV
ARBOR ST
SKYLARK DR
MURRAY AV
TANGLEWOOD AV
FERN AV
BRIAR RD
UPPER BRIAR
HERBING LN
BLACK LOG RD
OAK KNOLL RD
RANCHERIA RD
FERN WY
EVERGREEN DR
RIDGEWOOD DR
GREENWOOD WY
RIDGECREST RD
RANCHERIA RD
BLUE RIDGE RD
MADRONE WY
LAUREL WY
DIABLO
LIVE OAK
WOODLAND RD
VINEYARD WY
GOODHILL
ORCHARD WY
BUCKEYE WY
KENT LN
STADIUM AV
STADIUM WY
MC ALLISTER AV
ROSEBANK AV
ACACIA AV
LILAC AV
SHERWOOD CT
LANCASTER AV
BERENS DR
EDNA CT
KENTDALE LN
MANOR RD
CTE COMODA
VISTA GRANDE
CTE ELENA
CTE ANITA
CTE BALBOA
TIOGA LN
NADINA WY
LOS CERROS DR
CTE LOS SOMBRAS
ALMENAR
BRETANO WY
CTE MORADA
LA CUESTA DR
CTE BARISTO
PASEO WY
CTE LOYOLA
CTE PRECITA
VIA ALTURA
CTE LODATO
CHE PARRO
CTE LENOSA
VIA HIDALGO
CTE DEL NORTE
CTE SOLANO
EL PORTAL DR
CTE ENCANTO
VIA CASITAS
CTE ORIENTAL
VIA HOLON
CTE ORTEGA
VIA BELARDO
UPPER
CASITAS
BAYVIEW RD
TAMALPAIS RD
CTE REAL
CREEKSIDE
CRYSTAL CREEK
CANDY CREEK WY
CREEK CIR
VIEW
LARKSPUR PLAZA DR
CROSS CREEK PL
RIVIERA CIR
CTE DEL BAYO
CTE DEL CORONADO
VIA LA BRISA
LUCKY DR
MADERA
CORTE
GREGORY
LADERMAN LN
SCOTT PL
GRETCHEN PL
MARK PL
MIDWAY RD
GARDEN WY
RANCH
NIVEN LN
SOUTH GREEN
CHANTICLEER
DOLLIVER PK
BON AIR

MARIN CO

DETAIL

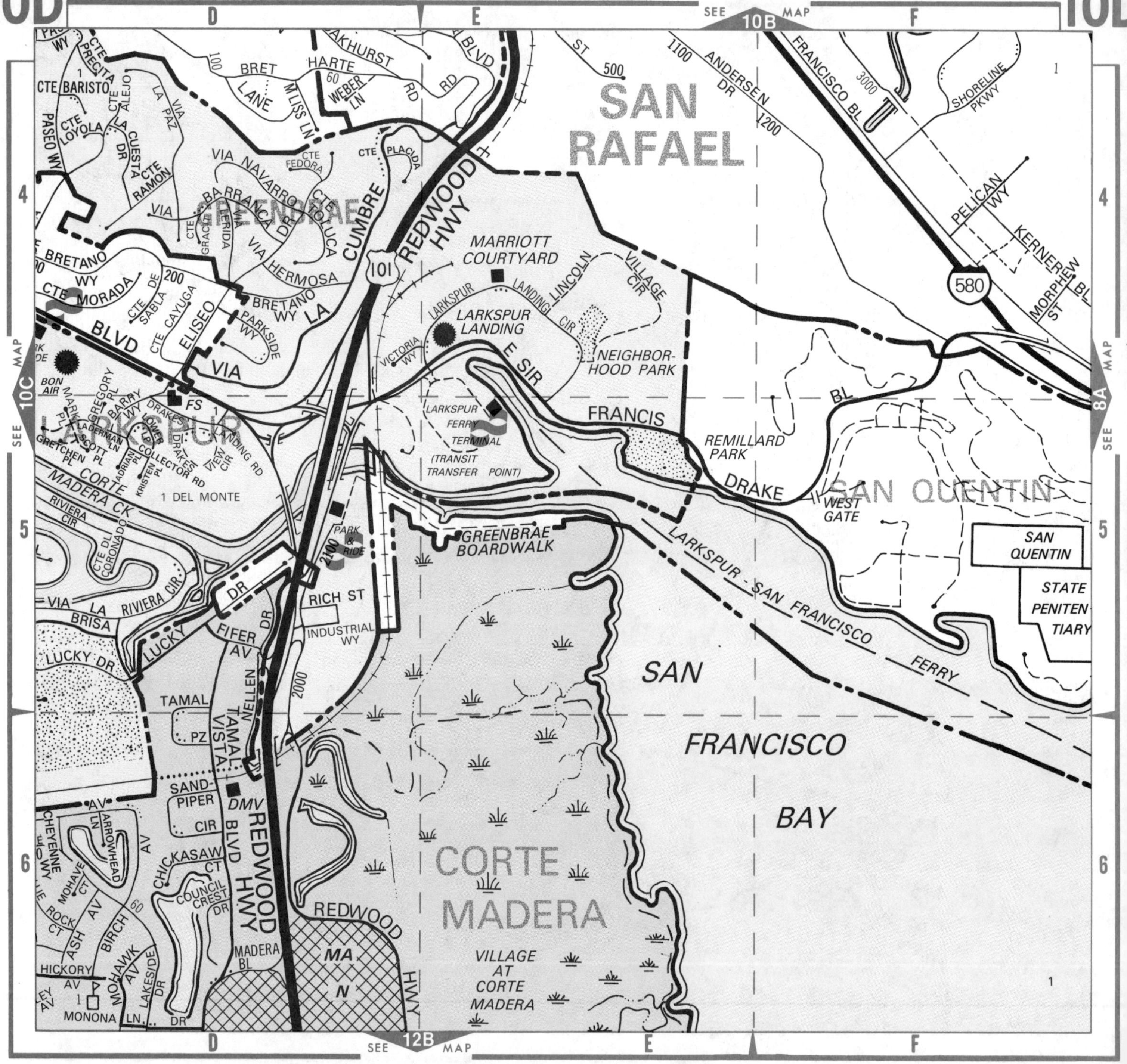

SEE 10B MAP
SEE 10C MAP
SEE 8A MAP
SEE 12B MAP

D
E
F
4
5
6

SAN RAFAEL
GREENBRAE
LARKSPUR
SAN QUENTIN
CORTE MADERA
SAN FRANCISCO BAY

MARRIOTT COURTYARD
LARKSPUR LANDING
NEIGHBOR-HOOD PARK
LARKSPUR FERRY TERMINAL (TRANSIT TRANSFER POINT)
REMILLARD PARK
WEST GATE
SAN QUENTIN STATE PENITENTIARY
GREENBRAE BOARDWALK
PARK & RIDE
BON AIR
FS
DMV
VILLAGE AT CORTE MADERA
1 DEL MONTE
LARKSPUR - SAN FRANCISCO FERRY

REDWOOD HWY
101
580
SIR FRANCIS DRAKE BL
ANDERSEN DR
FRANCISCO BL
SHORELINE PKWY
PELICAN WY
KERNER BL
MORPHEW ST
BRET HARTE RD
OAKHURST
BRET LANE
M'LISS LN
WEBER LN
LA CUMBRE
LARKSPUR LANDING CIR
LINCOLN VILLAGE CIR
VICTORIA WY
E SIR
VIA NAVARRO
VIA BARRANCA
CTE PLACIDA
CTE FEDORA
CTE TOLUCA
CTE GRACIA
VIA LERIDA
VIA HERMOSA
BRETANO WY
CTE MORADA
CTE DE SABLA
CTE CAYUGA
VIA ELISEO
PARKSIDE WY
CTE BARISTO
CTE PRECITA
CTE ALEJO
VIA LA PAZ
CTE LOYOLA
LA CUESTA DR
CTE RAMON
PASEO WY
MAGNOLIA
GREGORY PL
BARRY
MARK PL
LADERMAN LN
SCOTT PL
GRETCHEN PL
ADRIAN PL
KRISTEN PL
LOWER DRAKES RD
DRAKES LANDING RD
COLLECTOR RD
VIEW CIR
CORTE MADERA CK
RIVIERA CIR
CTE DL CORONADO
VIA LA BRISA
RIVIERA CIR
DR
LUCKY DR
FIFER AV
RICH ST
INDUSTRIAL WY
NELLEN AV
TAMAL PZ
TAMAL VISTA BLVD
SANDPIPER CIR
CHICKASAW CT
COUNCIL CREST DR
CHEYENNE WY
ARROWHEAD LN
MOHAVE CT
ROCK CT
ASH AV
BIRCH AV
MOHAWK AV
LAKESIDE DR
HICKORY AV
MONONA LN
MADERA BL
REDWOOD HWY
MA
N

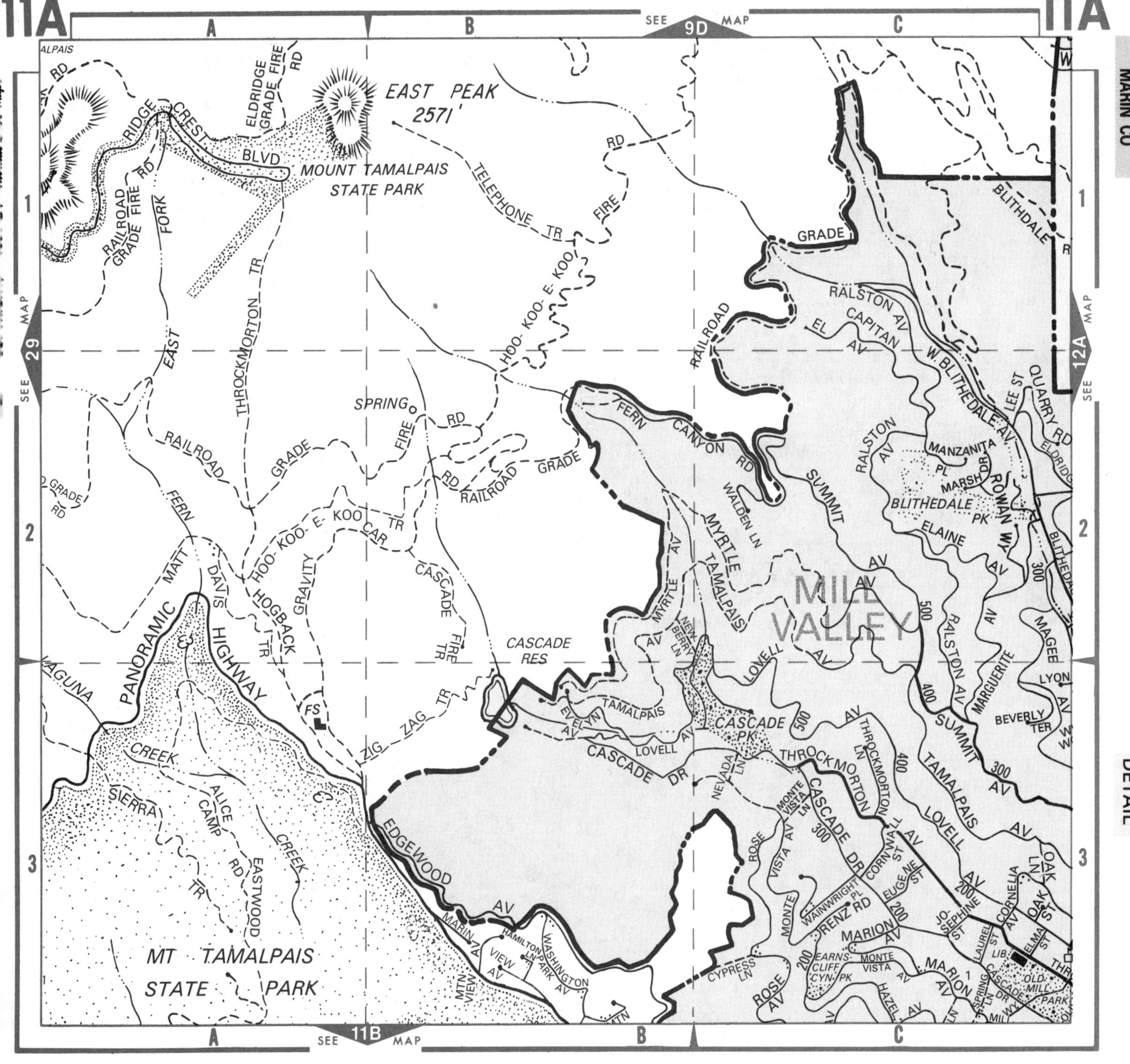

EAST PEAK
2571
MOUNT TAMALPAIS
STATE PARK
RIDGE CREST BLVD
ELDRIDGE GRADE FIRE RD
RAILROAD GRADE FIRE RD
EAST FORK
THROCKMORTON TR
TELEPHONE TR
HOO-KOO-E-KOO FIRE RD
HOO-KOO-E-KOO TR
RAILROAD GRADE
SPRING
FIRE RD
FERN CANYON RD
GRAVITY CAR
CASCADE FIRE TR
CASCADE RES
HOGBACK TR
MATT DAVIS
PANORAMIC HIGHWAY
ZIG ZAG TR
FS
LAGUNA
CREEK
SIERRA
ALICE CAMP RD
EASTWOOD
CREEK TR
MT TAMALPAIS
STATE PARK
EDGEWOOD AV
MARIN AV
MTN VIEW AV
HAMILTON LN
WASHINGTON PARK AV
MILL VALLEY
RALSTON AV
EL CAPITAN AV
W. BLITHEDALE AV
BLITHDALE
GRADE
RAILROAD
LEE ST
QUARRY RD
ELDRIDGE
MANZANITA PL
MARSH DR
BLITHEDALE PK
ROWAN WY
ELAINE AV
SUMMIT AV
WALDEN LN
MYRTLE AV
TAMALPAIS AV
NEWBERRY LN
LOVELL AV
MAGEE AV
MARGUERITE AV
LYON AV
BEVERLY TER
CASCADE PK
EVELYN AV
CASCADE DR
THROCKMORTON AV
THROCKMORTON LN
NEVADA LN
MONTE VISTA LN
ROSE
VISTA AV
WAINWRIGHT PL
RENZ RD
CORNWALL ST
EUGENE ST
JOSEPHINE ST
CORNELIA AV
OAK LN
OAK ST
ELMA ST
LAUREL ST
LIB
MARION AV
EARNSCLIFF PK
CYN
MONTE VISTA AV
HAZEL AV
SPRING LN
CASCADE DR
OLD MILL PARK
CYPRESS LN
ROSE AV
MILL WY
MTN
500
400
300
200
A
B
C
1
2
3
SEE 9D MAP
SEE 29 MAP
SEE 12A MAP
SEE 11B MAP
MARIN CO
DETAIL

11A

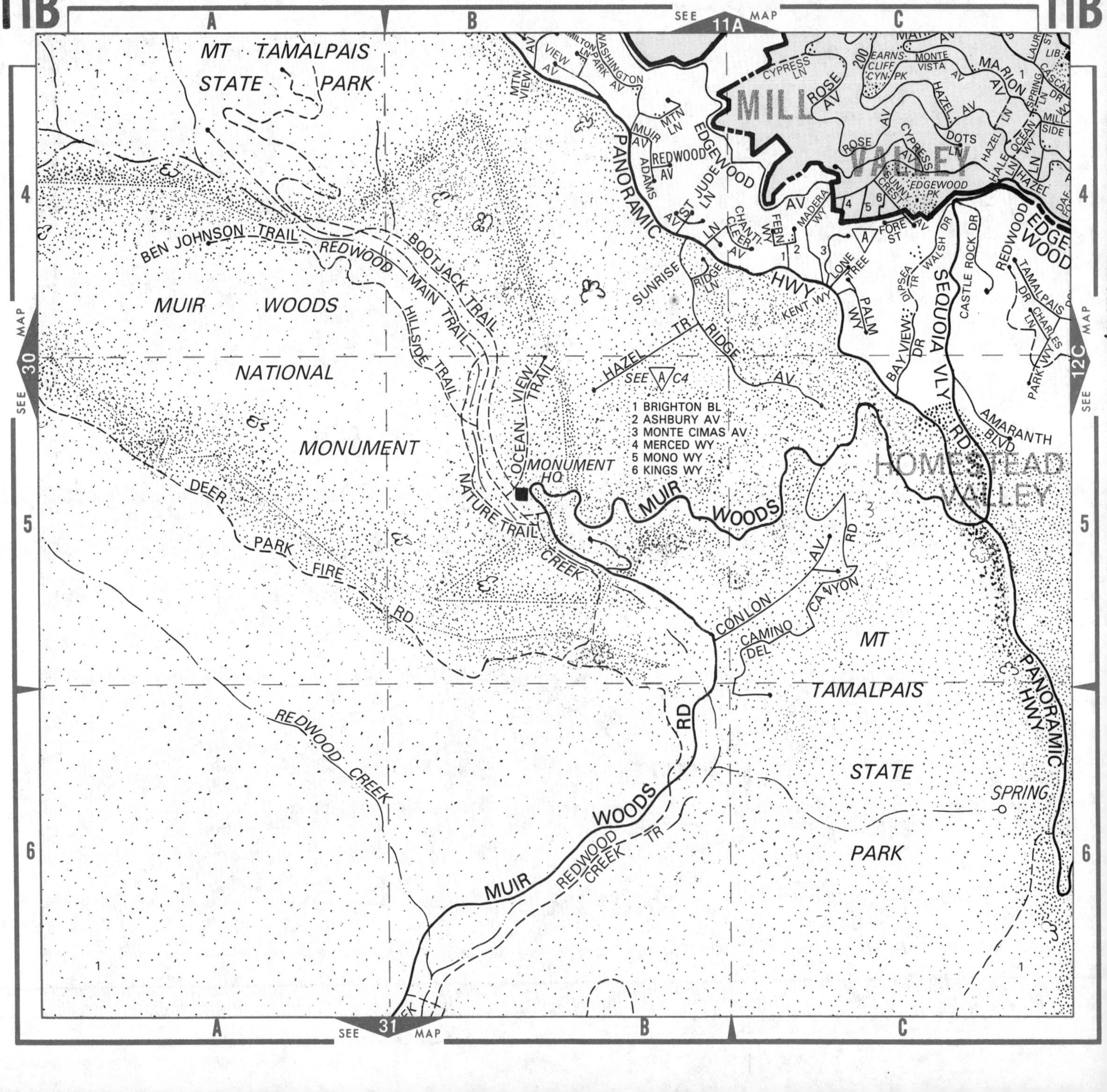

SEE 11A MAP

MARIN CO

MT TAMALPAIS STATE PARK

MUIR WOODS NATIONAL MONUMENT

MILL VALLEY

HOMESTEAD VALLEY

MT TAMALPAIS STATE PARK

BEN JOHNSON TRAIL
REDWOOD TRAIL
BOOTJACK TRAIL
MAIN TRAIL
HILLSIDE TRAIL
OCEAN VIEW TRAIL
NATURE TRAIL
DEER PARK FIRE RD
REDWOOD CREEK
MUIR WOODS RD
REDWOOD CREEK TR
MONUMENT HQ
HAZEL TR
SUNRISE
RIDGE LN
RIDGE AV
PANORAMIC HWY
CONLON AV
CAMINO DEL CANYON RD
SPRING
SEQUOIA VLY RD
AMARANTH BLVD
BAY VIEW DR
DIPSEA TR
WALSH DR
CASTLE ROCK DR
REDWOOD
EDGEWOOD
TAMALPAIS DR
CHARLES LN
PARK WY
KENT WY
PALM WY
LONE TREE
FORE ST
MADERA WY
FERN WY
CHANTICLEER AV
ST JUDE LN
EDGEWOOD AV
EDGEWOOD PK
REDWOOD AV
ADAMS
MUIR AV
MTN LN
MTN VIEW AV
VIEW AV
MILTON LN
PARK AV
WASHINGTON AV
CYPRESS LN
ROSE AV
CYPRESS AV
SUNNY CREST
EARNS CLIFF
CYN PK
MONTE VISTA AV
MARION AV
HAZEL AV
DOTS LN
HAZEL LN
HALE LN
OCEAN WY
SPRING LN
MILL SIDE
CASCADE DR
LAUREL
LIB

SEE A C4

1 BRIGHTON BL
2 ASHBURY AV
3 MONTE CIMAS AV
4 MERCED WY
5 MONO WY
6 KINGS WY

SEE 30 MAP

SEE 12C MAP

DETAIL

SEE 31 MAP

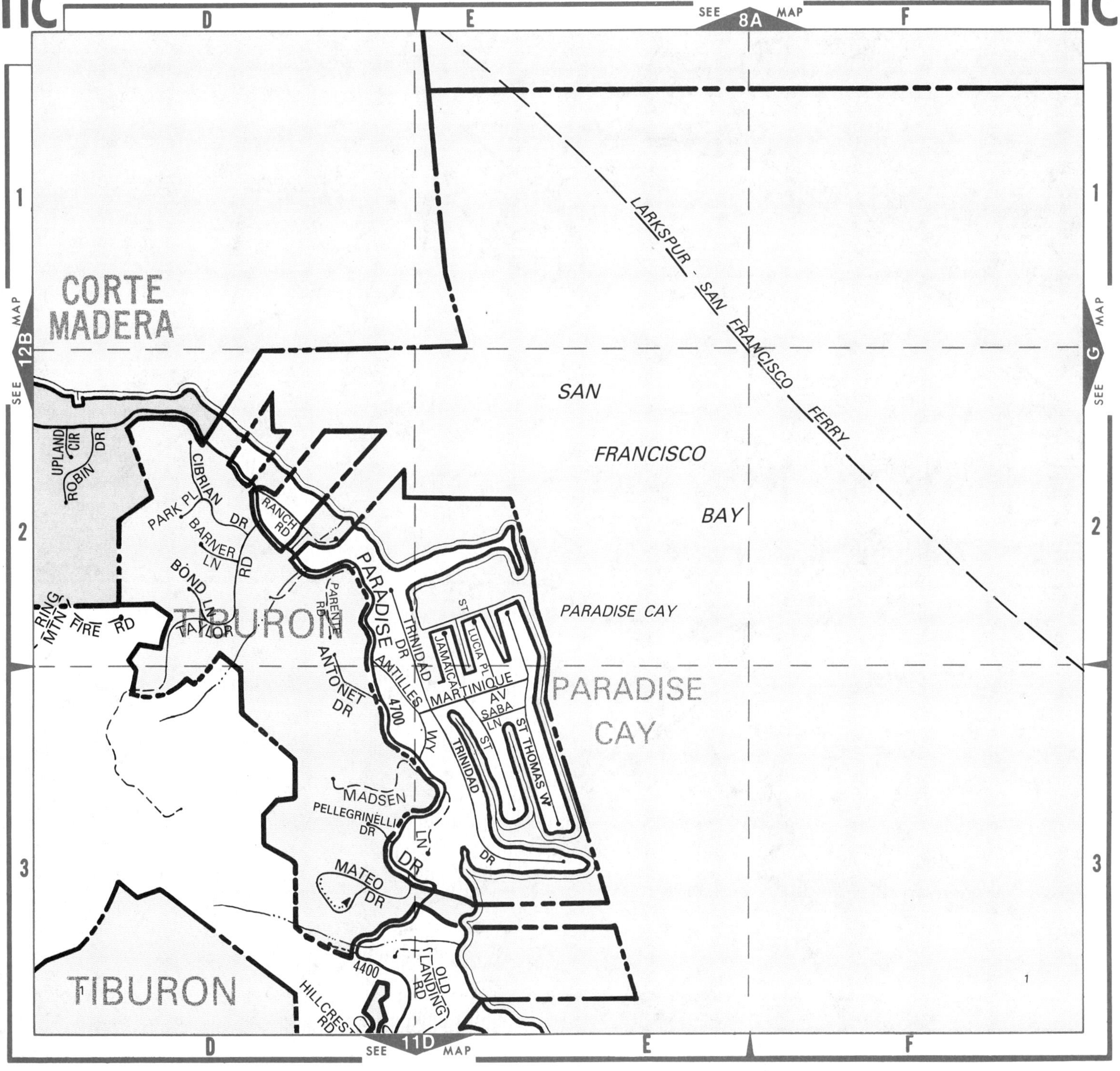

SEE 8A MAP

SEE 12B MAP

SEE G MAP

SEE 11D MAP

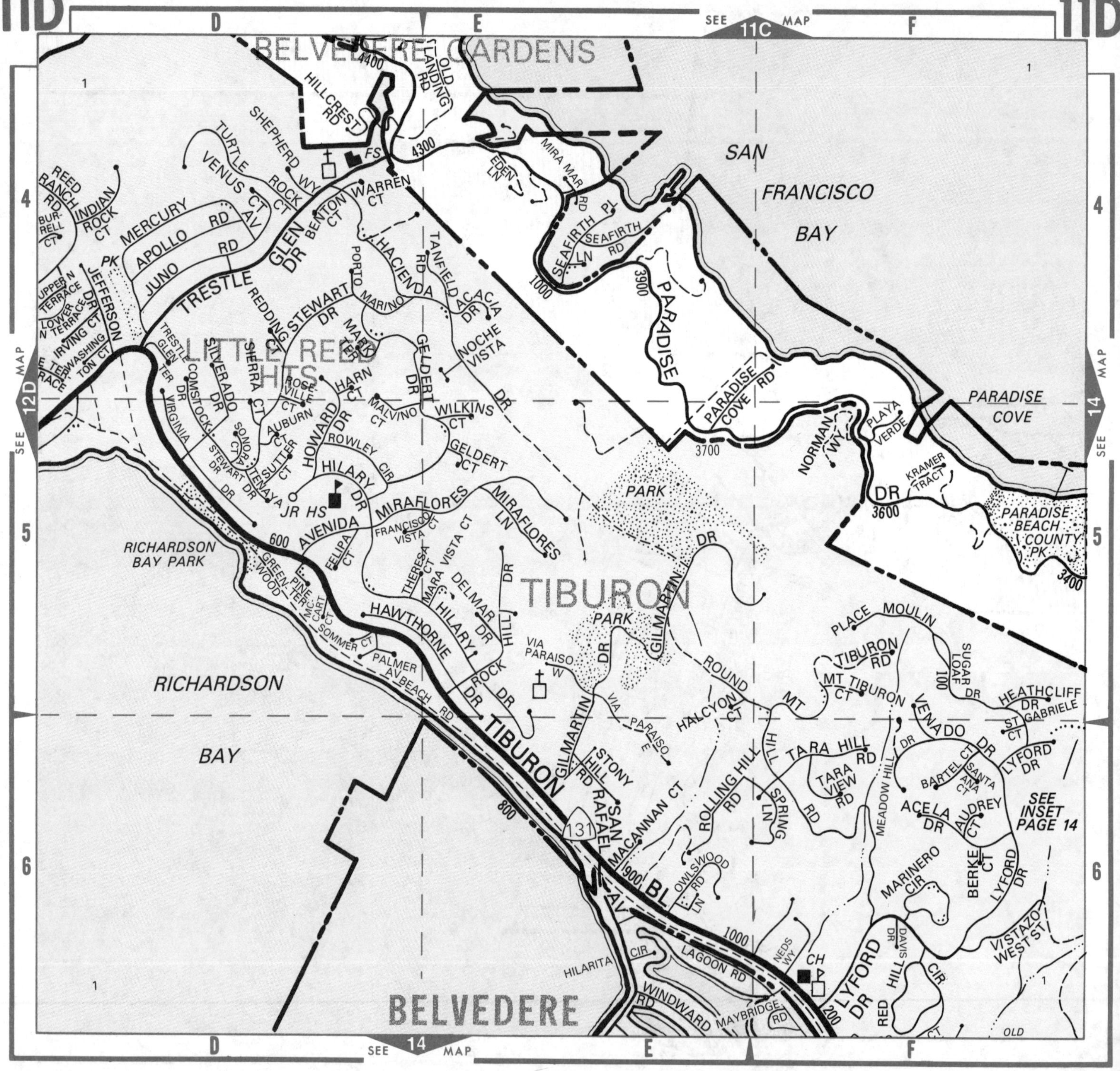

D E F

SEE 11C MAP

BELVEDERE GARDENS

SAN FRANCISCO BAY

LITTLE REED HTS

TIBURON

RICHARDSON BAY PARK

RICHARDSON BAY

PARADISE COVE

PARADISE BEACH COUNTY PK

PARK

BELVEDERE

HILLCREST RD
OLD LANDING RD
SHEPHERD WY
TURTLE ROCK CT
VENUS CT
AV
REED RANCH RD
BURRELL CT
INDIAN ROCK CT
MERCURY
APOLLO RD
JUNO RD
TRESTLE GLEN DR
WARREN CT
BENTON CT
EDEN LN
MIRA MAR RD
SEAFIRTH PL
SEAFIRTH LN
SEAFIRTH RD
PARADISE DR
PARADISE COVE RD
NORMAN WY
PLAYA VERDE
KRAMER TRACT
UPPER N TERRACE
LOWER N TERRACE
JEFFERSON DR
PK
IRVING CT
WASHINGTON CT
TERRACE
TRESTLE GLEN TER
VIRGINIA
SILVERADO DR
COMSTOCK
SIERRA CT
SONORA CT
STEWART DR
TENAYA
SUTTER CT
AUBURN CT
ROSEVILLE CT
REDDING CT
STEWART DR
PORTO MARINO
HACIENDA
TANFIELD RD
ACACIA DR
MARK
GELDERT DR
NOCHE VISTA DR
HARN CT
MALVINO CT
WILKINS CT
GELDERT CT
HOWARD DR
ROWLEY CIR
HILARY DR
JR HS
MIRAFLORES AVENIDA
MIRAFLORES LN
FRANCISCO VISTA CT
FELIPA CT
THERESA CT
MARA VISTA CT
DELMAR DR
HILL DR
HILARY
HAWTHORNE
ROCK DR
GREENWOOD BEACH RD
PINE TER
MC CART CT
SOMMER CT
PALMER AV
VIA PARAISO W
VIA PARAISO E
GILMARTIN DR
ROUND HALCYON CT
MT
HILL
STONY HILL RD
TIBURON BL
SAN RAFAEL AV
131
MACANNAN CT
ROLLING HILL RD
SPRING LN
TARA HILL RD
TARA VIEW RD
OWLSWOOD LN
PLACE MOULIN
TIBURON RD
MT TIBURON CT
SUGAR LOAF DR
VENADO DR
HEATHCLIFF DR
GABRIELE
ST CT
LYFORD DR
MEADOW HILL
BARTEL CT
SANTA ANA CT
ACELA DR
AUDREY CT
BERKE CT
MARINERO CIR
VISTAZO WEST ST
HILARITA CIR
LAGOON RD
NEDS WY
WINDWARD RD
MAYBRIDGE RD
CH
RED HILL CIR
DAVIS DR
LYFORD DR
OLD
CT

4400 4300 1000 3900 3700 3600 3400 100 600 800 900 1000 200

1

4 5 6

SEE INSET PAGE 14

SEE 12D MAP

SEE 14 MAP

DETAIL

SEE 14 MAP

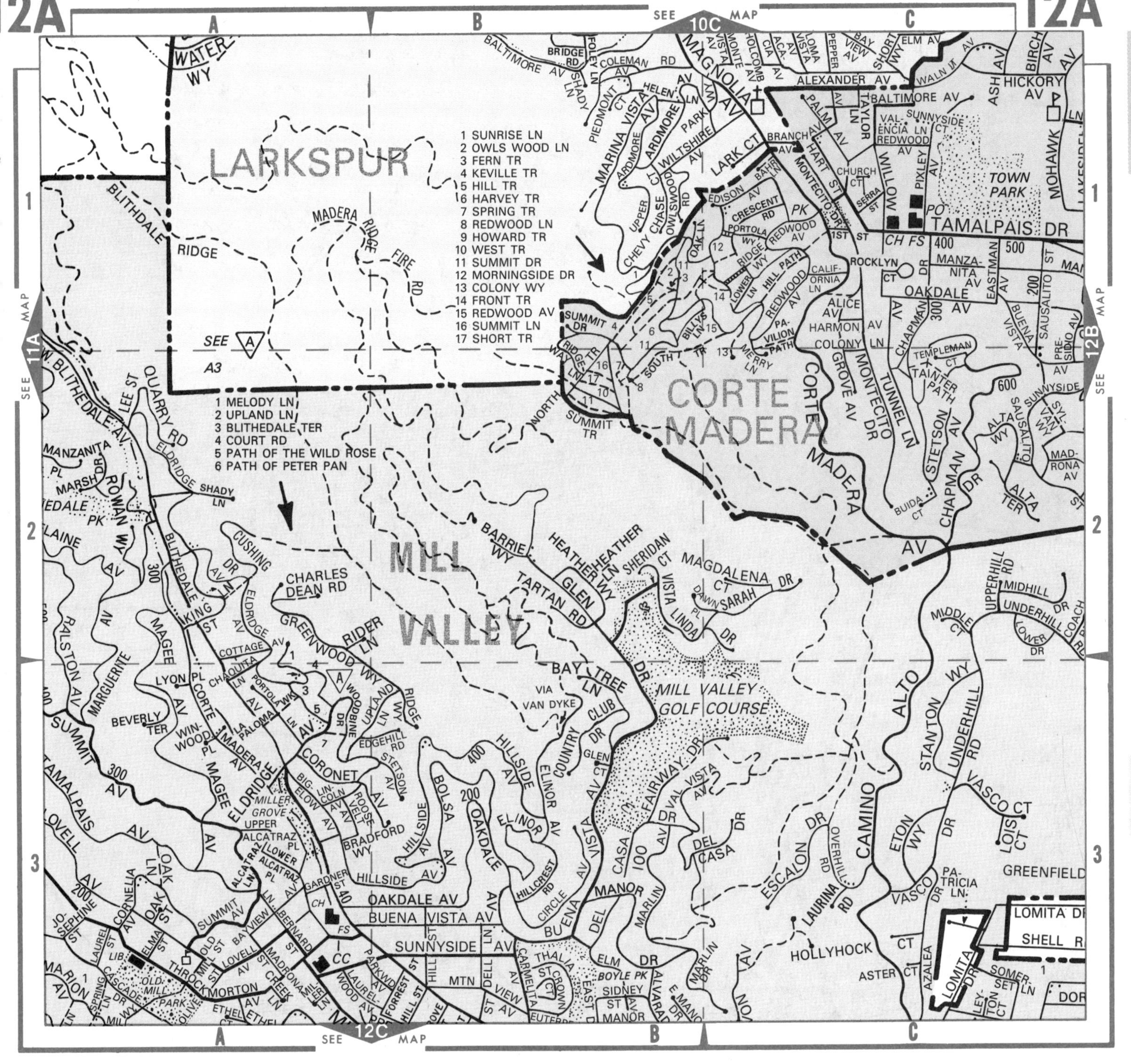
12A
SEE 10C MAP
SEE 11A MAP
SEE 12B MAP
SEE 12C MAP
MARIN CO
DETAIL
LARKSPUR
CORTE MADERA
MILL VALLEY
MILL VALLEY GOLF COURSE
TOWN PARK
BOYLE PK
1 SUNRISE LN
2 OWLS WOOD LN
3 FERN TR
4 KEVILLE TR
5 HILL TR
6 HARVEY TR
7 SPRING TR
8 REDWOOD LN
9 HOWARD TR
10 WEST TR
11 SUMMIT DR
12 MORNINGSIDE DR
13 COLONY WY
14 FRONT TR
15 REDWOOD AV
16 SUMMIT LN
17 SHORT TR
1 MELODY LN
2 UPLAND LN
3 BLITHEDALE TER
4 COURT RD
5 PATH OF THE WILD ROSE
6 PATH OF PETER PAN
SEE A A3
BALTIMORE AV
WATER WY
BLITHEDALE RIDGE
MADERA RIDGE FIRE RD
MAGNOLIA AV
ALEXANDER AV
TAMALPAIS DR
CORTE MADERA AV
CHAPMAN DR
CAMINO ALTO
OAKDALE AV
BUENA VISTA AV
SUNNYSIDE AV
THROCKMORTON AV
MILLER AV
E. BLITHEDALE AV
W. BLITHEDALE AV
SUMMIT AV
CORTE MADERA AV
ELDRIDGE AV
MAGEE AV
CASCADE DR
GREENWOOD WY
HEATHER WY
TARTAN RD
BAY TREE LN
SHERIDAN CT
MAGDALENA CT
VISTA LINDA DR
SARAH DR
FAIRWAY DR
COUNTRY CLUB DR
HILLSIDE AV
ELINOR AV
ESCALON DR
LAURINA RD
HOLLYHOCK
STANTON WY
UNDERHILL RD
VASCO CT
LOIS CT
GREENFIELD
LOMITA DR
SHELL RD
ETON WY
OVERHILL RD
DEL CASA DR
VAL VISTA AV
MANOR DR
ALVARADO
MARLIN DR
HILLCREST RD
CORONET AV
CHARLES DEAN RD
RIDER LN
CUSHING DR
KING ST
QUARRY RD
LEE ST
ROWAN WY
MARSH DR
MANZANITA PL
RALSTON AV
MARGUERITE AV
BEVERLY TER
LYON PL
COTTAGE AV
UPLAND WY
WOODBINE DR
EDGEHILL RD
BOLSA AV
BRADFORD WY
TUNNEL LN
MONTECITO DR
GROVE AV
STETSON AV
TEMPLEMAN CT
TAINTER PATH
SAUSALITO ST
BUENA VISTA
OAKDALE AV
MANZANITA AV
ROCKLYN CT
EASTMAN AV
MOHAWK AV
HICKORY AV
BIRCH AV
PIXLEY AV
WILLOW AV
SUNNYSIDE CT
REDWOOD AV
LARK CT
WILTSHIRE AV
ARDMORE AV
MARINA VISTA AV
CHEVY CHASE
PIEDMONT CT
COLEMAN RD
FOLEY LN
BRIDGE RD
SHADY LN
SUMMIT DR
NORTH SUMMIT TR
SOUTH TR
BARRIE WY
GLEN LN
HEATHER LN
VIA VAN DYKE
LOMITA DR
SOMERSET LN
AZALEA
ASTER CT
PATRICIA LN
MIDHILL DR
UPPERHILL RD
LOWER DR
MIDDLE CT
ALTA WY
ALTA TER
MADRONA AV
BUIDA CT
HARMON AV
COLONY LN
ALICE AV
CALIFORNIA LN
PAVILION PATH
MERRY LN
BILLYS LN
HILL PATH
REDWOOD WY
RIDGE WY
CRESCENT RD
EDISON AV
OAK LN
PORTOLA WY
CH FS
PO
CH FS CC LIB
OLD MILL PARK
JOSEPHINE ST
CORNELIA AV
OAK ST
ELMA ST
LAUREL ST
LOVELL AV
MADRONA ST
BERNARD ST
GARDNER ST
HILLSIDE AV
ALCATRAZ
PARKWOOD
FORREST ST
HILL ST
MTN VIEW AV
DELL
CARMELITA
THALIA ST
CROWN CT
ELM
SIDNEY
ST MANOR
MARION
A B C 1 2 3

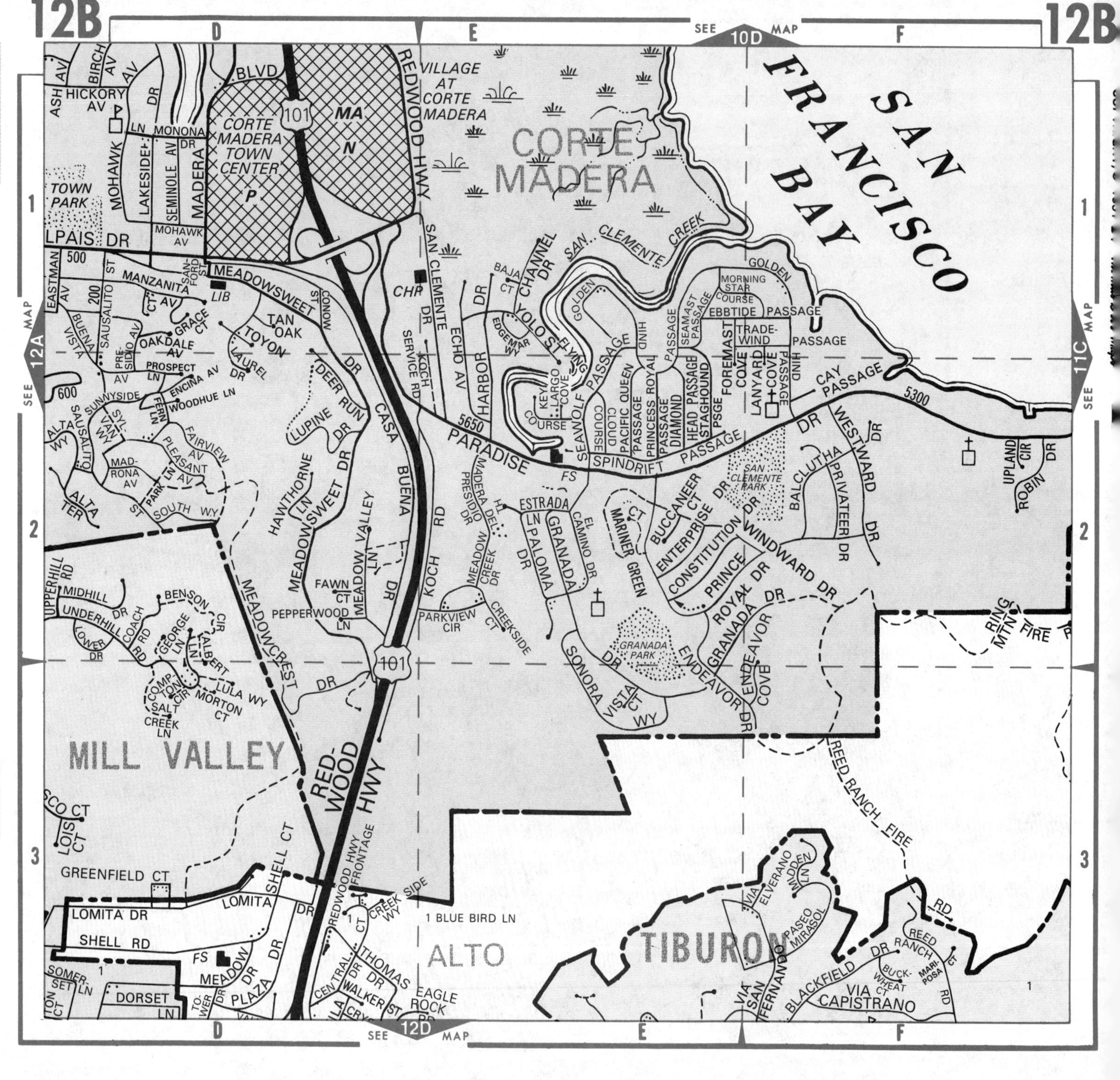

SEE 10D MAP
SEE 12A MAP
SEE 11C MAP
SEE 12D MAP
D
E
F
1
2
3
SAN FRANCISCO BAY
CORTE MADERA
VILLAGE AT CORTE MADERA
CORTE MADERA TOWN CENTER
MILL VALLEY
TIBURON
ALTO
TOWN PARK
SAN CLEMENTE PARK
GRANADA PARK
REDWOOD HWY
101
CASA BUENA DR
PARADISE DR
MEADOWSWEET DR
SAN CLEMENTE DR
SAN CLEMENTE CREEK
TAMALPAIS DR
MEADOWCREST DR
SPINDRIFT PASSAGE
CAY PASSAGE
GOLDEN HIND PASSAGE
WINDWARD DR
CONSTITUTION DR
ENTERPRISE DR
BUCCANEER CT
PRINCE ROYAL DR
GRANADA DR
ENDEAVOR DR
ENDEAVOR COVE
SONORA VISTA WY
MARINER GREEN CT
WESTWARD DR
PRIVATEER DR
BALCLUTHA DR
UPLAND CIR
ROBIN DR
RING MTN FIRE RD
REED RANCH FIRE RD
REED RANCH RD
BLACKFIELD DR
VIA CAPISTRANO
VIA SAN FERNANDO
PASEO MIRASOL
VIA ELVERANO
MADDEN LN
BUCKWHEAT CT
MARIPOSA CT
EAGLE ROCK RD
THOMAS DR
WALKER ST
CENTRAL DR
REDWOOD HWY FRONTAGE RD
CREEKSIDE CT
1 BLUE BIRD LN
LOMITA DR
SHELL RD
SHELL CT
GREENFIELD CT
MEADOW DR
PLAZA DR
DORSET LN
SOMERSET LN
FS
LIB
CHP
5650
5300
500
600
200

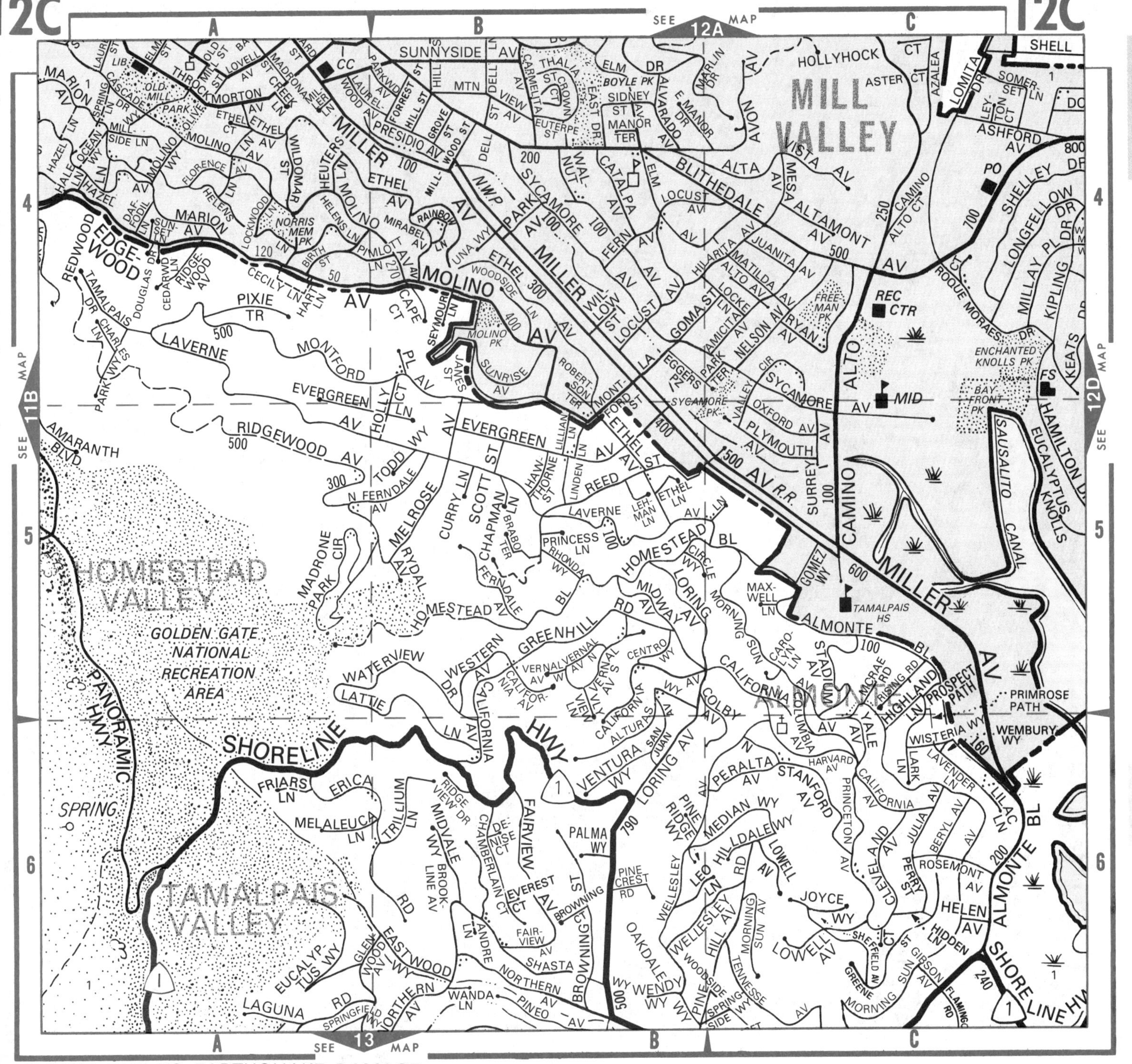

CLOSED DUE TO EARTHQUAKE DAMAGE

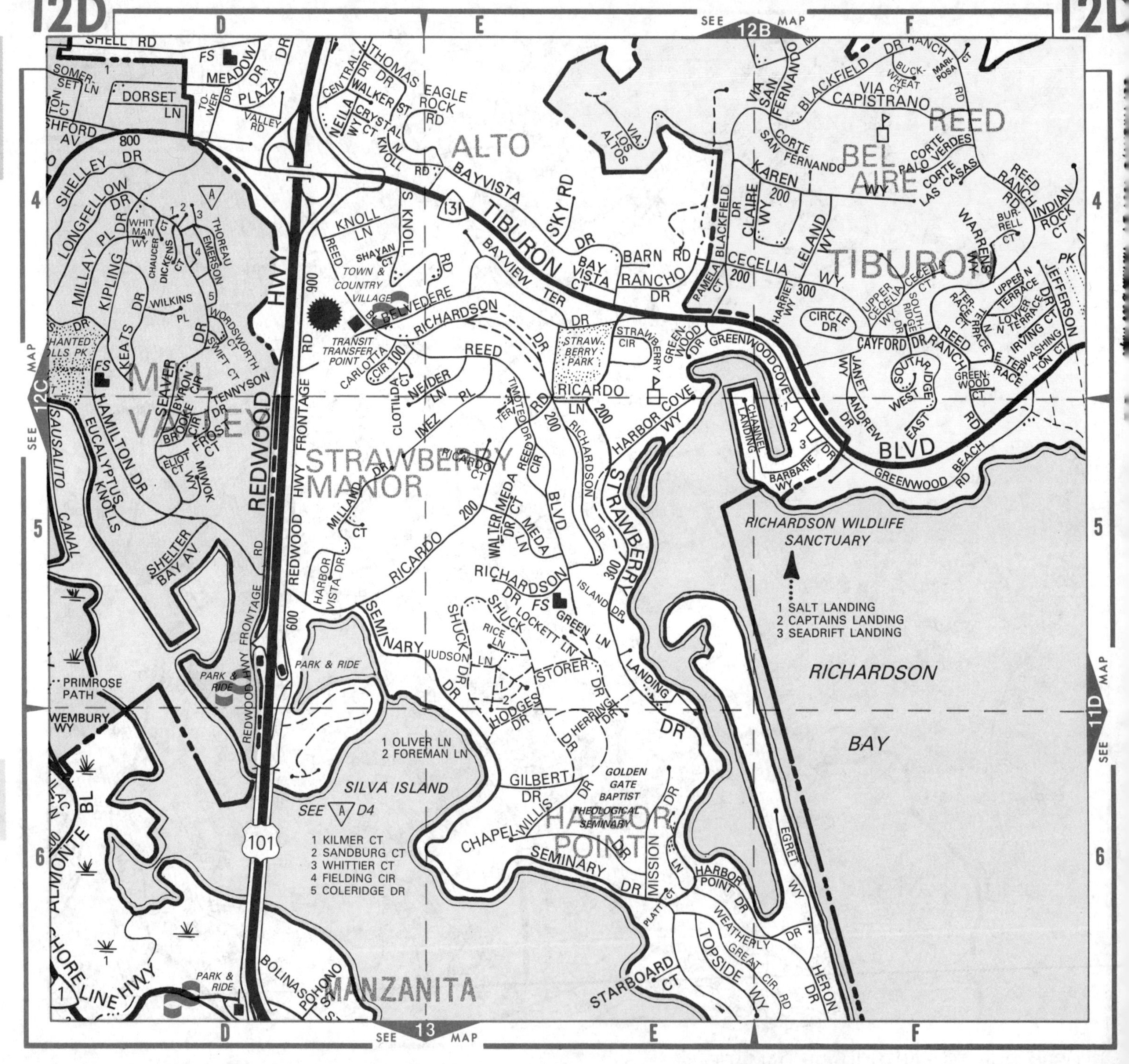

MARIN CO
DETAIL
SEE 12B MAP
SEE 12C MAP
SEE 11D MAP
SEE 13 MAP
ALTO
REED
BEL AIRE
TIBURON
MILL VALLEY
STRAWBERRY MANOR
HARBOR POINT
MANZANITA
RICHARDSON WILDLIFE SANCTUARY
1 SALT LANDING
2 CAPTAINS LANDING
3 SEADRIFT LANDING
RICHARDSON BAY
SILVA ISLAND
SEE A D4
1 KILMER CT
2 SANDBURG CT
3 WHITTIER CT
4 FIELDING CIR
5 COLERIDGE DR
1 OLIVER LN
2 FOREMAN LN
GOLDEN GATE BAPTIST THEOLOGICAL SEMINARY
TRANSIT TRANSFER POINT
TOWN & COUNTRY VILLAGE
STRAWBERRY PARK
PARK & RIDE
PRIMROSE PATH
REDWOOD HWY
TIBURON BLVD
SHORELINE HWY
101
131
1
SHELL RD
MEADOW DR
PLAZA DR
DORSET LN
SHELLEY DR
LONGFELLOW DR
MILLAY PL
KIPLING DR
KEATS DR
WILKINS PL
THOREAU
EMERSON
WORDSWORTH CT
TENNYSON
SEAVER DR
BYRON CIR
FROST CT
EUCALYPTUS KNOLLS
HAMILTON DR
SAUSALITO CANAL
SHELTER BAY AV
REDWOOD HWY FRONTAGE RD
THOMAS DR
WALKER ST
EAGLE ROCK RD
BAYVISTA
KNOLL LN
BAYVIEW TER
BELVEDERE
RICHARDSON DR
REED RD
RICARDO RD
STRAWBERRY DR
SEMINARY DR
GREENWOOD BEACH RD
GREENWOOD COVE DR
HARBOR COVE WY
CHANNEL LANDING
BARBARIE WY
BLACKFIELD DR
CECELIA WY
LELAND WY
CLAIRE WY
KAREN WY
VIA CAPISTRANO
CORTE SAN FERNANDO
REED RANCH RD
INDIAN ROCK CT
JEFFERSON
CAYFORD DR
SOUTH RIDGE
STARBOARD CT
TOPSIDE WY
HERON DR
EGRET WY
WEATHERLY DR
GILBERT DR
CHAPEL
MISSION DR
HARBOR POINT DR
BOLINAS
POHONO ST
ALMONTE BL
WEMBURY WY

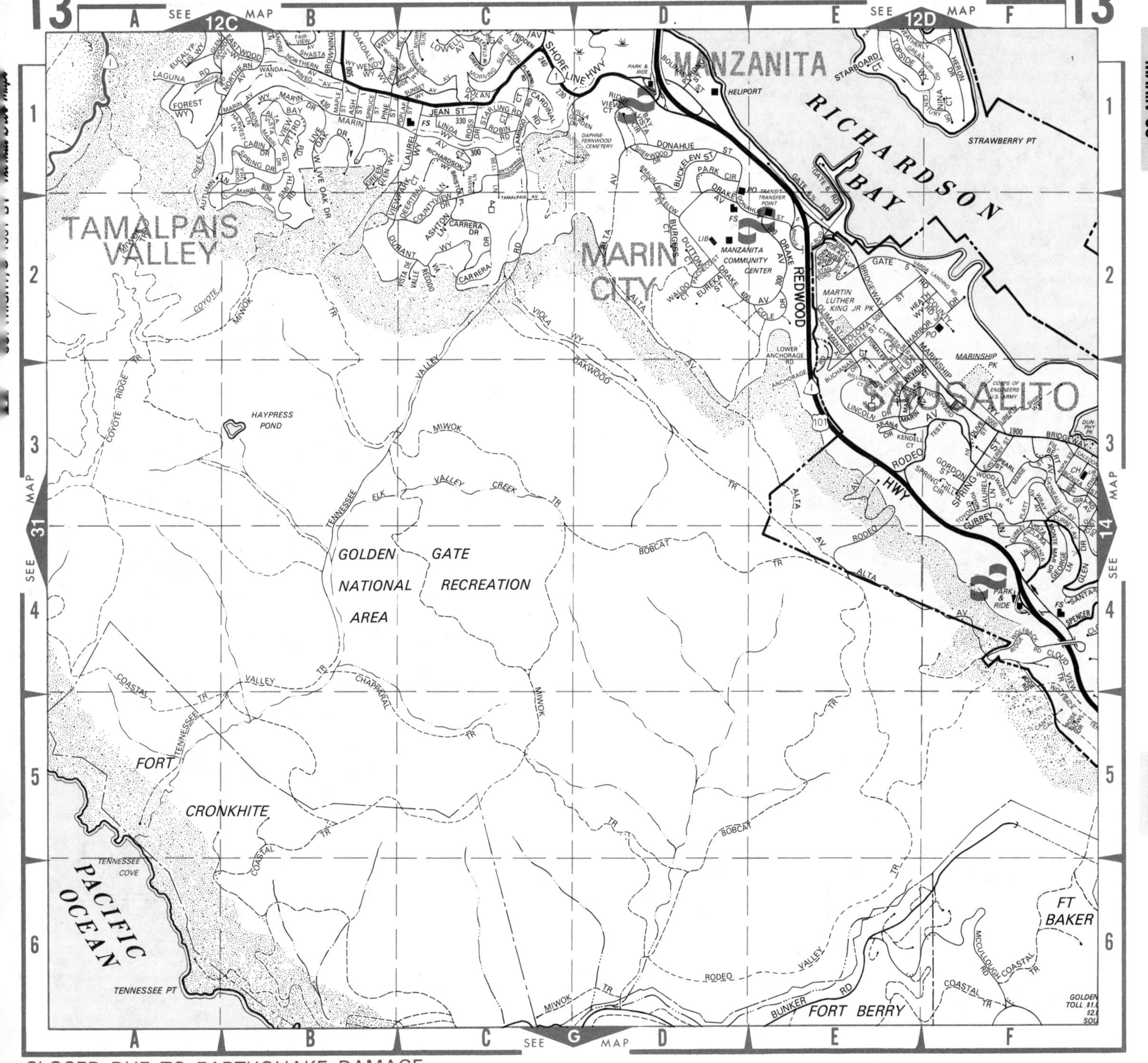

CLOSED DUE TO EARTHQUAKE DAMAGE

SEE MAP 11D

MARIN CO

RICHARDSON BAY

BELVEDERE

SAUSALITO

TIBURON

HILL HAVEN

RACCOON STRAIT

ANGEL ISLAND

ANGEL ISLAND STATE PARK

SAN FRANCISCO BAY

MARIN CO

SAN FRANCISCO CO

SEE INSET BELOW

SEE A D1
1 ESPERANZA AV
2 CAZADERO LN

1 TOWER POINT LN
2 RESERVA LN

1 HUMBOLT ST
2 PARK ST
3 EL PORTAL

FOR CONTINUATION SEE MAP 11D

INSET MAP

FOR CONTINUATION SEE GRID D1

GOLDEN GATE BRIDGE
TOLL $1.00 SUN – THURS
$2.00 FRI – SAT
SOUTHBOUND ONLY

DETAIL

SEE 13 MAP

SEE G MAP

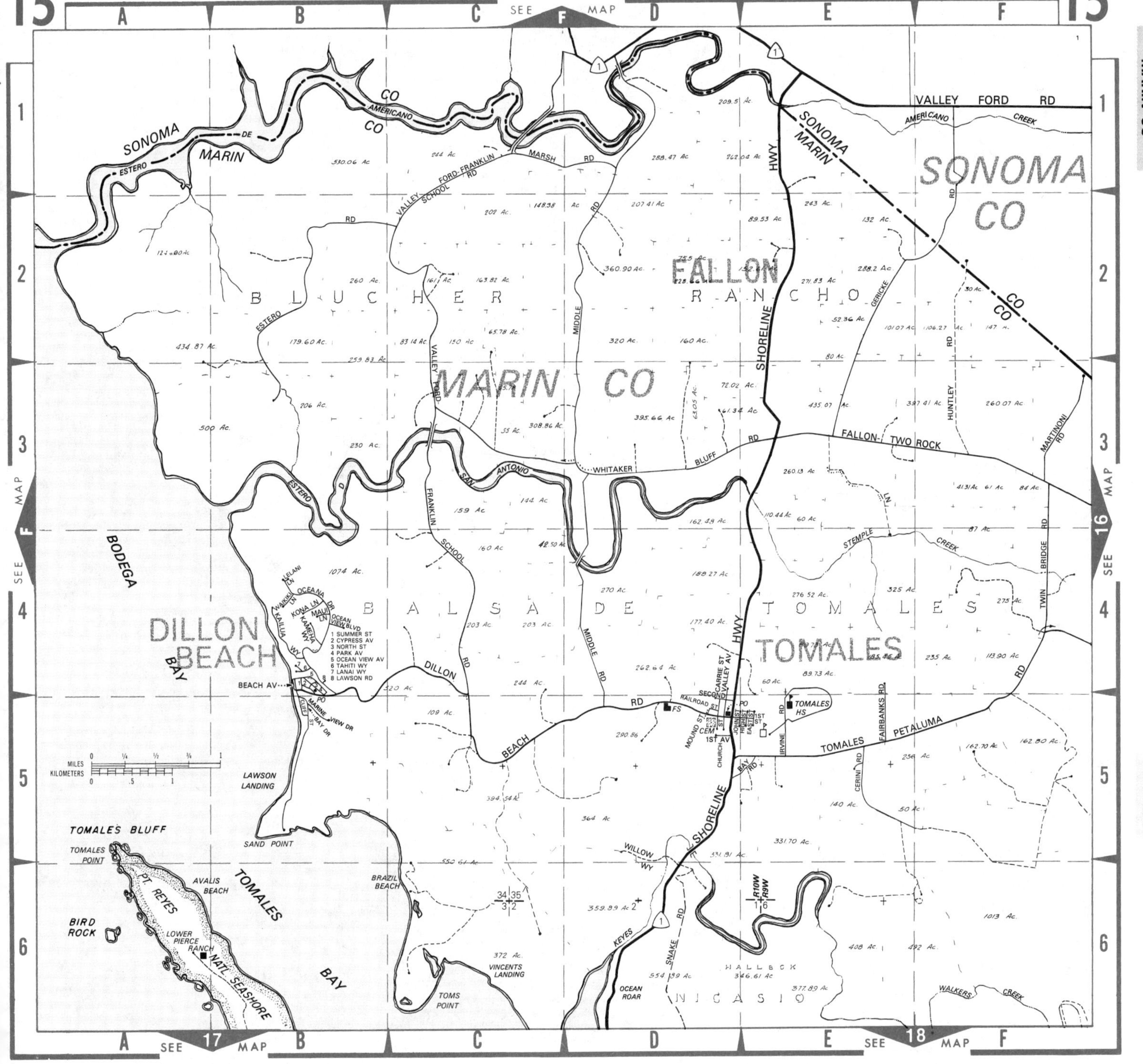
SEE F MAP
SONOMA CO
MARIN CO
ESTERO AMERICANO
VALLEY FORD RD
AMERICANO CREEK
SONOMA
MARIN
SONOMA CO
VALLEY FORD-FRANKLIN SCHOOL RD
MARSH RD
BLUCHER
FALLON
RANCHO
MARIN CO
SHORELINE HWY
MIDDLE RD
GERICKE RD
HUNTLEY
FALLON-TWO ROCK RD
WHITAKER BLUFF RD
MARTINONI RD
ESTERO SAN ANTONIO
FRANKLIN SCHOOL
STEMPLE CREEK
TWIN BRIDGE RD
BODEGA BAY
DILLON BEACH
BALSA DE TOMALES
TOMALES
DILLON BEACH RD
LELANI LN
OCEANA DR
KONA LN
MAUI LN
KAMEHA WY
KAILUA WY
WAIKIKI LN
OCEAN VIEW BLVD
1 SUMMER ST
2 CYPRESS AV
3 NORTH ST
4 PARK AV
5 OCEAN VIEW AV
6 TAHITI WY
7 LANAI WY
8 LAWSON RD
BEACH AV
MARINE VIEW DR
BAY DR
CLIFF ST
FS
CEM
PO
TOMALES HS
SECOND
CARRIE ST
VALLEY AV
RAILROAD ST
MOUND ST
CHURCH ST
1ST AV
TOMALES PETALUMA RD
IRVINE RD
FAIRBANKS RD
CERINI RD
BAY RD
LAWSON LANDING
SAND POINT
TOMALES BLUFF
TOMALES POINT
AVALIS BEACH
BIRD ROCK
LOWER PIERCE RANCH
PT. REYES NATL SEASHORE
TOMALES BAY
BRAZIL BEACH
VINCENTS LANDING
TOMS POINT
WILLOW WY
KEYES
SNAKE RD
OCEAN ROAR
HALLECK
NICASIO
WALKERS CREEK
R10W R9W
MILES 0 1/4 1/2 3/4 1
KILOMETERS 0 .5 1
SEE 16 MAP
SEE 17 MAP
SEE 18 MAP
MARIN CO
DETAIL

MARIN CO

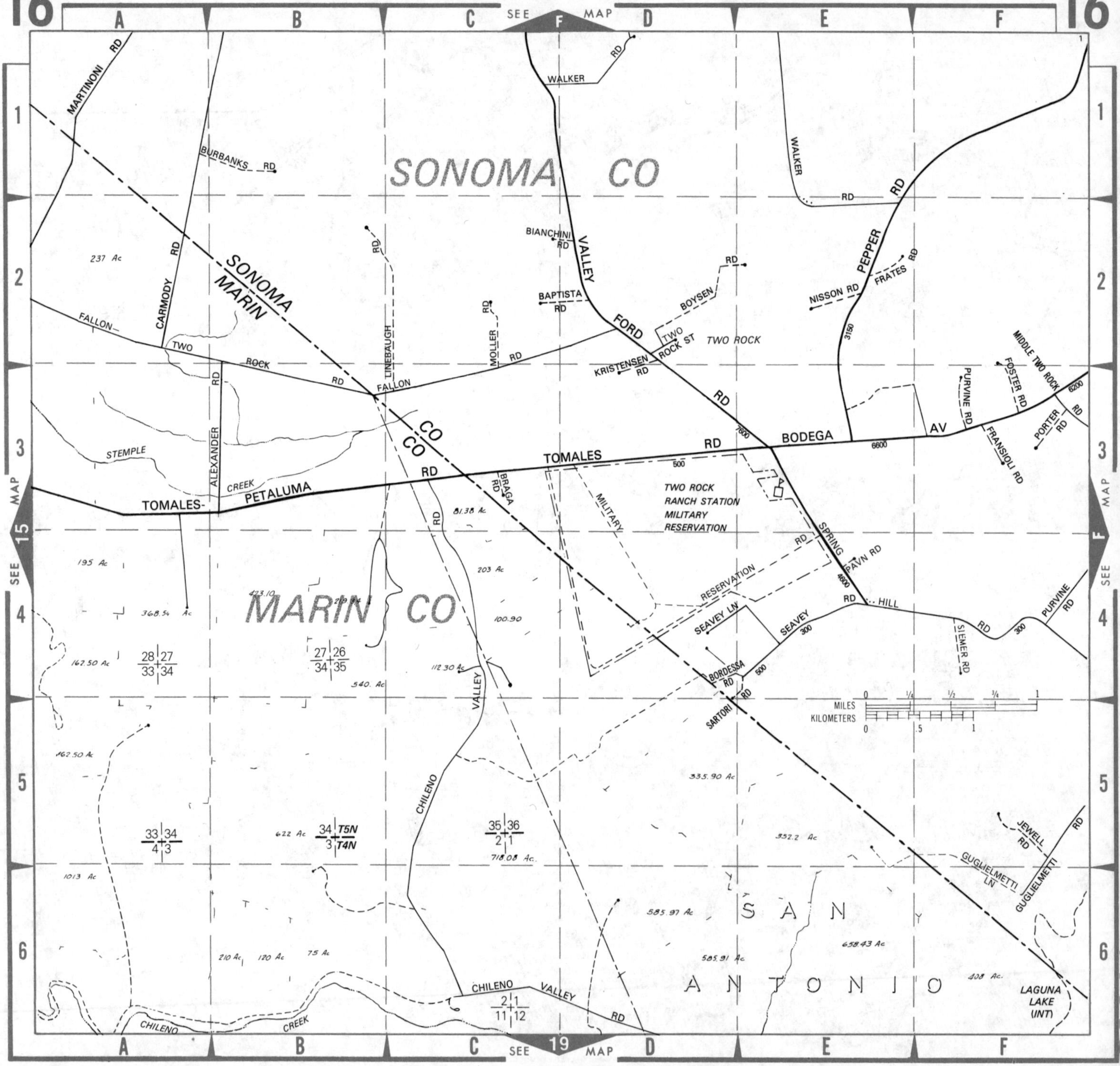
SEE F MAP
SEE 15 MAP
SEE F MAP
SEE 19 MAP
A
B
C
D
E
F
1
2
3
4
5
6
SONOMA CO
MARIN CO
SONOMA MARIN CO CO
MARTINONI RD
BURBANKS RD
WALKER RD
WALKER
VALLEY FORD RD
BIANCHINI RD
BAPTISTA RD
BOYSEN RD
NISSON RD
FRATES RD
PEPPER RD
3150
CARMODY RD
FALLON TWO ROCK RD
FALLON
LINEBAUGH RD
MOLLER RD
TWO ROCK ST
TWO ROCK
KRISTENSEN RD
MIDDLE TWO ROCK
FOSTER RD
PURVINE RD
6200
RD
PORTER RD
FRANSIOLI RD
ALEXANDER RD
STEMPLE CREEK
TOMALES- PETALUMA RD
TOMALES RD
BODEGA AV
7600
6600
500
BRAGA RD
MILITARY
TWO ROCK RANCH STATION MILITARY RESERVATION
RESERVATION
SPRING RD
PAVN RD
4600
HILL RD
SEAVEY LN
SEAVEY
300
SIEMER RD
PURVINE RD
BORDESSA RD
SARTORI RD
MILES 0 1/4 1/2 3/4 1
KILOMETERS 0 .5 1
237 Ac
195 Ac
81.38 Ac
203 Ac
423.10
368.54 Ac
100.90
167.50 Ac
28 27 33 34
27 26 34 35
112.30 Ac
540. Ac
162.50 Ac
335.90 Ac
33 34 4 3
622 Ac
34 T5N 3 T4N
35 36 2 1
718.08 Ac.
352.2 Ac
JEWELL RD
GUGLIELMETTI LN
GUGLIELMETTI
RD
1013 Ac
585.97 Ac
SAN ANTONIO
658.43 Ac
585.91 Ac
210 Ac
120 Ac
75 Ac
408 Ac.
CHILENO VALLEY RD
CHILENO CREEK
LAGUNA LAKE (INT)

DETAIL

16

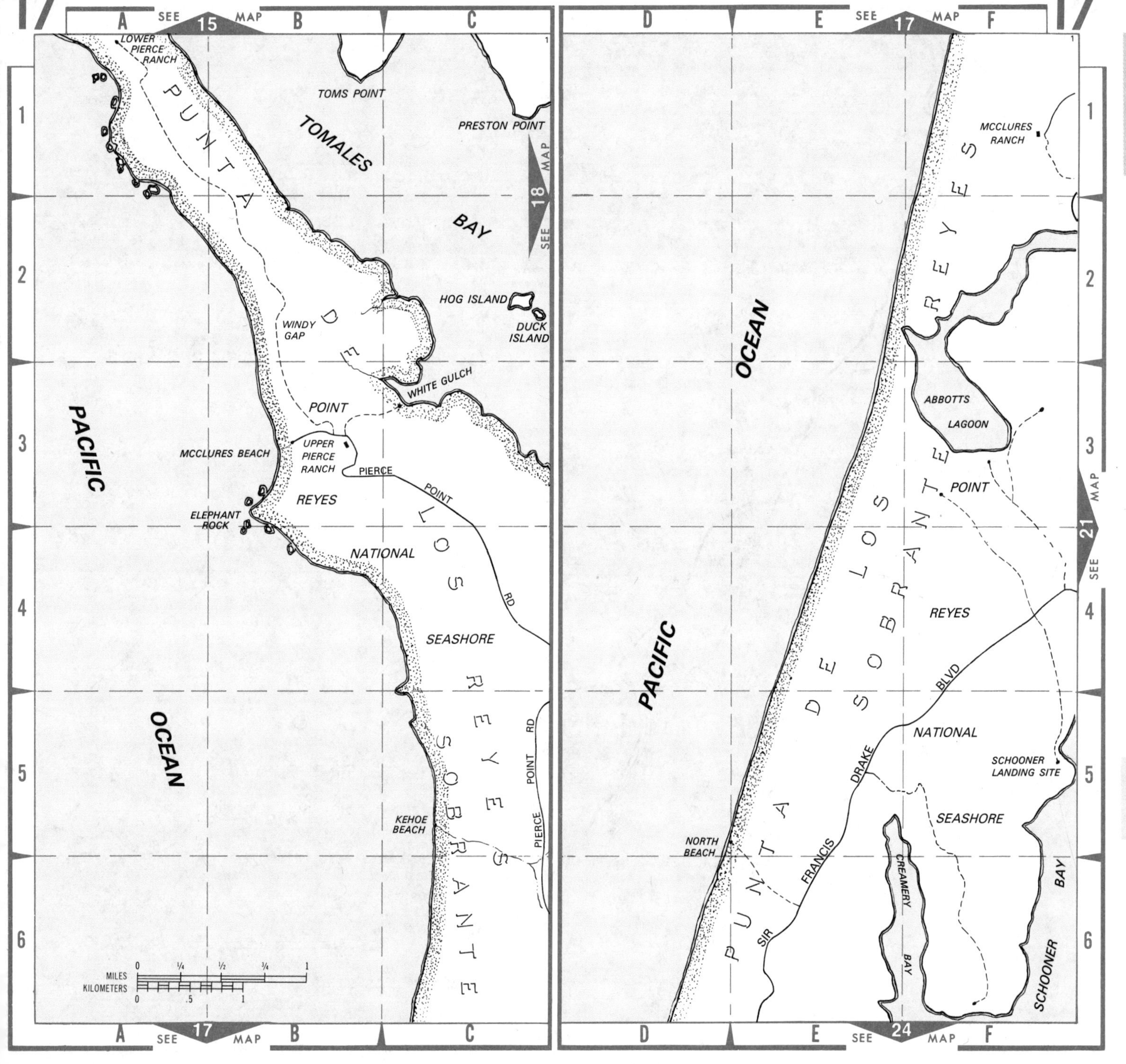

SEE 15 MAP
SEE 17 MAP
SEE 18 MAP
SEE 21 MAP
SEE 17 MAP
SEE 24 MAP
MARIN CO
DETAIL
LOWER PIERCE RANCH
TOMS POINT
PRESTON POINT
TOMALES
BAY
PUNTA DE LOS REYES
HOG ISLAND
DUCK ISLAND
WINDY GAP
WHITE GULCH
POINT
PACIFIC
OCEAN
MCCLURES BEACH
UPPER PIERCE RANCH
PIERCE POINT RD
REYES
ELEPHANT ROCK
NATIONAL
SEASHORE
PUNTA DE LOS REYES SOBRANTE
KEHOE BEACH
PIERCE POINT RD
MILES
KILOMETERS
MCCLURES RANCH
ABBOTTS LAGOON
POINT
REYES
NATIONAL
SEASHORE
SIR FRANCIS DRAKE BLVD
SCHOONER LANDING SITE
NORTH BEACH
CREAMERY BAY
SCHOONER BAY

18

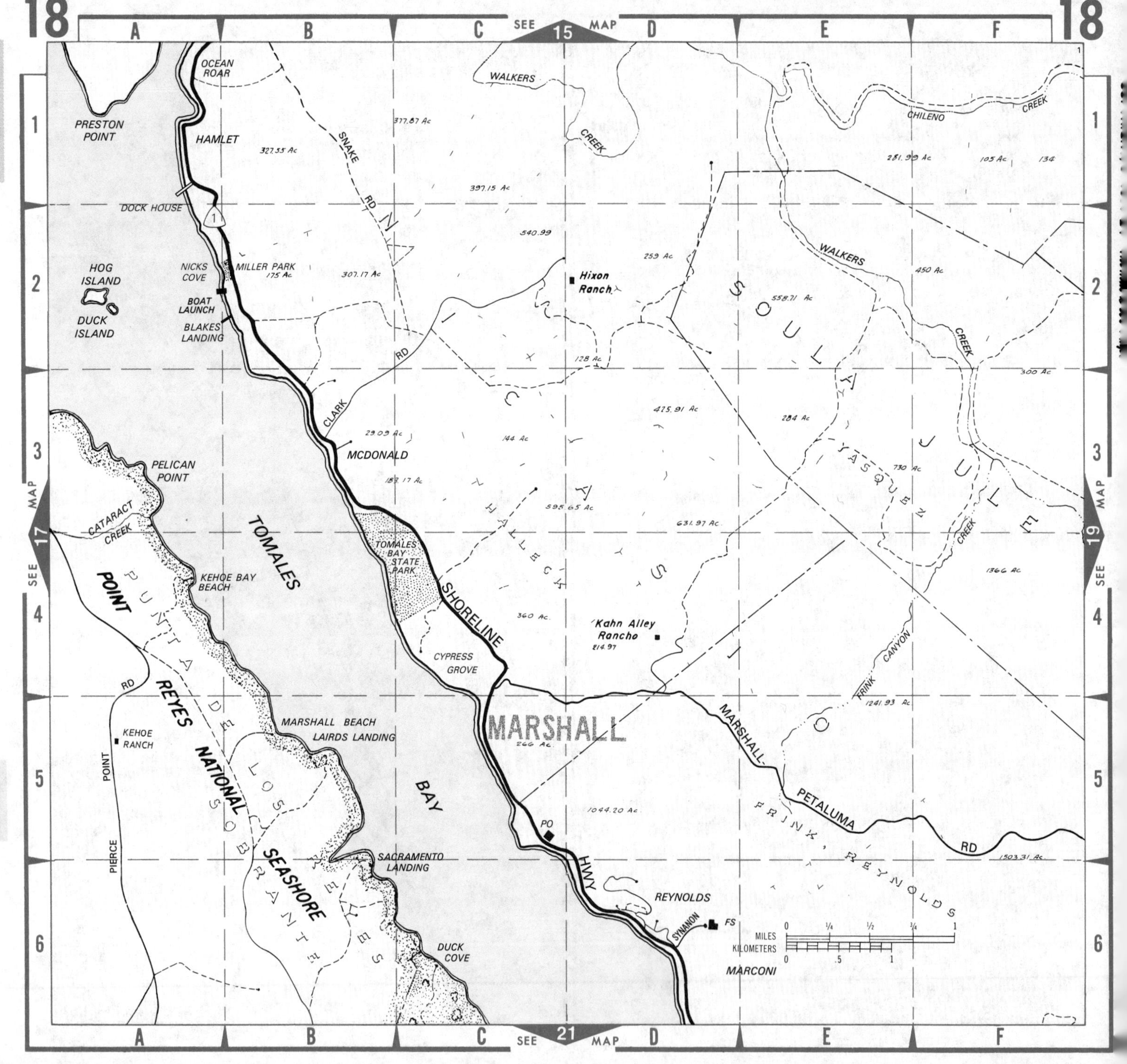
MARIN CO
SEE 15 MAP
A
B
C
D
E
F
1
2
3
4
5
6
OCEAN ROAR
PRESTON POINT
HAMLET
WALKERS
CREEK
CHILENO
CREEK
SNAKE RD
377.87 Ac
327.55 Ac
397.15 Ac
281.93 Ac
105 Ac
134
DOCK HOUSE
1
540.99
259 Ac
WALKERS
450 Ac
HOG ISLAND
DUCK ISLAND
NICKS COVE
MILLER PARK
175 Ac
307.17 Ac
Hixon Ranch
558.71 Ac
BOAT LAUNCH
BLAKES LANDING
CREEK
RD
128 Ac
300 Ac
CLARK
29.09 Ac
MCDONALD
144 Ac
425.91 Ac
284 Ac
730 Ac
PELICAN POINT
183.17 Ac
595.65 Ac
631.97 Ac
CATARACT CREEK
TOMALES
TOMALES BAY STATE PARK
SHORELINE
KEHOE BAY BEACH
POINT
1366 Ac
360 Ac
Kahn Alley Rancho
214.97
CYPRESS GROVE
RD
FRINK CANYON
MARSHALL
MARSHALL
266 Ac
1241.93 Ac
KEHOE RANCH
REYES NATIONAL
MARSHALL BEACH
LAIRDS LANDING
POINT
BAY
PETALUMA
1044.20 Ac
PO
RD
1503.31 Ac
PIERCE
SEASHORE
SACRAMENTO LANDING
HWY
REYNOLDS
SYNANON
FS
MILES
KILOMETERS
0
1/4
1/2
3/4
1
0
.5
1
DUCK COVE
MARCONI
SEE 17 MAP
SEE 19 MAP
SEE 21 MAP
DETAIL

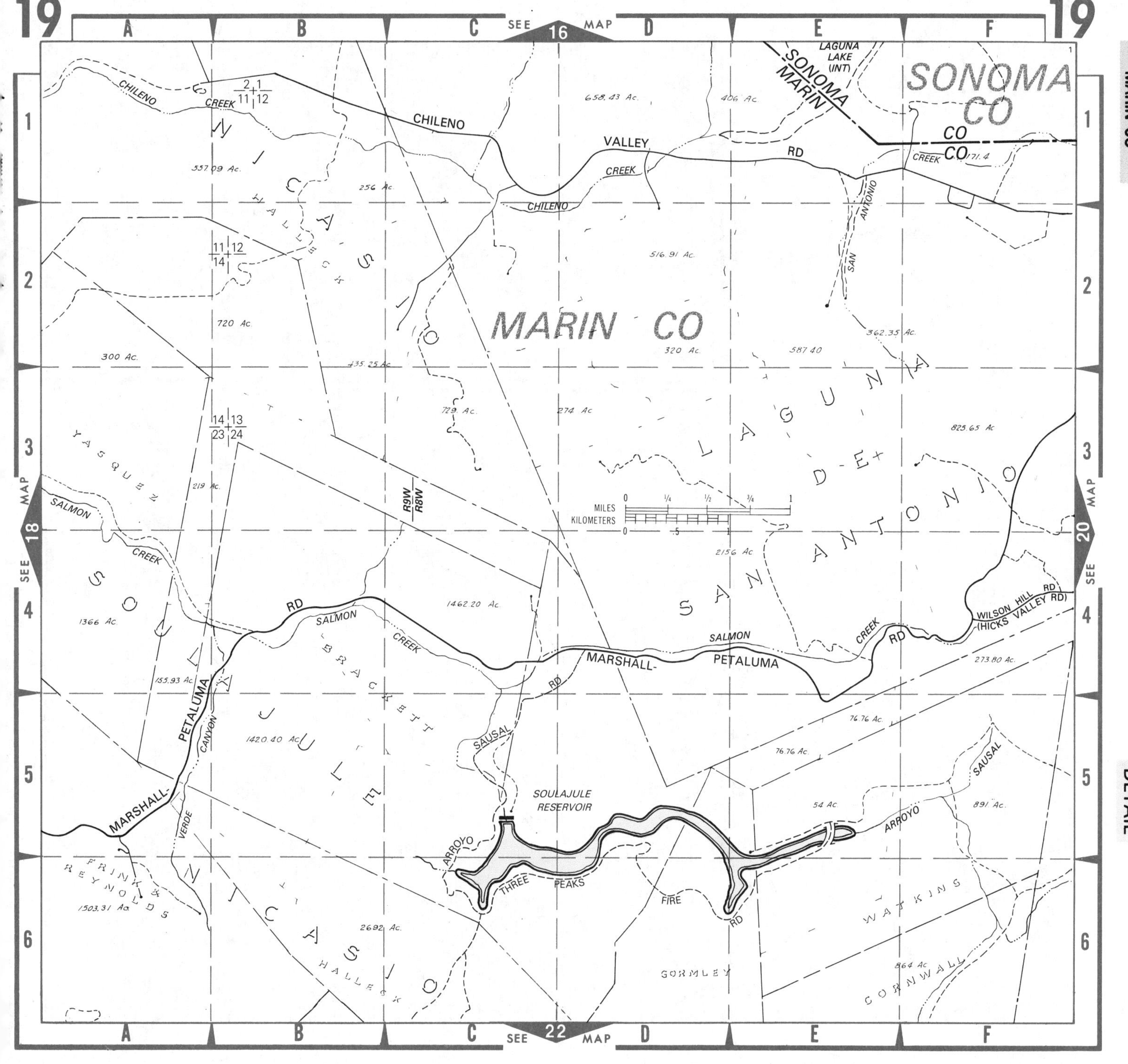
SEE MAP 16
SEE MAP 18
SEE MAP 20
SEE MAP 22
MARIN CO
DETAIL
SONOMA CO
MARIN CO
LAGUNA LAKE (INT)
SONOMA
MARIN
CHILENO VALLEY RD
CHILENO CREEK
SAN ANTONIO
LAGUNA DE SAN ANTONIO
NICASIO
HALLECK
YASQUEN
SOULAJULE
SALMON CREEK
MARSHALL-PETALUMA RD
WILSON HILL RD (HICKS VALLEY RD)
BRACKETT
SAUSAL
SOULAJULE RESERVOIR
ARROYO
THREE PEAKS FIRE RD
CANYON
VERDE
FRINK & REYNOLDS
WATKINS
CORNWALL
GORMLEY
R9W R8W
MILES
KILOMETERS
658.43 Ac.
406 Ac.
557.09 Ac.
256 Ac.
171.4
516.91 Ac.
720 Ac.
300 Ac.
435.25 Ac.
320 Ac.
587.40
362.35 Ac.
729 Ac.
274 Ac.
825.65 Ac.
219 Ac.
2156 Ac.
1366 Ac.
1462.20 Ac.
155.93 Ac.
273.80 Ac.
1420.40 Ac.
76.76 Ac.
54 Ac.
891 Ac.
1503.31 Ac.
2692 Ac.
864 Ac.

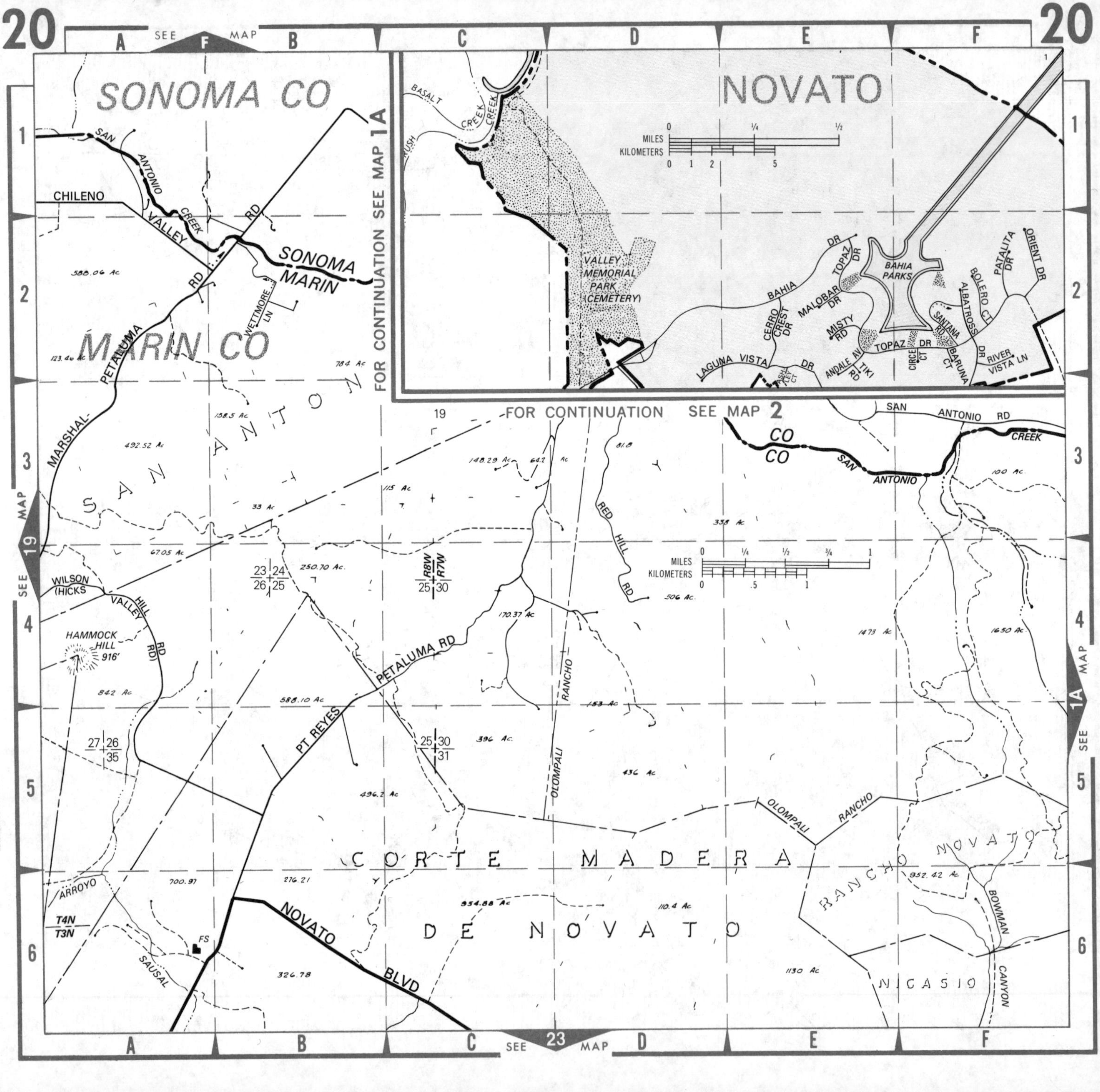

SEE F MAP
A B C D E F
1 2 3 4 5 6
MARIN CO
DETAIL
SONOMA CO
MARIN CO
NOVATO
FOR CONTINUATION SEE MAP 1A
FOR CONTINUATION SEE MAP 2
SEE 19 MAP
SEE 1A MAP
SEE 23 MAP
SAN ANTONIO CREEK
CHILENO VALLEY RD
SONOMA
MARIN
WETTMORE LN
PETALUMA
MARSHAL-PETALUMA RD
SAN ANTON
WILSON (HICKS VALLEY HILL RD)
HAMMOCK HILL 916'
RED HILL RD
PETALUMA RD
PT REYES
OLOMPALI RANCHO
CORTE MADERA DE NOVATO
RANCHO NOVATO
NICASIO
NOVATO BLVD
ARROYO
SAUSAL
T4N
T3N
FS
BOWMAN CANYON
SAN ANTONIO RD
CO
CO
SAN ANTONIO CREEK
BASALT
CREEK
RUSH
VALLEY MEMORIAL PARK (CEMETERY)
BAHIA
BAHIA PARKS
TOPAZ DR
MALOBAR DR
CERRO CREST DR
MISTY RD
LAGUNA VISTA DR
ANDALE AV
TIKI RD
CIRCE CT
BARUNA CT
SANTANA RD
ALBATROSS
BOLERO CT
PATALITA DR
ORIENT DR
RIVER VISTA LN
MILES 0 1/4 1/2
KILOMETERS 0 1 2 5
MILES 0 1/4 1/2 3/4 1
KILOMETERS 0 .5 1
R8W R7W
23 24 26 25
25 30
27 26 35
25 30 31
19
588.06 Ac
123.4 Ac
784 Ac
138.5 Ac
492.52 Ac
33 Ac
67.05 Ac
148.29 Ac
64.2 Ac
81.8
115 Ac
338 Ac
100 Ac
250.70 Ac
506 Ac
170.37 Ac
1473 Ac
1650 Ac
842 Ac
588.10 Ac
153 Ac
396 Ac
436 Ac
496.2 Ac
700.97
276.21
354.88 Ac
110.4 Ac
952.42 Ac
326.78
1130 Ac

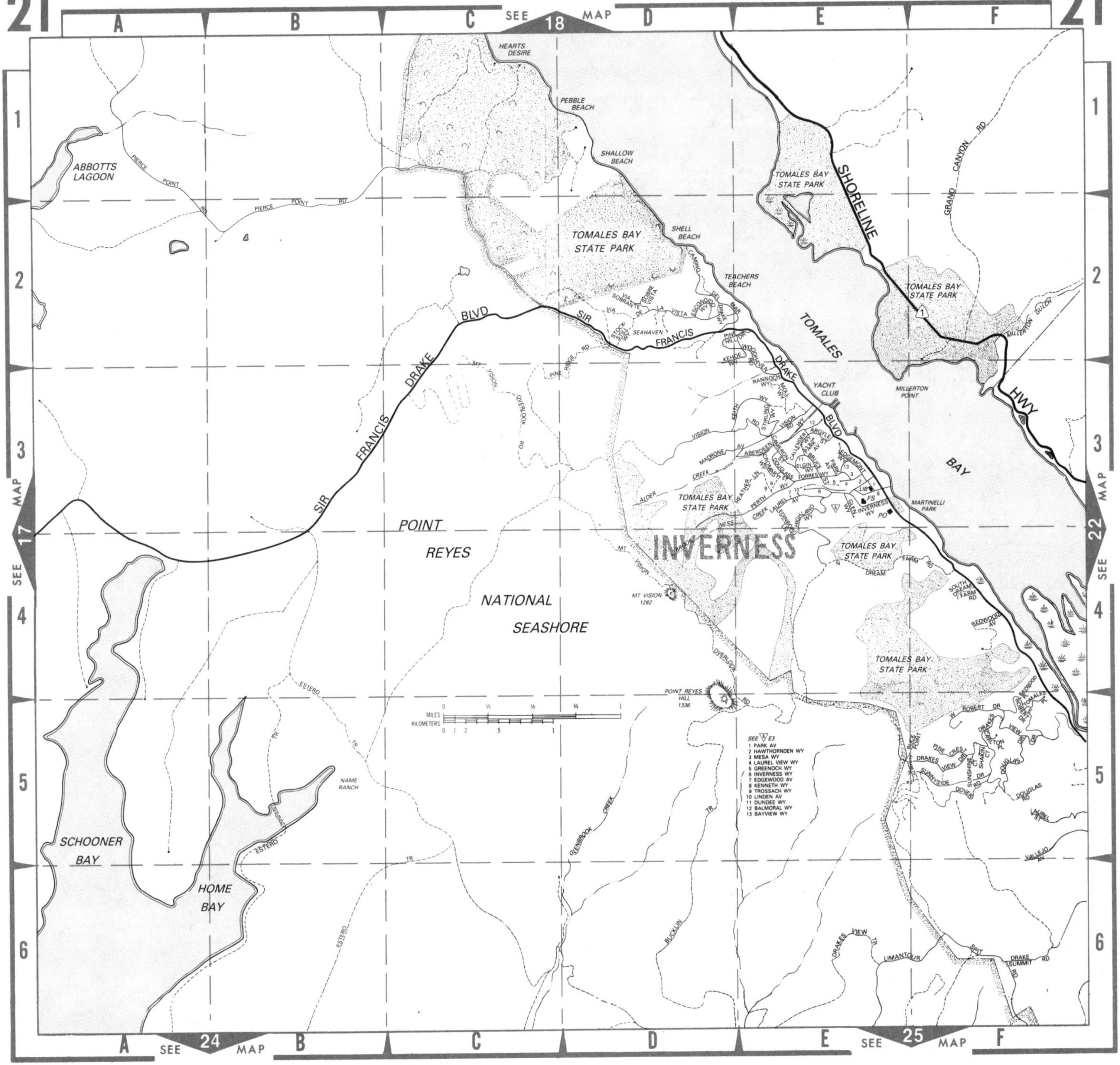

SEE 18 MAP

SEE 17 MAP

SEE 22 MAP

MARIN CO

DETAIL

A B C D E F

1 2 3 4 5 6

HEARTS DESIRE
PEBBLE BEACH
SHALLOW BEACH
ABBOTTS LAGOON
PIERCE POINT RD
TOMALES BAY STATE PARK
SHELL BEACH
TEACHERS BEACH
SHORELINE HWY
GRAND CANYON RD
MILLERTON GULCH
MILLERTON POINT
TOMALES BAY
YACHT CLUB
SIR FRANCIS DRAKE BLVD
PINE RIDGE RD
MT VISION OVERLOOK RD
MARTINELLI PARK
INVERNESS
POINT REYES NATIONAL SEASHORE
MT VISION 1282
POINT REYES HILL 1336
SOUTH DREAM FARM RD
REDWOOD AV
ESTERO TR
NAME RANCH
SCHOONER BAY
HOME BAY
GENBROOK CREEK
BUCKLIN TR
DRAKES VIEW TR
LIMANTOUR SPIT
DRAKE SUMMIT RD
VALLEJO AV
DOUGLAS RD
LAUREL ST

MILES 0 ¼ ½ ¾ 1
KILOMETERS 0 1 2 .5 1

SEE E3
1 PARK AV
2 HAWTHORNDEN WY
3 MESA WY
4 LAUREL VIEW WY
5 GREENOCH WY
6 INVERNESS WY
7 EDGEWOOD AV
8 KENNETH WY
9 TROSSACH WY
10 LINDEN AV
11 DUNDEE WY
12 BALMORAL WY
13 BAYVIEW WY

SEE 24 MAP

SEE 25 MAP

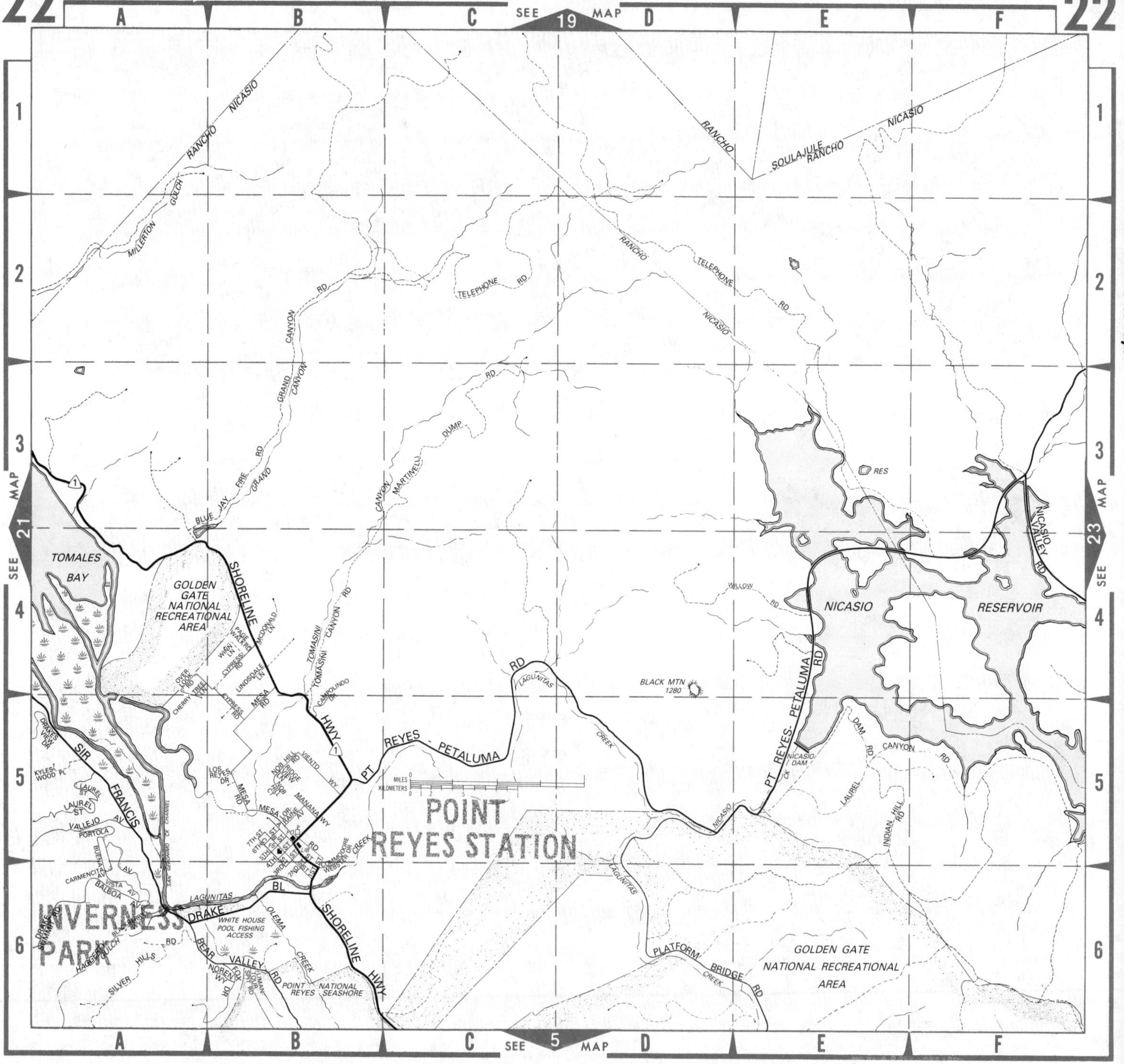

SEE 19 MAP

SEE 21 MAP

SEE 23 MAP

SEE 5 MAP

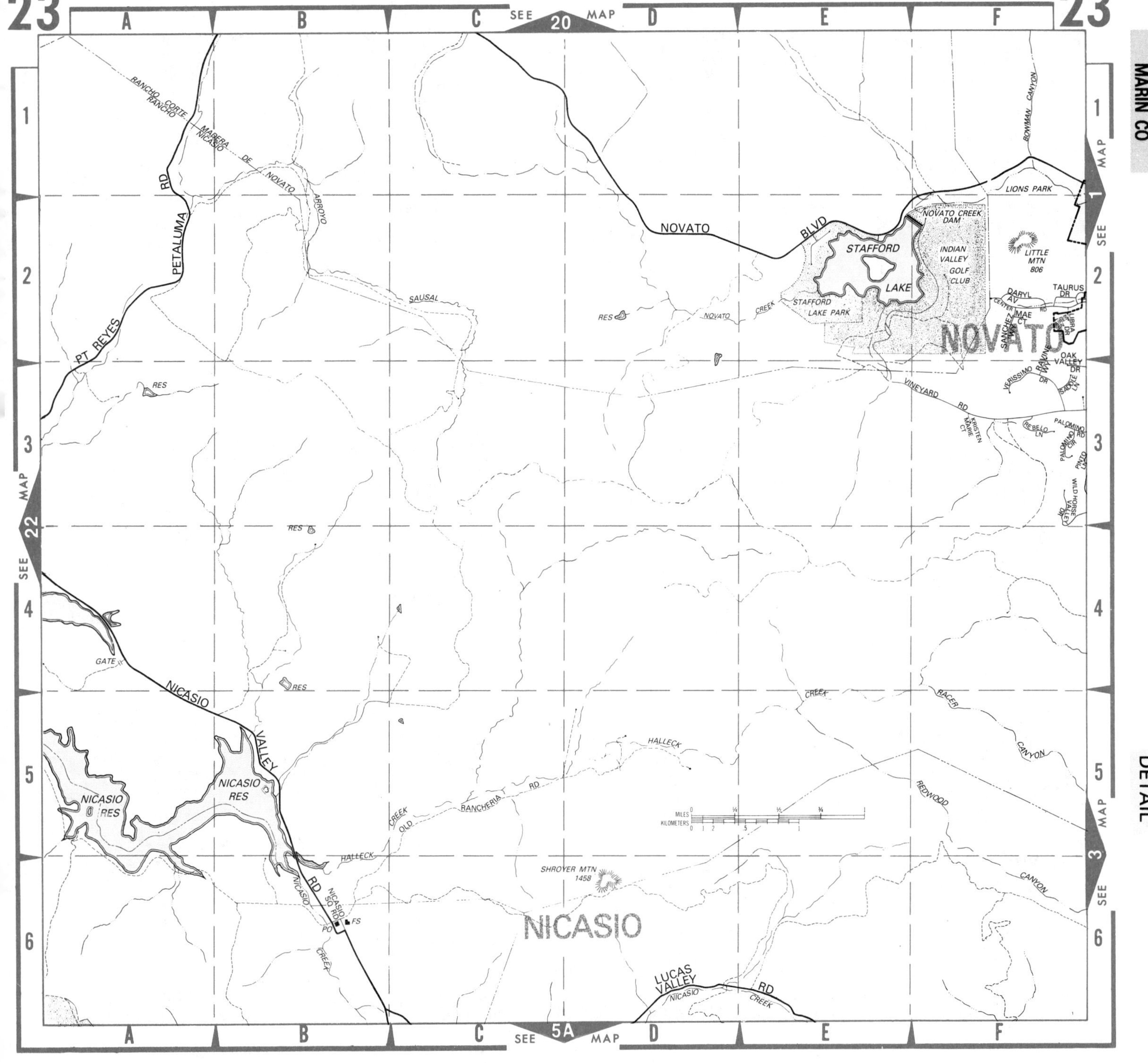

SEE MAP 20
SEE MAP 1
SEE MAP 22
SEE MAP 3
SEE MAP 5A
A
B
C
D
E
F
1
2
3
4
5
6
RANCHO CORTE MADERA DE NOVATO
RANCHO NICASIO
PETALUMA RD
PT REYES
ARROYO
SAUSAL
NOVATO BLVD
NOVATO CREEK
NOVATO CREEK DAM
STAFFORD LAKE
STAFFORD LAKE PARK
INDIAN VALLEY GOLF CLUB
LITTLE MTN 806
LIONS PARK
DARYL AV
TAURUS DR
CENTER RD
MAE CT
SANCHEZ WY
RAVINE WY
NOVATO
OAK VALLEY DR
VERISSIMO DR
SADDLE LN
VINEYARD RD
KRISTEN MARIE CT
REBELO LN
PALOMINO RD
PALOMINO CIR
PINTO LN
WILD HORSE VALLEY DR
BOWMAN CANYON
RES
GATE
NICASIO VALLEY RD
NICASIO RES
HALLECK CREEK
OLD RANCHERIA RD
CREEK
RACER CANYON
REDWOOD CANYON
SHROYER MTN 1458
NICASIO
NICASIO SQ RD
PO
FS
NICASIO CREEK
LUCAS VALLEY RD
MILES
KILOMETERS

SEE 17 MAP
SEE 21 MAP
SEE 25 MAP

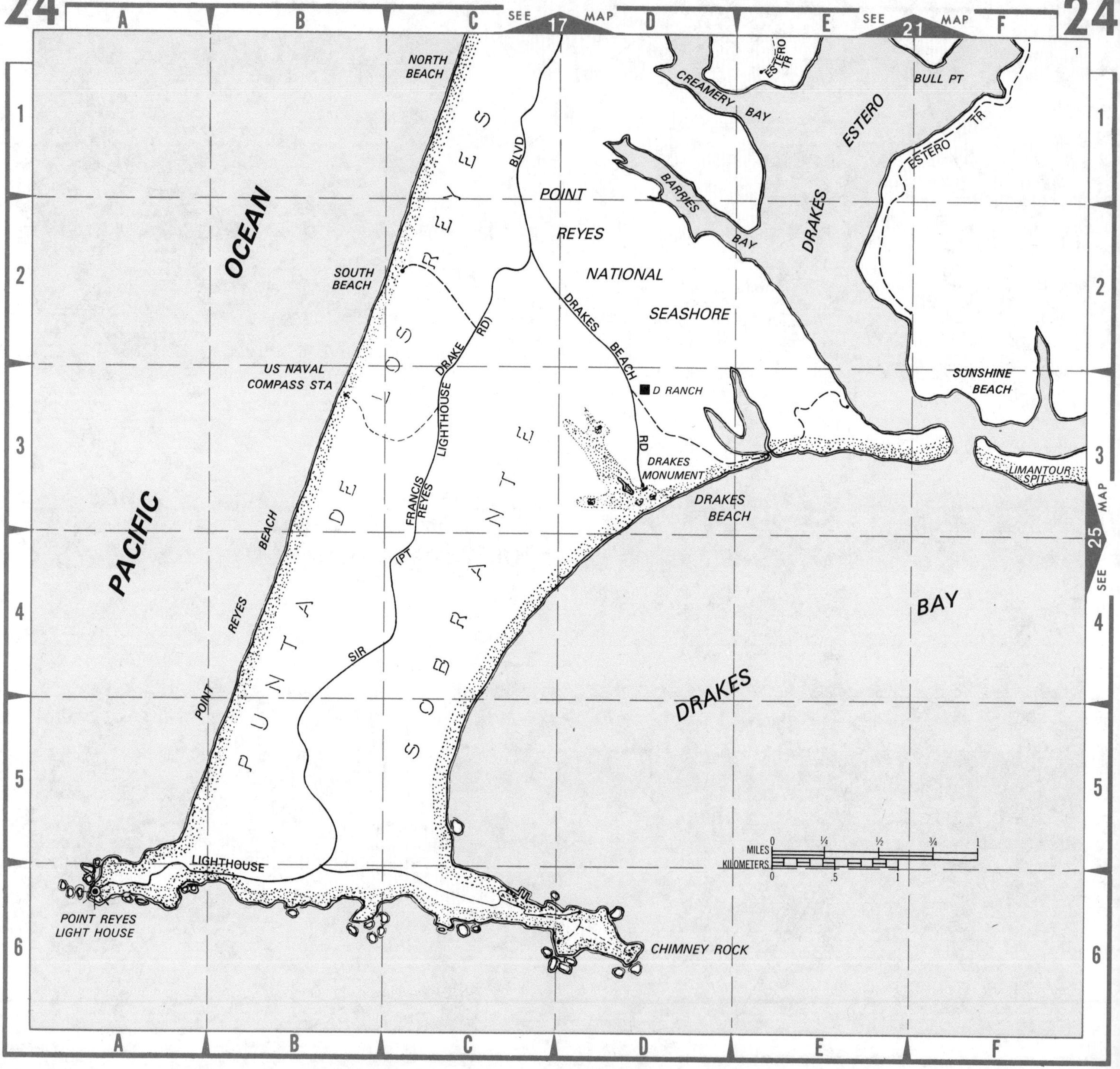

DETAIL

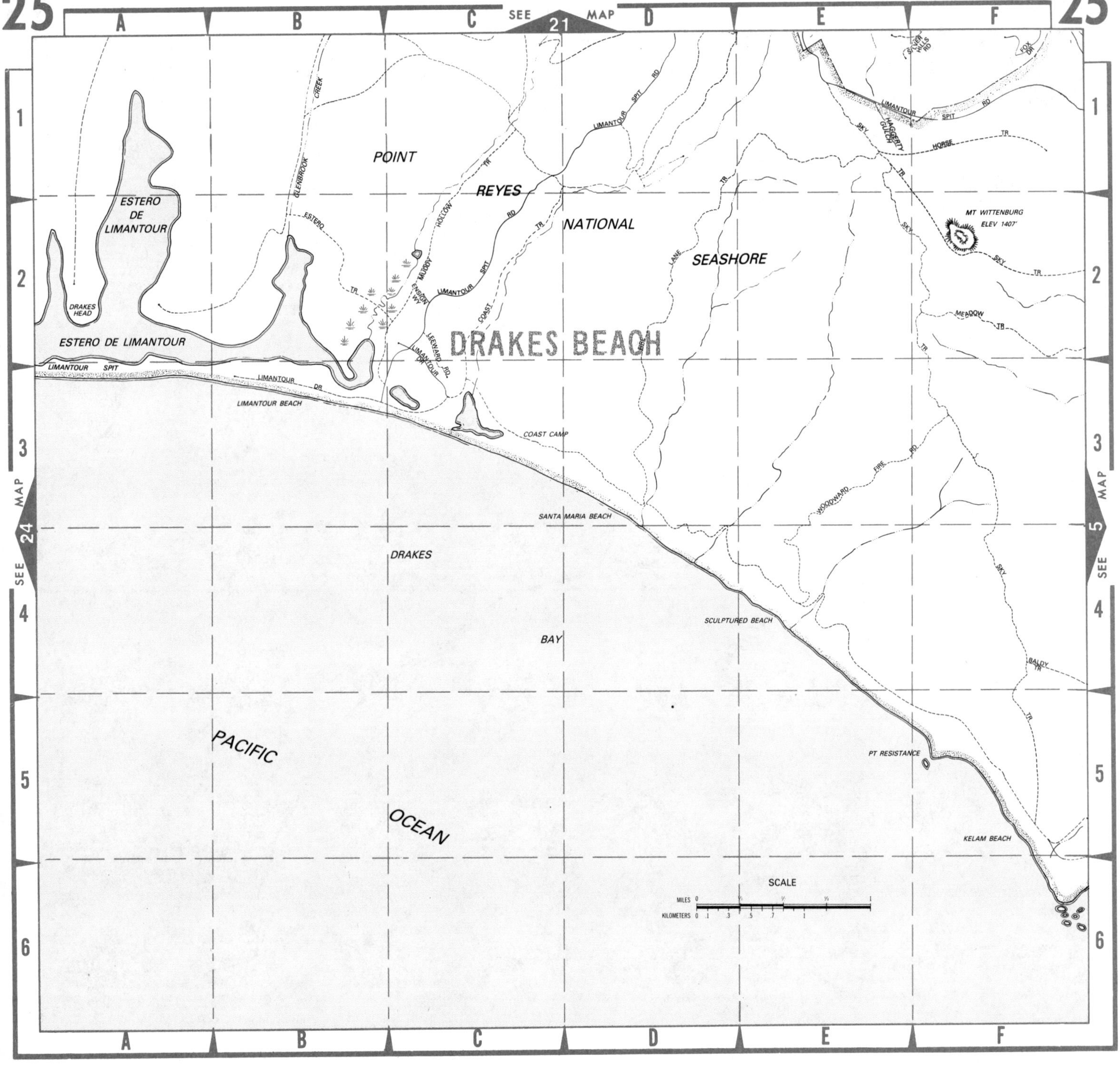

SEE MAP 21

SEE MAP 24

SEE MAP 5

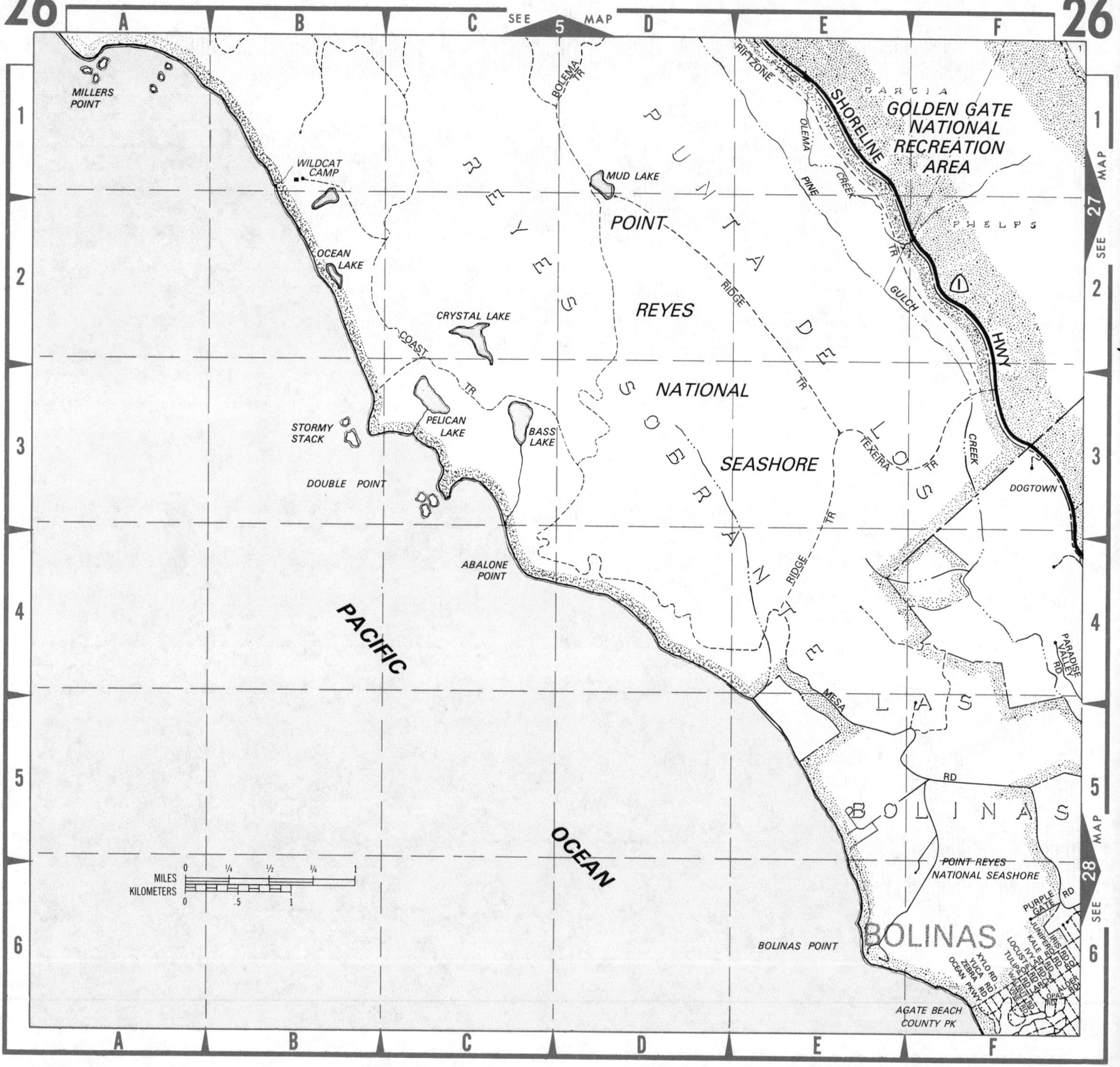

SEE 5 MAP

MARIN CO

MILLERS POINT

WILDCAT CAMP

MUD LAKE

OCEAN LAKE

CRYSTAL LAKE

PELICAN LAKE

BASS LAKE

STORMY STACK

DOUBLE POINT

ABALONE POINT

POINT REYES NATIONAL SEASHORE

PUNTA DE LOS REYES SOBRANTE

LAS BOLINAS

GOLDEN GATE NATIONAL RECREATION AREA

GARCIA

PHELPS

SHORELINE HWY

1

RIFTZONE

BOLEMA TR

OLEMA CREEK

PINE GULCH CREEK

TR

COAST TR

RIDGE TR

TEXEIRA TR

RIDGE TR

CREEK

DOGTOWN

PARADISE VALLEY RD

MESA RD

POINT REYES NATIONAL SEASHORE

PURPLE GATE RD

BOLINAS

BOLINAS POINT

AGATE BEACH COUNTY PK

IRIS RD, JUNIPER RD, KALE RD, IVY RD, LARCH RD, LOCUST RD, TULIP RD, VINE RD, WALNUT RD, XYLO RD, YUCA RD, ZEBRA RD, OCEAN PKWY, ALDER RD, OPAL RD

PACIFIC OCEAN

MILES 0 1/4 1/2 3/4 1

KILOMETERS 0 .5 1

SEE 27 MAP

SEE 28 MAP

DETAIL

26

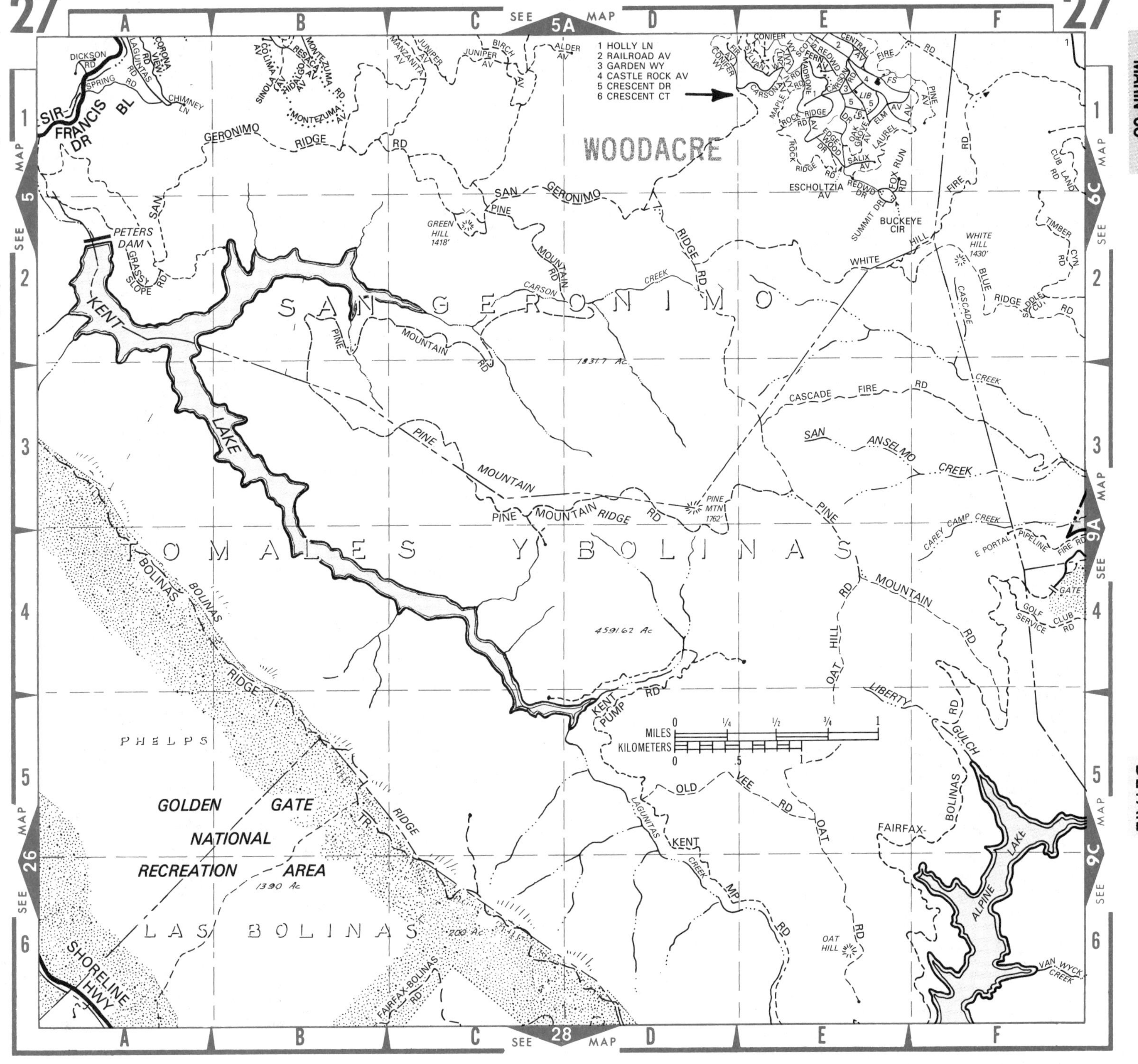
SEE 5A MAP
SEE 28 MAP
SEE 5 MAP
SEE 26 MAP
SEE 6C MAP
SEE 9A MAP
SEE 9C MAP
MARIN CO
DETAIL
1 HOLLY LN
2 RAILROAD AV
3 GARDEN WY
4 CASTLE ROCK AV
5 CRESCENT DR
6 CRESCENT CT
WOODACRE
SAN GERONIMO
TOMALES Y BOLINAS
GOLDEN GATE NATIONAL RECREATION AREA
LAS BOLINAS
PHELPS
SIR FRANCIS DRAKE BL
SHORELINE HWY
KENT LAKE
ALPINE LAKE
PETERS DAM
GREEN HILL 1418'
WHITE HILL 1430'
PINE MTN 1762'
OAT HILL
SAN GERONIMO RIDGE RD
PINE MOUNTAIN RD
PINE MOUNTAIN RIDGE RD
CASCADE FIRE RD
SAN ANSELMO CREEK
CAREY CAMP CREEK
OAT HILL RD
LIBERTY GULCH RD
BOLINAS RIDGE
OLD VEE RD
KENT PUMP RD
LAGUNITAS CREEK
FAIRFAX-BOLINAS RD
VAN WYCK CREEK
WHITE HILL FIRE RD
BLUE RIDGE RD
ESCHOLTZIA AV
BUCKEYE CIR
MILES
KILOMETERS
1831.7 Ac
4591.62 Ac
1390 Ac
200 Ac

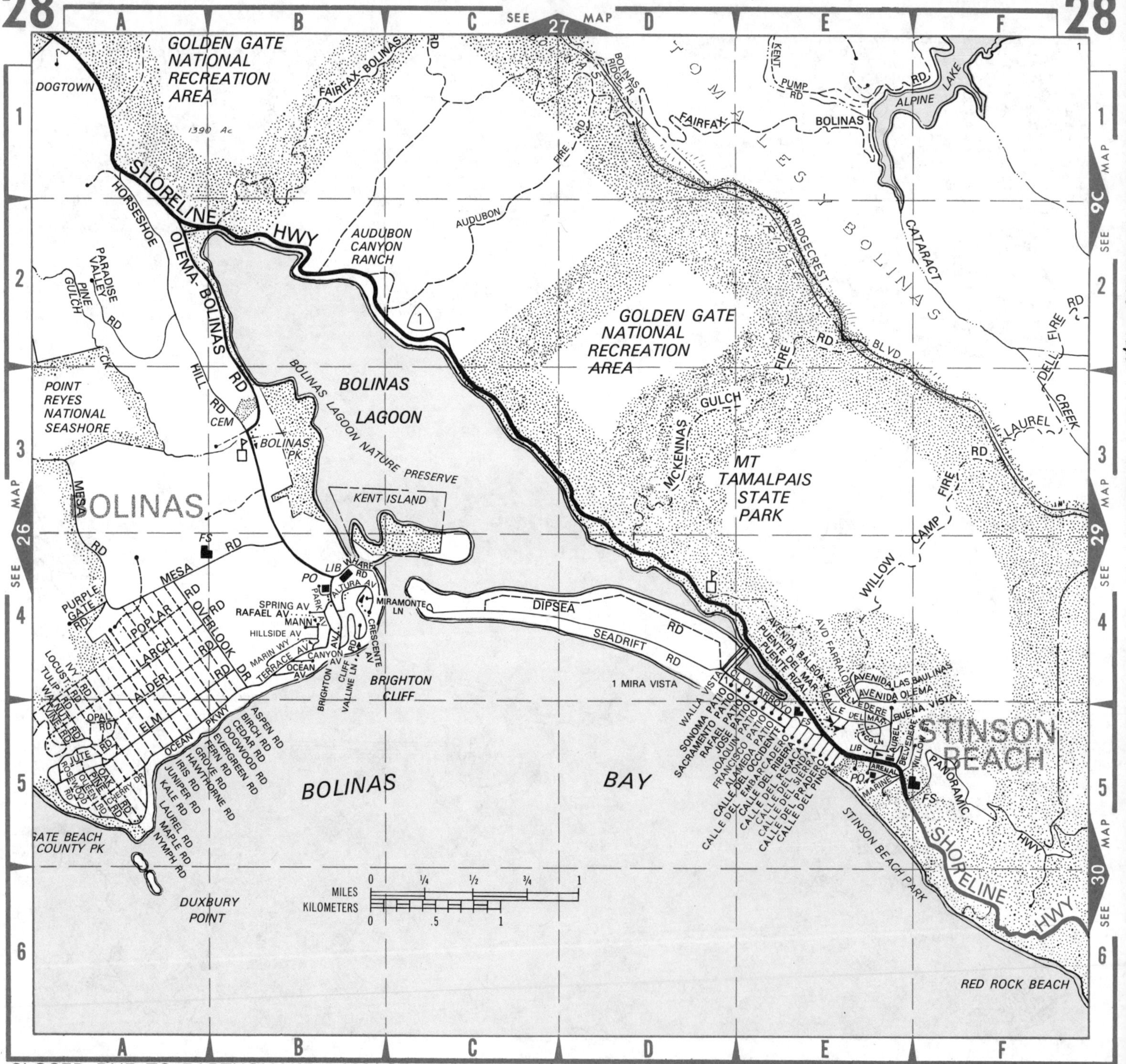

A B C D E F
1 2 3 4 5 6

CLOSED DUE TO EARTHQUAKE DAMAGE

29

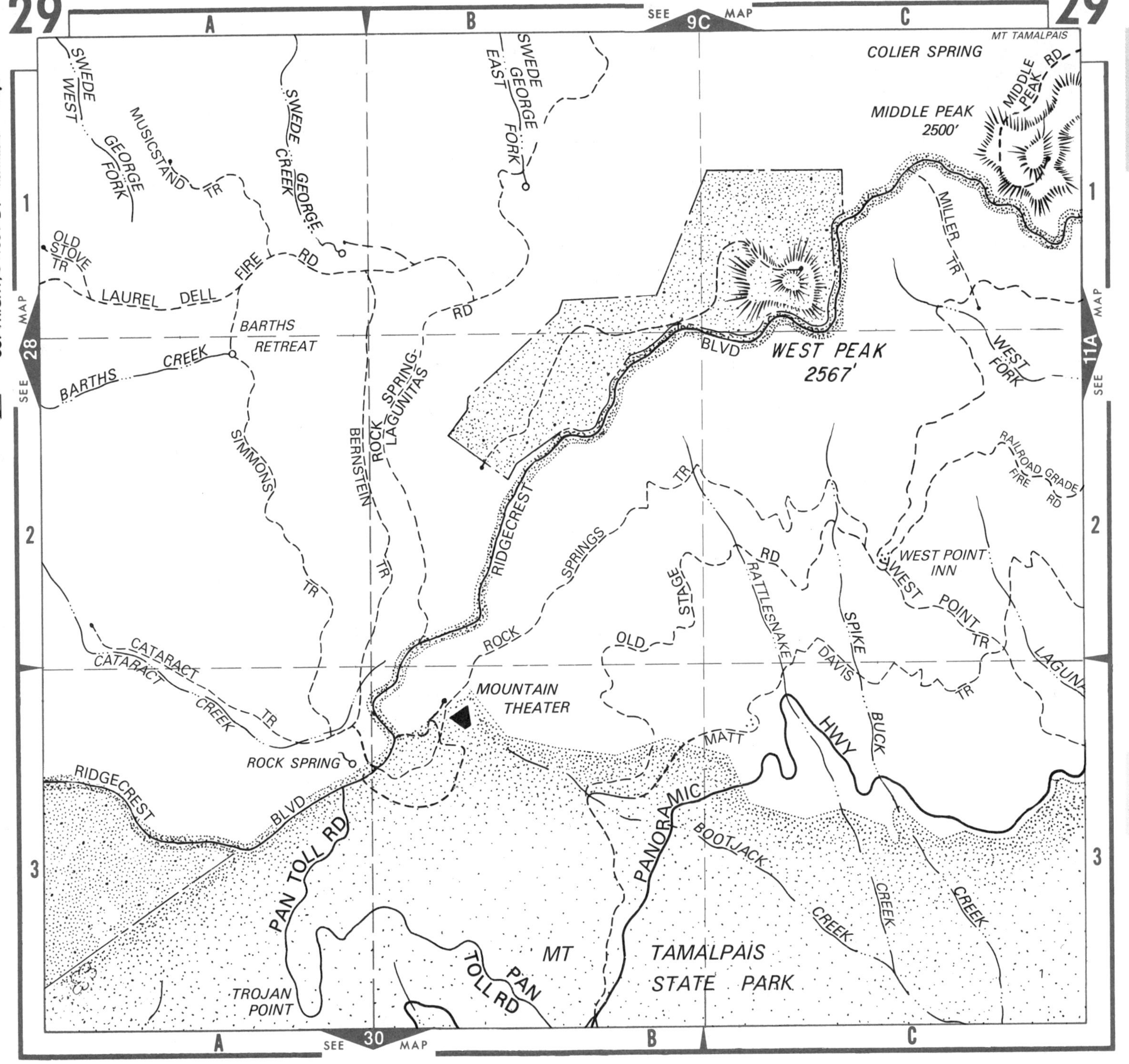

SEE 9C MAP
A
B
C
1
2
3
SEE 28 MAP
SEE 11A MAP
SEE 30 MAP
MARIN CO
DETAIL
MT TAMALPAIS
COLIER SPRING
MIDDLE PEAK RD
MIDDLE PEAK
2500'
WEST PEAK
2567'
SWEDE WEST GEORGE FORK
SWEDE GEORGE EAST FORK
SWEDE GEORGE CREEK
MUSICSTAND TR
OLD STOVE TR
LAUREL DELL FIRE RD
BARTHS RETREAT
BARTHS CREEK
SIMMONS TR
BERNSTEIN TR
ROCK SPRING-LAGUNITAS RD
RIDGECREST BLVD
MILLER TR
WEST FORK
RAILROAD GRADE FIRE RD
ROCK SPRINGS TR
OLD STAGE RD
RATTLESNAKE
WEST POINT INN
WEST POINT TR
SPIKE BUCK
DAVIS
LAGUNA
CATARACT TR
CATARACT CREEK
MOUNTAIN THEATER
MATT
ROCK SPRING
HWY
PANORAMIC
PAN TOLL RD
BOOTJACK CREEK
CREEK
MT TAMALPAIS STATE PARK
TROJAN POINT

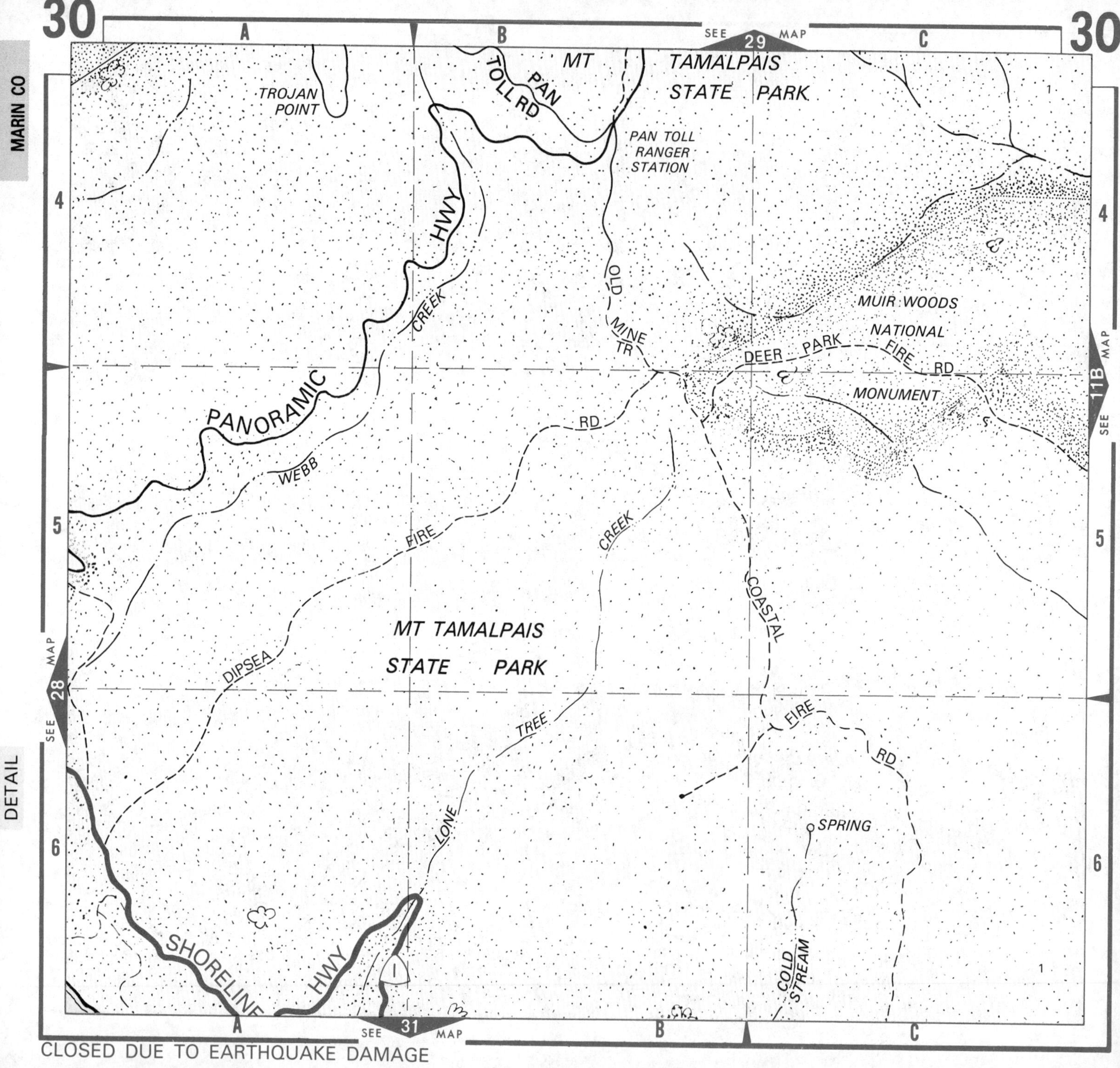

CLOSED DUE TO EARTHQUAKE DAMAGE

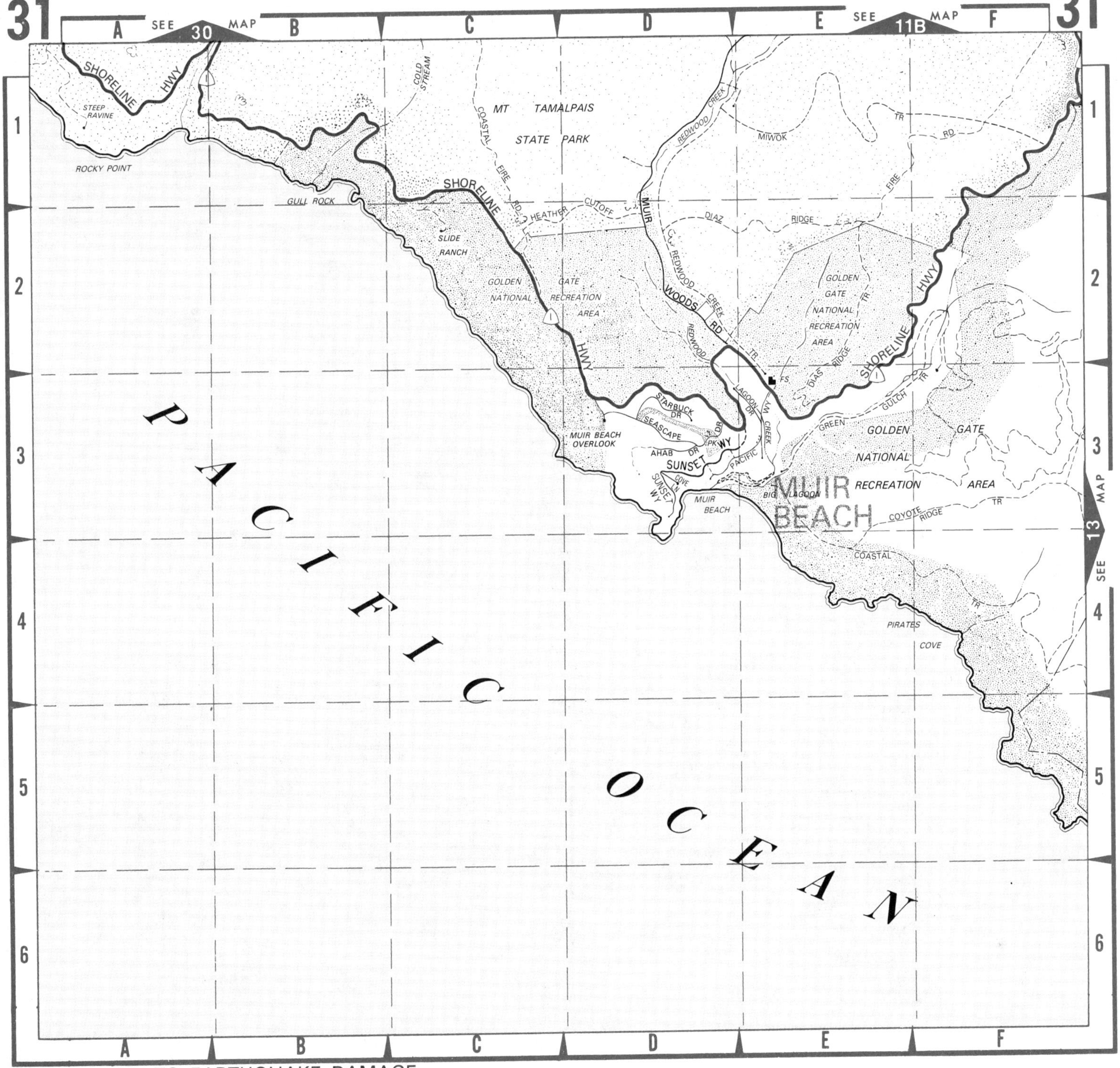

SEE 30 MAP

SEE 11B MAP

MARIN CO

A B C D E F

1 2 3 4 5 6

SHORELINE HWY
STEEP RAVINE
ROCKY POINT
GULL ROCK
COLD STREAM
MT TAMALPAIS STATE PARK
COASTAL FIRE RD
HEATHER CUTOFF
SLIDE RANCH
GOLDEN GATE NATIONAL RECREATION AREA
REDWOOD CREEK
MIWOK TR
RD
FIRE
MUIR WOODS RD
DIAZ RIDGE
REDWOOD CREEK TR
STARBUCK DR
SEASCAPE DR
AHAB DR
SUNSET WY
PK
COVE LN
PACIFIC WY
LAGOON DR
CREEK
FS
MUIR BEACH OVERLOOK
MUIR BEACH
BIG LAGOON
GREEN GULCH TR
COYOTE RIDGE TR
COASTAL TR
PIRATES COVE

PACIFIC OCEAN

SEE 13 MAP

DETAIL

A B C D E F

CLOSED DUE TO EARTHQUAKE DAMAGE

1991 MARIN COUNTY STREET INDEX

STREET	CITY	PAGE	GRID
A			
A ST	MCO	22	B5
A ST	N	4	C3
A ST	SR	10A	C1
ABERDEEN RD	N	4	D2
ABERDEEN WY	MCO	21	E3
ACACIA AV	BVDR	14	C2
ACACIA AV	L	10C	C6
ACACIA AV	L	12A	C1
ACACIA AV	MCO	10C	B4
ACACIA AV	SR	7D	D6
ACACIA CT	N	1	A1
ACACIA CT	N	1A	A6
ACACIA DR	TIB	11D	E4
ACACIA RD	F	6C	C5
ACADIA LN	SR	7A	C2
ACAPULCO CT	N	4	B2
ACE CT	F	6C	C4
ACELA DR	TIB	11D	F6
ACME CT	N	4	B1
ACORN CT	N	4	A4
ACORN WY	MCO	9D	F4
ADAMS AV	MCO	11B	B4
ADAMS CT	N	1	E4
ADAMS ST	N	1	E4
ADELE ST	N	1	F4
ADOBE CT	N	1A	D6
ADOBESTONE CT	MCO	4	B5
ADRIAN PL	L	10D	D5
ADRIAN WY	MCO	7B	D3
ADRIENNE ST	N	1	F3
AGATHA CT	SA	6D	E6
AGRESTE AV	MCO	14	E1
AGUA VISTA DR	SR	10B	E2
AHAB DR	MCO	31	D3
AIRPORT RD	MCO	1A	F4
AJAX ST	L	10C	B5
ALAMDA D L LOMA	MCO	4	A2
ALAMDA DL PRADO	MCO	4	B2
ALAMEDA PATIO	MCO	28	D5
ALAMEDA, THE	MCO	6D	E4
ALAMEDA, THE	SA	6D	E5
ALAMITOS WY	F	6C	B4
ALAMO WY	MCO	5A	A4
ALASDAIR CT	SR	6B	F3
ALBATROSS DR	N	2	C1
ALBATROSS DR	N	20	F2
ALBERT LN	MV	12B	D2
ALBERT PARK LN	SR	10A	C2
ALBION CT	N	2	A5
ALBION ST	MCO	10B	E3
ALCATRAZ AV	BVDR	14	C2
ALCATRAZ LN	MV	12A	A3
ALDER AV	MCO	5A	C5
ALDER AV	MCO	27	C1
ALDER AV	SA	6D	E6
ALDER CT	F	6D	D6
ALDER PL	N	1	B1
ALDER PL	N	1A	A6
ALDER RD	MCO	28	A4
ALDERNEY RD	SA	6D	E6
ALDERWOOD WY	SR	8	A4
ALEXANDER AV	L	10C	B6
ALEXANDER AV	L	12A	C1
ALEXANDER AV	MCO	14	B5
ALEXANDER AV	SR	7C	A6
ALEXANDER AV	SR	10A	A1
ALEXANDER AV	SLTO	14	B5
ALHAMBRA AV	MCO	5A	A4
ALHAMBRA CIR	F	6C	B4
ALICE AV	CM	12A	C1
ALICE ST	N	1	F3
ALICE ST	SR	10B	D1
ALICE WY	SA	6D	E5
ALICE ESTW C RD	MCO	11A	A3
ALLEMAND AV	SA	6D	F6
ALLEMAND AV	SA	9B	D1
ALLEN AV	R	9B	F3
ALLEN CT	SR	7C	B6
ALLENSBY LN	SR	8	A5
ALLYN AV	SA	6D	D6
ALLYN AV	SA	9B	D1
ALMENAR DR	MCO	10C	C4
ALMENAR DR N	L	10A	C3
ALMOND CT	N	2	B5
ALMONTE BLVD	MCO	12C	C5

STREET	CITY	PAGE	GRID
ALOMA WY	F	6C	B4
ALPINE ST	SR	7C	A6
ALPINE TER	SA	6D	F6
ALPINE TER	SA	7C	A6
ALPINE LILY PL	MCO	3	C5
ALTA AV	MCO	5A	A4
ALTA AV	MCO	13	E4
ALTA AV	SLTO	13	E4
ALTA ST	L	10C	B5
ALTA TER	CM	12B	D2
ALTA WY	CM	12A	C2
ALTAMIRA AV	MCO	10A	A3
ALTAMONT AV	MV	12C	C4
ALTA VISTA AV	MV	12C	C4
ALTA VISTA CT	N	4	D4
ALTA VISTA AV	SA	9B	F1
ALTA VISTA RD	MCO	13	B1
ALTA VISTA WY	MCO	10B	E2
ALTA VISTA WY	SR	10B	E2
ALTENA ST	MCO	10B	E3
ALTER LN	N	1	E1
ALTO AV	MV	12C	C4
ALTO AV	SA	6D	F6
ALTO AV	SR	7C	A6
ALTO ST	SR	10B	E2
ALTURA AV	MCO	28	B4
ALTURA WY	L	10C	C4
ALTURA WY	MCO	10C	C4
ALTURA WY	SR	10A	C3
ALTURAS WY	MCO	12C	B5
ALVARADO AV	MV	12C	B4
ALVINA AV	SR	10A	C2
ALYSSUM CT	N	1	E1
AMALFI PL	SR	10B	E2
AMANDA LN	N	1	B2
AMARANTH BLVD	MCO	11B	C5
AMBER CT	N	1	A3
AMBERWOOD LN	SA	7C	A6
AMES AV	R	9B	F2
AMICITA AV	MV	12C	C4
ANA CT	SR	7A	A3
ANCHOR ST	MCO	14	B4
ANCHORAGE CT	SR	7C	A4
ANCHORAGE RD	SLTO	13	E3
ANCHO VISTA AV	SA	9B	F1
ANDALE AV	N	2	C1
ANDERSEN DR	SR	10B	E3
ANDERSEN DR	SR	10D	E4
ANDRE LN	MCO	12C	B6
ANDREAS CIR	N	1	B1
ANDREAS CT	N	1A	B6
ANDREW DR	TIB	12D	F5
ANDREWS CT	N	4	C4
ANGEL CT	N	1	C3
ANGELA AV	SA	6D	D4
ANGELICA CT	N	1	A3
ANGELICA CT	SR	7D	D5
ANNE CT	N	1	D2
ANNIE LN	MCO	11A	B3
ANTILLES WY	MCO	11C	E3
ANTOINETTE LN	N	2	B5
ANTON WY	MCO	2	D1
ANTONETTE AV	SR	10A	C2
ANTONETTE DR	TIB	11C	D2
APACHE RD	CM	10C	C6
APOLLO CT	N	1	B2
APOLLO RD	TIB	11D	D4
APPLEBERRY DR	MCO	6B	F1
APPLEBERRY LN	MCO	3	F6
APPLEBERRY LN	MCO	4	A6
AQUA VISTA DR	SR	10B	E1
AQUINAS DR	SR	7D	D5
AQUINAS FIRE RD	SR	7D	D5
ARAM CT	N	1	D3
ARANA CIR	SLTO	13	E3
ARBOLEDA CIR	F	6C	B4
ARBOR CIR	N	1	C2
ARBOR ST	L	10C	A5
ARCH ST	L	10C	B6
ARCHANGEL CT	F	6C	C5
ARCHANGEL WY	SR	7C	A4
ARCHIBALD LN	MCO	2	B1
ARDMORE AV	L	10C	B6
ARDMORE AV	L	12A	B1
ARDMORE PKWY	L	10C	C6
ARENAL AV	MCO	28	E5
AREQUIPA FR RD	MCO	6A	A3
ARGUELLO CIR	SR	7D	F6

STREET	CITY	PAGE	GRID
ARGUELLO CIR	SR	10B	F1
ARGYLE ST	MCO	21	E3
ARIAS ST	SR	7A	A3
ARIES LN	N	1	A2
ARLENE TER	SR	6B	E3
ARLENE WY	N	2	A6
ARLINGTON CIR	N	1	F6
ARLINGTON CT	N	1	F6
ARLINGTON DR	N	1	F6
ARMORY DR	SR	7C	C4
ARMSBY CIR	R	9B	F3
ARMSTRONG AV	N	1	F2
ARONIA LN	N	1	E1
ARROWHEAD LN	CM	10C	C6
ARROWHEAD LN	N	1	E6
ARROYO AV	SA	6D	E5
ARROYO DR	MCO	10A	B3
ARROYO LN	N	1	E4
ARROYO RD	F	6C	C5
ARROYO RD	MCO	5A	A4
ARR SAUSAL RD	MCO	19	C5
ARTHUR ST	N	1	E4
ASCALON RD	MCO	5A	B4
ASH AV	CM	10C	C6
ASH AV	CM	12A	C1
ASH AV	F	6C	A6
ASH AV	F	9A	A1
ASH AV	SA	6D	E6
ASH ST	MCO	10A	B3
ASH ST	MCO	13	B1
ASH WY	MCO	7B	D2
ASHBURY AV	MCO	11B	B5
ASHFORD AV	MV	12C	C4
ASHLEY CT	N	2	C1
ASHLEY CT	N	20	E2
ASHTON LN	MCO	13	C2
ASHWOOD CT	SR	8	B5
ASPEN DR	N	1	B1
ASPEN DR	N	1A	B6
ASPEN RD	MCO	28	B5
ASTER CT	MV	12A	C3
ATHERTON AV	MCO	1	F1
ATHERTON AV	MCO	2	B1
ATHERTON AV	N	1	F1
ATHERTON AV	N	2	B1
ATHERTN OAKS DR	MCO	2	C2
ATWOOD AV	SLTO	14	A4
AUBURN CT	TIB	11D	D5
AUBURN ST	MCO	10B	D3
AUBURNVALE WY	R	10A	A2
AUDREY CT	TIB	11D	F6
AUDUBON FIRE RD	MCO	28	C1
AUREO WY	F	6C	B4
AUSTIN AV	SA	9B	E2
AUTUMN LN	MCO	13	A2
AVENIDA BALBOA	MCO	28	E4
AVD FARRALONE	MCO	28	E4
AVD LS BAULINAS	MCO	28	E4
AVD MIRAFLORES	TIB	11D	D5
AVENIDA OLEMA	MCO	28	E4
AV DEL NORTE	SA	9B	F1
AV OF THE FLAGS	SR	7A	B3
AVICHI KNOLL DR	N	1	E4
AVON AV	MV	12C	C4
AVON ST	L	10C	B6
AYALA CT	SR	7C	B4
AZALEA AV	F	6C	C5
AZALEA DR	MV	12C	C4
AZTEC AV	MCO	5A	B5
B			
B ST	MCO	22	B5
B ST	N	4	C3
B ST	SR	10A	C1
BACA VISTA	N	1	C2
BACHELORS RD	MCO	2	E2
BADGER CT	N	4	A3
BAHAMA REEF	MCO	2	D6
BAHIA CIR	SR	10B	F2
BAHIA DR	N	2	B1
BAHIA DR	N	20	E2
BAHIA LN	SR	10B	F2
BAHIA PL	SR	10B	F2
BAHIA WY	SR	10B	F2
BAHR LN	CM	12A	C1
BAJA CT	CM	12B	E1
BAJA WY	F	6C	B4

STREET	CITY	PAGE	GRID
BALBOA AV	MCO	21	F6
BALBOA AV	MCO	22	A6
BALBOA AV	SR	7D	F6
BALBOA AV	SR	10B	F1
BALCLUTHA DR	CM	12B	F2
BALD HL FIRE RD	MCO	9B	D2
BALDWIN CT	SR	10A	C3
BALDY TR	MCO	5	A4
BALMORAL WY	MCO	21	E3
BALRA DR	N	1	E5
BALTIMORE AV	CM	10C	C6
BALTIMORE AV	CM	12A	C1
BALTIMORE AV	L	10C	B6
BALTIMORE AV	L	12A	B1
BALTIMORE AV W	L	10C	B6
BALTUS LN	MCO	6B	E3
BAMBOO TER	SR	6B	F2
BANCHERO WY	F	6C	B4
BANK ST	F	6C	C5
BANK ST	SA	9B	F1
BANTA CT	N	4	B1
BARBARIE WY	MCO	12D	F5
BARBER AV	SA	9B	F1
BARBERRY LN	SR	6B	F2
BARCELONA DR	N	4	C1
BARKER AV	F	6C	C6
BARKER AV	F	9A	C1
BARKSDALE CT	N	4	C4
BARN RD	BVDR	14	C2
BARN RD	MCO	12D	E4
BARNER LN	TIB	11C	D2
BARONE LN	MCO	13	B1
BARRANCA RD	MCO	5A	A4
BARRIE WY	MV	12A	B2
BARRY WY	L	10C	C5
BARRY WY	L	10D	D5
BARTEL CT	TIB	11D	F6
BARUNA CT	N	2	C1
BATTERY DREW TR	TIB	14	F4
BAXTERS CT	SR	10B	D2
BAY CT	SR	10B	F1
BAY DR	MCO	15	B5
BAY RD	F	6C	C5
BAY RD	MCO	13	B1
BAY RD	MCO	15	D5
BAY ST	SR	10B	D2
BAY ST	SLTO	14	A3
BAY WY	SR	8	A6
BAY WY	SR	10B	F1
BAY CANYON AV	MCO	2	E2
BAYHILLS DR	MCO	7B	E3
BAYO VISTA AV	L	10C	A4
BAYO VISTA AV	MCO	10C	A4
BAYO VISTA WY	SR	7C	B6
BAYO VISTA WY	SR	10A	B1
BAYPOINT DR	SR	10B	F2
BAYSIDE CT	N	2	A5
BAY TREE LN	MV	12A	B2
BAYTREE LN	SA	6D	D4
BAYTREE RD	MCO	7C	B5
BAYTREE HOLLOW	MCO	1	F1
BAY VIEW AV	BVDR	14	C2
BAYVIEW AV	L	10C	C6
BAYVIEW AV	L	12A	C1
BAYVIEW AV	MV	12A	A3
BAYVIEW DR	MCO	8	A5
BAY VIEW DR	MCO	11B	C5
BAYVIEW RD	L	10C	B5
BAYVIEW RD	MCO	8	A5
BAYVIEW RD	MCO	10C	B5
BAYVIEW ST	MCO	2	F3
BAYVIEW ST	SR	10A	B2
BAYVIEW TER	MCO	12D	E4
BAY VIEW WY	MCO	21	E3
BAY VISTA CIR	MCO	13	D1
BAY VISTA CT	MCO	12D	E4
BAYVISTA DR	MCO	12D	E4
BAYWOOD AV	R	10A	A1
BAYWOOD CIR	N	3	F2
BAYWOOD PL	MCO	21	F4
BAYWOOD RD	F	6D	D6
BAYWOOD TER	SR	10A	C3
BAYWOOD TER	SR	10B	D3
BEACH AV	MCO	15	B4
BEACH DR	MCO	8	B6
BEACH RD	BVDR	14	C2
BEACH RD	MCO	14	C2
BEACH RD	TIB	14	D1

STREET	CITY	PAGE	GRID
BEACH PARK RD	SR	10B	D2
BEALE ST	SR	10B	F2
BEAR CREEK RD	N	1	A3
BEAR VALLEY RD	MCO	5	A1
BEAR VALLEY RD	MCO	22	B6
BEATTIE AV	MCO	2	E2
BECKY CT	N	3	F1
BEDFORD COVE	SR	10B	F2
BEE ST	SLTO	13	F3
BEE ST	SLTO	14	A3
BEECHNUT CT	SR	6B	E2
BEECHWOOD CT	SR	8	A5
BELL LN	MCO	13	C1
BELLAGIO RD	R	10A	A2
BELLAM BLVD	SR	10B	E3
BELLA VISTA AV	BVDR	14	C2
BELLA VISTA AV	SA	6D	F6
BELLE AV	F	6D	D5
BELLE AV	SA	9B	F2
BELLE AV	SR	7D	D6
BELLE AV	SR	10B	D1
BELLE RIVE PL	L	10C	A6
BELLEVUE AV	BVDR	14	C2
BELLEVUE AV	SR	8	A6
BELLEVUE AV	SR	10B	F1
BELLOREID AV	SR	7C	A6
BELLOREID AV	SR	10A	A1
BEL MARIN KEYS	MCO	2	C6
BEL MARIN KEYS	N	2	B6
BEL MARIN KEYS	N	4	B1
BELMONT AV	F	6D	D5
BELVEDERE AV	BVDR	14	C2
BELVEDERE AV	MCO	28	E5
BELVEDERE DR	MCO	12D	E4
BELVEDERE ST	SR	10B	E2
BELVEDERE WY	BVDR	14	B2
BEN JOHNSON TR	MCO	11B	A4
BENNIT AV	SA	6D	D5
BENSON CIR	MV	12B	D2
BENTON CT	MCO	11D	D4
BENTON CT	TIB	11D	D4
BENTON LN	N	1	D1
BERENS DR	MCO	10C	B4
BERKE CT	TIB	11D	F6
BERKELEY AV	SA	6D	E5
BERLIN AV	SA	6D	E6
BERMUDA HARBOUR	MCO	2	C6
BERNARD LN	MV	12A	A3
BERNARD ST	MV	12A	A3
BERNSTEIN TR	MCO	29	A2
BERRY LN	R	9B	F3
BERRY LN	R	10A	A3
BERRY TER	F	6C	C5
BERYL AV	MCO	12C	C6
BERYL LN	SR	7C	B6
BETA ST	L	10C	B6
BETTY LN	N	1	D3
BEVERLEY WY	SA	6D	E5
BEVERLY TER	MV	12A	A3
BEYER CT	N	1	D2
BIGELOW AV	MV	12A	A3
BIG ROCK RDG FR	MCO	1A	C3
BILLOU ST	SR	10B	D3
BILLYS LN	CM	12A	B1
BINFORD RD	MCO	1	F1
BINFORD RD	MCO	1A	F6
BINFORD RD	N	1	F1
BIRCH AV	CM	10C	C6
BIRCH AV	CM	10D	D6
BIRCH AV	CM	12A	C1
BIRCH AV	MCO	5A	C5
BIRCH AV	MCO	27	C1
BIRCH RD	MCO	28	B5
BIRCH ST	MV	12C	A4
BIRCH WY	MCO	7B	D2
BIRCHWOOD CT	SR	6B	F2
BIRCHWOOD DR	N	2	A5
BIRD CT	N	1	D4
BIRDIE DR	N	3	F1
BIRDIE DR	N	4	A1
BISCAYNE CT	SR	8	C3
BISCAYNE DR	SR	8	B3
BISHOP CT	N	2	A3
BLACKBERRY LN	F	6D	D6
BLACKBERRY LN	MCO	3	F6
BLACKBERRY LN	MCO	4	A6
BLACKBERRY WY	MCO	22	A6
BLACKFIELD DR	TIB	12D	E4

STREET	CITY	PAGE	GRID
BLACKHAWK DR	SA	6D	E5
BLACK JOHN RD	MCO	1A	F5
BLACK JOHN RD	N	1A	E6
BLACK LOG RD	MCO	10C	A5
BLACK OAK LN	N	1	D4
BLACKSTONE DR	MCO	4	A5
BLACKSTONE LN	MCO	4	A5
BLANCA DR	N	1	A3
BLANDING LN	BVDR	14	C3
BLITHEDALE AV	MV	11A	C2
BLITHEDALE AV	MV	12C	B4
BLITHEDALE AV	MV	12D	D4
BLITHEDALE AV W	MV	11A	C2
BLITHEDALE TER	MV	12A	A3
BLITHDLE RDG FR	MCO	9D	F6
BLOGETT LN	N	1	E3
BLOOM LN	MCO	1	C5
BLOSSOM CT	SR	10B	D3
BLOSSOM DR	SR	10B	D3
BLUE BIRD LN	MCO	12B	D3
BLUE JAY FR RD	MCO	22	B3
BLUE BLOSSOM CT	MCO	3	C5
BLUE OAK CT	MCO	3	D5
BLUE RIDGE RD	MCO	5A	F6
BLUE RIDGE RD	MCO	6C	A5
BLUE RIDGE RD	MCO	9D	F5
BLUE RIDGE RD	MCO	10C	A5
BLUE RIDGE RD	MCO	27	F2
BLUE ROCK CT	CM	10C	C6
BOBCAT TR	MCO	13	D4
BOGEY LN	N	3	F2
BOLANOS DR	SR	6B	E2
BOLEMA TR	MCO	5	D6
BOLEMA TR	MCO	26	D1
BOLERO CT	N	20	F2
BOLINAS AV	R	9B	E2
BOLINAS AV	SA	9B	F2
BOLINAS RD	F	6C	C6
BOLINAS RD	MCO	9A	A1
BOLINAS ST	MCO	13	D1
BOLINAS RG F TR	MCO	27	A4
BOLLING DR	N	4	C4
BOLSA AV	MV	12A	B3
BON AIR RD	L	10C	B5
BON AIR RD	MCO	10C	B4
BOND LN	TIB	11C	D2
BOND ST	L	10C	B5
BONITA ST	SLTO	13	F3
BONITA ST	SLTO	14	A3
BONNIE BANKS WY	SR	8	A6
BONNIE BRAE DR	N	3	F2
BONNIE BRAE DR	SR	7C	C6
BONNIE BRAE DR	SR	10A	C1
BON TEMPE P RD	MCO	9A	A3
BOOKER AV	SLTO	14	A4
BOOTJACK TR	MCO	11B	B4
BORGES CT	N	1	D3
BOSQUE AV	MCO	9A	A1
BOTHIN RD	F	6C	C4
BOULDER LN	SA	6D	F6
BOULEVARD CT	N	1	D3
BOULEVARD TER	N	1	D3
BOVIN WY	L	10C	A6
BRABO TER	MCO	12C	B5
BRACKEN CT	SR	8	B4
BRADCLIFF CT	SR	7D	D5
BRADFORD WY	MV	12A	B3
BRADLEY AV	N	1	D3
BRANCH AV	L	12A	C1
BRASSIE CT	N	3	F1
BRAUN CT	MCO	13	D1
BRENNFLECK AV	SA	6D	E6
BRENTWOOD DR	SR	8	A4
BRET AV	SR	10B	D2
BRET CT	N	1	D3
BRETANO WY	L	10D	D4
BRETANO WY	MCO	10D	D4
BRET HARTE LN	SR	10B	D3
BRET HARTE RD	MCO	10B	D3
BRET HARTE RD	SR	10B	D3
BRIAR RD	L	10C	A5
BRIAR RD	MCO	10C	A5
BRIARWOOD CT	N	2	A5
BRIARWOOD DR	SR	8	A4
BRIDGE AV	SA	6D	F6
BRIDGE AV	SA	9B	F1
BRIDGE BLVD	MCO	13	E2
BRIDGE CT	F	6D	D6

STREET	CITY	PAGE	GRID
BRIDGE RD	L	10C	B6
BRIDGE RD	L	12A	B1
BRIDGE RD	MCO	2	E1
BRIDGE RD	MCO	9B	F3
BRIDGE RD	MCO	10A	A3
BRIDGE RD	R	9B	F3
BRIDGE RD	R	10A	A3
BRIDGE WY	SA	9B	D1
BRIDGEGATE DR	MCO	3	D5
BRIDGEWATER DR	SR	7A	C3
BRIDGEWAY	SLTO	13	E2
BRIDGEWAY	SLTO	14	A3
BRIDLE PATH LN	N	1A	D5
BRIGHTON AV	MCO	28	B5
BRIGHTON BLVD	MCO	11B	B5
BRISTOL PL	MCO	13	C1
BRITTON AV	BVDR	14	B1
BRITTON CT	N	1	C2
BROADMOOR AV	SA	6D	E5
BROADMOOR CT	N	3	F2
BROADMOOR CT	SA	6D	E5
BROADVIEW CT	SR	10B	E1
BROADVIEW DR	SR	10B	E1
BROADWAY	F	6C	C5
BROADWAY	MCO	10A	B3
BRODEA WY	SR	10B	E1
BROOK LN	SA	6D	E5
BROOKDALE AV	SR	7D	D6
BROOKE CIR	MV	12D	D5
BROOKE DR	N	1	A3
BROOKE DR W	N	1	A3
BROOKLINE AV	MCO	12C	B6
BROOKMEAD CT	SA	6D	E5
BROOKMONT CIR	SA	6D	E5
BROOKS ST	SR	10A	C1
BROOKSIDE CT	N	1	C3
BROOKSIDE CT	SA	6D	E5
BROOKSIDE DR	SA	6D	E5
BROOKWOOD LN	R	9B	F3
BROWN CT	N	1	E5
BROWN DR	N	1	D5
BROWNING CT	MCO	12C	B6
BROWNING ST	MCO	12C	B6
BROWNING ST	MCO	13	B1
BRUCE ST	MCO	21	E3
BRUNO ST	N	1	E3
BRUSHWOOD LN	SR	10A	C3
BRYAN LN	N	1	D2
BRYCE CANYON RD	SR	7A	C2
BRYN MAWR DR	SR	7C	C6
BUCCANEER CT	CM	12B	E2
BUCHANAN CT	SLTO	13	E3
BUCHANAN DR	SLTO	13	E3
BUCHANAN ST	N	1	E4
BUCKELEW ST	MCO	13	D2
BUCKEYE CIR	MCO	5A	F6
BUCKEYE CIR	MCO	27	E2
BUCKEYE CT	N	4	A4
BUCKEYE RD	BVDR	14	B1
BUCKEYE WY	MCO	9D	F4
BUCKEYE WY	MCO	10C	A4
BUCKLIN TR	MCO	21	D6
BUCK POINT	MCO	21	E5
BUCKWHEAT CT	TIB	12D	F4
BUENA VISTA	N	1	C2
BUENA VISTA	N	4	E4
BUENA VISTA AV	CM	12B	D2
BUENA VISTA AV	MCO	9A	B1
BUENA VISTA AV	MCO	22	A5
BUENA VISTA AV	MCO	28	E5
BUENA VISTA AV	MV	12A	B3
BUENA VISTA LN	SA	6D	F6
BUGIEA LN	MCO	2	A1
BUGIEA LN	N	2	A1
BUIDA CT	CM	12A	C2
BULKLEY AV	SLTO	14	A2
BULLFROG FR RD	MCO	9A	B2
BUNGALOW AV	SA	6D	F6
BUNGALOW AV	SA	7C	A6
BUNGALOW AV	SA	9B	F1
BUNGALOW AV	SA	10A	A1
BUNGALOW AV	SR	10A	C2
BUNKER RD	MCO	13	E6
BURBANK LN	MCO	15	E3
BURDELL CT	N	4	B4
BURDELL MTN RDG	MCO	1A	A3
BURDETT LN	F	6D	D5
BURGESS CT	MCO	13	D2

STREET	CITY	PAGE	GRID
BURKSHIRE SQ	SA	6D	E4
BURMA RD	N	4	E3
BURNINGTREE DR	N	3	F2
BURNT RDG FR RD	MCO	1	B6
BURNT RDG FR RD	MCO	3	C1
BURRELL CT	TIB	11D	D4
BURRELL CT	TIB	12D	F4
BUTTE ST	SLTO	13	E2
BUTTERFIELD DR	N	1A	D6
BUTTERFIELD LN	MCO	6B	E3
BUTTERFIELD RD	MCO	6B	D3
BUTTERFIELD RD	SA	6D	E4
BUTTERFLY LN	MCO	10A	A3
BUTTERNUT DR	SR	6B	F2
BYRON CIR	MV	12D	D5
C			
C ST	MCO	22	B5
C ST	N	4	C3
C ST	SR	10A	C2
CABIN DR	MCO	13	B1
CABLE	SLTO	14	A4
CABRILLO CT	SR	6B	E2
CABRO CT	N	1	B4
CADDY CT	N	3	F2
CAIN LN	N	1	E3
CAJA CT	MCO	4	A6
CALAFIA CT	SR	6B	E2
CALAVISTA DR	SR	10A	B2
CALEDONIA ST	SLTO	13	F3
CALEDONIA ST	SLTO	14	A3
CALETA AV	SA	6D	E4
CALICO LN	N	1	C3
CALIENTE REAL	N	4	E3
CALIFORNIA AV	MCO	12C	C6
CALIFORNIA AV	SR	7C	A6
CALIFORNIA LN	CM	12A	C1
CALIF CONDOR WY	N	4	B4
CALLE ARBOLEDA	MCO	4	B2
CALLE D LA MESA	MCO	4	A1
CALLE D L ARROYO	MCO	28	D4
CALLE D L SELVA	MCO	4	B2
CL DL EMBARCDRO	MCO	28	D5
CALLE DEL MAR	MCO	28	E5
CL DL OCCIDENTE	MCO	28	D5
CALLE DEL ONDA	MCO	28	E5
CALLE DEL PINOS	MCO	28	E5
CL DEL PRADERO	MCO	28	E5
CL DEL RESACA	MCO	28	E5
CL DEL RIBERA	MCO	28	E5
CL DEL SIERRA	MCO	28	E5
CALLE EMPINADO	MCO	4	B2
CALLENDER WY	MCO	21	E3
CALLE PASEO	MCO	4	B2
CALUMET AV	SA	6D	E6
CALYPSO SHORES	MCO	2	D5
CAMA LN	N	1	F6
CAMBRIDGE CT	N	1	F5
CAMBRIDGE HTS	N	1	F5
CAMBRIDGE ST	N	1	F6
CAMERON ST	MCO	21	E3
CAMINO DR	N	4	D4
CAMINO ALTO	MV	12A	C3
CAMINO ALTO	MV	12C	C5
CAMINO ALTO CT	MV	12C	C4
CM DE HERRERA	SA	6D	D4
CAMINO DL CANON	MCO	11B	C6
CAMINO DEL MAR	MCO	21	D2
CM MARGARITA	MCO	5A	E2
CAMPBELL CT	N	1	C3
CAMPOLINDO DR	MCO	22	B4
CAMPUS DR E	N	1	E1
CAMPUS DR E	N	1A	E6
CAMPUS DR W	N	1	E1
CAMPUS DR W	N	1A	E6
CANADA CT	SR	7C	B4
CANAL ST	MCO	10B	E2
CANAL ST	SR	10B	E2
CANAL TER	MCO	2	F3
CANDELERO RD	MCO	5A	B5
CANDY CREEK WY	L	10C	B5
CANE ST	L	10C	B6
CANTERA WY	MCO	8	D3
CANTOGAL	SLTO	13	F5
CANYON AV	MCO	28	B4
CANYON RD	F	6C	B6
CANYON RD	N	1	D4

STREET	CITY	PAGE	GRID
CANYON RD	R	10A	A2
CANYON RD	SA	6D	D6
CANYON RD	SA	9B	D1
CANYON OAK DR	SR	3	F6
CANYON OAK DR	SR	6B	F1
CAPE CT	MCO	12C	B4
CAPETOWN CT	N	2	A6
CAPILANO DR	N	3	E2
CAPRI CT	SR	10B	E2
CAPTAINS CV DR	SR	7A	C2
CAPTAINS LANDNG	MCO	12D	F5
CARDINAL CT	MCO	13	C1
CARDINAL RD	MCO	13	C1
CAREY DR	MCO	7B	D3
CARIBE ISLE	MCO	2	D5
CARISA CT	N	1	C1
CARLOS DR	SR	7A	B2
CARLOTA CIR	MCO	12D	D4
CARLSBAD CT	SR	7A	C2
CARLSON AV	SA	6D	D4
CARLSON CT	SA	6D	D4
CARLTON PL	MCO	21	F5
CARMEL CT	MCO	7C	C4
CARMEL CT	N	1	E2
CARMEL DR	N	1	E2
CARMEL WY	MCO	6D	F5
CARMELITA AV	MV	12C	B4
CARMEN CT	N	1	C1
CARMENCITA AV	MCO	22	A5
CARMODY RD	MCO	16	A2
CARNOUSTIE DR	N	3	F2
CARNOUSTIE HTS	N	3	F2
CAROB WY	N	1	E1
CAROLINA AV	SA	7C	A6
CAROLYN LN	MCO	12C	C5
CAROLYN WY	N	1	D1
CARRERA DR	MCO	13	C2
CARRIE ST	MCO	15	D4
CARROLL CT	SR	6B	F3
CARSON RD	MCO	5A	E5
CARSON RD	MCO	27	E1
CASA AV	N	4	E3
CASA BUENA DR	CM	12B	D2
CASA BUENA DR	MCO	12B	D2
CASA GRNDE REAL	N	4	E4
CASCADE DR	F	6C	C6
CASCADE DR	F	9A	B1
CASCADE DR	MV	11A	C3
CASCADE DR	MV	12C	A4
CASCADE DR	SR	7D	E5
CASCADE WY	MV	11B	C4
CASCADE WY	MV	12C	A4
CASCADE FIRE RD	MCO	6C	A6
CASCADE FIRE RD	MCO	27	E3
CASCADE FIRE TR	MCO	11A	B2
CASPAR PL	N	2	A6
CASTLE CT	N	2	A2
CASTLE ROCK AV	MCO	5A	E5
CASTLE ROCK AV	MCO	27	D1
CASTLE ROCK DR	MCO	11B	C4
CASTLEWOOD DR	SR	8	B5
CASTLEWOOD DR W	SR	8	A5
CASTRO AV	SR	10B	E3
CASTRO ST	MCO	5A	A4
CASUAL CT	N	1	A3
CATALINA BLVD	SR	10B	F2
CATALPA AV	MV	12C	B4
CATARACT TR	MCO	29	A2
CATSKILL CT	MCO	6B	D3
CAVALLA CAY	MCO	2	C6
CAVALLERO CT	MCO	2	C2
CAYFORD DR	TIB	12D	F4
CAY PASSAGE	CM	12B	F2
CAZADERO LN	BVDR	14	B1
CAZNEAU AV	SLTO	13	F3
CAZNEAU AV	SLTO	14	A3
CECELIA CT	TIB	12D	F4
CECELIA WY	TIB	12D	F4
CECIL RD	MCO	5A	C5
CECILY LN	MCO	12C	A4
CEDAR AV	L	10C	B5
CEDAR AV	MCO	2	E3
CEDAR AV	MCO	10A	A3
CEDAR LN	SR	8	A6
CEDAR PL	N	1	B1
CEDAR PL	N	1A	A5
CEDAR RD	MCO	28	B5
CEDAR ST	SA	9B	F1

STREET	CITY	PAGE	GRID
CEDARBERRY LN	MCO	3	F6
CEDARBERRY LN	MCO	4	A6
CEDAR HILL DR	SR	3	F6
CEDAR HILL DR	SR	7A	A1
CEDARWOOD LN	MCO	12C	A4
CEDARWOOD LN	N	2	A5
CELESTE CT	N	1	B2
CEMETERY RD	MCO	6D	F6
CEMETERY RD	SA	6D	F6
CENTER BLVD	SA	6D	E6
CENTER BLVD	SA	9B	E1
CENTER RD	MCO	1	A2
CENTER RD	MCO	23	F2
CENTER RD	N	1	D3
CENTER ST	SR	7C	B6
CENTER ST	SR	10A	B1
CENTRAL AV	MCO	5A	E5
CENTRAL AV	MCO	27	E1
CENTRAL AV	SLTO	14	A4
CENTRAL CT	MCO	12B	D3
CENTRAL DR	MCO	12D	D4
CENTRO WY	MCO	12C	B5
CENTRO EAST ST	TIB	14	D1
CENTRO WEST ST	TIB	14	D1
CENTURY DR	MCO	13	F1
CERINI RD	MCO	15	E5
CERMENHO CT	SR	7C	A4
CERRO CREST DR	N	2	C1
CERRO CREST DR	N	20	E2
CHALDA CT	MCO	7B	D3
CHAMBERLAIN AV	N	1	D4
CHAMBERLAIN CT	MCO	12C	B6
CHAMBERLAIN CT	N	1	D4
CHANNEL DR	CM	12B	E1
CHANNEL DR	MCO	2	D1
CHANNEL LANDING	MCO	12D	F5
CHANNING WY	SR	7A	B3
CHANNING WY	SLTO	14	A4
CHANTICLEER AV	L	10C	C6
CHANTICLEER AV	MCO	11B	B4
CHAPARRAL CT	N	4	B4
CHAPARRO AV	MCO	5A	A4
CHAPEL DR	MCO	12D	E6
CHAPMAN DR	CM	12A	C2
CHAPMAN LN	MCO	12C	B5
CHAPPERAL TR	MCO	13	B5
CHAQUITA LN	MV	12A	A3
CHARLES LN	MCO	5A	A5
CHARLES LN	MCO	11B	C4
CHARLES DEAN RD	MV	12A	A2
CHARLOTTE DR	SR	10B	E2
CHARMAINE CT	N	4	B4
CHARRO WY	F	6C	B4
CHASE ST	N	1	F2
CHATEAU PL	SR	8	B4
CHAUCER CT	MV	12D	D4
CHEDA LN	N	2	A6
CHEDA KNOLLS DR	N	1	F6
CHERNE LN	SA	6D	D4
CHERRY CT	N	1	F2
CHERRY DR	MCO	28	A5
CHERRY ST	N	1	F2
CHERRY HILL DR	SR	7A	A1
CHERRY TREE LN	MCO	22	A5
CHESTER AV	F	6D	D5
CHESTNUT AV	R	9B	F3
CHESTNUT AV	SR	7C	B6
CHEVY CHASE CT	L	12A	B1
CHEYENNE WY	CM	10C	C6
CHIAPAS AV	MCO	5A	A5
CHICKASAW CT	CM	10D	D6
CHICKN SHK F RD	N	3	F3
CHILENO VLY RD	MCO	16	C5
CHILENO VLY RD	MCO	19	D1
CHILENO VLY RD	MCO	20	A1
CHIMNEY LN	MCO	5A	A5
CHIMNEY LN	MCO	27	A1
CHITMAN PL	SA	9B	E2
CHRISTOPHER CT	N	1	B2
CHULA VISTA DR	SR	7C	C6
CHURCH CT	CM	12A	C1
CHURCH ST	MCO	15	D5
CIBRIAN DR	TIB	11C	D2
CIELO DR	L	10A	C3
CIELO LN	N	4	C3
CIJOS ST	SR	10A	C1
CINNAMN TEAL LN	N	4	A4
CINTURA AV	MCO	5A	A4

STREET	CITY	PAGE	GRID
CINTURA AV E	MCO	5A	A4
CINTURA AV W	MCO	5A	A5
CIRCE CT	N	2	C1
CIRCLE AV	MV	12A	B3
CIRCLE DR	R	9B	F2
CIRCLE DR	SA	7C	A6
CIRCLE DR	SA	10A	A1
CIRCLE DR	SR	10A	A1
CIRCLE DR	TIB	12D	F4
CIRCLE RD	MCO	7C	B5
CIRCLE WY	MCO	12C	B5
CIR V ACCESS RD	MCO	6A	A3
CITRON AV	L	10C	B5
CITRUS PL	N	1	A1
CITRUS PL	N	1A	A6
CITY HALL AV	SA	9B	F1
CIVIC CENTER DR	SR	7A	B3
CIVIC CENTER DR	SR	7C	B4
CLAIRE CT	N	1	F6
CLAIRE CT	N	3	F1
CLAIRE WY	TIB	12D	E4
CLARITA CT	N	1	B3
CLARK RD	MCO	18	B3
CLARK ST	SR	10A	B2
CLAUS CIR	F	6C	C5
CLAUS DR	F	6C	C5
CLAUSING AV	N	1	F3
CLAUSING CT	N	1	F3
CLAY CT	N	4	B4
CLAYTON CT	N	1	E2
CLAYTON ST	SR	10A	B2
CLEMENTE CT	N	1	C1
CLEO ST	N	1	E4
CLEVELAND AV	MCO	12C	C6
CLEVELAND CT	MCO	12C	C6
CLIFF RD	BVDR	14	C2
CLIFF RD	MCO	28	B4
CLIFF ST	MCO	15	B5
CLORINDA AV	SR	10A	B2
CLOTILDA CT	MCO	12D	D4
CLOUD VIEW CIR	SLTO	14	A4
CLOUD VIEW RD	SLTO	14	A4
CLOUD VIEW TR	SLTO	13	F5
CLOUD VIEW TR	SLTO	14	A5
CLOVER HILL CT	SR	7A	A1
CLUB VIEW	N	4	D4
CLYDE AV	SR	7D	D6
COACH RD	MV	12B	D2
COAST TR	MCO	5	A5
COAST TR	MCO	26	C2
COASTAL TR	MCO	13	A4
COASTAL TR	MCO	31	E4
COASTAL FIRE RD	MCO	30	C5
COASTAL FIRE RD	MCO	31	C1
COAST OAK WY	SR	6B	F1
COBBLESTONE CT	N	1A	E5
COBBLESTONE DR	MCO	4	B5
COLBY AV	MCO	12D	D5
COLE DR	MCO	13	E2
COLEMAN AV	L	10C	B6
COLEMAN AV	L	12A	B1
COLEMAN DR	SR	7C	C6
COLERIDGE DR	MV	12D	D6
COLIMA AV	MCO	5A	B5
COLIMA AV	MCO	27	B1
COLLECTOR RD	L	10D	D5
COLLEEN CT	N	1	C2
COLLEGE AV	MCO	10A	A3
COLLEGE AV	MCO	10C	A4
COLLEGE CT	L	10C	A4
COLOMA ST	MCO	13	E2
COLONY LN	CM	12A	C2
COLONY WY	CM	12A	B1
COLUMBIA AV	MCO	12C	C6
COLUMBINE LN	N	2	A6
COMMERCIAL BLVD	N	4	B1
COMMERCIAL PL	SR	10A	C1
CMDR WEBSTER DR	MCO	22	B5
COMMUNITY RD	BVDR	14	C1
COMPTON CIR	MV	12B	D3
COMSTOCK DR	TIB	11D	D5
CONCHITA CT	N	1	A3
CONCORD CT	N	1	C2
CONCRTE PIPE RD	MCO	9A	B1
CONIFER PL	N	1	B1
CONIFER PL	N	1A	A6
CONIFER WY	MCO	5A	E5
CONIFER WY	MCO	27	D1

STREET	CITY	PAGE	GRID
CONLON AV	MCO	11B	C5
CONOW ST	CM	12B	D1
CONSTANCE DR	SR	7C	B4
CONSTITUTION DR	CM	12B	E2
CONVENT CT	SR	7D	D5
COOGAN AV	SA	6D	F6
COOLIDGE AV	F	6D	D6
COOPER LN	SLTO	14	A4
CORDONE DR	SA	6D	E6
COREE LN	F	6C	C6
CORINTHIAN CT	N	2	A5
CORINTHIAN CT	TIB	14	C1
CORNELIA AV	MV	11A	C3
CORNELIA AV	MV	12A	A3
CORNELL AV	L	10C	B5
CORNWALL ST	MV	11A	C3
CORONA AV	MCO	5A	A5
CORONA AV	MCO	27	A1
CORONA CT	N	1	C1
CORONADO CT	N	1A	C6
CORONET AV	MV	12A	A3
CORONET WY	MCO	9D	E5
CORRILLO DR	SR	7C	B4
CORTE ALEGRA	MCO	10A	C3
CORTE ALEJO	L	10D	D4
CORTE ALMADEN	SR	7A	A2
CORTE ALTA	MCO	4	B2
CORTE AMADO	L	10A	C3
CORTE ANITA	MCO	10C	C4
CORTE ARRIBA	MCO	4	B2
CORTE BALBOA	MCO	10C	C4
CORTE BARISTO	L	10A	C3
CTE CAPISTRANO	SR	7A	B1
CORTE CAYUGA	MCO	10D	D4
CORTE COLINA	MCO	4	B2
CORTE COMODA	MCO	10C	B4
CORTE CORDOVA	MCO	10A	C3
CORTE DEL BAYO	L	10C	C5
CORTE DEL CERRO	MCO	4	B2
CTE DL CORONADO	L	10D	D5
CORTE DEL NORTE	L	10C	C4
CORTE DEL REY	SR	7A	A1
CORTE DE SABLA	CO	10D	D4
CORTE DORADO	MCO	10A	C3
CORTE ELENA	MCO	10A	C3
CORTE ENCANTO	L	10C	C4
CORTE ESCUELA	MCO	4	A2
CORTE FEDORA	L	10D	D4
CORTE GRACITAS	L	10D	D4
CORTE LA PAZ	SR	7A	A2
CORTE LAS CASAS	TIB	12D	F4
CORTE LENOSA	L	10C	C4
CORTE LODATO	L	10C	C4
CORTE LODATO	MCO	10C	C4
CTE LOS SOMBRAS	MCO	10	C4
CORTE LOYOLA	L	10D	D4
CORTE MADERA	L	10C	C5
CORTE MADERA AV	CM	12A	C2
CORTE MADERA AV	MV	12A	A3
CORTE MESA DR	SR	7C	C5
CORTE MIGUEL	SR	7A	A1
CORTE MORADA	MCO	10D	D4
CORTE NORTE	MCO	4	A2
CORTE ORIENTAL	L	10C	C4
CORTE ORTEGA	L	10C	C4
CORTE PACHECO	SR	7C	A4
CTE PALOS VERDS	TIB	12D	F4
CORTE PATENCIO	MCO	10A	C3
CORTE PLACIDA	L	10D	D4
CORTE PRECITA	L	10B	D3
CORTE RAMON	L	10D	D4
CORTE REAL	L	10C	C5
CORTE ROBLE	MCO	4	A2
CORTES CT	SR	6B	E1
CTE SAN BENITO	SR	7A	A2
CTE SN FERNANDO	TIB	12D	F4
CORTE SARATOGA	SR	7A	A1
CORTE SERENO	MCO	10A	C3
CORTE SOLANO	L	10C	C4
CORTE SUR	MCO	4	A3
CORTE TOLUCA	L	10D	D4
CORTE VERANO	SR	7A	A1
CORTEZ AV	MCO	5A	B5
CORTEZ CIR	N	4	D4
COTTAGE AV	MV	12A	A2
COTTAGE AV	SA	6D	F6
COTTAGE AV	SA	7C	A6
COTTAGE AV	SA	9B	F1

1991 MARIN COUNTY STREET INDEX

STREET	CITY	PAGE	GRID
COTTAGE AV	SA	10A	A1
COTTAGE AV	SR	10A	B1
COTTONWOOD DR	SR	8	B4
COTTONWOOD PL	N	1	B1
COTTONWOOD PL	N	1A	A6
COUNCIL CRST DR	CM	10D	D6
COUNTRY LN	N	1	C1
COUNTRY CLUB DR	MCO	12A	B3
COUNTRY CLUB DR	MV	12A	B3
COUNTRY CLUB DR	N	3	F2
COUNTY RD 3	SLTO	13	F2
COUNTYVIEW DR	MCO	13	C2
COURT LN	F	6C	C6
COURT RD	MV	12A	A2
COURT RD	N	1	E3
COURT ST	SR	10A	C1
COURTRIGHT RD	SR	10A	C2
COVE LN	MCO	31	D3
COVE PL	BVDR	14	C2
COVE RD	BVDR	14	C1
COWBARN LN	N	2	A6
COYOTE RIDGE TR	MCO	13	A3
COYOTE RIDGE TR	MCO	31	E3
CRAIG CT	N	4	B1
CRANE DR	MCO	6B	D2
CRATER LAKE WY	SR	7A	C2
CREAMERY RD	MCO	5A	C5
CRECIENTA DR	SLTO	13	F4
CRECIENTA LN	SLTO	13	F4
CREEK LN	MV	12C	A4
CREEK RD	F	6C	C6
CREEK RD	SA	6D	D6
CREEK TR	SA	6D	D4
CREEKSIDE CT	L	10C	B5
CREEKSIDE CT	N	1	D2
CREEKSIDE CT	CM	12B	E2
CREEKSIDE DR	L	10C	B5
CREEKSIDE DR	MCO	3	C5
CREEK SIDE WY	MCO	12B	D3
CREEK VIEW CIR	L	10C	B5
CRESCENT AV	SLTO	14	A5
CRESCENT AV LWR	MCO	14	A4
CRESCENT CIR	F	6C	C4
CRESCENT CT	MCO	5A	E5
CRESCENT CT	MCO	27	D1
CRESCENT CT	N	1	D3
CRESCENT DR	MCO	5A	E5
CRESCENT DR	MCO	27	D1
CRESCENT DR	N	4	D3
CRESCENT DR	SR	7C	B6
CRESCENT DR E	SR	10A	B1
CRESCENT DR W	SR	10A	A1
CRESCENT LN	F	6C	C6
CRESCENT LN	SA	9B	E1
CRESCENT RD	CM	12A	C1
CRESCENT RD	SA	9B	E1
CRESCENTE AV	MCO	28	B4
CREST RD	BVDR	14	B2
CREST RD	F	6D	D6
CREST RD	MCO	2	D1
CREST RD	R	10A	A1
CREST RD	SA	10A	A1
CRESTA CIR	SR	7A	C1
CRESTA DR	SR	7A	C1
CRESTA WY	SR	7A	C1
CRESTHAVEN DR	MCO	7B	D3
CREST VIEW DR	MCO	7B	D3
CRESTWOOD DR	SR	7C	A5
CRICKLEWOOD DR	N	2	A5
CROMARY WY	MCO	21	E3
CROOKED AV	SA	6D	F6
CROOKED AV	SA	7C	A6
CROSS CREEK PL	L	10C	B5
CROSSCREEK WY	N	2	A2
CROSSROADS CT	N	2	A6
CROWN AV	MCO	10B	E1
CROWN CT	MV	12C	B4
CROWN RD	MCO	9D	F5
CROWN FIRE RD	MCO	9D	E4
CROWN POINT	MCO	10B	E1
CRYSTAL CT	MCO	12D	D4
CRYSTAL CK CT	L	10C	B5
CUB LAND RD	MCO	6C	A4
CUB LAND RD	MCO	27	F1
CULLODEN PK RD	SR	7C	B6
CULLODEN PK RD	SR	10A	B1
CULVER ST	SR	10B	D2
CURLEW WY	N	4	B4
CURREY AV	SLTO	14	A3
CURREY LN	SLTO	13	F4
CURRY LN	MCO	12C	B5
CURTIS AV	SR	7C	C6
CURTIS AV	SR	10A	C1
CUSHING AV	MCO	7A	C3
CUSHING DR	MV	12A	A2
CYNTHIA CT	MCO	6C	C4
CYPRESS AV	MCO	10A	B3
CYPRESS AV	MCO	15	B4
CYPRESS AV	MV	11B	C4
CYPRESS AV	N	1	E3
CYPRESS CT	N	1	D3
CYPRESS DR	F	6C	C6
CYPRESS LN	MV	11B	C4
CYPRESS PL	SLTO	13	E2
CYPRESS RD	MCO	22	B4
CYPRESS RD	SA	6D	F6
D			
D ST	N	4	C2
D ST	SR	10A	C2
DAFFODIL LN	MV	12C	A4
DAISY MAE CT	N	1	C2
DAM RD	MCO	22	E5
DANBERRY LN	MCO	3	F6
DANBERRY LN	MCO	6B	F1
DANBERRY LN	MCO	7A	A1
DANIELLE DR	SR	6B	E3
DARTMOUTH AV	L	10C	B4
DARYL AV	MCO	23	F2
DAVENPORT CT	SR	7C	B6
DAVENPORT CT	SR	10A	B1
DAVID CT	N	1	D3
DAVID CT	SR	7D	D5
DAVIDOR LN	N	1	D1
DAVIDSON ST	N	1	F3
DAVIDSON ST	N	2	A3
DAVIS DR	TIB	11D	F6
DAWES CT	N	1	E4
DAWES ST	N	1	E4
DAWN LN	MCO	13	C1
DAWN PL	MV	12A	B2
DAYS ISLAND RD	MCO	2	F3
DE ANZA WY	SR	7C	B4
DEBORAH CT	N	4	A1
DEBES RANCH RD	MCO	7C	B5
DE BURGH DR	MCO	6B	D3
DEEPSTONE DR	MCO	4	B5
DEER TR	MCO	1	C5
DEERFIELD LN	N	1	E4
DEER HOLLOW RD	MCO	6D	E4
DEER ISLAND LN	MCO	2	B3
DEER PARK AV	SR	7D	E6
DEER PARK AV	SR	10B	E1
DEER PARK LN	F	6C	C6
DEER PARK LN	F	6D	D6
DEER PARK LN	SA	6D	D6
DEER PK FIRE RD	MCO	11B	A5
DEER PK FIRE RD	MCO	30	C4
DEER RUN	MCO	12B	D2
DEERTRAIL LN	MCO	13	C2
DEER VALLEY RD	SR	7A	B1
DE FORD DR	SR	6B	F3
DE LA GUERRA RD	SR	6B	E1
DEL CASA DR	MV	12A	C3
DEL GANADO RD	MCO	6B	E1
DEL GANADO RD	SR	6B	E1
DEL HARO WY	SR	7C	A4
DELL LN	MV	12A	B3
DELL LN	MV	12C	B4
DELL ST	MV	12C	B4
DELLWOOD CT	SR	8	B5
DEL MAR AV	N	1	D3
DELMAR DR	TIB	11D	E5
DEL MONTE	L	10D	D5
DE LONG AV	N	1	E3
DEL ORO LAGOON	MCO	2	D6
DEL PRESIDIO BL	SR	7A	B3
DE LUCA PL	SR	10B	D2
DENISE CT	MCO	12C	B6
DENISE CT	N	1	F2
DENLYN ST	N	1	F5
DENNING AV	SR	6D	F4
DESCANSO WY	MCO	7B	D2
DEUCE CT	F	6C	B4
DEVILS GLCH FR	MCO	5	E2
DEVON DR	SR	6D	F4
DEVON DR	SR	7C	A4
DEVONSHIRE DR	N	1	B2
DE WITT DR	R	9B	F3
DIABLO AV	N	1	E3
DIABLO CT	N	1	E3
DIABLO DR	MCO	9D	F4
DIABLO DR	MCO	10C	A4
DIAMOND HD PASG	CM	12B	E2
DIANE LN	L	10C	C6
DIANNE WY	SR	10A	C3
DIAS WY	SR	7C	A4
DIAS RIDGE TR	MCO	31	E3
DIAZ RIDGE F RD	MCO	31	D1
DIBBLEE RD	R	9B	E3
DICKENS CT	MV	12D	D4
DICKSON DR	N	3	F1
DICKSON DR	N	4	A1
DICKSON RD	MCO	5	F4
DICKSON RD	MCO	5A	A5
DICKSON RD	MCO	27	A1
DIEGO DR	SR	6B	E2
DIGITAL DR	N	4	C1
DILLON BEACH RD	MCO	15	B4
DIPSEA RD	MCO	28	C4
DIPSEA TR	MCO	11B	C4
DIPSEA FIRE RD	MCO	30	A5
DIVISO ST	TIB	14	D1
DIXON RDG FIRE	MCO	5A	F3
DIXON RDG FIRE	MCO	6A	A1
DOCKSIDE CIR	SR	7A	C2
DODIE ST	SR	10B	E3
DOGWOOD CT	N	2	A4
DOGWOOD RD	MCO	28	B5
DOHERTY DR	L	10C	C5
DOLAN AV	MCO	13	C1
DOLORES ST	SR	10B	D3
DOLPHIN ISLE	MCO	2	D6
DOMINGA AV	F	6C	C6
DOMINIC DR	N	1	B2
DOMINICAN DR	SR	7D	D5
DONAHUE ST	MCO	13	D1
DONNA ST	N	1	F4
DON TIMOTEO CT	SR	7C	A4
DOOLEY CT	N	1	D1
DORETHEA ST	MCO	13	B1
DORIAN WY	SR	7D	F6
DORIAN WY	SR	8	A5
DORIS AV	N	1	C3
DORSET LN	MV	12D	D4
DOTS LN	MV	11B	C4
DOUGLAS DR	MCO	12C	A4
DOUGLAS DR	MCO	21	F5
DOUGLASS ST	MCO	21	E3
DOVE PL	N	4	B4
DOVER DR	MCO	21	F5
DOW LN	MCO	1	C3
DOW LN	N	1	C3
DRAKE AV	MCO	13	D2
DRAKE WY	MCO	21	D2
DRAKES BEACH RD	MCO	24	D2
DRAKES COVE	SR	7C	B4
DRAKES LNDNG RD	L	10D	D5
DRAKE SUMMIT RD	MCO	22	A6
DRAKES VIEW CIR	L	10D	D5
DRAKES VIEW DR	MCO	21	F5
DRAKES VIEW DR	MCO	22	A5
DRAKES VIEW TR	MCO	21	E6
DRAKEWOOD LN	N	1	E5
DRAKEWOOD PL	N	1	E5
DREAM FARM RD N	MCO	21	E4
DREAM FARM RD S	MCO	21	F4
DRIFTWOOD AV	N	1	D1
DRIFTWOOD CT	SR	8	B4
DUARTE CT	N	4	B4
DU BOIS ST	SR	10B	D2
DUFF LN	R	9B	E3
DUFFY PL	SR	10B	D2
DUNAND AV	SR	10A	B1
DUNDEE WY	MCO	21	E3
DUNFRIES TER	SR	8	A5
DUNLIN CT	MCO	4	B5
DUNN LN	SLTO	13	E3
DURAN DR	SR	6B	E1
DURANT WY	MCO	13	C2
DURHAM RD	SA	6D	E5
DUSEL CT	N	4	C3
DUTCH VALLEY LN	MCO	6A	C2
DUTTON CT	MCO	13	D2
DUXBURY COVE	SR	10B	F2
E			
E ST	N	4	D3
E ST	SR	10A	C1
EAGLE DR	N	3	F1
EAGLE GAP CT	N	4	B3
EAGLE GAP RD	N	4	B3
EAGLE ROCK RD	MCO	12D	E4
EAGLES RD	MCO	6C	A5
EAMES CT	N	1	B2
EAST CT	N	1	E3
EAST CT	SA	6D	D5
EAST DR	MV	12C	B4
EAST RD	R	9B	F3
EAST ST	MCO	15	E5
EAST ST	SR	10A	B1
EAST TER	TIB	11D	D4
EAST TER	TIB	12D	F4
EASTERBY ST	SLTO	13	F3
EASTMAN AV	CM	12A	C1
EAST VIEW AV	MCO	14	C2
EAST VIEW AV	TIB	14	C2
EASTWOOD WY	MCO	12C	B6
EASTWOOD WY	MCO	13	B1
EASY CT	N	1	C2
EBBTIDE AV	SLTO	13	E2
EBBTIDE PASSAGE	CM	12B	F1
EBRIGHT FIRE RD	MCO	1	B5
ECHO AV	CM	12B	E2
ECHO CT	SA	9B	E1
ECHO PL	L	10C	A6
ECHO PL	SR	7C	A6
EDEN ST	L	10C	B6
EDEN ROC DR	SLTO	13	E2
EDGEHILL RD	MV	12A	B3
EDGEHILL WY	MCO	7C	C4
EDGEMAR WY	CM	12B	E1
EDGEMONT WY	MCO	21	E3
EDGEWATER CT	SR	7A	C3
EDGEWATER RD	BVDR	11D	E6
EDGEWATER RD	BVDR	14	B1
EDGEWOOD AV	MCO	11A	B3
EDGEWOOD AV	MCO	12C	A4
EDGEWOOD AV	MCO	21	E3
EDGEWOOD AV	MV	11A	B3
EDGEWOOD AV	MV	11B	C4
EDGEWOOD DR	MCO	5A	E5
EDGEWOOD DR	MCO	27	E1
EDGEWOOD WY	SR	7C	B6
EDINBORO LN	MCO	21	E3
EDISON AV	CM	12A	C1
EDNA CT	MCO	10A	B3
EDWARD AV	MCO	7A	C3
EDWARD CT	SR	7D	D6
EDWARD CT	SR	10B	D1
EDWARDS AV	SLTO	14	B5
EGGERS PZ	MV	12C	B4
EGLIN LN	N	4	C3
EGRET WY	MCO	12D	F6
ELAINE AV	MV	11A	C2
ELAINE AV	MV	12A	A2
ELAINE WY	SR	10B	E2
EL ARROYO PL	N	4	C2
EL BONITO	N	4	D3
EL CAMINO	SR	7C	C6
EL CAMINO AV	SR	10A	B1
EL CAMINO DR	CM	12B	E2
EL CAMINO BUENO	R	9B	F2
EL CAMINO BUENO	R	10A	A2
EL CAPITAN AV	MV	11A	C1
EL CAPITAN DR	MCO	3	D5
EL CERRITO	MCO	5A	A4
EL CERRITO AV	SA	6D	E6
EL CERRITO AV	SR	7C	B6
EL CONDOR CT	SR	7A	A3
ELDA CT	SR	6B	F3
ELDA DR	SR	6B	F3
ELDERBERRY CT	MCO	2	C2
ELDERBERRY LN	MCO	3	F6
ELDERBERRY LN	MCO	6B	F1
EL DORADO CT	N	1	A4
ELDORADO WY	MCO	11B	C4
ELDRIDGE AV	MV	12A	C4
ELDRIDGE CT	N	1	F5
ELDRIDGE RD	MCO	9D	D4
ELDRIDGE ST	N	1	F5
ELDRIDGE GR RD	MCO	9B	D3
ELDRIDG GR F RD	MCO	9D	D5
ELDRIDG GR F RD	MCO	11A	A1
ELEGANT TERN RD	N	4	B4
ELENA CIR	SR	7A	A2
ELENA CT	N	1	C1
EL FAISAN DR	SR	7A	A3
ELFORD ST	SR	10A	C2
ELF OWL CT	N	4	B4
ELGIN WY	MCO	21	E3
ELINOR AV	MV	12A	B3
ELIOT CT	MV	12D	D5
ELISEO DR	L	10D	D4
ELISEO DR	MCO	10D	D4
ELISEO DR S	L	10C	C5
ELIZABETH PL	MCO	21	E5
ELIZABETH WY	SR	7C	B6
ELK HORN WY	SA	6D	E5
ELKIN CT	SR	7C	A6
ELKIN CT	SR	10A	A1
ELLEN CT	MCO	4	A6
ELLEN CT	MCO	7A	A1
ELLEN DR	MCO	4	A6
ELLEN DR	MCO	7A	A1
ELLIS LN	MCO	1	D1
ELLSWORTH LN	MCO	6A	C3
ELM AV	L	10C	C6
ELM AV	L	12A	C1
ELM AV	MCO	5A	E5
ELM AV	MCO	10A	A3
ELM AV	MCO	27	E1
ELM AV	MV	12C	C4
ELM AV	SA	6D	E6
ELM CT	SA	6D	E6
ELM CT	SA	9B	E1
ELM DR	N	1	E2
ELM RD	MCO	28	A5
ELM ST	SR	7D	D6
ELMA ST	MV	12A	A3
EL MIRADOR	MCO	5A	E1
EL MONTE	SLTO	14	A4
ELMWOOD CT	N	1	F2
ELMWOOD CT	SR	7C	B5
EL NOVATO CIR	N	1	E2
EL NOVATO CT	N	1	E2
EL PAVO RL CIR	SR	7A	A3
EL PORTAL	SLTO	14	B4
EL PORTAL DR	L	10C	C4
EL PRADO AV	SR	7C	B4
ELSIE LN	F	6C	C5
ELVIA CT	MCO	4	B6
EMBARCADERO WY	SR	10B	E2
EMERSON DR	MV	12D	D4
EMERYSTONE TER	MCO	4	B5
EMLIN LN	MCO	10A	A3
ENA CT	N	1	C3
ENCINA AV	CM	12B	D2
ENCINA CT	N	1	E1
ENCINA PL	SA	9B	E2
ENCINAL AV	MCO	9A	B2
ENDEAVOR COVE	CM	12B	F2
ENDEAVOR DR	CM	12B	E2
ENFRENTE RD	MCO	4	B1
ENGLISH CT	N	1	B3
ESENADA DR	N	4	B1
ENSIGN WY	MCO	25	C2
ENT CT	N	4	C3
ENTERPRISE DR	CM	12B	E2
ENTERPRISE CONC	MCO	13	C1
ENTRADA DR	N	4	B1
ENTRANCE RD	N	4	C3
ENTRATA AV	SA	9B	F1
EQUESTRIAN CT	MCO	1	F1
ERICA CT	N	1	B2
ERICA RD	MCO	12C	A6
ERIN DR	MCO	4	B6
ERLA LOUISE DR	MCO	2	C3
ESCALLE LN	L	10C	B5
ESCALLONIA DR	N	1	E1
ESCALON DR	MV	12A	C3
ESCHOLTZIA AV	MCO	5A	E6
ESCHOLTZIA AV	MCO	27	E1
ESCOLTA	N	4	D3
ESCONDIDA LN	MCO	5A	A4
ESCONDIDO WY	MCO	21	D2
ESMEYER DR	SR	6B	F3
ESMEYER DR	SR	7A	A3
ESPALDA CT	SR	10A	B1
ESPERANZA AV	TIB	14	D1
ESPERANZA ST	MCO	4	D1
ESPERANZA ST	TIB	14	B1
ESQUIRE CT	N	4	A1
ESSEX LN	SA	6D	F6
ESSEX LN	SA	9B	F1
ESSEX ST	SA	6D	F6
ESSEX ST	SA	9B	F1
ESTADO CT	N	1A	C6
ESTADO WY	N	1A	C6
ESTANCIA WY	MCO	7B	D2
ESTATES CT	SR	10A	B2
ESTATES DR	N	1	C2
ESTATES DR	MCO	6A	C2
ESTELLE AV	L	10C	A4
ESTELLE AV	MCO	10C	A4
ESTERO RD	MCO	15	B2
ESTERO TR	MCO	21	B4
ESTERO TR	MCO	24	E1
ESTERO TR	MCO	25	B2
ESTERO WY	SR	7C	A4
ESTRADA LN	MCO	12B	E2
ESTRELLA CT	N	1	C1
ESTRELLA WY	N	1	C1
ETHEL AV	MCO	12C	B5
ETHEL AV	MV	12C	B4
ETHEL CT	MV	12C	A4
ETHEL LN	MCO	12C	B5
ETHEL LN	MV	12C	A4
ETON WY	MCO	12A	C3
ETON WY	MV	12A	C3
ETTA CT	MCO	4	B6
EUCALYPTUS AV	N	1	B2
EUCALYPTUS LN	SR	7D	E6
EUCALYPTUS LN	SR	10B	E1
EUCALYPTUS RD	BVDR	14	C2
EUCALYPTUS WY	MCO	12C	A6
EUCALYPTUS WY	MCO	13	A1
EUCALYPTUS KNLS	MV	12D	D5
EUGENE ST	MV	11A	C3
EUREKA ST	MCO	13	D2
EUTERPE ST	MV	12C	B4
EVA ST	SR	10A	C2
EVELYN AV	MV	11A	B3
EVEREST CT	MCO	12C	B6
EVERGREEN AV	MCO	12C	B5
EVERGREEN DR	MCO	9D	F5
EVERGREEN DR	MCO	10C	A4
EVERGREEN LN	MCO	12C	A5
EVERGREEN RD	MCO	28	B5
EVERGREEN FR RD	MCO	9D	F5
EXCELSIOR LN	SLTO	14	A4
EYE ST	SR	7C	B6
F			
F ST	N	4	D3
F ST	SR	10A	B1
FABIAN CT	N	1	B2
FAIR DR	SR	7C	C5
FAIRBANKS RD	MCO	15	E5
FAIRFAX ST	SR	10B	E2
FAIRFX BOLNS RD	MCO	27	B6
FAIRFX BOLNS RD	MCO	28	B1
FAIRFAX RDG RD	MCO	6C	B4
FAIRHAVEN WY	N	2	A6
FAIRHILLS DR	SR	7C	B6
FAIRVIEW AV	CM	12B	D2
FAIRVIEW AV	MCO	12C	B6
FAIRVIEW AV	MCO	13	B1
FAIRVIEW CT	SA	6D	D5
FAIRWAY DR	MCO	7D	E6
FAIRWAY DR	MCO	10B	E1
FAIRWAY DR	MV	12A	B3
FAIRWAY DR	N	3	F2
FAIRWAY DR	N	4	A1
FAIRWOOD CT	SR	8	B4
FALLEN LEAF	R	9B	F2
FALLEN LEAF WY	N	4	D5
FALLN TWO RK RD	MCO	15	E3
FALLN TWO RK RD	MCO	16	A2
FARM RD	MCO	7C	B5
FARVUE ST	N	1	C4
FAWN CT	MCO	6B	E3
FAWN CT	MCO	12B	D2
FAWN DR	MCO	6B	E3
FAWN RIDGE	F	6C	C6

1991 MARIN COUNTY STREET INDEX

STREET	CITY	PAGE	GRID
FAWNRIDGE CT	N	1A	D6
FAY DR	MCO	10A	B3
FELIPA CT	TIB	11D	D5
FELIZ DR	N	1	C1
FELIZ RD	N	1	C1
FERN AV	BVDR	14	C2
FERN AV	MCO	5A	E5
FERN AV	MCO	27	E1
FERN AV	MV	12C	B4
FERN LN	CM	12B	D2
FERN LN	SA	6D	E6
FERN RD	MCO	10C	A5
FERN RD	MCO	28	B5
FERN TR	CM	12A	B1
FERN WY	MCO	10C	A5
FERN WY	MCO	11B	C4
FERNANDO DR	N	1	F3
FERNANDO DR	N	2	A3
FERNBRIDGE PL	N	2	A6
FERN CANYON RD	MV	11A	B2
FERNDALE AV	MCO	12C	B5
FERNHILL AV	R	9B	F2
FERNWOOD DR	SA	9B	E1
FERNWOOD DR	SR	8	B4
FERNWOOD LN	MCO	5A	C1
FERNWOOD WY	SR	8	B5
FERRIS DR	N	1	D1
FIELDING CIR	MV	12D	D6
FIELDSTONE DR	N	1A	D6
FIFER AV	CM	10D	D5
FILBERT AV	SLTO	13	F3
FILBERT AV	SLTO	14	A3
FIR AV	MCO	5A	C5
FIR AV	MCO	5A	E5
FIR AV	MCO	27	D1
FIR TR	F	6C	C5
FIRE RD	MCO	5A	E5
FISH GULCH RD	MCO	9A	C3
FLAG ST	L	10C	B6
FLAGSTONE TER	MCO	4	B5
FLAMINGO LN	SR	8	B4
FLAMINGO RD	MCO	12C	C6
FLAMINGO RD	MCO	13	C1
FLAMOUTH CV	SR	10B	F2
FLAXBERRY LN	MCO	3	F6
FLAXBERRY LN	MCO	6B	F1
FLEETWOOD CT	N	1	B3
FLICKER DR	N	4	B4
FLINT CT	N	1	E6
FLORENCE AV	MV	12C	A4
FLORENCE AV	SA	6D	D6
FLORIBEL AV	SA	6D	E6
FLORIBEL AV	SA	9B	E1
FLYING CLD CRSE	CM	12B	E2
FOLEY LN	L	10C	B6
FOLEY LN	L	12A	B1
FOLIUM AV	MCO	5A	A5
FONTANA	N	1	E1
FOOTHILL RD	SA	6D	E6
FORBES AV	SA	7C	A6
FORBES AV	SA	10A	A1
FORBES AV	SR	7C	B6
FORBES AV	SR	10A	B1
FORD WY	N	1	F4
FOREMAN LN	MCO	12D	D6
FOREMAST COVE	CM	12B	E2
FOREST AV	MCO	11B	C4
FOREST DR	MCO	5A	B5
FOREST WY	MCO	13	A1
FORRES WY	MCO	21	E3
FORREST AV	F	6D	D6
FORREST AV	SA	6D	D6
FORREST CT	MCO	6D	E4
FORREST LN	SR	6B	F3
FORREST RD	N	1	D4
FORREST ST	MV	12C	B4
FORREST TER	F	6C	C6
FOSS AV	SA	9B	E1
FOSTER AV	MCO	10A	B3
FOSTER LN	SR	7C	B6
FOSTER LN	SR	10A	B1
FOWLER CT	SR	6B	F3
FOX CT	N	1	E3
FOX DR	MCO	22	B6
FOX DR	MCO	25	F1
FOX LN	MCO	6B	E3
FOX HOLLOW PL	N	1A	E6
FOX RUN RD	MCO	5A	F6

STREET	CITY	PAGE	GRID
FOX RUN RD	MCO	27	E1
FRANCES AV	L	10C	A4
FRANCES AV	SA	6D	D6
FRANCES LN	SA	6D	F6
FRANCES LN	SA	7C	A6
FRANCES ST	SR	10A	C2
FRANCIS AV	F	6D	D6
FRANCIS AV	MCO	10C	A4
FRANCISCO BLVD	SR	8A	E3
FRANCISCO BLVD	SR	10B	D2
FRANCISCO BLVD	SR	10D	F4
FRANCISCO PATIO	MCO	28	D5
FRANCSCO VIS CT	TIB	11D	D5
FRANKLIN AV	N	1	F3
FREDA LN	SA	6D	F6
FREDSON CT	N	1	C3
FREITAS, M T PY	SR	6B	F2
FREITAS, M T PY	SR	7A	A2
FREMONT RD	SR	10A	B1
FRESA AV	MCO	9A	B1
FRIARS LN	MCO	12C	A6
FRIAR TUCK LN	SR	8	A4
FRIENDLY LN	N	1	D2
FRONT ST	N	1	E3
FRONT ST	SR	10B	E2
FRONT TR	CM	12A	B1
FRONTAGE RD	N	1	E3
FROST CT	MV	12D	D5
FROSTY LN	N	2	B6
FRUSTUCK AV	F	6C	C6
G			
G ST	SR	7C	B6
G ST	SR	10A	B1
GAGE LN	MCO	1	C5
GALERITA WY	MCO	7B	D2
GALLEON WY	SR	6B	E1
GALLI DR	N	4	B1
GALWAY LN	SR	6B	F1
GARDEN AV	MCO	7C	C4
GARDEN AV	R	9B	F2
GARDEN CT	N	1	E3
GARDEN LN	SR	10A	C1
GARDEN WY	L	10C	C6
GARDEN WY	MCO	5A	E5
GARDEN WY	MCO	12C	A6
GARDEN WY	MCO	27	D1
GARDEN ROCK RD	MCO	6A	C2
GARDNER ST	MV	12A	A3
GARFIELD ST	N	1	E4
GARNER CT	N	1	D5
GARNER DR	N	1	E5
GARY PL	SR	10B	E3
GARY WY	MCO	6A	C3
GATE 5 RD	SLTO	13	E2
GATE 6 RD	MCO	13	E1
GATE 6 RD	MCO	13	E2
GATE 6 1/2 RD	MCO	13	E2
GAZINA CT	N	1	E1
GEARY AV	F	6D	D5
GEARY AV	MCO	10A	A3
GEARY DR	MCO	10A	A3
GEARY LN	F	6D	D5
GELDERT CT	TIB	11D	E5
GELDERT DR	TIB	11D	D4
GENEVA WY	MCO	7B	D3
GEORGE LN	MV	12B	D2
GEORGE LN	SLTO	13	F4
GEORGE LN	SLTO	14	A4
GEORGE ST	N	1	E3
GERICKE RD	MCO	15	E2
GERLACK RD	SA	9B	D1
GERMAINE PL	N	3	E1
GERSTLE CT	SR	10A	B2
GERTRUDE LN	N	1	B2
GIBSON AV	MCO	12C	C6
GIBSON AV	MCO	13	C1
GILBERT DR	MCO	12D	E6
GILBERT ST	MCO	10B	D3
GILMARTIN DR	TIB	11D	E6
GIRARD AV	SLTO	13	F3
GIRARD AV	SLTO	14	A3
GLACIER WY	SR	7A	C2
GLEN AV	SR	10A	C2
GLEN CT	MV	12A	B3
GLEN CT	SLTO	14	A4
GLEN DR	F	6A	B3

STREET	CITY	PAGE	GRID
GLEN DR	F	6C	B4
GLEN DR	MCO	7B	E3
GLEN DR	MV	12A	B2
GLEN DR	SLTO	13	F4
GLEN DR	SLTO	14	A4
GLEN LN	MCO	2	D2
GLEN RD	MCO	2	D2
GLEN RD	SA	6D	D6
GLEN TR	MCO	5	A5
GLEN WY	L	10C	A6
GLEN WY	MCO	21	E3
GLENAIRE DR	SR	10B	D3
GLEN FIRE RD	MCO	6A	B3
GLENHILL CT	N	1	D3
GLEN PARK AV	SR	7D	D5
GLENSIDE WY	MCO	7C	B5
GLENWOOD AV	MCO	12C	A6
GLENWOOD AV	MCO	13	A1
GLENWOOD AV	R	9B	E2
GLENWOOD DR	SR	7C	C6
GLORIA DR	SR	10A	B2
GLOUCESTER CV	SR	10B	F2
GOING LN	N	1	B3
GOLDEN GATE AV	BVDR	14	C2
GOLDEN GATE DR	SR	10B	E3
GOLDEN GATE PL	N	1	E2
GOLDEN HINDE BL	SR	7C	A4
GOLDN HIND PSGE	CM	12B	E1
GOLDEN IRIS TER	MCO	3	D5
GOLDEN LILY PL	MCO	3	D5
GOLDFINCH CT	N	1	B3
GOLD HILL FR RD	SR	7D	E5
GOLD HILL GRADE	SR	7D	E5
GOLD MINER CT	N	1	D3
GOLF AV	SR	7C	C4
GOLF LN	SA	6D	F6
GOLF LN	SR	7C	A6
GOLF CLUB SV RD	MCO	9A	A2
GOLF CLUB SV RD	MCO	27	F4
GOMEZ WY	MV	12C	C5
GOODHILL RD	MCO	9D	F4
GOODHILL RD	MCO	10C	A4
GORDON ST	SLTO	13	F3
GOTHIC DR	N	1	D3
GRACE CT	CM	12B	D1
GRACELAND DR	SR	7C	C6
GRADY FIRE RD	MCO	3	B4
GRANADA DR	CM	12B	E2
GRAND AV	SR	7D	D6
GRAND AV	SR	10B	D1
GRAND CT	SR	7D	D6
GRAND CANYON RD	MCO	21	F1
GRAND CANYON RD	MCO	22	B3
GRANDE PASEO	MCO	4	B6
GRANDE VISTA	N	1	C2
GRANDVIEW AV	MCO	2	E3
GRANGE WY	SR	8A	E3
GRANLEE RD	MCO	7B	D3
GRANT AV	N	1	E2
GRANT ST	MCO	5A	E5
GRASS CT	N	4	C3
GRASSY SLOPE RD	MCO	5A	A6
GRASSY SLOPE RD	MCO	27	A2
GRAVITY CAR RD	MCO	11A	A2
GREAT CIRCLE DR	MCO	12D	E6
GREEN LN	MCO	12D	E5
GREEN WY	SR	10B	D1
GREENBERRY LN	MCO	3	F6
GREENBERRY LN	MCO	6B	F1
GREENBRAE BRDWK	MCO	10D	E5
GREENE ST	MCO	12C	C6
GREENE ST	MCO	13	C1
GREENFIELD AV	SA	9B	F1
GREENFIELD AV	SA	10A	A1
GREENFIELD AV	SR	10A	A1
GREENFIELD CT	MCO	12B	D3
GREENFIELD CT	MV	12B	D3
GREENFIELD CT	SA	9B	F1
GREENFIELD CT	SA	10A	A1
GREEN GLEN WY	MCO	13	B1
GREEN GULCH TR	MCO	31	E3
GREENHILL RD	MCO	12C	B5
GREEN OAK DR	N	4	C4
GREEN OAK PL	N	4	C4
GREENOCH WY	MCO	21	E3
GREENPICHER TR	MCO	5	C5
GREEN POINT LN	MCO	2	E2
GREENSBURGH LN	MCO	6A	C2

STREET	CITY	PAGE	GRID
GREENSIDE WY	SR	8	C3
GREEN VALLEY CT	MCO	6B	E3
GREENWOOD AV	SR	10A	B2
GREENWOOD CT	TIB	12D	F4
GREENWOOD DR	MCO	12D	E4
GREENWOOD DR	N	1	F5
GREENWOOD WY	MCO	9D	F5
GREENWOOD WY	MCO	10C	A5
GREENWOOD WY	MV	12A	B2
GREENWD BAY DR	MCO	12D	E4
GREENWD BCH RD	TIB	11D	D5
GREENWD BCH RD	TIB	12D	F5
GREENWOOD CV DR	MCO	12D	E4
GREGG PL	N	3	F1
GREGORY DR	MCO	6A	C3
GREGORY DR	MCO	6C	C4
GREGORY PL	L	10C	C5
GREGORY PL	L	10D	D5
GRETCHEN PL	L	10C	C5
GRETCHEN PL	L	10D	D5
GROVE AV	CM	12A	C2
GROVE LN	N	1	D3
GROVE LN	SA	6D	E6
GROVE LN	SA	9B	E1
GROVE RD	MCO	28	A5
GROVE ST	MV	12C	B4
GROVE ST	SR	10A	B2
GROVE HILL AV	SA	6D	F6
GUADALUPE PL	MCO	5A	B4
GUISELA CT	MCO	2	D1
GUM TREE CT	N	1	B2
GUSTAFSON CT	N	1	B2
H			
H LN	MCO	2	B1
H ST	SR	7C	B6
H ST	SR	10A	B1
HACIENDA AV	MCO	5A	A4
HACIENDA CT	SR	7C	C5
HACIENDA DR	TIB	11D	D4
HACIENDA WY	MCO	7B	D2
HALCYON CT	TIB	11D	E5
HALE LN	MV	12C	A4
HALF MOON RD	N	1	D4
HAMILTON CT	SR	7C	C5
HAMILTON DR	MV	12D	D5
HAMILTON DR	N	2	B6
HAMILTON DR	N	4	B1
HAMILTON LN	MCO	11B	B4
HAMMONDALE CT	SR	7C	C5
HAMPSHIRE WY	N	1	D1
HAMPTON AV	SA	6D	E6
HAMPTON LN	MCO	2	D2
HANCOCK ST	N	1	F3
HANEY LN	SR	7C	A6
HANGAR AV	N	4	D2
HANKEN DR	MCO	10A	A3
HANNA RANCH RD	N	2	B5
HANOVER CT	N	1	B2
HANSEN RD	N	1	C3
HAPPY LN	SR	7C	A6
HARBOR DR	CM	12B	E2
HARBOR DR	MCO	2	E2
HARBOR DR	SLTO	13	F2
HARBOR DR W	SLTO	13	E3
HARBOR ST	SR	10B	D2
HARBOR COVE WY	MCO	12D	E5
HARBOR OAK DR	TIB	14	C1
HARBOR POINT DR	MCO	12D	E6
HARBOR VIEW CT	MCO	10B	E2
HARBOR VISTA DR	MCO	12D	D5
HARCOURT ST	SR	7C	B6
HARCOURT ST	SR	10A	B1
HARDING DR	N	1	D5
HARKLE RD	N	1	F3
HARMON AV	CM	12A	C1
HARN CT	TIB	11D	D4
HARRIET WY	TIB	12D	F4
HARRIS HILL DR	N	1	C3
HARRISON AV	SLTO	14	A4
HARRISON CT	N	1	E4
HART AV	CM	12A	C1
HART LN	MCO	12C	A4
HART ST	CM	12A	C1
HART ST	SR	10A	B1
HARTE AV	SR	10B	D3
HARVARD AV	MCO	12C	C6

STREET	CITY	PAGE	GRID
HARVARD DR	L	10C	B4
HARVEST LN	MCO	13	A1
HARVEY TR	CM	12A	B1
HARVEY TR	L	12A	B1
HATCH RD	MCO	1	B3
HATZIC CT	L	10C	A6
HAVENWOOD RD	MCO	2	E2
HAVERHILL CT	N	1	B2
HAWKINS WY	L	10C	C6
HAWK RIDGE CT	N	4	B4
HAWTHORN WY	MCO	7B	D2
HAWTHORNDEN WY	MCO	21	E3
HAWTHORNE AV	L	10C	B6
HAWTHORNE AV	SA	6D	D5
HAWTHORNE CT	F	6C	C4
HAWTHORNE DR	TIB	11D	D5
HAWTHORNE LN	CM	12B	D2
HAWTHORNE LN	MCO	12B	D2
HAWTHORNE RD	MCO	28	A5
HAWTHORNE ST	MCO	12C	B5
HAWTHORNE TER	N	1	A1
HAWTHORNE TER	N	1A	A5
HAWTHORNE WY	N	1	B2
HAYDEN AV	N	1	E3
HAYES ST	N	1	E4
HAYES ST	SR	10A	B1
HAZEL AV	L	10C	B6
HAZEL AV	MCO	5A	A4
HAZEL AV	MV	11B	C4
HAZEL AV	MV	12C	A4
HAZEL AV	SA	6D	E6
HAZEL AV	SA	9B	E1
HAZEL CT	SR	10B	D3
HAZEL LN	MV	12C	A4
HAZEL RD	F	6C	C6
HAZEL TR	MCO	11B	B5
HAZELWOOD LN	SR	8	A4
HEARFIELD LN	SR	7D	D6
HEARTHSTONE CT	N	4	B5
HEARTWOOD CT	SR	8	A4
HEATH WY	SLTO	13	E2
HEATHCLIFF DR	TIB	11D	F5
HEATHER LN	MCO	21	D3
HEATHER LN	MV	12A	B2
HEATHER LN	N	1	B2
HEATHER WY	L	10C	C6
HEATHER WY	MV	12A	B2
HEATHER WY	SR	7A	A2
HEATHER CUTOFF	MCO	31	C2
HEATHERSTONE DR	MCO	4	B5
HEATHERSTONE LN	MCO	4	B4
HECHT AV	SLTO	14	A4
HECTOR LN	N	4	B2
HELEN AV	MCO	12C	C6
HELEN LN	L	12A	B1
HELENS LN	MV	12C	A4
HEMLOCK	MCO	5A	B4
HEMLOCK AV	MCO	2	F3
HEPBURN HTS RD	SR	7C	A6
HERBING LN	MCO	10C	A5
HERITAGE DR	SR	8	C4
HERMIT LN	MCO	10A	A3
HERON CT	MCO	8A	E4
HERON DR	MCO	12D	F6
HERON DR	MCO	13	F1
HERRERA CT	SA	6D	D4
HERRERA DR	F	6A	B3
HERRING DR	MCO	12D	E6
HETHERTON ST	SR	10B	D1
HEUTERS LN	MV	12C	A4
HIBISCUS WY	SR	7A	A2
HICKORY AV	CM	10C	C6
HICKORY AV	CM	12A	C1
HICKORY LN	SR	7A	A2
HICKORY RD	F	6C	C6
HICKOX RD	N	1	C2
HICKS VALLEY RD	MCO	19	F4
HICKS VALLEY RD	MCO	20	A4
HIDALGO AV	MCO	5A	B5
HIDALGO AV	MCO	27	B1
HIDDEN LN	MCO	12C	C6
HIDDEN OAKS DR	N	1	D1
HIDDEN VLY LN	MCO	6B	E3
HIGH ST	MCO	15	E5
HIGH ST	SR	10B	D2
HIGHLAND AV	MCO	7D	E6
HIGHLAND AV	SR	7D	E6
HIGHLAND AV	SR	10B	E1

STREET	CITY	PAGE	GRID
HIGHLAND CT	L	10C	B6
HIGHLAND DR	N	3	F1
HIGHLAND DR	N	4	A1
HIGHLAND LN	MCO	12C	C5
HIGHLAND WY	MCO	21	E3
HILARITA AV	MV	12C	C4
HILARITA CIR	BVDR	11D	E6
HILARITA CIR	BVDR	14	B1
HILARY CT	N	1	D3
HILARY DR	TIB	11D	E5
HILL AV	F	6D	D5
HILL AV	MCO	5A	E5
HILL DR	MCO	10A	B2
HILL PATH	CM	12A	C1
HILL RD	N	1	D3
HILL RD	R	9B	F3
HILL ST	MV	12C	B4
HILL TR	CM	12A	B1
HILLCREST AV	L	10C	A4
HILLCREST AV	MCO	10C	A4
HILLCREST AV	SA	9B	E1
HILLCREST CT	SA	6D	D5
HILLCREST DR	SR	7C	C6
HILLCREST DR	SR	10A	C1
HILLCREST RD	MCO	11D	D4
HILLCREST RD	MV	12A	B3
HILLCREST RD	TIB	11D	D4
HILLDALE DR	SA	7C	A6
HILLDALE WY	MCO	12C	C6
HILLGIRT DR	R	9B	F2
HILLSIDE AV	F	6C	C6
HILLSIDE AV	MCO	9B	F3
HILLSIDE AV	MCO	10A	A3
HILLSIDE AV	MCO	28	B4
HILLSIDE AV	MV	12A	B3
HILLSIDE AV	R	9B	F3
HILLSIDE AV	SA	6D	E6
HILLSIDE AV	SA	9B	E1
HILLSIDE AV	SR	8	A6
HILLSIDE AV	SR	10A	A1
HILLSIDE AV W	SA	9B	F1
HILLSIDE DR	F	6D	D6
HILLSIDE RD	MCO	10A	B3
HILLSIDE TER	MCO	2	E2
HILLSIDE TR	MCO	11B	A4
HILLSWOOD DR	N	1	E5
HILLTOP AV	MCO	5A	C5
HILLVIEW AV	SR	10B	D3
HINGHAM COVE	SR	10B	F2
HI VISTA RD	SLTO	14	B5
HOAG AV	SR	10B	E2
HODGES DR	MCO	12D	E6
HOGBACK	MCO	11A	A2
HOLCOMB AV	L	10C	C6
HOLLY AV	L	10C	B6
HOLLY AV	MCO	2	F3
HOLLY DR	SR	7A	A2
HOLLY LN	MCO	5A	E5
HOLLY LN	MCO	27	D1
HOLLY RD	F	6C	B5
HOLLY ST	MCO	12C	B5
HOLLYHOCK CT	MV	12A	C3
HOLMES AV	MCO	7A	C3
HOLSTEIN RD	SA	6D	E4
HOLSTROM CIR	N	1	C2
HOMESTEAD BLVD	MCO	12C	B5
HONEY LN	SA	6D	F6
HONEYSUCKLE CT	MCO	3	D5
HOO-KOO-E-KOO F	MCO	9D	E6
HOO-KOO-E-KOO F	MCO	11A	B1
HOOPER LN	SA	6D	D6
HORSE TR	MCO	25	F1
HORSESHOE HL RD	MCO	28	A2
HOSPITAL RD	N	4	D3
HOTALING CT	MCO	10A	B3
HOTCHKIN DR	N	1	E3
HOWARD DR	TIB	11D	D5
HOWARD TR	CM	12A	B2
HOWARD TR	L	12A	B2
H RANCH RD	MCO	1	A5
HUBBELL CT	SR	10B	D1
HUCKLEBERRY RD	MCO	3	F6
HUCKLEBERRY RD	MCO	6B	F1
HUMBOLDT AV	SA	6D	D6
HUMBOLDT ST	SR	7C	B6
HUMBOLDT ST	SLTO	14	A3
HUMMINGBIRD WY	N	4	B3
HUNE CT	N	1	B2

1991 MARIN COUNTY STREET INDEX

STREET	CITY	PAGE	GRID
HUNTLEY RD	MCO	15	F3
HYACINTH WY	SR	7A	A2
HYANNIS COVE	SR	10B	F2
HYLAND DR	MCO	2	E2

I

STREET	CITY	PAGE	GRID
ICHABOD CT	MCO	6B	D2
IDA ST	SR	10A	B1
IDALIA CT	SA	9B	E1
IDALIA RD	SA	9B	E1
IDLEWOOD CT	SA	6D	D4
IDLEWOOD PL	SR	7C	B6
IDLEWOOD RD	MCO	9D	F5
IDYLBERRY RD	MCO	3	D5
IDYLBERRY RD	MCO	4	A6
IGNACIO BLVD	MCO	4	B2
IGNACIO BLVD	N	1	E6
IGNACIO BLVD	N	3	F1
IGNACIO BLVD	N	4	B2
IGNACIO LN	N	4	B1
IGNACIO VLY CIR	N	4	A1
IKE CT	N	1	D1
INDIAN RD	MCO	7C	B5
INDIAN WY	N	1	E6
INDIAN FIRE RD	MCO	9D	E6
INDIAN HILL RD	MCO	22	E5
INDIAN HILLS DR	N	1	E6
INDIAN ROCK CT	SA	6D	E5
INDIAN ROCK CT	TIB	12D	F4
INDIAN ROCK RD	SA	6D	E5
INDIAN SPGS RD	MCO	1	B4
INDIAN TRAIL CT	MCO	1	C4
INDIAN VLY RD	MCO	1	D5
INDIAN VLY RD	N	1	D5
INDUSTRIAL WY	L	10D	D5
INDUSTRIAL WY	N	1	E2
INEZ PL	MCO	12D	E5
INMAN AV	MCO	10A	B3
INVERNESS DR	SR	8	A5
INVERNESS DR	SR	10B	F1
INVERNESS WY	MCO	21	E3
INYO AV	F	6D	D5
INYO CIR	N	2	A6
IOLANTHUS AV	MCO	2	F2
IRENE DR	N	1	C3
IRENE ST	SR	10B	E3
IRIS LN	SR	6B	E3
IRIS RD	MCO	26	F6
IRIS RD	MCO	28	A5
IRON SPRINGS RD	F	6C	B4
IRON SPRINGS RD	MCO	6C	B4
IRONSTONE CT	MCO	4	B5
IRONWOOD DR	SR	8	A4
IRVIN RD	MCO	15	E5
IRVING CT	TIB	11D	D4
IRVING CT	TIB	12D	F4
IRVING DR	MCO	6B	D2
IRWIN ST	MCO	10B	D3
IRWIN ST	SR	10B	D3
ISABELLA CT	N	1	C1
ISLAND DR	MCO	12D	E5
ISLAND DR	SA	10A	A1
ISLA VISTA LN	SR	10B	F2
ISLE ROYALE CT	SR	7A	C2
IVY AV	MCO	5A	E5
IVY DR	R	9B	E2
IVY LN	F	6C	C6
IVY LN	MCO	27	E1
IVY LN	SA	6D	D6
IVY LN	SA	9B	D1
IVY LN	SR	10A	C2
IVY LN	MCO	5A	E5
IVY RD	MCO	26	F6
IVY RD	MCO	28	A4
IVY WK	SA	6D	E5

J

STREET	CITY	PAGE	GRID
J ST	SR	7C	B6
JACINTO WY	N	1A	D6
JACK CT	N	1	C3
JACKSON CT	N	1	D5
JACKSON DR	N	1	D5
JACOBY ST	SR	10B	E3
JADE CT	N	1	E2
JAFCO CT	N	4	B1
JAMAICA ST	MCO	11C	E2
JAMES BLACK CIR	N	4	B4
JAN WY	N	1	C2
JANES ST	MV	12C	B4
JANET WY	TIB	12D	F4
JASMINE LN	MCO	3	D5
JEAN ST	MCO	13	C1
JEFFERSON AV	MCO	7C	C4
JEFFERSON CT	N	1	E5
JEFFERSON DR	TIB	11D	D4
JEFFERSON DR	TIB	12D	F4
JEFFREY CT	N	1	D1
JENNIFER LN	N	1	C3
JENSEN WY	SR	7C	A6
JERSEY AV	SA	6D	F6
JERSEY AV	SA	7C	A6
JESSUP ST	SR	10A	B1
JEWELL CT	SR	10B	E1
JEWELL ST	SR	7D	D6
JEWELL ST	SR	10B	E1
JOAN AV	N	1	E3
JOAQUIN PATIO	MCO	28	D5
JOHN ST	MCO	15	D5
JOHNSON ST	N	1	E4
JOHNSON ST	SLTO	14	A4
JOHNSTONE CT	MCO	4	B5
JOHNSTONE DR	MCO	4	B5
JONES PL	SR	10A	B1
JONES ST	SA	9B	F1
JONES WY	L	10C	B6
JORDAN AV	SA	6D	F6
JORDAN AV	SA	7C	A6
JORDAN AV	SA	10A	A1
JORDAN ST	SR	10A	C2
JOSEFA CT	N	4	B4
JOSE PATIO	MCO	28	D5
JOSEPH CT	SR	7A	B2
JOSEPHINE ST	MV	11A	C3
JOSEPHINE ST	MV	12A	A3
JOSEPHINE ST	SLTO	14	B4
JOYCE ST	N	1	F4
JOYCE WY	MCO	12C	C6
JUANITA AV	MV	12C	C4
JUANITA aV	TIB	14	C1
JUANITA CT	N	1	C1
JUAREZ AV	MCO	5A	B5
JUDGE HALEY DR	SR	7C	C4
JUDITH CT	N	1	F6
JUDSON LN	MCO	12D	E5
JULES DR	N	1	C2
JULIA AV	MCO	12C	C6
JULIA ST	SR	10A	C1
JUNE LN	MCO	2	B1
JUNIPER AV	MCO	5A	C5
JUNIPER AV	MCO	27	C1
JUNIPER CT	F	6D	D5
JUNIPER PL	N	1	B1
JUNIPER PL	N	1A	A5
JUNIPER RD	MCO	26	F6
JUNIPER RD	MCO	28	A5
JUNIPERBERRY DR	MCO	4	A6
JUNIPERBERRY DR	MCO	6B	F1
JUNIPERBERRY DR	MCO	7A	A1
JUNIPERO SER AV	SR	7D	F6
JUNIPERO SER AV	SR	10B	F1
JUNO RD	TIB	11D	D4
JUTE RD	MCO	28	A5

K

STREET	CITY	PAGE	GRID
K ST	SR	7C	B6
KADEN CT	N	1	E5
KADEN DR	N	1	E5
KAEHLER ST	N	1	E2
KAILUA WY	MCO	15	B4
KALE RD	MCO	26	F6
KALE RD	MCO	28	A5
KAMEHA WY	MCO	15	B4
KAREN WY	TIB	12D	F4
KARL AV	SA	6D	E6
KARLA CT	N	1	F6
KARLA CT	N	2	A6
KARLA CT	N	3	F1
KARLA CT	N	4	A1
KATHLEEN DR	N	1	A2
KATHY CT	N	1	E6
KATHY CT	N	3	E1
KATLAS CT	N	1	C1
KATRINA LN	MCO	6B	D3
KATYA CT	N	3	F1
KAVON CT	N	1	F5
KEATS DR	MV	12D	D4
KEEL CT	SR	7A	C2
KEENA LN	N	1	C3
KEHOE WY	MCO	21	D2
KEITH WY	MCO	21	D3
KELLY DR E	N	4	C3
KELLY DR W	N	4	C3
KEMP AV	SA	9B	E1
KENDELL CT	SLTO	13	E3
KENDON LN	N	1	B2
KENDRICK AV	SA	6D	D4
KENILWORTH CT	N	2	B1
KENNETH WY	MCO	21	E3
KENSINGTON CT	SA	9B	E2
KENSINGTON RD	SA	9B	E2
KENT AV	F	6D	D5
KENT AV	MCO	10A	A3
KENT LN	MCO	10C	A4
KENT WY	MCO	11B	C4
KENTDALE LN	MCO	10A	B3
KENT PUMP RD	MCO	27	D5
KENT PUMP RD	MCO	28	E1
KENWOOD CT	N	1	F1
KERNBERRY DR	MCO	3	F6
KERNBERRY DR	MCO	4	A6
KERNER BLVD	SR	10B	E2
KEVILLE TR	CM	12A	B1
KEY LARGO CRSE	CM	12B	E2
KEY LARGO COVE	CM	12B	E2
KEYSTONE CT	MCO	4	B5
KIENTZ LN	SA	9B	F1
KILGORE CT	SA	6D	E5
KILGORE LN	MCO	12C	C6
KILMER CT	MV	12D	D6
KING LN	MV	12A	A2
KING ST	L	10C	B6
KING ST	MV	12A	A2
KINGFISHER CT	N	4	B4
KINGS WY	MCO	11B	B5
KINROSS DR	SR	7D	F6
KINROSS DR	SR	8	A5
KINROSS DR	SR	10B	F1
KIPLING CT	MV	12D	D4
KIPLING DR	MV	12C	C5
KIPLING DR	MV	12D	D5
KLAMATH WY	N	2	B5
KLARE AV	SA	6D	E5
KNICKERBCKER LN	MCO	6B	D3
KNIGHT CT	N	2	A2
KNIGHT DR	SR	8	B4
KNOCKNABOUL WY	SR	6B	F1
KNOLL LN	MCO	12D	D4
KNOLL RD	SA	6D	F6
KNOLL RD	SA	7C	A6
KNOLL RD	SR	10A	B2
KNOLL RD N	CM	12B	D3
KNOLL RD N	MCO	12B	D3
KNOLL RD S	MCO	12D	D4
KNOLL WY	MCO	7C	B4
KNOLLTOP CT	N	2	A2
KNOLLTOP WY	N	2	A2
KNOLLWOOD DR	SR	8	C3
KNUTTE CT	MCO	1	B3
KOCH RD	CM	12B	E2
KOCH SERVICE RD	CM	12B	E2
KONA LN	MCO	15	B4
KRISTEN PL	L	10D	D5
KRSTEN MARIE CT	MCO	23	F3
KRISTIN LN	N	1	D2
KRISTY CT	N	1	D3
KYLESWOOD PL	MCO	22	A5

L

STREET	CITY	PAGE	GRID
LA ALONDRA CT	SR	7A	A3
LA BREA WY	MCO	7B	D2
LA COSTA CT	N	1	A3
LA CRESCENTA DR	N	4	C2
LA CRESCENTA WY	SR	10B	E2
LA CUESTA	MCO	5A	A4
LA CUESTA DR	L	10C	C4
LADERMAN LN	L	10C	C5
LADERMAN LN	L	10D	D5
LA GOMA ST	MV	12C	B4
LAGOON CT	SR	7A	C3
LAGOON DR	MCO	31	E3
LAGOON PL	SR	8	B4
LAGOON RD	BVDR	11D	E6
LAGOON RD	BVDR	14	C1
LAGOON RD	SR	8	B4
LAGOON FIRE RD	MCO	9C	A6
LAGOON VIEW DR	TIB	14	D1
LAGOON VISTA	TIB	14	D1
LAGUNA RD	MCO	12C	A6
LAGUNA RD	MCO	13	A1
LAGUNA VISTA DR	N	2	B1
LAGUNA VISTA DR	N	20	D2
LAGUNITAS RD	MCO	5A	A5
LAGUNITAS RD	MCO	9B	F3
LAGUNITAS RD	MCO	27	A1
LAGUNITAS RD	R	9B	F3
LAGUNITS SCH RD	MCO	5A	C4
LAKESIDE DR	CM	10D	D6
LAKESIDE DR	CM	12B	D1
LAKEVIEW CT	N	1	F4
LAKEVIEW RD	MCO	9C	C4
LAKEVIEW RD	MCO	9D	D4
LA LOMA CT	SR	10B	D3
LAMBERT WY	N	1	C1
LA MERIDA CT	N	1A	B6
LAMONT AV	N	1	E3
LANAI WY	MCO	15	B4
LANCASTER AV	MCO	10C	B4
LANGLEY LN	N	4	C3
LANHAM DR	N	4	C2
LA NOCHE CT	N	1	C1
LANSDALE AV	F	6D	D5
LANYARD COVE	CM	12B	F2
LA PALOMA LN	MV	12A	A3
LA PASADA	MCO	7B	D2
LA PERDIZ CT	SR	7A	A3
LA PLACITA CT	N	1A	B6
LA PLAYA WY	MCO	7B	D2
LARCH DR	N	2	A6
LARCH RD	MCO	28	A4
LARK CT	L	12A	C1
LARK LN	MCO	12C	C6
LARKSPUR LN	N	2	A6
LARKSPUR ST	SR	10B	E2
LARKSPUR BRDWLK	L	10C	C5
LARKSPUR LANDNG	L	10D	E4
LARKSPUR PZ DR	L	10C	B5
LA ROSA WY	L	10C	C6
LAS CASAS DR	SR	7D	F6
LAS CASAS DR	SR	10B	F1
LAS COLINDAS RD	SR	6B	F1
LAS COLINDAS RD	SR	7A	A2
LAS FLORES AV	SR	7C	B4
LAS GALLINAS AV	MCO	4	B6
LAS GALLINAS AV	SR	7A	A3
LAS GALLINAS AV	SR	7C	B4
LAS HUERTAS CT	SR	7C	B4
LAS LOMAS	N	4	E4
LAS LOMAS LN	TIB	14	D2
LAS OVEJAS AV	SR	6B	E2
LAS PALMAS AV	N	4	C2
LAS PAVADAS AV	SR	7A	A3
LAS RAPOSAS RD	SR	6B	F1
LASSEN LN	N	2	B5
LAS TARDES CT	N	1	C1
LAS TRELLIS DR	MCO	6B	F3
LATHAM ST	SR	10A	B1
LATTIE LN	MCO	12C	B6
LAURA LN	MCO	6C	C4
LAUREL AV	BVDR	14	C2
LAUREL AV	CM	12B	D2
LAUREL AV	L	10C	B6
LAUREL AV	MCO	1	B4
LAUREL AV	MCO	2	F3
LAUREL AV	MCO	5A	F5
LAUREL AV	MCO	10A	A3
LAUREL AV	MCO	21	E3
LAUREL AV	MCO	27	E1
LAUREL AV	MCO	28	E5
LAUREL AV	SA	6D	E6
LAUREL AV	SA	9B	E1
LAUREL DR	F	9A	B1
LAUREL LN	CM	12A	B1
LAUREL LN	SLTO	13	F3
LAUREL PL	SR	10A	C1
LAUREL RD	MCO	28	A5
LAUREL ST	MCO	21	F5
LAUREL ST	MCO	22	A5
LAUREL ST	MV	11A	C3
LAUREL ST	MV	12A	A3
LAUREL WY	MCO	9D	F4
LAUREL WY	MCO	10C	A4
LAUREL WY	MCO	13	C1
LAUREL CYN RD	MCO	22	E5
LAUREL CYN RD	SR	7C	C5
LAUREL DL FR RD	MCO	28	F3
LAUREL DL FR RD	MCO	29	A1
LAUREL GROVE AV	MCO	10A	A2
LAUREL GROVE AV	R	9B	F2
LAUREL GROVE AV	R	10A	A2
LAUREL VIEW WY	MCO	21	E3
LAURELWOOD AV	MV	12C	A4
LAURELWOOD CT	SR	8	A3
LAUREN AV	N	1	E3
LAURIE CT	N	1	C2
LAURIE DR	N	1	C2
LAURINA RD	MV	12A	C3
LAVENDER LN	MCO	12C	C6
LAVERNE AV	MCO	12C	B5
LAVERNE LN	MCO	12C	C5
LA VISTA WY	SR	7D	D6
LA VUELTA AV	MCO	5A	A5
LAWRENCE DR	N	1	F2
LAWRENCE DR	N	2	A2
LAWSON RD	MCO	15	B4
LEA CT	N	2	A3
LEA DR	N	2	A3
LEA DR	SR	6B	F3
LEAFWOOD CIR	SR	7C	B6
LEAFWOOD DR	N	1	F5
LEAFWOOD HTS	N	1	F5
LE CLAIRE CT	SR	7A	A3
LEE ST	MV	11A	C2
LEE ST	MV	12A	A2
LEESE LN	N	1	D1
LEEWARD RD	BVDR	14	C1
LEEWARD RD	MCO	25	C3
LEGEND RD	MCO	6B	D3
LEHMAN LN	MCO	12C	B5
LEIBERT LN	MCO	2	F2
LEISURE ACRS RD	MCO	1	C5
LEITH LN	SR	8	A6
LELAND CT	N	1	D3
LELAND WY	TIB	12D	F4
LELANI LN	MCO	15	B4
LENGLEN AV	SR	6B	F3
LEO LN	MCO	12C	B6
LEONA DR	MCO	7B	D3
LESLIE CT	N	1	C2
LEVERONI CT	N	4	C1
LEYTON CT	MV	12C	C4
LIBERTY ST	L	10C	C6
LIBERTY SHIP WY	SLTO	13	F3
LIBRA DR	MCO	1	A2
LIBRA DR	N	1	A2
LIBRARY PL	SA	9B	F1
LIDO LN	SR	10B	E2
LIDO RD	N	4	E3
LIGHTHOUSE RD	MCO	24	B6
LILAC AV	MCO	10C	B4
LILAC LN	MCO	12C	C6
LILIAN LN	SR	7C	C5
LILLIAN CT	SA	6D	D4
LILLIAN LN	MCO	12C	B5
LILY AV	SA	9B	E2
LIMANTOUR DR	MCO	25	B3
LIMANTOUR SP RD	MCO	5	A1
LIMANTOUR SP RD	MCO	21	F6
LIMANTOUR SP RD	MCO	22	B6
LIMANTOUR SP RD	MCO	25	C2
LIMESTONE GRADE	MCO	4	B5
LINARES AV	MCO	5A	B4
LINCOLN AV	MCO	28	E5
LINCOLN AV	MV	12A	A3
LINCOLN AV	SA	9B	F1
LINCOLN AV	SR	7C	C5
LINCOLN AV	SR	7D	D6
LINCOLN AV	SR	10A	C2
LINCOLN CT	SA	9B	F1
LINCOLN DR	SLTO	13	E3
LINCOLN VLG CIR	L	10D	E4
LINDA AV	MCO	7C	C4
LINDA CT	N	1	A3
LINDA WY	MCO	13	C1
LINDARO ST	SR	10A	C2
LINDA VISTA AV	TIB	14	D1
LINDEN AV	MCO	21	E3
LINDEN LN	MCO	12C	B5
LINDEN LN	SR	7C	C6
LINDEN LN	SR	7D	D6
LINDENWOOD CT	SR	8	A4
LINDSAY CT	N	2	C1
LINDSDALE LN	MCO	22	B4
LINDVIEW	SR	7D	D6
LINNET CT	MCO	4	B5
LISA CT	MCO	4	B6
LISA DR	MCO	6A	C3
LISA DR	MCO	6B	D3
LISBON ST	SR	10B	E2
LITCHENBERG RD	MCO	1A	B1
LITHO ST	SLTO	13	F3
LITHO ST	SLTO	14	A3
LITTLE CREEK LN	N	1A	E6
LIVE OAK AV	F	6D	D5
LIVE OAK DR	MCO	13	B1
LIVE OAK WY	MCO	9D	F4
LIVINGSTON CT	N	4	C3
LOBO VISTA	N	1	C2
LOCHINVAR RD	SR	7D	F6
LOCHINVAR RD	SR	8	A5
LOCHINVAR RD	SR	10B	F1
LOCH LOMOND DR	SR	8	A6
LOCHNESS LN	SR	8	A5
LOCKE LN	MV	12C	C4
LOCKETT LN	MCO	12D	E5
LOCKSLY LN	SR	8	A6
LOCKSLY LN	SR	10B	F1
LOCKTON LN	MCO	2	D2
LOCKWOOD DR	SR	8	A4
LOCKWOOD DR W	SR	8	A4
LOCKWOOD LN	MV	12C	A4
LOCUST AV	L	10C	B6
LOCUST AV	MCO	10A	A3
LOCUST AV	MV	12C	B4
LOCUST AV	R	9B	F2
LOCUST AV	SR	7D	D6
LOCUST RD	MCO	28	A4
LOCUST RD	SLTO	14	A3
LOCUST ST	SLTO	14	A3
LODGE LN	SR	10A	B2
LOGAN ST	N	1	F2
LOGANBERRY DR	MCO	3	F6
LOGANBERRY DR	MCO	4	A6
LOIS CT	MV	12A	C3
LOLETA LN	N	2	A6
LOLITA LN	N	2	A6
LOMA AV	TIB	14	D1
LOMA ALTA FIRE	MCO	3	A5
LOMA ALTA FIRE	MCO	6A	A1
LOMA LINDA AV	R	10A	A2
LOMA LINDA RD	R	9B	F2
LOMA LINDA RD	SR	10B	E2
LOMA ROBLES DR	SA	6D	F6
LOMA VISTA AV	L	10C	C6
LOMA VISTA AV	L	12A	C1
LOMA VISTA PL	SR	10B	E2
LOMBA VISTA	N	1	C2
LOMITA DR	MCO	12C	C4
LOMITA DR	MV	12C	C4
LONE TREE AV	MCO	11B	C4
LONGFELLOW DR	MV	12D	D4
LONGVIEW AV	SA	6D	F6
LONGVIEW AV	SA	7C	A6
LONGWOOD DR	SA	7C	A6
LONGWOOD DR	SR	7C	A6
LOOTENS PL	SR	10A	C1
LORETTA LN	MCO	5A	C5
LORING AV	MCO	12C	B6
LORRAINE AV	MCO	22	B5
LORRAINE CT	N	1	A2
LOS ALONDRAS CT	N	1	E3
LOS ALTOS DR	SR	7C	A5
LOS ANGELES AV	SA	6D	F6
LOS CEDROS DR	N	1	B3
LOS CERROS DR	MCO	10C	C4
LOS DIAS CT	N	1	C1
LOS GAMOS DR	SR	7A	B2
LOS GAMOS RD	SR	7A	B2
LOS PADRES CIR	N	2	A6
LOS PINOS	MCO	5A	D2
LOS PINOS SPUR	MCO	5A	E2
LS RANCHITOS RD	SR	7A	B3
LOS REYES DR	MCO	22	B5
LOS ROBLES DR	SR	10A	B2
LOS ROBLES RD	N	4	B2

STREET	CITY	PAGE	GRID
LOTUS CT	N	1	E1
LOUIS DR	N	1	F3
LOUISE AV	N	1	B3
LOUISE ST	SR	10B	E2
LOVE CT	F	6C	B4
LOVEJOY WY	N	4	C3
LOVELL AV	MV	11A	C3
LOVELL AV	MV	12A	A3
LOVELL AV	SR	10B	D2
LOVERS LN	N	1	D4
LOWELL AV	MCO	7B	D3
LOWELL AV	MCO	12C	C6
LOWELL AV	MCO	13	C1
LOWER DR	MV	12B	D2
LOWER LN	CM	12A	C1
LOWER LP	L	10D	D5
LOWER TER N	TIB	12D	F4
LWR ALCATRAZ PL	MV	12A	A3
LWR ANCHORAGE RD	SLTO	13	E3
LWR CRESCENT AV	SLTO	14	A4
LOYOLA	CM	12B	E2
LUCAS PARK DR	SR	7A	A1
LUCAS VALLEY RD	MCO	3	B5
LUCAS VALLEY RD	MCO	4	A6
LUCAS VALLEY RD	MCO	5A	C1
LUCAS VALLEY RD	MCO	6B	F1
LUCAS VALLEY RD	MCO	7A	B1
LUCAS VALLEY RD	MCO	23	D6
LUCIA LN	MCO	5A	A4
LUCKY DR	CM	10D	D5
LUCKY DR	L	10C	C5
LUISA CT	SR	7A	A3
LUIZ CT	MCO	3	D5
LUIZ FIRE RD	MCO	3	C4
LUKE LN	N	4	C3
LULA WY	MV	12B	D3
LUNA LN	SA	6D	F6
LUNADA CT	MCO	10B	E1
LUNNY LN	SR	10A	B1
LUPINE CIR	N	1	F6
LUPINE CT	SR	8	B4
LUPINE DR	MCO	12B	D2
LUZANNE CIR	MCO	6B	D2
LYFORD DR	TIB	11D	F6
LYFORD DR	TIB	14	C1
LYNN CT	SR	10B	D3
LYNWOOD DR	N	1	F5
LYON PL	MV	12A	A3
M			
MABEL AV	MCO	28	B4
MABRY WY	MCO	7B	D2
MAC ANNAN CT	TIB	11D	E6
MACHIN AV	N	1	E3
MADELINE CT	N	1	D3
MADELINE LN	MCO	10B	F1
MADERA AV	R	10A	A1
MADERA AV	SA	6D	F6
MADERA BLVD	CM	10D	D6
MADERA BLVD	CM	12B	D1
MADERA ST	SR	10B	F3
MADERA WY	MCO	11B	C4
MADERA WY	MV	11B	C4
MDRA DL PRESDIO	CM	12B	E2
MADISON AV	MCO	7C	C4
MADISON CT	N	1	E5
MADRID CT	N	4	B2
MADRONA AV	BVDR	14	C2
MADRONA AV	CM	12B	D2
MADRONA AV	R	9B	F3
MADRONA ST	MV	12C	A4
MADRONA ST	SR	10A	B2
MADRONE AV	L	10C	B6
MADRONE AV	MCO	5A	E5
MADRONE AV	MCO	10A	B3
MADRONE AV	MCO	21	D3
MADRONE AV	MCO	27	E1
MADRONE AV	N	1	F2
MADRONE AV	R	10A	B3
MADRONE AV	SA	6D	E6
MADRONE AV	SA	9B	E1
MADRONE CT	F	6C	C6
MADRONE RD	F	6C	C6
MADRONE WY	MCO	9D	F4
MADRONE WY	MCO	10C	A4
MADRONE PK CIR	MCO	12C	A5
MADSEN LN	MCO	11C	E3
MAE CT	MCO	23	F2
MAESTRO RD	MCO	1	B4
MAGDALENA CT	MV	12A	C2
MAGEE AV	MV	12A	A3
MAGEE LN	MV	12A	A3
MAGNOLIA AV	L	10C	B5
MAGNOLIA AV	L	12A	C1
MAGNOLIA AV	MCO	10C	A4
MAGNOLIA AV	SA	9B	F1
MAGNOLIA AV	SR	7D	E6
MAGNOLIA PL	N	1	B1
MAGNOLIA PL	N	1A	A6
MAHLSTEDT PL	N	1	E3
MAHOGANY DR	SR	6B	E2
MAILLIARD OVAL	MCO	5A	E5
MAIN CT	F	6C	C5
MAIN CT	F	6D	D5
MAIN DR	MCO	8	B5
MAIN DR	SR	7A	C1
MAIN DR	SR	7B	D1
MAIN DR	SR	8	A5
MAIN ST	MCO	8A	E4
MAIN ST	MCO	13	C1
MAIN ST	SLTO	14	A4
MAIN ST	TIB	14	C2
MAIN TR	MCO	11B	B4
MAJORCA CT	MCO	4	B6
MAKIN GRADE	R	10A	B2
MAKIN GRADE	SR	10A	B2
MALLARD RD	BVDR	14	C1
MALOBAR DR	N	20	E2
MALONE LN	SR	6D	F4
MALVINO CT	TIB	11D	D5
MANANA WY	MCO	22	B5
MANCHESTER CT	N	2	B5
MANDERLY RD	MCO	10B	F1
MANDERLY RD	SR	7D	F6
MANDERLY RD	SR	8	A5
MANITOU DR	MCO	6A	C2
MANN DR	MCO	10A	B3
MANN DR	MCO	28	B4
MANN DR	SR	7D	F6
MANOR DR	MV	12C	B4
MANOR RD	F	6C	C5
MANOR RD	MCO	10C	B4
MANOR TER	MV	12C	B4
MANOR VIEW	MCO	6A	C3
MANUEL DR	N	1	F3
M T FREITAS PKY	SR	6B	F2
M T FREITAS PKY	SR	7A	A2
MANZANITA AV	CM	12A	C1
MANZANITA AV	F	6C	C5
MANZANITA AV	MCO	2	E2
MANZANITA AV	MCO	5A	B5
MANZANITA AV	MCO	8	A5
MANZANITA AV	MCO	27	C1
MANZANITA CT	CM	12B	D1
MANZANITA CT	F	6C	C5
MANZANITA PL	MV	11A	C2
MANZANITA PL	MV	12A	A2
MANZANITA RD	F	6C	C5
MANZANO CT	N	1	C1
MAPLE AV	F	6D	D5
MAPLE AV	L	10C	B6
MAPLE AV	MCO	10A	A3
MAPLE DR	N	1	F2
MAPLE LN	SA	6D	E5
MAPLE RD	MCO	5A	E5
MAPLE RD	MCO	27	E1
MAPLE RD	MCO	28	A5
MAPLE ST	MCO	13	B1
MAPLE ST	SR	7C	C6
MAPLE ST	SR	10A	C1
MAPLE HILL DR	SR	7A	A1
MAPLEWOOD DR	SR	8	A4
MARA VISTA CT	TIB	11D	E5
MARCY CT	N	1	D3
MAR EAST ST	TIB	14	D1
MARGARET CT	N	2	B5
MARGARITA DR	MCO	7D	F6
MARGARITA DR	MCO	10B	F1
MARGARITA DR	SR	7D	F6
MARGARITA TER	N	2	A5
MARGORY CT	N	1	C2
MARGUERITE AV	MV	11A	C3
MARGUERITE AV	MV	12A	A3
MARIA CT	N	1	C1
MARIA LORETO CT	N	4	B4
MARIAN CT	SR	10B	E2
MARIE ST	SLTO	13	F3
MARIELE DR	MCO	6A	C3
MARIN AV	MCO	5A	E5
MARIN AV	MCO	13	C1
MARIN AV	MCO	27	E1
MARIN AV	SLTO	13	E3
MARIN DR	MCO	13	B1
MARIN RD	N	4	C2
MARIN ST	SR	10A	B2
MARIN WY	MCO	13	B1
MARIN WY	MCO	28	B4
MARINA CT	MCO	10B	E2
MARINA WY	N	1	E4
MARINA WY	SR	10B	F1
MARINA COURT DR	MCO	10B	E2
MARINA COURT DR	SR	10B	E2
MARINA VISTA AV	CM	12A	B1
MARINA VISTA AV	L	12A	B1
MARIN BAY PK CT	SR	8	D3
MARIN CENTER DR	SR	7A	B3
MARINDA CT	F	6C	C5
MARINDA DR	F	6C	C5
MARINE DR	MCO	8	B6
MARINE WY	MCO	28	E5
MARINER WY	TIB	14	C1
MARINER GRN CT	CM	12B	F2
MARINER GRN DR	CM	12B	F2
MARINERO CIR	TIB	11D	F6
MARINERS CIR	SR	7A	C3
MARINE VIEW DR	MCO	15	B5
MARINITA AV	SR	10B	D1
MARIN OAKS DR	N	3	F1
MARINSHIP AV	SLTO	13	E2
MARINSHIP WY	SLTO	13	F3
MARIN VALLEY DR	N	4	C4
MARIN VIEW AV	MCO	11A	B3
MARIN VIEW AV	MCO	11B	B4
MARIN VIEW DR	N	4	C4
MARINWOOD AV	MCO	4	B6
MARION AV	MV	11B	C4
MARION AV	MV	12C	A4
MARION AV	N	1	D2
MARION AV	SLTO	14	A5
MARION CT	N	1	D2
MARION OAKS CT	N	1	D2
MARIPOSA AV	SA	9B	F1
MARIPOSA CT	TIB	12D	F4
MARIPOSA LN	N	1	F6
MARIPOSA RD	SR	10A	C2
MARK DR	SR	7A	B2
MARK PL	L	10C	C5
MARK PL	L	10D	D4
MARK TER	TIB	11D	D4
MARKET ST	SR	10B	E3
MARK TWAIN AV	MCO	7A	C3
MARLIN AV	MV	12A	B3
MARLIN DR	MV	12C	C4
MARQUARD AV	SR	10A	B1
MARSH DR	MV	12A	A2
MARSH DR	N	2	B5
MARSH RD	MCO	15	C1
MARSH RD	TIB	14	C1
MARSHALL WY	MCO	5A	B4
MARSHL PETLM RD	MCO	18	D4
MARSHL PETLM RD	MCO	19	A5
MARSHL PETLM RD	MCO	20	A2
MARTENS BLVD	SR	10A	C2
MARTHA LN	SA	6D	D4
MARTIN DR	N	4	C2
MARTINELLI D RD	MCO	22	C3
MARTINEZ CT	N	1	C1
MARTINIQUE AV	MCO	11C	E3
MARTINONI RD	MCO	15	F3
MARTLING RD	MCO	6B	D3
MAR WEST ST	TIB	14	C1
MARY ST	SR	10B	D1
MARY JANE LN	N	1	C3
MATEO DR	TIB	11C	D3
MATHER RD	MCO	6A	C2
MATILDA AV	MV	12C	C4
MATT DAVIS TR	MCO	29	C3
MAUI LN	MCO	15	B4
MAXWELL LN	MCO	12C	C5
MAYBRIDGE RD	BVDR	11D	F6
MAYBRIDGE RD	BVDR	14	C1
MAYWOOD WY	SR	7C	B5
MCALLISTER AV	MCO	10C	B4
MCCART CT	TIB	11D	D5
MCCLAY AV	MCO	1	C4
MCCLAY RD	N	1	C3
MCCLELLAND DR	N	2	A3
MCCOY RD	SR	10A	C3
MCCULLOUGH RD	MCO	13	F6
MCDONALD LN	MCO	22	B4
MCINNIS PKWY	SR	7A	B3
MC INTOSH CT	N	4	B4
MCKENNAS G F RD	MCO	28	D3
MCKENNEY DR	F	6A	B3
MCKENZIE	MCO	8A	E4
MCKEON CT	N	1	C2
MCNEAR DR	SR	8	B4
MCNEARS RD	MCO	8	C4
MCRAE RD	MCO	12C	C5
MEADOW AV	MCO	10A	B3
MEADOW AV	SR	10B	D3
MEADOW CT	SA	6D	E5
MEADOW DR	MCO	7B	D3
MEADOW DR	MCO	12B	D3
MEADOW DR	MV	12B	D3
MEADOW TR	MCO	5	A2
MEADOW TR	MCO	25	F2
MEADOW WY	F	9A	B1
MEADOW WY	MCO	5A	C4
MEADOW WY	MCO	9A	B1
MEADOWBROOK CT	N	1	B3
MEADOWCREEK DR	CM	12B	E2
MEADOWCREST DR	MCO	12B	D3
MEADOWCREST RD	N	1A	E6
MEADOWCROFT DR	SA	6D	E5
MEADOW HILL DR	TIB	11D	F6
MEADOWLARK CT	N	1	B3
MEADOW OAKS DR	SR	7C	A4
MEADOWOOD DR	L	10C	C6
MEADOWSWEET DR	CM	12B	D2
MEADOWSWEET DR	MCO	12B	D2
MEADOW VLY LN	MCO	12B	D2
MEADOW VIEW DR	N	4	C4
MEDA CT	MCO	12D	E5
MEDA LN	MCO	12D	E5
MEDIAN WY	MCO	12C	C6
MEDICAL PLAZA	N	1	D4
MEDWAY RD	MCO	10B	E2
MEDWAY RD	SA	6D	D5
MEDWAY RD	SR	10B	E2
MEERNAA AV	F	6C	C6
MEERNAA AV	F	9A	C1
MEISNER CT	N	1	A2
MEISNER DR	N	1	A2
MELALEUCA LN	MCO	12C	A6
MELODY LN	MV	12A	A2
MELROSE AV	MCO	12C	B5
MELVILLE AV	SA	9B	E2
MEMORIAL DR	SR	7C	B4
MENDOCINO LN	N	1	B2
MENKE LN	MCO	12A	C2
MERCED AV	SA	6D	E6
MERCED WY	MV	11B	B5
MERCURY AV	TIB	11D	D4
MERIAM DR	MCO	7A	C3
MERIDIAN LN	SR	7D	D5
MERRITT DR	N	1	E6
MERRY LN	CM	12A	C1
MERRYDALE RD	SR	7A	B3
MERRYDALE RD	SR	7C	B4
MERWIN AV	F	6C	C5
MESA AV	MV	12C	C4
MESA RD	MCO	22	B5
MESA RD	MCO	26	E5
MESA RD	MCO	28	A3
MESA WY	MCO	21	E3
MESA VERDE WY	SR	7A	C2
MEYER PL	MCO	10A	A3
MEYER RD	SR	10A	C3
MICHAEL WY	SA	6D	D4
MICHELE CIR	N	1	A2
MIDDEN LN	TIB	12B	F3
MIDDLE CT	MV	12A	C2
MIDDLE RD	MCO	15	D2
MIDDLE PEAK RD	MCO	9D	D6
MIDDLE PEAK RD	MCO	29	C1
MIDHILL DR	MV	12B	D2
MIDVALE WY	MCO	12C	B6
MIDWAY	R	10A	A1
MIDWAY AV	MCO	12C	B5
MIDWAY BLVD	N	1	F6
MIDWAY BLVD	N	2	A5
MIDWAY CT	N	1	F5
MIDWAY CT	N	2	A5
MIDWAY LN	F	6C	C5
MIDWAY RD	L	10C	C6
MILANO PL	SR	8	B4
MILL RD	N	1	B3
MILL ST	SR	10B	E2
MILLAND CT	MCO	12D	D5
MILLAND DR	MCO	12D	D5
MILLARD RD	L	10C	B6
MILLAY PL	MV	12C	C4
MILLBRAE AV	SA	6D	F6
MILLER AV	MV	12C	B4
MILLER AV	SLTO	14	A4
MILLER LN	MV	12C	A4
MILLER LN	SLTO	14	A4
MILLER TR	MCO	29	C1
MILLER CREEK RD	MCO	4	A6
MILLER CREEK RD	MCO	7A	A1
MILLER RANCH CT	MCO	4	B5
MILLSIDE LN	MV	11B	C4
MILLSIDE LN	MV	12C	A4
MILLSTONE DR	MCO	4	B5
MILLWOOD CT	SR	8	A4
MILLWOOD ST	MV	12C	B4
MIMOSA AV	L	10C	B5
MING CT	N	2	B3
MINNIE ST	SR	10A	B1
MINOR CT	SR	6D	F4
MIRABEL AV	MV	12C	B4
MIRABELLA AV	N	1	E2
MIRACLE MILE	SA	6D	F6
MIRACLE MILE	SA	7C	A6
MIRACLE MILE	SA	9B	F1
MIRADA AV	SR	7C	B4
MIRAFLORES AV	SR	10A	B1
MIRAFLORES LN	TIB	11D	E5
MIRAMAR AV	SR	10A	B1
MIRAMAR RD	MCO	11D	E4
MIRAMAR RD	TIB	11D	E4
MIRAMONTE LN	MCO	28	B4
MIRANDA CT	N	1	D3
MIRA VISTA	MCO	28	D5
MISSION AV	SR	10B	E1
MISSION DR	MCO	12D	E6
MISTLETOE AV	MCO	2	E3
MISTLETOE LN	MCO	2	E2
MISTY RD	N	2	C1
MITCHELL BLVD	SR	7A	B2
MITCHELL DR	F	6A	B3
MITCHELL DR	F	6C	C4
MITCHELL LN	F	6C	B4
MIWOK DR	SA	6D	E5
MIWOK TR	MCO	13	C3
MIWOK TR	MCO	31	E1
MIWOK WY	MV	12D	D5
MLISS LN	SR	10D	D4
MOCKINGBIRD CT	N	1	B3
MODOC PL	N	2	B5
MOHAVE CT	CM	10C	C6
MOHAWK AV	CM	10D	D6
MOHAWK AV	CM	12B	D1
MOITOZA LN	TIB	14	D1
MOLINO AV	MV	12C	B4
MOLINO LN	MV	12C	A4
MOLINO WY	MV	12C	A4
MOLL WY	MCO	21	E3
MONCADA WY	MCO	10B	E1
MONCADA WY	SR	7D	E6
MONO AV	F	6D	D5
MONO LN	SA	6D	E5
MONO WY	MCO	11B	B5
MONONA DR	CM	10D	D6
MONONA DR	CM	12B	D1
MONONA LN	CM	10D	D6
MONONA LN	CM	12B	D1
MONROE CT	N	1	E4
MONTECILLO RD	SR	6B	F2
MONTECILLO RD	SR	7A	A3
MONTE CIMAS AV	MCO	11B	B5
MONTECITO DR	CM	12A	C2
MONTECITO RD	MCO	10B	E1
MONTEGO KEY	MCO	2	C5
MONTE MAR DR	SLTO	13	F4
MONTE MAR DR	SLTO	14	A4
MONTE MARIA AV	N	1	F5
MONTEREY AV	SA	6D	F6
MONTEREY TER	SA	6D	F6
MONTEVIDEO WY	SR	7A	A1
MONTE VISTA	MCO	10A	B3
MONTE VISTA AV	L	10C	C6
MONTE VISTA AV	L	12A	C1
MONTE VISTA AV	MV	11A	C3
MONTE VISTA AV	N	1	C2
MONTE VISTA LN	MV	11A	C3
MONTE VISTA RD	F	6C	C4
MONTEZUMA AV	MCO	27	B1
MONTEZUMA AV	MCO	5A	B5
MONTEZUMA RD	MCO	27	B1
MONTFORD AV	MCO	12C	A4
MONTFORD PL	MCO	12C	B4
MONTURA WY	N	3	E1
MOODY CT	SR	7C	A5
MOORING RD	SR	10B	E2
MORA AV	MCO	9A	A1
MORA LN	N	1	D4
MORELOS AV	MCO	5A	B4
MORGAN DR	N	4	A1
MORGAN LN	MCO	10B	F1
MORNINGSIDE DR	CM	12A	C2
MORNINGSIDE DR	SA	6D	E5
MORNING STR CRS	CM	12B	F1
MORNING SUN AV	MCO	12C	C6
MORPHEW ST	SR	8A	E3
MORPHEW ST	SR	10D	F4
MORRISON RD	R	10A	B2
MORTON CT	MV	12B	D3
MORTON LN	SA	6D	E6
MOSS LN	SA	6D	F6
MOSSWOOD CT	N	1	B3
MOUND ST	MCO	15	D5
MOUNTAIN LN	MCO	11B	B4
MTN KING RD	MCO	5A	A3
MOUNTAIN VW AV	MCO	5A	A5
MOUNTAIN VW AV	MCO	11A	B3
MOUNTAIN VW AV	MCO	11B	B4
MOUNTAIN VW AV	MV	12C	B4
MOUNTAIN VW AV	SA	6D	E5
MOUNTAIN VW AV	SR	7D	D6
MOUNTAIN VW DR	MCO	11A	B3
MOUNTAIN VW DR	TIB	14	D1
MOUNTAIN VW RD	F	6C	C5
MOUNTAIN VW RD	MCO	27	A1
MT BURNEY CT	MCO	3	D5
MT DANA DR	MCO	3	E6
MT DARWIN CT	MCO	3	E6
MT DIABLO CIR	MCO	3	E6
MT DIABLO RD	MCO	3	E6
MT FORAKER CT	MCO	3	D5
MT FORAKER DR	MCO	3	D5
MT HOOD CT	MCO	3	D6
MT LASSEN DR	MCO	3	E6
MT LYELL DR	MCO	3	D5
MT MCKINLEY RD	MCO	3	D6
MT MUIR CT	MCO	3	E6
MT PALOMAR CT	MCO	3	E6
MT RAINIER CT	MCO	3	D5
MT RAINIER DR	MCO	3	D5
MT SHASTA CT	MCO	3	E6
MT SHASTA DR	MCO	3	E6
MT SUSITNA CT	MCO	3	E6
MT TALLAC CT	MCO	3	D6
MT TENAYA CT	MCO	3	E6
MT TENAYA DR	MCO	3	E6
MT TIBURON CT	TIB	11D	F5
MT TIBURON RD	TIB	11D	F5
MT VISN OVLK RD	MCO	21	C2
MT WHITNEY CT	MCO	3	D5
MT WHITNEY DR	MCO	3	D5
MT WITTENBRG CT	MCO	3	D6
MUDDY HOLLOW TR	MCO	25	C2
MUIR AV	MCO	11B	B4
MUIR BCH OVERLK	MCO	31	D2
MUIR WOODS RD	MCO	11B	B6
MUIR WOODS RD	MCO	31	D2
MULBERRY TER	MCO	3	F6
MULBERRY TER	MCO	4	A6
MURIEL PL	F	6C	C5
MURPHY LN	MCO	2	E2
MURRAY AV	L	10C	A5
MURRAY AV	MCO	10C	A5
MURRAY LN	L	10C	A4
MURRAY LN	MCO	10C	A4
MUSICSTAND TR	MCO	29	A1
MYRTLE AV	L	10C	B6

1991 MARIN COUNTY STREET INDEX

STREET	CITY	PAGE	GRID
MYRTLE AV	MV	11A	C2
MYRTLE AV	SR	7C	C5
MYRTLE LN	SA	9B	E1
MYRTLE PL	N	1	A1
MYRTLE PL	N	1A	A5
N			
NADINA WY	N	10C	C4
NANCY DR	MCO	1	B3
NANDINA CT	N	1	E1
NANTUCKET CV	SR	10B	F2
NAPA AV	F	6D	D5
NAPA ST	SLTO	13	F3
NAPA ST	SLTO	14	A3
NAPIER LN	MV	11A	C3
NARRAGANSETT CV	SR	10B	F2
NASSAU CT	N	3	E2
NATURE TR	MCO	11B	B5
NAVAJO LN	CM	10C	C6
NAVE CT	N	1	E3
NAVE DR	N	4	C2
NEAME AV	SR	7C	A6
NEDS WY	TIB	14	C1
NEIDER LN	MCO	12D	E4
NEILA WY	MCO	12D	D4
NELLEN DR	CM	10D	D6
NELLEN DR	L	10D	D6
NELSON AV	MV	12C	C4
NEVADA LN	MV	11A	C3
NEVADA ST	SR	7C	A6
NEVADA ST	SLTO	13	E3
NEWBERRY LN	MV	11A	B2
NEWBERRY TER	MCO	3	F6
NEWCASTLE CT	SR	7C	C4
NEWELL RD	R	10A	A1
NEWHALL DR	SR	7D	D6
NEWPORT BLVD	SR	10B	F2
NEWPORT WY	SR	10B	F2
NICASIO SQ RD	MCO	23	B6
NICASIO VLY RD	MCO	5A	B1
NICASIO VLY RD	MCO	22	F4
NICASIO VLY RD	MCO	23	A4
NIGHTINGALE LN	SR	8	B4
NIGHTINGALE RD	L	10C	A6
NINA CT	MCO	13	F1
NINA DR	N	1	B3
NINESTONE CT	MCO	4	A5
NIVEN WY	L	10C	C6
NOB HILL CT	MCO	22	B5
NOB HILL RD	MCO	22	B5
NOBLE LN	SLTO	14	B4
NOCHE VISTA	TIB	11D	E4
NOGALES CT	N	1	D2
NOKOMIS AV	SA	6D	E6
NOREN WY	MCO	22	B6
NORMA CT	N	1	C2
NORMAN DR	N	4	A1
NORMAN WY	TIB	11D	F5
NORTH CIR	N	4	D3
NORTH RD	R	9B	F3
NORTH ST	MCO	15	B4
NORTH ST	SLTO	14	A4
NORTH TER	TIB	12D	F4
NORTH TR	CM	12A	B2
NORTHERN AV	MCO	12C	B6
NORTHERN AV	MCO	13	B1
NORTHGATE DR	SR	7A	A3
NORTH POINT CIR	BVDR	14	B1
NORTH RIDGE TR	TIB	14	F2
NORTHVIEW CT	MCO	7B	D3
NORTON AV	MCO	2	F2
NORWOOD AV	R	9B	F2
NOVA LN	N	1	C1
NOVA ALBION WY	SR	7A	A3
NOVATO BLVD	MCO	1	B1
NOVATO BLVD	MCO	20	B6
NOVATO BLVD	MCO	23	D2
NOVATO BLVD	N	2	A6
NOVATO ST	SR	10B	E2
NOVATO LANDG CT	N	1	F3
NUGENT LN	N	1	E2
NUNAN LN	SR	7D	D6
NUNAN LN	SR	10B	D1
NUNES DR	N	1A	E5
NUNES FIRE RD	MCO	3	D6
NUNES FIRE RD	MCO	6B	D1
NUNES FIRE RD	SR	6B	D1
NYE ST	SR	7C	C6
NYE ST	SR	10A	C1
NYMPH RD	MCO	28	A5
O			
OAK AV	BVDR	14	B2
OAK AV	MCO	2	F3
OAK AV	MCO	10A	B3
OAK AV	SA	9B	E1
OAK AV	SR	10A	C2
OAK DR	MCO	8	B6
OAK LN	CM	12A	B1
OAK LN	MV	12A	A3
OAK LN	SR	8	A6
OAK LN	SLTO	14	A4
OAK RD	F	6C	B6
OAK RD	L	10C	A6
OAK RD	MCO	28	A5
OAK ST	MV	12A	A3
OAK WY	N	1	F2
OAK WY	R	9B	F2
OAK CREST CT	N	2	A4
OAK CREST DR	MCO	6D	E4
OAKCREST DR	MCO	7B	D3
OAKCREST ST	MCO	7B	D3
OAKDALE AV	CM	12A	C1
OAKDALE AV	CM	12B	D1
OAKDALE AV	MV	12A	B3
OAKDALE AV	SR	7D	D5
OAKDALE WY	MCO	12C	B6
OAK FOREST RD	N	4	B3
OAK GROVE AV	MCO	5A	E5
OAK GROVE AV	MCO	27	E1
OAK HILL DR	SA	6D	F6
OAKHURST RD	MCO	10B	D3
OAK KNOLL AV	SA	6D	D6
OAK KNOLL CT	MCO	2	D2
OAK KNOLL DR	MCO	6B	E3
OAK KNOLL DR W	MCO	6B	D3
OAK KNOLL DR W	MCO	6D	D4
OAK KNOLL RD	L	10C	A4
OAK KNOLL RD	MCO	10C	A4
OAK KNOLL RD	N	1	B2
OAKLAND AV	SA	6D	E5
OAK MANOR DR	F	6C	C4
OAK MANOR DR	MCO	6C	C4
OAKMONT AV	SR	7C	C5
OAKMONT CT	SR	7C	C5
OAK MOUNTAIN CT	MCO	3	D5
OAK MOUNTAIN DR	MCO	3	D5
OAK PARK WY	N	1	F2
OAKRIDGE RD	MCO	7C	B4
OAK RIDGE TER	MCO	2	C2
OAK SPRINGS DR	SA	6D	D4
OAK TREE CT	SR	6B	F1
OAK TREE LN	F	6C	C4
OAK VALLEY DR	MCO	23	F2
OAK VALLEY DR	N	1	A3
OAK VIEW CT	N	1	E6
OAK VIEW DR	MCO	7C	B5
OAKWOOD AV	SA	6D	D5
OAKWOOD DR	N	4	D3
OAKWOOD DR	SR	7C	B5
OAKWOOD TR	MCO	13	D3
OAT HILL RD	MCO	27	E5
OBERTZ LN	N	3	F2
OCEAN AV	MCO	28	B4
OCEAN PKWY	MCO	26	F6
OCEAN PKWY	MCO	28	A5
OCEAN WY	MV	12C	A4
OCEANA DR	MCO	15	B4
OCEANO PL	N	4	B1
OCEAN VIEW AV	MCO	15	B4
OCEAN VIEW BLVD	MCO	15	B4
OCEAN VIEW TR	MCO	11B	B5
OCTAVIA ST	SR	10A	C2
OLD FRFX BLN RD	MCO	9A	B3
OLD LANDING RD	MCO	11D	E4
OLD LUCAS VL RD	SR	3	E6
OLD LUCAS VL RD	SR	6B	E1
OLD MILL ST	MV	12A	A3
OLD MINE TR	MCO	30	B4
OLD PINE TR	MCO	5	A3
OLD PINE TR	MCO	25	F3
OLD RANCH RD	MCO	1	C5
OLD RANCHRIA RD	MCO	23	C5
OLD STAGE RD	MCO	29	B2
OLD STOVE TR	MCO	29	A1
OLD VEE RD	MCO	27	D5
OLEANDER DR	SR	7A	B2
OLEANDER LN	N	1	F3
OLEMA RD	F	6C	B4
OLEMA RD	MCO	6C	B4
OLEMA BOLINS RD	MCO	28	A2
OLIMA ST	MCO	13	E2
OLIVA CT	N	1	C1
OLIVA DR	N	1	C2
OLIVE AV	L	10C	B6
OLIVE AV	MCO	2	B3
OLIVE AV	N	1	E2
OLIVE AV	R	9B	E2
OLIVE AV	SA	6D	E6
OLIVE AV	SA	9B	E1
OLIVE AV	SR	7D	D6
OLIVE AV	SR	10B	D1
OLIVE ST	MV	12C	A4
OLIVE ST	N	1	E2
OLIVE ST	SLTO	13	F3
OLIVER LN	MCO	12D	D5
OLYMPIA WY	N	3	E1
OLYMPIC WY	SR	7A	C2
ONYX ST	L	10C	B6
OPAL RD	MCO	26	F6
OPAL RD	MCO	28	A5
OPAL ST	L	10C	B5
OPALSTONE TER	MCO	4	A5
ORANGE AV	L	10C	B6
ORANGE AV	N	1	F2
ORANGE AV W	N	1	F2
ORANGE CT	MCO	10B	E3
ORANGE ST	MCO	10B	D3
ORANGE BLOSM LN	SR	7A	A2
ORCHARD WY	MCO	5A	C5
ORCHARD WY	MCO	10C	A4
ORCHARD WY	N	1	D3
ORCHID DR	SR	7A	A2
ORIENT DR	N	20	F2
ORIOLE CIR	N	4	B4
ORMOND CT	N	1	D3
ORO CT	N	1	A3
ORRIS TER	SR	7A	B2
OVER ST	L	10C	B5
OVERHILL RD	MV	12A	C3
OVERLOOK DR	MCO	28	A4
OVERLOOK RD	MCO	22	A4
OWENS DR	N	4	A1
OWLSWOOD LN	CM	12A	B1
OWLSWOOD LN	TIB	11D	E6
OWLSWOOD RD	L	12A	B1
OWLSWOOD RD	TIB	11D	E6
OXFORD AV	MCO	12C	C5
OXFORD AV	MV	12C	C5
OXFORD DR	MCO	7B	D3
P			
PACHECO AV	F	6D	D5
PACHECO AV	MCO	1	D4
PACHECO ST	MCO	13	D2
PACHECO ST	SR	10B	D1
PACHECO CK DR	N	4	A3
PACIFIC WY	MCO	31	E3
PACIFIC QN PSG	CM	12B	E2
PAGE WALK RD	MCO	22	B4
PALADINI RD	N	1	C2
PALAZZI CT	SA	6D	E6
PALM AV	CM	10C	C6
PALM AV	CM	12A	C1
PALM AV	L	10C	B6
PALM AV	MCO	10A	B3
PALM AV	SA	6D	F6
PALM AV	SA	9B	D1
PALM AV	SR	7D	D6
PALM AV	SR	10B	D1
PALM CT	L	10C	C6
PALM DR	MCO	1	F2
PALM DR	N	4	D3
PALM LN	MCO	1	F1
PALM WY	MCO	11B	C4
PALMA WY	MCO	12C	B6
PALMER AV	TIB	11D	D5
PALMER DR	MCO	4	A1
PALMER DR	N	4	A1
PALMERA WY	MCO	7B	D2
PALMO CT	N	1A	C6
PALMO WY	N	1A	C6
PALOMA AV	SR	7D	D6
PALOMA AV	SR	10A	C1
PALOMA DR	CM	12B	E2
PALOMA WK	MV	12A	A3
PALOMINO CIR	MCO	1	A3
PALOMINO RD	MCO	1	A3
PAMARON WY	N	4	C1
PAMELA CT	TIB	12D	E4
PANORAMA DR	N	4	D4
PANORAMIC HWY	MCO	11A	A3
PANORAMIC HWY	MCO	28	F5
PANORAMIC HWY	MCO	29	B3
PANORAMIC HWY	MCO	30	A5
PAN TOLL RD	MCO	29	A3
PAN TOLL RD	MCO	30	B4
PAPER MIL CK RD	N	4	B3
PAR LN	N	3	F2
PARADISE CT	N	1	D2
PARADISE DR	CM	12B	E2
PARADISE DR	MCO	11C	D2
PARADISE DR	MCO	11D	E4
PARADISE DR	MCO	14	D2
PARADISE DR	MCO	14	E5
PARADISE DR	TIB	14	D2
PARADISE CV RD	MCO	11D	E5
PARADISE VLY RD	MCO	28	A2
PARENTE RD	TIB	11C	D2
PARK AV	MCO	15	B4
PARK AV	MCO	21	E3
PARK AV	MCO	28	B4
PARK AV	MV	12C	B4
PARK AV	N	1	E2
PARK CIR	MCO	13	D1
PARK CT	N	1	E2
PARK DR	R	9B	E2
PARK DR	SA	6D	E6
PARK LN	CM	12B	D2
PARK LN	F	6C	C5
PARK LN	SA	6D	F6
PARK LN	SR	7C	A6
PARK PL	TIB	11C	D2
PARK RD	F	6C	C5
PARK ST	L	10C	B5
PARK ST	MCO	5A	E5
PARK ST	SLTO	14	B4
PARK ST	SR	10B	D1
PARK TER	MV	12C	C4
PARK WK	SA	6D	E5
PARK WY	L	10C	C6
PARK WY	L	12A	B1
PARK WY	MCO	11B	C4
PARK WY	MCO	12C	A5
PARK WY	SA	6D	F6
PARK WY	SA	7C	A6
PARK WY	SA	9B	F1
PARK WY	SA	10A	A1
PARK CREST CT	N	2	A5
PARKER LN	F	6D	D5
PARK RIDGE RD	SR	7A	A2
PARKSIDE CT	SA	6D	E5
PARKSIDE WY	L	10D	D4
PARKVIEW CIR	CM	12B	E2
PARKWOOD AV	MV	12C	B4
PARKWOOD DR	N	1	F5
PARRAL WY	MCO	5A	B5
PARTRIDGE CT	N	1A	D6
PARTRIDGE CT	SR	8	C3
PARTRIDGE DR	N	1A	D6
PARTRIDGE DR	SR	8	C3
PASADENA AV	MCO	6D	F5
PASEO WY	L	10C	C4
PASEO MIRASOL	TIB	12B	F3
PASTEL CT	N	1	E4
PASTEL LN	N	1	F4
PASTORI AV	F	6D	D6
PATALITA DR	N	20	F2
PTH OF PETR PAN	MV	12A	A2
PATH OF WILD RS	MV	12A	A2
PATH 1	L	10C	B6
PATH 2	L	10C	B6
PATH 3	L	10C	A6
PATRICIA LN	MCO	12A	C3
PATRICIA LN	MV	12A	C3
PATRICIA WY	SR	6B	E1
PATTERSON LN	N	4	C4
PAUL DR	SR	7A	B2
PAVADAS AV	MCO	6B	F3
PAVILION PATH	CM	12A	C1
PAXTON VILLA CT	N	1	D3
PEACH ST	N	1	F2
PEACHSTONE TER	MCO	4	B5
PEACOCK CT	SR	8	B4
PEACOCK DR	SR	8	B4
PEACOCK LN	SR	8	B5
PEACOCK MANOR	SR	8	C3
PEARCE RD	SR	10A	C2
PEARL ST	SLTO	13	F1
PEBBLE BEACH DR	N	4	A2
PECAN DR	SR	6B	E2
PEDRINI LN	MCO	5A	A5
PEDRINI WY	MCO	5A	A5
PELICAN LN	N	4	B4
PELICAN RD	BVDR	14	B2
PELICAN WY	SR	10D	F4
PELLEGRNELLI DR	TIB	11C	D3
PENINSULA RD	BVDR	14	C1
PENNY LN	F	6C	B4
PENNY LN	L	10C	A6
PENNY TER	MCO	8A	E4
PENNY ROYAL LN	SR	6B	E2
PENSACOLA CT	N	3	E3
PEPPER AV	L	12A	C1
PEPPER WY	SR	7C	B6
PEPPER HART AV	CM	10C	C6
PEPPER HART AV	L	10C	C6
PEPPERWOOD LN	MCO	12B	D2
PERALTA AV	MCO	12C	C6
PERRY ST	MCO	12C	C6
PERRY WALK AV	SR	10A	C3
PERTH WY	MCO	21	E3
PETLUMA V FD RD	MCO	15	E1
PETER CT	N	1	F4
PETRA AV	MCO	5A	A5
PHEASANT CT	SR	8	B3
PHILIP TER	MCO	2	E2
PHOENIX RD	MCO	9D	E5
PICADILLY CT	SR	7C	A4
PICNIC AV	SR	10A	C2
PICO CT	SR	6B	E2
PICO VISTA	N	1	C2
PIEDMONT CT	L	10C	B6
PIEDMONT RD	L	10C	B6
PIEDMONT RD	L	12A	B1
PIERCE DR	N	1	E5
PIERCE LN	N	1	E5
PIERCE POINT RD	MCO	17	C3
PIERCE POINT RD	MCO	18	A5
PIERCE POINT RD	MCO	21	B1
PIGEON HOLLW RD	MCO	10B	E1
PIGEON HOLLW RD	SR	10B	E1
PIKES PEAK DR	MCO	3	E6
PILGRIM WY	SR	7C	C5
PILLSBURY LN	MCO	1	B4
PIMENTEL CT	N	2	B6
PIMLOTT LN	MV	12C	B4
PINE AV	BVDR	14	C3
PINE AV	MCO	5A	F5
PINE AV	MCO	27	E1
PINE AV	N	1	E3
PINE CT	MCO	10A	B3
PINE DR	F	6C	A6
PINE DR	F	9A	B1
PINE LN	SR	6B	F2
PINE RD	MCO	28	A5
PINE ST	MCO	13	B1
PINE ST	SA	9B	F1
PINE ST	SR	7C	B6
PINE ST	SR	10A	B1
PINE ST	SLTO	14	A3
PINE TER	TIB	11D	D5
PINECONE CT	SR	8	A3
PINE CREST	MCO	21	F5
PINE CREST RD	MCO	12C	B6
PINE HILL CT	SR	7A	A1
PINE HILL RD	MCO	12C	C6
PINE HILL RD	MCO	13	C1
PINE HILL RD	MCO	21	D2
PINEO AV	MCO	12C	B6
PINEO AV	MCO	13	B1
PINE MOUNTAIN RD	MCO	5A	C6
PINE MOUNTAIN RD	MCO	27	C2
PINE RIDGE RD	MCO	21	D3
PINE RIDGE WY	MV	12C	B6
PINE TREE CT	SR	7C	B4
PINE VIEW LN	N	1	D1
PINEWOOD DR	MCO	4	A6
PINEWOOD LN	N	2	A5
PINTO LN	MCO	1	A3
PINYON PL	N	1	B1
PINYON PL	N	1A	A6
PIOMBO CT	F	6C	C5
PIOMBO PL	SR	8A	E3
PIONEER CT	N	1	D2
PIPELINE FR RD	MCO	6A	A3
PIPER CT	F	6C	C4
PIPER CT	N	1	C3
PIPER LN	F	6C	C4
PIPER LN	MCO	6C	C4
PIPING ROCK RD	N	3	D3
PIVATO CT	N	1	F3
PIXIE TR	MCO	12C	A4
PIXLEY AV	CM	10C	C6
PIXLEY AV	CM	12A	C1
PIZARO	MCO	5A	B4
PLACE MOULIN	TIB	11D	F5
PLATA CT	MCO	1	B4
PLATFORM BRG RD	MCO	5	C1
PLATFORM BRG RD	MCO	22	D6
PLATT AV	SLTO	13	F3
PLATT CT	MCO	12D	E6
PLAYA DEL REY	SR	10B	F2
PLAYA VERDE	MCO	11D	F5
PLAZA DR	MCO	12D	D4
PLAZA AMAPOLA	N	1	E3
PLAZA DEMIRA	N	1	E4
PLAZA HERMOSA	N	1	E3
PLAZA LINDA	N	1	E3
PLAZA LOMA	N	1	E3
PLEASANT AV	CM	12B	D2
PLEASANT LN	SR	10A	C2
PLEASNT VIEW RD	MCO	1	C3
PLUM ST	N	1	F2
PLUM ST	N	2	A2
PLUMAS AV	SA	6D	E6
PLUMAS AV	SA	9B	E1
PLUMAS CIR	N	2	B5
PLUM TREE LN	SR	7D	D6
PLYMOUTH AV	MV	12C	C5
PLYMOUTH CV	SR	10B	F2
POCO PASO	MCO	7C	B5
POHONO ST	MCO	13	D1
PT GALLINAS RD	MCO	7B	E2
PT REYS LTHS RD	MCO	24	C3
PT RY PETLUM RD	MCO	20	B5
PT RY PETLUM RD	MCO	22	C5
PT RY PETLUM RD	MCO	23	A2
PT SAN PEDRO RD	MCO	8	A6
PT SAN PEDRO RD	MCO	10B	E1
PT SAN PEDRO RD	SR	8	C4
PT SAN PEDRO RD	SR	8	A6
POLHEMUS WY	L	10C	A6
POMANDER WK	BVDR	14	C2
POMEROY RD	R	10A	A1
PONTE FIRE RD	N	3	F4
POPLAR AV	MCO	10A	A3
POPLAR AV	R	9B	F3
POPLAR AV	R	10A	A3
POPLAR DR	MCO	10A	B3
POPLAR DR	N	1	B1
POPLAR DR	N	1A	A5
POPLAR RD	MCO	26	F6
POPLAR RD	MCO	28	A5
POPLAR ST	MCO	13	C1
PTL PIPE F RD E	MCO	9A	A1
PTL PIPE F RD E	MCO	27	F4
PORTEOUS AV	F	6C	C6
PORTEOUS AV	F	9A	C1
PORTEOUS AV	MCO	9A	C1
PORTERO LN	MCO	5A	A4
PORTO BELLO	SR	10B	E2
PORTOFINO RD	SR	10B	E2
PORTOLA AV	MCO	5A	A4
PORTOLA AV	MCO	7C	C4
PORTOLA AV	MCO	22	A5
PORTOLA DR	SR	10B	F1
PORTOLA LN	MV	12A	A3
PORTOLA WY	CM	12A	C1
PORTO MARINO DR	TIB	11D	D4
PORTSMOUTH CV	SR	10B	F2
POSADA DEL SOL	N	4	B2
POST ST	L	10C	B5
POWER LN	F	6C	C6
PRAIRIE FALC DR	N	4	B4

1991 MARIN COUNTY STREET INDEX

STREET	CITY	PAGE	GRID
PRESIDIO AV	CM	12B	D1
PRESIDIO AV	MV	12C	B4
PRESTWICK CT	N	3	E2
PRIMROSE PATH	MCO	12C	C5
PRINCE ROYAL DR	CM	12B	E2
PRINCE ROYL PSG	CM	12B	E2
PRINCESS LN	MCO	12C	B5
PRINCESS LN	SLTO	14	B4
PRINCESS ST	SLTO	14	B4
PRINCETON AV	MCO	12C	C6
PRIVATEER DR	CM	12B	F2
PROFESNL CTR PY	SR	7A	B2
PROSPECT AV	SA	9B	F1
PROSPECT AV	SLTO	14	A4
PROSPECT DR	SR	7C	C6
PROSPECT LN	CM	12B	D2
PROSPECT PL	N	1	F3
PROSPECT PATH	MCO	12C	C5
PUEBLO DR	MCO	4	B6
PUENTE DEL MAR	MCO	28	E4
PUENTE RIZAL	MCO	28	E4
PUFFIN CT	N	4	A4
PURPLE GATE RD	MCO	28	A4
Q			
QUAIL CT	MCO	4	B5
QUAIL CT	N	4	B4
QUAIL RIDGE	MCO	9B	F3
QUAIL RIDGE	R	9B	F3
QUAIL WY	MCO	6D	E4
QUARRY RD	MV	12A	A2
QUARRY RD	SR	7C	B6
QUARRY RD	SR	10A	B1
QUEEN RD	MCO	28	A5
QUEENSTONE DR	MCO	4	A5
QUEENSTONE F RD	MCO	3	E4
QUERCUS CT	N	2	A3
QUEVA VISTA	N	1	C2
QUIETWOOD DR	MCO	4	A6
QUINCE CT	N	2	A6
QUISISANA DR	MCO	10A	B3
R			
RACCOON RD	N	4	A3
RACOON LN	TIB	14	D1
RACQUET CT	N	1	B3
RACQUET CLUB DR	SR	7C	A6
RADIO INTELG RD	N	4	D2
RAE LN	N	1	B2
RAFAEL AV	MCO	28	B4
RAFAEL DR	SR	7D	D6
RAFAEL DR	SR	10B	D1
RAFAEL WY	MCO	7B	D2
RAFAEL PATIO	MCO	28	D5
RAILROAD AV	MCO	2	F3
RAILROAD AV	MCO	5A	E5
RAILROAD AV	MCO	27	D1
RAILROAD AV	N	1	F2
RAILROAD AV	SR	10B	F2
RAILROAD ST	MCO	15	D5
RAILRD GRD F RD	MCO	29	C2
RAINBOW LN	MV	12C	A4
RAINBOW RD	MCO	7C	B5
RALLY CT	F	6C	B4
RALSTON AV	MV	11A	C2
RALSTON AV	MV	12A	A2
RAMONA AV	MCO	5A	B4
RAMONA CT	N	1	C1
RAMONA WY	N	1	C1
RAMONA WY	SA	6D	D6
RANCH LN	L	10C	C6
RANCH RD	MCO	7C	B5
RANCH RD	MCO	11C	D2
RANCH RD	TIB	11C	D2
RANCHERIA RD	MCO	10C	A5
RANCHITOS RD	SR	7C	C5
RANCHO DR	MCO	12D	E4
RANCHO DR	SA	6D	D4
RANDALL FIRE TR	MCO	5	E6
RANDOLPH DR	N	4	C3
RANNOCH WY	MCO	21	E3
RANSOME DR	N	3	F1
RAPOSA VISTA	N	1	C2
RAVEN RD	MCO	6B	D3
RAVINE WY	MCO	9D	E4
RAVINE WY	MCO	23	F3

STREET	CITY	PAGE	GRID
RAY CT	MCO	6D	F5
RAY CT	SA	6D	D4
RAY CT	SR	6D	F5
RAY CT	SR	7C	A5
RAYMOND AV	SA	9B	E1
READE LN	SLTO	14	B4
REBECCA WY	N	2	A2
REBELO LN	MCO	23	F3
REDBUD CT	N	1	E1
REDDING CT	TIB	11D	D4
REDDING WY	SR	10B	D3
RED HAWK RD	N	4	B4
RED HILL AV	SA	6D	F6
RED HILL AV	SA	7C	A6
RED HILL AV	SA	9B	F1
RED HILL AV	SA	10A	A1
RED HILL CIR	TIB	11D	F6
RED HILL CIR	TIB	14	C1
RED HILL RD	MCO	20	D3
RED MOUNTAIN RD	MCO	3	D5
REDONDA AV	MCO	5A	A5
RED ROCK WY	MCO	7C	C5
REDWOOD AV	CM	12A	B1
REDWOOD AV	L	10C	A6
REDWOOD AV	MCO	11B	B4
REDWOOD AV	MCO	21	F4
REDWOOD BLVD	N	1	E1
REDWOOD BLVD	N	1	E3
REDWOOD BLVD	N	1A	E6
REDWOOD BLVD	N	2	A5
REDWOOD DR	MCO	5A	E6
REDWOOD DR	MCO	10A	A3
REDWOOD DR	MCO	27	E1
REDWOOD DR	R	9B	F3
REDWOOD DR	R	10A	A3
REDWOOD DR	SR	7A	B1
REDWOOD DR	SR	10A	B2
REDWOOD DR N	SR	4	B6
REDWOOD DR N	SR	7A	B1
REDWOOD HWY	CM	10D	D6
REDWOOD HWY	CM	12B	D3
REDWOOD HWY	MCO	1A	E2
REDWOOD HWY	MCO	4	B5
REDWOOD HWY	MCO	7C	C4
REDWOOD HWY	MCO	10B	D2
REDWOOD HWY	MCO	12D	D5
REDWOOD HWY	MCO	13	E2
REDWOOD HWY	MCO	14	A5
REDWOOD HWY	N	1	F4
REDWOOD HWY	N	2	A5
REDWOOD HWY	N	4	B4
REDWOOD HWY	SR	7A	B2
REDWOOD HWY	SR	7D	D6
REDWOOD HWY	SLTO	13	E2
REDWOOD LN	CM	12A	B2
REDWOOD LN	L	12A	B2
REDWOOD LN	MV	12C	A4
REDWOOD RD	F	6C	C5
REDWOOD RD	N	1	E3
REDWOOD RD	R	10A	A2
REDWOOD RD	SA	6D	E6
REDWOOD RD	SA	9B	E1
REDWOOD CY F RD	MCO	3	A2
REDWOOD CK TR	MCO	11B	B6
REDWOOD CK TR	MCO	31	D2
REDWD HY FRT RD	SR	7A	B2
REED BLVD	MCO	12D	E4
REED CIR	MCO	12D	E5
REED ST	MCO	12C	B5
REED RANCH RD	TIB	11D	D4
REED RANCH RD	TIB	12D	F4
REED RCH FR RD	MCO	12B	F3
REGALIA DR	MCO	1	B2
REGENT CT	N	1	D3
REGINA WY	SR	6B	F3
REICHERT AV	N	1	E3
REICHERT CT	N	1	F3
RENA CT	N	1	C2
RENAISSANCE RD	N	2	E3
RENATA CT	N	1	F6
RENZ RD	MV	11A	C3
RESACA AV	MCO	5A	B5
RESACA AV	MCO	27	B1
RESERVA LN	TIB	14	D2
RESERVOIR AV	N	1	C2
RESERVOIR DR	N	1	F2
RESERVOIR RD	N	4	D2
RESERVOIR RD	SR	10A	B2

STREET	CITY	PAGE	GRID
RHINESTONE TER	MCO	4	B5
RHONDA WY	MCO	12C	B5
RICARDO CT	MCO	12D	E5
RICARDO LN	MCO	12D	E5
RICARDO RD	MCO	12D	E5
RICA VISTA	N	1	C2
RICE DR	SR	10B	D2
RICE LN	L	10C	C6
RICE LN	MCO	12D	F5
RICH ST	L	10D	D5
RICHARDSON CT	MCO	13	C2
RICHARDSON DR	MCO	12D	E5
RICHARDSON ST	SLTO	14	A4
RICHARDSON WY	MCO	13	C1
RICHIE LN	N	1	C3
RICHMOND RD	SA	9B	F2
RIDER LN	MV	12A	A2
RIDGE AV	MCO	8	A5
RIDGE AV	MCO	11B	B4
RIDGE AV	SR	10B	D1
RIDGE LN	MCO	11B	B4
RIDGE RD	F	6C	C5
RIDGE RD	MCO	13	F4
RIDGE RD	N	1	C4
RIDGE RD	SA	6D	E5
RIDGE RD	SLTO	13	F4
RIDGE RD	TIB	14	D1
RIDGE TR	MCO	5	C6
RIDGE TR	MCO	26	D2
RIDGE WK	SA	6D	E5
RIDGE WY	CM	12A	C1
RIDGE WY	MCO	12A	B3
RIDGE WY	MV	12A	B3
RIDGECREST BLVD	MCO	11A	A1
RIDGECREST BLVD	MCO	28	E2
RIDGECREST BLVD	MCO	29	A3
RIDGECREST RD	MCO	9D	F5
RIDGECREST RD	MCO	10C	A5
RIDGEVIEW CT	MCO	13	D1
RIDGE VIEW CT	N	1	F5
RIDGE VIEW DR	MCO	12C	B6
RIDGE VIEW DR	N	4	C4
RIDGE VIEW HTS	N	1	F5
RIDGE VIEW LN	MCO	22	B5
RIDGEWAY	L	10C	A6
RIDGEWAY AV	F	6D	D5
RIDGEWAY LN	CM	12A	B1
RIDGEWAY LN	L	10C	A6
RIDGEWOOD AV	MCO	12C	A4
RIDGEWOOD DR	SR	7C	A5
RIDGEWOOD DR N	MCO	9D	F4
RIDGEWOOD RD S	MCO	9D	F5
RIDGEWOOD RD S	MCO	10C	A5
RIDGEWOOD FR RD	SR	7C	A4
RIFTZONE TR	MCO	5	B3
RIFTZONE TR	MCO	26	E1
RINCON WY	MCO	7B	D2
RING MTN FR RD	MCO	11C	D2
RING MTN FR RD	MCO	12B	F2
RISING RD	MCO	12C	C5
RISING RD	N	1	D1
RITA CT	N	2	A2
RITTER ST	SR	10A	C1
RIVERA ST	SA	6D	E5
RIVER OAKS RD	SR	7C	A6
RIVER VISTA LN	N	2	D1
RIVIERA CIR	L	10C	C5
RIVIERA CIR	L	10D	D5
RIVIERA CIR S	L	10C	C5
RIVIERA DR	SR	8	C4
RIVIERA PL	SR	8	C4
ROBERT CT	SR	7C	A6
ROBERT DR E	MCO	21	F5
ROBERT DR W	MCO	21	F5
ROBT DOLLR SCNC	SR	7C	C6
ROBT DOLLR SCNC	SR	10A	C1
ROBERTS AV	SR	10A	C2
ROBERTSON TER	MV	12C	B4
ROBIN DR	CM	11C	D2
ROBIN DR	CM	12B	F2
ROBIN DR	TIB	11C	D2
ROBIN RD	MCO	13	C1
ROBINHOOD DR	SR	8	A4
ROBINHOOD LN	N	2	A2
ROBLAR DR	N	4	C1
ROBLE CT	SA	6D	E5
ROBLE RD	SR	10A	B1
ROCA CT	N	1	B3

STREET	CITY	PAGE	GRID
ROCCA AV	F	6D	D5
ROCK RD	MCO	9B	F3
ROCK RD	R	9B	F3
ROCKEN LN	N	1	B3
ROCK HILL DR	TIB	11D	E5
ROCKLYN CT	CM	12A	C1
ROCKPORT COVE	SR	10B	F2
ROCKPORT WY	N	2	A6
ROCK RIDGE RD	F	6C	C5
ROCKRIDGE RD	L	10C	B5
ROCK RIDGE RD	MCO	5A	E6
ROCK RIDGE RD	MCO	27	E1
ROCK ROSE CT	MCO	3	C5
ROCKROSE WY	N	1	E1
ROCK SPG LAG RD	MCO	9C	B6
ROCK SPG LAG RD	MCO	29	B2
ROCK SPRINGS TR	MCO	29	B2
ROCKY RIDGE RD	MCO	9C	B4
RODEO AV	MCO	5A	A5
RODEO AV	SLTO	13	F4
RODEO VALLEY TR	MCO	13	D6
ROGER AV	SA	6D	F6
ROGER DR	SR	7D	D5
ROLLING HILL RD	TIB	11D	E6
ROLLINGWOOD DR	SR	8	A4
ROMAR CT	N	1	E2
ROMERO CT	N	1	C1
ROOSEVELT AV	MCO	7C	C4
ROOSEVELT AV	MV	12A	A3
ROQUE MORAES CT	MV	12C	C4
ROQUE MORAES DR	MV	12C	C4
ROSAL WY	MCO	7B	D2
ROSALIA DR	N	1	F2
ROSARIO RD	MCO	5A	B5
ROSE AV	MV	11A	C3
ROSE AV	SA	9B	E2
ROSE CT	SLTO	14	A4
ROSE ST	MCO	10B	D3
ROSE ST	N	1	F2
ROSEBANK AV	MCO	10C	B4
ROSEBANK LN	MCO	10C	B4
ROSE BOWL DR	SLTO	13	F5
ROSE COURT TER	MCO	2	B3
ROSEMARY CT	N	1	E1
ROSEMONT AV	MCO	12C	C6
ROSEMONT AV	SA	6D	D5
ROSEVILLE CT	TIB	11D	D5
ROSEWOOD CT	SR	8	B5
ROSEWOOD DR	N	2	A4
ROSEWOOD RD	MCO	28	A5
ROSS AV	SA	9B	E1
ROSS DR	MCO	13	C1
ROSS DR	SLTO	13	E2
ROSS RD	MCO	13	E2
ROSS ST	SR	10A	C2
ROSS COMMON	R	10A	A3
ROSS STREET TER	SR	10A	B2
ROSS VALLEY DR	SR	10A	A1
ROUND HILL RD	TIB	11D	E5
ROUNDTREE BLVD	MCO	4	B6
ROUNDTREE WY	MCO	4	B6
ROWAN WY	MV	11A	C2
ROWAN WY	MV	12A	A2
ROWLAND AV	SA	6D	E6
ROWLAND AV	SA	9B	E1
ROWLAND BLVD	N	1	E5
ROWLAND BLVD	N	2	A4
ROWLAND CT	N	1	E5
ROWLAND WY	N	1	F4
ROWLAND WY	N	2	A4
ROWLEY CIR	TIB	11D	D5
ROY CT	N	1	A2
ROYAL CT	SR	10B	E2
RUBEN CT	N	1	A2
RUBICON CT	MCO	3	D5
RUBICON DR	MCO	3	D5
RUDNICK AV	N	2	A2
RUHLMAN LN	N	1	C1
RUHLMAN RD	N	1	C1
RUSH CREEK PL	N	1	E1
RUSH LANDING RD	N	1	E1
RUSH LANDING RD	N	1A	F6
RUSSEL AV	MCO	10A	B3
RUSTIC WY	SR	7C	B5
RUTH CT	N	1	D2
RUTHERFORD AV	SA	6D	D5
RYAN AV	MV	12C	C4
RYDAL AV	MCO	12C	B5

STREET	CITY	PAGE	GRID
S			
SABA LN	MCO	11C	E3
SACRAMENTO AV	MCO	6D	F5
SACRAMENTO AV	MCO	13	E2
SACRAMENTO AV	SLTO	13	E2
SACRAMENTO WY	SLTO	14	A4
SACRAMNTO PATIO	MCO	28	D5
SADDLE LN	MCO	1	A3
SADDLE LN	MCO	23	F3
SADDLE CUT	MCO	6C	A5
SADDLE CUT	MCO	27	F2
SADDLEBROOK CT	N	1	C3
SADY LN	F	6D	D5
SAGE CT	N	1	D1
SAGE CT	N	1A	D6
SAGEBRUSH CT	SR	8	B4
SAGE GROUSE RD	N	4	B4
SAGHALIE LN	SLTO	14	A4
SAILMAKER CT	SR	7A	C2
ST ANDREWS DR	N	3	D2
ST BERNARD LN	TIB	14	D1
ST BERNARD RD	TIB	14	D1
ST FRANCIS LN	N	1	B2
ST FRANCIS LN	SR	7D	E6
ST GABRIELE CT	TIB	11D	F6
ST JOHN CT	N	1	B2
ST JUDE RD	MCO	11B	B4
ST LUCIA PL	MCO	11AC	E2
ST PAUL CIR	N	1	D2
ST THOMAS WY	MCO	11AC	E3
ST VINCENTS DR	MCO	4	C5
SAIS AV	SA	6D	E6
SALEM COVE	SR	10B	F2
SALINAS AV	SA	6D	F5
SALIX AV	MCO	5A	E6
SALIX AV	MCO	27	E1
SALT CREEK LN	MCO	2	D3
SALT CREEK LN	MV	12B	D3
SALT LANDING	MCO	12D	F5
SALVADOR WY	SR	7A	A1
SALVATORE DR	N	4	B1
SAMOA LN	N	2	A5
SAMROSE DR	N	2	B2
SAN ALESO WY	N	1	B1
SAN ANDREAS DR	N	1	B1
SAN ANDREAS DR	N	1A	B6
SAN ANSELMO AV	SA	6D	E6
SAN ANSELMO AV	SA	9B	F1
SAN ARDO CT	N	1A	B6
SAN BENITO WY	N	1	B1
SAN BLAS CT	N	1A	B6
SAN CARLOS AV	SLTO	14	A4
SAN CARLOS WY	N	1	B1
SANCHEZ RD	MCO	5A	B4
SANCHEZ WY	MCO	23	F2
SAN CLEMENTE DR	CM	12B	E1
SANDALWOOD CT	SR	6B	E3
SANDBURG CT	MV	12D	D6
SAN DIEGO AV	SA	6D	E6
SAN DOMINGO WY	N	1A	B6
SANDPIPER CIR	CM	10D	D5
SANDPIPER CT	N	4	B4
SANDPIPER CT	SR	7A	C3
SANDSTONE CT	MCO	4	B5
SAN FELIPE WY	N	1	B1
SANFORD ST	CM	12B	D1
SN FRANCISCO BL	MCO	6D	F5
SN FRANCISCO BL	SA	6D	E5
SAN GABRIEL DR	F	6D	D5
SN GERNMO RG RD	MCO	5A	A6
SN GERNMO RG RD	MCO	27	A2
SN GERNMO VL DR	MCO	5A	D5
SAN GREGORIO CT	N	1	B3
SAN JOAQUIN CT	N	1	A3
SAN JOAQUIN PL	N	1	A2
SAN JOSE BLVD	N	3	F1
SAN JOSE BLVD	N	4	A1
SAN JOSE DR	N	4	D3
SAN JUAN AV	MCO	12C	B6
SAN JUAN CT	N	1	B1
SAN LUIS CT	N	1	C1
SAN LUIS WY	N	1	C1
SAN MARCOS CT	N	1	B1
SAN MARCOS PL	SR	8	C4
SAN MARIN DR	N	1	B1
SAN MARIN DR	N	1A	B6

STREET	CITY	PAGE	GRID
SAN MARINO CT	MCO	8	D3
SAN MARINO CT	SR	8	C4
SAN MARINO DR	SR	8	C4
SAN MARINO PL	SR	8	C4
SAN MATEO CT	SR	6B	F3
SAN MATEO WY	N	1A	C6
SAN MIGUEL CT	F	6C	C5
SAN MIGUEL CT	N	1	B1
SAN MIGUEL WY	N	1	B1
SAN PABLO AV	MCO	7C	C4
SAN PABLO AV	N	4	D3
SAN PABLO WY	N	4	C2
SAN PAULO WY	N	4	C1
SAN PEDRO CT	MCO	7B	D3
SAN PEDRO RD N	MCO	7A	C3
SAN PEDRO RD N	MCO	7B	D3
SAN PEDRO RD N	MCO	7C	C4
SAN PEDRO RD N	MCO	7D	D4
SAN PEDRO RD N	SR	7C	C4
SAN PEDRO RD N	SR	8	A2
SAN QUENTIN TER	MCO	8A	E4
SAN RAFAEL AV	BVDR	11D	E6
SAN RAFAEL AV	BVDR	14	C1
SAN RAFAEL AV	SA	6D	F6
SAN RAFAEL AV	SR	10A	B2
SAN RAFAEL AV	TIB	11D	E6
SAN RAFAEL ST	MCO	2	E3
SAN RAMON WY	N	1	B1
SAN SEBASTIAN	N	4	C1
SANTA ANA CT	TIB	11D	F6
STA BARBARA AV	MCO	6D	F5
STA BARBARA AV	SA	6D	E5
SANTA CLARA CT	SR	6B	F3
SANTA CRUZ AV	SA	6D	E5
STA GABRIELA CT	N	1	B1
STA GABRIELA CT	N	1A	B6
STA MARGARTA DR	SR	7C	A6
STA MARGARTA DR	SR	10A	A1
SANTA MARIA CT	N	1	B3
SANTA MARIA DR	N	1	A3
SANTA MARIA DR	N	1	B3
SANTANA RD	N	2	C1
SANTANA RD	N	20	F2
SANTA ROSA AV	SLTO	14	A4
STA VICTORIA CT	N	1	B1
STA VICTORIA CT	N	1A	B6
SANTA YNEZ CIR	N	1	B2
SANTA YORMA CT	N	1	B1
SANTA YORMA CT	N	1A	B6
SANTIAGO CT	MCO	4	B6
SANTIAGO WY	SR	7A	A1
SANTOLINA DR	N	1	E1
SAO AUGUSTNE WY	SR	7A	B3
SAO AUGUSTNE WY	SR	7C	B4
SARAH DR	MV	12A	C2
SAUNDERS AV	SA	6D	E6
SAUSALITO BLVD	SLTO	14	A5
SAUSALITO ST	CM	12B	D2
SAUSALITO LATRL	MCO	14	A6
SAVANNA CIR	N	1	E5
SAVANNAH AV	SA	6D	E6
SAVANNAH AV	SA	9B	E1
SAVANNAH RD	SA	9B	E1
SCENIC AV	SA	6D	D6
SCENIC AV	SA	9B	E1
SCENIC AV	SR	7C	B6
SCENIC AV	SR	10A	B1
SCENIC DR	N	4	C4
SCENIC LN	SLTO	13	F3
SCENIC RD	F	6C	C5
SCENIC TER	F	6C	C5
SCETTRINI FR RD	SR	7D	D5
SCHAAF CT	SR	7C	A6
SCHIRADO PL	MCO	10B	E1
SCHMIDT LN	MCO	7B	D3
SCHOOL RD	MCO	2	C2
SCHOOL ST	F	6C	C5
SCIACCA LN	MCO	2	C2
SCOTIA LN	N	2	A5
SCOTT AV	N	1	E3
SCOTT CIR	N	4	C3
SCOTT LN	L	10C	B6
SCOTT PL	L	10C	C5
SCOTT PL	L	10D	D5
SCOTT ST	MCO	5A	E5
SCOTT ST	MCO	12C	B5
SCOTTSDALE WY	N	1	F5
SCOTT TANK F RD	MCO	9A	B1

1991 MARIN COUNTY STREET INDEX

STREET	CITY	PAGE	GRID
SCOWN LN	N	1	E2
SEA WY	SR	10B	F1
SEACAPE DR	MCO	31	D3
SEADRIFT RD	MCO	28	D4
SEADRIFT LANDNG	MCO	12D	F5
SEAFIRTH LN	TIB	11D	E4
SEAFIRTH PL	TIB	11D	E4
SEAFIRTH RD	TIB	11D	E4
SEAGULL ROW	N	1	E4
SEAMAST PASSAGE	CM	12B	E1
SEARLESS LN	SA	6D	F6
SEARS POINT HWY	MCO	2	C4
SEASCAPE DR	N	2	A6
SEAVER DR	MV	12D	D4
SEA VIEW AV	MCO	10B	E1
SEA VIEW AV W	MCO	10B	E1
SEA VIEW AV W	SR	10B	E1
SEAWOLF PASSAGE	CM	12B	E2
SEIBEL ST	SR	10A	C2
SELFRIDGE WY	N	4	C3
SEMINARY DR	MCO	12D	E6
SEMINARY RD	SA	9B	F2
SEMINOLE AV	CM	12B	D1
SENTINEL CT	SR	10A	B1
SEQUIERA RD	MCO	3	F6
SEQUIERA RD	MCO	6B	F1
SEQUOIA DR	N	4	E4
SEQUOIA DR	SA	6D	F6
SEQUOIA DR	SA	7C	A6
SEQUOIA DR	SA	9B	F1
SEQUOIA DR	SA	10A	A1
SEQUOIA RD	F	6C	C5
SEQUOIA GLEN LN	N	2	A5
SEQUOIA VLY RD	MCO	11B	C4
SERENO WY	N	1A	D6
SERRA ST	CM	12A	C1
SERRA WY	SR	6B	E2
SEVILLE DR	MCO	4	B6
SEVILLE WY	N	4	C2
SEYMOUR LN	MCO	12C	B4
SHADY LN	L	10C	B6
SHADY LN	L	12A	B1
SHADY LN	MV	12A	A2
SHADY LN	N	1	C1
SHADY LN	R	9B	F2
SHAFER DR	N	1	F6
SHAFER DR	N	3	F1
SHAKIN CT	MCO	21	F5
SHANLEY LN	R	9B	F2
SHANNON CT	N	1	E6
SHANNON LN	SR	7C	A5
SHARI CT	N	1	F6
SHARILYN LN	N	1	B2
SHASTA LN	N	1	E3
SHASTA WY	MCO	12C	B6
SHASTA WY	MCO	13	B1
SHAVER ST	SR	10A	B1
SHAVER GRADE RD	MCO	9A	B3
SHAVER GR F RD	MCO	9B	D3
SHAW DR	SA	6D	F6
SHAYAN CT	MCO	12D	D4
SHEFFIELD AV	MCO	12C	C6
SHEFFIELD AV	MCO	13	C1
SHEILA CT	N	1	B2
SHEILA CT	SA	6D	D4
SHELDRAKE CT	MCO	4	B5
SHELL CT	MCO	12B	D3
SHELL RD	MCO	12B	D3
SHELLEY DR	MV	12C	C4
SHELTER BAY AV	MV	12D	D5
SHEMRAN CT	F	6C	B4
SHENANDOAH PL	SR	7A	C2
SHEPHERD WY	TIB	11D	D4
SHERIDAN CT	MV	12A	B2
SHERMAN AV	N	1	E3
SHERMAN ST	F	6D	D5
SHERWOOD CT	MCO	10C	B4
SHERWOOD DR	MCO	13	D1
SHERWOOD PL	N	2	A2
SHEVELIN RD	N	1	E6
SHIELDS LN	N	1	C3
SHON CT	N	1	E5
SHON DR	N	1	E6
SHORELINE HWY	MCO	5	B2
SHORELINE HWY	MCO	11D	D6
SHORELINE HWY	MCO	12D	D6
SHORELINE HWY	MCO	13	D1
SHORELINE HWY	MCO	15	D5
SHORELINE HWY	MCO	18	C4
SHORELINE HWY	MCO	21	E2
SHORELINE HWY	MCO	22	B4
SHORELINE HWY	MCO	26	E1
SHORELINE HWY	MCO	28	A1
SHORELINE HWY	MCO	30	A6
SHORELINE HWY	MCO	31	A1
SHORELINE PKWY	SR	10B	F3
SHORELINE PKWY	SR	10D	F4
SHORES CT	SR	7A	C3
SHORT LN	L	10C	C6
SHORT TR	CM	12A	B1
SHORT WY	L	10C	C6
SHORT WY	L	12A	C1
SHUCK DR	MCO	12D	E5
SIDNEY CT	MCO	7B	D3
SIDNEY ST	MV	12C	B4
SIENNA WY	SR	7D	D5
SIERRA AV	SA	6D	E6
SIERRA CIR	SR	10A	B2
SIERRA CT	TIB	11D	D5
SIERRA TR	MCO	11A	B3
SIERRA VISTA	N	1	C2
SIGNAL WY	MCO	6D	F6
SILK OAK CIR	SR	8	B4
SILVA CT	MCO	1	B3
SILVEIRA PKWY	SR	7A	C1
SILVERADO DR	TIB	11D	D4
SILVER HILLS RD	MCO	22	A6
SILVER HILLS RD	MCO	25	F1
SILVER LACE CT	MCO	3	D5
SILVER PINE TER	MCO	3	D5
SILVIO LN	N	2	A6
SIMMONS CT	N	1	D2
SIMMONS LN	N	1	C2
SIMMONS TR	MCO	29	A2
SIMMS ST	SR	10B	E3
SINALOA CT	MCO	1	B3
SINOLA AV	MCO	5A	B5
SINOLA AV	MCO	27	B1
SIRARD LN	SR	7C	A6
SIR FRANCIS D BL	F	6C	C4
SIR FRANCIS D BL	L	10C	B4
SIR FRANCIS D BL	MCO	5	D1
SIR FRANCIS D BL	MCO	5A	C4
SIR FRANCIS D BL	MCO	6A	A2
SIR FRANCIS D BL	MCO	10A	A3
SIR FRANCIS D BL	MCO	10D	D4
SIR FRANCIS D BL	MCO	17	E6
SIR FRANCIS D BL	MCO	21	D2
SIR FRANCIS D BL	MCO	24	B4
SIR FRANCIS D BL	R	9B	F2
SIR FRANCIS D BL	R	10A	B3
SIR FRANCIS D BL	SA	6D	D5
SIR FRANCIS D BL	SA	9B	F2
SKEET RANGE RD	N	4	C2
SKY RD	MCO	12D	E4
SKY TR	MCO	5	A5
SKY TR	MCO	25	E1
SKYLAND WY	R	10A	A2
SKYLARK DR	L	10C	B5
SKYLINE	SA	6D	D5
SKY OAKS RD	MCO	9A	B1
SKY OAKS RD	MCO	9C	C4
SKY TRAIL FR RD	MCO	3	B1
SKYVIEW RD	R	10A	A2
SKYVIEW TER	SR	7A	A1
SLEEPY HOLLW DR	MCO	6B	E3
SLOWDOWN CT	MCO	1	C4
SMITH LN	SA	9B	F1
SMITH RD	MCO	13	B1
SMITH RANCH RD	SR	7A	B1
SMITH RANCH RD	SR	7B	D1
SMITH RDG FIRE	MCO	6A	A1
SNAKE RD	MCO	15	D6
SNAKE RD	MCO	18	B1
SNOWBERRY CT	SR	8	B4
SOBRE VISTA	MCO	21	D2
SOLANO ST	TIB	14	D1
SOLANO ST	SR	7C	B6
SOLAR CT	SR	10B	D3
SOMERSET DR	N	1	D1
SOMERSET LN	MCO	12C	C4
SOMERSET LN	MV	12C	C4
SOMERSET PL	N	1	D1
SOMMER CT	TIB	11D	E5
SONOMA AV	SA	6D	E6
SONOMA ST	SR	10B	E2
SONOMA PATIO	MCO	28	D5
SONORA CT	TIB	11D	D5
SONORA WY	CM	12B	E3
SORRENTO WY	SR	10B	F2
SOTELO WY	N	1A	C6
SOUTH CIR	N	4	D4
SOUTH ST	SLTO	14	A5
SOUTH TR	CM	12A	B2
SOUTH WY	CM	12B	D2
SOUTHERN HTS BL	SR	10A	C3
STHRN MARN LINE	MCO	9C	C4
STHRN MARN LINE	MCO	9D	D4
SOUTH GREEN	L	10C	C6
SOUTH OAK AV	SA	9B	E1
SOUTHRIDGE DR	TIB	12D	F4
SOUTHRIDGE DR E	TIB	12D	F4
SOUTHRIDGE DR W	MCO	12D	F4
SOUTHRIDGE DR W	TIB	12D	F4
SOUTH SHRE F RD	MCO	9C	C5
SOUTH SIDE RD	MCO	29	A3
SOUTHVIEW TER	SA	6D	F6
SOUTHVIEW TER	SA	7C	A6
SOUTHWOOD AV	R	9B	F2
SPANISH TR RD	TIB	14	D1
SPAULDING ST	SA	6D	F6
SPAULDING ST	SA	9B	F1
SPENCER AV	SLTO	13	F4
SPENCER AV	SLTO	14	A4
SPENCER CT	SLTO	14	A4
SPINDRIFT PSG	CM	12B	E2
SPINNAKER DR	SLTO	14	B3
SPINOSA WY	N	1	E1
SPRING AV	MCO	28	B4
SPRING DR	MCO	13	A1
SPRING DR	MCO	13	B1
SPRING LN	F	6D	D6
SPRING LN	F	9B	D1
SPRING LN	L	10C	B5
SPRING LN	MV	12C	A4
SPRING LN	TIB	11D	F6
SPRING RD	MCO	5A	A5
SPRING RD	MCO	9B	F3
SPRING RD	MCO	27	A1
SPRING RD	R	9B	F3
SPRING ST	SR	10A	C3
SPRING ST	SLTO	13	F3
SPRING TR	CM	12A	C2
SPRINGFIELD WY	MCO	12C	A6
SPRINGFIELD WY	MCO	13	B1
SPRING GROVE AV	SA	10A	A1
SPRING GROVE AV	SR	10A	A1
SPRING GROVE LN	SR	10A	A1
SPRING HILL CIR	SLTO	13	E3
SPRINGSIDE WY	MCO	12C	C6
SPRINGSIDE WY	MCO	13	C1
SPRUCE AV	F	6D	D6
SPRUCE AV	SA	6D	D6
SPRUCE PL	N	1	B1
SPRUCE PL	N	1A	A6
SPRUCE RD	F	6C	C5
SPRUCE ST	MCO	13	B1
STACY CT	N	1	C3
STADIUM AV	MCO	10C	A4
STADIUM AV	MCO	12C	C5
STAGHOUND PSG	CM	12B	E2
STANFORD AV	MV	12C	C6
STANFORD CT	L	10C	B4
STANFORD CT	N	1	D3
STANFORD WY	SLTO	13	E2
STANGLAND AV	SR	10A	C2
STANTON WY	MV	12A	C3
STARBOARD CT	MCO	12D	E6
STARBUCK DR	MCO	31	D3
STARLING CT	MCO	13	C1
STARLING RD	MCO	13	C1
STASIA CT	N	1	A2
STASIA DR	N	1	A2
STATE ACCESS RD	N	4	C2
STELLA LN	L	10C	A4
STETSON AV	CM	12A	C2
STETSON AV	MCO	10A	A3
STETSON AV	MV	12A	B3
STEVEN CT	MCO	6A	C3
STEVEN WY	MCO	7B	D3
STEVENS PL	SR	10B	D1
STEWART DR	SR	7C	C6
STEWART DR	SR	10A	C1
STEWART DR	TIB	11D	D5
STEWART TR	MCO	5	C5
STIRLING WY	MCO	21	E3
STIRRUP LN	MCO	1	A3
STITTS CT	N	1	D2
STOCKSTILL WY	MCO	21	D2
STONE CT	SA	6D	E5
STONE DR	N	1	F6
STONE WK	SA	6D	E5
STONEHAVEN CT	N	1	A2
STONY HILL RD	TIB	11D	E6
STORER DR	MCO	12D	E5
STORY BOOK CT	N	1	D3
STRAITS VIEW DR	TIB	14	D1
STRAWBERRY CIR	MCO	12D	E4
STRAWBERRY CT	MCO	12D	E5
STRAWBERRY DR	MCO	12D	E5
STRAWBERRY DR E	MCO	12D	E5
STRAWBERRY LN	MCO	12D	E6
STRAWBRRY LNDNG	MCO	12D	E5
STURDIVANT AV	SA	9B	F1
STURDIVANT AV	SA	10A	A1
STUYVESANT DR	MCO	6B	D3
SUFFIELD AV	SA	6D	D5
SUGAR LOAF DR	TIB	11D	F5
SULGRAVE LN	SR	8	C3
SULLIVAN AV	MCO	2	E2
SULLIVAN RD	MCO	2	E2
SULPHUR SPA	MCO	6A	C2
SUMAC CT	N	1	D1
SUMAC CT	N	1A	D6
SUMMER AV	F	6C	C6
SUMMER AV	F	6D	D6
SUMMER ST	MCO	15	B4
SUMMERHILL CT	SR	7C	B4
SUMMERHILL WY	SR	7C	B4
SUMMERS AV	N	1	F2
SUMMERS AV	N	2	A3
SUMMIT AV	MCO	7D	E6
SUMMIT AV	MCO	10B	E1
SUMMIT AV	MV	11A	C3
SUMMIT AV	MV	12A	A3
SUMMIT AV	SR	10B	F1
SUMMIT AV	SR	10B	E1
SUMMIT DR	CM	12A	B2
SUMMIT DR	MCO	5A	E6
SUMMIT DR	MCO	8	B6
SUMMIT LN	CM	12A	B1
SUMMIT RD	F	6D	D6
SUMMIT RD	MCO	7B	E3
SUMMIT RD	SA	6D	D6
SUMMIT TR	CM	12A	B2
SUN LN	N	1	B2
SUNDANCE WY	N	1A	D6
SUNNY DR	SA	6D	F6
SUNNYBRAE LN	N	2	A5
SUNNYCREST AV	MCO	11B	C4
SUNNYCREST AV	MV	11B	C4
SUNNYHILL RD	N	1	E2
SUNNY HILLS DR	SA	6D	F6
SUNNY OAKS DR	MCO	7B	D2
SUNNYSIDE	R	9B	F2
SUNNYSIDE	R	10A	A2
SUNNYSIDE AV	CM	12B	D2
SUNNYSIDE AV	MV	12A	B3
SUNNYSIDE AV	SA	9B	E2
SUNNYSIDE CT	CM	10C	C6
SUNNYSIDE CT	CM	12A	C1
SUNNYSIDE DR	MCO	21	F5
SUNRISE AV	MV	12C	B4
SUNRISE LN	L	12A	B1
SUNRISE LN	MCO	11B	B4
SUNRISE LN	N	4	D4
SUNSET CT	N	1	F5
SUNSET DR	N	4	D3
SUNSET LN	MV	12C	A4
SUNSET PKWY	N	1	F5
SUNSET TR	MCO	2	C2
SUNSET TR	TIB	14	E3
SUNSET WY	MCO	13	C1
SUNSET WY	MCO	31	D3
SUNSET WY	SR	7C	A6
SUNSHINE AV	SLTO	14	A4
SUNSHINE CT	MCO	21	F5
SUNSHINE LN	MCO	5A	C5
SUNVIEW AV	SA	6D	E5
SURF WY	N	1	D1
SURFWOOD CIR	SR	8	B5
SURREY AV	MV	12C	C5
SURREY LN	SR	6B	F2
SUSAN CT	N	2	A6
SUSAN WY	N	2	A6
SUSSEX CT	SR	7C	B4
SUTRO AV	MCO	1	A2
SUTRO AV	N	1	A2
SUTRO CT	N	1	A2
SUTTER CT	TIB	11D	D5
SUTTON LN	MCO	2	D1
SWEETBRIAR LN	SLTO	14	A4
SWEETSER AV	N	1	E2
SWIFT CT	MV	12D	D4
SYCAMORE AV	L	10C	B6
SYCAMORE AV	MV	12C	B4
SYCAMORE AV	SA	6D	F6
SYCAMORE AV	SA	9B	F1
SYCAMORE DR	N	1	A1
SYCAMORE DR	N	1A	A5
SYL DOR LN	MCO	1	C3
SYLVAN LN	R	9B	F2
SYLVAN WY	CM	12B	D2
SYLVAN WY	MCO	5A	E5
SYLVAN WY	MCO	7B	D3
SYLAN WY	MCO	27	E1
SYLVESTRIS DR	MCO	5A	C5
SYLVIA CIR	N	1	C2
SYLVIA WY	SR	6B	E3
SYNANON	MCO	18	D6
SYOSSET LN	MCO	1	B4
T			
TAFT CT	N	1	E4
TAHITI WY	MCO	15	B4
TAHOE CIR	N	2	B5
TAHOE PL	SR	7A	C2
TAMAL AV	SA	6D	E6
TAMAL PZ	CM	10D	D5
TAMAL RD	MCO	5A	B4
TAMALPAIS AV	BVDR	14	B1
TAMALPAIS AV	L	10C	B5
TAMALPAIS AV	MCO	13	C2
TAMALPAIS AV	MV	11A	C2
TAMALPAIS AV	MV	12A	A3
TAMALPAIS AV	N	1	D3
TAMALPAIS AV	SA	9B	F1
TAMALPAIS AV	SR	10A	C1
TAMALPAIS AV	TIB	14	C2
TAMALPAIS DR	CM	12A	C1
TAMALPAIS DR	CM	12B	D1
TAMALPAIS DR	MCO	11B	C4
TAMALPAIS DR	MCO	12C	A4
TAMALPAIS RD	F	6C	C5
TAMALPAIS RD	MCO	10C	C4
TAMAL VISTA BL	CM	10D	D6
TAMAL VISTA BL	L	10D	D6
TAMAL VISTA BL	MCO	10D	D6
TAMAL VISTA DR	SR	7C	A6
TAMAL VISTA LN	MCO	10A	C3
TAMARACK DR	MCO	6B	F3
TAMARACK PL	N	1	B1
TAMARACK PL	N	1A	A6
TAMARACK RD	MCO	5A	C5
TAMARIN LN	MCO	2	D2
TAMPA DR	SR	7C	C6
TANBARK CT	N	1	D1
TANBARK CT	N	1A	D6
TANBARK TER	SR	6B	F2
TANFIELD RD	TIB	11D	E4
TANGLEWOOD AV	MCO	10C	A5
TANGLEWOOD LN	MCO	1	B5
TAN OAK	CM	12B	D1
TAN OAK CIR	SR	6B	F1
TAPPAN CT	MCO	6A	C2
TAPPAN RD	MCO	6A	C2
TARA LN	N	1	D1
TARA HILL RD	TIB	11D	F6
TARA VIEW RD	TIB	11D	F6
TARRAGON DR	SR	6B	F2
TARRANT CT	SR	7C	C5
TARRY RD	MCO	6A	C2
TARTAN RD	MV	12A	B2
TAURUS DR	MCO	1	A2
TAYLOR AV	MCO	5A	E5
TAYLOR DR	F	6C	C5
TAYLOR LN	CM	12A	C1
TAYLOR LN	L	10C	C6
TAYLOR LN	L	12A	C1
TAYLOR RD	TIB	11C	D2
TAYLOR ST	SA	6D	E6
TAYLOR ST	SR	10A	C2
TAYLOR PARK RD	MCO	5	F4
TAYLOR PARK RD	MCO	5A	A5
TEABERRY LN	MCO	14	E5
TEAKWOOD CT	SR	8	B5
TEAL RD	BVDR	14	C2
TELEPHONE RD	MCO	22	C2
TELEPHONE TR	MCO	11A	B1
TEMPLEMAN CT	CM	12A	C2
TENAYA DR	TIB	11D	D5
TENAYA LN	N	1	D4
TENNESSEE AV	MCO	12C	C6
TENNESSEE AV	MCO	13	C1
TENNESSEE VLY RD	MCO	13	C3
TENNESSE VLY TR	MCO	13	A5
TENNYSON DR	MV	12D	D5
TERMINAL RD	N	4	E3
TERRACE AV	MCO	10A	B3
TERRACE AV	MCO	28	B4
TERRACE AV	SA	10A	A1
TERRACE AV	SR	10A	A1
TERRACE CT	TIB	12D	F4
TERRACE LN	SR	10A	B1
TERRADILLO AV	SR	10B	D1
TERRA LINDA DR	SR	6B	F3
TERRY CIR	N	1	F6
TESTA ST	SLTO	13	F3
TETON CT	SR	7A	C2
TEXEIRA TR	MCO	26	E3
THALIA ST	MV	12C	B4
THE ALAMEDA	SA	6D	E4
THERESA CT	N	1	B2
THERESA CT	TIB	11D	E5
THERESA DR	SA	6D	D4
THISTLE DR	SR	6B	F2
THOMAS CT	N	1	B2
THOMAS CT	R	9B	F3
THOMAS CT	SR	7C	B6
THOMAS CT	SR	10A	B1
THOMAS DR	MCO	12B	D3
THOREAU CIR	MV	12D	D4
THORNDALE DR	SR	7A	A3
THORNHILL CT	N	3	E2
THORNTON CT	N	1	D1
THORNWOOD TER	SR	6B	F2
THREE PKS F RD	MCO	19	C6
THROCKMORTON AV	MV	11A	C3
THROCKMORTON AV	MV	12C	A4
THROCKMORTON LN	MV	11A	C3
THROCKMORTON TR	MCO	11A	A2
THUNDERBIRD CT	N	3	E3
THUNDERBIRD DR	N	3	E3
THYME PL	SR	6B	F2
TIBURON BLVD	BVDR	14	C1
TIBURON BLVD	MCO	10B	D3
TIBURON BLVD	MCO	12D	F4
TIBURON BLVD	TIB	11D	E6
TIBURON BLVD	TIB	12D	F4
TIBURON BLVD	TIB	14	C1
TIBURON ST	SR	10B	E2
TIERRA VISTA WY	SR	7C	B6
TIERRA VISTA WY	SR	10A	B1
TIKI RD	N	2	C1
TILDEN CIR	SR	7C	A6
TILDEN CT	N	1	E5
TIMBER CYN RD	MCO	5A	F6
TIMBER CYN RD	MCO	6C	A4
TIMBER CYN RD	MCO	27	F1
TIMOTEO DR	MCO	12D	E5
TIMOTEO TER	MCO	12D	E5
TIMOTHY CT	N	4	B4
TIMOTHY DR	SA	6D	D4
TIOGA CT	MCO	3	D5
TIOGA LN	MCO	10C	C4
TODD WY	MCO	12C	B5
TOMAHAWK CT	N	1	E6
TOMAHAWK DR	SA	6D	E5
TOMALES PL	MCO	21	F5
TOMALES ST	SLTO	13	E2
TOMALS PETAL RD	MCO	15	E5
TOMALS PETAL RD	MCO	16	A3
TOMASINI CYN RD	MCO	22	B4
TOPAZ DR	N	20	E2
TOPAZ RD	N	2	C1
TOPSIDE WY	MCO	12D	E6
TOUCHSTONE CT	MCO	4	A5

STREET	CITY	PAGE	GRID
TOUSSIN AV	MCO	10A	A3
TOWER DR	MCO	12D	D4
TOWER POINT LN	TIB	14	D2
TOYON	CM	12B	D1
TOYON AV	BVDR	14	C2
TOYON CT	SLTO	13	F3
TOYON DR	F	6C	B6
TOYON DR	SA	6D	E5
TOYON LN	SLTO	13	F3
TOYON WY	N	2	A3
TOYON WY	SR	10A	B2
TOYON FIRE RD	MCO	6C	B5
TRADEWIND PSG	CM	12B	F1
TRALEE WY	SR	6B	F1
TRAXLER RD	SA	6D	D5
TREANOR ST	SR	10A	C2
TREE LN	N	1	C3
TREE LN	N	1	D2
TREEHAVEN DR	SR	7C	B6
TREE TOP WY	MCO	9D	E4
TRELLIS DR	MCO	6B	F3
TRELLIS DR	SR	7A	A3
TRESTLE GLEN DR	TIB	11D	D4
TRESTLE GN TER	TIB	11D	D4
TRILLIUM LN	MCO	12C	B6
TRINIDAD DR	MCO	11C	E3
TRINITY DR	N	2	B5
TRINITY WY	SR	7A	A3
TRISH DR	MCO	1	A2
TRISH DR	N	1	A2
TROST RD	SR	10A	B1
TRUMAN CT	N	1	D5
TRUMAN DR	N	1	D5
TRUMBULL AV	N	1	B3
TRUMBULL CT	N	1	B3
TUDOR CT	SR	7C	C4
TULANE DR	L	10C	B5
TULIP RD	MCO	28	A5
TUNNEL LN	CM	12A	C2
TUNSTEAD AV	SA	9B	F1
TURNAGAIN RD	MCO	9D	F4
TURNER DR	N	1	E6
TURNER DR	N	3	E1
TURNEY ST	SLTO	14	A3
TURTLE ROCK CT	TIB	11D	D4
TWAIN HARTE LN	SR	10A	C3
TWEED TER	SR	8	A5
TWELVEOAK HL DR	SR	3	F6
TWELVEOAK HL DR	SR	7A	A1
TWIN BRIDGE RD	MCO	15	F4
TWIN OAKS AV	SR	7C	B6
TYLER ST	N	1	E4
U			
ULLOA CT	N	1	E6
UNA WY	MV	12C	B4
UNDERHILL RD	MV	12A	C3
UNDERHILL RD	MV	12B	D2
UNION ST	SR	10B	D1
UNIONSTONE DR	MCO	4	A5
UNIONSTONE LN	MCO	4	A5
UPLAND AV	MV	12A	B3
UPLAND CIR	CM	11C	D2
UPLAND CIR	CM	12B	F2
UPLAND LN	MV	12A	A2
UPLAND LN	N	2	A2
UPLAND RD	MCO	9D	F4
UPPER RD	MCO	7B	E2
UPPER RD	R	9B	E2
UPPER TER N	TIB	12D	F4
UPPER AMES AV	R	9B	F2
UPR ALCATRZ PL	MV	12A	A3
UPPER ARDMORE	L	12A	B1
UPPER BRIAR RD	MCO	10C	A5
UPPR CECELIA WY	TIB	12D	F4
UPR FREMONT DR	SR	10A	B1
UPPERHILL RD	MV	12A	C2
UPPER OAK DR	SR	3	F6
UPPER OAK DR	SR	6B	F1
UPR RIDGEWAY AV	F	6D	D5
UPPER TOYON DR	MCO	10A	B3
UPPER TOYON DR	SR	10A	B2
V			
VALENCIA AV	SR	10B	D1
VALENCIA CT	N	1	D2

STREET	CITY	PAGE	GRID
VALENCIA LN	CM	12A	C1
VALESCO CT	N	4	B4
VALLEJO AV	MCO	21	F5
VALLEJO AV	MCO	22	A5
VALLEJO AV	N	1	E2
VALLEJO WY	SR	6B	E2
VALLEY AV	MCO	15	D4
VALLEY CIR	MCO	12C	C4
VALLEY CIR	MV	12C	C5
VALLEY DR	N	4	C4
VALLEY RD	F	6C	C6
VALLEY RD	MCO	12D	D4
VALLEY RD	SA	6D	D5
VALLEY ST	SLTO	14	A5
VALLEY WY	L	10C	A6
VALLEY WY	MCO	5A	C5
VLY F FR SCH RD	MCO	15	C2
VALLEY OAK CT	N	1	F5
VALLEYSTONE DR	MCO	4	A5
VALLEY VIEW AV	SR	7C	B5
VALLEY VIEW LN	MCO	12C	B5
VALLINE LN	MCO	28	B5
VAL VISTA AV	MV	12A	B3
VAN BUREN CT	N	1	E5
VAN HOOTEN CT	MCO	6B	D3
VAN RIPPER CT	MCO	6B	D3
VAN TASSEL CT	MCO	6B	D2
VAN WINKLE DR	MCO	6A	C2
VARBORG TER	SA	6D	E4
VARDA LANDNG RD	SLTO	13	E2
VASCO CT	MV	12A	C3
VASCO DR	MV	12A	C3
VENADO DR	TIB	11D	F6
VENDOLA DR	MCO	7A	C2
VENDOLA DR	MCO	7B	D2
VENETIA MEADOW	MCO	7B	D3
VENTURA WY	MCO	12C	B6
VENUS CT	TIB	11D	D4
VERA CRUZ AV	N	4	C2
VERA SCHULTZ DR	SR	7C	C4
VERDAD WY	N	1A	C6
VERDI ST	SR	10B	E3
VEREDA PATH	TIB	14	D1
VERISSIMO DR	MCO	1	A3
VERISSIMO DR	MCO	23	F3
VERNAL AV	MCO	12C	B5
VIA BARRANCA	L	10D	D4
VIA BELARDO	L	10C	C4
VIA CAPISTRANO	TIB	12D	F4
VIA CASITAS	L	10C	C4
VIA CASITAS LWR	L	10C	C4
VIA CASITAS UPR	L	10C	C4
VIA CHEPARRO	L	10C	C4
VIA CHEPARRO	MCO	10C	C4
VIA DE LA VISTA	MCO	21	D2
VIA DEL PLANO	MCO	4	B2
VIA ELVERANO	TIB	12B	F3
VIA ESCONDIDA	MCO	4	B2
VIA HERBOSA	MCO	4	B2
VIA HERMOSA	L	10D	D4
VIA HIDALGO	L	10C	C4
VIA HIDALGO	MCO	10C	C4
VIA HOLON	L	10C	C5
VIA HORQUETA	SR	7A	A2
VIA LA BRISA	L	10C	C5
VIA LA CUMBRE	L	10D	D4
VIA LA CUMBRE	MCO	10D	D4
VIA LA PAZ	L	10D	D4
VIA LERIDA	L	10D	D4
VIA LERIDA	MCO	10D	D4
VIA LOS ALTOS	TIB	12D	E4
VIA MONTEBELLO	SR	8	C4
VIA NAVARRO	L	10D	D4
VIA PARAISO E	TIB	11D	E6
VIA PARAISO W	TIB	11D	E5
VIA RECODO	MCO	13	C2
VIA SN FERNANDO	TIB	12B	F3
VIA SESSI	SR	10A	C1
VIA SOBRANTE	MCO	21	D2
VIA VAN DYKE	MV	12A	B3
VIA VAN VUREN	SR	7C	B4
VICTOR CT	N	1	D3
VICTORIA WY	L	10D	D4
VIDA CT	N	1	B4
VIEJO WY	N	1A	D6
VIENTO WY	MCO	22	B5
VIEW ST	L	10C	B6
VIEWPARK CT	MCO	13	B2

STREET	CITY	PAGE	GRID
VIEW POINT RD	MCO	13	B1
VILLA AV	SR	7C	C5
VILLA CT	MCO	10A	B3
VILLA PL	N	1	D2
VILLA GARDEN DR	MCO	13	D1
VILLAGE CIR	N	2	A5
VILLAGE CIR	SR	7C	C4
VILLAGE CT	SR	7C	A4
VILLA MARIA	N	1	D3
VILLA VISTA CT	MCO	1	A3
VINCENT LN	N	2	B2
VINE AV	SA	9B	E2
VINE RD	MCO	26	F6
VINE RD	MCO	28	A5
VINE ST	L	10C	B5
VINEYARD AV	SA	9B	E2
VINEYARD CT	N	1	B3
VINEYARD DR	SR	7C	C5
VINEYARD RD	MCO	23	F3
VINEYARD RD	N	1	B3
VINEYARD WY	MCO	10C	A4
VIOLA WY	MCO	13	C2
VIOX WY	SR	10A	B1
VIRGINIA AV	N	1	D2
VIRGINIA DR	TIB	11D	D5
VIRGINIA ST	N	1	D2
VISCAINO WY	SR	7A	A3
VISION RD	MCO	21	E3
VISTA AV	MCO	5A	A4
VISTA CT	CM	12B	E3
VISTA DR	MCO	10A	B2
VISTA DR	R	10A	B2
VISTA LN	SA	6D	D6
VISTA WY	F	6D	D4
VISTA CLARA	SLTO	13	F4
VISTA DEL MAR	MCO	14	D1
VISTA DEL MAR	SR	10B	E3
VISTA DEL MAR	TIB	14	D1
VISTA DEL VALLE	MCO	13	C2
VISTA GRANDE	MCO	10C	C4
VISTA LINDA DR	MV	12A	C2
VISTA WOOD WY	SR	7C	A5
VISTAZO EAST ST	TIB	14	D1
VISTAZO WEST ST	TIB	11D	F6
VISTAZO WEST ST	TIB	14	D1
VIVIAN CT	N	1	A3
VIVIAN ST	SR	10B	E2
VOGELSANG DR	MCO	3	E5
VON CT	MCO	6A	C3
W			
WAIKIKI LN	MCO	15	B4
WAINWRIGHT PL	MV	11A	C3
WAKEROBIN LN	SR	6B	F2
WALDEN	MV	11A	C2
WALDO CT	MCO	13	D2
WALKER ST	MCO	12D	D4
WALLACE CT	N	1	E5
WALLACE WY	SR	6B	F3
WALLA VISTA	MCO	28	D5
WALNUT AV	CM	10C	C6
WALNUT AV	CM	12A	C1
WALNUT AV	L	10C	B6
WALNUT AV	MV	12C	B4
WALNUT AV	R	9B	F3
WALNUT CT	N	1	A1
WALNUT CT	N	1A	A6
WALNUT RD	F	6C	A6
WALNUT RD	F	9A	A1
WALNUT RD	MCO	28	A5
WALSH DR	MCO	11B	C4
WALSH LN	F	6C	C5
WALSH LN	MCO	2	F2
WALTER DR	MCO	12D	E5
WALTER LN	SR	10A	C1
WALTER PL	SR	7C	B4
WALTERS RD	R	9B	F2
WALTERS RD	R	10A	A2
WANDA LN	MCO	13	B1
WARD ST	L	10C	B6
WARD ST E	L	10C	B6
WAREHOUSE RD	N	4	C2
WARNER CT	SR	10A	C2
WARREN CT	TIB	11D	D4
WARREN CT	TIB	11D	E4
WARRENS WY	TIB	11D	D4
WARRENS WY	TIB	12D	F4

STREET	CITY	PAGE	GRID
WASHINGTON AV	MCO	7C	C4
WASHINGTON CT	TIB	11D	D4
WASHINGTON CT	TIB	12D	F4
WASHINGTON ST	N	1	E5
WASHINGTN PK AV	MCO	11B	B4
WATER WY	L	10C	A6
WATER WY	L	12A	A1
WATER WY	MCO	12A	A1
WATERSIDE CIR	SR	7A	C3
WATERVIEW DR	MCO	12C	B5
WATT AV	SR	7D	D6
WATT AV	SR	10B	D1
WAVERLY RD	SA	9B	E2
WEATHERLY DR	MCO	12D	E6
WEATHERLY DR	MCO	13	E1
WEBER LN	MCO	10D	D4
WELCH ST	SR	10A	B2
WELCOME LN	SR	7D	D6
WELLBROCK HGTS	SR	6B	F3
WELLESLEY AV	MCO	12C	C6
WELLESLEY AV	MCO	13	B1
WELLESLEY CT	MCO	12C	B6
WELLINGTON AV	R	9B	F2
WELLINGTON AV	R	10A	A1
WEMBURY WY	MCO	12C	C6
WENDY WY	MCO	13	B1
WENTWORTH LN	N	3	E2
WERNEN CT	N	1	D3
WESSEN LN	F	6C	C6
WEST CT	N	1	E3
WEST CT	SA	6D	D5
WEST CT	SLTO	14	A5
WEST LN	SA	6D	F6
WEST RD	R	9B	F3
WEST ST	SR	10A	B1
WEST ST	SLTO	14	A5
WEST TR	CM	12A	B2
WEST TR	L	12A	B2
WESTBRAE DR	F	6C	C4
WEST END AV	SR	10A	B1
WESTERN AV	MCO	12C	B5
WESTERN DR	N	1	C2
WEST GATE WY	SA	6D	F6
WESTOVER CIR	N	4	C4
WEST POINT TR	MCO	29	C2
WESTRIDGE LN	N	2	A2
WEST SHORE RD	BVDR	14	B2
WESTWARD DR	CM	12B	F2
WESTWOOD AV	SR	10A	A1
WESTWOOD DR	MCO	9D	F4
WESTWOOD DR	N	1	F2
WESTWOOD DR	SR	10A	A1
WETTMORE LN	MCO	20	B2
WHARF CIR	SR	7A	C2
WHARF RD	MCO	28	B4
WHITAKER BLF RD	MCO	15	D3
WHITE WY	SA	9B	E1
WHITE HILL F RD	MCO	5A	F6
WHITE HILL F RD	MCO	6A	A3
WHITE HILL F RD	MCO	27	E2
WHITEPLAINS CT	MCO	6A	C2
WHITEWOOD DR	SR	6B	F2
WHITEWOOD DR	SR	7A	A2
WHITMAN WY	MV	12D	D4
WHITTIER AV	MCO	7A	C3
WHITTIER CT	MV	12D	D6
WILDER RD	MCO	6A	C3
WILDER RD	MCO	6B	D3
WILDER RD	MCO	6C	C4
WILDER RD	MCO	6D	D4
WLD HRSE VLY DR	MCO	1	A4
WILD OAK DR	N	4	C4
WILDOMAR ST	MV	12C	A4
WILDWOOD WY	SR	7C	C6
WILKINS CT	TIB	11D	E5
WILKINS PL	MV	12D	D4
WILKINS ST	SR	10A	C1
WILLIAM AV	L	10C	C6
WILLIAM CT	SLTO	13	E3
WILLIAMS ST	SR	7D	D6
WILLIAMSON CT	N	1	C3
WILLIS DR	MCO	12D	E6
WILLIS LN	F	6C	C6
WILLOW AV	CM	12A	C1
WILLOW AV	F	6D	D5
WILLOW AV	L	10C	B5
WILLOW AV	L	12A	C1
WILLOW AV	R	9B	F3

STREET	CITY	PAGE	GRID
WILLOW AV	SR	7C	B4
WILLOW CT	N	2	A3
WILLOW LN	SLTO	13	E3
WILLOW RD	MCO	22	E4
WILLOW ST	MCO	28	E5
WILLOW ST	MV	12C	B4
WILLOW ST	SR	10A	C2
WILLOW WK	SA	6D	E5
WILLOW WY	MCO	15	D6
WILLOW WY	SA	6D	E5
WILLOW CP FR RD	MCO	28	E4
WILLOW HILL RD	R	9B	F3
WILMAC AV	N	1	C2
WILSON AV	MCO	1	B3
WILSON AV	N	1	B3
WILSON CT	N	1	E3
WILSON WY	L	10C	A6
WILSON HILL CT	N	1	E3
WILSON HILL RD	MCO	19	F4
WILSON HILL RD	MCO	20	A4
WILTSHIRE AV	L	10C	C6
WILTSHIRE AV	L	12A	C1
WIMBLEDON CT	N	4	A2
WIMBLEDON LN	F	6C	B4
WIMBLEDON WY	SR	6D	F6
WIMBLEDON WY	SR	7C	A6
WINDEMERE CT	N	1	D4
WINDING WY	R	10A	A2
WINDMILL PL	N	1A	E6
WINDSOR AV	SR	7C	B6
WINDSTONE DR	MCO	4	B5
WINDWARD DR	CM	12B	E2
WINDWARD RD	BVDR	11D	E6
WINDWARD RD	BVDR	14	B1
WINDWARD WY	SR	10B	F3
WINGED FOOT DR	N	3	F2
WINGED FOOT DR	N	4	A2
WINN LN	MCO	22	B4
WINSHIP AV	R	9B	F2
WINTERGREEN CT	N	1	E1
WINTERGREEN TER	SR	6B	F2
WINTERGREEN TER	SR	7A	A2
WINWOOD PL	MV	12A	A3
WISTERIA CT	N	1	E1
WISTERIA WY	MCO	12C	C6
WISTERIA WY	SR	6B	F2
WOLFBACK TER	SLTO	14	A5
WOLFBACK RDG RD	SLTO	13	F4
WOLFE AV	SR	10A	C2
WOLFE CANYON RD	MCO	10A	C3
WOLFE GLEN WY	MCO	10A	B3
WOLFE GRADE	MCO	10A	B3
WOLFE GRADE	SR	10A	B3
WOMACK CT	N	1	C2
WOOD CT	SA	6D	E5
WOOD LN	F	6C	C6
WOOD LN	F	9A	C1
WOODBINE DR	MV	12A	A3
WOODBINE DR	SR	6B	F2
WOODGATE PL	N	1A	E6
WOODHAVEN RD	MCO	21	E2
WOODHAVEN RD	R	9B	E2
WOOD HOLLOW DR	N	1A	E6
WOODHUE LN	CM	12B	D2
WOODLAND AV	SA	9B	F1
WOODLAND AV	SR	10A	C2
WOODLAND AV	SR	10B	D2
WOODLAND CT	N	1	F6
WOODLAND CT	F	6C	B6
WOODLAND DR	F	6C	B6
WOODLAND PL	SR	10A	C2
WOODLAND RD	F	6C	B6
WOODLAND RD	F	9A	B1
WOODLAND RD	MCO	9D	F4
WOODLAND RD	MCO	10C	A4
WOODLEAF CT	N	1A	D6
WOODOAKS DR	MCO	7B	D3
WOODROSE CT	SR	8	B3
WOODRUFF RD	SA	9B	F1
WOODRUFF RD	SA	10A	A1
WOODS ST	SR	10A	B2
WOODSIDE AV	MCO	12C	C6
WOODSIDE AV	MCO	13	C1
WOODSIDE CT	SA	6D	D4
WOODSIDE DR	SA	6D	D4
WOODSIDE LN	MV	12C	B4
WOODSIDE WY	R	9B	F3
WOODSIDE WY	SR	8	B4

STREET	CITY	PAGE	GRID
WOODSTOCK CT	SR	7C	A4
WOODVIEW LN	MCO	2	D2
WOODWARD AV	SLTO	13	F3
WOODWARD CT	MV	12D	D4
WOODWORTH FR RD	MCO	25	E3
WORN SPGS FR RD	MCO	9B	D2
WORTHINGTON LN	SR	7D	D6
WRAY AV	SLTO	13	F3
WRAY LN	SLTO	13	F3
WREDEN AV	F	6C	C5
WYWORRY CT	N	1	C3
X			
XYLO RD	MCO	26	F6
Y			
YALE AV	L	10C	B4
YALE AV	MCO	12C	C6
YARROW LN	N	1	F6
YELLOWSTONE CT	SR	7A	C2
YOLANDA DR	SA	6D	E6
YOLO ST	CM	12B	E1
YOSEMITE RD	SR	7A	C1
YOUNG CT	N	1	F6
YOUNG CT	N	3	F1
YUCA RD	MCO	26	F6
YUKON CT	N	1	E4
YUKON WY	N	1	E4
Z			
ZANCO WY	N	1	D3
ZANDRA PL	N	1	F2
ZANDRA PL	N	2	A2
ZEBRA RD	MCO	26	F6
ZEPHYR CT	MCO	3	D6
ZIG ZAG TR	MCO	11A	B3
ZION CT	SR	7A	C2
NUMERICAL STREETS			
1ST AV	MCO	15	D5
1ST ST	CM	12A	C1
1ST ST	MCO	15	E5
1ST ST	MCO	22	B6
1ST ST	N	1	E3
1ST ST	SR	10A	C1
2ND	MCO	15	D4
2ND ST	MCO	22	B6
2ND ST	N	1	E2
2ND ST	N	4	D2
2ND ST	SR	10A	C1
2ND ST	SR	10B	D1
2ND ST	SLTO	14	A5
3RD ST	MCO	22	B6
3RD ST	N	1	E2
3RD ST	N	4	D3
3RD ST	SR	10A	C1
3RD ST	SR	10B	D1
3RD ST	SLTO	14	A5
4TH ST	MCO	22	B5
4TH ST	N	1	E2
4TH ST	N	4	D2
4TH ST	SR	7C	A6
4TH ST	SR	10A	C1
4TH ST	SR	10B	D1
4TH ST	SLTO	14	A5
5TH AV	SR	7C	B6
5TH AV	SR	10A	C1
5TH ST	MCO	22	B5
5TH ST	N	1	E2
5TH ST	N	4	D3
6TH ST	MCO	22	B5
6TH ST	N	1	E2
6TH ST	N	4	D3
7TH ST	MCO	22	B5
7TH ST	N	1	D2
7TH ST	N	4	D3
8TH ST	MCO	22	B5
8TH ST	N	1	D2
8TH ST	N	4	D3
9TH ST	N	4	D3
10TH ST	N	4	D3
11TH ST	N	4	D3

1991 MARIN COUNTY POINTS OF INTEREST

PAGE	GRID	NAME	ADDRESS	CITY	PHONE
		AIRPORTS (SEE TRANSPORTATION)			
		BED & BREAKFAST INNS			
5	A1	BEAR VALLEY	88 BEAR VALLEY RD	OLEMA	663 1777
22	A5	BLACKTHORNE INN	266 VALLEJO AV	INVERNESS	663 8621
21	D2	GRAY WHALE	12781 SIR FRANCS DK BL	INVERNESS	669 1330
22	A6	HOLLY TREE INN	3 SILVER HILLS RD	PT REYES STA	663 1554
22	B5	JASMINE COTTAGE	BOX 56	PT REYES STA	663 1166
10A	B2	OLE RAFAEL	SAN RAFAEL AV	SAN RAFAEL	453 0414
10A	B2	PANAMA HOTEL B & B	4 BAYVIEW ST	SAN RAFAEL	457 3993
31	E3	PELICAN INN	10 PACIFIC WY	MUIR BEACH	383 6000
21	E3	TEN INVERNESS WAY	10 INVERNESS WY	INVERNESS	669 1648
22	B4	THIRTY-NINE CYPRESS	39 CYPRESS RD	PT REYES STA	663 1709
		BUILDINGS			
10A	C1	JOHNSON REYNOLD C BLDG	1299 4TH ST	SAN RAFAEL	
7C	C4	MARIN CO CIVIC CENTER	N SAN PEDRO RD	SAN RAFAEL	499 6211
7C	C4	MARIN CO COURT HOUSE	CIVIC CENTER	SAN RAFAEL	499 6211
12B	D1	SANFORD TERRACE	645 TAMALPAIS DR	CORTE MADERA	
13	F3	THIRTY-THIRTY BRIDGEWY	3030 BRIDGEWAY	SAUSALITO	332 3800
		CEMETERIES			
20	D2	BAHIA VALLEY MEM PARK	650 BUGEIA LN	NOVATO	897 9609
13	D1	DAPHNE FERNWOOD	301 TENNESSEE VLY RD	MILL VALLEY	383 7100
7A	B3	MT OLIVET	LOS RANCHITOS RD	SAN RAFAEL	479 9020
6D	F5	MT TAMALPAIS	2500 W 5TH AV	SAN RAFAEL	459 2500
5	B2	OLEMA	SHORELINE HWY	OLEMA	
		CHAMBERS OF COMMERCE AND VISITORS BUREAUS			
14	C2	BELVEDERE-TIBURON PEN	96 B MAIN ST	TIBURON	435 5633
10C	B5	LARKSPUR		LARKSPUR	924 3330
7C	C4	MARIN COUNTY	30 N SAN PEDRO RD	SAN RAFAEL	472 7470
12A	A3	MILL VALLEY	38 MILLER AV	MILL VALLEY	388 9700
1	E3	NOVATO	807 DE LONG AV	NOVATO	897 1164
6D	E6	SAN ANSELMO	1000 SIR FRANCIS DRAKE	SAN ANSELMO	454 2510
10B	D1	SAN RAFAEL	1030 B ST	SAN RAFAEL	454 4163
13	F3	SAUSALITO	333 CALEDONIA AV	SAUSALITO	332 0505
		CITY HALLS			
14	C1	BELVEDERE	450 SAN RAFAEL AV	BELVEDERE BAY	435 3838
12A	C1	CORTE MADERA	300 TAMALPAIS DR	CORTE MADERA	924 1700
6C	C5	FAIRFAX	142 BOLINAS RD	FAIRFAX	453 1584
10C	B6	LARKSPUR	400 MAGNOLIA AV	LARKSPUR	924 2405
12A	A3	MILL VALLEY	26 CORTE MADERA AV	MILL VALLEY	388 4033
1	E3	NOVATO	901 SHERMAN AV	NOVATO	897 4313
9B	F2	ROSS	31 SIR FRANCIS DRAKE	ROSS	453 1453
9B	F1	SAN ANSELMO	525 SAN ANSELMO AV	SAN ANSELMO	258 4600
10A	C1	SAN RAFAEL	1400 5TH AV	SAN RAFAEL	485 3066
14	A3	SAUSALITO	420 LITHO	SAUSALITO	332 0310
14	C1	TIBURON	1155 TIBURON BLVD	TIBURON	435 0956
		COLLEGES			
10A	A3	COLLEGE OF MARIN	COLLEGE AV	KENTFIELD	457 8811
7D	A2	DOMINICAN COLLEGE	1520 GRAND AV	SAN RAFAEL	457 4440
1	E6	INDIAN VALLEY COLLEGES	1800 IGNACIO BLVD	NOVATO	883 2211
9B	E2	SF THEOLOGICAL SEMINRY	2 KENSINGTON RD	SAN ANSELMO	258 6500
		GOLF COURSES			
23	F2	INDIAN VLY GOLF CLUB	NOVATO BLVD	NOVATO	897 1118
9B	E3	LAGUNITAS COUNTRY CLUB	LAGUNITAS & GLENWOOD	ROSS	453 8706
3	E2	MARIN COUNTRY CLUB	500 COUNTRY CLUB DR	NOVATO	453 5220
9A	A1	MEADOW COUNTRY CLUB	1001 BOLINAS RD	FAIRFAX	453 3274
12A	B3	MILL VALLEY	280 BUENA VISTA AV	MILL VALLEY	388 9982
8	B3	PEACOCK GAP CNTRY CLUB	333 BISCAYNE DR	SAN RAFAEL	453 4940
5A	D4	SAN GERONIMO NATIONAL	5500 SIR FRANCS DRK BL	SAN GERONIMO	488 4030
		HOSPITALS			
		*EMERGENCY SERVICES	AVAILABLE		
7A	A3	*KAISER-PERMANENTE MED	99 MONTECILLO RD	SAN RAFAEL	499 2000
10C	B4	* MARIN GENERAL	250 BON AIR RD	SAN RAFAEL	925 7000
1	D4	*NOVATO COMMUNITY	1625 HILL RD	NOVATO	897 3111
		HOTELS			
7A	B2	CLARION HOTEL	1010 NORTHGATE DR	SAN RAFAEL	479 8800
10D	E4	MARRIOTT COURTYARD	2500 LARKSPUR LNDG CIR	LARKSPUR	925 1800

PAGE	GRID	NAME	ADDRESS	CITY	PHONE
9B	F1	SAN ANSELMO	339 SAN ANSELMO AV	SAN ANSELMO	453 3532
14	B4	SAUSALITO	16 EL PORTAL	SAUSALITO	332 4155
		LIBRARIES			
14	D2	BELVEDERE-TIBURON	BEACH RD	BELVEDERE	435 1361
28	B4	BOLINAS	WHARF RD	BOLINAS	868 1171
12B	D1	CORTE MADERA REGIONAL	707 MEADOWSWEET DR	CORTE MADERA	924 4844
6C	C5	FAIRFAX	2097 SIR FRANCS DRK BL	FAIRFAX	453 8092
21	E3	INVERNESS	15 PARK AV	INVERNESS	669 1288
10C	B6	LARKSPUR	400 MAGNOLIA AV	LARKSPUR	924 1990
13	D2	MARIN CITY	630 DRAKE AV ANNEX B	MARIN CITY	332 1128
7C	C4	MARIN COUNTY CIVIC CTR	CIVIC CENTER	SAN RAFAEL	499 6056
12A	A3	MILL VALLEY	375 THROCKMORTON AV	MILL VALLEY	388 4245
1	D2	NOVATO	1720 NOVATO BLVD	NOVATO	897 1141
22	B5	POINT REYES	4TH & A STS	PT REYES STN	663 8375
9B	F1	SAN ANSELMO	110 TUNSTEAD AV	SAN ANSELMO	258 4656
5A	A5	SAN GERONIMO	7282 SIR FRANCS DRK BL	LAGUNITAS	488 0430
10A	C1	SAN RAFAEL	1100 E ST	SAN RAFAEL	485 3323
14	A3	SAUSALITO	420 LITHO	SAUSALITO	332 2325
28	E5	STINSON BEACH	3470 SHORELINE HWY	STINSON BEACH	868 0252
		MOTELS			
12B	D1	CORTE MADERA INN	1815 REDWOOD HWY	CORTE MADERA	924 1502
12D	D6	HOWARD JOHNSON	160 SHORELINE HWY	MILL VALLEY	332 5700
14	C1	TIBURON LODGE	1651 TIBURON BLVD	TIBURON	435 3133
		PARKS & BEACHES			
28	A5	AGATE BEACH		BOLINAS	
10A	C2	ALBERT PARK	B & TREANOR STS	SAN RAFAEL	
14	E3	ANGEL ISLAND STATE PK	ANGEL ISLAND	TIBURON	435 1915
14	E4	ARROYO AVICHI PARK	HILL ST	NOVATO	
10B	D2	BEACH PARK	FRANCISCO BLVD	SAN RAFAEL	
24	B4	BEAR VALLEY VIS CENTER	POINT REYES	MARIN COUNTY	
2	E2	BLACK PT BOAT LAUNCH	HARBOR DR	BLACK POINT	
28	B3	BOLINAS LAGOON NAT PRE		BOLINAS	
10A	C1	BOYD MEMORIAL PARK	B ST & MISSION AV	SAN RAFAEL	
12C	B4	BOYLE PARK	E BLITHEDALE AV & E DR	MILL VALLEY	
15	C6	BRAZIL BEACH	TOMALES BAY	CAMP TOMALES	
10B	D3	BRET HARTE PARK	IRWIN ST NEAR HAZEL CT	SAN RAFAEL	
8	A2	CHINA CAMP STATE PARK	NORTH SAN PEDRO RD	SAN RAFAEL	456 0766
9A	C1	DEER PARK	PORTEOUS AV	FAIRFAX	
15	B4	DILLON BEACH	DILLON RD	DILLON BEACH	
24	D3	DRAKES BEACH	DRAKES BEACH RD	INVERNESS	669 1250
10A	B2	GERSTLE PARK	SAN RAFAEL & CLARK ST	SAN RAFAEL	
11B	A6	GLDN GATE NAT REC AREA		MARIN COUNTY	
12B	E2	GRANADA PARK	GRANADA DR	CORTE MADERA	
7D	E1	HARRY A BARBIER PARK	MOUNTAIN VIEW AV	SAN RAFAEL	
6B	F1	JERRY RUSSOM MEM PARK	OLD LUCAS VALLEY RD	SAN RAFAEL	
7B	D1	JOHN F MCINNIS CO PARK	SMITH RANCH RD	SAN RAFAEL	
17	C5	KEHOE BEACH	PT REYES NATL SEASHORE	MARIN COUNTY	
25	F5	KELAM BEACH	PT REYES NATL SEASHORE	MARIN COUNTY	
25	B3	LIMANTOUR BEACH	PT REYES NATL SEASHORE	MARIN COUNTY	
23	F1	LIONS PARK	NOVATO BLVD	NOVATO	
6B	F3	MARIA B FREITAS MEM PK	MONTECILLO RD	SAN RAFAEL	
8	D3	MCNEARS BEACH PARK	PT SAN PEDRO RD	SAN RAFAEL	
18	B2	MILLER PARK	NICKS COVE AT TOM BAY	HAMLET	
11B	C5	MT TAMALPASI STATE PK	801 PANORAMIC HWY	MILL VALLEY	388 2070
11B	A4	MUIR WOODS NAT MONUMNT	MUIR WOODS RD	MILL VALLEY	388 2595
9B	E3	NATALIE C GREEN PARK	LAGUNITAS RD	ROSS	
24	C1	NORTH BEACH	PT REYES NATL SEASHORE	MARIN COUNTY	
14	D1	OLD ST HILARYS HIS PRE	MAR WEST ST	TIBURON	
7A	A2	OLEANDER PARK	OLEANDER DR	SAN RAFAEL	
11D	F5	PARADISE BEACH PARK	PARADISE DR	TIBURON	
10B	F2	PICKLEWEED PARK	SORRENTO WY	SAN RAFAEL	
1	C2	PIONEER MEMORIAL PARK	NOVATO BLVD	NOVATO	
10C	C5	PIPER PARK	LARKSPUR-DOHERTY DR	LARKSPUR	
24	C3	PT REYES NATL SEASHORE	POINT REYES	MARIN COUNTY	663 1092
1A	D3	RANCHO OLOMPALI HIS PK		MARIN COUNTY	
28	F6	RED ROCK BEACH	GLDN GATE NAT REC AREA	MARIN COUNTY	
9B	F3	ROSS COMMON PARK	LAGUNITAS RD	ROSS	
5	E3	SAMUEL P TAYLOR STATE	SIR FRANCIS DRAKE BLVD	LAGUNITAS	488 9897
12B	F2	SAN CLEMENT PARK	PARADISE DR	CORTE MADERA	
6B	D2	SANTA MARGARITA VLY PK	DE LA GUERRA RD	SAN RAFAEL	
25	D3	SANTA MARIA BEACH	PT REYES NATL SEASHORE	MARIN COUNTY	
10B	F2	SCHOEN PARK	CANAL ST & BAHIA LN	SAN RAFAEL	
25	E4	SCULPTURED BEACH	PT REYES NATL SEASHORE	MARIN COUNTY	
6D	F5	SORICH RANCH PARK	SAN FRANCISCO BLVD	SAN ANSELMO	
24	B2	SOUTH BEACH	PT REYES NATL SEASHORE	MARIN COUNTY	
23	E2	STAFFORD LAKE PARK	NOVATO BLVD	NOVATO	
28	F6	STINSON STATE BEACH PK	SHORELINE HWY	STINSON BEACH	
12D	E4	STRAWBERRY PARK	BELVEDERE DR & RICARDO	STRAWBRRY MNR	
24	F3	SUNSHINE BEACH	PT REYES NATL SEASHORE	MARIN COUNTY	
7C	B6	SUN VALLEY PARK	SOLANO ST	SAN RAFAEL	

1991 MARIN COUNTY POINTS OF INTEREST

PAGE	GRID	NAME	ADDRESS	CITY	PHONE
6B	F2	TERRA LINDA PARK	670 DEL GANADO DR	SAN RAFAEL	
14	E5	TIBURON UPLNDS NAT RES	PARADISE DR	TIBURON	
21	D2	TOMALES BAY STATE PARK	PIERCE POINT RD	INVERNESS	669 1140
8	A4	VICTOR JONES PARK	ROBINHOOD & MAPLEWD DR	SAN RAFAEL	

POINTS OF INTEREST

PAGE	GRID	NAME	ADDRESS	CITY	PHONE
14	E2	ANGEL ISLAND FERRY TRM	ANGEL ISLAND	MARIN COUNTY	
29	B3	CUSHING MEM THEATER	MT TAMALPAIS	MARIN COUNTY	
24	D3	DRAKES BAY GOLDN HINDE	DRAKES BEACH RD	DRAKES BAY	
7D	D6	FRST MDWS PERFORM ARTS	1500 GRAND AV	SAN RAFAEL	459 5407
13	B4	GLDN GATE NAT REC AREA		MARIN COUNTY	556 0560
10A	A2	MARIN ART & GARDEN CTR	SIR FRANCIS DRAKE BLVD	ROSS	454 5597
7C	C4	MARIN COUNTY CIVIC CTR	CIVIC CENTER DR	SAN RAFAEL	499 6211
10A	C1	MARIN CO HIST SOC MUS	1125 B ST	SAN RAFAEL	454 8538
10A	C2	MARIN MUS OF NAT SCI	76 ALBERT PARK LN	SAN RAFAEL	454 6961
10A	C1	MISSION SAN RAFAEL	1104 FIFTH AV	SAN RAFAEL	454 8141
14	D1	OLD ST HILARY CHURCH	ESPERANZA ST	TIBURON	
12D	F5	RICHARDSON BAY AUDUBON	GREENWOOD BEACH RD	TIBURON	
13	F3	SN FRANCISCO BAY MODEL	2100 BRIDGEWAY	SAUSALITO	332 3870
14	B3	SAUSALITO FERRY TERMNL	ANCHOR SPINNAKER DR	SAUSALITO	
14	F5	TIBURON MARINE LAB	PARADISE RD	TIBURON	
14	A6	VISTA POINT	N END GOLDEN GATE BRDG	MARIN COUNTY	

POST OFFICES

PAGE	GRID	NAME	ADDRESS	CITY	PHONE
14	D2	BELVEDERE-TIBURON	6 BEACH RD	BELVEDERE	435 1041
28	B4	BOLINAS	20 BRIGHTON AV	BOLINAS	868 1314
7C	C4	CIVIC CENTER STATION	2 CIVIC CENTER	SANTA VENETIA	479 2530
12A	C1	CORTE MADERA	7 PIXLEY AV	CORTE MADERA	924 4463
15A	B4	DILLON BEACH	52 CYPRESS WY	DILLON BEACH	878 2343
6D	D5	FAIRFAX	773 CENTER BLVD	FAIRFAX	453 3146
5A	B4	FOREST KNOLLS	6 CASTRO ST	FOREST KNOLLS	488 0533
21	E3	INVERNESS	12781 SIR FRCS DRAKE	INVERNESS	669 1675
10C	A4	KENTFIELD	822 COLLEGE AV	KENTFIELD	454 9627
5A	A5	LAGUNITAS	7120 SIR FRANCS DRK BL	LAGUNITAS	488 9708
10C	B6	LARKSPUR	120 WARD AV	LARKSPUR	924 4792
12C	C4	MILL VALLEY	751 E BLITHEDALE AV	MILL VALLEY	388 8656
10A	C1	MISSION RAFAEL STATION	910 D ST	SAN RAFAEL	453 1153
1	E4	NOVATO	1537 S NOVATO BLVD	NOVATO	897 3171
5	B2	OLEMA	10155 HIGHWAY 1	OLEMA	663 1761
22	B5	POINT REYES STATION	11260 HIGHWAY 1	PT REYES STA	663 1305
9B	F3	ROSS	1 ROSS COMMON	ROSS	454 4123
9B	F1	SAN ANSELMO	121 SAN ANSELMO AV	SAN ANSELMO	453 0830
5A	C5	SAN GERONIMO	630 SN GERNOIMO VLY DR	SAN GERONIMO	488 4644
8A	E4	SAN QUENTIN	1 MAIN ST	SAN QUENTIN	456 4741
10B	E3	SAN RAFAEL	40 BELLAM BLVD	SAN RAFAEL	453 0727
13	F1	SAUSALITO	150 HARBOR	SAUSALITO	332 4656
28	E5	STINSON BEACH	15 CALLE DEL MAR	STINSON BEACH	868 1504
6B	F2	TERRA LINDA STATION	603 DEL GANADO RD	TERRA LINDA	479 1850
14	C1	TIBURON	7 BEACH RD	BELVEDERE	435 1041
15	D5	TOMALES	27005 HIGHWAY 1	TOMALES	878 2364
5A	E5	WOODACRE	183 SN GERONIMO VLY DR	WOODACRE	488 9337

SCHOOLS - PRIVATE ELEMENTARY

PAGE	GRID	NAME	ADDRESS	CITY	PHONE
6B	E1	BIG WISDOM FREE ELEM	1055 LAS OVEJAS	SAN RAFAEL	492 0550
7C	C4	BRANDEIS-HILLEL	170 N SAN PEDRO RD	SAN RAFAEL	472 1833
1	F5	CHRISTIAN LIFE	1370 S NOVATO BLVD	NOVATO	892 5713
12B	E2	LYCEE FRCS D SN FRNSCO	50 EL CAMINO DR	CORTE MADERA	668 1833
12B	F2	MARIN COUNTY DAY ELEM	5221 PARADISE DR	CORTE MADERA	924 3743
12B	F2	MARIN HORIZON SCHOOL	330 GOLDEN HIND PSSAGE	CORTE MADERA	924 4202
12A	C1	MARIN PRIMARY	20 MAGNOLIA AV	LARKSPUR	924 2608
3	F6	MARIN WALDORF	755 IDYLBERRY RD	SAN RAFAEL	479 8190
12C	C6	MT TAMALPAIS	100 HARVARD AV	MILL VALLEY	383 9434
1	D2	OUR LADY OF LORETTO	1811 VIRGINIA AV	NOVATO	892 8621
9B	F1	ST ANSELM	40 BELLE AV	SAN ANSELMO	454 8667
11D	E5	ST HILARY	765 HILARY DR	TIBURON	435 2224
7A	A3	ST ISABELLA	1 TRINITY WY	SAN RAFAEL	479 3727
4	B5	ST MARK'S EPISCOPAL	375 BLACKSTONE DR	SAN RAFAEL	472 7911
10C	B6	ST PATRICK	120 KING ST	LARKSPUR	924 0501
10A	C1	ST RAPHAEL	1100 5TH AV	SAN RAFAEL	454 4455
6C	C5	ST RITA	102 MARINDA DR	FAIRFAX	456 1003
6B	D2	SAN DOMENICO LOWER	1500 BUTTERFIELD RD	SAN ANSELMO	454 0200

SCHOOLS - PRIVATE HIGH

PAGE	GRID	NAME	ADDRESS	CITY	PHONE
12D	E6	G G BAPTST THEOLG SEMY	SEMINARY DR	MILL VALLEY	388 8080
9B	E2	KATHERINE BRANSON H S	39 FERNHILL AV	ROSS	454 3612
10A	B1	MARIN ACADEMY	5TH & COTTAGE AV	SAN RAFAEL	924 3743
10C	B4	MARIN CATHOLIC HIGH	675 SIR FRANCIS DRK BL	KENTFIELD	461 8844
6B	D2	SAN DOMENICO	1500 BUTTERFIELD RD	SAN RAFAEL	454 0200

SCHOOLS - PUBLIC ELEMENTARY

PAGE	GRID	NAME	ADDRESS	CITY	PHONE
10C	B4	ANTHONY G BACICH	25 MCALLISTER AV	KENTFIELD	461 0680
10B	F2	BAHIA VISTA	125 BAHIA WY	SAN RAFAEL	485 2415
13	E3	BAYSIDE/M L KING	630 NEVADA ST	SAUSALITO	332 1024
12D	F4	BEL AIRE	277 KAREN WY	TIBURON	388 7100
28	B3	BOLINAS-STINSON	HORSESHOE HILL RD	BOLINAS	868 1603
6D	E5	BROOKSIDE	116 BUTTERFIELD RD	SAN ANSELMO	453 2948
6B	E3	BROOKSIDE ANNEX	46 GREEN VALLEY CT	SAN ANSELMO	454 7409
7D	D6	COLEMAN	140 RAFAEL DR	SAN RAFAEL	485 2420
3	E6	DIXIE	1175 IDYLBERRY RD	SAN RAFAEL	479 6200
7B	D3	GALLINAS	177 N SAN PEDRO RD	SAN RAFAEL	485 2425
8	B5	GLENWOOD	25 CASTLEWOOD DR	SAN RAFAEL	485 2430
4	C3	HAMILTON	601 BOLLING DR	NOVATO	883 4691
5A	C4	LAGUNITAS	SIR FRANCIS DRAKE BLVD	SAN GERONIMO	488 9437
4	A2	LOMA VERDE	399 ALAMEDA DE LA LOMA	NOVATO	883 4681
1	D3	LU SUTTON	1800 CENTER RD	NOVATO	897 3196
1	F5	LYNWOOD	1320 LYNWOOD DR	NOVATO	897 4161
6C	C4	MANOR	150 OAK MANOR DR	FAIRFAX	453 1544
10D	D6	NEIL CUMMINS	58 MOHAWK AV	CORTE MADERA	924 1393
12A	A3	OLD MILL	352 THROCKMORTON AV	MILL VALLEY	389 7727
1	F2	OLIVE	629 PLUM ST	NOVATO	897 2131
12C	B4	PARK	360 E BLITHEDALE AV	MILL VALLEY	389 7735
1	A2	PLEASANT VALLEY	755 SUTRO AV	NOVATO	897 5104
1	E4	RANCHO	1430 JOHNSTON ST	NOVATO	897 3101
11D	F6	REED	1199 TIBURON BLVD	TIBURON	435 3302
9B	F3	ROSS	LAGUNITAS RD	ROSS	457 2705
5A	C4	SAN GERONIMO VALLEY	SIR FRANCIS DRAKE BLVD	SAN GERONIMO	488 9421
1	B1	SAN RAMON	45 SAN RAMON WY	NOVATO	897 1196
12D	E4	STRAWBERRY POINT	117 E STRAWBERRY DR	MILL VALLEY	389 7733
7C	A5	SUN VALLEY	75 HAPPY LN	SAN RAFAEL	485 2440
13	C2	TAMALPAIS VALLEY	350 BELL LN	MILL VALLEY	389 7731
15	E5	TOMALES	TOMALES-PETALUMA RD	TOMALES	878 2214
7A	A3	VALLECITO	50 NOVA ALBION WY	SAN RAFAEL	479 0212
9B	E1	WADE THOMAS	ROSS & KENSINGTON RD	SAN ANSELMO	454 4603
22	B5	WEST MARIN	HWY 1 & MESA RD	PT REYES STA	663 1014

SCHOOLS - PUBLIC JUNIOR HIGH

PAGE	GRID	NAME	ADDRESS	CITY	PHONE
10A	C2	DAVIDSON MIDDLE	280 WOODLAND AV	SAN RAFAEL	485 2400
11D	D5	DEL MAR	105 AVD MIRA FLORES	TIBURON	435 1468
10C	C5	HALL MIDDLE	200 DOHERTY DR	LARKSPUR	924 0733
10A	A3	KENT MIDDLE	250 STADIUM WY	KENTFIELD	454 0651
4	A6	MILLER CREEK	2255 LAS GALLINAS AV	SAN RAFAEL	479 1660
12C	C5	MILL VALLEY MIDDLE	425 SYCAMORE AV	MILL VALLEY	389 7711
1	E6	SAN JOSE	1000 SUNSET PKWY	NOVATO	883 7831
1	C3	SINALOA	2045 VINEYARD RD	NOVATO	897 2111
6A	B3	WHITE HILL	101 GLEN DR	FAIRFAX	454 8390

SCHOOLS - PUBLIC HIGH

PAGE	GRID	NAME	ADDRESS	CITY	PHONE
1	E4	NOVATO	625 ARTHUR ST	NOVATO	898 2125
10C	C5	REDWOOD	DOHERTY DR	LARKSPUR	924 6200
1	B1	SAN MARIN	15 SAN MARIN DR	NOVATO	898 2121
10B	D1	SAN RAFAEL	185 MISSION AV	SAN RAFAEL	485 2330
6D	E6	SIR FRANCIS DRAKE	1327 SIR FRANCS DRK BL	SAN ANSELMO	453 8770
12C	C5	TAMALPAIS	CM ALTO & MILLER AV	MILL VALLEY	388 3292
7C	A4	TERRA LINDA	320 NOVA ALBION WY	SAN RAFAEL	485 2370
15	E5	TOMALES	1ST AV	TOMALES	878 2286

SHOPPING CENTERS

PAGE	GRID	NAME	ADDRESS	CITY	PHONE
12B	D1	CORTE MADERA TOWN CTR	706 TAMALPAIS DR	CORTE MADERA	
7A	B3	NORTHGATE MALL	5800 NORTHGATE MALL	SAN RAFAEL	479 5955
10D	D6	VILLAGE-CORTE MADERA	1852 REDWOOD HWY	CORTE MADERA	924 8557
14	B4	VILLAGE FAIR	777 BRIDGEWAY	SAUSALITO	332 1902

TRANSPORTATION

PAGE	GRID	NAME	ADDRESS	CITY	PHONE
10D	E5	LARKSPUR FERRY	E SIR FRANCIS DRAKE BL	LARKSPUR	
1A	F4	MARIN CO - GNOSS FIELD	451 AIRPORT RD	NOVATO	897 5185
10C	C4	PARK & RIDE	SIR F DRAKE & ELISEO	LARKSPUR	
10D	D5	PARK & RIDE	HWY 101 & LUCKY DR	LARKSPUR	
12D	D5	PARK & RIDE	HWY 101 & SEMINARY DR	MARIN COUNTY	
12D	D6	PARK & RIDE	HWY 101	MARIN COUNTY	
1	F1	PARK & RIDE	HWY 101 & ATHERTON AV	NOVATO	
4	C4	PARK & RIDE	HY 101 & ALMDA DL PRDO	NOVATO	
7A	B1	PARK & RIDE	HWY 101 & LUCAS VLY RD	SAN RAFAEL	
7C	C5	PARK & RIDE	LINCOLN AV & WILSON	SAN RAFAEL	
10B	D1	PARK & RIDE	4TH & HETHERTON	SAN RAFAEL	
13	F4	PARK & RIDE	HWY 101 & SPENCER	SAUSALITO	
14	B4	SAUSALITO FERRY	HUMBOLT ST & BAY ST	SAUSALITO	
14	D2	TIBURON FERRY	PARADISE DR	TIBURON	
12D	D4	TRANSIT TRANSFER POINT	REED BL & BELVEDERE DR	MARIN COUNTY	
13	E2	TRANSIT TRANSFER POINT	DRAKE AV & DONAHUE ST	MARIN COUNTY	
1	E2	TRANSIT TRANSFER POINT	PT REDWOOD BL&GRANT AV	NOVATO	
6D	F6	TRANSIT TRANSFER POINT	CENTER BL & BRIDGE AV	SAN ANSELMO	

1991 GOLDEN GATE TRANSIT INFORMATION

Introduction

Golden Gate Transit provides bus and ferry service between San Francisco and Marin and Sonoma Counties. The Golden Gate Transit service area extends from the San Francisco Central Business District on the south, to the City of Santa Rosa in Sonoma County on the north. Santa Rosa is approximately 50 miles north of San Francisco.

Park-and-Ride Facilities

There are approximately twenty Park-and Ride facilities located throughout the Golden Gate Transit service area. Parking is complimentary and each facility is served by Golden Gate Transit buses which provide commute services into San Francisco.

Free Personalized Trip Planning, Maps, Timetables Telephone information

Your public transit itinerary can be planned for you by telephone by calling our information operators any weekday from 6:00 am to 10:00 pm and on weekends and holidays from 6:30 am to 10:00 pm. When the operator answers your call, please have paper and pencil and the following information ready:

- Your departure point(address or nearest intersection)
- Your destination(address or nearest intersection)
- Day and time you wish to travel

Please telephone using one of the following numbers:

415-332-6600 from San Francisco
415-453-2100 from Marin County
707-544-1323 from Sonoma County

Map and Timetable information pamphlets can be mailed to you upon request.

Ferry Service

Golden Gate Transit operates two ferry routes: between Larkspur and San Francisco and between Sausalito and San Francisco. Service is provided daily (except on Thanksgiving, Christmas, and New Years days). Feeder bus service is available during the peak commute periods to the ferry terminals providing direct connections with ferry arrivals and departures.

Bus Service

Golden Gate Transit operates approximately 50 bus routes between San Francisco, Marin, and Sonoma Counties via the Golden Gate Bridge. Service is provided daily with expanded service during peak commute periods.

Stadium Services

Golden Gate Transit offers some bus service, on an advance reservation basis, to Candlestick Park for home games of the San Francisco Forty-Niners and Giants.

INDEX

SAN FRANCISCO COUNTY

1991 Thomas Guide®

SAN FRANCISCO

TABLE OF CONTENTS

Copyright, © 1991 by THOMAS BROS. MAPS.
esign, maps, index and text of this publication are copyrighted. It is
wful to copy or reproduce any part thereof for personal use or resale.

Corporate Office & Showroom
31 Cowan, Irvine, CA 92714 (714) 863-1984; toll-free, 1-800-899-MAPS
Retail Stores
603 W. 7th St., Los Angeles, CA 90017 (213) 627-4018
550 Jackson St., San Francisco, CA 94133 (415) 981-7520

GOLDEN GATE	TBM 4025	*$33.95*
SAN FRANCISCO	TBM 3035	*$12.95*
SAN FRANCISCO-ALAMEDA-CONTRA COSTA	TBM 4030	*$29.95*
SAN FRANCISCO-SAN MATEO	TBM 4026	*$19.95*

B HOW TO USE THE THOMAS GUIDE PAGE AND GRID SYSTEM

Finding Your Destination

- Use the Street Index to find the page number and grid location of a street name.
- Use the Cities and Communities or Points of Interest Index to find the page number and grid of a specific destination.

Planning Your Route

- Use the Key Maps or the Foldout Map to go from city to city, or to find what page your destination is on.
- Follow a street page to page by using the "See Map" page number in the border of each page.

Cross Street Index

- A special index has been prepared for all streets in San Francisco. This index lists each street, followed by all the cross streets in block number order. Most cross street names include the lowest house address starting at the intersection.

COMO USAR EL SISTEMA DE PAGINA Y CUADRADO DEL THOMAS GUIDE

Encontrando Su Destinación

- Se puede usar el Indice de Calle para encontrar el número de página y locación del cuadrado del nombre de la calle.
- Se puede usar los Indices de las Ciudades y las Comunidades, o de Puntos de Interés para encontrar el número de página y el cuadrado de la destinación específica.

Planeando Su Ruta

- Se puede usar el Mapa Clave o el Mapa Doblado para viajar de ciudad a ciudad, o para encontrar la página de su destinación.
- Se puede usar el número de página con las palabras "See Map" se encuentran al borde de cada página para seguir una calle de página a página.

El Indice de Calles Que Cruzan

- Un índice especial se ha preparado para todas las calles de San Francisco. Este índice tiene una lista de cada calle y todas las calles que cruzan en el orden de los números de las cuadras de casas. Lo más de los nombres de las calles que cruzan incluye la dirección lo más baja de una casa empezando en el cruce de caminos.

LIST OF ABBREVIATIONS

AL .... ALLEY
AR .... ARROYO
ARR .... ARROYO
AV .... AVENUE
AVD .... AVENIDA
AVD D LS .... AVENIDA DE LOS
BCH .... BEACH
BL .... BOULEVARD
BLVD .... BOULEVARD
CEM .... CEMETERY
CIR .... CIRCLE
CK .... CREEK
CL .... CALLE
CL DL .... CALLE DEL
CL D LS .... CALLE DE LAS / CALLE DE LOS
CL EL .... CALLE EL
CLJ .... CALLEJON
CL LA .... CALLE LA
CL LS .... CALLE LAS / CALLE LOS
CM .... CAMINO
CM D .... CAMINO DE
CM D LA .... CAMINO DE LA
CM D LS .... CAMINO DE LAS / CAMINO DE LOS
CMTO .... CAMINITO
CN .... CANAL
COM .... COMMON
CR .... CRESCENT
CRES .... CRESCENT
CSWY .... CAUSEWAY
CT .... COURT
CTE .... CORTE
CTO .... CUT OFF
CTR .... CENTER
CV .... COVE
CY .... CANYON
CYN .... CANYON
D .... DE
DL .... DEL
DR .... DRIVE
DS .... DOS
E .... EAST
EST .... ESTATE
EXPWY .... EXPRESSWAY
EXT .... EXTENSION
FRWY .... FREEWAY
FRW .... FREEWAY
FY .... FREEWAY
GN .... GLEN
GRDS .... GROUNDS
GRN .... GREEN
GRV .... GROVE
HTS .... HEIGHTS
HWY .... HIGHWAY
HY .... HIGHWAY
JCT .... JUNCTION
KPN .... KEY PENNINSULA NORTH
KPS .... KEY PENNINSULA SOUTH
L .... LA
LN .... LANE
LP .... LOOP
LS .... LAS, LOS
MDW .... MEADOW
MHP .... MOBILE HOME PARK
MNR .... MANOR
MT .... MOUNT
MTN .... MOUNTAIN
MTWY .... MOTORWAY
MTY .... MOTORWAY
N .... NORTH
PAS .... PASEO
PAS DE .... PASEO DE
PAS DL .... PASEO DEL
PAS D LS .... PASEO DE LAS / PASEO DE LOS
PGD .... PLAYGROUND
PK .... PARK
PK .... PEAK
PKWY .... PARKWAY
PL .... PLACE
PT .... POINT
PY .... PARKWAY
PZ .... PLAZA
RCH .... RANCH
RCHO .... RANCHO
RD .... ROAD
RDG .... RIDGE
RES .... RESERVOIR
RIV .... RIVER
RV .... RIVER
RO .... RANCHO
S .... SOUTH
SN .... SAN
SPG .... SPRING
SPGS .... SPRINGS
SQ .... SQUARE
SRA .... SIERRA
ST .... SAINT
ST .... STREET
STA .... SANTA
STA .... STATION
TER .... TERRACE
THTR .... THEATER
TK TR .... TRUCK TRAIL
TR .... TRAIL
VIA D .... VIA DE
VIA D LS .... VIA DE LAS / VIA DE LOS
VIA DL .... VIA DEL
VIS .... VISTA
VLG .... VILLAGE
VLY .... VALLEY
VW .... VIEW
W .... WEST
WK .... WALK
WY .... WAY

LEGEND

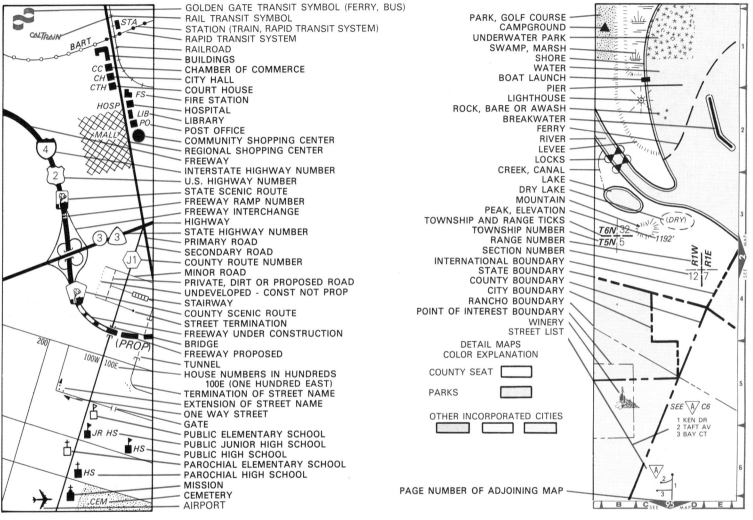

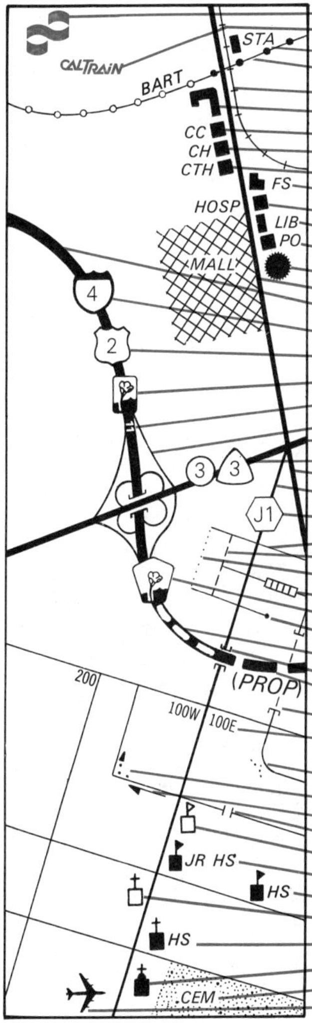

GOLDEN GATE TRANSIT SYMBOL (FERRY, BUS)
RAIL TRANSIT SYMBOL
STATION (TRAIN, RAPID TRANSIT SYSTEM)
RAPID TRANSIT SYSTEM
RAILROAD
BUILDINGS
CHAMBER OF COMMERCE
CITY HALL
COURT HOUSE
FIRE STATION
HOSPITAL
LIBRARY
POST OFFICE
COMMUNITY SHOPPING CENTER
REGIONAL SHOPPING CENTER
FREEWAY
INTERSTATE HIGHWAY NUMBER
U.S. HIGHWAY NUMBER
STATE SCENIC ROUTE
FREEWAY RAMP NUMBER
FREEWAY INTERCHANGE
HIGHWAY
STATE HIGHWAY NUMBER
PRIMARY ROAD
SECONDARY ROAD
COUNTY ROUTE NUMBER
MINOR ROAD
PRIVATE, DIRT OR PROPOSED ROAD
UNDEVELOPED - CONST NOT PROP
STAIRWAY
COUNTY SCENIC ROUTE
STREET TERMINATION
FREEWAY UNDER CONSTRUCTION
BRIDGE
FREEWAY PROPOSED
TUNNEL
HOUSE NUMBERS IN HUNDREDS
100E (ONE HUNDRED EAST)
TERMINATION OF STREET NAME
EXTENSION OF STREET NAME
ONE WAY STREET
GATE
PUBLIC ELEMENTARY SCHOOL
PUBLIC JUNIOR HIGH SCHOOL
PUBLIC HIGH SCHOOL
PAROCHIAL ELEMENTARY SCHOOL
PAROCHIAL HIGH SCHOOL
MISSION
CEMETERY
AIRPORT

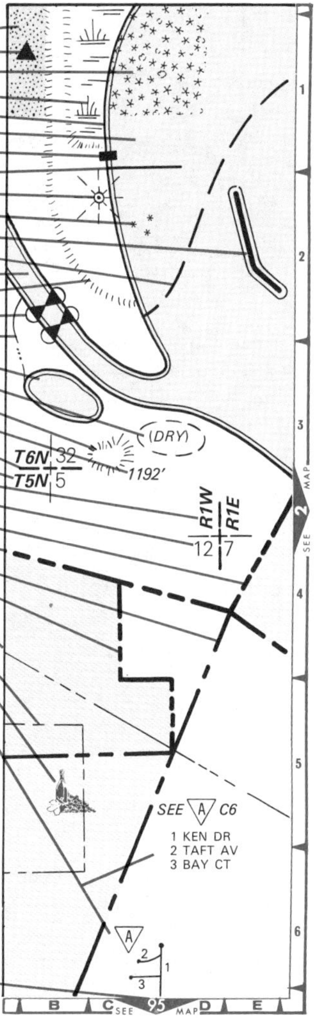

PARK, GOLF COURSE
CAMPGROUND
UNDERWATER PARK
SWAMP, MARSH
SHORE
WATER
BOAT LAUNCH
PIER
LIGHTHOUSE
ROCK, BARE OR AWASH
BREAKWATER
FERRY
RIVER
LEVEE
LOCKS
CREEK, CANAL
LAKE
DRY LAKE
MOUNTAIN
PEAK, ELEVATION
TOWNSHIP AND RANGE TICKS
TOWNSHIP NUMBER
RANGE NUMBER
SECTION NUMBER
INTERNATIONAL BOUNDARY
STATE BOUNDARY
COUNTY BOUNDARY
CITY BOUNDARY
RANCHO BOUNDARY
POINT OF INTEREST BOUNDARY
WINERY
STREET LIST

DETAIL MAPS
COLOR EXPLANATION

COUNTY SEAT

PARKS

OTHER INCORPORATED CITIES

PAGE NUMBER OF ADJOINING MAP

SEE A C6
1 KEN DR
2 TAFT AV
3 BAY CT

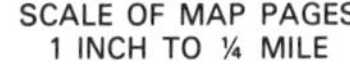

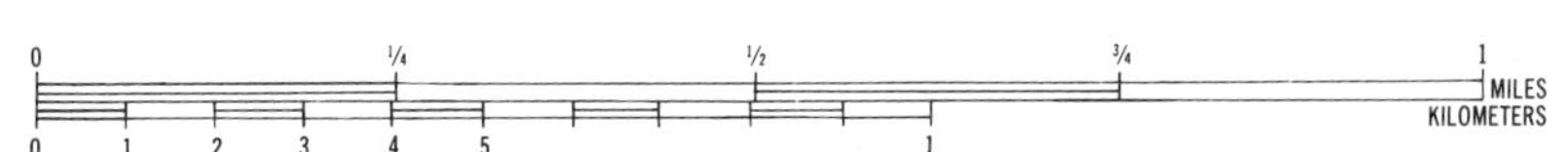

MAJOR DEPARTMENT STORES

BK	BULLOCKS
EC	EMPORIUM CAPWELL
MA	MACYS
N	NORDSTROM
NM	NEIMAN MARCUS

DOWNTOWN SAN FRANCISCO

NO.	POINTS OF INTEREST	PG.	GD.
1	BROOKS HALL	D	B1
40	CHINATOWN	E	B2
2	CITY HALL	D	B1
3	CIVIC AUDITORIUM	D	B1
4	CIVIC CENTER	D	B1
41	COIT TOWER	E	B1
5	DAVIES SYMPHONY HALL	D	A1
61	DONATELLO HOTEL	E	B3
42	EMBARCADERO CENTER	E	C2
20	FAIRMONT HOTEL	E	B3
6	FEDERAL BUILDING	D	B1
43	FERRY BUILDING - EMBARCADERO	E	C2
39	FISHERMANS WHARF	E	A1
21	FOUR SEASONS CLIFT HOTEL	E	B3
38	GEARY THEATER	E	B3
44	GHIRARDELLI SQUARE	E	A1
8	GOLDEN GATE THEATER	D	B1
58	GOLDEN GATEWAY CENTER	E	C2
25	GRAND HYATT - UNION SQUARE	E	B3
9	GREYHOUND BUS TERMINAL	D	B1
10	HALL OF JUSTICE	D	C2
19	HERBST THEATER	D	A1
22	HILTON ON HILTON SQUARE	E	B3
62	HOLIDAY INN - CIVIC CENTER	D	B1
23	HOLIDAY INN - FINANCIAL DISTRICT	E	B2
63	HOLIDAY INN - FISHERMANS WHARF	E	A1
24	HOLIDAY INN - UNION SQUARE	E	B3
55	HOTEL NIKKO	E	B3
54	HOTEL PORTMAN	E	B3
64	HOWARD JOHNSON	E	A1
53	HYATT - PARK	E	C2
26	HYATT REGENCY	E	C2
45	JACKSON SQUARE	E	B2
56	JUSTIN HERMAN PLAZA	E	C2
46	LOMBARD STREET	E	A1
12	MAIN LIBRARY	D	B1
13	MAIN POST OFFICE	D	B1
59	MANDARIN HOTEL	E	C2
57	MARITIME PLAZA	E	C2
27	MARK HOPKINS HOTEL	E	B3
37	MARRIOTT - FISHERMANS WHARF	E	A1
51	MARRIOTT - MOSCONE CENTER	E	B3
28	MERIDIEN HOTEL	E	B3
7	MOSCONE CONVENTION CENTER	D	C1
19	MUSEUM OF MODERN ART	D	A1
47	NOB HILL	E	A3
15	OLD MINT	D	C1
16	OPERA HOUSE	D	A1
17	ORPHEUM THEATER	D	B1
29	PARC FIFTY FIVE	E	B3
65	RAMADA HOTEL - FISHERMANS WHARF	E	A1
30	RAPHAEL HOTEL	E	B3
48	SAN FRANCISCO ART INSTITUTE	E	A1
31	SHERATON - FISHERMANS WHARF	E	A1
32	SHERATON - PALACE HOTEL	E	C3
33	SIR FRANCIS DRAKE HOTEL	E	B3
34	STANFORD COURT HOTEL	E	B3
18	STATE BUILDING	D	B1
52	THE CANNERY	E	A1
50	THOMAS BROS. MAPS	E	B2
49	UNION SQUARE	E	B3
36	VILLA FLORENCE HOTEL	E	B3
16	WAR MEMORIAL	D	A1
35	WESTIN ST FRANCIS	E	B3

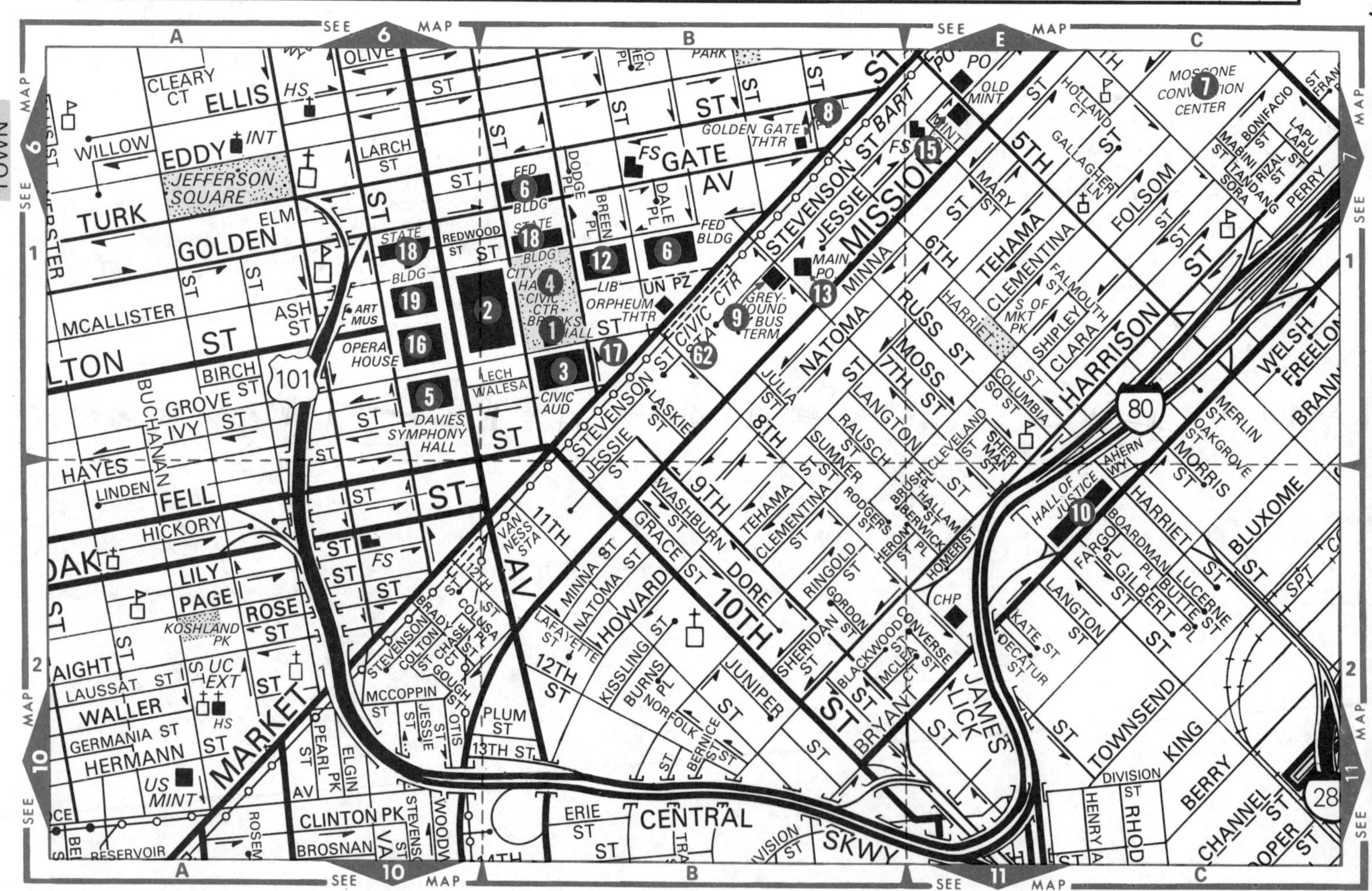

CLOSED DUE TO EARTHQUAKE DAMAGE

DOWNTOWN

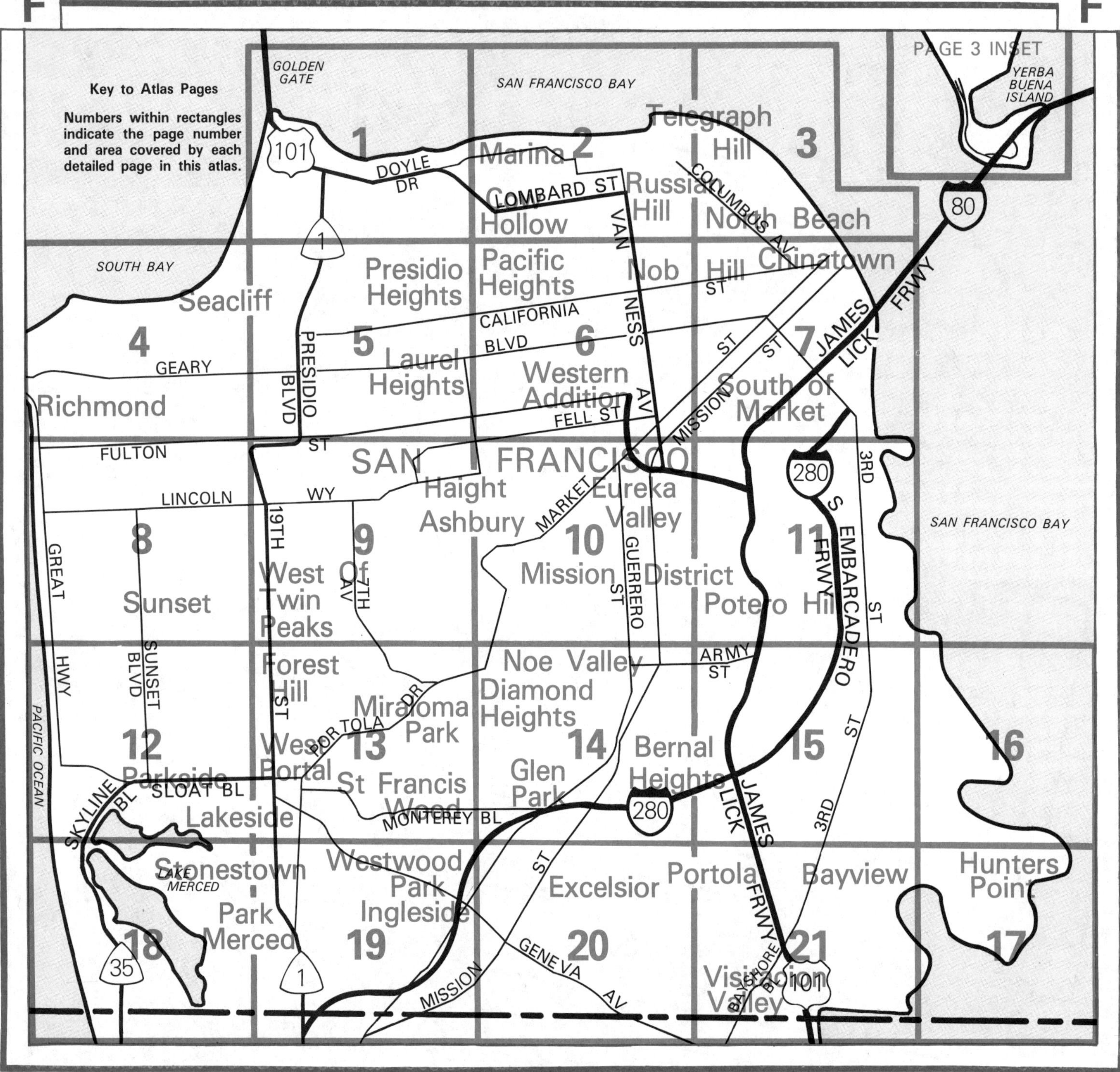
F
F
Key to Atlas Pages
Numbers within rectangles indicate the page number and area covered by each detailed page in this atlas.
PAGE 3 INSET
YERBA BUENA ISLAND
GOLDEN GATE
SAN FRANCISCO BAY
SOUTH BAY
PACIFIC OCEAN
SAN FRANCISCO BAY
LAKE MERCED
1
2
3
4
5
6
7
8
9
10
11
12
13
14
15
16
17
18
19
20
21
101
1
80
280
35
Marina
Telegraph Hill
Russian Hill
North Beach
Cow Hollow
Presidio Heights
Pacific Heights
Nob Hill
Chinatown
Seacliff
Laurel Heights
Western Addition
South of Market
Richmond
SAN FRANCISCO
Haight Ashbury
Eureka Valley
West Of Twin Peaks
Sunset
Mission District
Potero Hill
Forest Hill
Noe Valley
Miraloma Park
Diamond Heights
West Portal
Parkside
St Francis Wood
Glen Park
Bernal Heights
Lakeside
Stonestown
Westwood Park
Ingleside
Excelsior
Portola
Bayview
Hunters Point
Park Merced
Visitacion Valley
DOYLE DR
LOMBARD ST
VAN NESS AV
COLUMBUS AV
CALIFORNIA ST
GEARY BLVD
PRESIDIO BLVD
FELL ST
FULTON ST
MISSION ST
JAMES LICK FRWY
LINCOLN WY
MARKET ST
19TH AV
7TH AV
GUERRERO ST
S EMBARCADERO FRWY
3RD ST
GREAT HWY
SUNSET BLVD
ARMY ST
PORTOLA DR
SLOAT BL
SKYLINE BL
MONTEREY BL
GENEVA AV
BAYSHORE BL
MISSION

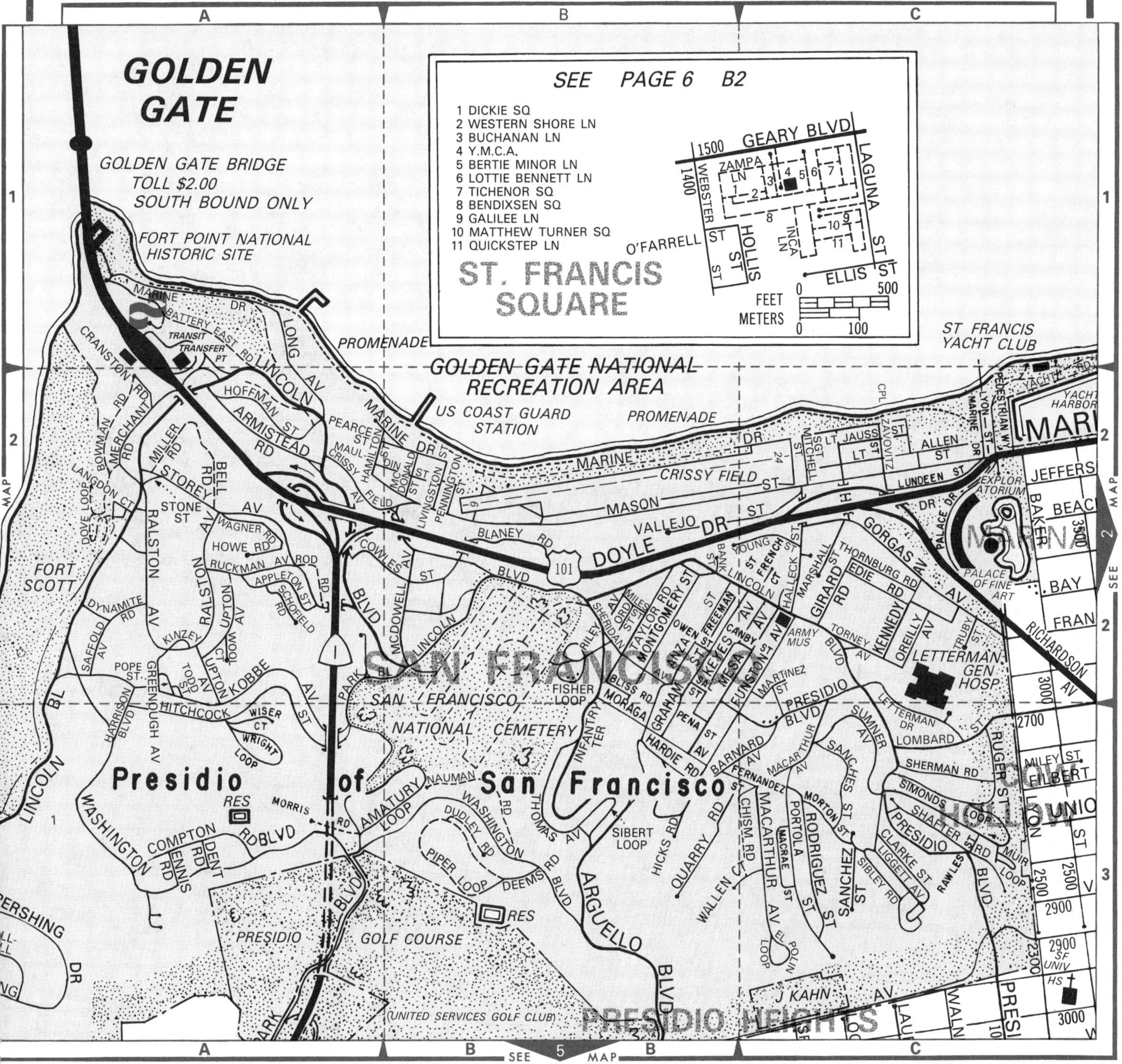

GOLDEN GATE

SEE PAGE 6 B2

1 DICKIE SQ
2 WESTERN SHORE LN
3 BUCHANAN LN
4 Y.M.C.A.
5 BERTIE MINOR LN
6 LOTTIE BENNETT LN
7 TICHENOR SQ
8 BENDIXSEN SQ
9 GALILEE LN
10 MATTHEW TURNER SQ
11 QUICKSTEP LN

ST. FRANCIS SQUARE

GEARY BLVD
1500
1400
ZAMPA LN
WEBSTER ST
LAGUNA ST
O'FARRELL ST
HOLLIS ST
INCA LN
ELLIS ST
FEET 0 500
METERS 0 100

GOLDEN GATE BRIDGE
TOLL $2.00
SOUTH BOUND ONLY

FORT POINT NATIONAL HISTORIC SITE

GOLDEN GATE NATIONAL RECREATION AREA

PROMENADE

US COAST GUARD STATION

CRISSY FIELD

ST FRANCIS YACHT CLUB

YACHT HARBOR

MARINA

EXPLORATORIUM

PALACE OF FINE ART

LETTERMAN GEN HOSP.

ARMY MUS

FORT SCOTT

SAN FRANCISCO

SAN FRANCISCO NATIONAL CEMETERY

Presidio of San Francisco

RES

PRESIDIO GOLF COURSE

(UNITED SERVICES GOLF CLUB)

PRESIDIO HEIGHTS

COW HOLLOW

J KAHN

SF UNIV

HS

MARINE DR
BATTERY EAST RD
TRANSIT TRANSFER PT
LONG AV
LINCOLN BLVD
HOFFMAN ST
ARMISTEAD RD
CRANSTON RD
MERCHANT RD
BOWMAN RD
LANGDON CT
DOVE LOOP
MILLER RD
BELL RD
STOREY AV
STONE ST
WAGNER RD
HOWE RD
RUCKMAN AV
ROD RD
APPLETON ST
SCHOFIELD RD
RALSTON AV
UPTON AV
DYNAMITE RD
SAFFOLD AV
KINZEY
POPE ST.
GREENOUGH AV
TODD ST
KOBBE AV
HARRISON BLVD
HITCHCOCK ST
WISER CT
WRIGHT LOOP
WASHINGTON BLVD
COMPTON RD
ENNIS RD
DENT RD
MORRIS RD
PERSHING DR
PARK BLVD
CRISSY FIELD AV
MAULDIN
HAMILTON ST
McDONALD ST
LIVINGSTON ST
PENNINGTON ST
PEARCE ST
COWLES ST
McDOWELL AV
BLANEY RD
MASON ST
VALLEJO ST
DOYLE DR
101
AMATURY LOOP
NAUMAN RD
DUDLEY RD
PIPER LOOP
DEEMS RD
THOMAS AV
FISHER LOOP
INFANTRY TER
SHERIDAN AV
RILEY AV
ORD ST
MILES ST
TAYLOR RD
MONTGOMERY ST
ANZA ST
OWEN ST
FREEMAN ST
CANBY ST
KEYES AV
MESA ST
FUNSTON AV
BLISS RD
MORAGA AV
GRAHAM ST
PENA ST
HARDIE RD
BARNARD AV
MARTINEZ ST
PRESIDIO BLVD
SIBERT LOOP
HICKS RD
QUARRY RD
ARGUELLO BLVD
WALLEN CT
CHISM RD
FERNANDEZ
MACARTHUR AV
MACRAE ST
PORTOLA ST
EL POLIN LOOP
RODRIGUEZ ST
MORTON ST
SANCHEZ ST
SIBLEY RD
SANCHES ST
SUMNER AV
LETTERMAN DR
LOMBARD ST
SHERMAN RD
SIMONDS LOOP
SHAFTER RD
PRESIDIO BLVD
CLARKE ST
LIGGETT AV
RAWLES
RUGER ST
MUIR LOOP
YOUNG ST
FRENCH CT
BANK ST
HALLECK ST
MARSHALL ST
GIRARD RD
THORNBURG RD
EDIE RD
GORGAS AV
KENNEDY
OREILLY AV
TORNEY AV
TRUBY ST
MARINE DR
24 ST
SGT MITCHELL ST
LT JAUSS ST
ZAVOVITZ ST
ALLEN ST
LUNDEEN ST
LYON ST
PEDESTRIAN WY
PALACE DR
YACHT RD
JEFFERSON
BEACH
BAKER
BAY
FRANCISCO
RICHARDSON AV
MILEY ST
FILBERT
UNION
3500
3000
2700
2500
2900
2300
CPL

A B C
1 2 3

SEE MAP 2

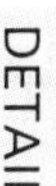

SEE 5 MAP

A
B
C
SAN FRANCISCO BAY
SEE A C1
1 RICHARD HENRY DANA PL
ANGEL ISLAND FERRY
ALCATRAZ FERRY
VALLEJO
SAN FRANCISCO MARITIME NATIONAL HISTORICAL PARK
MUNICIPAL PIER
GOLDEN GATE NATIONAL RECREATION CENTER
FISHERMAN'S WHARF
41
43
45
GOLDEN GATE YACHT CLUB
PIER 1
PIER 2
PIER 3
AQUATIC PARK
NATIONAL MARITIME MUSEUM BUILDING
PROMENADE
YACHT HARBOR
MARINA GREEN
GAS HOUSE COVE
FORT MASON CTR
FORT MASON
POPE RD
SCHOFIELD RD
MACARTHUR AV
GGNRA PK HQ
GHIRARDELLI SQ
THE CANNERY
THE ANCHORAGE
CONRAD PK
MARINA BLVD
CERVANTES BLVD
MARINA
JEFFERSON ST
BEACH ST
BAY ST
NORTH POINT ST
FRANCISCO ST
CHESTNUT ST
LOMBARD
101
GREENWICH
FILBERT
UNION
GREEN
VALLEJO
BROADWAY
PACIFIC
JACKSON
WASHINGTON
CLAY
SACRAMENTO
CALIFORNIA ST
GEORGE R MOSCONE REC CTR
SAN FRANCISCO
MAGNOLIA ST
MOULTON ST
HARRIS PL
RICHARDSON AV
COW HOLLOW
PACIFIC HEIGHTS
RUSSIAN HILL
ALTA PLAZA
LAFAYETTE PK
CALIF HIST SOC MUS
CONVENT OF SACRED HEART HS
UNIV OF THE PACIFIC
SF UNIV HS
BAKER
BRODERICK
DIVISADERO
SCOTT
PIERCE
STEINER
FILLMORE
WEBSTER
BUCHANAN
LAGUNA
OCTAVIA
GOUGH
FRANKLIN
VAN NESS AV
POLK ST
LARKIN
HYDE
LEAVENWORTH
JONES
TAYLOR
MASON
COLUMBUS AV
SEE PAGE E
BROADWAY TUNNEL
SEE 6 MAP
SEE 1 MAP DETAIL
SEE 3 MAP DETAIL

CLOSED DUE TO EARTHQUAKE DAMAGE

SEE MAP 1

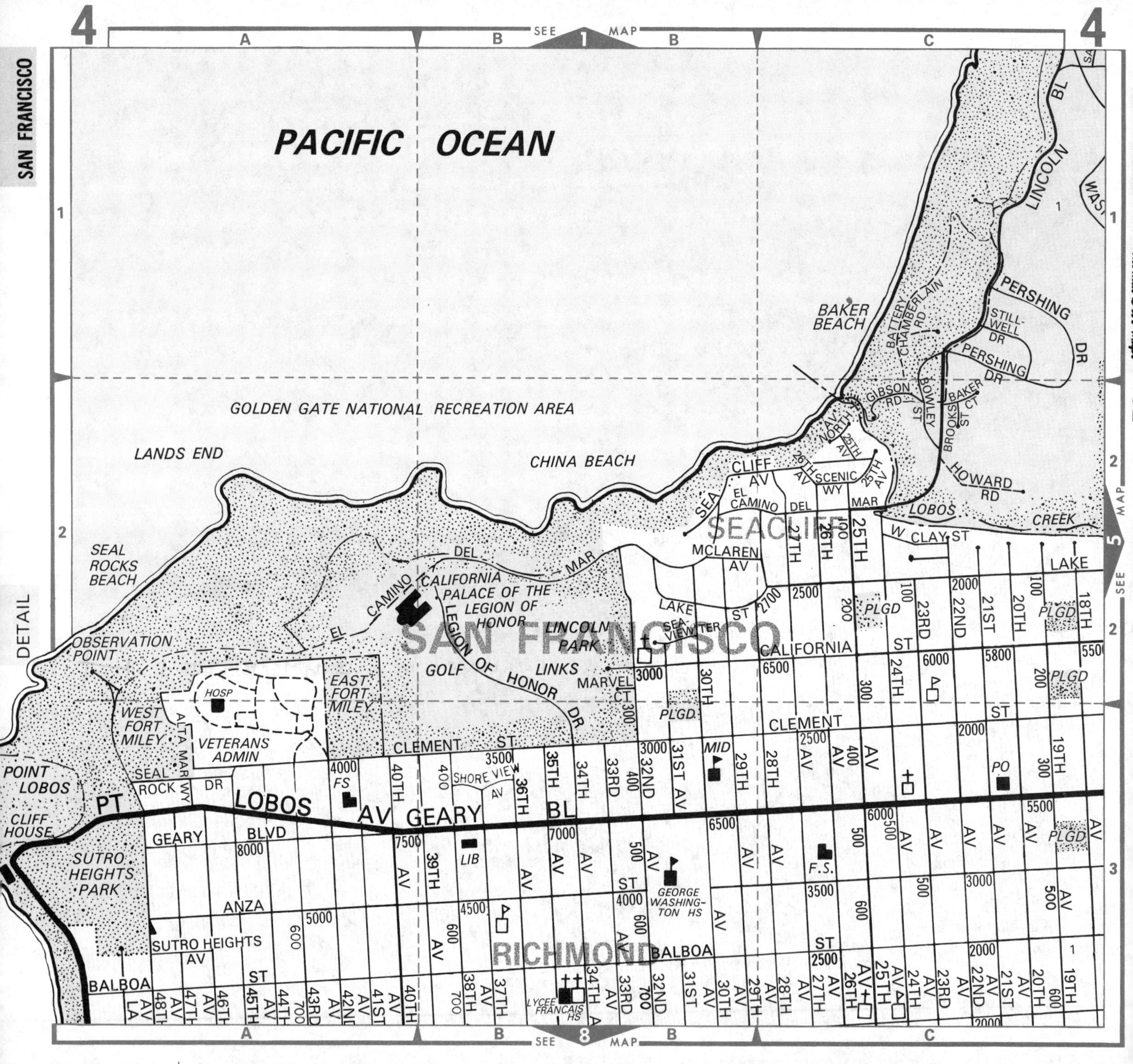

SEE MAP 5
SEE MAP 8

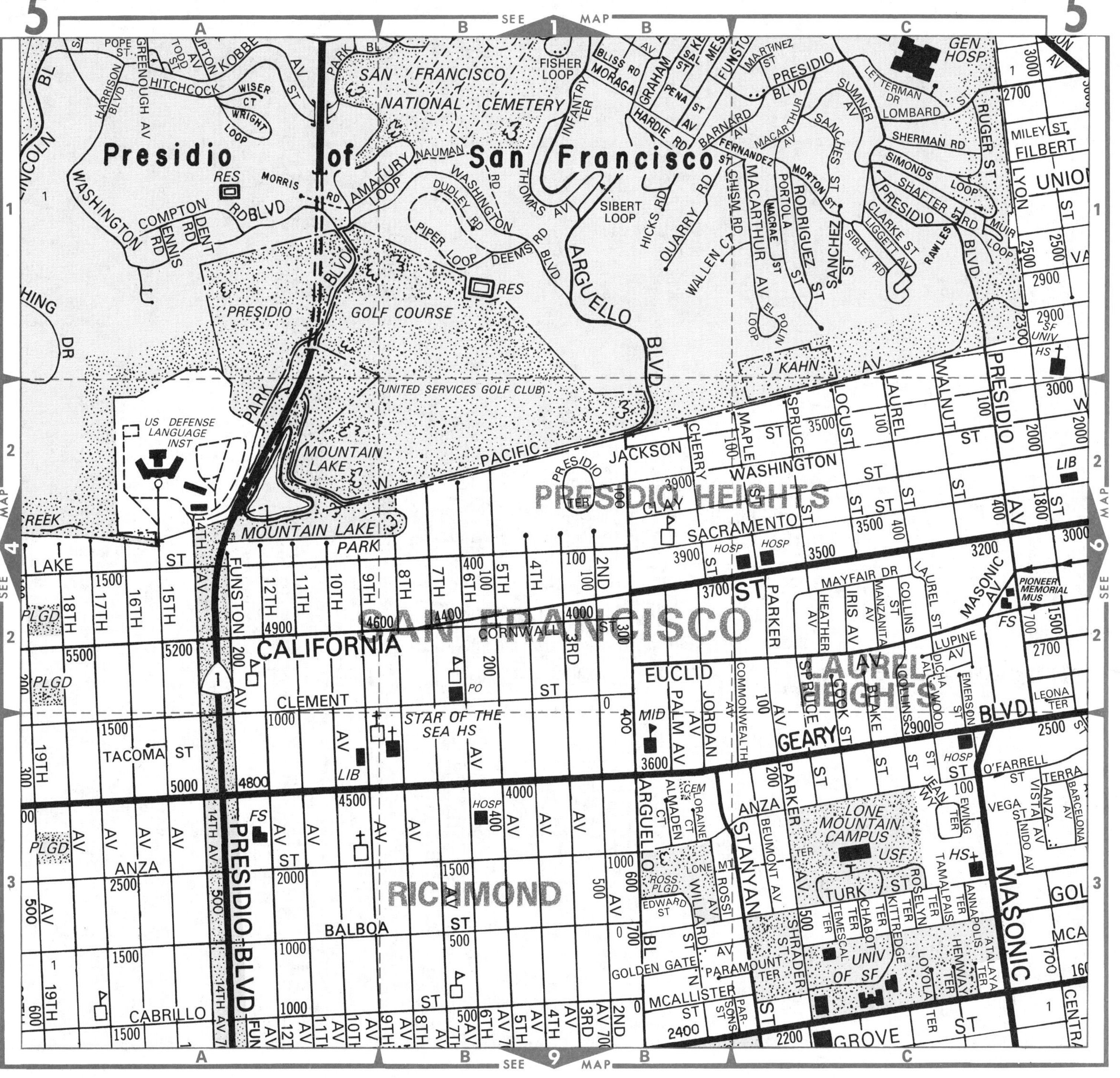

SEE MAP 4
SEE MAP 6
DETAIL
COPYRIGHT © 1991 BY Thomas Bros. Maps

SEE MAP 2
SEE MAP 5
SEE MAP 7
SEE MAP 10
A
B
C
1
2
3
COW HOLLOW
PACIFIC HEIGHTS
SAN FRANCISCO
WESTERN ADDITION
RUSSIAN HILL
GREENWICH
FILBERT
UNION
GREEN
VALLEJO
BROADWAY
PACIFIC
JACKSON
WASHINGTON
CLAY
SACRAMENTO
CALIFORNIA
PINE
BUSH
SUTTER
POST
GEARY
O'FARRELL
ELLIS
EDDY
TURK
GOLDEN GATE
MCALLISTER
FULTON
GROVE
HAYES
FELL
LYON
BRODERICK
DIVISADERO
SCOTT
PIERCE
STEINER
FILLMORE
WEBSTER
BUCHANAN
LAGUNA
OCTAVIA
GOUGH
FRANKLIN
VAN NESS AV
POLK
LARKIN
HYDE
LEAVENWORTH
JONES
TAYLOR
MASONIC
PRESIDIO AV
CENTRAL FRWY
MISSION ST
ALTA PLAZA
LAFAYETTE PK
HAMILTON SQ
RAYMOND KIMBELL PLGD
JEFFERSON SQ
HAYWARD PLGD
ALAMO SQ
JAPAN CENTER
ST FRANCIS SQ
CONVENT OF SACRED HEART HS
CALIF HIST SOC MUS
UNIV OF THE PACIFIC
ARCHIVES FOR THE PERFORMING ARTS
PIONEER MEMORIAL MUS
PODIATRIC MEDICAL CENTER
CATHEDRAL HS
SACRED HEART HS
ST ROSE HS
DREW HS
STATE BLDG
FED BLDG
CITY HALL
CIVIC CNTR
CIVIC AUD
OPERA HOUSE
DAVIS SYMPHONY HALL
ART MUS
ALAMO PARK HS
CIVIC CTR STA
VAN NESS STA
SEE PAGE D
SEE PAGE E
101
BROADWAY TUNNEL

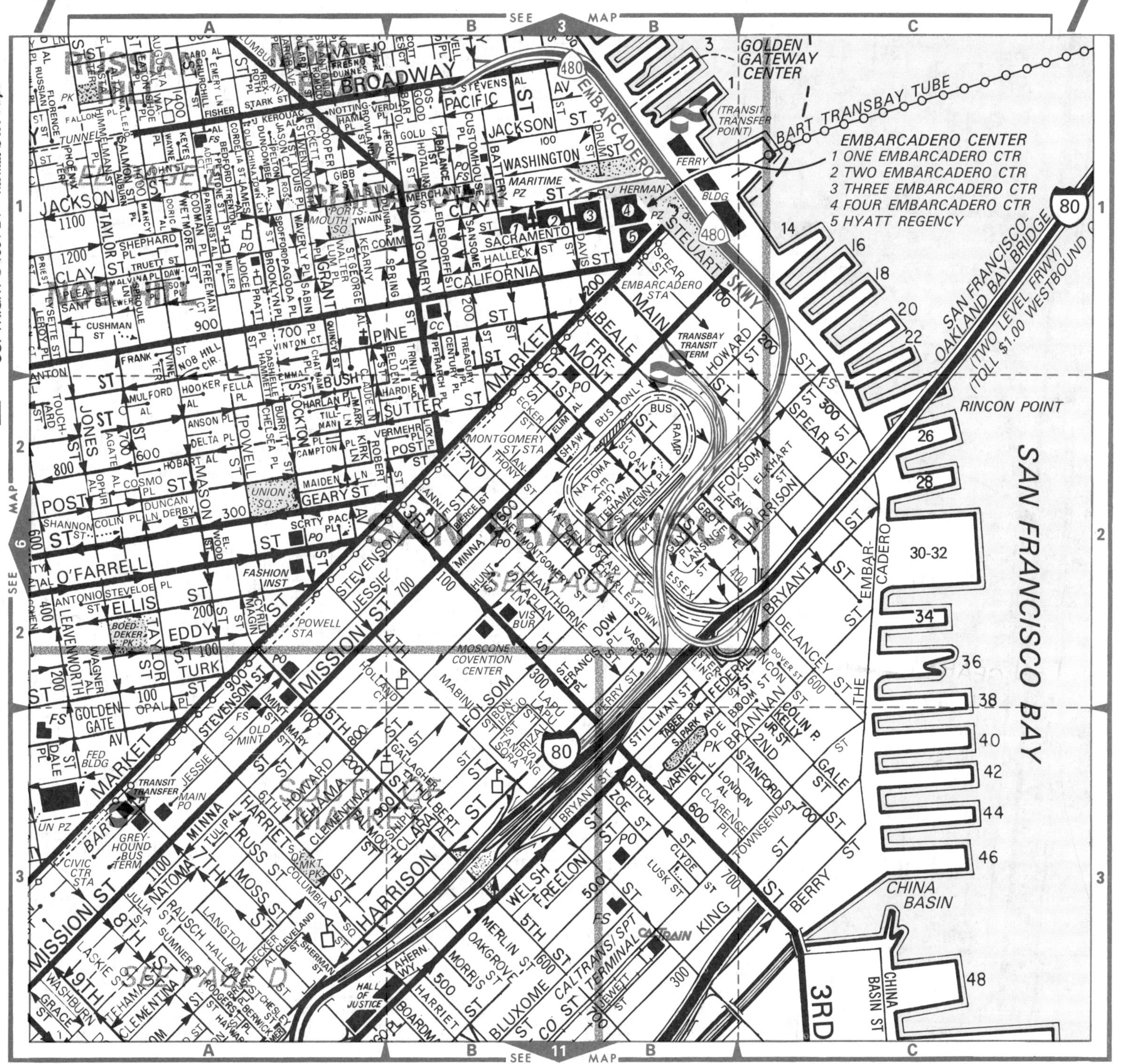

CLOSED DUE TO EARTHQUAKE DAMAGE

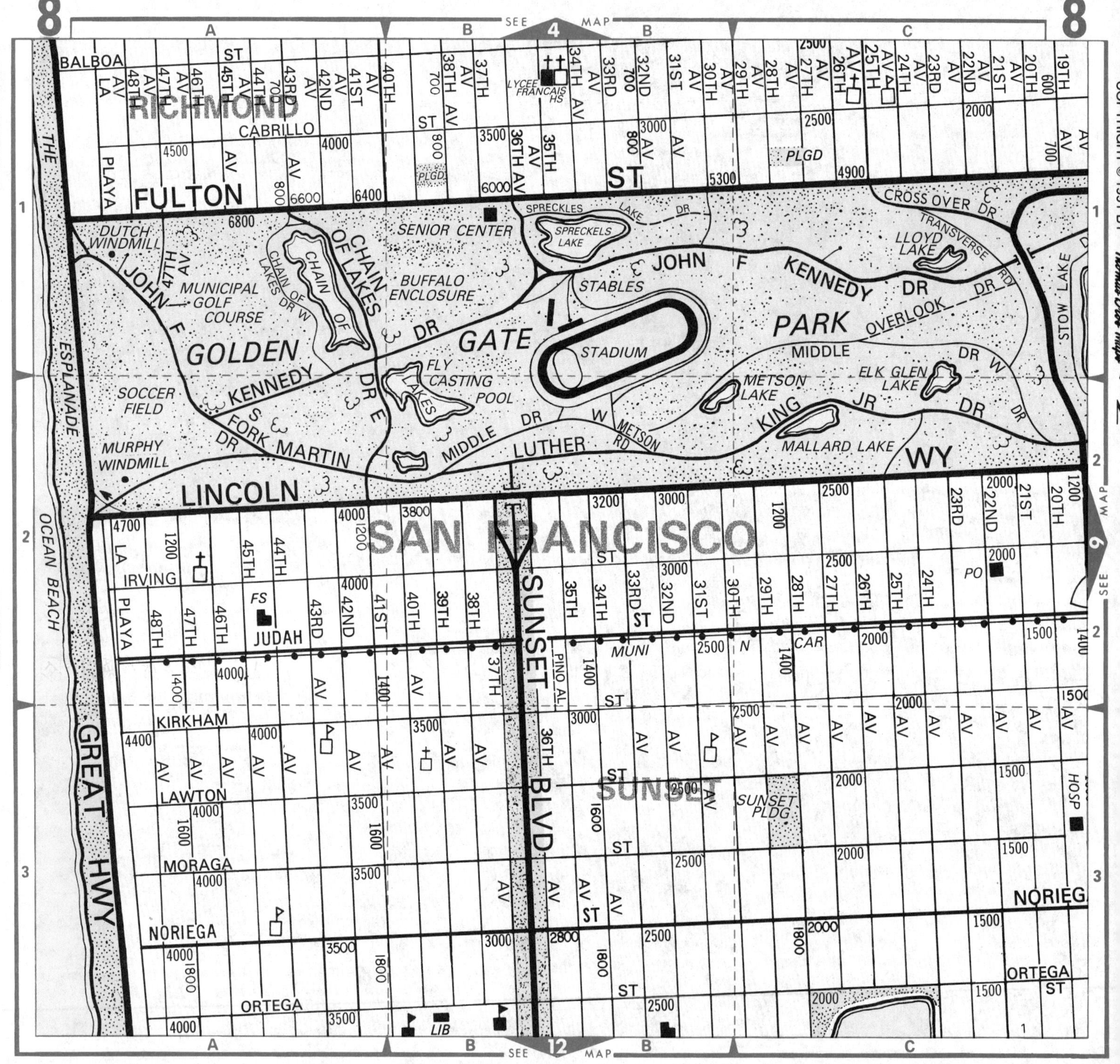
SEE MAP 4
A
B
C
RICHMOND
BALBOA ST
CABRILLO
FULTON ST
LA PLAYA
LYCEE FRANCAIS HS
PLGD
CROSS OVER DR
TRANSVERSE RD
SPRECKLES LAKE DR
SPRECKELS LAKE
SENIOR CENTER
DUTCH WINDMILL
MUNICIPAL GOLF COURSE
CHAIN OF LAKES
CHAIN OF LAKES DR W
BUFFALO ENCLOSURE
STABLES
STADIUM
LLOYD LAKE
JOHN F KENNEDY DR
GOLDEN GATE PARK
OVERLOOK DR
MIDDLE DR W
ELK GLEN LAKE
METSON LAKE
METSON RD
FLY CASTING POOL
LAKES
SOCCER FIELD
S FORK DR
MARTIN LUTHER KING JR DR
MIDDLE DR
MALLARD LAKE
MURPHY WINDMILL
STOW LAKE DR
LINCOLN WY
THE ESPLANADE
OCEAN BEACH
GREAT HWY
SAN FRANCISCO
IRVING ST
FS
JUDAH ST
MUNI N CAR
PINO AL
PO
KIRKHAM ST
LAWTON ST
SUNSET
SUNSET PLDG
SUNSET BLVD
MORAGA ST
NORIEGA ST
ORTEGA ST
HOSP
LIB
SEE MAP 9
SEE MAP 12
DETAIL

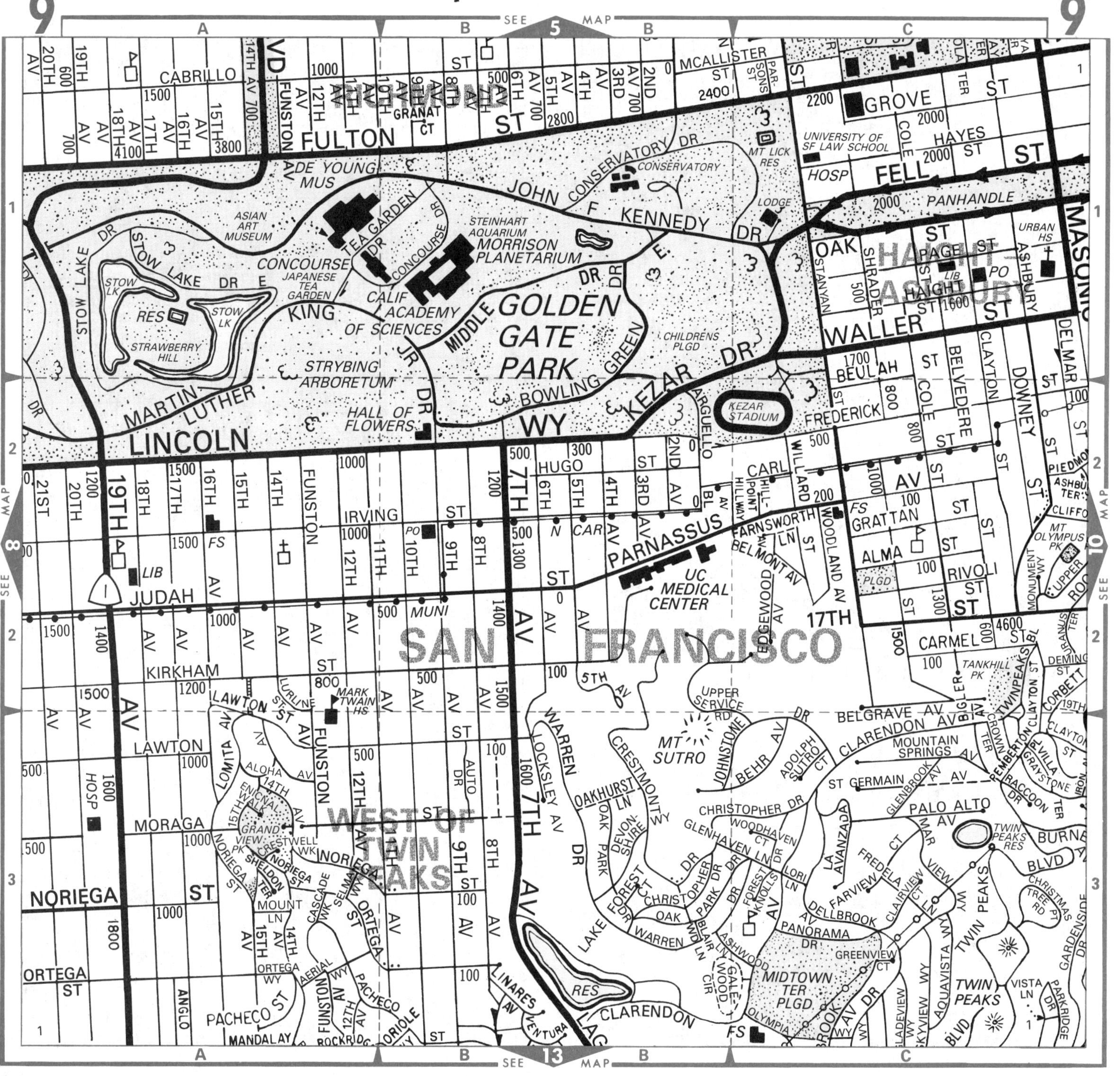
SEE 5 MAP
SEE 13 MAP
SEE 8 MAP
SEE 10 MAP
DETAIL
RICHMOND
GOLDEN GATE PARK
SAN FRANCISCO
WEST OF TWIN PEAKS
HAIGHT - ASHBURY
FULTON ST
CABRILLO
MCALLISTER ST
GROVE
HAYES ST
FELL ST
PANHANDLE
OAK
PAGE ST
HAIGHT ST
WALLER ST
BEULAH ST
FREDERICK
CARL
GRATTAN
ALMA
RIVOLI ST
17TH ST
CARMEL ST
PARNASSUS
IRVING ST
JUDAH
MUNI
KIRKHAM ST
LAWTON
MORAGA
NORIEGA ST
ORTEGA ST
PACHECO ST
MANDALAY
CLARENDON
LINCOLN WY
MARTIN LUTHER KING JR DR
JOHN F KENNEDY DR
CONSERVATORY DR
MIDDLE DR
KEZAR DR
BOWLING GREEN
STOW LAKE DR
DE YOUNG MUS
ASIAN ART MUSEUM
TEA GARDEN DR
CONCOURSE
JAPANESE TEA GARDEN
STEINHART AQUARIUM
MORRISON PLANETARIUM
CALIF ACADEMY OF SCIENCES
STRYBING ARBORETUM
HALL OF FLOWERS
CHILDRENS PLGD
KEZAR STADIUM
CONSERVATORY
MT LICK RES
LODGE
STRAWBERRY HILL
STOW LK
RES
UNIVERSITY OF SF LAW SCHOOL
HOSP
URBAN HS
LIB
PO
FS
UC MEDICAL CENTER
MT SUTRO
UPPER SERVICE RD
MARK TWAIN HS
TANKHILL PK
MT OLYMPUS PK
TWIN PEAKS RES
TWIN PEAKS
TWIN PEAKS BLVD
MIDTOWN TER PLGD
CLARENDON AV
BELGRAVE AV
MOUNTAIN SPRINGS AV
ST GERMAIN AV
PALO ALTO AV
CHRISTOPHER DR
GLENHAVEN LN
WOODHAVEN CT
PANORAMA DR
DELLBROOK AV
CRESTMONT DR
OAKHURST LN
WARREN DR
LOCKSLEY AV
LAGUNA HONDA BLVD
LAKE FOREST CT
JOHNSTONE DR
BEHR AV
ADOLPH SUTRO CT
FUNSTON AV
7TH AV
9TH AV
19TH AV
STANYAN
COLE
CLAYTON
ASHBURY
MASONIC
BELVEDERE
DOWNEY
DELMAR
WILLARD
WOODLAND AV
EDGEWOOD AV
ARGUELLO
LINARES AV
VENTURA
LOMITA AV
ALOHA AV
GRAND VIEW PK
NORIEGA
CASCADE WK
SELMA WY
AERIAL WY
ORIOLE
ANGLO
ROCKRIDGE

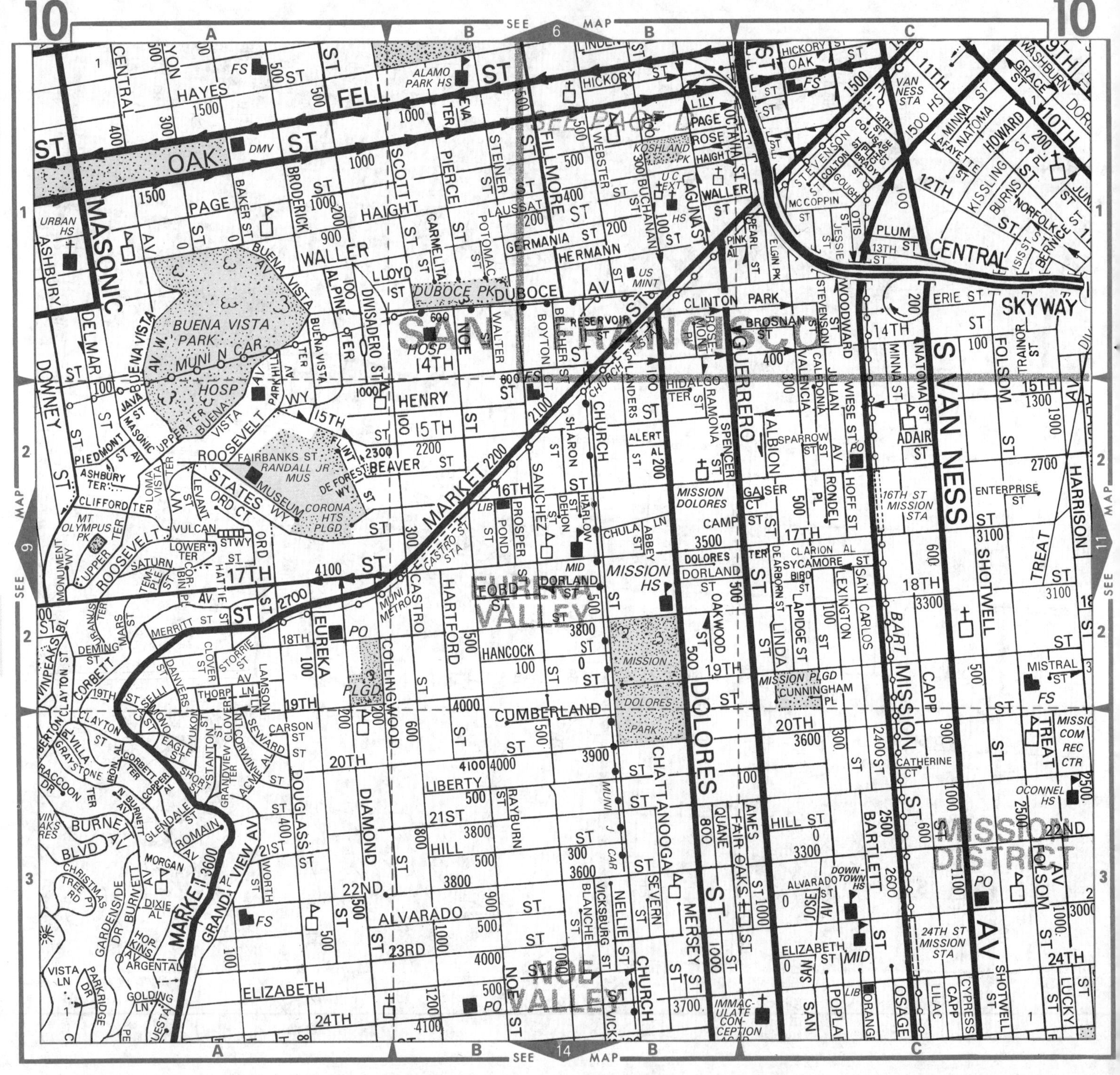
SEE 6 MAP
SEE 14 MAP
SEE 9 MAP
SEE 11 MAP
SEE PAGE D
SAN FRANCISCO
EUREKA VALLEY
NOE VALLEY
MISSION DISTRICT
BUENA VISTA PARK
DUBOCE PK
MISSION DOLORES PARK
CORONA HTS PLGD
MT OLYMPUS PK
KOSHLAND PK
MISSION PLGD
MISSION DOLORES
MISSION HS
ALAMO PARK HS
URBAN HS
US MINT
UC EXT
DMV
RANDALL JR MUS
MUSEUM
HOSP
MISSION COM REC CTR
OCONNEL HS
DOWN-TOWN HS
IMMACULATE CONCEPTION ACAD
VAN NESS STA
16TH ST MISSION STA
24TH ST MISSION STA
CHURCH ST STA
CASTRO ST STA
MUNI METRO
MUNI N CAR
MUNI J CAR
BART
SKYWAY
CENTRAL
MARKET
MASONIC
OAK ST
FELL ST
HAYES ST
PAGE
HAIGHT
WALLER
DUBOCE AV
14TH
15TH
16TH
17TH
18TH
19TH
20TH
21ST
22ND
23RD
24TH
DIVISADERO ST
CASTRO
NOE
SANCHEZ
CHURCH
DOLORES ST
GUERRERO ST
VALENCIA
MISSION ST
S VAN NESS AV
FOLSOM
HARRISON
FILLMORE
LAGUNA ST
OCTAVIA ST
ROOSEVELT WY
STATES WY
CLAYTON ST
CORBETT
DOUGLASS
DIAMOND
COLLINGWOOD
HARTFORD
EUREKA
GRAND VIEW AV
BURNETT AV
ELIZABETH
ALVARADO
HILL
LIBERTY
CUMBERLAND
HANCOCK
CHATTANOOGA
SHOTWELL
CAPP
BARTLETT
TREAT
PO
FS
LIB
PLGD

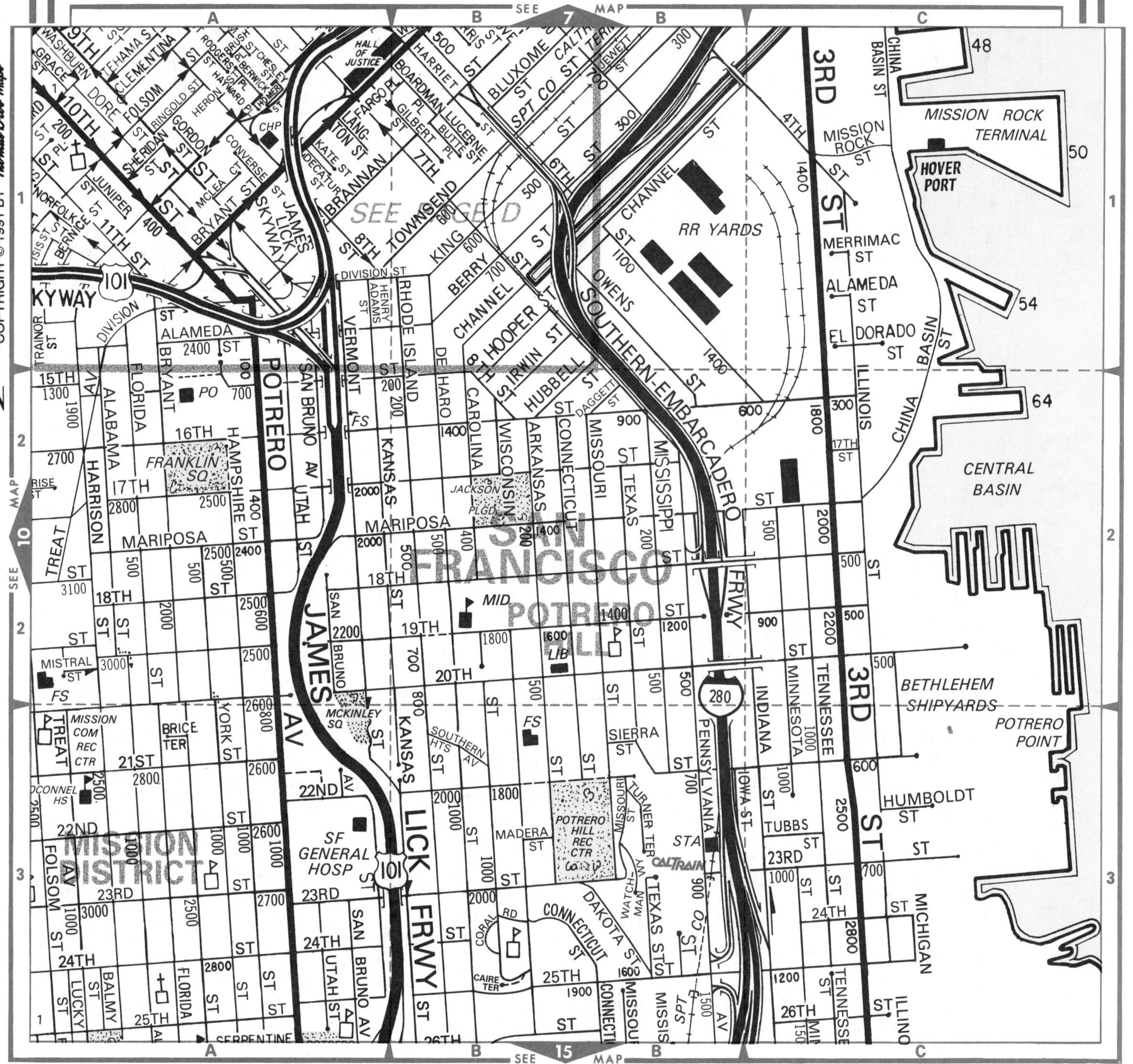

COPYRIGHT © 1991 BY Thomas Bros. Maps

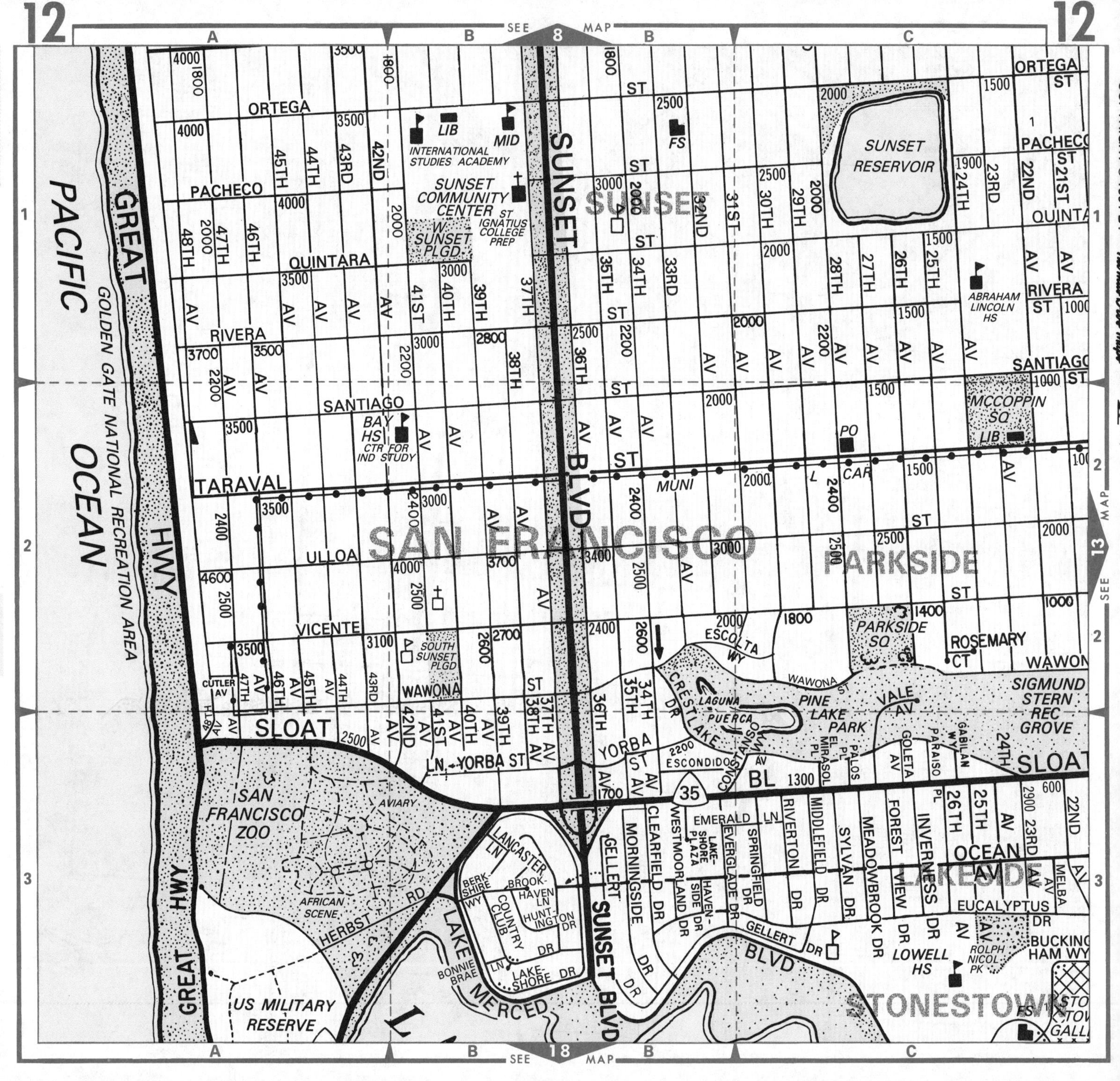
SEE 8 MAP
PACIFIC OCEAN
GOLDEN GATE NATIONAL RECREATION AREA
GREAT HWY
SUNSET
SAN FRANCISCO
PARKSIDE
LAKESIDE
STONESTOWN
SUNSET BLVD
ORTEGA
PACHECO
QUINTARA
RIVERA
SANTIAGO
TARAVAL
ULLOA
VICENTE
WAWONA
SLOAT
INTERNATIONAL STUDIES ACADEMY
LIB
MID
FS
SUNSET COMMUNITY CENTER
ST IGNATIUS COLLEGE PREP
W SUNSET PLGD
SUNSET RESERVOIR
ABRAHAM LINCOLN HS
MCCOPPIN SQ
BAY HS
CTR FOR IND STUDY
PO
MUNI L CAR
SOUTH SUNSET PLGD
PARKSIDE SQ
ROSEMARY CT
ESCOLTA WY
LAGUNA PUERCA
CRESTLAKE DR
PINE LAKE PARK
VALE AV
SIGMUND STERN REC GROVE
YORBA ST
ESCONDIDO
CONSTANSO WY
EL MIRASOL PL
PALOS PL
GOLETA AV
PARAISO PL
GABILAN WY
SAN FRANCISCO ZOO
AVIARY
AFRICAN SCENE
HERBST RD
LANCASTER LN
BERKSHIRE WY
BROOKHAVEN LN
COUNTRY CLUB DR
HUNTINGTON DR
LAKESHORE DR
BONNIE BRAE LN
LAKE MERCED BLVD
US MILITARY RESERVE
EMERALD LN
GELLERT DR
MORNINGSIDE DR
CLEARFIELD DR
WESTMOORLAND DR
LAKESHORE PLAZA
HAVENSIDE DR
EVERGLADE DR
SPRINGFIELD DR
RIVERTON DR
MIDDLEFIELD DR
SYLVAN DR
MEADOWBROOK DR
FOREST VIEW DR
INVERNESS DR
OCEAN AV
EUCALYPTUS DR
MELBA AV
BUCKINGHAM WY
LOWELL HS
ROLPH NICOL PK
CUTLER AV
35
SEE 13 MAP
SEE 18 MAP
DETAIL

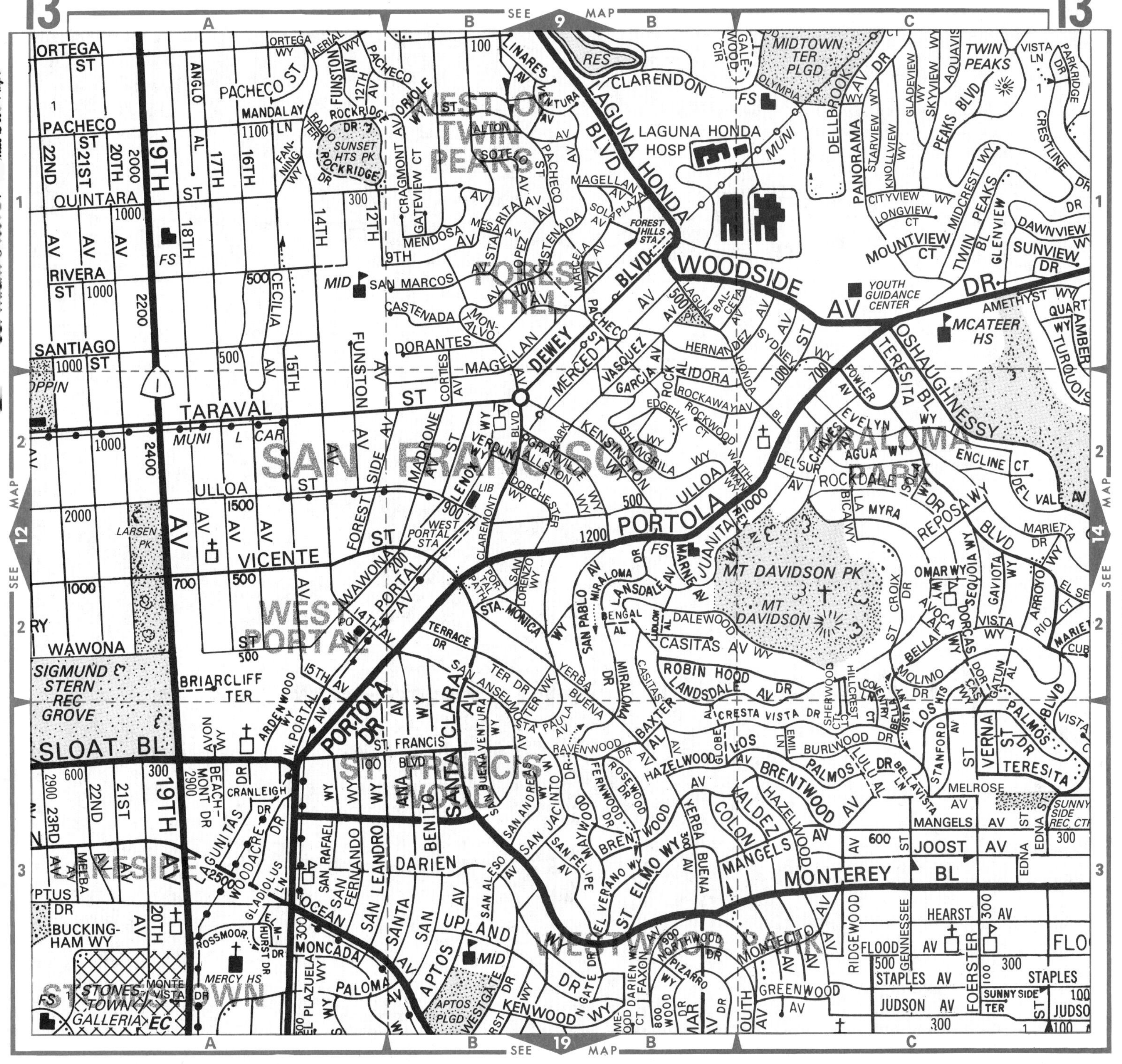
SEE MAP 9
SEE MAP 19
SEE MAP 12
SEE MAP 14
DETAIL
SAN FRANCISCO
WEST OF TWIN PEAKS
FOREST HILL
WEST PORTAL
ST. FRANCIS WOOD
MIRALOMA PARK
WESTWOOD PARK
LAKESIDE
STONESTOWN
MIDTOWN TER PLGD
LAGUNA HONDA HOSP
YOUTH GUIDANCE CENTER
MCATEER HS
MT DAVIDSON PK
MT DAVIDSON
SIGMUND & STERN REC GROVE
LARSEN PK
SUNSET HTS PK
APTOS PLGD
MERCY HS
STONESTOWN GALLERIA
SUNNY SIDE REC CTR
TWIN PEAKS
FOREST HILLS STA
WEST PORTAL STA
MUNI L CAR
19TH AV
SLOAT BL
TARAVAL ST
ULLOA ST
VICENTE ST
WAWONA ST
PORTOLA DR
LAGUNA HONDA BLVD
WOODSIDE AV
O'SHAUGHNESSY BLVD
MONTEREY BL
OCEAN AV
JUNIPERO SERRA BLVD
TWIN PEAKS BL
DEWEY BLVD
CLARENDON AV
QUINTARA ST
PACHECO ST
RIVERA ST
SANTIAGO ST
ORTEGA ST
MAGELLAN AV
DORANTES AV
SAN MARCOS AV
CASTENADA AV
KENSINGTON WY
TERESITA BL
JUANITA WY
MIRALOMA DR
SANTA CLARA AV
ST. FRANCIS BLVD
HAZELWOOD AV
BRENTWOOD AV
DARIEN WY
UPLAND DR
KENWOOD WY
JOOST AV
MANGELS AV
FLOOD AV
STAPLES AV
JUDSON AV
HEARST AV
GREENWOOD AV

SEE 10 MAP
SEE 20 MAP
SEE 13 MAP
SEE 15 MAP
DETAIL
NOE VALLEY
DIAMOND HEIGHTS
GLEN CANYON PARK
SAN FRANCISCO
BERNAL HEIGHTS
GLEN PARK
CHRISTOPHER PLGD
DOUGLASS PLGD
BILLY GOAT HILL PK
WALTER HAAS PK
POLICE ACADEMY
GLEN PARK REC CTR
DOROTHY ERSKINE PK
SUNNY SIDE REC CTR
MONTEREY CONSERVATORY
ST MARYS PARK
HOLLY PARK
BERNAL HTS PK
IMMACULATE CONCEPTION ACAD
ST PAUL HS
JURI COMMONS PK
GLEN PARK STA
RES
ELIZABETH
24TH
JERSEY
25TH
CLIPPER
26TH
ARMY
27TH
DUNCAN
28TH
VALLEY
29TH
DAY
30TH
DIAMOND
CASTRO
NOE ST
SANCHEZ
CHURCH
DOLORES ST
GUERRERO ST
MISSION ST
DIAMOND HEIGHTS BL
GOLD MINE DR
BERKELEY WY
O'SHAUGHNESSY BL
BOSWORTH
CHENERY
MONTEREY BL
280
FRWY
ALEMANY BLVD
SILVER AV
CORTLAND
PRECITA AV
SANTA MARINA
FAIRMOUNT ST
RANDALL
ARLINGTON
FLOOD AV
CIRCULAR AV
JOOST AV
MANGELS
STAPLES
JUDSON
TRUMBULL
TULANE
CRESCENT
RICHLAND
HIGHLAND
TOMPKINS
OGDEN AV
BENTON
JUSTIN
A
B
C
1
2
3

SEE MAP 11

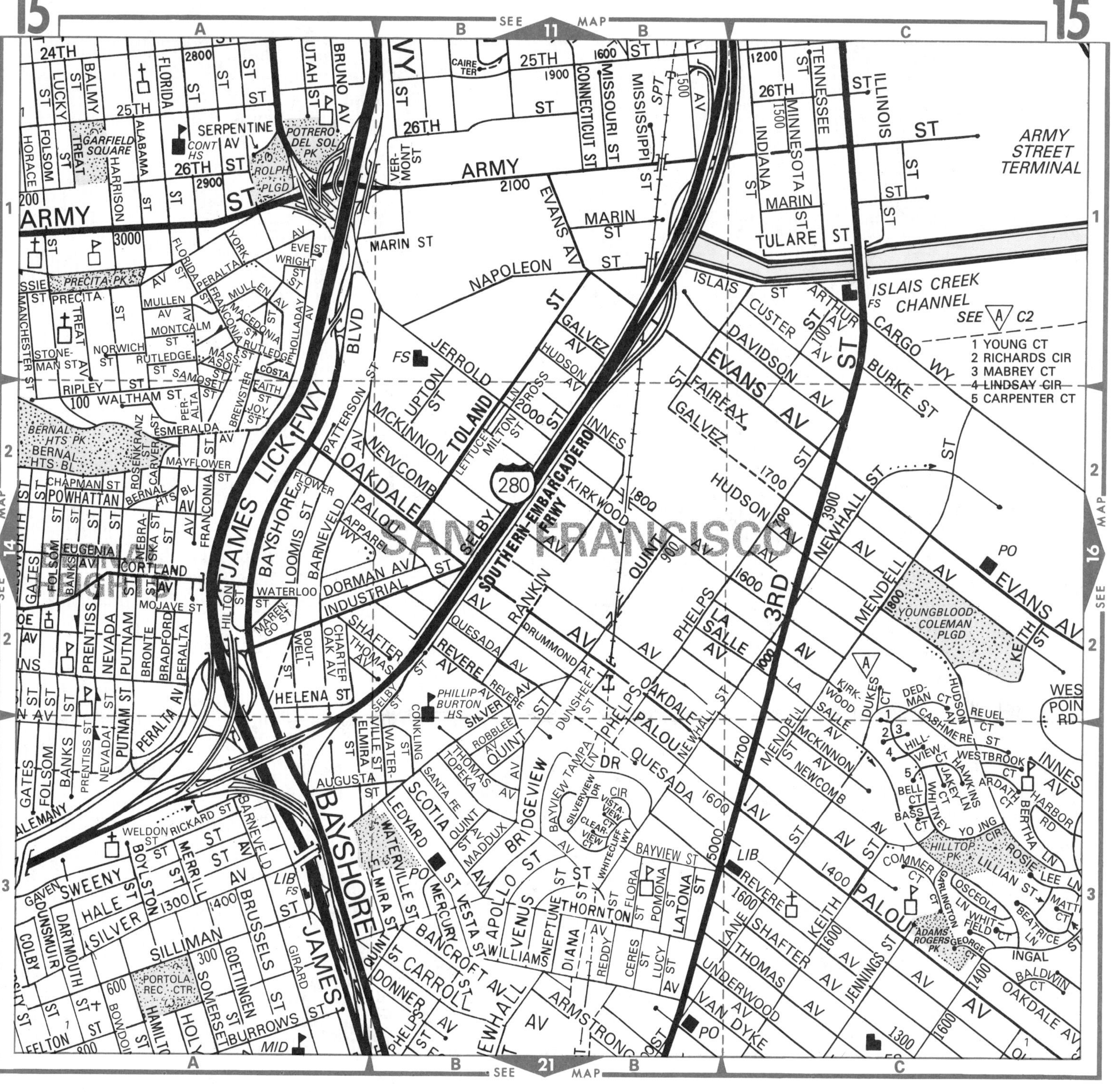

SEE MAP 14
SEE MAP 16
SEE MAP 21
SEE DETAIL

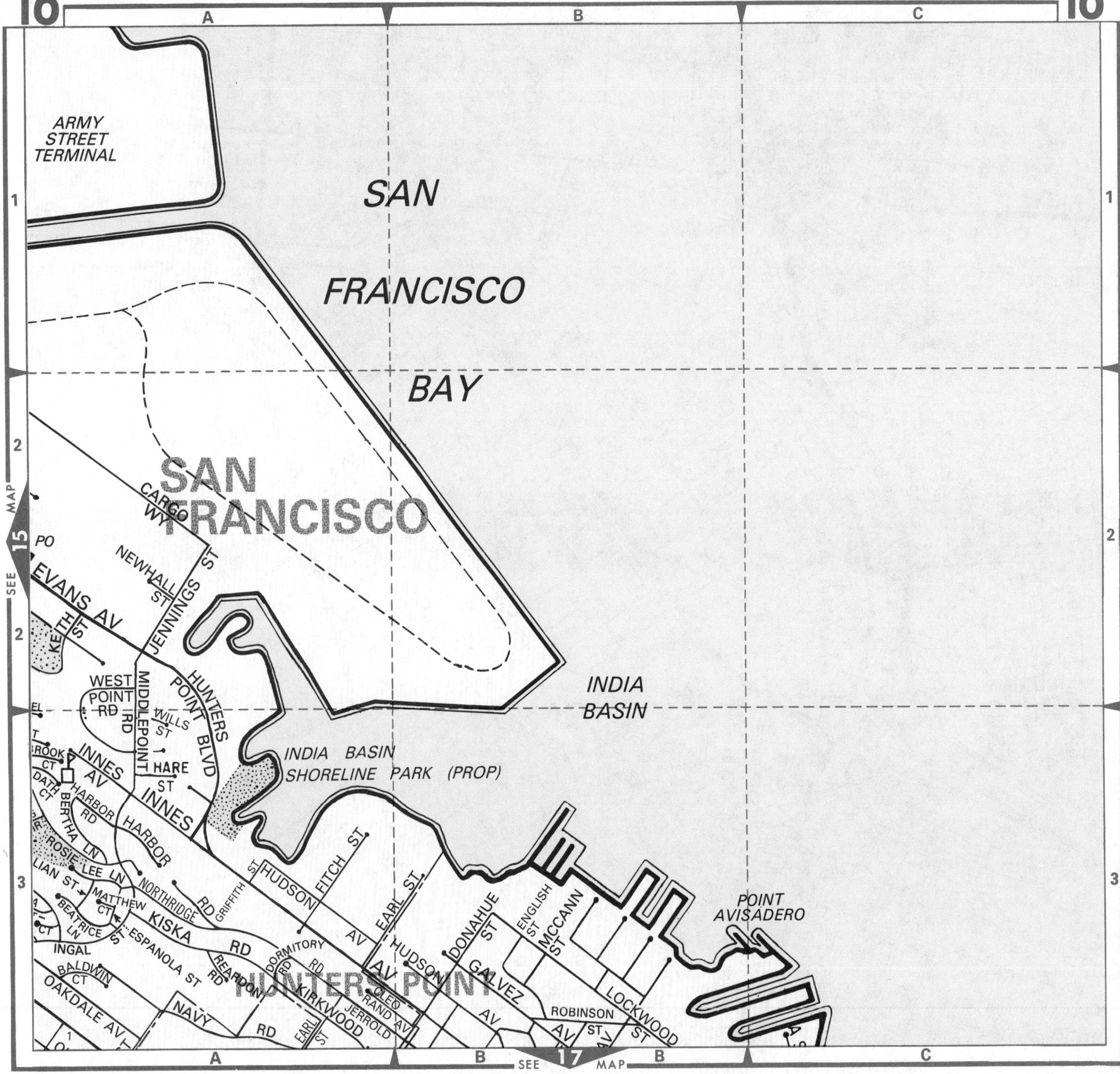

A B C

1

ARMY STREET TERMINAL

SAN FRANCISCO BAY

SAN FRANCISCO

CARGO WY
EVANS AV
NEWHALL ST
JENNINGS ST
KEITH ST
HUNTERS POINT BLVD
WEST POINT RD
MIDDLEPOINT RD
WILLS ST
HARE ST
INNES AV
INNES
HARBOR RD
HARBOR
BERTHA LN
DATH CT
ROSIE LEE LN
NORTHRIDGE RD
MATTHEW CT
BEATRICE LN
KISKA RD
ESPANOLA ST
INGAL
BALDWIN CT
OAKDALE AV
REARDON RD
DORMITORY RD
GRIFFITH ST
HUDSON AV
FITCH ST
EARL ST
KIRKWOOD
JERROLD AV
NAVY RD
DONAHUE ST
GALVEZ AV
ENGLISH ST
MCCANN ST
ROBINSON ST
LOCKWOOD ST

INDIA BASIN

INDIA BASIN SHORELINE PARK (PROP)

POINT AVISADERO

HUNTERS POINT

2

3

DETAIL

SEE 15 MAP

SEE 17 MAP

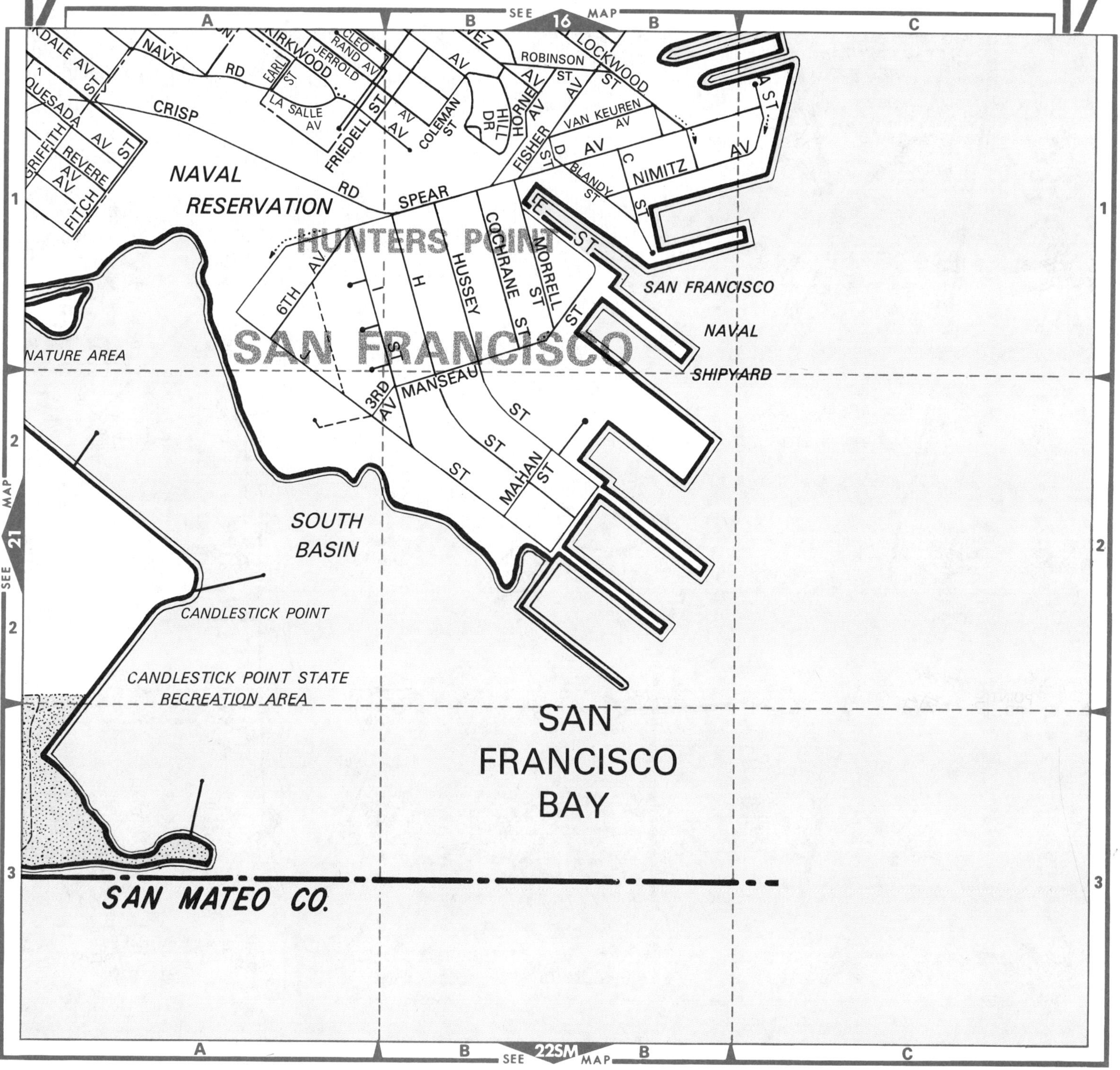

A B B C

NAVY RD
KIRKWOOD
CLEO RAND AV
JERROLD AV
EARL ST
LA SALLE AV
QUESADA AV
CRISP RD
GRIFFITH AV
REVERE AV
FITCH ST
FRIEDELL ST
COLEMAN ST
HILL DR
HORNE AV
ROBINSON ST
LOCKWOOD ST
FISHER AV
VAN KEUREN AV
D ST
C ST
BLANDY ST
NIMITZ AV
A ST
SPEAR AV
NAVAL RESERVATION
HUNTERS POINT
6TH AV
J ST
I ST
H ST
HUSSEY ST
COCHRANE ST
MORRELL ST
E ST
SAN FRANCISCO
SAN FRANCISCO NAVAL SHIPYARD
NATURE AREA
3RD AV
MANSEAU ST
MAHAN ST
SOUTH BASIN
CANDLESTICK POINT
CANDLESTICK POINT STATE RECREATION AREA
SAN FRANCISCO BAY
SAN MATEO CO.

1 2 3

SEE 21 MAP

DETAIL

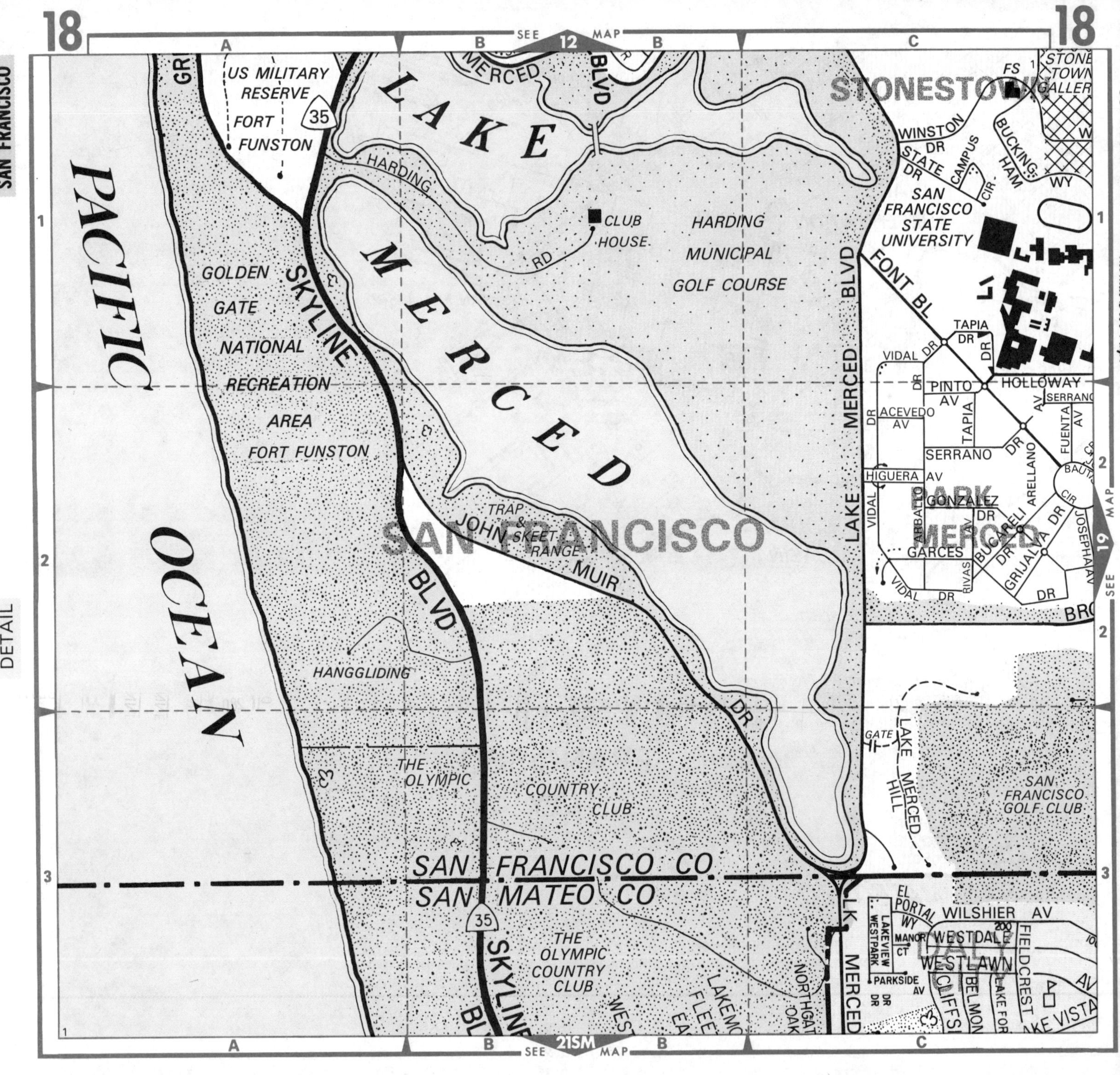
SEE 12 MAP
US MILITARY RESERVE
FORT FUNSTON
35
LAKE MERCED
MERCED
BLVD
HARDING
RD
CLUB HOUSE
HARDING MUNICIPAL GOLF COURSE
STONESTOWN
WINSTON DR
STATE DR
CAMPUS CIR
BUCKINGHAM WY
SAN FRANCISCO STATE UNIVERSITY
FONT BL
TAPIA DR
VIDAL DR
PINTO AV
HOLLOWAY
SERRANO
ACEVEDO AV
TAPIA
FUENTA
ARELLANO
HIGUERA AV
GONZALEZ DR
PARK MERCED
ARBALLO
BUCARELI DR
GRIJALVA DR
JOSEPHA AV
GARCES
RIVAS
PACIFIC OCEAN
GOLDEN GATE NATIONAL RECREATION AREA FORT FUNSTON
SKYLINE BLVD
SAN FRANCISCO
TRAP & SKEET RANGE
JOHN MUIR DR
LAKE MERCED BLVD
HANGGLIDING
GATE
LAKE MERCED HILL
SAN FRANCISCO GOLF CLUB
THE OLYMPIC COUNTRY CLUB
SAN FRANCISCO CO
SAN MATEO CO
EL PORTAL WY
WILSHIER AV
LAKEVIEW
WESTPARK
MANOR CT
WESTDALE
WESTLAWN
FIELDCREST
PARKSIDE AV
DALY CITY
CLIFFSIDE
BELMONT
LAKE FOREST
LAKE VISTA
NORTHGATE
OAK
LAKEMONT
FLEET
EAST
WEST
LK MERCED
DETAIL
SEE 19 MAP
SEE 21SM MAP

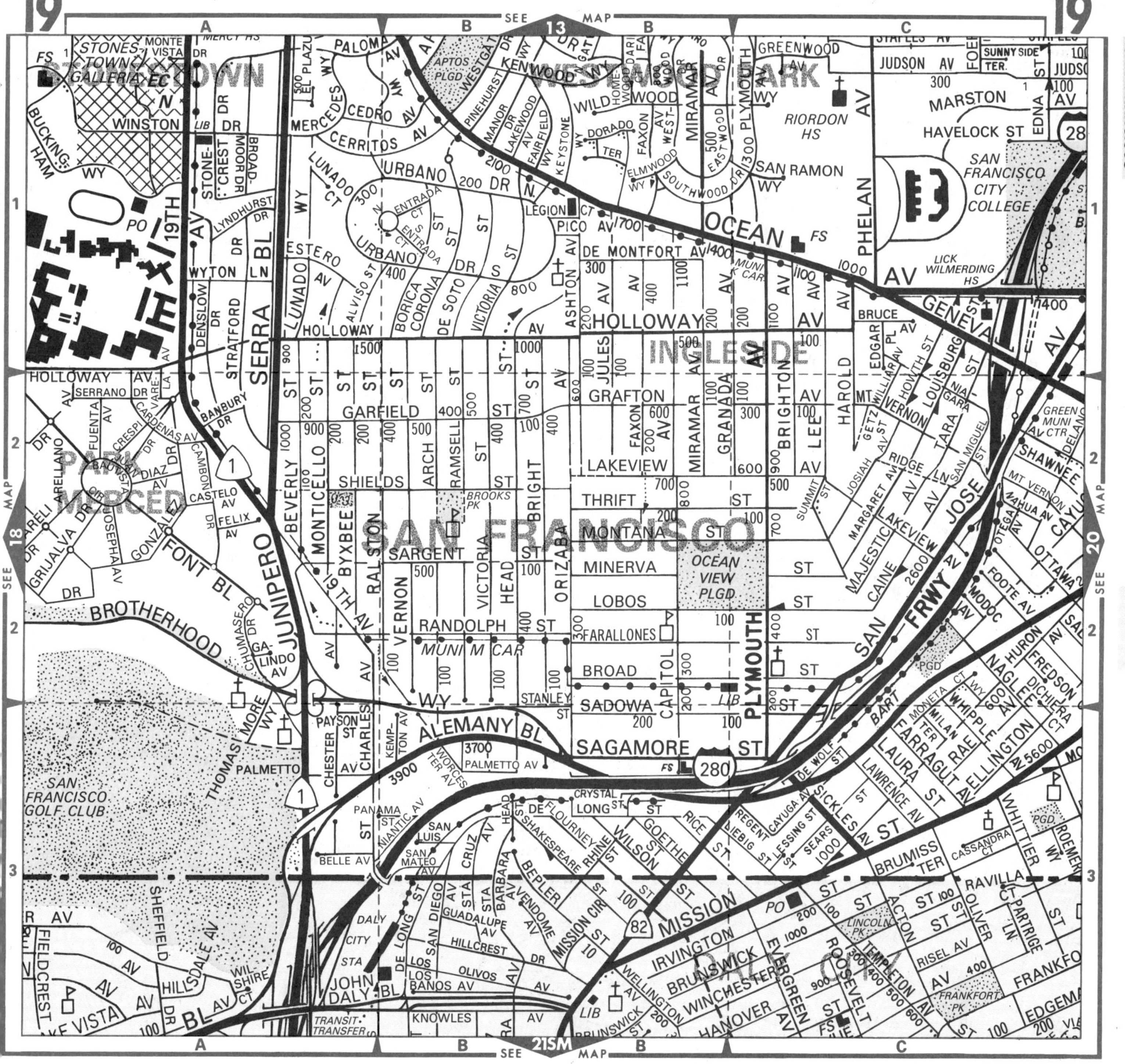

SAN FRANCISCO

DETAIL

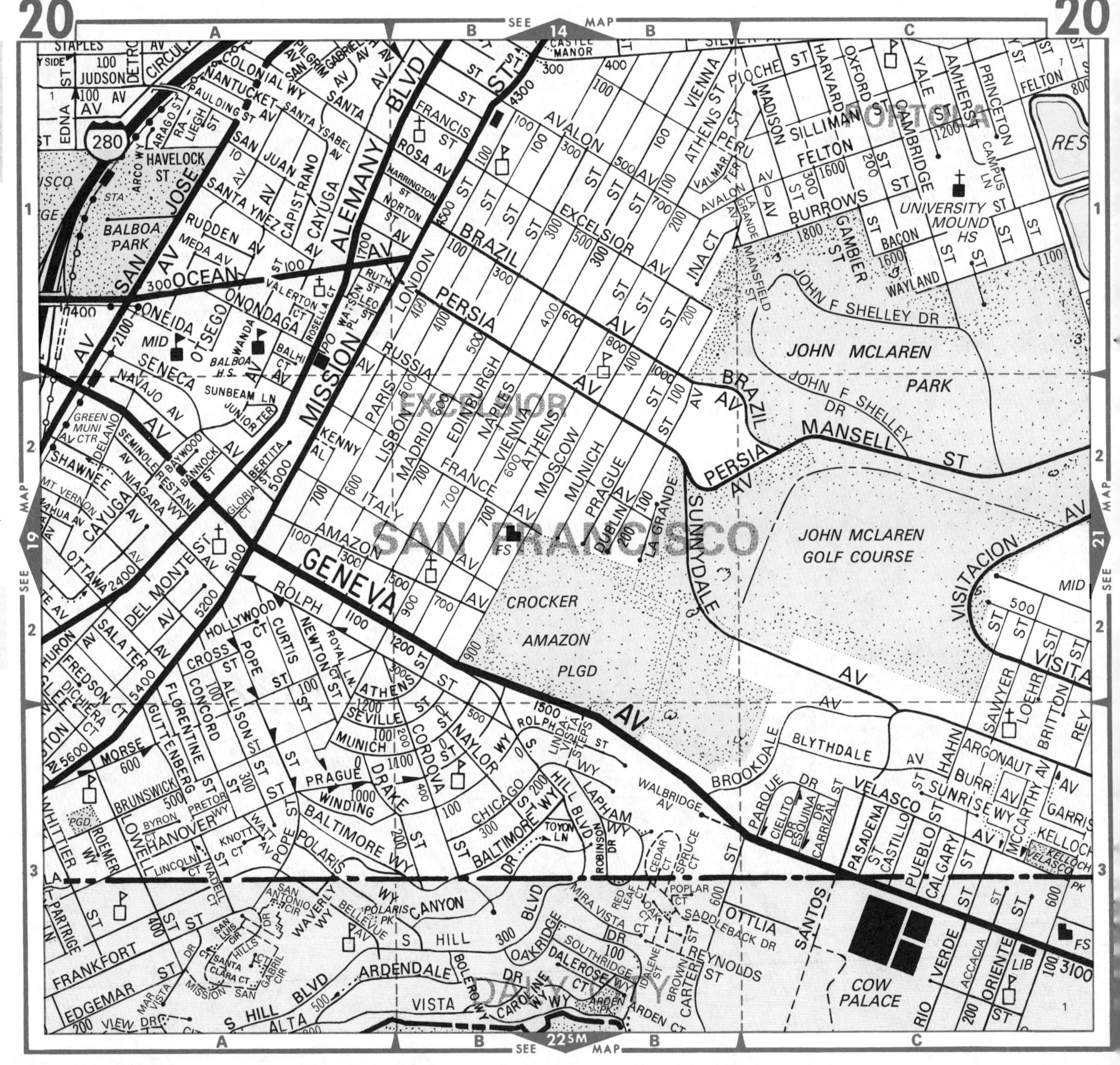
SEE 14 MAP
SEE 22SM MAP
SEE MAP 19 DETAIL
SEE MAP 21 DETAIL
A
B
C
1
2
3
SAN FRANCISCO
EXCELSIOR
PORTOLA
DALY CITY
JOHN MCLAREN PARK
JOHN MCLAREN GOLF COURSE
CROCKER AMAZON PLGD
BALBOA PARK
UNIVERSITY MOUND HS
BALBOA H.S.
COW PALACE
GREEN MUNI CTR
CASTLE MANOR
RES
FS
LIB
MID
PGD.
280
MISSION ST
ALEMANY BLVD
SAN JOSE AV
GENEVA AV
OCEAN AV
BRAZIL AV
PERSIA AV
EXCELSIOR AV
AVALON AV
RUSSIA AV
FRANCE AV
ITALY AV
AMAZON AV
SUNNYDALE AV
MANSELL ST
JOHN F SHELLEY DR
VISITACION AV
BURROWS ST
FELTON ST
SILLIMAN ST
CAMBRIDGE ST
ROLPH ST
NAYLOR ST
CORDOVA ST
DRAKE ST
PRAGUE ST
WINDING WY
BALTIMORE WY
POLARIS WY
HANOVER ST
BRUNSWICK ST
MORSE ST
LOWELL ST
WHITTIER ST
EDGEMAR AV
FRANKFORT ST
VISTA GRANDE AV
S HILL BLVD
CANYON DR
OAKRIDGE DR
SOUTHRIDGE DR
SADDLEBACK DR
REYNOLDS ST
SANTOS ST
VELASCO AV
BLYTHDALE AV
BROOKDALE AV
LAPHAM WY
HILL BLVD
ONONDAGA AV
ONEIDA AV
SENECA AV
OTTAWA AV
NIAGARA AV
CAYUGA AV
DEL MONTE ST
LONDON ST
PARIS ST
LISBON ST
MADRID ST
EDINBURGH ST
NAPLES ST
VIENNA ST
ATHENS ST
MOSCOW ST
MUNICH ST
PRAGUE ST
DUBLIN ST
LA GRANDE AV

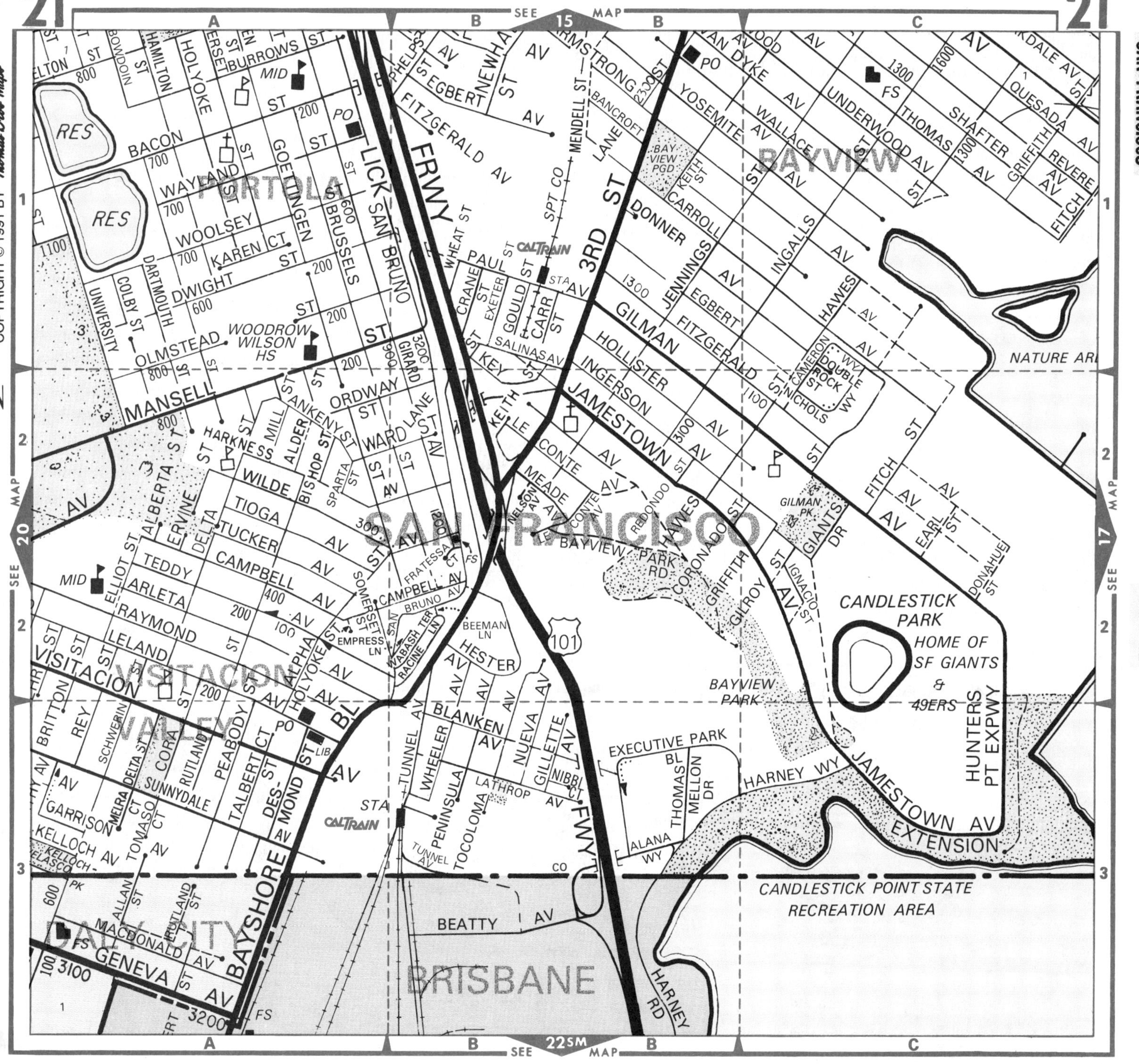
SEE 15 MAP
SEE 22SM MAP
SEE 20 MAP
SEE 17 MAP
DETAIL
A
B
C
1
2
3
PORTOLA
BAYVIEW
SAN FRANCISCO
VISITACION VALLEY
DALY CITY
BRISBANE
CANDLESTICK PARK
HOME OF SF GIANTS & 49ERS
CANDLESTICK POINT STATE RECREATION AREA
BAYVIEW PARK
EXECUTIVE PARK
NATURE AREA
GILMAN PK
BAY VIEW PGD
WOODROW WILSON HS
MID
PO
FS
LIB
STA
CALTRAIN
RES
SPT CO
BAYSHORE FRWY
101
BAYSHORE BL
3RD ST
SAN BRUNO AV
MANSELL ST
GENEVA AV
JAMESTOWN AV
JAMESTOWN AV EXTENSION
HUNTERS PT EXPWY
HARNEY WY
HARNEY RD
BEATTY AV
TUNNEL AV
BLANKEN AV
VISITACION AV
SUNNYDALE AV
LELAND AV
RAYMOND AV
ARLETA AV
TEDDY AV
CAMPBELL AV
TUCKER AV
TIOGA AV
WILDE AV
SILVER AV
BACON ST
WAYLAND ST
WOOLSEY ST
DWIGHT ST
OLMSTEAD ST
BURROWS ST
GOETTINGEN ST
BRUSSELS ST
UNIVERSITY ST
COLBY ST
DARTMOUTH ST
HAMILTON ST
HOLYOKE ST
BOWDOIN ST
GILMAN AV
HOLLISTER AV
INGERSON AV
FITZGERALD AV
EGBERT AV
DONNER AV
CARROLL AV
YOSEMITE AV
WALLACE AV
UNDERWOOD AV
THOMAS AV
SHAFTER AV
QUESADA AV
REVERE AV
VAN DYKE AV
INGALLS ST
JENNINGS ST
HAWES ST
FITCH ST
GIANTS DR
GILROY ST
GRIFFITH ST
CORONADO ST
REDONDO ST
BAYVIEW PARK RD
PAUL AV
SALINAS AV
KEY AV
LE CONTE AV
MEADE AV
HESTER AV
WHEELER AV
NUEVA AV
GILLETTE AV
PENINSULA AV
TOCOLOMA AV
LATHROP AV
THOMAS MELLON DR
ALANA WY
BRITTON ST
REY ST
SCHWERIN ST
DELTA ST
CORA ST
RUTLAND ST
PEABODY ST
TALBERT ST
DESMOND ST
GARRISON AV
KELLOCH AV
MACDONALD AV
ALLAN ST
ALPHA ST
ELLIOT ST
ALBERTA ST
ERVINE ST
HARKNESS AV
ORDWAY ST
WARD ST
ANKENY ST
ALDER ST
BISHOP ST
SPARTA ST
SOMERSET ST
GIRARD ST
CRANE ST
EXETER ST
GOULD ST
CARR ST
WHEAT ST
MENDELL ST
ARMSTRONG AV
BANCROFT AV
LANE ST
KEITH ST
PHELPS ST
NEWHALL ST
CAMERON WY
DOUBLE ROCK ST
NICHOLS WY
EARL ST
DONAHUE ST
IGNACIO ST
EMPRESS LN
WABASH TER
RACINE LN
BEEMAN LN
FRATESSA CT
KAREN CT
NIBBI CT
DE WOLF ST
MILL ST
LEBAN ST

22
SAN FRANCISCO
1991 SAN FRANCISCO
ZIP CODE
POSTAL
ZONES
FOR ZIP CODE INDEX REFER TO COUNTY
COMMUNITIES INDEX, PAGE 30
0 1000 2000
FEET
GOLDEN GATE
GOLDEN GATE BRIDGE
TOLL $2.00
SOUTH BOUND ONLY
FORT POINT
FORT POINT NATIONAL
HISTORIC SITE
GOLDEN GATE NATIONAL
RECREATION AREA
US COAST GUARD
STATION
PROMENADE
CRISSY FIELD
ST FRANCIS
YACHT CLUB
GOLDEN GATE
YACHT CLUB
MARINA
94123
FORT SCOTT
Presidio of San Francisco
SAN FRANCISCO
NATIONAL CEMETERY
94129
PRESIDIO
GOLF COURSE
BAKER
BEACH
GOLDEN GATE NATIONAL RECREATION AREA
LANDS END
CHINA BEACH
SEAL
ROCKS
BEACH
OBSERVATION
POINT
POINT
LOBOS
CLIFF
HOUSE
SUTRO
HEIGHTS
PARK
CALIFORNIA
PALACE OF THE
LEGION OF
HONOR
LINCOLN
PARK
WEST
FORT
MILEY
VETERANS
ADMIN
EAST
FORT
MILEY
US DEFENSE
LANGUAGE
INST
MOUNTAIN LAKE
PARK
94121
94118
94115
94117
94122
94143
94114
LONE
MOUNTAIN
CAMPUS
USF
UNIV
OF SF
GOLDEN GATE PARK
STADIUM
MUNICIPAL
GOLF
COURSE
BUFFALO
ENCLOSURE
CHAIN OF LAKES
SPRECKELS
LAKE
LLOYD
LAKE
FLY
CASTING
POOL
METSON
LAKE
ELK GLEN
LAKE
MALLARD LAKE
STOW LAKE
STRAWBERRY
HILL
ASIAN
ART
MUSEUM
DE YOUNG
MUS
CONSERVATORY
MORRISON
PLANETARIUM
CALIF
ACADEMY
OF SCIENCES
STRYBING
ARBORETUM
HALL OF
FLOWERS
KEZAR
STADIUM
SOCCER
FIELD
MURPHY
WINDMILL
DUTCH
WINDMILL
OCEAN BEACH
ESPLANADE
UC
MEDICAL
CENTER
BUENA VISTA
PARK
FULTON
LINCOLN
GEARY
CALIFORNIA
CLEMENT
BALBOA
CABRILLO
ANZA
JUDAH
IRVING
KIRKHAM
SUNSET
PRESIDIO BLVD
MASONIC
LOMBARD
ZIP

SAN FRANCISCO BAY
SAN FRANCISCO MARITIME NATIONAL HISTORICAL PARK
MUNICIPAL PIER
AQUATIC PARK
FISHERMAN'S WHARF
ALCATRAZ FERRY
ANGEL ISLAND FERRY
VALLEJO
SAUSALITO-LARKSPUR FERRY
FORT MASON
GHIRARDELLI
THE EMBARCADERO
GOLDEN GATEWAY CENTER
BART TRANSBAY TUBE
EMBARCADERO CENTER
1 ONE EMBARCADERO CTR
2 TWO EMBARCADERO CTR
3 THREE EMBARCADERO CTR
4 FOUR EMBARCADERO CTR
5 HYATT REGENCY
SAN FRANCISCO-OAKLAND BAY BRIDGE
(TWO LEVEL FRWY)
(TOLL $1.00 WESTBOUND ONLY)
RINCON POINT
SAN FRANCISCO BAY
CHINA BASIN
MISSION ROCK TERMINAL
HOVER PORT
CENTRAL BASIN
RR YARDS
MOSCONE CONVENTION CENTER
CIVIC CNTR
CITY HALL
LAFAYETTE PK
JAPAN CENTER
94123
94133
94147 P.O. BOXES
94111
94104
94108
94109
94105
94102
94103
94107
94141 P.O. BOXES
94110
INSET OF TREASURE ISLAND NAVAL RESERVATION
94130
1 KEPPLER CT
2 HUTCHINS CT
3 HALYBURTON CT
YERBA BUENA ISLAND
SCALE OF INSET
1 INCH TO 2200 FT.
FEET
METERS
SEE SAN FRANCISCO ATLAS PAGE 3 GRID C2

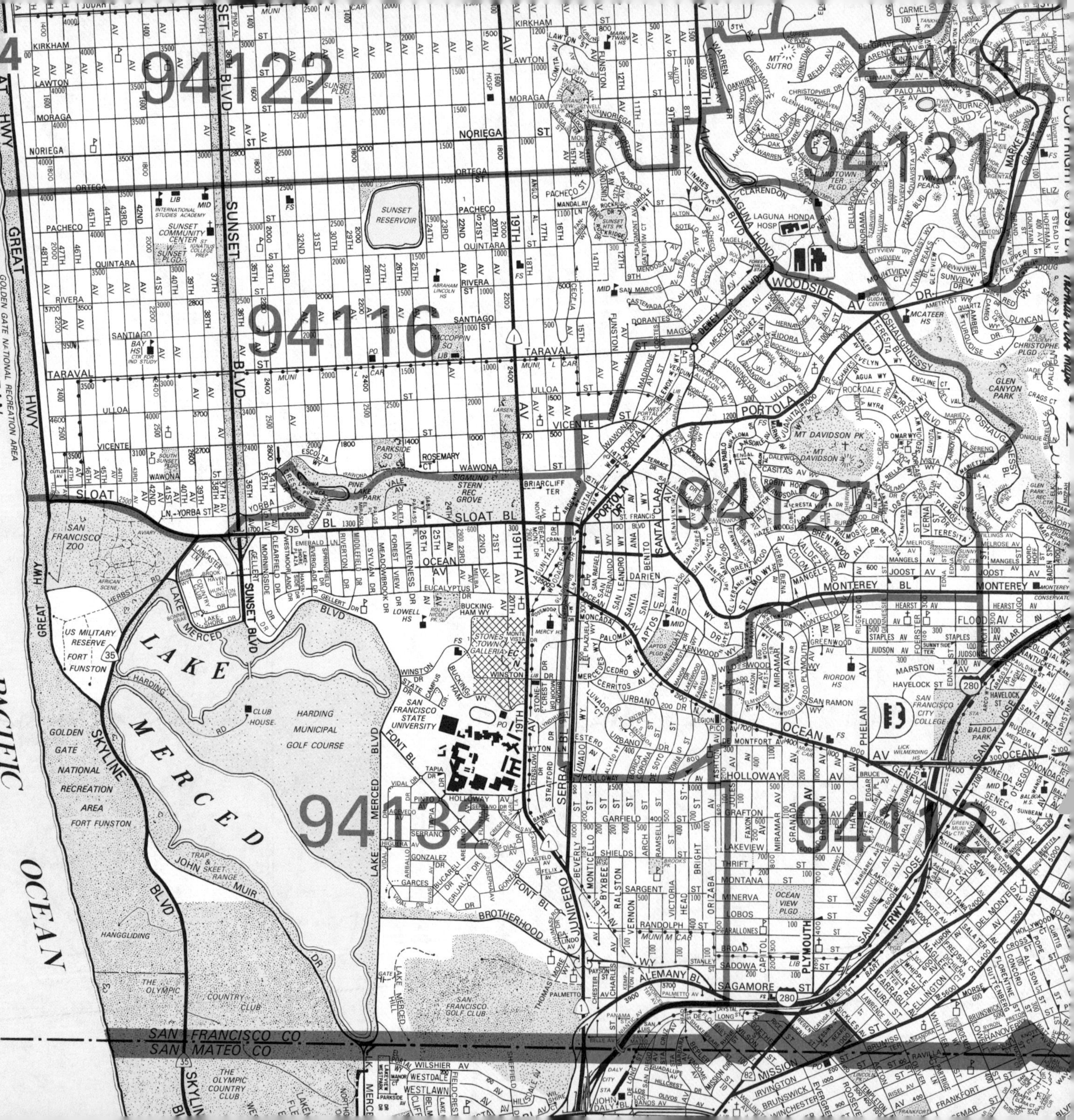
94122
94116
94132
94127
94131
94112
94114
PACIFIC OCEAN
GOLDEN GATE NATIONAL RECREATION AREA
GREAT HWY
SUNSET BLVD
19TH AV
SLOAT BL
OCEAN AV
SUNSET RESERVOIR
SAN FRANCISCO ZOO
LAKE MERCED
HARDING MUNICIPAL GOLF COURSE
SAN FRANCISCO STATE UNIVERSITY
STONESTOWN GALLERIA
US MILITARY RESERVE
FORT FUNSTON
GOLDEN GATE NATIONAL RECREATION AREA FORT FUNSTON
HANGGLIDING
THE OLYMPIC COUNTRY CLUB
SAN FRANCISCO GOLF CLUB
SKYLINE BLVD
JOHN MUIR DR
LAKE MERCED BLVD
JUNIPERO SERRA BL
PORTOLA DR
MONTEREY BL
ALEMANY BL
SAN JOSE AV
MISSION ST
GENEVA AV
MT DAVIDSON
MT DAVIDSON PK
MT SUTRO
TWIN PEAKS
LAGUNA HONDA HOSP
GLEN CANYON PARK
SAN FRANCISCO CITY COLLEGE
BALBOA PARK
RIORDON HS
LOWELL HS
MERCY HS
ABRAHAM LINCOLN HS
MCCOPPIN SQ
PARKSIDE SQ
SIGMUND STERN REC GROVE
PINE LAKE PARK
OCEAN VIEW PLGD
TARAVAL
NORIEGA
ORTEGA
KIRKHAM
LAWTON
MORAGA
PACHECO
QUINTARA
RIVERA
SANTIAGO
ULLOA
VICENTE
WAWONA
WOODSIDE AV
SAN FRANCISCO CO
SAN MATEO CO

ZIP

94110
94107
94124
94131
94112
94134
SAN FRANCISCO BAY
SAN FRANCISCO BAY
INDIA BASIN
INDIA BASIN SHORELINE PARK (PROP)
ISLAIS CREEK CHANNEL
ARMY STREET TERMINAL
BETHLEHEM SHIPYARDS
POTRERO POINT
POINT AVISADERO
NAVAL RESERVATION
SAN FRANCISCO NAVAL SHIPYARD
NATURE AREA
SOUTH BASIN
CANDLESTICK POINT
CANDLESTICK POINT STATE RECREATION AREA
CANDLESTICK PARK HOME OF SF GIANTS & 49ERS
BAYVIEW PARK
JOHN MCLAREN PARK
JOHN MCLAREN GOLF COURSE
CROCKER AMAZON PLGD
COW PALACE
SAN MATEO CO.
SF GENERAL HOSP
JAMES LICK FRWY
BAYSHORE BLVD
SOUTHERN EMBARCADERO FRWY
HUNTERS PT EXPWY
JAMESTOWN AV EXTENSION
ARMY ST
3RD ST
MISSION ST
DOLORES ST
GUERRERO ST
GENEVA AV
SILVER AV
EVANS AV
ZIP

26
SAN FRANCISCO
ZIP
MUNICIPAL PIER
SAN FRANCISCO MARITIME NATIONAL HISTORICAL PARK
45
43
35
PIER 39
BALCLUTHA SHIP
AQUATIC PARK
NATIONAL MARITIME MUSEUM BUILDING
THE EMBARCADERO ST
FISHERMAN'S WHARF
JEFFERSON ST
THE CANNERY
THE ANCORAGE
BEACH ST
FORT MASON
POPE RD
SCHOFIELD RD
MACARTHUR AV
GHIRARDELLI SQUARE
NORTH POINT ST
BERGEN PL
BAY ST
RES
NORTHVIEW CT
FRANCISCO ST
CHESTNUT ST
LOMBARD ST
GREENWICH ST
FILBERT ST
UNION ST
GREEN ST
VALLEJO ST
BROADWAY
PACIFIC
JACKSON ST
GOUGH ST
OCTAVIA ST
FRANKLIN ST
VAN NESS
POLK ST
LARKIN ST
HYDE ST
LEAVENWORTH ST
JONES ST
TAYLOR ST
MASON ST
POWELL ST
STOCKTON ST
GRANT AV
KEARNY ST
COLUMBUS AV
101
BLACKSTONE CT
GRENARD TER
CULEBRA TER
IMPERIAL AV
OCTAGON HOUSE
BONITA ST
ROCKLAND ST
MONTCLAIR TER
SOUTHARD PL
BRET HARTE TER
LURMONT TER
HOUSTON ST
WATER ST
VANDEWATER ST
VALPARAISO ST
ROACH ST
JANSEN ST
NEWELL ST
VENARD ST
SCOTLAND ST
ALADDIN TER
KENT ST
ATTRIDGE AL
BLACK PL
SHARP PL
HAVENS ST
HASTINGS TER
ALLEN ST
MOORE PL
EASTMAN ST
RUSSELL ST
WARNER PL
DELGADO PL
HAMLIN ST
MACONDRAY LN
MARION PL
REDFIELD AL
RUSSIAN HILL PL
FLORENCE ST
ALTA VISTA TER
WEBB PL
WINTER PL
AUGUST AL
VIA BUFANO
EATON PL
WASHOE PL
VALLEJO TER
FALLON PL
GLOVER ST
WALDO AL
CYRUS PL
CHARING CROSS
TUNNEL
BERNARD ST
WHITE ST
MORRELL ST
MCCORMICK ST
LYNCH ST
WALL PL
BURGOYNE ST
PHOENIX TER
HIMMELMAN PL
SALMON ST
AUBURN ST
MARCY PL
CABLE CAR BARN
REED
PREST
TAYL
SPROUL
TRUETT ST
59
60
LIB
WORDEN ST
MIDWAY ST
PFEIFFER ST
BELLAIR PL
JULIUS ST
WHITING ST
LA FERRERA TER
WINTHROP ST
FIELDING ST
TUSCANY AL
EDGARDO PL
KRAMER PL
CHILD ST
TELEGRAPH PL
TELEGRAPH
EDITH ST
GERKE AL
PARDEE AL
BRYANT AL
KRAUSGRILL PL
MEDAU PL
JASPER PL
BOB KAUFMAN AL
GENOA PL
NOBLES AL
WASHINGTON SQ
PO
CADELL PL
BANNAM PL
VARENNES ST
SONOMA ST
POLLARD PL
SAN ANTONIO PL
ROMOLO PL
MARGRAVE PL
PRICE ROW
CLUB FUGAZI
CARD AL
NORTH BEACH MUSEUM
CHURCHILL ST
EMERY LN
CORDELIA ST
KENNETH REXROTH PL
KEROUAC AL
BROAD
FISHER AL
STARK ST
WAYNE PL
KEYES
JOHN ST
ADELE CT
TRENTON ST
BEDFORD PL
DUMCOMBE AL
PELTON PL
JASON CT
ROSS AL
ST LOUIS AL
BECKETT ST
WENTWORTH PL
COOPER AL
CHINATOWN
OLD CHINATOWN LN
SPOFFORD LN
WAVERLY PL
WALTER LUM PL
DORIC AL
WETMORE
CODMAN PL
STONE ST
PARKHURST AL
SHEPHARD PL
JOICE
STOCK
GRANT
COM

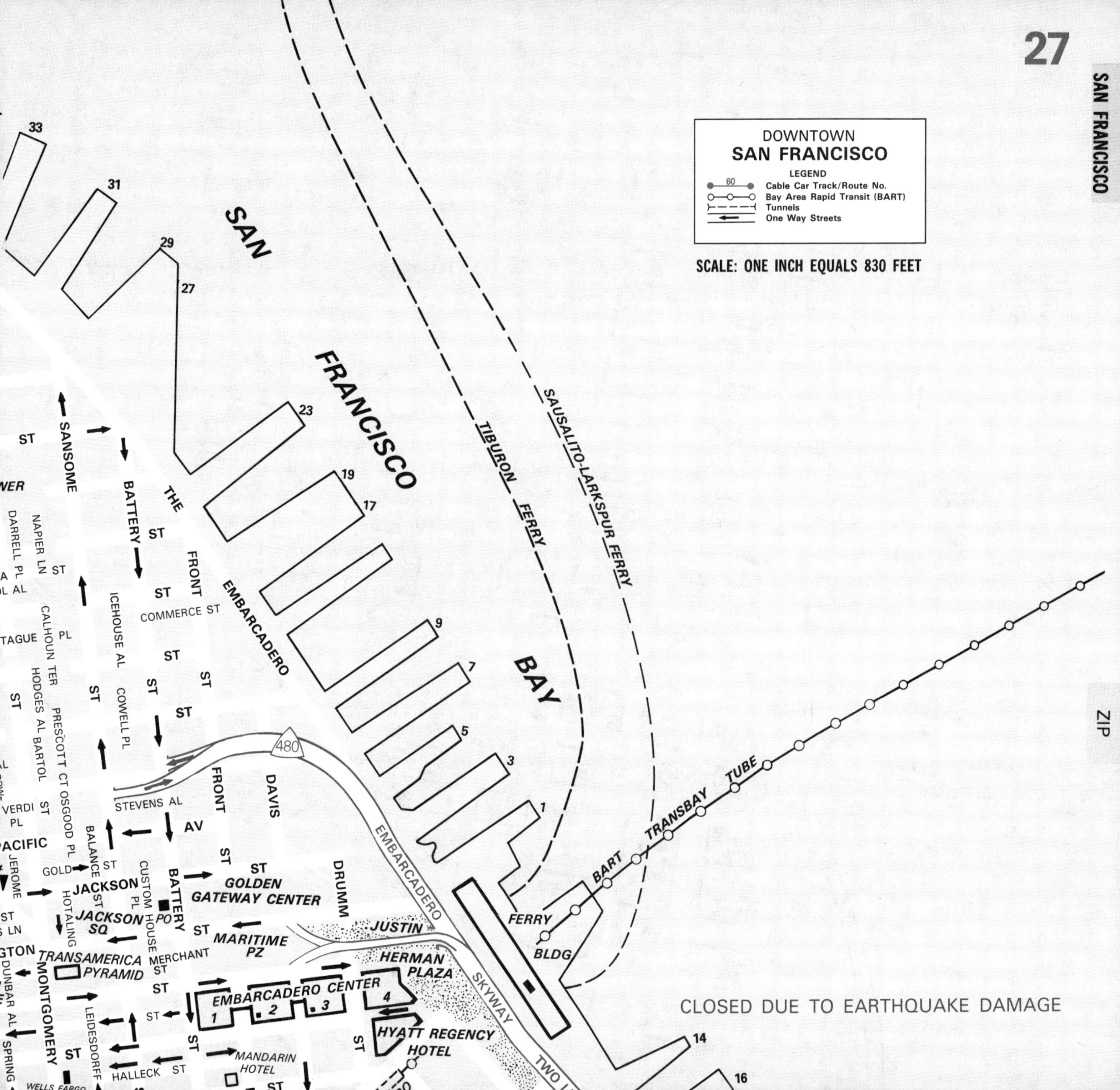
DOWNTOWN
SAN FRANCISCO
LEGEND
60
Cable Car Track/Route No.
Bay Area Rapid Transit (BART)
Tunnels
One Way Streets
SCALE: ONE INCH EQUALS 830 FEET
SAN FRANCISCO BAY
TIBURON FERRY
SAUSALITO-LARKSPUR FERRY
BART TRANSBAY TUBE
CLOSED DUE TO EARTHQUAKE DAMAGE
ZIP
33
31
29
27
23
19
17
9
7
5
3
1
14
16
THE EMBARCADERO
EMBARCADERO SKYWAY
TWO
480
FERRY BLDG
SANSOME ST
BATTERY ST
FRONT ST
COMMERCE ST
ICEHOUSE AL
NAPIER LN
DARRELL PL
CALHOUN TER
HODGES AL
PRESCOTT CT
BARTOL ST
OSGOOD PL
COWELL PL
STEVENS AL
DAVIS ST
DRUMM ST
VERDI PL
PACIFIC AV
BALANCE ST
GOLD ST
JEROME AL
JACKSON ST
HOTALING ST
CUSTOM HOUSE PL
PO
JACKSON SQ
GOLDEN GATEWAY CENTER
MARITIME PZ
JUSTIN HERMAN PLAZA
TRANSAMERICA PYRAMID
MERCHANT ST
MONTGOMERY ST
DUNBAR AL
LEIDESDORFF ST
EMBARCADERO CENTER
1
2
3
4
HYATT REGENCY HOTEL
MANDARIN HOTEL
HALLECK ST
SPRING
WELLS FARGO

HASS-LILIENTHAL HOUSE
WASHINGTON
CLAY
SACRAMENTO
CALIFORNIA
61
LAFAYETTE PARK
PINE
NORRIS
EUREKA PL
BUSH
SUTTER
FRANK
FERN
HEMLOCK
DANIEL BURHAM CT
POST
CEDAR
PETER YORKE WY
CATHEDRAL HILL HOTEL
GEARY
ST MARYS CATHEDRAL
STARR
KING WY
MYRTLE
O'FARRELL
OLIVE
ELLIS
CLEARY CT
WILLOW
EDDY
WILLOW ST
LARCH
TURK
ELM
JEFFERSON SQUARE
HAYWARD PLGD
GOLDEN GATE
REDWOOD ST
MCALLISTER
ASH ST
FULTON
BIRCH ST
GROVE
HAYES
FELL
LINDEN ST
LECH WALESA
CENTRAL FRWY
101
OCTAVIA
GOUGH
FRANKLIN
VAN NESS
LARKIN
POLK
HYDE
LEAVENWORTH
LAGUNA
MEACHAM PL
ADA CT
HARLEM
AMITY AL
MABEL AL
COHEN PL
DODGE PL
BREEN PL
DALE PL
WAGNER AL
KIMBALL PL
GOLDEN CT
LEROY PL
LYSETTE ST
HELEN ST
ACORN AL
TROY AL
PANTON AL
TOUCHARD ST
JONES
GRACE CATHEDRAL
PLEASANT ST
MALVINA PL
EWER PL
CUSHMAN ST
MASON
FAIRMONT HOTEL
MARK HOPKINS
STANFORD COURT
NOB HILL CIR
VINE TER
FRANK ST
MULFORD AL
HOOKER AL
FELLA PL
POWELL
MILLER PL
PRATT PL
D HAMMETT ST
CHELSEA PL
BURRITT ST
TUNNEL
BROOKLYN PL
SABIN PL
VINTON CT
CHATHAM PL
EMMA ST
HARLAN
ANSON PL
DELTA PL
HOLIDAY INN
HYATT HOTEL
CAMPTON
GUMPS
SIR FRANCIS DRAKE HOTEL
SAKS
FRANK LLOYD WRIGHT BLDG
MAIDEN
UNION SQUARE
PORTMAN HOTEL
HOBART AL
COSMO
OPHIR AL
AGATE AL
DUNCAN LN
ST FRANCIS HOTEL
COLIN PL
DERBY
CURRAN THTR
GEARY THTR
ELWOOD ST
CLIFT HOTEL
HOTEL NIKKO
HILTON HOTEL
SHANNON ST
STEVELOE PL
ANTONIO ST
C MAGNIN ST
60
PO
VISITOR INFO CENTER
PARC FIFTY FIVE
HALLIDIE PLAZA
AIRLINES BUS TERMINAL
POWELL ST STATION
PIONEER
EC
OPAL PL
GOLDEN GATE THTR
AV
OLD MINT
MINT ST
MARY
BART & MUNI METRO
FEDERAL BLDG
STATE BLDG
REDWOOD ST
FED BLDG
MAIN LIB
JAMES ROLPH JR CIVIC CENTER
HERBST THTR
ART MUSEUM
CITY HALL
WAR MEMORIAL OPERA HOUSE
BROOKS HALL
CIVIC AUDITORIUM
DAVIES SYMPHONY HALL
ORPHEUM THTR
CIVIC CENTER STATION
STEVENSON
GREYHOUND BUS TERMINAL
MAIN POST OFFICE
JESSIE
MARKET
6TH
7TH
8TH
9TH
5TH
HOWARD
TEHAMA
CLEMENTINA
TULIP AL
RUSS
MINNA
NATOMA
MOSS ST
S OF MKT PK
HARRIET
JULIA ST
LASKE ST
LANGTON ST
RAUSCH ST
SUMNER ST
DECKER AL
CLEVELAND ST
SHERMAN ST
COLUMBIA
ZIP

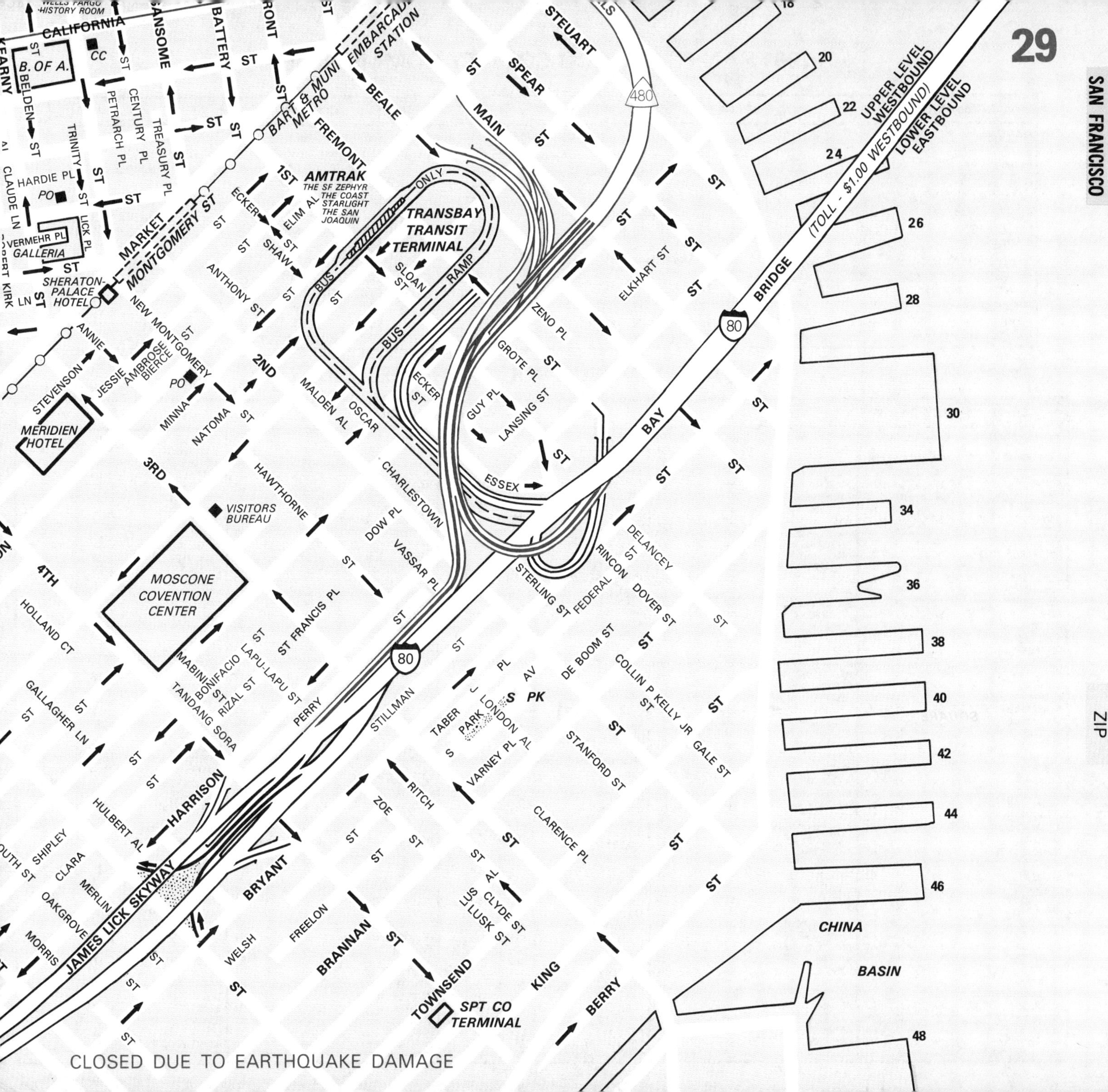
WELLS FARGO HISTORY ROOM
CALIFORNIA
KEARNY
B. OF A.
CC
BELDEN
SANSOME
BATTERY
FRONT
ST
EMBARCADERO STATION
BART & MUNI METRO
STEUART
SPEAR
MAIN
BEALE
FREMONT
480
CENTURY PL
PETRARCH PL
TREASURY PL
TRINITY
HARDIE PL
PO
CLAUDE LN
LICK PL
VERMEHR PL
GALLERIA
MARKET
MONTGOMERY ST
SHERATON-PALACE HOTEL
KIRK LN
1ST
ECKER
ELIM AL
AMTRAK
THE SF ZEPHYR
THE COAST STARLIGHT
THE SAN JOAQUIN
TRANSBAY TRANSIT TERMINAL
ONLY
BUS
RAMP
SHAW
SLOAN ST
ANTHONY ST
NEW MONTGOMERY ST
ANNIE
JESSIE
AMBROSE BIERCE
STEVENSON
MERIDIEN HOTEL
MINNA
NATOMA
2ND
MALDEN AL
OSCAR
ECKER ST
ZENO PL
GROTE PL
GUY PL
LANSING ST
ELKHART ST
ESSEX
BRIDGE
BAY
80
UPPER LEVEL WESTBOUND
LOWER LEVEL EASTBOUND
(TOLL - $1.00 WESTBOUND)
18
20
22
24
26
28
30
34
36
38
40
42
44
46
48
3RD
VISITORS BUREAU
HAWTHORNE
CHARLESTOWN
DOW PL
VASSAR PL
4TH
MOSCONE COVENTION CENTER
HOLLAND CT
ST FRANCIS PL
DELANCEY
RINCON
STERLING ST
FEDERAL
DOVER ST
DE BOOM ST
COLLIN P KELLY JR
GALE ST
MABINI ST
BONIFACIO
LAPU-LAPU ST
RIZAL ST
TANDANG SORA
PERRY
STILLMAN
TABER
PARK
J LONDON AL
S PK
AV
PL
VARNEY PL
STANFORD ST
GALLAGHER LN
HARRISON
HULBERT AL
RITCH
ZOE
CLARENCE PL
SHIPLEY
CLARA
MERLIN
OAKGROVE
MORRIS
JAMES LICK SKYWAY
BRYANT
FREELON
WELSH
BRANNAN
LUS
CLYDE ST
LUSK ST
TOWNSEND
SPT CO TERMINAL
KING
BERRY
CHINA BASIN
CLOSED DUE TO EARTHQUAKE DAMAGE
ZIP

1991 SAN FRANCISCO COUNTY COMMUNITIES

ESTIMATED POPULATION 727,000 AREA IN SQUARE MILES 44.75

COMMUNITY NAME	ZIP CODE	PAGE	COMMUNITY NAME	ZIP CODE	PAGE	COMMUNITY NAME	ZIP CODE	PAGE
BAYVIEW	94124	21	MARINA	94123	1	RUSSIAN HILL	94133	2
BERNAL HEIGHTS	94110	14	MIRALOMA PARK	94127	13	ST FRANCIS WOOD	94127	13
CHINATOWN	94108	3	MISSION DISTRICT	94110	11	SAN FRANCISCO	94101	3
COW HOLLOW	94123	2	NOB HILL	94108	7	-SAN FRANCISCO COUNTY		
DIAMOND HEIGHTS	94131	14	NOE VALLEY	94114	14	SEACLIFF	94121	4
EUREKA VALLEY	94114	10	NORTH BEACH	94133	3	SOUTH OF MARKET	94103	7
EXCELSIOR	94112	20	PACIFIC HEIGHTS	94115	6	STONESTOWN	94132	19
FOREST HILL	94116	13	PARK MERCED	94132	19	SUNSET	94122	8
GLEN PARK	94131	14	PARKSIDE	94116	12	TELEGRAPH HILL	94133	3
HAIGHT-ASHBURY	94117	9	PORTOLA	94134	20	VISITACION VALLEY	94134	21
HUNTER'S POINT	94124	17	POTRERO HILL	94107	11	WESTERN ADDITION	94115	6
INGLESIDE	94112	19	PRESIDIO HEIGHTS	94118	5	WEST OF TWIN PEAKS	94122	9
LAKESIDE	94132	12	PRESDIO OF SN FRANCSCO	94129	5	WEST PORTAL	94127	13
LAUREL HEIGHTS	94118	5	RICHMOND	94121	8	WESTWOOD PARK	94127	13

1991 SAN FRANCISCO COUNTY STREET INDEX

STREET	CITY	PAGE	GRID
A			
A ST	SF	17	C1
A ST	SF	10	B2
A ST	SF	14	A3
A ST	SF	20	C3
A ST	SF	18	C2
A ST	SF	10	A3
ACADIA ST	SF	14	A3
ACORN AL	SF	6	C1
ACTNO ST	SF	19	C3
ADA CT	SF	6	C2
ADAIR ST	SF	10	C2
ADDISON ST	SF	14	B2
ADELE CT	SF	3	A3
ADMIRAL AV	SF	14	B3
ADOLPH SUTRO CT	SF	9	C3
AERIAL WY	SF	9	A3
AGATE AL	SF	7	A2
AGNON AV	SF	14	C3
AGUA WY	SF	13	C2
AHERN WY	SF	7	B3
ALABAMA ST	SF	11	A1
ALABAMA ST	SF	15	A1
ALADDIN TER	SF	3	A2
ALAMEDA ST	SF	11	A1
ALANA WY	SF	21	B3
ALBERTA ST	SF	21	A2
ALBION ST	SF	10	C2
ALDER ST	SF	21	A2
ALEMANY BLVD	SF	14	C3
ALEMANY BLVD	SF	19	B3
ALEMANY BLVD	SF	20	A1
ALERT AL	SF	10	B2
ALHAMBRA ST	SF	2	A2
ALLAN ST	SF	21	A3
ALLEN ST	SF	2	C3
ALLISON ST	SF	20	A2
ALLSTON WY	SF	13	B2
ALMA ST	SF	9	C2
ALMADEN CT	SF	5	B3
ALOHA AV	SF	9	A3
ALPHA ST	SF	21	A2
ALPINE TER	SF	10	A1
ALTA ST	SF	3	A2
ALTA MAR WY	SF	4	A3
ALTA VISTA TER	SF	2	C3
ALTON AV	SF	13	B1
ALVARADO ST	SF	10	A3
ALVISO ST	SF	19	A1
AMATISTA LN	SF	14	B2
AMATURY LOOP	SF	1	B3

STREET	CITY	PAGE	GRID
AMAZON AV	SF	20	A2
AMBER DR	SF	14	A1
AMBROSE BRCE ST	SF	7	B2
AMES ST	SF	10	C3
AMETHYST WY	SF	13	C1
AMHERST ST	SF	20	C1
AMITY AL	SF	6	C2
ANDERSON ST	SF	14	C2
ANDOVER ST	SF	14	C3
ANGLO AL	SF	13	A1
ANKENY ST	SF	21	A2
ANNAPOLIS TER	SF	5	C3
ANNIE ST	SF	7	B2
ANSON PL	SF	7	A2
ANTHONY ST	SF	7	B2
ANTONIO ST	SF	6	C2
ANZA ST	SF	1	B2
ANZA ST	SF	4	A3
ANZA ST	SF	5	C3
ANZAVISTA AV	SF	6	A3
APOLLO ST	SF	15	B3
APPAREL WY	SF	15	A2
APPLETON AV	SF	14	C2
APPLETON ST	SF	1	A2
APTOS AV	SF	13	B3
AQUAVISTA WY	SF	9	C3
ARAGO ST	SF	20	A1
ARBALLO DR	SF	18	C2
ARBOL LN	SF	6	A3
ARBOR ST	SF	14	A2
ARCH ST	SF	19	B1
ARCO WY	SF	20	A1
ARDATH CT	SF	15	C3
ARDENWOOD WY	SF	13	A3
ARELLANO AV	SF	19	A2
ARGENT AL	SF	10	A3
ARGONAUT AV	SF	20	C3
ARGUELLO BLVD	SF	5	B1
ARGUELLO BLVD	SF	9	B2
ARKANSAS ST	SF	11	B2
ARLETA AV	SF	21	A2
ARLINGTON ST	SF	14	B3
ARMISTEAD RD	SF	1	A2
ARMSTRONG AV	SF	21	B1
ARMY ST	SF	14	A1
ARMY ST	SF	15	A1
ARNOLD AV	SF	14	C3
ARROYO WY	SF	13	C2
ARTHUR AV	SF	15	C1
ASH ST	SF	6	C3
ASHBURTON PL	SF	7	A2
ASHBURY ST	SF	9	C1
ASHBURY TER	SF	10	A2

STREET	CITY	PAGE	GRID
ASHTON AV	SF	19	B1
ASHWOOD LN	SF	9	C3
ATALAYA TER	SF	5	C3
ATHENS ST	SF	20	B2
ATTRIDGE AL	SF	2	C2
AUBURN ST	SF	3	A3
AUGUST AL	SF	3	A2
AUGUSTA ST	SF	15	A3
AUTO DR	SF	9	B3
AVALON AV	SF	20	B1
AVENUE B	SF	3	C2
AVENUE C	SF	3	C1
AVENUE D	SF	3	C1
AVENUE E	SF	3	C1
AVENUE F	SF	3	C1
AVENUE H	SF	3	C1
AVENUE I	SF	3	C1
AVENUE M	SF	3	C1
AVENUE N	SF	3	C1
AVENUE NORTH	SF	4	C2
AV OF THE PALMS	SF	3	C1
AVERY ST	SF	6	B2
AVILA ST	SF	2	A2
AVOCA AL	SF	13	C2
AVON WY	SF	13	A3
AZTEC ST	SF	14	C1
B			
BACHE ST	SF	14	C3
BACON ST	SF	20	C1
BACON ST	SF	21	A1
BADEN ST	SF	14	A3
BADGER ST	SF	14	B3
BAKER CT	SF	4	C2
BAKER ST	SF	2	A2
BAKER ST	SF	6	A2
BAKER ST	SF	10	A1
BALANCE ST	SF	3	A3
BALBOA ST	SF	4	B3
BALBOA ST	SF	5	A3
BALCETA AV	SF	13	B1
BALDWIN CT	SF	15	C3
BALHI CT	SF	20	A1
BALMY ST	SF	11	A3
BALTIMORE WY	SF	20	B3
BANBURY DR	SF	19	A2
BANCROFT AV	SF	15	B3
BANCROFT AV	SF	21	B1
BANK ST	SF	1	B2
BANKS ST	SF	15	A2
BANNAM PL	SF	3	A2
BANNOCK ST	SF	20	A2
BARCELONA AV	SF	6	A3

STREET	CITY	PAGE	GRID
BARNARD AV	SF	1	C3
BARNEVELD AV	SF	15	A2
BARTLETT ST	SF	10	C3
BARTLETT ST	SF	14	C1
BARTOL ST	SF	3	A2
BASS CT	SF	15	C3
BATTERY ST	SF	3	B2
BATTERY CMBR RD	SF	4	C1
BATTERY EAST RD	SF	1	A1
BAXTER AL	SF	13	B3
BAY ST	SF	2	B2
BAY ST	SF	3	A2
BAYSHORE BLVD	SF	15	A2
BAYSHORE BLVD	SF	21	A3
BAYSIDE DR	SF	3	C1
BAYVIEW CIR	SF	15	B3
BAYVIEW ST	SF	15	B3
BAYWIEW PARK RD	SF	21	B2
BAYWOOD CT	SF	20	A2
BEACH ST	SF	2	A2
BEACH ST	SF	3	A2
BEACHMONT DR	SF	13	A3
BEACON ST	SF	14	B2
BEALE ST	SF	7	B1
BEATRICE LN	SF	15	C3
BEAUMONT AV	SF	5	C3
BEAVER ST	SF	10	A2
BECKETT ST	SF	3	A3
BEDFORD PL	SF	3	A3
BEEMAN LN	SF	21	B2
BEHR AV	SF	9	C3
BEIDEMAN ST	SF	6	A3
BELCHER ST	SF	10	B1
BELDEN ST	SF	7	A1
BELGRAVE AV	SF	9	C2
BELL CT	SF	15	C3
BELL RD	SF	1	A2
BELLAIR PL	SF	3	A2
BELLAVISTA LN	SF	13	C3
BELLA VISTA WY	SF	13	C2
BELLE AV	SF	19	A3
BELLEVUE AV	SF	20	A3
BELMONT AV	SF	9	C2
BELVEDERE ST	SF	9	C1
BEMIS ST	SF	14	B2
BENDIXSEN SQ	SF	1	B1
BENGAL AL	SF	13	B2
BENNINGTON ST	SF	14	C2
BENTON AV	SF	14	B3
BEPLER ST	SF	19	B3
BERGEN PL	SF	2	C2
BERKELEY WY	SF	14	A2
BERKSHIRE WY	SF	12	B3

STREET	CITY	PAGE	GRID
BERNAL HTS BLVD	SF	14	C2
BERNARD ST	SF	2	C3
BERNICE ST	SF	11	A1
BERRY ST	SF	7	C3
BERRY ST	SF	11	B1
BERTHA LN	SF	15	C3
BERTIE MINOR LN	SF	1	B1
BERTITA ST	SF	20	A2
BERWICK PL	SF	11	A1
BESSIE ST	SF	14	C1
BEULAH ST	SF	9	C2
BEVERLY ST	SF	19	A2
BIGELOW CT	SF	3	C1
BIGLER AV	SF	9	C3
BIRCH ST	SF	6	B3
BIRD ST	SF	10	C2
BISHOP ST	SF	21	A2
BLACK PL	SF	2	C2
BLACKSTONE CT	SF	2	B2
BLAIRWOOD LN	SF	9	B3
BLAKE ST	SF	5	C2
BLANCHE ST	SF	10	B3
BLANDY ST	SF	17	B1
BLANEY RD	SF	1	B2
BLANKEN AV	SF	21	B3
BLISS RD	SF	1	B3
BLUXOME ST	SF	7	B3
BLYTHDALE AV	SF	20	C3
BOARDMAN PL	SF	11	B1
BOB KAUFMAN AL	SF	3	A2
BOCANA ST	SF	14	C2
BONIFACIO ST	SF	7	B3
BONITA ST	SF	2	C3
BONNIE BRAE LN	SF	12	B3
BONVIEW ST	SF	14	C2
BORICA ST	SF	19	B1
BOSWORTH ST	SF	14	A3
BOUTWELL ST	SF	15	A2
BOWDOIN ST	SF	21	A1
BOWLEY ST	SF	4	C1
BOWLING GRN DR	SF	9	B1
BOWMAN RD	SF	1	A2
BOYLSTON ST	SF	15	A3
BOYNTON CT	SF	10	B1
BRADFORD ST	SF	15	A2
BRADY ST	SF	10	C1
BRANNAN ST	SF	7	B3
BRANNAN ST	SF	11	A1
BRANT AL	SF	3	A2
BRAZIL AV	SF	20	B1
BREEN PL	SF	6	C3
BRENTWOOD AV	SF	13	C3
BRET HARTE TER	SF	2	C2

1991 SAN FRANCISCO COUNTY STREET INDEX

STREET	CITY	PAGE	GRID
BREWSTER ST	SF	15	A2
BRIARCLIFF TER	SF	13	A2
BRICE TER	SF	11	A3
BRIDGEVIEW DR	SF	15	B3
BRIGHT ST	SF	19	B1
BRIGHTON AV	SF	19	C2
BRITTON ST	SF	21	A3
BROAD ST	SF	19	B2
BROADMOOR DR	SF	19	A1
BROADWAY	SF	2	A3
BROADWAY	SF	3	A3
BRODERICK ST	SF	2	A3
BRODERICK ST	SF	6	A2
BRODERICK ST	SF	10	A1
BROMLEY PL	SF	2	B3
BROMPTON AV	SF	14	A3
BRONTE ST	SF	15	A2
BROOK ST	SF	14	B2
BROOKDALE AV	SF	20	B3
BROOKHAVEN LN	SF	12	B3
BROOKLYN PL	SF	3	A3
BROOKS ST	SF	4	C2
BROSNAN ST	SF	10	C1
BROTHERHOOD WY	SF	19	A2
BRUCE AV	SF	19	C1
BRUMISS TER	SF	19	C3
BRUNSWICK ST	SF	19	B3
BRUNSWICK ST	SF	20	A3
BRUSH PL	SF	11	A1
BRUSSELS ST	SF	15	A3
BRYANT ST	SF	7	C2
BRYANT ST	SF	11	A1
BUCARELI DR	SF	18	C2
BUCHANAN LN	SF	1	B1
BUCHANAN ST	SF	2	B3
BUCHANAN ST	SF	6	B3
BUCKINGHAM WY	SF	19	A1
BUENA VISTA AV	SF	10	A1
BUENA VISTA TER	SF	10	A1
BURGOYNE ST	SF	2	C3
BURKE ST	SF	15	C2
BURLWOOD DR	SF	13	C3
BURNETT AV	SF	10	A3
BURNETT AV	SF	14	A2
BURNETT AV N	SF	10	A3
BURNHAM DANL CT	SF	6	B2
BURNS PL	SF	10	C1
BURNSIDE AV	SF	14	A3
BURR AV	SF	20	C3
BURRITT ST	SF	7	A2
BURROWS ST	SF	20	C1
BURROWS ST	SF	21	A1
BUSH ST	SF	6	A2
BUSH ST	SF	7	A1
BUTTE PL	SF	11	B1
BYINGTON ST	SF	6	B2
BYRON CT	SF	20	A3
BYXBEE ST	SF	19	A2
C			
C ST	SF	17	B1
CABRILLO ST	SF	8	A1
CABRILLO ST	SF	9	A1
CADELL PL	SF	3	A2
CAINE AV	SF	19	C2
CAIRE TER	SF	11	B3
CALEDONIA ST	SF	10	C1
CALGARY ST	SF	20	C3
CALHOUN TER	SF	3	A2
CALIFORNIA AV	SF	3	C2
CALIFORNIA ST	SF	3	B3
CALIFORNIA ST	SF	4	C2
CALIFORNIA ST	SF	5	A2
CALIFORNIA ST	SF	6	A2
CAMBON DR	SF	19	A2
CAMBRIDGE ST	SF	14	C3
CAMBRIDGE ST	SF	20	C1
CAMELLIA AV	SF	14	B3
CAMEO WY	SF	14	A1
CAMERON WY	SF	21	C2

STREET	CITY	PAGE	GRID
CAMP ST	SF	10	B2
CAMPBELL AV	SF	21	A2
CAMPTON PL	SF	7	A2
CAMPUS CIR	SF	18	C1
CAMPUS LN	SF	20	C1
CANBY ST	SF	1	C2
CANYON DR	SF	20	B3
CAPISTRANO AV	SF	20	A1
CAPITOL AV	SF	19	B3
CAPP ST	SF	10	C2
CAPP ST	SF	14	C1
CAPRA WY	SF	2	A2
CARD AL	SF	3	A3
CARDENAS AV	SF	19	A2
CARGO WY	SF	15	C1
CARL ST	SF	9	C2
CARMEL ST	SF	9	C2
CARMELITA ST	SF	10	B1
CARNELIAN WY	SF	14	A1
CAROLINA ST	SF	11	B2
CARPENTER CT	SF	15	C1
CARR ST	SF	21	B1
CARRIE ST	SF	14	B3
CARRIZAL ST	SF	20	C3
CARROLL AV	SF	15	B3
CARROLL AV	SF	21	B1
CARSON ST	SF	10	A3
CARTER ST	SF	20	B3
CARVER ST	SF	15	A2
CASA WY	SF	2	A2
CASCADE WK	SF	13	A1
CASELLI AV	SF	10	A3
CASHMERE ST	SF	15	C3
CASITAS AV	SF	13	B2
CASSANDRA CT	SF	19	C3
CASTELO AV	SF	19	A2
CASTENADA AV	SF	13	B1
CASTILLO ST	SF	20	C3
CASTLE ST	SF	3	A2
CASTLE MANOR AV	SF	14	B3
CASTRO ST	SF	10	B2
CASTRO ST	SF	14	B1
CATHERINE CT	SF	10	C3
CAYUGA AV	SF	19	C3
CAYUGA AV	SF	20	A2
CECILIA AV	SF	13	A1
CEDAR CT	SF	20	B3
CEDAR ST	SF	6	C2
CEDRO AV	SF	19	A1
CENTRAL AV	SF	10	A1
CENTRAL FRWY	SF	6	C3
CENTRAL SKWY	SF	10	C1
CENTURY PL	SF	7	B1
CERES ST	SF	15	B3
CERRITOS AV	SF	19	A1
CERVANTES BLVD	SF	2	A2
CHABOT TER	SF	5	C3
CHAIN OF L DR E	SF	8	A1
CHAIN OF L DR W	SF	8	A1
CHANNEL ST	SF	11	B1
CHAPMAN ST	SF	15	A2
CHARING CRSS ST	SF	2	C3
CHARLES ST	SF	14	B2
CHARLESTOWN PL	SF	7	B2
CHARLTON CT	SF	2	B3
CHARTER OAK AV	SF	15	A2
CHASE CT	SF	10	C1
CHATHAM PL	SF	7	A1
CHATTANOOGA ST	SF	10	B3
CHAVES AV	SF	13	C2
CHELSEA PL	SF	7	A2
CHENERY ST	SF	14	B2
CHERRY ST	SF	5	B2
CHESLEY ST	SF	11	A1
CHESTER AV	SF	19	A3
CHESTNUT ST	SF	2	A2
CHESTNUT ST	SF	3	A2
CHICAGO WY	SF	20	B3
CHILD ST	SF	3	A2
CHILTON AV	SF	14	A3
CHINA BASIN ST	SF	11	C1

STREET	CITY	PAGE	GRID
CHISM RD	SF	1	C3
CHRISTMAS TR PT	SF	10	A3
CHRISTOPHER DR	SF	9	B3
CHULA LN	SF	10	B2
CHUMASERO DR	SF	19	A2
CHURCH ST	SF	10	B2
CHURCH ST	SF	14	B1
CHURCHILL ST	SF	3	A3
CIELITO DR	SF	20	C3
CIRCULAR AV	SF	14	A3
CITY VIEW WY	SF	13	C1
CLAIRVIEW CT	SF	9	C3
CLARA ST	SF	7	B3
CLAREMONT BLVD	SF	13	B2
CLARENCE PL	SF	7	B3
CLARENDON AV	SF	9	C3
CLARION AL	SF	10	C2
CLARKE ST	SF	1	C3
CLAUDE LN	SF	7	A1
CLAY ST	SF	3	A3
CLAY ST	SF	5	C2
CLAYTON ST	SF	9	C1
CLAYTON ST	SF	10	A3
CLEARFIELD DR	SF	12	B3
CLEARVIEW CT	SF	15	B3
CLEARY CT	SF	6	B2
CLEMENT ST	SF	4	A3
CLEMENT ST	SF	5	A2
CLEMENTINA ST	SF	7	B2
CLEMENTINA ST	SF	11	A1
CLEO RAND AV	SF	16	A3
CLEVELAND ST	SF	7	A3
CLIFFORD TER	SF	10	A2
CLINTON PARK	SF	10	B1
CLIPPER ST	SF	14	A1
CLIPPER TER	SF	14	A1
CLOVER LN	SF	10	A3
CLOVER ST	SF	10	A2
CLYDE ST	SF	7	B3
COCHRANE ST	SF	17	B1
CODMAN PL	SF	3	A3
COHEN PL	SF	6	C2
COLBY ST	SF	15	A3
COLBY ST	SF	21	A1
COLE ST	SF	9	C2
COLEMAN ST	SF	17	B1
COLERIDGE ST	SF	14	C2
COLIN PL	SF	7	A2
COLIN KELLY ST	SF	7	C3
COLLEGE AV	SF	14	B3
COLLEGE TER	SF	14	B3
COLLIER	SF	3	A3
COLLINGWOOD ST	SF	10	A2
COLLINS ST	SF	5	C2
COLON AV	SF	13	B3
COLONIAL WY	SF	20	A1
COLTON ST	SF	10	C1
COLUMBIA SQ ST	SF	7	A3
COLUMBUS AV	SF	2	C2
COLUSA PL	SF	10	C1
COMERFORD ST	SF	14	B1
COMMER CT	SF	15	C3
COMMERCE ST	SF	3	B2
COMMERCIAL ST	SF	3	A3
COMMONWEALTH AV	SF	5	C2
COMPTON RD	SF	1	A3
CONCORD ST	SF	20	A2
CONCOURSE DR	SF	9	B1
CONGDON	SF	14	B3
CONGO ST	SF	14	A3
CONKLING ST	SF	15	B3
CONNECTICUT ST	SF	11	B2
CONRAD ST	SF	14	A2
CONSERVATORY DR	SF	9	B1
CONSTANSO WY	SF	12	C3
CONVERSE ST	SF	11	A1
COOK ST	SF	5	C2
COOPER AL	SF	3	A3
COPPER AL	SF	10	A3
CORA ST	SF	21	A3
CORAL RD	SF	11	B3

STREET	CITY	PAGE	GRID
CORALINO LN	SF	14	A1
CORBETT AV	SF	10	A3
CORBIN PL	SF	10	A2
CORDELIA ST	SF	3	A3
CORDOVA ST	SF	20	B3
CORNWALL ST	SF	5	B2
CORONA ST	SF	19	B1
CORONADO ST	SF	21	B2
CPL ZAVOVITZ ST	SF	1	C2
CORTES AV	SF	13	B2
CORTLAND AV	SF	14	C2
CORTLAND AV	SF	15	A2
CORWIN ST	SF	10	A3
COSMO PL	SF	7	A2
COSO AV	SF	14	C1
COSTA ST	SF	15	A1
COTTAGE ROW	SF	6	B2
COTTER ST	SF	14	A3
COUNTRY CLUB DR	SF	12	B3
COVENTRY CT	SF	13	C2
COVENTRY LN	SF	13	C2
COWELL PL	SF	3	B2
COWLES ST	SF	1	A2
CRAGMONT AV	SF	13	B1
CRAGS CT	SF	14	A2
CRAN PL	SF	6	B3
CRANE ST	SF	21	B1
CRANLEIGH DR	SF	13	A3
CRANSTON RD	SF	1	A2
CRAUT ST	SF	14	B3
CRESCENT AV	SF	14	C3
CRESPI DR	SF	19	A2
CRESTA VISTA DR	SF	13	B3
CRESTLAKE DR	SF	12	B2
CRESTLINE DR	SF	13	C1
CRESTMONT DR	SF	9	B3
CRESTWELL WK	SF	9	A3
CRISP RD	SF	17	A1
CRISSY FIELD AV	SF	1	A2
CROSS ST	SF	20	A2
CROSS OVER DR	SF	8	C1
CROWN TER	SF	9	C3
CRYSTAL ST	SF	19	B3
CUBA AL	SF	14	A2
CUESTA CT	SF	14	A1
CULEBRA TER	SF	2	C2
CUMBERLAND ST	SF	10	B3
CUNNINGHAM PL	SF	10	C3
CURTIS ST	SF	20	A2
CUSHMAN ST	SF	3	A3
CUSTER AV	SF	15	C1
CUSTOM HOUSE PL	SF	3	A3
CUTLER AV	SF	12	A2
CUVIER ST	SF	14	B3
CYPRESS ST	SF	14	C1
CYRIL MAGIN ST	SF	7	A2
CYRUS PL	SF	2	C3
D			
D ST	SF	17	B1
DAGGETT ST	SF	11	B1
DAKOTA ST	SF	11	B3
DALE PL	SF	6	C3
DALEWOOD WY	SF	13	B2
DANL BURNHAM CT	SF	6	B2
DANTON ST	SF	14	B3
DANVERS ST	SF	10	A2
DARIEN WY	SF	13	B3
DARRELL PL	SF	3	A2
DARTMOUTH ST	SF	15	A3
DARTMOUTH ST	SF	21	A1
DASHEL HAMMT ST	SF	7	A1
DAVIDSON AV	SF	15	C1
DAVIS ST	SF	3	B3
DAWNVIEW WY	SF	14	A1
DAWSON PL	SF	3	A3
DAY ST	SF	14	B2
DEARBORN ST	SF	10	C2
DE BOOM ST	SF	7	B3
DECATUR ST	SF	11	A1

STREET	CITY	PAGE	GRID
DECKER AL	SF	7	A3
DEDMAN CT	SF	15	C2
DEEMS RD	SF	1	B3
DEFOREST WY	SF	10	A2
DE HARO ST	SF	11	B1
DEHON ST	SF	10	B2
DELANCEY ST	SF	7	C2
DELANO AV	SF	20	A2
DELGADO PL	SF	2	C3
DELLBROOK AV	SF	9	C3
DELLBROOK AV	SF	13	C1
DELMAR ST	SF	10	A1
DEL MONTE ST	SF	20	A2
DE LONG ST	SF	19	B3
DEL SUR AV	SF	13	C2
DELTA PL	SF	7	A2
DELTA ST	SF	21	A2
DEL VALE AV	SF	13	C2
DEMING ST	SF	10	A2
DEMONTFORT AV	SF	19	B1
DENSLOWE DR	SF	19	A2
DENT RD	SF	1	A3
DERBY ST	SF	7	A2
DESMOND ST	SF	21	A3
DE SOTO ST	SF	19	B1
DETROIT ST	SF	14	A3
DEVONSHIRE WY	SF	9	B3
DEWEY BLVD	SF	13	B1
DE WOLF ST	SF	19	C3
DIAMOND ST	SF	10	A2
DIAMOND ST	SF	14	A2
DIAMOND HTS BL	SF	14	A1
DIANA ST	SF	15	B3
DIAZ AV	SF	19	A2
DICHA AL	SF	5	C2
DICHIERA CT	SF	19	C3
DICKIE SQ	SF	1	B1
DIGBY ST	SF	14	B2
DIVISADERO ST	SF	2	A3
DIVISADERO ST	SF	6	A3
DIVISADERO ST	SF	10	A1
DIVISION ST	SF	11	A1
DIXIE AL	SF	10	A3
DODGE PL	SF	6	C2
DOLORES ST	SF	10	B1
DOLORES ST	SF	14	B1
DOLORES TER	SF	10	B2
DONAHUE ST	SF	16	B3
DONAHUE ST	SF	17	A1
DONNER AV	SF	15	B3
DONNER AV	SF	21	B1
DORADO TER	SF	19	B1
DORANTES AV	SF	13	B1
DORCAS WY	SF	13	C2
DORCHESTER WY	SF	13	B2
DORE ST	SF	11	A1
DORIC AL	SF	3	A3
DORLAND ST	SF	10	B2
DORMAN AV	SF	15	A2
DORMITORY RD	SF	16	A3
DOUBLE ROCK ST	SF	21	C1
DOUGLASS ST	SF	10	A3
DOUGLASS ST	SF	14	A1
DOVE LOOP	SF	1	A2
DOVER ST	SF	7	C2
DOW PL	SF	7	B2
DOWNEY ST	SF	9	C2
DOYLE DR	SF	1	B2
DRAKE ST	SF	20	A3
DRUMM ST	SF	3	B3
DRUMMOND AL	SF	15	B2
DUBLIN ST	SF	20	B2
DUBOCE AV	SF	10	B1
DUDLEY RD	SF	1	B3
DUKES CT	SF	15	C2
DUNBAR AL	SF	3	A3
DUNCAN ST	SF	14	B1
DUNCOMBE AL	SF	3	A3
DUNNES AL	SF	3	A3
DUNSHEE AL	SF	15	B3
DUNSMUIR ST	SF	15	A3

1991 SAN FRANCISCO COUNTY STREET INDEX

STREET	CITY	PAGE	GRID
DWIGHT ST	SF	21	A1
DYNAMITE RD	SF	1	A2
E			
E ST	SF	17	B1
EAGLE ST	SF	10	A3
EARL ST	SF	17	A1
EASTMAN ST	SF	2	C2
EASTWOOD DR	SF	19	B1
EATON PL	SF	3	A3
ECKER ST	SF	7	B1
EDDY ST	SF	6	A3
EDDY ST	SF	7	A2
EDGAR PL	SF	19	C1
EDGARDO PL	SF	3	A2
EDGEHILL WY	SF	13	B2
EDGEWOOD AV	SF	9	C2
EDIE RD	SF	1	C2
EDINBURGH ST	SF	20	B2
EDITH ST	SF	3	A2
EDNA ST	SF	19	C1
EDWARD ST	SF	5	B3
EGBERT AV	SF	21	B1
EL CM DEL MAR	SF	4	A2
EL DORADO ST	SF	11	C1
ELGIN PARK	SF	10	C1
ELIM AL	SF	7	B1
ELIZABETH ST	SF	10	A3
ELIZABETH ST	SF	14	A1
ELK ST	SF	14	A3
ELKHART ST	SF	7	C2
ELLERT ST	SF	14	C2
ELLICK LN	SF	3	A3
ELLINGTON AV	SF	19	C3
ELLIOT ST	SF	21	A2
ELLIS ST	SF	6	A3
ELLIS ST	SF	7	A2
ELLSWORTH ST	SF	14	C2
ELM ST	SF	6	B3
ELMHURST DR	SF	13	A3
ELMIRA ST	SF	15	A2
EL MIRASOL PL	SF	12	C3
ELMWOOD WY	SF	19	B1
EL PLAZUELA WY	SF	19	A1
EL POLIN LOOP	SF	1	C3
EL SERENO CT	SF	14	A2
ELSIE ST	SF	14	C2
EL VERANO WY	SF	13	B3
ELWOOD ST	SF	7	A2
EMBRCADERO SKWY	SF	3	B3
EMBARCADERO THE	SF	3	A2
EMERALD LN	SF	12	B3
EMERSON ST	SF	5	C2
EMERY LN	SF	3	A3
EMIL LN	SF	13	C3
EMMA ST	SF	7	A1
EMMET PL	SF	3	A3
EMMETT CT	SF	14	C1
EMPRESS LN	SF	21	A2
ENCANTO AV	SF	6	A3
ENCINAL WK	SF	9	A3
ENCLINE CT	SF	13	C2
ENGLISH ST	SF	16	B3
ENNIS RD	SF	1	A3
ENTERPRISE ST	SF	10	C2
ENTRADA CT N	SF	19	B1
ENTRADA CT S	SF	19	B1
ERIE ST	SF	10	C1
ERKSON CT	SF	6	A2
ERVINE ST	SF	21	A2
ESCOLTA WY	SF	12	B2
ESCONDIDO AV	SF	12	B3
ESMERALDA AV	SF	14	C2
ESMERALDA AV	SF	15	A2
ESPANOLA ST	SF	16	A3
ESPLANADE THE	SF	8	A1
ESQUINA DR	SF	20	C3
ESSEX ST	SF	7	B2
ESTERO AV	SF	19	A1
EUCALYPTUS DR	SF	12	C3

STREET	CITY	PAGE	GRID
EUCLID AV	SF	5	B2
EUGENIA AV	SF	14	C2
EUREKA PL	SF	6	C2
EUREKA ST	SF	10	A2
EVA TER	SF	10	B1
EVANS AV	SF	15	C2
EVE ST	SF	15	A1
EVELYN WY	SF	13	C2
EVERGLADE DR	SF	12	B3
EVERSON ST	SF	14	B2
EWER PL	SF	3	A3
EWING TER	SF	5	C3
EXCELSIOR AV	SF	20	B1
EXECUTIVE PK BL	SF	21	B3
EXETER ST	SF	21	B1
EXPOSITION DR	SF	3	C1
F			
FAIR AV	SF	14	C1
FAIRBANKS ST	SF	10	A2
FAIRFAX AV	SF	15	B1
FAIRFIELD WY	SF	19	B1
FAIRMOUNT ST	SF	14	B2
FAIR OAKS ST	SF	10	B3
FAITH ST	SF	15	A1
FALLON PL	SF	3	A3
FALMOUTH ST	SF	7	A3
FANNING WY	SF	13	A1
FARALLONES ST	SF	19	B2
FARGO PL	SF	11	A1
FARNSWORTH LN	SF	9	C2
FARNUM ST	SF	14	B2
FARRAGUT AV	SF	19	C3
FARVIEW CT	SF	9	C3
FAXON AV	SF	19	B1
FEDERAL ST	SF	7	B2
FELIX AV	SF	19	A2
FELL ST	SF	6	C3
FELL ST	SF	9	C1
FELL ST	SF	10	A1
FELLA PL	SF	7	A1
FELTON ST	SF	20	C1
FENTON LN	SF	14	A1
FERN ST	SF	6	B2
FERNANDEZ ST	SF	1	C3
FERNWOOD DR	SF	13	B3
FIELDING ST	SF	3	A2
FILBERT ST	SF	2	A3
FILBERT ST	SF	3	A2
FILLMORE ST	SF	2	A3
FILLMORE ST	SF	6	B3
FILLMORE ST	SF	10	B1
FISHER AL	SF	3	A3
FISHER AV	SF	17	B1
FISHER LOOP	SF	1	B3
FITCH ST	SF	21	C2
FITZGERALD AV	SF	21	B1
FLINT ST	SF	10	A2
FLOOD AV	SF	14	A3
FLORA ST	SF	15	B3
FLORENCE ST	SF	3	A3
FLORENTINE ST	SF	20	A2
FLORIDA ST	SF	11	A1
FLORIDA ST	SF	15	A1
FLOURNOY ST	SF	19	B3
FLOWER ST	SF	15	A2
FOERSTER ST	SF	13	C3
FOLGER AL	SF	6	B2
FOLSOM ST	SF	7	B2
FOLSOM ST	SF	10	C1
FOLSOM ST	SF	11	A1
FOLSOM ST	SF	15	A2
FONT BLVD	SF	18	C1
FONT BLVD	SF	19	A2
FOOTE AV	SF	19	C2
FORD ST	SF	10	B2
FOREST KNLS DR	SF	9	C3
FOREST SIDE AV	SF	13	A2
FOREST VIEW DR	SF	12	C3
FORTUNA AV	SF	6	A3

STREET	CITY	PAGE	GRID
FOUNTAIN ST	SF	14	A1
FOWLER AV	SF	13	C1
FRANCE AV	SF	20	B2
FRANCIS ST	SF	20	B1
FRANCISCO ST	SF	2	A2
FRANCISCO ST	SF	3	A2
FRANCONIA ST	SF	15	A2
FRANK ST	SF	7	A1
FRANKLIN ST	SF	2	B2
FRANKLIN ST	SF	6	B1
FRANK NORRIS ST	SF	6	B2
FRATESSA CT	SF	21	B2
FREDELA LN	SF	9	C3
FREDERICK ST	SF	9	C2
FREDSON CT	SF	20	A2
FREELON ST	SF	7	B3
FREEMAN CT	SF	3	A3
FREEMAN ST	SF	1	B2
FREMONT ST	SF	7	B1
FRENCH CT	SF	1	C2
FRESNO ST	SF	3	A3
FRIEDELL ST	SF	17	A1
FRONT ST	SF	3	B2
FUENTE AV	SF	19	A2
FULTON ST	SF	6	A3
FULTON ST	SF	8	A1
FULTON ST	SF	9	A1
FUNSTON AV	SF	1	C3
FUNSTON AV	SF	5	A2
FUNSTON AV	SF	9	A2
FUNSTON AV	SF	13	A1
G			
GABILAN WY	SF	12	C3
GAISER CT	SF	10	B2
GALE ST	SF	7	C3
GALEWOOD CIR	SF	9	C3
GALILEE LN	SF	1	B1
GALINDO AV	SF	19	A2
GALLAGHER LN	SF	7	A3
GALVEZ AV	SF	15	B2
GALVEZ AV	SF	16	A3
GAMBIER ST	SF	20	C1
GARCES DR	SF	18	C2
GARCIA AV	SF	13	B2
GARDEN ST	SF	6	A2
GARDENSIDE DR	SF	10	A3
GARDNER PL	SF	7	A2
GARFIELD ST	SF	19	A2
GARLINGTON CT	SF	15	C3
GARRISON AV	SF	21	A3
GATES ST	SF	15	A2
GATEVIEW AV	SF	3	C1
GATEVIEW CT	SF	13	B1
GATUN AL	SF	13	C2
GAVEN ST	SF	15	A3
GAVIOTA WY	SF	13	C2
GEARY BLVD	SF	5	C3
GEARY ST	SF	6	C2
GEARY ST	SF	7	A2
GELLERT DR	SF	12	B3
GENEBERN WY	SF	14	B3
GENEVA AV	SF	19	C1
GENEVA AV	SF	20	A2
GENNESSEE ST	SF	13	C3
GENOA PL	SF	3	A2
GEORGE CT	SF	15	C3
GERKE AL	SF	3	A2
GERMANIA ST	SF	10	B1
GETZ ST	SF	19	C2
GIANTS DR	SF	21	C2
GIBB ST	SF	3	A3
GIBSON RD	SF	4	C2
GILBERT ST	SF	11	A1
GILLETTE AV	SF	21	B3
GILMAN AV	SF	21	B1
GILROY ST	SF	21	B2
GIRARD RD	SF	1	C2
GIRARD ST	SF	15	A3
GLADEVIEW WY	SF	13	C1

STREET	CITY	PAGE	GRID
GLADIOLUS LN	SF	13	A3
GLADSTONE DR	SF	14	C3
GLADYS ST	SF	14	C2
GLENBROOK AV	SF	9	C3
GLENDALE ST	SF	10	A3
GLENHAVEN LN	SF	10	A3
GLENVIEW DR	SF	13	C1
GLOBE AL	SF	13	B3
GLORIA CT	SF	20	A2
GLOVER ST	SF	2	C3
GODEUS ST	SF	14	C2
GOETHE ST	SF	19	B3
GOETTINGEN ST	SF	15	A3
GOETTINGEN ST	SF	21	A1
GOLD ST	SF	3	A3
GOLDEN CT	SF	2	C3
GOLDEN GATE AV	SF	5	B3
GOLDEN GATE AV	SF	6	A3
GOLDING LN	SF	10	A3
GOLD MINE DR	SF	14	A2
GOLETA AV	SF	12	C3
GONZALEZ DR	SF	18	C2
GONZALEZ DR	SF	19	A2
GORDON ST	SF	11	A1
GORGAS AV	SF	1	C2
GORHAM ST	SF	14	B3
GOUGH ST	SF	6	B1
GOUGH ST	SF	10	C1
GOULD ST	SF	21	B1
GRACE ST	SF	10	C1
GRAFTON AV	SF	19	B2
GRAHAM ST	SF	1	B3
GRANADA AV	SF	19	B2
GRANAT CT	SF	9	B1
GRAND VIEW AV	SF	10	A3
GRAND VIEW AV	SF	14	A1
GRANDVIEW TER	SF	10	A3
GRANT AV	SF	3	A2
GRANT AV	SF	7	A1
GRANVILLE WY	SF	13	B2
GRATTAN ST	SF	9	C2
GRAYSTONE TER	SF	9	C3
GREAT HWY	SF	8	A3
GREAT HWY	SF	12	A1
GREEN ST	SF	2	A3
GREEN ST	SF	3	B2
GREENOUGH AV	SF	1	A2
GREENVIEW CT	SF	9	B3
GREENWICH ST	SF	2	A3
GREENWICH ST	SF	3	B2
GREENWICH TER	SF	2	C2
GREENWOOD AV	SF	19	C1
GRENARD TER	SF	2	B2
GRIFFITH ST	SF	21	C2
GRIJALVA DR	SF	19	A2
GROTE PL	SF	7	B2
GROVE ST	SF	6	A3
GROVE ST	SF	9	C1
GUERRERO ST	SF	10	C1
GUERRERO ST	SF	14	C1
GUTTENBERG ST	SF	20	A3
GUY PL	SF	7	B2
H			
H ST	SF	17	B1
HAHN ST	SF	20	C3
HAIGHT ST	SF	9	C1
HAIGHT ST	SF	10	A1
HALE ST	SF	15	A3
HALLAM ST	SF	7	A3
HALLECK ST	SF	1	C2
HALLECK ST	SF	3	B3
HALYBURTON CT	SF	3	C1
HAMERTON AV	SF	14	A3
HAMILTON ST	SF	1	A2
HAMILTON ST	SF	21	A1
HAMLIN ST	SF	2	C3
HAMPSHIRE ST	SF	11	A2
HANCOCK ST	SF	10	B2
HANOVER ST	SF	20	A3

STREET	CITY	PAGE	GRID
HARBOR RD	SF	16	A3
HARDIE PL	SF	7	A1
HARDIE RD	SF	1	B3
HARDING RD	SF	18	A1
HARE ST	SF	16	A3
HARKNESS AV	SF	21	A2
HARLAN PL	SF	7	A1
HARLEM AL	SF	6	C2
HARLOW ST	SF	10	B2
HARNEY WY	SF	21	B3
HAROLD AV	SF	19	C2
HARPER ST	SF	14	B2
HARRIET ST	SF	7	A3
HARRIET ST	SF	11	B1
HARRINGTON ST	SF	20	A1
HARRIS PL	SF	2	B2
HARRISON BLVD	SF	1	A3
HARRISON ST	SF	7	A3
HARRISON ST	SF	11	A2
HARRISON ST	SF	15	A1
HARRY ST	SF	14	B2
HARTFORD ST	SF	10	B2
HARVARD ST	SF	20	C1
HASTINGS TER	SF	2	C2
HATTIE ST	SF	10	A2
HAVELOCK ST	SF	19	C1
HAVENS ST	SF	2	C2
HAVENSIDE DR	SF	12	B3
HAWES ST	SF	21	C1
HAWKINS LN	SF	15	C3
HAWTHORNE ST	SF	7	B2
HAYES ST	SF	6	A3
HAYES ST	SF	9	C1
HAYWARD PL	SF	11	A1
HAZELWOOD AV	SF	13	C3
HEAD ST	SF	19	B2
HEARST AV	SF	13	C3
HEATHER AV	SF	5	C2
HELEN ST	SF	6	C1
HELENA ST	SF	15	A2
HEMLOCK ST	SF	6	B2
HEMWAY TER	SF	5	C3
HENRY ST	SF	10	B2
HENRY ADAMS ST	SF	11	A1
HERBST RD	SF	18	A3
HERMANN ST	SF	10	B1
HERNANDEZ AV	SF	13	B1
HERON ST	SF	11	A1
HESTER AV	SF	21	B2
HEYMAN AV	SF	14	C2
HICKORY ST	SF	10	B1
HICKS RD	SF	1	B3
HIDALGO TER	SF	10	B2
HIGH ST	SF	14	A1
HIGHLAND AV	SF	14	B2
HIGUERA AV	SF	18	C2
HILIRITAS AV	SF	14	A2
HILL BLVD S	SF	20	B3
HILL DR	SF	17	B1
HILL ST	SF	10	B3
HILLCREST CT	SF	13	C3
HILLPOINT AV	SF	9	C2
HILLVIEW CT	SF	15	C3
HILLWAY AV	SF	9	C2
HILTON ST	SF	15	A2
HIMMELMAN PL	SF	2	C3
HITCHCOCK ST	SF	1	A2
HOBART AL	SF	7	A2
HODGES AL	SF	3	A2
HOFF ST	SF	10	C2
HOFFMAN AV	SF	14	A1
HOFFMAN ST	SF	1	A2
HOLLADAY AV	SF	15	A1
HOLLAND CT	SF	7	A2
HOLLIS ST	SF	6	B2
HOLLISTER AV	SF	21	B1
HOLLOWAY AV	SF	19	B1
HOLLY PARK CIR	SF	14	C2
HOLLYWOOD CT	SF	20	A2
HOLYOKE ST	SF	21	A1
HOMER ST	SF	11	A1

INDEX

1991 SAN FRANCISCO COUNTY STREET INDEX

STREET	CITY	PAGE	GRID
HOMESTEAD ST	SF	14	A1
HOMEWOOD CT	SF	19	B1
HOOKER AL	SF	7	A1
HOOPER ST	SF	11	B1
HOPKINS AV	SF	10	A3
HORACE ST	SF	15	A1
HORNE AV	SF	17	B1
HOTALING PL	SF	3	B3
HOUSTON ST	SF	2	C2
HOWARD RD	SF	4	C2
HOWARD ST	SF	7	A3
HOWARD ST	SF	10	C1
HOWE RD	SF	1	A2
HOWTH ST	SF	19	C2
HUBBELL ST	SF	11	B2
HUDSON AV	SF	15	B1
HUDSON AV	SF	16	C3
HUGO ST	SF	9	B2
HULBERT AL	SF	7	B3
HUMBOLDT ST	SF	11	C3
HUNT ST	SF	7	B2
HUNTERS PT BLVD	SF	16	A2
HUNTERS PT EXWY	SF	21	C2
HUNTINGTON DR	SF	12	B3
HURON AV	SF	19	C2
HUSSEY ST	SF	17	B1
HUTCHINS CT	SF	3	C1
HYDE ST	SF	2	C2
HYDE ST	SF	6	C2
I			
I ST	SF	17	A1
ICEHOUSE AL	SF	3	B2
IDORA AV	SF	13	B2
IGNACIO ST	SF	21	C2
ILLINOIS ST	SF	11	C1
ILLINOIS ST	SF	15	C1
ILS LN	SF	3	A3
IMPERIAL AV	SF	2	B2
INA CT	SF	20	B1
INDIANA ST	SF	11	C2
INDIANA ST	SF	15	C1
INDUSTRIAL ST	SF	15	A2
INFANTRY TER	SF	1	B3
INGALLS ST	SF	16	A3
INGALLS ST	SF	21	C1
INGERSON AV	SF	21	B1
INNES AV	SF	15	B1
INNES AV	SF	16	A3
INVERNESS DR	SF	12	C3
IOWA ST	SF	11	C3
IRIS AV	SF	5	C2
IRON AL	SF	10	A3
IRVING ST	SF	8	A2
IRVING ST	SF	9	A2
IRWIN ST	SF	11	B2
ISDRA DUNCAN LN	SF	7	A2
ISIS ST	SF	10	C1
ISLAIS ST	SF	15	C1
ISOLA WY	SF	13	C2
ITALY AV	SF	20	A2
IVY ST	SF	6	B3
J			
J ST	SF	17	A1
JACK KEROUAC AL	SF	3	A3
JACK LONDON AL	SF	7	B3
JACKSON PL	SF	3	B3
JACKSON ST	SF	2	A3
JACKSON ST	SF	3	A3
JACKSON ST	SF	5	B2
JADE PL	SF	14	A2
JAKEY CT	SF	15	C3
JAMES AL	SF	3	A3
JAMES LICK FRWY	SF	15	A2
JAMES LICK FRWY	SF	21	A1
JAMES LICK SKWY	SF	11	A1
JAMESTOWN AV	SF	21	B2
JANSEN ST	SF	2	C2

STREET	CITY	PAGE	GRID
JARBOE AV	SF	14	C2
JASON CT	SF	3	A3
JASPER PL	SF	3	A2
JAVA ST	SF	10	A2
JEAN WY	SF	5	C3
JEFFERSON ST	SF	2	A2
JENNINGS ST	SF	15	C3
JENNINGS ST	SF	16	A2
JENNINGS ST	SF	21	B1
JEROME AL	SF	3	A3
JERROLD AV	SF	15	B1
JERROLD AV	SF	16	A3
JERSEY ST	SF	14	A1
JESSIE ST	SF	6	C3
JESSIE ST	SF	7	A2
JESSIE ST	SF	10	C1
JEWETT ST	SF	11	B1
JOHN ST	SF	3	A3
J F KENNEDY DR	SF	8	A1
J F KENNEDY DR	SF	9	B1
J F SHELLEY DR	SF	20	C1
JOHN MUIR DR	SF	18	B2
JOHNSTONE DR	SF	9	C3
JOICE ST	SF	3	A3
JONES ST	SF	2	C2
JONES ST	SF	7	A2
JOOST AV	SF	13	C3
JORDAN AV	SF	5	C2
JOSEPHA AV	SF	19	A2
JOSIAH AV	SF	19	C2
JOY ST	SF	15	A2
JUAN BATSTA CIR	SF	19	A2
JUANITA WY	SF	13	B2
JUDAH ST	SF	8	A2
JUDAH ST	SF	9	A2
JUDSON AV	SF	19	C1
JULES AV	SF	19	B1
JULIA ST	SF	7	A3
JULIAN AV	SF	10	C1
JULIUS ST	SF	3	A2
JUNIOR TER	SF	20	A2
JUNIPER ST	SF	11	A1
JUNIPRO SRRA BL	SF	19	A2
JURI ST	SF	14	C1
JUSTIN DR	SF	14	B3
K			
KANSAS ST	SF	11	A1
KAPLAN LN	SF	7	B2
KAREN CT	SF	21	A1
KATE ST	SF	11	A1
KEARNY ST	SF	3	A2
KEARNY ST	SF	7	A1
KEITH ST	SF	15	C2
KEITH ST	SF	21	B2
KELLOCH AV	SF	21	A3
KEMPTON AV	SF	19	B3
KENNEDY AV	SF	1	C2
KENNTH RXRTH PL	SF	3	A3
KENNY AL	SF	20	A2
KENSINGTON WY	SF	13	B2
KENT ST	SF	3	A2
KENWOOD WY	SF	19	B1
KEPPLER CT	SF	3	C1
KERN ST	SF	14	B3
KEY AV	SF	21	B2
KEYES AL	SF	3	A3
KEYES AV	SF	1	B2
KEYSTONE WY	SF	19	B1
KEZAR DR	SF	9	B2
KIMBALL PL	SF	2	C3
KING ST	SF	7	B3
KING ST	SF	11	B1
KINGSTON ST	SF	14	C2
KINZEY ST	SF	1	A2
KIRKHAM ST	SF	8	A3
KIRKHAM ST	SF	9	A2
KIRKWOOD AV	SF	15	B2
KIRKWOOD AV	SF	17	A1
KISKA RD	SF	16	A3

STREET	CITY	PAGE	GRID
KISSLING ST	SF	10	C1
KITTREDGE TER	SF	5	C3
KNOLLVIEW WY	SF	13	C1
KNOTT CT	SF	20	A3
KOBBE AV	SF	1	A3
KOHLER	SF	3	A2
KRAMER PL	SF	3	A2
KRAUSGRILL PL	SF	3	A2
KRONQUIST CT	SF	14	B1
L			
LA AVANZADA	SF	9	C3
LA BICA WY	SF	13	C2
LAFAYETTE ST	SF	10	C1
LA FERRERA TER	SF	3	A2
LA GRANDE AV	SF	20	B2
LAGUNA ST	SF	2	B3
LAGUNA ST	SF	6	B3
LAGUNA ST	SF	10	B1
LAGUNA HONDA BL	SF	13	B1
LAGUNITAS DR	SF	13	A3
LAIDLEY ST	SF	14	B2
LAKE ST	SF	4	B2
LAKE ST	SF	5	A2
LAKE FOREST CT	SF	9	B3
LAKE MERCED BL	SF	12	B3
LAKE MERCED BL	SF	18	C2
LK MERCED HILL	SF	18	C3
LAKE SHORE DR	SF	12	B3
LAKE SHORE PZ	SF	12	B3
LAKEVIEW AV	SF	19	B2
LAKEWOOD AV	SF	19	B1
LAMARTINE ST	SF	14	B3
LAMSON LN	SF	10	A3
LANCASTER LN	SF	12	B3
LANDERS ST	SF	10	B2
LANE ST	SF	15	C3
LANE ST	SF	21	B2
LANGDON CT	SF	1	A2
LANGTON ST	SF	7	A3
LANGTON ST	SF	11	A1
LANSDALE AV	SF	13	B2
LANSING ST	SF	7	B2
LAPHAM WY	SF	20	B3
LAPIDGE ST	SF	10	C2
LA PLAYA	SF	8	A1
LAPU LAPU ST	SF	7	B3
LARCH ST	SF	6	A3
LARKIN ST	SF	2	C2
LARKIN ST	SF	6	C2
LA SALLE AV	SF	15	C2
LA SALLE AV	SF	17	A1
LASKIE ST	SF	7	A3
LATHROP AV	SF	21	B3
LATONA ST	SF	15	B3
LAURA ST	SF	19	C3
LAUREL ST	SF	5	C1
LAUSSAT ST	SF	10	B1
LAWRENCE AV	SF	19	C3
LAWTON ST	SF	8	A3
LAWTON ST	SF	9	A3
LEAVENWORTH ST	SF	2	C2
LEAVENWORTH ST	SF	6	C2
LEAVENWORTH ST	SF	7	A3
LECH WALESA	SF	6	C3
LE CONTE AV	SF	21	B2
LEDYARD ST	SF	15	B3
LEE AV	SF	19	C2
LEESE ST	SF	14	C2
LEGION CT	SF	19	B1
LEGION HONOR DR	SF	4	C1
LEIDESDORFF ST	SF	3	B3
LELAND AV	SF	21	A2
LENOX WY	SF	13	B2
LEO ST	SF	20	B1
LEONA TER	SF	6	A2
LEROY PL	SF	2	C3
LESSING ST	SF	19	C3
LESTER CT	SF	3	C1
LETTERMAN DR	SF	1	C2

STREET	CITY	PAGE	GRID
LETTUCE LN	SF	15	B2
LEVANT ST	SF	10	A2
LEXINGTON ST	SF	10	C2
LIBERTY ST	SF	10	B3
LICK PL	SF	7	B2
LIEBIG ST	SF	19	C3
LIEUT ALLEN ST	SF	1	C2
LIEUT JAUSS ST	SF	1	C2
LIGGETT AV	SF	1	C3
LILAC ST	SF	14	C1
LILLIAN ST	SF	15	C3
LILY ST	SF	10	B1
LINARES AV	SF	9	B3
LINCOLN BLVD	SF	1	A3
LINCOLN BLVD	SF	4	C1
LINCOLN CT	SF	20	A3
LINCOLN WY	SF	8	A2
LINCOLN WY	SF	9	A2
LINDA ST	SF	10	C2
LINDA VIS STEPS	SF	7	B3
LINDEN ST	SF	6	B3
LINDSAY CIR	SF	15	C1
LIPPARD AV	SF	14	A3
LISBON ST	SF	20	A2
LIVINGSTON ST	SF	1	B2
LLOYD ST	SF	10	A1
LOBOS ST	SF	19	B2
LOCKSLEY AV	SF	9	B3
LOCKWOOD ST	SF	17	B1
LOCUST ST	SF	5	C2
LOEHR ST	SF	20	C3
LOMA VISTA TER	SF	10	A2
LOMBARD ST	SF	1	C3
LOMBARD ST	SF	2	A2
LOMBARD ST	SF	3	A2
LOMITA AV	SF	9	A3
LONDON ST	SF	20	A1
LONE MTN TER	SF	5	C3
LONG AV	SF	1	A2
LONGVIEW CT	SF	13	C1
LOOMIS ST	SF	15	A2
LOPEZ AV	SF	13	B1
LORAINE CT	SF	5	B3
LORI LN	SF	9	C3
LOS PALMOS DR	SF	13	C3
LOTTIE BNNET LN	SF	1	B1
LOUISBURG ST	SF	19	C2
LOWELL ST	SF	20	A3
LOWER TER	SF	10	A2
LOYOLA TER	SF	5	C3
LUCERNE ST	SF	11	B1
LUCKY ST	SF	15	A1
LUCY ST	SF	15	B3
LUDLOW AL	SF	13	B2
LULU AL	SF	13	C3
LUM, WALTER PL	SF	3	A3
LUM, WALTER PL	SF	7	A1
LUNADO CT	SF	19	A1
LUNADO WY	SF	19	A1
LUNDEEN ST	SF	1	C2
LUNDYS LN	SF	14	C2
LUPINE AV	SF	5	C2
LURLINE ST	SF	9	A3
LURMONT TER	SF	2	C2
LUSK ST	SF	7	B3
LYELL ST	SF	14	B3
LYNCH ST	SF	2	C3
LYNDHURST DR	SF	19	A1
LYON ST	SF	1	C3
LYON ST	SF	6	A1
LYON ST	SF	10	A1
LYSETTE ST	SF	2	C3
M			
MABEL AL	SF	6	C2
MABINI ST	SF	7	B2
MABREY CT	SF	15	C1
MACARTHUR AV	SF	1	C3
MAC ARTHUR AV	SF	2	B2
MACEDONIA ST	SF	15	A1

STREET	CITY	PAGE	GRID
MACONDRAY LN	SF	2	C3
MACRAE ST	SF	1	C2
MADDUX AV	SF	15	B3
MADERA ST	SF	11	B3
MADISON ST	SF	20	C1
MADRID ST	SF	20	B2
MADRONE AV	SF	13	B2
MAGELLAN AV	SF	13	B1
MAGNOLIA ST	SF	2	B2
MAHAN ST	SF	17	B2
MAIDEN LN	SF	7	A2
MAIN ST	SF	7	B1
MAJESTIC AV	SF	19	C2
MALDEN AL	SF	7	B2
MALLORCA WY	SF	2	A2
MALTA DR	SF	14	A3
MALVINA PL	SF	3	A3
MANCHESTER ST	SF	14	C1
MANDALAY LN	SF	13	A1
MANGELS AV	SF	13	C3
MANOR DR	SF	19	B1
MANSEAU ST	SF	17	B2
MANSELL ST	SF	20	C2
MANSELL ST	SF	21	A2
MANSFIELD ST	SF	20	C1
MANZANITA AV	SF	5	C2
MAPLE ST	SF	5	C2
MARCELA AV	SF	13	B1
MARCY PL	SF	3	A3
MARENGO ST	SF	15	A2
MARGARET AV	SF	19	C2
MARGRAVE PL	SF	3	A2
MARIETTA DR	SF	13	C2
MARIETTA DR	SF	14	A2
MARIN ST	SF	15	C1
MARINA BLVD	SF	2	A2
MARINE DR	SF	1	B2
MARINER DR	SF	3	C1
MARION PL	SF	2	C2
MARIPOSA ST	SF	11	A2
MARK LN	SF	7	A1
MARKET ST	SF	7	A3
MARKET ST	SF	10	B2
MARK TWAIN PL	SF	3	A3
MARNE AV	SF	13	B2
MARS ST	SF	10	A2
MARSHALL ST	SF	1	C2
MARSILLY ST	SF	14	B3
MARSTON AV	SF	19	C1
MARTHA AV	SF	14	A3
MARTINEZ ST	SF	1	C3
MARTN L KING DR	SF	8	A2
MARTN L KING DR	SF	9	A2
MARVEL CT	SF	4	B2
MAR VIEW WY	SF	9	C3
MARX MEADOW DR	SF	8	C1
MARY ST	SF	7	A3
MASON CT	SF	3	C1
MASON ST	SF	1	B2
MASON ST	SF	3	A2
MASON ST	SF	7	A2
MASONIC AV	SF	5	C3
MASONIC AV	SF	10	A1
MASSASOIT ST	SF	15	A1
MASSETT PL	SF	7	B2
MATEO ST	SF	14	B2
MATTHEW CT	SF	16	A3
MTTHW TURNER SQ	SF	1	B1
MAULDIN ST	SF	1	A2
MAYFAIR DR	SF	5	C2
MAYFLOWER ST	SF	15	A2
MAYNARD ST	SF	14	B3
MAYWOOD DR	SF	13	B3
MCALLISTER ST	SF	5	C3
MCALLISTER ST	SF	6	A3
MCCANN ST	SF	16	B3
MCCARTHY AV	SF	20	C3
MCCOPPIN ST	SF	10	C1
MCCORMICK ST	SF	2	C3
MCDONALD ST	SF	1	B2
MCDOWELL AV	SF	1	B2

1991 SAN FRANCISCO COUNTY STREET INDEX

STREET	CITY	PAGE	GRID
MCDOWELL AV	SF	2	B2
MCKINNON AV	SF	15	B2
MCLAREN AV	SF	4	B2
MCLEA CT	SF	11	A1
MEACHAM PL	SF	6	C2
MEADE AV	SF	21	B2
MEADOWBROOK DR	SF	12	C3
MEDA AV	SF	20	A1
MEDAU PL	SF	3	A2
MELBA AV	SF	13	A3
MELRA CT	SF	21	A3
MELROSE AV	SF	13	C3
MENDELL ST	SF	15	B2
MENDELL ST	SF	21	B1
MENDOSA AV	SF	13	B1
MERCATO CT	SF	14	A3
MERCED AV	SF	13	B2
MERCEDES WY	SF	19	A1
MERCHANT RD	SF	1	A2
MERCHANT ST	SF	3	B3
MERCURY ST	SF	15	B3
MERLIN ST	SF	7	B3
MERRILL ST	SF	15	A3
MERRIMAC ST	SF	11	C1
MERRITT ST	SF	10	A2
MERSEY ST	SF	10	B3
MESA AV	SF	1	C2
MESA AV	SF	13	B1
METSON RD	SF	8	C2
MICHIGAN ST	SF	11	C3
MIDCREST WY	SF	13	C1
MIDDLE DR E	SF	9	B1
MIDDLE DR W	SF	8	C2
MIDDLEFIELD DR	SF	12	C3
MIDDLE POINT RD	SF	16	A2
MIDWAY ST	SF	3	A2
MIGUEL ST	SF	14	B2
MILAN TER	SF	19	C3
MILES ST	SF	1	B2
MILEY ST	SF	5	C1
MILL ST	SF	21	A2
MILLER PL	SF	3	A3
MILLER RD	SF	1	A2
MILTON ST	SF	14	B3
MILTON ROSS ST	SF	15	B2
MINERVA ST	SF	19	B2
MINNA ST	SF	7	A3
MINNA ST	SF	10	C1
MINNESOTA ST	SF	11	C2
MINNESOTA ST	SF	15	C1
MINT ST	SF	7	A3
MIRABEL AV	SF	14	C1
MIRALOMA DR	SF	13	B2
MIRAMAR AV	SF	19	B2
MISSION ST	SF	6	C3
MISSION ST	SF	7	A2
MISSION ST	SF	10	C2
MISSION ST	SF	14	B3
MISSION ST	SF	20	A2
MISSION ROCK ST	SF	11	B1
MISSISSIPPI ST	SF	11	B2
MISSISSIPPI ST	SF	15	B1
MISSOURI ST	SF	11	B2
MISSOURI ST	SF	15	B1
MISTRAL ST	SF	11	A2
MIZPAH ST	SF	14	A3
MODOC AV	SF	19	C2
MOFFITT ST	SF	14	B2
MOJAVE ST	SF	15	A2
MOLIMO DR	SF	13	C2
MONCADA WY	SF	13	A3
MONETA CT	SF	19	C3
MONETA WY	SF	19	C3
MONO ST	SF	10	A3
MONTAGUE PL	SF	3	A2
MONTALVO AV	SF	13	B1
MONTANA ST	SF	19	B2
MONTCALM AV	SF	15	A1
MONTCLAIR TER	SF	2	C2
MONTECITO AV	SF	13	C3
MONTEREY BLVD	SF	13	C3
MONTE VISTA DR	SF	19	A1
MONTEZUMA ST	SF	14	C1
MONTGOMERY ST	SF	1	B2
MONTGOMERY ST	SF	3	A2
MONTGOMERY ST	SF	7	B1
MONTICELLO ST	SF	19	A2
MONUMENT WY	SF	9	C2
MOORE PL	SF	2	C2
MORAGA AV	SF	1	B3
MORAGA ST	SF	8	A3
MORAGA ST	SF	9	A3
MORELAND ST	SF	14	B2
MORGAN AL	SF	10	A3
MORNINGSIDE DR	SF	12	B3
MORRELL ST	SF	2	C3
MORRELL ST	SF	17	B1
MORRIS RD	SF	1	A3
MORRIS ST	SF	7	B3
MORSE ST	SF	20	A3
MORTON ST	SF	1	C2
MOSCOW ST	SF	20	B2
MOSS ST	SF	7	A3
MOULTON ST	SF	2	A2
MOULTRIE ST	SF	14	C2
MOUNT LN	SF	9	A3
MTN SPRINGS AV	SF	9	C3
MOUNT VERNON AV	SF	19	C2
MOUNTVIEW CT	SF	13	C1
MUIR LOOP	SF	1	C3
MULFORD AL	SF	7	A1
MULLEN AV	SF	15	A1
MUNICH ST	SF	20	B2
MURRAY ST	SF	14	B3
MUSEUM WY	SF	10	A2
MYRA WY	SF	13	C2
MYRTLE ST	SF	6	C2
N			
NADELL CT	SF	20	A3
NAGLEE AV	SF	19	C2
NAHUA AV	SF	19	C2
NANTUCKET AV	SF	20	A1
NAPIER LN	SF	3	A2
NAPLES ST	SF	20	B2
NAPOLEON ST	SF	15	B1
NATICK ST	SF	14	B3
NATOMA ST	SF	7	A3
NATOMA ST	SF	10	C1
NAUMAN RD	SF	1	B3
NAVAJO AV	SF	20	A1
NAVY RD	SF	16	A3
NAYLOR ST	SF	20	B3
NEBRASKA ST	SF	15	A2
NELLIE ST	SF	10	B3
NELSON AV	SF	21	B2
NEPTUNE ST	SF	15	B3
NEVADA ST	SF	15	A2
NEWBURG ST	SF	14	A1
NEWCOMB AV	SF	15	B2
NEWELL ST	SF	2	C2
NEWHALL ST	SF	15	B3
NEWHALL ST	SF	21	B1
NEWMAN ST	SF	14	C2
NEW MONTGMRY ST	SF	7	B2
NEWTON ST	SF	20	A2
NEY ST	SF	14	B3
NIAGARA AV	SF	19	C2
NIANTIC AV	SF	19	B3
NIBBI CT	SF	21	B3
NICHOLS WY	SF	21	C2
NIDO AV	SF	5	C3
NIMITZ AV	SF	17	B1
NOB HILL CIR	SF	7	A1
NOBLES AL	SF	3	A2
NOE ST	SF	10	B1
NOE ST	SF	14	B1
NORDHOFF ST	SF	14	A3
NORFOLK ST	SF	10	C1
NORIEGA ST	SF	8	A3
NORIEGA ST	SF	9	A3
NORMANDIE TER	SF	2	A3
NORTH GATE DR	SF	13	B3
NORTH POINT DR	SF	3	C1
NORTH POINT ST	SF	2	A2
NORTH POINT ST	SF	3	A2
NORTHRIDGE RD	SF	16	A3
NORTH VIEW CT	SF	2	C2
NORTHWOOD DR	SF	13	B3
NORTON ST	SF	20	A1
NORWICH ST	SF	15	A1
NOTTINGHAM PL	SF	3	A3
NUEVA AV	SF	21	B3
O			
OAK ST	SF	10	A1
OAKDALE AV	SF	15	B2
OAK GROVE ST	SF	7	B3
OAKHURST LN	SF	9	B3
OAK PARK DR	SF	9	B3
OAKWOOD ST	SF	10	B2
OCEAN AV	SF	19	B1
OCTAVIA ST	SF	2	B2
OCTAVIA ST	SF	6	B3
OCTAVIA ST	SF	10	B1
OFARRELL ST	SF	6	A3
OFARRELL ST	SF	7	A2
OGDEN AV	SF	14	C2
OLD CHINATWN LN	SF	3	A3
OLIVE ST	SF	6	C2
OLIVER ST	SF	19	C3
OLMSTEAD ST	SF	21	A2
OLYMPIA WY	SF	13	C1
OMAR WY	SF	13	C2
ONEIDA AV	SF	20	A1
ONIQUE LN	SF	14	A2
ONONDAGA AV	SF	20	A1
OPAL PL	SF	7	A2
OPALO LN	SF	14	A2
OPHIR AL	SF	6	C2
ORA WY	SF	14	A2
ORANGE AL	SF	14	C1
ORBEN PL	SF	6	B2
ORD CT	SF	10	A2
ORD ST	SF	1	B2
ORD ST	SF	10	A2
ORDWAY ST	SF	21	A2
OREILLY AV	SF	1	C2
ORIENTE ST	SF	20	C3
ORIOLE WY	SF	13	B1
ORIZABA AV	SF	19	B2
ORTEGA ST	SF	12	A1
ORTEGA ST	SF	14	C1
ORTEGA WY	SF	9	A3
OSAGE AL	SF	14	C1
OSCAR AL	SF	7	B2
OSCEOLA LN	SF	15	C3
OSGOOD PL	SF	3	B3
OSHAUGHNESSY BL	SF	13	C1
OSHAUGHNESSY BL	SF	14	A2
OTEGA AV	SF	19	C2
OTIS ST	SF	10	C1
OTSEGO AV	SF	20	A1
OTTAWA AV	SF	20	A2
OVERLOOK DR	SF	8	C1
OWEN ST	SF	1	B2
OWENS ST	SF	11	B1
OXFORD ST	SF	20	C1
OZBORN CT	SF	3	C1
P			
PACHECO ST	SF	9	A3
PACHECO ST	SF	12	A1
PACHECO ST	SF	13	A1
PACIFIC AV	SF	2	A3
PACIFIC AV	SF	3	B3
PACIFIC AV W	SF	5	B2
PAGE ST	SF	9	C1
PAGE ST	SF	10	B1
PAGODA PL	SF	7	A1
PALACE DR	SF	1	C2
PALM AV	SF	5	B2
PALMETTO AV	SF	19	B3
PALO ALTO AV	SF	9	C3
PALOMA AV	SF	19	A1
PALOS PL	SF	12	C3
PALOU AV	SF	15	B2
PANAMA ST	SF	19	A3
PANORAMA DR	SF	9	C3
PANORAMA DR	SF	13	C1
PANTON AL	SF	6	C1
PARADISE AV	SF	14	A3
PARAISO PL	SF	12	C3
PARAMOUNT TER	SF	5	C3
PARDEE AL	SF	3	A2
PARIS ST	SF	20	A2
PARK BLVD	SF	1	A3
PARK ST	SF	14	B2
PARKER AV	SF	5	C2
PARK HILL AV	SF	10	A2
PARKHURST AL	SF	3	A3
PK PRESIDIO BL	SF	5	A3
PARKRIDGE DR	SF	14	A1
PARNASSUS AV	SF	9	B2
PARQUE DR	SF	20	C3
PARSONS ST	SF	9	C1
PASADENA ST	SF	20	C3
PATTEN RD	SF	1	B2
PATTERSON ST	SF	15	A2
PATTON ST	SF	14	C2
PAUL AV	SF	21	B1
PAULDING ST	SF	20	A1
PAYSON ST	SF	19	A3
PEABODY ST	SF	21	A3
PEARCE ST	SF	1	A2
PEARL ST	SF	10	C1
PEDESTRIAN WY	SF	1	C2
PELTON PL	SF	3	A3
PEMBERTON PL	SF	9	C3
PENA ST	SF	1	B3
PENINSULA AV	SF	21	B3
PENNINGTON ST	SF	1	B2
PENNSYLVANIA AV	SF	11	B3
PERALTA AV	SF	15	A2
PEREGO TER	SF	14	A1
PERINE PL	SF	6	A2
PERRY ST	SF	7	B2
PERSHING DR	SF	4	C1
PERSIA AV	SF	20	B1
PERU AV	SF	20	B1
PETERS AV	SF	14	C2
PETER YORKE WY	SF	6	B2
PETRARCH PL	SF	7	B1
PFEIFFER ST	SF	3	A2
PHELAN AV	SF	19	C1
PHELPS ST	SF	15	B2
PHELPS ST	SF	21	B1
PHOENIX TER	SF	2	C3
PICO AV	SF	19	B1
PIEDMONT ST	SF	10	A2
PIERCE ST	SF	2	A3
PIERCE ST	SF	6	A3
PIERCE ST	SF	10	B1
PILGRIM AV	SF	14	A3
PINAR LN	SF	6	A3
PINE ST	SF	3	B3
PINE ST	SF	6	A2
PINEHURST WY	SF	19	B1
PINK AL	SF	10	B1
PINO AL	SF	8	C2
PINTO AV	SF	18	C2
PIOCHE ST	SF	20	B1
PIPER LOOP	SF	1	B3
PIXLEY ST	SF	2	A3
PIZARRO WY	SF	13	B3
PLAZA ST	SF	13	B1
PLEASANT ST	SF	2	C3
PLUM ST	SF	10	C1
PLYMOUTH AV	SF	19	C3
POINT LOBOS AV	SF	4	A3
POLARIS WY	SF	20	A3
POLK ST	SF	2	C2
POLK ST	SF	6	A3
POLLARD PL	SF	3	A2
POMONA ST	SF	15	B3
POND ST	SF	10	B2
POPE RD	SF	2	B2
POPE ST	SF	1	A3
POPE ST	SF	20	A2
POPLAR ST	SF	14	C1
POPPY LN	SF	14	A2
PORTAL PATH	SF	13	B2
PORTER ST	SF	14	C3
PORTOLA DR	SF	13	B2
PORTOLA ST	SF	1	C2
POST ST	SF	6	A2
POST ST	SF	7	A2
POTOMAC ST	SF	10	B1
POTRERO AV	SF	11	A3
POWELL ST	SF	3	A1
POWELL ST	SF	7	A2
POWERS AV	SF	14	C1
POWHATTAN AV	SF	15	A2
PRADO ST	SF	2	A2
PRAGUE ST	SF	20	B2
PRECITA AV	SF	14	C1
PRENTISS ST	SF	15	A2
PRESCOTT CT	SF	3	B2
PRESIDIO AV	SF	5	C1
PRESIDIO BLVD	SF	1	C3
PRESIDIO TER	SF	5	B2
PRETOR WY	SF	20	A3
PRICE ROW	SF	3	A2
PRIEST ST	SF	2	C3
PRINCETON ST	SF	20	C1
PROSPECT AV	SF	14	C2
PROSPER ST	SF	10	B2
PUEBLO ST	SF	20	C3
PUTNAM ST	SF	15	A2
Q			
QUANE ST	SF	10	B3
QUARRY RD	SF	5	B1
QUARTZ WY	SF	14	A1
QUESADA AV	SF	15	B2
QUICKSTEP LN	SF	1	B1
QUINCY ST	SF	3	A3
QUINT ST	SF	15	B2
QUINTARA ST	SF	12	A1
QUINTARA ST	SF	13	A1
R			
RACCOON DR	SF	9	C3
RACINE LN	SF	21	B2
RADIO TER	SF	13	A1
RAE AV	SF	19	C3
RALEIGH ST	SF	20	A1
RALSTON AV	SF	1	A2
RALSTON ST	SF	19	A2
RAMONA ST	SF	10	B2
RAMSELL ST	SF	19	B2
RANDALL ST	SF	14	B2
RANDOLPH ST	SF	19	B2
RANKIN ST	SF	15	B2
RAUSCH ST	SF	7	A3
RAVENWOOD DR	SF	13	B3
RAWLES ST	SF	1	C3
RAYBURN ST	SF	10	B3
RAYCLIFF TER	SF	2	A3
RAYMOND AV	SF	21	A2
REARDON RD	SF	16	A3
REDDY ST	SF	15	B3
REDFIELD AL	SF	2	C2
REDONDO ST	SF	21	B2
RED ROCK WY	SF	14	A1
REDWOOD ST	SF	6	B3
REED ST	SF	2	C3
REEVES CT	SF	3	C1
REGENT ST	SF	19	C3
RENO PL	SF	3	A2

1991 SAN FRANCISCO COUNTY STREET INDEX

STREET	CITY	PAGE	GRID
REPOSA WY	SF	13	C2
RESERVOIR ST	SF	10	B1
RESTANI WY	SF	20	A2
RETIRO WY	SF	2	A2
REUEL CT	SF	15	C2
REVERE AV	SF	15	B2
REX AV	SF	13	B2
REY ST	SF	21	A3
RHINE ST	SF	19	B3
RHODE ISLAND ST	SF	11	B1
RICE ST	SF	19	B3
RCHD H DANA PL	SF	2	B1
RICHARDS CIR	SF	15	C1
RICHARDSON AV	SF	1	C2
RICHLAND AV	SF	14	C2
RICKARD ST	SF	15	A3
RICO WY	SF	2	A2
RIDGE LN	SF	19	C2
RIDGEWOOD AV	SF	13	C3
RILEY AV	SF	1	B2
RINCON ST	SF	7	C2
RINGOLD ST	SF	11	A1
RIO CT	SF	13	C2
RIO VERDE ST	SF	20	C3
RIPLEY ST	SF	15	A1
RITCH ST	SF	7	B3
RIVAS AV	SF	18	C2
RIVERA ST	SF	12	A1
RIVERA ST	SF	13	A1
RIVERTON DR	SF	12	C3
RIVOLI ST	SF	9	C2
RIZAL ST	SF	7	B3
ROACH ST	SF	2	C2
ROANOKE ST	SF	14	B2
ROBBLEE AV	SF	15	B3
ROBINHOOD DR	SF	13	B2
ROBINSON DR	SF	20	B3
ROBINSON ST	SF	17	B1
ROCK AL	SF	13	B2
ROCKAWAY AV	SF	13	B2
ROCKDALE DR	SF	13	C2
ROCKLAND ST	SF	2	C3
ROCKRIDGE DR	SF	13	A1
ROCKWOOD CT	SF	13	B2
ROD RD	SF	1	A2
RODGERS ST	SF	11	A1
RODRIGUEZ ST	SF	1	C3
ROEMER WY	SF	19	C3
ROLPH ST	SF	20	A2
ROMAIN ST	SF	10	A3
ROME ST	SF	19	C2
ROME ST	SF	20	C2
ROMOLO ST	SF	3	A3
RONDEL PL	SF	10	C2
ROOSEVELT WY	SF	10	A2
ROSCOE ST	SF	14	C3
ROSE ST	SF	10	B1
ROSELLA CT	SF	20	A1
ROSELYN TER	SF	5	C3
ROSEMARY CT	SF	12	C2
ROSEMONT PL	SF	10	B1
ROSENKRANZ ST	SF	15	A2
ROSEWOOD DR	SF	13	B3
ROSIE LEE LN	SF	15	C3
ROSS AL	SF	3	A3
ROSSI AV	SF	5	C3
ROSSMOOR DR	SF	13	A3
ROTTECK ST	SF	14	B3
ROUSSEAU ST	SF	14	B3
ROWLAND ST	SF	7	A1
ROYAL LANE CT	SF	20	A2
RUCKMAN AV	SF	1	A2
RUDDEN AV	SF	20	A1
RUGER ST	SF	1	C3
RUSS ST	SF	7	A3
RUSSELL ST	SF	2	C3
RUSSIA AV	SF	20	A1
RUSSIAN HILL PL	SF	2	C3
RUTH ST	SF	20	A1
RUTLAND ST	SF	21	A3
RUTLEDGE ST	SF	15	A1

S

STREET	CITY	PAGE	GRID
SABIN PL	SF	3	A3
SACRAMENTO ST	SF	2	C3
SACRAMENTO ST	SF	3	A3
SACRAMENTO ST	SF	5	B2
SACRAMENTO ST	SF	6	A3
SADOWA ST	SF	19	B3
SAFFOLD RD	SF	1	A3
SAFIRA LN	SF	14	A1
SAGAMORE ST	SF	19	B3
ST CHARLES AV	SF	19	A3
ST CROIX DR	SF	13	C2
ST ELMO WY	SF	13	B3
ST FRANCIS BLVD	SF	13	B3
ST FRANCIS PL	SF	7	B2
ST GEORGE AL	SF	3	A3
ST GERMAIN AV	SF	9	C3
ST JOSEPHS AV	SF	6	A3
ST LOUIS PL	SF	3	A3
ST MARYS AV	SF	14	B3
SAL ST	SF	1	B3
SALA TER	SF	20	A2
SALINAS AV	SF	21	B1
SALMON ST	SF	3	A3
SAMOSET ST	SF	15	A1
SAMPSON AV	SF	21	B3
SAN ALESO AV	SF	13	B3
SAN ANDREAS WY	SF	13	B3
SAN ANSELMO AV	SF	13	B2
SAN ANTONIO PL	SF	3	A2
SAN BENITO WY	SF	13	B3
SAN BRUNO AV	SF	11	A2
SAN BRUNO AV	SF	15	A3
SAN BRUNO AV	SF	21	A1
SN BUENAVNTR WY	SF	13	B3
SAN CARLOS ST	SF	10	C2
SANCHEZ ST	SF	1	C3
SANCHEZ ST	SF	5	C1
SANCHEZ ST	SF	10	B2
SAN DIEGO AV	SF	19	B3
SAN FELIPE AV	SF	13	B3
SAN FERNANDO WY	SF	13	A3
SAN GABRIEL AV	SF	20	A1
SAN JACINTO WY	SF	13	B3
SAN JOSE AV	SF	14	B2
SAN JOSE AV	SF	19	C2
SAN JOSE AV	SF	20	A1
SAN JUAN AV	SF	20	A1
SAN LEANDRO WY	SF	13	A3
SAN LORENZO WY	SF	13	B2
SAN LUIS AV	SF	19	B3
SAN MARCOS AV	SF	13	B1
SAN MATEO AV	SF	19	B3
SAN MIGUEL ST	SF	19	C2
SAN PABLO AV	SF	13	B2
SAN RAFAEL WY	SF	13	A3
SAN RAMON WY	SF	19	C1
SANSOME ST	SF	3	B2
SANTA ANA AV	SF	13	B3
STA BARBARA AV	SF	19	B3
SANTA CLARA AV	SF	13	B3
SANTA CRUZ AV	SF	19	B3
SANTA FE AV	SF	15	B3
SANTA MARINA ST	SF	14	C2
SANTA MONICA WY	SF	13	B2
SANTA PAULA AV	SF	13	B3
SANTA RITA AV	SF	13	B1
SANTA ROSA AV	SF	20	A1
SANTA YNEZ AV	SF	20	A1
SANTA YSABEL AV	SF	20	A1
SANTIAGO ST	SF	12	A1
SANTIAGO ST	SF	13	A1
SANTOS ST	SF	20	C3
SARGENT ST	SF	19	B2
SATURN ST	SF	10	A2
SAWYER ST	SF	20	C3
SCENIC WY	SF	4	C2
SCHOFIELD RD	SF	1	A2
SCHOFIELD RD	SF	2	B2

STREET	CITY	PAGE	GRID
SCHOOL AL	SF	3	A2
SCHWERIN ST	SF	21	A3
SCOTIA AV	SF	15	B3
SCOTLAND ST	SF	3	A2
SCOTT ST	SF	2	A3
SCOTT ST	SF	6	A3
SCOTT ST	SF	10	A1
SEA CLIFF AV	SF	4	B2
SEAL ROCK DR	SF	4	A3
SEARS ST	SF	19	C3
SEAVIEW TER	SF	4	B2
SECURITY PAC PL	SF	7	A2
SELBY ST	SF	15	B2
SELMA WY	SF	9	A3
SEMINOLE AV	SF	20	A2
SENECA AV	SF	20	A1
SEQUOIA WY	SF	13	C2
SGT MITCHELL ST	SF	1	C2
SERPENTINE AV	SF	15	A1
SERRANO DR	SF	18	C2
SERRANO DR	SF	19	A2
SERVICE ST	SF	2	A3
SEVERN ST	SF	10	B3
SEVILLE ST	SF	20	A3
SEWARD ST	SF	10	A3
SEYMOUR ST	SF	6	A3
SHAFTER AV	SF	15	C3
SHAFTER AV	SF	21	C1
SHAFTER RD	SF	1	C3
SHAKESPEARE ST	SF	19	B3
SHANGRILA WY	SF	13	B2
SHANNON ST	SF	7	A2
SHARON ST	SF	10	B2
SHARP PL	SF	2	C3
SHAW AL	SF	7	B2
SHAWNEE AV	SF	20	A2
SHELDON TER	SF	9	A3
SHEPHARD PL	SF	3	A3
SHERIDAN AV	SF	1	B2
SHERIDAN ST	SF	11	A1
SHERMAN RD	SF	1	C3
SHERMAN ST	SF	7	A3
SHERWOOD CT	SF	13	C3
SHIELDS ST	SF	19	A2
SHIPLEY ST	SF	7	A3
SHORE VIEW AV	SF	4	B3
SHORT ST	SF	10	A3
SHOTWELL ST	SF	10	C2
SHOTWELL ST	SF	14	C1
SHRADER ST	SF	5	C3
SHRADER ST	SF	9	C1
SIBERT LOOP	SF	1	B3
SIBLEY RD	SF	1	C3
SICKLES AV	SF	19	C3
SIERRA ST	SF	11	B3
SILLIMAN ST	SF	15	A3
SILLIMAN ST	SF	20	C1
SILVER AV	SF	14	B3
SILVER AV	SF	15	A3
SILVERVIEW DR	SF	15	B3
SIMONDS LOOP	SF	1	C3
SKYLINE BLVD	SF	18	A1
SKYVIEW WY	SF	9	C3
SLOAN AL	SF	7	B2
SLOAT BLVD	SF	12	A3
SOLA AV	SF	13	B1
SOMERSET ST	SF	15	C3
SOMERSET ST	SF	21	A1
SONOMA ST	SF	3	A2
SONORA LN	SF	6	A3
SOTELO AV	SF	13	B1
SOUTH DR	SF	8	A2
SOUTHERN HTS AV	SF	11	B3
SOUTH HILL BLVD	SF	20	B3
SOUTH PARK AV	SF	7	B3
S VAN NESS AV	SF	10	C1
SOUTHWOOD DR	SF	19	B1
SPARROW ST	SF	10	C2
SPARTA ST	SF	21	A2
SPEAR AV	SF	17	B1
SPEAR ST	SF	7	B1

STREET	CITY	PAGE	GRID
SPENCE ST	SF	10	B2
SPOFFORD ST	SF	3	A3
SPRECKLES LK DR	SF	8	C1
SPRING ST	SF	3	A3
SPRINGFIELD DR	SF	12	C3
SPROULE LN	SF	3	A3
SPRUCE CT	SF	20	B3
SPRUCE ST	SF	5	C2
STANDISH AV	SF	14	A3
STANFORD ST	SF	7	C3
STANFORD HTS AV	SF	13	C3
STANLEY ST	SF	19	B2
STANTON ST	SF	10	A3
STANYAN ST	SF	5	C3
STANYAN ST	SF	9	C1
STAPLES AV	SF	13	C3
STARK ST	SF	3	A3
STARR KING WY	SF	6	C2
STARVIEW WY	SF	13	C1
STATE DR	SF	18	C1
STATES ST	SF	10	A2
STEINER ST	SF	2	A3
STEINER ST	SF	6	B3
STEINER ST	SF	10	B1
STERLING ST	SF	7	B2
STEUART ST	SF	7	B1
STEVELOE PL	SF	7	A2
STEVENS AL	SF	3	B3
STEVENSON ST	SF	6	C3
STEVENSON ST	SF	7	A3
STEVENSON ST	SF	10	C1
STILL ST	SF	14	B3
STILLINGS AV	SF	14	A3
STILLMAN ST	SF	7	B3
STILWELL DR	SF	4	C1
STOCKTON ST	SF	3	A2
STOCKTON ST	SF	7	A1
STONE ST	SF	1	A2
STONE ST	SF	3	A3
STONECREST DR	SF	19	A1
STONEMAN ST	SF	15	A1
STONEYBROOK AV	SF	14	C3
STONEYFORD AV	SF	14	C3
STOREY AV	SF	1	A2
STORRIE ST	SF	10	A2
STOW LAKE DR	SF	9	A1
STOW LAKE DR E	SF	9	A1
STRATFORD DR	SF	19	A2
SUMMIT ST	SF	19	C2
SUMNER AV	SF	1	C3
SUMNER ST	SF	7	A3
SUNBEAM LN	SF	20	A2
SUNGLOW LN	SF	14	C3
SUNNYDALE AV	SF	20	B2
SUNNYDALE AV	SF	21	A3
SUNNYSIDE TER	SF	19	C1
SUNRISE WY	SF	20	C3
SUNSET BLVD	SF	8	B2
SUNSET BLVD	SF	12	B1
SUNVIEW DR	SF	14	A1
SURREY ST	SF	14	A3
SUSSEX ST	SF	14	B2
SUTRO HTS AV	SF	4	A3
SUTTER ST	SF	6	A3
SUTTER ST	SF	7	A2
SWEENY ST	SF	15	A3
SWISS AV	SF	14	A3
SYCAMORE ST	SF	10	C2
SYDNEY WY	SF	13	C1
SYLVAN DR	SF	12	C3

T

STREET	CITY	PAGE	GRID
TABER PL	SF	7	B3
TACOMA ST	SF	5	A3
TALBERT CT	SF	21	A3
TALBERT ST	SF	21	A3
TAMALPAIS TER	SF	5	C3
TAMPA LN	SF	15	B3
TANDANG SORA	SF	7	B3
TAPIA DR	SF	18	C1

STREET	CITY	PAGE	GRID
TARA ST	SF	19	C2
TARAVAL ST	SF	12	A2
TARAVAL ST	SF	13	A2
TAYLOR RD	SF	1	B2
TAYLOR ST	SF	2	C1
TAYLOR ST	SF	7	A1
TAYLOR ST	SF	7	A2
TEDDY AV	SF	21	A2
TEHAMA ST	SF	7	A3
TELEGRAPH PL	SF	3	A2
TELEGRAPH HL BL	SF	3	A2
TEMESCAL TER	SF	5	C3
TEMPLE ST	SF	10	A2
TENNESSEE ST	SF	11	C2
TENNESSEE ST	SF	15	C1
TENNY PL	SF	7	B2
TERESITA BLVD	SF	13	C1
TERRACE DR	SF	13	B2
TERRACE WALK	SF	13	B2
TERRA VISTA AV	SF	6	A3
TEXAS ST	SF	11	B2
THE ESPLANADE	SF	8	A1
THERESA ST	SF	14	A3
THOMAS AV	SF	1	B3
THOMAS AV	SF	15	C3
THOMAS AV	SF	21	C1
THOMAS MELLN DR	SF	21	B3
THOMAS MORE WY	SF	19	A3
THOR AV	SF	14	B3
THORNBURG RD	SF	1	C2
THORNE WY	SF	15	B3
THORNTON AV	SF	15	B3
THORP LN	SF	10	A3
THRIFT ST	SF	19	B2
TICHENOR SQ	SF	1	B1
TIFFANY AV	SF	14	C1
TILLMAN PL	SF	7	A2
TINGLEY ST	SF	14	B3
TIOGA AV	SF	21	A2
TOCOLOMA AV	SF	21	B3
TODD ST	SF	1	A2
TOLAND ST	SF	15	B2
TOLEDO WY	SF	2	A2
TOMASO CT	SF	21	A3
TOMPKINS AV	SF	14	C2
TOPAZ WY	SF	14	A2
TOPEKA AV	SF	15	B3
TORNEY AV	SF	1	C2
TORRENS CT	SF	2	C3
TOUCHARD ST	SF	6	C1
TOWNSEND ST	SF	7	C3
TOWNSEND ST	SF	11	A1
TOYON LN	SF	20	B3
TRAINOR ST	SF	10	C1
TRANSVERSE RD	SF	8	C1
TREASURY PL	SF	3	B3
TREAT AV	SF	11	A2
TREAT AV	SF	15	A1
TRENTON ST	SF	3	A3
TRINITY ST	SF	7	B1
TROY AL	SF	2	C3
TRUBY ST	SF	1	C2
TRUETT ST	SF	3	A3
TRUMBULL ST	SF	14	B3
TUBBS ST	SF	11	C3
TUCKER AV	SF	21	A2
TULANE ST	SF	14	C3
TULARE ST	SF	15	C1
TULIP AL	SF	7	A3
TUNNEL AV	SF	21	B3
TURK ST	SF	5	C3
TURK ST	SF	6	A3
TURK ST	SF	7	A2
TURNER TER	SF	11	B3
TURQUOISE WY	SF	14	A2
TUSCANY AL	SF	3	A2
TWIN PEAKS BLVD	SF	9	C3

U

STREET	CITY	PAGE	GRID
ULLOA ST	SF	12	A2

1991 SAN FRANCISCO COUNTY STREET INDEX

STREET	CITY	PAGE	GRID
ULLOA ST	SF	13	A2
UNDERWOOD AV	SF	21	C1
UNION ST	SF	2	A3
UNION ST	SF	3	A2
UNITED NATNS PZ	SF	6	C3
UNIVERSITY ST	SF	20	C1
UNIVERSITY ST	SF	21	A1
UPLAND DR	SF	13	B3
UPPER TER	SF	10	A2
UPR SERVICE RD	SF	9	B2
UPTON AV	SF	1	A2
UPTON ST	SF	15	B2
URANUS TER	SF	9	C2
URBANO DR N	SF	19	B1
URBANO DR S	SF	19	B1
UTAH ST	SF	11	A3

V

STREET	CITY	PAGE	GRID
VALDEZ AV	SF	13	C3
VALE AV	SF	12	C3
VALENCIA ST	SF	10	C1
VALENCIA ST	SF	14	C1
VALERTON CT	SF	20	A1
VALLEJO ST	SF	1	B2
VALLEJO ST	SF	2	C3
VALLEJO ST	SF	3	A3
VALLEJO TER	SF	3	A3
VALLETA CT	SF	14	A2
VALLEY ST	SF	14	B1
VALMAR TER	SF	20	B1
VALPARAISO ST	SF	2	C2
VAN BUREN ST	SF	14	A3
VANDEWATER ST	SF	3	A2
VAN DYKE AV	SF	21	B1
VAN KEUREN AV	SF	17	B1
VAN NESS AV	SF	2	B2
VAN NESS AV	SF	6	C2
VARELA AV	SF	19	A1
VARENNES ST	SF	3	A2
VARNEY PL	SF	7	B3
VASQUEZ AV	SF	13	B2
VASSAR PL	SF	7	B2
VEGA ST	SF	5	C3
VELASCO AV	SF	20	C3
VENARD AL	SF	3	A2
VENTURA AV	SF	13	B1
VENUS ST	SF	15	B3
VERDI PL	SF	3	A3
VERDUN WY	SF	13	B2
VERMEHR PL	SF	7	A2
VERMONT ST	SF	11	A1
VERMONT ST	SF	15	B1
VERNA ST	SF	13	C3
VERNON ST	SF	19	B2
VERONA PL	SF	7	B2
VESTA ST	SF	15	B3
VIA BUFANO	SF	3	A2
VICENTE ST	SF	12	A2
VICENTE ST	SF	13	A2
VICKSBURG ST	SF	10	B3
VICKSBURG ST	SF	14	B1
VICTORIA ST	SF	19	B2
VIDAL DR	SF	18	C2
VIENNA ST	SF	20	B2
VILLA TER	SF	10	A3
VINE TER	SF	7	A1
VINTON CT	SF	3	A3
VIRGIL ST	SF	14	C1
VIRGINIA AV	SF	14	C2
VISITACION AV	SF	20	C2
VISITACION AV	SF	21	A3
VISTA LN	SF	10	A3
VISTA VERDE CT	SF	14	A3
VISTAVIEW CT	SF	15	B3
VULCAN STAIRWAY	SF	10	A2

W

STREET	CITY	PAGE	GRID
WABASH TER	SF	21	B2
WAGNER AL	SF	6	C2
WAGNER AL	SF	7	A2
WAGNER RD	SF	1	A2
WAITHMAN WY	SF	13	B2
WALBRIDGE ST	SF	20	B3
WALDO AL	SF	3	C3
WALESA, LECH	SF	6	C3
WALL PL	SF	3	C3
WALLACE AV	SF	21	B1
WALLEN CT	SF	1	C3
WALLER ST	SF	9	C1
WALLER ST	SF	10	A1
WALNUT ST	SF	5	C1
WALTER ST	SF	10	B1
WALTER LUM PL	SF	3	A3
WALTER LUM PL	SF	7	A1
WALTHAM ST	SF	15	A1
WANDA ST	SF	20	A1
WARD ST	SF	21	A2
WARNER PL	SF	3	C3
WARREN DR	SF	9	B3
WASHBURN ST	SF	11	A1
WASHINGTON BLVD	SF	1	B3
WASHINGTON ST	SF	3	B3
WASHINGTON ST	SF	5	C2
WASHINGTON ST	SF	6	A2
WASHOE PL	SF	3	A3
WATCHMAN WY	SF	11	B3
WATER ST	SF	2	C2
WATERLOO ST	SF	15	A2
WATERVILLE ST	SF	15	B2
WATSON PL	SF	20	A1
WATT AV	SF	20	A3
WAVERLY PL	SF	3	A3
WAWONA ST	SF	12	B3
WAWONA ST	SF	13	A2
WAYLAND ST	SF	20	C1
WAYLAND ST	SF	21	A1
WAYNE PL	SF	3	A3
WEBB PL	SF	3	A2
WEBSTER ST	SF	2	B3
WEBSTER ST	SF	6	B3
WEBSTER ST	SF	10	B1
WELDON ST	SF	15	A3
WELSH ST	SF	7	B3
WENTWORTH PL	SF	3	A3
WESTBROOK CT	SF	15	C3
WEST CLAY ST	SF	4	C2
WESTRN SHORE LN	SF	1	B1
WESTGATE DR	SF	13	B3
WESTMOORLAND DR	SF	12	B3
WEST POINT RD	SF	16	A2
WEST PORTAL AV	SF	13	A2
WESTSIDE DR	SF	3	C1
WEST VIEW AV	SF	14	C3
WESTWOOD DR	SF	19	B1
WETMORE ST	SF	3	A3
WHEAT ST	SF	21	B1
WHEELER AV	SF	21	B3
WHIPPLE AV	SF	19	C3
WHITE ST	SF	2	C3
WHITECLIFF WY	SF	15	B3
WHITFIELD CT	SF	15	C3
WHITING ST	SF	3	A2
WHITNEY ST	SF	14	B2
WHITNEY YNG CIR	SF	15	C3
WHITTIER ST	SF	19	C3
WIESE ST	SF	10	C2
WILDE AV	SF	21	A2
WILDER ST	SF	14	B3
WILDWOOD WY	SF	19	B1
WILLARD ST	SF	9	C2
WILLARD ST N	SF	5	B3
WILLIAMS AV	SF	15	B3
WILLIAR AV	SF	19	C2
WILLOW ST	SF	6	B3
WILLS ST	SF	16	A2
WILMOT ST	SF	6	B2
WILSON ST	SF	19	B3
WINDING WY	SF	20	A3
WINDSOR PL	SF	3	A2
WINFIELD ST	SF	14	C2
WINSTON DR	SF	19	A1
WINTER PL	SF	3	A2
WINTHROP ST	SF	3	A2
WISCONSIN ST	SF	11	B2
WISER CT	SF	1	A3
WOOD ST	SF	5	C2
WOODACRE DR	SF	13	A3
WOODHAVEN CT	SF	9	C3
WOODLAND AV	SF	9	C2
WOODSIDE AV	SF	13	B1
WOODWARD ST	SF	10	C1
WOOL CT	SF	1	A2
WOOL ST	SF	14	C2
WOOLSEY ST	SF	21	A1
WORCESTER AV	SF	19	B3
WORDEN ST	SF	3	A2
WORTH ST	SF	10	A3
WRIGHT LOOP	SF	1	A3
WRIGHT ST	SF	15	A1
WYTON LN	SF	19	A1

Y

STREET	CITY	PAGE	GRID
YACHT RD	SF	1	C2
YALE ST	SF	20	C1
YERBA BUENA AV	SF	13	B2
YORBA LN	SF	12	B3
YORBA ST	SF	12	B3
YORK ST	SF	11	A2
YORK ST	SF	15	A1
YOSEMITE AV	SF	21	B1
YOUNG ST	SF	1	C2
YOUNG CT	SF	15	C1
YUKON ST	SF	10	A3

Z

STREET	CITY	PAGE	GRID
ZENO PL	SF	7	B2
ZIRCON PL	SF	14	B2
ZOE ST	SF	7	B3

NUMERICAL STREETS

STREET	CITY	PAGE	GRID
1ST ST	SF	3	C2
1ST ST	SF	7	B1
2ND AV	SF	5	B2
2ND AV	SF	9	B2
2ND ST	SF	3	C1
2ND ST	SF	7	B2
3RD AV	SF	5	B2
3RD AV	SF	9	B2
3RD AV	SF	17	A2
3RD ST	SF	3	C1
3RD ST	SF	7	B2
3RD ST	SF	11	C1
3RD ST	SF	15	C2
3RD ST	SF	21	B1
4TH AV	SF	5	B2
4TH AV	SF	9	B2
4TH ST	SF	3	C1
4TH ST	SF	7	B2
4TH ST	SF	11	C1
5TH AV	SF	5	B2
5TH AV	SF	9	B2
5TH ST	SF	3	C1
5TH ST	SF	7	A2
6TH AV	SF	5	B2
6TH AV	SF	9	B2
6TH AV	SF	17	A1
6TH ST	SF	3	C1
6TH ST	SF	7	A3
6TH ST	SF	11	B1
7TH AV	SF	5	B2
7TH AV	SF	9	B2
7TH ST	SF	7	A3
7TH ST	SF	11	B1
8TH AV	SF	5	B2
8TH AV	SF	9	B2
8TH ST	SF	3	C1
8TH ST	SF	7	A3
8TH ST	SF	11	A1
9TH AV	SF	5	B2
9TH AV	SF	9	B3
9TH AV	SF	13	B1
9TH ST	SF	3	C1
9TH ST	SF	11	A1
10TH AV	SF	5	A2
10TH AV	SF	9	B2
10TH AV	SF	13	B1
10TH ST	SF	3	C1
10TH ST	SF	11	A1
11TH AV	SF	5	A2
11TH AV	SF	9	B2
11TH ST	SF	3	C1
11TH ST	SF	10	C1
12TH AV	SF	5	A2
12TH AV	SF	9	A3
12TH AV	SF	13	B1
12TH ST	SF	3	C1
12TH ST	SF	10	C1
13TH ST	SF	3	C1
13TH ST	SF	10	C1
14TH AV	SF	5	A2
14TH AV	SF	9	A2
14TH AV	SF	13	A1
14TH ST	SF	10	B1
15TH AV	SF	5	A2
15TH AV	SF	9	A3
15TH AV	SF	13	A1
15TH ST	SF	10	A2
15TH ST	SF	11	A2
16TH AV	SF	5	A2
16TH AV	SF	9	A2
16TH AV	SF	13	A1
16TH ST	SF	10	B2
16TH ST	SF	11	A2
17TH AV	SF	5	A2
17TH AV	SF	9	A2
17TH ST	SF	9	C2
17TH ST	SF	10	A2
17TH ST	SF	11	A2
18TH AV	SF	5	A3
18TH AV	SF	9	A2
18TH AV	SF	13	A1
18TH ST	SF	10	A2
18TH ST	SF	11	A2
19TH AV	SF	5	A3
19TH AV	SF	9	A2
19TH AV	SF	13	A1
19TH AV	SF	19	A1
19TH ST	SF	10	A2
19TH ST	SF	11	A2
20TH AV	SF	4	C2
20TH AV	SF	9	A2
20TH AV	SF	13	A1
20TH ST	SF	10	A3
20TH ST	SF	11	A2
21ST AV	SF	4	C2
21ST AV	SF	9	A2
21ST AV	SF	13	A1
21ST ST	SF	10	B3
21ST ST	SF	11	A3
22ND AV	SF	4	C2
22ND AV	SF	8	C3
22ND AV	SF	13	A1
22ND ST	SF	10	A3
22ND ST	SF	11	A3
23RD AV	SF	4	C2
23RD AV	SF	8	C2
23RD AV	SF	12	C1
23RD AV	SF	13	A3
23RD ST	SF	10	B3
23RD ST	SF	11	A3
24TH AV	SF	4	C2
24TH AV	SF	8	C3
24TH AV	SF	12	C1
24TH ST	SF	10	A3
24TH ST	SF	11	A3
24TH ST	SF	14	A1
25TH AV	SF	4	C2
25TH AV	SF	8	C3
25TH AV	SF	12	C1
25TH ST	SF	14	A1
25TH ST	SF	15	A1
26TH AV	SF	4	C2
26TH AV	SF	8	C3
26TH AV	SF	12	C1
26TH ST	SF	14	A1
26TH ST	SF	15	A1
27TH AV	SF	4	C2
27TH AV	SF	8	C3
27TH AV	SF	12	C1
27TH ST	SF	14	A1
28TH AV	SF	4	C3
28TH AV	SF	8	C3
28TH AV	SF	12	C1
28TH ST	SF	14	B1
29TH AV	SF	4	C3
29TH AV	SF	8	C3
29TH AV	SF	12	C1
29TH ST	SF	14	B2
30TH AV	SF	4	B3
30TH AV	SF	8	C2
30TH AV	SF	12	C1
30TH ST	SF	14	B2
31ST AV	SF	4	B2
31ST AV	SF	8	B2
31ST AV	SF	12	C1
32ND AV	SF	4	B3
32ND AV	SF	8	B2
32ND AV	SF	12	B1
33RD AV	SF	4	B3
33RD AV	SF	8	B2
33RD AV	SF	12	B1
34TH AV	SF	4	B3
34TH AV	SF	8	B2
34TH AV	SF	12	B1
35TH AV	SF	4	B3
35TH AV	SF	8	B2
35TH AV	SF	12	B1
36TH AV	SF	4	B3
36TH AV	SF	8	B3
36TH AV	SF	12	B1
37TH AV	SF	4	B3
37TH AV	SF	8	B2
37TH AV	SF	12	B1
38TH AV	SF	4	B3
38TH AV	SF	8	B2
38TH AV	SF	12	B1
39TH AV	SF	4	B3
39TH AV	SF	8	B2
39TH AV	SF	12	B1
40TH AV	SF	4	A3
40TH AV	SF	8	B2
40TH AV	SF	12	B1
41ST AV	SF	4	A3
41ST AV	SF	8	A1
41ST AV	SF	12	B1
42ND AV	SF	4	A3
42ND AV	SF	8	A2
42ND AV	SF	12	A1
43RD AV	SF	4	A3
43RD AV	SF	8	A2
43RD AV	SF	12	A1
44TH AV	SF	4	A3
44TH AV	SF	8	A1
44TH AV	SF	12	A1
45TH AV	SF	4	A3
45TH AV	SF	8	A1
45TH AV	SF	12	A1
46TH AV	SF	4	A3
46TH AV	SF	8	A1
46TH AV	SF	12	A1
47TH AV	SF	4	A3
47TH AV	SF	8	A1
47TH AV	SF	12	A1
48TH AV	SF	4	A3
48TH AV	SF	8	A2
48TH AV	SF	12	A1

1991 SAN FRANCISCO COUNTY POINTS OF INTEREST

PAGE	GRID	NAME	ADDRESS	CITY	PHONE
		AIRPORTS & AIRLINES			
7	A2	AIR CALIFORNIA	460 POST ST		433 2660
7	A2	AIR CANADA	350 POST ST		761 0733
7	A2	ALASKA AIRLINES	275 POST ST		931 8888
7	A2	AMERICAN AIRLINES	CALIFORNIA & POWELL ST		398 4434
7	A2	BRITISH AIRWAYS	345 POWELL ST		877 0622
7	A2	CANADIAN PACIFIC AIR	343 POWELL ST		877 5960
7	A2	CHINA AIRLINES	391 SUTTER ST		989 3300
7	B1	CONTINENTAL AIRLINES	433 CALIFORNIA ST		397 8818
7	A2	DELTA AIRLINES	250 STOCKTON ST		552 5700
7	A1	EASTERN AIRLINES	CALIFORNIA & POWELL ST		474 5858
7	A2	JAPAN AIRLINES	POWELL & O FARRELL STS		982 8141
7	A2	LTU	360 POST ST		989 6640
7	A2	LUFTHANSA	360 POST ST		645 3880
7	A2	MEXICANA AIRLINES	421 POWELL ST		982 1424
7	A2	NORTHWEST ORIENT	350 POST ST		392 2163
7	A2	PACIFIC SOUTHWEST, PSA	212 STOCKTON ST		956 8636
7	A2	PAN AMERICAN	222 STOCKTON ST		221 1111
7	A2	PHILIPPINE AIRLINES	447 SUTTER		391 0470
7	A2	QANTAS AIRWAYS	360 POST ST		761 8000
		S F INT AIRPORT	AIRPORT WY	SSF	761 0800
7	A2	SINGAPORE AIRLINES	476 POST ST		781 7304
7	A2	TRANS WORLD AIRLINES	433 CALIFORNIA		864 5731
7	A2	UNITED AIRLINES	POST & POWELL		397 2100
7	A2	WESTERN	287 GEARY ST		761 3300
7	A2	WORLD AIRWAYS	320 20TH ST		577 2500
		BUILDINGS			
7	A2	A/AARON BUSINESS SERV	260 KEARNY ST		
7	B1	ADAM GRANT	114 SANSOME ST		981 0375
7	B2	AETNA LIFE & CASUALTY	600 MARKET ST		
7	B1	ALCOA, THE	1 MARITIME PLAZA		434 2000
7	B2	ALEXANDER	155 MONTGOMERY ST		981 5074
7	B1	AMERICAN INTERNATIONAL	206 SANSOME ST		
7	B2	AMERICAN SAVINGS	MARKET & KEARNY STS		362 8220
7	B2	BANKERS INVESTMENT	742 MARKET ST		781 2836
7	B1	BANK OF AMERICA CENTER	555 CALIFORNIA ST		765 3174
7	B1	BECHTEL	50 BEALE ST		768 1234
7	A2	BOARD OF TRADE	989 MARKET ST		421 6302
7	A2	BROOKS BROTHERS	209 POST ST		
6	C3	BROOKS HALL	HYDE & FULTON STS		974 4000
6	C2	BUILDERS EXCHANGE	850 S VAN NESS AV		282 8220
7	B1	CAL COMMERCIAL UNION	315 MONTGOMERY ST		
7	B2	CALIFORNIA PACIFIC	105 MONTGOMERY ST		
6	C3	CALIFORNIA STATE	350 MCALLISTER ST		
7	B2	CALL	74 NEW MONTGOMERY ST		
6	C2	CATHEDRAL HILL	1255 POST ST		776 8200
7	B2	CENTRAL TOWER	703 MARKET ST		982 1935
7	B2	CHANCERY	564 MARKET ST		
3	A3	CHINESE CULTURAL CTR	750 KEARNY ST		
7	A2	CHRONICLE	5TH & MISSION STS		777 1111
6	C3	CITY HALL	400 VAN NESS AV		554 4000
6	C3	CIVIC AUDITORIUM	99 GROVE ST		974 4000
6	C3	CIVIC CENTER	VAN NESS & POLK ST		
3	A2	CLUB FUGAZI	678 GREEN ST		
7	A2	COMMERCIAL	833 MARKET ST		362 4915
7	B1	COMMERCIAL BLOCK	149 CALIFORNIA ST		
7	A2	CORDES, W F	126 POST ST		
20	C3	COW PALACE	GENEVA AV & SANTOS ST		469 6000
7	A2	CROCKER CENTER	POST ST & KEARNY ST		
7	B2	CROCKER NATIONAL BANK	1 MONTGOMERY ST		399 7564
7	B2	CROCKER PLAZA	600 MARKET ST		434 4753
7	B1	CROWN ZELLERBACH	1 BUSH ST		951 5209
7	A2	CURRAN THEATER	445 GEARY ST		
7	B1	CUSTOMS HOUSE	555 BATTERY ST		556 4440
7	B1	DANT MANAGEMENT CORP	260 CALIFORNIA ST		397 5404
6	C3	DAVIES SYMPHONY HALL	GROVE ST & VAN NESS AV		431 5400
5	A2	DEFENSE LANGUAGE INST	1804 14TH AV-PRESIDIO		221 0369
7	A1	DE MARIA ENTERPRISES	222 COLUMBUS AV		
10	A1	DEPT MOTOR VEHICLES	1377 FELL ST		557 1179
7	B1	DOLLAR, J HAROLD	351 CALIFORNIA ST		
3	B3	DOLLAR, ROBERT	311 CALIFORNIA ST		392 8454
7	A2	EIGHT THIRTY MARKET	830 MARKET ST		
7	A2	ELEVATED SHOPS	150 POWELL ST		781 5185
7	B1	1 EMBARCADERO CENTER	EMBARCADERO CENTER		772 0500
7	B1	2 EMBARCADERO CENTER	EMBARCADERO CENTER		772 0500
7	B1	3 EMBARCADERO CENTER	EMBARCADERO CENTER		772 0500
7	B2	EQUITABLE LIFE ASSUR	120 MONTGOMERY ST		781 6200
7	B1	EXCHANGE BLOCK	369 PINE ST		421 0422
7	B1	EXECUTIVE TOWERS	503 MARKET ST		
6	C3	FEDERAL	450 MCALLISTER		556 6600
7	B1	FERRY	FOOT OF MARKET ST		
7	B1	FIFTEEN CALIFORNIA ST	15 CALIFORNIA ST		
7	B2	FIFTY HAWTHORNE	50 HAWTHORNE ST		
7	B1	FIRST INTERSTATE BANK	405 MONTGOMERY ST		544 5000
7	B2	FIVE FREMONT CENTER	MISSION & FREMONT STS		
7	A2	FLOOD	870 MARKET ST		982 3298
7	B2	FORTY FOUR MONTGOMERY	44 MONTGOMERY ST		392 2433
7	A2	FOUR FIFTY SUTTER	450 SUTTER ST		421 7221
7	B1	FOUR SEVENTEEN MONTGMY	417 MONTGOMERY ST		392 2470
6	C3	FOX PLAZA	1390 MARKET ST		626 6900
11	A1	GALLERIA	101 HENRY ADAMS ST		863 3388
7	A2	GEARY THEATER	450 GEARY ST		771 3880
7	A3	GOLDEN GATE	25 TAYLOR ST		775 3890
7	A3	GOLDEN GATE THEATER	GOLDEN GT AV&TAYLOR ST		775 8800
7	A3	GRANT	1095 MARKET ST		621 8139
7	A2	GUNST, ELKAN	323 GEARY ST		421 4762
7	A1	HARTFORD OFFICES	650 CALIFORNIA ST		781 0260
6	C3	HEALTH CENTER	260 KEARNY ST		
7	B2	HEARST	3RD & MARKET STS		777 0600
6	C3	HERBST THEATER	VAN NESS & GROVE ST		392 4400
7	B2	HOBART	582 MARKET ST		362 8783
7	B2	HOLBROOK	58 SUTTER ST		
7	A2	HOWARD	209 POST ST		
7	B1	INSURANCE CENTER CORP	450 SANSOME ST		981 0660
7	B1	INSURANCE EXCHANGE	433 CALIFORNIA ST		362 0529
7	A1	INTERNATIONAL	601 CALIFORNIA ST		981 7878
7	B1	KOHL	400 MONTGOMERY ST		392 2470
7	A2	KOHLER & CHASE	26 O'FARRELL ST		
7	A3	LOEW'S WARFIELD	988 MARKET ST		771 9858
7	B2	MACK MILTON ASSOC LTD	116 NEW MONTGOMERY ST		546 9380
7	B1	MFG'S AGENTS EXHIBIT	200 DAVIS ST		
6	C3	MARSHALL SQUARE	1182 MARKET ST		
7	B1	MARVIN	24 CALIFORNIA ST		
15	C3	MASONIC	1111 CALIFORNIA ST		776 4702
6	C2	MEDICAL	909 HYDE ST		673 1317
6	C1	MEDICAL ARTS	2000 VAN NESS AV		474 9292
7	A2	MEDICO/DENTAL	490 POST ST		781 1427
7	B2	MERCANTILEL CENTER	86 3RD ST		
7	B2	MERCHANTS' EXCHANGE	465 CALIFORNIA ST		421 7730
7	B1	MILLS	220 MONTGOMERY ST		421 1444
7	B1	MILLS TOWER	200 BUSH ST		
10	C3	MISSION MEDICAL/DENTAL	2480 MISSION		
7	B2	MONADNOCK	681 MARKET ST		781 1361
7	B2	MOSCONE CONVENTION CTR	747 HOWARD ST		974 4000
7	A2	NATIVE SONS	414 MASON ST		392 0943
7	B2	ONE ELEVEN SUTTER	111 SUTTER ST		477 3274
7	B1	ONE JACKSON PLACE	633 BATTERY ST		362 1800
7	B1	ONE METROPOLITAN PLAZA	425 MARKET ST		495 7333
7	A2	ONE SIXTY FIVE POST	165 POST ST		
6	C3	ORPHEUM THEATER	1192 MARKET ST		
7	A2	PACIFIC	821 MARKET ST		
7	B2	PACIFIC BELL	140 NEW MONTGOMERY ST		811 9000
7	A1	PACIFIC MUTUAL LIFE	600 CALIFORNIA ST		
6	C3	PERFORMING ARTS CENTER	GROVE ST & VAN NESS AV		621 6600
7	A2	PHELAN	760 MARKET ST		392 7552
3	A3	PHOENIX THEATER	430 BROADWAY		
7	A2	PHYSICIANS'	516 SUTTER ST		
7	A2	POETZ	449 POWELL ST		
6	C3	PROFESSIONAL/LEGAL CTR	335 HAYES ST		
6	C3	PUBLIC UTILITIES COMM	505 VAN NESS AV		
7	B2	RIALTO	116 NEW MONTGOMERY ST		421 0704
7	B1	RITCHIE & RITCHIE	120 BUSH ST		
7	B1	ROYAL INSURANCE	201 SANSOME ST		
7	B1	RUSS	235 MONTGOMERY ST		421 7424
7	A2	SACHS	133 GEARY ST		
7	A2	ST PAUL	285 GEARY ST		421 7454

1991 SAN FRANCISCO COUNTY POINTS OF INTEREST

PAGE	GRID	NAME	ADDRESS	CITY	PHONE
21	B1	SALES MART	1485 BAYSHORE BLVD		467 0707
7	A3	SAN CHRISTINA	1026 MARKET ST		
7	B2	S F FEDERAL SAVINGS	POST ST & KEARNY ST		
7	B1	S F STOCK EXCHANGE	301 PINE ST		
7	B1	SANTA MARINA	112 MARKET ST		
7	A2	SCHROTH	240 STOCKTON ST		
7	B2	SEVENTY NINE NEW MONTG	79 NEW MONTGOMERY ST		
7	B2	SHARON	55 NEW MONTGOMERY ST		982 9281
7	B2	SHELDON	9 FIRST ST		
7	B1	SHELL	100 BUSH ST		986 0647
7	A2	SHREVE & CO	POST ST & GRANT AV		781 2065
7	B2	605 MARKET STREET	605 MARKET ST		495 0239
7	B2	SIX SIXTY MARKET ST	660 MARKET ST		788 4820
7	B2	SIXTY EIGHT POST	80 POST ST		
7	B1	SIXTY FOUR PINE ST	64 PINE ST		
7	B1	SOUTHERN PACIFIC	1 MARKET ST		541 1000
7	B1	STANDARD OIL	225 BUSH ST		894 7700
7	B1	THREE FORTY MARKET ST	340 MARKET ST		
7	B1	343 SANSOME	343 SONSOME ST		
7	B1	THREE TWENTY CALIF ST	320 CALIFORNIA ST		397 6943
7	B2	TIDEWATER	55 NEW MONTGOMERY ST		
11	A1	TRADE SHOW CENTER	2 HENRY ADAMS ST		864 1500
7	B1	TRANSAMERICA (PYRAMID)	600 MONTGOMERY ST		983 4000
6	A2	2299 POST MEDICAL CTR	2299 POST ST		
7	B1	200 BUSH INVENTMENT CO	200 BUSH ST		
3	B3	UNION BANK	50 CALIFORNIA ST		774 6000
3	B3	UNION CARBIDE	1 CALIFORNIA ST		
6	B1	UNION STREET PLAZA	2001 UNION ST		931 2445
6	C1	VAN NESS PACIFIC MED	2107 VAN NESS AV		885 6808
6	C2	VAN NESS POST CENTER	1255 POST ST		
6	C3	VETERANS' WAR MEMORIAL	MCALLISTER & VAN NESS		
21	A3	VISITACION MED & DENTL	5 PEABODY ST		239 5500
6	C3	WAR MEMRL OPERA HOUSE	VAN NESS AV & GROVE ST		864 3330
7	B1	WELLS FARGO	464 CALIFORNIA ST		396 0123
7	B2	WESIX	390 FIRST ST		
6	C3	WEST COAST LIFE	1275 MARKET ST		552 6200
7	A2	WESTPHAL	545 SUTTER ST		
7	A2	WILSON	973 MARKET ST		
6	C3	WOODBRIDGE	228 MCALLISTER ST		
		CHAMBER OF COMMERCE			
7	B2	SAN FRANCISCO	465 CALIFORNIA ST		392 4511
7	B2	SF CONVENTION/VIS BUR	201 3RD ST		976 6900
		COLLEGES & UNIVERSITIES			
19	C1	CITY COLLEGE OF S F	50 PHELAN AV		239 3000
7	A2	FASHION INSTITUTE	55 STOCKTON ST		433 6691
7	B2	GOLDEN GATE UNIVERSITY	550 MISSION ST		442 7225
18	C1	SAN FRANCISCO STATE U	1600 HOLLOWAY AV		469 1111
14	B3	SIMPSON COLLEGE	801 SILVER AV		334 7400
9	B2	UNIVERSITY OF CAL, S F	501 PARNASSUS AV		476 9000
10	B1	UC EXTENSION CENTER	55 LAGUNA ST		552 3016
6	C3	UC/HASTINGS COL OF LAW	198 MCALLISTER ST		565 4600
6	B2	UNIV OF THE PACIFIC	2155 WEBSTER ST		929 6450
5	C3	UNIVERSITY OF S F	PARKER&GOLDEN GATE AVS		666 6886
		GOLF COURSES			
18	B1	FLEMING (PUBLIC)	HARDING & SKYLINE BLVD		661 1865
8	A1	GOLDEN GATE PARK (PUB)	47TH AV & FULTON ST		751 8987
18	B1	HARDING PARK (PUBLIC)	HARDING & SKYLINE BLVD		664 4690
4	B3	LINCOLN PARK (PUBLIC)	CLEMENT ST & 33RD AV		221 9911
20	C2	MCLAREN, JOHN (PUBLIC)	MCLAREN PARK		587 2425
5	A1	PRESIDIO GOLF CLUB	PARK PRESIDIO BLVD		751 1322
19	A3	S F GOLF & COUNTRY CLB	JUNIPERO SERRA BLVD		585 0480
		HOSPITALS			
		*EMERGENCY SERVICES	AVAILABLE		
5	C2	*CHILDREN'S HOSPITAL	3700 CALIFORNIA ST		387 8700
3	A3	CHINESE HOSPITAL	835 JACKSON ST		982 2400
6	A3	*KAISER FOUNDATION HOS	2425 GEARY BLVD		929 4000
5	B3	*KAISER-FRENCH HOSP	4131 GEARY BLVD		666 8800

PAGE	GRID	NAME	ADDRESS	CITY	PHONE
13	B1	*LAGUNA HONDA HOSP	375 LAGUNA HONDA BL		664 1580
5	C2	*MARSHAL HALE MEM HOSP	3773 SACRAMENTO ST		386 7000
6	A2	*MOUNT ZION HOSPITAL	1600 DIVISADERO ST		567 6600
2	B3	*PACIFIC PRESBYTERIAN	2333 BUCHANAN ST		563 4321
5	C3	*PACIFIC PRESBYTERIAN	2750 GEARY BLVD		921 6171
10	B1	*RALPH DAVIES MED CTR	CASTRO & DUBOCE		565 6779
6	C2	*ST FRANCIS MEMORIAL	900 HYDE ST		775 4321
14	C1	*ST LUKE'S HOSPITAL	3555 ARMY ST		647 8600
9	C1	*ST MARY'S HOSPITAL	450 STANYAN ST		668 1000
11	A3	*S F GENERAL HOSPITAL	1001 POTRERO AV		821 8200
9	A3	SHRINERS CRIPLD CHILD	1701 19TH AV		665 1100
9	B2	*UCSF MEDICAL CENTER	501 PARNASSUS AV		476 1000
4	A2	V A MEDICAL CENTER	4150 CLEMENT ST		221 4810
		HOTELS & MOTELS			
7	A3	AMERICANIA	121 7TH ST		626 0200
7	A2	CAMPTON PLACE	340 STOCKTON ST		781 5555
6	C2	CATHEDRAL HILL	VAN NESS AV & GEARY ST		776 8200
7	A2	DONATELLO, THE	POST ST & MASON		441 7100
7	A1	FAIRMONT	CALIFORNIA & MASON STS		772 5000
7	A2	FOUR SEASONS CLIFT	GEARY & TAYLOR STS		775 4700
6	C2	GROSVENOR INN	1050 VAN NESS AV		673 4711
		HILTON	SN FRANCISCO INT AIRPT		589 0770
7	A2	HILTON ON HILTON SQ	333 O'FARRELL ST		771 1400
7	A3	HOLIDAY INN, CIVIC CTR	50 8TH ST		626 6103
7	A1	HOLIDAY INN, FINAN DIS	750 KEARNY ST		433 6600
2	C2	HOLIDAY INN,FISHERMN W	1300 COLUMBUS AV		771 9000
6	C2	HOLIDAY INN,GOLDEN GTE	1500 VAN NESS AV		441 4000
7	A2	HOLIDAY INN, UNION SQ	480 SUTTER ST		398 8900
2	C2	HOWARD JOHNSONS	580 BEACH ST		775 3800
7	A2	HOTEL NIKKO OF S F	150 POWELL ST		421 9037
7	A2	HYATT ON UNION SQ	345 STOCKTON ST		398 1234
7	B1	HYATT REGENCY	5 EMBARCADERO CENTER		788 1234
6	B2	KYOTO INN	1800 SUTTER ST		921 4000
7	B1	MANDARIN OF S F	222 SANSOME ST		885 0999
2	C2	MARRIOTT-FISHERMNS WHF	1250 COLUMBUS AV		775 7555
7	A2	MARRIOTT-MOSCONE CTR	785 MARKET ST		896 1600
6	B2	MIYAKO	1625 POST ST		922 3200
7	A1	MARK HOPKINS	CALIFORNIA & MASON STS		392 3434
7	B2	MERIDIEN	50 THIRD ST		974 6400
2	C2	PARK FIFTY FIVE	590 BAY ST		885 4700
7	B1	PARK HYATT	400 COMMERCIAL ST		392 1234
7	A2	PORTMAN HOTEL	414 MASON ST		398 2525
7	A2	RAMADA RENAISSANCE	55 CYRL MAGNIN ST/EDDY		392 8000
7	A2	RAPHAEL	386 GEARY ST		986 2000
3	A1	SHERATON FISHERMNS WHF	2500 MASON ST		362 5500
7	B2	SHERATON PALACE	2 NEW MONTGOMERY ST		392 8600
7	A2	SIR FRANCIS DRAKE	SUTTER & POWELL STS		392 7755
7	A1	STANFORD COURT	905 CALIFORNIA ST		989 3500
9	C1	STANYAN PARK HOTEL	750 STANYAN ST		751 1000
3	A1	TRAVELODGE AT WHARF	250 BEACH ST		392 6700
6	C2	TRAVELODGE CIVIC CTR	655 ELLIS ST		771 3000
6	C2	TRAVELODGE DOWNTOWN	790 ELLIS ST		775 7612
2	C2	TRAVELODGE FISHERM WHF	1201 COLUMBUS AV		776 7070
2	A2	TRAVELODGE GOLDEN GATE	2230 LOMBARD ST		922 3900
10	C1	TRAVELODGE S F CENTRAL	1707 MARKET ST		621 6775
7	A3	TRAVELODGE YERBA BUENA	240 7TH ST		861 6469
2	B2	VAGABOND INN - MIDTOWN	2550 VAN NESS AV		776 7500
7	A2	VILLA FLORENCE	225 POWELL ST		397 7700
7	A2	WESTIN ST FRANCIS	POWELL & GEARY STS		397 7000
		LIBRARIES			
15	C3	ANNA WADEN	5075 3RD ST		468 1323
4	B3	ANZA	550 37TH AV		752 1960
14	C2	BERNAL	500 CORTLAND AV		285 1744
7	A1	BUSINESS	530 KEARNY ST		558 3946
7	A1	CHINATOWN	1135 POWELL ST		989 6770
10	B2	EUREKA VLY-HARVEY MILK	3555 16TH ST		626 1132
20	B1	EXCELSIOR	4400 MISSION ST		586 4075
14	B3	GLEN PARK	653 CHENERY ST		586 4144
2	B3	GOLDEN GATE	1801 GREEN ST		346 9273
19	B1	INGLESIDE	387 ASHTON ST		586 4156
6	C3	MAIN LIBRARY	CIVIC CENTER		558 3191

1991 SAN FRANCISCO COUNTY POINTS OF INTEREST

PAGE	GRID	NAME	ADDRESS	CITY	PHONE
2	B2	MARINA	CHESTNUT & WEBSTER		346 9336
19	A1	MERCED	155 WINSTON DR		586 4246
10	C3	MISSION	3359 24TH ST		824 2810
14	B1	NOE VALLEY	451 JERSEY ST		285 2788
3	A2	NORTH BEACH	2000 MASON ST		391 9473
19	B2	OCEAN VIEW	111 BROAD ST		586 4193
12	B1	ORTEGA	3223 ORTEGA ST		681 1848
9	C1	PARK	1833 PAGE ST		752 4620
12	C2	PARKSIDE	1200 TARAVAL ST		566 4647
15	A3	PORTOLA	2434 SAN BRUNO AV		468 2232
11	B2	POTRERO	1616 20TH ST		285 3022
6	A2	PRESIDIO BRANCH	3150 SACRAMENTO ST		558 5035
5	A3	RICHMOND	351 9TH AV		752 1240
9	A2	SUNSET	1305 18TH AV		566 4552
21	A3	VISITACION	45 LELAND AV		239 5270
6	A2	WESTERN ADDITION	1550 SCOTT		346 9531
13	B2	WEST PORTAL	190 LENOX WY		566 4584

POST OFFICES

PAGE	GRID	NAME	ADDRESS	CITY	PHONE
15	B3	BAYVIEW	2111 LANE ST		822 7619
14	C2	BERNAL	30 29TH ST		695 1703
7	A1	CHINATOWN	867 STOCKTON ST		956 3566
6	C3	CITY HALL	CIVIC CENTER		621 6325
14	A1	DIAMOND HEIGHTS	5262 DIAMOND HTS BLVD		550 6412
6	C3	FEDERAL BUILDING	450 GOLDEN GATE AV		621 7505
9	B2	FISK	1317 9TH AV		759 1901
4	C3	GEARY	5654 GEARY BL		752 0231
15	C2	GENERAL MAIL FACILITY	1300 EVANS AV		550 5247
1	C2	LETTERMAN	PRESIDIO MILITARY		563 7195
2	A2	MARINA	2055 LOMBARD ST		563 4674
21	A1	MCLAREN	2755 SAN BRUNO AV		467 3560
11	A2	MISSION ANNEX	1600 BRYANT ST		621 8646
10	B3	NOE VALLEY	4083 24TH ST		821 0776
3	A2	NORTH BEACH	1640 STOCKTON ST		956 3581
12	C2	PARKSIDE	1800 TARAVAL ST		759 1601
1	C2	PRESIDIO	PRESIDIO MILITARY		563 4975
7	B1	RINCON CENTER	180 STEAURT ST		543 3340
19	A1	STONESTOWN	565 BUCKINGHAM WY		759 1660
8	C2	SUNSET	1314 22ND AV		759 1707
7	A2	SUTTER	150 SUTTER ST		956 3169
3	C1	TREASURE ISLAND	TREASURE ISLAND		956 1520
21	A3	VISITACION	68 LELAND AV		331 1150
13	A2	WEST PORTAL	317 W PORTAL AV		759 1811
7	A2	NO 23 THE EMPORIUM	835 MARKET ST		543 2606
10	C2	NO 40 BELL BAZAAR	3030 16TH ST		621 6053
7	A2	NO 57 MACYS	STOCKTON & O'FARRELL		956 3570
6	B2	A	1550 STEINER ST		563 5954
3	B3	B	555 BATTERY ST		956 3140
6	C2	C	1198 S VAN NESS AV		285 7382
7	B3	E	460 BRANNAN ST		543 7729
20	A1	F	15 ONONDAGA AV		334 0709
10	A2	G	4304 18TH ST		621 5317
9	C1	J	554 CLAYTON ST		621 7445
6	C2	O	1414 VAN NESS AV		441 6941

SCHOOLS - PRIVATE ELEMENTARY

PAGE	GRID	NAME	ADDRESS	CITY	PHONE
15	C3	ALL HALLOWS	1601 LANE ST		822 8780
19	A2	BRANDEIS-HILLEL DAY	655 BROTHERHOOD WY		334 9841
4	B2	BURKE, KATHERINE D	7070 CALIFORNIA ST		751 0177
6	B3	CATHEDRAL INTERMEDIATE	1016 EDDY ST		567 1082
7	A1	CATHEDRAL SCH FOR BOYS	1275 SACRAMENTO ST		771 6600
6	B1	CONVENT SACRED HEART	2200 BROADWAY ST		563 2900
20	B1	CORPUS CHRISTI	75 FRANCIS ST		587 7014
20	A1	DISCOVERY CENTER	65 OCEAN AV		333 6609
20	B2	EPIPHANY	600 ITALY AV		587 6900
10	B1	FIRST BAPTIST CHURCH	42 WALLER ST		863 1691
10	B1	FRENCH AMER INTERNATL	220 BUCHANAN ST		626 8564
6	B1	HAMLIN	2129 VALLEJO ST		922 0600
8	C1	HEBREW ACADEMY OF S F	763 25TH AV		752 7490
8	B3	HOLY NAME	1560 40TH AV		731 4077
15	A1	IMMACULATE CONCEPTION	1550 TREAT AV		824 6860
8	A2	LITTLE LIGHTS BAPTIST	4508 IRVING ST		564 8357
4	B3	LYCEE FRANCAIS DE S F	3301 BALBOA ST		668 1833
10	B2	MISSION DOLORES	3371 16TH ST		861 7673
6	B2	MORNING STAR	1911 PINE ST		921 4436
10	B2	NOTRE DAME ELEMENTARY	333 DOLORES ST		552 3590
7	A1	NOTRE DAME VICTOIRES	659 PINE ST		421 0069
20	C3	OUR LADY OF VISITACION	785 SUNNYDALE AV		239 7840
10	B1	SACRED HEART ELEM	660 OAK ST		621 8035
9	A2	ST ANNE	1320 14TH AV		664 7977
14	C1	ST ANTHONY	299 PRECITA AV		648 2008
13	C2	ST BRENDAN	234 ULLOA ST		731 2665
2	C3	ST BRIGID	2250 FRANKLIN ST		673 4523
13	A2	ST CECILIA	660 VICENTE ST		731 8400
10	C2	ST CHARLES	3250 18TH ST		861 7652
6	B2	ST DOMINIC	2445 PINE ST		346 9500
21	A1	ST ELIZABETH	450 SOMERSET ST		468 3247
19	B1	ST EMYDIUS	301 DE MONTFORT AV		333 4877
13	C3	ST FINN BARR	419 HEARST AV		333 1800
12	B2	ST GABRIEL	2550 41ST AV		566 0314
10	B3	ST JAMES	321 FAIR OAKS ST		647 8972
14	A3	ST JOHN	925 CHENERY ST		584 8383
10	C1	ST JOSEPH	220 10TH ST		431 1206
7	A1	ST MARY CHINESE DAY	902 STOCKTON ST		362 7394
19	C2	ST MICHAEL	55 FARALLONES ST		585 4781
4	C3	ST MONICA	5920 GEARY BLVD		751 9564
14	B2	ST PAUL	1660 CHURCH ST		648 2055
21	B2	ST PAUL OF SHIPWRECK	1060 KEY AV		467 1798
6	C3	ST PAULUS LUTHERAN	888 TURK ST		673 0497
15	A1	ST PETER	1266 FLORIDA ST		647 8662
3	A2	SAINTS PETER & PAUL	632 FILBERT ST		421 5219
10	A3	ST PHILIP	665 ELIZABETH ST		824 8467
13	A3	ST STEPHEN	401 EUCALYPTUS DR		664 8331
4	B3	ST THOMAS THE APOSTLE	3801 BALBOA ST		221 2711
19	A3	ST THOMAS MORE	50 THOMAS MORE WY		377 0100
2	A3	ST VINCENT DE PAUL	2356 GREEN ST		346 5505
7	A1	SF CHINESE PARENT COMM	843 STOCKTON ST		391 5564
19	C3	S F CHRISTIAN ELEM	25 WHITTIER ST		586 1117
6	B2	SAN FRANCISCO DAY	2266 CALIFORNIA ST		563 6355
20	A2	S F JUNIOR ACADEMY	66 GENEVA AV		585 5550
15	A3	S F MONTESSORI	300 GAVEN ST		239 5065
6	A2	SAN FRANCISCO WALDORF	2938 WASHINGTON ST		931 2750
2	A3	TOWN SCHOOL FOR BOYS	2750 JACKSON ST		921 3747
5	B3	STAR OF THE SEA ELEM	360 9TH AV		221 8558
6	B1	STUART HALL FOR BOYS	2252 BROADWAY		563 2900
13	A3	WEST PORTAL LUTHERAN	200 SLOAT BLVD		665 6330
5	B3	ZION LUTHERAN	495 9TH AV		221 7500

SCHOOLS - PRIVATE HIGH

PAGE	GRID	NAME	ADDRESS	CITY	PHONE
6	B2	CATHEDRAL HIGH SCHOOL	1100 ELLIS ST		567 7400
6	B1	CONVENT SACRED HT HIGH	2222 BROADWAY ST		563 2900
10	B1	FRENCH AMERICAN INTNL	220 BUCHANAN ST		626 8564
6	A2	DREW COLLEGE PREP	2901 CALIFORNIA ST		346 4831
14	C1	IMMAC CONCEPTION ACAD	3625 24TH ST		824 2052
19	C1	LICK-WILMERDING	775 OCEAN AV		333 4021
4	B3	LYCEE FRANCAIS DE SF	3301 BALBOA ST		668 1833
13	A3	MERCY HIGH (GIRLS)	3250 19TH AV		334 0525
5	C3	PRESENTATION (GIRLS)	2350 TURK ST		387 4720
19	C1	RIORDAN HIGH (BOYS)	175 PHELAN AV		586 8200
6	C2	SACRED HEART HS	1055 ELLIS ST		775 6626
12	B1	ST IGNATIUS	2001 37TH AV		731 7500
14	B3	ST JOHN URSULINE HIGH	4056 MISSION ST		586 6333
14	B2	ST PAUL'S GIRLS HIGH	317 29TH ST		648 0505
6	A2	ST ROSE ACADEMY	2475 PINE ST		346 7035
5	C1	SF UNIVERSITY HS	3065 JACKSON ST		346 8400
5	B3	STAR OF THE SEA ACAD	350 9TH AV		752 6024
10	A1	URBAN	1563 PAGE ST		626 2919

SCHOOLS - PUBLIC ELEMENTARY

PAGE	GRID	NAME	ADDRESS	CITY	PHONE
4	C2	ALAMO	250 23RD AV		752 8244
10	A3	ALVARADO	625 DOUGLASS ST		826 1650
9	A1	ARGONNE	675 17TH AV		751 6717
11	A3	BRYANT	1050 YORK ST		647 4959
15	A1	BUENA VISTA	2641 25TH ST		821 1852
8	C1	CABRILLO	735 24TH AV		752 9237
7	A3	CARMICHAEL, BESSIE	55 SHERMAN ST		863 2442

1991 SAN FRANCISCO COUNTY POINTS OF INTEREST

PAGE	GRID	NAME	ADDRESS	CITY	PHONE
15	C3	CARVER, GEO WASHINGTON	1360 OAKDALE AV		822 6391
7	B1	CHINESE EDUCATION CTR	657 MERCHANT ST		982 9550
9	C3	CLARENDON	500 CLARENDON AV		661 0770
20	B1	CLEVELAND	455 ATHENS ST		585 0845
6	A2	COBB, WILLIAM L	2725 CALIFORNIA ST		567 0700
13	A3	COMMODORE SLOAT	50 DARIEN WY		564 0311
7	A1	COMMODORE STOCKTON	950 CLAY ST		781 7045
10	A1	DE AVILA, WILLIAM	1351 HAIGHT ST		626 0181
10	A3	DOUGLAS	4235 19TH ST		863 5184
15	C3	DRAKE, SIR FRANCIS	350 HARBOR RD		282 8390
15	B3	DREW, CHARLES R	50 POMONA ST		822 9770
10	B3	EDISON	3531 22ND ST		821 4510
21	A2	EL DORADO	70 DELTA ST		467 6050
14	B2	FAIRMOUNT	65 CHENERY ST		285 3828
7	B3	FILIPINO EDUCATION CTR	824 HARRISON ST		543 8430
15	A1	FLYNN, LEONARD	3125 ARMY ST		648 8727
3	A2	GARFIELD	420 FILBERT ST		982 2823
14	A3	GLEN PARK	151 LIPPARD AV		333 6388
6	A3	GOLDEN GATE	1601 TURK ST		931 0449
9	C2	GRATTAN	165 GRATTAN ST		681 8822
20	B3	GUADALUPE	859 PRAGUE ST		334 1975
21	C2	HARTE, BRET	1035 GILMAN AV		822 5271
10	C3	HAWTHORNE	825 SHOTWELL ST		824 0896
14	C3	HILLCREST	810 SILVER AV		585 3202
9	A2	JEFFERSON	1725 IRVING ST		664 0342
8	A3	KEY, FRANCIS SCOTT	1530 43RD AV		664 2062
11	B3	KING, STARR	1215 CAROLINA ST		282 8615
4	B3	LAFAYETTE	4545 ANZA ST		387 3322
12	C3	LAKESHORE	220 MIDDLEFIELD DR		664 6768
8	B3	LAWTON	1570 31ST AV		564 5500
5	B2	LILIENTHAL, CLAIRE	3950 SACRAMENTO ST		751 9630
20	A3	LONGFELLOW	755 MORSE ST		587 2400
10	C2	MARSHALL	1575 15TH ST		626 9180
5	B3	MCCOPPIN, FRANK	651 6TH AV		752 9825
10	A2	MCKINLEY	1025 14TH ST		626 3055
13	C2	MIRALOMA	175 OMAR WY		587 4028
11	A3	MISSION EDUCATION CTR	2641 25TH ST		826 8330
20	B1	MONROE	260 MADRID ST		334 0754
10	C3	MOSCONE, GEORGE R	2355 FOLSOM ST		647 8526
10	B1	MUIR, JOHN	380 WEBSTER ST		621 0600
6	B2	NEW TRADITIONS CTR	1501 OFARRELL ST		922 1850
19	B2	ORTEGA, JOSE	400 SARGENT ST		587 7529
3	A3	PARKER, JEAN	840 BROADWAY		421 2988
5	B2	PEABODY, GEORGE	251 6TH AV		565 9574
6	C2	REDDING	1421 PINE ST		673 7931
14	C2	REVERE, PAUL	555 TOMPKINS AV		282 2875
14	C2	REVERE, PAUL ANNEX	610 TOMPKINS AV		648 1776
10	A3	ROOFTOP ALT	445 BURNETT ST		285 1977
10	B2	SANCHEZ	325 SANCHEZ ST		626 4527
20	B1	SN FRANCISCO COMMUNITY	125 EXCELSIOR ST		239 1870
14	C2	SERRA, JUNIPERO	625 HOLLY PARK CIR		285 0252
19	B2	SHERIDAN	431 CAPITOL AV		586 2200
2	B3	SHERMAN	1651 UNION ST		776 5500
6	C1	SPRING VALLEY	1451 JACKSON ST		474 5637
12	B1	STEVENSON, ROBT LOUIS	2051 34TH AV		564 4159
13	C3	SUNNYSIDE	250 FOERSTER ST		585 8127
5	A2	SUTRO	235 12TH AV		752 4203
6	C3	SWETT, JOHN	727 GOLDEN GATE AV		863 6474
21	A1	TAYLOR, E R	423 BURROWS ST		468 1912
3	C1	TREASURE ISLAND	13TH ST & AV E	TREASURE ISL	421 5412
12	B2	ULLOA	2650 42ND AV		564 4240
21	A2	VISITACION VALLEY	55 SCHWERIN ST		239 7396
11	B2	WEBSTER, DANIEL	465 MISSOURI ST		826 6195
6	B2	WEILL, RAPHAEL	1501 O'FARRELL ST		922 0757
13	B2	WEST PORTAL	5 LENOX WY		731 0340
2	C2	YICK WO	2245 JONES ST		474 2833
		SCHOOLS - PUBLIC MIDDLE			
13	B3	APTOS	105 APTOS AV		586 6194
20	B2	BURBANK, LUTHER	325 LA GRANDE AV		586 1650
20	A1	DENMAN, JAMES	241 ONEIDA AV		586 0840
10	B2	EVERETT	450 CHURCH ST		431 0822
3	A2	FRANCISCO	2190 POWELL ST		392 8214
6	A2	FRANKLIN, BENJAMIN	1430 SCOTT ST		565 9654

PAGE	GRID	NAME	ADDRESS	CITY	PHONE
12	B1	GIANNINI, A P	3151 ORTEGA ST		664 4575
13	A1	HOOVER, HERBERT	2290 14TH AV		564 1226
21	A1	KING, MARTIN LUTHER	350 GIRARD ST		468 7290
14	B1	LICK, JAMES	1220 NOE ST		648 8080
10	C3	MANN, HORACE	3351 23RD ST		826 4504
2	A2	MARINA	3500 FILLMORE ST		565 9577
11	B2	POTRERO HILL	655 DE HARO ST		647 1011
4	B3	PRESIDIO	450 30TH AV		752 9696
5	B3	ROOSEVELT	460 ARGUELLO BL		386 1600
20	C2	VISITACION VALLEY	450 RAYMOND AV		239 6550
		SCHOOLS - PUBLIC HIGH			
6	B3	ALAMO PARK	1099 HAYES ST		565 9756
20	A1	BALBOA	1000 CAYUGA AV		333 2777
12	A2	BAY	2325 41ST AV		753 8703
12	A2	CTR INDEPENDENT STUDY	3045 SANTIAGO ST		546 7717
15	B3	BURTON, PHILLIP	45 CONKLING ST		826 9090
10	C3	DOWNTOWN	110 BARTLETT ST		565 9610
2	B2	GALILEO	1150 FRANCISCO ST		771 3150
12	B1	INTERNTL STUDIES ACAD	1920 41ST AV		566 3800
12	C1	LINCOLN, ABRAHAM	2162 24TH AV		566 1618
12	C3	LOWELL	1101 EUCALYPTUS DR		566 7900
9	A2	MARK TWAIN	1541 12TH AV		731 3380
13	C1	MCATEER, J EUGENE	555 PORTOLA DR		824 6001
10	B2	MISSION	3750 18TH ST		552 5800
2	B3	NEWCOMER	2340 JACKSON ST		922 1190
10	C3	O'CONNELL, JOHN	2905 21ST ST		648 1326
15	A1	SUNSHINE	2730 BRYANT ST		647 1516
5	C3	WALLENBERG, RAOUL	40 VEGA ST		346 7466
4	B3	WASHINGTON, GEORGE	600 32ND AV		387 0550
21	A1	WILSON, WOODROW	400 MANSELL ST		239 6200
		SHOPPING CENTERS			
2	C2	ANCHORAGE, THE	2800 LEAVENWORTH ST		775 6000
2	C2	CANNERY, THE	2801 LEAVENWORTH ST		771 3112
7	B2	CROCKER GALLERIA	50 POST ST		
3	B3	EMBARCADERO CENTER	SACRAMENTO & CLAY		772 0500
2	C2	GHIRARDELLI SQUARE	POLK & NORTH POINT		775 5500
6	B2	JAPAN CENTER	POST & LAGUNA		567 6076
3	A1	PIER 39	EMBARCADERO		981 7437
19	A1	STONESTOWN GALLERIA	EUCALYPTUS DR&19TH AV		564 4000
		TRANSPORTATION			
7	C3	RAIL STA (CALTRAIN)	4TH ST & TOWNSEND ST		495 4546
11	B3	RAIL STA (CALTRAIN)	22ND ST & PENNSYLVANIA		
21	B1	RAIL STA (CALTRAIN)	PAUL AV & GOULD ST		
21	B3	RAIL STA (CALTRAIN)	TUNNEL AV & VISITACION		
1	A1	TRANSIT TRANSFER POINT	TOLL PLAZA		
3	B3	TRANSIT TRANSFER POINT	EMBARCADERO & MARKT ST		
7	A3	TRANSIT TRANSFER POINT	7TH ST & MARKET ST		
7	B1	TRANSIT TRANSFER POINT	1ST ST & MISSION ST		
		U S GOVERNMENT OFFICES			
7	B1	AGRICULTURE DEPT	630 SANSOME ST		556 6464
1	C2	ARMY DEPT	PRESIDIO OF S F		561 2211
6	C3	CIVIL SERVICE COM	450 GOLDEN GATE AV		556 6667
7	B1	COAST GUARD	630 SANSOME ST		556 3530
3	B3	CUSTOMS HOUSE	555 BATTERY ST		556 4440
6	C3	FED BUREAU INVESTIGATN	450 GOLDEN GATE AV		553 7400
6	C3	FEDERAL OFFICE BLDG	450 GOLDEN GATE AV		556 6600
6	C3	FEDERAL OFC BLDG (OLD)	50 FULTON ST		
6	C3	INTERNAL REVENUE SERV	450 GOLDEN GATE AV		839 1040
3	C1	MARINES	TREASURE ISLAND		765 6074
7	B2	MARITIME COMMISSION	525 MARKET ST		974 9756
3	C1	NAVY DEPT	TREASURE ISLAND		765 9111
6	C3	SOCIAL SECURITY BOARD	FEDERAL OFFICE BLDG		956 3000
7	B2	VETERANS ADMINISTRATN	211 MAIN ST		495 8900
6	C3	WEATHER BUREAU	FEDERAL OFFICE BLDG		936 1212

1991 SAN FRANCISCO COUNTY POINTS OF INTEREST

ALCATRAZ ISLAND .... **San Francisco Bay**
1 3/4 miles from the San Francisco shoreline. Until recently, visitors could only look at Alcatraz or sail by at a cautious distance, speculating on what the inside of the legendary federal prison was actually like. *The Rock* has been a fortification, a U.S. military prison, an Army disciplinary barracks, and finally a maximum security federal penitentiary before it was phased out in 1963.
Tour Hours: Various times. Call for Information.
Closed: Thanksgiving, Christmas and New Year's Day.
Admission: $7.50 Adults, $7.00 Seniors (55 years & up), $4.00 Children (5 to 11 years), includes transportation.
Reservations: Ticketron or in person, Pier 41, San Francisco, **546-2896.**

AQUATIC PARK **2 B1**
The Aquatic Park, three blocks west of Fisherman's Wharf and north of Ghirardelli Square, contains the Hyde Street Pier and the architecturally unique Maritime Museum building.

BAKER BEACH **4 C1**

BALCLUTHA **3 A1**
A steel hulled, square rigged vessel built in Scotland in 1886, now survives as the last of the Cape Horn Fleet.

BART **3 B2**
The 75 Mile transbay Bay Area Rapid Transit links San Francisco's subway stations with East Bay terminals. For information, telephone **788-BART.**

CABLE CAR BARN AND MUSEUM **7 A1**
This red brick building, built in 1887, is the control center for the cable car system, and is also a museum and visitors' gallery with exhibits and photos of 19th century cable car operations. Located at Washington and Mason Streets.**474-1887.**
Hours: Daily, 10am-6pm, April-Oct; 10am-5pm, Nov-March.
Closed: Thanksgiving , Christmas and New Year's Day.
Admission: Free.

CALIFORNIA ACADEMY OF SCIENCES .... **See Golden Gate Park**

CALIFORNIA PALACE OF THE LEGION OF HONOR **4 B2**
This unique collection, displaying 16th to 20th century French art works, features paintings of prominent 18th and 19th century French artists. The sculpture collection of Rodin is of special significance. Decorative arts of Medieval and Renaissance periods are on display in the new gallery. Lincoln Park. Public Information is **750-3614.**
Hours: 10am-5pm, Wednesday through Sunday.
Admission: $4.00 Adults, $2.00 Seniors (65 and over) and Juniors (12 to 18 years). Children under 12 admitted free. Free first Wednesday of each month and Saturday morning from 10am to 12 noon.

CANDLESTICK PARK **21 C2**
This stadium is located 8 miles south of the city and is home to the 49er's Football Team and the Giants Baseball Team.

CHINATOWN **7 A1**
This bustling community is the largest Chinese settlement in the United States and a delight for tourists. A multitude of curio bazaars, exotic shops, restaurants and food markets line its main street, Grant Avenue and continue for eight blocks between Bush and Columbus.

CIVIC CENTER **6 C3**
Located at Van Ness Avenue and McAllister Street.

- City Hall
- Brooks Hall
- Performing Arts Center
  - Davies Symphony Hall
  - Opera House
  - Herbst Theatre
- Federal Building
- Civic Auditorium
- Public Library
- War Memorial Veterans Building and the San Francisco Museum of Modern Art. A selection of 20th century contemporary art is shown in the many galleries on the spacious third and fourth floors of the Veterans Building.

Hours: Tuesday, Wednesday and Friday, 10am to 5pm; Thursday, 10am to 9pm; Saturday and Sunday, 11am to 5pm. Closed Mondays and major holidays. **863-8800.**
Admission: $4.00 Adults, $1.50 Seniors & Juniors (under16). Free Tuesday, discount on Thursday.

CLIFF HOUSE **4 A3**
The famous Cliff House, a restaurant and gift shop, offers a magnificent view of the Seal Rocks and the Pacific Ocean. Located at 1066 to 1090 Point Lobos Avenue, Ocean Beach.

COIT MEMORIAL TOWER **3 A2**
The Tower, located on Telegraph Hill, was built as a memorial to the City's volunteer firefighters. An elevator ride to the top provides magnificent views of the skyline and bay.
Hours: 9am to 4pm.

EMBARCADERO CENTER **3 C2**
Four spectacular buildings, designed by architect John Portman, tower above three interconnecting levels of shops, restaurants, services and entertainment. Pedestrian bridges link the innovative Hyatt Regency and sculptures by Willi Gutmann, Louise Nevelson, and Nicolas Schoffer create a visually exciting environment.

FERRY BUILDING **3 B2**
A former commuter terminal building is now occupied by the Port Commission, the World Trade Center, a mineral exhibit and library.

FISHERMAN'S WHARF **2 C1**
This is the headquarters for the fishing fleet, harbor cruise boats, and sightseeing tours. Visitors enjoy outstanding seafood restaurants, shops, and outdoor seafood stores. Located at the foot of Taylor Street at Jefferson on the northern waterfront.

FORT POINT NATIONAL HISTORIC SITE **1 A1**
A three-tiered fort which required eight years to complete (1853-1861) surrounds a large courtyard. Guided tours provided. Presidio of San Francisco reached via Lincoln Boulevard to Long Avenue. **556-1693.**
Hours: 10am to 5pm daily, closed Thanksgiving, Christmas and New Year's.
Admission: Free

GOLDEN GATE BRIDGE **1 A1**
One of the longest single span suspension bridges in the world.
Admission: Auto toll collected southbound only, $2.00. Pedestrians free.

GOLDEN GATE PARK **8 C1**

- **California Academy of Sciences** **9 A1**
  It's In Golden Gate Park But It's Out of This World can identify only one place in San Francisco . . . The California Academy of Sciences. This magnet annually attracts more than 1,000,000 visitors of every age and interest and it keeps luring them back year after year. All under one roof are the STEINHART AQUARIUM, the new FISH ROUNDABOUT, the MORRISON PLANETARIUM and the HALLS OF SCIENCE. The WATTIS HALL OF MAN, depicting a series of life-like cultural habitat scenes, is a worthwhile exhibit for those with an interest in ecology, anthropology, or the exotic. The Fish Roundabout is unique in the United States. **752-8268.**
  Hours: 10am to 5pm daily (Open later in summer months).
  Admission: $4.00 Adults (18-64), $2.00 for Seniors and Students (12-17) and $1.00 for Children (6-11). First Wednesday of the month is free.
  Planetarium shows: $2.50 Adults, $1.25 Children (6-17). Children 5 and under, free. **750-7141.**
- **Strybing Arboretum and Botanical Gardens** **9 A1**
  Sixty acres of more than 6,000 species and varieties of plants.**661-0822.**
  Hours: Weekdays, 8am to 4:00pm. Weekends, Holidays, 10am to 5pm.
- **Asian Art Museum** **9 A1**
  The Avery Brundage Collection contains objects of art from Oriental civilizations. Special exhibits.
  Hours: 10am to 5pm, Wednesday through Sunday. **668-8921.**
  Admission: $4.00 Adults(18-64), $2.00 Seniors and Juniors (12-17). Children under 12 are free.
- **Conservatory of Flowers** **9 B1**
  Tropical plants and flower shows. **588-3973.**
  Hours: Open 9am to 5pm.
  Admission: $1.50
- **M.H. De Young Museum** **9 A1**
  This is the city's most diversified art museum. With more than 1,000,000 visitors annually, it is one of America's most popular. Permanent exhibition of fine and applied arts, special exhibits and educational services. **750-3600.**
  Hours: 10am to 5pm. Wednesday through Sunday.
  Admission: $4.00 Adults (18-65), $2.00 Seniors & Young Adults (12-17), all others free. One admission charge for De Young, Asian Art and Legion of Honor Museums on the same day.
- **Japanese Tea Garden** **9 A1**
  Superb example of a Japanese Garden. The fragile blossoms of 200 cherry

1991 SAN FRANCISCO COUNTY POINTS OF INTEREST

trees are at their peak blooming period the first week of April. Hours: Open daily: Summer, 9am to 6:30pm; Winter, 8:30am to 5:30pm. Admission: $2.00 Adults, $1.00 Seniors & Children (6-12).

- **Music Concourse** 9 A1
  Sunday afternoon concerts held in a peaceful, tree-sheltered setting.
- **Kezar Stadium** 9 B1
- **Stow Lake** 9 A1
  Row boats, paddle boats and electric boats for rent.
- **Golden Gate Equestrian Center** 8 B1
  Horseback Riding.
- **Golden Gate Golf Course** 8 A1
  Nine hole golf course, par 3. No reservations.
- **Children's Playground** 9 B2
  All types of playground equipment and an animal farm. Visitors of all ages are delighted by a 1912 Hershel-Spillman carousel.

GUINNESS MUSEUM OF WORLD RECORDS 2 C1
Tallest, fastest, greatest and smallest of literally hundreds of people, animals, things, whatever. 235 Jefferson Street at Fisherman's Wharf. **771-9890.**
Hours: Sunday through Thursday, 10am to 10pm; Friday & Saturday, 10am to midnight.
Admission: $5.95 Adults, $4.95 Seniors, $4.75 Students, $2.75 Children (5-12). Children under 5 years old admitted free.

JACKSON SQUARE 3 A2
The Square, originally known as the Barbary Coast, is entered from Jackson and Montgomery Streets. Decorator and specialty shops now occupy the 19th century buildings which have been preserved.

JAPAN CENTER 6 B2
Bounded by Geary, Laguna, Fillmore and Post Streets, this area includes a hotel, shopping center, restaurants and many interesting gift shops.

MISSION DOLORES 10 B2
Mission San Francisco de Asis at Dolores and 16th Streets. The sixth in a chain of missions established by Father Junipero Serra in 1776. **621-8203.**
Hours: 8am to 4pm daily.Closed on major holidays, half day on Good Friday. Restoration fee is $1.00, Children under 12 free.

MOSCONE CONVENTION CENTER 7 B2
The Center is located at Third and Howard Streets.

NATIONAL MARITIME MUSEUM 2 C1
Located at the Hyde Street Pier, Hyde and Jefferson Streets, the Museum has four vessels moored here that have much in common. They all played a significant part in Pacific Maritime History. Now a part of the National Park Service, they are fully restored and afloat. **556-6435.**
Hours: November through April, 10am to 5pm; May through October, 10am to 6pm. It is closed Christmas Day and New Year's Day.
Admission: $3.00, ages 17-61; Children free.

NATIONAL MARITIME MUSEUM BUILDING 2 B1
The Maritime Museum Building, now part of the National Park Service, is located at the foot of Polk Street at the Aquatic Park. It contains an exciting historical display of ship models, photographs, relics, paintings, maps and sailors' handicrafts. **556-2904.**
Hours: 10am to 5pm, Wednesday through Sunday, Admission free.

OCTAGON HOUSE 2 B2
Located at 2645 Gough Street at Union Street, this house, built in 1861, was one of five such residences in early San Francisco. Now the residence of the National Society of Colonial Dames of America, it is one of the few remaining examples of this style. **441-7512.**
Hours: Open the 2nd Sunday of the month and the second and fourth Thursday, 12 noon to 3pm. Closed January.
Admission: Donation.

OLD UNITED STATES MINT 7 A2
The Mint opened in 1874 to serve the West during the Gold Rush. Surviving the 1906 earthquake, this building now houses a museum of western exhibits and a solid gold bear. **744-6830.**
Hours: 10am to 4pm, Monday through Friday. Closed holidays & weekends.
Admission: Free, with tours beginning every hour.

PALACE OF FINE ARTS 1 C2
Built for the 1915 Panama Pacific International Exposition and later restored, this building now houses a science museum. *The Exploratorium* and a theater.

PERFORMING ARTS CENTER .... **See Civic Center**

PIER 39 .... 3 A1
An unique shopping and restaurant complex on the waterfront designed in the manner of a San Francisco street scene at the turn of the century.

PRESIDIO 1 A2
Sixth Army Headquarters established in 1776 by the Spaniards.

PRESIDIO ARMY MUSEUM 1 C2
At Lincoln Boulevard and Funston Avenue in the Presidio of San Francisco. The museum focuses on the role of the military in the history and development of San Francisco from 1776 to the present. **561-4115.**
Hours: 10am to 4pm, closed on Mondays and major holidays.
Admission: Free.

RIPLEY'S *BELIEVE IT OR NOT* MUSEUM 2 C1
175 Jefferson Street at Fisherman's Wharf. Cartoonist Robert L. Ripley's fascination with the unbelievable and unimaginable resulted in an enormous collection of oddities that is now on view in San Francisco. **771-6188.**
Hours: Sunday through Thursday, 10am to 10pm; Friday and Saturday, 10am to midnight.
Admission: $6.95 for Adults, $5.25 for Seniors and Juniors (13-17) and $3.75 for Children (5-12). Children under 5 admitted free.

SAN FRANCISCO VISITORS INFORMATION CENTER 7 A2
Service of San Francisco Convention & Visitors Bureau. The place to contact for anything you need to know about San Francisco. Brochures and information supplied free. Located in the Hallidie Plaza (Powell and Market Streets). **391-2000.** Business office is at 201 Third Street, **974-6900.** For a two minute recorded summary of daily activities and events, telephone **391-2001.** Benjamin H. Swig Pavilion.
Hours: Daily except Thanksgiving, Christmas and New Year's Day.

SAN FRANCISCO ZOO 12 A3
Colorful and unusual animals, Zebra Zephyr Guided Tours, a Children's Zoo and picnic areas provide enjoyment for young and old. **753-7083.**
Hours: 10am to 5pm. Daily, all year round.
Admission: $6.00 for Adults, $3.00 for Seniors and Juniors (12-15) and Children under 12 are free. The Children's Zoo is $1.00, under 2 free.

SEAL ROCKS 4 A3
Located 400 feet off-shore from the Cliff House Restaurant and Gift Shop, these miniature islands of the Sea Lions can be enjoyed all year round. Point Lobos Avenue at Ocean Beach.

SIGMUND STERN GROVE 12 C2
A natural Amphitheater sheltered by eucalyptus trees at Sloat Boulevard and 19th Avenue. Summer Sunday concerts at 2pm are free.

THOMAS BROS. MAPS 3 A3
Quality mapping since 1915. A unique *Old English Map House* featuring everything in maps. It is located at the entrance to Jackson Square which is noted for antique and decorator shops at Jackson and Columbus. **981-7520.**
Hours: 9am to 5pm, daily. Closed Saturday and Sunday.

YACHT HARBOR 1 C1
St. Francis Yacht Club at the foot of Divisadero Street. Regattas are held during the summer months.

HOW TO USE THE CROSS STREET INDEX

A special index has been prepared for all streets in San Francisco. This index lists each street, followed by all the crossing streets in house address order. Most crossing streets include the lowest house address starting at the intersection.

1991 SAN FRANCISCO COUNTY CROSS STREET INDEX

A

A ST SF 17 C1
N FROM NIMITZ AV E OF LOCKWOOD ST
ABBEY ST SF 10 B2
N FROM 17TH ST BETWEEN
DOLORES ST AND CHURCH ST
N TO CHULA LANE
ACADIA ST SF 14 A3
FROM MONTEREY BLVD TO A POINT
N OF JOOST AV
100 MONTEREY BLVD
200 JOOST AV
END PT N OF JOOST AV
ACCACIA ST SF 20 C3
FROM VELASCO AV TO COUNTY LINE
ACEVEDO AV SF 18 C2
W FROM ARBALLO DR N OF
HIGUERA AV TO VIDAL DR
ACME AL SF 10 A3
FROM SEWARD ST NEAR DOUGLASS ST
SW TO GRAND VIEW AV
ACORN AL SF 6 C1
SW FROM LEAVENWORTH ST BETWEEN
CALIFORNIA ST AND SACRAMENTO ST
ACTON ST SF 19 C3
FROM 5900 MISSION ST S TO
COUNTY LINE
ADA CT SF 6 C2
N FROM O'FARRELL ST TO AMITY AL
BETWEEN LEAVENWORTH ST
AND HYDE ST
ADAIR ST SF 10 C2
W FROM SOUTH VAN NESS AV BETWEEN
15TH ST AND 16TH ST W TO CAPP ST
ADDISON ST SF 14 B2
FROM BEMIS ST W TO
DIAMOND HEIGHTS BLVD
ADELE CT SF 3 A3
N FROM JACKSON ST BETWEEN
STOCKTON ST AND POWELL ST
ADMIRAL AV SF 14 B3
FROM 4150 MISSION ST W TO
ALEMANY BLVD
ADOLPH SUTRO CT SF 9 C3
W FROM JOHNSTONE DR
W BLK N OF CLARENDON AV
AERIAL WY SF 9 A3
W FROM ORTEGA ST TO 14TH AV
ORTEGA ST
PACHECO ST
FUNSTON AVE
END 14TH AV
AGATE AL SF 7 A2
N FROM POST ST BETWEEN JONES
ST AND TAYLOR ST
AGNON AV SF 14 C3
FROM 100 CRESCENT AV SW
TO JUSTIN DR
AGUA WY SF 13 C2
FROM TERESITA BLVD W TO
CHAVES AV
AHERN WY SF 7 B3
W OF SIXTH ST BETWEEN HARRISON
AND BRYANT ST
AHLERS CT SF 2 B3
S FROM FILBERT ST BETWEEN WEBSTER
AND BUCHANAN STS
AILEEN ST SF 10 B2
N FROM 15TH ST BETWEEN
RAMONA ST AND DOLORES ST
ALABAMA ST SF 11 A2
ALABAMA ST SF 15 A1
FROM ALAMEDA ST BETWEEN
FLORIDA ST AND HARRISON ST
S TO ESMERALDA AV
100 ALAMEDA ST
TREAT AV
200 15TH ST
300 16TH ST
400 17TH ST
500 MARIPOSA ST
600 18TH ST
700 19TH ST
800 20TH ST
900 21ST ST
1000 22ND ST
1100 23RD ST
1200 24TH ST
1300 25TH ST
1400 26TH ST
1500 ARMY ST
1600 PRECITA AV
MULLEN AV
MONTCALM ST
1700 NORWICH ST
RUTLEDGE ST
1800 RIPLEY ST
WALTHAM ST
END ESMERALDA AV
ALADDIN TER SF 2 C2
FROM TAYLOR E & W BETWEEN
UNION ST AND FILBERT ST
ALAMEDA ST SF 11 A1
W FROM ILLINOIS ST TO A POINT
E OF 3RD ST
FROM DE HARO ST W TO
HARRISON ST N OF 15TH ST
1700 DE HARO ST
1800 RHODE ISLAND ST
1900 KANSAS ST
2000 VERMONT ST
2100 SAN BRUNO AV
2200 UTAH ST
2300 POTRERO AV
2400 HAMPSHIRE ST
END BRYANT ST
FROM FLORIDA ST W
TREAT AV
2800 ALABAMA ST
END HARRISON ST
ALANA WY SF 21 B3
W FROM HARNEY WY
E OF JAMES LICK FWY (HWY 101)
ALBATROSS CT SF 16 A3
S FROM KISKA RD IN
HUNTERS PT NAVAL RES
ALBERTA ST SF 21 A2
N FROM CAMPBELL AV NEAR ELLIOT ST
ALBION ST SF 10 C2
S FROM 15TH ST BETWEEN
VALENCIA ST AND GUERRERO ST
S TO 17TH ST
2 15TH ST
100 16TH ST
END 17TH ST
ALDER ST SF 21 A2
FROM ANKENY ST S TO HARKNESS AV
BETWEEN MILL ST & BISHOP ST
ALEMANY BLVD SF 14 C3
ALEMANY BLVD SF 19 B3
ALEMANY BLVD SF 20 A1
SW FROM BAYSHORE BLVD
TO JUNIPERO SERRA BLVD
BAYSHORE BLVD
JAMES LICK FRWY
PUTNAM ST
FOLSOM ST
ELLSWORTH ST
I-280 FRWY
TRUMBULL ST
JUSTIN DR
CONGDON ST
ROUSSEAU ST
ADMIRAL AV
LYELL ST
SILVER AV
TINGLEY ST
THERESA ST
COTTER ST
FRANCIS ST
1600 SANTA ROSA AV
HARRINGTON ST
NORTON ST
1700 SAN JUAN AV
OCEAN AV
LEO ST
1900 ONONDAGA ST
2000 ONEIDA AV
2100 SENECA AV
2200 GENEVA AV
2300 NIAGARA AV
2400 MOUNT VERNON AV
HURON AV
OTTAWA AV
FOOTE AV
NAGLEE AV
FARRAGUT AV
LAURA ST
LAWRENCE AV
CAYUGA AV
DE WOLF ST
3100 SICKLES AV
REGENT ST
3150 SAN JOSE AV
SAGAMORE ST
ORIZABA AV
BROTHERHOOD WY
BRIGHT ST
HEAD ST
VICTORIA ST
RAMSELL ST
WORCESTER AV
ARCH ST
KEMPTON AV
ST CHARLES AV
END JUNIPERO SERRA BLVD
ALERT AL SF 10 B2
W FROM DOLORES ST BETWEEN
15TH ST AND 16TH ST TO
LANDERS ST
ALHAMBRA ST SF 2 A2
FROM CERVANTES BLVD NEAR
FILLMORE ST W TO AVILA ST
2 CERVANTES BLVD
100 MALLORCA WY
200 PIERCE ST
END AVILA ST
ALLAN ST SF 21 A3
N FROM 3100 GENEVA AV
2 BLKS W OF BAYSHORE BLVD
ALLEN ST SF 2 C2
W FROM WS HYDE ST BETWEEN UNION
ST AND FILBERT ST TO
EASTMAN ST
ALLISON ST SF 20 A2
SE FROM 5301 MISSION ST TO A
POINT NEAR THE COUNTY LINE
2 MISSION ST
100 CROSS ST
200 MORSE ST
300 BRUNSWICK ST
400 HANOVER ST
END PT S OF HANOVER ST
ALLSTON WY SF 13 B2
FROM 650 ULLOA ST NW TO
CLAREMONT BLVD
VASQUEZ AV END CLAREMONT BLVD
ALMA ST SF 9 C2
SW FROM BELVEDERE ST BETWEEN
GRATTAN ST AND RIVOLI ST
TO SANYAN ST
2 BELVEDERE ST
100 COLE ST
200 SHRADER ST
END STANYAN ST
ALMADEN CT SF 5 B3
N FROM ANZA ST BETWEEN
LORAINE CT AND ARGUELLO BLVD
TO A POINT S OF GEARY BLVD
ALOHA AV SF 9 A3
FROM 1601 FUNSTON AV W TO
LOMITA AV
ALPHA ST SF 21 A2
W FROM SAN BRUNO AV S FROM
GOETTINGEN ST TO LELAND AV
GOETTINGEN ST
GIRARD AV
BRUSSELS ST
34 TIOGA AV
58 TUCKER AV
CAMPBELL AV
200 TEDDY AV
300 ARLETA AV
400 RAYMOND AV
END LELAND AV
ALPINE TER SF 10 A1
S FROM WALLER ST BETWEEN BUENA
VISTA AV AND DIVISADERO
ST TO 14TH ST
2 WALLER ST
100 DUBOCE AV
END 14TH ST
ALTA ST SF 3 A2
E & W FROM MONTGOMERY ST BETWEEN
UNION AND FILBERT STS
ALTA MAR WY SF 4 A3
N FROM PT LOBOS AV BETWEEN
EL CAMINO DEL MAR ST AND
45TH AV TO SEAL ROCK DR
ALTA VISTA TER SF 3 A2
N FROM VALLEJO ST BETWEEN
MASON ST AND TAYLOR ST
ALTON AV SF 13 B1
W FROM CASTENADA AV TO 9TH AV
2 CASTENADA AV
100 PACHECO ST
END 9TH AV
ALVARADO ST SF 10 B3
W FROM SAN JOSE AV BETWEEN
22ND AND 23RD STS TO
GUERRERO ST AND W FROM
SANCHEZ ST TO DIAMOND ST AND
W FROM DOUGLASS ST TO
GRAND VIEW AV
2 SAN JOSE AV
GUERRERO ST
400 SANCHEZ ST
500 NOE ST
CASTRO ST
DIAMOND ST
ALVISO ST SF 19 A1
N FROM HOLLOWAY AV BETWEEN
MONTICELLO ST AND BORICA ST
AMATISTA LN SF 14 B2
N FROM BEMIS ONE BLK
W OF MIGUEL ST
AMATURY LOOP SF 1 B3
N OF WASHINGTON BLVD
IN PRESIDIO
AMAZON AV SF 20 A2
E FROM 5101 MISSION ST BETWEEN
ITALY AV AND GENEVA AV
TO MOSCOW ST
2 MISSION ST
100 LONDON ST
200 PARIS ST
300 LISBON ST
400 MADRID ST
500 EDINBURGH ST
600 NAPLES ST
700 VIENNA ST
800 ATHENS ST
END MOSCOW ST
AMBER DR SF 14 A1
W FROM DUNCAN 2 BLKS W OF
DOUGLASS
CAMEO WY
AMBROSE BRCE ST SF 7 B2
SW FROM NEW MONTGOMERY ST
BETWEEN JESSIE ST AND MISSION
ST W TO ANNIE ST
AMES ST SF 10 C3
S FROM 21ST ST BETWEEN
FAIR OAKS AND GUERRERO STS
TO 23RD ST
AMETHYST WY SF 13 C1
W FROM AMBER DR
AMHERST ST SF 20 C1
S FROM SILVER AV BETWEEN
YALE STS TO WAYLAND ST
BURROWS ST S FROM BACON ST
TO WAYLAND ST
2 SILVER AV

1991 SAN FRANCISCO COUNTY CROSS STREET INDEX

100 SILLIMAN ST
200 FELTON ST
BURROWS ST
BACON ST
END WAYLAND ST
AMITY AL SF 6 C2
E FROM ADA CT NEAR HYDE ST
AND O'FARRELL ST
ANDERSON ST SF 14 C2
S FROM BERNAL HEIGHTS BLVD
BETWEEN ELLSWORTH & MOULTRIE STS
TO A POINT S OF CRESCENT AV
2 ESMERALDA AV
100 POWHATTAN AV
200 EUGENIA AV
300 CORTLAND AV
400 JARBOE AV
500 TOMPKINS AV
600 OGDEN AV
700 CRESCENT AV
END PT S OF CRESCENT AV
ANDOVER ST SF 14 C3
S FROM A POINT N OF POWHATTAN ST
BETWEEN WOOL ST AND MOULTRIE ST
TO A POINT S OF BENTON AV
2 ESMERALDA AV
BERNAL HEIGHTS AV
100 POWHATTAN AV
200 EUGENIA AV
300 CORTLAND AV
400 ELLERT ST
450 NEWMAN ST
TOMPKINS AV
500 HIGHLAND AV
600 PARK ST
OGDEN AV
RICHLAND AV
700 CRESCENT AV
BENTON AV
END PT S OF BENTON AV
ANGLO AL SF 13 A1
S FROM ORTEGA ST BETWEEN 17TH AV
AND 18TH AV TO A POINT S
OF PACHECO ST
ANKENY ST SF 21 A2
FROM DELTA ST E TO SPARTA ST
ANNAPOLIS TER SF 5 C3
S FROM TURK ST BETWEEN MASONIC
AV AND TAMALPAIS TER TO
GOLDEN GATE AV
ANNIE ST SF 7 B2
SE FROM MARKET ST BETWEEN NEW
MONTGOMERY ST AND 3RD ST
TO MISSION ST
ANSON PL SF 7 A2
E FROM POWELL ST BETWEEN SUTTER
ST AND BUSH ST
ANTHONY ST SF 7 B2
FROM POINT N OF JESSIE ST
BETWEEN ECKER AND 2ND STS SE
TO MISSION ST
ANTONIO ST SF 6 C2
W FROM JONES ST BETWEEN
ELLIS AND O'FARRELL STS
ANZA ST SF 1 B2
IN PRESIDIO
ANZA ST SF 4 A3
ANZA ST SF 5 C3
FROM MASONIC AV BETWEEN GEARY
BLVD AND BALBOA ST W TO
48TH AV
100 MASONIC AV
WOOD ST
JEAN WY
COLLINS ST
BLAKE ST
COOK ST
SPRUCE ST
PARKER AV
BEAUMONT AV
STANYAN ST
ROSSI AV
LORAINE CT
ALMADEN CT
1000 ARGUELLO BLVD
1100 2ND AV
1200 3RD AV
1300 4TH AV
1400 5TH AV
1500 6TH AV
1600 7TH AV
1700 8TH AV
1800 9TH AV
1900 10TH AV
2000 11TH AV
2100 12TH AV
2000 FUNSTON AV
PARK PRESIDIO BLVD
2300 14TH AV
2400 15TH AV
2500 16TH AV
2600 17TH AV
2700 18TH AV
2800 19TH AV
2900 20TH AV
3000 21ST AV
3100 22ND AV
3200 23RD AV
3300 24TH AV
3400 25TH AV
3500 26TH AV
3600 27TH AV
3700 28TH AV
3800 29TH AV
30TH AV
4000 32ND AV
4100 33RD AV
4200 34TH AV
4300 35TH AV
4400 36TH AV
4500 37TH AV
4600 38TH AV
4700 39TH AV
4800 40TH AV
4900 41ST AV
5000 42ND AV
5100 43RD AV
5200 44TH AV
5300 45TH AV
5400 46TH AV
5500 47TH AV
END 48TH AV
ANZAVISTA AV SF 6 A3
S FROM O'FARRELL ST TO
BAKER ST
O'FARRELL ST
TERRA VISTA AV
VEGA ST
BARCELONA AV
ARBOL LN
ENCANTO AV
FORTUNA AV
END BAKER ST
APOLLO ST SF 15 B3
S FROM TOPEKA AV TO
WILLIAMS AV
APPAREL WY SF 15 A2
E FROM BARNEVELD AV BETWEEN
PALOU AV AND DORMAN AV
APPLETON AV SF 14 C2
SE FROM 3601 MISSION ST BETWEEN
SANTA MARINA ST AND HIGHLAND AV
TO HOLLY PARK CIR
APPLETON ST SF 1 A2
IN PRESIDIO S AND W
FROM RUCKMAN AV
APTOS AV SF 13 B3
N FROM 2200 OCEAN AV TO DARIEN WY
2 OCEAN AV
200 UPLAND DR
END DARIEN WY
AQUAVISTA WY SF 9 C3
S FROM MAR VIEW WY TO SKYVIEW WY
ARAGO ST SF 20 A1
S FROM PAULDING ST W OF
SAN JOSE AV TO HAVELOCK ST
ARBALLO DR SF 18 C2
N FROM TAPIA DR ENDING AT A POINT
N OF TAPIA DR CONTINUING SW FROM
TAPIA DR TO VIDAL DR
TAPIA DR
VIDAL DR
PINTO ST
ACEVEDO AV
SERRANO DR
HIGUERA AV
GONZALEZ DR
GARCES DR
END VIDAL DR
ARBOL LN SF 6 A3
N FROM TURK ST BETWEEN BAKER ST
AND CENTRAL AV TO A POINT S OF
ANZAVISTA AV
ARBOR ST SF 14 A2
W FROM DIAMOND ST TO BERKELY WY
ARCH ST SF 19 B2
S FROM ALEMANY BLVD BETWEEN
VERNON ST AND RAMSELL ST
N TO HOLLOWAY AV
ALEMANY BLVD
100 BROTHERHOOD WY
200 RANDOLPH ST
300 SARGENT ST
400 SHIELDS ST
500 GARFIELD ST
END HOLLOWAY AV
ARCO WY SF 20 A1
N FROM HAVELOCK ST BETWEEN
ARAGO ST AND 280 FREEWAY
ARDATH CT SF 15 C3
E FROM HUDSON AV BETWEEN
WESTBROOK CT AND
WHITNEY YOUNG CIR
ARDENWOOD WY SF 13 A3
N FROM SLOAT BLVD BETWEEN 19TH
AV AND WEST PORTAL AV
ARELLANO AV SF 19 A2
S FROM HOLLOWAY AV BETWEEN
CARDENAS AV AND TAPIA DR
TO SERRANO DR
ARGENT AL SF 10 A3
W FROM MARKET ST N OF 23RD
ST TO CORBETT AV
ARGONAUT AV SF 20 C3
W FROM GARRISON AV S OF
SUNNYDALE AV TO VELASCO AV
MC CARTHY AV
BURR AV
END VELASCO AV
ARGUELLO BLVD SF 1 B3
ARGUELLO BLVD SF 5 B1
ARGUELLO BLVD SF 9 B2
S FROM SHERIDAN AV
IN THE PRESIDIO TO PARNASSUS
BETWEEN 3RD AV AND HILLWAY AV
2 PACIFIC AV
SHERIDAN AV
MORAGA AV
HARDIE RD
SIBERT LOOP
WASHINGTON BLVD
RACH
50 JACKSON ST
100 WASHINGTON ST
PRESIDIO TER
150 CLAY ST
LAKE ST
200 SACRAMENTO ST
300 CALIFORNIA ST
CORNWALL ST
400 EUCLID AV
CLEMENT ST
500 GEARY BLVD
ANZA ST
600 EDWARD ST
BALBOA ST
700 TURK ST
750 GOLDEN GATE AV
CABRILLO ST
800 MCALLISTER ST
FULTON ST
END CONSERVATORY DR E
CONTINUING S FROM KEZAR DR IN
GOLDEN GATE PARK
KEZAR DR
LINCOLN WY
1200 FREDERICK ST
HUGO ST
1300 CARL ST
IRVING ST
END PARNASSUS AV
ARKANSAS ST SF 11 B2
S FROM 16TH ST BETWEEN
CONNECTICUT ST AND WISCONSIN ST
TO 23RD ST
2 16TH ST
100 17TH ST
200 MARIPOSA ST
300 18TH ST
400 19TH ST
500 20TH ST
700 22ND ST
MADERA ST
END 23RD ST
ARLETA AV SF 21 A2
NW FROM BAYSHORE BLVD TO
ELLIOTT ST BETWEEN TEDDY AV &
RAYMOND AV
BAYSHORE BLVD
100 ALPHA ST
200 RUTLAND ST
300 DELTA ST
END ELLIOT ST
ARLINGTON ST SF 14 B3
SW FROM RANDALL ST BETWEEN
SAN JOSE AV AND CHENERY ST TO
BOSWORTH ST
RANDALL ST
FAIRMOUNT ST
CHARLES ST
300 MIGUEL ST
MATEO ST
ST MARYS AV
ROANOKE ST
NATICK ST
END BOSWORTH ST
ARMISTEAD RD SF 1 A2
IN THE PRESIDIO
ARMSTRONG AV SF 21 B1
FROM HAWES ST BETWEEN YOSEMITE AV
AND BANCROFT AV NW TO NEWHALL ST
HAWES ST
INGALLS ST
JENNINGS ST
KEITH ST
3RD ST
LANE ST
END MENDELL ST
FROM RAILROAD TRACKS
END NEWHALL ST
ARMY ST SF 14 A1
ARMY ST SF 15 A1
FROM A POINT E OF MICHIGAN ST
W TO DOUGLASS ST
1000 3RD ST
TENNESSEE ST
MINNESOTA ST
INDIANA ST
PENNSYLVANIA ST
MISSOURI ST
CONNECTICUT ST
EVANS AV
KANSAS ST
VERMONT ST
JAMES LICK FRWY
2800 POTRERO AV
2850 HAMPSHIRE ST
2900 YORK ST
2950 BRYANT ST
3000 FLORIDA ST
3050 ALABAMA ST
3100 HARRISON ST
3200 FOLSOM ST
SHOTWELL ST
3300 SOUTH VAN NESS
CAPP ST
3400 MISSION ST
3450 BARTLETT ST
3500 VALENCIA ST
3600 SAN JOSE AV
3700 GUERRERO ST
3800 DOLORES ST
3900 CHURCH ST
4000 SANCHEZ ST
4100 NOE ST
4200 CASTRO ST
4300 DIAMOND ST
END DOUGLASS ST
ARNOLD AV SF 14 C3
S FROM CRESCENT AV BETWEEN
ROSCOE ST AND AGNON AV
ARROYO WY SF 13 C2
S FROM MARIETTA DR TO
BELLA VISTA WY
ARTHUR AV SF 15 C1
SE FROM ISLAIS ST TO 3RD ST
ASH ST SF 6 C3
W FROM GOUGH ST BETWEEN
FULTON ST AND MCALLISTER ST
W TO BUCHANAN ST
BUCHANAN ST
GOUGH ST
500 OCTAVIA ST
600 LAGUNA ST
END BUCHANAN ST
ASHBURTON PL SF 7 A2
E FROM GRANT AV BETWEEN
POST ST AND SUTTER ST
ASHBURY ST SF 9 C1
S FROM FULTON ST BETWEEN
MASONIC AV AND CLAYTON ST
ENDING AT CLAYTON ST
2 FULTON ST
100 GROVE ST
200 HAYES ST
FELL ST
400 OAK ST
500 PAGE ST
600 HAIGHT ST
WALLER ST
800 FREDERICK ST
930 PIEDMONT ST
1000 CLIFFORD ST
DOWNEY ST
END CLAYTON ST
ASHBURY TER SF 10 A2
S FROM PIEDMONT ST AND E TO
UPPER TER
ASHTON AV SF 19 B1
BETWEEN JULES ST AND
ORIZABA ST N FROM
LAKEVIEW AV TO OCEAN AV
2 LAKEVIEW AV
100 GRAFTON AV
200 HOLLOWAY AV
HEAD ST
300 DE MONTFORD AV
PICO AV
END OCEAN AV
ASHWOOD LN SF 9 C3
NW FROM CLARENDON AV BETWEEN
OLYMPIC WY AND PANORAMA DR
ATALAYA TER SF 5 C3
N FROM 1850 FULTON ST
ATHENS ST SF 20 B2
W FROM MADISON ST CONTINUING
TO NAPLES ST

1991 SAN FRANCISCO COUNTY CROSS STREET INDEX

2 MADISON ST
100 PERU AV
200 AVALON AV
300 EXCELSIOR AV
400 BRAZIL AV
500 PERSIA AV
600 RUSSIA AV
700 FRANCE AV
800 ITALY AV
900 AMAZON AV
1000 GENEVA AV
1100 ROLPH ST
1200 CORDOVA ST
END NAPLES ST
ATTRIDGE AL SF 2 C2
N FROM FILBERT ST BETWEEN
JONES ST AND LEAVENWORTH ST
AUBURN ST SF 3 A3
N FROM JACKSON ST BETWEEN
MASON ST AND TAYLOR ST
N TO PACIFIC AV
AUGUST AL SF 3 A2
N FROM GREEN ST BETWEEN
POWELL ST AND MASON ST
AUGUSTA ST SF 15 A3
FROM SILVER AV BETWEEN
SILVER AV AND HELENA ST
W TO SAN BRUNO AV
2 SILVER AV
WATERVILLE ST
100 EL MIRA ST
200 CHARTER OAK AV
300 BOUTWELL ST
BAY SHORE BLVD
400 STEUBEN ST
END SAN BRUNO AV
AUTO DR SF 9 B3
S FROM LAWTON TO MORAGA ST
BETWEEN 8TH AV AND 9TH AV
AVALON AV SF 20 B1
FROM MISSION ST 1 BLK N OF
EXCELSIOR AV SE TO PERU AV
2 MISSION ST
100 LONDON ST
200 PARIS ST
300 LISBON ST
400 MADRID ST
500 EDINBURGH ST
600 NAPLES ST
700 VIENNA ST
800 ATHENS ST
MOSCOW ST
LA GRANDE AV
END PERU ST
AVENUE B SF 3 C2
NW FROM CALIFORNIA AV TO 3RD ST,
BETWEEN AV A & AV C,
TREASURE ISLAND
AVENUE C SF 3 C1
NW FROM CALIFORNIA AV TO SW
EXTENSION OF 4TH ST BETWEEN
AV B & AV D, TREASURE ISLAND
AVENUE D SF 3 C1
NW FROM CALIFORNIA AV TO 12TH ST
BETWEEN AV C & AV F,
TREASURE ISLAND
CALIFORNIA AV
3RD ST
9TH ST
11TH ST
END 12TH ST
AVENUE E SF 3 C1
NW FROM 9TH ST TO 13TH ST BETWEEN
AV D & AV H, TREASURE ISLAND
9TH ST
11TH ST
12TH ST
END 13TH ST
AVENUE F SF 3 C1
NW FROM CALIFORNIA AV TO 3RD ST,
& FROM UNNAMED ST TO 9TH ST
BETWEEN AV D & AV H,
TREASURE ISLAND
AVENUE H SF 3 C1
NW FROM CALIFORNIA AV TO 13TH ST,
TREASURE ISLAND
CALIFORNIA AV
3RD ST
4TH ST
6TH ST
9TH ST
11TH ST
12TH ST
END 13TH ST
AVENUE I SF 3 C1
NW FROM 6TH ST TO PARKING LOT
ADJOINING AV M, TREASURE ISLAND
6TH ST
9TH ST
11TH ST
13TH ST
END AV M
AVENUE M SF 3 C1
NW FROM CALIFORNIA AV TO
PARKING LOT ADJOINING AV I,
TREASURE ISLAND
CALIFORNIA AV
3RD ST
4TH ST
5TH ST
6TH ST
8TH ST
9TH ST
10TH ST
11TH ST
13TH ST
END AV I
AVENUE N SF 3 C1
N FROM SE CORNER OF TREASURE
ISLAND TO 3RD ST THEN NW TO POINT
N OF 13TH ST
CALIFORNIA AV
3RD ST
4TH ST
5TH ST
8TH ST
10TH ST
13TH ST
AVENUE NORTH SF 4 C2
N FROM 25TH AV
AV OF THE PALMS SF 3 C1
NW FROM 1ST ST AT ENTRANCE OF
TREASURE ISLAND, TO 9TH ST
1ST ST
CALIFORNIA AV
3RD ST
END 9TH ST
AVERY ST SF 6 B2
N FROM GEARY ST BETWEEN
FILLMORE ST AND
STEINER ST TO POST ST
AVILA ST SF 2 A2
N FROM 2250 CHESTNUT ST
TO MARINA BLVD
2 CHESTNUT ST
100 ALHAMBRA ST
200 CAPRA WY
300 PRADO ST
END MARINA BLVD
AVOCA AL SF 13 C2
SE FROM CRESTA VISTA DR BETWEEN
OMAR WY AND MYRA WY TO
ROCKDALE DR
AVON WY SF 13 A3
N FROM SLOAT BLVD BETWEEN
JUNIPERO SERRA & 19TH AV
AZTEC ST SF 14 C1
FROM COSO AV E TO SHOTWELL ST

B

BACHE ST SF 14 C3
S FROM CRESCENT AV BETWEEN
ANDOVER ST AND PORTER ST
BACON ST SF 20 C1
BACON ST SF 21 A1
FROM BAYSHORE BLVD BETWEEN
BURROWS ST & WAYLAND ST W TO
HARVARD ST
BAYSHORE BLVD
100 SAN BRUNO AV
200 GIRARD ST
300 BRUSSELS ST
400 GOETTINGEN ST
500 SOMERSET ST
600 HOLYOKE ST
HAMILTON ST
BOWDOIN ST
UNIVERSITY ST
PRINCETON ST
CAMPUS LN
AMHERST ST
1500 CAMBRIDGE ST
1600 OXFORD ST
END HARVARD ST
BADEN ST SF 14 A3
FROM CIRCULAR AV BETWEEN
ACADIA ST AND CONGO ST
N TO MARTHA ST
2 CIRCULAR AV
100 HEARST AV
200 MONTEREY BLVD
300 JOOST AV
400 MANGELS AV
END MARTHA ST
BADGER ST SF 14 B3
N FROM CAYUGA AV BETWEEN
LAMARTINE ST & GORMAN ST
BAKER CT SF 4 C2
E FROM LINCOLN BLVD
BAKER ST SF 2 A2
BAKER ST SF 6 A2
BAKER ST SF 10 A1
N FROM S HAIGHT ST BETWEEN
BRODERICK ST AND LYON ST
N TO THE BAY
2 HAIGHT ST
100 PAGE ST
200 OAK ST
300 FELL ST
400 HAYES ST
500 GROVE ST
600 FULTON ST
700 MCALLISTER ST
800 GOLDEN GATE AV
TURK ST
ANZAVISTA AV
PINAR LN
ELLIS ST
1300 GEARY ST
1400 POST ST
1500 SUTTER ST
1600 BUSH ST
1700 PINE ST
1800 CALIFORNIA ST
1900 SACRAMENTO ST
2000 CLAY ST
2100 WASHINGTON ST
2200 JACKSON ST
2300 PACIFIC AV
END BROADWAY
2500 VALLEJO ST
2600 GREEN ST
2700 UNION ST
2800 FILBERT ST
MILEY ST
2900 GREENWICH ST
3000 LOMBARD ST
3100 CHESTNUT ST
RICHARDSON AV
3200 FRANCISCO ST
3300 BAY ST
3400 NORTH POINT ST
3500 BEACH ST
3600 JEFFERSON ST
3700 MARINA BLVD
BALANCE ST SF 3 B3
N FROM S JACKSON ST BETWEEN
SANSOME ST AND
MONTGOMERY ST N TO GOLD ST
BALBOA ST SF 4 B3
BALBOA ST SF 5 A3
FROM ARGUELLO BLVD BETWEEN
ANZA ST AND CABRILLO ST W
TO GREAT HIGHWAY
2 ARGUELLO BLVD
100 2ND AV
200 3RD AV
300 4TH AV
400 5TH AV
500 6TH AV
600 7TH AV
700 8TH AV
800 9TH AV
900 10TH AV
1000 11TH AV
1100 12TH AV
FUNSTON AV
PARK PRESIDIO BL
1300 14TH AV
1400 15TH AV
1500 16TH AV
1600 17TH AV
1700 18TH AV
1800 19TH AV
1900 20TH AV
2000 21ST AV
2100 22ND AV
2200 23RD AV
2300 24TH AV
2400 25TH AV
2500 26TH AV
2600 27TH AV
2700 28TH AV
2800 29TH AV
2900 30TH AV
3000 31ST AV
3100 32ND AV
3200 33RD AV
3300 34TH AV
3400 35TH AV
3500 36TH AV
3600 37TH AV
3700 38TH AV
3800 39TH AV
3900 40TH AV
4000 41ST AV
4100 42ND AV
4200 43RD AV
4300 44TH AV
4400 45TH AV
4500 46TH AV
4600 47TH AV
4700 48TH AV
4800 LA PLAYA ST
END THE GREAT HIGHWAY
BALCETA AV SF 13 B1
FROM LAGUNA HONDA ST NE
TO WOODSIDE AV
BALDWIN CT SF 15 C3
NE OFF OAKDALE AV S OF INGALLS ST
BALHI CT SF 20 A1
E FROM CAYUGA AV BETWEEN
ONEIDA AV AND ONONDAGA AV
BALMY ST SF 11 A3
S FROM S 24TH ST BETWEEN
HARRISON ST AND TREAT AV
S TO 25TH ST
BALTIMORE WY SF 20 B3
NE FROM S CORDOVA ST TO
SOUTH HILL BLVD
BANBURY DR SF 19 A2
E FROM 19TH AV TO
STRATFORD DR S OF
HOLLOWAY AV
BANCROFT AV SF 15 B3
BANCROFT AV SF 21 B1
NW FROM HAWES ST BETWEEN
ARMSTRONG ST & CARROLL ST TO
MENDELL ST & NEWHALL ST
TO QUINT ST
HAWES ST
INGALLS ST
JENNINGS ST
KEITH ST
3RD ST
MENDELL ST
NEWHALL ST
PHELPS ST
END QUINT ST
BANK ST SF 1 B2
N FROM LINCOLN BLVD S OF DOYLE DR
BANKS ST SF 15 A2
S FROM BERNAL HTS BLVD BETWEEN
PRENTISS ST AND FOLSOM ST TO A
POINT S OF CRESCENT AV
2 BERNAL HTS BLVD
CHAPMAN ST
100 POWHATTAN AV
200 EUGENIA AV
300 CORTLAND AV
400 JARBOE AV
500 TOMPKINS AV
600 OGDEN AV
700 CRESCENT AV
END PT S OF CRESCENT
BANNAM PL SF 3 A2
N FROM S GREEN ST BETWEEN
GRANT AV AND STOCKTON ST
N TO UNION ST
BANNOCK ST SF 20 A2
N OFF S GENEVA AV TO
SENECA AV BETWEEN CAYUGA AV
AND ALEMANY BLVD
BARCELONA AV SF 6 A3
N FROM ANZAVISTA AV BETWEEN
ENCANTO AV AND ANZAVISTA AV TO
TERRA VISTA AV
BARNARD AV SF 1 C3
S OFF OF PRESIDIO BLVD
BARNEVELD AV SF 15 A2
S FROM JERROLD AV AND
SW TO SILVER AV
JERROLD AV
LOOMIS ST
MCKINNON AV
NEWCOMB AV
OAKDALE AV
PALOU AV
APPAREL WY
DORMAN AV
INDUSTRIAL ST
DICKENSON ST
600 SAN BRUNO AV
700 RICKARD ST
750 GAVEN ST
800 SWEENY ST
850 HALE ST
END SILVER AV
BARTLETT ST SF 10 C3
S FROM S 21ST ST BETWEEN
MISSION ST AND VALENCIA ST
TO ARMY ST
2 21ST ST
100 22ND ST
200 23RD ST
300 24TH ST
400 25TH ST
500 26TH ST
END ARMY ST
BARTOL ST SF 3 A2
FROM A POINT S OF
BROADWAY BETWEEN SANSOME ST
AND MONTGOMERY ST N TO
VALLEJO ST
BATTERY ST SF 3 B2
N FROM S MARKET ST BETWEEN

FRONT ST AND SANSOME ST
TO THE EMBARCADERO
2 MARKET ST
BUSH ST
100 PINE ST
200 CALIFORNIA ST
HALLECK ST
300 SACRAMENTO ST
COMMERCIAL ST
400 CLAY ST
MERCHANT ST
500 WASHINGTON ST
600 JACKSON ST
700 PACIFIC AV
800 BROADWAY
900 VALLEJO ST
1000 GREEN ST
COMMERCE ST
1100 UNION ST
1200 FILBERT ST
1300 GREENWICH ST
LOMBARD ST
END THE EMBARCADERO
BTRY CHMBRLN RD SF 4 C1
N FROM GIBSON RD AND NE
TO LINCOLN BLVD
BATTERY EAST RD SF 1 A1
BAXTER AL SF 13 B3
NE FROM YERBA BUENA AV
TO CASITAS AV BETWEEN
MIRALOMA DR AND HAZELWOOD AV
BAY ST SF 2 B2
BAY ST SF 3 A2
FROM THE EMBARCADERO BETWEEN
NORTH POINT AND FRANCISCO STS
W TO BAKER ST
2 THE EMBARCADERO
50 KEARNY ST
MIDWAY ST
200 STOCKTON ST
300 POWELL ST
400 MASON ST
500 TAYLOR ST
COLUMBUS AV
JONES ST
700 LEAVENWORTH ST
800 HYDE ST
900 LARKIN ST
1000 POLK ST
VAN NESS AV
FRANKLIN ST
GOUGH ST
OCTAVIA ST
1500 LAGUNA ST
1600 BUCHANAN ST
1700 WEBSTER ST
END FILLMORE ST
2100 SCOTT ST
2200 DIVISADERO ST
2300 BRODERICK ST
END BAKER ST
BAYSHORE BLVD SF 11 B3
BAYSHORE BLVD SF 15 A2
BAYSHORE BLVD SF 21 A3
S FROM ARMY TO CITY LIMITS
ARMY ST
MARIN ST
JERROLD AV
OAKDALE AV
COSGROVE ST
FLOWER ST
CORTLAND AV
WATERLOO ST
MARENGO ST
INDUSTRIAL ST
HELENA ST
LOOMIS ST
I-280 FRWY RAMPS
800 AUGUSTA ST
900 SILVER AV
1100 FELTON ST
QUINT ST
DONNER AV
EGBERT AV
1300 BACON ST
PHELPS ST
FITZGERALD AV
PAUL AV
WHEAT ST
CRANE ST
SALINAS AV
KEY AVE
LANE ST
3RD ST
JAMES LICK FRWY
2100 HESTER AV
TUNNEL AV
2400 BLANKEN AV
SOMERSET ST
ARLETA AV
RAYMOND AV
LELAND AV
2500 VISITACION AV
SUNNYDALE AV
CITY LIMITS
BAYSIDE DR SF 3 C1
LOOP EXTENDING NW FROM GATEVIEW
AV, TREASURE ISLAND
BAYVIEW ST SF 15 B3
W FROM S 3RD ST AT REVERE AV
TO NEWHALL ST
LATONA ST
POMONA ST
FLORA ST
BAYVIEW PARK RD SF 21 B2
S FROM KEY AV TO LE CONTE AV
BAYWOOD CT SF 20 A2
NE FROM GENEVA AV BETWEEN
BANNOCK ST AND CAYUGA AV
BEACH ST SF 2 A2
BEACH ST SF 3 A1
FROM THE EMBARCADERO BET
NORTH POINT ST AND
JEFFERSON ST W TO BAKER ST
THE EMBARCADERO
2 GRANT AV
100 STOCKTON ST
200 POWELL ST
300 MASON ST
400 TAYLOR ST
500 JONES ST
600 LEAVENWORTH ST
COLUMBUS AV
700 HYDE ST
800 LARKIN ST
END W OF POLK ST
1400 LAGUNA ST
1500 BUCHANAN ST
1600 WEBSTER ST
1700 FILLMORE ST
1800 RETIRO ST
1900 CERVANTES BLVD
MALLORCA WY
PIERCE ST
AVILA ST
2000 SCOTT ST
2100 DIVISADERO ST
2200 BRODERICK ST
END BAKER ST
BEACHMONT DR SF 13 A3
N FROM LAGUNITAS DR BETWEEN
19TH AV AND LAGUNITAS DR
TO SLOAT BLVD
BEACON ST SF 14 B2
E FROM DIAMOND BETWEEN
29TH ST AND ADDISON ST
BEALE ST SF 7 B1
SE FROM S MARKET ST BETWEEN
MAIN ST AND FREMONT ST
TO THE EMBARCADERO
2 MARKET ST
100 MISSION ST
200 HOWARD ST
300 FOLSOM ST
400 HARRISON ST
500 BRYANT ST
BRANNAN ST
END THE EMBARCADERO
BEATRICE LN SF 15 C3
TO KEYES AV S OF PRESIDIO BLVD
OFF INGALLS ST BETWEEN
LA SALLE AV & ROSIE LEE LN
BEAUMONT AV SF 5 C3
S FROM GEARY BLVD TO
TURK ST
BEAVER ST SF 10 A2
W FROM NOE ST BETWEEN
15TH ST & 16TH ST TO 15TH ST
WAY
BECKETT ST SF 3 A3
N FROM S JACKSON ST BETWEEN
KEARNY ST AND GRANT AV TO
PACIFIC AV
BEDFORD PL SF 3 A3
N FROM S JACKSON ST BETWEEN
STOCKTON ST AND POWELL ST
TO PACIFIC AV
BEEMAN LN SF 21 B2
S FROM SAN BRUNO AV TO
WABASH TER NEAR BAY SHORE BLVD
BEHR AV SF 9 C3
SE OF JOHNSTONE DR CIRCLES BACK
TO JOHNSTONE DR
BEIDEMAN ST SF 6 A3
N FROM S ELLIS ST BETWEEN
SCOTT ST AND DIVISADERO ST
N TO O'FARRELL ST
BELCHER ST SF 10 B1
S FROM S DUBOCE AV BETWEEN
CHURCH ST AND SANCHEZ ST
S TO 14TH ST
BELDEN ST SF 7 A1
N FROM S BUSH ST BETWEEN
MONTGOMERY ST AND KEARNY
ST TO PINE ST
BELGRAVE AV SF 9 C2
FROM POINT E OF COLE ST W TO
A POINT W OF STANYAN ST
BELL RD SF 1 A2
NW OFF STOREY AV TO MILLER RD
BELLAIR PL SF 3 A2
N FROM S CHESTNUT ST BETWEEN
GRANT AV AND STOCKTON ST
TO FRANCISCO ST
BELLAVISTA LN SF 13 C3
SE FROM LOS PALMOS DR TO
BELLA VISTA WY AT MELROSE AV
PALMOS DR
BELLA VISTA WY SF 13 C2
W FROM TERESITA BLVD TO
MELROSE AV
BELLE AV SF 19 A3
W FROM ST CHARLES AV BETWEEN
PALMETTO AV AND COUNTY LINE
BELLEVUE AV SF 20 A3
E OFF GUTENBERG ST TO WAVERLY WY
NEAR COUNTY LINE
BELMONT AV SF 9 C2
S OF PARNASSUS AV SE
FROM EDGEWOOD AV TO
WILLARD ST
BELVEDERE ST SF 9 C1
S FROM S HAIGHT ST BETWEEN
CLAYTON ST AND COLE ST S
TO CARMEL ST
2 HAIGHT ST
100 WALLER ST
FREDERICK ST
400 PARNASSUS AV
GRATTAN ST
ALMA ST
RIVOLI ST
600 17TH ST
END CARMEL ST
BEMIS ST SF 14 B2
FROM MIGUEL ST SE TO CASTRO ST
MIGUEL ST
100 ADDISON ST
MATEO ST
ROANOKE ST
END CASTRO ST
BENGAL AL SF 13 B2
E FROM MIRALOMA DR TO
LANSDALE AV S OF PORTOLA DR
BENNINGTON ST SF 14 C2
TO SIMONDS LOOP
S FROM EUGENIA AV TO HIGHLAND AV
2 EUGENIA AV
100 CORTLAND AV
200 ELLERT ST
300 NEWMAN ST
END HIGHLAND AV
BENTON AV SF 14 B3
NE FROM A POINT SW OF GENEBERN WY
TO ANDOVER ST
100 GENEBERN WY
200 COLLEGE AV
END JUSTIN DR
ARNOLD AV
400 ROSCOE ST
500 PORTER ST
600 BACHE ST
END ANDOVER ST
BEPLER ST SF 19 B3
NW FROM RHINE ST AT THE
COUNTY LINE
BERGEN PL SF 2 C2
W FROM S HYDE ST BETWEEN
BAY ST AND NORTH PT ST
BERKELEY WY SF 14 A2
W FROM DIAMOND HGTS BLVD
S OF GOLD MINE DR
BERKSHIRE WY SF 12 B3
E OFF LAKESHORE DR TO
COUNTRY CLUB DR
BERNAL HTS BLVD SF 14 C2
W S E AND N FROM
CARVER ST TO CARVER ST
CARVER ST
ESMERALDA AV
FOLSOM ST
MOULTRIE ST
ANDERSON ST
ELLSWORTH ST
GATES ST
FOLSOM ST
BANKS ST
PRENTISS ST
NEVADA ST
ROSENKRANZ ST
END CARVER ST
BERNARD ST SF 2 C3
W FROM S TAYLOR ST BETWEEN
PACIFIC AV AND BROADWAY
TO LEAVENWORTH ST
2 TAYLOR ST
100 JONES ST
END LEAVENWORTH ST
BERNICE ST SF 11 A1
S FROM S 12TH ST BETWEEN
FOLSOM ST AND HARRISON ST
BERRY ST SF 7 C3
BERRY ST SF 11 B1
FROM THE EMBARCADERO BETWEEN
KING ST AND CHANNEL ST SW TO
DE HARO ST
THE EMBARCADERO
2 2ND ST
100 3RD ST
200 4TH ST
300 5TH ST
400 6TH ST
500 7TH ST
END DE HARO ST
BERTHA LN SF 15 C3
N FROM HUDSON AV BETWEEN INGALLS
ST AND WHITNEY YOUNG CIR
TO HARBOR RD
BERTITA ST SF 20 A2
N FROM S SENECA AV BETWEEN
ALEMANY BLVD AND MISSION ST
BERWICK PL SF 11 A1
FROM A POINT NEAR HERON ST
BETWEEN 7TH ST AND 8TH ST SE
TO HARRISON ST
BESSIE ST SF 14 C3
S OF PRECITA AV FROM
FOLSOM ST W TO A POINT W OF
MANCHESTER ST
BEULAH ST SF 9 C2
FROM COLE ST BETWEEN WALLER ST
AND FREDERICK ST W TO
STANYAN ST
2 COLE ST
100 SHRADER ST
END STANYAN ST
BEVERLY ST SF 19 A2
N FROM 19TH AV BETWEEN
MONTICELLO ST AND JUNIPERO
SERRA BLVD TO HOLLOWAY AV
19TH AV
100 SHIELDS ST
200 GARFIELD ST
END HOLLOWAY AV
BIGELOW CT SF 3 C1
S FROM 13TH ST BETWEEN
HALYBURTON CT & AV E,
TREASURE ISLAND
BIGLER AV SF 9 C3
S FROM BELGRAVE AV TO TWIN
PEAKS BLVD
BIRCH ST SF 6 B3
W FROM S OCTAVIA ST BETWEEN
GROVE ST AND FULTON ST TO
LAGUNA ST
BIRD ST SF 10 C2
E FROM DEARBORN ST BETWEEN
17TH ST AND 18TH ST
BISHOP ST SF 21 A2
SW OF ANKENY ST BETWEEN
ALDER ST AND SPARTA ST TO
HARKNESS AV
BLACK PL SF 2 C2
N FROM S UNION ST BETWEEN
LEAVENWORTH ST & JONES ST
BLACKSTONE CT SF 2 B2
W FROM FRANKLIN ST BETWEEN
GREENWICH ST AND LOMBARD ST
BLACKWOOD ST SF 11 A1
E OFF S 9TH ST BETWEEN MCLEA CT
AND HARRISON ST
BLAIRWOOD LN SF 9 B3
N FROM WARREN DR BETWEEN
CHRISTOPHER DR AND ASHWOOD
LANE TO CRESTMONT DR
BLAKE ST SF 5 C2
FROM A POINT N OF GEARY BLVD
BETWEEN COLLINS ST AND COOK ST
TO ANZA ST
BLANCHE ST SF 10 B3
FROM A POINT N OF 23RD ST BETWEEN
VICKSBURG ST AND SANCHEZ ST
TO ELIZABETH ST
BLANDY ST SF 17 B1
SE FROM SPEAR AV BETWEEN
C ST AND E ST TO C ST
BLANEY RD SF 1 B2
S FROM A POINT N OF DOYLE DR
E OF CRISSY FIELD AV TO PATTEN RD
DOYLE DR
BLANKEN AV SF 21 B3
E FROM BAY SHORE BLVD TO
EXECUTIVE PARK BLVD
CRISSY FIELD AV
COWLES ST
END PATTEN RD
BAY SHORE BLVD

TUNNEL AV
WHEELER AV
PENINSULA AV
TOCOLOMA AV
NUEVA AV
GILLETTE AV
END EXECUTIVE PARK BL
BLISS RD SF 1 B3
E FROM TAYLOR RD BETWEEN
SHERIDAN AV & MORAGA AV
TO MONTGOMERY ST
BLUXOME ST SF 7 B3
SW FROM 4TH ST BETWEEN BRANNAN ST
AND TOWNSEND ST TO 6TH ST
BLYTHDALE AV SF 20 C3
E FROM BROOKDALE AV TO
HAHN ST N OF VELASCO AV
BOARDMAN PL SF 11 B1
SE FROM BRYANT ST BETWEEN 6TH ST
& 7TH ST TO BRANNAN ST
BOB KAUFMAN ST SF 3 A2
S OFF 451 FILBERT ST BETWEEN
GRANT AV AND VARENNES ST
BOCANA ST SF 14 C2
SW FROM A POINT N OF POWHATTAN AV
TO HOLLY PARK CIRCLE
POWHATTAN AV
200 EUGENIA AV
300 CORTLAND AV
ELLERT ST
END HOLLY PARK CIR
BONIFACIO ST SF 7 B3
SW FROM LAPU LAPU ST TO TANDANG
SORA BETWEEN FOLSOM ST
AND HARRISON ST
LAPU LAPU ST
MABINI ST
END TANDANG SORA
BONITA ST SF 2 C3
W FROM S POLK ST BETWEEN GREEN ST
AND VALLEJO ST
BONNIE BRAE LN SF 12 B3
NE OFF LAKESHORE DR TO
COUNTRY CLUB DR
BONVIEW ST SF 14 C2
SW FROM COO AV E OF ELSIE ST
TO CORTLAND AV
2 COSO AV
200 EUGENIA AV
END CORTLAND AV
BORICA ST SF 19 B1
N FROM HOLLOWAY AV BETWEEN
ALVISO ST AND CORONA ST TO
URBANO DR N
HOLLOWAY AV
URBANO DR S
N ENTRADA CT
END URBANO DR N
BOSWORTH ST SF 14 A3
W FROM MISSION ST S OF
ST MARYS AV TO A POINT NE OF
O'SHAUGNESSY BLVD
2 MISSION ST
100 MARSILLY ST
200 CUVIER ST
300 MILTON ST
400 ROSSEAU ST
ROTTECK ST
LYELL ST
500 ARLINGTON ST
600 DIAMOND ST
700 BROMPTON AV
800 LIPPARD AV
900 CHILTON AV
1000 HAMERTON AV
1100 BURNSIDE AV
CONGO ST
END O'SHAUGHNESSY BLVD
BOUTWELL ST SF 15 A2
S FROM INDUSTRIAL ST TO
BAY SHORE BLVD

BOWDOIN ST SF 15 A3
BOWDOIN ST SF 15 A3
BOWDOIN ST SF 21 A1
SE FROM A POINT N OF GAVEN ST W
OF BOYLSTON ST TO A POINT SE OF
MANSELL ST
GAVEN ST
SWEENY ST
HALE ST
400 SILVER AV
500 SILLIMAN ST
600 FELTON ST
END BURROWS ST
800 BACON ST
900 WAYLAND ST
1000 WOOLSEY ST
1100 DWIGHT ST
1200 OLMSTEAD ST
1300 MANSELL ST
END SE OF MANSELL ST
BOWLEY ST SF 4 C1
W FROM LINCOLN BLVD THEN CIRCLE
BACK TO LINCOLN BLVD
BOWLING GREEN DR SF 9 B1
SW FROM MIDDLE DR E TO SOUTH DR
BOWMAN RD SF 1 A2
W OF MERCHANT RD
BOYLSTON ST SF 15 A3
S FROM A POINT N OF GAVEN ST W OF
MERRILL ST TO SILLIMAN ST
GAVEN ST
SWEENEY ST
HALE ST
SILVER AV
END SILLIMAN ST
BOYNTON CT SF 10 B1
S FROM S 14TH ST BETWEEN
CHURCH ST AND SANCHEZ ST
BRADFORD ST SF 15 A2
S FROM ESMERALDA AV BETWEEN
PERALTA AV AND CARVER ST TO
TOMPKINS AV
2 ESMERALDA AV
MAYFLOWER ST
100 POWHATTAN AV
200 CORTLAND AV
MOJAVE ST
300 JARBOE AV
END TOMPKINS AV
BRADY ST SF 10 C1
SE FROM MARKET ST BETWEEN 12TH ST
AND GOUGH ST TO OTIS ST
BRANNAN ST SF 7 C3
BRANNAN ST SF 11 A1
FROM THE EMBARCADERO BETWEEN
BRYANT ST AND TOWNSEND ST
SW TO DIVISION ST
THE EMBARCADERO
2 BEALE ST
100 FREMONT ST
200 DELANCEY ST
COLIN P KELLY JR ST
300 2ND ST
STANFORD ST
CENTER PL
400 3RD ST
420 RITCH ST
ZOE ST
500 4TH ST
600 5TH ST
700 6TH ST
722 HARRIET ST
LUCERNE ST
BOARDMAN PL
BUTTE PL
GILBERT ST
800 7TH ST
900 8TH ST
1000 9TH ST
DORE ST
END DIVISION ST
BRANT AL SF 3 A2

S FROM S GREENWICH ST BETWEEN
STOCKTON ST AND POWELL ST
BRAZIL AV SF 20 B1
SE FROM S MISSION ST BETWEEN
EXCELSIOR AV AND PERSIA AV
TO MANSELL ST
2 MISSION ST
100 LONDON ST
200 PARIS ST
300 LISBON ST
400 MADRID ST
500 EDINBURGH ST
600 NAPLES ST
700 VIENNA ST
800 ATHENS ST
900 MOSCOW ST
1000 MUNICH ST
1100 PRAGUE ST
DUBLIN ST
END MANSELL ST
BREEN PL SF 6 C3
N FROM MCALLISTEER ST BETWEEN
HYDE ST AND LARKIN ST
BRENHAM PL SF 3 A3
N FROM S CLAY ST BETWEEN GRANT AV
AND KEARNY ST TO WASHINGTON ST
BRENTWOOD AV SF 13 C3
W FROM MELROSE AV TO MAYWOOD DR
MELROSE AV
MANGELS ST
100 HAZELWOOD AV
VALDEZ AV
COLON AV
200 YERBA BUENA AV
300 FERNWOOD DR
END MAYWOOD AV
BRET HARTE TER SF 2 C2
N FROM FRANCISCO ST BETWEEN
LEAVENWORTH ST AND JONES ST
BREWSTER ST SF 15 A2
SW FROM MONTCALM ST TO
ESMERALDA AV
2 MONTCALM ST
MACEDONIA ST
100 RUTLEDGE ST
COSTA ST
JOY ST
END ESMERALDA AV
BRIARCLIFF TER SF 13 A2
E FROM 19TH AV ONE BLK
N OF SLOAT BLVD
BRICE TER SF 11 A3
W FROM S BRYANT ST BETWEEN
20TH ST AND 21ST ST
BRIDGEVIEW DR SF 15 B3
N AND E FROM THORNTON AV
TO NEWHALL ST
THORNTON AV
TOPEKA AV
THORNE WY
TAMPA LN
END NEWHALL ST
BRIGHT ST SF 19 B2
S FROM ALEMANY BLVD, & N FROM
STANLEY ST TO HOLLOWAY AV BETWEEN
ORIZABA AV AND HEAD ST
ALEMANY BLVD
100 STANLEY ST
200 RANDOLPH ST
300 SARGENT ST
400 SHIELDS ST
500 GARFIELD ST
END HOLLOWAY AV
BRIGHTON AV SF 19 C2
N FROM LAKE VIEW AV BETWEEN LEE
AV AND PLYMOUTH AV TO OCEAN AV
2 LAKE VIEW AV
100 GRAFTON AV
200 HOLLOWAY AV
END OCEAN AV
BRITTON ST SF 21 A3

S FROM LELAND TO A POINT S OF
BROAD VISITACION AV
BROAD ST SF 19 B2
W FROM SAN JOSE AV BETWEEN
SADOWA ST AND FARRALLONES ST TO
ORIZABA AV
2 SAN JOSE AV
100 PLYMOUTH AV
200 CAPITOL AV
END ORIZABA AV
BROADMOOR DR SF 19 A1
S FROM STONECREST DR TO
STONECREST DR W OF
JUNIPERO SERRA BLVD
BROADWAY SF 2 A3
BROADWAY SF 3 A3
FROM THE EMBARCADERO BETWEEN
PACIFIC AV AND VALLEJO ST
W TO LYON ST
2 THE EMBARCADERO
50 DAVIS ST
100 FRONT ST
200 BATTERY ST
300 SANSOME ST
OSGOOD PL
BARTOL ST
400 MONTGOMERY ST
500 KEARNY ST
ROMOLO ST
COLUMBUS AV
600 GRANT AV
700 STOCKTON ST
CORDELIA ST
CHURCHILL ST
800 POWELL ST
WAYNE PL
900 MASON ST
HIMMELMAN PL
1000 TAYLOR ST
1100 JONES ST
1200 LEAVENWORTH ST
CYRUS PL
1300 HYDE ST
MORRELL PL
1400 LARKIN ST
1500 POLK ST
1600 VAN NESS AV
1700 FRANKLIN ST
1800 GOUGH ST
1900 OCTAVIA ST
2000 LAGUNA ST
2100 BUCHANAN ST
2200 WEBSTER ST
2300 FILLMORE ST
2400 STEINER ST
2500 PIERCE ST
2600 SCOTT ST
2700 DIVISADERO ST
2800 BRODERICK ST
2900 BAKER ST
END LYON ST
BRODERICK ST SF 2 A3
BRODERICK ST SF 6 A2
BRODERICK ST SF 10 A1
N FROM WALLER ST BETWEEN
DIVISADERO ST & BAKER ST
TO THE BAY
2 WALLER ST
100 HAIGHT ST
200 PAGE ST
300 OAK ST
400 FELL ST
500 HAYES ST
600 GROVE ST
700 FULTON ST
800 MCALLISTER ST
900 GOLDEN GATE AV
1000 TURK ST
1100 EDDY ST
1200 ELLIS ST
1300 O'FARRELL ST
1400 GEARY BLVD

1500 GARDEN ST
1500 POST ST
1600 SUTTER ST
1700 BUSH ST
1800 PINE ST
1900 CALIFORNIA ST
2000 SACRAMENTO ST
2100 CLAY ST
2200 WASHINGTON ST
2300 JACKSON ST
2400 PACIFIC AV
2500 BROADWAY
2600 VALLEJO ST
2700 GREEN ST
2800 UNION ST
2900 FILBERT ST
3000 GREENWICH ST
3100 LOMBARD ST
3200 CHESTNUT ST
3300 FRANCISCO ST
3400 BAY ST
3500 NORTH POINT ST
3600 BEACH ST
3700 JEFFERSON ST
END MARINA BLVD
BROMLEY PL SF 2 B3
E FROM S WEBSTER ST BETWEEN
JACKSON ST AND PACIFIC AV
BROMPTON AV SF 14 A3
S FROM CHENERY ST BETWEEN
DIAMOND ST AND LIPPARD AV
TO JOOST AV
2 CHENERY ST
KERN ST
100 BOSWORTH ST
END JOOST AVE
BRONTE ST SF 15 A2
S FROM S CORTLAND AV BETWEEN
BRADFORD ST AND PUTNAM ST
S TO TOMPKINS AV
2 CORTLAND AV
MOJAVE ST
100 JARBOE AV
END TOMPKINS AV
BROOK ST SF 14 B2
W FROM S MISSION ST BETWEEN
KINGSTON ST & RANDALL ST
TO JOSE AV
BROOKDALE AV SF 20 B3
NE FROM GENEVA AV TO
SANTOS ST N OF BLYTHDALE AV
BROOKHAVEN LN SF 12 B3
OFF HUNTINGTON DR E AND W
BROOKLYN PL SF 3 A3
S FROM S SACRAMENTO ST BETWEEN
GRANT AV & STOCKTON ST
BROOKS ST SF 4 C2
S FROM BAKER CT
BROSNAN ST SF 10 C1
W FROM S VALENCIA ST BETWEEN
CLINTON PARK AND 14TH ST
TO GUERRERO ST
BROTHERHOOD WY SF 19 A2
NW FROM ALEMANY BLVD TO
LAKE MERCED BLVD
ALEMANY BLVD
100 STANLEY ST
400 ARCH ST
ST CHARLES AV
JUNIPERO SERRA BL, HWY
CHUMASERO DR
THOMAS MORE WY
END LAKE MERCED BLVD
BRUCE AV SF 19 C1
E FROM 200 BLOCK OF HAROLD AV
BRUMISS TER SF 19 C3
E FROM ACTON ST BETWEEN
MISSION ST & BRUNSWICK ST
BRUNSWICK ST SF 19 B3
BRUNSWICK ST SF 20 A3
SW FROM NEWTON ST BETWEEN

MORSE ST & HANOVER ST
TO THE COUNTY LINE
2 NEWTON ST
100 CURTIS ST
200 POPE ST
300 ALLISON ST
400 CONCORD ST
FLORENTINE AV
500 GUTTENBERG ST
600 LOWELL ST
ROEMER WY
700 WHITTIER ST
800 OLIVER ST
END COUNTY LINE
BRUSH PL SF 11 A1
SW FROM HALLAM ST NEAR FOLSOM ST
BETWEEN 7TH ST AND 8TH ST
8TH ST
BRUSSELS ST SF 15 A3
BRUSSELS ST SF 21 A1
SE FROM SILVER AV BETWEEN
GIRARD ST AND GOETTINGEN
ST S TO CAMPBELL AV
2 SILVER AV
100 SILLIMAN ST
200 FELTON ST
END BURROWS ST
400 BACON ST
500 WAYLAND ST
600 WOOLSEY ST
700 DWIGHT ST
800 OLMSTEAD ST
900 MANSELL ST
1000 ORDWAY ST
1100 WARD ST
1200 HARKNESS ST
1300 WILDE ST
END CAMPBELL ST
BRYANT ST SF 7 C2
BRYANT ST SF 11 A1
BRYANT ST SF 15 A1
SW FROM THE EMBARCADERO BETWEEN
HARRISON ST AND BRANNAN ST
TO 11TH ST THEN S TO PRECITA AV
THE EMBARCADERO
50 MAIN ST
100 BEALE ST
300 DELANCEY ST
RINCON ST
STERLING ST
400 2ND ST
CENTER PL
500 3RD ST
RITCH ST
600 ZOE ST
600 4TH ST
STILLMAN ST
700 5TH ST
OAK GROVE ST
MORRIS ST
800 6TH ST
HARRIET ST
BOARDMAN PL
GILBERT ST
900 7TH ST
LANGTON ST
KATE ST
DECATUR ST
1000 8TH ST
CONVERSE ST
1100 9TH ST
DORE ST
1200 10TH ST
JUNIPER ST
1300 11TH ST
1400 DIVISION ST
1500 ALAMEDA ST
1600 15TH ST
1700 16TH ST
1800 17TH ST
1900 MARIPOSA ST
2000 18TH ST
2100 19TH ST
2200 20TH ST
BRICE TER
2300 21ST ST
2400 22ND ST
2500 23RD ST
2600 24TH ST
2700 25TH ST
2800 26TH ST
2900 ARMY ST
END PRECITA AV
BUCARELI DR SF 18 C2
SW FROM JUAN BAUTISTA
CIRCLE TO RIVAS AV N OF
BROTHERHOOD WY
BUCHANAN ST SF 2 B3
BUCHANAN ST SF 6 B3
BUCHANAN ST SF 10 B1
N FROM S MARKET ST AND
DUBOCE AV BETWEEN LAGUNA ST AND
WEBSTER ST TO MARINA BLVD
2 MARKET ST
DUBOCE AV
100 HERMANN ST
200 WALLER ST
250 LAUSSAT ST
300 HAIGHT ST
400 PAGE ST
LILY ST
500 OAK ST
550 HICKORY ST
600 FELL ST
638 LINDEN ST
700 HAYES ST
726 IVY ST
END GROVE ST
1300 EDDY ST
END WILLOW ST
1700 POST ST
1800 SUTTER ST
FERN ST
1900 BUSH ST
2000 PINE ST
2100 CALIFORNIA ST
2200 SACRAMENTO ST
2300 CLAY ST
2400 WASHINGTON ST
2500 JACKSON ST
2600 PACIFIC AV
2700 BROADWAY
2800 VALLEJO ST
2900 GREEN ST
3000 UNION ST
3100 FILBERT ST
HARRIS PL
3200 GREENWICH ST
MOULTON ST
3300 LOMBARD ST
MAGNOLIA ST
END CHESTNUT ST
GEORGE MOSCONE REC CTR
3600 BAY ST
3700 NORTH POINT ST
3800 BEACH ST
END MARINA BLVD
BUCKINGHAM WY SF 19 A1
NW FROM 19TH AV TO WINSTON DR
BUENA VISTA AV SF 10 A1
SURROUNDING BUENA VISTA PARK S
OF HAIGHT ST E OF MASONIC AV
EAST
HAIGHT ST
WALLER ST
DUBOCE AV
BUENA VISTA TER
PARK HILL AV
BUENA VISTA TER SF 10 A1
S FROM JUNCTION BUENA VISTA AV
& DUBOCE AV TO 15TH ST
2 BUENA VISTA AV
DUBOCE AV
100 14TH ST
ROOSEVELT WY
END 15TH ST
BURGOYNE ST SF 2 C3
S FROM S PACIFIC AV BETWEEN
LEAVENWORTH ST AND HYDE ST
BURKE ST SF 15 C2
FROM 3600 3RD ST
BURLWOOD DR SF 13 C3
E FROM LOS PALMOS DR BETWEEN
LOS PALMOS DR AND CRESTA VISTA DR
TO BELLA VISTA WY
BURNETT AV SF 10 A3
BURNETT AV SF 14 A1
SE FROM TWIN PEAKS BLVD
TO PORTOLA
TWIN PEAKS BLVD
GARDENSIDE DR
450 DIXIE AL
HOPKINS AV
GOLDING LN
FENTON LN
CRESTLINE DR
GLENVIEW DR
DAWNVIEW WY
END PORTOLA DR
BURNS PL SF 10 C1
W FROM S 11TH ST N OF FOLSOM ST
BURNSIDE AV SF 14 A3
N FROM MANGELS AV TO CHENERY ST
2 CHENERY ST
PARADISE AV
100 BOSWORTH ST
END MANGELS AV
BURR AV SF 20 C3
E FROM ARGONAUT AV N OF
VELASCO AV
BURRITT ST SF 7 A2
S FROM S BUSH ST BETWEEN
STOCKTON ST AND POWELL ST
BURROWS ST SF 20 C1
BURROWS ST SF 21 A1
E FROM LA GRANDE AV BETWEEN
FELTON & BACON ST TO A POINT
E OF SAN BRUNO AV
100 SAN BRUNO AV
200 GIRARD ST
300 BRUSSELS ST
400 GOETTINGEN ST
500 SOMERSET ST
600 HOLYOKE ST
700 HAMILTON ST
END BOWDOIN ST
RESERVOIR
UNIVERSITY ST
CAMPUS LN
END AMHERST ST
1500 CAMBRIDGE ST
1600 OXFORD ST
1700 HARVARD ST
1800 GAMBIER ST
1900 MADISON ST
PERU AV
MANSFIELD ST
END LA GRANDE AV
BUSH ST SF 6 A2
BUSH ST SF 7 A2
W FROM S MARKET ST BETWEEN
SUTTER ST AND PINE ST TO
PRESIDIO AV
2 MARKET ST
100 BATTERY ST
200 SANSOME ST
TREASURY PL
PETRARCH PL
300 MONTGOMERY ST
TRINITY ST
BELDEN ST
400 KEARNY ST
ST GEORGE AL
CLAUDE LN
MARK LN
500 GRANT AV
CHATHAM PL
600 STOCKTON ST
BURRITT ST
650 MONROE ST
CHELSEA PL
700 POWELL ST
800 MASON ST
900 TAYLOR ST
1000 JONES ST
1100 LEAVENWORTH ST
1200 HYDE ST
1300 LARKIN ST
1400 POLK ST
1500 VAN NESS AV
1600 FRANKLIN ST
1700 GOUGH ST
1800 OCTAVIA ST
1900 LAGUNA ST
2000 BUCHANAN ST
2100 WEBSTER ST
COTTAGE ROW
2200 FILLMORE ST
2300 STEINER ST
2400 PIERCE ST
2500 SCOTT ST
2600 DIVISADERO ST
2700 BRODERICK ST
2800 BAKER ST
2900 LYON ST
END PRESIDIO AV
BUTTE PL SF 11 B1
S FROM S BRANNAN ST BETWEEN
6TH ST AND 7TH ST
BYINGTON ST SF 6 B2
E FROM S FILLMORE ST BETWEEN
ELLIS ST AND O'FARRELL
BYRON CT SF 20 A3
E FROM LOWELL ST BETWEEN
BRUNSWICK ST AND HANOVER ST
BYXBEE ST SF 19 A2
N FROM RANDOLPH ST BETWEEN
MONTICELLO ST & RALSTON ST TO
HOLLOWAY AV
2 RANDOLPH ST
19TH AV
100 SARGENT ST
200 SHIELDS ST
300 GARFIELD ST
END HOLLOWAY AV

C

C ST SF 17 B1
S FROM SPEAR AV BETWEEN LOCKWOOD
AND BLANDY ST TO A POINT S OF
NIMITZ AV
SPEAR AV
NIMITZ AV
END BLANDY ST
CABRILLO ST SF 8 A1
CABRILLO ST SF 9 A1
W FROM ARGUELLO BLVD BETWEEN
BALBOA ST AND FULTON ST
W TO LA PLAYA
2 ARGUELLO BLVD
100 2ND AV
200 3RD AV
300 4TH AV
400 5TH AV
500 6TH AV
600 7TH AV
700 8TH AV
800 9TH AV
900 10TH AV
1000 11TH AV
1100 12TH AV
FUNSTON AV
PARK PRESIDIO BLVD
1300 14TH AV
1400 15TH AV
1500 16TH AV
1600 17TH AV
1700 18TH AV
1800 19TH AV
1900 20TH AV
2000 21ST AV
2100 22ND AV
2200 23RD AV
2300 24TH AV
2400 25TH AV
2500 26TH AV
2600 27TH AV
2700 28TH AV
2800 29TH AV
2900 30TH AV
3000 31ST AV
3100 32ND AV
3200 33RD AV
3300 34TH AV
3400 35TH AV
3500 36TH AV
3600 37TH AV
3700 38TH AV
3800 39TH AV
3900 40TH AV
4000 41ST AV
4100 42ND AV
4200 43RD AV
4300 44TH AV
4400 45TH AV
4500 46TH AV
4600 47TH AV
4700 48TH AV
END LA PLAYA ST
CADELL PL SF 3 A2
N FROM S S UNION ST BETWEEN
GRANT AV & STOCKTON ST
CAINE AV SF 19 C2
NE FROM LOBOS ST BETWEEN
MAJESTIC AV AND SAN JOSE AV
TO RIDGE LN
2 RIDGE LANE ST
100 LAKE VIEW AV
END LOBOS ST
CAIRE TER SF 11 B3
S FROM CAROLINA ST
CALEDONIA ST SF 10 C1
FROM A POINT N OF 15TH ST
BETWEEN JULIAN AV AND
VALENCIA ST S TO 16TH ST
CALGARY ST SF 20 C3
S FROM VELASCO AV TO
COUNTY LINE E OF PUEBLO ST
CALHOUN TER SF 3 A2
SANSOME ST AND MONTGOMERY ST TO
GREEN ST
CALIFORNIA AV SF 3 C2
NE FROM AV A TO AV N, TREASURE IS
AVENUE A
AVENUE B
AVENUE C
AVENUE D
AVENUE F
AVENUE H
AVENUE M
END AVENUE N
CALIFORNIA ST SF 3 B3
CALIFORNIA ST SF 4 C2
CALIFORNIA ST SF 5 A2
CALIFORNIA ST SF 6 A2
W FROM MARKET ST BETWEEN
PINE ST AND SACRAMENTO ST
A POINT W OF 32ND ST
2 MARKET ST
DRUMM ST
100 DAVIS ST
200 FRONT ST
300 BATTERY ST
400 SANSOME ST
LEIDESDORFF ST
500 MONTGOMERY ST

SPRING ST
600 KEARNY ST
QUINCY ST
700 GRANT AV
SABIN PL
800 STOCKTON ST
PRATT PL
JOICE ST
900 POWELL ST
1000 MASON ST
SPROULE LN
1100 TAYLOR ST
1200 JONES ST
LYSETTE ST
1300 LEAVENWORTH ST
HELEN ST
1400 HYDE ST
1500 LARKIN ST
1600 POLK ST
1700 VAN NESS AV
1800 FRANKLIN ST
1900 GOUGH ST
2000 OCTAVIA ST
2100 LAGUNA ST
2200 BUCHANAN ST
2300 WEBSTER ST
ORBEN PL
2400 FILLMORE ST
2500 STEINER ST
2600 PIERCE ST
2700 SCOTT ST
2800 DIVISADERO ST
2900 BRODERICK ST
3000 BAKER ST
3100 LYON ST
3200 PRESIDIO AV
3300 WALNUT ST
3400 LAUREL ST
3500 LOCUST ST
3600 SPRUCE ST
PARKER AV
3700 MAPLE ST
COMMONWEALTH AV
3800 CHERRY ST
JORDAN AV
PALM AV
3900 ARGUELLO BLVD
4000 2ND AV
4100 3RD AV
4200 4TH AV
4300 5TH AV
CORNWALL ST
4400 6TH AV
4500 7TH AV
4600 8TH AV
4700 9TH AV
4800 10TH AV
4900 11TH AV
5000 12TH AV
FUNSTON AV
PARK PRESIDIO BLVD
5200 14TH AV
5300 15TH AV
5400 16TH AV
5500 57TH AV
5600 18TH AV
5700 19TH AV
5800 20TH AV
5900 21ST AV
6000 22ND AV
6100 23RD AV
6200 24TH AV
6300 25TH AV
6400 26TH AV
6500 27TH AV
6600 28TH AV
6700 29TH AV
6800 30TH AV
6900 31ST AV
7000 32ND AV
END 33RD AV

CAMBON DR SF 19 A2
N FROM FONT BLVD BETWEEN
JUNIPERO SERRA BLVD AND
GONZALES DR
CAMBRIDGE ST SF 14 C3
CAMBRIDGE ST SF 20 C1
E FROM STONEYBROOK AV PARALLEL
TO I-280, THEN S TO
JOHN F SHELLEY DR
TRUMBULL ST
STONEYBROOK AV
STONEYFORD AV
GLADSTONE DR
WEST VIEW AV
SWEENY ST
SILVER AVE
PIOCHE ST
SILLIMAN ST
FELTON ST
BURROWS ST
BACON ST
WAYLAND ST
END JOHN F SHELLEY DR
CAMELLIA AV SF 14 B3
N FROM SILVER AV N TO
ADMIRAL AV
ADMIRAL AV
CASTLE MANOR AV
END SILVER AV
CAMEO WY SF 14 A1
SE FROM AMBER DR TO DUNCAN ST
CAMERON WY SF 21 C2
N FROM FITZGERALD AV BETWEEN
HAWES ST AND GRIFFITH ST
FITZGERALD AV
NICHOLS WY
DOUBLE ROCK ST
NICHOLS WY
END GRIFFITH ST
CAMP ST SF 10 B2
E FROM GUERRO ST BETWEEN
16TH ST AND 17TH ST TO
ALBION ST
CAMPBELL AV SF 21 A2
SW FROM SAN BRUNO AV TO
HOLLYOKE DR THEN NW TO ELLIOT ST
2 SAN BRUNO AV
100 BRUSSELS ST
200 GOETTINGEN ST
SOMERSET ST
HOLYOKE ST
400 ALPHA ST
500 RUTLAND ST
600 DELTA ST
ERVINE ST
ALBERTA ST
END ELLIOT ST
CAMPTON PL SF 7 A2
W FROM S GRANT AV BETWEEN
POST ST AND SUTTER ST
TO STOCKTON ST
CAMPUS CIR SF 18 C1
OFF STATE DR-SAN FRANCISCO
STATE UNIVERSITY
CAMPUS LN SF 20 C1
NORTH EXTENSION OF PRICETON ST
BETWEEN AMHERST & UNIVERSITY
CANBY ST SF 1 C2
NW FROM MESA AV TO KEYES AV
CANYON DR SF 20 B3
SW FROM SOUTH HILL BLVD TO
THE COUNTY LINE
CAPISTRANO AV SF 20 A1
SE FROM SAN JOSE AV AND THEN
S TO SANTA YNEZ ST BETWEEN
LOTTER ST & SANTA ROSA AV
AND SANTA ROSA AVE
2 SAN JOSE AV
100 SAN GABRIEL AV
200 SANTA ROSA AV
300 SANTA YSABEL AV
400 SAN JUAN AV
END SANTA YNEZ AV
CAPITOL AV SF 19 B3
FROM A POINT S OF SAGAMORE ST
BETWEEN PLYMOUTH AV & ORIZABA AV
N TO OCEAN AV
100 SAGAMORE ST
200 SADOWA ST
300 BROAD ST
400 FARALLONES ST
500 LOBOS ST
600 MINERVA ST
700 MONTANA ST
800 THRIFT ST
900 LAKE VIEW AV
1000 GRAFTON AV
1100 HOLLOWAY AV
1200 DE MONTFORD AV
END OCEAN AV
CAPP ST SF 10 C2
CAPP ST SF 14 C1
S FROM S 15TH ST BETWEEN
SO VAN NESS AV AND MISSION
ST TO MISSION ST
2 15TH ST
ADAIR ST
100 16TH ST
200 17TH ST
300 18TH ST
400 19TH ST
500 20TH ST
600 21ST ST
700 22ND ST
800 23RD ST
900 24TH ST
1000 25TH ST
1100 26TH ST
END MISSION ST
CAPRA WY SF 2 A2
W FROM MALLORCA WY TO SCOTT ST
2 MALLORCA WY
100 PIERCE ST
150 AVILA ST
END SCOTT ST
CARD AL SF 3 A3
W FROM S STOCKTON ST BETWEEN
VALLEJO ST AND GREEN ST
CARDENAS AV SF 19 A2
SE FROM HOLLOWAY AV BETWEEN
VARELA AV AND FUENTE AV
TO 19TH AV
CARGO WY SF 15 C1
CARGO WY SF 16 A2
SE FROM 3RD ST TO JENNINGS ST
CARL ST SF 9 C2
W FROM 857 CLAYTON ST S OF
FREDERICK ST TO ARGUELLO BLVD
2 CLAYTON ST
100 COLE ST
152 SHRADER ST
200 STANYAN ST
300 WILLARD ST
HILLWAY ST
END ARGUELLO BLVD
CARMEL ST SF 9 C2
W FROM CLAYTON ST TO SHRADER ST
2 CLAYTON ST
64 BELVEDERE ST
100 COLE ST
END SHRADER ST
CARMELITA ST SF 10 B1
S FROM WALLER ST BETWEEN
PIERCE ST AND SCOTT ST
TO DUBOCE PARK
CARNELIAN WY SF 14 A1
N FROM DIAMOND HEIGHTS BLVD
2 BLKS E OF PORTOLA DR
CAROLINA ST SF 11 B2
S FROM CHANNEL ST BETWEEN
WISCONSIT ST AND DE HARO ST
S TO KONA RD
2 CHANNEL ST
100 15TH ST
200 16TH ST
300 17TH ST
400 MARIPOSA ST
500 18TH ST
KOHALA RD
600 19TH ST
700 20TH ST
SOUTHERN HTS AV
900 22ND ST
1100 23RD ST
CORAL RD
END WISCONSIN ST
CARR ST SF 21 B1
S FROM PAUL AV BETWEEN 3RD ST
AND GOULD ST TO SALINAS AV
CARRIE ST SF 14 B3
S FROM CHENERY ST W OF
CASTRO ST TO WILDER ST
CARRIZAL ST SF 20 C3
S FROM VELASCO AV TO GENEVA AV
CARROLL AV SF 15 B3
CARROLL AV SF 21 B1
FROM FITCH ST NW TO THORNTON AV
FITCH ST
HAWES ST
INGALLS ST
JENNINGS ST
KEITH ST
3RD ST
MENDELL ST
NEWHALL ST
PHELPS ST
QUINT ST
END THORNTON AVE
CARSON ST SF 10 A3
W FROM S DOUGLASS ST BETWEEN
19TH ST AND SEWARD ST
CARTER ST SF 20 B3
SW FROM GENEVA AV TO COUNTY LINE
CARVER ST SF 15 A2
S FROM BERNAL HEIGHTS BLVD
CASA WY SF 2 A2
NW FROM RETIRO WY TO MARINA BLVD
CASCADE WK SF 19 A3
SW FROM ORTEGA ST TO FUNSTON AV
CASELLI AV SF 10 A3
FROM DOUGLASS ST NEAR
19TH ST TO MARKET ST
2 DOUGLASS ST
LAMSON LN
CLOVER LN
100 CLOVER ST
YUKON ST
200 DANVERS ST
300 MONO ST
END MARKET ST
CASHMERE ST SF 15 C3
N FROM LA SALLE AV N TO A POINT
E OF HUDSON AV
CASITAS AV SF 13 B2
E FROM LANDSDALE AV BETWEEN
OAKDALE WY & ROBINHOOD DR
CASSANDRA CT SF 19 C3
SE OFF S WHITTIER ST BETWEEN
MISSION ST & BRUNSWICK ST
CASTELO AV SF 19 A2
E FROM GONZALES DR BETWEEN
CARDENAS AV AND FONT BLVD
TO CAMBON DR
CASTENADA AV SF 13 B1
SW FROM S VENTURA AV TO A POINT
W OF MONTALVO
2 VENTURA AV
100 ALTON AV
MAGELLAN AV
200 PACHECO AV
LOPEZ AV
SAN MARCOS AV
300 SANTA RITA AV
MONTALVO AV
END W OF MONTALVO AV

CASTILLO ST SF 20 C3
S FROM VELASCO AV TO COUNTY LINE
CASTLE ST SF 3 A2
N FROM S GREEN ST BETWEEN
MONTGOMERY ST AND KEARNY ST
TO UNION ST
CASTLE MANOR AV SF 14 B3
W FROM 4200 MISSION ST
TO CAMELLIA AV
CASTRO ST SF 10 B2
CASTRO ST SF 14 B1
S FROM S WALLER ST W OF
NOE ST S TO CHENERY ST
WALLER ST
LLOYD ST
2 DUBOCE AV
100 14TH ST
HENRY ST
200 15TH ST
250 BEAVER ST
300 16TH ST
340 STATES ST
MARKET ST
400 17TH ST
500 18TH ST
600 19TH ST
700 20TH ST
LIBERTY ST
800 21ST ST
HILL ST
900 22ND ST
1000 ALVARADO ST
1100 23RD ST
1200 ELIZABETH ST
1300 24TH ST
1400 JERSEY ST
1500 25TH ST
1600 CLIPPER ST
1700 26TH ST
1800 ARMY ST
1900 27TH ST
2000 DUNCAN ST
2100 28TH ST
2200 VALLEY ST
2300 29TH ST
2400 DAY ST
2500 30TH ST
CONTINUED AT SUSSEX TO
CHENERY
CATHERINE CT SF 10 C3
E OFF 2425 MISSION ST
CAYUGA AV SF 19 C3
CAYUGA AV SF 20 A2
SW FROM A POINT NE OF ROUSSEAU ST
MISSION ST SW TO REGENT ST
REGENT ST
2 CUVIER ST
36 MILTON ST
68 ROSSEAU ST
S FROM UNION ST BETWEEN
100 ROTTECK ST
LYELL ST
DANTON ST
200 LAMARTINE ST
BADGER ST
300 GORHAM ST
400 TINGLEY ST
THERESA ST
COTTER ST
600 SANTA ROSA AV
800 SAN JUAN AV
SANTA YNEZ AV
900 OCEAN AV
VALERTON CT
ONONDAGA AV
BALHI CT
ONEIDA AV
SUNBEAM LN
JUNIOR TER
SENECA AV
NAVAJO AV

GENEVA AV
SEMINOLE AV
NIAGARA AV
SHAWNEE ST
MT VERNON AV
1600 OTTAWA AV
ROME ST
1700 FOOTE AV
MODOC AV
NAGLEE AV
MANDAN AV
WHIPPLE AV
LIPANI AV
2200 ALEMANY BLVD
SICKLES AV
END REGENT ST
CECILIA AV SF 13 A1
S FROM RIVERA ST ACROSS
SANTIAGO ST TO A POINT
ON 16TH AV N OF TARAVAL
CEDAR ST SF 6 C2
W FROM S LARKIN ST BETWEEN
GEARY ST AND POST ST TO
TO VAN NESS AV
600 LARKIN ST
100 POLK ST
END VAN NESS AV
CEDRO AV SF 19 A1
SW FROM S OCEAN AV TO MERCEDES WY
CENTRAL AV SF 6 A3
CENTRAL AV SF 10 A1
N FROM BUENA VISTA AV W
OF LYON ST TO TURK ST
2 BUENA VISTA AV
50 WALLER ST
100 HAIGHT ST
200 PAGE ST
OAK ST
400 FELL ST
500 HAYES ST
600 GROVE ST
700 FULTON ST
800 MCALLISTER ST
900 GOLDEN GATE AV
END TURK ST
CENTRAL FRWY SF 6 C3
CENTRAL SKYWAY SF 10 C1
CENTURY PL SF 7 B1
S FROM PINE ST BETWEEN
SANSOME ST & MONTGOMERY ST
CERES ST SF 15 B3
S FROM THORNTON AV TO WILLIAMS AV
CERRITOS AV SF 19 A1
SW FROM OCEAN AV SW TO
MERCEDES WY
2 OCEAN AVE
100 MONCADA WY
END MERCEDES WY
CERVANTES BLVD SF 2 A2
NW FROM FILLMORE ST AND
BAY ST TO MARINA BLVD
2 FILLMORE ST
ALHAMBRA ST
100 BEACH ST
200 PRADO ST
AVILA ST
END MARINA BLVD
CHABOT TER SF 5 C3
S FROM TURK ST BETWEEN
TEMESCAL TER AND
KITTREDGE TER TO
GOLDEN GATE AV
CHAIN OF L DR E SF 8 A1
IN GOLDEN GATE PARK
CHAIN OF L DR W SF 8 A1
IN GOLDEN GATE PARK
CHANNEL ST SF 11 B1
SW FROM THE BAY BETWEEN BERRY ST
AND HOOPER ST TO CAROLINA ST
CHAPMAN ST SF 15 A2
W FROM NEVADA ST BETWEEN
BERNAL HEIGHTS BLVD AND
POWHATTAN AV TO FOLSOM ST
CHARLES ST SF 14 B2
W FROM S ARLINGTONS ST
NEAR HIGHLAND AV TO CHENERY ST
CHARLESTOWN PL SF 7 B2
NW FROM S HARRISON ST BETWEEN
ESSEX ST AND 2ND ST
CHARLTON CT SF 2 B3
S FROM S UNION ST BETWEEN
LAGUNA ST AND BUCHANAN ST
CHARTER OAK AV SF 15 A2
S FROM INDUSTRIAL TO SILVER AV
BRUNO AVE S TO SILVER AV
2 INDUSTRIAL ST
100 HELENA ST
200 AUGUSTA ST
END SILVER AV
CHASE CT SF 10 C1
NE FROM COLUSA PL BETWEEN
OTIS ST AND COLTON ST W
CHATHAM PL SF 7 A1
N FROM W BUSH ST BETWEEN
GRANT AV & STOCKTON ST
CHATTANOOGA ST SF 10 B3
S FROM S 21ST ST BETWEEN
DOLORES ST AND CHURCH ST
TO JERSEY ST
2 21ST ST
100 22ND ST
200 23RD ST
300 24TH ST
400 JERSEY ST
CHAVES AV SF 13 C2
SW FROM EVELYN WY TO A POINT
SW OF ROCKDALE DR
CHELSEA PL SF 7 A2
S FROM S BUSH ST BETWEEN
STOCKTON ST AND POWELL ST
CHENERY ST SF 14 B2
S FROM 30TH ST NEAR CHURCH TO
CHARLES ST AND SW TO ELK ST
ST S AND S W TO ELK ST
2 30TH ST
100 RANDALL ST
200 FAIRMOUNT ST
CHARLES ST
300 MIGUEL LN
400 MATEO ST
500 ROANOKE ST
NATICK ST
600 CASTRO ST
CARRIE ST
700 DIAMOND ST
THOR ST
BROMPTON AV
LIPPARD AV
CHILTON AV
942 HAMERTON AV
BURNSIDE AV
1000 MIZPAH ST
END ELK ST
CHERRY ST SF 5 B2
S FROM A POINT N OF JACKSON ST
BETWEEN MAPLE ST AND
ARGUELLO BLVD TO CALIFORNIA ST
2 PRESIDIO
RESERVATION
100 JACKSON ST
200 WASHINGTON ST
300 CLAY ST
400 SACRAMENTO ST
END CALIFORNIA ST
CHESLEY ST SF 11 A1
SE FROM S HARRISON ST BETWEEN
7TH ST AND 8TH ST TO HOMER ST
BRYANT ST
CHESTER AV SF 19 A3
S FROM 19TH AV BETWEEN
ST CHARLES ST AND
JUNIPERO SERRA BLVD TO BELL AV
CHESTNUT ST SF 2 A2
CHESTNUT ST SF 3 A2
W FROM THE EMBARCADERO BETWEEN
LOMBARD ST AND FRANCISCO ST
TO LYON ST
2 SANSOME ST
100 MONTGOMERY ST
WINTHROP ST
200 KEARNY ST
300 GRANT AV
MIDWAY ST
BELLAIR PL
400 STOCKTON ST
500 POWELL ST
VENARD AL
600 MASON ST
700 COLUMBUS AV
TAYLOR ST
800 JONES ST
MONTCLAIR TER
1000 HYDE ST
1100 LARKIN ST
CULEBRA TER
1200 POLK ST
1300 VAN NESS AV
1400 FRANKLIN ST
1500 GOUGH ST
1600 OCTAVIA ST
LAGUNA ST
BUCHANAN ST
1900 WEBSTER ST
2000 FILLMORE ST
MALLORCA WY
2100 STEINER ST
2200 PIERCE ST
2300 SCOTT ST
2400 DIVISADERO ST
2500 BRODERICK ST
RICHARDSON AV
2600 BAKER ST
END LYON ST
CHICAGO WY SF 20 B3
FROM A POINT E OF LINDA
VISTA LN W AND SW TO CORDOVA ST
2 PT E OF LINDA
VISTA STEPS
100 LINDA VISTA STEPS
200 SOUTH HILL BLVD
300 NAYLOR ST
END CORDOVA ST
CHILD ST SF 3 A2
N FROM NS GREENWICH ST BETWEEN
KEARNY ST AND GRANT AV
TO LOMBARD ST
CHILTON AV SF 14 A3
SW FROM CHENERY ST BETWEEN
HAMERTON AV AND LIPPARD AV
TO A POINT N OF JOOST AV
2 CHENERY ST
100 BOSWORTH ST
END ACADIA ST
CHINA BASIN ST SF 11 C1
E FROM 3RD ST S OF CHANNEL
THEN S TO ILLINOIS ST
CHISM RD SF 1 C3
IN PRESIDIO
CHRISTMAS TR PT SF 9 C3
NE FROM TWIN PEAKS BLVD
CHRISTOPHER DR SF 9 B3
NE FROM WARREN DR BETWEEN
DEVONSHIRE WY & BLAIRWOOD LN
TO CLARENDON AV
CHULA LN SF 10 B2
W FROM S DOLORES ST BETWEEN
16TH ST AND 17TH ST TO CHURCH ST
CHUMASERO DR SF 19 A2
SE FROM FONT BLVD TO
BROTHERHOOD WY
CHURCH ST SF 10 B2
CHURCH ST SF 14 B1
S FROM HERMANN ST BETWEEN
DOLORES ST AND SANCHEZ ST
TO RANDALL ST
2 HERMANN ST
100 DUBOCE AVE
RESERVOIR ST
200 14TH ST
MARKET ST
300 15TH ST
400 16TH ST
CHULA LN
500 17TH ST
550 DORLAND ST
600 18TH ST
650 HANCOCK ST
700 19TH ST
748 CUMBERLAND ST
800 20TH ST
850 LIBERTY ST
900 21ST ST
950 HILL ST
1000 22ND ST
1100 23RD ST
1150 ELIZABETH ST
1200 24TH ST
1250 JERSEY ST
1300 25TH ST
1332 CLIPPER ST
1400 26TH ST
1450 ARMY ST
1500 27TH ST
1550 DUNCAN ST
1600 28TH ST
1650 VALLEY ST
1700 29TH ST
1750 DAY ST
1800 30TH ST
END RANDALL ST
CHURCHILL ST SF 3 A3
N FROM S BROADWAY BETWEEN
STOCKTON ST AND POWELL ST
TO VALLEJO ST
CIELITO DR SF 20 C3
S FROM PARQUE DR BETWEEN
PARQUE DR AND ESQUINA DR
TO GENEVA AV
CIRCULAR AV SF 14 A3
FROM JOOST AV AND DIAMOND ST
SW TO HAVELOCK ST
2 JOOST AV
100 MONTEREY BLVD
ACADIA ST
200 HEARST AV
BADEN ST
300 FLOOD AV
350 CONGO ST
400 STAPLES AV
DETROIT ST
600 MARSTON AV
END HAVELOCK ST
CITY VIEW WY SF 13 C1
E FROM PANORAMA DR AT
MIDCREST WY
CLAIRVIEW CT SF 9 C3
N FROM PANORAMA DR AT
DELLBROOK AV
CLARA ST SF 7 B3
SW FROM 4TH ST BETWEEN
FOLSOM ST & HARRISON ST TO 6TH ST
100 4TH ST
HULBERT AL
200 5TH ST
END 6TH ST
CLAREMONT BLVD SF 13 B2
S FROM JUNCTION OF TARAVAL ST AND
DEWEY BOLD TO PORTOLA DR
2 TARAVAL ST
GRANVILLE WY
ALLSTON WY
VERDUN WY
DORCHESTER WY
300 ULLOA ST
END PORTOLA DR
CLARENCE PL SF 7 B3
NW FROM TOWNSEND ST BETWEEN
2ND ST AND 3RD ST
CLARENDON AV SF 9 C3
SW FROM BIGLER AV TO
LAGUNA HONDA BLVD
CLARION AL SF 10 C2
W FROM S MISSION ST BETWEEN
17TH ST AND SYCAMORE ST
W TO VALENCIA ST
CLARKE ST SF 1 C3
IN PRESIDIO
CLAUDE LN SF 7 A1
N FROM S SUTTER ST BETWEEN
KEARNY ST AND GRANT AV
TO BUSH ST
CLAY ST SF 2 C3
CLAY ST SF 3 A3
CLAY ST SF 5 C2
W FROM THE EMBARCADERO BETWEEN
SACRAMENTO ST AND WASHINGTON ST
TO ARGUELLO BLVD
2 THE EMBARCADERO
100 DRUMM ST
200 DAVIS ST
400 BATTERY ST
500 SANSOME ST
LEIDESDORFF ST
600 MONTGOMERY ST
700 KEARNY ST
760 WALTER LUM PL
800 GRANT AVE
WAVERLY PL
SPOFFORD ST
900 STOCKTON ST
JOICE ST
PARKHURST AL
1000 POWELL ST
FREEMAN CT
CODMAN PL
TAY ST
WESTMORE PL
1100 MASON ST
YERBA BUENA ST
1200 TAYLOR ST
1300 JONES ST
PRIEST ST
REED ST
1400 LEAVENWORTH ST
1500 HYDE ST
TORRENS CT
1600 LARKIN ST
1700 POLK ST
1800 VAN NESS AV
1900 FRANKLIN ST
GOUGH ST
LAFAYETTE PARK
2200 LAGUNA ST
2300 BUCHANAN ST
2400 WEBSTER ST
2500 FILLMORE ST
STEINER ST
PIERCE ST
2800 SCOTT ST
2900 DIVISADERO ST
3000 BRODERICK ST
3100 BAKER ST
3200 LYON ST
3300 PRESIDIO AV
3400 WALNUT ST
3500 LAUREL ST
3600 LOCUST ST
3700 SPRUCE ST
3800 MAPLE ST
3900 CHERRY ST
END ARGUELLO BLVD
CLAYTON ST SF 9 C1
CLAYTON ST SF 10 A3
S FROM FULTON ST BETWEEN COLE ST
AND ASHBURY ST TO MARKET ST
2 FULTON ST
100 GROVE ST

1991 SAN FRANCISCO COUNTY CROSS STREET INDEX

200 HAYES ST
FELL ST
400 OAK ST
500 PAGE ST
600 HAIGHT ST
700 WALLER ST
800 FREDERICK ST
CARL ST
PARNASSUS AV
1100 ASHBURY ST
1200 17TH ST
1300 DEMING ST
1400 PEMBERTON PL
CORBETT ST
END MARKET ST
CLEARFIELD DR SF 12 B3
S FROM SLOAT BLVD BETWEEN
WESTMOORLAND DR & MORNINGSIDE DR
TO LAKE MERCED BLVD
CLEARY CT SF 6 B2
S FROM 1400 GEARY ST
S AND W TO LAGUNA ST
CLEMENT ST SF 4 A3
CLEMENT ST SF 5 A2
W FROM ARGUELLO BLVD BETWEEN
GEARY BLVD AND CORNWALL
ST TO 45TH AV
2 ARGUELLO BLVD
100 2ND AV
200 3RD AV
300 4TH AV
400 5TH AV
500 6TH AV
600 7TH AV
700 8TH AV
800 9TH AV
900 10TH AV
1000 11TH AV
1100 12TH AV
FUNSTON AV
PARK PRESIDIO BLVD
1300 14TH AV
1400 15TH AV
1500 16TH AV
1600 17TH AV
1700 18TH AV
1800 19TH AV
1900 20TH AV
2000 21ST AV
2100 22ND AV
2200 23RD AV
2300 24TH AV
2400 25TH AV
2500 26TH AV
2600 27TH AV
2700 28TH AV
2800 29TH AV
2900 30TH AV
3000 31ST AV
3100 32ND AV
3200 33RD AV
3300 34TH AV
3400 35TH AV
3500 36TH AV
3600 37TH AV
3700 38TH AV
3800 39TH AV
3900 40TH AV
4000 41ST AV
4100 42ND AV
4200 43RD AV
4300 44TH AV
END 45TH AV
CLEMENTINA ST SF 7 B2
CLEMENTINA ST SF 11 A1
W FROM S 1ST ST BETWEEN
TEHAMA ST AND FOLSOM ST
TO 9TH ST
2 1ST ST
ECKER ST
OSCAR AL

132 2ND ST
200 3RD ST
300 4TH ST
400 5TH ST
6TH ST
600 SUMNER ST
700 8TH ST
END 9TH ST
CLEO RAND AV SF 16 A3
NW FROM DONAHUE ST
BETWEEN JERROLD AV
AND INNES AV
CLEVELAND ST SF 7 A3
SW FROM S SHERMAN ST BETWEEN
FOLSOM ST AND HARRISON ST
TO 7TH ST
CLIFFORD TER SF 10 A2
NW FROM ROOSEVELT WY TO
ASHBURY ST
2 ROOSEVELT WY
100 UPPER TER
END ASHBURY ST
CLINTON PARK SF 10 C1
W FROM S STEVENSON ST
BETWEEN DUBOCE AV AND 14TH ST
TO DOLORES ST
2 STEVENSON ST
100 VALENCIA ST
200 GUERRERO ST
END DOLORES ST
CLIPPER ST SF 14 A1
W FROM S DOLORES BETWEEN
25TH ST AND 26TH ST TO PORTOLA DR
2 DOLORES ST
100 CHURCH ST
200 SANCHEZ ST
300 NOE ST
400 CASTRO ST
500 DIAMOND ST
600 DOUGLASS ST
HOMESTEAD ST
700 HOFFMAN AVE
FOUNTAIN ST
800 GRAND VIEW AVE
HIGH ST
END PORTOLA DR
CLIPPER TER SF 14 A1
OFF CLIPPER ST BETWEEN
GRAND VIEW AV AND HIGH ST
CLOVER LN SF 10 A3
S FROM CASSELLI AV W OF
DOUGLASS ST TO CORWIN ST
CLOVER ST SF 10 A2
S FROM 18TH ST W OF
DOUGLASS ST TO CASSELLI AV
CLYDE ST SF 7 B3
N FROM TOWNSEND ST BETWEEN
3RD ST AND 4TH ST TO BLUXOME ST
COCHRANE ST SF 17 B1
NW FROM MANSEAU ST TO SPEAR AV
CODMAN PL SF 3 A3
S FROM WASHINGTON ST BETWEEN
POWELL ST AND MASON ST TO CLAY ST
COHEN PL SF 6 C2
S FROM ELLIS ST BETWEEN
LEAVENWORTH ST AND HYDE ST
COLBY ST SF 15 A3
COLBY ST SF 21 A1
S FROM SWEENY ST BETWEEN
DARTMOUTH ST AND UNIVERSITY ST
TO MANSELL ST
SWEENY ST
SILVER AVE
100 SILLIMAN ST
FELTON ST
600 WOOLSEY ST
700 DWIGHT ST
800 OLMSTEAD ST
END MANSELL ST
COLE ST SF 9 C2
S FROM FULTON ST BETWEEN
CLAYTON ST AND SHRADER ST

TO POINT S OF CARMEL ST
2 FULTON ST
100 GROVE ST
200 HAYES ST
FELL ST
400 OAK ST
500 PAGE ST
600 HAIGHT ST
700 WALLER ST
BEULAH ST
800 FREDERICK ST
900 CARL ST
1000 PARNASSUS ST
1100 GRATTAN ST
1200 ALMA ST
1300 RIVOLI ST
1400 17TH ST
1500 CARMEL ST
END PT S OF CARMEL ST
COLEMAN ST SF 17 B1
SW FROM HUDSON ST E OF
FRIEDELL ST TO JERROLD AV
HUDSON ST
INNES AVE
END JERROLD AVE
COLERIDGE AV SF 14 C2
SW FROM COSO AV BETWEEN
MISSION ST AND PROSPECT AV
TO CORTLAND AV
2 COSO AV
POWERS AV
100 FAIR AV
ESMERALDA AV
200 VIRGINIA AV
250 GODEUS ST
HEYMAN ST
300 EUGENIA AV
KINGSTON AV
END CORTLAND AV
COLIN PL SF 7 A2
NE FROM JONES ST BETWEEN
GEARY ST AND POST ST
COLIN P KELLY ST SF 7 C3
NW FROM TOWNSEND ST BETWEEN
1ST ST AND 2ND ST TO BRANNAN ST
COLLEGE AV SF 14 B3
N FROM JUSTIN DR TO MISSION ST
TO E OF SAN JOSE AV
S TO ST MARYS AV
2 ST MARYS AV
200 MISSION ST
300 GENEBERN WY
JUSTIN DR
400 MURRAY ST
500 BENTON AV
END JUSTIN DR
COLLEGE TER SF 14 B3
NW FROM 3900 MISSION ST BETWEEN
COLLEGE AV AND ST MARY AV
COLLINGWOOD ST SF 10 A2
S FROM 17TH ST BETWEEN
CASTRO ST AND DIAMOND ST
S TO 22ND ST
2 MARKET ST
100 18TH ST
200 19TH ST
300 20TH ST
400 21ST ST
END 22ND ST
COLLINS ST SF 5 C2
S FROM MAYFAIR DR BETWEEN
WOOD ST AND BLAKE ST TO ANZA ST
COLON AV SF 13 B3
N FROM POINT S OF GREENWOOD AV
TO BRENTWOOD AV
2 PT S OF GREENWOOD
100 GREENWOOD AV
200 MONTECITO AV
300 MONTEREY BLVD
400 MANGELS AV
END BRENTWOOD ST

COLONIAL WY SF 20 A1
NW FROM 1800 SAN JOSE AV
COLTON ST SF 10 C1
NE FROM GOUGH ST BETWEEN
MARKET ST AND OTIS ST
COLUMBIA SQ ST SF 7 A3
SE FROM S FOLSOM ST BETWEEN
6TH ST AND 7TH ST TO
HARRISON ST
COLUMBUS AV SF 2 C2
COLUMBUS AV SF 3 A2
NW FROM JUCTION MONTGOMERY
ST AND WASHINGTON ST
TO BEACH ST
2 MONTGOMERY ST
WASHINGTON ST
GIBB ST
100 JACKSON ST
KEARNY ST
200 PACIFIC AV
ALDER ST
300 BROADWAY
338 GRANT AVE
400 VALLEJO ST
500 STOCKTON ST
GREEN ST
UNION ST
POWELL ST
GROVER PL
700 FILBERT ST
800 GREENWICH ST
830 MASON ST
900 LOMBARD ST
NEWELL ST
1000 TAYLOR ST
CHESTNUT ST
HOUSTON ST
1100 FRANCISCO ST
JONES ST
1200 BAY ST
1300 NORTH POINT ST
END BEACH ST
COLUSA PL SF 10 C1
SE FROM COLTON ST BETWEEN 12TH ST
AND BRADY ST TO CHASE ST
COMERFORD ST SF 14 B1
E FROM SANCHEZ ST BETWEEN
27TH ST & DUNCAN ST TO CHURCH ST
COMMER CT SF 15 C3
SOUTH FROM NEWCOMB AV TO
GARLINGTON CT
COMMERCE ST SF 3 B2
W FROM S FRONT ST BETWEEN
GREEN ST AND UNION ST
TO BATTERY ST
COMMERCIAL ST SF 3 A3
W FROM BATTERY ST BETWEEN
SACRAMENTO ST AND CLAY ST
TO GRANT AV
2 THE EMBARCADERO
100 DRUMM ST
200 DAVIS ST
300 FRONT ST
400 BATTERY ST
500 SANSOME ST
LEIDESDORFF ST
600 MONTGOMERY ST
700 KEARNY ST
END GRANT AVE
COMMONWEALTH AVSF 5 C2
S FROM CALIFORNIA ST TO
GEARY BLVD BETWEEN PARKER AV
AND JORDAN AV
2 CALIFORNIA ST
100 EUCLID AV
END GEARY BLVD
COMPTON RD SF 1 A3
NE FROM WASHINGTON BLVD
THEN SE TO WASHINGTON BLVD
CONCORD ST SF 20 A2
SW FROM MISSION ST BETWEEN
ALLISON ST AND FLORENTINE ST

TO HANOVER ST
2 MISSION ST
CROSS ST
100 MORSE ST
200 BRUNSWICK ST
END WATT AVE
CONCOURSE DR SF 9 B1
IN GOLDEN GATE PARK
CONGDON AV SF 14 B3
E OF CRAUT ST FROM CANAL
ST TO SILVER AV
2 CANAL ST
100 TRUMBULL ST
200 NEY ST
300 MAYNARD ST
END SILVER AVE
CONGO ST SF 14 A3
N FROM CIRCULAR AV AND
E TO BOSWORTH ST
2 CIRCULAR AV
100 FLOOD AV
200 HEARST AV
300 MONTEREY BLVD
400 JOOST AV
500 MANGELS AV
MELROSE AV
600 STILLINGS ST
END BOSWORTH ST
CONKLING ST SF 15 B3
N FROM SILVER AV NEAR AUGUSTA ST
CONNECTICUT ST SF 11 B2
S FROM 16TH ST BETWEEN
MISSOURI ST AND ARKANSAS ST
TO ARMY ST
2 16TH ST
100 17TH ST
200 MARIPOSA ST
300 18TH ST
400 19TH ST
500 20TH ST
700 22ND ST
WISCONSIN ST
1100 25TH ST
26TH ST
1300 ARMY ST
CONRAD ST SF 14 A2
W OF DIAMOND ST FROM
SUSSEX ST N TO DIAMOND
CONSERVATORY DR SF 9 B1
IN GOLDEN GATE PARK
CONSTANSO WY SF 12 C3
N FROM 1500 SLOAT BLVD
TO CRESTLAKE DR
CONVERSE ST SF 11 A1
NW FROM S BRYANT ST BETWEEN
8TH ST AND 9TH ST
COOK ST SF 5 C2
S FROM POINT N OF GEARY BLVD
BETWEEN BLAKE ST AND
SPRUCE ST TO ANZA ST
COOPER AL SF 3 A3
S FROM S JACKSON ST BETWEEN
KEARNY AND GRANT AV
COPPER AL SF 10 A3
FROM MARKET ST NEAR
SHORT ST SW TO BURNETT ST
2 MARKET ST
100 CORBETT ST
GRAYSTONE TER
END BURNETT ST
CORA ST SF 21 A3
S FROM LELAND AV BETWEEN
DELTA ST AND RUTLAND ST
TO A POINT N OF COUNTY LINE
CORAL CT SF 17 A1
N FROM KIRKWOOD AV IN
HUNTERS PT NAVAL RES
CORAL RD SF 11 B3
W OF CAROLINA ST BETWEEN
23RD ST AND 25TH ST
CORALINO LN SF 14 A1

S FROM CAMEO WY TO AMBER DR
CORBETT AV SF 10 A3
SW FROM 17TH ST AND
DOUGLASS ST AND S TO MARKET ST
2 DOUGLASS ST
17TH ST
100 ORD ST
130 HATTIE ST
200 CORBIN PL
DANVERS ST
300 MARS ST
19TH ST
400 PEMBERTON PL
CLAYTON ST
500 IRON AL
600 COPPER AL
YUKON ST
GLENDALE ST
GRAYSTONE TER
700 ROMAIN ST
MORGAN ST
800 DIXIE AL
ARGENT AL
900 HOPKINS ST
23RD ST
956 GOLDING AL
END 24TH ST
CORBIN PL SF 10 A2
S FROM 17TH ST E OF
TEMPLE ST TO CORBETT AV
CORDELIA ST SF 3 A3
N FROM S PACIFIC AV BETWEEN
STOCKTON ST AND POWELL ST
TO BROADWAY
CORDOVA ST SF 20 B3
SE FROM S ROLPH ST E OF
NAPLES ST TO BALTIMORE WY
2 ROLPH ST
100 ATHENS ST
200 SEVILLE ST
300 MUNICH ST
400 PRAGUE ST
CHICAGO WY
500 WINDING WY
END COUNTY LINE
CORNWALL ST SF 5 B2
W FROM ARGUELLO BLVD BETWEEN
CLLEMENT ST AND CALIFORNIA ST
TO CALIFORNIA ST
CALIFORNIA ST
2 ARGUELLO BLVD
100 2ND AV
200 3RD AV
300 4TH AV
400 5TH AV
END CALIFORNIA ST
CORONA ST SF 19 B1
N FROM HOLLOWAY AV TO
OCEAN AV BETWEEN DE SOTO ST
AND BORICO ST
2 HOLLOWAY AVE
100 URBANO DR
END PT N OF URBANO DR
CORONADO ST SF 21 B2
SW FROM INGERSON AV TO
JAMESTOWN AV BETWEEN HAWES AND
GRIFFITH ST
CPL ZAVOVITZ ST SF 1 C2
N FROM LUNDEEN ST
CORTES AV SF 13 B2
N FROM 100 TARAVAL ST TO
DORANTES ST
CORTLAND AV SF 14 C2
CORTLAND AV SF 15 A2
E FROM 3501 MISSION ST BETWEEN
KINGSTON AV AND SANTA MARINA ST
TO BAY SHORE BLVD
2 MISSION ST
COLERIDGE ST
100 PROSPECT ST
WINFIELD ST
200 ELSIE ST
BONVIEW ST
300 BOCANA ST
400 BENNINGTON ST
WOOL ST
500 ANDOVER ST
600 MOULTRIE ST
700 ANDERSON ST
800 ELLSWORTH ST
900 GATES ST
1000 FOLSOM ST
1100 BANKS ST
1200 PRENTISS ST
1300 NEVADA ST
1400 PUTNAM ST
NEBRASKA ST
BRONTE ST
1500 BRADFORD ST
1600 PERALTA ST
1700 HOLLADAY AV
HILTON ST
END BAY SHORE BLVD
CORWIN ST SF 10 A3
NW FROM DOUGLASS ST S OF 20TH ST
TO CLOVER LN
2 DOUGLASS ST
100 ACME AL
END CLOVER LN
COSGROVE ST SF 15 A2
SW FROM BAY SHORE BLVD
S OF OAKDALE AV
COSMO PL SF 7 A2
W FROM S TAYLOR ST BETWEEN
POST ST AND SUTTER ST
TO JONES ST
COSO AV SF 14 C1
FROM MISSION ST SE TO BOCANA AV
MISSION ST
PRECITA AV
BERNAL AV
MONTEZUMA ST
LUNDY LANE
150 PROSPECT ST
200 WINFIELD ST
AZTEC ST
ELSIE ST
BONVIEW ST
SHOTWELL ST
END BOCANA ST
COSTA ST SF 15 A1
SE FROM BREWSTER ST BETWEEN
RUTLEDGE ST AND FAITH ST
TO A POINT E OF HOLLADAY AV
COTTAGE ROW SF 6 B2
N FROM S SUTTER ST BETWEEN
WEBSTER ST AND FILLMORE ST
TO BUSH ST
COTTER ST SF 14 A3
SE FROM 4400 MISSION ST BETWEEN
THERESA ST AND FRANCIS ST
2 MISSION ST
100 ALEMANY BLVD
200 CAYUGA AV
END SAN JOSE AV
COUNTRY CLUB DR SF 12 B3
BETWEEN SUNSET BLVD AND
SKYLINE BLVD
S OF SLOAT BLVD
COVENTRY CT SF 13 C2
N FROM CRESTA VISTA DR
ONE BLK E OF BELLA VISTA
COVENTRY LN SF 13 C2
EXTENSION OF COVENTRY CT
COWELL PL SF 3 B2
S FROM S VALLEJO ST BETWEEN
BATTERY ST AND SANSOME ST
COWLES ST SF 1 A2
IN PRESIDIO
CRAGMONT AV SF 13 B1
S FROM ROCKRIDGE DR BETWEEN
10TH AV AND 12TH AV
TO QUINTARA ST
CRAGS CT SF 14 A2
NW FROM BERKELEY WY W OF
DIAMOND HEIGHTS BLVD
CRAN PL SF 6 B3
N FROM MCALLISTER ST BETWEEN
FILLMORE ST AND WEBSTER ST
CRANE ST SF 21 B1
S FROM PAUL AV BETWEEN WHEAT ST
AND EXETER ST
CRANLEIGH DR SF 13 A3
W FROM LAGUNITAS DR ONE
BLOCK W OR PORTOLA DR
CRANSTON RD SF 1 A2
IN PRESIDIO
NW FROM MERCHANT RD
CRAUT ST SF 14 B3
S FROM TRUMBULL ST
E OF MISSION ST TO SILVER AV
2 CANAL ST
100 TRUMBULL ST
200 NEY ST
300 MAYNARD ST
END SILVER AVE
CRESCENT AV SF 14 C3
E FROM MISSION ST S
OF RICHLAND ST TO PUTNAM ST
2 MISSION ST
LEESE ST
100 AGNON AVE
200 MURRAY ST
ARNOLD AVE
300 ROSCOE ST
PORTER ST
BACHE ST
400 ANDOVER ST
500 MOULTRIE ST
600 ANDERSON ST
700 ELLSWORTH ST
800 GATES ST
900 FOLSOM ST
1000 BANKS ST
1100 PRENTISS ST
NEVADA ST
PUTNAM ST
BRONTE ST
BRADFORD ST
CRESPI DR SF 19 A2
NE FROM JUAN BAUTISTA CIRCLE
BETWEEN GRIJALVA DR
AND FUENTE AV TO SERRANO DR
CRESTA VISTA DR SF 13 B3
W FROM BELLA VISTA WY TO BAXTER
AL & CASITAS AV, 4 BLKS N OF
MONTEREY BLVD
BELLA VISTA WY
COVENTRY CT
LULU AL
EMIL LN
GLOBE AL
BAXTER AL
END CASITAS AVE
CRESTLAKE DR SF 12 B2
FROM 800 SLOAT BLVD W
TO 34TH AV AND WAWONA ST
CRESTLINE DR SF 13 C1
W FROM BURNETT AV 3 BLKS
N OF PORTOLA DR TO PARKRIDGE DR
CRESTMONT DR SF 9 B3
W FROM CHRISTOPHER DR ONE
BLK FROM GLENHAVEN LN
CRESTWELL WK SF 9 A3
OFF JUNCTION OF NORIEGA
ST AND 15TH AV
CRISP RD SF 17 A1
N FROM SPEAR AV TO PALOU AV
IN HUNTERS PT NAVAL RESERVATION
CRISSY FIELD AV SF 1 A2
E FROM LINCOLN BLVD TO MASON ST
CROSS ST SF 20 A2
SW FROM POPE ST NEAR
MISSION ST TO CONCORD ST
CROSS OVER DR SF 8 C1
IN GOLDEN GATE PARK
CROWN TER SF 9 C3
S FROM S CLARENDON AV
TO PEMBERTON PL
CRYSTAL ST SF 19 B3
N FROM DE LONG ST TO ALEMANY BLVD
CUBA AL SF 14 A2
EAST FROM THE INTERSECTION OF
MARIETTA DR, MOLIMO DR AND
TERESITA BLVD
CUESTA CT SF 14 A1
ONE BLK N FROM CORBETT AND
MARKET ST JUNCTION
CULEBRA TER SF 2 C2
N FROM A POINT N OF LOMBARD ST
BETWEEN LARKIN ST AND POLK ST TO
A POINT S OF FRANCISCO ST
2 LOMBARD ST
100 CHESTNUT ST
END FRANCISCO ST
CUMBERLAND ST SF 10 B3
W FROM S GUERRERO ST BETWEEN
19TH ST AND 20TH ST
TO A POINT E OF NOE ST
3 GUERRERO ST
DOLORES ST
200 CHURCH ST
300 SANCHEZ ST
END NOE ST
CUNNINGHAM PL SF 10 C2
W FROM S VALENCIA ST BETWEEN
19TH ST AND 20TH ST
CURTIS ST SF 20 A2
S FROM S ROLPH ST BETWEEN
POPE ST AND NEWTON ST
TO PRAGUE ST
2 ROLPH ST
100 MORSE ST
200 BRUNSWICK ST
END PRAGUE ST
CUSHMAN ST SF 3 A3
FROM CALIFORNIA ST TO
SACRAMENTO ST BETWEEN MASON ST
AND TAYLOR ST
CUSTER AV SF 15 C1
NW FROM 3RD ST TO RANKIN ST
CUSTOM HOUSE PL SF 3 A3
N FROM S WASHINGTON ST BETWEEN
BATTERY ST AND SANSOME ST
TO JACKSON ST
CUTLER AV SF 12 A2
W FROM 47TH AV TO THE GREAT
HIGHWAY BETWEEN WAWONA ST
AND VICENTE ST
CUVIER ST SF 14 B3
S FROM SAN JOSE AV BETWEEN
MARSILLY ST AND MILTON ST
CYPRESS ST SF 14 C1
S FROM S 24TH ST BETWEEN
SOUTH VAN NESS AV AND
CAPP ST S TO 26TH ST
CYRUS PL SF 2 C3
S FROM S BROADWAY BETWEEN
LEAVENWORTH ST AND HYDE ST

D

D ST SF 17 B1
S FROM VAN KEUREN AV TO SPEAR AV
IN HUNTERS POINT
DAGGETT ST SF 11 B1
NE FROM 1000 16TH ST TO 7TH ST
300 7TH ST
END 16TH ST
DAKOTA ST SF 11 B3
SE FROM 23RD ST TO TEXAS ST
E OF CONNECTICUT ST
DALE PL SF 6 C3
S FROM S GOLDEN GATE AV BETWEEN
LEAVENWORTH ST AND HYDE ST
DALEWOOD WY SF 13 B2
W FROM MYRA ST TO LANSDALE AV
DANL BURNHAM CT SF 6 B2
BETWEEN VAN NESS AV AND
FRANKLIN ST
DANTON ST SF 14 B3
NW FROM CAYUGA AV W OF
LYELL ST
DANVERS ST SF 10 A2
S FROM CORBETT AV TO 19TH ST
2 CORBETT AVE
MERRITT ST
18TH ST
100 MARKET ST
200 CASELLI AVE
END 19TH ST
DARIEN WY SF 13 B3
E FROM JUNIPERO SERRA BLVD
TO KENWOOD WY
2 JUNIPERO SERRA BL
100 SAN RAFAEL WAY
200 SAN FERNANDO WAY
300 SAN LEANDRO WAY
400 SANTA ANA AVE
500 SAN BENITO WAY
APTOS AVE
600 SAN ALESO AVE
700 WESTGATE DR
800 MANOR DR
900 NORTH GATE DR
END KENWOOD WAY
DARRELL PL SF 3 A2
N FROM 200 FILBERT ST BETWEEN
MONTGOMERY ST AND SANSOME ST
DARTMOUTH ST SF 15 A3
DARTMOUTH ST SF 21 A1
S FROM SWEENY ST W OF BOWDOIN ST
TO A POINT S OF MANSELL ST
SWEENY ST
2 SILVER AVE
100 SILLIMAN ST
FELTON ST
RESERVOIR
600 WOOLSEY ST
700 DWIGHT ST
800 OLMSTEAD ST
END MANSELL ST
DASHEL HMMT ST SF 7 A1
N FROM 600 BUSH ST BETWEEN
STOCKTON ST AND POWELL ST
TO PINE ST
DAVIDSON AV SF 15 C1
S FROM POINT NW OF RANKIN ST
TO 3RD ST
DAVIS ST SF 3 B3
N FROM S MARKET ST BETWEEN
DRUMM ST AND FRONT ST
TO THE BAY
2 MARKET ST
PINE ST
100 CALIFORNIA ST
200 SACRAMENTO ST
COMMERCIAL ST
300 CLAY ST
400 WASHINGTON ST
500 JACKSON ST
600 PACIFIC AVE
700 BROADWAY
800 VALLEJO ST
GREEN ST
END THE EMBARCADERO
DAWNVIEW WY SF 14 A1
W FROM BURNETT AV TO GLENVIEW DR
DAWSON PL SF 3 A3
E FROM 1000 MASON ST BETWEEN
SACRAMENTO ST AND CLAY ST
DAY ST SF 14 B3
W FROM S SAN JOSE AV
BETWEEN 29TH ST AND 30TH ST
TO A POINT W OF CASTRO ST
2 SAN JOSE AVE
100 DOLORES ST

200 CHURCH ST
300 SANCHEZ ST
400 NOE ST
END CASTRO ST
DEARBORN ST SF 10 C2
FROM S S 17TH ST BETWEEN
VALENCIA ST AND GUERRERO ST
TO 18TH ST
DE BOOM ST SF 7 B3
E FROM S 2ND ST BETWEEN
BRYANT ST AND BRANNAN ST
DECATUR ST SF 11 A1
SE FROM S BRYANNT ST BETWEEN
7TH ST AND 8TH ST
DECKER AL SF 7 A3
W FROM S 7TH ST BETWEEN
FOLSOM ST AND HARRISON ST
DEDMAN CT SF 15 C2
W OFF CASHMERE ST ONE BLOCK S
OF HUDSON AV
DEEMS RD SF 1 B3
IN PRESIDIO
W FROM WASHINGTON BLVD
DEFOREST WY SF 10 A2
W FROM BEAVER ST W OF
CASTRO ST TO FLINT ST
DE HARO ST SF 11 B1
S FROM DIVISION BETWEEN RHODE
ISLAND ST AND CAROLINA ST
TO 26TH ST
2 DIVISION ST
BERRY ST
100 ALAMEDA ST
200 15TH ST
300 16TH ST
400 17TH ST
500 MARIPOSA ST
600 18TH ST
700 19TH ST
800 20TH ST
SOUTHERN HTS AVE
1000 22ND ST
1200 23RD ST
1300 24TH ST
1400 25TH ST
END 26TH ST
DEHON ST SF 10 B2
S FROM 3415 16TH ST BETWEEN
CHURST ST AND SANCHEZ ST
TOWARDS 17TH ST
DELANCEY ST SF 7 C2
S FROM BRYANT ST BETWEEN
RINCON ST AND BEALE ST
TO THE EMBARACADERO
500 BRYANT ST
FEDERAL ST
600 BRANNAN ST
TOWNSEND ST
END THE EMBARCADERO
DELANO AV SF 20 A2
E OF SAN JOSE AV S FROM
S SANTA YSABEL AV TO
OTTAWA AV
2 SANTA YSABEL AVE
100 SAN JUAN AVE
200 SANTA YNEZ AVE
RUDDEN AVE
MEDA AVE
400 OCEAN AVE
500 ONEIDA AVE
600 SENECA AVE
NAVAJO AVE
700 GENEVA AVE
SEMINOLE AVE
800 NIAGARA AVE
SHAWNEE AVE
900 MT VERNON AVE
NAHUA AVE
END OTTOWA AVE
DELGADO PL SF 2 C3
E FROM S HYDE ST BETWEEN
GREEN ST AND UNION ST
DELLBROOK AV SF 9 C3
DELLBROOK AV SF 13 C1
S OFF OLYMPIA WY E
AND N TO PALO ALTO AV
DELMAR ST SF 10 A1
S FROM S WALLER ST BETWEEN
MASONIC AV AND ASHBURY ST
TO PIEDMONT ST
2 WALLER ST
100 FREDERICK ST
END PIEDMONT ST
DEL MONTE ST SF 20 A2
N FROM OTTAWA AV TO A POINT
NE OF MT VERNON AV
W OF MISSION ST
5200 MISSION ST
2 NIAGARA AVE
100 MT VERNON AVE
END OTTAWA AVE
DE LONG ST SF 19 B3
W FROM SAN JOSE AV NEAR
COUNTY LINE TO JOHN DALY BLVD
2 SAN JOSE AVE
LIEBIG ST
RICE ST
GOETHE ST
RHINE ST
100 CRYSTAL ST
WILSON ST
200 ORIZABA AVE
FLOURNOY ST
300 HEAD ST
SHAKESPEARE ST
SANTA CRUZ AVE
SAN LUIS AV
SAN MATEO AV
END SAN DIEGO AV
DEL SUR AV SF 13 C2
E FROM 901 PORTOLA DR
TO CHAVES AV
DELTA PL SF 7 A2
NE FROM 600 MASON ST BETWEEN
SUTTER ST AND BUSH ST
DELTA ST SF 21 A2
BETWEEN ELLIOTT ST AND RUTLAND ST
S FROM ANKENY ST TO SUNNYDALE AV
2 WILDE AVE
TIOGA AVE
TUCKER AVE
100 CAMPBELL AVE
200 TEDDY AVE
300 ARLETA AVE
400 RAYMOND AVE
500 LELAND AVE
600 VISITACION AVE
END SUNNYDALE AVE
DEL VALE AV SF 13 C2
SE FROM EVELYN WY TO
OSHAUGHNESSY BLVD
DEMING ST SF 10 A2
E FROM CLAYTON ST TO A
POINT E OF URANUS TER
DE MONTFORT AV SF 19 B1
W FROM MIRAMAR AV TO ASHTON AV
2 MIRAMAR AVE
100 CAPITOL AVE
200 FAXON AVE
300 JULES AVE
END ASHTON AVE
DENSLOWE DR SF 19 A2
E FROM 19TH AV AND S TO
BANBURY DR PARALLEL WITH 19TH AV
DENT RD SF 1 A3
IN PRESIDIO S FROM
COMPTON RD TO WASHINGTON BLVD
DERBY ST SF 7 A2
W FROM S MASON ST BETWEEN
GEARY ST AND POST ST TO
TAYLOR ST
DESMOND ST SF 21 A3
W OF SAN BRUNO AV FROM
LELAND AV TO SUNNYDALE AV
DE SOTO ST SF 19 B1
BETWEEN CORONA ST AND
VICTORIA ST FROM HOLLOWAY
AV N TO URBANO DR
DETROIT ST SF 14 A3
N FROM CIRCULAR AV TO
STILLINGS AV
2 CIRCULAR AVE
100 JUDSON AVE
200 STAPLES AVE
300 FLOOD AVE
400 HEARST AVE
500 MONTEREY BLVD
600 JOOST AVE
700 MANGELS AVE
800 MELROSE AVE
END STILLINGS AVE
DEVONSHIRE WY SF 9 B3
E FROM WARREN DR BETWEEN
OAKHURST LN & CHRISTOPHER DR
TO CRESTMONT DR
DEWEY BLVD SF 13 B1
S FROM LAGUNA HONDA BLVD S
TO CLAREMONT BLVD
DE WOLF ST SF 19 C3
W FROM LAWRENCE ST NEAR
SAN JOSE AV TO SICKLES AV
DIAMOND ST SF 10 A3
DIAMOND ST SF 14 A2
S FROM S 17TH ST BETWEEN
COLLINGSWOOD ST AND
EUREKA ST TO CIRCULAR AV
2 17TH ST
MARKET ST
100 18TH ST
200 19TH ST
300 20TH ST
400 21ST ST
500 22ND ST
ALVARADO ST
600 23RD ST
700 ELIZABETH ST
800 24TH ST
900 JERSEY ST
1000 25TH ST
1100 CLIPPER ST
1200 26TH ST
1300 ARMY ST
1400 27TH ST
1500 DUNCAN ST
1600 28TH ST
1700 VALLEY ST
1800 29TH ST
2590 ARBOR ST
SUSSEX ST
SURREY ST
2790 CHENERY ST
2870 BOSWORTH ST
END CIRCULAR AV
DIAMOND HTS BL SF 14 A1
S FROM CLIPPER ST AT PORTOLA
DR TO ARBOR ST
DUNCAN ST
GOLDMINE DR
DIAMOND ST
ADDISON ST
BERKELEY WAY
END ARBOR ST
DIANA ST SF 15 B3
S FROM THORNTON AV TO
WILLIAMS AV
DIAZ AV SF 19 A2
W FROM GONZALES DR TO
JUAN BAUTISTA CIR
DICHA AL SF 5 C2
S FROM LUPINE AV W OF LAUREL ST
TO WOOD ST
DICHIERA CT SF 19 C2
N FROM ELLINGTON 3 BLKS E OF
MISSION ST
DIGBY ST SF 14 B2
S FROM ADDISON ST 3 BLKS E
OF DIAMOND HEIGHTS BLVD
TO EVERSON ST
DIKEMAN SF 7 A2
W FROM S 14TH ST BETWEEN
OFARRELL ST AND ELLIS ST
DIVISADERO ST SF 2 A3
DIVISADERO ST SF 6 A3
DIVISADERO ST SF 10 A1
FROM N S 14TH ST BET
SCOTT ST AND BRODERICK ST
TO MARINA BLVD
2 14TH ST
100 DUBOCE ST
200 WALLER ST
250 HAIGHT ST
300 PAGE ST
400 OAK ST
500 FELL ST
600 HAYES ST
700 GROVE ST
800 FULTON ST
900 MCALLISTER ST
1000 GOLDEN GATE AVE
1100 TURK ST
1200 EDDY ST
1300 ELLIS ST
1400 OFARRELL ST
1500 GEARY ST
GARDEN ST
1600 POST ST
1700 SUTTER ST
1800 BUSH ST
1900 PINE ST
2000 CALIFORNIA ST
2100 SACRAMENTO ST
2200 CLAY ST
2300 WASHINGTON ST
2500 PACIFIC AVE
2600 BROADWAY
2700 VALLEJO ST
2800 GREEN ST
2900 UNION ST
3000 FILBERT ST
3100 GREENWICH ST
3200 LOMBARD ST
3300 CHESTNUT ST
3400 FRANCISCO ST
3500 BAY ST
3600 NORTH POINT ST
3700 BEACH ST
3800 JEFFERSON ST
END MARINA BLVD
DIVISION ST SF 11 B1
W FROM KING ST AND DE HARO ST
TO FLORIDA ST
2 KING ST
DE HARO ST
100 TOWNSEND ST
KANSAS ST
VERMONT ST
SAN BRUNO AVE
200 9TH ST
UTAH ST
BRANNAN ST
POTRERO AVE
300 10TH ST
YORK ST
450 BRYANT ST
END FLORIDA ST
DIXIE AL SF 10 A3
W FROM CORBETT AV TO BURNETT AV
TO BURNETT AV
DODGE PL SF 6 C2
S FROM S TURK ST BETWEEN
HYDE ST AND LARKIN ST
DOLORES ST SF 10 B1
DOLORES ST SF 14 B1
S FROM S MARKET ST BETWEEN
GUERRERO ST AND CHURCH ST
TO SAN JOSE AV
2 MARKET ST
CLINTON PARK
100 14TH ST
HIDALGO TER
200 15TH ST
230 ALERT AL
300 16TH ST
CHULA LN
400 17TH ST
DOLORES TER
DORLAND ST
18TH ST
19TH ST
CUMBERLAND ST
700 20TH ST
750 LIBERTY ST
800 21ST ST
900 22ND ST
1000 23RD ST
1100 24TH ST
1150 JERSEY ST
1200 25TH ST
1250 CLIPPER ST
1300 26TH ST
1350 ARMY ST
1400 27TH ST
1450 DUNCAN ST
1500 28TH ST
1550 VALLEY ST
1600 29TH ST
1650 DAY ST
1700 30TH ST
END SAN JOSE AVE
DOLORES TER SF 10 B2
OFF 401 DOLORES ST BETWEEN
17TH ST AND DORLAND ST
DOLPHIN CT SF 17 A1
N FROM KIRKWOOD AV IN
HUNTERS PT
DONAHUE ST SF 16 B3
DONAHUE ST SF 17 A1
SW FROM LOCKWOOD TO A POINT S
OF KIRKWOOD AV
KING AVE
HUDSON AVE
INNES AVE
JERROLD AVE
END KIRKWOOD AVE
DONNER AV SF 15 B3
SE FROM BAYSHORE BLVD & QUINT ST
DONNER AV SF 21 B1
SE FROM 3RD ST, FROM JENNINGS ST
TO INGALLS ST, & FROM FITCH ST
DORADO TER SF 19 B1
N FROM OCEAN AV 2 BLOCKS W
OF MIRAMAR AV
DORANTES AV SF 13 B1
W FROM S MAGELLAN AV AND THEN
PARALLEL WITH MAGELLAN AV TO A
POINT W OF CORTES AV
DORCAS WY SF 13 C2
N FROM FOERSTER ST TO
BELLA VISTA DR
DORCHESTER WY SF 13 B2
NW FROM 1300 PORTOLA DR
TO CLAREMONT BLVD
PORTOLA DR
ULLOA ST
END CLAREMONT BLVD
DORE ST SF 11 A1
S FROM S HOWARD ST BETWEEN
9TH ST AND 10TH ST TO BRANNAN ST
2 HOWARD ST
100 FOLSOM ST
SHERIDAN ST
200 HARRISON ST
300 BRYANT ST
END BRANNAN ST
DORIC AL SF 3 A3
S FROM 901 JACKSON ST BETWEEN
POWELL ST AND MASON ST

DORLAND ST SF 10 B2
W FROM S GUERRERO ST BETWEEN
17TH ST AND 18TH ST W TO
SANCHEZ ST
2 GUERRERO ST
100 DOLORES ST
200 CHURCH ST
END SANCHEZ ST

DORMAN AV SF 15 A2
SW FROM PALOU ST BETWEEN
APPAREL WY AND INDUSTRIAL ST TO
BARNEVELD AV

DORMITORY RD SF 16 A3
S FROM NORTHRIDGE RD TO
KISKA RD

DOUBLE ROCK ST SF 21 C1
E FROM CAMERON WY
2 BLKS N OF FITZGERALD ST

DOUGLASS ST SF 10 A3
DOUGLASS ST SF 14 A1
S FROM A POINT N OF 17TH ST
TO 28TH ST
2 ORD CT
100 CORBETT AVE
17TH ST
MARKET ST
200 18TH ST
230 CASELLI AVE
300 19TH ST
324 CARSON ST
366 SEWARD ST
20TH ST
CORWIN ST
400 ROMAIN ST
500 21ST ST
600 22ND ST
ALVARADO ST
700 23RD ST
750 ELIZABETH ST
800 24TH ST
JERSEY ST
900 25TH ST
1000 CLIPPER ST
1100 26TH ST
1200 ARMY ST
1300 27TH ST
1400 DUNCAN ST
END 28TH ST

DOVE LOOP SF 1 A2
IN PRESIDIO

DOVER ST SF 7 C2
N FROM S BRANNAN ST BETWEEN
1ST ST AND 2ND ST

DOW PL SF 7 B2
SW FROM 2ND ST BETWEEN FOLSOM ST
AND HARRISON ST

DOWNEY ST SF 9 C2
S FROM S WALLER ST BETWEEN
ASHBURY ST AND CLAYTON ST
TO ASHBURY ST
2 WALLER ST
100 FREDERICK ST
END ASHBURY ST

DOYLE DR SF 1 B2
IN PRESIDIO

DRAKE ST SF 20 A3
S FROM S MUNICH ST TO
BALTIMORE WY
2 MUNICH ST
100 PRAGUE ST
200 WINDING WAY
END COUNTY LINE

DRUMM ST SF 3 B3
N FROM S MARKET ST BETWEEN
THE EMBARCADERO AND DAVIS ST
TO JACKSON ST
2 MARKET ST
CALIFORNIA ST
100 SACRAMENTO ST
COMMERCIAL ST
200 CLAY ST
300 WASHINGTON ST
400 JACKSON ST

DRUMMOND AL SF 15 B2
E FROM S QUINT ST BETWEEN
OAKDALE AV AND PALOU AV
TO DUNSHEE ST

DUBLIN ST SF 20 B2
S FROM S PERSIA AV E OF
PRAGUE ST TO A POINT S OF
RUSSIA ST
100 PERSIA AVE
200 RUSSIA AVE
END PT S OF RUSSIA AVE

DUBOCE AV SF 10 B1
FROM MISSION ST N OF 14TH
ST W TO BUENA VISTA AV
2 MISSION ST
OTIS ST
WOODWARD ST
STEVENSON ST
100 VALENCIA ST
132 ELGIN PARK
170 PEARL ST
200 GUERRERO ST
MARKET ST
300 BUCHANAN ST
392 WEBSTER ST
400 CHURCH ST
402 FILLMORE ST
BELCHER ST
SANCHEZ ST
STEINER ST
WALTER ST
NOE ST
700 SCOTT ST
CASTRO ST
800 DIVISADERO ST
900 ALPINE TERR
END BUENA VISTA AVE

DUDLEY RD SF 1 B3
IN PRESIDIO
S OF WASHINGTON BLVD

DUKES CT SF 15 C2
N OFF CASHMERE ST ONE BLOCK N
OF LA SALLE AV

DUNBAR AL SF 3 A3
S FROM WASHINGTON ST BETWEEN
MONTGOMERY ST AND KEARNY ST
TO MERCHANT ST

DUNCAN ST SF 14 B1
W FROM S TIFFANY AV BETWEEN
ARMY ST AND MISSION ST
TO DIAMOND HEIGHTS BLVD
TIFFANY AVE
SAN JOSE AVE
100 GUERRERO ST
200 DOLORES ST
300 CHURCH ST
400 SANCHEZ ST
500 NOE ST
600 CASTRO ST
NEWBERG ST
700 DIAMOND ST
800 DOUGLASS ST
END CLIPPER ST

DUNCOMBE AL SF 3 A3
N FROM S JACKSON ST BETWEEN
GRANT AV AND STOCKTON ST

DUNNES AL SF 3 A3
E FROM 1100 KEARNY ST BETWEEN
BROADWAY ST AND VALLEJO ST

DUNSHEE ST SF 15 B3
S FROM S DRUMMOND AL BETWEEN
PHELPS ST AND QUINT ST
TO PALOU AV

DUNSMUIR ST SF 15 A3
S FROM SWEENY ST BETWEEN
DARTMOUTH ST AND COLBY ST
TO SILVER AV

DWIGHT ST SF 21 A1
SW FROM SAN BRUNO AV S OF
WOOLSEY ST TO UNIVERSITY ST
2 SAN BRUNO AVE
100 GIRARD ST
200 BRUSSELS ST
300 GOTTINGEN ST
600 HAMILTON ST
700 BOWDOIN ST
800 DARTMOUTH ST
900 COLBY ST
END UNIVERSITY ST

DYNAMITE RD SF 1 A2
IN PRESIDIO
W FROM RALSTON AV

E

E ST SF 17 B1
SE FROM MORRELL ST TO MANSEAU
ST IN HUNTERS PT

EAGLE ST SF 10 A3
W FROM YUKON ST TO MARKET ST
2 YUKON ST
100 MONO ST
END MARKET ST

EARL ST SF 17 A1
SW FROM A POINT N OF INNES AV
TO NAVY RD

EASTMAN ST SF 2 C2
N FROM S GREEN ST BETWEEN
HYDE ST AND LARKIN ST
TO ALLEN ST
2 GREEN ST
RUSSELL ST
ROCKLAND ST
100 UNION ST
END ALLEN ST

EASTWOOD DR SF 19 B1
E AND N FROM MIRAMAR AV
TO MIRAMAR AV
2 MIRAMAR AVE
100 WILDWOOD AVE
MONTECITO AVE
END MIRAMAR AVE

EATON PL SF 3 A3
S FROM 701 GREEN ST BETWEEN
POWELL ST AND MASON ST

ECKER ST SF 7 B1
FROM STEVENSON STS TO
MISSION ST AND FROM
CLEMENTINA ST TO FOLSOM ST
BETWEEN 1ST ST AND 2ND ST

EDDY ST SF 6 A3
EDDY ST SF 7 A2
FROM MARKET ST & POWELL ST W
TO ST JOSEPHS AV
2 MARKET & POWELL STS
5TH ST
100 MASON ST
200 TAYLOR ST
300 JONES ST
WAGNER AL
400 LEAVENWORTH ST
500 HYDE ST
600 LARKIN ST
700 POLK ST
800 VAN NESS AVE
900 FRANKLIN ST
1000 GOUGH ST
1100 OCTAVIA ST
1200 LAGUNA ST
1300 BUCHANAN ST
1400 WEBSTER ST
1500 FILLMORE ST
1600 STEINER ST
BOURBIN ST
1700 PIERCE ST
FARREN ST
1800 SCOTT ST
1900 DIVISADERO ST
2000 BRODERICK ST
END ST JOSEPHS AV

EDGAR PL SF 19 C1
S FROM BRUCE AV NEAR
HAROLD AV

EDGARDO PL SF 3 A2
FROM 1701 GRANT AV BETWEEN
GREENWICH ST AND LOMBARD ST

EDGEHILL WY SF 13 B2
S FROM S GARCIA AV SW AND
NW TO GARCIA AV

EDGEWOOD AV SF 9 C2
S FROM FARNSWORTH LN W BLK W OF
WILLARD ST
100 FARNSWORTH ST
200 BELMONT AVE

EDIE RD SF 1 C2
IN PRESIDIO
S OF GORGAS AV

EDINBURGH ST SF 20 B2
SW FROM SILVER AV BETWEEN
MADRID ST AND NAPLES ST
TO GENEVA AV
2 SILVER AVE
100 PERU AVE
200 AVALON AVE
300 EXCELSIOR AVE
400 BRAZIL AVE
500 PERSIA AVE
600 RUSSIA AVE
700 FRANCE AVE
800 ITALY AVE
900 AMAZON AVE
END GENEVA AVE

EDITH ST SF 3 A2
FROM 1701 GRANT AV BETWEEN
GREENWICH ST AND LOMBARD ST

EDNA ST SF 19 C1
N FROM HAVELOCK ST TO
MELROSE AV BETWEEN DETROIT ST
AND FOERSTER ST
2 HAVELOCK ST
100 MARSTON AVE
200 JUDSON AVE
300 STAPLES AVE
400 FLOOD AVE
500 HEARST AVE
600 MONTEREY BLVD
700 JOOST AVE
800 MANGELS AVE
900 MELROSE AVE

EDWARD ST SF 5 B3
W FROM WILLARD ST TO
ARGUELLO BLVD N OF TURK ST

EGBERT AV SF 21 B1
SE FROM BAYSHORE BL NW
TO HAWEST ST
INGALLS ST
JENNINGS ST
KEITH ST
3RD ST
NEWHALL ST
PHELPS ST
END BAYSHORE BLVD

EL CAMINO DEL MAR RSF 4 A2
W FROM 24TH AV TO LINCOLN PARK
25TH AVE
300 26TH AVE
400 27TH AVE
28TH AVE
MCLAREN AVE
30TH AVE
LAKE ST
32ND AVE
GEARY BLVD
END 48TH AVE

EL DORADO ST SF 11 C1
E OF 1700 3RD ST

ELGIN PARK SF 10 C1
S FROM MCCOPPIN ST BETWEEN
VALENCIA ST AND MARKET ST
S TO DUBOCE AV

ELIM AL SF 7 B1
W FROM S 1ST ST BETWEEN
JESSIE ST AND MISSION ST

ELIZABETH ST SF 10 A3
W FROM S SAN JOSE AV BETWEEN
23RD ST AND 24TH ST TO BURNHAM ST
2 SAN JOSE AVE
GUERRERO ST
200 CHURCH ST
NELLIE ST
VICKSBURG ST
BLANCHE ST
400 SANCHEZ ST
500 NOE ST
600 CASTRO ST
700 DIAMOND ST
800 DOUGLASS ST
900 HOFFMAN AVE
MARKET ST
END GRAND VIEW AV

ELK ST SF 14 A3
N FROM BOSWORTH ST TO ARBOR ST

ELKHART ST SF 7 C2
W FROM S MAIN ST BETWEEN
FOLSOM ST AND HARRISON ST

ELLERT ST SF 14 C2
E FROM BOCANA ST NEAR HOLLY
PARK CIRCLE TO ANDOVER ST
2 BOCANA ST
100 BENNINGTON ST
END ANDOVER ST

ELLINGTON AV SF 19 C3
W OF MISSION ST NEAR
COUNTY LINE FROM S OF NIAGARA AV
AV SW TO MISSION ST
2 NIAGARA AVE
100 MT VERNON AVE
200 OTTAWA AVE
SALA TERR
300 FOOTE AVE
400 NAGLEE AVE
500 WHIPPLE AVE
END MISSION ST

ELLIOT ST SF 21 A2
BETWEEN DELTA ST AND BRITTON ST
S FROM CAPBELL AV TO LELAND AV
2 CAMPBELL AVE
100 TEDDY AVE
200 ARLETA AVE
300 RAYMOND AVE
END LELAND AVE

ELLIS ST SF 6 A3
ELLIS ST SF 7 A2
W FROM MARKET ST AND STOCKTON ST
TO ST JOSEPHS AV
2 MARKET & STOCKTON STS
100 POWELL ST
5TH ST
200 MASON ST
300 TAYLOR ST
400 JONES ST
500 LEAVENWORTH ST
COHEN PL
600 HYDE ST
700 LARKIN ST
800 POLK ST
900 VAN NESS AVE
1000 FRANKLIN ST
1100 GOUGH ST
1200 OCTAVIA ST
1300 LAGUNA ST
HOLLIS ST
1500 WEBSTER ST
FOLGER AL
1600 FILLMORE ST
1700 STEINER ST
BOURBIN ST
1800 PIERCE ST
FARREN ST
1900 SCOTT ST
BEIDEMAN ST
2000 DIVISADERO ST
2100 BRODERICK ST
END ST JOSEPHS AV

ELLSWORTH ST SF 14 C2
S FROM S BENRAL HTS BLVD
BETWEEN ANDERSON ST AND GATES ST
TO ALEMANY BLVD
2 ESMERALDA AVE
100 POWHATTAN AVE
200 EUGENIA AVE
300 CORTLAND AVE
400 JARBOE AVE
500 TOMPKINS AVE
600 OGDEN AVE
700 CRESCENT AVE
END PT S OF CRESCENT AV
ELM ST SF 6 B3
W FROM S POLK ST BETWEEN
GOLDEN GATE AV AND TURK ST
TO SCOTT ST
2 POLK ST
200 VAN NESS AVE
300 FRANKLIN ST
GOUGH ST
JEFFERSON SQUARE
PIERCE ST
END SCOTT ST
ELMHURST DR SF 13 A3
E AND S FROM ROSSMOOR DR
TO ROSSMOOR DR S OF OCEAN AV
ELMIRA ST SF 15 A3
FROM INDUSTRIAL ST S TO
THORNTON AV
INDUSTRIAL ST
TOLAND ST
100 HELENA ST
200 AUGUSTA ST
300 SILVER AVE
END THORNTON AVE
EL MIRASOL PL SF 12 C3
N FROM SLOAT BLVD TO CREST
LAKE DR
ELMWOOD WY SF 19 B1
N OF OCEAN AV AND W FROM
WESTWOOD DR
EL PLAZUELA WY SF 19 A1
E FROM 501 JUNIPERO SERRA BLVD
EL POLIN LOOP SF 1 C3
IN PRESIDIO
AT S END OF MACARTHUR ST
EL SERENO CT SF 14 A2
E FROM TERESITA BLVD TO
MARIETTA DR
ELSIE ST SF 14 C2
FROM COSO AV S OF ARMY ST TO
HOLLY PARK CIR
2 COSO AVE
100 ESMERALDA AVE
VIRGINIA AVE
200 EUGENIA AVE
300 CORTLAND AVE
320 SANTA MARINA AVE
APPLETON ST
END HOLLY PARK CIRCLE
EL VERANO WY SF 13 B3
N FROM 1100 MONTREY BLVD
TO ST ELMO WY
ELWOOD ST SF 7 A2
N FROM 200 O FARRELL ST BETWEEN
POWELL ST AND MASON ST
AND W TO MASON ST
EMBARCADERO SWY SF 3 B3
N FROM BAY BRIDGE TO
BROADWAY AND SANSOME ST
EMBARCADERO, THE SF 3 A2
EMBARCADERO, THE SF 7 C2
FROM BERRY ST PARALLEL
WITH THE SEA WALL TO TAYLOR ST
BERRY ST
KING ST
DELANCEY ST
TOWNSEND ST
FREMONT ST
BRANNAN ST
BEALE ST
MAIN ST
BRYANT ST
SPEAR ST
SF-OAKLAND BAY BR/I-80
HARRISON ST
STEUART ST
FOLSOM ST
HOWARD ST
MISSION ST
EMBARCADERO SKWY RAMPS
WASHINGTON ST
PACIFIC AVE
BROADWAY
VALLEJO ST
GREEN ST
FRONT ST
FILBERT ST
GREENWICH ST
LOMBARD ST
BATTERY ST
CHESTNUT ST
SANSOME ST
BAY ST
KEARNY ST
NORTH POINT ST
GRANT AV
BEACH ST
JEFFERSON ST
POWELL ST
END TAYLOR ST
EMERALD LN SF 12 B3
W FROM RIVERTON DR TO
EVERGLADE DR
S OF SLOAT BLVD
EMERSON ST SF 5 C2
N FROM GEARY BLVD
EMERY LN SF 3 A3
N FROM 700 VALLEJO ST BETWEEN
STOCKTON ST AND POWELL ST
EMIL LN SF 13 C3
S FROM CRESTA VISTA DR TO
LOS PALMOS DR BETWEEN GLOBE
AL AND LULU AL
EMMA ST SF 7 A1
E FROM 500 STOCKTON ST BETWEEN
BUSH ST AND PINE ST
EMMETT CT SF 14 C1
S FROM S PRECITA AV BETWEEN
COSO AV AND SHOTWELL ST
TO MIRABEL AV
EMPRESS LN SF 21 A2
NE FROM SAN BRUNO AV
3 BLKS N OF BAYSHORE BLVD
ENCANTO AV SF 6 A3
N FROM ANZAVISTA AV TO
TERRA VISTA AV NEAR FORTUNA ST
ENCINAL WK SF 9 A3
E FROM 15TH AV JUST N OF
MORAGA ST
ENCLINE CT SF 13 C2
FROM POINT E OF DEL VALE
AV TO MARIETTA DR S OF
O SHAUGHNESSY BLVD
ENGLISH ST SF 16 B3
HUNTERS POINT
SW FROM LOCKWOOD ST
ENNIS RD SF 1 A3
IN PRESIDIO
S FROM COMPTON ST
ENTERPRISE ST SF 10 C2
E FROM S FOLSOM ST BETWEEN
16TH ST AND 17TH ST
ENTRADA CT N SF 19 B1
ENTRADA CT S SF 19 B1
W FROM BORICA ST BETWEEN URBANO
DR N AND S
ERIE ST SF 10 C1
W FROM S FOLSOM ST BETWEEN
13TH ST AND 14TH ST TO
MISSION ST
2 FOLSOM ST
100 SOUTH VAN NESS AVE
END MISSION ST
ERKSON CT SF 6 A2
N FROM S POST ST BETWEEN
DIVISADERO ST AND BRODERICK ST
ERVINE ST SF 21 A2
BETWEEN ALBERTA ST AND DELTA ST
FROM CAMPBELL AV N TC WILDE AV
WILDE AV
ESCOLTA WY SF 12 B2
FROM 30TH AV W TO WAWONA
ST W OF 1901 VICENTE ST
ESCONDIDO AV SF 12 B3
FROM CONSTANSO WY W TO
34TH AV
ESMERALDA AV SF 14 C2
ESMERALDA AV SF 15 A2
FROM COLERIDGE ST SE AND
E TO HOLLADAY AV
2 COLERIDGE ST
LUNDYS LN
100 PROSPECT AVE
200 WINFIELD ST
300 ELSIE ST
400 BONVIEW ST
BOCANA ST
500 ANDOVER ST
600 MOULTRIE ST
650 ANDERSON ST
SHOTWELL ST
700 ELLSWORTH ST
750 GATES ST
800 FOLSOM ST
BANKS ST
PRENTISS ST
NEVADA ST
900 ROSENKRANS ST
BERNAL HTS BLVD
ALABAMA ST
BRADFORD ST
1000 PERALTA ST
1100 FRANCONIA ST
BREWSTER ST
END HOLLADAY AVE
ESPANOLA ST SF 16 A3
W OF INGALKLS ST BETWEEN ROSIE
LEE LN AND BEATRICE LN
ESQUINA DR SF 20 C3
S FROM PARQUE DR BETWEEN
CIELITO DR AND CARRIZAL ST
TO GENEVA AV
ESSEX ST SF 7 B2
S FROM S FOLSOM ST BETWEEN
1ST ST AND 2ND ST TO HARRISON
ESTERO AV SF 19 A1
SE FROM JUNIPERO SERRA
BLVD TO ALVISO ST
EUCALYPTUS DR SF 12 C3
W FROM JUNIPERO SERRA
BLVD S OF OCEAN AV TO
CLEARFIELD DR
EUCLID AV SF 5 B2
W FROM S PRESIDIO AV BETWEEN
CALIFORNIA ST AND GEARY BLVD
TO ARGUELLO BLVD
PRESIDIO AVE
MASONIC AVE
LAUREL ST
COLLINS ST
MANZANITA AVE
IRIS AVE
HEATHER AVE
SPRUCE ST
PARKER AVE
COMMONWEALTH AVE
JORDAN AVE
PALM AVE
ARGUELLO BLVD
EUGENIA AV SF 14 C2
SE FROM MISSION ST NEAR 30TH ST
AND E TO A POINT E OF
NEVADA ST
2 MISSION ST
100 COLERIDGE ST
200 PROSPECT AVE
300 WINFIELD ST
400 ELSIE ST
VIRGINIA AVE
500 BONVIEW ST
600 BOCANA ST
BENNINGTON ST
700 WOOL ST
800 ANDOVER ST
900 MOULTRIE ST
1000 ANDERSON ST
1100 ELLSWORTH ST
1200 GATES ST
1300 FOLSOM ST
1400 BANKS ST
1500 PRENTISS ST
END PT S OF PRENTISS ST
EUREKA PL SF 6 C2
E OFF S LARKIN BETWEEN BUSH ST
AND PINE ST
EUREKA ST SF 10 A2
S FROM S 17TH ST BETWEEN
DIAMOND ST AND DOUGLASS ST
TO 23RD ST
2 17TH ST
MARKET ST
100 18TH ST
200 19TH ST
300 20TH ST
400 21ST ST
500 22ND ST
END 23RD ST
EVA TER SF 10 B1
N FROM OAK ST BETWEEN
STEINER ST AND PIERCE ST
EVANS AV SF 15 B1
NW FROM JENNINGS ST TO ARMY ST
KEITH ST
MENDELL ST
NEWHALL ST
3RD ST
PHELPS ST
QUINT ST
RANKIN ST
SO-EMBARCADERO FRWY
NAPOLEON ST
TOLAND ST
MARIN ST
END ARMY ST
EVE ST SF 15 A1
END OF PERALTA AV
EVELYN WY SF 13 C2
NW FROM DEL VALE AV
TO 801 PORTOLA DR
EVERGLADE DR SF 12 B3
S FROM SOAT BLVD TO GELLERT DR
E OF HAVENSIDE DR
EVERSON ST SF 14 B2
E FROM ADDISON ST BETWEEN
DIGBY ST AND ADDISON ST
TO AMATISTA LN
EWER PL SF 3 A3
W FROM S MASON ST BETWEEN
SACRAMENTO ST AND CLAY ST
EWING TER SF 5 C3
W OF MASONIC AV S OF
ANZA ST AND N OF TURK ST
EXCELSIOR AV SF 20 B1
SW FROM MISSION ST BETWEEN
AVALON AV AND BRAZIL AV
TO PRAGUE ST
2 MISSION ST
100 LONDON ST
200 PARIS ST
300 LISBON ST
400 MADRID ST
500 EDINBURGH ST
600 NAPLES ST
700 VIENNA ST
800 ATHENS ST
900 MOSCOW ST
1000 MUNICH ST
END PRAGUE ST
EXECUTIVE PK BL SF 21 B3
N FROM ALANA WY E OF BAYSHORE FWY
THEN E & S TO HARNEY WY
EXETER ST SF 21 B1
S FROM PAUL AV BETWEEN GOULD ST
AND CRANE ST TO SALINAS AV
NEAR SAN BRUNO AV
EXPOSITION DR SF 3 C1
NW FROM 13TH ST TO GATEVIEW AV
TREASURE ISLAND

F

FAIR AV SF 14 C1
SE FROM 3201 MISSION ST OPPOSITE
VALENCIA ST TO PROSPECT ST
2 MISSION ST
100 COLERIDGE ST
LUNDY S LN
END PROSPECT ST
FAIRBANKS ST SF 10 A2
E FROM JUNCTION OF
ROOSEVELT & MUSEUM WYS
FAIRFAX AV SF 15 B1
FROM KEITH ST NW TO RANKIN ST
KEITH ST
MENDELL ST
NEWHALL ST
3RD ST
PHELPS ST
QUINT ST
END RANKIN ST
FAIRFIELD WY SF 19 B1
N FROM 1950 OCEAN AV TO
KENWOOD WY
FAIRMOUNT ST SF 14 B2
W FROM ARLINGTON ST TO
MIGUEL ST
ARLINGTON ST
100 CHENERY ST
200 WHITNEY ST
300 LAIDLEY ST
END MIGUEL ST
FAIR OAKS ST SF 10 B3
S FROM S 21ST ST BETWEEN
GUERRERO ST AND DOLORES ST
TO 26TH ST
2 21ST ST
100 22ND ST
200 23RD ST
300 24TH ST
400 25TH ST
END 26TH ST
FAITH ST SF 15 A1
NW FROM A POINT E OF HOLLADAY AV
TO A POINT W OF HOLLADAY AV
FALLON PL SF 3 A3
E FROM S TAYLOR ST BETWEEN
BROADWAY ST AND VALLEJO ST
FALMOUTH ST SF 7 A3
S FROM S FOLSOM ST BETWEEN
5TH ST AND 6TH ST TO
SHIPLEY ST
FANNING WY SF 13 A1
FROM 14TH AV TO JUNCTION
OF 15TH AV AND QUINTARA ST
FARALLONES ST SF 19 B2
W FROM SAN JOSE AV
TO ORIZABA AV BETWEEN
LOBOS ST AND BROAD ST
2 SAN JOSE AVE
100 PLYMOUTH AVE
200 CAPITOL AVE
END ORIZABA AVE
FARGO PL SF 11 A1
SW FROM BOARDMAN PL BETWEEN
BRYANT ST AND BRANNAN ST

FARNSWORTH LN SF 9 C2
W FROM WILLARD ST S OF
PARNASSUS AV
FARNUM ST SF 14 B2
SE FROM DIAMOND ST
ST W OF CASTRO ST
2 31ST ST
100 MORELAND ST
END MOFFIT ST
FARRAGUT AV SF 19 C3
NW FROM MISSION ST TO
ALAMANY BLVD
2 MISSION ST
100 HURON AVE
200 WINNIPEG AVE
END SAN JOSE AVE
FARVIEW CT SF 9 C3
W FROM MARVIEW WY TO
POINT SW OF FREDELA LN
FAXON AV SF 19 B1
N FROM MONTANA ST TO
MONTEREY BLVD
2 MONTANA ST
200 LAKE VIEW AVE
300 GRAFTON AVE
400 HOLLOWAY AVE
500 DE MONTFORD AVE
600 OCEAN AVE
700 ELMWOOD WAY
800 WILDWOOD WAY
900 PIZARRO WAY
KENWOOD WAY
END MONTEREY BLVD
FEDERAL ST SF 7 B2
W FROM S 1ST ST BETWEEN
BRYANT & BRANNAN STS TO 2ND ST
FELIX AV SF 19 A2
E FROM CAMBON DR
W OF JUNIPERO SERRA BLVD
FELL ST SF 6 C3
FELL ST SF 9 C1
FELL ST SF 10 A1
W FROM JUNCTION MARKET ST
AND POLK ST BETWEEN OAK ST
& HAYES ST TO STANYAN ST
2 MARKET ST
POLK ST
100 VAN NESS AVE
200 FRANKLIN ST
300 GOUGH ST
400 OCTAVIA ST
500 LAGUNA ST
600 BUCHANAN ST
700 WEBSTER ST
800 FILLMORE ST
900 STEINER ST
1000 PIERCE ST
1100 SCOTT ST
1200 DIVISADERO ST
1300 BRODERICK ST
1400 BAKER ST
1500 LYON ST
1600 CENTRAL AVE
1700 MASONIC AVE
1800 ASHBURY ST
1900 CLAYTON ST
2000 COLE ST
2100 SHRADER ST
END STANYAN ST
FELLA PL SF 7 A1
NE FROM 600 POWELL ST BETWEEN
BUSH ST AND PINE ST
FELTON ST SF 20 C1
W FROM SAN BRUNO AV BETWEEN
SILLIMAN ST AND BURROWS
ST TO PERU AV
2 BAY SHORE BLVD
100 GIRARD ST
200 BRUSSELS ST
300 GOETTINGEN ST
400 SOMERSET ST
500 HOLYOKE ST
600 HAMILTON ST
700 BOWDOIN ST
800 DARTMOUTH ST
900 COLBY ST
1000 UNIVERSITY ST
1100 PRINCETON ST
1200 AMHERST ST
1300 YALE ST
1400 CAMBRIDGE ST
1500 OXFORD ST
1600 HARVARD ST
1700 GAMBIER ST
1800 MADISON ST
END PERU AV
FENTON LN SF 14 A1
W FROM PORTOLA DR NEAR 25TH ST
TO BURNETT AV
FERN ST SF 6 B2
W FROM S LARKIN ST BETWEEN
SUTTER ST AND BUSH ST
TO GOUGH ST
2 LARKIN ST
100 POLK
200 VAN NESS AVE
300 FRANKLIN ST
END GOUGH ST
FERNANDEZ ST SF 1 C3
IN PRESIDIO
SE FROM BARNARD AV
FERNWOOD DR SF 13 B3
N FROM EL VERANO WY TO
RAVENWOOD DR
FIELDING ST SF 3 A2
FROM 1901 STOCKTON ST BETWEEN
LOMBARD AND CHESTNUT STS
TO POWELL ST
FILBERT ST SF 2 A3
FILBERT ST SF 3 A2
FROM THE BAY BETWEEN UNION ST
AND GREENWICH ST W TO
LYON ST
THE EMBARCADERO
2 FRONT ST
100 BATTERY ST
200 SANSOME ST
NAPIER PL
DARRELL PL
300 MONTGOMERY ST
400 KEARNY ST
GENOA PL
VARENNES ST
HARDWOOD AL
500 GRANT AVE
MEDAU PL
JASPER PL
KRAUSGRILL AL
600 STOCKTON ST
700 POWELL ST
COLUMBUS AVE
SCOTLAND ST
800 MASON ST
900 TAYLOR ST
ROACH ST
REDFIELD AL
1000 JONES ST
ATTRIDGE AL
1100 LEAVENWORTH ST
1200 HYDE ST
1300 LARKIN ST
1400 POLK ST
1500 VAN NESS AVE
1600 FRANKLIN ST
1700 GOUGH ST
1800 OCTAVIA ST
1900 LAGUNA ST
2000 BUCHANAN ST
AHLERS CT
2100 WEBSTER ST
2200 FILLMORE ST
2300 STEINER ST
2400 PIERCE ST
2500 SCOTT ST
2600 DIVISADERO ST
2700 BRODERICK ST
2800 BAKER ST
END LYON ST
FILLMORE ST SF 2 A3
FILLMORE ST SF 6 B3
FILLMORE ST SF 10 B1
N FROM S DUBOCE AV BETWEEN
WEBSTER ST AND STEINER ST
TO THE BAY
2 DUBOCE AVE
100 HERMANN ST
130 GERMAINIA ST
200 WALLER ST
LAUSSAT ST
300 HAIGHT ST
400 PAGE ST
500 OAK ST
600 FELL ST
700 HAYES ST
800 GROVE ST
900 FULTON ST
1000 MCALLISTER ST
1100 GOLDEN GATE AVE
1200 TURK ST
1300 EDDY ST
1400 ELLIS ST
BYINGTON ST
1500 O FARRELL ST
1600 GEARY ST
1700 POST ST
1800 SUTTER ST
1900 BUSH ST
WILMOT ST
2000 PINE ST
CALUMET PL
2100 CALIFORNIA ST
2200 SACRAMENTO ST
2300 CLAY ST
2400 WASHINGTON ST
JACKSON ST
PACIFIC AVE
BROADWAY
2800 VALLEJO ST
2900 GREEN ST
3000 UNION ST
3100 FILBERT ST
PIXLEY ST
3200 GREENWICH ST
MOULTON ST
3300 LOMBARD ST
3400 CHESTNUT ST
CERVANTES BLVD
3600 BAY ST
NORTH POINT ST
3800 BEACH ST
JEFFERSON ST
END MARINA BLVD
FISHER AL SF 3 A3
E FROM 1300 POWELL ST BETWEEN
PACIFIC AV AND BROADWAY
FISHER AV SF 17 B1
SW FROM ROBINSON E OF
HORNEL AV TO SPEAR AV
FISHER LOOP SF 1 B3
IN PRESIDIO
W OF INFANTRY TER
FITCH ST SF 16 A3
SW FROM INNES AV
FITCH ST SF 17 A1
FITCH ST SF 21 C2
SW FROM PALOU AV TO THOMAS AV &
FROM CARROL AV TO GILMAN AV
PALOU AV
QUESADA AV
REVERE AV
SHAFTER AV
THOMAS AV
UNDERWOOD AV
VAN DYKE AV
CARROL AV
DONNER AV
END GILMAN AV
FITZGERALD AV SF 21 B1
NW FROM A POINT E OF GRIFFITH ST
TO BAYSHORE BLVD
GRIFFITH ST
CAMERON WY
HAWES ST
INGALLS ST
JENNINGS ST
END 3RD ST
FLINT ST SF 10 A2
NW FROM 16TH ST NEAR CASTRO
ST TO A POINT NW OF DEFOREST WY
FLOOD AV SF 13 C3
FLOOD AV SF 14 A3
W FROM CIRCULAR AV BETWEEN
HEARST AV AND STAPLES AV
TO HAZELWOOD AV
2 CIRCULAR AVE
100 CONGO ST
200 DETROIT ST
300 EDNA ST
400 FOERSTER ST
500 GENNESSEE ST
PHELAN AVE
RIDGEWOOD ST
END HAZELWOOD AVE
FLORA ST SF 15 B3
FROM BAY VIEW ST BETWEEN
POMONA ST AND NEWHALL ST
S TO THORNTON AVE
FLORENCE ST SF 2 C3
S FROM VALLEJO ST BETWEEN
TAYLOR ST AND JONES ST
FLORENTINE ST SF 20 A2
S FROM 5401 MISSION ST
TO BRUNSWICK ST
2 MISSION ST
100 MORSE ST
END BRUNSWICK ST
FLORIDA ST SF 11 A1
FLORIDA ST SF 15 A1
S FROM A POINT N OF DIVISION ST
BETWEEN BRYANT ST AND
ALABAMA ST TO PERALTA AV
2 PT N OF DIVISION ST
DIVISION ST
100 ALAMEDA ST
200 15TH ST
300 16TH ST
400 17TH ST
500 MARIPOSA ST
600 18TH ST
700 19TH ST
800 20TH ST
900 21ST ST
1000 22ND ST
1100 23RD ST
1200 24TH ST
1300 25TH ST
1400 26TH ST
1500 ARMY ST
1600 PRECITA ST
END PERALTA AVE
FLOURNOY ST SF 19 B3
SE FROM DE LONG ST TO
COUNTY LINE
FLOWER ST SF 15 A2
FROM LOOMIS ST S OF
OAKDALE AV W TO BAYSHORE BLVD
FOERSTER ST SF 13 C3
N FROM JUDSON AV BETWEEN EDNA ST
AND GENESSEE ST TO
TERESITA BLVD
2 JUDSON AVE
100 STAPLES AVE
200 FLOOD AVE
300 HEARST AVE
400 MONTEREY BLVD
500 JOOST AVE
600 MANGELS AVE
700 MELROSE AVE
END TERESITA BLVD
FOLSOM ST SF 7 B2
FOLSOM ST SF 10 C1
FOLSOM ST SF 11 A1
FOLSOM ST SF 15 A2
SW FROM THE BAY BETWEEN HOWARD ST
AND HARRISON ST
AND TO A POINT S OF
CRESCENT AV
2 THE EMBARCADERO
50 STEUART ST
100 SPEAR ST
200 MAIN ST
300 BEALE ST
ZENO PL
400 FREMONT ST
BALDWIN CT
GROTE PL
500 1ST ST
ECKER ST
ESSEX ST
600 2ND ST
654 HAWTHORNE ST
HAMPTON PL
700 3RD ST
800 4TH ST
900 5TH ST
FALMOUTH ST
1000 6TH ST
HARRIET ST
COLUMBIA SQ
1078 RUSS ST
SHERMAN ST
MOSS ST
1100 7TH ST
LANGTON ST
HALLAM ST
1138 RAUSCH ST
RODGERS ST
1200 8TH ST
1300 9TH ST
DORE ST
1400 10TH ST
JUNIPER ST
1500 11TH ST
NORFOLK ST
1600 12TH ST
1700 13TH ST
1732 ERIE ST
1800 14TH ST
1900 15TH ST
2000 16TH ST
ENTERPRISE ST
2100 17TH ST
2200 18TH ST
2300 19TH ST
2400 20TH ST
2500 21ST ST
2600 22ND ST
2700 23RD ST
2800 24TH ST
2900 25TH ST
3000 26TH ST
3100 ARMY ST
3200 BESSIE ST
PRECITA AVE
3300 STONEMAN ST
3400 RIPLEY ST
3500 ESMERALDA AVE
BERNAL HTS BLVD
3600 POWHATTAN AVE
3700 EUGENIA AVE
3800 CORTLAND AVE
3900 JARBOE AVE
4000 TOMPKINS AVE
4100 OGDEN AVE
4200 CRESCENT AVE
END PT S OF CRESCENT AVE
FONT BLVD SF 18 C1

FONT BLVD SF 19 A2
FROM JUAN BAUTISTA CIR
NW TO LAKE MERCED BLVD
AND SE TO JUNIPERO SERRA BLVD

FOOTE AV SF 19 C2
NW FROM S MISSION ST NEAR
COUNTY LINE BETWEEN OTTAWA AV
& NAGLEE AV TO SAN JOSE AV
2 MISSION ST
100 ELLINGTON AVE
200 HURON AVE
ALEMANY BLVD
CAYUGA AVE
END SAN JOSE AVE

FORD ST SF 10 B2
W FROM S SANCHEZ ST BETWEEN
17TH ST AND 18TH ST TO
NOE ST

FOREST KNOLLS DR SF 9 C3
FROM CHRISTOPHER DR SOUTH
TO A POINT S OF GLENHAVEN LN
ONE BLK W OF CLARENDON AV

FOREST SIDE AV SF 13 A2
N FROM VICENTE ST TO
TARAVAL ST
VICENTE ST
ULLOA ST
END TARAVAL ST

FOREST VIEW DR SF 12 C3
S FROM SLOAT BLVD BETWEEN
MEADOWBROOK DR AND INVERNESS DR
TO EUCALYPTUS DR

FORTUNA AV SF 6 A3
N FROM ANZAVISTA AV BETWEEN
BAKER ST AND ENCANTO AV
TO TERRA VISTA AV

FOUNTAIN ST SF 14 A1
S FROM S 24TH ST BETWEEN
HOFFMAN AV AND GRAND VIEW AV
TO CLIPPER ST
2 24TH ST
100 25TH ST
END CLIPPER ST

FOWLER AV SF 13 C1
FROM 701 PORTOLA DR SW
OF TERESITA BLVD

FRANCE AV SF 20 B2
SE FROM 4901 MISSION ST S OF
RUSSIA AV TO A POINT E
OF MOSCOW ST
2 MISSION ST
100 LONDON ST
200 PARIS ST
300 LISBON ST
400 MADRID ST
500 EDINBURGH ST
600 NAPLES ST
700 VIENNA ST
800 ATHENS ST
MOSCOW ST
END PT S OF MOSCOW ST

FRANCIS ST SF 20 B1
NW FROM 4440 MISSION ST BETWEEN
COTTER ST AND SANTA ROSA AV
TO ALEMANY BLVD

FRANCISCO ST SF 2 A2
FRANCISCO ST SF 3 A2
W FROM MONTGOMERY ST BETWEEN
CHESTNUT & BAY STS TO LAGUNA ST &
FROM SCOTT ST TO THE PRESIDIO
50 MONTGOMERY ST
100 KEARNY ST
200 GRANT AVE
MIDWAY ST
BELLAIR PL
300 STOCKTON ST
WORDEN ST
400 POWELL ST
500 MASON ST
600 TAYLOR ST
COLUMBUS AVE
700 JONES ST
BRET HARTE TER
800 LEAVENWORTH ST
900 HYDE ST
RESERVOIR
1000 LARKIN ST
1100 POLK ST
1200 VAN NESS AVE
1300 FRANKLIN ST
1400 GOUGH ST
1500 OCTAVIA ST
LAGUNA ST
2200 SCOTT ST
2300 DIVISADERO ST
2400 BRODERICK ST
2500 BAKER ST
RICHARDSON AVE
END LYON ST

FRANCONIA ST SF 15 A2
S FROM 151 PERALTA AV TO
A POINS S OF POWHATTAN AV
2 PERALTA AVE
MULLEN AVE
200 MONTCALM ST
300 RUTLEDGE ST
MASSASOIT ST
SAMOSET ST
CABOT ST
STAR ST
400 ESMERALDA AVE
500 MAYFLOWER ST
END POWHATTAN AVE

FRANK ST SF 7 A1
W FROM 801 MASON ST BETWEEN
PINE ST AND CALIFORNIA ST

FRANKLIN ST SF 2 B2
FRANKLIN ST SF 6 B1
N FROM S MARKET ST BETWEEN
VAN NESS AV AND GOUGH ST
TO FORT MASON
2 MARKET ST
PAGE ST
LILY ST
100 OAK ST
HICKORY AVE
200 FELL ST
LINDEN ST
300 HAYES ST
IVY ST
400 GROVE ST
500 FULTON ST
600 MCALLISTER ST
REDWOOD ST
700 GOLDEN GATE AVE
730 ELM ST
800 TURK ST
LARCH ST
900 EDDY ST
WILLOW ST
1000 ELLIS ST
OLIVE ST
1100 O FARRELL ST
MYRTLE ST
1200 GEARY ST
1300 POST ST
HEMLOCK ST
1400 SUTTER ST
FERN ST
1500 BUSH ST
AUSTIN ST
1600 PINE ST
1700 CALIFORNIA ST
1800 SACRAMENTO ST
1900 CLAY ST
2000 WASHINGTON ST
2100 JACKSON ST
2200 PACIFIC AVE
2300 BROADWAY
2400 VALLEJO ST
2500 GREEN ST
2600 UNION ST
2700 FILBERT ST
2800 GREENWICH ST
BLACKSTONE ST
2900 LOMBARD ST
3000 CHESTNUT ST
3100 FRANCISCO ST
BAY ST
END FORT MASON

FRANK NORRIS ST SF 6 B2
W FROM S LARKIN ST BETWEEN
BUSH ST AND PINE ST CONTINUING
TO OCTAVIA ST
2 LARKIN ST
100 POLK ST
200 VAN NESS AV
300 FRANKLIN ST
400 GOUGH ST
END OCTAVIA ST

FRATESSA CT SF 21 B2
W FROM SAN BRUNO AV
1 BLK N OF CAMPBELL AV

FREDELA LN SF 9 C3
N FROM MARVIEW WY TO
FARVIEW CT

FREDERICK ST SF 9 C2
W FROM BUENA VISTA AV S OF
WALLER ST W TO ARGUELLO
AV
2 BUENA VISTA AVE
100 MASONIC AVE
124 DELMAR ST
200 ASHBURY ST
250 DOWNEY ST
300 CLAYTON ST
352 BELVEDERE ST
400 COLE ST
450 SHRADER ST
500 STANYAN ST
600 WILLIAR ST
END ARGUELLO BLVD

FREDSON CT SF 20 A2
SE FROM HURON AV BETWEEN
FOOTE AV AND NAGLEE AV

FREELON ST SF 7 B3
SW FROM ZOE ST BETWEEN
BRYANT ST AND BRANNAN ST
TO A POINT W OF 4TH ST
2 ZOE ST
100 4TH ST
END PT W OF 4TH ST

FREEMAN CT SF 3 A3
S FROM 1001 CLAY ST BETWEEN
POWELL ST AND MASON ST

FREEMAN ST SF 1 B2
IN PRESIDIO
SW OF LINCOLN BLVD

FREMONT ST SF 7 B1
SE FROM S MARKET ST BETWEEN
BEALE ST AND 1ST ST
TO THE EMBARCADERO
2 MARKET ST
100 MISSION ST
NATOMA ST
200 HOWARD ST
300 FOLSOM ST
END THE EMBARCADERO

FRENCH CT SF 1 C2
IN PRESIDIO
N FROM LINCOLN BLVD

FRESNO ST SF 3 A3
E FROM GRANT AV BETWEEN
BROADWAY AND VALLEJO ST

FRIEDELL ST SF 17 A1
IN HUNTERS PT
SW FROM HUDSON AV

FRONT ST SF 3 B2
N FROM S MARKET ST BETWEEN
DAVIS ST AND BATTERY ST
TO THE EMBARCADERO
2 MARKET ST
100 PINE ST
200 CALIFORNIA ST
HALLECK ST
300 SACRAMENTO ST
COMMERCIAL ST
400 CLAY ST
600 JACKSON ST
700 PACIFIC AVE
800 BROADWAY
900 VALLEJO ST
1000 GREEN ST
COMMERCE ST
1100 UNION ST
FILBERT ST
END THE EMBARCADERO

FUENTE AV SF 19 A2
N FROM JUAN BAUTISTA CIR
TO SERRANO DR

FULTON ST SF 6 A3
FULTON ST SF 8 A1
FULTON ST SF 9 A1
SW FROM HYDE ST BETWEEN
GROVE ST AND MCALLISTER ST
TO GREAT HIGHWAY
HYDE ST
CIVIC CENTER
200 VAN NESS AVE
300 FRANKLIN ST
400 GOUGH ST
500 OCTAVIA ST
600 LAGUNA ST
700 BUCHANAN ST
800 WEBSTER ST
900 FILLMORE ST
1000 STEINER ST
1100 PIERCE ST
1200 SCOTT ST
1300 DIVISADERO ST
1400 BRODERICK ST
1500 BAKER ST
1600 LYON ST
1700 CENTRAL AVE
1800 MASONIC AVE
ATAYLA TERR
ASHBURY ST
HEMWAY TERR
CLAYTON ST
LOYOLA TERR
COLE ST
2200 PARKER AVE
SHRADER ST
2300 STANYAN ST
2344 PARSONS ST
2400 WILLARD ST
2500 ARGUELLO BLVD
2600 2ND AVE
2700 3RD AVE
2800 4TH AVE
2900 5TH AVE
3000 6TH AVE
3100 7TH AVE
3200 8TH AVE
3300 9TH AVE
3400 10TH AVE
3500 11TH AVE
3600 12TH AVE
FUNSTON AVE
PARK PRESIDIO BLVD
3800 14TH AVE
3900 15TH AVE
4000 16TH AVE
4100 17TH AVE
4200 18TH AVE
4300 19TH AVE
4400 20TH AVE
4500 21ST AVE
4600 22ND AVE
4700 23RD AVE
4800 24TH AVE
4900 25TH AVE
5000 26TH AVE
5100 27TH AVE
5200 28TH AVE
5300 29TH AVE
5400 30TH AVE
5500 31ST AVE
5600 32ND AVE
5700 33RD AVE
5800 34TH AVE
5900 35TH AVE
6000 36TH AVE
6100 37TH AVE
6200 38TH AVE
6300 39TH AVE
6400 40TH AVE
6500 41ST AVE
6600 42ND AVE
6700 43RD AVE
6800 44TH AVE
6900 45TH AVE
7000 46TH AVE
7100 47TH AVE
7200 48TH AVE
7300 LA PLAYA ST
END GREAT HIGHWAY

FUNSTON AV SF 1 C3
FUNSTON AV SF 5 A2
FUNSTON AV SF 9 A2
FUNSTON AV SF 13 A1
S BETWEEN 12TH AV AND 14TH AV
FROM MOUNTAIN LAKE PARK
TO ULLOA ST
2 MOUNTAIN LAKE PARK
100 LAKE ST
200 CALIFORNIA ST
300 CLEMENT ST
400 GEARY BLVD
500 ANZA ST
600 BALBOA ST
700 CABRILLO ST
FULTON ST
GOLDEN GATE PARK
1200 LINCOLN WAY
1300 IRVING ST
1400 JUDAH ST
1500 KIRKHAM ST
LURLINE ST
ALOHA AVE
1600 LAWTON ST
1700 MORAGA ST
1800 NORIEGA ST
1900 ORTEGA ST
ROCKRIDGE DR
2400 TARAVAL ST
END ULLOA ST

G

GABILAN WY SF 12 C3
N FROM SLOAT BLVD E OF
PARAISO PL TO CRESTLAKE DR

GAISER CT SF 10 B2
E FROM S GUERRERO ST BETWEEN
16TH ST AND CAMP ST

GALE ST SF 7 C3
SE OFF TOWNSEND ST
TO KING ST

GALEWOOD CIR SF 9 C3
W FROM CLARENDON AV BETWEEN
ASHWOOD N & OLYMPIA WY

GALINDO AV SF 19 A2
E FROM CHUMASERO AV TO A POINT
W OF JUNIPERO SERRA BLVD

GALLAGHER LN SF 7 A3
S FROM TEHAMA ST BETWEEN 4TH ST &
5TH ST TO CLEMENTINA ST

GALVEZ AV SF 15 B2
N FROM MENDELL
ST TO TOLAND ST
PT S OF MENDELL ST
MENDELL ST
NEWHALL ST
3RD ST
PHELPS ST
QUINT ST

RANKIN ST
SELBY ST
END TOLAND ST
GALVEZ AV SF 16 A3
NW FROM HORNE AV TO A POINT
NW OF DONAHUE ST IN HUNTERS PT
GAMBIER ST SF 20 C1
S FROM SILVER AV TO BURROWS ST
2 SILVER AVE
100 PIOCHE ST
200 SILLIMAN ST
300 FELTON ST
END BURROWS ST
GARCES DR SF 18 C2
FROM A POINT S OF VIDAL DR
N AND E TO GONZALES DR
GARCIA AV SF 13 B2
SW FROM 401 VASQUEZ AV
AND NW TO MERCED AV
GARDEN ST SF 6 A2
W FROM S DIVISADERO ST BETWEEN
GEARY ST AND POST ST
TO BRODERICK ST
GARDENSIDE DR SF 10 A3
S FROM BURNETT AV TO
PARKRIDGE DR & BURNETT AV
GARFIELD ST SF 19 A2
W FROM ORIZABA AV BETWEEN
HOLLOWAY AV AND SHIELDS ST
TO JUNIPERO SERRA BLVD
2 ORIZABA AVE
100 BRIGHT ST
200 HEAD ST
300 VICTORIA ST
400 RAMSELL ST
500 ARCH ST
600 VERNON ST
700 RALSTON ST
800 BIXBY ST
900 MONTICELLO ST
1000 BEVERLY ST
END JUNIPERO SERRA BLVD
GARLINGTON CT SF 15 C3
S OFF LA SALLE AV ONE BLOCK E
OF NECOMB AV
GARRISON AV SF 21 A3
S FROM SUNNYDALE ONE
BLK W OF SCHWERIN ST
GATES ST SF 15 A2
FROM S BERNAL HTS BLVD
NEAR ELLSWORTH S TO POINT
S OF CRESCENT AVE
2 BERNAL HT BLVD
100 POWHATTAN AVE
GATEVIEW AV SF 3 C1
NW FROM 13TH ST & AV H TO
LESTER CT ON TREASURE ISLAND
13TH ST
EXPOSITION DR
MARINER DR
NORTH POINT DR
BAYSIDE DR
MARINER DR
OZBORN CT
REEVES CT
MASON CT
13TH ST
END LESTER CT
GATEVIEW CT SF 13 B1
N FROM MENDOSA AV BETWEEN
QUINTARA ST AND 9TH AV
GAVEN ST SF 15 A3
W FROM 2300 SAN BRUNO AV
TO A POINT N OF COLBY ST
GAVIOTA WY SF 13 C2
S FROM TERESITA BLVD TO
BELLA VISTA WY
GEARY BLVD SF 4 B3
GEARY BLVD SF 5 C2
GEARY BLVD SF 6 A2
GEARY BLVD SF 7 A2

W FROM MARKET TO
PT LOBOS AV AT 40TH AV
1100 VAN NESS AVE
1200 FRANKLIN ST
1300 GOUGH ST
1500 LAGUNA ST
1700 WEBSTER ST
1800 FILLMORE ST
STEINER
2100 SCOTT ST
2200 DIVISADERO ST
2400 BAKER ST
2500 LYON ST
2600 PRESIDIO
2800 EMERSON ST
2900 WOOD ST
3000 COLLINS ST
3100 BLAKE ST
3200 COOK ST
BOYCE ST
PARKER AVE
COMMONWEALTH AVE
STANYAN ST
3500 JORDAN AVE
3600 PALM AVE
3700 ARGUELLO BLVD
3800 2ND AVE
3900 3RD AVE
4000 4TH AVE
4100 5TH AVE
4200 6TH AVE
4300 7TH AVE
4400 8TH AVE
4500 9TH AVE
4600 10TH AVE
4700 11TH AVE
4800 12TH AVE
FUNSTON AVE
PARK PRESIDIO BLVD
5000 14TH AVE
5100 15TH AVE
5200 16TH AVE
5300 17TH AVE
5400 18TH AVE
5500 19TH AVE
5600 20TH AVE
5700 21ST AVE
5800 22ND AVE
5900 23RD AVE
6000 24TH AVE
6100 25TH AVE
6200 26TH AVE
6300 27TH AVE
6400 28TH AVE
6500 29TH AVE
6600 30TH AVE
6700 31ST AVE
6800 32ND AVE
6900 33RD AVE
7000 34TH AVE
7100 35TH AVE
7200 36TH AVE
7300 37TH AVE
7400 38TH AVE
7500 39TH AVE
7600 40TH AVE
7700 41ST AVE
7800 42ND AVE
7900 43RD AVE
8000 44TH AVE
8100 45TH AVE
8200 46TH AVE
8300 47TH AVE
END 48TH AVE
2 MARKET ST
KEARNY ST
100 GRANT AVE
STOCKTON ST
300 POWELL ST
400 MASON ST
500 TAYLOR ST
SHANNON ST

600 JONES ST
700 LEAVENWORTH ST
800 HYDE ST
900 LARKIN ST
1000 POLK ST
END VAN NESS
GELLERT DR SF 12 B3
N AND S OF OCEAN AV E OF
SUNSET BLVD
GENEBERN WY SF 14 B3
SE OF MISSION ST AND SW FROM
COLLEGE AV S TO JUSTIN DR
DR
2 COLLEGE AVE
100 MURRAY ST
200 BENTON AVE
END JUSTIN DR
GENEVA AV SF 19 C1
GENEVA AV SF 20 A2
SE FROM OCEAN AV AND PHELAN AV TO
SANTOS ST
2 PT W OF HOWTH ST
100 HOWTH ST
200 LOUISBURG ST
TARA ST
500 SAN JOSE AVE
600 DELANO AVE
CAYUGA AVE
BAYWOOD CT
BANNOCK ST
ALEMANY BLVD
GLORIA CT
900 MISSION ST
LONDON ST
1000 PARIS ST
LISBON ST
1100 MADRID ST
EDINBURGH ST
1200 NAPLES ST
VIENNA ST
1300 ATHENS ST
MOSCOW ST
HILL BLVD S
1400 MUNICH ST
1500 PRAGUE ST
1600 LINDA VISTA STEPS
BROOKDALE AVE
WALBRIDGE ST
CARTER ST
PARQUE DR
CIELITO DR
ESQUINA DR
CARRIZAL ST
SANTOS ST
COUNTY LINE
GENNESSEE ST SF 13 C3
N FROM JUDSON AV BETWEEN
FOERSTER ST AND PHELAN AV
TO MELROSE AV
2 JUDSON AVE
100 STAPLES AVE
200 FLOOD AVE
300 HEARST AVE
400 MONTEREY ST
500 JOOST AVE
600 MANGELS AVE
END MELROSE AVE
GENOA PL SF 3 A2
N FROM 400 UNION ST BETWEEN
KEARNY ST AND GRANT AV
TO FILBERT ST
GEORGE CT SF 15 C3
W OFF INGALLS ST BETWEEN
LA SALLE AV AND OAKDALE AV
GERKE AL SF 3 A2
E FROM 1600 GRANT AV BETWEEN
FILBERT ST AND GREENWICH ST
GERMANIA ST SF 10 B1
W FROM S WEBSTER ST BETWEEN
HERMANN ST AND WALLER ST
TO STEINER ST

GETZ ST SF 19 C2
SW FROM MT VERNON AV W OF
HOWTH ST TO HAROLD AV
GIANTS DR SF 21 C2
SW FROM GILMAN AV
TO INGERSON AV
GIBB ST SF 3 A3
W FROM S COLUMBUS AV BETWEEN
WASHINGTON ST AND JACKSON ST
GIBSON RD SF 4 C2
OFF BOWLEY ST AT LINCOLN BLVD
GILBERT ST SF 11 B1
SE FROM S BRYANT ST BETWEEN
6TH ST AND 7TH ST TO
A POINT S OF BRANNAN ST
GILLETTE AV SF 21 B3
N FROM LATHROP AV TO A
POINT NE OF BLANKEN AV
GILMAN AV SF 21 B1
NW FROM WATER FRONT TO
3RD ST
GRIFFITH ST
INGALLS ST
JENNINGS ST
END 3RD ST
GILROY ST SF 21 B2
S FROM S INGERSON AV E
OF GRIFFITH ST TO
JAMESTOWN AV
GIRARD RD SF 1 C2
IN PRESIDIO
NE FROM LINCOLN BLVD
GIRARD ST SF 15 A3
S FROM SILVER AV S TO FRATESSA CT
BETWEEN SAN BRUNO AV
AND BRUSSELS ST
2 SILVER AVE
100 SILLIMAN ST
300 BURROWS ST
400 BACON ST
500 WAYLAND ST
600 WOOLSEY ST
700 DWIGHT ST
800 OLMSTEAD ST
900 MANSELL ST
1000 ORDWAY ST
1100 WARD ST
1200 HARKNESS AVE
1300 WILDE AVE
END SAN BRUNO AVE
GLADEVIEW WY SF 13 C1
N OFF SKYVIEW WY BETWEEN
KNOLLVIEW WY AND SKYVIEW WY
TO PANORAMA DR
GLADIOLUS LN SF 13 A3
S FROM EUCALYPTUS DR BETWEEN
19TH AV AND JUNIPERO SERRA BLVD
TO ELMHURST DR
GLADSTONE DR SF 14 C3
E AND N FROM MAYNARD ST
TO TRUMBULL ST
GLADYS ST SF 14 C2
S FROM SANTA MARINA ST NEAR
MISSION ST TO APPLETON ST
GLENBROOK AV SF 9 C3
SW FROM MOUNTAIN SPRINGS AV TO
PALO ALTO AV
STANYAN
GLENDALE ST SF 10 A3
W FROM MARKET ST BETWEEN COPPER
AL AND ROMAIN ST TO
CORBETT AV
GLENHAVEN LN SF 9 B3
FROM CHRISTOPHER DR EAST
GLENVIEW DR SF 13 C1
N FROM 400 PORTOLA DR TO
BURNETT AV
GLOBE AL SF 13 B3
N FROM HAZELWOOD AV
TO LANDSDALE AV
GLORIA CT SF 20 A2
NE FROM 840 GENEVE AV

GLOVER ST SF 2 C3
W FROM S JONES BETWEEN VALLEJO ST
AND BROADWAY TO
LEAVENWORTH ST
GODEUS ST SF 14 C2
FROM 3351 MISSION ST NEAR
30TH ST TO COLERIDGE ST
GOETHE ST SF 19 B3
NW FROM MISSION ST
TO DE LONG ST
2 COUNTY LINE
100 SAN JOSE AVE
END DE LONG ST
GOETTINGEN ST SF 15 A3
GOETTINGEN ST SF 21 A1
S FROM S SILVER AV TO
CAMPBELL AV
2 SILVER AVE
100 SILLIMAN ST
200 FELTON ST
300 BURROWS ST
400 BACON ST
500 WAYLAND ST
600 WOOLSEY ST
700 DWIGHT ST
800 OLMSTEAD ST
900 MANSELL ST
1000 ORDWAY ST
1100 WARD ST
1200 HARKNESS AVE
1300 ALPHA ST
END CAMPBELL AVE
GOLD ST SF 3 A3
W FROM 701 SANSOME ST BETWEEN
JACKSON ST AND PACIFIC AV
TO MONTGOMERY ST
GOLDEN CT SF 2 C3
S FROM S SACRAMENTO ST BETWEEN
JONES AND LEAVENWORTH STS
GOLDEN GATE AV SF 5 B3
GOLDEN GATE AV SF 6 A3
W FROM JUNCTION MARKET ST
AND TAYLOR ST BETWEEN
MCALLISTER AND TURK STS
TO ARGUELLO BLVD
2 MARKET ST
TAYLOR ST
100 JONES ST
200 LEAVENWORTH ST
DALE PL
300 HYDE ST
400 LARKIN ST
500 POLK ST
600 VAN NESS AVE
700 FRANKLIN ST
GOUGH ST
OCTAVIA ST
1000 LAGUNA ST
1100 BUCHANAN ST
CRAM PL
1200 WEBSTER ST
1300 FILLMORE ST
1400 STEINER ST
1500 PIERCE ST
1700 DIVISADERO ST
1800 BRODERICK ST
1900 BAKER ST
2000 LYON ST
2100 CENTRAL AVE
MASONIC AVE
ANNAPOLIS TERR
TAMALPAIS TERR
ROSLYN TERR
KITTREDGE TERR
CHABOT TERR
TEMESCAL TERR
PARKET AVE
2700 STANYAN ST
2800 WILLARD ST
END ARGUELLO BLVD
GOLDING LN SF 10 A3

W FROM MARKET ST OPPOSITE
ELIZABETH TO BURNETT AV
2 MARKET ST
100 CORBETT AVE
END BURNETT AVE
GOLD MINE DR SF 14 A2
W FROM DIAMOND HGTS BLVD
N & E TO DIAMOND HEIGHTS BLVD
GOLETA AV SF 12 C3
N FROM SLOAT BLVD BETWEEN
VALE AND PARAISO PL TO
CRESTLAKE DR
GONZALEZ DR SF 18 C2
GONZALEZ DR SF 19 A2
E FROM ARBALLO DR S OF
SERRANO DR TO CASTELO AV
GORDON ST SF 11 A1
N FROM S HARRISON ST BETWEEN
8TH ST AND 9TH ST
GORGAS AV SF 1 C2
IN PRESIDIO
S OF RICHARDSON AV
GORHAM ST SF 14 B3
W FROM CAYUGA AV
N OF TINGLEY ST
GOUGH ST SF 2 B3
GOUGH ST SF 6 B1
GOUGH ST SF 10 C1
N FROM S MARKET ST BETWEEN
FRANKLIN AND OCTAVIA STS
TO FORT MASON
2 MARKET ST
HAIGHT ST
ROSE ST
100 PAGE ST
LILY ST
200 OAK ST
HICKORY ST
300 FELL ST
LINDEN ST
400 HAYES ST
IVY ST
500 GROVE ST
600 FULTON ST
ASH ST
700 MCALLISTER ST
800 GOLDEN GATE AVE
ELM ST
900 TURK ST
1000 EDDY ST
WILLOW ST
1100 ELLIS ST
1300 GEARY ST
1400 POST ST
1500 SUTTER ST
FERN ST
1600 BUSH ST
AUSTIN ST
1700 PINE ST
1800 CALIFORNIA ST
1900 SACRAMENTO ST
2000 CLAY ST
2100 WASHINGTON ST
2200 JACKSON ST
2300 PACIFIC AVE
2400 BROADWAY
2500 VALLEJO ST
2600 GREEN ST
2700 UNION ST
2800 FILBERT ST
2900 GREENWICH ST
3000 LOMBARD ST
3100 CHESTNUT ST
3200 FRANCISCO ST
BAY ST
END FORT MASON
GOULD ST SF 21 B1
S FROM PAUL AV BETWEEN CARR AND
EXETER STS TO SALINAS AV
GRACE ST SF 10 C1
S FROM S MISSION ST BETWEEN
9TH AND 10TH STS TO
HOWARD ST
GRAFTON AV SF 19 B2
W FROM HAROLD AV TO ORIZABA AV
2 HAROLD AVE
100 LEE AVE
200 BRIGHTON AVE
300 PLYMOUTH AVE
400 GRANADA AVE
500 MIRAMAR AVE
600 CAPITOL AVE
700 FAXON AVE
800 JULES AVE
900 ASHTON AVE
END ORIZABA AVE
GRAHAM ST SF 1 B3
IN PRESIDIO
NE FROM MORAGA AV
GRANADA AV SF 19 B2
N FROM LAKE VIEW AV TO
SOUTHWOOD DR BETWEEN PLYMOUTH
AND MIRAMAR AVES
2 LAKE VIEW AVE
100 GRAFTON AVE
200 HOLLOWAY AVE
300 OCEAN AVE
END SOUTHWOOD DR
GRANAT CT SF 9 B1
E OFF S 9TH AV BETWEEN FULTON
ST AND CABRILLO ST
GRAND VIEW AV SF 10 A3
GRAND VIEW AV SF 14 A1
S FROM MARKET ST AND YUKON ST
TO 23RD ST
2 MARKET ST
STANTON ST
GRAND VIEW TERR
ACME AL
100 ROMAIN ST
200 21ST ST
246 MORGAN AL
HOFFMAN ST
ALVARADO ST
23RD ST
ELIZABETH ST
24TH ST
25TH ST
END CLIPPER ST
GRANDVIEW TER SF 10 A3
N FROM GRAND VIEW AV BETWEEN
ACME AL AND STANTON ST
GRANT AV SF 3 A2
GRANT AV SF 7 A1
N FROM S MARKET ST BETWEEN
KEARNY AND STOCKTON STS
TO BEACH ST
2 MARKET ST
OFARRELL ST
100 GEARY ST
MAIDEN LN
200 POST ST
ASHBURTON PL
CAMPTON PL
TILLMAN PL
300 SUTTER ST
HARLAN PL
400 BUSH ST
500 PINE ST
VINTON CT
600 CALIFORNIA ST
700 SACRAMENTO ST
COMMERCIAL ST
800 CLAY ST
900 WASHINGTON ST
1000 JACKSON ST
1100 PACIFIC AVE
ADLER ST
BROADWAY
1200 COLUMBUS AVE
FRESNO ST
1300 VALLEJO ST
1400 GREEN ST
1500 UNION ST
NOBLES AL
1600 FILBERT ST
GERKE AL
PARKEE AL
1700 GREENWICH ST
EDITH PL
EDGARDO PL
1800 LOMBARD ST
WHITING ST
1900 CHESTNUT ST
PFEIFFER ST
2000 FRANCISCO ST
GRANVILLE WY SF 13 B2
NW FROM 1200 PORTOLA DR TO
CLAREMONT BLVD
2 PORTOLA DR
100 ULLOA ST
END CLAREMONT BLVD
GRATTAN ST SF 9 C2
W FROM BELVEDERE ST NEAR
ALMA ST TO STANYAN ST
2 BELVEDERE ST
100 COLE ST
200 SHRADER ST
END STANYAN ST
GRAYSTONE TER SF 9 C3
S FROM S PEMBERTON PL TO
CORBETT AV
100 PEMBERTON PL
200 IRON AL
300 COPPER AL
END CORBETT AVE
GREAT HWY SF 8 A3
GREAT HWY SF 12 A1
S FROM TERMINATION OF POINT
LOBOS AV ALONG THE OCEAN
BEACH TO SLOAT BLVD
600 END OF PT LOBOS AVE
700 BALBOA ST
800 CABRILLO ST
FULTON ST
JFK DR
1200 LINCOLN WAY
1300 IRVING ST
1400 JUDAH ST
1500 KIRKHAM ST
1600 LAWTON ST
1700 MORAGA ST
1800 NORIEGA ST
1900 ORTEGA ST
2000 PACHECO ST
2100 QUINTARA ST
2200 RIVERA ST
2300 SANTIAGO ST
TARAVAL ST
ULLOA ST
VICENTE ST
WAWONA ST
END SLOAT BLVD
GREEN ST SF 2 A3
GREEN ST SF 3 B2
FROM THE EMBARCADERO BETWEEN
VALLEJO ST AND UNION ST
TO PRESIDIO RESERVATION
2 THE EMBARCADERO
DAVIS ST
50 FRONT ST
100 BATTERY ST
GAINES ST
200 SANSOME ST
CALHOUN ST
300 MONTGOMERY ST
CASTLE ST
WINDSOR PL
400 KEARNY ST
SONOMA ST
VARENNES ST
500 GRANT AVE
BANNAM PL
JASPER PL
600 COLUMBUS AVE
STOCKTON ST
700 POWELL ST
AUGUST AL
EATON PL
800 MASON ST
ALTA VISTA TER
900 TAYLOR ST
1000 JONES ST
1100 LEAVENWORTH ST
NEW ORLEANS AVE
1200 HYDE ST
EASTMAN ST
1300 LARKIN ST
1400 POLK ST
1500 VAN NESS AVE
1600 FRANKLIN ST
1700 GOUGH ST
1800 OCTAVIA ST
1900 LAGUNA ST
2000 BUCHANAN ST
2100 WEBSTER ST
2200 FILLMORE ST
2300 STEINER ST
2400 PIERCE ST
2500 SCOTT ST
2600 DIVISADERO ST
2700 BRODERICK ST
2800 BAKER ST
END LYON ST
GREENOUGH AV SF 1 A2
IN PRESIDIO
N FROM KOBBE AV
GREENVIEW CT SF 9 C3
E FROM S DELLBROOK ONE BLK S
OF PANORAMA DR
GREENWICH ST SF 2 A3
GREENWICH ST SF 3 B2
W FROM THE EMBARCADERO BETWEEN
FILBERT AND LOMBARD STS
TO PRESIDIO RESERVATION
2 THE EMBARCADERO
100 BATTERY ST
200 SANSOME ST
TELEGRAPH HILL BLVD
400 KEARNY ST
CHILD ST
500 GRANT AVE
KRAMER PL
600 STOCKTON ST
700 POWELL ST
GROVER PL
COLUMBUS AVE
800 MASON ST
JANSEN ST
900 TAYLOR ST
ROACH ST
1000 JONES ST
1100 LEAVENWORTH ST
GREENWICH TER
SOUTHARD PL
1200 HYDE ST
1300 LARKIN ST
1400 POLK ST
1500 VAN NESS AVE
1600 FRANKLIN ST
IMPERIAL AL
1700 GOUGH ST
1800 OCTAVIA ST
1900 LAGUNA ST
2000 BUCHANAN ST
2100 WEBSTER ST
2200 FILLMORE ST
2300 STEINER ST
2400 PIERCE ST
2500 SCOTT ST
2600 DIVISADERO ST
2700 BRODERICK ST
2800 BAKER ST
END LYON ST
GREENWOOD AV SF 19 C1
W FROM JUNCTION OF HAZELWOOD AV
OPPOSITE JUDSON AV TO
PLYMOUTH AV
2 HAZELWOOD AVE
50 VALDEZ AVE
100 COLON AVE
END PLYMOUTH AVE
GRENARD TER SF 2 B2
N FROM 1412 GREENWICH ST
GRIFFITH ST SF 21 C2
SW FROM NAVY RD TO
JAMESTOWN AV
NAVY RD
OAKDALE AVE
PALOU AVE
QUESADA AV
REVERE AV
SHAFTER AV
THOMAS AV
UNDERWOOD AV
VAN DYKE AV
CAMERON WY
FITZGERALD AVE
GILMAN AVE
INGERSON AV
END JAMESTOWN AVE
GRIJALVA DR SF 19 A2
SW FROM JUAN BAUTISTA CIR
TO GARCES DR
GROTE PL SF 7 B2
S FROM S FOLSOM ST BETWEEN
FREMONT ST AND 1ST ST
GROVE ST SF 6 A3
GROVE ST SF 9 C1
W FROM S MARKET ST AT HYDE ST
BETWEEN HAYES ST AND FULTON ST
TO STANYAN ST
MARKET ST
LARKIN ST
POLK ST
200 VAN NESS AVE
300 FRANKLIN ST
400 GOUGH ST
500 OCTAVIA ST
600 LAGUNA ST
700 BUCHANAN ST
800 WEBSTER ST
900 FILLMORE ST
STEINER ST
ALAMO SQUARE
1200 SCOTT ST
1300 DIVISADERO ST
1400 BRODERICK ST
1500 BAKER ST
1600 LYON ST
1700 CENTRAL AVE
1800 MASONIC AVE
1900 ASHBURY ST
2000 CLAYTON ST
2100 COLE ST
2200 SHRADER ST
END STANYAN ST
GUERRERO ST SF 10 C1
GUERRERO ST SF 14 C1
S FROM S MARKET ST BETWEEN
VALENCIA AND DOLORES STS
TO SAN JOSE AV
2 MARKET ST
100 DUBOCE AVE
132 CLINTON PARK
BROSNAN ST
200 14TH ST
300 15TH ST
400 16TH ST
GAISER CT
CAMP ST
500 17TH ST
DOLORES TER
550 DORLAND ST
600 18TH ST
700 19TH ST
800 20TH ST

850 LIBERTY ST
900 21ST ST
HILL ST
1000 22ND ST
ALVARADO ST
1100 23RD ST
ELIZABETH ST
1200 24TH ST
1300 25TH ST
JURI ST
1400 26TH ST
1454 ARMY ST
1500 27TH ST
1550 DUNCAN ST
1600 28TH ST
END SAN JOSE AVE
GUTTENBERG ST SF 20 A3
SE FROM 5501 MISSION ST
TO COUNTY LINE
2 MISSION ST
100 MORSE ST
200 BRUNSWICK ST
300 HANOVER ST
END COUNTY LINE
GUY PL SF 7 B2
W FROM S 1ST ST BETWEEN
FOLSOM ST AND HARRISON ST

H

H ST SF 17 B1
SE FROM SPEAR AV IN
HUNTERS POINT
HAHN ST SF 20 C3
N FROM SUNRISE WY TO LELAND AV
HAIGHT ST SF 9 C1
HAIGHT ST SF 10 A1
W FROM JUNCTION MARKET AND
GOUGH STS BETWEEN WALLER AND
PAGE STS TO STANYAN ST
2 MARKET ST
GOUGH ST
100 OCTAVIA ST
200 LAGUNA ST
300 BUCHANAN ST
400 WEBSTER ST
500 FILLMORE ST
600 STEINER ST
700 PIERCE ST
800 SCOTT ST
900 DIVISADERO ST
1000 BRODERICK ST
BUENA VISTA AVE
1100 BAKER ST
1200 LYON ST
BUENA VISTA AVE
1300 CENTRAL AVE
1400 MASONIC AVE
1500 ASHBURY ST
1600 CLAYTON ST
BELVEDERE ST
1700 COLE ST
1800 SHRADER ST
END STANYAN ST
HALE ST SF 15 A3
W FROM 2300 SAN BRUNO AV
TO BOWDOIN ST
2 SAN BRUNO AVE
100 BARNEVELD ST
200 MERRILL ST
300 BOYLSTON ST
END BOWDOIN ST
HALLAM ST SF 7 A3
S FROM S FOLSOM ST BETWEEN
7TH AND 8TH STS
HALLECK ST SF 1 C2
IN PRESIDIO
N FROM LINCOLN BLVD
HALLECK ST SF 3 B3
W FROM 201 FRONT ST BETWEEN
CALIFORNIA AND SACRAMENTO STS
TO LEIDESDORFF ST
2 FRONT ST
100 BATTERY ST
200 SANSOME ST
END LIEDESDORFF ST
HALYBURTON CT SF 3 C1
N FROM 13TH ST BET HUTCHINS CT &
BIGELOW CT, TREASURE ISLAND
HAMERTON AV SF 14 A3
BETWEEN BURNSIDE AV AND
CHILTON AV FROM CHENERY ST S
THEN N FROM MANGELS AV
HAMILTON ST SF 1 A2
IN PRESIDIO
S FROM MARINE DR
HAMILTON ST SF 21 A1
S FROM SILVER AV TO DELTA ST
2 SILVER AVE
100 SILLIMAN ST
200 FELTON ST
300 BURROWS ST
400 BACON ST
500 WAYLAND ST
600 WOOLSEY ST
700 DWIGHT ST
900 MANSELL ST
END DELTA ST
HAMLIN ST SF 2 C3
HAMPSHIRE ST SF 11 A2
S FROM ALAMEDA ST BETWEEN
PORTERO AV AND YORK ST
TO PERALTA AV
100 ALAMEDA ST
200 15TH ST
16TH ST
400 17TH ST
500 MARIPOSA ST
600 18TH ST
700 19TH ST
800 20TH ST
900 21ST ST
1000 22ND ST
1100 23RD ST
1200 24TH ST
1300 25TH ST
26TH ST
1500 ARMY ST
END PERALTA AVE
HANCOCK ST SF 10 B2
W FROM S CHURCH ST BETWEEN
18TH & 19TH STS TO NOE ST
2 CHURCH ST
100 SANCHEZ ST
END NOE ST
HANOVER ST SF 20 A3
SW FROM 300 BLOCK OF
POPE ST S OF BRUNSWICK ST
TO COUNTY LINE
50 POPE ST
100 ALLISON ST
200 WATT AVE
CONCORD ST
300 GUTTENBERG ST
400 LOWELL ST
END COUNTY LINE
HARBOR RD SF 16 A3
NW FROM NORTHRIDGE RD AND
INGALLS ST BETWEEN INNES AV
AND HUDSON AV
HARDIE PL SF 7 A1
E FROM 200 KEARNY ST BETWEEN
SUTTER ST AND BUSH ST
HARDIE RD SF 1 B3
IN PRESIDIO
S OF MORAGA AV
HARDING RD SF 18 A1
SE FROM SKYLINE BLVD S
FROM LAKE MERCED BLVD
HARE ST SF 16 A3
E FROM MIDDLE PT RD ONE BLK
N OF INNES AV
HARKNESS AV SF 21 A2
W FROM 3500 SAN BRUNO AV
BETWEEN WILDE AND WARD ST
TO DELTA ST
2 SAN BRUNO AVE
100 GIRARD ST
300 GOETTINGEN ST
SPARTA ST
BISHOP ST
RUTLAND ST
400 ALDER ST
MILL ST
DELTA ST
BOWDOIN ST
END MANSELL ST
HARLAN PL SF 7 A2
W FROM MARK LN BETWEEN BUSH
AND SUTTER STS
HARLEM AL SF 6 C2
N FROM S O FARRELL ST BETWEEN
LEAVENWORTH ST AND HYDE ST
HARLOW ST SF 10 B2
S FROM 3465 16TH ST BETWEEN
CHURCH ST AND SANCHEZ ST
TOWARDS 17TH ST
HARNEY WY SF 21 B3
SW FROM JAMESTOWN AV AT
CANDLESTICK PARK
HAROLD AV SF 19 C2
N FROM GETZ ST NEAR GRAFTON AV
TO OCEAN AV
2 GETZ ST
GRAFTON AVE
HOLLOWAY AVE
200 BRUCE ST
END OCEAN AVE
HARPER ST SF 14 B2
S FROM 30TH ST NEAR NOE ST
TO LAIDLEY ST
2 30TH ST
RANDALL ST
END LAIDLEY ST
HARRIET ST SF 7 A3
HARRIET ST SF 11 B1
SE FROM 1001 HOWARD ST BETWEEN
6TH AND 7TH STS TO A
POINT S OF BRANNAN ST
2 HOWARD ST
100 FOLSOM ST
200 HARRISON ST
300 BRYANT ST
400 BRANNAN ST
END PT S OF BRANNAN ST
HARRINGTON ST SF 20 A1
NW FROM S MISSION ST BETWEEN
SANTA ROSA ST AND NORTON ST
TO ALEMANY BLVD
HARRIS PL SF 2 B2
S FROM E S LAGUNA ST BETWEEN
FILBERT AND GREENWICH STS
HARRISON BLVD SF 1 A3
IN PRESIDIO
S OF KOBBE AV
HARRISON ST SF 7 A3
HARRISON ST SF 11 A2
HARRISON ST SF 15 A1
W FROM THE BAY BETWEEN FOLSOM
AND BRYANT STS AND S
TO RIPLEY ST
THE EMBARCADERO
2 STEUART ST
100 SPEAR ST
200 MAIN ST
300 BEALE ST
400 FREMONT ST
500 1ST ST
RINCON ST
ESSEX ST
STERLING ST
BRADLEY CT
600 2ND ST
VASSAR PL
650 HAWTHORNE ST
700 3RD ST
LAPU LAPU
800 4TH ST
900 5TH ST
MERLIN ST
OAK GROVE ST
MORRIS ST
1000 6TH ST
HARRIET ST
COLUMBIA SQUARE
SHERMAN ST
1100 7TH ST
1126 LANGTON ST
CHESLEY ST
BERWICK PL
HAYWARD ST
1200 8TH ST
GORDON ST
1300 9TH ST
DORE ST
1400 10TH ST
JUNIPER ST
1500 11TH ST
NORFOLK ST
1600 12TH ST
1700 13TH ST
1800 14TH ST
ALAMEDA ST
1900 15TH ST
16TH ST
2000 TREAT AVE
2100 17TH ST
MARIPOSA ST
2200 18TH ST
2300 19TH ST
2400 20TH ST
2500 21ST ST
2600 22ND ST
2700 23RD ST
2800 24TH ST
25TH ST
3000 26TH ST
3100 ARMY ST
3200 PRECITA AVE
3300 NORWICH ST
END RIPLEY ST
HARRY ST SF 14 B2
SW FROM LAIDLEY ST TO BEACON ST
HARTFORD ST SF 10 B2
S FROM S 17TH ST BETWEEN NOE
& CASTRO STS TO 20TH ST
2 17TH ST
100 18TH ST
200 19TH ST
END 20TH ST
HARVARD ST SF 20 C1
S FROM SILVER AV BETWEEN
OXFORD ST AND BAMBIER ST
TO BACON ST
2 SILVER AVE
100 PIOCHE ST
200 SILLIMAN ST
300 FELTON ST
400 BURROWS ST
END BACON ST
HASTINGS TER SF 2 C2
E FROM S HYDE ST BETWEEN
UNION ST AND FILBERT ST
HATTIE ST SF 10 A2
S FROM CORBETT AV W OF ORD ST
TO 18TH ST
HAVELOCK ST SF 19 C1
W FROM SAN JOSE AV 2
BLKS N OF OCEAN AV
TO A POINT W OF
EDNA ST
HAVENS ST SF 2 C2
W FROM S LEAVENWORTH ST
BETWEEN UNION AND FILBERT STS
HAVENSIDE DR SF 12 B3
S FROM OCEAN AV TO
EUCALYPTUS DR E OF
WESTMOORLAND DR
HAWES ST SF 21 C1
FROM PALOU AV SW TO JAMESTOWN AV
PALOU AVE
QUESADA AVE
REVERE AVE
SHAFTER AV
THOMAS AV
UNDERWOOD AV
VAN DYKE AV
YOSEMITE AV
ARMSTRONG AV
BANCROFT AV
CARROL AV
EGBERT AV
FITZGERALD AV
GILMAN AV
HOLLISTER AV
END JAMESTOWN AV
HAWTHORNE ST SF 7 B2
S FROM S HOWARD ST BETWEEN
2ND AND 3RD ST TO
HARRISON ST
HAYES ST SF 6 A3
HAYES ST SF 9 C1
W FROM JUNCTION MARKET ST
AND LARKIN ST BETWEEN FELL ST
& GROVE ST TO STANYAN ST
MARKET ST
LARKIN ST
100 POLK ST
200 VAN NESS AVE
300 FRANKLIN ST
400 GOUGH ST
500 OCTAVIA ST
600 LAGUNA ST
700 BUCHANAN ST
800 WEBSTER ST
900 FILLMORE ST
STEINER ST
PIERCE ST
1200 SCOTT ST
1300 DIVISADERO ST
1400 BRODERICK ST
1500 BAKER ST
1600 LYON ST
1700 CENTRAL AVE
1800 MASONIC AVE
1900 ASHBURY ST
2000 CLAYTON ST
2100 COLE ST
2200 SHRADER ST
END STANYAN ST
HAYWARD PL SF 11 A1
S FROM S HARRISON ST BETWEEN
7TH ST AND 8TH ST
HAZELWOOD AV SF 13 C3
E OF VALDEZ AV AND NW FROM
JUDSON AV TO YERBA BUENA AV
2 JUDSON AVE
GREENWOOD AVE
34 STAPLES AVE
66 FLOOD AVE
100 MONTECITO AVE
200 MONTEREY BLVD
JOOST AVE
300 MANGELS AVE
400 BRENTWOOD AVE
END YERBA BUENA AVE
HEAD ST SF 19 B2
W OF SAN JOSE AV NEAR
COUNTY LINE FROM
RANDOLPH N AND NE
TO ASHTON AV
400 RANDOLPH ST
500 SARGENT ST
600 SHIELDS ST
700 GARFIELD ST
800 HOLLOWAY AVE
END ASHTON AVE

HEARST AV SF 13 C3
HEARST AV SF 14 A3
W FROM CIRCULAR AV BETWEEN
MONTEREY BLVD AND FLOOD AV
TO RIDGEWOOD ST
2 CIRCULAR AVE
100 BADEN ST
200 CONGO ST
300 DETROIT ST
400 EDNA ST
500 FOERSTER ST
600 GENNESSEE ST
END RIDGEWOOD ST
HEATHER AV SF 5 C2
N FROM EUCLID AV TO
MAYFAIR DR W OF IRIS AV
HELEN ST SF 6 C1
S FROM S CALIFORNIA ST
BETWEEN LEAVENWORTH AND HYDE STS
HELENA ST SF 15 A2
E OF SAN BRUNO AV NEAR
SILVER AV N OF AUGUSTA ST
E FROM BAYSHORE BLVD
HEMLOCK ST SF 6 B2
W FROM S LARKIN ST BETWEEN
POST ST AND SUTTER ST
TO A POINT W OF LAGUNA ST
2 LARKIN ST
100 POLK ST
VAN NESS AVE
FRANKLIN ST
600 LAGUNA ST
END PT W OF LAGUNA ST
HEMWAY TER SF 5 C3
N FROM 1900 FULTON ST W OF
MASONIC AV
HENRY ST SF 10 B2
W FROM S SANCHEZ ST BETWEEN
14TH AND 15TH STS TO A
POINT W OF CASTRO ST
2 SANCHEZ ST
100 NOE ST
200 CASTRO ST
END PT W OF CASTRO ST
HERBST RD SF 12 A3
E FROM GREAT HIGHWAY TO
SKYLINE BLVD S OF SLOAT BLVD
HERMANN ST SF 10 B1
W FROM MARKET ST BETWEEN WALLER
ST AND DUBOCE AV TO STEINER ST
2 MARKET ST
LAGUNA ST
100 BUCHANAN ST
200 WEBSTER ST
CHURCH ST
300 FILLMORE ST
END STEINER ST
HERNANDEZ AV SF 13 B1
W FROM WOODSIDE AV TO
MERCED AV
2 WOODSIDE AVE
100 LAGUNA HONDA BLVD
200 VASQUEZ ST
END WOODSIDE AVE
HERON ST SF 11 A1
W FROM S BERWICK PL BETWEEN
FOLSOM AND HARRISON STS
TO 8TH ST
HESTER AV SF 21 B2
SE AND W FROM BAY SHORE
BLVD TO BAY SHORE BLVD
HEYMAN AV SF 14 C2
SE FROM 200 BLOCK COLERIDGE AV
TO PROSPECT AV
HICKORY ST SF 10 B1
W FROM S VAN NESS AV BETWEEN
OAK ST & FELL ST TO WEBSTER ST
2 VAN NESS AVE
100 FRANKLIN ST
200 GOUGH ST
300 OCTAVIA ST
LAGUNA ST
BUCHANAN ST
END WEBSTER ST
HICKS RD SF 1 B3
E OF ARGUELLO BLVD, PRESIDIO
HIDALGO TER SF 10 B2
E FROM S DOLORES BETWEEN 14TH ST
AND 15TH ST
HIGH ST SF 14 A1
S FROM 25TH ST W OF GRAND VIEW AV
TO CLIPPER ST
HIGHLAND AV SF 14 B2
E FROM ARLINGTON ST NEAR
CHARLES ST TO ANDOVER ST
ARLINGTON ST
100 MISSION ST
PATTON ST
300 HOLLY PARK CIR
BENNINGTON ST
END ANDOVER ST
HIGUERA AV SF 18 C2
W FROM ARBALLO DR TO
LAKE MERCED BLVD
HILIRITAS AV SF 14 A2
N FROM ARBOR ST TO DIAMOND ST
HILL BLVD S SF 20 B3
SE FROM S GENEVA TO COUNTY LINE
HILL DR SF 17 B1
HUNTERS POINT RES
HILL ST SF 10 B3
W FROM S VALENCIA ST BETWEEN
21ST ST & 22ND ST W TO CASTRO ST
2 VALENCIA ST
END GUERRERO ST
300 CHURCH ST
400 SANCHEZ ST
500 NOE ST
END CASTRO ST
HILLCREST CT SF 13 C3
S FROM MYRA WY E OF SHERWOOD CT
HILLPOINT AV SF 9 C2
N FROM PARNASSUS AV BETWEEN
WILLARD ST AND HILLWAY AV
HILLWAY AV SF 9 C2
N FROM PARNASSUS AV BETWEEN
WILLARD ST AND ARGUELLO BLVD
TO CARL ST
HILTON ST SF 15 A2
S FROM CORTLAND AV BETWEEN
BAYSHORE BLVD AND JAMES LICK FRWY
HIMMELMAN PL SF 2 C3
N FROM S PACIFIC AV BETWEEN
MASON ST & TAYLOR ST TO BROADWAY
HITCHCOCK ST SF 1 A2
E FROM HARRISON BLVD, PRESIDIO
HOBART AL SF 7 A2
E FROM S TAYLOR ST BETWEEN
POST ST AND SUTTER ST
HODGES AL SF 3 A2
N FROM 300 VALLEJO ST BETWEEN
SANSOME ST AND MONTGOMERY ST
HOFF ST SF 10 C2
S FROM S 16TH ST BETWEEN
MISSION ST AND VALENCIA ST
TO 17TH ST
HOFFMAN AV SF 10 A3
HOFFMAN AV SF 14 A1
S FROM GRAND VIEW AV TO
CLIPPER ST 1 BLK E OF MARKET ST
GRAND VIEW AV
2 22ND ST
100 ALVARADO ST
200 23RD ST
300 ELIZABETH ST
400 24TH ST
500 25TH ST
END CLIPPER ST
HOFFMAN ST SF 1 A2
S OF LINCOLN BLVD, PRESIDIO
HOLLADAY AV SF 15 A1
S FROM PERALTA AV S OF ARMY ST
TO MAYFLOWER ST
100 PERALTA AV
WRIGHT ST
YORK ST
300 RUTLEDGE ST
COSTA ST
FAITH ST
JOY ST
400 ESMERALDA AV
END MAYFLOWER ST
HOLLAND CT SF 7 A2
NW FROM S HOWARD ST BETWEEN
4TH ST AND 5TH ST
HOLLIS ST SF 6 B2
N FROM S ELLIS ST BETWEEN
LAGUNA ST AND WEBSTER ST TO
O'FARRELL ST
HOLLISTER AV SF 21 B1
FROM A POINT SE OF HAWES ST
NW TO 3RD ST
HAWES ST
INGALLS ST
JENNINGS ST
END 3RD ST
HOLLOWAY AV SF 19 B1
W FROM HAROLD AV TO TAPIA DR
2 HAROLD AV
100 LEE AV
200 BRIGHTON AV
300 PLYMOUTH AV
400 GRANADA AV
500 MIRAMAR AV
600 CAPITOL AV
700 FAXON AV
800 JULES AV
900 ASHTON AV
ORIZABA AV
BRIGHT ST
1100 HEAD ST
1200 VICTORIA ST
RAMSELL ST
1300 DE SOTO ST
ARCH ST
1400 CORONA ST
VERNON ST
1500 BORICA ST
RALSTON ST
1600 ALVISO ST
BIXBY ST
1700 MONTICELLO ST
1800 LUNADO WY
BEVERLY ST
JUNIPERO SERRA BLVD
STRATFORD DR
DENSLOWE DR
19TH AV
VARELA AV
CARDENAS AV
ARELLANO AV
END TAPIA DR
HOLLY PARK CIR SF 14 C2
SURROUNDING HOLLY PARK
ELSIE ST
BOCANA ST
NEWMAN ST
HIGHLAND AV
PARK ST
MURRAY ST
PARK ST
HIGHLAND AV
END APPLETON ST
HOLLYWOOD CT SF 20 A2
E OFF S POPE ST BETWEEN MORSE ST
AND MISSION ST
HOLYOKE ST SF 21 A1
S FROM SILVER AV BETWEEN
HAMILTON ST & SOMERSET ST TO
ANKENY ST, AND S FROM CAMPBELL AV
2 SILVER AV
END SILLIMAN ST
200 FELTON ST
300 BURROWS ST
400 BACON ST
500 WAYLAND ST
600 WOOLSEY ST
END KAREN CT
900 MANSELL ST
END ANKENY ST
CAMPBELL AV
HOMER ST SF 11 A1
SW FROM CHELSEY ST BETWEEN
HARRISON ST & BRYANT ST
AND 7TH ST AND 8TH ST
HOMESTEAD ST SF 14 A1
S FROM S 24TH ST BETWEEN
DOUGLASS ST AND HOFFMAN AV
TO CLIPPER ST
2 24TH ST
100 25TH ST
END CLIPPER ST
HOMEWOOD CT SF 19 B1
N FROM WILDWOOD WY BETWEEN
KEYSTONE WY & FAXON AV
HOOKER AL SF 7 A2
E FROM 700 MASON ST BETWEEN
PINE ST AND BUSH ST
HOOPER ST SF 11 B1
S FROM 1100 - 7TH ST
TO 8TH ST
HOPKINS AV SF 10 A3
NW FROM CORBETT AV NEAR 23RD ST
TO BURNETT AV
HORACE ST SF 15 A1
S FROM 25TH ST BETWEEN FOLSOM ST
AND SHOTWELL ST TO 26TH ST
HORNE AV SF 17 B1
SW FROM ROBINSON ST BETWEEN
FISHER AV AND COLEMAN ST
TO SPEAR AV
ROBINSON ST
GALVEZ AV
END SPEAR AV
HOTALING PL SF 3 B3
N FROM WASHINGTON ST BETWEEN
MONTGOMERY ST AND SANSOME ST
TO JACKSON ST
HOUSTON ST SF 2 C2
W FROM 1001 COLUMBUS AV BETWEEN
CHESTNUT ST AND FRANCISCO ST
TO JONES ST
HOWARD RD SF 4 C2
E FROM LINCOLN BLVD, PRESIDIO
HOWARD ST SF 7 A3
HOWARD ST SF 10 C1
SW FROM THE EMBARCADERO BETWEEN
MISSION ST AND FOLSOM ST
TO SOUTH VAN NESS AV
2 THE EMBARCADERO
50 STEUART ST
100 SPEAR ST
200 MAIN ST
300 BEALE ST
400 FREMONT ST
500 1ST ST
MALDEN AL
600 2ND ST
656 NEW MONTGOMERY ST
HAWTHORNE ST
700 3RD ST
800 4TH ST
HOLLAND CT
900 5TH ST
MARY ST
1000 6TH ST
HARRIET ST
RUSS ST
MOSS ST
1100 7TH ST
LANGTON ST
RAUSCH ST
SUMMER ST
1200 8TH ST
1300 9TH ST
WASHBURN ST
DORE ST
GRACE ST
1400 10TH ST
1500 11TH ST
LAFAYETTE ST
1600 12TH ST
END SOUTH VAN NESS AV
HOWE RD SF 1 A2
SW OF STOREY AV, PRESIDIO
HOWTH ST SF 19 C2
SW FROM 810 OCEAN AV TO RIDGE LN
2 OCEAN AV
100 GENEVA AV
200 NIAGARA AV
300 MT VERNON AV
END RIDGE LN
HUBBELL ST SF 11 B2
SW FROM 1300 7TH ST TO 16TH ST
HUDSON AV SF 15 B1
HUDSON AV SF 16 A3
NW FROM A POINT E OF INGALLS ST
TO TOLAND ST
INGALLS ST
BERTHA LN
WHITNEY YOUNG CIR
ARDATH CT
WESTBROOK CT
CASHMERE ST
REUEL CT
KEITH ST
MENDELL ST
NEWHALL ST
3RD ST
END PHELPS ST
SELBY ST
END TOLAND ST
HUGO ST SF 9 B2
FROM ARGUELLO BLVD BETWEEN
LINCOLN WY & IRVING ST TO 7TH AV
2 ARGUELLO BLVD
100 2ND AV
200 3RD AV
300 4TH AV
400 5TH AV
500 6TH AV
END 7TH AV
HULBERT AL SF 7 B3
N & S OFF CLARA ST BETWEEN
4TH ST AND 5TH ST
HUMBOLDT ST SF 11 C3
E FROM ILLINOIS ST BETWEEN
22ND ST AND 23RD ST
HUNT ST SF 7 B2
BETWEEN MISSION ST AND HOWARD ST
NORTHEAST FROM 3RD ST
HUNTERS PT BLVD SF 16 A2
SE FROM 1000 EVANS SE TO INNES ST
HUNTERS PT EXWY SF 21 C2
END OF JAMESTOWN AV AT
CANDLESTICK PARK
HUNTINGTON DR SF 12 B3
OFF COUNTRY CLUB DR
HURON AV SF 19 C2
SW FROM ALEMANY BL TO MISSION ST
ALEMANY BLVD
OTTAWA AV
SALA TER
FOOTE AV
FREDSON CT
NAGLEE AV
MONETA WY
WHIPPLE AV
MILAN TER
FARRAGUT AV
LAURA ST
LAWRENCE ST
SICKLES AV
END MISSION ST
HUSSEY ST SF 17 B1
SE FROM SPEAR AV, HUNTERS POINT
HUTCHINS CT SF 3 C1

N FROM 13TH ST BETWEEN KEPPLER CT
& HALYBURTON CT, TREASURE ISLAND
HYDE ST SF 2 C2
HYDE ST SF 6 C2
N FROM S MARKET AT GROVE ST
TO THE BAY
MARKET ST
GROVE ST
FULTON ST
2 MCALLISTER ST
100 GOLDEN GATE AV
200 TURK ST
300 EDDY ST
400 ELLIS ST
500 OFARRELL ST
MABEL AL
600 GEARY ST
700 POST ST
800 SUTTER ST
900 BUSH ST
1000 PINE ST
1100 CALIFORNIA ST
1200 SACRAMENTO ST
TROY AL
1300 CLAY ST
1400 WASHINGTON ST
1500 JACKSON ST
1600 PACIFIC AV
LYNCH ST
1700 BROADWAY ST
1800 VALLEJO ST
1900 GREEN ST
DELGADO PL
RUSSELL ST
WARNER PL
2000 UNION ST
ALLEN ST
HASTINGS TER
2100 FILBERT ST
2200 GREENWICH ST
2300 LOMBARD ST
2400 CHESTNUT ST
2500 FRANCISCO ST
2600 BAY ST
BERGIN PL
2700 NORTH POINT ST
2800 BEACH ST
2900 JEFFERSON

I

I ST SF 17 A1
SE FROM SPEAR AV TO J ST
IN HUNTERS POINT
ICEHOUSE AL SF 3 B2
N FROM 100 GREEN ST BETWEEN
BATTERY ST AND SANSOME ST
TO UNION ST
IDORA AV SF 13 B2
W FROM WOODSIDE AV TO GARCIA AV
IGNACIO ST SF 21 C2
S OF INGERSON AV OFF GILROY ST
ILLINOIS ST SF 11 C1
ILLINOIS ST SF 15 C1
S FROM 4TH ST TO TULARE ST
4TH ST
MERRIMAC ST
ALAMEDA ST
EL DORADO ST
16TH ST
17TH ST
MARIPOSA ST
18TH ST
19TH ST
20TH ST
22ND ST
HUMBOLDT ST
23RD ST
24TH ST
END 25TH ST
ARMY ST
MARIN ST
END TULARE ST
ILS LN SF 3 A3
OFF COLUMBUS AV BETWEEN
JACKSON ST AND WASHINGTON ST
IMPERIAL AV SF 2 B2
S FROM S GREENWICH ST BETWEEN
FRANKLIN ST AND GOUGH ST
INA CT SF 20 B1
EXTENSION OF MUNICH TO
LAGRANDE AV
INDIANA ST SF 11 C2
INDIANA ST SF 15 C1
S FROM MARIPOSA ST BETWEEN
MINNESOTA ST AND I-280
TO TULARE ST
500 MARIPOSA ST
600 18TH ST
700 19TH ST
800 20TH ST
1000 22ND ST
TUBBS ST
1200 23RD ST
1400 25TH ST
1500 26TH ST
1600 ARMY ST
MARIN ST
END TULARE ST
INDUSTRIAL ST SF 15 A2
SW FROM OAKDALE AV TO BAYSHORE BL
INFANTRY TER SF 1 B3
IN PRESIDIO
INGALLS ST SF 16 A3
INGALLS ST SF 21 C1
SW FROM INNES AV TO JAMESTOWN AV
INNES AV
HARBOR RD
HUDSON AV
NORTHRIDGE RD
ROSIE LEE LN
KISKA RD
BEATRICE LN
LA SALLE AV
WHITFIELD CT
GEORGE CT
OAKDALE AV
PALOU AV
QUESADA AV
REVERE AV
SHAFTER AV
THOMAS AV
UNDERWOOD ST
VAN DYKE AV
WALLACE AV
YOSEMITE AV
ARMSTRONG AV
BANCROFT AV
CARROLL AV
DONNER AV
EGBERT AV
FITZGERALD AV
GILMAN AV
HOLLISTER AV
INGERSON AV
END JAMESTOWN AV
INGERSON AV SF 21 B1
NW FROM GIANTS DR TO 3RD ST
GIANTS DR
GILROY ST
GRIFFITH ST
CORONADO ST
HAWES ST
REDONDO ST
INGALLS ST
JENNINGS ST
END 3RD ST
INNES AV SF 15 B1
INNES AV SF 16 A3
NW FROM COLEMAN ST TO
TO MILTON ROSS ST
COLEMAN ST
FRIEDELL ST
DONAHUE ST
EARL ST
FITCH ST
HUNTERS PT BLVD
END MIDDLE PT RD
MENDELL ST
3RD ST
NEWHALL ST
END PHELPS ST
RANKIN ST
END MILTON ROSS ST
INVERNESS DR SF 12 C3
S FROM SLOAT BLVD BETWEEN
FOREST VIEW DR AND 26TH AV
TO EUCALYPTUS DR
IOWA ST SF 11 C3
S FROM 22ND ST BETWEEN INDIANA AV
AND PENNSYLVANIA AV TO 23RD ST
700 22ND ST
900 23RD ST
IRIS AV SF 5 C2
N FROM EUCLID AV TO MAYFAIR DR
IRON AL SF 10 A3
S FROM CLAYTON ST
TO GRAYSTONE TER
IRVING ST SF 8 A2
IRVING ST SF 9 A2
W FROM ARGUELLO BLVD S OF
LINCOLN WY TO THE GREAT HIGHWAY
2 ARGUELLO BLVD
100 2ND AV
200 3RD AV
300 4TH AV
400 5TH AV
500 6TH AV
600 7TH AV
700 8TH AV
800 9TH AV
900 10TH AV
1000 11TH AV
1100 12TH AV
1200 FUNSTON AV
1300 14TH AV
1400 15TH AV
1500 16TH AV
1600 17TH AV
1700 18TH AV
1800 19TH AV
1900 20TH AV
2000 21ST AV
2100 22ND AV
2200 23RD AV
2300 24TH AV
2400 25TH AV
2500 26TH AV
2600 27TH AV
2700 28TH AV
2800 29TH AV
2900 30TH AV
3000 31ST AV
3100 32ND AV
3200 33RD AV
3300 34TH AV
3400 35TH AV
3500 36TH AV
SUNSET BLVD
3600 37TH AV
3700 38TH AV
3800 39TH AV
3900 40TH AV
4000 41ST AV
4100 42ND AV
4200 43RD AV
4300 44TH AV
4400 45TH AV
4500 46TH AV
4600 47TH AV
4700 48TH AV
END LA PLAYA ST
IRWIN ST SF 11 B2
S FROM 2700 7TH ST TO 8TH ST
TO 8TH ST
ISADORA DNCN LN SF 7 A2
W FROM TAYLOR ST BETWEEN
GEARY ST AND POST ST
ISIS ST SF 10 C1
S FROM 12TH ST BETWEEN FOLSOM ST
AND HARRISON ST TO 13TH ST
ISLAIS ST SF 15 C1
E FROM THE END OF NAPOLEON ST
TO ARTHUR AV
ISOLA WY SF 13 C2
SW FROM TERESITA BLVD
TO ROCKDALE DR
ITALY AV SF 20 A2
SE FROM 5001 MISSION ST S OF
FRANCE AV TO MOSCOW ST
2 MISSION ST
100 LONDON ST
200 PARIS ST
300 LISBON ST
400 MADRID ST
500 EDINBURGH ST
600 NAPLES ST
700 VIENNA ST
800 ATHENS ST
END MOSCOW ST
IVY ST SF 6 B3
W FROM FRANKLIN ST BETWEEN HAYES
ST AND GROVE ST W TO WEBSTER ST
200 FRANKLIN ST
300 GOUGH ST
500 LAGUNA ST
600 BUCHANAN ST
END WEBSTER ST

J

J ST SF 17 A1
S OFF SPEAR ST
SPEAR AV
6TH AV
3RD AV
I ST
MAHAN ST
JACK KEROUAC ST SF 3 A3
E FROM GRANT AV BETWEEN
PACIFIC AV AND BROADWAY
TO COLUMBUS AV
JACK LONDON ST SF 7 B3
S FROM S BRYANT ST BETWEEN
2ND ST AND 3RD ST TO BRANNAN ST
JACKSON ST SF 2 A3
JACKSON ST SF 3 A3
JACKSON ST SF 5 B2
W FROM THE BAY BETWEEN PACIFIC AV
AND WASHINGTON ST TO ARGUELLO BL
DRUMM ST
100 DAVIS ST
200 FRONT ST
300 BATTERY ST
CUSTOM HOUSE PL
400 SANSOME ST
BALANCE ST
HOTALING PL
500 MONTGOMERY ST
COLUMBUS AV
600 KEARNY ST
COOPER AL
WENTWORTH PL
BECKETT ST
700 GRANT AV
ST LOUIS PL
JASON CT
ROSS AL
DUNCOMBE AL
800 STOCKTON ST
BEDFORD PL
JAMES AL
STONE ST
ADELE CT
900 POWELL ST
DORIC AL
1000 MASON ST
MARCY PL
AUBURN ST
1100 TAYLOR ST
1200 JONES ST
1300 LEAVENWORTH ST
WALL PL
1400 HYDE ST
1500 LARKIN ST
1600 POLK ST
1700 VAN NESS AV
1800 FRANKLIN ST
1900 GOUGH ST
2000 OCTAVIA ST
2100 LAGUNA ST
2200 BUCHANAN ST
2300 WEBSTER ST
2400 FILLMORE ST
2500 STEINER ST
2600 PIERCE ST
2700 SCOTT ST
2800 DIVISADERO ST
2900 BRODERICK ST
3000 BAKER ST
3100 LYON ST
3200 PRESIDIO AV
3300 WALNUT ST
3400 LAUREL ST
3500 LOCUST ST
3600 SPRUCE ST
3700 MAPLE ST
3800 CHERRY ST
END ARGUELLO BLVD
JADE PL SF 14 A2
W FROM GOLDMINE DR 3 BLKS W
OF DIAMOND HEIGHTS BLVD
JAMES AL SF 3 A3
S FROM JACKSON ST BETWEEN
STOCKTON ST AND POWELL ST
JAMES LICK FRWY SF 15 A2
JAMES LICK FRWY SF 21 A1
JAMES LICK SKWY SF 11 A1
JAMESTOWN AV SF 21 C3
FROM HUNTERS PT EXPWY N W
TO SALINAS AV
HUNTERS PT EXPWY
HARNEY WY
GILROY ST
GRIFFITH ST
CORONADO ST
HAWES ST
REDONDO ST
INGALLS ST
JENNINGS ST
3RD ST
KEY ST
END SALINAS AV
JANSEN ST SF 2 C2
N FROM 800 GREENWICH ST BETWEEN
MASON & TAYLOR STS TO LOMBARD ST
JARBOE AV SF 14 C2
E FROM 300 MOULTRIE ST
TO PERALTA AV
100 MOULTRIE ST
200 ANDERSON ST
300 ELLSWORTH ST
400 GATES ST
500 FOLSOM ST
600 BANKS ST
700 PRENTISS ST
800 NEVADA ST
900 PUTNAM ST
1000 BRONTE ST
1100 BRADFORD ST
1200 PERALTA AV
JASON CT SF 3 A3
OFF 700 JACKSON ST BETWEEN
GRANT AV AND STOCKTON ST
JASPER PL SF 3 A3
N FROM 500 GREEN ST BETWEEN
GRANT AV AND STOCKTON ST

TO FILBERT ST
2 GREEN ST
100 UNION ST
END FILBERT ST
JAVA ST SF 10 A2
SW FROM BUENA VISTA AV
TO MASONIC AV
JEAN WY SF 5 C3
NW FROM EWING TER TO ANZA ST
S OF GEARY BLVD
JEFFERSON ST SF 2 A2
W FROM THE BAY N OF BEACH ST
TO THE PRESIDIO
2 POWELL ST
THE EMBARCADERO
100 MASON ST
200 TAYLOR ST
300 JONES ST
400 LEAVENWORTH ST
END HYDE ST
WEBSTER ST
END FILLMORE ST
1800 SCOTT ST
1900 DIVISADERO ST
2000 BRODERICK ST
END BAKER ST
JENNINGS ST SF 16 A2
JENNINGS ST SF 21 B1
SW FROM CARGO WY TO MEADE AV
CARGO WY
END HUNTERS POINT BLVD
PALOU AV
QUESADA AV
REVERE AV
SHAFTER AV
THOMAS AV
UNDERWOOD AV
VAN DYKE AV
WALLACE AV
YOSEMITE AV
ARMSTRONG AV
BANCROFT AV
CARROLL AV
DONNER AV
EGBERT AV
FITZGERALD AV
GILMAN AV
HOLLISTER AV
INGERSON AV
JAMESTOWN AV
KEY AV
LE CONTE AV
MEADE AV
END
JEROME AL SF 3 A3
S FROM 501 PACIFIC AV BETWEEN
MONTGOMERY ST AND KEARNY ST
JERROLD AV SF 15 B1
JERROLD AV SF 16 A3
JERROLD AV SF 17 A1
NW FROM MENDELL ST TO BAYSHORE BL
MENDELL ST
NEWHALL ST
3RD ST
PHELPS ST
QUINT ST
RANKIN ST
SELBY ST
MILTON ROSS ST
LETTUCE LN
TOLAND ST
UPTON ST
NAPOLEON ST
BARNEVELD AVE
BAY SHORE BLVD
JERSEY ST SF 14 A1
W FROM S DOLORES ST BETWEEN
24TH ST AND 25TH ST
TO DOUGLASS ST
2 DOLORES ST
CHATTANOOGA ST
100 CHURCH ST
VICKSBURG ST
200 SANCHEZ ST
300 NOE ST
400 CASTRO ST
500 DIAMOND ST
END DOUGLASS ST
JESSIE ST SF 6 C3
JESSIE ST SF 7 A2
JESSIE ST SF 10 C1
W FROM S 1ST ST BETWEEN MARKET ST
AND MISSION ST SW TO A POINT
S OF MCCOPPIN ST
2 1ST ST
ECKER ST
ANTHONY ST
100 2ND ST
NEW MONTGOMERY ST
188 ANNIE ST
END 3RD ST
300 4TH ST
END 5TH ST
400 MINT ST
END 6TH ST
END 7TH ST
800 9TH ST
900 10TH ST
JEWETT ST SF 7 B3
SW FROM 4TH ST BETWEEN KING ST
& TOWNSEND ST TO 5TH ST
JOHN ST SF 3 A3
W FROM 1201 POWELL ST BETWEEN
JACKSON ST AND PACIFIC AV
TO MASON ST
J F KENNEDY DR SF 8 A1
IN GOLDEN GATE PARK
J F KENNEDY DR SF 9 A1
IN GOLDEN GATE PARK
J F SHELLEY DR SF 20 C1
IN JOHN MCLAREN PARK
JOHN MUIR DR SF 18 B2
SE FROM SKYLINE BLVD TO
LAKE MERCED BLVD
JOHNSTONE DR SF 9 C3
N FROM CLARENDON AV ONE BLK
W OF STANYAN
JOICE ST SF 3 A3
N FROM 700 PINE BETWEEN
STOCKTON ST AND POWELL ST
TO CLAY ST
2 PINE ST
100 CALIFORNIA ST
200 SACRAMENTO ST
END CLAY ST
JONES ST SF 2 C2
JONES ST SF 7 A2
N FROM S MARKKET ST BETWEEN
TAYLOR ST AND LEAVENWORTH ST
TO THE BAY
2 MARKET ST
MCALLISTER ST
100 GOLDEN GATE AV
200 TURK ST
300 EDDY ST
400 ELLIS ST
ANTONIO ST
STEVELOE PL
500 OFARRELL ST
600 GEARY ST
COLIN PL
700 POST ST
COSMO PL
800 SUTTER PL
900 BUSH ST
1000 PINE
1100 CALIFORNIA ST
1200 SACRAMENTO ST
PLEASANT ST
1300 CLAY ST
1400 WASHINGTON ST
1500 JACKSON ST
1600 PACIFIC AV
BERNARD ST
1700 BROADWAY
GLOVER ST
1800 VALLEJO ST
1900 GREEN ST
MACONDRAY ST
2000 UNION ST
2100 FILBERT ST
VALPARAISO ST
2200 GREENWICH ST
2300 LOMBARD ST
2400 CHESTNUT ST
HOUSTON ST
2500 FRANCISCO ST
COLUMBUS AV
2600 BAY ST
2700 NORTH POINT ST
2800 BEACH ST
2900 JEFFERSON ST
END THE EMBARCADERO
JOOST AV SF 13 C3
N FROM CIRCULAR AV AND DIAMOND ST
TO HAZELWOOD AV
2 CIRCULAR AV
BROMPTON AV
LIPPARD AV
100 ACADIA ST
200 BADEN ST
300 CONGO ST
400 DETROIT ST
500 EDNA ST
600 FOERSTER ST
700 GENNESSEE ST
800 RIDGEWOOD AV
END HAZELWOOD AV
JORDAN AV SF 5 C2
S FROM S CALIFORNIA ST BETWEEN
COMMONWEALTH AV AND PALM AV
TO GEARY ST
2 CALIFORNIA ST
100 EUCLID AV
END GEARY ST
JOSEPHA AV SF 19 A2
S FROM JUAN BAUTISTA CIR
TO GONZALES DR
JOSIAH AV SF 19 C2
BETWEEN MARGARET AV AND LEE AV
CROSSING LAKE VIEW AV SW FROM
RIDGE LN
JOY ST SF 15 A2
FROM BREWSTER ST TO A POINT E OF
HOLLADAY AV
JUAN BATSTA CIR SF 19 A2
CIRCLE W OF JUNIPERO SERRA BLVD
N OF BROTHERHOOD WY
FONT BLVD
FUENTE AV
CRESPI DR
DIAZ AV
FONT BLVD
JOSEPHA AV
GRIJALVA DR
BUCARELI DR
JUANITA WY SF 13 B2
SW FROM TERESITA BLVD TO
MIRALOMA DR
2 TERESITA BLVD
FOWLER AV
100 EVELYN WY
200 DEL SUR AV
250 REX AV
300 MARNE AV
LANSDALE AV
END MIRALOMA DR
JUDAH ST SF 8 A2
JUDAH ST SF 9 A2
FROM 5TH AVE BET IRVING
AND KIRKHAM STS W TO
GREAT HIGHWAY
2 5TH AV
100 6TH AV
200 7TH AV
300 8TH AV
400 9TH AV
500 10TH AV
600 11TH AV
700 12TH AV
800 FUNSTON AV
900 14TH AV
1000 15TH AV
1100 16TH AV
1200 17TH AV
1300 18TH AV
1400 19TH AV
1500 20TH AV
1600 21ST AV
1700 22ND AV
1800 23RD AV
1900 24TH AV
2000 25TH AV
2100 26TH AV
2200 27TH AV
2300 28TH AV
2400 29TH AV
2500 30TH AV
2600 31ST AV
2700 32ND AV
2800 33RD AV
2900 34TH AV
3000 35TH AV
PINO AL
3100 36TH AV
SUNSET BLVD
3200 37TH AV
3300 38TH AV
3400 39TH AV
3500 40TH AV
3600 41ST AV
3700 42ND AV
3800 43RD AV
3900 44TH AV
4000 45TH AV
4100 46TH AV
4200 47TH AV
4300 48TH AV
LA PLAYA ST
END GREAT HIGHWAY
JUDSON AV SF 19 C1
FROM DETROIT ST BET
STAPLES AND MARSTON AVES
W TO HAZELWOOD AVE
100 DETROIT ST
200 EDNA ST
300 FOERSTER ST
400 GENNESSEE ST
500 PHELAN AV
END HAZELWOOD AV
JULES AV SF 19 B1
N FROM LAKE VIEW AV BETWEEN
FAXON AV AND ASHTON AV TO
OCEAN AV
2 LAKE VIEW AV
100 GRAFTON AV
200 HOLLOWAY AV
300 DE MONTFORD AV
END OCEAN AV
JULIA ST SF 7 A3
S FROM S MISSION ST BETWEEN
7TH ST & 8TH ST TO NATOMA ST
2 MISSION ST
44 MINNA ST
END NATOMA ST
JULIAN AV SF 10 C1
S FROM S 14TH ST BETWEEN
2 14TH ST
MISSION ST AND VALENCIA
ST TO 16TH ST
100 15TH ST
END 16TH ST
JULIUS ST SF 3 A2
N FROM 300 LOMBARD ST BETWEEN
KEARNY ST AND GRANT AV
JUNIOR TER SF 20 A2
E AND N FROM CAYUGA AV
NEAR ALEMANY BLVD
JUNIPER ST SF 11 A1
S FROM S FOLSOM ST BETWEEN
10TH ST AND 11TH ST
TO BRYANT ST
2 FOLSOM ST
100 HARRISON ST
END BRYANT ST
JUNIPRO SRRA BL SF 19 A2
S FROM ST FRANCIS BLVD TO
COUNTY LINE
ST FRANCIS BLVD
SLOAT BLVD
WOODACRE DR
MONTEREY BLVD
DARIEN WY
300 OCEAN AV
ROSSMOOR DR
MONCADA WY
PALOMA AV
STONECREST DR
EL PLAZUELA WY
WINSTON DR
MERCEDES WY
STONECREST DR
LYNDHURST DR
800 ESTERO AV
WYTON LN
HOLLOWAY AV
GARFIELD ST
1000 STRATFORD DR
SHIELDS ST
19TH AV
FONT BLVD
BROTHERHOOD WY
PALMETTO AV
COUNTY LINE
JURI ST SF 14 C1
W FROM SAN JOSE AV BETWEEN
25TH ST AND 26TH ST
JUSTIN DR SF 14 B3
S FROM 301 COLLEGE AV
AND W TO ALEMANY BLVD
2 COLLEGE AV
AGNON AV
100 MURRAY ST
200 BENTON AV
300 COLLEGE AV
400 GENEBERN WY
END ALEMANY BLVD

K

KANSAS ST SF 11 A1
S FROM DIVISION ST BETWEEN
RHODE ISLAND AND VERMONT
STS TO MARIN ST
2 DIVISION ST
100 ALAMEDA ST
200 15TH ST
300 16TH ST
400 17TH ST
500 MARIPOSA ST
600 18TH ST
700 19TH ST
END 20TH ST
1000 22ND ST
1200 23RD ST
1300 24TH ST
1400 25TH ST
END 26TH ST
1600 ARMY ST
END MARIN ST
KAPLAN LN SF 7 B2
FROM CLEMENTINA ST NEAR
3RD ST BET HOWARD ST
AND FOLSOM ST
KAREN CT SF 21 A1
S OF WOOLLSEY STREET BETWEEN
HAMILTON AND GOETTINGEN STREET

KATE ST SF 11 A1
S FROM S BRYANT ST BETWEEN
7TH ST AND 8TH ST
KEARNY ST SF 3 A2
KEARNY ST SF 7 A1
N FROM S MARKET ST BETWEEN
MONTGOMERY ST AND GRANT AV
TO THE EMBARCADERO
2 MARKET ST
GEARY ST
MAIDEN LN
100 POST ST
VER MEHR PL
200 SUTTER ST
HARDIE PL
300 BUSH ST
400 PINE ST
500 CALIFORNIA ST
600 SACRAMENTO ST
COMMERCIAL ST
700 CLAY ST
MERCHANT ST
800 WASHINGTON ST
900 JACKSON ST
COLUMBUS AV
1000 PACIFIC AV
NOTTINGHAM PL
1100 BROADWAY
DUNNES AL
FRESNO ST
1200 VALLEJO ST
1300 GREEN ST
1400 UNION ST
END FILBERT ST
1700 LOMBARD ST
END LA FERRERA TER
1900 FRANCISCO ST
2000 BAY ST
N POINT ST
END THE EMBARCADERO
KEITH ST SF 15 C2
KEITH ST SF 21 B2
FROM EVANS AV SW TO 3RD ST
EVANS AV
FAIRFAX AV
END HUDSON AV
NEWCOMB AV
1400 OAKDALE AV
1500 PALOU AV
1600 QUESADA AV
1700 REVERE AV
1800 SHAFTER AV
1900 THOMAS AV
2000 UNDERWOOD AV
2100 VAN DYKE AV
2200 WALLACE AV
2300 YOSEMITE AV
2400 ARMSTRONG AV
BANCROFT AV
END CARROLL AV
END 3RD ST
KELLOCH AV SF 21 A3
W FROM SCHWERIN ST TWO
BLKS S OF SUNNYDALE AV
KEMPTON AV SF 19 B3
N FROM ALEMANY BLVD TWO
BLKS E OF JUNIPERO SERRA
KENNEDY AV SF 1 C2
IN PRESIDIO
SW OF RICHARDSON AV
KNNTH REXRTH PL SF 3 A3
S FROM 601 VALLEJO ST BETWEEN
COLUMBUS AV & STOCKTON ST
KENNY AL SF 20 A2
FROM 4901 BLOCK OF
MISSION ST BETWEEN FRANCE AV
AND ITALY AV TO LONDON ST
KENSINGTON WY SF 13 B2
FROM 1096 PORTOLA DR TO
CLAREMONT BLVD
2 PORTOLA DR
100 ULLOA ST
300 VASQUEZ ST
MERCED AV
END CLAREMONT BLVD
KENT ST SF 3 A2
W FROM 1802 MASON ST BETWEEN
UNION ST AND FILBERT ST
KENWOOD WY SF 19 B1
W FROM FAXON AV N
OF WILDWOOD WY TO SAN ALESO AV
2 FAXON AV
DARIEN WY
100 KEYSTONE WY
200 FAIRFIELD WY
300 MANOR DR
400 PINEHURST WY
END WESTGATE DR
KEPPLER CT SF 3 C1
S FROM 13TH ST BETWEEN GATEVIEW
AV & HUTCHINS CT, TREASURE ISLAND
KERN ST SF 14 B3
W FROM DIAMOND ST TO
BROMPTON AV N OF BOSWORTH ST
KEY AV SF 21 B2
NW FROM A POINT S OF JENNINGS ST
TO LANE ST & BAYSHORE BLVD
SOUTH OF LE CONTE AV
LE CONTE AV
JENNINGS ST
3RD ST
KEITH ST
LANE ST
END BAY SHORE BLVD
KEYES AL SF 3 A3
N FROM 900 PACIFIC AV BETWEEN
POWELL ST AND MASON ST
KEYES AV SF 1 B2
IN PRESIDIO
S FROM LINCOLN BLVD
KEYSTONE WY SF 19 B1
N FROM 1900 OCEAN AV N TO
KENWOOD WY
KEZAR DR SF 9 B2
WESTERLY END OF WALLER ST
TO LINCOLN WY
KIMBALL PL SF 2 C3
N FROM 1400 SACRAMENTO ST AND S
BETWEEN LEAVENWORTH & HYDE STS
KING ST SF 11 B1
SW FROM THE BAY BETWEEN BERRY AND
TOWNSEND STS TO
DIVISION ST
2 THE EMBARCADERO
GALE ST
100 2ND ST
200 3RD ST
300 4TH ST
400 5TH ST
500 6TH ST
600 7TH ST
END DIVISION ST
KINGSTON ST SF 14 C2
E FROM 837 SAN JOSE AV TO
PROSPECT AV
2 SAN JOSE AV
100 MISSION ST
200 COLERIDGE AV
END PROSPECT AV
KINZEY ST SF 1 A2
IN PRESIDIO
N OF RALSTON AV
KIRKHAM ST SF 8 A3
KIRKHAM ST SF 9 A2
W FROM 4TH AV RO LA PLAYA
2 4TH AV
100 5TH AV
200 6TH AV
300 7TH AV
400 8TH AV
500 9TH AV
600 10TH AV
700 11TH AV
800 12TH AV
900 FUNSTON AV
1000 14TH AV
1100 15TH AV
1200 16TH AV
1300 17TH AV
1400 18TH AV
1500 19TH AV
1600 20TH AV
1700 21ST AV
1800 22ND AV
1900 23RD AV
2000 24TH AV
2100 25TH AV
2200 26TH AV
2300 27TH AV
2400 28TH AV
2500 29TH AV
2600 30TH AV
2700 31ST AV
2800 32ND AV
2900 33RD AV
3000 34TH AV
3100 35TH AV
PINO AL
3200 36TH AV
SUNSET BLVD
3300 37TH AV
3400 38TH AV
3500 39TH AV
3600 40TH AV
3700 41ST AV
3800 42ND AV
3900 43RD AV
4000 44TH AV
4100 45TH AV
4200 46TH AV
4300 47TH AV
4400 48TH AV
END GREAT HIGHWAY
KIRKWOOD AV SF 15 B2
NW FROM A POINT SW OF MENDELL
ST TO TOLAND ST
MENDELL ST
3RD ST
NEWHALL ST
END PHELPS ST
SOUTH OF RANKIN ST
RANKIN ST
SELBY ST
MILTON ROSS ST
LETTUCE LN
END TOLAND ST
SE FROM END TOLAND ST TO A POINT
SE OF FRIEDELL ST
KISKA RD SF 16 A3
FROM INGALLS ST TO KIRKWOOD
AV S OF NORTHRIDGE RD
KISSLING ST SF 10 C1
W FROM POINT E OF 11TH ST
BETWEEN HOWARD ST AND FOLSOM ST
TO 12TH ST
KITTREDGE TER SF 5 C3
S FROM TURK ST TO GOLDEN
GATE AV E OF CHABOT TER
KNOLLVIEW WY SF 13 C1
N FROM CITY VIEW WY
TO PANORAMA DR
3 BLKS N OF TWIN PEAKS BLVD
KNOTT CT SF 20 A3
W FROM WATT AV 1 BLK S
OF HANOVER ST
KOBBE AV SF 1 A3
IN PRESIDIO
N OF HITCHCOCK ST
18TH ST
KONA RD SF 15 B1
S FROM 2200 ARMY ST TO KANSAS ST
KRAMER PL SF 3 A2
S FROM 501 GREENWICH ST BETWEEN
GRANT AV AND STOCKTON ST
KRAUSGRILL PL SF 3 A2
N FROM 500 FILBERT ST BETWEEN
GRANT AV AND STOCKTON ST
KRONQUIST CT SF 14 B1
N FROM S 27TH ST BETWEEN
CASTRO AND DIAMOND STS

L

LA AVANZADA SF 9 C3
SW FROM PALO ALTO AV BETWEEN
GLENBROOK AV AND CLARENDON AV
LA BICA WY SF 13 C2
S FROM AGUA WY TO ST CROIX DR
LAFAYETTE ST SF 10 C1
SE FROM S MISSION ST BETWEEN
11TH AND 12TH STS TO HOWARD ST
LA FERRERA TER SF 3 A2
W FROM S KEARNY ST BETWEEN
LOMBARD AND CHESTNUT STS
LA GRANDE AV SF 20 B2
FROM PERU AV SW TO PERSIA AV
100 AVALON AV
INCA CT
MANSFIELD ST
END BURROWS ST
300 BRAZIL AV
DUBLIN ST
400 PERSIA AV
RUSSIA AV
END S OF RUSSIA AV
LAGUNA ST SF 2 B3
LAGUNA ST SF 6 B3
LAGUNA ST SF 10 B1
N FROM S MARKET ST BETWEEN
OCTAVIA ST AND BUCHANAN ST
TO BEACH ST
2 MARKET ST
HERMANN ST
100 WALLER ST
200 HAIGHT ST
230 ROSE ST
300 PAGE ST
312 LILY ST
400 OAK ST
550 HICKORY ST
500 FELL ST
516 LINDEN ST
600 HAYES ST
650 IVY ST
700 GROVE ST
750 BIRCH ST
600 FULTON ST
ASH ST
900 MCALLISTER ST
REDWOOD ST
1000 GOLDEN GATE AV
1100 TURK ST
1200 EDDY ST
1250 WILLOW ST
1300 ELLIS ST
1350 CLEARY CT
END GEARY ST
1600 POST ST
1650 HEMLOCK ST
1700 SUTTER ST
1750 FERN ST
1800 BUSH ST
1900 PINE ST
2000 CALIFORNIA ST
2100 SACRAMENTO ST
2200 CLAY ST
2300 WASHINGTON ST
2400 JACKSON ST
2500 PACIFIC AV
2600 BROADWAY
2700 VALLEJO ST
2800 GREEN ST
2900 UNION ST
3000 FILBERT ST
HARRIS PL
3100 GREENWICH ST
3200 LOMBARD ST
MAGNOLIA ST
3300 CHESTNUT ST
3400 FRANCISCO ST
BAY ST
NORTH POINT ST
END BEACH ST
LAGUNA HONDA BL SF 13 B1
SE FROM 7TH AV TO DEWEY BLVD
7TH AV
CLARENDON AV
PLAZA DR
END DEWEY BLVD
LAGUNITAS DR SF 13 A3
SW FROM SLOAT BLVD TO
OCEAN AV E OF 19TH AV
LAIDLEY ST SF 14 B2
S FROM S 30TH ST BETWEEN NOE
AND CASTRO STS TO CASTRO ST
2 30TH ST
NOE ST
100 HARRY ST
HARPER ST
200 FAIRMOUNT ST
300 MIGUEL ST
400 MATEO ST
500 ROANOKE ST
END CASTRO ST
LAKE ST SF 4 B2
LAKE ST SF 5 A2
W FROM ARGUELLO BLVD N OF
CALIFORNIA ST TO
EL CAMINO DEL MAR
2 ARGUELLO BLVD
100 2ND AV
200 3RD AV
300 4TH AV
400 5TH AV
500 6TH AV
600 7TH AV
700 8TH AV
800 9TH AV
900 10TH AV
1000 11TH AV
1100 12TH AV
FUNSTON AV
PARK PRESIDIO BLVD
1300 14TH AV
1400 15TH AV
1500 16TH AV
1600 17TH AV
1700 18TH AV
1800 19TH AV
1900 20TH AV
2000 21ST AV
2100 22ND AV
2200 23RD AV
2300 24TH AV
2400 25TH AV
2500 26TH AV
2600 27TH AV
2700 28TH AV
2800 29TH AV
2900 30TH AV
END EL CAMINO DEL MAR
LAKE FOREST CT SF 9 B3
N FROM OAK PARK DR BETWEEN
DEVONSHIRE & CHRISTOPHER DR
LAKE MERCED BL SF 12 B3
LAKE MERCED BL SF 18 C2
SE FROM SKYLINE BLVD
S TO ALEMANY BLVD
LAKE MERCED HILL SF 18 C3
E FROM LAKE MERCED BLVD
WITHIN SF GOLF CLUB
LAKE SHORE DR SF 12 B3
OFF OCEAN AV - S OF SLOAT
BLVD - CIRCULAR
LAKE SHORE PZ SF 12 B3
S FROM SLOAT BLVD E OF 34TH AV
LAKEVIEW AV SF 19 B2

NW FROM SAN JOSE AV AND
W TO ORIZABA AV
2 SAN JOSE AV
100 CAINE AV
200 MAJESTIC AV
300 MARGARET AV
400 JOSIAH AV
500 LEE AV
SUMMIT ST
550 BRIGHTON AV
600 PLYMOUTH AV
636 GRANADA AV
672 MIRAMAR AV
700 CAPITOL AV
730 FAXON AV
756 JULES AV
ASHTON AV
END ORIZABA AV
LAKEWOOD AV SF 19 B1
N FROM 2000 OCEAN AV TO
FAIRFIELD WY
LAMARTINE ST SF 14 B3
N FROM CAYUGA AV W OF
DANTON ST
LAMSON LN SF 10 A3
N FROM 19TH ST TO CASELLI AV
S OF MARKET ST
LANCASTER LN SF 12 B3
E FROM LAKESHORE DR ONE BLK
N OF LAKE MERCED BLVD
LANDERS ST SF 10 B2
S FROM S 14TH ST BETWEEN
DOLORES ST AND CHURCH ST
TO 16TH ST
2 14TH ST
100 15TH ST
ALERT AL
END 16TH ST
LANE ST SF 15 C3
LANE ST SF 21 B2
SW FROM LA SALLE AV TO ARMSTRONG
AV & FROM SALINAS AV TO
BAYSHORE BLVD
LA SALLE AV
MCKINNON AV
NEWCOMB AV
OAKDALE AV
PALOU AV
QUESADA AV
REVERE AV
SHAFTER AV
THOMAS AV
UNDERWOOD AV
VAN DYKE AV
3RD ST
WALLACE AV
YOSEMITE AV
END ARMSTRONG AV
SALINAS AV
KEY AV
BAYSHORE BLVD
LANGDON CT SF 1 A2
IN PRESIDIO
NW FROM LINCOLN BLVD
LANGTON ST SF 7 A3
S FROM S HOWARD ST BETWEEN
7TH AND 8TH STS TO HARRISON ST
2 HOWARD ST
100 FOLSOM ST
DECKER ST
200 HARRISON ST
LANSDALE AV SF 13 B2
S FROM JUANITA WY
LANSING ST SF 7 B2
W FROM S 1ST ST BETWEEN
FOLSOM ST AND HARRISON ST
LAPHAM WY SF 20 B3
SE OFF CHICAGO WY NE OF
SOUTH HILL BLVD
LAPIDGE ST SF 10 C2
S FROM S 18TH ST BETWEEN
VALENCIA ST AND GUERRERO ST
ST TO 19TH ST
LA PLAYA SF 8 A1
S FROM SUTRO HEIGHTS TO
JUDAH ST
600 SUTRO HEIGHTS
700 BALBOA ST
800 CABRILLO ST
FULTON ST
PARK
1200 LINCOLN WY
1300 IRVING ST
END JUDAH ST
LAPU LAPU ST SF 7 B3
SE FROM BONIFACIO ST TO
HATTISON ST BETWEEN
BONIFACIO ST
RIZAL ST
END HARRISON ST
LARCH ST SF 6 C3
W FROM S VAN NESS AV BETWEEN
TURK ST AND EDDY ST TO
FRANKLIN ST
200 VAN NESS AVE
END FRANKLIN ST
LARKIN ST SF 2 C2
LARKIN ST SF 6 C2
N FROM S MARKET ST BETWEEN
HYDE AND POLK STS TO
BEACH ST
2 MARKET ST
HAYES ST
GROVE ST
FULTON ST
300 MCALLISTER ST
REDWOOD ST
400 GOLDEN GATE AV
500 TURK ST
600 EDDY ST
WILLOW ST
700 ELLIS ST
OLIVE ST
800 OFARRELL ST
800 MYRTLE ST
900 GEARY ST
CEDAR ST
1000 POST ST
HEMLOCK ST
1100 SUTTER ST
FERN ST
1200 BUSH ST
EUREKA PL
AUSTIN ST
1300 PINE ST
1400 CALIFORNIA ST
1500 SACRAMENTO ST
1600 CLAY ST
1700 WASHINGTON ST
1800 JACKSON ST
1900 PACIFIC AV
2000 BROADWAY
2100 VALLEJO ST
2200 GREEN ST
ROCKLAND ST
2300 UNION ST
2400 FILBERT ST
2500 GREENWICH ST
2600 LOMBARD ST
2700 CHESTNUT ST
2800 FRANCISCO ST
2900 BAY ST
3000 NORTH POINT ST
END BEACH ST
LA SALLE AV SF 15 C2
FROM INGALLS ST NW TO PHELPS ST
INGALLS ST
WHITFIELD CT
OSCEOLA LN
GARLINGTON CT
NEWCOMB AV
LANE ST
CASHMERE ST
1600 MENDELL ST
1690 3RD ST
1700 NEWHALL ST
END PHELPS ST
LASKIE ST SF 7 A3
N FROM S MISSION ST BETWEEN
8TH ST AND 9TH ST
LATHAM PL SF 7 A2
W FROM S MASON ST BETWEEN
OFARRELL ST AND ELLIS ST
LATHROP AV SF 21 B3
E FROM TUNNEL AV TO US-101 FRWY
LATONA ST SF 15 B3
S FROM BAY VIEW ST BETWEEN 3RD ST
AND POMONA ST TO
THORNTON AV
LAURA ST SF 19 C3
BETWEEN LAWRENCE AV AND
FARRAGUT AV FROM 5700 MISSION ST
MISSION NW TO ALEMANY BLVD
LAUREL ST SF 5 C1
S OF PACIFIC AV BETWEEN
WALNUT ST AND LOCUST ST
TO EUCLID AV
100 JACKSON ST
200 WASHINGTON ST
300 CLAY ST
400 SACRAMENTO ST
CALIFORNIA ST
MAYFAIR DR
END EUCLID AV
LAUSSAT ST SF 10 B1
W FROM S BUCHANAN ST BETWEEN
WALLER ST AND HAIGHT ST
TO STEINER ST
2 BUCHANAN ST
WEBSTER ST
200 FILLMORE ST
END STEINER ST
LAWRENCE AV SF 19 C3
NW FROM 5800 BLOCK MISSION ST
NW TO SAN JOSE AV NEAR
COUNTY LINE
2 MISSION ST
100 HURON AV
SEARS ST
ALEMANY BLVD
END DE WOLF ST
LAWTON ST SF 8 A3
LAWTON ST SF 9 A3
W FROM LOCKSLEY AV S OF
KIRKHAM ST TO GREAT HIGHWAY
2 LOCKSLEY AV
100 7TH AV
200 8TH AV
300 9TH AV
400 10TH AV
500 11TH AV
600 12TH AV
700 FUNSTON AV
800 14TH AV
900 15TH AV
LOMITA AV
1000 16TH AV
1100 17TH AV
1200 18TH AV
1300 19TH AV
1400 20TH AV
1500 21ST AV
1600 22ND AV
1700 23RD AV
1800 24TH AV
1900 25TH AV
2000 26TH AV
2100 27TH AV
2200 28TH AV
2300 29TH AV
2400 30TH AV
2500 31ST AV
2600 32ND AV
2700 33RD AV
2800 34TH AV
2900 35TH AV
3000 36TH AV
SUNSET BLVD
3100 37TH AV
3200 38TH AV
3300 39TH AV
3400 40TH AV
3500 41ST AV
3600 42ND AV
3700 43RD AV
3800 44TH AV
3900 45TH AV
4000 46TH AV
4100 47TH AV
4200 48TH AV
END GREAT HIGHWAY
LEAVENWORTH ST SF 2 C2
LEAVENWORTH ST SF 6 C2
LEAVENWORTH ST SF 7 A3
N FROM MCALLISTER ST BETWEEN
HYDE STS TO THE BAY
FULTON ST
50 MCALLISTER ST
100 GOLDEN GATE AV
200 TURK ST
300 EDDY ST
400 ELLIS ST
500 O'FARRELL ST
600 GEARY ST
700 POST ST
800 SUTTER ST
900 BUSH ST
1000 PINE ST
PANTON AL
1100 CALIFORNIA ST
ACORN AL
1200 SACRAMENTO ST
1300 CLAY ST
1400 WASHINGTON ST
1500 JACKSON ST
1600 PACIFIC AV
LYNCH ST
BERNARD ST
1700 BROADWAY
GLOVER ST
WALDO AL
1800 VALLEJO ST
1900 GREEN ST
MACONDRAY ST
2000 UNION ST
HAVENS ST
2100 FILBERT ST
2200 GREENWICH ST
LURMONT TER
2300 LOMBARD ST
2400 CHESTNUT ST
2500 FRANCISCO ST
2600 BAY ST
NORTH POINT ST
2700 COLUMBUS AV
2800 BEACH ST
END JEFFERSON ST
LECH WALESA SF 6 C3
BETWEEN HAYES ST AND GROVE ST W
FROM POLK ST TO VAN NESS AV
LE CONTE AV SF 21 B2
NW FROM KEY AV TO KEITH ST
KEY AV
JENNINGS ST
3RD ST
END KEITH ST
LEDYARD ST SF 15 B3
SE FROM SILVER AV W OF
SCOTIA AV
LEE AV SF 19 C2
N FROM LAKE VIEW AV TO OCEAN AV
2 LAKE VIEW AV
100 GRAFTON AV
200 HOLLOWAY AV
END OCEAN AV
LEESE ST SF 14 C2
SE FROM PARK ST NEAR HIGHLAND AV
TO CRESCENT AV
PARK ST
100 RICHLAND AV
END CRESCENT AV
LEGION CT SF 19 B1
FROM OCEAN AV SW TO URBANO DR
LEGION HONOR DR SF 4 B2
FROM CLEMENT ST N TO
EL CAMINO DEL MAR BETWEEN 32ND AV
AND 36TH AV
LEIDESDORFF ST SF 3 B3
FROM 300 PINE ST BETWEEN
SANSOME ST AND MONTGOMERY ST
N TO CLAY ST
2 PINE ST
100 CALIFORNIA ST
HALLECK ST
200 SACRAMENTO ST
COMMERCIAL ST
END CLAY ST
LELAND AV SF 21 A2
BETWEEN RAYMOND AV AND
VISITACION AV FROM BAYSHORE BLVD
W TO HAHN ST
BAY SHORE BLVD
DESMOND ST
100 ALPHA ST
PEABODY ST
200 RUTLAND ST
CORA ST
300 DELTA ST
SCHWERIN ST
REY ST
400 ELLIOT ST
BRITTON ST
LOEHR ST
500 SAWYER ST
END HAHN ST
LENOX WY SF 13 B2
FROM 51 TARAVAL ST S TO
ULLOA ST
LEO ST SF 20 A1
W FROM 4700 BLOCK MISSION ST
BETWEEN ONONDAGA AV AND RUTH ST
LEONA TER SF 6 A2
W FROM LYON ST BETWEEN GEARY BLVD
AND POST ST
LEROY PL SF 2 C3
FROM SACRAMENTO ST N & S BETWEEN
JONES ST AND LEAVENWORTH ST
LESSING ST SF 19 C3
W OF MISSION ST NE FROM LIEBIG ST
BETWEEN MISSION ST & SAN JOSE AV
LESTER CT SF 3 C1
W FROM GATEVIEW AV, TREASURE ISLD
LETTERMAN DR SF 1 C3
S OF LETTERMAN GEN HOSP BETWEEN
PRESIDIO BLVD AND LOMBARD ST
LETTUCE LN SF 15 B2
S W FROM JERROLD AV BET
TOLAND ST AND SELBY ST
LEVANT ST SF 10 A2
N OF 17TH ST FROM LOWER TER
TO FAIRBANKS ST
LEXINGTON ST SF 10 C2
FROM SYCAMORE ST BETWEEN
VALENCIA ST AND MISSION ST
S TO 21ST ST
2 SYCAMORE AVE
100 18TH ST
200 19TH ST
300 20TH ST
END 21ST ST
LIBERTY ST SF 10 B3
W FROM S VALENCIA ST BETWEEN
20TH & 21ST STS W TO CASTRO ST
2 VALENCIA ST
100 GUERRERO ST
200 DOLORES ST
300 CHURCH ST

400 SANCHEZ ST
END RAYBURN ST
500 NOE ST
END CASTRO ST
LICK PL SF 7 B2
FROM POST ST BETWEEN KEARNY ST
AND MONTGOMERY ST N TO SUTTER ST
LIEBIG ST SF 19 C3
FROM SAN JOSE AV SE TO THE
COUNTY LINE BETWEEN REGENT ST
AND RICE ST
LT ALLEN ST SF 1 C2
N OF DOYLE DR BETWEEN
CPL ZAVOVITZ ST & SGT MITCHELL ST
LT JAUSS ST SF 1 C2
E OF CPL ZAVOVITZ ST BETWEEN
MARINE DR AND LT ALLEN ST
LIGGETT AV SF 1 C3
S FROM PRESIDIO BLVD BETWEEN
CLARKE ST AND SIBLEY RD
LILAC ST SF 14 C1
S FROM 24TH ST BETWEEN CAPP ST
AND MISSION ST S TO 26TH ST
LILLIAN ST SF 15 C3
W OF INGALLS ST BETWEEN
ROSIE LEE LN & BEATRICE LN
LILY ST SF 10 B1
W FROM S FRANKLIN ST BETWEEN
PAGE ST & OAK ST W TO BUCHANAN ST
2 FRANKLIN ST
100 GOUGH ST
200 OCTAVIA ST
300 LAGUNA ST
END BUCHANAN ST
LINARES AV SF 9 B3
FROM S END OF 8TH AV SE TO A
POINT E OF VENTURA AV
LINCOLN BLVD SF 1 A3
LINCOLN BLVD SF 4 C1
LINCOLN CT SF 20 A3
W OF NADELL CT TWO BLOCKS
S OF BRUNSWICK
LINCOLN WY SF 8 A2
LINCOLN WY SF 9 A2
S OF GOLDEN GATE PARK FROM
ARGUELLO BLVD W TO GREAT HIGHWAY
1 ARGUELLO BLVD
100 2ND AV
200 3RD AV
300 4TH AV
400 5TH AV
500 6TH AV
600 7TH AV
700 8TH AV
800 9TH AV
900 10TH AV
1000 11TH AV
1100 12TH AV
1200 FUNSTON AV
1300 14TH AV
1400 15TH AV
1500 16TH AV
1600 17TH AV
1700 18TH AV
1800 19TH AV
1900 20TH AV
2000 21ST AV
2100 22ND AV
2200 23RD AV
2300 24TH AV
2400 25TH AV
2500 26TH AV
2600 27TH AV
2700 28TH AV
2800 29TH AV
2900 30TH AV
3000 31ST AV
3100 32ND AV
3200 33RD AV
3300 34TH AV
3400 35TH AV
3500 36TH AV
SUNSET BLVD
3600 37TH AV
3700 38TH AV
3800 39TH AV
3900 40TH AV
4000 41ST AV
4100 42ND AV
4200 43RD AV
4300 44TH AV
4500 46TH AV
4600 47TH AV
4700 48TH AV
LA PLAYA ST
END GREAT HIGHWAY
LINDA ST SF 10 C2
S FROM 18TH ST BETWEEN
LAPIDGE ST AND GUERRERO ST
LINDA VISTA LN SF 20 B3
OFF GENEVA AV S TO CHICAGO WY
LINDEN ST SF 6 B3
W FROM FRANKLIN ST BETWEEN
FELL ST AND HAYES ST TO A
POINT W OF BUCHANAN ST
200 FRANKLIN ST
300 GOUGH ST
400 OCTAVIA ST
500 LAGUNA ST
600 BUCHANAN ST
LIPPARD AV SF 14 A3
FROM SURREY ST S TO JOOST AV
2 SURREY ST
CHENERY ST
100 BOSWORTH ST
END JOOST AV
LISBON ST SF 20 A2
FROM SILVER AV S W TO GENEVA AV
2 SILVER AV
PERU AV
100 AVALON AV
200 EXCELSIOR AV
300 BRAZIL AV
400 PERSIA AV
500 RUSSIA AV
600 FRANCE AV
700 ITALY AV
800 AMAZON AV
END GENEVA AV
LIVINGSTON ST SF 1 B2
N FROM MASON ST TO MARINE DR
LLOYD ST SF 10 A1
W FROM S SCOTT ST BETWEEN
DUBOCE AV AND WALLER ST
LOBOS ST SF 19 B2
W OF SAN JOSE AV NEAR THE
COUNTY LINE FROM CAINE ST
W TO ORIZABA AV
2 CAINE ST
100 PLYMOUTH AV
200 CAPITOL AV
END ORIZABA AV
LOCKSLEY AV SF 9 B3
S OFF KIRKHAM ST AND
ONE BLOCK E OF 7TH AV
LOCKWOOD ST SF 17 B1
SE FROM DONAHUE ST TO NIMITZ AV
LOCUST ST SF 5 C2
FROM PACIFIC AV BETWEEN LAUREL ST
AND SPRUCE ST S TO CALIFORNIA ST
2 PACIFIC AV
100 JACKSON ST
200 WASHINGTON ST
300 CLAY ST
400 SACRAMENTO ST
END CALIFORNIA ST
LOEHR ST SF 20 C3
W OF BAYSHORE BLVD N & S OF
VISITACION AV BETWEEN
BRITTON ST AND SAWYER ST
LOMA VISTA TER SF 10 A2
S FROM UPPER TER TO ROOSEVELT WY
LOMBARD ST SF 2 A2
LOMBARD ST SF 3 A2
FROM THE BAY BETWEEN GREENWICH ST
AND CHESTNUT ST W TO LYON ST
THE EMBARCADERO
2 BATTERY ST
100 SANSOME ST
200 MONTGOMERY ST
WINTHROP ST
300 KEARNY ST
CHILD ST
JULIUS ST
400 GRANT AV
500 STOCKTON ST
TUSCANY AL
600 POWELL ST
700 MASON ST
NEWELL ST
COLUMBUS AV
JANSEN ST
800 TAYLOR ST
900 JONES ST
1000 LEAVENWORTH ST
MONTCLAIR TER
1100 HYDE ST
1200 LARKIN ST
1300 POLK ST
1400 VAN NESS AV
1500 FRANKLIN ST
1600 GOUGH ST
1700 OCTAVIA ST
1800 LAGUNA ST
1900 BUCHANAN ST
2000 WEBSTER ST
2100 FILLMORE ST
2200 STEINER ST
2300 PIERCE ST
2400 SCOTT ST
2500 DIVISADERO ST
2600 BRODERICK ST
2700 BAKER ST
END LYON ST
LOMITA AV SF 9 A3
FROM LAWTON ST AND 15TH AV
S TO MORAGA ST
LONDON ST SF 20 B1
FROM AVALON AV SW TO GENEVA AV
AVALON AV
200 EXCELSIOR AV
300 BRAZIL AV
400 PERSIA AV
500 RUSSIA AV
600 FRANCE AV
700 ITALY AV
800 AMAZON AV
END GENEVA AV
LONE MTN TER SF 5 C3
E FROM ROSSI AV BETWEEN ANZA ST
AND TURK ST TO PARKER AV
LONG AV SF 1 A1
FROM MARINE DR S TO LINCOLN BLVD
LONGVIEW CT SF 13 C1
E FROM PANORAMA DR BETWEEN
CITYVIEW WY AND MOUNTVIEW CT
LOOMIS ST SF 15 A2
FROM INDUSTRIAL ST N OF
MCKINNON AV AT BARNEVELD AV
LOPEZ AV SF 13 B1
N FROM CASTENADA AV PARALLEL WITH
SANTA RITA AV N TO PACHECO ST
LORAINE CT SF 5 B3
N FROM ANZA ST BETWEEN ALMADEN CT
AND STANYAN ST
LORI LN SF 9 C3
E FROM CLARENDON AV ONE BLK
N OF PANORAMA
LOS PALMOS DR SF 13 C3
FROM TERESITA BLVD W TO
HAZELWOOD AV
TERESITA BLVD
VERNA ST
FOERSTER ST
STANFORD HEIGHTS AV
BELLA VISTA WY
LULU AL
EMIL LN
GLOBE AL
END HAZELWOOD AV
LOTTIE BENNT LN SF 4 A1
IN ST FRANCIS SQ S FROM GEARY BL
W OF LAGUNA ST
LOUISBURG ST SF 19 C2
FROM GENEVA AV W OF TARA ST
S TO RIDGE LN
100 GENEVA AV
200 NIAGARA AV
300 MT VERNON AV
END RIDGE LANE
LOWELL ST SF 20 A3
FROM 5600 BLOCK OF MISSION ST
SE TO COUNTY LINE
2 MISSION ST
100 MORSE ST
200 BRUNSWICK ST
BYRON ST
300 HANOVER ST
END COUNTY LINE
LOWER TER SF 10 A2
FROM SATURN ST N OF 17TH ST NEAR
ORD ST AND E OF ROOSEVELT WY
LOYOLA TER SF 5 C3
FROM 1900 FULTON ST N BETWEEN
HEMWAY TER AND KITTREDGE TER
LUCERNE ST SF 11 B1
BETWEEN 6TH ST AND 7TH ST FROM
BRANNAN ST S
LUCKY ST SF 15 A1
S FROM 24TH ST BET TREAT AV &
FOLSOM ST TO 26TH ST
LUCY ST SF 15 B3
FROM THRONTON AV BETWEEN 3RD ST
AND CERES ST S TO WILLIAMS AV
LUDLOW AL SF 13 B2
S FROM JUANITA WY TO CASITAS AV
S OF PORTOLA DR
LULU AL SF 13 C3
FROM A POINT N OF CRESTA VISTA DR
S TO MELROSE AV
CRESTA VISTA DR
BURLWOOD DR
LOS PALMOS DR
END MELROSE AV
LUNADO CT SF 19 A1
SE FROM LUNADO WY
S OF MERCEDES WY
LUNADO WY SF 19 A1
FROM HOLLOWAY AV N TO MERCEDES WY
2 HOLLOWAY AV
100 ESTERO AV
END MERCEDES WY
LUNDEEN ST SF 1 C2
N OF DOYLE DR BETWEEN
CPL ZAVOVITZ ST AND PEDESTRIAN WY
LUNDYS LN SF 14 C2
SW FROM COSO AV BETWEEN
COLERIDGE AV AND PROSPECT AV
TO VIRGINIA AV
2 COSO AV
FAIR AV
100 ESMERALDA AV
END VIRGINIA AV
LUPINE AV SF 5 C2
W OF MASONIC AV ONE BLOCK S
OF EUCLID AV
LURLINE ST SF 9 A3
FROM KIRKHAM ST AND 14TH AV S
E TO FUNSTON AV
LURMONT TER SF 2 C2
W FROM LEAVENWORTH ST BETWEEN
GREENWICH ST AND LOMBARD ST
LUSK ST SF 7 B3
NE OF TOWNSEND ST BETWEEN
CLYDE ST AND 4TH ST
LYELL ST SF 14 B3
FROM BOSWORTH ST W OF ROTTECK ST
ST S TO ALEMANY BLVD
LYNCH ST SF 2 C3
SW FROM LEAVENWORTH ST BETWEEN
PACIFIC AV AND BROADWAY
W TO HYDE ST
LYNDHURST DR SF 19 A1
SW FROM JUNIPERO SERRA BLVD
TO DENSLOWE DR
LYON ST SF 1 C3
LYON ST SF 6 A1
LYON ST SF 10 A1
NW FROM HAIGHT ST W OF
BAKER ST N TO MARINA BLVD
2 HAIGHT ST
100 PAGE ST
END OAK ST
300 FELL ST
400 HAYES ST
500 GROVE ST
600 FULTON ST
700 MCALLISTER ST
800 GOLDEN GATE AV
TURK ST
END ANZAVISTA AV
TERRA VISTA AV
OFARRELL ST
1300 GEARY ST
1400 POST ST
1500 SUTTER ST
1600 BUSH ST
1700 PINE ST
1800 CALIFORNIA ST
1900 SACRAMENTO ST
2000 CLAY ST
2100 WASHINGTON ST
2200 JACKSON ST
2300 PACIFIC AV
2400 BROADWAY
2500 VALLEJO ST
2600 GREEN ST
2700 UNION ST
2800 FILBERT ST
2900 GREENWICH ST
3000 LOMBARD ST
3100 CHESTNUT ST
3200 FRANCISCO ST
3300 BAY ST
END MARINA BLVD
LYSETTE ST SF 2 C3
S FROM SACRAMENTO ST BETWEEN
JONES ST AND LEAVENWORTH ST

M

MABEL AL SF 6 C2
OFF HYDE ST BETWEEN GEARY ST
AND O'FARRELL ST
MABINI ST SF 7 B2
SE FROM FOLSOM ST TO BONIFACIO ST
BETWEEN 3RD ST AND 4TH ST
MAC ARTHUR AV SF 1 C3
FROM PRESIDIO BL S TO EL POLIN LP
MAC ARTHUR AV SF 2 B2
IN FORT MASON N OF BAY ST
MACEDONIA ST SF 15 A1
FROM MONTCALM ST W OF
MULLEN AV SE TO BREWSTER ST
MACONDRAY ST SF 2 C3
FROM 1801 TAYLOR ST BETWEEN
GREEN ST AND UNION ST W TO
LEAVENWORTH ST
2 TAYLOR ST
100 JONES ST
END LEAVENWORTH ST
MACRAE ST SF 1 C3
S OF MACARTHUR ST W OF PORTOLA ST
MADDUX AV SF 15 B3
NE FROM SCOTIA AV TO REVERE AV
BETWEEN BRIDGEVIEW DR & QUINT ST
MADERA ST SF 11 B3

W FROM ARKANSAS ST BETWEEN
22ND ST & 23RD ST TO WISCONSIN ST
MADISON ST SF 20 C1
FROM SILVER AV S TO BURROWS ST
2 SILVER AV
100 ATHENS ST END
PIOCHE ST
VALMAR TER
200 SILLIMAN ST
300 FELTON ST
END BURROWS ST
MADRID ST SF 20 B2
FROM SILVER AV SW TO ROLPH ST
2 SILVER AV
100 PERU AV
200 AVALON AV
300 EXCELSIOR AV
400 BRAZIL AV
500 PERSIA AV
600 RUSSIA AV
700 FRANCE AV
800 ITALY AV
900 AMAZON AV
1000 GENEVA AV
END ROLPH ST
MADRONE AV SF 13 B2
FROM TARAVAL ST SW TO VICENTE ST
2 TARAVAL ST
100 ULLOA ST
END VICENTE ST
MAGELLAN AV SF 13 B1
NE FROM 12TH AV PARALLEL TO
DEWEY BLVD ENDING AT CASTANEDA AV
12TH AV
500 CORTES AV
400 MONTALVO AV
DORANTES AV
300 PACHECO AV
200 SOLA AV
PLAZA
100 MARCELA AV
END CASTENADA AV
MAGNOLIA ST SF 2 B2
BETWEEN LOMBARD ST & CHESTNUT ST
FROM LAGUNA ST W TO WEBSTER ST
MAHAN ST SF 17 B2
SW FROM HUSSEY ST TO J ST BETWEEN
MANSEAU ST AND THE BAY
MAIDEN LN SF 7 A2
W FROM S KEARNY ST BETWEEN
GEARY ST AND POST ST ENDING AT
STOCKTON ST
2 KEARNY ST
100 GRANT AV
END STOCKTON ST
MAIN ST SF 7 B1
S FROM MARKET ST BETWEEN SPEAR ST
AND BEALE ST SE TO THE BAY
2 MARKET ST
100 MISSION ST
200 HOWARD ST
300 FOLSOM ST
ELKHART ST
400 HARRISON ST
500 BRYANT ST
END THE EMBARCADERO
MAJESTIC AV SF 19 C2
BETWEEN CAINE ST AND MARGARET AV
CROSSING LAKEVIEW AV FROM
RIDGE LN S TO SUMMIT AV
2 RIDGE LANE
100 LAKE VIEW AV
END SUMMIT AV
MALDEN AL SF 7 B2
S FROM HOWARD ST BETWEEN 1ST ST
AND 2ND ST SE TO TEHAMA ST
MALLORCA WY SF 2 A2
FROM CHESTNUT ST AND FILLMORE ST
NW TO BEACH ST AND CERVANTES BLVD
2 CHESTNUT ST
100 TOLEDO WAY
200 ALHAMBRA ST
CAPRA WY
END BEACH ST
MALTA DR SF 14 A3
N FROM STILLINGS AV TO
OSHAUGHNESSY BLVD
MALVINA PL SF 3 A3
W FROM S MASON ST BETWEEN CLAY ST
AND SACRAMENTO ST
MANCHESTER ST SF 14 C1
S OF ARMY ST FROM BESSIE ST TO
RIPLEY ST BETWEEN FOLSOM ST
AND SHOTWELL ST
2 BESSIE ST
100 STONEMAN ST
END RIPLEY ST
MANDALAY LN SF 13 A1
FROM PACHECO ST AND 15TH AV
E TO 14TH AV
MANGELS AV SF 13 C3
FROM HAMERTON AV N OF JOOST AV
W TO PLYMOUTH AV
HAMERTON AV
BURNSIDE AV
100 BADEN ST
NORDHOFF ST
200 CONGO ST
300 DETROIT ST
400 EDNA ST
500 FOERSTER ST
600 GENNESSEE ST
700 RIDGEWOOD AV
750 BRENTWOOD AV
800 HAZELWOOD AV
850 VALDEZ AV
900 COLON AV
END PLYMOUTH AV
MANOR DR SF 19 B1
FROM 2060 OCEAN AV N TO DARIEN WY
2 OCEAN AV
100 KENWOOD WY
200 UPLAND DR
END DARIEN WY
MANSEAU ST SF 17 B2
BETWEEN SPEAR AV AND MAHAN ST
MANSELL ST SF 20 C2
MANSELL ST SF 21 A2
FROM 3200 BLOCK OF SAN BRUNO AV
S OF OLMSTEAD ST
W TO JOHN MCLAREN PARK
2 SAN BRUNO AV
100 GIRARD ST
200 BRUSSELS ST
300 GOETTINGEN ST
400 SOMERSET ST
500 HOLYOKE ST
600 HAMILTON ST
700 BOWDOIN ST
800 DARTMOUTH ST
COLBY ST
UNIVERSITY ST
VISITACION AV
JOHN F SHELLEY DR
END PERSIA AV & BRAZIL AV
MANSFIELD ST SF 20 C1
FROM LA GRANDE AV S TO BURROWS ST
MANZANITA AV SF 5 C2
S FROM MAYFAIR DR TO EUCLID AV
W OF COLLINS ST
MAPLE ST SF 5 C2
FROM PRESIDIO RESERVATION
BETWEEN SPRUCE ST AND CHERRY ST
S TO CALIFORNIA ST
2 PRESIDIO RESERVATION
100 JACKSON ST
200 WASHINGTON ST
300 CLAY ST
400 SACRAMENTO ST
END CALIFORNIA ST
MARCELA AV SF 13 B1
E FROM PACHECO ST PARALLEL WITH
CASTANEDA AV TO MAGELLAN AV
PACHECO ST
SOLA AV
END MAGELLAN AV
MARCY PL SF 3 A3
S FROM S JACKSON ST BETWEEN
MASON ST AND TAYLOR ST
MARENGO ST SF 15 A2
E OF JAMES LICK FRWY FROM
WATERLOO ST S TO BAYSHORE BLVD
MARGARET AV SF 19 C2
BETWEEN MAJESTIC AV AND JOSIAH AV
CROSSING LAKE VIEW AV FROM
RIDGE LN TO SUMMIT AV
MARGRAVE PL SF 3 A2
FROM 500 VALLEJO ST BETWEEN
KEARNY ST AND GRANT AV
MARIETTA DR SF 13 C2
MARIETTA DR SF 14 A2
FROM TERESITA BL SE TO CUBA AL
MARIN ST SF 15 C1
ONE BLK S OF ARMY ST FROM A POINT
E OF MICHIGAN ST TO BAYSHORE BLVD
MARINA BLVD SF 2 C3
FROM BEACH ST AND BUCHANAN ST NW
AND W TO LYON ST
100 BUCHANAN ST
BEACH ST
WEBSTER ST
FILLMORE ST
RETIRO WY
CASA WY
AVILA ST
SCOTT ST
DIVISADERO ST
BRODERICK ST
BAKER ST
END LYON ST
MARINE DR SF 1 B2
W FROM LYON ST ALONG THE COAST TO
MARINER DR SF 3 C1
W FROM GATEVIEW AV 1 BLK NW OF
FORT POINT NATIONAL HISTORIC SITE
13TH ST, REJOINING GATEVIEW NEAR
BAYSIDE DR, TREASURE ISLAND
MARION PL SF 2 C2
N FROM 900 UNION ST BETWEEN
JONES ST AND TAYLOR ST
MARIPOSA ST SF 11 A2
FROM THE BAY BETWEEN 17TH ST
& 18TH ST W TO HARRISON ST
400 ILLINOIS ST
500 3RD ST
600 TENNESSEE ST
700 MINNESOTA ST
800 INDIANA ST
900 IOWA ST
1000 PENNSYLVANIA AV
1100 MISSISSIPPI ST
1200 TEXAS ST
1300 MISSOURI ST
1400 CONNECTICUT ST
ARKANSAS ST
WISCONSIN ST
1700 CAROLINA ST
1800 DE HARO ST
1900 RHODE ISLAND ST
2000 KANSAS ST
2100 VERMONT ST
2200 SAN BRUNO AV
2300 UTAH ST
2400 POTRERO AV
2500 HAMPSHIRE ST
2600 YORK ST
2700 BRYANT ST
2800 FLORIDA ST
2900 ALABAMA ST
END HARRISON ST
MARK LN SF 7 A1
S FROM 401 BUSH ST BETWEEN
KEARNY ST & GRANT AV TO SUTTER ST
MARKET ST SF 7 A3
MARKET ST SF 10 B2
FROM THE BAY SW TO THE JUNCTION
OF 17TH ST AND CASTRO ST, THEN W
TO 24TH ST AND PORTOLA DR
THE EMBARCADERO
STEUART ST
SPEAR ST
CALIFORNIA ST
200 DRUMM ST
MAIN ST
300 DAVIS ST
PINE ST
BEALE ST
400 FRONT ST
FREMONT ST
BUSH ST
500 BATTERY ST
1ST ST
ECKER ST
546 SANSOME ST
SUTTER ST
600 MONTGOMERY ST
NEW MONTGOMERY ST
ANNIE ST
700 KEARNY ST
GEARY ST
3RD ST
750 GRANT AVE
O'FARRELL ST
4TH ST
800 STOCKTON ST
ELLIS ST
900 POWELL ST
EDDY ST
5TH ST
TURK ST
950 MASON ST
6TH ST
1000 TAYLOR ST
GOLDEN GATE AV
1100 JONES ST
MCALLISTER ST
7TH ST
1200 HYDE ST
8TH ST
GROVE ST
1300 LARKIN ST
HAYES ST
9TH ST
10TH ST
1400 POLK ST
FELL ST
11TH ST
1500 VAN NESS AV
12TH ST
1600 FRANKLIN ST
ROSE ST
BRADY ST
HAIGHT ST
1700 GOUGH ST
VALENCIA ST
MCCOPPIN ST
1800 OCTAVIA ST
PEARL ST
GUERRERO ST
1900 LAGUNA ST
HERMANN ST
2000 DUBOCE AV
DOLORES ST
RESERVOIR ST
14TH ST
2100 CHURCH ST
15TH ST
2200 SANCHEZ ST
2300 16TH ST
NOE ST
17TH ST
2400 CASTRO ST
2500 COLLINGWOOD ST
2600 DIAMOND ST
2700 EUREKA ST
2800 DOUGLASS ST
2900 ORD ST
3000 HATTIE ST
MERRITT ST
3100 DANVERS ST
3200 MONO ST
3300 IRON AL
CASELLI AV
EAGLE ST
SHORT ST
3460 COPPER AL
3500 GLENDALE ST
STANTON ST
GRANDVIEW AV
3700 MORGAN AL
3800 DIXIE AL
3878 ARGENT AL
3950 GOLDING LN
MARLIN CT SF 17 A1
SW FROM NAVY RD IN
HUNTERS PT NAVAL RES
MARNE AV SF 13 B2
FROM 1099 PORTOLA DR S TO
JUANITA AV
MARS ST SF 10 A2
S FROM 17TH ST TO CORBETT AV
MARSHALL ST SF 1 C2
SW FROM GORGAS AV IN THE PRESIDIO
MARSILLY ST SF 14 B3
W OF MISSION ST FROM ST MARYS AV
S TO A POINT S OF BOSWORTH ST
MARSTON AV SF 19 C1
FROM CIRCULAR AV W BETWEEN
JUDSON AV AND HAVELOCK ST
MARTHA AV SF 14 A3
FROM CONGO ST SE TO A POINT NEAR
BURNSIDE AV
MARTINEZ ST SF 1 C2
E FROM FUNSTON AV
N OF PRESIDIO BLVD
MARTIN L KING DR SF 8 A2
MARTIN L KING DR SF 9 A2
IN GOLDEN GATE PARK W FROM
E MIDDLE DR TO THE GREAT HWY
E MIDDLE DR
CONCOURSE DR
TEA GARDEN DR
STOW LAKE DR E
19TH AV
MIDDLE DR W
METSON RD
MIDDLE DR W
CHAIN OF LAKES DR E
THE GREAT HWY
MARVEL CT SF 4 B2
W FROM 32ND AV 2 BLKS N OF
GEARY BLVD
MAR VIEW WY SF 9 C3
E FROM PANORAMA DR BETWEEN
CLAIRVIEW CT AND GLADEVIEW WY
MARX MEADOW DR SF 8 C1
NE FROM JFK DR TO CROSS OVER DR
IN GOLDEN GATE PARK
MARY ST SF 7 A3
S FROM S MISSION ST BETWEEN
5TH ST & 6TH ST SE TO HOWARD ST
2 MISSION ST
30 MINNA ST
70 NATOMA ST
END HOWARD ST
MASON CT SF 3 C1
W FROM GATEVIEW AV BETWEEN
OZBORN CT & LESTER CT
ON TREASURE ISLAND
MASON ST SF 1 B2
E FROM HAMILTON ST TO LYON ST
N OF DOYLE DR
MASON ST SF 3 A2
MASON ST SF 7 A2
N FROM S MARKET ST BETWEEN
POWELL ST & TAYLOR ST
N TO THE BAY

SAN FRANCISCO

INDEX

2 MARKET ST
TURK ST
100 EDDY ST
200 ELLIS
300 OFARRELL ST
ELWOOD ST
400 GEARY ST
DERBY ST
500 POST ST
600 SUTTER ST
DELTA PL
700 BUSH ST
HOOKER AL
800 PINE ST
FRANK ST
900 CALIFORNIA ST
1000 SACRAMENTO ST
EWER PL
DAWSON PL
MALVINA PL
1100 CLAY ST
TRUETT ST
SHEPHARD PL
1200 WASHINGTON ST
1300 JACKSON ST
JOHN ST
1400 PACIFIC AV
1500 BROADWAY
1600 VALLEJO ST
1700 GREEN ST
WINTER PL
WEBB PL
1800 UNION ST
KENT ST
1900 FILBERT ST
VALPARAISO ST
GREENWICH ST
2000 COLUMBUS AV
2100 LOMBARD ST
2200 CHESTNUT ST
WATER ST
2300 FRANCISCO ST
2400 BAY ST
2500 NORTH POINT ST
2600 BEACH ST
END JEFFERSON ST
MASONIC AV SF 5 C3
MASONIC AV SF 10 A1
FROM PINE ST W OF CENTRAL AV
S TO UPPER TERRACE
PINE ST
EUCLID AV
GEARY BLVD
ANZA ST
EWING TER
300 TURK ST
400 GOLDEN GATE AV
500 MCALLISTER ST
600 FULTON ST
700 GROVE ST
800 HAYES ST
FELL ST
1000 OAK ST
1100 PAGE ST
1200 HAIGHT ST
1300 WALLER ST
1400 FREDERICK ST
1500 JAVA ST
PIEDMONT ST
END UPPER TERRACE
MASSASOIT ST SF 15 A1
FROM FRANCONIA ST N W TO
RUTLEDGE ST
MATEO ST SF 14 B2
FROM BEMIS ST SE TO SAN JOSE AV
2 BEMIS ST
100 LAIDLEY ST
200 CHENERY ST
300 ARLINGTON ST
END SAN JOSE AV
MATTHEW CT SF 16 A3
OFF ESPANOLA ST BETWEEN
BEATRICE LN AND ROSIE LEE LN
MAULDIN ST SF 1 A2
FROM HAMILTON ST SE TO
LIVINGSTON ST BETWEEN MASON ST
AND MARINE DR
MAYFAIR DR SF 5 C2
W FROM LAUREL ST TO SPRUCE ST
S OF CALIFORNIA ST
MAYFLOWER ST SF 15 A2
FROM HOLLADAY AV NEAR
POWHATTAN AV W TO CARVER ST
MAYNARD ST SF 14 B3
FROM 4200 BLOCK MISSION ST NEAR
SILVER AV TO TRUMBULL ST
22 MISSION ST
100 CRAUT ST
200 CONGDON ST
END TRUMBULL ST
MAYWOOD DR SF 13 B3
FROM YERBA BUENA AV S TO
EL VERANO WY
MCALLISTER ST SF 5 C3
MCALLISTER ST SF 6 A3
FROM THE JUNCTION OF MARKET ST
AND JONES ST BETWEEN FULTON ST &
GOLDEN GATE AV W TO ARGUELLO BLVD
2 MARKET ST
JONES ST
7TH ST N
100 LEAVENWORTH ST
200 HYDE ST
BREEN PL
300 LARKIN ST
400 POLK ST
500 VAN NESS AV
600 FRANKLIN ST
700 GOUGH ST
800 OCTAVIA ST
900 LAGUNA ST
1100 WEBSTER ST
CRAN PL
1200 FILLMORE ST
1300 STEINER ST
1400 PIERCE ST
1500 SCOTT ST
1600 DIVISADERO ST
1700 BRODERICK ST
1800 BAKER ST
1900 LYON ST
2000 CENTRAL AV
END MASONIC AV
PARKER AV
2600 STANYAN ST
PARSONS ST
2700 WILLARD ST
END ARGUELLO BLVD
MCCANN ST SF 16 B3
S FROM LOCKWOOD TO ENGLISH ST
MCCARTHY AV SF 20 C3
S FROM ARGONAUT 1 BLK TO BURR AV
MCCOPPIN ST SF 10 C1
FROM OTIS ST BETWEEN GOUGH ST
& DUBOCE AV W TO MARKET ST
2 OTIS ST
JESSIE ST
STEVENSON ST
100 VALENCIA ST
ELGIN PARK
END MARKET ST
MCCORMICK ST SF 2 C3
S FROM PACIFIC AV BETWEEN HYDE ST
AND LARKIN ST
MCDONALD ST SF 1 B2
N FROM MASON ST BETWEEN
HAMILTON ST & LIVINGSTON ST
MCDOWELL AV SF 1 B2
N FROM LINCOLN BLVD TO
CRISSY FIELD AV IN PRESIDIO
MCDOWELL AV SF 2 B2
N FROM SCHOFIELD RD TO THE BAY
MCKINNON AV SF 15 B2
FROM A POINT S OF LANE ST
NW TO BARNEVELD AV
PT S OF LANE ST
LANE ST
MENDELL ST
3RD ST
NEWHALL ST
PHELPS ST
END QUINT ST
RANKIN ST
SELBY ST
TOLAND ST
UPTON ST
END BARNEVELD AV
MCLAREN AV SF 4 B2
W FROM 28TH AV N OF LAKE ST
TO EL CAMINO DEL MAR
MCLEA CT SF 11 A1
E FROM S 9TH ST BETWEEN BRYANT ST
AND HARRISON ST
MEACHAM PL SF 6 C2
S FROM S POST ST BETWEEN HYDE ST
AND LARKIN ST
MEADE AV SF 21 B2
NW FROM LE CONTE AV TO 3RD ST
LE CONTE AV
JENNINGS ST
END 3RD ST
MEADOWBROOK DR SF 12 C3
S FROM SLOAT BLVD TO
EUCALYPTUS DR E OF SYLVAN DR
MEDA AV SF 20 A1
NW FROM OTSEGO AV BETWEEN
OCEAN AV & SANTA YNEZ AV W TO
DELANO AV
MEDAU PL SF 3 A2
N FROM 500 FILBERT ST BETWEEN
GRANT AV AND STOCKTON ST
MELBA AV SF 13 A3
S FROM OCEAN AV TO
EUCALYPTUS DR BETWEEN 22ND AV
AND 23RD AV
MELRA CT SF 21 A3
S FROM SUNNYDALE AV
AT DELTA ST
MELROSE AV SF 13 C3
FROM CONGO ST N OF MANGELS AV
W TO LULU AV
2 CONGO ST
100 DETROIT ST
200 EDNA ST
300 FOERSTER ST
400 GENNESSEE ST
END LULU AL
MENDELL ST SF 15 C2
MENDELL ST SF 21 B1
FROM CARGO WY SW TO PALOU AV
AND THEN S FROM WILLIAMS AV
TO CARROLL AV
CARGO WY
NEWHALL ST
EVANS AV
FAIRFAX AV
GALVEZ AV
HUDSON AV
INNES AV
JERROLD AV
KIRKWOOD AV
LA SALLE AV
MCKINNON AV
NEWCOMB AV
OAKDALE AV
PALOU AV
WILLIAMS AV
YOSEMITE AV
ARMSTRONG AV
BANCROFT AV
END CARROLL AV
MENDOSA AV SF 13 B1
W FROM S 9TH AV TO POINT E
OF 12TH AV
MERCATO CT SF 14 A3
N FROM MALTA DR ONE BLK N OF
STILLINGS AV
MERCED AV SF 13 B2
FROM LAGUNA HONDA BLVD SW
TO KENSINGTON WY
2 LAGUNA HONDA BLVD
100 PACHECO ST
END KENSINGTON WY
MERCEDES WY SF 19 A1
W FROM JUNIPERO SERRA BLVD
N TO PALOMA AV
MERCHANT RD SF 1 A2
N FROM LINCOLN BLVD TO
A POINT S OF DOYLE DR
MERCHANT ST SF 3 B3
FROM BATTERY ST BETWEEN CLAY ST
AND WASHINGTON ST W TO
KEARNY ST
400 BATTERY ST
500 SANSOME ST
600 MONTGOMERY ST
END KEARNY ST
MERCURY ST SF 15 B3
S FROM THORNTON AV W OF VESTA ST
MERLIN ST SF 7 B3
S FROM HARRISON ST BETWEEN
5TH ST AND 6TH ST
MERRILL ST SF 15 A3
S FROM GAVEN ST BETWEEN
BARNEVELD AV AND BOYLSTON
ST S TO SILVER AV
MERRIMAC ST SF 11 C1
E FROM 1500 3RD ST
MERRITT ST SF 10 A2
W FROM MARKET ST TO DANVERS ST
MERSEY ST SF 10 B3
FROM PT N OF 23RD ST BETWEEN
DOLORES ST AND CHATTANOOGA
ST S TO 24TH ST
MESA AV SF 1 C2
SW FROM LINCOLN BLVD TO MORAGA AV
BETWEEN FUNSTON AV AND KEYES AV
MESA AV SF 13 B1
W FROM S SANTA RITA AV
TO 2200 9TH AV
METSON RD SF 8 B2
MICHIGAN ST SF 11 C3
S FROM 20TH ST TO MARIN ST
E OF 3RD ST
20TH ST
22TH ST
24TH ST
25TH ST
ARMY ST
MARIN ST
MIDCREST WY SF 13 C1
1 BLK W OF TWIN PEAKS
BLVD E OF PANORAMA DR
MIDDLE DR E SF 9 B1
IN GOLDEN GATE PARK SW FROM
JFK DR TO MARTIN L KING DR
MIDDLE DR W SF 8 C2
FROM A POINT N OF 39TH AV E
TO A POINT N OF 20TH AV
IN GOLDEN GATE PARK
TRANSVERSE RD
OVERLOOK DR
METSON RD
MARTIN L KING DR
MIDDLEFIELD DR SF 12 C3
S FROM SLOAT BLVD
BETWEEN SYLVAN DR AND
RIVERTON DR
MIDDLE POINT RD SF 16 A2
S FROM EVANS AV TO INNES AV
MIDWAY ST SF 3 A2
FROM 200 FRANCISCO ST BETWEEN
GRANT AV AND STOCKTON ST
N TO BAY ST
MIGUEL ST SF 14 B2
FROM BEACON ST SE TO POINT
S OF ARLINGTON ST
2 BEACON ST
100 BEMIS ST
FAIRMOUNT ST
200 LAIDLEY ST
300 CHENERY ST
400 ARLINGTON ST
END PT S OF ARLINGTON ST
MILAN TER SF 19 C3
S FROM MONETA WY W OF
WHIPPLE AV TO HURON AV
MILES ST SF 1 B2
IN PRESIDIO BETWEEN ORD ST AND
TAYLOR RD S OF LINCOLN BLVD
MILEY ST SF 5 C1
E FROM S BAKER ST BETWEEN
FILBERT ST AND GREENWICH ST
MILL ST SF 21 A2
S OF MANSELL ST FROM
ANKENY ST TO HARKNESS AV
MILLER PL SF 3 A3
N FROM 900 SACRAMENTO ST BETWEEN
STOCKTON ST AND POWELL ST
MILLER RD SF 1 A2
IN PRESIDIO E OF LINCOLN BLVD
N OF STOREY AV
MILTON ST SF 14 B3
S FROM SAN JOSE AV BETWEEN
CUVIER ST
AND ROUSSEAU ST
MILTON ROSS ST SF 15 B2
N E FROM KIRKWOOD AV TO INNES
AV BETWEEN TOLAND ST AND SELBY ST
MINERVA ST SF 19 B2
W OF SAN JOSE AV FROM SUMMIT AV
BETWEEN MONTANA ST AND LOBOS ST
W TO ORIZABA AV
2 SUMMIT AV
100 PLYMOUTH AV
200 CAPITOL AV
END ORIZABA AV
MINNA ST SF 7 A3
MINNA ST SF 10 C1
SW FROM 1ST ST BETWEEN MISSION ST
AND HOWARD ST TO 15TH ST
2 1ST ST
SHAW AL
100 2ND ST
130 NEW MONTGOMERY ST
200 3RD ST
300 4TH ST
400 5TH ST
MARY ST
500 6TH ST
RUSS ST
600 7TH ST
JULIA ST
700 8TH ST
9TH ST
900 10TH ST
1000 11TH ST
LAFAYETTE ST
1300 14TH ST
END 15TH ST
MINNESOTA ST SF 11 C2
MINNESOTA ST SF 15 C1
S FROM MARIPOSA ST BETWEEN
TENNESSEE ST AND INDIANA ST
S TO ARMY ST
500 MARIPOSA ST
600 18TH ST
700 19TH ST
800 20TH ST
KENTUCKY PL
1000 22ND ST
1200 23RD ST
1300 24TH ST
1400 25TH ST
1500 26TH ST
END ARMY ST
MINT ST SF 7 A3

W FROM W 5TH ST BETWEEN
MISSION ST AND STEVENSON ST
MIRABEL AV SF 14 C1
E FROM COSO AV TO SHOTWELL
ST S OF ARMY ST
MIRALOMA DR SF 13 B2
S FROM 1151 PORTOLA DR TO
YERBA BUENA AV
MIRAMAR AV SF 19 B2
N FROM LAKE VIEW AV TO
MONTEREY BLVD
2 LAKE VIEW AV
100 GRAFTON AV
200 HOLLOWAY AV
DE MONTFORD AV
300 OCEAN AV
400 SOUTHWOOD DR
500 EASTWOOD DR
WESTWOOD DR
600 WILDWOOD DR
700 EASTWOOD DR
WESTWOOD DR
800 NORTHWOOD DR
END MONTEREY BLVD
MISSION ST SF 6 C3
MISSION ST SF 7 A2
MISSION ST SF 10 C2
MISSION ST SF 14 B3
MISSION ST SF 20 A2
FROM THE BAY BETWEEN HOWARD ST
& MARKET ST SW TO COUNTY LINE
2 THE EMBARCADERO
50 STEUART ST
100 SPEAR ST
200 MAIN ST
300 BEALE ST
400 FREMONT ST
500 1ST ST
ECKER ST
SHAW AL
ANTHONY ST
600 2ND ST
638 NEW MONTGOMERY ST
ANNIE ST
700 3RD ST
800 4TH ST
900 5TH ST
MINT ST
MARY ST
1000 6TH ST
1100 7TH ST
JULIA ST
1200 8TH ST
LASKIE ST
1300 9TH ST
WASHBURN ST
GRACE ST
1400 10TH ST
1500 11TH ST
LAFAYETTE ST
1600 OTIS ST
VAN NESS AVE
12TH ST
PLUM ST
13TH ST
1700 DUBOCE ST
ERIE ST
1800 14TH ST
1900 15TH ST
2000 16TH ST
2100 17TH ST
2120 CLARION AL
2146 SYCAMORE ST
2200 18TH ST
2300 19TH ST
2400 20TH ST
CATHERINE CT
2500 21ST ST
2600 22ND ST
2700 23RD ST
2800 24TH ST
2900 25TH ST
3000 26TH ST
CAPP ST
3100 ARMY ST
COSO AVE
POWERS AV
3200 VALENCIA ST
FAIR AVE
3300 29TH ST
VIRGINIA AV
GODEUS ST
3400 30TH ST
EUGENIA AV
3438 KINGSTON ST
CORTLAND AV
3500 BROOK ST
SANTA MARINA ST
3600 RANDALL ST
APPLETON AV
3700 HIGHLAND AV
LEESE ST
3750 PARK ST
3800 RICHLAND AV
CRESCENT AV
3900 COLLEGE AV
COLLEGE TER
3990 ST MARYS AV
4000 BOSWORTH ST
MURRAY ST
ALEMANY BLVD
TRUMBALL ST
NEY ST
MAYNARD ST
CASTLE MANOR AV
SILVER AV
4300 TINGLEY ST
AVALON AV
4350 THERESA ST
4400 COTTER ST
4434 FRANCIS ST
EXCELSIOR AV
4500 SANTA ROSA AV
4550 HARRINGTON ST
BRAZIL AV
4600 NORTON ST
SAN JUAN AV
OCEAN AV
4700 RUTH ST
PERSIA AV
4723 LEO ST
RUSSIA AV
4800 ONONDAGA AV
FRANCE AV
KENNEY AL
ITALY AV
SENECA AV
AMAZON AV
5100 GENEVA AV
ROLPH ST
5200 NIAGARA AV
POPE ST
5300 MT VERNON AV
ALLISON ST
CONCORD ST
5400 OTTAWA AV
FLORENTINE ST
5500 FOOTE AV
GUTENBERG ST
5600 NAGLEE AV
LOWELL ST
MORSE ST
5650 WHIPPLE AV
WHITTIER ST
5700 FARRAGUT AV
LAURA ST
OLIVER ST
5800 LAWRENCE AV
ACTON ST
5900 SICKLES AV
HURON AV
END COUNTY LINE
MISSION ROCK ST SF 11 B1
AT JCT OF 4TH AND 3RD ST AT
PIER 50
MISSISSIPPI ST SF 11 B2
MISSISSIPPI ST SF 15 B1
FROM 16TH ST BETWEEN TEXAS ST AND
PENNSYLVANIA AV S TO ARMY ST
2 16TH ST
100 17TH ST
200 MARIPOSA ST
300 18TH ST
400 19TH ST
500 20TH ST
700 22ND ST
1000 25TH ST
END ARMY ST
MISSOURI ST SF 11 B2
MISSOURI ST SF 15 B1
FROM 16TH ST BETWEEN TEXAS AND
CONNECTICUT ST S TO ARMY ST
2 16TH ST
100 17TH ST
200 MARIPOSA ST
300 18TH ST
400 19TH ST
500 20TH ST
SIERRA ST
700 22ND ST
900 23RD ST
END ARMY ST
MISTRAL ST SF 11 A2
E FROM TREAT AV TO HARRISON ST
BETWEEN 19TH ST AND 20TH ST
MIZPAH ST SF 14 A3
BETWEEN SWISS AV AND ELK AV
FROM CHENERY ST N TO
SUSSEX ST
MODOC AV SF 19 C2
N FROM CAYUGA AV BETWEEN
FOOTE AV AND NAGLEE AV
MOFFITT ST SF 14 B2
BETWEEN MORELAND ST AND SUSSEX ST
N FROM CASTRO ST
MOJAVE ST SF 15 A2
W FROM PERALTA AV S OF
CORTLAND AV TO BRONTE ST
MOLIMO DR SF 13 C2
FROM BELLA VISTA DR W TO POINT
WEST OF MYRA WY
MONCADA WY SF 13 A3
N FROM URBANO DR TO
JUNIPERO SERRA BLVD
2 URBANO DR
100 CERRITOS AV
200 CEDRO AV
300 PALOMA AV
END JUNIPERO SERRA BLVD
MONETA CT SF 19 C3
NW FROM MONETA WY
MONETA WY SF 19 C3
N FROM HURON AV BETWEEN
NAGLEE AV AND WHIPPLE AV
MONO ST SF 10 A3
FROM MARKET ST N AND W TO
CASELLI AV
2 MARKET ST
100 EAGLE ST
END CASELLI AV
MONTAGUE PL SF 3 A2
E FROM 1201 MONTGOMERY ST
BETWEEN GREEN ST AND UNION ST
MONTALVO AV SF 13 B1
FROM DEWEY BLVD N TO CASTENADA AV
MONTANA ST SF 19 B2
W FROM SUMMIT AV BETWEEN
THRIFT ST AND MINERVA ST TO
ORIZABA AV
2 SUMMIT AV
100 PLYMOUTH AV
200 CAPITOL AV
FAXON AV
END ORIZABA AV
MONTCALM AV SF 15 A1
FROM YORK ST W TO ALABAMA ST
YORKS
MULLEN AVE
200 FRANCONIA ST
300 PERALTA AV
END ALABAMA ST
MONTCLAIR TER SF 2 C2
N FROM LOMBARD ST BETWEEN HYDE ST
AND LEAVENWORTH ST
MONTECITO AV SF 13 C3
FROM MONTEREY BLVD SW TO
EASTWOOD DR
2 MONTEREY BLVD
100 HAZELWOOD AV
200 VALDEZ AV
300 COLON AV
400 PLYMOUTH AV
NORTHWOOD AV
END EASTWOOD DR
MONTEREY BLVD SF 13 C3
FROM CIRCULAR AVE AND SAN
JOSE AVE W THROUGH
WESTWOOD PARK AND ST
FRANCIS WOOD TO JUNIPERO
SERRA BLVD
2 CIRCULAR AVE
100 ACADIA ST
200 BADEN ST
300 CONGO ST
400 DETROIT ST
542 EDNA ST
600 FOERSTER ST
700 GENNESSEE ST
800 RIDGEWOOD AV
MONTECITO AV
856 HAZELWOOD AV
900 VALDEZ AV
930 COLON AV
950 PLYMOUTH ST
MIRAMAR AV
1000 YERBA BUENA AV
FAXON AV
1100 ST ELMO WY
1200 SAN FELIPE AV
NO GATE DR
1400 SAN JACINTO WY
1500 SAN ANDREAS WY
SAN ALESO AV
1600 SANTA CLARA AV
1700 SAN BENITO WY
1800 SANTA ANA AV
1900 SAN LEANDRO WY
2000 SAN FERNANDO WY
2100 SAN RAFAEL WY
END JUNIPERO SERRA BLVD
MONTE VISTA DR SF 19 A1
W FROM 19TH AV S OF
EUCALYPTUS DR
MONTEZUMA ST SF 14 C1
FROM COSO AV E TO
SHOTWELL ST
MONTGOMERY ST SF 1 B2
SW FROM LINCOLN BLVD TO
SHERIDAN AV BETWEEN TAYLOR RD AND
ANZA ST
MONTGOMERY ST SF 3 A2
MONTGOMERY ST SF 7 B1
N FROM MARKET ST BETWEEN SANSOME
ST AND KEARNY ST TO FRANCISCO ST
2 MARKET ST
POST ST
100 SUTTER ST
200 BUSH ST
300 PINE ST
400 CALIFORNIA ST
500 SACRAMENTO ST
COMMERCIAL ST
600 CLAY ST
MERCHANT ST
700 WASHINGTON ST
COLUMBUS AV
800 JACKSON ST
GOLD ST
900 PACIFIC AV
VERDI PL
1000 BROADWAY
1100 VALLEJO ST
1200 GREEN ST
MONTAGUE PL
1300 UNION ST
SCHOOL AL
ALTA ST
1400 FILBERT ST
1500 GREENWICH ST
1600 LOMBARD ST
1700 CHESTNUT ST
END FRANCISCO ST
MONTICELLO ST SF 19 A2
N FROM RANDOLPH ST TO ESTERO AV
2 BLKS E OF JUNIPERO SERRA BLVD
19TH AV
100 SARGENT ST
200 SHIELDS ST
300 GARFIELD ST
400 HOLLOWAY AV
END ESTERO AV
MONUMENT WY SF 9 C2
N FROM 17TH ST E OF ROOSEVELT WY
MOORE PL SF 2 C2
N FROM UNION ST BETWEEN HYDE
ST AND LARKIN ST
MORAGA AV SF 1 B3
IN PRESIDIO NE FROM INFANTRY TER
TO FUNSTON AV
MORAGA ST SF 8 A3
MORAGA ST SF 9 A3
FROM LOCKSLEY AV S OF
LAWTON ST W TO GREAT HWY
2 LOCKSLEY AV
100 7TH AV
200 8TH AV
AUTO DR
300 9TH AV
400 10TH AV
500 11TH AV
600 12TH AV
700 FUNSTON AV
800 14TH AV
900 15TH AV
1000 16TH AV
1100 17TH AV
1200 18TH AV
1300 19TH AV
1400 20TH AV
1500 21ST AV
1600 22ND AV
1700 23RD AV
1800 24TH AV
1900 25TH AV
2000 26TH AV
2100 27TH AV
2200 28TH AV
2300 29TH AV
2400 30TH AV
2500 31ST AV
2600 32ND AV
2700 33RD AV
2800 34TH AV
2900 35TH AV
3000 36TH AV
SUNSET BLVD
3100 37TH AV
3200 38TH AV
3300 39TH AV
3400 40TH AV
3500 41ST AV
3600 42ND AV
3700 43RD AV
3800 44TH AV
3900 45TH AV
4000 46TH AV
4100 47TH AV

4200 48TH AV
END GREAT HIGHWAY
MORELAND ST SF 14 B2
W FROM FARNUM ST TO DIAMOND ST
MORGAN AL SF 10 A3
FROM GRAND VIEW AV W TO
CORBETT AV
MORNINGSIDE DR SF 12 B3
N AND S OF OCEAN AV BETWEEN
GELLERT DR AND CLEARFIELD DR
MORREEL ST SF 17 B1
S FROM SPEAR AV TO MANSEAU ST
MORRELL ST SF 2 C3
N FROM PACIFIC AV BETWEEN
HYDE ST AND LARKIN ST N TO
BROADWAY
MORRIS RD SF 1 A3
IN PRESIDIO W FROM AMATURY LOOP
MORRIS ST SF 7 B3
S FROM HARRISON ST BETWEEN
5TH ST AND 6TH ST SE TO
POINT S OF BRYANT ST
MORSE ST SF 20 A3
FROM ROLPH ST S W TO
MISSION ST N W OF
BRUNSWICK ST
2 ROLPH ST
ROYAL DR
100 NEWTON ST
200 CURTIS ST
300 POPE ST
400 ALLISON ST
500 CONCORD ST
FLORENTINE ST
600 GUTENBERG ST
700 LOWELL ST
END MISSION ST
MORTON ST SF 1 C3
IN PRESIDIO SE FROM RODGIGUEZ ST
TO SANCHEZ ST
MOSCOW ST SF 20 B2
FROM MADISON ST SW TO AMAZON AV
100 AVALON AV
200 EXCELSIOR AV
300 BRAZIL AV
400 PERSIA AV
500 RUSSIA AV
600 FRANCE AV
700 ITALY AV
800 AMAZON AV
END GENEVA AV
MOSS ST SF 7 A3
S FROM HOWARD ST BETWEEN 6TH ST
AND 7TH ST SE TO FOLSOM ST
MOULTON ST SF 2 B2
W FROM BUCHANAN ST BETWEEN
GREENWICH ST AND LOMBARD ST
W TO STEINER ST
2 BUCHANAN ST
100 WEBSTER ST
200 FILLMORE ST
END STEINER ST
MOULTRIE ST SF 14 C2
S FROM BERNAL HEIGHTS BLVD
TO A POINT S OF CRESCENT AV
100 BERNAL HEIGHTS BLVD
200 POWHATTAN AV
300 EUGENIA AV
400 CORTLAND AV
500 JARBOE AV
600 TOMPKINS AV
700 OGDEN AV
800 CRESCENT AV
END PT S OF CRESCENT AV
MOUNT LN SF 9 A3
FROM NORIEGA ST AND 15TH
AV E TO 14TH AV
MOUNTAIN SPGS AV SF 9 C3
FROM TWIN PEAKS BLVD S OF
CLARENDON AV TO PT W OF
STANYAN ST

MOUNT VERNON AV SF 19 C2
FROM MISSION ST BETWEEN OTTAWA AV
AND NIAGARA AV NW TO HAROLD AV
MISSION ST
ELLINGTON AV
DEL MONTE ST
ALEMANY BLVD
ROME ST
CAYUGA AV
DELANO AV
OTEGA AV
SAN JOSE AV
SAN MIGUEL ST
TARA ST
LOUISBURG ST
HOWTH ST
WILLIAR AV
END HAROLD AV
MOUNTVIEW CT SF 13 C1
2 BLKS N OF TWIN PEAKS
BLVD E FROM PANORAMA DR
MUIR LOOP SF 1 C3
IN PRESIDIO S OF SIMONDS LOOP
E OF SHAFTER RD
MULFORD AL SF 7 A2
E FROM TAYLOR ST BETWEEN
BUSH ST AND PINE ST
MULLEN AV SF 15 A1
E FROM ALABAMA ST BETWEEN
PRECITA AV AND MONTCALM ST
TO BREWSTER ST
MUNICH ST SF 20 B2
SW FROM EXCELSIOR AV TO CROCKER
AMAZON PLGD, & FROM HILL BLVD TO
NAPLES ST
200 EXCELSIOR AV
300 BRAZIL AV
400 PERSIA AV
500 RUSSIA AV
CROCKER AMAZON PLGD
900 HILL BLVD
1000 ROLPH ST
NAYLOR ST
1100 CORDOVA ST
DRAKE ST
END NAPLES ST
MURRAY ST SF 14 B3
TO HOLLY PARK CIRCLE
2 MISSION ST
100 GENEBERN WY
200 COLLEGE AV
300 JUSTIN DR
400 CRESCENT AV
500 RICHLAND AV
END HOLLY PARK CIRCLE
MUSEUM WY SF 10 A2
S FROM ROOSEVELT WAY
AND FAIRBANKS ST
MYRA WY SF 13 C2
FROM ROCKDALE DR SW TO
POINT S OF MOLINO DR
MYRTLE ST SF 6 C2
W FROM LARKIN ST BETWEEN
O FARRELL ST AND GEARY ST
2 LARKIN ST
100 POLK ST
200 VAN NESS AVE
END FRANKLIN ST

N

NADELL CT SF 20 A3
E FROM GUTTENBERG 2 BLKS S
OF BRUNSWICK
NAGLEE AV SF 19 C2
FROM 5600 BLOCK OF MISSION
ST NW TO SAN JOSE AV
2 MISSION ST
100 ELLINGTON AV
RAE AV
200 HURON AV
ALEMANY BLVD

CAYUGA AV
END SAN JOSE AVE
NAHUA AV SF 19 C2
SE FROM MT VERNON AV TO
DELANO AV N OF OTTAWA AV
NANTUCKET AV SF 20 A1
W FROM 1800 SAN JOSE AV
NAPIER LN SF 3 A2
N FROM 200 FILBERT ST BETWEEN
SANSOME ST AND MONTGOMERY ST
NAPLES ST SF 20 B2
FROM SILVER AV SW
THROUGH CROCKER AMAZON
TRACT TO CURTIS ST
2 SILVER AV
100 PERU AV
200 AVALON AV
300 EXCELSIOR AV
400 BRAZIL AV
500 PERSIA AV
600 RUSSIA AV
700 FRANCE AV
800 ITALY AV
900 AMAZON AV
1000 GENEVA AV
1100 ROLPH ST
ATHENS ST
ROYAL LN
SEVILLE ST
NEWTON ST
MUNICH ST
END CURTIS ST
NAPOLEON ST SF 15 B1
W FROM ISLAIS ST TO JERROLD AV
NATICK ST SF 14 C3
S FROM CHENERY ST TO SAN JOSE AV
NATOMA ST SF 7 A3
NATOMA ST SF 10 C1
FROM W S FREMONT ST BETWEEN
MISSION AND HOWARD ST SW
TO 15TH ST
2 FREMONT ST
20 1ST ST
100 2ND ST
144 NEW MONTGOMERY ST
TO A POINT N OF 3RD ST
400 5TH ST
MARY ST
500 6TH ST
RUSS ST
600 7TH ST
700 8TH ST
9TH ST
WASHBURN ST
GRACE ST
900 10TH ST
1000 11TH ST
LAFAYETTE ST
1300 14TH ST
END 15TH ST
NAUMAN RD SF 1 B3
IN PRESIDIO N FROM WASHINGTON
BLVD TO A POINT E OF AMATURY LOOP
NAUTILUS CT SF 17 A1
N FROM KIRKWOOD AV IN
HUNTERS PT NAVAL RES
NAVAJO AV SF 20 A1
FROM A POINT NW OF DELANO AV S E
TO CAYUGA AV
NAVY RD SF 16 A3
NAVY RD SF 17 A1
FROM A POINT NW OF GRIFFITH ST
SE TO EARL ST
GRIFFITH ST
EARL ST
END KIRKWOOD AV
NAYLOR ST SF 20 B3
S FROM MUNICH ST E OF CORDOVA ST
SE TO BALTIMORE WY
2 MUNICH ST
100 PRAGUE ST

200 WINDING WY
300 CHICAGO WY
END BALTIMORE WY
NEBRASKA ST SF 15 A2
FROM POWHATTAN ST S TO
CORTLAND AV
NELLIE ST SF 10 B3
N FROM ELIZABETH ST TO
POINT N OF 23RD ST W OF
CHURCH ST
NELSON AV SF 21 B2
SW FROM MEADE AV
NEPTUNE ST SF 15 B3
FROM THORNTON AV S TO WILLIAMS AV
NEVADA ST SF 15 A2
FROM BERNAL HEIGHTS BLVD BETWEEN
PRENTISS ST AND ROSENKRANZ ST
S TO CRESCENT AV
BERNAL HEIGHTS BLVD
100 POWHATTAN AV
200 CORTLAND AV
300 JARBOE AV
400 TOMPKINS AV
500 OGDEN AV
END CRESCENT AV
NEWBURG ST SF 14 A1
FROM 27TH ST BETWEEN CASTRO ST
AND DIAMOND ST S TO DUNCAN ST
NEWCOMB AV SF 15 B2
FROM WHITNEY YOUNG CIR N OF
OAKDALE AV NW TO BARNEVELD AV
SOUTH RIDGE RD
LANE ST
MENDELL ST
3RD ST
NEWHALL ST
PHELPS ST
QUINT ST
RANKIN ST
SELBY ST
TOLAND ST
END BARNEVELD AV
NEWELL ST SF 2 C2
N FROM 700 LOMBARD ST BETWEEN
MASON ST AND TAYLOR ST
NEWHALL ST SF 15 B3
NEWHALL ST SF 21 B1
FROM JENNINGS ST NW TO MENDELL
ST & W TO EVANS AV THEN SW TO
EGBERT AV
JENNINGS ST
MENDELL ST
EVANS AV
FAIRFAX AV
GALVEZ AV
HUDSON AV
INNES AV
3RD ST
JERROLD AV
KIRKWOOD AV
LA SALLE AV
MCKINNON AV
NEWCOMB AV
OAKDALE AV
PALOU AV
QUESADA AV
REVERE AV
BAY VIEW AV
TOPEKA AV
WILLIAMS AV
YOSEMITE AV
ARMSTRONG AV
CARROLL AV
END EGBERT AV
NEWMAN ST SF 14 C2
E FROM HOLLY PARK CIRCLE BETWEEN
ELLERT ST AND HIGHLAND AV
TO ANDOVER ST
2 HOLLY PARK CIRCLE
100 BENNINGTON ST
END ANDOVER ST
NEW MONTGMRY ST SF 7 B2

S FROM MARKET ST BETWEEN 2ND ST
AND 3RD ST SE TO HOWARD ST
2 MARKET ST
STEVENSON ST
JESSIE ST
ALDRICH AL
100 MISSION ST
140 MINNA ST
NATOMA ST
END HOWARD ST
NEWTON ST SF 20 A2
S FROM S ROLPH ST NE OF
CURTIS ST SE TO NAPLES ST
2 ROLPH ST
100 MORSE ST
BRUNSWICK ST
END NAPLES ST
NEY ST SF 14 B3
E FROM S MISSION ST TO TRUBULL ST
2 MISSION ST
100 CRAUT ST
200 CONGDON ST
END TRUMBULL ST
NIAGARA AV SF 19 C2
N FROM 5200 BLOCK MISSION ST
BETWEEN GENEVA AV AND MOUNT
VERNON AV TO EDGAR PL
2 MISSION ST
ALEMANY BLVD
CAYUGA AV
300 DELANO AV
400 SAN JOSE AV
500 SAN MIGUEL AV
600 TARA ST
700 LOUISBURG ST
800 HOWTH ST
WILLIAR AV
END EDGAR PL
NIANTIC AV SF 19 B3
SW FROM PANAMA ST TO
ST CHARLES AV RUNNING
PARALLEL WITH SOUTHERN FRWY
NIBBI CT SF 21 B3
E FROM GILLETTE AV
NICHOLS WY SF 21 C2
E FROM CAMERON WY ONE
BLK N OF FITZGERALD ST
NIDO AV SF 5 C3
N FROM TURK ST TO VEGA ST
BETWEEN ANZAVISTA AV AND
MASONIC AV
NIMITZ AV SF 17 B1
E FROM BLANDY ST TO A ST S
OF SPEAR AV IN HUNTERS POINT
NOB HILL CIR SF 7 A1
NE CORNER OF PINE ST AND MASON ST
NOBLES AL SF 3 A2
FROM 1500 GRANT AV BETWEEN
UNION ST AND FILBERT ST
NOE ST SF 10 B1
NOE ST SF 14 B1
S FROM DUBOCE AV BETWEEN
SANCHEZ ST AND CASTRO ST S
TO LAIDLEY ST
2 DUBOCE AV
100 14TH ST
150 HENRY ST
200 15TH ST
250 BEAVER ST
16TH ST
300 MARKET ST
400 17TH ST
FORD ST
500 18TH ST
HANCOCK ST
600 19TH ST
700 20TH ST
750 LIBERTY ST
800 21ST ST
850 HILL ST
900 22ND ST

950 ALVARADO ST
1000 23RD ST
1050 ELIZABETH ST
1100 24TH ST
1150 JERSEY ST
1200 25TH ST
1250 CLIPPER ST
1300 26TH ST
1350 ARMY ST
1400 27TH ST
1500 28TH ST
1550 VALLEY ST
1600 29TH ST
1650 DAY ST
1700 30TH ST
END LAIDLEY ST
NORDHOFF ST SF 14 A3
BETWEEN BADEN AV AND CONGO AV
FROM STILLINGS ST S ONE BLK
NORFOLK ST SF 10 C1
S FROM FOLSOM ST BETWEEN
11TH ST AND 12TH ST SE TO
HARRISON ST
NORIEGA ST SF 8 A3
NORIEGA ST SF 9 A3
FROM 8TH AV S OF MORAGA
ST W TO GREAT HIGHWAY
2 7TH AV
100 8TH AV
200 9TH AV
300 10TH AV
400 11TH AV
500 12TH AV
600 FUNSTON AV
700 14TH AV
800 15TH AV
900 16TH AV
1000 17TH AV
1100 18TH AV
1200 19TH AV
1300 20TH AV
1400 21ST AV
1500 22ND AV
1600 23RD AV
1700 24TH AV
1800 25TH AV
1900 26TH AV
2000 27TH AV
2100 28TH AV
2200 29TH AV
2300 30TH AV
2400 31ST AV
2500 32ND AV
2600 33RD AV
2700 34TH AV
2800 35TH AV
2900 36TH AV
SUNSET BLVD
3000 37TH AV
3100 38TH AV
3200 39TH AV
3300 40TH AV
3400 41ST AV
3500 42ND AV
3600 43RD AV
3700 44TH AV
3800 45TH AV
3900 46TH AV
3000 47TH AV
4100 48TH AV
END GREAT HIGHWAY
NORMANDIE TER SF 2 A3
N FROM BROADWAY BETWEEN SCOTT ST
AND DIVISADERO ST TO VALLEJO ST
NORTH GATE DR SF 13 B3
FROM 1199 MONTEREY BLVD S
TO UPLAND DR
NORTH POINT DR SF 3 C1
LOOP EXTENDING N FROM GATEVIEW AV
2 BLKS NW OF 13TH ST, TREASURE
ISLAND

NORTH POINT ST SF 2 A2
NORTH POINT ST SF 3 A2
FROM THE BAY BETWEEN BAY ST AND
BEACH ST W TO BAKER ST
THE EMBARCADERO
2 KEARNY ST
100 GRANT AV
200 STOCKTON ST
300 POWELL ST
400 MASON ST
500 TAYLOR ST
JONES ST
700 COLUMBUS AV
LEAVENWORTH ST
800 HYDE ST
900 LARKIN ST
1000 POLK ST
VAN NESS AV
FORT MASON
1500 LAGUNA ST
1600 BUCHANAN ST
WEBSTER ST
1266 FILLMORE ST
2100 SCOTT ST
2200 DIVISADERO ST
2300 BRODERICK ST
END BAKER ST
NORTHRIDGE RD SF 16 A3
E FROM INGALLS ST TO JERROLD AV
NORTH VIEW CT SF 2 C2
S FROM BAY ST BETWEEN POLK ST AND
LARKIN ST
NORTHWOOD DR SF 13 B3
WESTERLY FROM MONTECITO
AV TO PIZARRO WY S OF
MONTEREY BLVD
2 MONTECITO AV
100 MIRAMAR AV
END PIZARRO WY
NORTON ST SF 20 A1
FROM 4600 BLOCK MISSION ST
BETWEEN HARRINGTON ST AND
SAN JUAN ST
NORWICH ST SF 15 A1
W FROM S ALABAMA ST NEAR
RIPLEY ST W TO POINT NEAR
TREAT AV
NOTTINGHAM PL SF 3 A3
FROM 1000 KEARNY ST BETWEEN
PACIFIC AV AND BROADWAY
NUEVA AV SF 21 B3
FROM LATHROP AV NE TO A POINT
NE OF BLANKEN AV

O

OAK ST SF 10 A1
FROM JUNCTION MARKET ST
AND VAN NESS AV BETWEEN PAGE ST
AND FELL ST W TO STANYAN ST
2 MARKET ST
VAN NESS AV
100 FRANKLIN ST
200 GOUGH ST
300 OCTAVIA ST
400 LAGUNA ST
500 BUCHANAN ST
600 WEBSTER ST
700 FILLMORE ST
800 STEINER ST
EVA TERR
900 PIERCE ST
1000 SCOTT ST
1100 DIVISADERO ST
1200 BRODERICK ST
BAKER ST
LYON ST
CENTRAL AV
MASONIC AV
ASHBURY ST
CLAYTON ST
COLE ST

SHRADER ST
END STANYAN ST
OAKDALE AV SF 15 B2
FROM GRIFFITH ST NW TO
BAYSHORE BLVD
GRIFFITH ST
BALDWIN CT
INGALLS ST
KEITH ST
LANE ST
MENDELL ST
3RD ST
NEWHALL ST
PHELPS ST
QUINT ST
RANKIN ST
SELBY ST
INDUSTRIAL ST
TOLAND ST
BARNEVELD AVE
LOOMIS ST
PATTERSON ST
END BAY SHORE BLVD
OAK GROVE ST SF 7 B3
S FROM S HARRISON ST BETWEEN
5TH ST AND 6TH ST SE TO BRYANT ST
OAKHURST LN SF 9 B3
FROM WARREN AV E BETWEEN
LOCKSLEY AV AND DEVONSHIRE WY
OAK PARK DR SF 9 B3
S FROM GLENHAVEN LN AND
WARREN DR W OF CLARENDON AV
OAKWOOD ST SF 10 B2
S FROM 18TH ST BETWEEN
GUERRERO AND DOLORES ST
OCEAN AV SF 19 C1
FROM 4700 MISSION ST W TO
COUNTRY CLUB DR
2 MISSION ST
PERSIA AV
WATSON PL
ALEMANY BLVD
100 SANTA YNEZ AV
CAYUGA AV
WANDA ST
200 OTSEGO AV
ONONDAGA ST
300 DELANO AV
400 SAN JOSE AV
TARA ST
920 HOWTH ST
1000 PHELAN AV
HAROLD AV
LEE AV
BRIGHTON AV
1300 PLYMOUTH AV
1400 GRANADA AV
1500 MIRAMAR AV
1600 CAPITOL AV
1700 FAXON AV
1800 JULES AV
ASHTON AV
KEYSTONE WY
FAIRFIELD WY
VICTORIA ST
2100 LAKEWOOD AV
MANOR DR
PINEHURST WY
CORONA ST
CERRITOS AV
WEST GATE DR
CEDRO AV
2200 APTOS AV
SAN BENITO WY
PALOMA AV
SANTA ANA AV
SAN LEANDRO WY
SAN FERNANDO WY
JUNIPERO SERRA BLVD
EUCALYPTUS DR
2500 WOODACRE DR

LAGUNITAS DR
19TH AV
20TH AV
21ST AV
22ND AV
MELBA AV
23RD AV
24TH AV
25TH AV
26TH AV
INVERNESS DR
FOREST VIEW DR
MEADOWBROOK DR
SYLVAN DR
MIDDLEFIELD DR
RIVERTON DR
SPRINGFIELD DR
EVERGLADE DR
HAVENSIDE DR
WESTMOORLAND DR
CLEARFIELD DR
MORNINGSIDE DR
GELLERT DR
SUNSET BLVD
LAKE SHORE DR
END COUNTRY CLUB DR
OCTAVIA ST SF 2 B2
OCTAVIA ST SF 6 B3
OCTAVIA ST SF 10 B1
N FROM MARKET ST BETWEEN
GOUGH AND LAGUNA ST N TO
FORT MASON
2 MARKET ST
WALLER ST
100 HAIGHT ST
ROSE ST
200 PAGE ST
LILY ST
300 OAK ST
HICKORY ST
400 FELL ST
LINDEN ST
500 HAYES ST
IVY ST
600 GROVE ST
BIRCH ST
700 FULTON ST
ASH ST
800 MCALLISTER ST
GOLDEN GATE AV
1600 SUTTER ST
1700 BUSH ST
AUSTIN ST
1800 PINE ST
1900 CALIFORNIA ST
SACRAMENTO ST
2200 WASHINGTON ST
2300 JACKSON ST
2400 PACIFIC AV
2500 BROADWAY
2600 VALLEJO ST
2700 GREEN ST
2800 UNION ST
2900 FILBERT ST
3000 GREENWICH ST
3100 LOMBARD ST
3200 CHESTNUT ST
3300 FRANCISCO ST
END FORT MASON
OFARRELL ST SF 6 A3
OFARRELL ST SF 7 A2
FROM JUNCTION MARKET ST
AND GRANT AV BETWEEN ELLIS ST
AND GEARY ST W TO MASONIC AV
2 MARKET ST
GRANT AVE
SAVINGS UNION PL
100 STOCKTON ST
200 POWELL ST
CYRIL MAGIN ST
ELWOOD ST
300 MASON ST

400 TAYLOR ST
SHANNON ST
500 JONES ST
600 LEAVENWORTH ST
HARLAM AL
ADA CT
700 HYDE ST
800 LARKIN ST
900 POLK ST
1000 VAN NESS AV
FRANKLIN ST
HOLLIS ST
1600 WEBSTER ST
1700 FILLMORE ST
STEINER ST
PIERCE ST
2000 SCOTT ST
BEIDEMAN ST
2100 DIVISADERO ST
2200 BRODERICK ST
ST JOSEPHS AV
LYON ST
ANZAVISTA AV
END MASONIC AV
OGDEN AV SF 14 C2
E FROM 601 ANDOVER ST TO
PUTNAM ST
2 ANDOVER ST
100 MOULTRIE ST
200 ANDERSON ST
300 ELLSWORTH ST
400 GATES ST
500 FOLSOM ST
600 BANKS ST
700 PRENTISS ST
800 NEVADA ST
END PUTNAM ST
OLD CHINA TN LN SF 3 A3
N FROM WASHINGTON ST BETWEEN
STOCKTON ST AND GRANT AV
OLIVE ST SF 6 C2
W FROM LARKIN ST BETWEEN
ELLIS ST AND O FARRELL ST
2 LARKIN ST
100 POLK ST
200 VAN NESS AV
END FRANKLIN ST
OLIVER ST SF 19 C3
SE FROM 5800 MISSION ST
NEAR COUNTY LINE
OLMSTEAD ST SF 21 A2
SW FROM 3100 SAN BRUNO AV S
OF DWIGHT ST TO UNIVERSITY ST
2 SAN BRUNO AV
100 GIRARD ST
200 BRUSSELS ST
300 GOETTINGEN ST
700 BOWDOIN ST
800 DARTMOUTH ST
900 COLBY ST
END UNIVERSITY ST
OLYMPIA WY SF 13 C1
W OFF PANORAMA DR TO
CLARENDON AV
OMAR WY SF 13 C2
W FROM SEQUOIA WY TO MYRA WY
ONEIDA AV SF 20 A1
FROM ALEMANY BLVD NW TO
SAN JOSE AV
ALEMANY BLVD
100 CAYUGA AV
200 OTSEGO AV
300 DELANO AV
END SAN JOSE AV
ONIQUE LN SF 14 A2
W FROM GOLD MINE DR TO
TO BERKELEY WY
ONONDAGA AV SF 20 A1
NW FROM 4800 MISSION ST
TO OCEAN AV
2 MISSION ST

1991 SAN FRANCISCO COUNTY CROSS STREET INDEX

ALEMANY BLVD
ROSELLA CT
100 CAYUGA AV
WANDA ST
200 OTSEGO AV
END OCEAN AV
OPAL PL SF 7 A2
E FROM S TAYLOR ST BETWEEN
MARKET ST AND TURK ST
OPALO LN SF 14 A2
N FROM GOLD MINE DR ONE
BLK W OF DIAMOND HEIGHTS BLVD
OPHIR AL SF 6 C2
N FROM POST ST BETWEEN JONES
ST AND TAYLOR ST
ORA WY SF 14 A2
S FROM GOLD MINE DR TWO
BLKS W OF DIAMOND HEIGHTS BLVD
ORANGE AL SF 14 C1
S FROM POINT N OF 24TH ST
BETWEEN VALENCIA ST AND BARTLETT
ST TO 26TH ST
ORBEN PL SF 6 B2
N FROM PINE ST BETWEEN
WEBSTER ST AND FILLMORE ST
TO CALIFORNIA ST
ORD CT SF 10 A2
FROM DOUGLASS ST WESTERLY
N OF VULCAN ST
ORD ST SF 1 B2
IN PRESIDIO N OF SHERIDAN AV
TO MILES ST
ORD ST SF 10 A2
N FROM 18TH ST ONE BLK
W OF DOUGLASS
MARKET ST
100 17TH ST
126 CORBETT AV
SATURN ST
VALCAN ST
END ORD CT
ORDWAY ST SF 21 A2
W FROM 3300 SAN BRUNO AV S
OF MANSELL ST TO ANKENY ST
2 SAN BRUNO AV
100 GIRARD ST
200 BRUSSELS ST
300 GOETTINGEN ST
400 SOMERSET ST
END ANKENY ST
OREILLY AV SF 1 C2
IN PRESIDIO N FROM TORNEY AV
TO EDIE RD
ORIENTE ST SF 20 C3
S FROM VELASCO ST TO
COUNTY LINE E OF ACACIA ST
ORIOLE WY SF 13 B1
FROM PACHECO ST BETWEEN 10TH AV
AND 11TH AV SW TO ROCKRIDGE DR
ORIZABA AV SF 19 B2
W OF SAN JOSE AV FROM DE LONG ST
N TO HOLLOWAY AV
2 DE LONG ST
50 PALMETTO AV
100 SAGAMORE ST
150 SADOWA ST
STANLEY ST
200 BROAD ST
250 FARALLONES ST
RANDOLPH ST
300 LOBOS ST
350 MINERVA ST
SARGENT ST
400 MONTANA ST
450 THRIFT ST
SHIELDS ST
500 LAKE VIEW AV
GARFIELD ST
600 GRAFTON AV
END HOLLOWAY AV
ORTEGA ST SF 12 A1
ORTEGA ST SF 9 B3
W FROM POINT E OF 8TH AV S
OF NORIEGA ST TO THE OCEAN
100 8TH AV
200 9TH AV
300 10TH AV
400 11TH AV
AERIAL WY
SELMA WY
CASCADE WK
700 14TH AV
600 FUNSTON AV
800 15TH AV
900 16TH AV
1000 17TH AV
1100 18TH AV
1200 19TH AV
1300 20TH AV
1400 21ST AV
1500 22ND AV
1600 23RD AV
1700 24TH AV
1800 25TH AV
1900 26TH AV
2000 27TH AV
2100 28TH AV
2200 29TH AV
2300 30TH AV
2400 31ST AV
2500 32ND AV
2600 33RD AV
2700 34TH AV
2800 35TH AV
2900 36TH AV
SUNSET BLVD
3000 37TH AV
3100 38TH AV
3200 39TH AV
3300 40TH AV
3400 41ST AV
3500 42ND AV
3600 43RD AV
3700 44TH AV
3800 45TH AV
3900 46TH AV
4000 47TH AV
4100 48TH AV
END GREAT HIGHWAY
ORTEGA WY SF 9 A3
E FROM ORTEGA ST AND 15TH
AV TO 14TH AV
OSAGE AL SF 14 C1
FROM POINT N OF 24TH ST
BETWEEN MISSION ST AND
BARTLETT ST S TO 26TH ST
OSCAR AL ♠ SF 7 B2
N FROM CLEMENTINA ST BETWEEN
1ST ST AND 2ND ST
OSCEOLA LN SF 15 C3
LOOP EXTENDING S FROM LA SALLE AV
GARLINGTON CT AND WHITFIELD CT
OSGOOD PL SF 3 B3
N FROM 400 PACIFIC AV BETWEEN
SANSOME ST AND MONTGOMERY
ST TO BROADWAY
OSHAUGHNESSY BL SF 13 C1
OSHAUGHNESSY BL SF 14 A2
FROM 600 PORTOLA DR S TO
BOSWORTH ST
PORTOLA DR
EVELYN WY
DEL VALE AV
MALTA DR
END BOSWORTH ST
OTEGA AV SF 19 C2
SW FROM MOUNT VERNON AV E OF
SAN JOSE AV TO OTTAWA AV
OTIS ST SF 10 C1
FROM MISSION AND 12TH STS
SW TO MCCOPPIN ST THEN
S TO MISSION ST AND DUBOCE AV
2 12TH ST
MISSION ST
70 BRADY ST
GOUGH ST
100 MCCOPPIN ST
MISSION ST
END DUBOCE AV
OTSEGO AV SF 20 A1
FROM SANTA YSABEL AV SW
TO ONEIDA AV
2 SANTA YSABEL AV
100 SAN JUAN AV
200 SANTA YNEZ AV
RUDDEN AV
MEDA AV
300 OCEAN AV
400 ONONDAGA AV
END ONEIDA AV
OTTAWA AV SF 20 A2
NW FROM 5400 MISSION ST
TO SAN JOSE AV NEAR
COUNTY LINE
2 MISSION ST
24 ELLINGTON AV
DEL MONTE ST
100 HURON AV
ALEMANY BLVD
ROME ST
CAYUGA AV
DELANO AV
OTEGA AV
END SAN JOSE AV
OVERLOOK DR SF 8 C1
IN GOLDEN GATE PARK N FROM MIDDLE
DR W TO TRANSVERSE RD
OWEN ST SF 1 B2
IN PRESIDIO SE FROM ANZA ST
TO GRAHAM ST
OWENS ST SF 11 B1
SW FROM CHANNEL ST
AND S TO 16TH ST
OXFORD ST SF 20 C1
FROM SILVER AV S TO WAYLAND ST
2 SILVER AV
PIOCHE ST
100 SILLIMAN ST
200 FELTON ST
300 BURROWS ST
400 BACON ST
END WAYLAND ST
OZBORN CT SF 3 C1
NW FROM GATEVIEW AV 1 BLK SW OF
BAYSIDE DR, TREASURE ISLAND

P

PACHECO ST SF 9 A3
PACHECO ST SF 12 A1
PACHECO ST SF 13 A1
FROM MERCED AV N AND NW TO
JUNCTION OF PACHECO ST
PROPER THEN WESTERLY TO
THE OCEAN
2 MERCED AV
100 DEWEY BLVD
200 MAGELLAN AV
266 MARCELA AV
DORANTES AV
300 CASTENADA AV
325 LOPEZ AV
400 ALTON AV
500 9TH AV
600 10TH AV
700 11TH AV
ORIOLE WY
800 12TH AV
900 FUNSTON AV
1000 14TH AV
1100 15TH AV
1200 16TH AV
1300 17TH AV
1400 18TH AV
1500 19TH AV
1600 20TH AV
1700 21ST AV
1800 22ND AV
1900 23RD AV
2000 24TH AV
SUNSET RESERVOIR
2400 28TH AV
2500 29TH AV
2600 30TH AV
2700 31ST AV
2800 32ND AV
2900 33RD AV
3000 34TH AV
3100 35TH AV
3200 36TH AV
SUNSET BLVD
37TH AV
SUNSET COMMUNITY CTR
3700 41ST AV
3800 42ND AV
3900 43RD AV
4000 44TH AV
4100 45TH AV
4200 46TH AV
4300 47TH AV
END 48TH AV
PACIFIC AV SF 2 A3
PACIFIC AV SF 3 B3
FROM THE BAY BET JACKSON
& BROADWAY W TO THE PRESIDIO
2 THE EMBARCADERO
50 DRUMM ST
100 DAVIS ST
200 FRONT ST
300 BATTERY ST
400 SANSOME ST
OSGOOD PL
500 MONTGOMERY ST
JEROME AL
KEARNY ST
600 COLUMBUS AV
BECKETT ST
700 GRANT AV
JASON CT
PELTON PL
800 STOCKTON ST
CORDELIA ST
TRENTON ST
900 POWELL ST
KEYES AL
WAYNE PL
1000 MASON ST
AUBURN ST
SALMON ST
HIMMELMANN PL
1100 TAYLOR ST
PHOENIX TER
1200 JONES ST
1300 LEAVENWORTH ST
BURGOYNE PL
1400 HYDE ST
MORRELL PL
MCCORMICK ST
1500 LARKIN ST
1600 POLK ST
1700 VAN NESS AV
1800 FRANKLIN ST
1900 GOUGH ST
2000 OCTAVIA ST
2100 LAGUNA ST
2200 BUCHANAN ST
2300 WEBSTER ST
2400 FILLMORE ST
2500 STEINER ST
2600 PIERCE ST
2700 SCOTT ST
2800 DIVISADERO ST
RAYCLIFF TER
2900 BRODERICK ST
3000 BAKER ST
3100 LYON ST
3200 PRESIDIO AV
WALNUT ST
LAUREL ST
LOCUST ST
END PRESIDIO
PACIFIC AV W SF 5 B2
BEGINNING WALNUT
LAUREL ST
LOCUST ST
SPRUCE ST
MAPLE ST
CHERRY ST
ARGUELLO BLVD
END 8TH AV
PAGE ST SF 9 C1
PAGE ST SF 10 B1
FROM JUNCTION MARKET ST
AND FRANKLIN ST BETWEEN HEIGHT ST
AND OAK ST W TO STANYAN ST
2 MARKET ST
FRANKLIN ST
100 GOUGH ST
200 OCTAVIA ST
300 LAGUNA ST
400 BUCHANAN ST
500 WEBSTER ST
600 FILLMORE ST
700 STEINER ST
800 PIERCE ST
900 SCOTT ST
1000 DIVISADERO ST
1100 BRODERICK ST
1200 BAKER ST
1300 LYON ST
1400 CENTRAL AV
1500 MASONIC AV
1600 ASHBURY ST
1700 CLAYTON ST
1800 COLE ST
1900 SHRADER ST
END STANYAN ST
PAGODA PL SF 7 A1
N FROM 1800 SACRAMENTO ST BETWEEN
STOCKTON ST AND GRANT AV
PALACE DR SF 1 C2
S FROM MARINA BLVD AROUND
THE PALACE OF FINE ARTS
TO BAY ST
PALM AV SF 5 B2
FROM CALIFORNIA ST S TO
GEARY BLVD BETWEEN JORDAN AV
AND ARGUELLO BLVD
2 CALIFORNIA ST
100 EUCLID AV
END GEARY BLVD
PALMETTO AV SF 19 B3
W FROM HEAD ST TO
JUNIPERO SERRA BLVD
SERRA BLVD
300 HEAD ST
VICTORIA ST
RAMSELL ST
WORCESTER AV
600 ST CHARLES AV
700 CHESTER AV
END JUNIPERO SERRA BLVD
PALO ALTO AV SF 9 C3
E FROM LA AVANZADA TO A POINT
W OF BURNETT AV
PALOMA AV SF 19 A1
W FROM OCEAN AV TO
JUNIPERO SERRA BLVD
2 OCEAN AV
100 MONCADA WY
MERCEDES WY
END JUNIPERO SERRA BLVD
PALOS PL SF 12 C3
N FROM SLOAT BLVD BETWEEN
VALE AV AND EL MIRASOL PL
PALOU AV SF 15 B2
FROM FITCH ST NW TO BARNEVELD AV

FITCH ST
1000 GRIFFITH ST
1100 HAWES ST
1200 INGALLS ST
1300 JENNINGS ST
1400 KEITH ST
1500 LANE ST
1600 3RD ST
MENDELL ST
1700 NEWHALL ST
1800 PHELPS ST
DUNSHEE ST
1900 QUINT ST
SILVER AV
2000 RANKIN ST
2100 SELBY ST
INDUSTRIAL ST
DORMAN AV
END BARNEVELD AV
PANAMA ST SF 19 A3
W OF SO EMBARCADERO FRWY
FROM NIANTIC AV
PANORAMA DR SF 9 C3
PANORAMA DR SF 13 C1
N FROM TWIN PEAKS BLVD TO
CLARENDON AV 1 BLK N OF
PORTOLA DR
PANTON AL SF 6 C1
E FROM LEAVENWORTH ST BETWEEN
CALIFORNIA ST AND PINE ST
PARADISE AV SF 14 A3
SE FROM ELK ST BETWEEN
CHENERY ST AND BOSWORTH ST
TO BURNSIDE AV
PARAISO PL SF 12 C3
FROM SLOAT BLVD N TO
CRESTLAKE DR
PARAMOUNT TER SF 5 C3
W FROM STANYAN ST BETWEEN
GOLDEN GATE AV AND MCALLISTER ST
PARDEE AL SF 3 A2
FROM 1601 GRANT AV BETWEEN
FILBERT ST AND GREENWICH ST
PARIS ST SF 20 A2
FROM AVALON AV SW TO ROLPH ST
AVALON ST
200 EXCELSIOR AV
300 BRAZIL AV
400 PERSIA AV
500 RUSSIA AV
600 FRANCE AV
700 ITALY AV
800 AMAZON AV
900 GENEVA AV
END ROLPH ST
PARK BLVD SF 5 A2
IN PRESIDIO PARALLEL TO
PARK PRESIDIO BLVD
PARK ST SF 14 B2
FROM SAN JOSE AV TO ANDOVER ST
MISSION ST
100 LEESE ST
300 HOLLY PARK CIRCLE
END ANDOVER ST
PARKER AV SF 5 C2
S FROM CALIFORNIA ST OPPOSITE
MAPLE ST S TO FULTON ST
CALIFORNIA ST
EUCLID AV
200 GEARY BLVD
ANZA ST
600 TURK ST
GOLDEN GATE AV
MCALLISTER ST
END FULTON ST
PARK HILL AV SF 10 A2
N FROM ROOSEVELT WY BETWEEN
BUENA VISTA AV AND BUENA
VISTA TER
PARKHURST AL SF 3 A3
N FROM 900 CLAY ST BETWEEN
STOCKTON ST AND POWELL ST
PARK PRESIDIO BL SF 5 A3
N FROM FULTON ST TO LAKE ST
BETWEEN FUNSTON AV AND 14TH AV
FULTON ST
CABRILLO ST
BALBOA ST
ANZA ST
GEARY BLVD
CLEMENT ST
CALIFORNIA ST
END LAKE ST
PARKRIDGE DR SF 14 A1
N FROM BURNETT AV 4
BLKS N OF PORTOLA DR
PARNASSUS AV SF 9 B2
FROM CLAYTON ST BETWEEN CARL ST
AND GRATTON ST W TO 5TH AV
W TO 5TH AVE
2 CLAYTON ST
BELVEDERE ST
100 COLE ST
164 SHRADER ST
200 STANYAN ST
WOODLAND AV
300 WILLARD ST
HILL POINT ST
374 HILLWAY ST
400 ARGUELLO BLVD
500 2ND AV
600 3RD AV
700 4TH AV
END 5TH AV
PARQUE DR SF 20 C3
N FROM CARRIZAL ST TO GENEVA AV
PARSONS ST SF 9 C1
N FROM FULTON ST BETWEEN
STANYAN ST AND WILLARD ST
PASADENA ST SF 20 C3
FROM VELASCO AV TO GENEVA AV
PATTEN RD SF 1 B2
IN PRESIDIO E FROM MCDOWELL AV
TO LINCOLN BLVD
PATTERSON ST SF 15 A2
E OF BAYSHORE BLVD FROM
FLOWER ST NE
PATTON ST SF 14 C2
FROM APPLETON AV S TO
HIGHLAND AV E OF MISSION ST
PAUL AV SF 21 B1
FROM 3RD ST AND GILMAN AV
NW TO SAN BRUNO AV
3RD ST
CARR ST
GOULD ST
EXETER ST
CRANE ST
500 WHEAT ST
BAYSHORE BLVD
END SAN BRUNO AV
PAULDING ST SF 20 A1
FROM W S SAN JOSE AV BETWEEN
NANTUCKET AV AND HAVELOCK ST
PAYSON ST SF 19 A3
N OF PALMETTO AV FROM ST CHARLES
AV TO CHESTER AV
PEABODY ST SF 21 A3
W OF BAYSHORE BLVD FROM LELAND AV
COUNTY LINE
PEARCE ST SF 1 A2
IN PRESIDIO E FROM HAMILTON ST
BETWEEN MARINE DR AND HAMILTON ST
PEARL ST SF 10 C1
S FROM MARKET ST BETWEEN
ELGIN PARK AND GUERRERO ST
S TO DUBOCE AV
PEDESTRIAN WY SF 1 C2
N FROM MARINA BLVD AT
ST FRANCIS YACHT CLUB
PELTON PL SF 3 A3
N FROM 700 PACIFIC AV BETWEEN
GRANT AV AND STOCKTON ST
PEMBERTON PL SF 9 C3
SW FROM CLAYTON ST AND CORBETT AV
TO BURNETT AV
PENA ST SF 1 B3
IN PRESIDIO NW FROM MESA AV
PENINSULA AV SF 21 B3
BETWEEN WHEELER AV AND TOCOLOMA
AV FROM HESTER AV TO
POINT S OF LATHROP AV
PENNINGTON ST SF 1 B2
IN PRESIDIO N FROM MASON ST
TO MAULDIN ST
PENNSYLVANIA AV SF 11 B3
FROM 16TH ST BETWEEN IOWA ST AND
MISSISSIPPI ST S TO ARMY ST
16TH ST
100 17TH ST
200 MARIPOSA ST
300 18TH ST
400 19TH ST
500 20TH ST
700 22ND ST
900 23RD ST
1100 25TH ST
END ARMY ST
PERALTA AV SF 15 A1
FROM HOLLADAY AV S OF
ARMY ST SW AND S T A POINT S
OF OGDEN AV
2 HOLLADAY AV
16 HAMPSHIRE ST
100 YORK ST
FRANCONIA ST
200 FLORIDA ST
220 MULLEN ST
300 MONTCALM ST
400 RUTLEDGE ST
SAMOSET ST
500 RIPLEY ST
ESMERALDA AV
MAYFLOWER ST
700 POWHATTAN AV
800 CORTLAND AV
MOJAVE ST
900 JARBOE AV
TOMPKINS AV
END PUTNAM ST
PEREGO TER SF 14 A1
E FROM BURNETT 4 BLKS N OF
PORTOLA DR
PERINE PL SF 6 A2
W FROM STEINER ST BETWEEN
CALIFORNIA ST AND SACRAMENTO ST
TO PIERCE ST
PERRY ST SF 7 B2
FROM POINT W OF 2ND ST BETWEEN
HARRISON ST AND BRYANT ST
SW TO 5TH ST
2 PT W OF 2ND ST
100 3RD ST
200 4TH ST
END 5TH ST
PERSHING DR SF 4 C1
IN PRESIDIO
PERSIA AV SF 20 B1
FROM OCEAN AV BETWEEN
ALEMANY BLVD AND MISSION ST SE TO
BRAZIL AV AND MANSELL ST
OCEAN AV
2 MISSION ST
100 LONDON ST
200 PARIS ST
300 LISBON ST
400 MADRID ST
500 EDINBURGH ST
600 NAPLES ST
700 VIENNA ST
800 ATHENS ST
900 MOSCOW ST
1000 MUNICH ST
1100 PRAGUE ST
DUBLIN ST
LA GRANDE AV
SUNNYDALE AV
END MANSELL ST & BRAZIL AV
PERU AV SF 20 B1
SE FROM LISBON ST TO BURROWS ST
100 LISBON ST
200 MADRID ST
300 EDINBURG ST
400 NAPLES ST
500 VIENNA ST
600 ATHENS ST
VALMAR TER
AVALON AV
FELTON ST
END BURROWS ST
PETERS AV SF 14 C2
SW FROM FAIR AV BETWEEN
MISSION ST AND COLERIDGE ST
PETER YORKE WY SF 6 B2
N FROM GEARY ST BETWEEN GOUGH ST
AND FRANKLIN ST
PETRARCH PL SF 7 B1
FROM 301 PINE ST BETWEEN
SANSOME ST AND MONTGOMERY ST
PFEIFFER ST SF 3 A2
FROM POINT E OF GRANT AV BETWEEN
CHESTNUT ST AND FRANCISCO ST W TO
STOCKTON ST
2 POINT E OF GRANT AV
100 GRANT AV
BELLAIR PL
END STOCKTON ST
PHELAN AV SF 19 C1
FROM OCEAN AV N TO FLOOD AV
W OF BALBOA PARK
2 OCEAN AV
200 JUDSON AV
300 STAPLES AV
END FLOOD AV
PHELPS ST SF 15 B2
PHELPS ST SF 21 B1
S FROM DAVIDSON AV AND 3RD ST TO
BAYSHORE BLVD
DAVIDSON AV
400 EVANS AV
500 FAIRFAX AV
600 GALVEZ AV
700 HUDSON AV
800 INNES AV
900 JERROLD AV
1000 KIRKWOOD AV
1100 LA SALLE AV
1200 MCKINNON AV
1300 NEWCOMB AV
1400 OAKDALE AV
1500 PALOU AV
1600 QUESADA AV
2500 BANCROFT AV
2600 CARROLL AV
2700 DONNER AV
2800 EGBERT AV
END BAYSHORE BLVD
PHOENIX TER SF 2 C3
S OF PACIFIC AV BETWEEN
TAYLOR ST AND JONES ST
PICO AV SF 19 B1
FROM ASHTON AV W BETWEEN
HOLLOWAY AV AND OCEAN AV
PIEDMONT ST SF 10 A2
FROM MASONIC AV S OF FREDERICK ST
W TO ASHBURY ST
2 MASONIC AV
100 DELMAR ST
END ASHBURY ST
PIERCE ST SF 2 A3
PIERCE ST SF 6 A1
PIERCE ST SF 10 B1
FROM DUBOCE PARK BETWEEN
STEINER ST AND SCOTT ST N TO
BEACH ST
2 DUBOCE PARK
100 WALLER ST
200 HAIGHT ST
300 PAGE ST
400 OAK ST
500 FELL ST
HAYES
ALAMO SQUARE
800 FULTON ST
900 MCALLISTER ST
1000 GOLDEN GATE AV
ELM ST
1100 TURK ST
1200 EDDY ST
1300 ELLIS ST
O'FARRELL ST
HAMILTON SQUARE
1600 POST ST
1700 SUTTER ST
1800 BUSH ST
1900 PINE ST
2000 CALIFORNIA ST
PERINE PL
2100 SACRAMENTO ST
CLAY ST
ALTA PLAZA
2400 JACKSON ST
2500 PACIFIC AV
2600 BROADWAY
2700 VALLEJO ST
2800 GREEN ST
2900 UNION ST
3000 FILBERT ST
3100 GREENWICH ST
3200 LOMBARD ST
3300 CHESTNUT ST
TOLEDO WY
3400 ALHAMBRA ST
3500 CAPRA WY
END BEACH ST
PILGRIM AV SF 14 A3
S FROM MONTEREY BLVD TO
SAN JOSE AV
PINE ST SF 3 B3
PINE ST SF 6 A2
FROM JUNCTION MARKET ST
AND DAVIS ST BETWEEN BUSH ST
AND CALIFORNIA ST W TO
PRESIDIO AV
2 MARKET ST
DAVIS ST
100 FRONT ST
200 BATTERY ST
CENTURY PL
300 SANSOME ST
LEIDESDORFF ST
EXCHANGE PL
PETRARCH PL
400 MONTGOMERY ST
BELDEN ST
500 KEARNY ST
ST GEORGE AL
QUINCY ST
600 GRANT AV
700 STOCKTON ST
JOICE ST
MONROE ST
800 POWELL ST
900 MASON ST
VINE TERR
1000 TAYLOR ST
1100 JONES ST
TOUCHARD ST
1200 LEAVENWORTH ST
1300 HYDE ST
1400 LARKIN ST
1500 POLK ST
1600 VAN NESS AV
1700 FRANKLIN ST
1800 GOUGH ST
1900 OCTAVIA ST
2000 LAGUNA ST

2100 BUCHANAN ST
2200 WEBSTER ST
ORBEN PL
2300 FILLMORE ST
2400 STEINER ST
2500 PIERCE ST
2600 SCOTT ST
2700 DIVISADERO ST
2800 BRODERICK ST
2900 BAKER ST
3000 LYON ST
END PRESIDIO AV
PINEHURST WY SF 19 B1
FROM 2000 OCEAN AV N TO UPLAND DR
2 OCEAN AV
100 KENWOOD WY
END UPLAND DR
PINK AL SF 10 B1
FROM PEARL ST BETWEEN MARKET ST AND DUBOCE AV
PINO AL SF 8 C2
FROM JUDAH ST BETWEEN 35TH AV AND 36TH AV
PINTO AV SF 18 C2
W FROM TAPIA DR NEAR FONT BLVD TO ARBALLO DR
PIOCHE ST SF 20 B1
FROM CAMBRIDGE ST W TO MADISON ST
100 CAMBRIDGE ST
200 OXFORD ST
300 HARVARD ST
400 GAMBIER ST
END MADISON ST
PIPER LOOP SF 1 B3
IN PRESIDIO LOOP EXTENDING NW FROM WASHINGTON BLVD
PIXLEY ST SF 2 A3
W FROM BUCHANAN ST BETWEEN FILBERT ST AND GREENWICH ST TO STEINER ST
2 BUCHANAN ST
100 WEBSTER ST
200 FILLMORE ST
END STEINER ST
PIZARRO WY SF 13 B3
FROM WESTWOOD DR TO FAXON AV JUST S OF MONTEREY BLVD
PLAZA ST SF 13 B1
E FROM MAGELLAN AV TO LAGUNA HONDA BLVD
PLEASANT ST SF 2 C3
W FROM TAYLOR ST BETWEEN SACRAMENTO ST AND CLAY ST W TO JONES ST
PLUM ST SF 10 C1
E FROM MISSION ST TO S VAN NESS AV BETWEEN 12TH ST AND 13TH ST
PLYMOUTH AV SF 19 C2
FROM SAN JOSE AV AT JUNCTION OF PALMETTO AV N TO YERBA BUENA AV
SAN JOSE AV
100 SAGAMORE ST
200 SADOWA ST
300 BROAD ST
400 FARALLONES ST
500 LOBOS ST
600 MINERVA ST
700 MONTANA ST
800 THRIFT ST
900 LAKEVIEW AV
1000 GRAFTON AV
1100 HOLLOWAY AV
1200 OCEAN AV
1300 SAN RAMON WY
1400 WILDWOOD WY
GREENWOOD AV
1500 MONTECITO AV
1600 MONTEREY BLVD
MANGELS AV

END YERBA BUENA AV
POINT LOBOS AV SF 4 A3
FROM JUNCTION OF GEARY BLVD AND 40TH AV NW W AND S TO GREAT HIGHWAY
GEARY BLVD
40TH AV
41ST AV
42ND AV
100 43RD AV
200 44TH AV
300 45TH AV
400 46TH AV
ALTA MAR WY
500 47TH AV
600 48TH AV
END GREAT HIGHWAY
POLARIS WY SF 20 A3
E FROM POPE ST 2 BLKS S OF HANOVER ST
POLK ST SF 2 C2
POLK ST SF 6 C3
N FROM MARKET ST BETWEEN VAN NESS AV AND LARKIN ST N TO BEACH ST
2 MARKET ST
FELL ST
HAYES ST
LECH WALESA
GROVE ST
MCALLISTER ST
430 REDWOOD ST
500 GOLDEN GATE AV
ELM ST
600 TURK ST
700 EDDY ST
730 WILLOW ST
800 ELLIS ST
830 OLIVE ST
900 OFARRELL ST
930 MYRTLE ST
1000 GEARY ST
1030 CEDAR ST
1100 POST ST
1130 HEMLOCK ST
1200 SUTTER ST
1230 FERN ST
1300 BUSH ST
1330 AUSTIN ST
1400 PINE ST
1500 CALIFORNIA ST
1600 SACRAMENTO ST
1700 CLAY ST
1800 WASHINGTON ST
1900 JACKSON ST
2000 PACIFIC AV
2100 BROADWAY
2200 VALLEJO ST
BONITA ST
2300 GREEN ST
2400 UNION ST
2500 FILBERT ST
2600 GREENWICH ST
2700 LOMBARD ST
2800 CHESTNUT ST
2900 FRANCISCO ST
3000 BAY ST
3100 NORTH POINT ST
END BEACH ST
POLLARD PL SF 3 A2
FROM 500 VALLEJO ST BETWEEN KEARNY ST AND GRANT AV
POMONA ST SF 15 B3
FROM BAY VIEW ST BETWEEN LATONA ST AND FLORA ST S TO THORNTON AV
POND ST SF 10 B2
S FROM 16TH ST BETWEEN NOE ST AND SANCHEZ ST TO 17TH ST
POPE RD SF 2 B2
IN FORT MASON N FROM SHOFIELD RD
POPE ST SF 1 A2

IN PRESIDIO N FROM KOBBE AV BETWEEN GREENOUGH AV AND TODD ST
POPE ST SF 20 A2
FROM 5200 MISSION OPPOSITE NIAGARA AV S TO BELLEVUE WY
2 MISSION ST
HOLLYWOOD CT
100 CROSS ST
200 MORSE ST
300 BRUNSWICK ST
HANOVER ST
BALTIMORE WY
POLARIS WY
END BELLEVUE WY
POPLAR ST SF 14 C1
FROM POINT N OF 24TH ST BETWEEN VALENCIA ST AND SAN JOSE AV S TO 26TH ST
2 PT N OF 24TH ST
100 24TH ST
200 25TH ST
END 26TH ST
POPPY LN SF 14 A2
NE FROM CONRAD ST TO A POINT W OF CASTRO ST N OF SUSSEX ST BEMIS ST AND N OF SUSSEX ST
PORTAL PATH SF 13 B2
S FROM PORTOLA DR TO SANTA MONICA AV W OF SAN LORENZO WY
PORTER ST SF 14 C3
S FROM CRESCENT AV BETWEEN ROSCOE ST AND BACHE ST
PORTOLA DR SF 13 B2
FROM DIAMOND HEIGHTS BLVD AND SW TO JUNIPERO SERRA BLVD
DIAMOND HEIGHTS BLVD
TURQUOISE WY
O'SHAUGHNESSY BLVD
TERESITA BLVD
700 WOODSIDE AV
800 SYDNEY WY
FOWLER AV
EVELYN WY
900 LAGUNA HONDA BLVD
DEL SUR AV
1000 WAITHMAN PL
REX AV
MARNE AV
1100 KENSINGTON WY
MIRALOMA DR
1200 GRANVILLE WY
SAN PABLO AV
SANTA PAULA AV
1300 DORCHESTER WY
SAN LORENZO WY
1370 CLAREMONT BLVD
PORTAL PATH
1400 VICENTE ST
SANTA CLARA AV
1500 14TH AV
TERRACE DR
SANTA ANA AV
SAN ANSELMO AV
SAN LEANDRO WY
1600 15TH AV
SAN FERNANDO WY
END JUNIPERO SERRA BLVD
PORTOLA ST SF 1 C3
IN PRESIDIO S FROM MACARTHUR ST PARALLEL TO RODRIGUEZ ST
POST ST SF 6 A2
POST ST SF 7 A2
FROM JUNCTION MARKET ST AND MONTGOMERY ST BETWEEN GEARY ST AND SUTTER ST W TO PRESIDIO AV
2 MARKET ST
MONTGOMERY ST
LICK PL
100 KEARNY ST
ROBERT KIRK LN

200 GRANT AV
300 STOCKTON ST
400 POWELL ST
500 MASON ST
600 TAYLOR ST
AGATE AL
SHANNON ST
OPHIR AL
700 JONES ST
800 LEAVENWORTH ST
900 HYDE ST
MEACHAM PL
1000 LARKIN ST
1100 POLK ST
1200 VAN NESS AV
1300 FRANKLIN ST
1400 GOUGH ST
1600 LAGUNA ST
1700 BUCHANAN ST
1800 WEBSTER ST
1900 FILLMORE ST
AVERY ST
2000 STEINER ST
2100 PIERCE ST
2200 SCOTT ST
2300 DIVISADERO ST
ERKSON CT
2400 BRODERICK ST
2500 BAKER ST
2600 LYON ST
END PRESIDIO AV
POTOMAC ST SF 10 B1
FROM 549 WALLER ST S TO DUBOCE PARK BETWEEN STEINER ST AND PIERCE ST
POTRERO AV SF 11 A3
FROM DIVISION ST BETWEEN UTAH ST AND HAMPSHIRE ST S TO ARMY ST
2 DIVISION ST
100 ALAMEDA ST
200 15TH ST
300 16TH ST
400 17TH ST
500 MARIPOSA ST
600 18TH ST
700 19TH ST
800 20TH ST
900 21ST ST
1000 22ND ST
1100 23RD ST
1200 24TH ST
1300 25TH ST
END ARMY ST
POWELL ST SF 3 A1
POWELL ST SF 7 A2
N FROM MARKET ST BETWEEN STOCKTON ST AND MASON ST N TO THE EMBARCADERO
2 MARKET ST
EDDY ST
100 ELLIS ST
200 OFARRELL ST
GEARY ST
400 POST ST
500 SUTTER ST
ANSON PL
600 BUSH ST
FELLA PL
700 PINE ST
800 CALIFORNIA ST
900 SACRAMENTO ST
1000 CLAY ST
1100 WASHINGTON ST
1200 JACKSON ST
JOHN ST
1300 PACIFIC AV
FISHER AL
1400 BROADWAY
1500 VALLEJO ST
1600 GREEN ST
1700 UNION ST
COLUMBUS AV

1800 FILBERT ST
1900 GREENWICH ST
2000 LOMBARD ST
FIELDING ST
2100 CHESTNUT ST
2200 FRANCISCO ST
VANDEWATER ST
2300 BAY ST
2400 NORTH POINT ST
2500 BEACH ST
JEFFERSON ST
END THE EMBARCADERO
POWERS AV SF 14 C1
FROM MISSION ST S OF PRECITA AV SE TO COLERIDGE ST
POWHATTAN AV SF 15 A2
FROM BOCANA ST BETWEEN EUGENIA AV AND ESMERALDA AV E TO HOLLADAY AV
BOCANA ST
2 WOOL ST
100 ANDOVER ST
200 MOULTRIE ST
300 ANDERSON ST
400 ELLSWORTH ST
500 GATES ST
600 FOLSOM ST
700 BANKS ST
800 PRENTISS ST
900 NEVADA ST
ROSENKRANZ ST
1000 NEBRASKA ST
1100 BRADFORD ST
1200 PERALTA AV
FRANCONIA ST
END HOLLADAY AV
PRADO ST SF 2 A2
W FROM CERVANTES BLVD TO SCOTT ST
PRAGUE ST SF 20 B2
FROM EXCELSIOR AV BETWEEN MUNICH ST AND DUBLIN ST SW TO HANOVER ST
2 EXCELSIOR AV
100 BRAZIL AV
200 PERSIA AV
300 RUSSIA AV
CROCKER AMAZON PLGD
GENEVA AV
HILL BLVD
700 ROLPH ST
800 NAYLOR ST
900 CORDOVA ST
1000 DRAKE ST
1100 CURTIS ST
WINDING WY
END POPE ST & HANOVER ST
PRECITA AV SF 14 C1
FROM COSO AV S OF ARMY ST E TO ARMY ST AND YORK ST
100 COSO AV
EMMETT CT
252 SHOTWELL ST
300 FOLSOM ST
400 HARRISON ST
500 ALABAMA ST
600 FLORIDA ST
BRYANT ST
700 YORK ST
HAMPSHIRE ST
END ARMY ST
PRENTISS ST SF 15 A2
FROM BERNAL HEIGHTS BLVD BETWEEN BANKS ST AND NEVADA ST S TO POINT S OF CRESCENT AV
2 BERNAL HTS BLVD
CHAPMAN ST
100 POWHATTAN AV
200 EUGENIA AV
300 CORTLAND AV
400 JARBOE AV
500 TOMPKINS AV

600 OGDEN AV
700 CRESCENT AV
END PT S OF CRESCENT AV

PRESCOTT CT SF 3 B2
FROM 301 VALLEJO ST BETWEEN
SANSOME ST AND MONTGOMERY ST

PRESIDIO AV SF 5 C1
W OF LYON ST FROM PRESIDIO
RESERVATION S TO GEARY BLVD
2 PACIFIC AV
100 JACKSON ST
200 WASHINGTON ST
300 CLAY ST
400 SACRAMENTO ST
500 CALIFORNIA ST
600 PINE ST
700 BUSH ST
800 SUTTER ST
900 POST ST
END GEARY BLVD

PRESIDIO BLVD SF 1 C3
IN PRESIDIO N FROM PACIFIC AV TO
MESA AV

PRESIDIO TER SF 5 B2
LOOP EXTENDING FROM W END OF
WASHINGTON ST S OF PRESIDIO

PRETOR WY SF 20 A3
E FROM GUTTENBERG ST 3 BLKS S OF
MISSION ST

PRICE ROW SF 3 A2
S FROM 501 UNION ST BETWEEN
GRANT AV AND STOCKTON ST

PRIEST ST SF 2 C3
S FROM WASHINGTON ST TO
A POINT N OF CLAY ST
AND LEAVENWORTH ST

PRINCETON ST SF 20 C1
FROM SILVER AV TO WAYLAND ST
2 SILVER AV
100 SILLIMAN ST
200 FELTON ST
BACON ST
END WAYLAND ST

PROSPECT AV SF 14 C2
S FROM COSO AV BETWEEN
WINFIELD ST AND COLERIDGE ST TO
SANTA MARINA ST
2 COSO AV
FAIR AV
100 ESMERALDA AV
200 VIRGINIA AV
HEYMAN AV
300 EUGENIA AV
KINGSTON ST
400 CORTLAND AV
END SANTA MARINA ST

PROSPER ST SF 10 B2
S FROM 16TH ST BETWEEN SANCHEZ ST
AND NOE ST TO 17TH ST

PUEBLO ST SF 20 C3
FROM VELASCO AV TO COUNTY LINE

PUTNAM ST SF 15 A2
S FROM CORTLAND AV BETWEEN
BRONTE ST AND NEVADA ST S TO
CRESCENT AV
2 CORTLAND AV
100 JARBOE AV
200 TOMPKINS AV
300 OGDEN AV
END CRESCENT AVE

Q

QUANE ST SF 10 B3
S FROM 21ST ST BETWEEN
DOLORES ST AND FAIR OAKS ST
TO 24TH ST

QUARRY RD SF 5 B1
E OF ARGUELLO S FROM FERNANDEZ ST
IN THE PRESIDIO

QUARTZ WY SF 14 A1
W OF AMBER DR JUST S OF
PORTOLA DR

QUESADA AV SF 15 B2
FROM FITCH ST NW TO INDUSTRIAL ST
BETWEEN PALOU AV AND REVERE AV
FITCH ST
GRIFFITH ST
1200 HAWES ST
1300 INGALLS ST
1400 JENNINGS ST
1500 KEITH ST
1600 LANE ST
1700 3RD ST
1800 NEWHALL ST
1900 PHELPS ST
2000 QUINT ST
SILVER AV
2100 RANKIN ST
2200 SELBY ST
END INDUSTRIAL ST

QUINCY ST SF 3 A3
FROM A POINT S OF PINE ST BETWEEN
KEARNY ST AND GRANT AV N
TO CALIFORNIA ST

QUINT ST SF 15 B2
FROM CARGO WY SW TO REVERE AV
AND BANCROFT AV S TO BAYSHORE BL
2 CARGO WY
200 CUSTER AV
300 DAVIDSON AV
400 EVANS AV
500 FAIRFAX AV
600 GALVEZ AV
700 HUDSON AV
800 INNES AV
900 JERROLD AV
1000 KIRKWOOD AV
1200 MCKINNON AV
1300 NEWCOMB AV
1400 OAKDALE AV
1500 PALOU AV
1600 QUESADA AV
REVERE AV
THOMAS AV
TOPEKA AV
SANTA FE ST
SCOTIA ST
2500 BANCROFT AV
2600 CARROLL AV
END BAYSHORE BLVD

QUINTARA ST SF 12 A1

QUINTARA ST SF 13 A1
FROM A POINT E OF 10TH AV S
OF PACHECO ST W TO THE
GREAT HIGHWAY
2 PT E OF 10TH AV
100 10TH AV
CRAGMONT AV
300 12TH AV
FUNSTON AV
14TH AV
600 15TH AV
700 16TH AV
800 17TH AV
900 18TH AV
1000 19TH AV
1100 20TH AV
1200 21ST AV
1300 22ND AV
1400 23RD AV
1500 24TH AV
1600 25TH AV
1700 26TH AV
1800 27TH AV
1900 28TH AV
2000 29TH AV
2100 30TH AV
2200 31ST AV
2300 32ND AV
2400 33RD AV
2500 34TH AV
2600 35TH AV
2700 36TH AV
SUNSET BLVD
2800 37TH AV
3000 39TH AV
3100 40TH AV
3200 41ST AV
3300 42ND AV
3400 43RD AV
3500 44TH AV
3600 45TH AV
3700 46TH AV
3800 47TH AV
3900 48TH AV
END GREAT HIGHWAY

R

RACCOON DR SF 9 C3
FROM PEMBERTON PL S TO
PALO ALTO AV

RACINE LN SF 21 B2
SW FROM BEEMAN LN TO BRUNO AV
W OF BAYSHORE BLVD

RADIO TER SF 13 A1
FROM ROCKRIDGE ST NW TO 14TH AV

RAE AV SF 19 C3
SW FROM NAGLEE AV TO FARRAGUT AV
2 NAGLEE AV
100 WHIPPLE AV
END FARRAGUT AV

RALEIGH ST SF 20 A1
FROM PAULDING ST TO A POINT N
OF HAVELOCK ST

RALSTON AV SF 1 A2
LOOP EXTENDING S FROM STOREY AV
IN THE PRESIDIO

RALSTON ST SF 19 A2
FROM HOLLOWAY AV TO A POINT S OF
RANDOLPH ST
400 GARFIELD ST
300 SHIELDS ST
200 SARGENT ST
100 RANDOLPH ST

RAMONA ST SF 10 B2
S FROM 14TH ST TO 15TH ST BETWEEN
GUERRERO ST AND DOLORES ST

RAMSELL ST SF 19 B2
S FROM HOLLOWAY AV BETWEEN
ARCH ST & VICTORIA ST TO A POINT
S OF RANDOLPH ST, AND FROM
ALEMANY BLVD TO PALMETTO AV AND
WORCESTER AV
2 PALMETTO & WORCESTER AV
100 ALEMANY BLVD
200 RANDOLPH ST
300 SARGENT ST
400 SHIELDS ST
500 GARFIELD ST
END HOLLOWAY AV

RANDALL ST SF 14 B2
FROM 3550 MISSION ST S OF
30TH ST W TO HARPER ST
2 MISSION ST
32 SAN JOSE AV
100 CHENERY ST
150 CHURCH ST
200 WHITNEY ST
250 SANCHEZ ST
END HARPER ST

RANDOLPH ST SF 19 B2
W OF SAN JOSE AV NEAR COUNTY LINE
W FROM ORIZABA AV BETWEEN
STANLEY ST AND SARGENT ST W TO A
POINT W OF CHESTER AV
2 ORIZABA AV
100 BRIGHT ST
200 HEAD ST
300 VICTORIA ST
400 RAMSELL ST
500 ARCH ST
600 VERNON ST
700 RALSTON ST
19TH AV
900 CHESTER AV
END PT W OF CHESTER AV

RANKIN ST SF 15 B2
FROM ISLAIS SW TO REVERE AV
BETWEEN QUINT ST & SELBY ST
2 ISLAIS ST
CUSTER AV
DAVIDSON AV
300 EVANS AV
400 FAIRFAX AV
500 GALVEZ AV
700 INNES AV
800 JERROLD AV
900 KIRKWOOD AV
1100 MCKINNON AV
1200 NEWCOMB AV
1300 OAKDALE AV
1400 PALOU AV
1500 QUESADA AV
1600 REVERE AV

RAUSCH ST SF 7 A3
S FROM HOWARD ST BETWEEN 7TH ST
& 8TH ST SE TO FOLSOM ST

RAVENWOOD DR SF 13 B3
FROM 200 YERBA BUENA AV SW
TO MAYWOOD DR

RAWLES ST SF 1 C3
FROM PRESIDIO BL TO SIMONDS LOOP
IN THE PRESIDIO

RAYBURN ST SF 10 B3
S FROM LIBERTY ST TO 21ST ST
BETWEEN SANCHEZ ST AND NOE ST

RAYCLIFF TER SF 2 A3
N FROM PACIFIC AV BETWEEN
BRODERICK ST & DIVISADERO ST

RAYMOND AV SF 21 A2
FROM BAY SHORE BLVD W TO
A POINT W OF SAWYER ST
BAY SHORE BLVD
100 ALPHA ST
200 RUTLAND ST
300 DELTA ST
400 ELLIOT ST
500 SAWYER ST
END PT W OF SAWYER ST

REARDON RD SF 16 A3
S FROM KISKA RD IN HUNTERS PT

REDDY ST SF 15 B3
FROM THORNTON AV S TO WILLIAMS AV

REDFIELD AL SF 2 C2
FROM 1901 TAYLOR ST BETWEEN
UNION ST AND FILBERT ST
TURNING N TO FILBERT ST

REDONDO ST SF 21 B2
SW FROM INGERSON ST TO
JAMESTOWN ST BETWEEN HAWES ST
AND INGALLS ST

RED ROCK WY SF 14 A1
E FROM DUNCAN ONE BLK S OF
DIAMOND HEIGHTS BLVD

REDWOOD ST SF 6 C3
W FROM POLK ST BETWEEN
MCALLISTER ST AND GOLDEN GATE AV
TO A POINT W OF LAGUNA
100 POLK ST
200 VAN NESS AV
300 FRANKLIN ST
600 LAGUNA ST

REED ST SF 2 C3
N FROM CLAY ST BETWEEN JONES ST
AND LEAVENWORTH ST N TO
WASHINGTON ST

REEVES CT SF 3 C1
SE FROM GATEVIEW AV 1 BLK SW OF
BAYSIDE DR, TREASURE ISLAND

REGENT ST SF 19 C3
FROM CAYUGA AV NW TO SAN JOSE AV
BETWEEN SICKLES AV AND LIEBIG ST

RENO PL SF 3 A2
S FROM 301 GREEN ST BETWEEN
MONTGOMERY ST AND KEARNY ST

REPOSA WY SF 13 C2
FROM MARIETTA DR SW TO MYRA WY

RESERVOIR ST SF 10 B1
W FROM MARKET ST BETWEEN 14TH ST
& DUBOCE AV TO CHURCH ST

RESTANI WY SF 20 A2
NW OFF ALEMANY BLVD BETWEEN
GENEVA AV AND NIAGARA AV

RETIRO WY SF 2 A2
FROM BEACH ST N AND NE TO
MARINA BLVD

REUEL CT SF 15 C2
E FROM HUDSON AV JUST N OF
CASHMERE ST

REVERE AV SF 15 B2
N FROM FITCH ST W TO
INDUSTRIAL ST
FITCH ST
GRIFFITH ST
1200 HAWES ST
1300 INGALLS ST
1400 JENNINGS ST
1500 KEITH ST
1600 LANE ST
1700 3RD ST
1800 NEWHALL ST
2000 SILVER AV
2100 RANKIN ST
2200 SELBY ST
END INDUSTRIAL ST

REX AV SF 13 C2
OFF PORTOLA DR S TO JUANITA WY

REY ST SF 21 A3
W OF BAYSHORE BLVD N FROM
SUNNYDALE AV TO LELAND AV

RHINE ST SF 19 B3
S FROM DE LONG ST SW TO
SHAKESPEARE ST

RHODE ISLAND ST SF 11 B1
FROM DIVISION ST BETWEEN
DE HARO ST AND KANSAS ST S TO
26TH ST
2 DIVISION ST
8TH ST
100 ALAMEDA ST
200 15TH ST
300 16TH ST
400 17TH ST
500 MARIPOSA ST
600 18TH ST
700 19TH ST
800 20TH ST
S HEIGHTS AV
1000 22ND ST
1200 23RD ST
1300 24TH ST
1400 25TH ST
END 26TH ST

RICE ST SF 19 B3
FROM THE COUNTY LINE NW TO
DE LONG ST
2 COUNTY LINE
100 SAN JOSE AVE
END DE LONG ST

RICHARDSON AV SF 1 C2
NW FROM LOMBARD ST TO A
POINT NW OF LYON ST

RICHLAND AV SF 14 C2
E FROM SAN JOSE AV TO ANDOVER ST
SAN JOSE AVE
100 MISSION ST
200 LEESE ST
300 MURRAY ST
END ANDOVER ST

RICKARD ST SF 15 A3
W FROM SAN BRUNO AV NEAR
EMBARCADERO FRWY

RICO WY SF 2 A2
FROM RETIRO WY NW TO AVILA ST

RIDGE LN SF 19 C2

FROM SAN JOSE AV S OF
MOUNT VERNON AV W TO JOSIAH AV
RIDGEWOOD AV SF 13 C3
FROM FLOOD AV W OF GENESEE ST
N TO MANGLES AV
2 FLOOD AV
100 HEARST AV
200 MONTEREY BLVD
300 JOOST AV
END MANGLES AV
RILEY AV SF 1 B2
N FROM SHERIDAN AV TO LINCOLN BL
IN THE PRESIDIO
RINCON ST SF 7 C2
FROM HARRISON ST BETWEEN 1ST ST
& 2ND ST SE TO FEDERAL ST
2 HARRISON ST
100 BRYANT ST
END FEDERAL ST
RINGOLD ST SF 11 A1
W FROM 8TH ST BETWEEN FOLSOM ST
& HARRISON ST SW TO 9TH ST
RIO CT SF 14 A2
OFF TERESITA BLVD E TO
EL SERRENO CT
RIO VERDE ST SF 20 C3
FROM VELASCO AV S TO
COUNTY LINE
RIPLEY ST SF 15 A2
FROM MANCHESTER ST S OF
STONEMAN ST E TO PERALTA AV
MANCHESTER ST
100 FOLSOM ST
HARRISON ST
200 ALABAMA ST
END PERALTA AV
RITCH ST SF 7 B3
S FROM BRYANT ST BETWEEN 3RD ST
& 4TH ST SE TO TOWNSEND ST
200 BRYANT ST
300 BRANNAN ST
END TOWNSEND ST
RIVAS AV SF 18 C2
S FROM GONZALES DR TO VIDAL DR
E OF ARABALLO DR
RIVERA ST SF 12 A1
RIVERA ST SF 13 A1
FROM 14TH AV S OF QUINTARA ST
W TO GREAT HIGHWAY
400 14TH AV
500 15TH AV
600 16TH AV
700 17TH AV
800 18TH AV
900 19TH AV
1000 20TH AV
1100 21ST AV
1200 22ND AV
1400 24TH AV
1500 25TH AV
1600 26TH AV
1700 27TH AV
1800 28TH AV
1900 29TH AV
2000 30TH AV
2100 31ST AV
2200 32ND AV
2300 33RD AV
2400 34TH AV
2500 35TH AV
2600 36TH AV
SUNSET BLVD
2700 37TH AV
2800 38TH AV
2900 39TH AV
3000 40TH AV
3100 41ST AV
3200 42ND AV
3300 43RD AV
3400 44TH AV
3500 45TH AV
3600 46TH AV
3700 47TH AV
3800 48TH AV
END GREAT HIGHWAY
RIVERTON DR SF 12 C3
S FROM SLOAT BLVD BETWEEN
SPRINGFIELD DR & MIDDLEFIELD DR
RIVOLI ST SF 9 C2
FROM BELVEDERE ST BETWEEN ALMA ST
AND 17TH ST TO STANYAN ST
2 BELVEDERE ST
100 COLE ST
200 SHRADER ST
END STANYAN ST
RIZAL ST SF 7 B3
SW FROM LAPU LAPU ST TO
TANDANG SORA BETWEEN FOLSOM ST
AND HARRISON ST
ROACH ST SF 2 C2
N FROM 900 FILBERT ST BETWEEN
TAYLOR ST AND JONES ST N TO
GREENWICH ST
ROANOKE ST SF 14 B2
FROM BEMIS ST SE TO A POINT S OF
ARLINGTON ST
2 BEMIS ST
100 LAIDLEY ST
200 CHENERY ST
300 ARLINGTON ST
ROBBLEE AV SF 15 B3
W FROM MADDUX AV TO THOMAS AV
S OF SILVER AV
ROBINHOOD DR SF 13 B2
SW OF MT DAVIDSON PK FROM
LANDSDALE AV TO LANDSDALE AV
ROBINSON DR SF 20 B3
S OFF LAPHAM WY TO COUNTY LINE
ROBINSON ST SF 17 B1
E FROM GALVEZ AV TO LOCKWOOD
IN HUNTERS POINT NAVAL
RESERVATION
ROCK AL SF 13 B2
N FROM ROCKAWAY AV TO
IDORA ST E OF GARCIA AV
ROCKAWAY AV SF 13 B2
W FROM LAGUNA HONDA BLVD
N OF PORTOLA DR
ROCKDALE DR SF 13 C2
FROM JUANITA WY SE TO
BELLA VISTA DR
ROCKLAND ST SF 2 C3
E FROM LARKIN ST BETWEEN
GREEN ST AND UNION ST
ROCKRIDGE DR SF 13 A1
FROM 12TH AV NEAR PACHECO ST
A CIRCLE AROUND SUNSET HTS PK
ROCKWOOD CT SF 13 B2
S FROM ROCKAWAY AV W OF ULLOA ST
ROD RD SF 1 A2
E OF RUCKMAN AV, IN THE PRESIDIO
RODGERS ST SF 11 A1
S FROM FOLSOM ST BETWEEN 7TH ST
AND 8TH ST
RODRIGUEZ ST SF 1 C3
S FROM MACARTHUR ST BETWEEN
PORTOLA ST AND SANCHEZ ST
IN THE PRESIDIO
ROEMER WY SF 20 A3
BETWEEN WHITTIER ST AND LOWELL ST
S FROM BRUNSWICK ST
ROLPH ST SF 20 A2
FROM 5201 MISSION ST S OF
GENEVA AV E TO A POINT E OF
LINDA VISTA STEPS
2 MISSION ST
100 CURTIS ST
PARIS ST
200 NEWTON ST
MADRID ST
MORSE ST
NAPLES ST
300 CORDOVA ST
400 ATHENS ST
SEVILLE ST
500 MUNICH ST
PRAGUE ST
600 SOUTH HILL BLVD
700 LINDA VISTA STEPS
END E OF LINDA VISTA STEPS
ROMAIN ST SF 10 A3
FROM DOUGLASS ST NEAR 20TH ST
W TO MARKET ST THEN SW TO
CORBETT AV
2 DOUGLASS ST
100 GRAND VIEW AV
200 MARKET ST
END CORBETT AV
ROME ST SF 19 C2
ROME ST SF 20 A2
SW FROM NIAGARA AV 1 BLK W OF
ALEMANY BLVD
ROMOLO ST SF 3 A3
N FROM 500 BROADWAY BETWEEN
GRANT AV AND KEARNY ST TO
VALLEJO ST
RONDEL PL SF 10 C2
S FROM 16TH ST BETWEEN HOFF ST
AND VALENCIA ST
ROOSEVELT WY SF 10 A2
FROM INTERSECTION OF 14TH ST &
ALPINE TER SW TO 17TH ST
2 14TH ST
100 BUENA VISTA TER
200 PARK HILL AV
15TH ST
400 LOMA VISTA TER
CLIFFORD TER
484 LOWER TER
560 SATURN ST
END 17TH ST
ROSCOE ST SF 14 C3
S FROM CRESCENT AV 3 BLKS E OF
MISSION ST TO BENTON AV
ROSE ST SF 10 B1
N FROM MARKET ST BETWEEN PAGE ST
AND HAIGHT ST W TO LAGUNA ST
2 MARKET ST
100 GOUGH ST
200 OCTAVIA ST
END LAGUNA ST
ROSELLA CT SF 20 A1
N FROM ONONDAGA 1 BLK W OF
ALEMANY BLVD
ROSELYN TER SF 5 C3
N FROM GOLDEN GATE AV TO TURK ST
ROSEMARY CT SF 12 C2
E FROM 25TH AV ONE BLK S OF
VICENTE ST
ROSEMONT PL SF 10 B1
N FROM 14TH ST BETWEEN
GUERRERO ST AND DOLORES ST
ROSENKRANZ ST SF 15 A2
S FROM BERNAL HTS BLVD TO
POWHATTAN AV
ROSEWOOD DR SF 13 B3
FROM RAVENWOOD DR S TO
BRENTWOOD AV
ROSIE LEE LN SF 15 C3
OFF INGALLS ST BETWEEN HUDSON AV
AND BEATRICE LN
ROSS AL SF 3 A3
FROM 800 WASHINGTON ST BETWEEN
GRANT AV AND STOCKTON ST
N TO JACKSON ST
ROSSI AV SF 5 C3
N FROM TURK ST TO ANZA ST
E OF ARGUELLO BLVD
ROSSMOOR DR SF 13 A3
E FROM 19TH AV TO JUNIPERO
SERRA BLVD S OF EUCALYPTUS DR
ROTTECK ST SF 14 B3
FROM BOSWORTH ST W OF
ROUSSEAU ST S TO CAYUGA AV
ROUSSEAU ST SF 14 B3
FROM SAN JOSE AV BETWEEN
MILTON ST AND ROTTECK ST S TO
ALEMANY BLVD
100 BOSWORTH ST
END ALEMANY BLVD
ROWLAND ST SF 7 A1
S FROM BROADWAY
ROYAL LANE CT SF 20 A2
N FROM NAPLES 2 BLKS S OF
GENEVA AV
RUCKMAN AV SF 1 A2
E FROM RALSTON AV TO STOREY AV
IN THE PRESIDIO
RUDDEN AV SF 20 A1
FROM 250 DELANO AV TO OSTEGO AV
BETWEEN SANTA YNEZ AV & OCEAN AV
RUGER ST SF 1 C3
S FROM LOMBARD ST, SIMONDS LOOP
IN THE PRESIDIO
RUSS ST SF 7 A3
S FROM MINNA ST BETWEEN 6TH ST
AND 7TH ST SE TO FOLSOM ST
2 MINNA ST
48 NATOMA ST
100 HOWARD ST
END FOLSOM ST
RUSSELL ST SF 2 C3
W FROM HYDE ST BETWEEN GREEN ST
AND UNION ST TO EASTMAN ST
EASTMAN ST
RUSSIA AV SF 20 A1
FROM 4801 MISSION ST SE TO
LA GRANDE AV
2 MISSION ST
100 LONDON ST
200 PARIS ST
300 LISBON ST
400 MADRID ST
500 EDINBURGH ST
600 NAPLES ST
700 VIENNA ST
800 ATHENS ST
900 MOSCOW ST
1000 MUNICH ST
1100 PRAGUE ST
1200 DUBLIN ST
END LA GRANDE AV
RUSSIAN HILL PL SF 2 C3
N FROM VALLEJO ST BETWEEN
JONES ST AND TAYLOR ST
RUTH ST SF 20 A1
FROM 4700 MISSION ST BETWEEN
OCEAN AV AND LEO ST
RUTLAND ST SF 21 A3
FROM HARKNESS AV S TO A POINT S
OF SUNNYDALE AV
2 HARKNESS AV
100 WILDE AV
200 TIOGA AV
300 TUCKER AV
400 CAMPBELL AV
500 TEDDY AV
600 ARLETA AV
700 RAYMOND AV
800 LELAND AV
900 VISITACION AV
END SUNNYDALE AV
RUTLEDGE ST SF 15 A1
FROM HOLLADAY AV W TO
1700 ALABAMA ST
2 HOLLADAY AV
100 BREWSTER ST
FRANCONIA ST
PERALTA AV
END ALABAMA ST

S

SABIN PL SF 3 A3
N FROM 700 CALIFORNIA ST BETWEEN
GRANT AV AND STOCKTON ST
SACRAMENTO ST SF 2 C3
SACRAMENTO ST SF 3 A3
SACRAMENTO ST SF 5 B2
SACRAMENTO ST SF 6 A3
FROM THE BAY BETWEEN CALIFORNIA
AND CLAY STS W TO ARGUELLO BLVD
100 DRUMM ST
200 DAVIS ST
300 FRONT ST
400 BATTERY ST
500 SANSOME ST
LEIDESDORFF ST
600 MONTGOMERY ST
SPRING ST
700 KEARNY ST
800 GRANT AVE
WAVERLY PL
PAGODA PL
BROOKLYN PL
900 STOCKTON ST
JOICE ST
MILLER PL
1000 POWELL ST
1100 MASON ST
CUSHMAN ST
1200 TAYLOR ST
1300 JONES ST
LYSETTE ST
LEROY PL
GOLDEN CT
1400 LEAVENWORTH ST
KIMBALL PL
1500 HYDE ST
1600 LARKIN ST
1700 POLK ST
1800 VAN NESS AV
1900 FRANKLIN ST
GOUGH ST
OCTAVIA ST
2200 LAGUNA ST
2300 BUCHANAN ST
2400 WEBSTER ST
2500 FILLMORE ST
2600 STEINER ST
2700 PIERCE ST
2800 SCOTT ST
2900 DIVISADERO ST
3000 BRODERICK ST
3100 BAKER ST
3200 LYON ST
3300 PRESIDIO AV
3400 WALNUT ST
3500 LAUREL ST
3600 LOCUST ST
3700 SPRUCE ST
3800 MAPLE ST
3900 CHERRY ST
END ARGUELLO BLVD
SADOWA ST SF 19 B2
W OF SAN JOSE AV TO ORIZABA AV
2 SAN JOSE AV
100 PLYMOUTH AV
200 CAPITOL AV
END ORIZABA AV
SAFFOLD RD SF 1 A2
E OF LINCOLN BLVD BETWEEN
KOBBE AV AND DYNAMITE RD
IN THE PRESIDIO
SAFIRA LN SF 14 A1
E FROM DIAMOND HEIGHTS BLVD
TO 27TH ST
SAGAMORE ST SF 19 B3
W FROM SAN JOSE AV TO ALEMANY BL
2 SAN JOSE AV
100 PLYMOUTH AV
200 CAPITOL AV
ORIZABA AV
END ALEMANY BLVD
ST CHARLES AV SF 19 A3
FROM 19TH AV NEAR RANDOLPH ST
S TO BELLE AV

1991 SAN FRANCISCO COUNTY CROSS STREET INDEX

ST CROIX DR SF 13 C2
S FROM LA BREA WY TO MYRA WY
ST ELMO WY SF 13 B3
FROM 1000 MONTEREY BLVD N
TO YERBA BUENA AV
ST FRANCIS BLVD SF 13 B3
E FROM JUNIPERO SERRA BLVD
BETWEEN PORTOLA DR AND
MONTEREY BLVD OPPOSITE SLOAT BLVD
TO SAN ANSELMO AV
2 JUNIPERO SERRA BLVD
SAN RAFAEL WY
100 SAN FERNANDO WY
200 SAN LEANDRO WY
300 SANTA ANA AV
400 SAN BENITO WY
500 SANTA CLARA AV
600 SAN BUENAVENTURA WY
END SAN ANSELMO AV
ST FRANCIS PL SF 7 B2
FROM 3RD ST BETWEEN
FOLSOM ST AND HARRISON ST
ST GEORGE AL SF 3 A3
FROM 400 BUSH ST BETWEEN GRANT AV
AND KEARNY ST N TO PINE ST
ST GERMAIN AV SF 9 C3
W FROM TWIN PEAKS BLVD
ONE BLK S FROM MOUNTAIN SPRINGS
OFF GLENBROOK AV
ST JOSEPHS AV SF 6 A3
N FROM TURK ST BETWEEN BAKER ST
AND BRODERICK ST N TO GEARY BLVD
2 TURK ST
100 EDDY ST
200 ELLIS ST
300 OFARRELL ST
END GEARY BLVD
ST LOUIS PL SF 3 A3
FROM 701 JACKSON ST BETWEEN
GRANT AV AND STOCKTON ST
ST MARYS AV SF 14 B3
W FROM 3990 MISSION ST S
OF COLLEGE AV TO ARLINGTON ST
2 MISSION ST
MARSILLY ST
100 COLLEGE AV
END ARLINGTON ST
SAL ST SF 1 B2
S OF LINCOLN BLVD BETWEEN
GRAHAM ST AND KEYES AV, PRESIDIO
SALA TER SF 20 A2
FROM HURON AV SE TO ELLINGTON AV
SALINAS AV SF 21 B1
FROM 3RD ST OPPOSITE INGERSON AV
W TO SAN BRUNO AV
2 3RD ST
100 CARR ST
150 GOULD ST
JAMESTOWN AVE
200 EXETER ST
KEY ST
BAYSHORE BLVD
SALMON ST SF 3 A3
N FROM PACIFIC AV BETWEEN
MASON ST AND TAYLOR ST N
TO BROADWAY
SAMOSET ST SF 15 A1
W FROM FRANCONIA ST TO PERALTA AV
SAN ALESO AV SF 13 B3
N FROM UPLAND DR TO MONTEREY BLVD
DARIEN WY
END MONTEREY BLVD
SAN ANDREAS WY SF 13 B3
FROM THE JUNCTION OF
SAN ANSELMO AV & ST FRANCIS BLVD
S TO 1500 MONTEREY BLVD
SAN ANSELMO AV SF 13 B2
S FROM PORTOLA DR TO MONTEREY BL
SAN BENITO WY SF 13 B3
S FROM SAN ANSELMO AV BETWEEN
SANTA CLARA AV AND SANTA ANA AV
S TO OCEAN AV
2 SAN ANSELMO AV
100 ST FRANCIS BLVD
200 MONTEREY BLVD
300 DARIEN WY
END OCEAN AV
SAN BRUNO AV SF 11 A2
SAN BRUNO AV SF 15 A3
SAN BRUNO AV SF 21 A1
FROM DIVISION ST BETWEEN UTAH ST
AND VERMONT ST S TO COUNTY LINE
2 DIVISION ST
100 ALAMEDA ST
200 15TH ST
300 16TH ST
400 17TH ST
MARIPOSA ST
1200 23RD ST
1300 24TH ST
1400 25TH ST
ARMY ST
ALEMANY
RICKARD ST
2300 GAVEN ST
SWEENY ST
HALE ST
2400 SILVER AV
2450 SILLIMAN ST
2500 FELTON ST
2600 BURROWS ST
2700 BACON ST
2800 WAYLAND ST
2900 WOOLSEY ST
3000 DWIGHT ST
3100 OLMSTEAD ST
3200 MANSELL ST
3300 ORDWAY ST
3500 HARKNESS AV
3600 WILDE AV
FRATESSA CT
CAMPBELL AV
BEEMAN LN
SOMERSET ST
EMPRESS LN
WABASH TER
RACINE LN
END BAYSHORE BLVD
SN BUENAVNTRA WY SF 13 B3
FROM SAN ANSELMO AV TO
ST FRANCIS BLVD E OF
SANTA CLARA AV
SAN CARLOS ST SF 10 C2
FROM SYCAMORE ST BETWEEN
MISSION ST AND VALENCIA ST
S TO 21ST ST
2 SYCAMORE ST
100 18TH ST
200 19TH ST
300 20TH ST
END 21ST ST
SANCHES ST 1 C3
S OF PRESIDIO BLVD BETWEEN
MACARTHUR ST AND MORTON ST
IN THE PRESIDIO
SANCHEZ ST SF 5 C1
S FROM MORTON ST, PRESIDIO
SANCHEZ ST SF 10 B2
S FROM DUBOCE AV BETWEEN
CHURCH ST AND NOE ST
TO RANDALL ST
2 DUBOCE AV
100 14TH ST
150 HENRY ST
15TH ST
200 MARKET ST
300 16TH ST
400 17TH ST
DORLAND ST
450 FORD ST
500 18TH ST
550 HANCOCK ST
600 19TH ST
650 CUMBERLAND ST
700 20TH ST
750 LIBERTY ST
800 21ST ST
850 HILL ST
900 22ND ST
950 ALVARADO ST
1000 23RD ST
1050 ELIZABETH ST
1100 24TH ST
1150 JERSEY ST
1200 25TH ST
1252 CLIPPER ST
1300 26TH ST
1350 ARMY ST
1400 27TH ST
1450 DUNCAN ST
1500 28TH ST
1550 VALLEY ST
1600 29TH ST
1650 DAY ST
1700 30TH ST
END RANDALL ST
SAN DIEGO AV SF 19 B3
W OF SANTA CRUZ AV FROM
DE LONG ST TO THE COUNTY LINE
SAN FELIPE AV SF 13 B3
N FROM 1100 MONTEREY BLVD TO
SAN JACINTO WY
SAN FERNANDO WY SF 13 A3
S FROM PORTOLA DR BETWEEN
SAN RAFAEL WY AND SAN LEANDRO WY
TO OCEAN AV
2 PORTOLA DR
100 ST FRANCIS BLVD
200 MONTEREY BLVD
300 DARIEN WY
END OCEAN AV
SAN GABRIEL AV SF 20 A1
SW FROM CAPISTRANO AV TO
SANTA ROSA AV ONE BLK E OF
SAN JOSE AV
SAN JACINTO WY SF 13 B3
S FROM THE JUNCTION OF
SANTA PAULA AV AND SAN ANSELMO AV
TO MONTEREY BLVD
SAN JOSE AV SF 10 C3
SAN JOSE AV SF 14 B2
SAN JOSE AV SF 19 C2
SAN JOSE AV SF 20 A1
S FROM 22ND ST BETWEEN
VALENCIA ST AND GUERRERO ST
TO THE COUNTY LINE
2 22ND ST
50 ALVARADO ST
100 23RD ST
ELIZABETH ST
200 24TH ST
300 25TH ST
JURI ST
400 26TH ST
500 ARMY ST
550 27TH ST
600 DUNCAN ST
658 GUERRERO ST
672 VALLEY ST
700 29TH ST
DAY ST
800 30TH ST
KINGSTON ST
BROOK ST
DOLORES ST
RANDALL ST
CHARLES ST
HIGHLAND AV
PARK ST
RICHLAND AV
CRESCENT AV
MATEO ST
ST MARYS AV
CUVIER ST
MILTON ST
ROUSSEAU ST
CIRCULAR AV
BOSWORTH ST
GORHAM ST
TINGLEY ST
THERESA ST
COTTER ST
CAPISTRANO AV
STANDISH AV
PILGRM AV
1800 SANTA ROSA AV
COLONIAL WY
SANTA YSABEL AV
NANTUCKET AV
1884 PAULDING ST
SAN JUAN AV
HAVELOCK ST
SANTA YNEZ AV
BALBOA PARK
2100 OCEAN AV
ONEIDA AV
SENECA AV
GENEVA AV
2400 NIAGARA AV
2500 MOUNT VERNON AV
2524 RIDGE LN
2600 LAKEVIEW AV
NAGLEE ST
2700 FARRALLONES ST
2800 BROAD ST
2900 SADOWA ST
SICKLES AV
3000 PLYMOUTH AV
SAGAMORE ST
ALEMANY BLVD
REGENT ST
3100 LIEBIG ST
DE LONG ST
RICE ST
3200 GOETHE ST
END COUNTY LINE
SAN JUAN AV SF 20 A1
FROM MISSION ST AND OCEAN AV
NW TO SAN JOSE AV
2 MISSION ST
100 ALEMANY BLVD
200 CAYUGA AV
300 CAPISTRANO AV
400 OTSEGO AV
500 DELANO AV
END SAN JOSE AV
SAN LEANDRO WY SF 13 A3
S FROM PORTOLA DR BETWEEN
SAN FERNANDO WY AND SANTA ANA AV
TO OCEAN AV
2 PORTOLA DR
100 ST FRANCIS BLVD
200 MONTEREY BLVD
300 DARIEN WY
END OCEAN AV
SAN LORENZO WY SF 13 B2
S FROM PORTOLA DR BETWEEN
SANTA CLARA AV AND SANTA PAULA AV
TO SANTA MONICA AV
SAN LUIS AV SF 19 B3
W FROM DE LONG ST NEAR
THE COUNTY LINE
SAN MARCOS AV SF 13 B1
NW FROM DORANTES AV
SAN MATEO AV SF 19 B3
W FROM DE LONG ST NEAR
THE COUNTY LINE
SAN MIGUEL ST SF 19 C2
S FROM NIAGARA AV BETWEEN TARA ST
AND SAN JOSE AV S TO RIDGE LN
300 NIAGARA AV
400 MOUNT VERNON AV
END RIDGE LANE
SAN PABLO AV SF 13 B2
S FROM PORTOLA DR TO
YERBA BUENA AV
SAN RAFAEL WY SF 13 A3
S FROM ST FRANCIS BLVD BETWEEN
JUNIPERO SERRA BLVD AND
SAN FERNANDO WY TO DARIEN WY
2 ST FRANCIS BLVD
100 MONTEREY BLVD
END DARIEN WY
SAN RAMON WY SF 19 C1
N OF OCEAN AV FROM EASTWOOD DR
SANSOME ST SF 3 B2
N FROM MARKET ST BETWEEN
BATTERY ST AND MONTGOMERY ST
TO THE BAY
2 MARKET ST
SUTTER ST
100 BUSH ST
200 PINE ST
300 CALIFORNIA ST
HALLECK ST
400 SACRAMENTO ST
COMMERCIAL ST
500 CLAY ST
MERCHANT ST
600 WASHINGTON ST
700 JACKSON ST
GOLD ST
800 PACIFIC AV
STEVENS AL
900 BROADWAY
1000 VALLEJO ST
1100 GREEN ST
1200 UNION ST
1300 FILBERT ST
1400 GREENWICH ST
1500 LOMBARD ST
CHESTNUT ST
END THE EMBARCADERO
SANTA ANA AV SF 13 B3
S FROM PORTOLA DR BETWEEN
SAN BENITO WY AND SAN LEANDRO WY
TO OCEAN AV
2 PORTOLA DR
100 ST FRANCIS BLVD
200 MONTEREY BLVD
300 DARIEN WY
END OCEAN AV
SANTA BARBARA AV SF 19 B3
S FROM DE LONG ST TO COUNTY LINE
MERLA CT
SANTA CLARA AV SF 13 B3
S FROM PORTOLA DR BETWEEN
SAN BENITO WY AND
SAN BUENAVENTURA WY TO
MONTEREY BLVD
2 PORTOLA DR
YERBA BUENA AV
100 TERRACE DR
200 SAN ANSELMO AV
300 ST FRANCIS BLVD
END MONTEREY BLVD
SANTA CRUZ AV SF 19 B3
S FROM DE LONG ST NEAR
THE COUNTY LINE
SANTA FE AV SF 15 B3
SE FROM SILVER AV TO QUINT ST
BETWEEN TOPEKA ST AND SCOTIA AV
SANTA MARINA ST SF 14 C2
FROM 3525 MISSION ST NEAR
CORTLAND AV E TO ELSIE ST
2 MISSION ST
GLADYS ST
PROSPECT AV
END ELSIE ST
SANTA MONICA WY SF 13 B2
FROM SANTA CLARA AV S OF
PORTOLA DR E TO SAN PABLO AV
SANTA CLARA AV
100 SANTA PAULA AV
END SAN PABLO AV
SANTA PAULA AV SF 13 B3
S FROM 1251 PORTOLA DR TO

SAN ANSELMO AV
2 PORTOLA DR
SANTA MONICA WY
100 YERBA BUENA AV
END SAN ANSELMO AV
SANTA RITA AV SF 13 B1
S FROM SOTELO AV W OF LOPEZ AV
TO SAN MARCOS AV
2 SOTELO AV
50 MESA AV
END SAN MARCOS AV
SANTA ROSA AV SF 20 A1
FROM 4500 MISSION ST BETWEEN
FRANCIS ST AND HARRINGTON ST
TO A POINT W OF SAN JOSE AV
2 MISSION ST
100 ALEMANY BLVD
CAYUGA AV
200 CAPISTRANO AV
SAN GABRIEL AV
300 SAN JOSE AV
SANTA YNEZ AV SF 20 A1
FROM CAYUGA AV BETWEEN
SAN JUAN AV AND OCEAN AV NW TO
SAN JOSE AV
2 CAYUGA AV
CAPISTRANO AV
100 OTSEGO ST
200 DELANO AV
END SAN JOSE AV
SANTA YSABEL AV SF 20 A1
SE FROM SAN JOSE AV TO
CAPISTRANO AV BETWEEN
SANTA ROSA AV AND SAN JUAN AV
SANTIAGO ST SF 12 A1
SANTIAGO ST SF 13 A1
W FROM 14TH AV TO GREAT HIGHWAY
BETWEEN RIVERA ST AND TARAVAL ST
300 14TH AV
400 15TH AV
CECILIA AV
500 16TH AV
600 17TH AV
700 18TH AV
800 19TH AV
900 20TH AV
1000 21ST AV
1100 22ND AV
1300 24TH AV
1400 25TH AV
1500 26TH AV
1600 27TH AV
1700 28TH AV
1800 29TH AV
1900 30TH AV
2000 31ST AV
2100 32ND AV
2200 33RD AV
2300 34TH AV
2400 35TH AV
2500 36TH AV
SUNSET BLVD
2600 37TH AV
2700 38TH AV
2800 39TH AV
2900 40TH AV
3000 41ST AV
3100 42ND AV
3200 43RD AV
3300 44TH AV
3400 45TH AV
3500 46TH AV
3600 47TH AV
3700 48TH AV
END GREAT HIGHWAY
SANTOS ST SF 20 C3
FROM SUNNYVALE AV TO COUNTY LINE
SARGENT ST SF 19 B2
W FROM ORIZABA AV TO 19TH AV
2 ORIZABA AV
100 BRIGHT ST
200 HEAD ST
300 VICTORIA ST
400 RAMSELL ST
500 ARCH ST
600 VERNON ST
700 RALSTON ST
800 BIXBY ST
900 MONTICELLO ST
END 19TH AV
SATURN ST SF 10 A2
FROM ROOSEVELT WY N OF 17TH ST
E TO LOWER TERRACE
ROOSEVELT WY
100 TEMPLE ST
END LOWER TERRACE
SAWYER ST SF 20 C3
FROM RAYMOND AV S TO
VISITACION AV
200 RAYMOND AV
300 LELAND AV
400 VISITACION AV
SCENIC WY SF 4 C2
FROM 25TH AV W TO 26TH AV BETWEEN
EL CAMINO DEL MAR AND SEACLIFF AV
SCHOFIELD RD SF 1 A2
S FROM APPLETON ST, PRESIDIO
SCHOFIELD RD SF 2 B2
N OF MACARTHUR AV, FORT MASON
SCHOOL AL SF 3 A2
E FROM 1301 MONTGOMERY ST BETWEEN
UNION ST & FILBERT ST
SCHWERIN ST SF 21 A3
S FROM LELAND AV
6 BLKS W OF BAYSHORE BLVD
SCOTIA AV SF 15 B3
FROM SILVER AV SE TO THORNTON AV
SCOTLAND ST SF 3 A2
FROM 700 FILBERT ST BETWEEN
POWELL ST AND MASON ST N
TO COLUMBUS AV
SCOTT ST SF 2 A3
SCOTT ST SF 6 A3
SCOTT ST SF 10 B1
N FROM DUBOCE AV BETWEEN
PIERCE ST AND DIVISADERO ST
TO MARINA BLVD
2 DUBOCE AV
LLOYD ST
100 WALLER ST
200 HAIGHT ST
300 PAGE ST
400 OAK ST
500 FELL ST
HAYES ST
GROVE ST
800 FULTON ST
900 MCALLISTER ST
1000 GOLDEN GATE AV
ELM ST
1100 TURK ST
1200 EDDY ST
1300 ELLIS ST
1400 OFARRELL ST
GEARY BLVD
1600 POST ST
1700 SUTTER ST
1800 BUSH ST
1900 PINE ST
2000 CALIFORNIA ST
2100 SACRAMENTO ST
CLAY ST
WASHINGTON ST
2400 JACKSON ST
2500 PACIFIC AV
2600 BROADWAY
2700 VALLEJO ST
2800 GREEN ST
2900 UNION ST
3000 FILBERT ST
3100 GREENWICH ST
3200 LOMBARD ST
3300 CHESTNUT ST
FRANCISCO ST
3400 ALHAMBRA ST
BAY ST
3500 CAPRA WY
NORTH POINT ST
3700 BEACH ST
3800 PRADO ST
JEFFERSON ST
CERVANTES BLVD
END MARINA BLVD
SEA CLIFF AV SF 4 B2
S FROM 25TH AV W TO 30TH AV N OF
EL CAMINO DEL MAR
SEAL ROCK DR SF 4 A3
W FROM 45TH AV TO
EL CAMINO DEL MAR N OF
POINT LOBOS AV
SEARS ST SF 19 C3
S FROM LAWRENCE ST TO A POINT
S OF SICKLES AV
SEAVIEW TER SF 4 B2
FROM 249 30TH AV W TO A POINT
W OF 31ST AV
SECURITY PAC PL SF 7 A2
N FROM OFARRELL ST W OF GRANT AV
SELBY ST SF 15 B2
FROM ISLAIS ST SW TO
WATERVILLE ST
200 EVANS AV
400 GALVEZ AV
500 HUDSON AV
600 INNES AV
700 JERROLD AV
KIRKWOOD AV
MCKINNON AV
NEWCOMB AV
1200 OAKDALE AV
1300 PALOU AV
1400 QUESADA AV
1500 REVERE AV
END WATERVILLE ST
SELMA WY SF 9 A3
FROM NORIEGA ST AT 12TH AV
SW TO ORTEGA ST
SEMINOLE AV SF 20 A2
FROM 750 DELANO AV E TO CAYUGA AV
SENECA AV SF 20 A1
FROM MISSION ST NW TO SAN JOSE AV
MISSION ST
BERTITA ST
ALEMANY BLVD
BANNOCK ST
CAYUGA AV
DELANO AV
END SAN JOSE AV
SEQUOIA WY SF 13 C2
FROM TERESITA BLVD S TO
BELLA VISTA WY
SGT MITCHELL SF 1 C2
N FROM MASON ST TO LT ALLEN ST
IN THE PRESIDIO
SERPENTINE AV SF 15 A1
E FROM POTRERO AV 1 BLK S
OF 25TH ST
SERRANO DR SF 18 C2
SERRANO DR SF 19 A2
W FROM GRIJALVA DR TO
ARBALLO DR S OF HOLLOWAY AV
SERVICE ST SF 2 A3
W FROM STEINER ST BETWEEN
LOMBARD ST AND GREENWICH ST
SEVERN ST SF 10 B3
N FROM 23RD ST BETWEEN
CHATTANOOGA ST AND CHURCH ST
SEVILLE ST SF 20 A3
S FROM ROLPH ST BETWEEN ATHENS ST
AND MUNICH ST W TO NAPLES ST
TO NAPLES ST
2 ROLPH ST
100 CORDOVA ST
END NAPLES ST
SEWARD ST SF 10 A3
FROM 358 DOUGLASS ST NW TO
19TH ST
2 DOUGLASS ST
ACME ALLEY
END 19TH ST
SEYMOUR ST SF 6 A3
FROM GOLDEN GATE AV BETWEEN
SCOTT ST AND DIVISADERO ST N
TO TURK ST
SHAFTER AV SF 15 C3
SHAFTER AV SF 21 C1
FROM FITCH ST NW TO 3RD ST AND
FROM SELBY ST TO INDUSTRIAL ST
FITCH ST
GRIFFITH ST
1200 HAWES ST
1300 INGALLS ST
1400 JENNINGS ST
1500 KEITH ST
1600 LANE ST
3RD ST
2200 SELBY ST
INDUSTRIAL ST
SHAFTER RD SF 1 C3
NW FROM RAWLES ST, PRESIDIO
SHAKESPEARE ST SF 19 B3
FROM DE LONG ST SE TO COUNTY LINE
SHANGRILA WY SF 13 B2
FROM 300 ULLOA ST N TO
EDGEHILL WY E OF KENSINGTON WY
SHANNON ST SF 7 A2
N FROM O'FARRELL ST BETWEEN
TAYLOR ST AND JONES ST TO POST ST
2 O'FARRELL ST
100 GEARY ST
END POST ST
SHARON ST SF 10 B2
S FROM 15TH ST BETWEEN CHURCH ST
AND SANCHEZ ST TO 16TH ST
SHARP PL SF 2 C2
S FROM UNION ST BETWEEN HYDE ST
AND LEAVENWORTH ST
SHAW AL SF 7 B2
S FROM MISSION ST BETWEEN 1ST ST
AND 2ND ST TO MINNA ST
SHAWNEE AV SF 20 A2
FROM SAN JOSE AV SE TO CAYUGA AV
SHEPHARD PL SF 3 A3
E FROM 1100 MASON ST BETWEEN
CLAY ST AND WASHINGTON ST
SHERIDAN AV SF 1 B2
S FROM LINCOLN BLVD TO TAYLOR RD
IN THE PRESIDIO
SHERIDAN ST SF 11 A1
FROM 9TH ST BETWEEN FOLSOM ST AND
HARRISON ST SW TO 10TH ST
SHERMAN RD SF 1 C3
S OF LOMBARD ST BETWEEN
LINCOLN BLVD AND RUGER ST
IN THE PRESIDIO
SHERMAN ST SF 7 A3
S FROM FOLSOM ST BETWEEN 6TH ST
AND 7TH ST SE TO HARRISON ST
SHERWOOD CT SF 13 C3
S FROM LANSDALE AV ONE
BLK E OF ROBINHOOD DR
SHIELDS ST SF 19 A2
FROM ORIZABA AV W TO
JUNIPERO SERRA BLVD
2 ORIZABA AV
100 BRIGHT ST
200 HEAD ST
300 VICTORIA ST
400 RAMSELL ST
500 ARCH ST
600 VERNON ST
700 RALSTON ST
800 BIXBY ST
900 MONTICELLO ST
1000 BEVERLY ST
END JUNIPERO SERRA BLVD
SHIPLEY ST SF 7 A3
FROM 4TH ST BETWEEN FOLSOM ST AND
CLARA ST SW TO 6TH ST
100 4TH ST
200 5TH ST
FALMOUTH ST
END 6TH ST
SHORE VIEW AV SF 4 B3
S FROM 36TH AV BETWEEN CLEMENT ST
AND GEARY BLVD W TO 38TH AV
SHORT ST SF 10 A3
FROM YUKON ST W TO MARKET ST
OFF 3401 MARKET ST
SHOTWELL ST SF 10 C2
SHOTWELL ST SF 14 C1
S FROM 14TH ST BETWEEN FOLSOM ST
AND S VAN NESS AV TO
BERNAL HEIGHTS BLVD
2 14TH ST
100 15TH ST
200 16TH ST
300 17TH ST
400 18TH ST
500 19TH ST
600 20TH ST
700 21ST ST
800 22ND ST
900 23RD ST
1000 24TH ST
1100 25TH ST
1200 26TH ST
1300 ARMY ST
PRECITA AV
BESSIE ST
MIRABEL AV
1420 MONTEZUMA ST
BERNAL HTS BLVD
SHRADER ST SF 9 C1
S FROM FULTON ST BETWEEN COLE ST
AND STANYAN ST TO BELGRAVE AV
2 FULTON ST
100 GROVE ST
200 HAYES ST
FELL ST
400 OAK ST
500 PAGE ST
600 HAIGHT ST
700 WALLER ST
800 BEULAH ST
FREDERICK ST
1000 CARL ST
1100 PARNASSUS AV
1200 GRATTAN ST
1300 ALMA ST
1400 RIVOLI ST
1500 17TH ST
1550 CARMEL ST
END BELGRAVE AV
SIBERT LOOP SF 1 B3
N FROM ARGUELLO BLVD, PRESIDIO
SIBLEY RD SF 1 C3
S FROM MORTON ST BETWEEN
LIGGETT AV AND SANCHEZ ST
IN THE PRESIDIO
SICKLES AV SF 19 C3
FROM 5900 MISSION ST NW TO
SAN JOSE AV NEAR THE COUNTY LINE
2 MISSION ST
100 HURON AV
SEARS ST
CAYUGA AV
ALEMANY BLVD
DE WOLF ST
END SAN JOSE AV
SIERRA ST SF 11 B3
FROM TEXAS ST TO MISSOURI ST
BETWEEN 20TH ST AND 22ND ST
SILLIMAN ST SF 15 A3
SILLIMAN ST SF 20 C1
FROM 2450 SAN BRUNO AV S OF
SILVER AV W TO VALMAR TER

2 SAN BRUNO AV
100 GIRARD ST
200 BRUSSELS ST
300 GOETTINGEN ST
400 SOMERSET ST
500 BOYSTON ST
600 HAMILTON ST
700 BOWDOIN ST
800 DARTMOUTH ST
900 COLBY ST
1000 UNIVERSITY ST
1100 PRINCETON ST
1200 AMHERST ST
1300 YALE ST
1400 CAMBRIDGE ST
1500 OXFORD ST
1600 HARVARD ST
1700 GAMBIER ST
1800 MADISON ST
END VALMAR TER
SILVER AV SF 14 B3
SILVER AV SF 15 A3
FROM ALEMANY BL E TO SAN BRUNO AV
THEN NE TO PALOU AV
200 ALEMANY BLVD
CAMELLIA AV
300 MISSION ST
LISBON ST
400 CRAUT ST
MADRID ST
EDINBURGH ST
500 CONGDON ST
NAPLES ST
VIENNA ST
MADISON ST
GAMBIER ST
HARVARD ST
SUNGLOW LN
OXFORD ST
CAMBRIDGE ST
YALE ST
AMHERST ST
1000 PRINCETON ST
UNIVERSITY ST
COLBY ST
DUNSMUIR ST
DARTMOUTH ST
1200 BOWDOIN ST
HAMILTON ST
BOYLSTON ST
1300 SOMERSET ST
MERRILL ST
1400 GOETTINGEN ST
BRUSSELS ST
1500 BARNEVELD AV
GIRARD ST
SAN BRUNO AV
BAYSHORE BLVD
CHARTER OAK AV
1700 ELMIRA ST
LEDYARD ST
WATERVILLE ST
SCOTIA AV
CONKLING ST
SANTA FE AV
TOPEKA AV
THOMAS AV
REVERE AV
QUESADA AV
END PALOU AV & QUINT ST
SIMONDS LOOP SF 1 C3
E FROM PRESIDIO BLVD JUST S OF
SHERMAN RD, IN THE PRESIDIO
SKYLINE BLVD SF 18 A1
S FROM SLOAT BLVD TO THE
COUNTY LINE E OF LAKE MERCED BLVD
SKYVIEW WY SF 9 C3
N FROM TWIN PEAKS BLVD TO
MAR VIEW WY
SLOAN AL SF 7 B2
OFF TENNY PL NEAR 201 1ST ST

BETWEEN HOWARD ST AND FOLSOM ST
SLOAT BLVD SF 12 A3
FROM PORTOLA DR W TO
GREAT HIGHWAY
2 PORTOLA DR
CRANLEIGH DR
ARDENWOOD WY
LAGUNITAS DR
BEACHMONT DR
100 AVON WY
300 19TH AV
20TH AV
500 21ST AV
700 23RD AV
24TH AV
25TH AV
GABILAN WY
800 CRESTLAKE DR
26TH AV
1000 PARAISO PL
SYLVAN DR
1300 EL MIRASOL PL
MIDDLEFIELD DR
RIVERTON DR
SPRINGFIELD DR
1600 CONSTANSO WAY
EVERGLADE DR
LAKESHORE PLAZA
1700 34TH AV
CLEARFIELD DR
35TH AV
1800 36TH AV
SUNSET BLVD
37TH AV
39TH AV
SKYLINE BLVD
41ST AV
42ND AV
43RD AV
2600 44TH AV
2700 45TH AV
2800 46TH AV
2800 47TH AV
48TH AV
END GREAT HIGHWAY
SOLA AV SF 13 B1
FROM MAGELLAN AV NW TO MARCELA AV
JUST S OF LAGUNA HONDA BLVD
SOMERSET ST SF 15 A3
SOMERSET ST SF 21 A1
S FROM SILVER AV TO KAREN CT
MANSELL ST TO ANKENY ST & FROM
CAMPBELL AV TO BAYSHORE BLVD
BETWEEN GOETTINGEN & HOLYOKE STS
2 SILVER AV
100 SILLIMAN ST
200 FELTON ST
300 BURROWS ST
400 BACON ST
500 WAYLAND ST
600 WOOLSEY ST
KAREN CT
900 MANSELL ST
ANKENY ST
CAMPBELL AV
SAN BRUNO AV
WABASH TER
TEDDY AV
RACINE LN
BAYSHORE BLVD
SONOMA ST SF 3 A2
FROM 400 GREEN ST BETWEEN
KEARNY ST AND GRANT AV N
TO UNION ST
SONORA LN SF 6 A3
S FROM O'FARRELL ST TO
ELLIS ST E OF ANZAVISTA AV
SOTELO AV SF 13 B1
E FROM 9TH AV S OF ALTON AV
E & S TO LOPEZ AV
SOUTHARD PL SF 2 C2
N FROM GREENWICH ST BETWEEN

LEAVENWORTH ST AND HYDE ST
SOUTHERN HTS AV SF 11 B3
FROM CAROLINA ST BETWEEN 20TH ST
AND 22ND ST TO RHODE ISLAND ST
2 CAROLINA ST
100 DE HARO ST
SOUTH GOUGH ST
END RHODE ISLAND ST
SOUTH HILL BLVD SF 20 B3
S FROM GENEVA AV SE TO
THE COUNTY LINE
SOUTH PARK AV SF 7 B3
W FROM 2ND ST BETWEEN BRANT ST
AND BRANNAN ST SW TO 3RD ST
S VAN NESS AV SF 10 C1
S FROM 13TH ST TO ARMY ST
BETWEEN SHOTWELL ST AND CAPP ST
200 13TH ST
251 ERIE ST
300 14TH ST
400 15TH ST
ADAIR ST
500 16TH ST
600 17TH ST
18TH ST
19TH ST
900 20TH ST
1000 21ST ST
1100 22ND ST
1200 23RD ST
24TH ST
1400 25TH ST
26TH ST
END ARMY ST
SOUTHWOOD DR SF 19 B1
W FROM PLYMOUTH AV TO FAXON AV
PLYMOUTH AV
2 SAN RAMON WY
100 MIRAMAR WY
ELMWOOD WY
END FAXON AV
SPARROW ST SF 10 C2
E FROM VALENCIA ST BETWEEN
15TH ST & 16TH ST TO CALEDONIA ST
SPARTA ST SF 21 A2
E OF BISHOP ST FROM ANKENY ST
S TO HARKNESS AV
SPEAR AV SF 17 B1
E FROM J ST TO A ST, HUNTERS PT
SPEAR ST SF 7 B1
S FROM MARKET ST BETWEEN
STEUART ST AND MAIN ST SE
TO THE BAY
2 MARKET ST
100 MISSION ST
200 HOWARD ST
300 FOLSOM ST
400 HARRISON ST
BRYANT ST
END BAY OF S F
SPENCER ST SF 10 B2
N FROM 16TH ST BETWEEN
GUERRERO ST & DOLORES ST
SPOFFORD ST SF 3 A3
FROM 800 CLAY ST BETWEEN GRANT AV
AND STOCKTON ST N TO
WASHINGTON ST
SPRECKLES LK DR SF 8 B1
S OF FULTON ST BETWEEN 36TH AV
AND 30TH AV IN GOLDEN GATE PARK
SPRING ST SF 3 A3
FROM CALIFORNIA ST BETWEEN
MONTGOMERY ST AND KEARNY ST
N TO SACRAMENTO ST
SPRINGFIELD DR SF 12 C3
S FROM SLOAT BLVD BETWEEN
RIVERTON DR AND EVERGLADE DR
SPROULE LN SF 3 A3
S FROM CLAY ST BETWEEN MASON ST
AND TAYLOR ST
SPRUCE ST SF 5 C2

FROM PRESIDIO RESERVATION
BETWEEN LOCUST ST AND MAPLE ST
S TO ANZA ST
2 PRESIDIO RESERVATION
100 JACKSON ST
200 WASHINGTON ST
300 CLAY ST
400 SACRAMENTO ST
CALIFORNIA ST
MAYFAIR DR
EUCLID AV
GEARY BLVD
END ANZA ST
STANDISH AV SF 14 A3
W OFF 1700 SAN JOSE AV
STANFORD ST SF 7 C3
S FROM BRANNAN ST BETWEEN 2ND ST
AND 3RD ST S TO TOWNSEND ST
STANFORD HTS AV SF 13 C3
FROM LOS PALMOS DR S TO
MELROSE AV
STANLEY ST SF 19 B2
W OF SAN JOSE AV NEAR THE
COUNTY LINE FROM ORIZABA AV
W TO HEAD ST
STANTON ST SF 10 A3
N FROM MARKET ST BETWEEN YUKON ST
AND GRANDVIEW TER
STANYAN ST SF 5 C3
STANYAN ST SF 9 C1
FROM GEARY BLVD S TO
MOUNTAIN SPRINGS AV
GEARY BLVD
ANZA ST
LONE MTN TER
2 TURK ST
GOLDEN GATE AV
PARAMOUNT TER
100 MCALLISTER ST
200 FULTON ST
300 HAYES ST
FELL ST
400 OAK ST
500 PAGE ST
600 HAIGHT ST
700 WALLER ST
800 BEULAH ST
900 FREDERICK ST
1000 CARL ST
1100 PARNASSUS AV
1134 GRATTAN ST
1174 ALMA ST
1200 RIVOLI ST
1226 17TH ST
1300 BELGRAVE AV
CLAREDON AV
END MOUNTAIN SPRINGS AV
STAPLES AV SF 13 C3
W FROM CIRCULAR AV BETWEEN
FLOOD AV AND JUDSON AV TO
HAZELWOOD AV
2 CIRCULAR AV
100 DETROIT ST
200 EDNA ST
300 FOERSTER ST
400 GENNESSE ST
500 PHELAN AV
END HAZELWOOD AV
STARK ST SF 3 A3
FROM 1200 STOCKTON ST BETWEEN
PACIFIC AV AND BROADWAY
STARR KING WY SF 6 C2
S FROM GEARY ST BETWEEN GOUGH ST
AND FRANKLIN ST
STARVIEW WY SF 13 C1
NE FROM PANORAMA DR 6 BLKS N OF
PORTOLA DR
STATE DR SF 18 C1
E FROM LAKE MERCED BLVD
BETWEEN FONT BLVD AND WINSTON DR
STATES ST SF 10 A2
W FROM CASTRO ST BETWEEN 16TH ST

AND 17TH ST W TO LEVANT ST
2 CASTRO
200 DOUGLASS ST
END LEVANT ST
STEINER ST SF 2 A3
STEINER ST SF 6 B3
STEINER ST SF 10 B1
S FROM DUBOCE AV BETWEEN
FILLMORE ST AND PIERCE ST
N TO CHESTNUT ST
2 DUBOCE AV
100 HERMANN ST
130 GERMANIA ST
200 WALLER ST
230 LAUSSAT ST
300 HAIGHT ST
400 PAGE ST
500 OAK ST
600 FELL ST
700 HAYES ST
800 GROVE ST
900 FULTON ST
1000 MCALLISTER ST
1100 GOLDEN GATE AV
1200 TURK ST
1300 EDDY ST
1400 ELLIS ST
1500 O'FARRELL ST
1600 GEARY BLVD
1700 POST ST
1800 SUTTER ST
1900 BUSH ST
WILMOT ST
2000 PINE ST
2100 CALIFORNIA ST
PERINE PL
2200 SACRAMENTO ST
2300 CLAY ST
2400 WASHINGTON ST
2500 JACKSON ST
2600 PACIFIC AV
2700 BROADWAY
2800 VALLEJO ST
2900 GREEN ST
3000 UNION ST
3100 FILBERT ST
3150 PIXLEY ST
3200 GREENWICH ST
3250 MOULTON ST
SERVICE ST
3300 LOMBARD ST
END CHESTNUT ST
STERLING ST SF 7 B2
S FROM HARRISON ST BETWEEN 1ST ST
AND 2ND ST SE TO BRYANT ST
STEUART ST SF 7 B1
S FROM MARKET ST BETWEEN
THE EMBARCADERO AND SPEAR ST
SE TO THE BAY
2 MARKET ST
100 MISSION ST
200 HOWARD ST
300 FOLSOM ST
HARRISON ST
END BAY OF S F
STEVELOE PL SF 7 A2
E FROM JONES ST BETWEEN ELLIS ST
AND O'FARRELL ST
STEVENS AL SF 3 B3
E FROM SANSOME ST BETWEEN
BROADWAY AND PACIFIC AV
STEVENSON ST SF 6 C3
STEVENSON ST SF 7 A3
STEVENSON ST SF 10 C1
S FROM 1ST ST BETWEEN MARKET ST
AND JESSIE ST SW TO 14TH ST
2 1ST ST
ECKER ST
100 2ND ST
NEW MONTGOMERY ST
192 ANNIE ST

200 3RD ST
4TH ST
400 5TH ST
500 6TH ST
600 7TH ST
700 8TH ST
800 9TH ST
10TH ST
1100 12TH ST
1200 BRADY ST
GOUGH ST
1300 MCCOPPIN ST
DUBOCE AV
1400 CLINTON PARK
END 14TH ST
STILL ST SF 14 B3
E FROM ADMIRAL AV TO ROUSSEAU ST
PARALLEL TO I-280 FRWY
STILLINGS AV SF 14 A3
E FROM 600 TERESITA BLVD
TO MARTHA AV
STILLMAN ST SF 7 B3
W FROM 2ND ST BETWEEN BRYANT ST
AND HARRISON ST SW TO 4TH ST
2 2ND ST
100 3RD ST
END 4TH ST
STILWELL DR SF 4 C1
E FROM LINCOLN BLVD TO
PERSHING DR, IN THE PRESIDIO
STOCKTON ST SF 3 A2
STOCKTON ST SF 7 A1
N FROM MARKET ST BETWEEN GRANT AV
AND POWELL ST TO THE EMBARCADERO
2 MARKET ST
ELLIS ST
100 OFARRELL ST
200 GEARY ST
MAIDEN LN
300 POST ST
CAMPTON PL
400 SUTTER ST
500 BUSH ST
EMMA ST
600 PINE ST
700 CALIFORNIA ST
800 SACRAMENTO ST
900 CLAY ST
1000 WASHINGTON ST
1100 JACKSON ST
1200 PACIFIC AV
STARK ST
1300 BROADWAY
1400 VALLEJO ST
CARD AL
COLUMBUS AV
1500 GREEN ST
1600 UNION ST
1700 FILBERT ST
1800 GREENWICH ST
1900 LOMBARD ST
FIELDING ST
2000 CHESTNUT ST
PFEIFFER ST
2100 FRANCISCO ST
2200 BAY ST
2300 NORTH POINT ST
2400 BEACH ST
END THE EMBARCADERO
STONE ST SF 1 A2
BETWEEN RALSTON AV AND STOREY AV
IN THE PRESIDIO
STONE ST SF 3 A3
N FROM 900 WASHINGTON ST BETWEEN
STOCKTON ST AND POWELL ST
N TO JACKSON ST
STONECREST DR SF 19 A1
LOOP EXTENDING W FROM JUNIPERO
SERRA BLVD N & E OF 19TH AV
STONEMAN ST SF 15 A1
FROM 3300 FOLSOM ST W TO
SHOTWELL ST
STONESTOWN SF 13 A3
N FROM 20TH AV NEAR WINSTON DR
STONEYBROOK AV SF 14 C3
S FROM CAMBRIDGE ST TO
GLADSTONE DR NEAR SILVER AV
STONEYFORD AV SF 14 C3
S FROM CAMBRIDGE ST TO
GLADSTONE DR NEAR SILVER AV
STOREY AV SF 1 A2
SE FROM LINCOLN BL, IN PRESIDIO
STORRIE ST SF 10 A2
NE FROM 18TH ST
STOW LAKE DR SF 9 A1
S FROM JOHN F KENNEDY DR IN
GOLDEN GATE PARK
STOW LAKE DR E SF 9 A1
S FROM STOW LAKE DR TO MARTIN L
KING DR IN GOLDEN GATE PARK
STRATFORD DR SF 19 A1
SE FROM LYNDHURST DR TO
JUNIPERO SERRA BLVD E OF
DENSLOWE DR
SUMMIT ST SF 19 C2
FROM MAJESTIC AV W OF SAN JOSE AV
NW TO LAKE VIEW AV
SUMNER AV SF 1 C3
E FROM MACARTHUR ST TO
PRESIDIO BLVD, IN THE PRESIDIO
SUMNER ST SF 7 A3
S FROM HOWARD ST BETWEEN 7TH ST
AND 8TH ST TO CLEMENTINA ST
SUNBEAM LN SF 20 A2
E FROM CAYUGA AV BETWEEN
ONEIDA AV AND JUNIOR TER
SUNGLOW LN SF 14 C3
S FROM GLADSTONE DR TO
SILVER AV NEAR CAMBRIDGE ST
SUNNYDALE AV SF 20 B2
SUNNYDALE AV SF 21 A3
FROM PERSIA ST S TO COUNTY LINE
SANTOS ST
HAHN ST
SAWYER ST
GARRISON AV
REY ST
SCHWERIN ST
DELTA ST
CORA ST
RUTLAND ST
PEABODY ST
TALBERT ST
DESMOND ST
BAY SHORE BLVD
END COUNTY LINE
SUNNYSIDE TER SF 13 C3
E FROM FOERSTER ST BETWEEN
STAPLES AV AND JUDSON AV
SUNRISE WY SF 20 C3
FROM POINT E OF SAWYER ST
TO POINT W OF HAHN ST N OF
VELASCO AV
SUNSET BLVD SF 8 B2
SUNSET BLVD SF 12 B1
S FROM LINCOLN WY BETWEEN
36TH AV AND 37TH AV TO OCEAN AV
LINCOLN WAY
IRVING ST
JUDAH ST
KIRKHAM ST
LAWTON ST
MORAGA ST
NORIEGA ST
ORTEGA ST
PACHECO ST
QUINTARA ST
RIVERA ST
SANTIAGO ST
TARAVAL ST
ULLOA ST
VICENTE ST
WAWONA ST
YORBA ST
SLOAT BLVD
END OCEAN AV
SUNVIEW DR SF 13 C1
N FROM PORTOLA DR
SURREY ST SF 14 A3
FROM CHENERY ST NW TO SWISS AV
LIPPARD AV
292 VAN BUREN ST
END SWISS AV
SUSSEX ST SF 14 B2
NW FROM CASTRO ST NEAR BEMIS ST
TO ELK ST
2 CASTRO ST
100 DIAMOND ST
VAN BUREN ST
300 CONRAD ST
400 SWISS AVE
MIZPAH ST
END ELK ST
SUTRO HTS AV SF 4 A3
BETWEEN ANZA ST AND BALBOA ST
FROM 46TH AV TO 48TH AV
SUTTER ST SF 6 A3
SUTTER ST SF 7 A2
FROM THE JUNCTION OF MARKET ST
AND SANSOME ST BETWEEN POST ST
& BUSH ST W TO PRESIDIO AV
2 MARKET ST
SANSOME ST
100 MONTGOMERY ST
TRINITY ST
LICK PL
200 KEARNY ST
CLAUDE LN
MARK LN
300 GRANT AV
400 STOCKTON ST
500 POWELL ST
600 MASON ST
700 TAYLOR ST
800 JONES ST
900 LEAVENWORTH ST
1000 HYDE ST
1100 LARKIN ST
1200 POLK ST
1300 VAN NESS AV
1400 FRANKLIN ST
1500 GOUGH ST
1600 OCTAVIA ST
1700 LAGUNA ST
1800 BUCHANAN ST
1900 WEBSTER ST
COTTAGE ROW
2000 FILLMORE ST
2100 STEINER ST
2200 PIERCE ST
2300 SCOTT ST
2400 DIVISADERO ST
2500 BRODERICK ST
2600 BAKER ST
2700 LYON ST
END PRESIDIO AVE
SWEENY ST SF 15 A3
FROM SAN BRUNO AV NEAR ISLAIS CK
W TO CAMBRIDGE ST
2 SAN BRUNO AV
100 BARNEVELD ST
200 MERRILL ST
300 BOYLSTON ST
BOWDOIN ST
DARTMOUTH ST
DUNSMUIR ST
COLBY ST
UNIVERSITY ST
PRINCETON ST
END CAMBRIDGE ST
SWISS AV SF 14 A3
BETWEEN CONRAD ST AND MIZPAH AV
FROM ARBOR ST TO SURREY ST
2 ARBOR ST
50 SUSSEX ST
END SURREY ST
SYCAMORE ST SF 10 C2
W FROM MISSION ST BETWEEN 17TH ST
AND 18TH ST TO VALENCIA ST
SYDNEY WY SF 13 C1
FROM IDORA AV S ACROSS
ULLOA ST TO PORTOLA DR
SYLVAN DR SF 12 C3
S FROM SLOAT BLVD TO OCEAN AV
E OF MIDDLEFIELD DR

T

TABER PL SF 7 B3
FROM 2ND ST BETWEEN BRYANT ST AND
SOUTH PARK AV SW TO 3RD ST
TACOMA ST SF 5 A3
W FROM 15TH AV BETWEEN
GEARY BLVD AND CLEMENT ST
TALBERT CT SF 21 A3
N FROM TALBERT ST & VISITACION AV
2 BLKS W OF BAYSHORE BLVD
TALBERT ST SF 21 A3
SW FROM VISITACION AV TO COUNTY
LINE, 2 BLKS W OF BAYSHORE BLVD
TAMALPAIS TER SF 5 C3
N FROM GOLDEN GATE AV TO TURK ST
BETWEEN ANNAPOLIS TER AND
ROSLYN TER
TAMPA LN SF 15 B3
S FROM QUESADA AV TO
BRIDGEVIEW DR BETWEEN QUINT ST
AND NEWHALL ST
TANDANG SORA SF 7 B3
SE FROM BONIFACIO ST TO RIZAL ST
BETWEEN 3RD ST AND 4TH ST
TAPIA DR SF 18 C1
S FROM ARBALLO DR TO SERRANO DR
E OF LAKE MERCED BLVD
TARA ST SF 19 C2
S FROM GENEVA AV TO RIDGE LN
1 BLK W OF I-280 FRWY
100 GENEVA AV
200 NIAGARA AV
300 MT VERNON AV
END RIDGE LN
TARAVAL ST SF 12 A2
TARAVAL ST SF 13 A2
W FROM DEWEY BLVD TO 48TH AV
BETWEEN SANTIAGO ST & ULLOA ST
2 DEWEY BLVD
LENOX WY
WAWONA ST
100 CORTES ST
MADRONE AV
FOREST SIDE AV
200 12TH AV
300 FUNSTON AV
400 14TH AV
500 15TH AV
600 16TH AV
700 17TH AV
800 18TH AV
900 19TH AV
1000 20TH AV
1100 21ST AV
22ND AV
23RD AV
1400 24TH AV
1500 25TH AV
1600 26TH AV
1700 27TH AV
1800 28TH AV
1900 29TH AV
2000 30TH AV
2100 31ST AV
2200 32ND AV
2300 33RD AV
35TH AV
2500 35TH AV
2600 36TH AV
SUNSET BLVD
2700 37TH AV
2800 38TH AV
2900 39TH AV
3000 40TH AV
3100 41ST AV
3200 42ND AV
3300 43RD AV
3400 44TH AV
3500 45TH AV
3600 46TH AV
3700 47TH AV
END 48TH AV
TAYLOR RD SF 1 B2
S FROM LINCOLN BLVD TO BLISS RD
BETWEEN ORD ST AND MONTGOMERY ST
IN THE PRESIDIO
TAYLOR ST SF 2 C1
TAYLOR ST SF 7 A1
N FROM MARKET ST BETWEEN MASON ST
AND JONES ST TO THE BAY
2 MARKET ST
GOLDEN GATE AV
OPAL PL
100 TURK ST
200 EDDY ST
300 ELLIS ST
400 O'FARRELL ST
500 GEARY ST
DERBY PL
ADELAIDE PL
600 POST ST
COSMO PL
HOBART AL
700 SUTTER ST
800 BUSH ST
MULFORD AL
900 PINE ST
1000 CALIFORNIA ST
1100 SACRAMENTO ST
PLEASANT ST
1200 CLAY ST
1300 WASHINGTON ST
1400 JACKSON ST
1500 PACIFIC AV
BERNARD ST
1600 BROADWAY
FALLON PL
1700 VALLEJO ST
1800 GREEN ST
MACONADRAY ST
1900 UNION ST
ALADDIN TER
2000 FILBERT ST
VALPARAISO ST
2100 GREENWICH ST
2200 LOMBARD ST
COLUMBUS AV
2300 CHESTNUT ST
WATER ST
2400 FRANCISCO ST
2500 BAY ST
2600 NORTH POINT ST
2700 BEACH ST
2800 JEFFERSON ST
END THE EMBARCADERO
TEA GARDEN DR SF 9 A1
S FROM JOHN F KENNEDY DR TO
MARTN L KING DR IN GOLDEN GATE PK
TEDDY AV SF 21 A2
FROM 4100 SAN BRUNO AV BETWEEN
CAMPBELL AV AND ARLETA AV
W TO ELLIOT ST
2 SAN BRUNO AV
100 ALPHA ST
200 RUTLAND ST
300 DELTA ST
400 ELLIOT ST
TEHAMA ST SF 7 A3
W FROM 1ST ST BETWEEN HOWARD ST
AND CLEMENTINA ST SW TO 9TH ST

2 1ST ST
MALDEN AL
100 2ND ST
400 5TH ST
6TH ST
700 8TH ST
END 9TH ST
TELEGRAPH PL SF 3 A2
N OF GREENWICH ST BETWEEN
KEARNY ST AND GRANT AV
TELEGRAPH HL BL SF 3 A2
S FROM LOMBARD ST TO
FILBERT ST AND N TO
GREENWICH ST
TEMESCAL TER SF 5 C3
N FROM GOLDEN GATE AV TO
TURK ST BETWEEN PARKER AV AND
CHABOT TER
TEMPLE ST SF 10 A2
FROM 17TH ST N TO SATURN ST 1 BLK
E OF ROOSEVELT WY
TENNESSEE ST SF 11 C2
TENNESSEE ST SF 15 C1
FROM MARIPOSA ST BETWEEN 3RD ST
AND MINNESOTA ST S TO TULARE ST
600 MARIPOSA ST
700 18TH ST
800 19TH ST
900 20TH ST
1100 22ND ST
TUBBS ST
1200 23RD ST
24TH ST
1500 25TH ST
1600 26TH ST
ARMY ST
MARIN ST
END TULARE ST
TENNY PL SF 7 B2
E FROM 1ST ST BETWEEN HOWARD ST
AND FOLSOM ST
TERESITA BLVD SF 13 C1
FROM 561 PORTOLA DR S TO
FOERSTER ST
PORTOLA DR
100 FOWLER AV
200 EVELYN WY
MARIETTA DR
AGUA WY
300 ISOLA WY
REPOSA WY
SEQUOIA WY
400 GAVIOTA WY
500 ARROYO WY
EL SERENO CT
RIO CT
BELLA VISTA WAY
MARIETTA DR
CUBA AL
FOERSTER ST
600 LOS PALMOS DR
STILLINGS AV
MELROSE AV
EDNA ST
VERNA ST
END FOERSTER ST
TERRACE DR SF 13 B2
FROM 1499 PORTOLA DR SE TO A
POINT E OF SANTA CLARA AV
TERRACE WALK SF 13 B2
SW FROM YERBA BUENA AV TO
SAN ANSELMO AV W OF
SANTA PAULA AV
TERRA VISTA AV SF 6 A3
E FROM ANZAVISTA AV TO
ST JOSEPHS AV BETWEEN
O'FARRELL ST AND TURK ST
TEXAS ST SF 11 B2
FROM 17TH ST BETWEEN MISSOURI ST
AND MISSISSIPPI ST S TO 25TH ST
100 17TH ST
200 MARIPOSA ST
300 18TH ST
400 19TH ST
500 20TH ST
SIERRA ST
900 23RD ST
1100 25TH ST
THERESA ST SF 14 A3
FROM 4400 MISSION ST BETWEEN
TINGLEY ST AND COTTER ST TO
SAN JOSE AV
2 MISSION ST
ALEMANY BLVD
200 CAYUGA AV
END SAN JOSE AV
THOMAS AV SF 1 B3
FROM INFANTRY TER S TO
SIBERT LOOP IN THE PRESIDIO
THOMAS AV SF 15 A2
THOMAS AV SF 21 C1
FROM FITCH ST NW TO 3RD ST AND
FROM MADDUX AV TO A POINT W OF
SELBY ST
FITCH ST
GRIFFITH ST
HAWES ST
1300 INGALLS ST
1400 JENNINGS ST
1500 KEITH ST
1600 LANE ST
3RD ST
2000 MADDUX AV
QUINT ST
ROBBLEE AV
2100 SILVER AV
SELBY ST
END PT W OF SELBY ST
THOMAS MELLON DR SF 21 B3
N FROM ALANA WY AND HARNEY WY
TO EXECUTIVE PARK BLVD
THOMAS MORE WY SF 19 A3
S OF BROTHERHOOD WY 2 BLKS W OF
JUNIPERO SERRA BLVD
THOR AV SF 14 B3
N FROM CHENERY ST TO SURREY ST
THORNBURG RD SF 1 C2
NW FROM KENNEDY AV TO GIRARD RD
IN THE PRESIDIO
THORNE WY SF 15 B3
SE FROM BRIDGEVIEW DR BETWEEN
BRIDGEVIEW DR & TOPEKA AV
THORNTON AV SF 15 B3
FROM 5200 3RD ST W TO BAYSHORE BL
2 3RD ST
LATONA ST
LUCY ST
100 POMONA ST
CERES ST
FLORA ST
REDDY ST
TOPEKA AV
DIANA ST
NEPTUNE ST
VENUS ST
APOLLO ST
BRIDGEVIEW DR
600 SCOTIA ST
VESTA ST
MERCURY ST
700 WATERVILLE ST
QUINT ST
ELMIRA ST
CARROLL AV
END BAYSHORE BLVD
THORP LN SF 10 A3
N FROM 19TH ST AND CLOVER ST
THRIFT ST SF 19 B2
S FROM SUMMIT ST TO ORIZABA AV
2 SUMMIT ST
100 PLYMOUTH AV
200 CAPITOL AV
FAXON AV
END ORIZABA AV
TIFFANY AV SF 14 C1
FROM THE JUNCTION OF VALENCIA ST
AND DUNCAN ST SW TO 29TH ST
TILLMAN PL SF 7 A2
W FROM 201 GRANT AV BETWEEN
SUTTER ST AND POST ST
TINGLEY ST SF 14 B3
FROM 4300 MISSION ST NEAR
SILVER AV NW TO SAN JOSE AV
2 MISSION ST
100 ALEMANY BLVD
200 CAYUGA AV
END SAN JOSE AV
TIOGA AV SF 21 A2
BETWEEN TUCKER AV AND WILDE AV
FROM ALPHA ST W TO DELTA ST
TOCOLOMA AV SF 21 B3
BETWEEN PENINSULA AV AND NUEVA AV
TODD ST SF 1 A2
FROM POPE ST TO HITCHCOCK ST
IN THE PRESIDIO
TOLAND ST SF 15 B2
FROM EVANS AV SW TO OAKDALE AV
2 EVANS AV
200 GALVEZ AV
300 HUDSON AV
400 INNES AV
JERROLD AV
KIRKWOOD AV
MCKINNON AV
NEWCOMB AV
OAKDALE AV
TOLEDO WY SF 2 A2
W FROM MALLORCA WY TO PIERCE ST
TOMASO CT SF 21 A3
W OF BAYSHORE BLVD
S OF SUNNYDALE AV
TOMPKINS AV SF 14 C2
FROM ANDOVER ST BETWEEN JARBOE AV
& OGDEN AV E TO PERALTA AV
2 ANDOVER ST
100 MOULTRIE ST
200 ANDERSON ST
300 ELLSWORTH ST
400 GATES ST
500 FOLSOM ST
600 BANKS ST
700 PRENTISS ST
800 NEVADA ST
900 PUTNAM ST
1000 BRONTE ST
1100 BRADFORD ST
END PERALTA AV
TOPAZ WY SF 14 A2
S FROM GOLDMINE DR 2 BLKS W
OF DIAMOND ST
TOPEKA AV SF 15 B3
S FROM SILVER AV TO
THRONTON AV E OF SANTA FE AV
TORNEY AV SF 1 C2
SE FROM LINCOLN BLVD TO
LETTERMAN HOSPITAL IN PRESIDIO
TORRENS CT SF 2 C3
N FROM CLAY ST BETWEEN HYDE ST
AND LARKIN ST
TOUCHARD ST SF 6 C1
S FROM 1101 PINE ST BETWEEN
JONES ST AND LEAVENWORTH ST
TOWNSEND ST SF 7 C3
TOWNSEND ST SF 11 B1
FROM THE BAY BETWEEN BRANNAN ST
AND KING ST SW TO 8TH ST
BAY OF S F
2 DELANCEY ST
GALE ST
COLIN P KELLY JR ST
100 2ND ST
STANFORD ST
CLARENCE PL
200 3RD ST
236 RITCH ST
CLYDE ST
LUSK ST
300 4TH ST
400 5TH ST
500 6TH ST
600 7TH ST
700 8TH ST
END DIVISION ST
TOYON LN SF 20 B3
E FROM BALTIMORE WY TO
SOUTH HILL BLVD
TRAINOR ST SF 10 C1
N FROM 14TH ST BETWEEN FOLSOM ST
AND HARRISON ST
TRANSVERSE RD SF 8 C1
S FROM CROSSOVER DR TO
MIDDLE DR W IN GOLDEN GATE PARK
TREASURY PL SF 3 B3
N FROM 200 BUSH ST BETWEEN
SANSOME ST AND MONTGOMERY ST
TREAT AV SF 11 A2
TREAT AV SF 15 A1
FROM FLORIDA ST SW TO 18TH ST
THEN S BETWEEN FOLSOM ST AND
HARRISON ST TO A POINT S
OF PRECITA AV
2 FLORIDA ST
ALAMEDA ST
100 ALABAMA ST
200 15TH ST
300 HARRISON ST
16TH ST
400 17TH ST
18TH ST
600 19TH ST
MISTRAL ST
700 20TH ST
800 21ST ST
900 22ND ST
1000 23RD ST
1100 24TH ST
1200 25TH ST
1300 26TH ST
PRECITA AV
END PT S OF PRECITA AV
TRENTON ST SF 3 A3
FROM 900 WASHINGTON ST BETWEEN
STOCKTON ST AND POWELL ST
N TO JACKSON ST
2 WASHINGTON ST
100 JACKSON ST
TRINITY ST SF 7 B1
FROM 100 SUTTER ST BETWEEN
MONTGOMERY ST AND KEARNY ST
N TO BUSH ST
TROCADERO DR SF 12 C2
E FROM THE JUNCTION OF WAWONA ST
AND CRESTLAKE IN PINE LAKE PARK
TROY AL SF 2 C3
W FROM 1201 HYDE ST BETWEEN
CLAY ST AND SACRAMENTO ST
TRUBY ST SF 1 C2
S FROM GORGAS AV IN THE PRESIDIO
TRUETT ST SF 3 A3
W FROM MASON ST BETWEEN CLAY ST
AND WASHINGTON ST
TRUMBULL ST SF 14 B3
FROM 4101 MISSION ST NEAR
SILVER AV TO CAMBRIDGE ST
2 MISSION ST
100 CRAUT ST
200 CONGDON ST
NEY ST
MAYNARD ST
STONEYBROOK AV
STONEYFORD AV
GLADSTONE DR
CAMBRIDGE ST
TUBBS ST SF 11 C3
E FROM INDIANA ST TO TENNESSEE ST
BETWEEN 22ND ST AND 23RD ST
TUCKER AV SF 21 A2
W FROM ALPHA ST TO DELTA ST
BETWEEN CAMPBELL AV & TIOGA AV
TULANE ST SF 14 C3
W FROM PRINCETON ST BETWEEN
SWEENY ST AND SILVER AV
TULARE ST SF 15 C1
FROM 3RD ST W TO INDIANA ST
TULIP AL SF 7 A3
OFF RUSS ST BETWEEN MINNA ST
AND NATOMA ST
TUNNEL AV SF 21 B3
FROM BAY SHORE BLVD S TO A
POINT S OF THE COUNTY LINE
TURK ST SF 5 C3
TURK ST SF 6 A3
TURK ST SF 7 A2
FROM THE JUNCTION OF MARKET ST
& MASON ST BETWEEN GOLDEN GATE AV
AND EDDY ST W TO ARGUELLO BLVD
2 MARKET ST
MASON ST
100 TAYLOR ST
200 JONES ST
300 LEAVENWORTH ST
400 HYDE ST
DODGE PL
500 LARKIN ST
600 POLK ST
700 VAN NESS AVE
800 FRANKLIN ST
GOUGH ST
LAGUNA ST
1300 WEBSTER ST
1400 FILLMORE ST
STEINER ST
1600 PIERCE ST
1700 SCOTT ST
SEYMOUR AVE
1800 DIVISADERO ST
1900 BRODERICK ST
1938 ST JOSEPHS AV
2000 BAKER ST
2100 LYON ST
2200 CENTRAL AV
2300 MASONIC AV
ANNAPOLIS TER
TAMALPAIS TER
ROSELYN TER
KITTREDGE TER
CHABOT TER
TEMESCAL TER
PARKER AV
BEAUMONT AV
STANYAN ST
ROSSI AV
3100 WILLARD ST
END ARGUELLO BLVD
TURNER TER SF 11 B3
SE OFF MISSOURI ST BETWEEN
22ND ST AND 23RD ST
TURQUOISE WY SF 14 A2
SW FROM AMBER DR ONE BLK S
OF DUNCAN ST
TUSCANY AL SF 3 A2
S FROM 501 LOMBARD ST BETWEEN
STOCKTON ST AND POWELL ST
TWIN PEAKS BLVD SF 9 C3
FROM CARMEL ST AND CLAYTON ST
S AND SW TO BURNETT AV
100 CARMEL ST
CLAYTON ST
200 CLARENDON AV
MT SPRING AV
ST GERMAIN AV
RACCOON DR
BURNETT AV
300 PALO ALTO AV
VISTA LN
END PORTOLA DR

U

ULLOA ST SF 12 A2
ULLOA ST SF 13 A2
FROM WOODSIDE AV SW AND W TO THE GREAT HWY S OF TARAVAL ST OF TARAVAL ST
2 WOODSIDE AV
SYDNEY WY
300 LAGUNA HONDA BLVD
ROCKAWAY AV
WAITHMAN WY
SHANGRILA WY
500 KENSINGTON WY
600 GRANVILLE WY
650 ALLSTON WY
700 DORCHESTER WY
800 CLAREMONT BLVD
900 LENOX WY
WEST PORTAL AV
1000 WAWONA ST
1100 MADRONE AV
1200 FORESTSIDE AV
1202 FUNSTON AV
1300 14TH AV
1400 15TH AV
1500 16TH AV
1600 17TH AV
1700 18TH AV
1800 19TH AV
1900 20TH AV
2000 21ST AV
2100 22ND AV
2200 23RD AV
2300 24TH AV
2400 25TH AV
2500 26TH AV
2600 27TH AV
2700 28TH AV
2800 29TH AV
2900 30TH AV
3000 31ST AV
3100 32ND AV
3200 33RD AV
3300 34TH AV
3400 35TH AV
36TH AV
SUNSET BLVD
3600 37TH AV
3700 38TH AV
3800 39TH AV
3900 40TH AV
4000 41ST AV
4100 42ND AV
4200 43RD AV
4300 44TH AV
4400 45TH AV
4500 46TH AV
4600 47TH AV
48TH AV
END GREAT HIGHWAY
UNDERWOOD AV SF 21 C1
FROM HAWES ST NW TO 3RD ST
HAWES ST
INGALLS ST
JENNINGS ST
1500 KEITH ST
1600 LANE ST
END 3RD ST
UNION ST SF 2 A3
UNION ST SF 3 A2
FROM THE EMBARCADERO BETWEEN GREEN & FILBERT STS W TO LYON ST
2 THE EMBARCADERO
50 FRONT ST
100 BATTERY ST
KEHOUSE AL
200 SANSOME ST
CALHOUN ST
300 MONTGOMERY ST
CASTLE ST
400 KEARNY ST
GENOA PL
SONOMA ST
VARENNES ST
500 GRANT AV
BANNAM PL
CADELL AL
550 JASPER PL
PRICE ROW
STOCKTON ST
COLUMBUS AV
700 POWELL ST
800 MASON ST
900 TAYLOR ST
MARION PL
1000 JONES ST
BLACK PL
1100 LEAVENWORTH ST
SHARP PL
1200 HYDE ST
EASTMAN ST
MOORE PL
1300 LARKIN ST
1400 POLK ST
1500 VAN NESS AV
1600 FRANKLIN ST
1700 GOUGH ST
1800 OCTAVIA ST
1900 LAGUNA ST
CHARLTON CT
2000 BUCHANAN ST
2100 WEBSTER ST
2200 FILLMORE ST
2300 STEINER ST
2400 PIERCE ST
2500 SCOTT ST
2600 DIVISADERO ST
2700 BRODERICK ST
2800 BAKER ST
END LYON ST
UNITD NATIONS PZ SF 6 C3
E FROM HYDE ST BETWEEN GROVE ST AND MCALLISTER ST W TO MARKET ST
UNIVERSITY ST SF 21 A1
FROM SWEENY ST S TO MANSELL ST
SWEENY ST
2 SILVER AV
100 SILLIMAN ST
200 FELTON ST
BURROW ST
BACON ST
500 WAYLAND ST
600 WOOLSEY ST
700 DWIGHT ST
800 OLMSTEAD ST
END MANSELL ST
UPLAND DR SF 13 B3
FROM KENWOOD WY WESTERLY TO SAN BENITO WY
KENWOOD WY
NORTH GATE DR
MANOR DR
PINEHURST WY
WESTGATE DR
SAN ALESO AV
APTOS AV
END SAN BENITO WY
UPPER TER SF 10 A2
FROM BUENA VISTA AV SW TO MONUMENT WY
2 BUENA VISTA AV
100 MASONIC AV
ASHBURY TER
200 CLIFFORD TER
END MONUMENT WY
UPPER SERVICE RD SF 9 B2
N FROM JOHNSTONE DR IN SUTRO FOREST
UPTON AV SF 1 A2
N FROM KOBBE AV TO RUCKMAN AV IN THE PRESIDIO
UPTON ST SF 15 B2
S FROM JERROLD AV TO MCKINNON AV N OF TOLAND ST
URANUS TER SF 9 C2
S FROM 17TH ST TO DEMING ST BETWEEN MARS ST & CLAYTON ST
URBANO DR N SF 19 B1
URBANO DR S SF 19 B1
A CIRCULAR STREET STARTING S OF OCEAN AV CROSSING VICTORIA ST, DE SOTO ST, CORONA ST AND BORICO ST, BOTH E AND W
LEGION CT
2 PICO AV
100 VICTORIA ST
DE SOTO ST
200 CORONA ST
BORICA
ALVISO ST
300 MONCADA WY
500 BORICO ST
600 CORONA ST
700 DE SOTO ST
800 VICTORIA ST
UTAH ST SF 11 A3
FROM DIVISION ST BETWEEN SAN BRUNO AV AND POTRERO AV S TO 18TH ST & FROM 23RD ST TO A POINT S OF 25TH ST
2 DIVISION ST
100 ALAMEDA ST
200 15TH ST
300 16TH ST
400 17TH ST
500 MARIPOSA ST
18TH ST
1200 23RD ST
1300 24TH ST
1400 25TH ST
END PT S OF 25TH ST

V

VALDEZ AV SF 13 C3
N FROM GREENWOOD AV BETWEEN COLON AV AND HAZELWOOD AV TO BRENTWOOD ST
2 GREENWOOD AVE
100 MONTECITO AVE
200 MONTEREY BLVD
300 MANGELS AVE
END BRENTWOOD ST
VALE AV SF 12 C3
N FROM SLOAT BLVD TO TROCADERO DR
VALENCIA ST SF 10 C1
VALENCIA ST SF 14 C1
S FROM MARKET ST BETWEEN MISSION ST AND GUERRERO ST S TO MISSION ST
2 MARKET ST
100 MC COPPIN ST
200 DUBOCE AVE
240 CLINTON PARK
260 BROSNAN ST
300 14TH ST
400 15TH ST
500 16TH ST
600 17TH ST
CLARION AL
SYCAMORE ST
700 18TH ST
800 19TH ST
CUNNINGHAM PL
900 20TH ST
950 LIBERTY ST
1000 21ST ST
1050 HILL ST
1100 22ND ST
1200 23RD ST
1300 24TH ST
1400 25TH ST
1500 26TH ST
153 ARMY ST
DUNCAN ST
1600 TIFFANY ST
END MISSION ST
VALERTON CT SF 20 A1
SE FROM CAYUGA AV BETWEEN ONONDAGA AV AND OCEAN AV
VALLEJO ST SF 1 B2
W FROM SGT MITCHELL ST, PRESIDIO
VALLEJO ST SF 2 C3
VALLEJO ST SF 3 A3
FROM THE EMBARCADERO BETWEEN BROADWAY & GREEN ST W TO LYON ST
2 THE EMBARCADERO
50 DAVIS ST
100 FRONT ST
200 BATTERY ST
COWELL PL
300 SANSOME ST
PRESCOTT CT
HODGES AL
BARTOL ST
400 MONTGOMERY ST
500 KEARNY ST
SAN ANTONIO ST
ROMOLO ST
POLLARD PL
MARGRAVE PL
600 GRANT AVE
COLUMBUS AVE
TRACY PL
700 STOCKTON ST
EMERY LN
CHURCHILL ST
800 POWELL ST
WASHOE PL
900 MASON ST
VALLEJO TER
VISTA TER
1000 TAYLOR ST
FLORENCE ST
RUSSIAN HILL PL
1100 JONES ST
1200 LEAVENWORTH ST
1300 HYDE ST
WHITE ST
1400 LARKIN ST
1500 POLK ST
1600 VAN NESS AV
1700 FRANKLIN ST
1800 GOUGH ST
1900 OCTAVIA ST
2000 LAGUNA ST
2100 BUCHANAN ST
2200 WEBSTER ST
2300 FILLMORE ST
2400 STEINER ST
2500 PIERCE ST
2600 SCOTT ST
NORMANDY TER
2700 DIVISADERO ST
2800 BRODERICK ST
2900 BAKER ST
END LYON ST
VALLEJO TER SF 3 A3
OFF 927 VALLEJO ST BETWEEN MASON ST AND TAYLOR ST
VALLETA CT SF 14 A2
NW FROM MALTA DR ONE BLK N OF STILLINGS AV
VALLEY ST SF 14 B1
W FROM SAN JOSE AV BETWEEN 28TH ST AND 29TH ST TO DIAMOND ST
2 SAN JOSE AVE
100 DOLORES ST
200 CHURCH ST
300 SANCHEZ ST
400 NOE ST
500 CASTRO ST
END DIAMOND ST
VALMAR TER SF 20 B1
S OFF 600 PERU AV
VALPARAISO ST SF 2 C2
FROM 1901 MASON ST BETWEEN FILBERT ST AND GREENWICH ST W TO TAYLOR ST AND FROM ROACH ST TO JONES ST
VAN BUREN ST SF 14 A3
W OF DIAMOND ST S FROM SUSSEX ST TO SURREY ST
VANDEWATER ST SF 3 A2
W FROM 2201 POWELL ST BETWEEN BAY ST & FRANCISCO ST W TO MASON ST
VAN DYKE AV SF 21 B1
N FROM HAWES ST TO 3RD ST
HAWES ST
INGALLS ST
JENNINGS ST
1500 KEITH ST
1600 LANE ST
END 3RD ST
VAN KEUREN AV SF 17 B1
E FROM FISHER AV TO LOCKWOOD ST N OF SPEAR AV
VAN NESS AV SF 2 B2
VAN NESS AV SF 6 C2
N FROM MARKET ST BETWEEN POLK ST AND FRANKLIN ST TO BEACH ST
2 MARKET ST
OAK ST
HICKORY ST
100 FELL ST
LINDEN ST
200 HAYES ST
LECH WALESA
GROVE ST
500 MC ALLISTER ST
530 REDWOOD ST
600 GOLDEN GATE AV
630 ELM ST
700 TURK ST
LARCH ST
800 EDDY ST
830 WILLOW ST
900 ELLIS ST
930 OLIVE ST
1000 O FARRELL ST
1030 MYRTLE ST
1100 GEARY ST
1130 CEDAR ST
1200 POST ST
1230 HEMLOCK ST
1300 SUTTER ST
1330 FERN ST
1400 BUSH ST
1430 AUSTIN ST
1500 PINE ST
1600 CALIFORNIA ST
1700 SACRAMENTO ST
1800 CLAY ST
1900 WASHINGTON ST
2000 JACKSON ST
2100 PACIFIC AV
2200 BROADWAY
2300 VALLEJO ST
2400 GREEN ST
2500 UNION ST
2600 FILBERT ST
2700 GREENWICH ST
2800 LOMBARD ST
2900 CHESTNUT ST
3000 FRANCISCO ST
3100 BAY ST
3200 NORTH POINT ST
END BEACH ST
VARELA AV SF 19 A1
S FROM HOLLOWAY AV TO SERRANO DR W OF 19TH AV
VARENNES ST SF 3 A2
N FROM 400 GREEN ST BETWEEN KEARNY ST AND GRANT AV TO

FILBERT ST
2 GREEN ST
100 UNION ST
END FILBERT ST
VARNEY PL SF 7 B3
SW FROM CENTER PL BETWEEN
SOUTH PARK AV AND BRANNAN ST
TO 3RD ST
VASQUEZ AV SF 13 B2
FROM WOODSIDE AV SW TO
KENSINGTON WY
2 WOODSIDE AV
50 LAGUNA HONDA BLVD
100 HERNANDEZ AV
GARCIA AV
END ENSINGTON WY
VASSAR PL SF 7 B2
S FROM HARRISON ST BETWEEN 2ND ST
AND 3RD ST
VEGA ST SF 5 C3
W FROM ANZAVISTA AV TO MASONIC AV
BETWEEN TURK ST AND O'FARRELL ST
VELASCO AV SF 20 C3
FROM SCHWERIN ST AND THE
COUNTY LINE W TO CARRIZAL ST
VENARD AL SF 3 A2
S FROM 501 CHESTNUT ST BETWEEN
POWELL ST AND MASON ST
VENTURA AV SF 13 B1
SE FROM LINARES AV TO
CASTENADA AV
VENUS ST SF 15 B3
FROM THORNTON AV S TO WILLIAMS AV
VERDI PL SF 3 A3
W FROM 901 MONTGOMERY ST BETWEEN
PACIFIC AV AND BROADWAY
VERDUN WY SF 13 B2
FROM CLAREMONT BLVD S OF
TARAVAL ST W TO LENOX WY
VERMEHR PL SF 7 A2
E FROM 100 KEARNY ST BETWEEN
POST ST AND SUTTER ST
VERMONT ST SF 11 A1
VERMONT ST SF 15 B1
FROM DIVISION ST BETWEEN
SAN BRUNO AV AND KANSAS ST
S TO 26TH ST
2 DIVISION ST
100 ALAMEDA ST
200 15TH ST
300 16TH ST
400 17TH ST
500 MARIPOSA ST
600 18TH ST
700 19TH ST
20TH ST
900 21ST ST
1000 22ND ST
1200 23RD ST
1300 24TH ST
1400 25TH ST
END 26TH ST
VERNA ST SF 13 C3
S FROM LOS PALMOS DR
TO MELROSE AV E OF FOERSTER ST
VERNON ST SF 19 B2
W OF SAN JOSE AV AND S FROM
HOLLOWAY AV TO A POINT S OF
RANDOLPH ST
100 RANDOLPH ST
200 SARGENT ST
300 SHIELDS ST
400 GARFIELD ST
END HOLLOWAY AVE
VESTA ST SF 15 B3
S FROM THORNTON AV TO WILLIAMS AV
& PHELPS ST
VIA BUFANO SF 3 A2
S FROM 701 GREENWICH ST TO
COLUMBUS AV
VICENTE ST SF 12 A2
VICENTE ST SF 13 A2
W FROM PORTOLA DR TO GREAT HWY
1 BLK S OF ULLOA ST
2 PORTOLA DR
100 WEST PORTAL AVE
200 WAWONA ST
MADRONE AVE
260 FOREST SIDE AVE
300 14TH AVE
400 15TH AVE
500 16TH AVE
600 17TH AVE
700 18TH AVE
800 19TH AVE
900 20TH AVE
1000 21ST AVE
1100 22ND AVE
1200 23RD AVE
1300 24TH AVE
1400 25TH AVE
1500 26TH AVE
1600 27TH AVE
1700 28TH AVE
1800 29TH AVE
1900 30TH AVE
2000 31ST AVE
2100 32ND AVE
2200 33RD AVE
2300 34TH AVE
2400 35TH AVE
2500 36TH AVE
SUNSET BLVD
2600 37TH AVE
2700 38TH AVE
2800 39TH AVE
2900 40TH AVE
3000 41ST AVE
3100 42ND AVE
3200 43RD AVE
3300 44TH AVE
3400 45TH AVE
3500 46TH AVE
3600 47TH AVE
END GREAT HIGHWAY
VICKSBURG ST SF 10 B3
VICKSBURG ST SF 14 B1
S FROM 22ND ST BETWEEN CHURCH ST
AND SANCHEZ ST TO 25TH ST
VICTORIA ST SF 19 B2
N FROM PALMETTO AV TO ALEMANY BL
& FROM S OF RANDOLPH ST
TO OCEAN AV
2 PALMETTO AVE
ALEMANY BLVD
200 RANDOLPH ST
300 SARGENT ST
400 SHIELDS ST
500 GARFIELD ST
600 HOLLOWAY AVE
700 URBANO DR S
URBANO DR N
END OCEAN AVE
VIDAL DR SF 18 C2
S FROM FONT BLVD TO RIVAS DR
VIENNA ST SF 20 B2
FROM SILVER AV SW TO GENEVA AV
2 SILVER AVE
100 PERU AVE
200 AVALON AVE
300 EXCELSIOR AVE
400 BRAZIL AVE
500 PERSIA AVE
600 RUSSIA AV
700 FRANCE AVE
800 ITALY AVE
900 AMAZON AVE
END GENEVA AVE
VILLA TER SF 10 A3
SE FROM TWIN PEAKS BLVD TO
GRAYSTONE TER
2 TWIN PEAKS BLVD
100 PEMBERTON PL
END GRAYSTONE TER
VINE TER SF 7 A1
N FROM PINE ST BETWEEN MASON ST
AND TAYLOR ST
VINTON CT SF 3 A3
W FROM 501 GRANT AV BETWEEN
PINE ST AND CALIFORNIA ST
VIRGIL ST SF 14 C1
S FROM 25TH ST BETWEEN SOUTH
VAN NESS AV & SHOTWELL ST
VIRGINIA AV SF 14 C2
SE FROM 3351 MISSION ST NEAR
30TH ST TO ELSIE ST AND
EUGENIA AV
2 MISSION ST
100 COLERIDGE AV
LUNDYS LANE
200 PROSPECT AV
300 WINFIELD ST
400 ELSIE ST
END EUGENIA AV
VISITACION AV SF 20 C2
VISITACION AV SF 21 A3
FROM A POINT E OF BAYSHORE BLVD
NEAR COUNTY LINE TO MANSELL ST
BAYSHORE BLVD
700 DESMOND ST
TALBERT CT
900 PEABODY ST
948 RUTLAND ST
CORA ST
DELTA ST
SCHWERIN ST
REY ST
BRITTON ST
LOEHR ST
SAWYER ST
HAHN ST
END MANSELL ST
VISTA LN SF 10 A3
W FROM BURNETT AV 5
BLKS N OF PORTOLA DR
VISTA VERDE CT SF 14 A3
N FROM STILLINGS AV BETWEEN
TERESITA BLVD & MALTA DR
VULCAN ST SF 10 A2
FROM POINT W OF ORD ST TO
LEVANT ST N OF LOWER TER

W

WABASH TER SF 21 B2
NE FROM SAN BRUNO AV TO
BEEMAN LN W OF BAYSHORE BLVD
WAGNER AL SF 6 C2
WAGNER AL SF 7 A3
S FROM EDDY ST BETWEEN JONES ST
AND LEAVENWORTH ST
WAGNER RD SF 1 A2
FROM STOREY AV SE TO HOWE RD
IN THE PRESIDIO
WAITHMAN WY SF 13 B2
FROM 1000 PORTOLA DR N TO ULLOA S
WALBRIDGE ST SF 20 B3
W FROM THE INTERSECTION OF
GENEVA AV AND PARQUE DR
WALDO AL SF 2 C3
W FROM LEAVENWORTH ST BETWEEN
BROADWAY AND VALLEJO ST
WALL PL SF 2 C3
N FROM JACKSON ST BETWEEN HYDE ST
AND LEAVENWORTH ST
WALLACE AV SF 21 B1
FROM POINT S OF INGALLS ST
NW TO 3RD ST
INGALLS ST
JENNINGS ST
KEITH ST
LANE ST
END 3RD ST
WALLEN CT SF 1 B3
SW FROM MACARTHUR ST, PRESIDIO
WALLER ST SF 9 C1
WALLER ST SF 10 A1
FROM THE JUNCTION OF MARKET ST
& OCTAVIA ST W TO STANYAN ST
2 MARKET ST
8 OCTAVIA ST
LAGUNA ST
200 BUCHANAN ST
300 WEBSTER ST
400 FILLMORE ST
500 STEINER ST
POTOMAC ST
600 PIERCE ST
CARMELITA ST
700 SCOTT ST
800 DIVISADERO ST
ALPINE TER
900 BRODERICK ST
1100 BUENA VISTA AVE
1200 CENTRAL AVE
1300 MASONIC AVE
DELMAR ST
1400 ASHBURY ST
DOWNEY ST
1500 CLAYTON ST
1550 BELVEDERE ST
1600 COLE ST
1700 SHRADER ST
END STANYAN ST
WALNUT ST SF 5 C1
FROM PACIFIC AV BETWEEN
PRESIDIO AV AND LAUREL ST S TO
CALIFORNIA ST
2 PACIFIC AVE
100 JACKSON ST
200 WASHINGTON ST
300 CLAY ST
400 SACRAMENTO ST
END CALIFORNIA ST
WALTER ST SF 10 B1
S FROM DUBOCE AV BETWEEN
SANCHEZ ST & NOE ST TO 14TH ST
WALTER LUM PL SF 3 A3
WALTHAM ST SF 15 A2
W FROM ALABAMA ST NEAR
ESMERALDA AV
WANDA ST SF 20 A1
N FROM ONONDAGA AV BETWEEN
CAYUGA AV AND OTSEGO AV N TO
OCEAN AV
WARD ST SF 21 A2
W FROM SAN BRUNO AV TO SPARTA ST
BETWEEN ORDWAY ST AND HARKNESS AV
WARNER PL SF 2 C2
E FROM HYDE ST BETWEEN GREEN ST
AND UNION ST
WARREN DR SF 9 B3
SE FROM LAWTON ST & LOCKSLEY AV
PARALLEL TO 7TH AV
WASHBURN ST SF 11 A1
S FROM MISSION ST BETWEEN 9TH ST
AND 10TH ST SE TO HOWARD ST
WASHINGTON BLVD SF 1 B3
E FROM LINCOLN BL TO ARGUELLO BL
IN THE PRESIDIO
WASHINGTON ST SF 2 A3
WASHINGTON ST SF 3 B3
WASHINGTON ST SF 5 C2
WASHINGTON ST SF 6 A2
WASHINGTON ST SF 7 B1
FROM THE EMBARCADERO BETWEEN
CLAY ST AND JACKSON ST W
TO ARGUELLO BLVD
2 THE EMBARCADERO
100 DRUMM ST
200 DAVIS ST
400 BATTERY ST
CUSTOM HOUSE PL
500 SANSOME ST
HOTALING PL
MONTGOMERY ST
600 COLUMBUS AVE
DUNBAR AL
700 KEARNY ST
WALTER LUM PL
WENTWORTH PL
800 GRANT AVE
WAVERLY PL
ROSS AL
OLD CHINA TOWN LN
SPOFFORD ST
900 STOCKTON ST
TRENTON ST
STONE ST
1000 POWELL ST
CODMAN PL
WETMORE ST
1100 MASON ST
1200 TAYLOR ST
1300 JONES ST
PRIEST ST
REED ST
1400 LEAVENWORTH ST
1500 HYDE ST
1600 LARKIN ST
1700 POLK ST
1800 VAN NESS AV
1900 FRANKLIN ST
2000 GOUGH ST
2100 OCTAVIA ST
2200 LAGUNA ST
2300 BUCHANAN ST
2400 WEBSTER ST
2500 FILLMORE ST
STEINER ST
2800 SCOTT ST
2900 DIVISADERO ST
3000 BRODERICK ST
3100 BAKER ST
3200 LYON ST
3300 PRESIDIO AVE
3400 WALNUT ST
3500 LAUREL ST
3600 LOCUST ST
3700 SPRUCE ST
3800 MAPLE ST
3900 CHERRY ST
END ARGUELLO BLVD
WASHOE PL SF 3 A3
S FROM 800 VALLEJO ST BETWEEN
POWELL ST AND MASON ST
WATCHMAN WY SF 11 B3
SE OFF MISSOURI ST BETWEEN
22ND ST & 23RD ST
WATER ST SF 2 C2
FROM 2201 MASON ST BETWEEN
CHESTNUT ST AND FRANCISCO ST
W TO TAYLOR ST
WATERLOO ST SF 15 A2
FROM E S BAY SHORE BLVD
N OF INDUSTRIAL ST
WATERVILLE ST SF 15 B2
FROM SELBY ST E OF ELMIRA ST S TO
THORNTON AV
2 HELENA ST
SILVER AVE
END THORNTON AVE
WATSON PL SF 20 A1
SW FROM OCEAN AV 1 BLK E OF
ALEMANY BLVD
WATT AV SF 20 A3
S FROM HANOVER ST TO
BELLEVUE ST E OF GUTTENBERG ST
WAVERLY PL SF 3 A3
FROM 800 SACRAMENTO ST BETWEEN
GRANT AV AND STOCKTON ST
N TO WASHINGTON ST
2 SACRAMENTO ST
100 CLAY ST
END WASHINGTON ST
WAWONA ST SF 12 B3
WAWONA ST SF 13 A2

FROM TARAVAL ST S AND W TO
GREAT HIGHWAY
2 TARAVAL ST
100 ULLOA ST
200 VICENTE ST
300 14TH AVE
400 15TH AVE
500 16TH AVE
600 17TH AVE
18TH AV
800 19TH AVE
900 20TH AVE
1000 21ST AVE
1100 22ND AVE
1200 23RD AVE
1300 24TH AVE
1400 25TH AVE
26TH AVE
1700 28TH AVE
1900 30TH AVE
2200 33RD AVE
2300 34TH AVE
2400 35TH AVE
2500 36TH AVE
SUNSET BLVD
2600 37TH AVE
2700 38TH AVE
2800 39TH AVE
2900 40TH AVE
3000 41ST AVE
3100 42ND AVE
3200 43RD AVE
3300 44TH AVE
3400 45TH AVE
3500 46TH AVE
3600 47TH AVE
48TH AV
END GREAT HIGHWAY
WAYLAND ST SF 20 C1
WAYLAND ST SF 21 A1
FROM SAN BRUNO AV S OF BACON ST
W TO OXFORD ST
100 SAN BRUNO AV
200 GIRARD ST
300 BRUSSELS ST
400 GOETTINGEN ST
500 SOMERSET ST
600 HOLYOKE ST
700 HAMILTON ST
800 BOWDOIN ST
1100 UNIVERSITY ST
1200 PRINCETON ST
1300 AMHERST ST
1400 YALE ST
1500 CAMBRIDGE ST
END OXFORD ST
WAYNE PL SF 3 A3
FROM 900 PACIFIC AV BETWEEN
POWELL ST AND MASON ST N TO
BROADWAY
WEBB PL SF 3 A2
W FROM 1701 MASON ST BETWEEN
GREEN ST AND UNION ST
WEBSTER ST SF 2 B3
WEBSTER ST SF 6 B3
WEBSTER ST SF 10 B1
N FROM DUBOCE AV BETWEEN
BUCHANAN ST AND FILLMORE ST
TO A POINT N OF MARINA BLVD
2 DUBOCE AV
50 HERMANN ST
GERMANIA ST
100 WALLER ST
LAUSSAT ST
200 HAIGHT ST
300 PAGE ST
LILY ST
400 OAK ST
HICKORY ST
500 FELL ST
512 LINDEN ST
600 HAYES ST
614 IVY ST
700 GROVE ST
800 FULTON ST
900 MCALLISTER ST
1000 GOLDEN GATE AV
1100 TURK ST
1200 EDDY ST
1300 ELLIS ST
1400 O FARRELL ST
1500 GEARY ST
1600 POST ST
1700 SUTTER ST
1800 BUSH ST
WILMOT ST
1900 PINE ST
2000 CALIFORNIA ST
2100 SACRAMENTO ST
2200 CLAY ST
2300 WASHINGTON ST
2400 JACKSON ST
BROMLEY PL
2500 PACIFIC AVE
2600 BROADWAY
2700 VALLEJO ST
2800 GREEN ST
2900 UNION ST
3000 FILBERT ST
PIXLEY ST
3100 GREENWICH ST
MOULTON ST
3200 LOMBARD ST
MAGNOLIA ST
CHESTNUT ST
BAY ST
NORTH POINT ST
3700 BEACH ST
JEFFERSON ST
3800 MARINA BLVD
END PT N OF MARINA BLVD
WELSH ST SF 7 B3
W FROM ZOE ST BETWEEN BRANT ST
& BRANNAN ST SW TO 5TH ST
2 ZOE ST
100 4TH ST
END 5TH ST
WENTWORTH PL SF 3 A3
FROM 733 WASHINGTON ST BETWEEN
KEARNY ST AND GRANT AV N
TO JACKSON ST
WESTBROOK CT SF 15 C3
BETWEEN CASHMERE ST AND ARDATH CT
OFF HUDSON AV
WEST CLAY ST SF 4 C2
W FROM 22ND AV ONE BLOCK N
OF LAKE ST
WESTGATE DR SF 13 B3
FROM 2100 OCEAN AV N TO
MONTEREY BLVD
2 OCEAN AV
100 KENWOOD WY
200 UPLAND DR
300 DARIEN WY
END MONTEREY BLVD
WESTMOORLAND DR SF 12 B3
S FROM OCEAN AV TO EUCALYPTUS DR
WEST POINT RD SF 16 A2
A LOOP EXTENDING W FROM
MIDDLEPOINT RD
WEST PORTAL AV SF 13 A2
FROM ULLOA ST SW TO PORTOLA DR
2 ULLOA ST
100 VICENTE ST
300 14TH AVE
400 15TH AVE
END PORTOLA DR
WEST VIEW AV SF 14 C3
E FROM CAMBRIDGE ST BETWEEN
SWEENY ST AND ALEMANY BLVD
WESTWOOD DR SF 19 B1
W & N FROM MIRAMAR AV TO
MIRAMAR AV
2 MIRAMAR AVE
100 WILDWOOD AVE
PIZARRO WAY
END MIRAMAR AVE
WETMORE ST SF 3 A3
FROM 1000 CLAY ST BETWEEN
POWELL ST AND MASON ST N
TO WASHINGTON ST
WHEAT ST SF 21 B1
FROM PAUL AV BETWEEN CRANE ST
& BAYSHORE BLVD S TO SALINAS AV
WHEELER AV SF 21 B3
FROM HESTER AV TO A POINT S OF
LATHROP AV
WHIPPLE AV SF 19 C3
FROM MISSION ST NW TO SAN JOSE AV
NEAR THE COUNTY LINE
WHITE ST SF 2 C3
N FROM VALLEJO ST BETWEEN HYDE ST
AND LARKIN ST
WHITFIELD CT SF 15 C3
OFF LA SALLE AV BETWEEN
OSEOLA LN AND INGALLS ST
WHITING ST SF 3 A2
E FROM 1800 GRANT AV BETWEEN
LOMBARD ST & CHESTNUT ST
WHITNEY ST SF 14 B2
FROM 30TH ST E OF SANCHEZ ST
S TO CHENERY ST
2 30TH ST
100 RANDALL ST
200 FAIRMOUNT ST
END CHENERY ST
WHITNEY YOUNG CIR RSF 15 C3
S FROM CASHMERE ST TO HUDSON AV
WHITTIER ST SF 19 C3
SE FROM 5701 MISSION ST
2 MISSION ST
CASSANDRA CT
100 BRUNSWICK ST
COUNTY LINE
WIESE ST SF 10 C2
FROM 1601 15TH ST BETWEEN
MISSION ST & JULIAN AV S TO
16TH ST
WILDE AV SF 21 A2
FROM 3600 SAN BRUNO AV BETWEEN
CAMPBELL AV & HARNESS AV W TO
ERVINE ST
2 SAN BRUNO AVE
100 GIRARD ST
200 BRUSSELS ST
300 GOETTINGEN ST
400 RUTLAND ST
DELTA ST
END ERVINE ST
WILDER ST SF 14 B3
FROM POINT E OF CARRIE ST
S OF CHENERY ST W TO DIAMOND ST
WILDWOOD WY SF 19 B1
FROM A POINT E OF PLYMOUTH AV
BETWEEN GREENWOOD AV AND
SAN RAMON WY W TO A POINT W
OF FAXON AV
100 PLYMOUTH AVE
200 EASTWOOD DR
300 MIRAMAR AVE
400 WESTWOOD DR
500 FAXON AVE
HOMEWOOD CT
END PT W OF HOMEWOOD CT
WILLARD ST SF 9 C2
FROM GOLDEN GATE PARK S TO
WOODLAND AV
1200 FREDERICK ST
1300 CARL ST
1400 PARNASSUS AVE
FARNSWORTH ST
1500 BELMONT AVE
END WOODLAND AVE
WILLARD ST N SF 5 B3
FROM EDWARD ST E OF
ARGUELLO BLVD SW TO FULTON ST
2 EDWARD ST
100 TURK ST
200 GOLDEN GATE AVE
300 MCALLISTER ST
END FULTON ST
WILLIAMS AV SF 15 B3
FROM 3RD ST NEAR VAN DYKE AV
W TO PHELPS ST & VESTA ST
2 3RD ST
34 LUCY ST
66 CERES ST
MENDELL ST
100 REDDY ST
150 DIANA ST
200 NEPTUNE ST
NEWHALL ST
250 VENUS ST
300 APOLLO ST
PHELPS ST
END VESTA ST
WILLIAR AV SF 19 C2
W OF 2400 SAN JOSE AV OFF
800 NIAGARA AV S TO MT VERNON AV
WILLOW ST SF 6 B3
W FROM LARKIN ST BETWEEN EDDY ST
AND ELLIS ST W TO BUCHANAN ST
2 LARKIN ST
100 POLK ST
200 VAN NESS AVE
300 FRANKLIN ST
GOUCH ST
600 LAGUNA ST
END BUCHANAN ST
WILLS ST SF 16 A3
E FROM MIDDLE POINT RD IN
HUNTERS POINT
WILMOT ST SF 6 B2
W FROM WEBSTER ST BETWEEN BUSH ST
& PINE ST W TO STEINER ST
2 WEBSTER ST
100 FILLMORE ST
END STEINER ST
WILSON ST SF 19 B3
FROM MISSION ST S OF COUNTY LINE
NW TO DE LONG ST
COUNTY LINE
200 RHINE ST
END DE LONG ST
WINDING WY SF 20 A3
FROM ROLPH ST AND SOUTH HILL BLVD
SW AND WESTERLY TO PRAGUE ST
TO PRAGUE ST
2 ROLPH ST
100 NAYLOR ST
200 CORDOVA ST
300 DRAKE ST
END PRAGUE ST
WINDSOR PL SF 3 A2
N FROM 300 GREEN ST BETWEEN
MONTGOMERY ST AND KEARNY ST
WINFIELD ST SF 14 C2
FROM COSO AV BETWEEN PROSPECT AV
AND ELSIE ST SW TO CORTLAND AV
2 COSO AVE
100 ESMERALDA AVE
200 VIRGINIA AVE
300 EUGENIA AVE
END CORTLAND AVE
WINSTON DR SF 19 A1
W FROM JUNIPERO SERRA BLVD
TO LAKE MERCED BLVD
WINTER PL SF 3 A2
E OFF 1700 MASON ST BETWEEN
UNION ST AND GREEN ST
WINTHROP ST SF 3 A2
N FROM 200 LOMBARD ST BETWEEN
MONTGOMERY ST AND KEARNY ST
TO CHESTNUT ST
WISCONSIN ST SF 11 B2
FROM 16TH ST BETWEEN ARKANSAS ST
& CAROLINA ST S TO 26TH ST
100 16TH ST
17TH ST
300 MARIPOSA ST
500 19TH ST
600 20TH ST
800 22ND ST
MADERA ST
1000 23RD ST
CONNECTICUT ST
1200 25TH ST
26TH ST
WISER CT SF 1 A3
E FROM THE INTERSECTION OF
HITCHCOCK ST AND WRIGHT LOOP
IN THE PRESIDIO
WOOD ST SF 5 C2
FROM A POINT E OF EMERSON ST
W & S BETWEEN EMERSON ST AND
COLLINS ST S TO ANZA ST
PT E OF EMERSON ST
EMERSON ST
GEARY BLVD
END ANZA ST
WOODACRE DR SF 13 A3
NE FROM OCEAN AV TO
JUNIPERO SERRA BLVD NEAR
PORTOLA DR
WOODHAVEN CT SF 9 C3
W FROM FOREST KNOLLS DR 1
BLK S OF CHRISTOPHER DR
WOODLAND AV SF 9 C2
FROM 249 PARNASSUS AV BETWEEN
STANYAN ST AND WILLARD ST
S TO WILLARD ST
WOODSIDE AV SF 13 B1
FROM PORTOLA DR W TO DEWEY BLVD
WOODWARD ST SF 10 C1
S FROM DUBOCE AV BETWEEN
MISSION ST AND VALENCIA ST
TO 14TH ST
WOOL CT SF 1 A2
S FROM UPTON AV, IN THE PRESIDIO
WOOL ST SF 14 C2
FROM POWHATTAN AV AND BOCANA ST
S TO CORTLAND AV
2 BOCANA ST
POWHATTAN AVE
100 EUGENIA AVE
END CORTLAND AVE
WOOLSEY ST SF 21 A1
FROM SAN BRUNO AV S OF WAYLAND ST
W TO UNIVERSITY ST
100 SAN BRUNO AVE
200 GIRARD ST
300 BRUSSELS ST
400 GOETTINGEN ST
500 SOMERSET ST
600 HOLYOKE ST
700 HAMILTON ST
800 BOWDOIN ST
900 DARTMOUTH ST
1000 COLBY ST
END UNIVERSITY ST
WORCESTER AV SF 19 B3
SE FROM ALEMANY BLVD TO
PALMETTO AV
WORDEN ST SF 3 A2
N FROM 300 FRANCISCO ST BETWEEN
STOCKTON ST AND POWELL ST
WORTH ST SF 10 A3
FROM 4301 21ST ST S TO
22ND ST W OF DOUGLASS ST
WRIGHT LOOP SF 1 A3
S FROM HITCHCOCK ST, PRESIDIO
WRIGHT ST SF 15 A1
W FROM HOLLADAY AV
TO MONTCALM ST
WYTON LN SF 19 A1
W FROM JUNIPERO SERRA BLVD
TO 19TH AV N OF HOLLOWAY AV

Y

YALE ST SF 20 C1
S FROM SILVER AV TO WAYLAND ST
2 SILVER AVE
100 SILLIMAN ST
200 FELTON ST
END 500 WAYLAND ST
YERBA BUENA AV SF 13 B2
SE FROM SANTA CLARA AV TO MONTEREY BLVD
2 SANTA CLARA AVE
SANTA MONICA WY
TERRACE WK
100 SANTA PAULA AVE
SAN PABLO AV
MIRALOMA DR
MAYWOOD DR
200 RAVENWOOD DR
BAXTER AL
HAZELWOOD AV
300 BRENTWOOD AVE
400 ST ELMO WAY
END MONTEREY BLVD
YORBA LN SF 12 B3
W FROM 40TH AV TO 41ST AV BETWEEN SLOAT BLVD AND WAWONA ST
YORBA ST SF 12 B3
FROM CRESTLAKE DR W TO 40TH AV
2200 CRESTLAKE DR
2300 34TH AVE
2400 35TH AVE
2500 36TH AVE
SUNSET BLVD
2600 37TH AVE
2700 38TH AVE
2800 39TH AVE
END 40TH AV
YORK ST SF 11 A2
YORK ST SF 15 A1
FROM A POINT S OF MARIPOSA ST BETWEEN HAMPSHIRE ST & BRYANT ST S TO HOLLADAY AV
500 MARIPOSA ST
600 18TH ST
700 19TH ST
800 20TH ST
900 21ST ST
1000 22ND ST
1100 23RD ST
1200 24TH ST
1300 25TH ST
1400 26TH ST
ARMY ST
1500 PRECITA AVE
1600 PERALTA AVE
1700 WRIGHT ST
END HOLLADAY AVE
YOSEMITE AV SF 21 B1
FROM HAWES ST NW TO NEWHALL ST
HAWES ST
INGALLS ST
JENNINGS ST
1600 KEITH ST
1700 3RD ST
LANE ST
MENDELL ST
END NEWHALL ST
YOUNG ST SF 1 C2
W OF HALLECK ST, IN THE PRESIDIO
YUKON ST SF 10 A3
FROM CASELLI AV S TO GRAND VIEW AV
2 CASELLI AVE
100 EAGLE ST
END GRAND VIEW AVE

Z

ZENO PL SF 7 B2
S FROM FOLSOM ST BETWEEN BEALE ST AND FREMONT ST
ZIRCON PL SF 14 B2
S FROM 29TH ST BETWEEN BACON ST AND CASTRO ST
ZOE ST SF 7 B3
S FROM BRYANT ST BETWEEN 3RD ST AND 4TH ST TO BRANNAN ST

NUMERICAL STREETS

1ST ST SF 3 C1
NE FROM AVENUE A AT ENTRANCE TO TREASURE ISLAND
1ST ST SF 7 B1
S FROM MARKET ST BETWEEN 2ND ST AND FREMONT ST TO THE EMBARCADERO
2 MARKET ST
STEVENSON ST
JESSIE ST
ELIM ALLEY
100 MISSION ST
MINNA ST
NATOMA ST
200 HOWARD ST
TEHEMA ST
TENNY PL
CLEMENTINA ST
300 FOLSOM ST
GUY PL
LANSING ST
END HARRISON ST
2ND AV SF 5 B2
2ND AV SF 9 B2
FROM POINT N OF LAKE ST S TO PARNASSUS AV
NUMBERS THE SAME AS 19TH AV
2ND ST SF 7 B2
S FROM MARKET ST BETWEEN 1ST ST & 3RD ST SE TO THE BAY
2 MARKET ST
STEVENSON ST
JESSIE ST
100 MISSION ST
MINNA ST
NATOMA ST
200 HOWARD ST
TEHAMA ST
CLEMENTINA ST
300 FOLSOM ST
DOW PL
400 HARRISON ST
STILLMAN ST
500 BRYANT ST
TABER PL
FEDERAL ST
SOUTH PARK AV
DE BOOM ST
600 BRANNAN ST
700 TOWNSEND ST
KING ST
BERRY ST
END BAY OF S F
3RD AV SF 5 B2
3RD AV SF 9 B2
FROM POINT N OF LAKE ST S TO PARNASSUS AV
NUMBERS THE SAME AS 19TH AV
3RD AV SF 17 A2
SE FROM SPEAR AV TO MAHAN ST
3RD STIN HUNTERS POIN T
3RD ST SF 3 C1
NE FROM AVENUE A TO AVENUE B AND FROM AVENUE D TO AVENUE N TREASURE ISLAND
AV A
AV B
AV D
AV F
AV H
AV M
END AV N
3RD ST SF 7 B2
3RD ST SF 11 C1
3RD ST SF 15 C2
3RD ST SF 21 B1
SE FROM MARKET ST BETWEEN 2ND ST & 4TH ST TO CHANNEL, THEN S & SW TO BAYSHORE BLVD
2 MARKET ST
STEVENSON ST
ALDRICH ST
100 MISSION ST
134 MINNA ST
HUNT ST
200 HOWARD ST
CLEMENTINA ST
300 FOLSOM ST
ST FRANCIS PL
400 HARRISON ST
PERRY ST
STILLMAN ST
500 BRYANT ST
TABER PL
SOUTH PARK AV
VARNEY PL
600 BRANNAN ST
700 TOWNSEND ST
800 KING ST
900 BERRY ST
CHIN BASIN ST
ROCK ST
4TH ST
1800 16TH ST
1900 17TH ST
2000 MARIPOSA ST
2100 18TH ST
2200 19TH ST
2300 20TH ST
2500 22ND ST
2700 23RD ST
2800 24TH ST
2900 25TH ST
3000 26TH ST
3100 ARMY ST
3200 MARIN ST
3300 TULARE ST
3400 ARTHUR AVE
CARGO WY
BURKE ST
3600 CUSTER AVE
3700 DAVIDSON AVE
PHELPS ST
3800 EVANS AVE
3900 FAIRFAX AVE
4000 GALVEZ AVE
4100 HUDSON AVE
4200 INNES AVE
NEWHALL ST
4300 JERROLD AVE
4400 KIRKWOOD AVE
4500 LA SALLE AVE
4600 MCKINNON AVE
4700 NEWCOMB AVE
4800 OAKDALE AVE
MENDELL ST
4900 PALOU AVE
5000 QUESADA AVE
REVERE AVE
5100 BAYVIEW ST
SHAFTER AVE
THOMAS AVE
5200 THORNTON AVE
UNDERWOOD AVE
VAN DYKE AVE
5300 WILLIAMS AVE
LANE ST
WALLACE AVE
5500 YOSEMITE AVE
5600 ARMSTRONG AVE
5700 BANCROFT AVE
5800 CARROLL AVE
DONNER AVE
EGBERT AVE
FITZGERALD AV
GILMAN AVE
6200 PAUL AVE
HOLLISTER AVE
INGERSON AVE
6300 SALINAS AVE
6400 JAMESTOWN AVE
6500 KEY AVE
6600 LE CONTE AVE
KEITH ST
6700 MEADE AVE
END BAYSHORE BLVD
4TH AV SF 5 B2
4TH AV SF 9 B2
FROM 100 LAKE ST S TO PARNASSUS AV
NUMBERS THE SAME AS 19TH AV
4TH ST SF 3 C1
NE FROM AVENUE H TO AVENUE N TREASURE ISLAND
AV H
AV M
END AV N
4TH ST SF 7 B2
4TH ST SF 11 C1
S FROM MARKET ST BETWEEN 3RD ST AND 5TH ST SE TO 3RD ST
2 MARKET ST
PIONEER CT
STEVENSON ST
JESSIE ST
100 MISSION ST
134 MINNA ST
200 HOWARD ST
CLEMENTINA ST
300 FOLSOM ST
SHIPLEY ST
CLARA ST
400 HARRISON ST
PERRY ST
STILLMAN ST
500 BRYANT ST
WELSH ST
FREELON ST
600 BRANNAN ST
BLUXOME ST
700 TOWNSEND ST
JEWETT ST
800 KING ST
900 BERRY ST
CHANNEL
MISSION ROCK ST
END 3RD ST
5TH AV SF 5 B2
5TH AV SF 9 B2
FROM PRESIDIO RESERVATION S TO LOCKSLEY AV
NUMBERS THE SAME AS 19TH AV
5TH ST SF 3 C1
NE FROM AVENUE M TO AVENUE N, ONE BLK NW OF 4TH ST, TREASURE ISLAND
5TH ST SF 7 A2
S FROM MARKET ST BETWEEN 4TH ST AND 6TH ST SE TO CHANNEL
2 MARKET ST
STEVENSON ST
MINT ST
JESSIE ST
100 MISSION ST
136 MINNA ST
NATOMA ST
200 HOWARD ST
TEHAMA ST
268 CLEMENTINA ST
300 FOLSOM ST
SHIPLEY ST
368 CLARA ST
400 HARRISON ST
500 BRYANT ST
WELSH ST
600 BRANNAN ST
BLUXOME ST
700 TOWNSEND ST
JEWETT ST
800 KING ST
900 BERRY ST
END CHANNEL
6TH AV SF 5 B2
6TH AV SF 9 B2
FROM PRESIDIO S TO LOCKSLEY AV
NUMBERS THE SAME AS 19TH AV
6TH AV SF 17 A1
NE FROM J ST TO SPEAR AV
6TH ST SF 3 C1
NE FROM AVENUE H TO AVENUE M TREASURE ISLAND
AV H
AV I
END AV M
6TH ST SF 7 A3
6TH ST SF 11 B1
S FROM MARKET ST BETWEEN 5TH ST AND 7TH ST TO 16TH ST
2 MARKET ST
32 STEVENSON ST
JESSIE ST
100 MISSION ST
132 MINNA ST
162 NATOMA ST
200 HOWARD ST
TEHAMA ST
CLEMENTINA ST
300 FOLSOM ST
SHIPLEY ST
CLARA ST
400 HARRISON ST
AHERN WY
500 BRYANT ST
600 BRANNAN ST
BLUXOME ST
700 TOWNSEND ST
800 KING ST
900 BERRY ST
1000 CHANNEL
END 16TH ST
7TH AV SF 5 B2
7TH AV SF 9 B2
FROM PRESIDIO S TO CLARENDON AV & LAGUNA HONDA BLVD
NUMBERS THE SAME AS 19TH AV
7TH ST SF 7 A3
7TH ST SF 11 B1
S FROM MARKET ST BETWEEN 6TH ST AND 8TH ST TO 17TH ST AND PENNSYLVANIA AV
2 MARKET ST
STEVENSON ST
JESSIE ST
100 MISSION ST
134 MINNA ST
168 NATOMA ST
200 HOWARD ST
300 FOLSOM ST
DECKER AL
CLEVELAND ST
400 HARRISON ST
500 BRYANT ST
600 BRANNAN ST
700 TOWNSEND ST
800 KING ST
900 BERRY ST
1000 CHANNEL
1100 HOOPER ST
1200 IRWIN ST
1300 HUBBELL ST
1400 DAGGETT ST
1500 16TH ST
MISSISSIPPI ST
17TH ST
END PENNSYLVANIA AVE
8TH AV SF 5 B2
8TH AV SF 9 B2

FROM MOUNTAIN LAKE PARK S
TO PACHECO ST
NUMBERS SAME AS 19TH AV
8TH ST SF 3 C1
NE FROM AVENUE I TO AVENUE N
TREASURE ISLAND
AV I
AV M
END AV N
8TH ST SF 7 A3
8TH ST SF 11 B1
S FROM MARKET ST BETWEEN 7TH ST
& 9TH ST SE TO TOWNSEND ST
2 MARKET ST
STEVENSON ST
100 MISSION ST
MINNA ST
NATOMA ST
200 HOWARD ST
TEHAMA ST
CLEMENTINA ST
300 FOLSOM ST
320 RINGOLD ST
HERON ST
400 HARRISON ST
500 BRYANT ST
600 BRANNAN ST
END TOWNSEND ST
9TH AV SF 5 B2
9TH AV SF 9 B3
9TH AV SF 13 B1
FROM MOUNTAIN LAKE PARK S
TO 12TH AV
NUMBERS THE SAME AS 19TH AV
9TH ST SF 3 C1
NE FROM AVENUE D TO AVENUE M
TREASURE ISLAND
AV D
AV E
AV F
AV H
AV I
END AV M
9TH ST SF 11 A1
S FROM MARKET ST BETWEEN 8TH ST
& 10TH ST SE TO DIVISION ST
2 MARKET ST
STEVENSON ST
JESSIE ST
100 MISSION ST
MINNA ST
NATOMA ST
200 HOWARD ST
TEHAMA ST
CLEMENTINA ST
300 FOLSOM ST
RINGOLD ST
SHERIDAN ST
400 HARRISON ST
BLACKWOOD ST
MCLEA CT
500 BRYANT ST
600 BRANNAN ST
END DIVISION ST
10TH AV SF 5 A2
10TH AV SF 9 B2
10TH AV SF 13 B1
FROM MOUNTAIN LAKE PARK S
TO MENDOSA AV
NUMBERS SAME AS 19TH AV
10TH ST SF 3 C1
NE FROM AVENUE M TO AVENUE N
BETWEEN 9TH ST & 11TH
TREASURE ISLAND
10TH ST SF 10 C1
S FROM MARKET ST BETWEEN 9TH ST
& 11TH ST SE TO DIVISION ST
2 MARKET ST
STEVENSON ST
JESSIE ST
100 MISSION ST
MINNA ST
NATOMA ST
200 HOWARD ST
300 FOLSOM ST
SHERIDAN ST
400 HARRISON ST
500 BRYANT ST
END DIVISION ST
11TH AV SF 5 A2
11TH AV SF 9 B2
FROM MOUNTAIN LAKE PARK S
TO PACHECO ST
NUMBERS SAME AS 19TH AV
11TH ST SF 3 C1
NE FROM AV D TO AV M, TREASURE
ISLAND
AV D
AV E
AV H
AV I
END AV M
11TH ST SF 10 C1
S FROM MARKET ST BETWEEN 10TH ST
AND 12TH ST SE TO BRYANT ST
AND DIVISION ST
2 MARKET ST
100 MISSION ST
MINNA ST
NATOMA ST
200 HOWARD ST
238 KISSLING ST
298 BURNS PL
300 FOLSOM ST
400 HARRISON ST
BRYANT ST
END DIVISION ST
12TH AV SF 5 A2
12TH AV SF 9 A3
12TH AV SF 13 B1
FROM MOUNTAIN LAKE PARK S
TO TARAVAL ST NUMBERS THE
SAME AS 19TH AV
12TH ST SF 3 C1
NE FROM AVENUE B TO AVENUE H
TREASURE ISLAND
AV B
AV D
AV E
END AV H
12TH ST SF 10 C1
S FROM MARKET ST BETWEEN 11TH ST
AND BRADY ST SE TO HARRISON ST
2 MARKET ST
STEVENSON ST
100 MISSION ST
200 HOWARD ST
KISSLING ST
300 FOLSOM ST
ISIS ST
BERNICE ST
END HARRISON ST
13TH ST SF 3 C1
E FROM GATEVIEW AV TO AVENUE E,
THEN NE TO AV N, TREASURE ISLAND
GATEVIEW AV
KEPPLER CT
HUTCHINS CT
HALYBURTON CT
BIGELOW CT
AV E
AV H & GATEVIEW AV
EXPOSITION DR
AV I
AV M
END AV N
13TH ST SF 10 C1
W OFF CENTRAL SKYWAY TO
MISSION ST
14TH AV SF 5 A2
14TH AV SF 9 A2
14TH AV SF 13 A1
FROM PRESIDIO S TO PORTOLA DR
NUMBERS SAME AS 19TH AV
14TH ST SF 10 B1
W FROM HARRISON ST BETWEEN
13TH ST AND 15TH ST TO
BUENA VISTA TER
2 HARRISON ST
TRAINOR ST
100 FOLSOM ST
SHOTWELL ST
S VAN NESS AV
NATOMA ST
MINNA ST
300 MISSION ST
328 WOODWARD ST
JULIAN AVE
STEVENSON ST
400 VALENCIA ST
500 GUERRERO ST
RAMONA AVE
ROSEMONT PL
600 DOLORES ST
LANDERS ST
MARKET ST
700 CHURCH ST
750 BELCHER ST
BOYNTON CT
800 SANCHEZ ST
850 WALTER ST
900 NOE ST
1000 CASTRO ST
1034 DIVISADERO ST
1058 ALPINE TER
END BUENA VISTA TERR
15TH AV SF 5 A2
15TH AV SF 9 A3
15TH AV SF 13 A1
FROM PRESIDIO RESERVATION
S TO PORTOLA DR
NUMBERS SAME AS 19TH AV
15TH ST SF 10 A2
15TH ST SF 11 A2
FROM CAROLINA ST BETWEEN 16TH ST
& ALAMEDA ST W TO PARKHILL AV
2 CAROLINA ST
100 DE HARO ST
200 RHODE ISLAND ST
300 KANSAS ST
400 VERMONT ST
500 SAN BRUNO AVE
600 UTAH ST
700 POTRERO AVE
1000 BRYANT ST
FLORIDA ST
ALABAMA ST
1300 HARRISON ST
1400 FOLSOM ST
1450 SHOTWELL ST
S VAN NESS AV
1536 NATOMA ST
CAPP ST
1572 MINNA ST
1600 MISSION ST
WIESE ST
1660 JULIAN AVE
1680 CALEDONIA ST
1700 VALENCIA ST
ALBION ST
1800 GUERRERO ST
1840 RAMONA AVE
AILEEN ST
1900 DOLORES ST
1950 LANDERS ST
2000 CHURCH ST
SHARON ST
MARKET ST
2100 SANCHEZ ST
2200 NOE ST
2300 CASTRO ST
BEAVER ST
2500 BUENA VISTA TER
END PARKHILL AV
16TH AV SF 5 A3
16TH AV SF 9 A2
16TH AV SF 13 A1
FROM PRESIDIO S TO WAWONA ST
NUMBERS SAME AS 19TH AV
16TH ST SF 10 B2
16TH ST SF 11 A2
FROM THE BAY BETWEEN 15TH ST
& 17TH ST W TO FLINT ST
300 ILLINOIS ST
3RD ST
600 6TH ST
OWENS ST
PENNSYLVANIA AV
BARSTOW ST
MISSISSIPPI ST
900 7TH ST
1000 DAGGETT ST
MISSOURI ST
CONNECTICUT ST
1100 HUBBELL ST
ARKANSAS ST
1200 8TH ST
1300 WISCONSIN ST
1400 CAROLINA ST
1500 DE HARO ST
1600 RHODE ISLAND ST
1700 KANSAS ST
1800 VERMONT ST
1900 SAN BRUNO AVE
2000 UTAH ST
2100 POTRERO AVE
2200 HAMPSHIRE ST
2300 YORK ST
2400 BRYANT ST
2500 FLORIDA ST
2600 ALABAMA ST
TREAT AVE
2700 HARRISON ST
2800 FOLSOM ST
2850 SHOTWELL ST
2900 SOUTH VAN NESS AVE
2950 CAPP ST
3000 MISSION ST
3050 WIESE ST
HOFF ST
3060 JULIAN AVE
RONDEL PL
CALEDONIA ST
3100 VALENCIA ST
ALBION ST
3200 GUERRERO ST
SPENCER ST
3300 DOLORES ST
3350 LANDERS ST
3400 CHURCH ST
HARLOW ST
3450 SHARON ST
DEHON ST
3500 SANCHEZ ST
PROSPER ST
POND ST
3600 NOE ST
MARKET ST
3700 CASTRO ST
FLINT ST
END 1 BLK BEYOND
17TH AV SF 5 A2
17TH AV SF 9 A2
FROM PRESIDIO S TO WAWONA ST
NUMBERS SAME AS 19TH AV
17TH ST SF 9 C2
17TH ST SF 10 A2
17TH ST SF 11 A2
FROM PENNSYLVANIA AV BETWEEN
16TH ST AND MARIPOSA ST W
TO STANYAN ST
1000 PENNSYLVANIA AVE
1100 MISSISSIPPI ST
1200 TEXAS ST
1300 MISSOURI ST
1400 CONNECTICUT ST
1500 ARKANSAS ST
1600 WISCONSIN ST
1700 CAROLINA ST
1800 DE HARO ST
1900 RHODE ISLAND ST
2000 KANSAS ST
2100 VERMONT ST
2200 SAN BRUNO AVE
2300 UTAH ST
2400 POTRERO AVE
HAMPSHIRE ST
2700 BRYANT ST
2800 FLORIDA ST
2900 ALABAMA ST
3000 HARRISON ST
TREAT AVE
3100 FOLSOM ST
3150 SHOTWELL ST
3200 SOUTH VAN NESS AVE
3250 CAPP ST
3300 MISSION ST
3338 HOFF ST
3400 VALENCIA ST
3444 ALBION ST
DEARBORN ST
3500 GUERRERO ST
3600 DOLORES ST
ABBEY ST
3700 CHURCH ST
3800 SANCHEZ ST
3854 PROSPER ST
3870 POND ST
3900 NOE ST
HARTFORD ST
MARKET ST
4000 CASTRO ST
COLLINGWOOD ST
DIAMOND ST
EUREKA ST
4200 DOUGLASS ST
CORBETT AVE
4300 ORD ST
CORBIN PL
4400 TEMPLE ST
MARS ST
URANUS TERR
ROOSEVELT WY
MONUMENT WY
ASHBURY ST
4600 CLAYTON ST
4700 BELVEDERE ST
4800 COLE ST
4900 SHRADER ST
END STANYAN ST
18TH AV SF 5 A2
18TH AV SF 9 A2
18TH AV SF 13 A1
FROM PRESIDIO S TO WAWONA ST
NUMBERS SAME AS 19TH AV
18TH ST SF 10 A2
18TH ST SF 11 A2
FROM THE BAY BETWEEN MARIPOSA ST
& 19TH ST W TO DANVERS ST
AT MARKET ST
500 ILLINOIS ST
600 3RD ST
700 TENNESSEE ST
800 MINNESOTA ST
900 INDIANA ST
1000 IOWA ST
1100 PENNSYLVANIA AVE
1200 MISSISSIPPI ST
1300 TEXAS ST
1400 MISSOURI ST
1500 CONNECTICUT ST
1600 ARKANSAS ST
1800 CAROLINA ST
1900 DE HARO ST
2000 RHODE ISLAND ST
2100 KANSAS ST
2200 VERMONT ST

2300 SAN BRUNO AVE
2400 UTAH ST
2500 POTRERO AVE
2600 HAMPSHIRE ST
2700 YORK ST
2800 BRYANT ST
2900 FLORIDA ST
3000 ALABAMA ST
3100 HARRISON ST
TREAT AVE
3200 FOLSOM ST
3250 SHOTWELL ST
3300 SOUTH VAN NESS AVE
3350 CAPP ST
3400 MISSION ST
3426 SAN CARLOS ST
3466 LEXINGTON ST
3500 VALENCIA ST
LAPIDGE ST
DEARBORN ST
LINDA ST
3600 GUERRERO ST
OAKWOOD ST
3700 DOLORES ST
3800 CHURCH ST
3900 SANCHEZ ST
4000 NOE ST
4050 HARTFORD ST
4100 CASTRO ST
4200 COLLINGWOOD ST
4300 DIAMOND ST
4400 EUREKA ST
4500 DOUGLASS ST
4548 ORD ST
4600 HATTIE ST
CLOVER ST
END DANVERS ST

19TH AV SF 5 A3
19TH AV SF 9 A2
19TH AV SF 13 A1
19TH AV SF 19 A1
FROM PRESIDIO S TO PT S OF RANDOLPH ST
2 PRESIDIO
100 LAKE ST
200 CALIFORNIA ST
300 CLEMENT ST
400 GEARY BLVD
500 ANZA ST
600 BALBOA ST
700 CABRILLO ST
FULTON ST
MARTIN L KING DR
1200 LINCOLN WY
1300 IRVING ST
1400 JUDAH ST
1500 KIRKHAM ST
1600 LAWTON ST
1700 MORAGA ST
1800 NORIEGA ST
1900 ORTEGA ST
2000 PACHECO ST
2100 QUINTARA ST
2200 RIVERA ST
2300 SANTIAGO ST
2400 TARAVAL ST
2500 ULLOA ST
2600 VICENTE ST
2700 WAWONA ST
BRIARCLIFF TER
SLOAT BLVD
OCEAN AVE
EUCALYPTUS DR
ROSSMOOR DR
MONTE VISTA DR
WINSTON DR
BUCKINGHAM WY
DENSLOWE DR
WYTON LANE
HOLLOWAY AVE
CRESPI DR
BANBURY DR
CARDENAS AVE
JUNIPERO SERRA BLVD
BEVERLY ST
SARGENT ST
MONTICELLO ST
CHESTER AVE
BYXBEE ST
RANDOLPH ST
ST CHARLES AV
VERNON ST

19TH ST SF 10 A2
19TH ST SF 11 B2
FROM THE BAY BETWEEN 18TH ST AND 20TH ST W TO CORBETT AV
500 ILLINOIS ST
600 3RD ST
700 TENNESSEE ST
800 MINNESOTA ST
900 INDIANA ST
SO EMBARCADERO FRWY
1100 PENNSYLVANIA AVE
1200 MISSISSIPPI ST
1300 TEXAS ST
1400 MISSOURI ST
1500 CONNECTICUT ST
1600 ARKANSAS ST
1700 WISCONSIN ST
1800 CAROLINA ST
1900 DE HARO ST
2000 RHODE ISLAND ST
2100 KANSAS ST
2200 VERMONT ST
2300 SAN BRUNO AVE
2500 POTRERO AVE
2600 HAMPSHIRE ST
2700 YORK ST
2800 BRYANT ST
2900 FLORIDA ST
3000 ALABAMA ST
3100 HARRISON ST
3150 TREAT AVE
3200 FOLSOM ST
3250 SHOTWELL ST
3300 SOUTH VAN NESS AVE
3350 CAPP ST
3400 MISSION ST
3428 SAN CARLOS ST
3464 LEXINGTON ST
3500 VALENCIA ST
3546 LAPIDGE ST
LINDA ST
3600 GUERRERO ST
OAKWOOD ST
DOLORES ST
3800 CHURCH ST
3900 SANCHEZ ST
4000 NOE ST
4050 HARTFORD ST
4100 CASTRO ST
4200 COLLINGWOOD ST
4300 DIAMOND ST
4400 EUREKA ST
4500 DOUGLASS ST
LAMSON LN
SEWARD ST
4612 CLOVER LANE
YUKON ST
DANVERS ST
CASELLI AV
MARKET ST
END CORBETT AVE

20TH AV SF 4 C2
20TH AV SF 9 A2
20TH AV SF 13 A1
FROM PRESIDIO S TO BUCKINGHAM WY
NUMBERS SAME AS 19TH AV

20TH ST SF 10 A3
20TH ST SF 11 A2
FROM THE BAY BETWEEN 19TH ST & 21ST ST W TO DOUGLASS ST
500 MICHIGAN ST
600 ILLINOIS ST
700 3RD ST
800 TENNESSEE ST
900 MINNESOTA ST
1000 INDIANA ST
1100 IOWA ST
1200 PENNSYLVANIA AVE
1300 MISSISSIPPI ST
1400 TEXAS ST
1500 MISSOURI ST
1600 CONNECTICUT ST
1700 ARKANSAS ST
1800 WISCONSIN ST
1900 CAROLINA ST
2000 DE HARO ST
2100 RHODE ISLAND ST
2200 KANSAS ST
2300 VERMONT ST
2400 SAN BRUNO AVE
2600 POTRERO AVE
2700 HAMPSHIRE ST
2800 YORK ST
2900 BRYANT ST
3000 FLORIDA ST
3100 ALABAMA ST
3200 HARRISON ST
3250 TREAT AVE
3300 FOLSOM ST
3350 SHOTWELL ST
3400 SOUTH VAN NESS AVE
3450 CAPP ST
3500 MISSION ST
3532 SAN CARLOS ST
3572 LEXINGTON ST
3600 VALENCIA ST
3700 GUERRERO ST
DOLORES ST
3900 CHURCH ST
4000 SANCHEZ ST
4100 NOE ST
4150 HARTFORD ST
4200 CASTRO ST
4300 COLLINGWOOD ST
4400 DIAMOND ST
4500 EUREKA ST
END DOUGLASS ST

21ST AV SF 4 C2
21ST AV SF 9 A2
21ST AV SF 13 A1
FROM PRESIDIO S TO EUCALYPTUS DR
NUMBERS SAME AS 19TH AV

21ST ST SF 10 B3
21ST ST SF 11 A3
FROM POTRERO AV BETWEEN 20TH ST & 22ND ST W TO GRAND VIEW AV
2600 POTRERO AVE
2650 HAMPSHIRE ST
2700 YORK ST
2750 BRYANT ST
2800 FLORIDA ST
2850 ALABAMA ST
2900 HARRISON ST
2950 TREAT AVE
3000 FOLSOM ST
3050 SHOTWELL ST
3100 SOUTH VAN NESS AVE
3150 CAPP ST
3200 MISSION ST
3238 SAN CARLOS ST
BARTLETT ST
3266 LEXINGTON ST
3300 VALENCIA ST
3400 GUERRERO ST
AMES ST
FAIR OAKS ST
QUANE ST
3500 DOLORES ST
CHATTANOOGA ST
3600 CHURCH ST
3700 SANCHEZ ST
RAYBURN ST
3800 NOE ST
3900 CASTRO ST
4000 COLLINGWOOD ST
4100 DIAMOND ST
4200 EUREKA ST
4300 DOUGLASS ST
WORTH ST
END GRAND VIEW AVE

22ND AV SF 4 C2
22ND AV SF 8 C2
22ND AV SF 13 A1
FROM PRESIDIO S TO EUCALYPTUS DR
NUMBERS SAME AS 19TH AV

22ND ST SF 10 A3
22ND ST SF 11 A3
FROM THE BAY BETWEEN 21ST ST & 23RD ST W TO GRAND VIEW AV
50 MICHIGAN
600 ILLINOIS ST
700 3RD ST
800 TENNESSEE ST
900 MINNESOTA ST
1000 INDIANA ST
1100 IOWA ST
1200 PENNSYLVANIA AVE
1300 MISSISSIPPI ST
1500 MISSOURI ST
1600 CONNECTICUT ST
1700 ARKANSAS ST
1800 WISCONSIN ST
1900 CAROLINA ST
2000 DE HARO ST
2100 RHODE ISLAND ST
KANSAS ST
2400 SAN BRUNO AVE
UTAH ST
2600 POTRERO AVE
2650 HAMPSHIRE ST
2700 YORK ST
2750 BRYANT ST
2800 FLORIDA ST
2850 ALABAMA ST
2900 HARRISON ST
2950 TREAT AVE
3000 FOLSOM ST
3050 SHOTWELL ST
3100 SOUTH VAN NESS AVE
CAPP ST
3200 MISSION ST
3250 BARTLETT ST
3300 VALENCIA ST
SAN JOSE AVE
3400 GUERRERO ST
3426 AMES ST
3450 FAIR OAKS ST
QUANE ST
3500 DOLORES ST
3550 CHATTANOOGA ST
3600 CHURCH ST
VICKSBURG ST
3700 SANCHEZ ST
3800 NOE ST
3900 CASTRO ST
3966 COLLINGWOOD ST
4000 DIAMOND ST
4100 EUREKA ST
4200 DOUGLASS ST
WORTH ST
HOFFMAN AVE
END GRAND VIEW AVE

23RD AV SF 4 C2
23RD AV SF 8 C2
23RD AV SF 12 C1
23RD AV SF 13 A3
FROM LAKE ST S TO EUCALYPTUS DR
NUMBERS SAME AS 19TH AV

23RD ST SF 10 A3
23RD ST SF 11 A3
FROM THE BAY BETWEEN 22ND ST & 24TH ST W TO CORBETT AV
700 ILLINOIS ST
800 3RD ST
900 TENNESSEE ST
1000 MINNESOTA ST
1100 INDIANA ST
1200 IOWA ST
1300 PENNSYLVANIA AVE
1600 MISSOURI ST
1700 DAKOTA ST
1800 ARKANSAS ST
1900 WISCONSIN ST
2000 CAROLINA ST
2100 DE HARO ST
2200 RHODE ISLAND ST
2300 KANSAS ST
2400 VERMONT ST
SAN BRUNO AVE
UTAH ST
2700 POTRERO ST
2750 HAMPSHIRE ST
2800 YORK ST
2850 BRYANT ST
2900 FLORIDA ST
2950 ALABAMA ST
3000 HARRISON ST
3050 TREAT AVE
3100 FOLSOM ST
3150 SHOTWELL ST
3200 SOUTH VAN NESS AVE
3250 CAPP ST
3300 MISSION ST
3350 BARTLETT ST
3400 VALENCIA ST
3500 SAN JOSE AVE
3600 GUERRERO ST
3628 AMES ST
3650 FAIR OAKS ST
QUANE ST
3700 DOLORES ST
MERSEY ST
3750 CHATTANOOGA ST
SEVERN ST
3800 CHURCH ST
NELLIE ST
3850 VICKSBURG ST
BLANCHE ST
3900 SANCHEZ ST
4000 NOE ST
4100 CASTRO ST
4200 DIAMOND ST
4250 EUREKA ST
4300 DOUGLASS ST
4400 HOFFMAN AVE
GRAND VIEW AVE
4500 MARKET ST
END CORBETT AVE

24TH AV SF 4 C2
24TH AV SF 8 C2
24TH AV SF 12 C1
FROM PRESIDIO S TO EUCALYPTUS DR
100 PRESIDIO
W CLAY
200 LAKE ST
300 CALIFORNIA ST
400 CLEMENT ST
500 GEARY BLVD
600 ANZA ST
700 BALBOA ST
800 CABRILLO ST
FULTON ST
1200 LINCOLN WY
1300 IRVING ST
1400 JUDAH ST
1500 KIRKHAM ST
1600 LAWTON ST
1700 MORAGA ST
1800 NORIEGA ST
1900 ORTEGA ST
2000 PACHECO ST
2100 QUINTARA ST
2200 RIVERA ST
SANTIAGO ST
2400 TARAVAL ST

1991 SAN FRANCISCO COUNTY CROSS STREET INDEX

2500 ULLOA ST
2600 VICENTE ST
WAWONA ST
SLOAT BLVD
OCEAN AV
END EUCALYPTUS DR
24TH ST SF 10 A3
24TH ST SF 11 A3
FROM THE BAY TO MINNESOTA ST AND
FROM DE HARO ST BETWEEN 23RD ST
AND 25TH ST W TO PORTOLA DR
MICHIGAN ST
ILLINOIS ST
3RD ST
TENNESSEE ST
MINNESOTA ST
2100 DE HARO ST
2200 RHODE ISLAND ST
KANSAS ST
2400 VERMONT ST
2500 SAN BRUNO AVE
2600 UTAH ST
2700 POTRERO AVE
2750 HAMPSHIRE ST
2800 YORK ST
2850 BRYANT ST
2900 FLORIDA ST
2950 ALABAMA ST
3000 HARRISON ST
BALMY ST
3050 TREAT AVE
LUCKY ST
3100 FOLSOM ST
3150 SHOTWELL ST
3200 SOUTH VAN NESS AVE
CYPRESS ST
3250 CAPP ST
LILAC ST
3300 MISSION ST
OSAGE AL
3350 BARTLETT ST
ORANGE AL
3400 VALENCIA ST
POPLAR ST
3500 SAN JOSE AVE
3600 GUERRERO ST
3652 FAIR OAKS ST
QUANE ST
3700 DOLORES ST
MERSEY ST
3750 CHATTANOOGA ST
3800 CHURCH ST
3850 VICKSBURG ST
3900 SANCHEZ ST
4000 NOE ST
4100 CASTRO ST
4200 DIAMOND ST
4300 DOUGLASS ST
HOMESTEAD ST
4400 HOFFMAN AVE
FOUNTAIN ST
4500 GRAND VIEW
END PORTOLA DR
25TH AV SF 4 C2
25TH AV SF 8 C3
25TH AV SF 12 C1
S FROM SEACLIFF AV TO EUCALYPTUS
DR NUMBERS SAME AS 24TH AV
25TH ST SF 14 A1
25TH ST SF 15 A1
FROM MICHIGAN ST BETWEEN 24TH ST
AND 26TH ST W TO PORTOLA DR
MICHIGAN ST
ILLINOIS ST
900 3RD ST
1000 TENNESSEE ST
1000 MINNESOTA ST
1200 INDIANA ST
1300 IOWA ST
1400 PENNSYLVANIA AVE
1500 MISSISSIPPI ST
1600 TEXAS ST
1800 CONNECTICUT ST
2000 WISCONSIN ST
PALI RD
2200 DE HARO ST
2300 RHODE ISLAND ST
KANSAS ST
2500 VERMONT ST
2600 SAN BRUNO AVE
2700 UTAH ST
2800 POTRERO AVE
2850 HAMPSHIRE ST
2900 YORK ST
2950 BRYANT ST
3000 FLORIDA ST
3050 ALABAMA ST
3100 HARRISON ST
BALMY ST
3150 TREAT AVE
LUCKY ST
3200 FOLSOM ST
HORACE ST
3250 SHOTWELL ST
VIRGIL AVE
3300 SOUTH VAN NESS AVE
3326 CYPRESS ST
3350 CAPP ST
LILAC ST
3400 MISSION ST
OSAGE AL
3450 BARTLETT ST
ORANGE AL
3590 VALENCIA ST
POPLAR ST
3600 SAN JOSE AVE
3700 GUERRERO ST
3750 FAIR OAKS ST
3800 DOLORES ST
3900 CHURCH ST
3950 VICKSBURG ST
4000 SANCHEZ ST
4100 NOE ST
4200 CASTRO ST
4300 DIAMOND ST
4400 DOUGLASS ST
4500 HOMESTEAD ST
4600 HOFFMAN AVE
4700 FOUNTAIN ST
4800 GRAND VIEW
HIGH ST
END PORTOLA DR
26TH AV SF 4 C2
26TH AV SF 8 C2
26TH AV SF 12 C1
S FROM SEACLIFF AV TO EUCALYPTUS
DR NUMBERS SAME AS 24TH AV
26TH ST SF 14 A1
26TH ST SF 15 A1
FROM 3RD ST BETWEEN 25TH ST AND
ARMY ST W TO DOUGLASS ST
800 3RD ST
900 TENNESSEE ST
1000 MINNESOTA ST
1100 INDIANA ST
CONNECTICUT ST
WISCONSIN ST
PALI RD
DE HARO ST
RHODE ISLAND ST
KANSAS ST
VERMONT ST
2800 HAMPSHIRE ST
2900 YORK ST
2950 BRYANT ST
3000 FLORIDA ST
3050 ALABAMA ST
3100 HARRISON ST
3150 TREAT AVE
LUCKY ST
3200 FOLSOM ST
HORACE ST
3250 SHOTWELL ST
VIRGIL AVE
3300 SOUTH VAN NESS AVE
CYPRESS ST
3350 CAPP ST
LILAC ST
3400 MISSION ST
OSAGE AL
3450 BARTLETT ST
ORANGE ST
3500 VALENCIA ST
POPLAR ST
3600 SAN JOSE AVE
3700 GUERRERO ST
3750 FAIR OAKS ST
3800 DOLORES ST
3900 CHURCH ST
4000 SANCHEZ ST
4100 NOE ST
4200 CASTRO ST
4300 DIAMOND ST
END DOUGLASS ST
27TH AV SF 4 C2
27TH AV SF 12 C1
FROM SEACLIFF AV S TO VICENTE ST
NUMBERS SAME AS 24TH AV
27TH ST SF 14 A1
W FROM SAN JOSE AV BETWEEN
ARMY ST AND DUNCAN ST W TO
DIAMOND HEIGHTS BLVD
2 SAN JOSE AVE
100 GUERRERO ST
200 DOLORES ST
300 CHURCH ST
400 SANCHEZ ST
500 NOE ST
600 CASTRO ST
NEWBURG ST
KRONQUIST CT
700 DIAMOND ST
END 800 DOUGLASS ST
28TH AV SF 4 C3
28TH AV SF 8 C2
28TH AV SF 12 C1
FROM EL CAMINO DEL MAR S TO
WAWONA ST
NUMBERS SAME AS 24TH AV
28TH ST SF 14 B1
W FROM GUERRERO ST BETWEEN
DUNCAN ST AND VALLEY ST TO
DOUGLASS ST
2 GUERRERO ST
100 DOLORES ST
CHURCH ST
300 SANCHEZ ST
400 NOE ST
500 CASTRO ST
600 DIAMOND ST
END 700 DOUGLASS ST
29TH AV SF 4 B3
29TH AV SF 8 C2
29TH AV SF 12 C1
FROM MCLAREN AV S TO VICENTE ST
NUMBERS SAME AS 24TH AV
29TH ST SF 14 B2
FROM 3300 MISSION ST BETWEEN
DAY ST & VALLEY ST
W TO DIAMOND ST
2 MISSION ST
80 TIFFANY AVE
100 SAN JOSE AVE
200 DOLORES ST
300 CHURCH ST
400 SANCHEZ ST
500 NOE ST
600 CASTRO ST
ZIRCON PL
END 700 DIAMOND ST
30TH AV SF 4 B3
30TH AV SF 8 C2
30TH AV SF 12 C1
FROM EL CAMINO DEL MAR S TO
WAWONA ST
NUMBER SAME AS 24TH AV
30TH ST SF 14 B2
FROM 3400 MISSION S OF 29TH ST
W TO CASTRO ST
2 MISSION ST
100 SAN JOSE AVE
200 DOLORES ST
CHENERY ST
300 CHURCH ST
WHITNEY ST
400 SANCHEZ ST
HARPER ST
500 NOE ST
LAIDLEY ST
END CASTRO ST
31ST AV SF 4 B2
31ST AV SF 8 B2
31ST AV SF 12 C1
FROM SEA VIEW TER S TO
ESCOLTA WY
SEA VIEW TERR
300 CALIFORNIA ST
400 CLEMENT ST
500 GEARY BLVD
700 BALBOA ST
800 CABRILLO ST
FULTON ST
1200 LINCOLN WY
1300 IRVING ST
1400 JUDAH ST
1500 KIRKHAM ST
1600 LAWTON ST
1700 MORAGA ST
1800 NORIEGA ST
1900 ORTEGA ST
2000 PACHECO ST
2100 QUINTARA ST
2200 RIVERA ST
2300 SANTIAGO ST
2400 TARAVAL ST
2500 ULLOA ST
2600 VICENTE ST
END ESCOLTA WY
32ND AV SF 4 B3
32ND AV SF 8 B2
32ND AV SF 12 B1
FROM EL CAMINO DEL MAR S TO
VICENTE ST
NUMBERS ARE THE SAME AS 31ST AV
33RD AV SF 4 B3
33RD AV SF 8 B2
33RD AV SF 12 B1
FROM CLEMENT ST S TO WAWONA ST
NUMBERS SAME AS 31ST AV
34TH AV SF 4 B3
34TH AV SF 8 B2
34TH AV SF 12 B1
FROM CLEMENT ST S TO SLOAT BLVD
NUMBERS SAME AS 31ST AV
35TH AV SF 4 B3
35TH AV SF 8 B2
35TH AV SF 12 B1
FROM CLEMENT ST S TO SLOAT BLVD
NUMBERS SAME AS 31ST AV
36TH AV SF 4 B3
36TH AV SF 8 B3
36TH AV SF 12 B1
FROM CLEMENT ST S TO SLOAT BLVD
NUMBERS SAME AS 31ST AV
37TH AV SF 4 B3
37TH AV SF 8 B2
37TH AV SF 12 B1
FROM SHORE VIEW TER S TO SLOAT BL
NUMBERS SAME AS 31ST AV
38TH AV SF 4 B3
38TH AV SF 8 B2
38TH AV SF 12 B1
FROM CLEMENT ST S TO YORBA ST
400 CLEMENT ST
SHORE VIEW AVE
500 GEARY BLVD
600 ANZA ST
700 BALBOA ST
800 CABRILLO ST
FULTON ST
1200 LINCOLN WY
1300 IRVING ST
1400 JUDAH ST
1500 KIRKHAM ST
1600 LAWTON ST
1700 MORAGA ST
1800 NORIEGA ST
1900 ORTEGA ST
2100 QUINTARA ST
2200 RIVERA ST
2300 SANTIAGO ST
2400 TARAVAL ST
2500 ULLOA ST
2600 VICENTE ST
2700 WAWONA ST
END YORBA ST
39TH AV SF 4 B3
39TH AV SF 8 B2
39TH AV SF 12 B1
FROM CLEMENT ST S TO SLOAT
BLVD NUMBERS SAME AS 38TH AV
40TH AV SF 4 A3
40TH AV SF 8 B2
40TH AV SF 12 B1
FROM CLEMENT ST S TO YORBA ST
NUMBERS SAME AS 38TH AV
41ST AV SF 4 A3
41ST AV SF 8 A1
41ST AV SF 12 B1
FROM CLEMENT ST S TO SLOAT BLVD
NUMBERS SAME AS 38TH AV
42ND AV SF 4 A3
42ND AV SF 8 A2
42ND AV SF 12 A1
FROM CLEMENT ST S TO SLOAT BLVD
NUMBERS SAME AS 38TH AV
43RD AV SF 4 A3
43RD AV SF 8 A2
43RD AV SF 12 A1
FROM CLEMENT ST S TO SLOAT BLVD
NUMBERS SAME AS 38TH AV
44TH AV SF 4 A3
44TH AV SF 8 A1
44TH AV SF 12 A1
FROM CLEMENT ST S TO SLOAT BLVD
NUMBERS SAME AS 38TH AV
45TH AV SF 4 A3
45TH AV SF 8 A1

COPYRIGHT © 1991 BY Thomas Bros maps

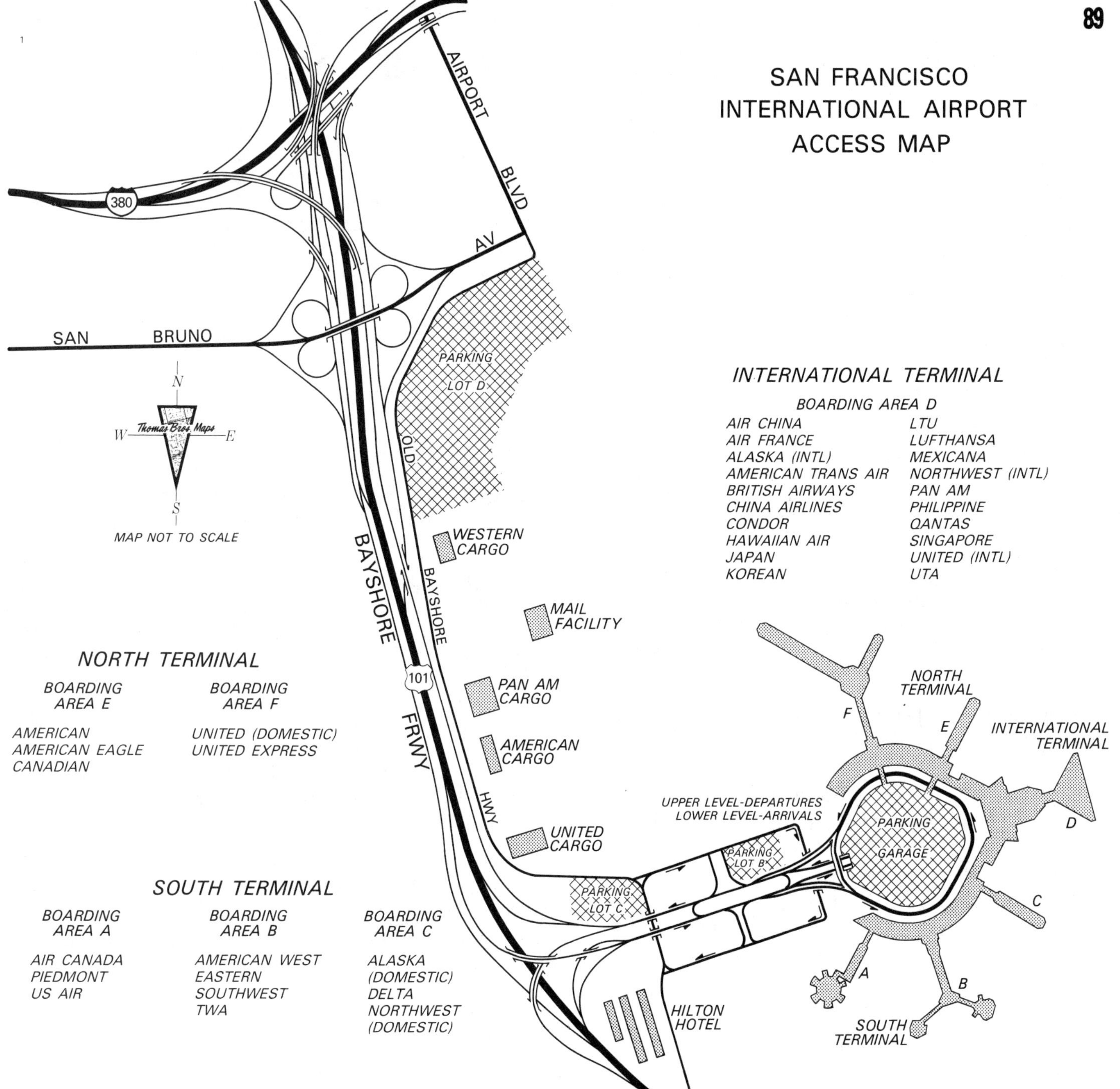
SAN FRANCISCO
INTERNATIONAL AIRPORT
ACCESS MAP
AIRPORT BLVD
AV
380
SAN BRUNO
PARKING LOT D
OLD BAYSHORE HWY
BAYSHORE FRWY
101
N
W
E
S
Thomas Bros. Maps
MAP NOT TO SCALE
WESTERN CARGO
MAIL FACILITY
PAN AM CARGO
AMERICAN CARGO
UNITED CARGO
UPPER LEVEL-DEPARTURES
LOWER LEVEL-ARRIVALS
PARKING LOT B
PARKING LOT C
PARKING GARAGE
HILTON HOTEL
NORTH TERMINAL
INTERNATIONAL TERMINAL
SOUTH TERMINAL
A
B
C
D
E
F
INTERNATIONAL TERMINAL
BOARDING AREA D
AIR CHINA
AIR FRANCE
ALASKA (INTL)
AMERICAN TRANS AIR
BRITISH AIRWAYS
CHINA AIRLINES
CONDOR
HAWAIIAN AIR
JAPAN
KOREAN
LTU
LUFTHANSA
MEXICANA
NORTHWEST (INTL)
PAN AM
PHILIPPINE
QANTAS
SINGAPORE
UNITED (INTL)
UTA
NORTH TERMINAL
BOARDING AREA E
AMERICAN
AMERICAN EAGLE
CANADIAN
BOARDING AREA F
UNITED (DOMESTIC)
UNITED EXPRESS
SOUTH TERMINAL
BOARDING AREA A
AIR CANADA
PIEDMONT
US AIR
BOARDING AREA B
AMERICAN WEST
EASTERN
SOUTHWEST
TWA
BOARDING AREA C
ALASKA
(DOMESTIC)
DELTA
NORTHWEST
(DOMESTIC)

COPYRIGHT © 1991 BY

1991 GOLDEN GATE TRANSIT INFORMATION

COPYRIGHT © 1991 BY Thomas Bros. Maps

Introduction

Golden Gate Transit provides bus and ferry service between San Francisco and Marin and Sonoma Counties. The Golden Gate Transit service area extends from the San Francisco Central Business District on the south, to the City of Santa Rosa in Sonoma County on the north. Santa Rosa is approximately 50 miles north of San Francisco.

Park-and Ride Facilities

There are approximately twenty Park-and-Ride facilities located throughout the Golden Gate Transit service area. Parking is complimentary and each facility is served by Golden Gate Transit buses which provide commute services into San Francisco.

Free Personalized Trip Planning, Maps, Timetables and Telephone Information

Your public transit itinerary can be planned for you by telephone by calling our information operators any weekday from 6:00 a.m. to 10:00 p.m. and on weekends and holidays from 6:30 a.m. to 10:00 p.m. When the operator answers your call, please have paper and pencil and the following information ready:

- Your departure point (address or nearest intersection)
- Your destination (address or nearest intersection)
- Day and time you wish to travel

Please telephone using one of the following numbers:

415-332-6600 from San Francisco
415-453-2100 from Marin County
707-544-1323 from Sonoma County

Map and Timetable information pamphlets can be mailed to you upon request.

Ferry Service

Golden Gate Transit operates two ferry routes: between Larkspur and San Francisco. Service is provided daily (except on Thanksgiving, Christmas, and New Years days). Feeder bus service is available during the peak commute periods to the ferry terminals providing direct connections with ferry arrivals and departures.

Bus Service

Golden Gate Transit operates approximately 50 bus routes between San Francisco, Marin, and Sonoma Counties via the Golden Gate Bridge. Service is provided daily with expanded service during peak commute periods.

Stadium Services

Golden Gate Transit offers some bus service on an advance reservation basis, to Candlestick Park for home games of the San Francisco Forty-Niners and Giants.

CalTrain Information

For information regarding fares, tickets, schedules or train / bus connections or any questions and / or comments concerning CalTrain service please call:

The Peninsula Commute Service

Hotline .... **(415) 557-8661**
Toll free (Voice or TDD) .... **(415) 558-8661**

Monday thru Friday 7:00 a.m. to 5:00p.m.

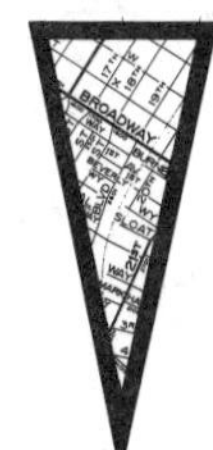

SAN MATEO COUNTY

1991 Thomas Guide®

TABLE OF CONTENTS

Copyright, © 1991 by THOMAS BROS. MAPS.
Design, maps, index and text of this publication are copyrighted. It is unlawful to copy or reproduce any part thereof for personal use or resale.

Corporate Office & Showroom
17731 Cowan, Irvine, CA 92714 (714) 863-1984; toll-free, 1-800-899-MAPS
Retail Stores
603 W. 7th St., Los Angeles, CA 90017 (213) 627-4018
550 Jackson St., San Francisco, CA 94133 (415) 981-7520

GOLDEN GATE COMBINATION	TBM 4025	***$33.95***
SANTA CLARA-SAN MATEO	TBM 4036	***$21.95***
SAN FRANCISCO-SAN MATEO	TBM 4026	***$19.95***
SAN MATEO	TBM 3036	***$12.95***

HOW TO USE THE THOMAS GUIDE PAGE AND GRID SYSTEM

Finding Your Destination

- Use the Street Index to find the page number and grid location of a street name.
- Use the Cities and Communities or Points of Interest Index to find the page number and grid of a specific destination.

Planning Your Route

- Use the Key Maps or the Foldout Map to go from city to city, or to find what page your destination is on.
- Follow a street page to page by using the "See Map" page number in the border of each page.

COMO USAR EL SISTEMA DE PAGINA Y CUADRADO DEL THOMAS GUIDE

Encontrando Su Destinación

- Se puede usar el Indice de Calle para encontrar el número de página y locación del cuadrado del nombre de la calle.
- Se puede usar los Indices de las Ciudades y las Comunidades, o de Puntos de Interés para encontrar el número de página y el cuadrado de la destinación específica.

Planeando Su Ruta

- Se puede usar el Mapa Clave o el Mapa Doblado para viajar de ciudad a ciudad, o para encontrar la página de su destinación.
- Se puede usar el número de página con las palabras "See Map" se encuentran al borde de cada página para seguir una calle de página a página.

COPYRIGHT © 1991 BY Thomas Bros. Maps

LIST OF ABBREVIATIONS

AL	ALLEY
AR	ARROYO
ARR	ARROYO
AV	AVENUE
AVD	AVENIDA
AVD D LS	AVENIDA DE LOS
BCH	BEACH
BL	BOULEVARD
BLVD	BOULEVARD
CEM	CEMETERY
CIR	CIRCLE
CK	CREEK
CL	CALLE
CL DL	CALLE DEL
CL D LS	CALLE DE LAS CALLE DE LOS
CL EL	CALLE EL
CLJ	CALLEJON
CL LA	CALLE LA
CL LS	CALLE LAS CALLE LOS
CM	CAMINO
CM D	CAMINO DE
CM D LA	CAMINO DE LA
CM D LS	CAMINO DE LAS CAMINO DE LOS
CMTO	CAMINITO
CN	CANAL
COM	COMMON
CR	CRESCENT
CRES	CRESCENT
CSWY	CAUSEWAY
CT	COURT
CTE	CORTE
CTO	CUT OFF
CTR	CENTER
CV	COVE
CY	CANYON
CYN	CANYON
D	DE
DL	DEL
DR	DRIVE
DS	DOS
E	EAST
EST	ESTATE
EXPWY	EXPRESSWAY
EXT	EXTENSION
FRWY	FREEWAY
FRW	FREEWAY
FY	FREEWAY
GN	GLEN
GRDS	GROUNDS
GRN	GREEN
GRV	GROVE
HTS	HEIGHTS
HWY	HIGHWAY
HY	HIGHWAY
JCT	JUNCTION
KPN	KEY PENINSULA NORTH
KPS	KEY PENINSULA SOUTH
L	LA
LN	LANE
LP	LOOP
LS	LAS, LOS
MDW	MEADOW
MHP	MOBILE HOME PARK
MNR	MANOR
MT	MOUNT
MTN	MOUNTAIN
MTWY	MOTORWAY
MTY	MOTORWAY
N	NORTH
PAS	PASEO
PAS DE	PASEO DE
PAS DL	PASEO DEL
PAS D LS	PASEO DE LAS PASEO DE LOS
PGD	PLAYGROUND
PK	PARK
PK	PEAK
PKWY	PARKWAY
PL	PLACE
PT	POINT
PY	PARKWAY
PZ	PLAZA
RCH	RANCH
RCHO	RANCHO
RD	ROAD
RDG	RIDGE
RES	RESERVOIR
RIV	RIVER
RV	RIVER
RO	RANCHO
S	SOUTH
SN	SAN
SPG	SPRING
SPGS	SPRINGS
SQ	SQUARE
SRA	SIERRA
ST	SAINT
ST	STREET
STA	SANTA
STA	STATION
TER	TERRACE
THTR	THEATER
TK TR	TRUCK TRAIL
TR	TRAIL
VIA D	VIA DE
VIA D LS	VIA DE LAS VIA DE LOS
VIA DL	VIA DEL
VIS	VISTA
VLG	VILLAGE
VLY	VALLEY
VW	VIEW
W	WEST
WK	WALK
WY	WAY

COPYRIGHT © 1991 BY Thomas Bros Maps

LEGEND

samTrans
CALTRAIN
BART
STA
CC
CH
CTH
FS
HOSP
LIB
PO
MALL
4
2
3
3
J1
200
(PROP)
100W
100E
JR HS
HS
HS
CEM

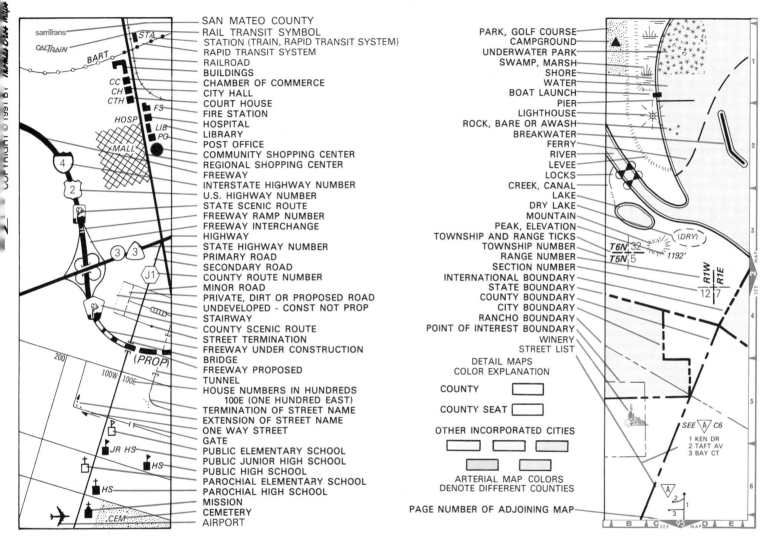

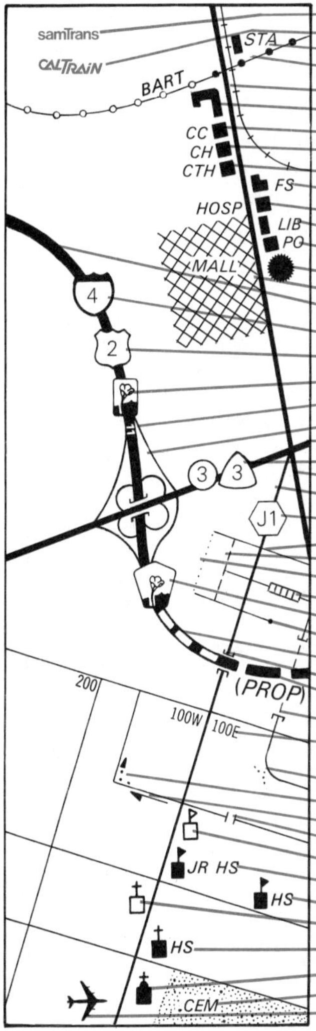

- SAN MATEO COUNTY
- RAIL TRANSIT SYMBOL
- STATION (TRAIN, RAPID TRANSIT SYSTEM)
- RAPID TRANSIT SYSTEM
- RAILROAD
- BUILDINGS
- CHAMBER OF COMMERCE
- CITY HALL
- COURT HOUSE
- FIRE STATION
- HOSPITAL
- LIBRARY
- POST OFFICE
- COMMUNITY SHOPPING CENTER
- REGIONAL SHOPPING CENTER
- FREEWAY
- INTERSTATE HIGHWAY NUMBER
- U.S. HIGHWAY NUMBER
- STATE SCENIC ROUTE
- FREEWAY RAMP NUMBER
- FREEWAY INTERCHANGE
- HIGHWAY
- STATE HIGHWAY NUMBER
- PRIMARY ROAD
- SECONDARY ROAD
- COUNTY ROUTE NUMBER
- MINOR ROAD
- PRIVATE, DIRT OR PROPOSED ROAD
- UNDEVELOPED - CONST NOT PROP
- STAIRWAY
- COUNTY SCENIC ROUTE
- STREET TERMINATION
- FREEWAY UNDER CONSTRUCTION
- BRIDGE
- FREEWAY PROPOSED
- TUNNEL
- HOUSE NUMBERS IN HUNDREDS 100E (ONE HUNDRED EAST)
- TERMINATION OF STREET NAME
- EXTENSION OF STREET NAME
- ONE WAY STREET
- GATE
- PUBLIC ELEMENTARY SCHOOL
- PUBLIC JUNIOR HIGH SCHOOL
- PUBLIC HIGH SCHOOL
- PAROCHIAL ELEMENTARY SCHOOL
- PAROCHIAL HIGH SCHOOL
- MISSION
- CEMETERY
- AIRPORT

- PARK, GOLF COURSE
- CAMPGROUND
- UNDERWATER PARK
- SWAMP, MARSH
- SHORE
- WATER
- BOAT LAUNCH
- PIER
- LIGHTHOUSE
- ROCK, BARE OR AWASH
- BREAKWATER
- FERRY
- RIVER
- LEVEE
- LOCKS
- CREEK, CANAL
- LAKE
- DRY LAKE
- MOUNTAIN
- PEAK, ELEVATION
- TOWNSHIP AND RANGE TICKS
- TOWNSHIP NUMBER
- RANGE NUMBER
- SECTION NUMBER
- INTERNATIONAL BOUNDARY
- STATE BOUNDARY
- COUNTY BOUNDARY
- CITY BOUNDARY
- RANCHO BOUNDARY
- POINT OF INTEREST BOUNDARY
- WINERY
- STREET LIST

DETAIL MAPS
COLOR EXPLANATION

COUNTY

COUNTY SEAT

OTHER INCORPORATED CITIES

ARTERIAL MAP COLORS
DENOTE DIFFERENT COUNTIES

PAGE NUMBER OF ADJOINING MAP

1
2
3
4
5
6
(DRY)
T6N
T5N
32
5
1192'
R1W
R1E
12
7
SEE MAP 2
SEE A C6
1 KEN DR
2 TAFT AV
3 BAY CT
A
B
C
SEE 95 MAP
D
E

0
1/4
1/2
3/4
1
2
MILES
KILOMETERS
0 .1 .2
.5
1
2

SCALE OF MULTIPLE MAP PAGES
1 INCH TO 1 MILE

SCALE OF SINGLE MAP PAGES
1 INCH TO ½ MILE

0
1/4
1/2
3/4
1
2
MILES
KILOMETERS
0 .1 .2
.5
1
2

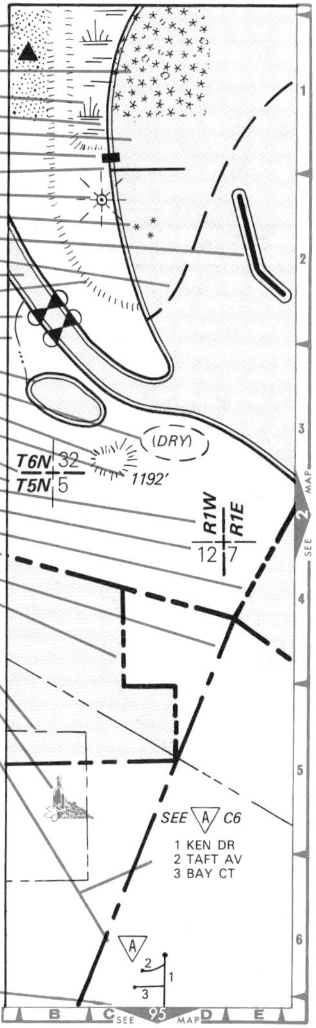

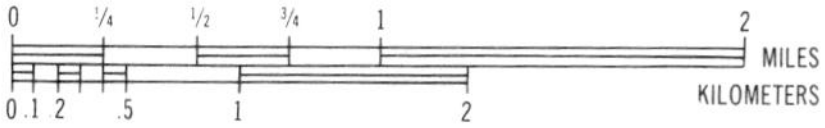

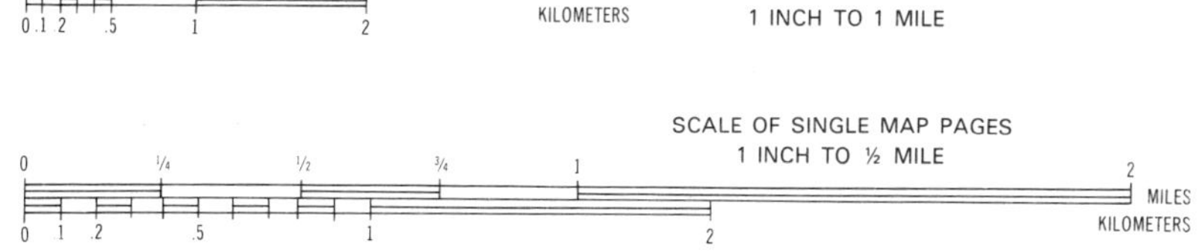

MAJOR DEPARTMENT STORES

EC	EMPORIUM CAPWELL
MA	MACYS
ME	MERVYNS
MW	MONTGOMERY WARD
NM	NEIMAN MARCUS
N	NORDSTROM
P	JC PENNEY
S	SEARS

MALL
EC MW NM

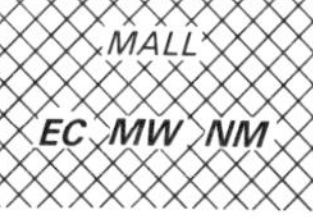

1991 SAN MATEO COUNTY
CITIES AND COMMUNITIES INDEX

ESTIMATED POPULATION INCORPORATED CITIES	583,840
ESTIMATED POPULATION UNINCORPORATED AREAS	57,160
ESTIMATED TOTAL COUNTY POPULATION	641,000

COMMUNITY NAME	ABBR.	ZIP CODE	AREA SQ. MI.	ESTIMATED POPULATION	PAGE
ALPINE HILLS		94025			47
* ATHERTON	A	94027	6.00	7,975	37
BAYSHORE		94005			22
* BELMONT	BLMT	94002	4.00	25,150	33
* BRISBANE	BR	94005	15.00	3,070	24
BROADMOOR VILLAGE		94015			23
* BURLINGAME	B	94010	6.10	27,400	28
BURLINGAME HILLS		94010			28
* COLMA	CLMA	94014	2.50	730	23
* DALY CITY	DC	94014	7.40	86,400	21
DEVONSHIRE		94070			33
EAST MENLO		94025			38
* EAST PALO ALTO	EPA	94303	2.50	18,950	38
EL GRANADA		94018			30A
EMERALD LAKE		94062			36
FARM HILLS		94061			36
* FOSTER CITY	FCTY	94404	4.04	30,150	29A
* HALF MOON BAY	HMB	94019	8.00	9,375	34
* HILLSBOROUGH	H	94010	6.25	11,300	28
HILLSDALE		94403			32
KINGS MOUNTAIN		94062			41
LADERA		94025			43
LA HONDA		94020			50
LINDA MAR		94044			27A
LINDENWOOD		94025			37
LOMA MAR		94021			49A
LOS TRANCOS WOODS		94025			51
MENLO OAKS		94025			37
* MENLO PARK	MP	94025	19.00	28,500	37
* MILLBRAE	M	94030	10.00	21,150	26
MIRAMAR		94019			34
MONTARA		94037			30

COMMUNITY NAME	ABBR.	ZIP CODE	AREA SQ. MI.	ESTIMATED POPULATION	PAGE
MOSS BEACH		94038			30
NORTH FAIR OAKS		94063			37
* PACIFICA	P	94044	12.50	38,450	25
PALOMAR PARK		94062			36
PESCADERO		94060			56
* PORTOLA VALLEY	PV	94028	10.00	4,540	47
PORTOLA VALLEY RANCH		94025			47
PRINCETON BY THE SEA		94018			30
* REDWOOD CITY	RC	94061	33.60	63,200	36
REDWOOD SHORES		94065			33
ROCKAWAY BEACH		94044			20
* SAN BRUNO	SBR	94066	5.87	35,750	26
* SAN CARLOS	SC	94070	4.50	27,500	33
SAN GREGORIO		94074			48
* SAN MATEO	SM	94401	14.60	85,600	29
- -SAN MATEO COUNTY	SMCO		552.0	641,000	
SAN PEDRO TERRACE		94044			20
SERRAMONTE		94015			23
SHARON HEIGHTS		94025			43
SHARP PARK		94044			25
SKYLINE		94062			35
SKY LONDA		94062			46
* SOUTH SAN FRANCISCO	SSF	94080	9.50	52,900	24
THE HIGHLANDS		94402			32
VALLEMAR		94044			25
VISTA VERDE		94025			51
WESTBOROUGH		94080			23
WEST MENLO PARK		94025			43
WESTRIDGE		94025			47
* WOODSIDE	W	94062	14.00	5,750	42
WOODSIDE HIGHLANDS		94025			46
WOODSIDE HILLS		94062			42

*INDICATES INCORPORATED CITY

EY TO ATLAS PAGES
JUMBERS WITHIN THE REC-
TANGLES INDICATE THE PAGE
JUMBER AND AREA COVERED
Y EACH DETAIL PAGE IN THIS
TLAS.
SCALE
0 1 2 3 4 5 MILES
E
SAN MATEO
AREA
SAN FRANCISCO CO
SAN MATEO CO
ALAMEDA CO
SAN MATEO CO
SANTA CLARA CO
SAN MATEO CO
SANTA CRUZ CO
DALY CITY
COLMA
BRISBANE
Bayshore
PACIFICA
SOUTH SAN FRANCISCO
SAN BRUNO
SAN FRANCISCO INTERNATIONAL AIRPORT
Rockaway Beach
SAN ANDREAS LAKE
MILLBRAE
San Pedro Terrace
Linda Mar
BURLINGAME
SAN MATEO
HILLSBOROUGH
FOSTER CITY
Montara
Moss Beach
The Highlands
LOWER CRYSTAL SPRINGS RES
BELMONT
Redwood Shores
DUMBARTON BRIDGE
Princeton By The Sea
El Granada
SAN CARLOS
EAST PALO ALTO
Miramar
HALF MOON BAY
UPPER CRYSTAL SPRINGS RES
REDWOOD CITY
ATHERTON
MENLO PARK
PALO ALTO
Skyline
Kings Mtn
WOODSIDE
Stanford
Ladera
PORTOLA VALLEY
Sky Londa
LOS ALTOS HILLS
La Honda
San Gregorio
Loma Mar
Pescadero
South Shore
Bay Farm Island
OAKLAND INTERNATIONAL AIRPORT
Mulford Gardens
SAN LEANDRO
Sheffield Village
Castro Valley
San Lorenzo
HAYWARD
YOUNGER FRWY
SAN MATEO TOLL BRIDGE
UNION CITY
Alvarado
NEWARK
FREMONT
Centerville
Mission San Jose
Warm Springs
SAN RAMON
Dougherty
DUBLIN
Santa Rita
LIVERMO
PLEASANTON
Kilkare
Sunol
Scotts Corner
SAN ANTONIO RES
CALAVERAS RES
MILPITAS
Alviso
MOUNTAIN VIEW
LOS ALTOS
SUNNYVALE
SANTA CLARA
East San Jose
Alum Rock
SAN JOSE
CUPERTINO
Monte Vista
Rancho Rinconade
CAMPBELL
SARATOGA
MONTE SERENO
LOS GATOS
LEXINGTON RES
New Almaden
CALERO RES
Idylwild
Aldercroft Heights
Chemeketa Park
Holy City
Redwood Estates
Boulder Creek
Brookdale

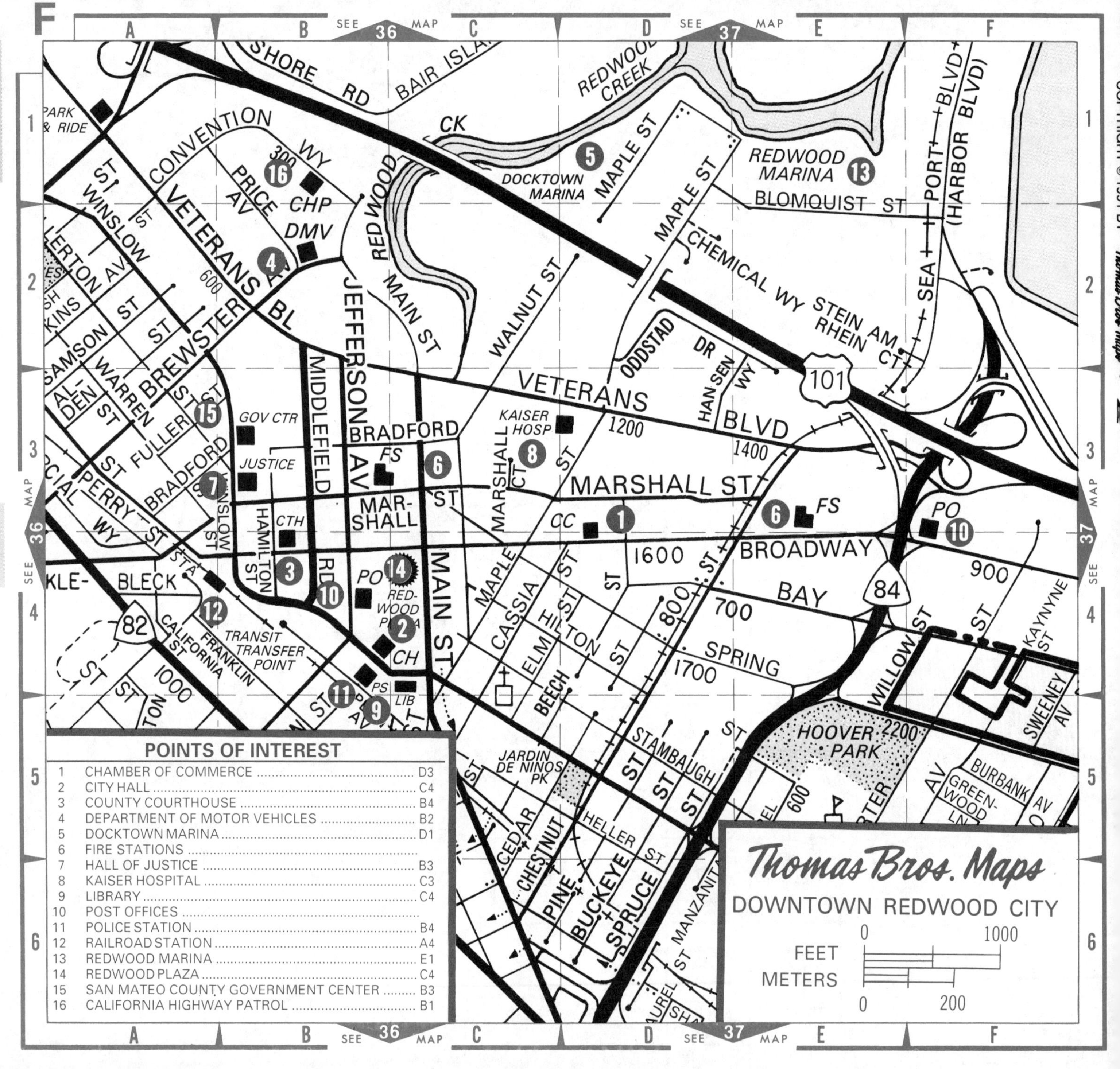
SAN MATEO
AREA
SEE MAP 36
SEE MAP 37
A
B
C
D
E
F
1
2
3
4
5
6
Thomas Bros. Maps
DOWNTOWN REDWOOD CITY
FEET
METERS
0
1000
200
POINTS OF INTEREST
1 CHAMBER OF COMMERCE D3
2 CITY HALL C4
3 COUNTY COURTHOUSE B4
4 DEPARTMENT OF MOTOR VEHICLES B2
5 DOCKTOWN MARINA D1
6 FIRE STATIONS ....
7 HALL OF JUSTICE B3
8 KAISER HOSPITAL C3
9 LIBRARY C4
10 POST OFFICES ....
11 POLICE STATION B4
12 RAILROAD STATION A4
13 REDWOOD MARINA E1
14 REDWOOD PLAZA C4
15 SAN MATEO COUNTY GOVERNMENT CENTER B3
16 CALIFORNIA HIGHWAY PATROL B1
PARK & RIDE
SHORE RD
BAIR ISLAND
REDWOOD CREEK
CK
CONVENTION WY
300
CHP
DMV
PRICE AV
REDWOOD
DOCKTOWN MARINA
MAPLE ST
REDWOOD MARINA
BLOMQUIST ST
PORT BLVD (HARBOR BLVD)
SEA
CHEMICAL WY
STEIN AM RHEIN CT
ODDSTAD DR
HANSEN WY
101
WINSLOW ST
VETERANS BL
600
BREWSTER AV
JEFFERSON AV
MAIN ST
WALNUT ST
SAMSON ST
ALDEN ST
WARREN ST
FULLER ST
VETERANS BLVD
1200
1400
KAISER HOSP
GOV CTR
JUSTICE
MIDDLEFIELD RD
BRADFORD
FS
MARSHALL CT
MARSHALL ST
BRADFORD ST
PERRY ST
WY
CTH
HAMILTON ST
CC
BROADWAY
1600
PO
900
84
BAY
700
800
KLE-BLECK
STA
82
CALIFORNIA ST
FRANKLIN
TRANSIT TRANSFER POINT
REDWOOD PLAZA
CH
PS
LIB
1000
MAPLE
CASSIA
ELM
HILTON ST
BEECH
SPRING
1700
WILLOW ST
KAYNYNE ST
SWEENEY AV
HOOVER PARK
2200
STAMBAUGH ST
JARDIN DE NINOS PK
CEDAR
CHESTNUT
HELLER ST
PINE
BUCKEYE
SPRUCE
MANZANITA ST
LAUREL
600
BURBANK AV
GREENWOOD LN
COPYRIGHT © 1991 BY Thomas Bros. Maps

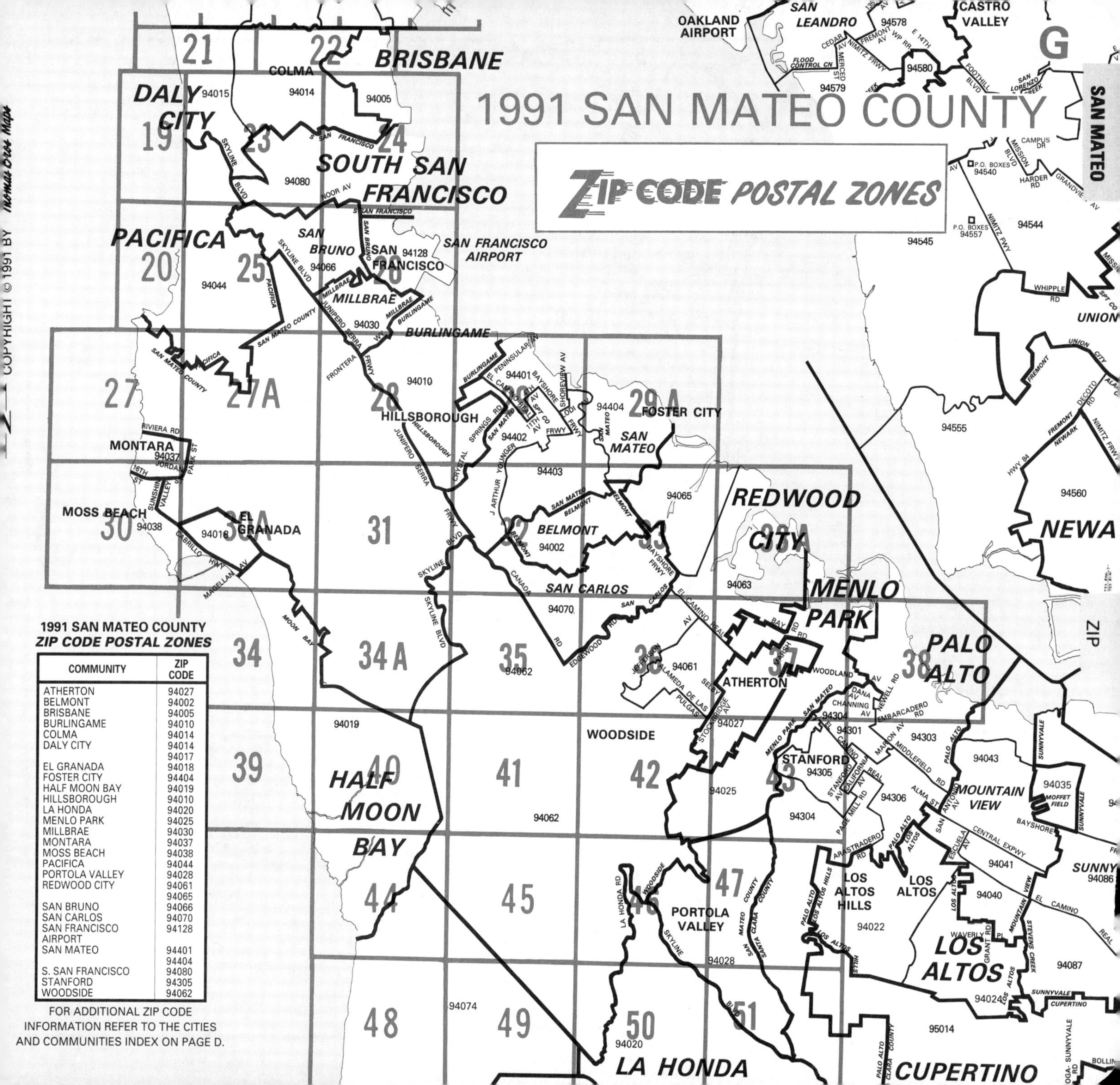

COMMUNITY	ZIP CODE
ATHERTON	94027
BELMONT	94002
BRISBANE	94005
BURLINGAME	94010
COLMA	94014
DALY CITY	94014
	94017
EL GRANADA	94018
FOSTER CITY	94404
HALF MOON BAY	94019
HILLSBOROUGH	94010
LA HONDA	94020
MENLO PARK	94025
MILLBRAE	94030
MONTARA	94037
MOSS BEACH	94038
PACIFICA	94044
PORTOLA VALLEY	94028
REDWOOD CITY	94061
	94065
SAN BRUNO	94066
SAN CARLOS	94070
SAN FRANCISCO AIRPORT	94128
SAN MATEO	94401
	94404
S. SAN FRANCISCO	94080
STANFORD	94305
WOODSIDE	94062

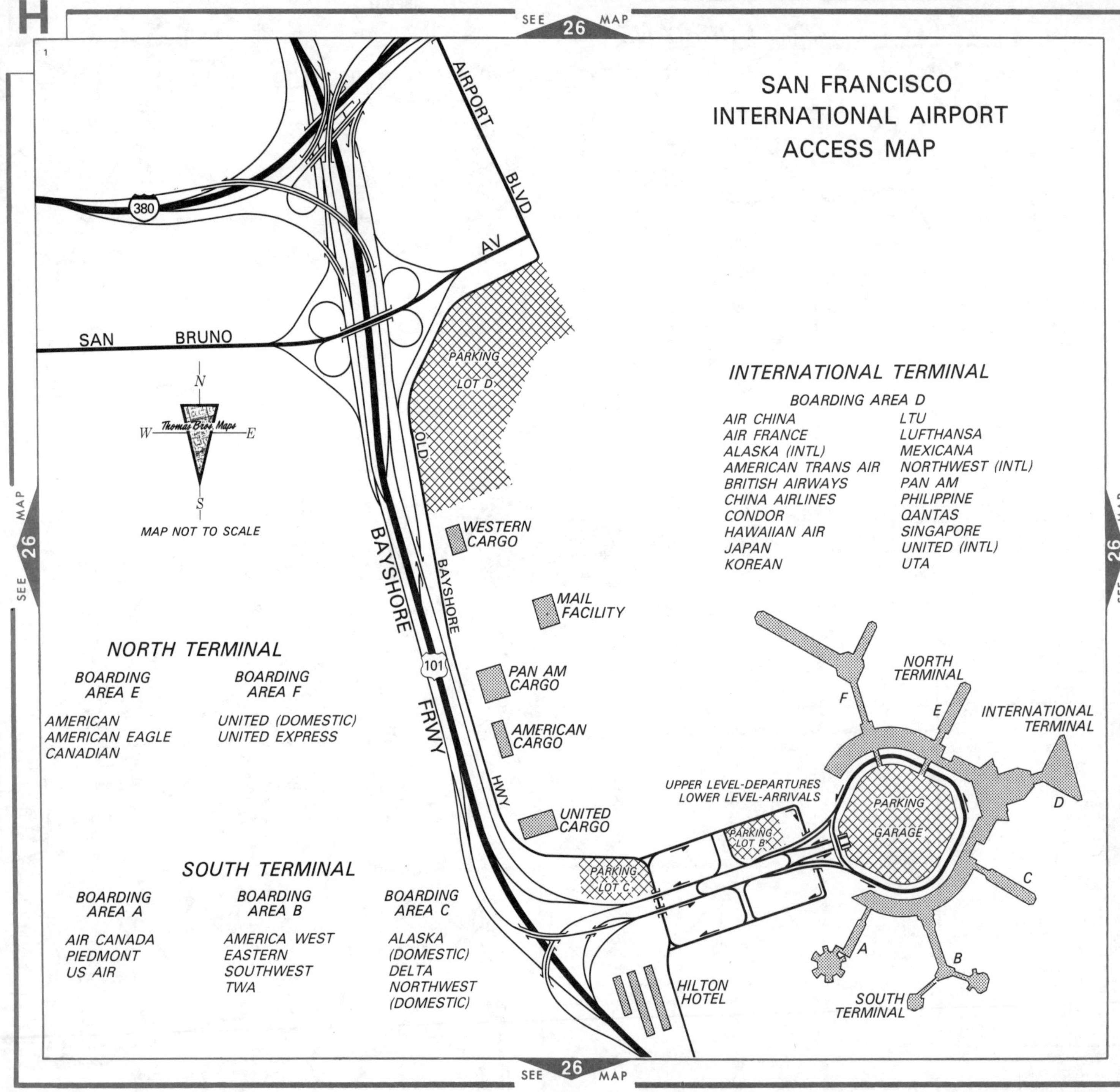

SEE 26 MAP
SEE 26 MAP
SEE 26 MAP
SEE 26 MAP

COPYRIGHT © 1991 BY Thomas Bros. Maps

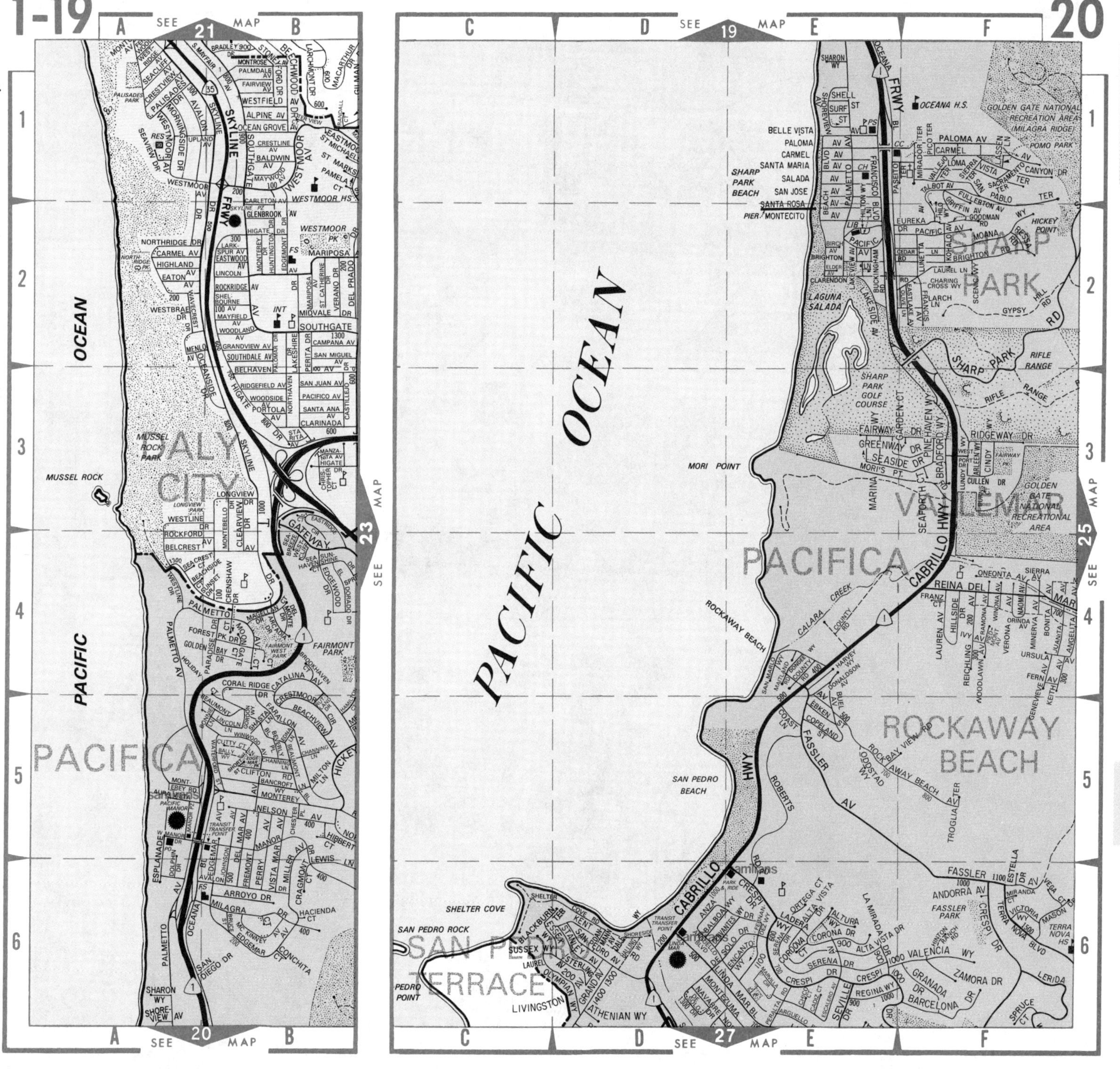

COPYRIGHT © 1991 BY Thomas Bros Maps

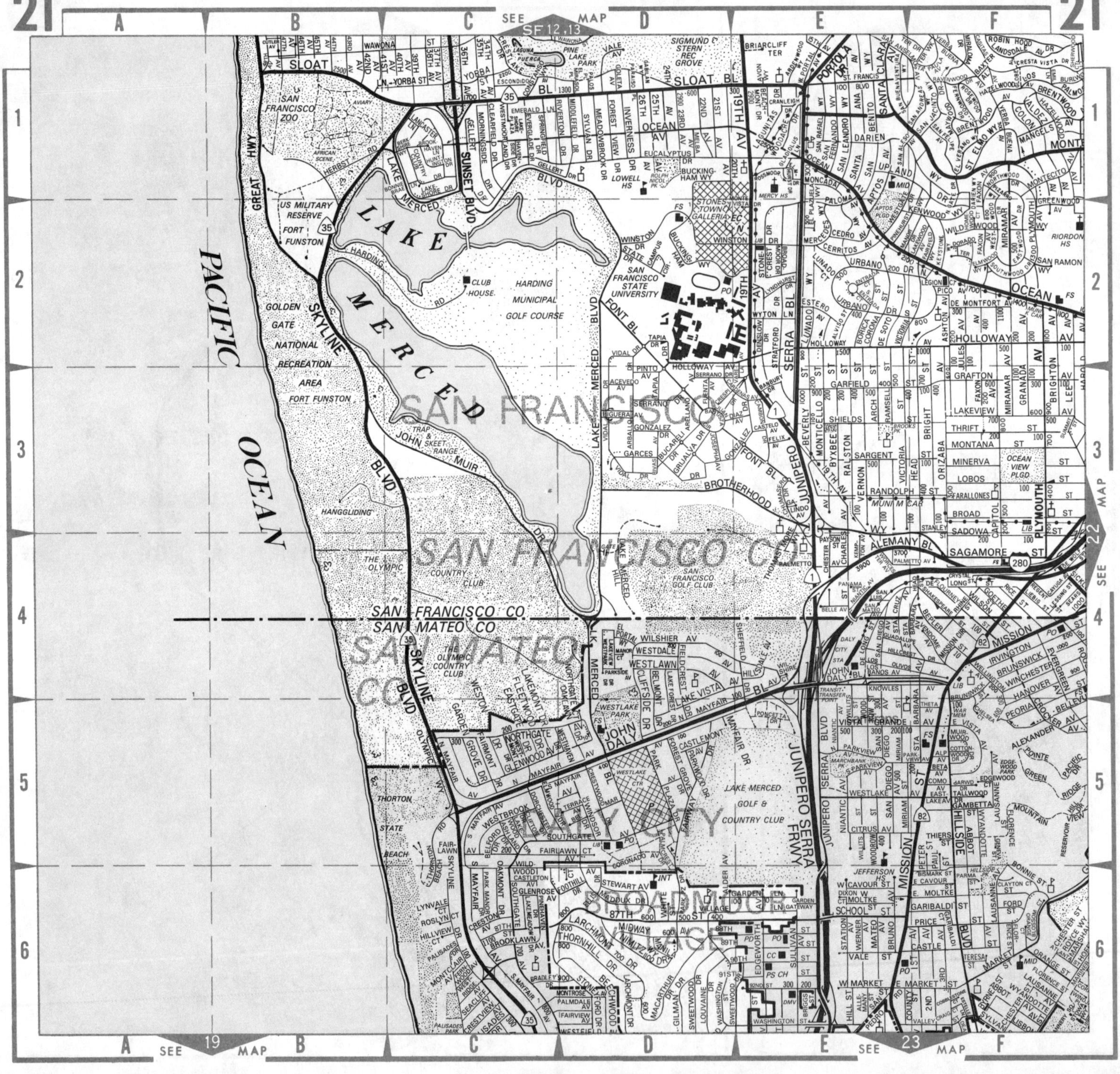

SEE SF 12,13 MAP

PACIFIC OCEAN

LAKE MERCED

SAN FRANCISCO

SAN FRANCISCO CO

SAN FRANCISCO CO
SAN MATEO CO

SAN MATEO CO

DALY CITY

BROADMOOR VILLAGE

SAN FRANCISCO ZOO

US MILITARY RESERVE FORT FUNSTON

GOLDEN GATE NATIONAL RECREATION AREA FORT FUNSTON

HARDING MUNICIPAL GOLF COURSE

SAN FRANCISCO STATE UNIVERSITY

STONESTOWN GALLERIA

SIGMUND STERN REC GROVE

PINE LAKE PARK

LOWELL HS

MERCY HS

RIORDON HS

OCEAN VIEW PLGD

APTOS PLGD

TRAP & SKEET RANGE

HANGGLIDING

THE OLYMPIC COUNTRY CLUB

SAN FRANCISCO GOLF CLUB

LAKE MERCED GOLF & COUNTRY CLUB

WESTLAKE PARK

WESTLAKE SHOPPING CTR

THORNTON STATE BEACH

JUNIPERO SERRA FRWY

SKYLINE BLVD

GREAT HWY

JOHN MUIR DR

SLOAT BL

OCEAN AV

ALEMANY BL

MISSION ST

JOHN DALY BL

SEE 22 MAP

DETAIL

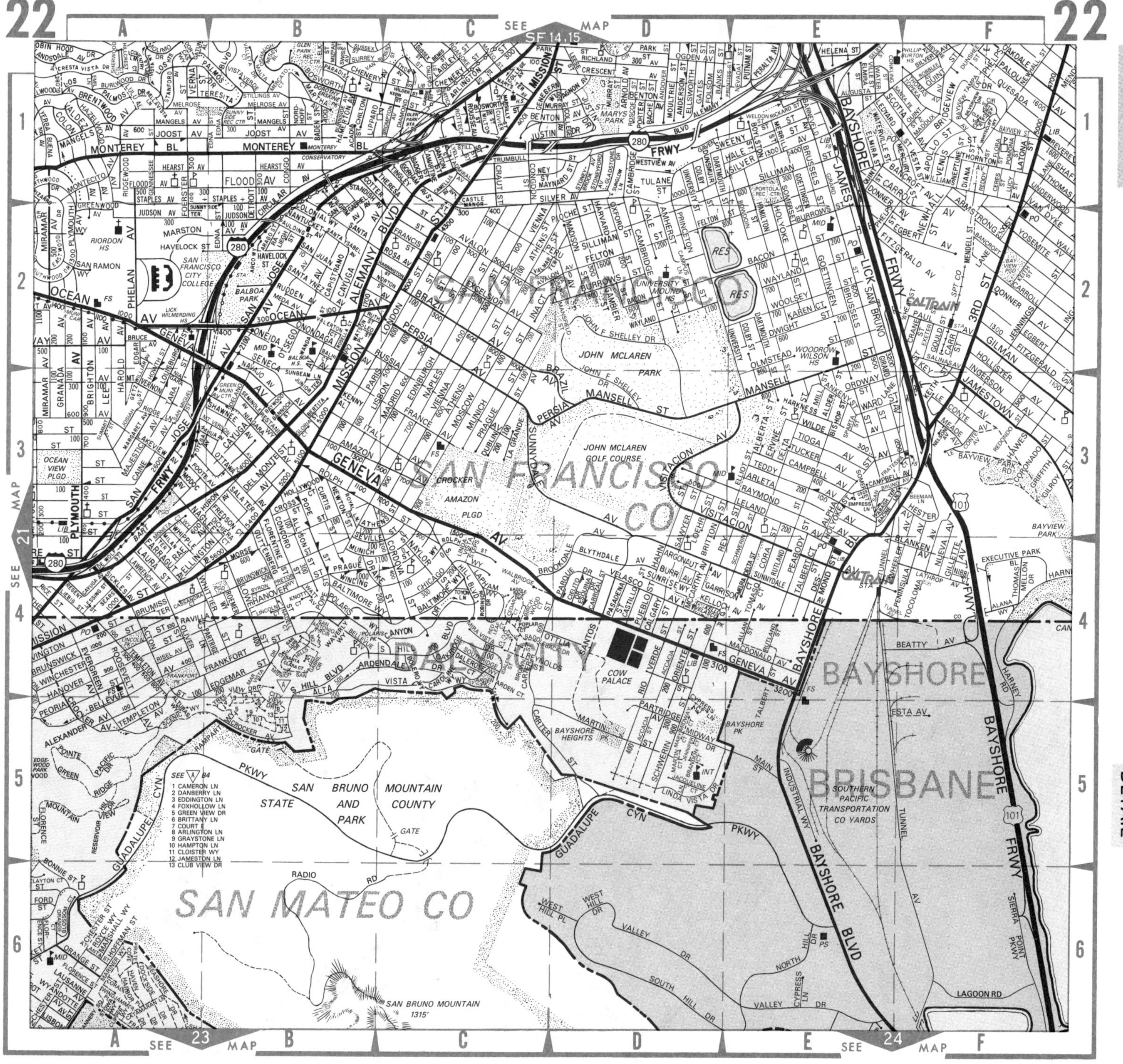

COPYRIGHT © 1991 BY Thomas Bros Maps

SEE 21 MAP

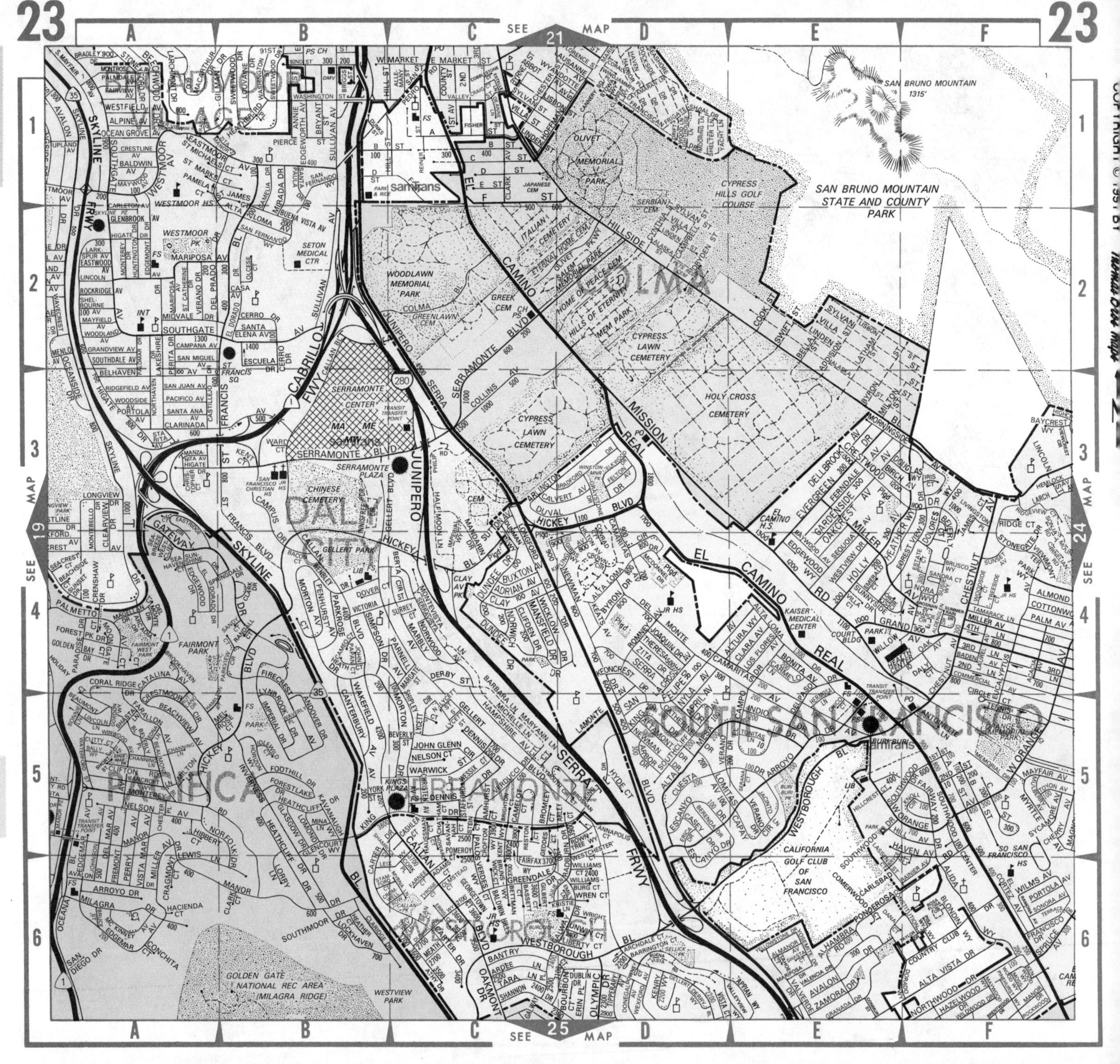

COPYRIGHT © 1991 BY Thomas Bros Maps

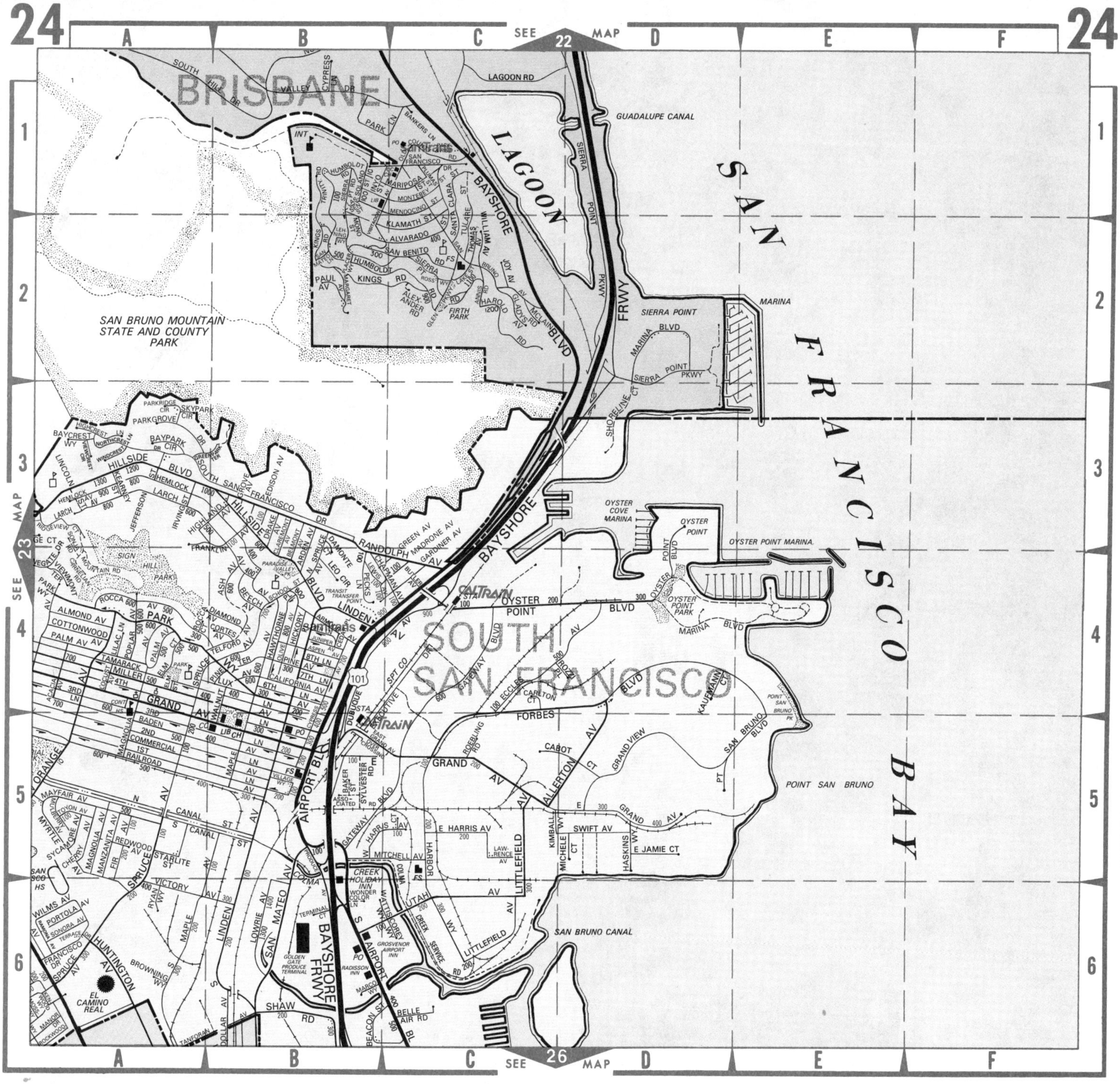

BRISBANE
LAGOON
SAN FRANCISCO BAY
SAN BRUNO MOUNTAIN
STATE AND COUNTY
PARK
SOUTH
SAN FRANCISCO

SOUTH HILL DR
VALLEY DR
CYPRESS LN
LAGOON RD
GUADALUPE CANAL
SIERRA POINT PKWY
BANKERS LN
PARK LN
SAN FRANCISCO AV
HUMBOLDT RD
MARIPOSA ST
MONTEBELLO ST
MENDOCINO ST
KLAMATH ST
ALVARADO ST
SAN BENITO RD
SIERRA ST
KINGS RD
PAUL AV
ALEXANDER RD
FIRTH PARK
HAROLD AV
GLADYS AV
McLAIN RD
TULARE ST
SANTA CLARA ST
WILLIAM AV
JOY AV
BAYSHORE BLVD
FRWY
SIERRA POINT
MARINA
MARINA BLVD
SIERRA POINT PKWY
SHORELINE CT

PARKRIDGE CIR
SKYPARK CIR
PARKGROVE CIR
BAYCREST WY
HIGHCREST LN
NORTHCREST LN
WINDCREST LN
BAYPARK CIR
HILLSIDE BLVD
LINCOLN
HEMLOCK AV
LARCH AV
SOUTH SAN FRANCISCO DR
EDISON AV
JEFFERSON
IRVING ST
HIGHLAND AV
FRANKLIN
SIGN HILL PARK
RANDOLPH AV
GREEN AV
MADRONE AV
GARDNER AV
DAMONTE
LEO CIR
SPRUCE AV
ARDEN AV
BELMONT AV
DRAKE AV
CLAREMONT AV
PARADISE VALLEY PARK
SCHOOL ST
ASH AV
BEECH AV
ROCCA AV
DIAMOND AV
PARK WY
ALMOND AV
COTTONWOOD AV
PALM AV
TAMARACK LN
MILLER AV
GRAND AV
BADEN AV
2ND LN
COMMERCIAL AV
1ST LN
RAILROAD AV
3RD LN
4TH LN
MAGNOLIA AV
WALNUT AV
MAPLE AV
LINDEN AV
HAWTHORNE
HICKORY
OLIVE
PINE AV
CALIFORNIA AV
JUNIPER AV
ASPEN AV
8TH LN
7TH LN
6TH LN
CYPRESS AV
LUX AV
TELFORD AV
CORTES AV
AIRPORT BLVD
VILLAGE WY

OYSTER POINT BLVD
OYSTER COVE MARINA
OYSTER POINT MARINA
OYSTER POINT
OYSTER POINT PARK
MARINA BLVD
GATEWAY BLVD
DUBUQUE AV
SPT CO
CALTRAIN
CARLTON CT
ECCLES AV
FORBES BLVD
KAUFMANN CT
POINT SAN BRUNO PK
POINT SAN BRUNO
SAN BRUNO BLVD
GRAND VIEW DR
CABOT RD
ALLERTON AV
ROEBLING RD
GRAND AV
E GRAND AV
LITTLEFIELD AV
E HARRIS AV
HARRIS CT
LAWRENCE AV
SWIFT AV
KIMBALL WY
MICHELE CT
HASKINS WY
E JAMIE CT
MITCHELL AV
HARBOR WY
UTAH AV
SAN BRUNO CANAL
COLMA CREEK
HOLIDAY INN
WONDER COLOR
BAKER WY
SYLVESTER RD
ASSOCIATED RD
101

MAYFAIR AV
N CANAL ST
S CANAL ST
MYRTLE AV
SYCAMORE AV
CHERRY AV
MAGNOLIA AV
MANZANITA AV
FIR AV
REDWOOD AV
STARLITE ST
SPRUCE AV
VICTORY AV
RYAN WY
LOWRIE AV
SAN MATEO AV
BAYSHORE FRWY
GOLDEN GATE PRODUCE TERMINAL
AIRPORT BLVD
GROSVENOR AIRPORT INN
RADISSON INN
MARCO WY
BEACON ST
BELLE AIR RD
SHAW RD
DOLLAR AV
TANFORAN AV
HUNTINGTON AV
EL CAMINO REAL
BROWNING WY
WILMS AV
PORTOLA AV
SONORA AV
TERRACE AV
FRANCISCO DR
SOUTH SAN FRANCISCO HS
MANOR DR
ROCKWOOD DR
ORANGE AV

COPYRIGHT © 1991 BY Thomas Bros. Maps

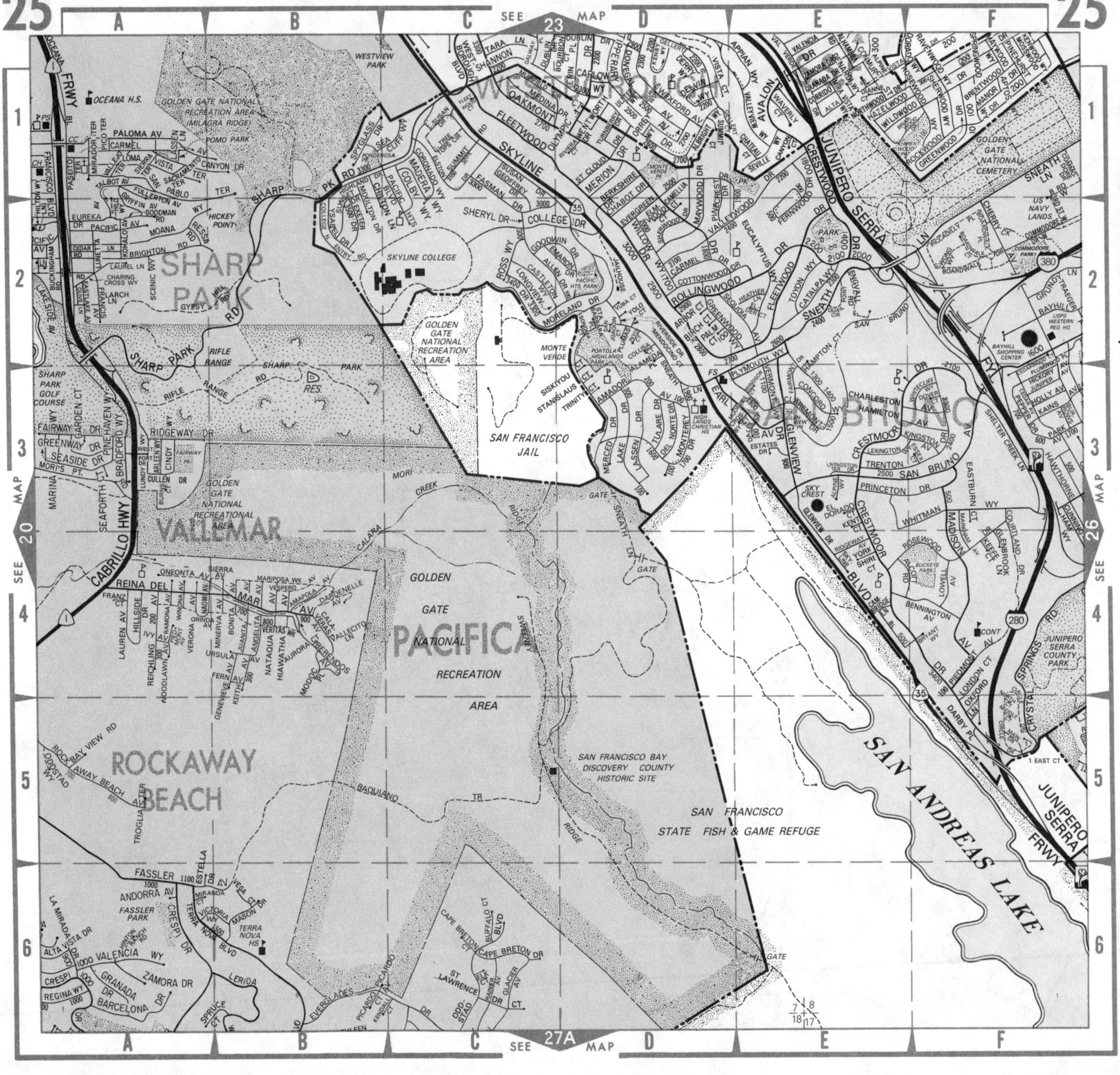

SEE 23 MAP

SEE 20 MAP

SEE 26 MAP

SEE 27A MAP

DETAIL

A B C D E F

1 2 3 4 5 6

WESTBOROUGH

SHARP PARK

VALLEMAR

PACIFICA

ROCKAWAY BEACH

SAN BRUNO

SKYLINE COLLEGE

GOLDEN GATE NATIONAL RECREATION AREA (MILAGRA RIDGE)

GOLDEN GATE NATIONAL RECREATION AREA

SAN FRANCISCO JAIL

SHARP PARK GOLF COURSE

SHARP PARK RIFLE RANGE

GOLDEN GATE NATIONAL CEMETERY

US NAVY LANDS

BAYHILL SHOPPING CENTER

USPS WESTERN REG HQ

JUNIPERO SERRA COUNTY PARK

SAN FRANCISCO BAY DISCOVERY COUNTY HISTORIC SITE

SAN FRANCISCO STATE FISH & GAME REFUGE

SAN ANDREAS LAKE

OCEANA H.S.

TERRA NOVA HS

HIGHLANDS CHRISTIAN HS

FASSLER PARK

BUCKEYE PARK

WESTVIEW PARK

CABRILLO HWY

OCEANA FRWY

JUNIPERO SERRA FRWY

SKYLINE BLVD

SHARP PARK RD

SNEATH LN

CRESTMOOR DR

JUNIPERO SERRA BLVD

REINA DEL MAR AV

FASSLER AV

ROCKAWAY BEACH AV

BAQUIANO TR

COPYRIGHT © 1991 BY Thomas Bros. Maps

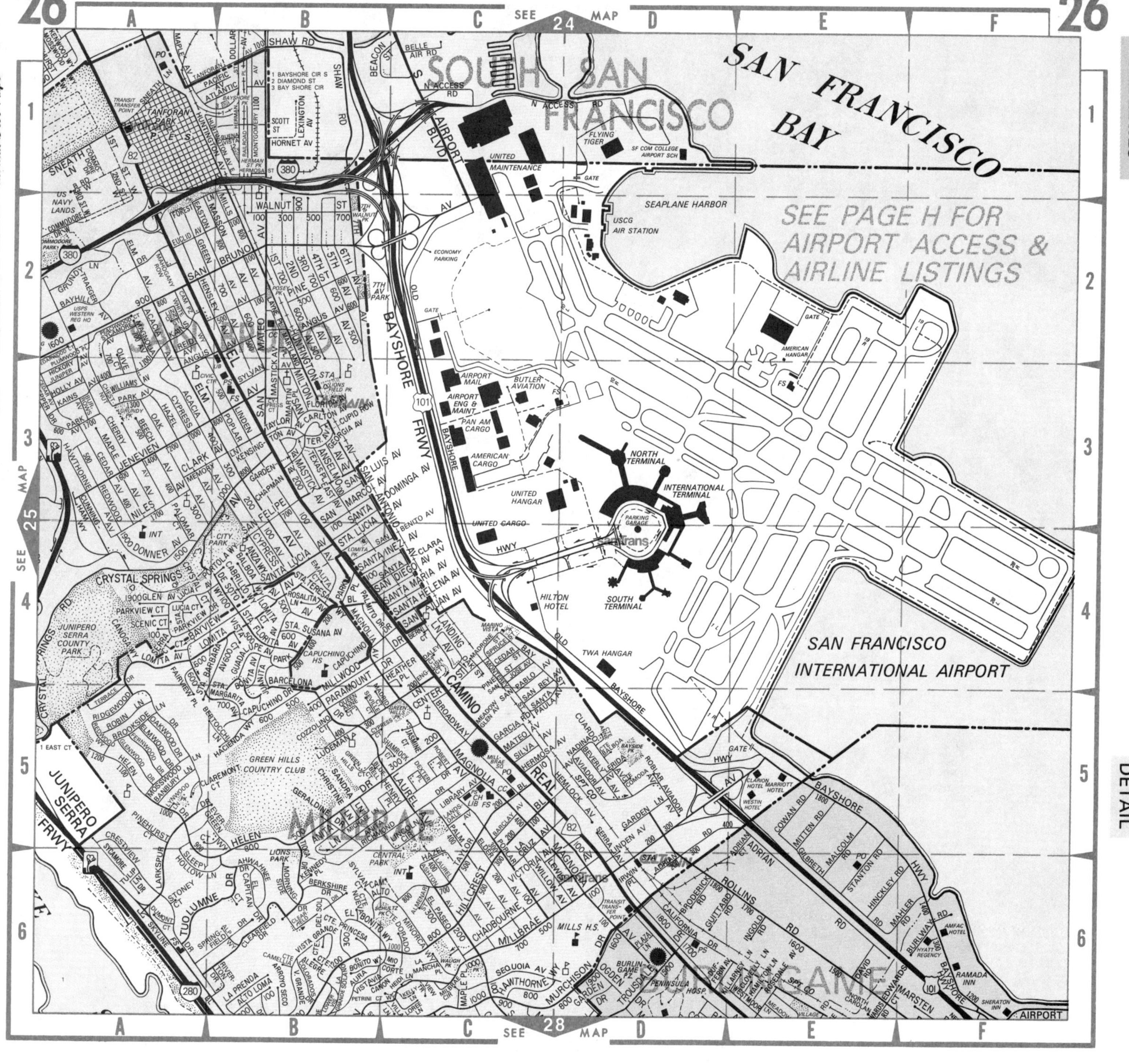
SOUTH SAN FRANCISCO
SAN FRANCISCO BAY
SEE PAGE H FOR AIRPORT ACCESS & AIRLINE LISTINGS
SAN BRUNO
MILLBRAE
BURLINGAME
SAN FRANCISCO INTERNATIONAL AIRPORT
NORTH TERMINAL
INTERNATIONAL TERMINAL
SOUTH TERMINAL
SEAPLANE HARBOR
USCG AIR STATION
UNITED MAINTENANCE
AMERICAN HANGAR
UNITED HANGAR
TWA HANGAR
HILTON HOTEL
GREEN HILLS COUNTRY CLUB
JUNIPERO SERRA COUNTY PARK
CRYSTAL SPRINGS
BAYSHORE FRWY
JUNIPERO SERRA FRWY
CAMINO REAL
SEE MAP 24
SEE MAP 25
SEE MAP 28
SAN MATEO
DETAIL

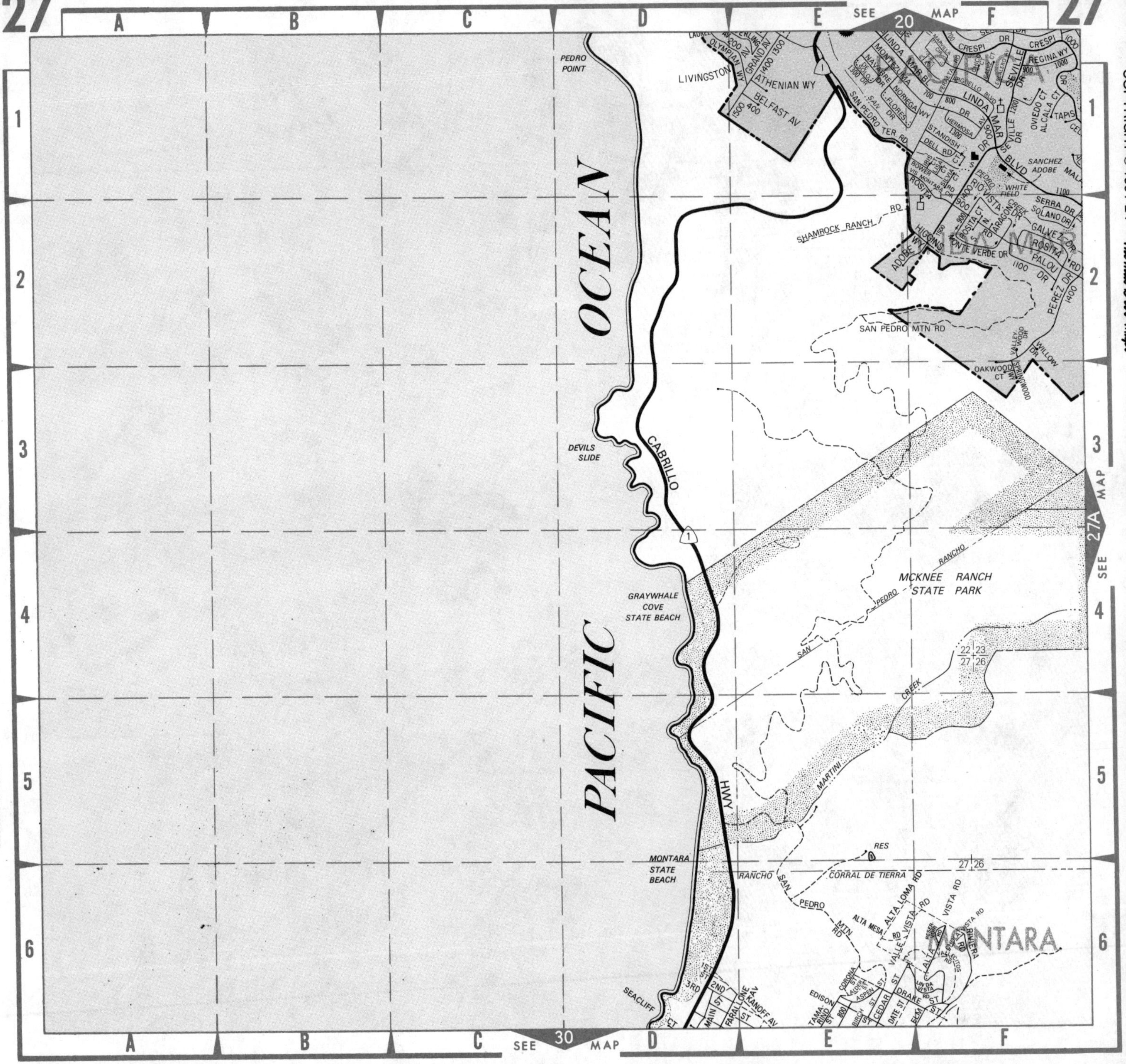

A B C D E F
SEE 20 MAP
SAN MATEO
DETAIL
1 2 3 4 5 6
PACIFIC OCEAN
PEDRO POINT
LIVINGSTON
ATHENIAN WY
BELFAST AV
CRESPI DR
LINDA MAR BLVD
SEVILLE DR
SAN PEDRO TER RD
SANCHEZ ADOBE
SHAMROCK RANCH RD
HIGGINS WY
MONTE VERDE DR
SERRA DR
GALVEZ DR
PALOU DR
PEREZ DR
SAN PEDRO MTN RD
OAKWOOD CT
SPRINGWOOD
WILLOW
DEVILS SLIDE
CABRILLO HWY
GRAYWHALE COVE STATE BEACH
MCKNEE RANCH STATE PARK
SAN PEDRO RANCHO
MARTINI CREEK
SEE 27A MAP
RES
MONTARA STATE BEACH
RANCHO SAN PEDRO
CORRAL DE TIERRA
ALTA LOMA RD
ALTA MESA RD
ALTA VISTA RD
VALLE VISTA
VISTA RD
RIVIERA
MONTARA
SEACLIFF CT
MAIN ST
FARALLONE AV
KANOFF AV
EDISON ST
CEDAR ST
DATE ST
DRAKE ST
ELM ST
SEE 30 MAP

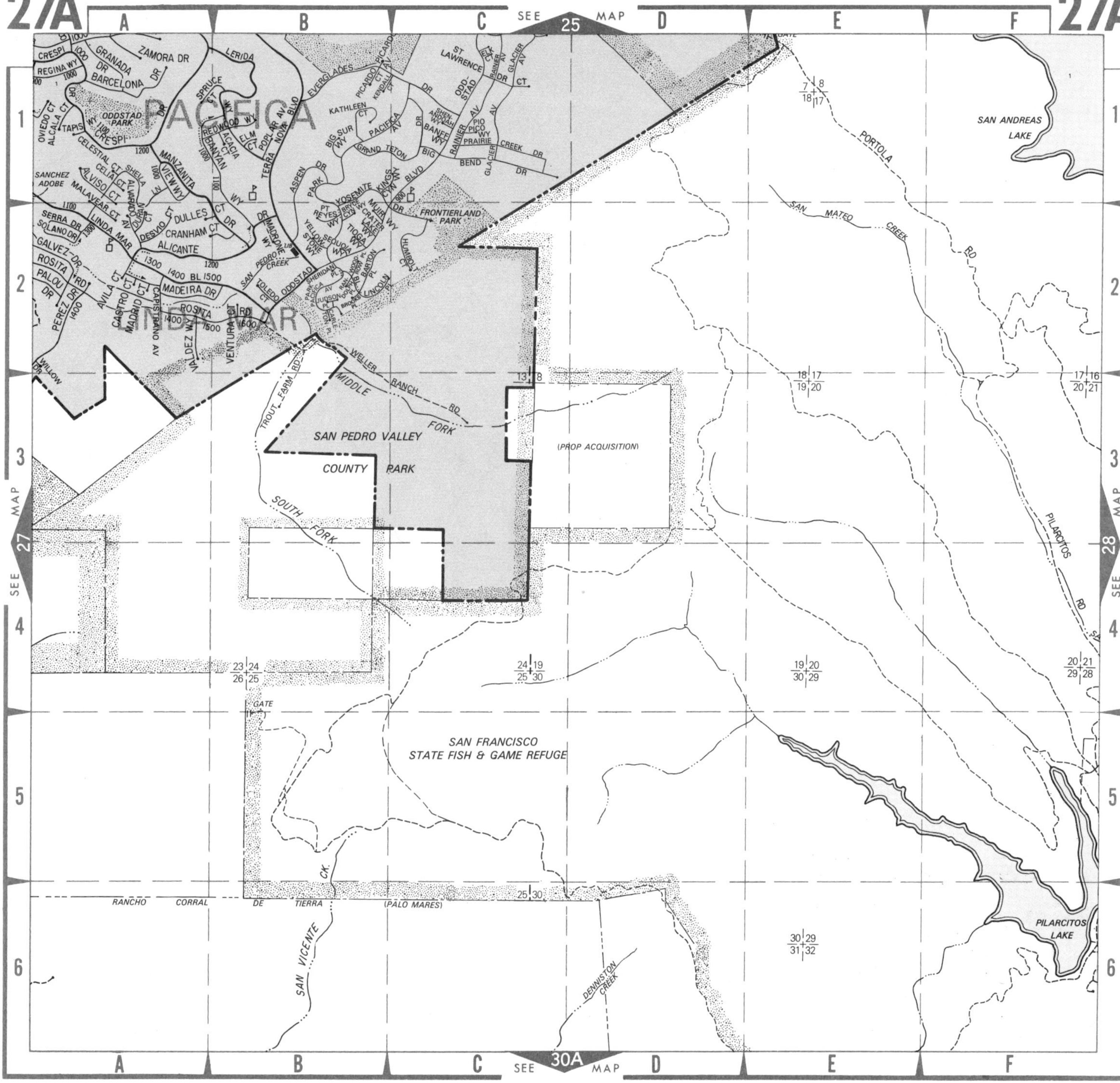

COPYRIGHT © 1991 BY Thomas Bros Maps

SEE 26 MAP

28

A B C D E F

1 2 3 4 5 6

MILLBRAE

BURLINGAME

BURLINGAME HILLS

HILLSBOROUGH

SAN ANDREAS LAKE

SAN FRANCISCO STATE FISH & GAME REFUGE

FELIZ RANCHO

BURLINGAME COUNTRY CLUB

CRYSTAL SPRINGS GOLF COURSE

LOWER CRYSTAL SPRINGS RESERVOIR

PILARCITOS LAKE

MILLS CANYON PARK

SPENCER LAKE

JUNIPERO SERRA FRWY

SKYLINE BLVD

SKYLINE FRONTAGE RD

BLACK MTN RD

PILARCITOS RD

SAN MATEO CREEK

SAWYER CAMP COUNTY HISTORIC TR (BIKEWAY)

AIRPORT BLVD

BAYSIDE PARK

RAMADA INN

SHERATON INN

EL CAMINO REAL

PENINSULA HOSP.

MERCY HS

BAYSHORE FRWY

SEE 27A MAP

SEE 29 MAP

SEE 31 MAP

DETAIL

COPYRIGHT © 1991 BY Thomas Bros. Maps

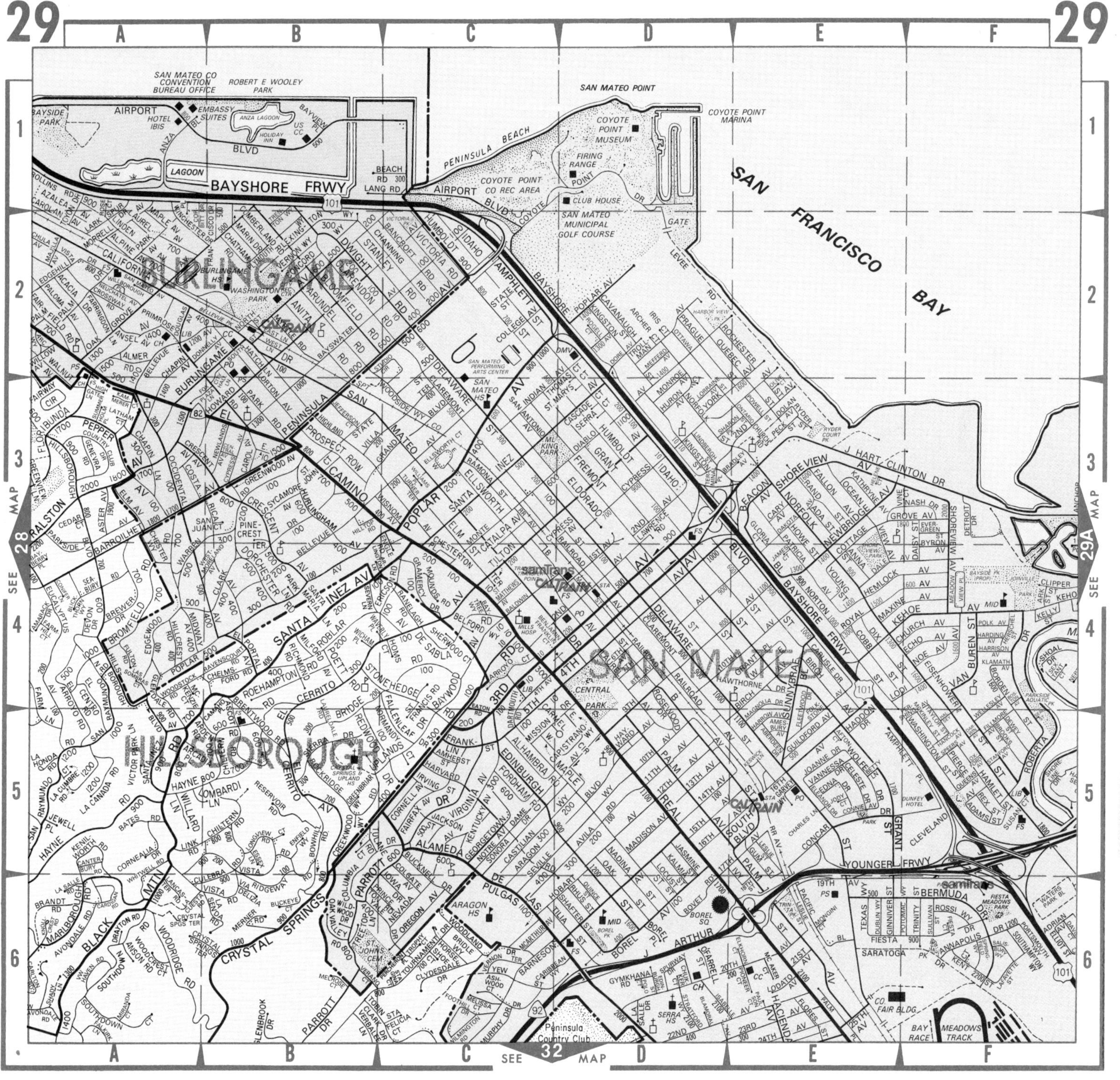

COPYRIGHT © 1991 BY Thomas Bros Maps

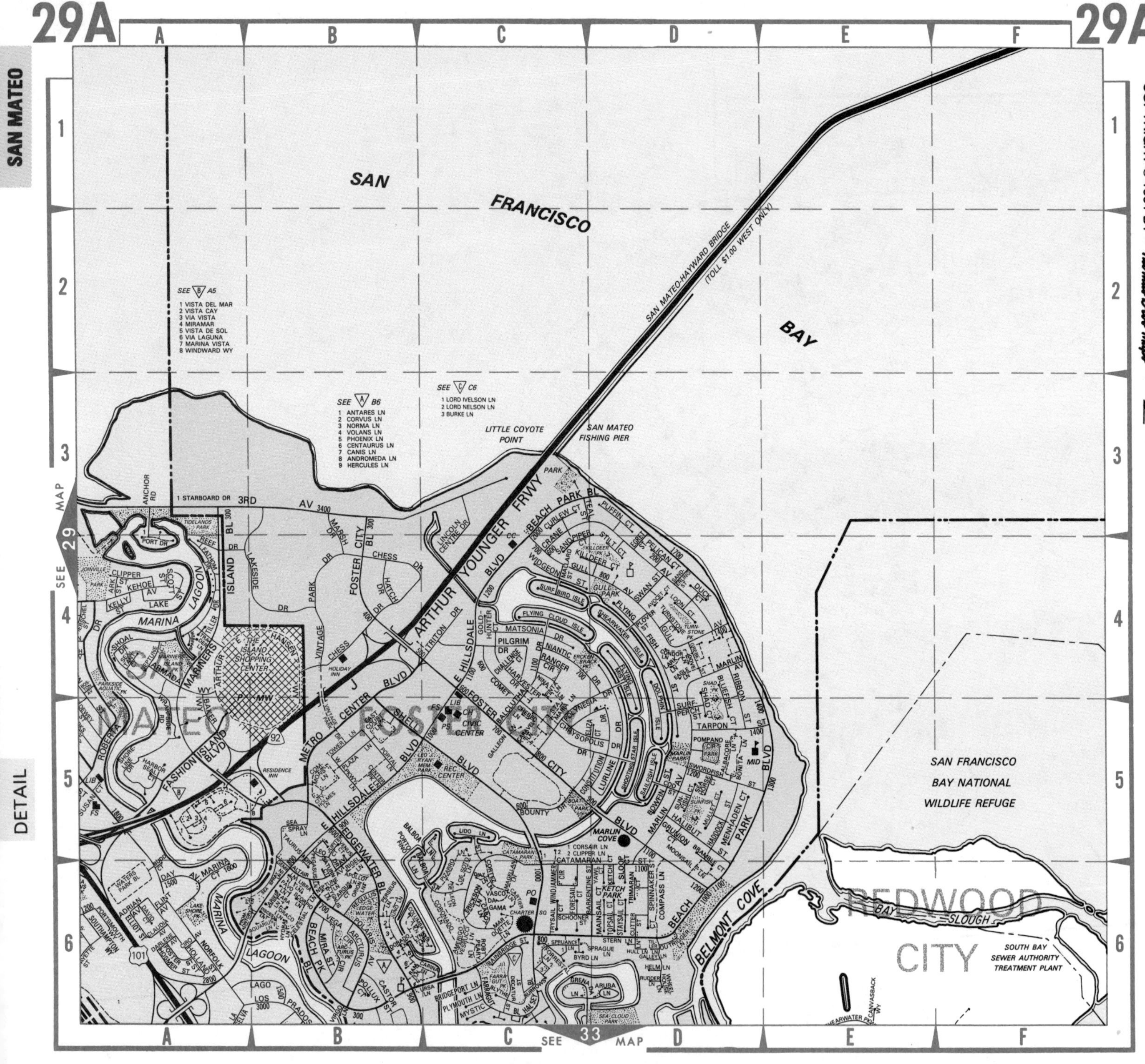
29A
29A
SAN MATEO
DETAIL
COPYRIGHT © 1991 BY Thomas Bros Maps
SAN
FRANCISCO
BAY
SAN MATEO-HAYWARD BRIDGE
(TOLL $1.00 WEST ONLY)
SEE B A5
1 VISTA DEL MAR
2 VISTA CAY
3 VIA VISTA
4 MIRAMAR
5 VISTA DE SOL
6 VIA LAGUNA
7 MARINA VISTA
8 WINDWARD WY
SEE A B6
1 ANTARES LN
2 CORVUS LN
3 NORMA LN
4 VOLANS LN
5 PHOENIX LN
6 CENTAURUS LN
7 CANIS LN
8 ANDROMEDA LN
9 HERCULES LN
SEE C C6
1 LORD IVELSON LN
2 LORD NELSON LN
3 BURKE LN
LITTLE COYOTE POINT
SAN MATEO FISHING PIER
SEE 29 MAP
SEE 33 MAP
SAN MATEO
FOSTER CITY
REDWOOD CITY
SAN FRANCISCO BAY NATIONAL WILDLIFE REFUGE
SOUTH BAY SEWER AUTHORITY TREATMENT PLANT
BELMONT CAVE
BAY SLOUGH
MARINA LAGOON
LAGOON
3RD AV
J ARTHUR YOUNGER FRWY
E HILLSDALE BLVD
FOSTER CITY BLVD
METRO CENTER BLVD
BEACH PARK BL
EDGEWATER BL
MARINER'S ISLAND BLVD
FASHION ISLAND BLVD
CIVIC CENTER
THE ISLAND SHOPPING CENTER
MARLIN COVE
HOLIDAY INN
RESIDENCE INN
REC CENTER
MARLIN PARK
KETCH PARK
1 STARBOARD DR
1 CORSAIR LN
2 CLIPPER LN

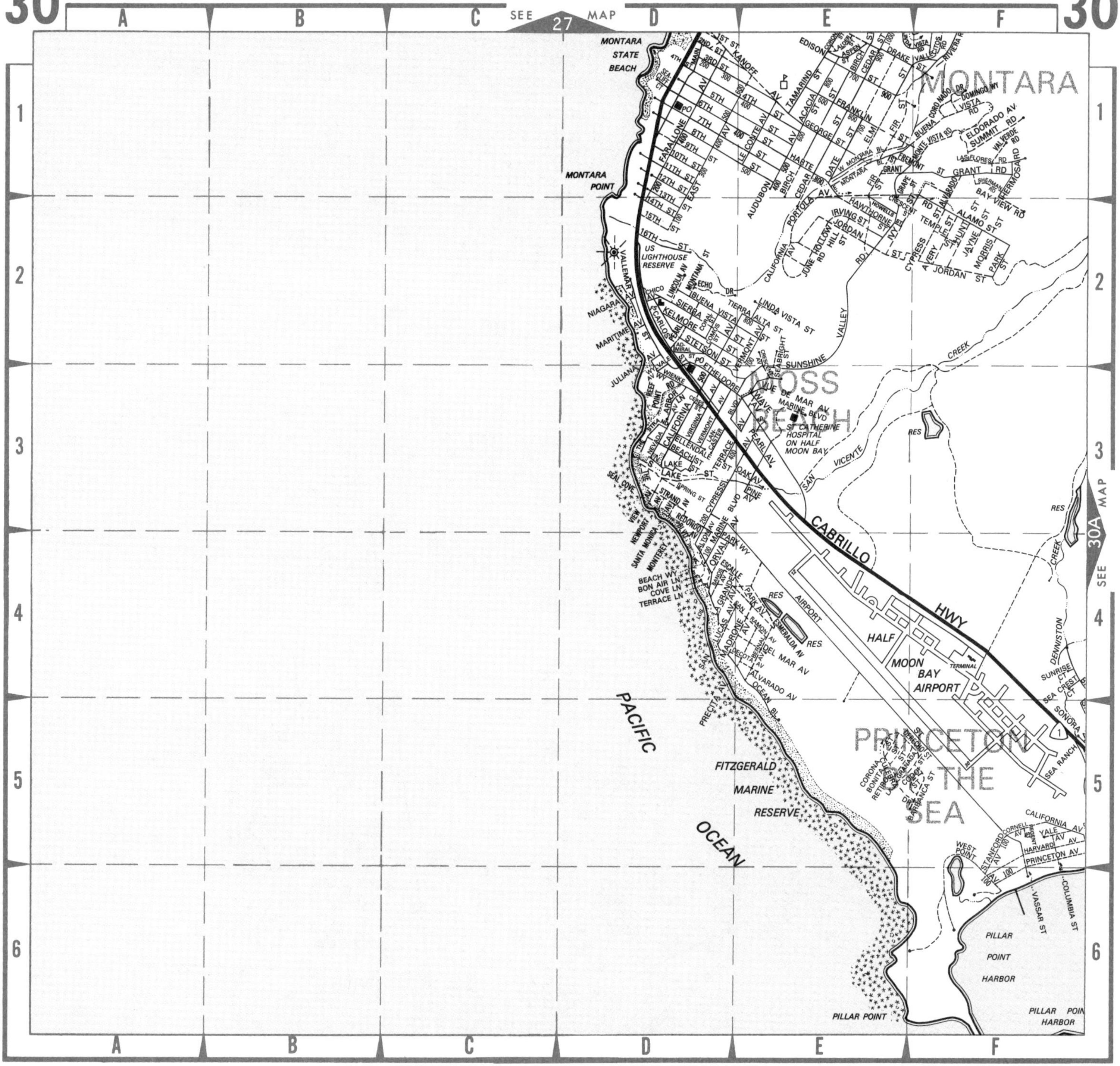

SEE MAP 27

SEE MAP 30A

MONTARA

MOSS BEACH

PRINCETON BY THE SEA

MONTARA STATE BEACH

MONTARA POINT

US LIGHTHOUSE RESERVE

ST CATHERINE HOSPITAL ON HALF MOON BAY

HALF MOON BAY AIRPORT

CABRILLO HWY

PACIFIC OCEAN

FITZGERALD MARINE RESERVE

PILLAR POINT

PILLAR POINT HARBOR

WEST POINT

SAN MATEO

DETAIL

COPYRIGHT © 1991 BY Thomas Bros. Maps

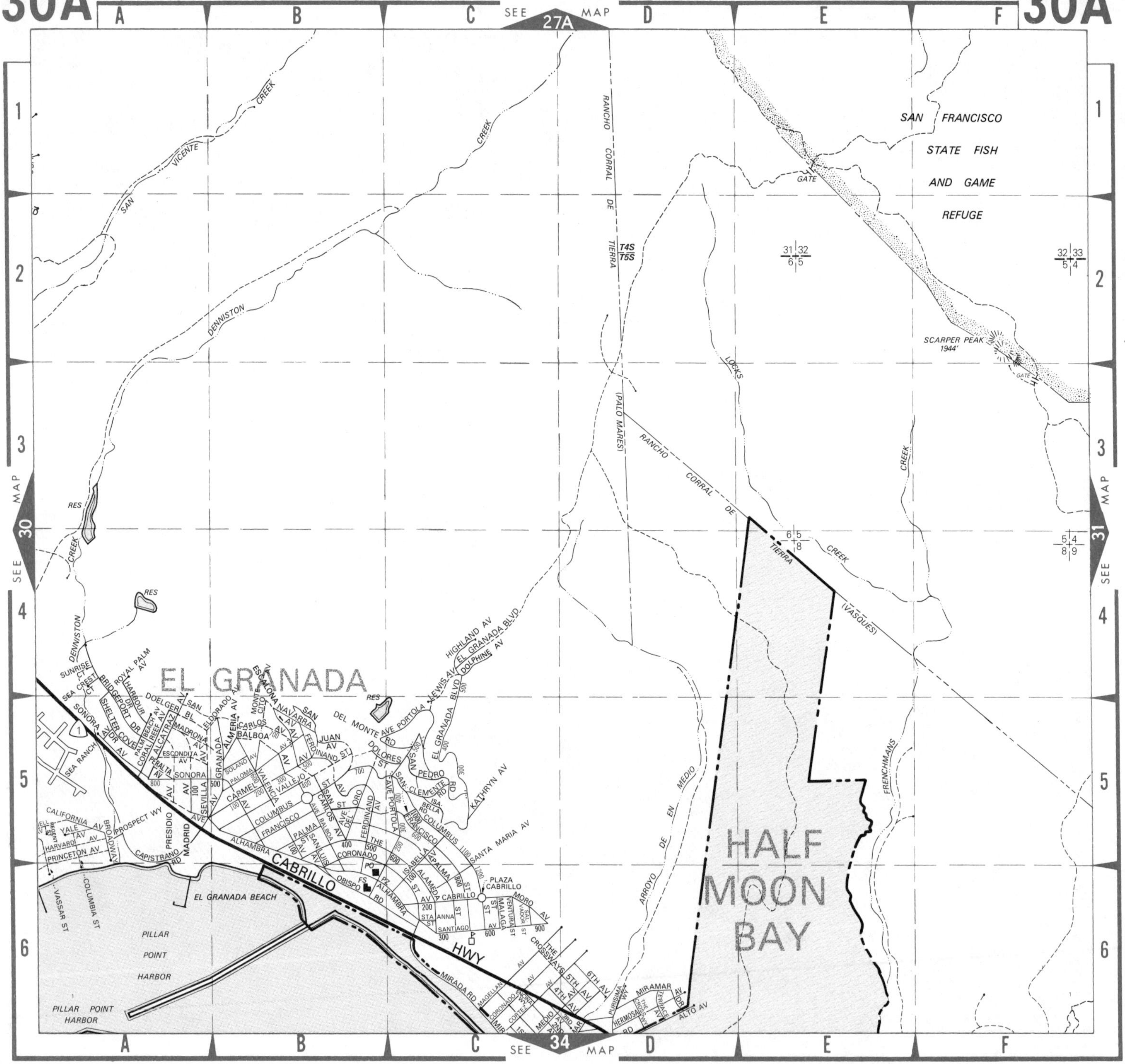

30A

SEE 27A MAP
SEE 30 MAP
SEE 31 MAP
SEE 34 MAP

COPYRIGHT © 1991 BY Thomas Bros. Maps

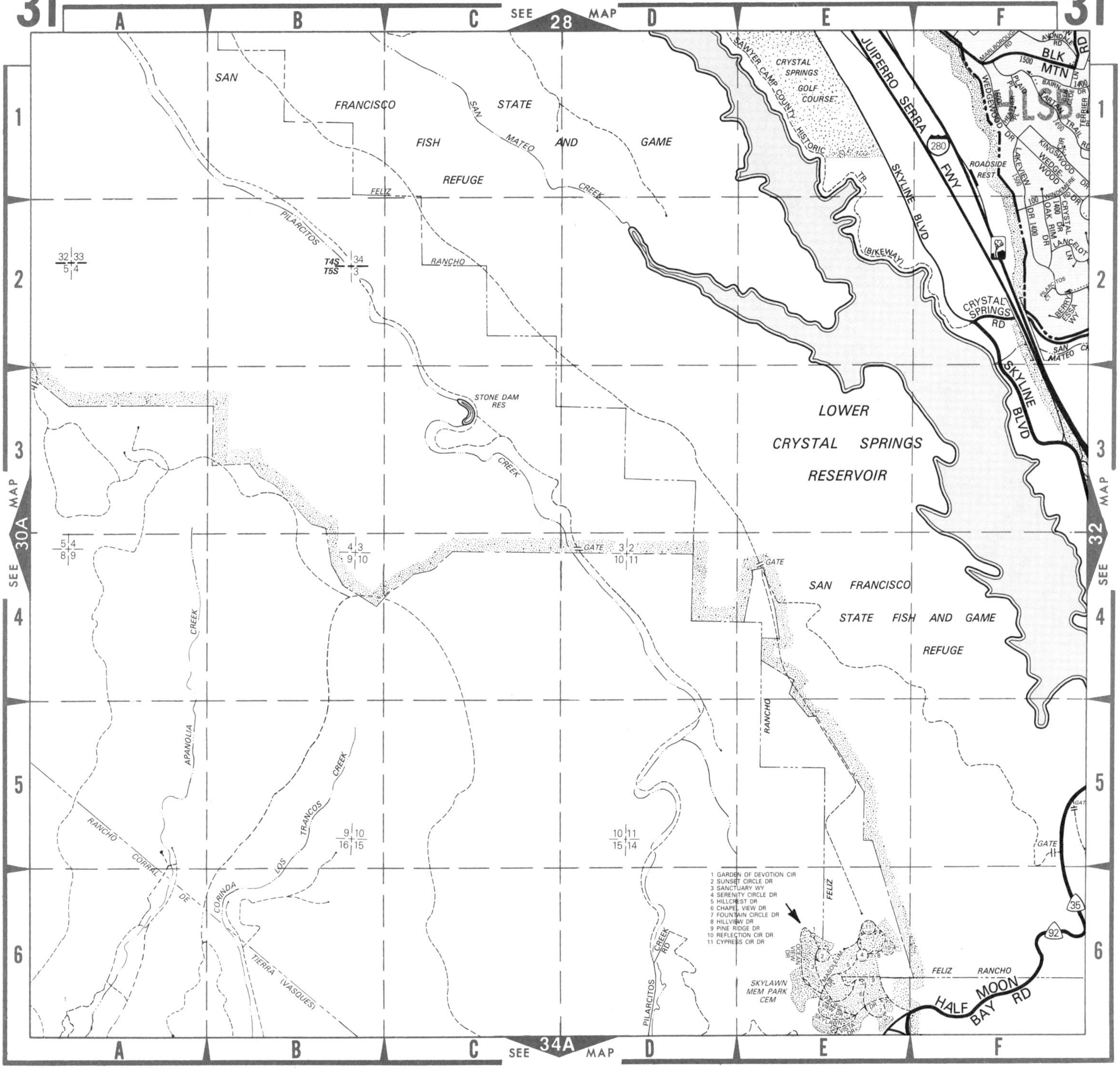

SEE 28 MAP

SAN FRANCISCO STATE FISH AND GAME REFUGE

SAN MATEO CREEK

PILARCITOS CREEK

STONE DAM RES

FELIZ

RANCHO

CRYSTAL SPRINGS GOLF COURSE

SAWYER CAMP COUNTY HISTORIC TR

(BIKEWAY)

JUIPERRO SERRA FWY

280

SKYLINE BLVD

ROADSIDE REST

CRYSTAL SPRINGS RD

HLSB

BLK MTN RD

LOWER CRYSTAL SPRINGS RESERVOIR

SAN FRANCISCO STATE FISH AND GAME REFUGE

GATE

APANOLIA CREEK

LOS TRANCOS CREEK

RANCHO CORRAL DE TIERRA (VASQUES)

CORINDA

PILARCITOS CREEK RD

FELIZ RANCHO

HALF MOON BAY RD

92

35

SKYLAWN MEM PARK CEM

OCEAN VIEW DR

1 GARDEN OF DEVOTION CIR
2 SUNSET CIRCLE DR
3 SANCTUARY WY
4 SERENITY CIRCLE DR
5 HILLCREST DR
6 CHAPEL VIEW DR
7 FOUNTAIN CIRCLE DR
8 HILLVIEW DR
9 PINE RIDGE DR
10 REFLECTION CIR DR
11 CYPRESS CIR DR

SAN MATEO

DETAIL

SEE 30A MAP

SEE 32 MAP

SEE 34A MAP

COPYRIGHT © 1991 BY Thomas Bros. Maps

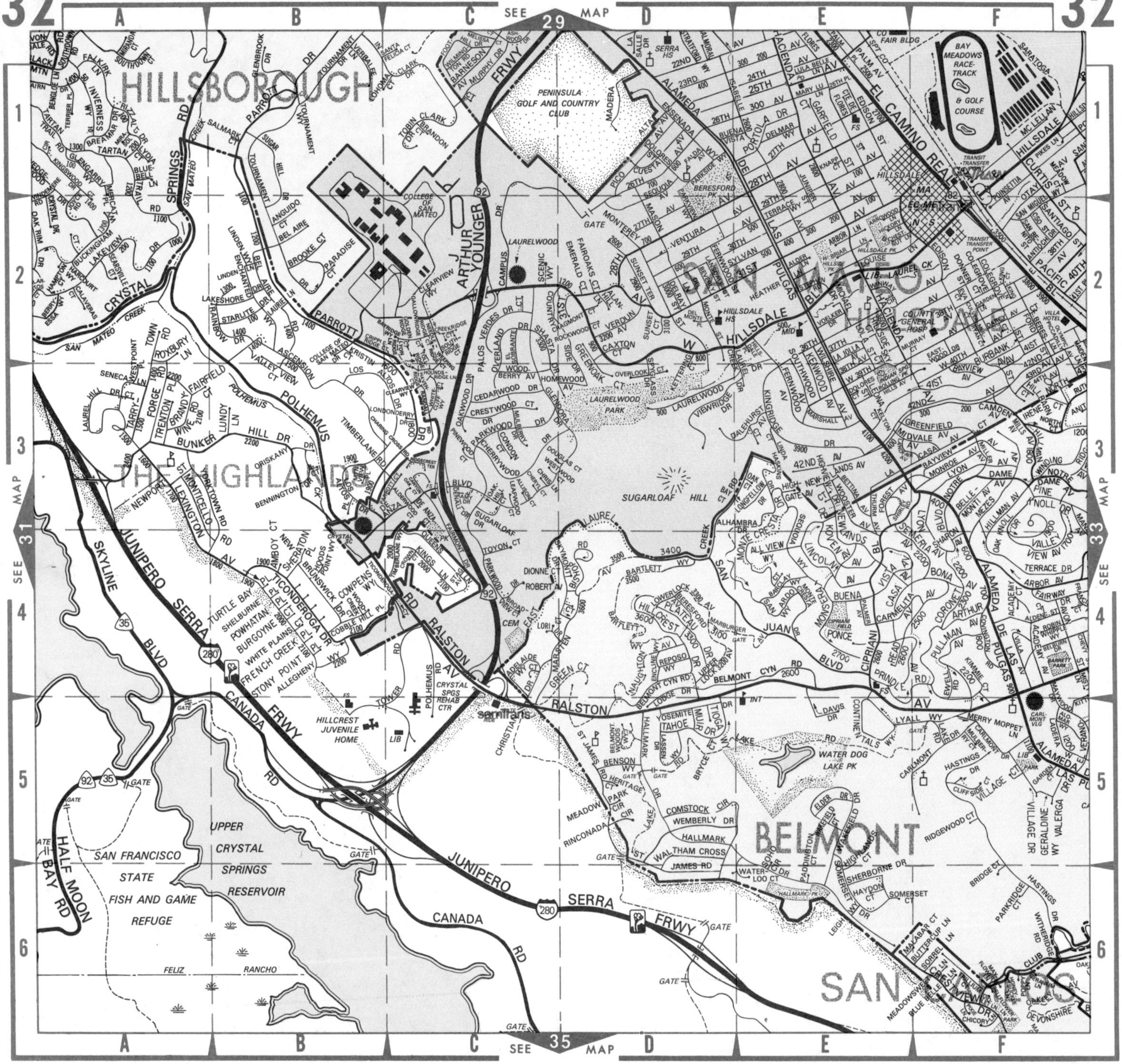

SEE 29 MAP

A B C D E F

1 2 3 4 5 6

HILLSBOROUGH

SAN MATEO

HILLSDALE

THE HIGHLANDS

BELMONT

SAN CARLOS

PENINSULA GOLF AND COUNTRY CLUB

BAY MEADOWS RACE-TRACK & GOLF COURSE

COLLEGE OF SAN MATEO

SUGARLOAF HILL

LAURELWOOD PARK

WATER DOG LAKE PK

UPPER CRYSTAL SPRINGS RESERVOIR

SAN FRANCISCO STATE FISH AND GAME REFUGE

HILLCREST JUVENILE HOME

CRYSTAL SPGS REHAB CTR

JUNIPERO SERRA FRWY

J ARTHUR YOUNGER FRWY

EL CAMINO REAL

ALAMEDA DE LAS PULGAS

RALSTON AV

HILLSDALE BL

POLHEMUS RD

CRYSTAL SPRINGS RD

SKYLINE BLVD

HALF MOON BAY RD

CANADA RD

FELIZ RANCHO

SEE 31 MAP

SEE 33 MAP

SEE 35 MAP

COPYRIGHT © 1991 BY Thomas Bros. Maps

DETAIL

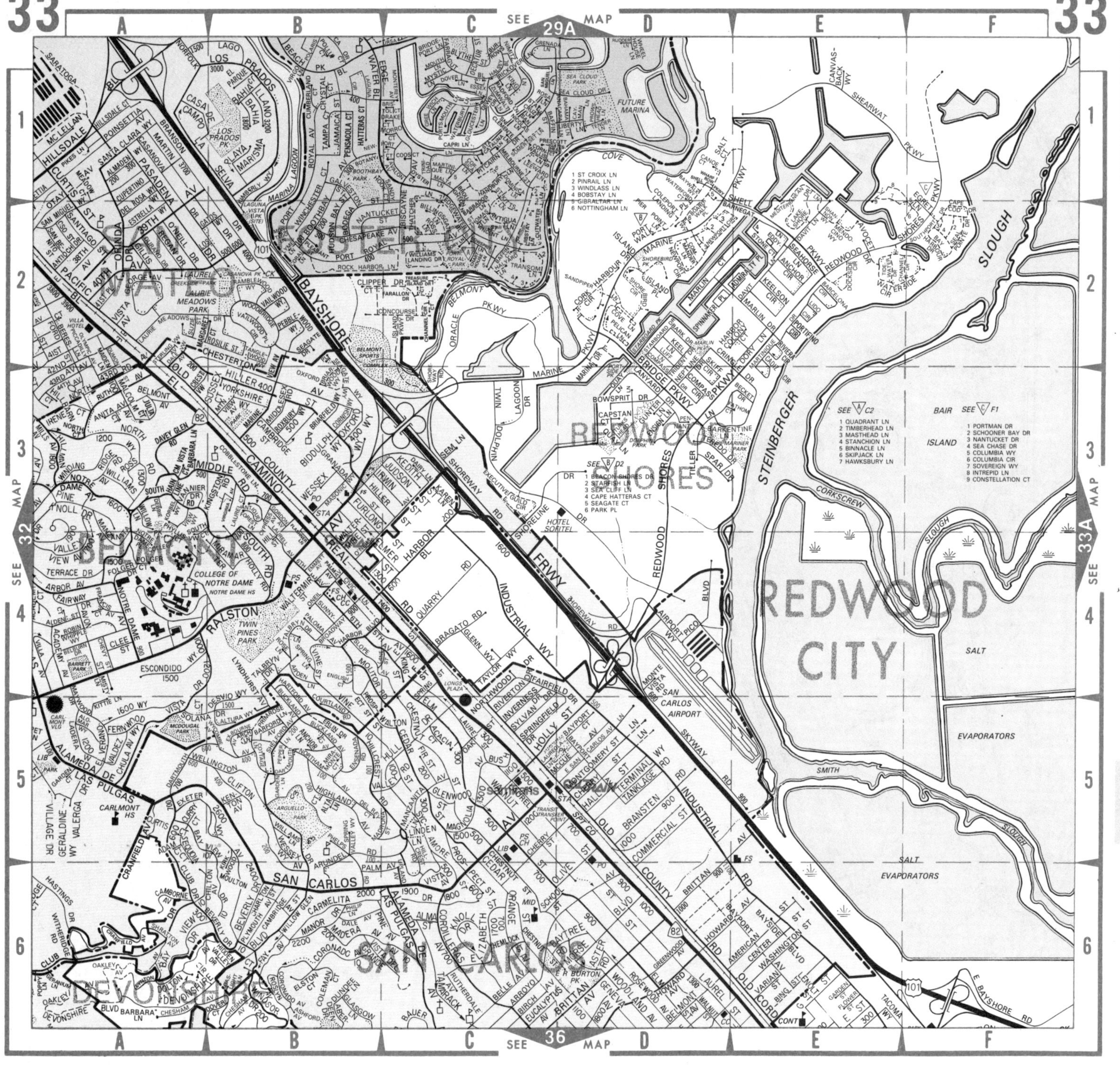
SEE MAP 29A
SEE MAP 32
SEE MAP 33A
SEE MAP 36
SAN MATEO
FOSTER CITY
BELMONT
REDWOOD SHORES
REDWOOD CITY
SAN CARLOS
DEVONSHIRE
BAYSHORE FRWY
EL CAMINO REAL
SAN CARLOS AIRPORT
COLLEGE OF NOTRE DAME
TWIN PINES PARK
LAURIE MEADOWS PARK
BELMONT SPORTS COMPLEX
HOTEL SOFITEL
CARLMONT HS
BAIR ISLAND
SALT EVAPORATORS
STEINBERGER SLOUGH
CORKSCREW SLOUGH
SMITH SLOUGH
FUTURE MARINA
1 ST CROIX LN
2 PINRAIL LN
3 WINDLASS LN
4 BOBSTAY LN
5 GIBRALTAR LN
6 NOTTINGHAM LN
SEE B D2
1 BEACON SHORES DR
2 STARFISH LN
3 SEA CLIFF LN
4 CAPE HATTERAS CT
5 SEAGATE CT
6 PARK PL
SEE A C2
1 QUADRANT LN
2 TIMBERHEAD LN
3 MASTHEAD LN
4 STANCHION LN
5 BINNACLE LN
6 SKIPJACK LN
7 HAWKSBURY LN
SEE C F1
1 PORTMAN DR
2 SCHOONER BAY DR
3 NANTUCKET DR
4 SEA CHASE DR
5 COLUMBIA WY
6 COLUMBIA CIR
7 SOVEREIGN WY
8 INTREPID LN
9 CONSTELLATION CT

SEE 33 MAP

SEE 37 MAP

34

A B C D E F

SEE 30A MAP

SEE 34A MAP

SEE 39 MAP

1 2 3 4 5 6

COPYRIGHT © 1991 BY Thomas Bros Maps

HARBOR

PILLAR POINT HARBOR

MIRAMAR BEACH

MIRAMAR

HALF MOON BAY

NAPLES BEACH

DUNES BEACH

VENICE BEACH

FRANCIS BEACH

PACIFIC OCEAN

HALF MOON BAY STATE BEACHES

HALF MOON BAY

MIRADA RD

MAGELLAN AV

CORONADO AV

CORTEZ AV

1ST AV

2ND AV

3RD AV

4TH AV

5TH AV

6TH AV

MEDIO AV

ALAMEDA AV

MIRAMAR DR

MIRADA RD

PURISIMA WY

MIRAMAR DR

HERMOSA AV

TERRACE AV

ALTO AV

SAN ANDREAS

VENTURA ST

VALENCIA ST

GUERRERO AV

SANTA ROSA AV

LONG ISLAND AV

NAPLES AV

BALBOA BLVD

ROOSEVELT BL

WASHINGTON BL

PULLMAN AV

CHAMPS ELYSEES

YOUNG AV

AVIGNON PL

LE BLANC CT

TOURAINE LN

TOULOUSE CT

BORDEAUX LN

LE MANS WY

MARSEILLE PL

FRANCAIS AV

RUISSEAU

FRENCHMANS CREEK COM PK

FRENCHMANS CREEK RD

FRENCHMANS CREEK

CABRILLO HWY

VENICE BLVD

WAVE AV

BEACH AV

CASA DEL MAR DR

JUDITH CT

MARIE ST

ANTOINETTE LN

ST JOSEPH AV

ST JOHN AV

PILARCITOS AV

KEHOE AV

LORYN LN

HAWSER LN

MIZZEN LN

SPINNAKER LN

BRIG CT

BARK CT

TILLER CT

KEEL CT

SPINDRIFT

VENDOME AV

CHANNING BL

BELVEDERE AV

GOLDEN GATE AV

BANCROFT AV

DWIGHT AV

GRANDVIEW BL

PACIFIC AV

TERRACE AV

SILVER AV

HIGHLAND AV

QUARTZ ST

RALSTON AV

CHESTERFIELD AV

ST JAMES ST

GRAND BL

BELLEVILLE BL

PILARCITOS CREEK

ALSTON

MAIN ST

LEWIS

FOSTER

HALF MOON BAY HS

CATHOLIC CEM

CEM

HALF MOON BAY RD (SAN MATEO RD)

PO

PARK AV

PINE AV

OAK AV

CYPRESS AV

WILLOW AV

LAUREL AV

PINE AV

CHURCH ST

PURISIMA ST

MILL ST

KELLY AV

PS

SAN BENITO ST

MIRAMONTES AV

INT

FS

CC

CORREAS ST

BALBOA BLVD

OCEAN AV

POTTER AV

LORAINE AV

ALSACE AV

VALDEZ

GARCIA

AV CENTRAL

GRANELLI AV

AMESPORT LANDING

LIB

MYRTLE ST

FILBERT ST

RAILROAD AV

1ST AV

SPRUCE ST

POPLAR ST

2ND AV

3RD AV

4TH AV

METZGAR ST

GROVE ST

MAGNOLIA ST

JOHNSTON ST

PABLO

CARROYO

VASQUES

MONTE VISTA LN

BLOOM LN

ARNOLD WY

SUZANNE CT

RIDGWAY

DONALD CT

COLONEL WY

ARROYO LEON CREEK

SEYMOUR ST

ARLETA WY

MAIN ST

HIGGINS PURISIMA RD

WAVECREST RD

1

92

1

300 400 500 600 700 800 1000 1200 200

A B C D E F

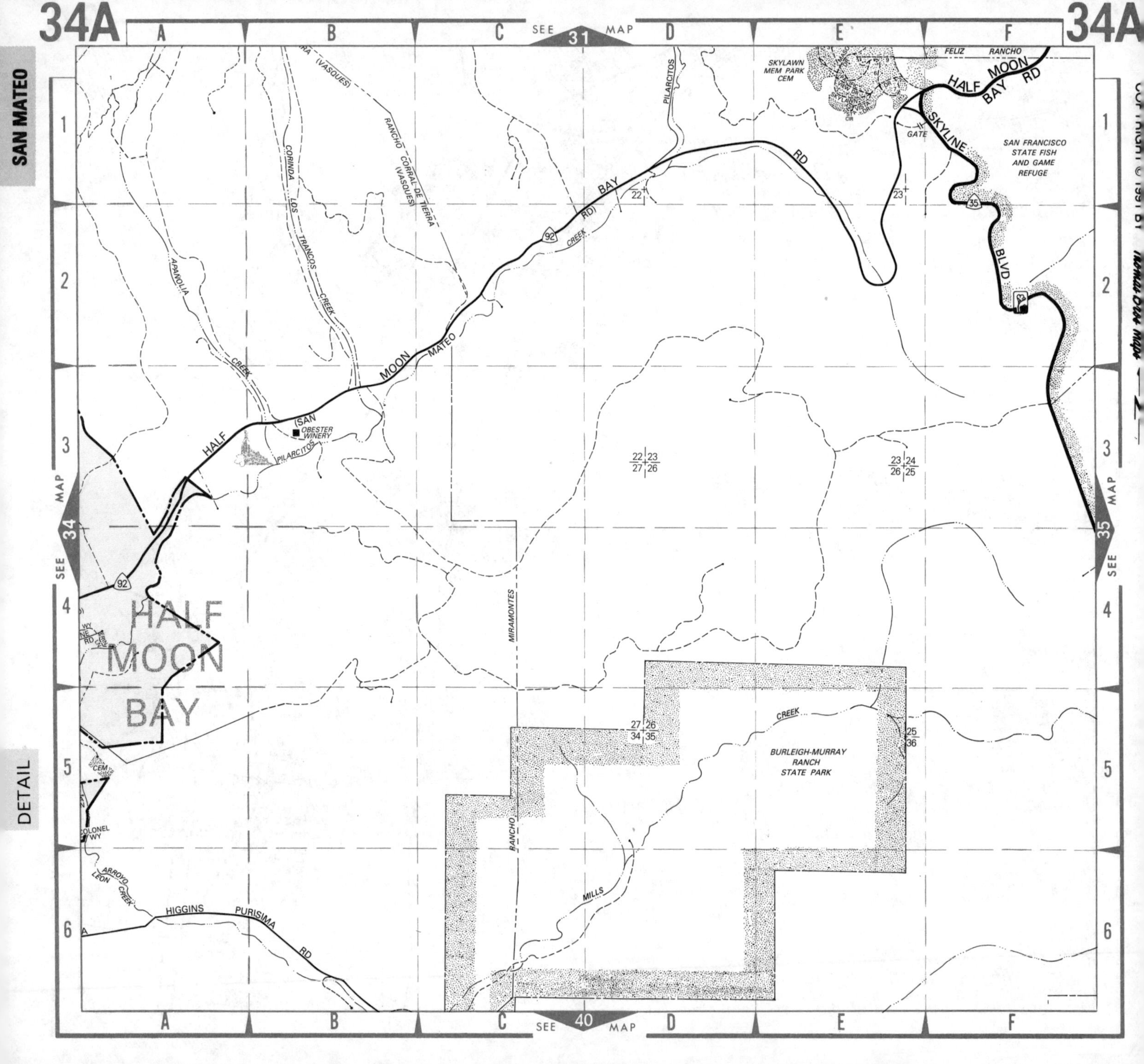
SEE MAP 31
SEE MAP 34
SEE MAP 35
SEE MAP 40
HALF MOON BAY RD
SKYLINE BLVD
SKYLAWN MEM PARK CEM
FELIZ RANCHO
GATE
SAN FRANCISCO STATE FISH AND GAME REFUGE
PILARCITOS
RD
BAY
RD)
CREEK
HALF MOON (SAN MATEO
OBESTER WINERY
PILARCITOS
APANOLIA CREEK
CORINDA LOS TRANCOS CREEK
RANCHO CORRAL DE TIERRA (VASQUES)
(VASQUES)
MIRAMONTES
HALF MOON BAY
BURLEIGH-MURRAY RANCH STATE PARK
CREEK
RANCHO
MILLS
CEM
COLONEL WY
ARROYO LEON CREEK
HIGGINS PURISIMA RD

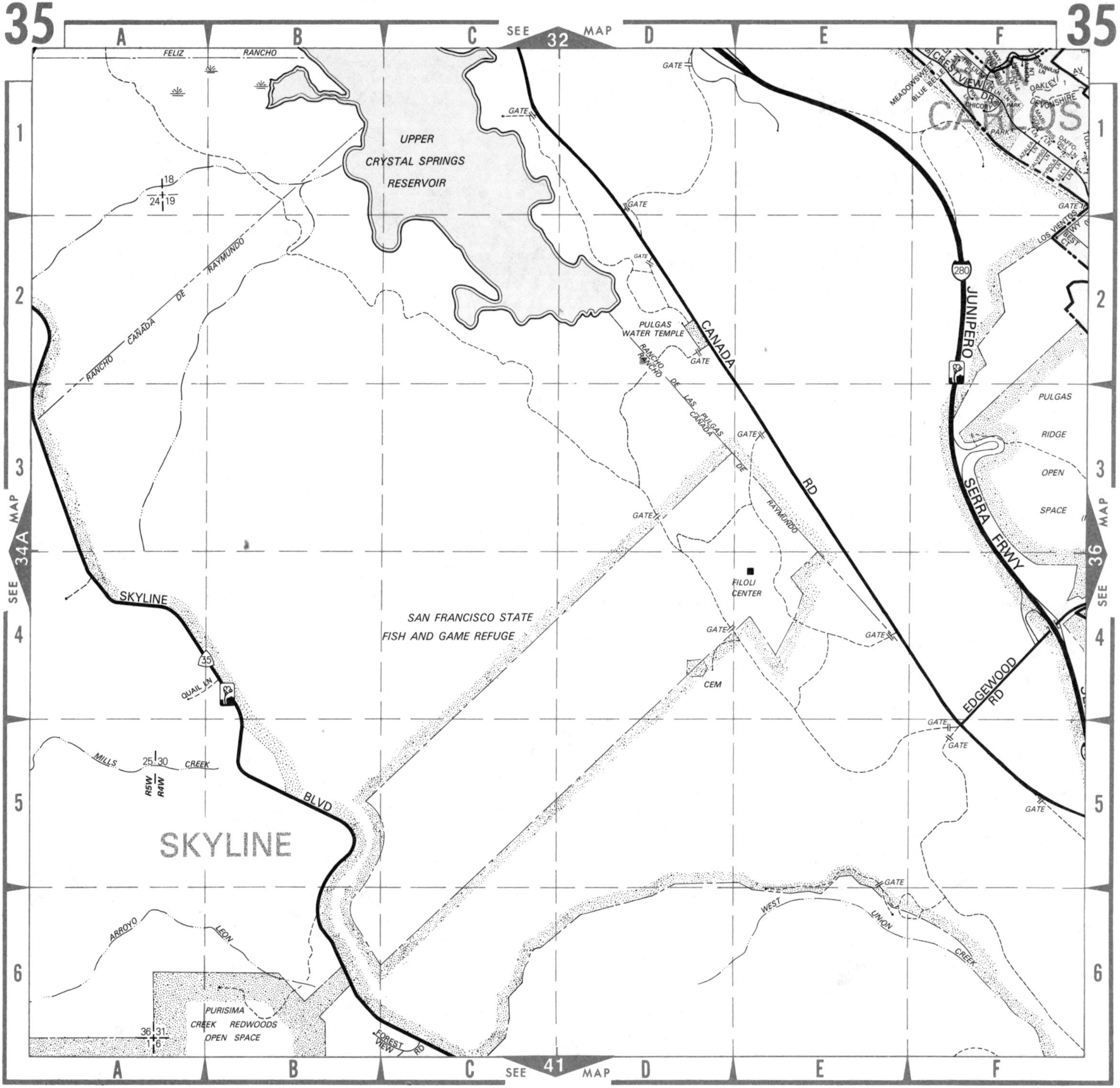

SEE 32 MAP

SEE 34A MAP

SEE 36 MAP

SEE 41 MAP

COPYRIGHT © 1991 BY Thomas Bros. Maps

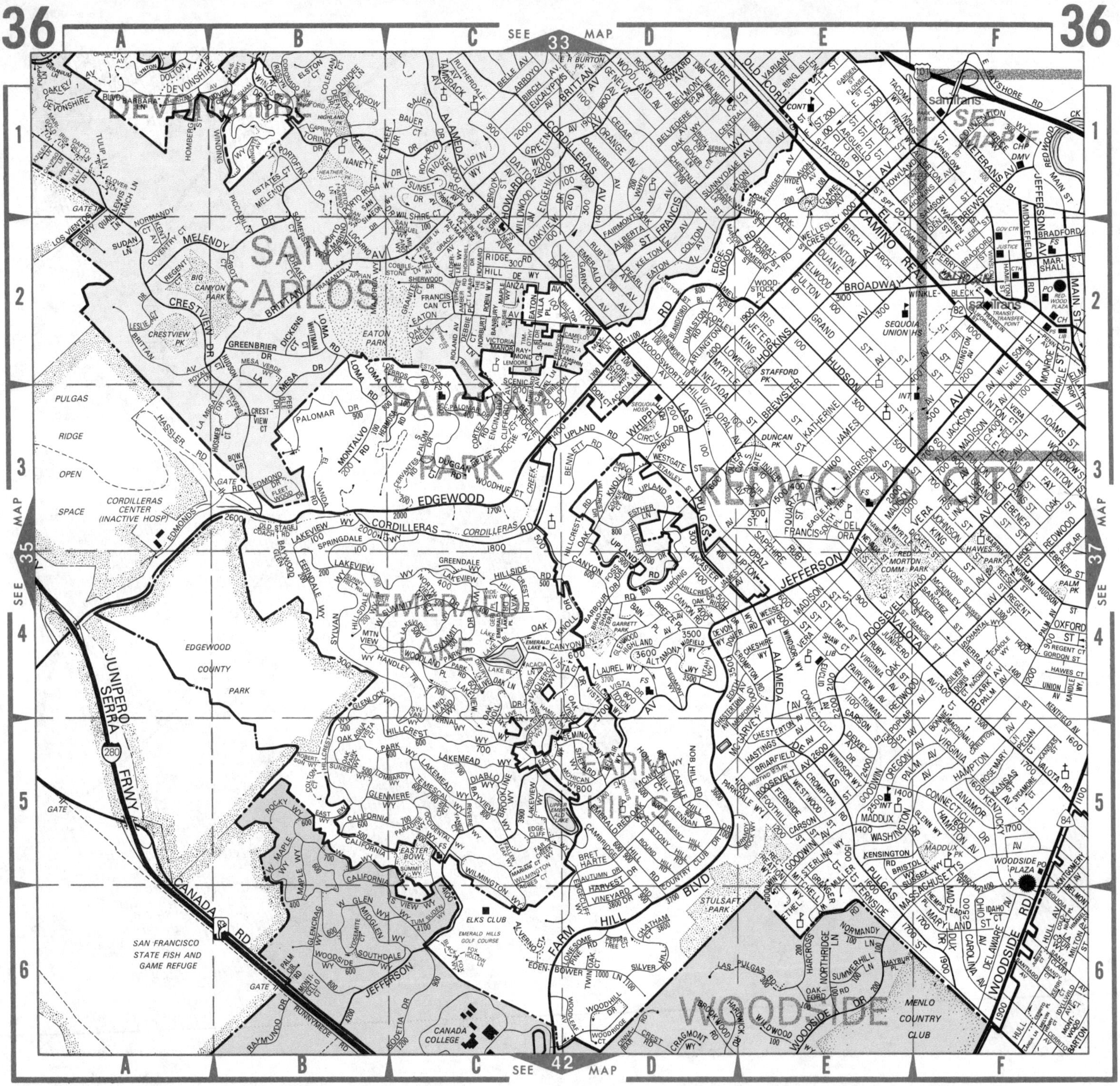
SEE MAP 33
SEE MAP 35
SEE MAP 37
SEE MAP 42
SAN CARLOS
DEVONSHIRE
REDWOOD CITY
PALOMAR PARK
EMERALD LAKE
FARM HILLS
WOODSIDE
EDGEWOOD COUNTY PARK
PULGAS RIDGE OPEN SPACE
CORDILLERAS CENTER (INACTIVE HOSP)
SAN FRANCISCO STATE FISH AND GAME REFUGE
CANADA COLLEGE
MENLO COUNTRY CLUB
EMERALD HILLS GOLF COURSE
ELKS CLUB
STULSAFT PARK
SEQUOIA UNION HS
WOODSIDE PLAZA
JUNIPERO SERRA FRWY
CANADA RD
EDGEWOOD RD
FARM HILL BLVD
EL CAMINO REAL
ALAMEDA DE LAS PULGAS
WOODSIDE RD
JEFFERSON AV
BROADWAY
CRESTVIEW DR
BAYSHORE RD
SEE MAP F
samTrans
A B C D E F
1 2 3 4 5 6

COPYRIGHT © 1991 BY Thomas Bros Maps

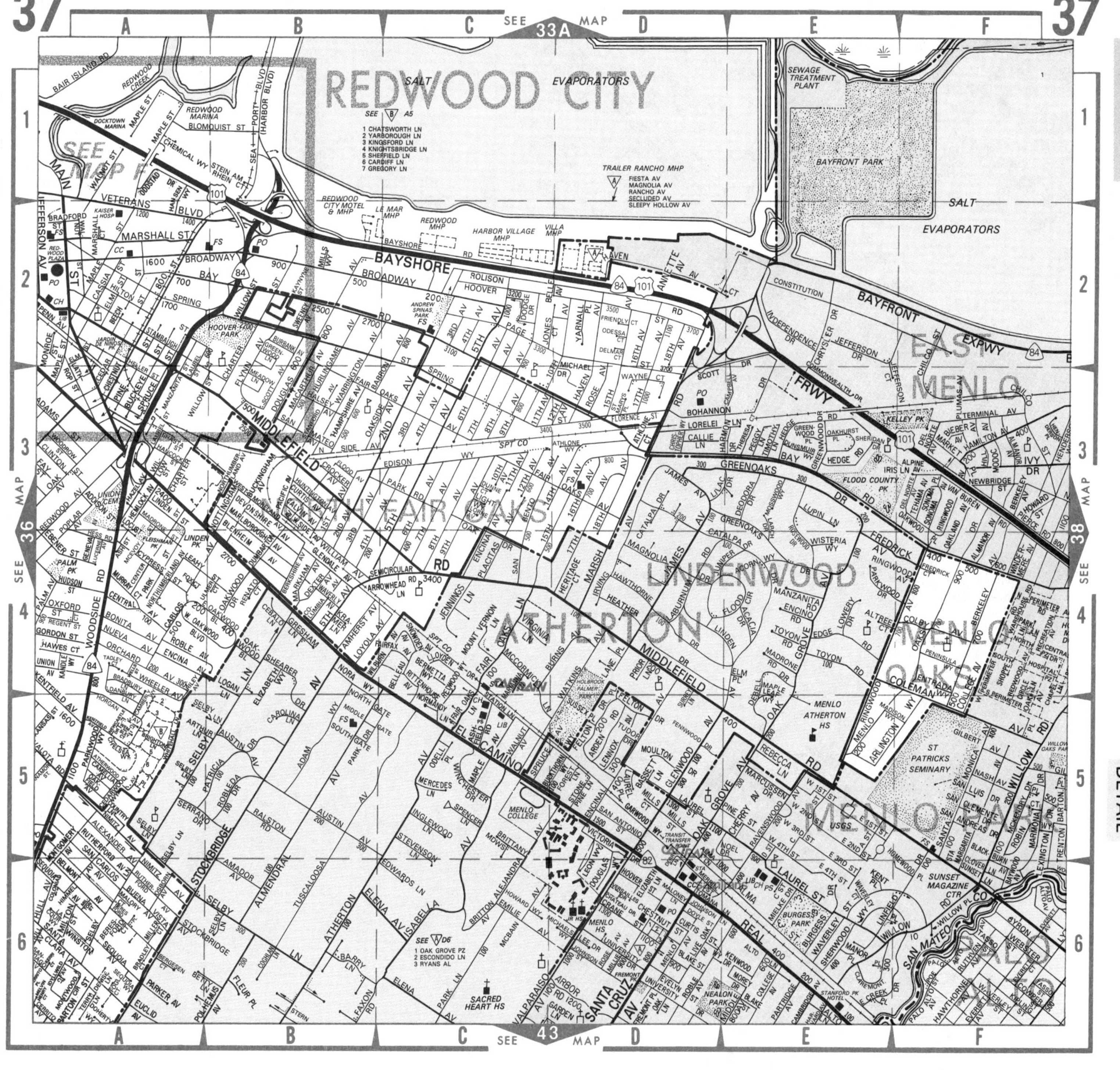
SEE MAP 33A
SEE MAP 36
SEE MAP 38
SEE MAP 43
SAN MATEO
DETAIL
REDWOOD CITY
SALT EVAPORATORS
SEWAGE TREATMENT PLANT
BAYFRONT PARK
SEE MAP F
SEE B A5
1 CHATSWORTH LN
2 YARBOROUGH LN
3 KINGSFORD LN
4 KNIGHTSBRIDGE LN
5 SHEFFIELD LN
6 CARDIFF LN
7 GREGORY LN
TRAILER RANCHO MHP
FIESTA AV
MAGNOLIA AV
RANCHO AV
SECLUDED AV
SLEEPY HOLLOW AV
REDWOOD CITY MOTEL & MHP
LE MAR MHP
REDWOOD MHP
HARBOR VILLAGE MHP
VILLA MHP
REDWOOD MARINA
DOCKTOWN MARINA
BAIR ISLAND RD
REDWOOD CREEK
VETERANS BLVD
MARSHALL ST
BROADWAY
BAYSHORE RD
BAYFRONT EXPWY
EAST MENLO
HOOVER PARK
NORTH FAIR OAKS
LINDENWOOD
ATHERTON
MIDDLEFIELD RD
EL CAMINO REAL
FLOOD COUNTY PK
MENLO OAKS
MENLO ATHERTON HS
ST PATRICKS SEMINARY
MENLO PARK
MENLO COLLEGE
SUNSET MAGAZINE CTR
BURGESS PARK
NEALON PARK
STANFORD PK HOTEL
SACRED HEART HS
HOLBROOK PALMER PARK
PALO ALTO
SEE A D6
1 OAK GROVE PZ
2 ESCONDIDO LN
3 RYANS AL
SANTA CRUZ AV
SAN MATEO DR
WOODSIDE RD
STOCKBRIDGE
ALAMEDA DE LAS PULGAS
SELBY LN
ATHERTON AV
ELENA AV
VALPARAISO AV
UNIVERSITY
WILLOW RD
RINGWOOD AV
GREENOAKS DR
FREDRICK AV
SPT CO

SEE 105AL MAP

SALT EVAPORATORS

SAN FRANCISCO BAY NATIONAL WILDLIFE REFUGE

RAVENSWOOD SLOUGH

TO DUMBARTON BRIDGE (TOLL $1.00 WEST ONLY)

RAVENSWOOD OPEN SPACE PRESERVE

SAN FRANCISCO BAY NATIONAL WILDLIFE REFUGE

ALAMEDA CO
SAN MATEO CO

SALT EVAPORATORS

SAN FRANCISCO BAY

BAYFRONT EXPWY

UNIVERSITY AV

RAVENSWOOD OPEN SPACE PRESERVE

MENLO PARK

EAST MENLO

COOLEY LANDING

EAST PALO ALTO

SAN MATEO CO
SANTA CLARA CO

SAND POINT

SAN FRANCISQUITO CREEK

PALO ALTO AIRPORT

BAYLANDS NATURE INTERPRETIVE CENTER

BOAT LAUNCH

HOOKS POINT

PALO ALTO YACHT HARBOR

PALO ALTO MUNICIPAL GOLF COURSE

BYXBEE REC AREA

BAYLANDS ATHLETIC CENTER

BAYSHORE FRWY

WILLOW RD

MIDDLEFIELD RD

EMBARCADERO RD

PALO ALTO

SEE 37 MAP

SEE 38ASC MAP

SEE 44SC MAP

SEE MAP 34
SEE MAP 40

COPYRIGHT © 1991 BY Thomas Bros. Maps

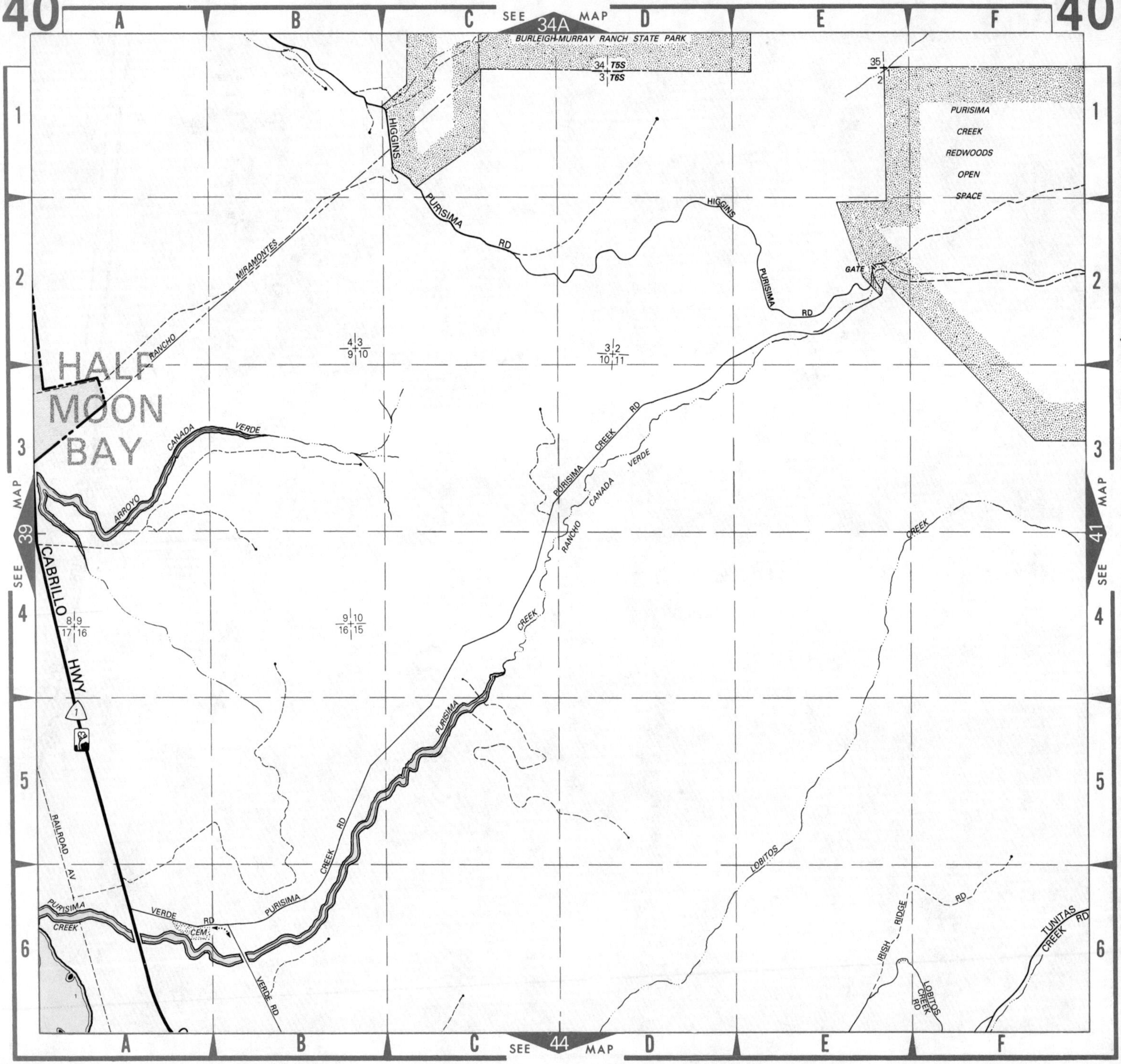

SEE 34A MAP

SEE 39 MAP
SEE 41 MAP
SEE 44 MAP

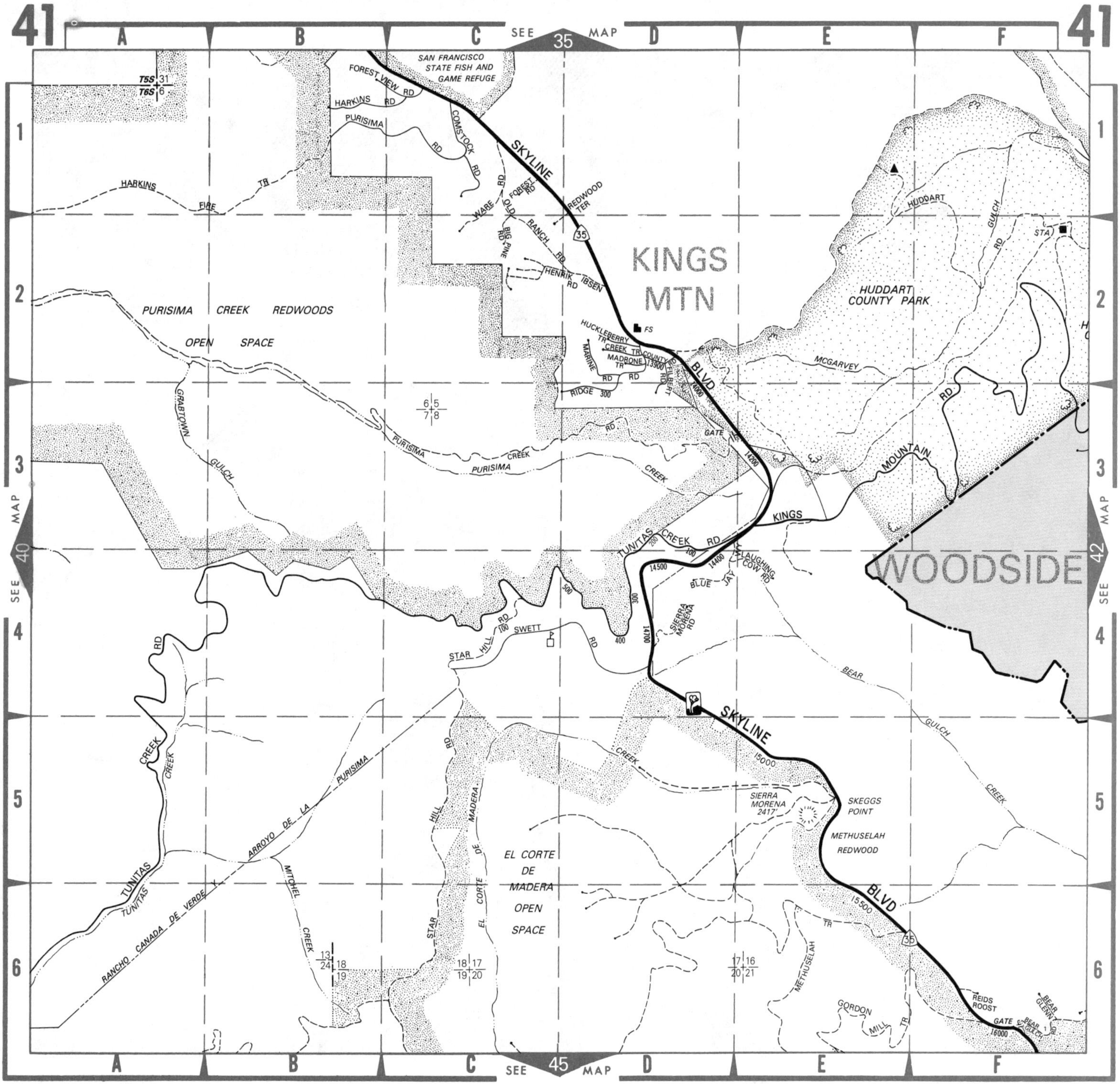
SEE MAP 35
KINGS MTN
WOODSIDE
PURISIMA CREEK REDWOODS OPEN SPACE
HUDDART COUNTY PARK
SAN FRANCISCO STATE FISH AND GAME REFUGE
EL CORTE DE MADERA OPEN SPACE
SKYLINE BLVD
KINGS MOUNTAIN RD
TUNITAS CREEK RD
SKEGGS POINT
METHUSELAH REDWOOD
SIERRA MORENA 2417'
SEE MAP 40
SEE MAP 42
SEE MAP 45

COPYRIGHT © 1991 BY Thomas Bros Maps

SAN MATEO

DETAIL

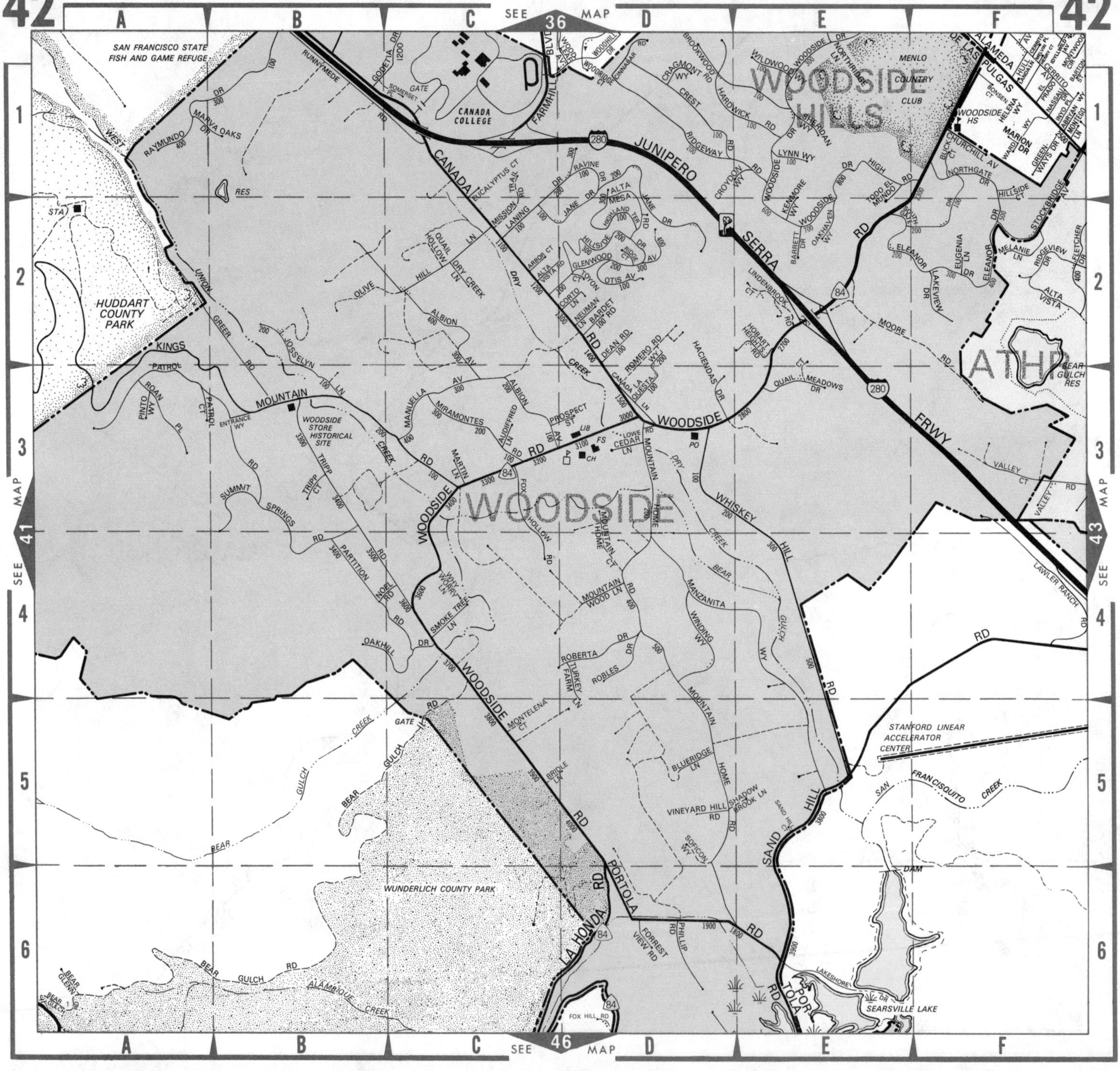

SEE MAP 41

SEE MAP 43

COPYRIGHT © 1991 BY Thomas Bros Maps

SAN FRANCISCO STATE FISH AND GAME REFUGE
HUDDART COUNTY PARK
CANADA COLLEGE
WOODSIDE HILLS
MENLO COUNTRY CLUB
WOODSIDE HS
WOODSIDE
WOODSIDE STORE HISTORICAL SITE
ATHR
BEAR GULCH RES
STANFORD LINEAR ACCELERATOR CENTER
WUNDERLICH COUNTY PARK
SEARSVILLE LAKE
DAM
SAN FRANCISQUITO CREEK

JUNIPERO SERRA FRWY 280
CANADA RD
WOODSIDE RD 84
KINGS MOUNTAIN RD
LA HONDA RD
PORTOLA RD
SAND HILL RD
WHISKEY HILL RD
MOUNTAIN HOME RD
ALAMEDA DE LAS PULGAS
FARMHILL BLVD
UNION
GREER RD
JOSSELYN LN
ALBION AV
MANUELLA AV
MIRAMONTES
AUDIFFRED RD
PROSPECT ST
TRIPP RD
TRIPP CT
PARTITION RD
NOEL DR
SUMMIT SPRINGS RD
PATROL RD
PATROL CT
PINTO WY
ROAN PL
ENTRANCE WY
RAYMUNDO DR
MARVA OAKS DR
WEST UNION
RUNNYMEDE RD
GODETIA DR
SOMERSET PL
EUCALYPTUS CT
MISSION TRAIL CT
LANING DR
QUAIL HOLLOW
DRY CREEK LN
HILL LN
OLIVE
ALTA MESA RD
JANE DR
RAVINE DR
HIGHLAND TER
HILLSIDE DR
GLENWOOD AV
RIDGE CT
OTIS AV
ARBOR CT
ALTA VISTA RD
TOYON
CORTO LN
NEUMAN LN
BARDET RD
DEAN RD
ROMERO RD
LA QUESTA WY
HACIENDAS DR
HOBART HEIGHTS RD
QUAIL MEADOWS DR
MOORE RD
LOWE CEDAR LN
FOX HOLLOW RD
MOUNTAIN HOME CT
MOUNTAIN WOOD LN
WHY WORRY LN
SMOKE TREE LN
OAKHILL DR
MANZANITA
WINDING WY
BEAR GULCH WY
ROBERTA DR
ROBLES DR
TURKEY FARM LN
MONTELENA CT
BRIDLE LN
BLUERIDGE LN
VINEYARD HILL RD
SHADOW BROOK LN
SOFICON WY
FORREST VIEW RD
PHILLIP RD
LAKESHORE DR
FOX HILL RD
BEAR GULCH RD
ALAMBIQUE CREEK
LAWLER RANCH RD
VALLEY CT
VALLEY RD
CRAGMONT WY
BROOKWOOD RD
WILDWOOD WY
NORTHRIDGE LN
SHERIDAN WY
HARDWICK RD
CREST RD
RIDGEWAY RD
CROYDON WY
LYNN WY
KENMORE WY
WOODSIDE DR
OAKHAVEN WY
BARRETT DR
HIGH RD
TODO EL MUNDO
SOUTHGATE
NORTHGATE DR
CHURCHILL AV
HILLSIDE CT
STOCKBRIDGE AV
ELEANOR DR
EUGENIA LN
LAKEVIEW DR
MELANIE LN
RIDGEVIEW DR
FLETCHER DR
ALTA VISTA
LINDENBROOK RD
HELENA WY
MARION DR
GREEN WAYS DR
WOODHILL DR
WOODRIDGE CT
CINNABAR RD

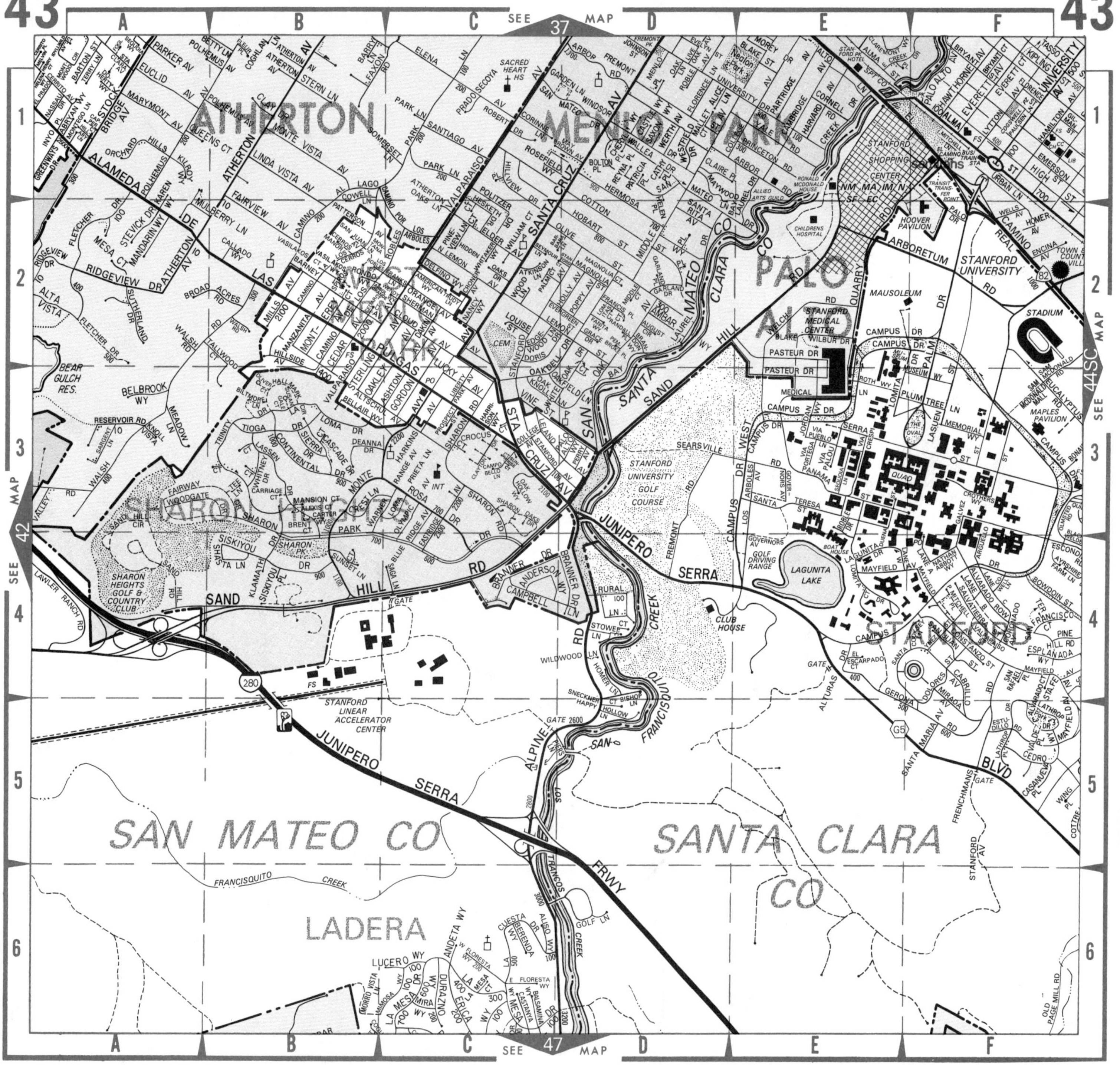

SEE 37 MAP

COPYRIGHT © 1991 BY Thomas Bros. Maps

SEE 42 MAP

SEE 44SC MAP

ATHERTON

MENLO PARK

WEST MENLO PARK

PALO ALTO

SHARON HEIGHTS

STANFORD

STANFORD UNIVERSITY

STANFORD SHOPPING CENTER

STANFORD MEDICAL CENTER

STANFORD UNIVERSITY GOLF COURSE

STANFORD LINEAR ACCELERATOR CENTER

SHARON HEIGHTS GOLF & COUNTRY CLUB

SACRED HEART HS

CHILDRENS HOSPITAL

RONALD MCDONALD HOUSE

ALLIED ARTS GUILD

HOOVER PAVILION

MAPLES PAVILION

STADIUM

MAUSOLEUM

QUAD

THE OVAL

LAGUNITA LAKE

BOAT HOUSE

GOLF DRIVING RANGE

CLUB HOUSE

BEAR GULCH RES.

CEM

TOWN & COUNTRY VILLAGE

SAN MATEO CO

SANTA CLARA CO

LADERA

JUNIPERO SERRA FRWY

SAND HILL RD

ALAMEDA DE LAS PULGAS

SANTA CRUZ AV

EL CAMINO REAL

ALPINE RD

SAN FRANCISQUITO CREEK

LOS TRANCOS CREEK

CAMPUS DR

ARBORETUM RD

SEE 47 MAP

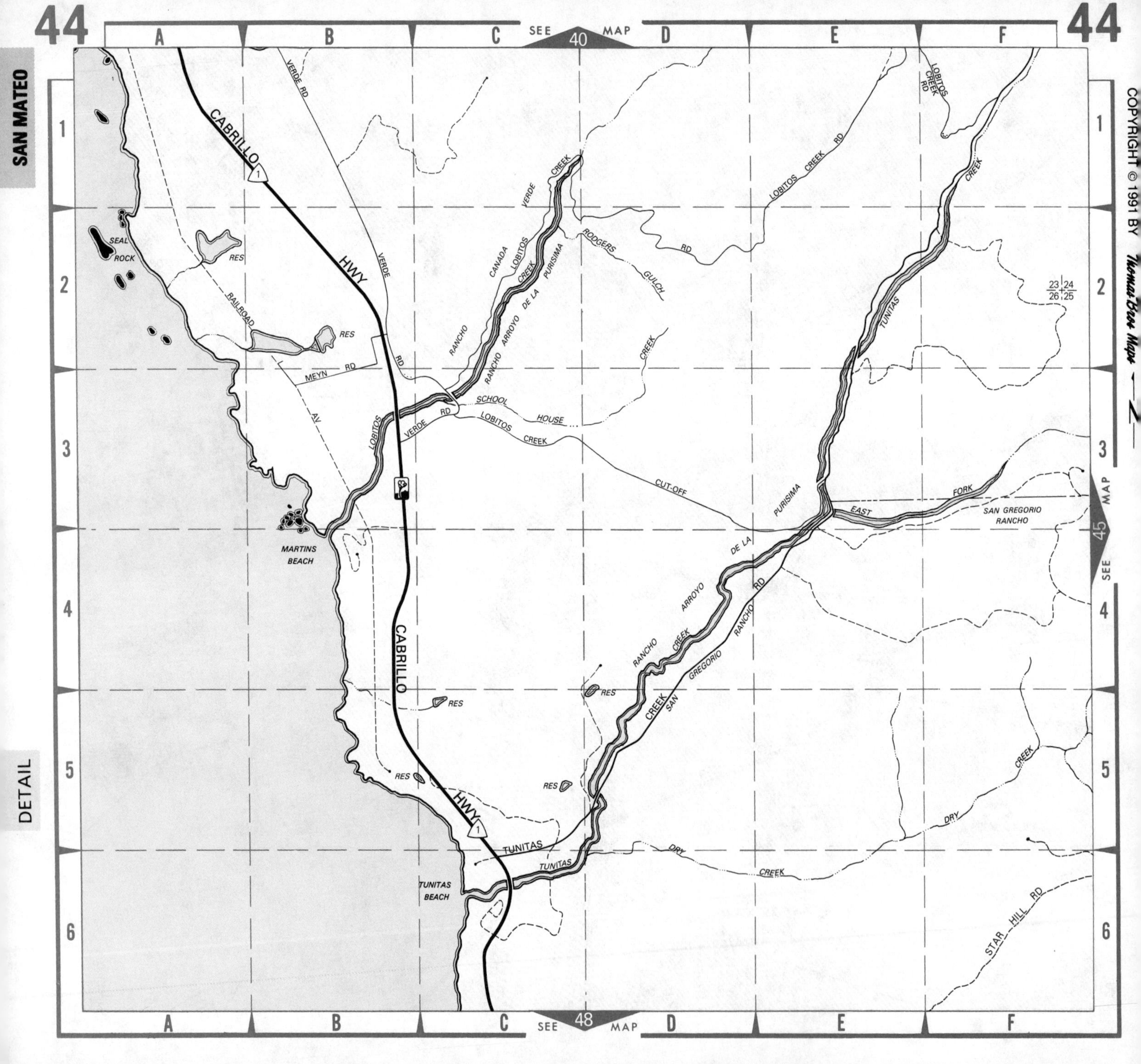

COPYRIGHT © 1991 BY Thomas Bros Maps

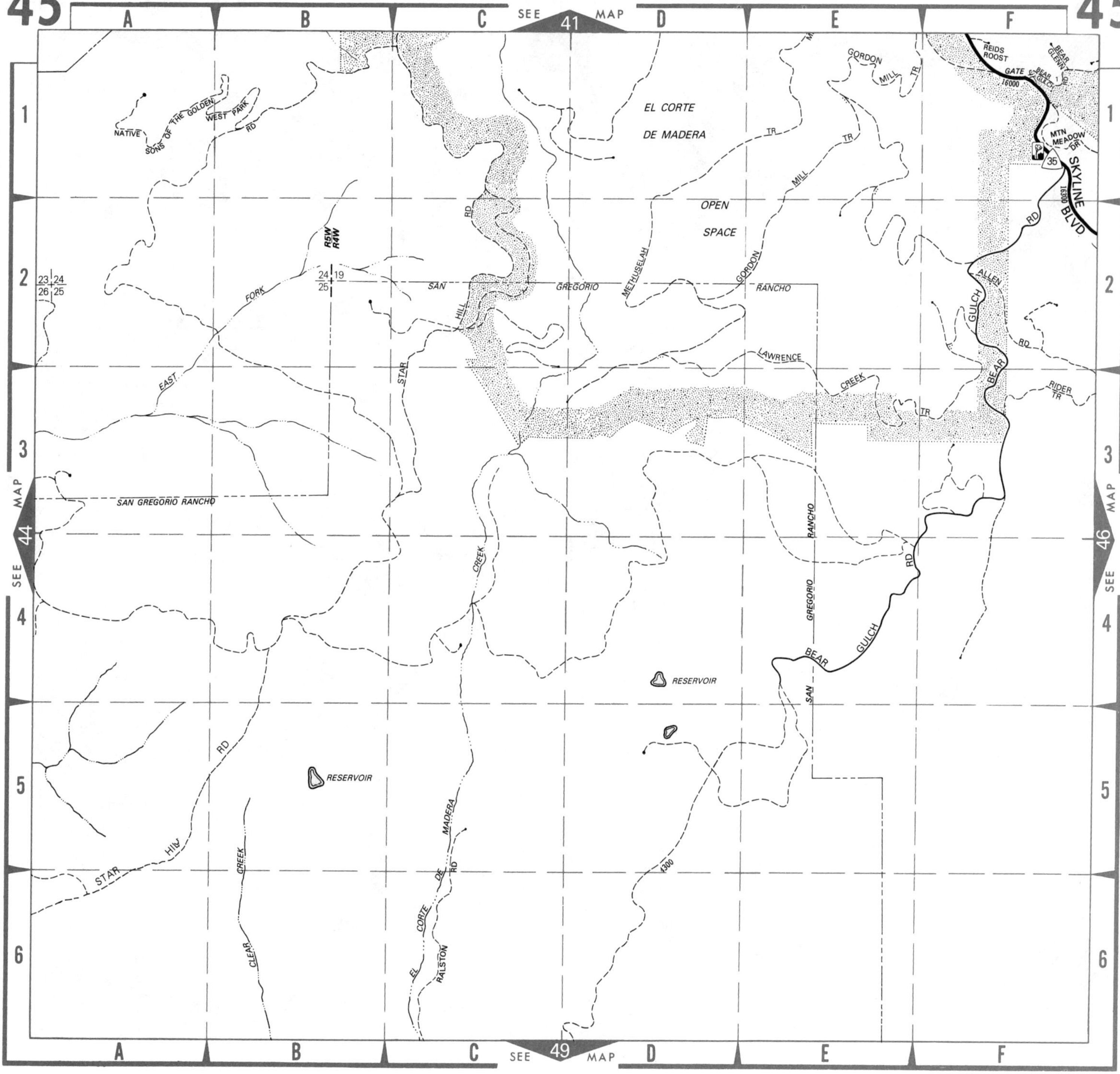
SEE MAP 41
SEE MAP 44
SEE MAP 46
SEE MAP 49
A B C D E F
1 2 3 4 5 6
NATIVE SONS OF THE GOLDEN WEST PARK RD
EL CORTE DE MADERA OPEN SPACE
GORDON MILL TR
REIDS ROOST
GATE
BEAR GULCH
BEAR GLENN RD
16000
MTN MEADOW DR
35
SKYLINE BLVD
16300
RD
R5W R4W
23 24 26 25
24 19 25
EAST FORK
SAN GREGORIO RANCHO
STAR HILL RD
METHUSELAH
GORDON
ALLEN RD
GULCH
BEAR
LAWRENCE CREEK TR
RIDER TR
CREEK
RESERVOIR
BEAR GULCH RD
SAN GREGORIO RANCHO
RESERVOIR
STAR HILL RD
CLEAR CREEK
EL CORTE DE MADERA CREEK
RALSTON RD
1300

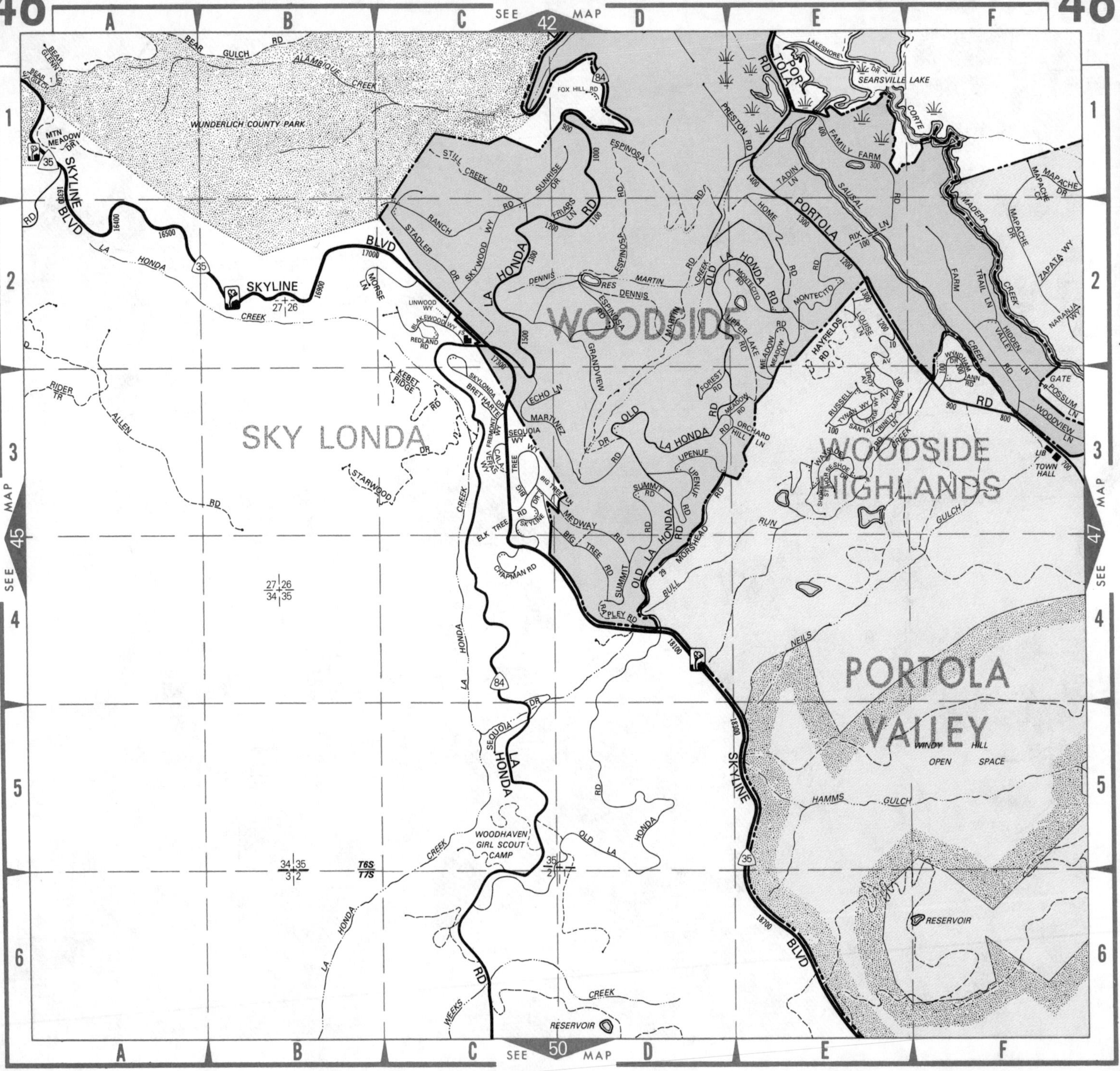

SEE MAP 42
SEE MAP 45
SEE MAP 47
SEE MAP 50

COPYRIGHT © 1991 BY Thomas Bros. Maps

DETAIL

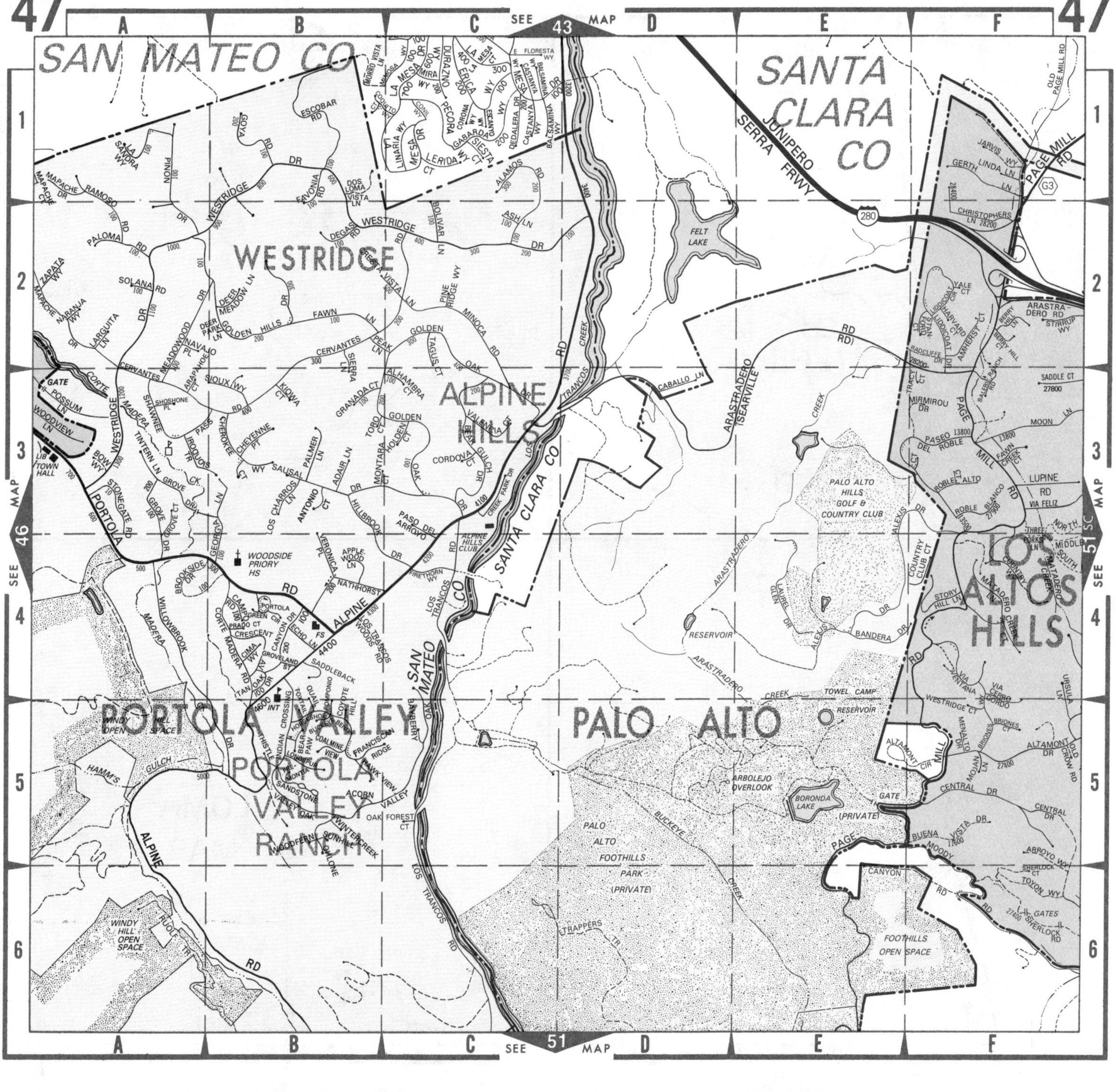

COPYRIGHT © 1991 BY Thomas Bros Maps

SAN MATEO CO
SANTA CLARA CO
WESTRIDGE
ALPINE HILLS
PORTOLA VALLEY
PORTOLA VALLEY RANCH
PALO ALTO
LOS ALTOS HILLS
FELT LAKE
PALO ALTO HILLS GOLF & COUNTRY CLUB
WOODSIDE PRIORY HS
ALPINE HILLS CLUB
LIB TOWN HALL
RESERVOIR
TOWEL CAMP RESERVOIR
ARBOLEJO OVERLOOK
BORONDA LAKE
GATE (PRIVATE)
PALO ALTO FOOTHILLS PARK (PRIVATE)
FOOTHILLS OPEN SPACE
WINDY HILL OPEN SPACE
JUNIPERO SERRA FRWY
280
G3
PAGE MILL RD
OLD PAGE MILL RD
ALPINE RD
PORTOLA RD
WESTRIDGE DR
ARASTRADERO RD
ARASTRADERO (SEARSVILLE) RD
LOS TRANCOS RD
LOS TRANCOS CREEK
SAN MATEO CO
BUCKEYE CREEK
ARASTRADERO CREEK
HAMM'S GULCH
TRAPPERS TR
RUOLF TR
CANYON RD
MOODY RD
CENTRAL DR
BUENA VISTA DR
ALTAMONT DR
ALTAMONT CIR
ESCOBAR RD
GOYA RD
PINON DR
LA SANDRA WY
RAMOSO RD
MAPACHE DR
PALOMA RD
ZAPATA WY
SOLANA DR
NARANJA WY
LARGUITA LN
FAVONIA RD
DOS LOMA VISTA LN
DEGAS RD
BOLIVAR LN
ALAMOS RD
ASH LN
VISTA LN
PINE RIDGE WY
MINOCA RD
FAWN LN
GOLDEN HILLS DR
DEER MEADOW LN
DEER PARK LN
NAVAJO PL
MEADOWOOD DR
ARAPAHOE CT
CERVANTES RD
PEAK LN
SIERRA LN
GOLDEN OAK DR
TAGUS CT
ALHAMBRA CT
GRANADA CT
TORO CT
MONTARA CT
HOLDEN CT
CORDOVA CT
VALENCIA CT
BEN GULCH
SIOUX WY
KIOWA CT
SHOSHONE PL
SHAWNEE PASS
CHEROKEE LN
CHEYENNE PT
IROQUOIS TR
TINTERN LN
SAUSAL DR
PALMER LN
ADAIR LN
ANTONIO CT
LOS CHARROS LN
HILLBROOK DR
PASO DEL ARROYO
VERONICA PL
APPLEWOOD LN
FIRETHORN WY
NATHHORST AV
CORTE MADERA RD
POSSUM LN
WOODVIEW LN
BOW WY
STONEGATE RD
GROVE DR
GROVE CT
GEORGIA LN
BROOKSIDE DR
WILLOWBROOK DR
MADERA DR
CAMPO
PORTOLA GREEN CIR
PRADO CT
CRESCENT
CANYON DR
ECHO LN
CIMA WY
GROVELAND ST
TAN OAK DR
SADDLEBACK DR
QUAIL
COYOTE HILL
BANBERRY
FRANCISCAN RIDGE
HAWK VIEW
COALMINE VIEW
INDIAN CROSSING
THISTLE
BEAR PAW
SANDSTONE
ACORN
VALLEY OAK
OAK FOREST CT
WINTERCREEK
SUNHILL
WOODFERN
CHALONE
LOS TRANCOS WOODS RD
CABALLO LN
LAUREL GLEN DR
ALEXIS DR
BANDERA DR
COUNTRY CLUB CT
JARVIS WY
GERTH LN
LINDA LN
CHRISTOPHERS LN
YALE CT
HARVARD CT
LIDDICOAT CIR
STANFORD CT
AMHERST CT
RADCLIFFE DR
BERRY HILL
ARASTRADERO RD
STIRRUP WY
SADDLE CT
MIRMIROU DR
PASEO DEL ROBLE
MOON LN
FAWN CREEK CT
LUPINE RD
ROBLE ALTO
ROBLE BLANCO
VIA FELIZ
NORTH MIDDLE SOUTH
THREE FORKS LN
STORY HILL LN
MATADERO CREEK
MATADERO CT
VIA VENTANA
VIA CERRO CORDO
WESTRIDGE CT
MENALTO DR
BRIONES CT
MOJAN LN
OLD CROW RD
URSULA LN
ARROYO WY
SHERLOCK CT
TOYON WY
GATES
SHERLOCK RD
LA MESA DR
MORRO VISTA
DURAZNO WY
ERICA WY
MIRA WY
PECORA WY
CORONA WY
GABARDA WY
SIESTA CT
LERIDA CT
LINARIA WY
CONIL WY
ESCANDIDO WY
MESA CT
DEDALERA DR
CASTANYA WY
BALSAMINA WY
FLORESTA WY

SAN MATEO

SAN GREGORIO

SAN GREGORIO STATE BEACH

RESERVOIR

STAR HILL RD

STAGE RD

LA HONDA RD

SAN GREGORIO CREEK

SEASIDE SCHOOL RD

CABRILLO HIGHWAY

COYOTE CREEK

CLEAR CREEK

BEAR GULCH RD

EL CORTE MADERA CREEK

RALSTON RD

SAN GREGORIO RANCHO

BOGESS CREEK

HARRINGTON CREEK

HONDA RD

SAN GREGORIO RANCHO

KINGSTON CREEK

POMPONIO STATE BEACH

POMPONIO CREEK RD

OLD STAGE RD

PESCADERO RANCHO

LITTLE LAGOON

BIG LAGOON

POMPONIA RESERVOIR

LOMA MAR

SAN MATEO COUNTY MEMORIAL PARK

PESCADERO STATE BEACH

PESCADERO CREEK RD

PESCADERO CREEK

BUENA VISTA

REDWOOD DR

SYLVAN WY

LOMA MAR AV

BAKER RD

GUTHRIE RD

BLOOMQUIST CREEK

PETERS CREEK

RD

DEARBORN PARK RD

ROURKE RD

LOWER DEARBORN

PESCADERO CREEK COUNTY PARK

PESCADERO

NORTH ST

DETAIL

SEE MAP 50

SEE MAP 50A

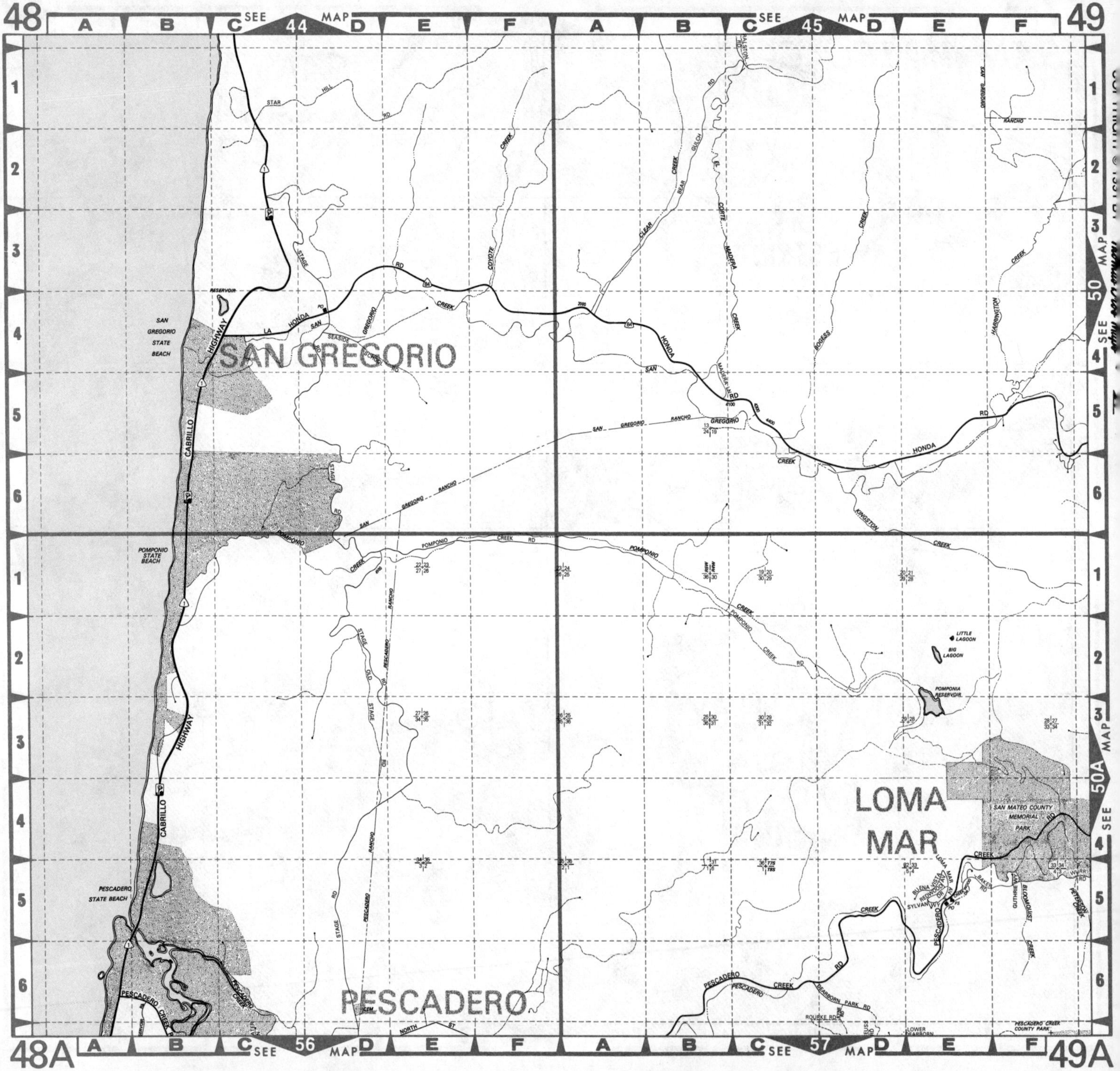

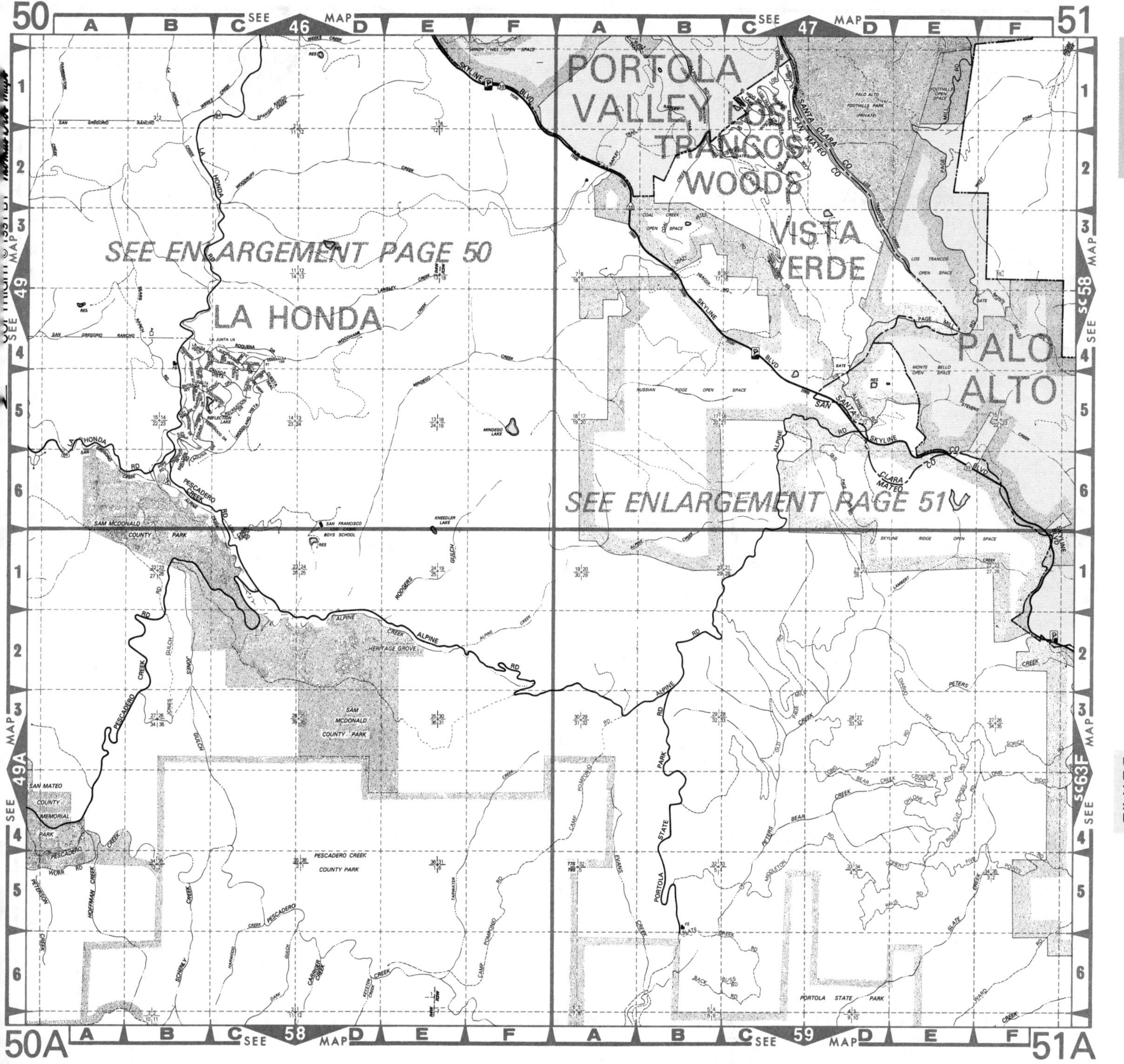

SAN MATEO
PORTOLA VALLEY
LOS TRANCOS WOODS
VISTA VERDE
PALO ALTO
LA HONDA
SEE ENLARGEMENT PAGE 50
SEE ENLARGEMENT PAGE 51
SKYLINE BLVD
LA HONDA RD
PESCADERO CREEK RD
ALPINE RD
PORTOLA STATE PARK RD
PAGE MILL RD
SAM McDONALD COUNTY PARK
PESCADERO CREEK COUNTY PARK
SAN MATEO COUNTY MEMORIAL PARK
HERITAGE GROVE
PORTOLA STATE PARK
MINDEGO LAKE
SKYLINE RIDGE OPEN SPACE
RUSSIAN RIDGE OPEN SPACE
LOS TRANCOS OPEN SPACE
MONTE BELLO OPEN SPACE
PALO ALTO FOOTHILLS PARK (PRIVATE)
SAN FRANCISCO BOYS SCHOOL
SEE MAP 46
SEE MAP 47
SEE MAP 49
SEE MAP 49A
SEE MAP 58
SEE MAP 59
SEE SC 58
SEE SC 63F
DETAIL

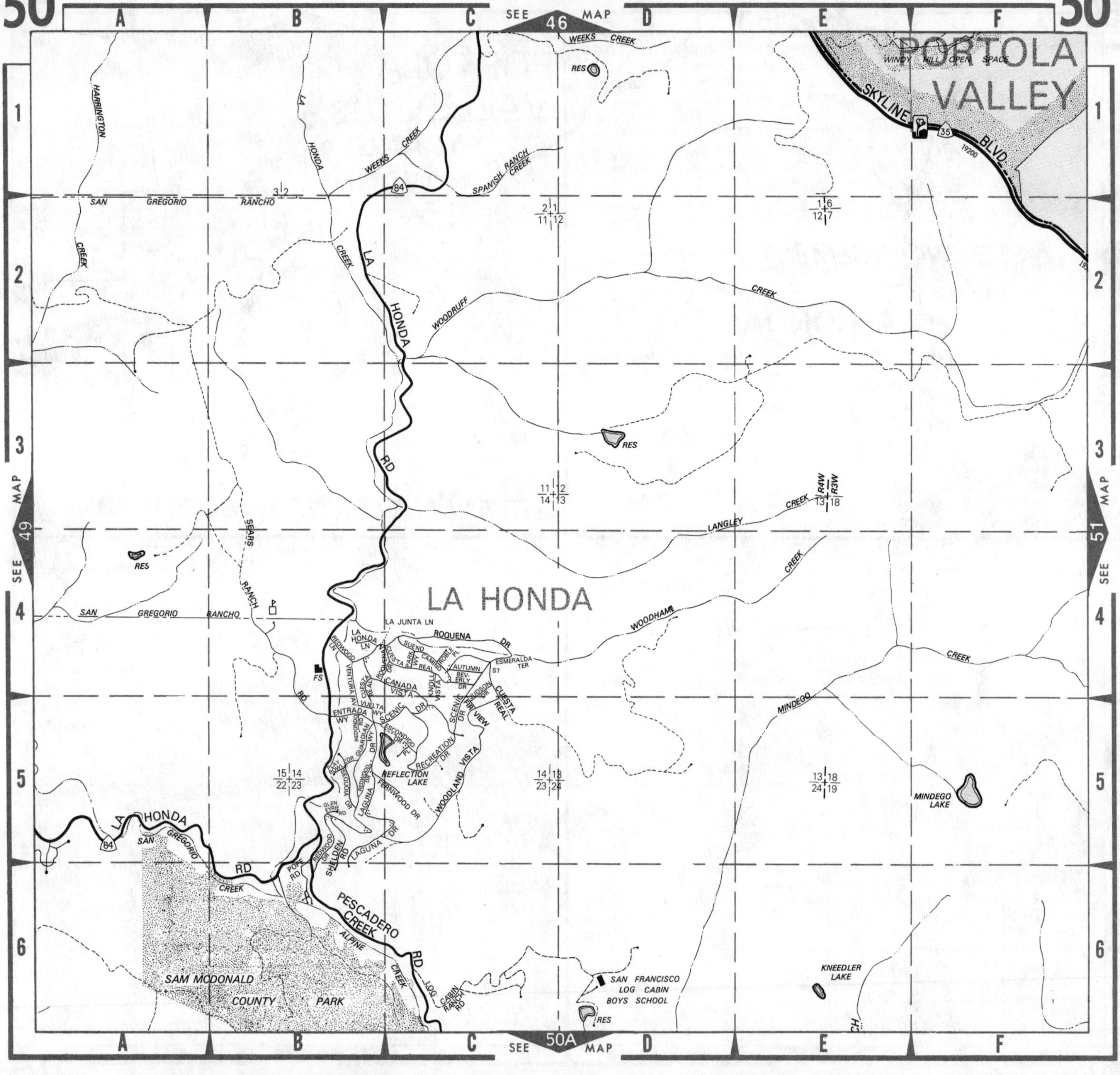
SEE MAP 46
SEE MAP 49
SEE MAP 51
SEE MAP 50A
A B C D E F
1 2 3 4 5 6
PORTOLA VALLEY
WINDY HILL OPEN SPACE
SKYLINE BLVD.
35
1920
WEEKS CREEK
RES
HARRINGTON CREEK
LA HONDA CREEK
SPANISH RANCH CREEK
84
SAN GREGORIO RANCHO
LA HONDA RD
WOODRUFF CREEK
RES
R4W R3W
LANGLEY CREEK
SEARS RANCH RD
RES
LA HONDA
WOODHAMS CREEK
MINDEGO CREEK
MINDEGO LAKE
LA JUNTA LN
LA HONDA LN
ROQUENA DR
REDWOOD LN
SUENO
CAMINO
ROBLE
PL
CUESTA REAL
ESMERALDA TER
AUTUMN ST
BEV-ERLY DR
CANADA VISTA
HUDSON DR
VENTURA AV
VUELTA
ENTRADA WY
SCENIC DR
FIR VIEW
ESCONDIDO DR
FS
REFLECTION LAKE
RECREATION DR
WOODLAND VISTA
FERNWOOD DR
LAGUNA DR
GLEN EYRIE RD
SEQUOIA DR
SHELDEN RD
POPE RD
LA HONDA RD
SAN GREGORIO CREEK
PESCADERO CREEK RD
ALPINE CREEK
LOG CABIN RANCH RD
SAM MCDONALD COUNTY PARK
SAN FRANCISCO LOG CABIN BOYS SCHOOL
KNEEDLER LAKE
RES

DETAIL

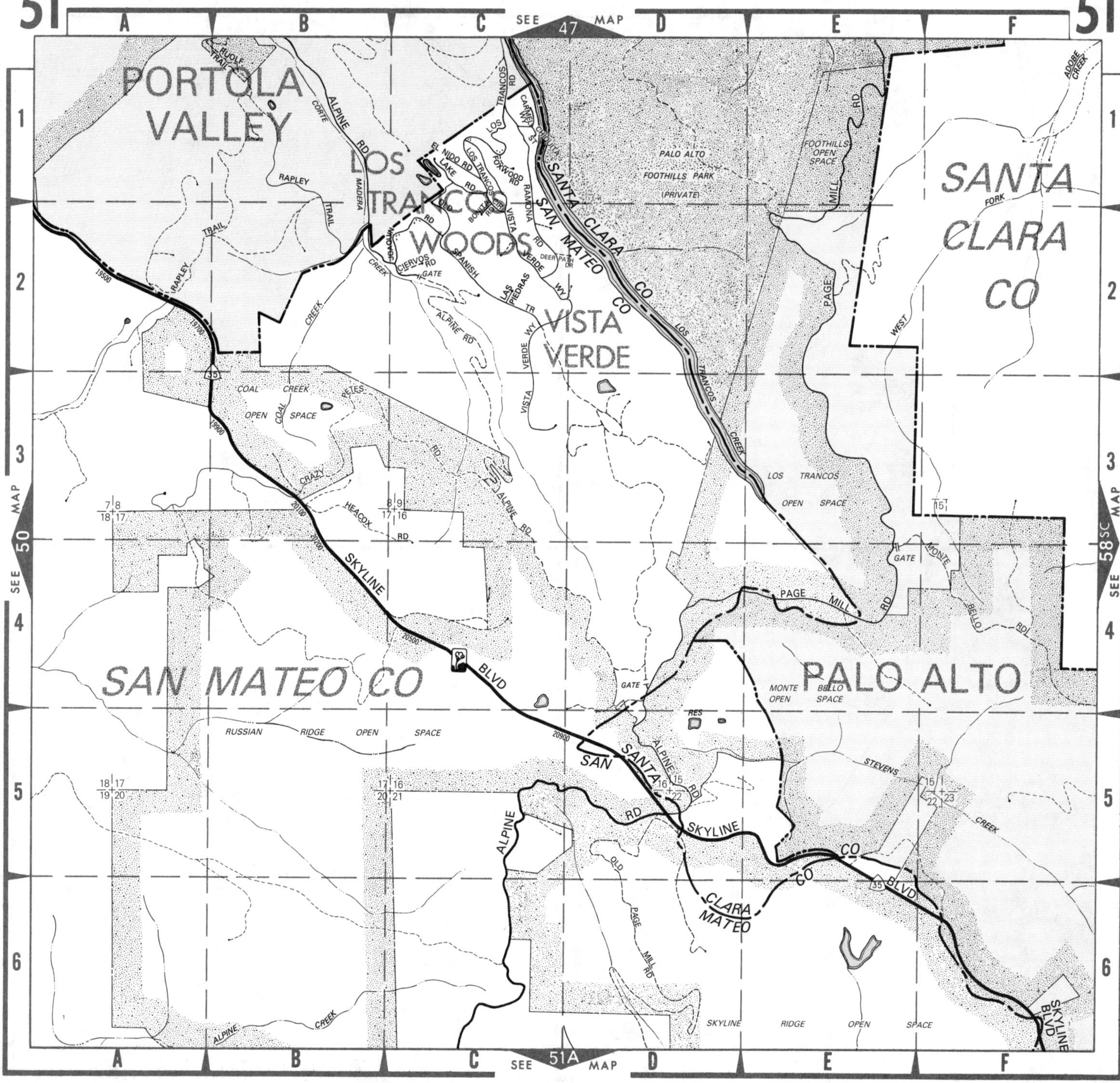

SEE 47 MAP

PORTOLA VALLEY

LOS TRANCOS WOODS

VISTA VERDE

SANTA CLARA CO

SAN MATEO CO

PALO ALTO

PALO ALTO FOOTHILLS PARK (PRIVATE)

FOOTHILLS OPEN SPACE

COAL CREEK OPEN SPACE

LOS TRANCOS OPEN SPACE

MONTE BELLO OPEN SPACE

RUSSIAN RIDGE OPEN SPACE

SKYLINE RIDGE OPEN SPACE

SKYLINE BLVD

ALPINE RD

PAGE MILL RD

OLD PAGE MILL RD

LOS TRANCOS RD

LOS TRANCOS CREEK

MONTE BELLO RD

STEVENS CREEK

ALPINE CREEK

ADOBE CREEK

WEST FORK

CORTE MADERA

RAPLEY TRAIL

RUOLF TRAIL

CRAZY PETES RD

HEACOX RD

CIERVOS RD

SPANISH

LAS PIEDRAS TR

VISTA VERDE WY

DEER PATH DR

RAMONA RD

FOXWOOD RD

EL NIDO RD

LAKE RD

OLD RD

BONITA RD

CARMEL WY

TRANCOS RD

GATE

RES

1 2 3 4 5 6

SEE 50 MAP

SEE 58SC MAP

SEE 51A MAP

COPYRIGHT © 1991 BY Thomas Bros. Maps

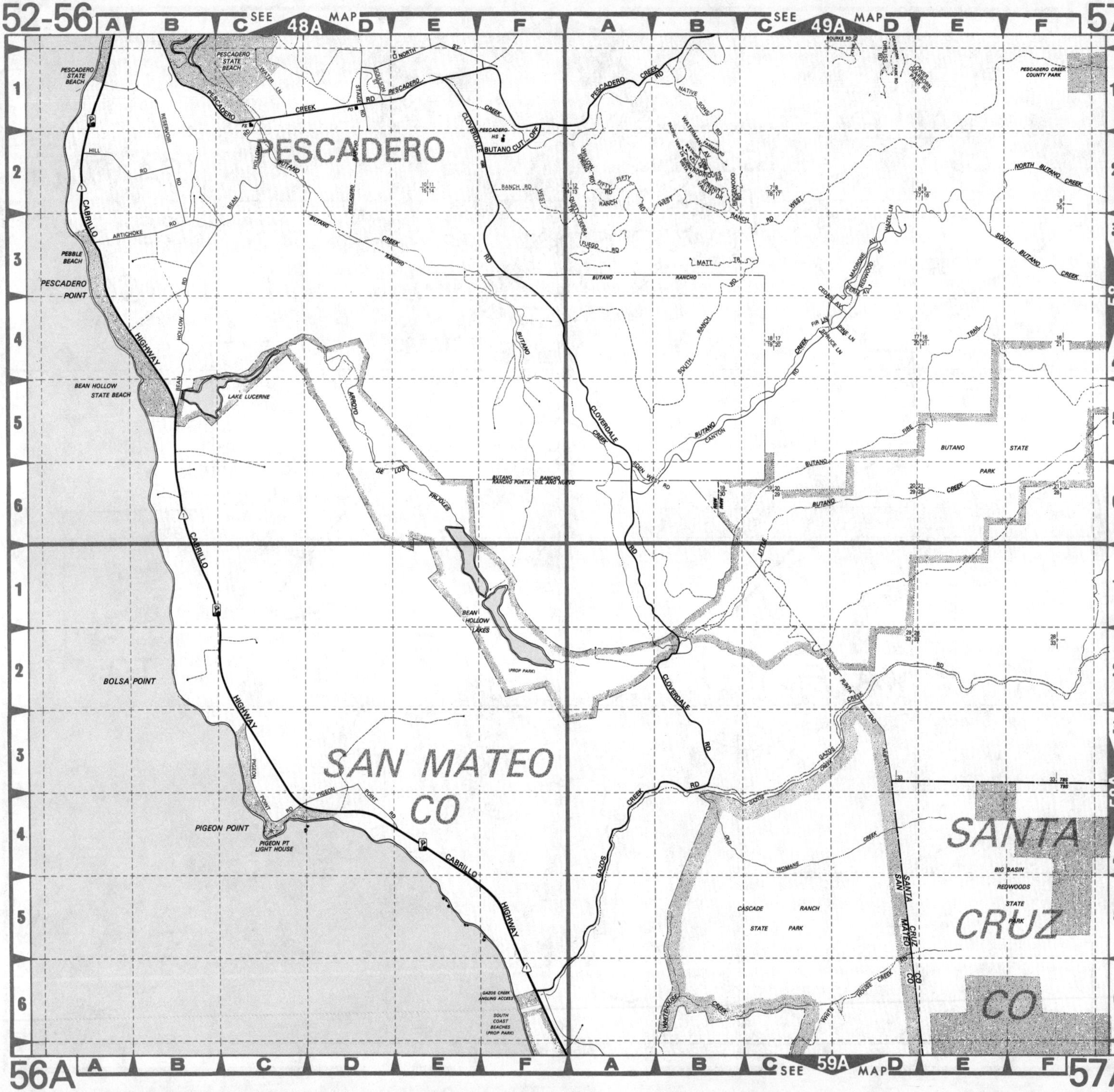

SAN MATEO

DETAIL

PESCADERO

PESCADERO STATE BEACH

PESCADERO CREEK COUNTY PARK

PEBBLE BEACH

PESCADERO POINT

BEAN HOLLOW STATE BEACH

LAKE LUCERNE

BOLSA POINT

PIGEON POINT

PIGEON PT LIGHT HOUSE

BEAN HOLLOW LAKES (PROP PARK)

SAN MATEO CO

SANTA CRUZ CO

BUTANO STATE PARK

CASCADE RANCH STATE PARK

BIG BASIN REDWOODS STATE PARK

GAZOS CREEK ANGLING ACCESS

SOUTH COAST BEACHES (PROP PARK)

CABRILLO HIGHWAY

PESCADERO CREEK RD

CLOVERDALE RD

BUTANO CUT OFF

STAGE RD

NORTH ST

WATER LN

HILL RD

RESERVOIR RD

ARTICHOKE RD

BEAN HOLLOW RD

BUTANO RANCH RD

BUTANO CREEK

ARROYO DE LOS FRIJOLES

BUTANO CANYON

BUTANO FIRE TRAIL

NORTH BUTANO CREEK

SOUTH BUTANO CREEK

LITTLE BUTANO CREEK

WEST RANCH RD

FIFTY FIFTY RD

FUEGO RD

TIERRA

MATT

NATIVE SONS RD

MADRONE AV

REDWOOD AV

CEDAR AV

FIR LN

PINE LN

SPRUCE LN

HAZEL LN

RANCHO PUNTA DEL ANO NUEVO

PIGEON POINT RD

GAZOS CREEK RD

OLD WOMANS CREEK

WHITEHOUSE CREEK

WHITE HOUSE CREEK RD

SANTA CRUZ CO

SAN MATEO CO

PESCADERO HS

COPYRIGHT © 1991 BY Thomas Bros. Maps

SEE 58 MAP

SEE 58A MAP

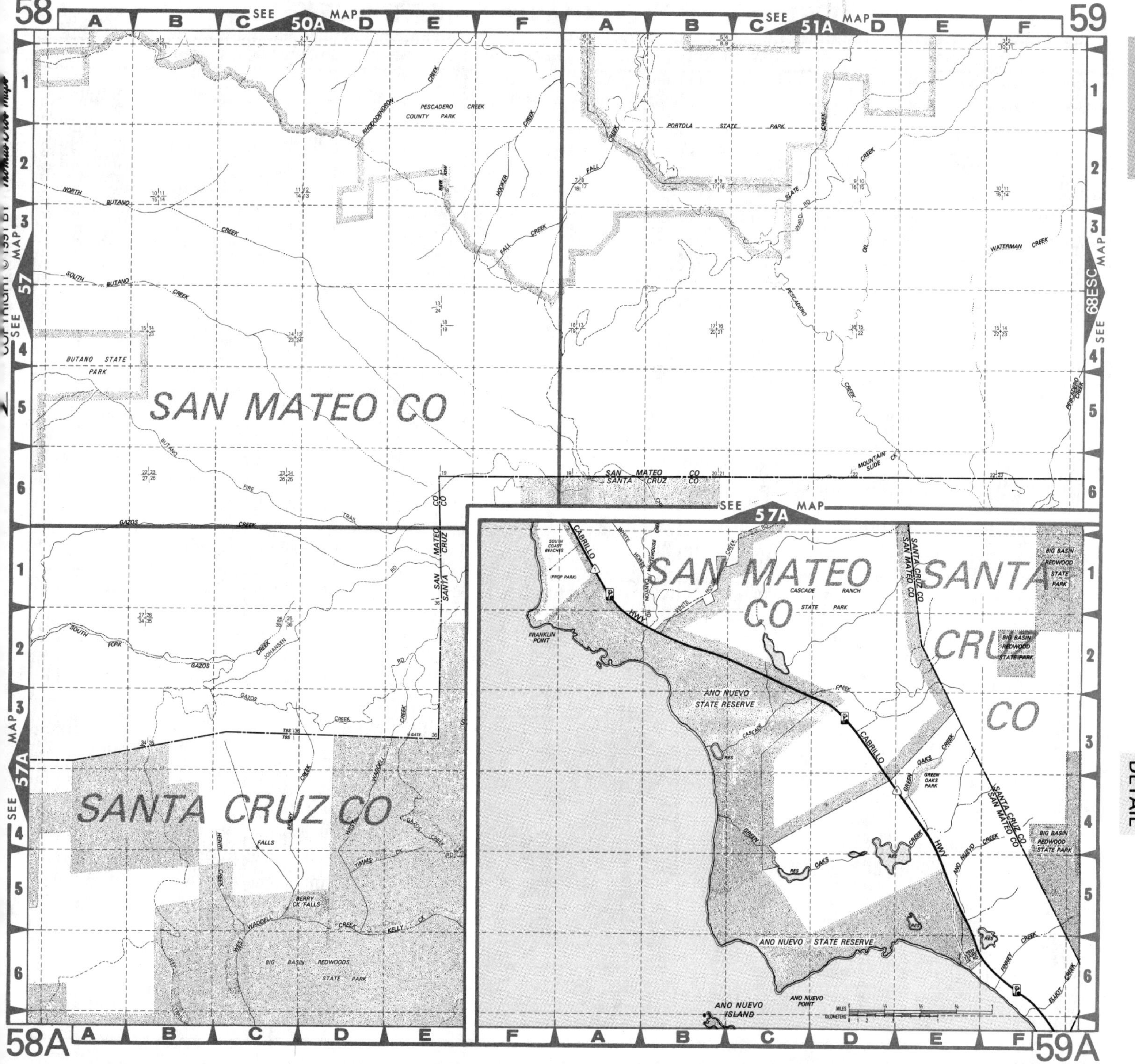
SEE MAP 50A
SEE MAP 51A
SEE MAP 57
SEE MAP 68ESC
SEE MAP 57A
SEE MAP 57A
PESCADERO CREEK COUNTY PARK
RHODODENDRON CREEK
PORTOLA STATE PARK
NORTH BUTANO CREEK
SOUTH BUTANO CREEK
BUTANO STATE PARK
SAN MATEO CO
BUTANO FIRE TRAIL
HOOKER CREEK
FALL CREEK
SLATE CREEK
WARD RD
OIL CREEK
WATERMAN CREEK
PESCADERO CREEK
MOUNTAIN SLIDE CK
SAN MATEO CO
SANTA CRUZ CO
GAZOS CREEK
SOUTH FORK GAZOS CREEK
JOHANSEN RD
SANTA CRUZ CO
WEST WADDELL CREEK
HENRY CREEK
BERRY CREEK
FALLS
BERRY CK FALLS
TIMMS CK
KELLY CK
BIG BASIN REDWOODS STATE PARK
CABRILLO HWY
SOUTH COAST BEACHES
FRANKLIN POINT
WHITEHOUSE CANYON RD
SAN MATEO CO
SANTA CRUZ CO
CASCADE RANCH STATE PARK
ANO NUEVO STATE RESERVE
CASCADE CREEK
GREEN OAKS CREEK
GREEN OAKS PARK
BIG BASIN REDWOOD STATE PARK
ANO NUEVO CREEK
FINNEY CREEK
ELLIOT CREEK
ANO NUEVO ISLAND
ANO NUEVO POINT
MILES
KILOMETERS
SAN MATEO
DETAIL

STREET	CITY	PAGE	GRID
A			
A ST	DC	23	C1
A ST	MP	37	E6
A ST	RC	36	E1
A ST	SMCO	23	C1
A ST	SSF	23	F5
ABBOT AV	DC	21	F6
ABBOT AV	DC	23	C1
ABELIA WY	EPA	38	D6
ABERDEEN DR	SC	36	B1
ABERDEEN DR	SM	29	E5
ABRYAN WY	SMCO	42	F1
ABRYAN WY	SMCO	43	A1
ACACIA AV	SBR	26	A3
ACACIA AV	SSF	23	F4
ACACIA AV	SSF	24	A4
ACACIA CT	P	27A	B1
ACACIA CT	SC	33	C5
ACACIA DR	A	37	E4
ACACIA DR	B	28	F2
ACACIA DR	B	29	A2
ACACIA LN	RC	36	D3
ACACIA LN	SMCO	36	C4
ACACIA ST	SMCO	30	E1
ACADEMY AV	BLMT	32	F4
ACADEMY AV	BLMT	33	A4
ACADEMY CT	BLMT	32	F4
ACCACIA ST	DC	22	D4
ACORN	PV	47	B5
ACORN DR	H	28	E2
ACORN WY	A	37	E4
ACTON ST	DC	22	A4
ADA ST	SM	29	E3
ADAIR LN	PV	47	B3
ADAM CT	SC	33	A5
ADAM WY	A	37	B5
ADAMS CT	MP	38	B3
ADAMS CT	SSF	23	C6
ADAMS DR	MP	38	B3
ADAMS ST	RC	36	F3
ADAMS ST	RC	37	A3
ADAMS ST	SM	29	F5
ADDISON AV	EPA	38	B4
ADDISON ST	CLMA	23	E2
ADDISON ST	RC	37	A3
ADELAIDE WY	BLMT	32	C4
ADELINE DR	SMCO	28	D2
ADMIRAL ST	SMCO	30	D2
ADMIRALTY PL	RC	33	E2
ADOBE DR	P	27	F2
ADRIAN AV	SM	29A	A6
ADRIAN AV	SSF	23	C4
ADRIAN CT	B	26	E5
ADRIAN RD	B	26	E6
ADRIAN RD	M	26	D6
AFTON CT	SM	29	E5
AGUA VISTA CT	SMCO	36	B5
AHWAHNEE DR	M	26	B6
AIRPORT BLVD	B	28	F1
AIRPORT BLVD	B	29	C1
AIRPORT BLVD	SM	29	C1
AIRPORT BLVD	SSF	24	B5
AIRPORT BLVD S	SMCO	26	C1
AIRPORT BLVD S	SSF	24	B6
AIRPORT BLVD S	SSF	26	C1
AIRPORT ST	SMCO	30	E4
AIRPORT WY	RC	33	D4
ALAMEDA AV	SMCO	34	C1
ALAMEDA PL	SBR	25	D2
ALMDA D LS PLGS	A	43	A1
ALMDA D LS PLGS	BLMT	32	D1
ALMDA D LS PLGS	BLMT	33	A5
ALMDA D LS PLGS	RC	36	E4
ALMDA D LS PLGS	SC	33	C6
ALMDA D LS PLGS	SC	36	C1
ALMDA D LS PLGS	SM	29	C5
ALMDA D LS PLGS	SM	32	D1
ALMDA D LS PLGS	SMCO	36	E4
ALMDA D LS PLGS	SMCO	42	F1
ALMDA D LS PLGS	SMCO	43	A1
ALAMEDA, THE	SMCO	30A	C6
ALAMO RD	SMCO	30	F2
ALAMO ST	SMCO	30	F2
ALAMOS RD	PV	47	C1
ALANHILL LN	SM	32	D2
ALASKA ST	CLMA	23	D2
ALBACORE LN	FCTY	29A	D5
ALBEMARLE WY	B	28	E1
ALBERNI ST	EPA	38	A3
ALBERTA AV	SC	36	D2
ALBERTA WY	H	28	F6
ALBION AV	W	42	C3
ALCALA CT	P	27	F1
ALCATRAZ AV	HMB	34	D1
ALCATRAZ AV	SMCO	30A	A5
ALCAZAR DR	B	28	C2
ALCOTT RD	SBR	25	F4
ALDEN CT	BLMT	32	F4
ALDEN CT	BLMT	33	A4
ALDEN ST	BLMT	32	F4
ALDEN ST	BLMT	33	A4
ALDEN ST	RC	36	F2
ALDENGLEN DR	SSF	23	F4
ALDER AV	SMCO	21	D6
ALDER LN	SM	32	E2
ALDER ST	SMCO	27	E6
ALDER ST	SMCO	30	E1
ALDERLEE WY	SC	36	C2
ALDERWOOD CT	SM	32	C3
ALEJANDRA AV	A	37	C6
ALEXANDER AV	DC	22	A5
ALEXANDER AV	RC	37	A5
ALEXANDER AV	SMCO	37	A5
ALEXANDER RD	BR	24	C2
ALEXIS CT	MP	43	B3
ALHAMBRA CT	PV	47	C3
ALHAMBRA DR	BLMT	32	E4
ALHAMBRA RD	SM	29	C5
ALHAMBRA RD	SSF	23	E6
ALHAMBRA RD	SSF	25	E1
ALICANTE DR	P	27A	A2
ALICE LN	MP	43	D1
ALIDA WY	SMCO	23	F6
ALIDA WY	SSF	23	F6
ALISO WY	SMCO	43	C6
ALLAN ST	DC	22	E4
ALLEGHENY WY	SMCO	32	B4
ALLEMANY ST	DC	23	C1
ALLEN DR	SBR	25	D2
ALLEN RD	SMCO	45	F2
ALLEN RD	SMCO	46	A3
ALLERTON AV	SSF	24	D5
ALLERTON ST	RC	36	F1
ALLISON CT	SM	32	C3
ALL VIEW WY	BLMT	32	E4
ALMA LN	MP	37	D5
ALMA ST	MP	37	E6
ALMA ST	MP	43	E1
ALMA ST	SC	33	C6
ALMADEN WY	SM	33	A1
ALMANOR AV	MP	37	F4
ALMANOR AV	MP	38	A3
ALMANOR AV	SSF	23	E6
ALMENOR ST	M	26	C6
ALMENDRAL AV	A	37	B6
ALMER RD	B	29	A2
ALMERIA AV	SMCO	30A	B5
ALMOND AV	SSF	23	F4
ALMOND AV	SSF	24	A4
ALMOND CT	EPA	38	C5
ALOMAR WY	BLMT	32	F5
ALOMAR WY	BLMT	33	A5
ALP AV	DC	21	F5
ALP WY	M	26	B6
ALPINE AV	B	29	A2
ALPINE AV	DC	19	B1
ALPINE AV	DC	23	A1
ALPINE AV	MP	37	F3
ALPINE CT	SSF	25	E1
ALPINE RD	MP	43	C5
ALPINE RD	PV	47	B4
ALPINE RD	PV	51	B1
ALPINE RD	SMCO	43	C6
ALPINE RD	SMCO	50A	E2
ALPINE RD	SMCO	51	C5
ALPINE RD	SMCO	51A	B3
ALPINE WY	SBR	25	E3
ALSACE LORAN AV	HMB	34	E5
ALSTON AV	HMB	34	D4
ALTA AV	SM	32	D1
ALTA LN	SC	33	B5
ALTAIR AV	FCTY	29A	B5
ALTA LOMA AV	DC	23	B2
ALTA LOMA DR	SSF	23	E4
ALTA LOMA RD	SMCO	27	E6
ALTA MESA DR	SSF	23	D5
ALTA MESA RD	SMCO	27	E6
ALTA MESA RD	W	42	D2
ALTAMONT DR	SSF	23	D5
ALTAMONT WY	RC	36	D4
ALTA VISTA	A	42	F2
ALTA VISTA	A	43	A2
ALTA VISTA DR	P	20	E6
ALTA VISTA DR	P	25	A6
ALTA VISTA DR	SSF	23	F6
ALTA VISTA DR	SSF	25	E1
ALTA VISTA RD	SMCO	27	F6
ALTA VISTA RD	W	42	C2
ALTA VISTA WY	DC	22	B4
ALTO AV	HMB	34	D1
ALTO AV	SMCO	34	D1
ALTO LN	MP	37	E6
ALTO LN	MP	43	E1
ALTO LOMA	M	26	B6
ALTO LOMA	M	28	B1
ALTON AV	SMCO	30	D4
ALTREE CT	A	37	F4
ALTREE CT	SMCO	37	F4
ALTSCHUL AV	SMCO	43	B3
ALTURA WY	BLMT	33	B5
ALTURA WY	P	20	E6
ALTURA WY	SSF	23	E4
ALTURAS DR	B	28	C3
ALTURAS WY	DC	22	A5
ALVARADO	SMCO	30	F2
ALVARADO AV	B	28	D2
ALVARADO AV	P	27A	A2
ALVARADO AV	SMCO	30	E4
ALVARADO ST	BR	24	C2
ALVERNO CT	RC	36	C6
ALVISO CT	P	27A	A1
AMADOR AV	A	37	B6
AMADOR AV	MP	37	F3
AMADOR AV	SBR	25	D3
AMAPOLA AV	P	25	B4
AMBAR WY	MP	43	D2
AMBER CT	SC	36	C2
AMBOY CT	SMCO	32	B4
AMERICAN ST	SC	33	E6
AMERICAN WY	SMCO	43	C2
AM VESPUCCI LN	FCTY	29A	C6
AMESBURY AV	SM	29	E5
AMESPORT LANDNG	HMB	34	F5
AMHERST AV	A	37	B4
AMHERST AV	SMCO	37	B4
AMHERST ST	SM	29	C5
AMHURST CT	DC	23	C5
AMPHLET BLVD	SM	29	C3
AMY DR	SM	32	C3
ANACAPA LN	FCTY	33	D1
ANAMOR ST	RC	36	F5
ANAMOR ST	RC	37	A5
ANCHOR CIR	RC	33	E2
ANCHOR DR	SM	29A	A3
ANCHOR LN	SC	33	B5
ANCHOR WY	HMB	39	F4
ANDERSON WY	MP	43	D4
ANDETA WY	SMCO	43	C6
ANDORRA AV	P	20	F6
ANDORRA AV	P	25	A6
ANDOVER DR	P	23	B5
ANDROMEDA LN	FCTY	29A	B3
ANGELITA AV	P	20	F4
ANGELITA AV	P	25	B4
ANGUIDO CT	H	32	B2
ANGUS AV	SBR	26	A3
ANITA AV	BLMT	33	A3
ANITA CT	BLMT	33	A3
ANITA DR	M	26	C5
ANITA LN	M	26	B5
ANITA RD	B	29	B2
ANN RD	PV	46	F3
ANNA ST	SM	29	E4
ANNAPOLIS CT	DC	23	D5
ANNAPOLIS CT	SMCO	23	D5
ANNAPOLIS DR	SM	29	F6
ANNAPOLIS ST	EPA	38	C3
ANNESCOURT DR	H	28	E3
ANNESCOURT PL	H	28	E3
ANNETTE AV	MP	37	D2
ANNIE ST	SMCO	23	B1
ANNIS RD	BR	24	C2
ANSEL AV	B	29	A2
ANSON RD	H	29	A6
ANTARES LN	FCTY	29A	B3
ANTIGUA LN	FCTY	33	C2
ANTIOCH DR	SM	32	F2
ANTIOCH DR	SM	33	A2
ANTIQUE FOREST	BLMT	33	B3
ANTOINETTE LN	HMB	34	E3
ANTOINETTE LN	SS	23	F5
ANTONIO CT	PV	47	B3
ANZA BL	B	29	A1
ANZA DR	P	20	D6
ANZA WY	SBR	26	B4
APOLLO LN	FCTY	29A	B6
APPIAN WY	SC	36	B2
APPIAN WY	SSF	23	D6
APPIAN WY	SSF	25	E1
APPLEWOOD LN	PV	47	B4
APRIL AV	SSF	23	D5
APTOS WY	SF	25	F1
AQUARIUS LN	FCTY	29A	A6
ARA LN	FCTY	29A	B6
ARAGON BLVD	SM	29	C5
ARAGON CT	P	27	F2
ARAPAHOE CT	PV	47	A3
ARASTRADERO RD	PA	47	D3
ARBOL GRANDE CT	SMCO	43	B2
ARBOR AV	BLMT	32	F4
ARBOR AV	BLMT	33	A4
ARBOR CT	SBR	25	D2
ARBOR CT	W	42	C2
ARBOR DR	SSF	23	D5
ARBOR LN	SM	32	E2
ARBOR LN	SMCO	30	D3
ARBOR RD	MP	37	D6
ARBOR RD	MP	43	D1
ARC WY	B	28	F2
ARC WY	B	29	A2
ARCADIA CT	P	23	A4
ARCADIA DR	DC	23	A4
ARCADIA DR	P	19	B4
ARCADIA DR	P	23	A4
ARCADIA PL	H	29	B5
ARCH LN	SC	33	B5
ARCH ST	RC	36	E2
ARCHDALE CT	SSF	23	D6
ARCHER CT	SM	29	D2
ARCTURUS CIR	FCTY	29A	B6
ARDEE LN	SSF	23	C6
ARDEN AV	SSF	24	B4
ARDEN CT	DC	22	C4
ARDEN CT	RC	36	F4
ARDEN LN	BLMT	33	B4
ARDEN RD	H	29	B5
ARDEN RD	MP	37	D5
ARDENDALE DR	DC	22	B4
ARGUELLO BLVD	P	20	E6
ARGUELLO BLVD	P	27	F1
ARGUELLO DR	B	28	C2
ARGUELLO ST	RC	36	E1
ARGUS CT	FCTY	29A	B6
ARIES LN	FCTY	29A	B6
ARIZONA WY	RC	36	F5
ARK ST	SM	29	F4
ARK ST	SM	29A	A4
ARLEEN WY	P	20	F3
ARLEEN WY	P	25	A3
ARLETA WY	HMB	34	F6
ARLEY CT	DC	23	D5
ARLINGTON DR	SSF	23	D3
ARLINGTON LN	DC	22	A5
ARLINGTON LN	SM	29	B4
ARLINGTON RD	RC	36	D2
ARLINGTON WY	SMCO	37	F5
ARMADA WY	SM	29A	A4
ARMOUR AV	SSF	24	B4
ARMSBY DR	H	28	E2
ARNOLD WY	HMB	34	F5
ARNOLD WY	MP	38	A4
ARROWHEAD LN	SMCO	37	C4
ARROWOOD LN	SM	32	E2
ARROYO AV	SC	33	C6
ARROYO AV	SC	36	C1
ARROYO CT	SM	29	C4
ARROYO DR	P	19	B6
ARROYO DR	P	23	A6
ARROYO DR	SSF	23	E5
ARROYO LEON DR	HMB	34	F5
ARROYO SECO	M	26	B6
ARROYO SECO	M	28	B1
ARTHUR AV	BLMT	32	F4
ARTHUR LN	A	37	A5
ART E HANSEN WY	SM	29A	A4
ARTICHOKE RD	SMCO	56	B3
ARUBA LN	FCTY	33	D1
ARUNDEL RD	B	29	B2
ARUNDEL RD	SC	33	B6
ASCENSION DR	SMCO	32	B3
ASCOT RD	H	29	B5
ASH AV	RC	37	A4
ASH AV	SSF	24	B4
ASH LN	PV	47	C2
ASHDOWN PL	HMB	39	E2
ASHFIELD RD	A	37	C5
ASHFORD AV	SC	33	B6
ASHFORD AV	SC	36	B1
ASHLAND DR	DC	21	C5
ASHTON AV	M	26	C6
ASHTON AV	M	28	C1
ASHTON AV	SMCO	43	C3
ASHWOOD CT	SM	29	C6
ASHWOOD DR	SM	29	C6
ASPEN AV	SSF	24	B4
ASPEN DR	P	27A	B2
ASPEN ST	SMCO	27	E6
ASPEN ST	SMCO	30	E1
ASSOCIATED RD	SSF	24	C5
ASTER AV	H	29	A3
ASTER RD	SC	33	D6
ASTER WY	EPA	38	D6
ATHENIAN WY	P	20	D6
ATHENIAN WY	P	27	E1
ATHERTON AV	A	37	B6

COPYRIGHT © 1991 BY Thomas Bros Maps

1991 SAN MATEO COUNTY STREET INDEX

STREET	CITY	PAGE	GRID
ATHERTON AV	A	43	B1
ATHERTON OKS LN	A	43	C1
ATHERWOOD AV	RC	37	A5
ATHERWOOD PL	RC	37	A5
ATHLONE AV	SMCO	37	D3
ATHLONE CT	SMCO	37	D3
ATHLONE WY	SMCO	37	D3
ATHY DR	SSF	23	C6
ATKINSON LN	MP	43	C2
ATLANTA ST	DC	21	F6
ATLANTA ST	DC	22	A6
ATLANTIC AV	SBR	26	B1
ATWATER DR	B	28	C2
AUDIFFRED LN	W	42	C3
AUDUBON AV	SMCO	30	E2
AUGUST CIR	MP	43	D2
AURA VISTA	M	26	B6
AURA VISTA	M	28	B1
AURA VISTA	P	19	A5
AURORA CT	P	25	B4
AUSTIN AV	A	37	B5
AUSTIN CT	DC	23	B4
AUTUMN DR	RC	36	D5
AUTUMN ST	SMCO	50	C4
AVALON AV	FCTY	33	C1
AVALON DR	DC	19	A1
AVALON DR	DC	23	A1
AVALON DR	P	19	B6
AVALON DR	P	23	A6
AVALON DR	SMCO	25	E1
AVALON DR	SSF	23	E6
AVALON DR	SSF	25	E1
AVENIDA DEL ORA	RC	36	E3
AVE ALHAMBRA	SMCO	30A	A5
AVE BALBOA	SMCO	30A	B5
AVE CABRILLO	SMCO	30A	C6
AVE DEL ORO	SMCO	30A	B5
AVE GRANADA	SMCO	30A	A5
AVE PORTOLA	SMCO	30A	B5
AVERY ST	SMCO	30	F2
AVIADOR AV	M	26	D5
AVIGNON PL	HMB	34	D2
AVILA CT	P	27A	A2
AVILA RD	SM	29	D5
AVOCET CT	FCTY	29A	D4
AVOCET DR	RC	33	E2
AVON ST	BLMT	32	F4
AVON ST	BLMT	33	A4
AVONDALE AV	RC	36	E1
AVONDALE RD	H	28	F6
AVONDALE RD	H	29	A6
AVONDALE RD	H	32	A1
AVONDALE RD W	H	28	F6
AVONDALE RD W	H	29	A6
AVONDALE RD W	H	31	F1
AVY AV	MP	43	C3
AVY AV	SMCO	43	C3
AZALEA AV	B	28	F1
AZALEA AV	B	29	A1
AZALEA LN	SC	35	F1
AZALIA DR	EPA	38	C5
B			
B RD W	SBR	25	F1
B RD W	SBR	26	A1
B ST	CLMA	23	C1
B ST	RC	36	E1
B ST	SM	29	C4
B ST	SMCO	23	C1
B ST	SSF	23	F5
BACK RD	SMCO	51A	B6
BACON CT	DC	23	B4
BADEN AV	SSF	23	F4
BADEN AV	SSF	24	A5
BAFFIN CT	FCTY	33	C2
BAFFIN ST	FCTY	33	C1

STREET	CITY	PAGE	GRID
BAHAMA LN	FCTY	33	D1
BAHIA	SM	33	B1
BAILEYANA RD	H	28	E3
BAIN PL	RC	36	D4
BAINBRIDGE ST	FCTY	29A	C6
BAIR ISLAND RD	RC	36	F1
BAIR ISLAND RD	RC	37	A1
BAIRN DR	H	31	F1
BAIRN DR	H	32	F1
BAKER RD	SMCO	49A	E5
BAKER ST	SSF	24	B5
BAKER WY	SM	29A	A5
BALBOA AV	B	28	E1
BALBOA AV	SMCO	30A	B5
BALBOA BLVD	HMB	34	E5
BALBOA LN	FCTY	29A	B5
BALBOA ST	FCTY	29A	B5
BALBOA WY	B	28	E1
BALBOA WY	P	20	D6
BALBOA WY	SBR	26	B4
BALCLUTHA DR	FCTY	29A	C5
BALDWIN AV	DC	19	B1
BALDWIN AV	DC	23	A1
BLADWIN AV	SM	29	C4
BALDWIN HLLS CT	SSF	23	C6
BALLY LN	P	19	B5
BALMORAL	SM	29	D6
BALSAMINA WY	SMCO	43	C6
BALSAMINA WY	SMCO	47	C1
BALTIMORE WY	DC	22	B4
BANBURY	SC	36	C2
BANBURY LN	M	26	A5
BANCROFT AV	HMB	34	E3
BANCROFT LN	P	23	A5
BANCROFT RD	B	29	C2
BANCROFT WY	P	19	B5
BANCROFT WY	P	23	A5
BANFF WY	P	27A	C1
BANKERS LN	BR	24	C1
BANTRY LN	SSF	23	C6
BANYAN WY	P	27A	A1
BAQUIANO TR	P	25	B5
BARBADOS LN	FCTY	33	C1
BARBARA LN	BLMT	33	A3
BARBARA LN	DC	23	C4
BARBARA LN	MP	43	D2
BARBARA LN	SMCO	33	A6
BARBARA WY	H	28	E5
BARBOUR DR	RC	36	D4
BARCELONA CIR	RC	33	E2
BARCELONA DR	M	26	B5
BARCELONA DR	P	20	F6
BARCELONA DR	P	25	A6
BARCELONA DR	P	27A	A1
BARCLAY AV	M	26	C5
BARCLAY WY	BLMT	32	E4
BARDET RD	W	42	D2
BARFORD AV	SC	33	B5
BARK CT	HMB	34	E2
BARK DR	RC	33	D2
BARKENTINE LN	RC	33	D3
BARKENTINE ST	FCTY	29A	C6
BARNEGAT LN	RC	33	D1
BARNESON AV	SM	29	C6
BARNESON AV	SM	32	C1
BARNEY AV	A	43	B2
BARNEY AV	SMCO	43	B2
BARNEY CT	SMCO	43	B2
BARRANCA ST	SMCO	30	F5
BARRETT DR	W	42	E2
BARRINGTON CT	SSF	23	D6
BARROILHET AV	B	29	A3
BARROILHET AV	H	28	F4
BARROILHET AV	H	29	A3
BARRON AV	SMCO	37	B3
BARRY LN	A	37	B6
BARTLETT WY	BLMT	32	D4
BARTON PL	MP	38	A5

STREET	CITY	PAGE	GRID
BARTON PL	P	27A	B2
BARTON ST	SMCO	36	F6
BARTON ST	SMCO	37	A6
BARTON ST	SMCO	42	F1
BARTON ST	SMCO	43	A1
BARTON WY	MP	38	A5
BASSETT CT	SSF	23	C6
BASSETT LN	A	37	D5
BATES RD	H	29	A5
BAUER CT	SC	36	C1
BAUER DR	SC	33	C6
BAUER DR	SC	36	C1
BAY CT	BLMT	32	E3
BAY RD	MP	37	E3
BAY RD	RC	37	B2
BAY RD	SMCO	37	B2
BAY RD	EPA	38	B4
BAY ST	M	26	C4
BAYBERRY	PV	47	C5
BAYBERRY PL	H	28	F4
BAYCREST WY	SSF	24	A3
BAYFRONT EXPWY	MP	37	F2
BAYFRONT EXPWY	MP	38	A2
BAY HARBOUR DR	RC	33	F2
BAY HILL CT	HMB	39	F2
BAYHILL DR	SBR	26	A2
BAY HILL PL	HMB	39	F2
BAY HILL RD	HMB	39	F2
BAY LAUREL DR	MP	43	D3
BAY LAUREL DR	SMCO	43	D3
BAYLOR ST	EPA	38	C3
BAYPARK CIR	SSF	24	A3
BAYPORT AV	SC	33	E6
BAYPORT CT	SC	33	D5
BAY RIDGE WY	SM	32	B2
BAYSHORE BLVD	BR	22	E5
BAYSHORE BLVD	BR	24	C2
BAYSHORE BLVD	DC	22	E4
BAYSHORE BLVD	SM	29	C2
BAY SHORE CIR	SBR	26	B1
BAY SHORE CIR S	SBR	26	B1
BAYSHORE FRWY	BLMT	33	B2
BAYSHORE FRWY	BR	24	F5
BAYSHORE FRWY	MP	37	D2
BAYSHORE FRWY	MP	38	C5
BAYSHORE FRWY	RC	33	B2
BAYSHORE FRWY	RC	37	C2
BAYSHORE FRWY	SC	33	B2
BAYSHORE FRWY	SM	29	B1
BAYSHORE FRWY	SM	33	B2
BAYSHORE FRWY	SMCO	26	C3
BAYSHORE FRWY	SMCO	33	B2
BAYSHORE FRWY	SMCO	37	D2
BAYSHORE FRWY	EPA	38	C5
BAYSHORE FRWY	SSF	24	C4
BAYSHORE HWY	B	26	E5
BAYSHORE HWY	B	28	F1
BAYSHORE RD	EPA	38	C5
BAYSHORE RD E	RC	36	F1
BAYSHORE RD E	RC	37	C2
BAYSIDE BLVD	SC	33	E6
BAYSWATER AV	B	29	B2
BAYSWATER AV	SM	29	B2
BAYTREE RD	SC	33	D6
BAYTREE WY	SM	29	C4
BAYVIEW AV	BLMT	32	F3
BAY VIEW AV	M	26	A5
BAYVIEW AV	M	26	B4
BAYVIEW AV	SM	32	F3
BAYVIEW CT	M	26	B4
BAYVIEW DR	SC	33	A5
BAY VIEW DR	SMCO	33	A5
BAYVIEW PL	B	29	B1
BAY VIEW RD	P	20	E5
BAY VIEW RD	P	25	A5
BAY VIEW RD	SMCO	30	F2
BAYVIEW WY	SMCO	36	C5

STREET	CITY	PAGE	GRID
BAYWALK WY	RC	33	D1
BAYWOOD AV	H	29	C4
BAYWOOD AV	MP	37	F6
BAYWOOD AV	MP	38	A5
BAYWOOD AV	SM	29	C4
BAYWOOD AV	SSF	23	E4
BAYWOOD GLEN	SMCO	36	B4
BEACH AV	P	25	A5
BEACH BLVD	P	20	E1
BEACH RD	B	29	C1
BEACH ST	SMCO	30	D3
BEACH WY	SMCO	30	D4
BEACH PARK BLVD	FCTY	29A	D6
BEACHSIDE CT	DC	19	A4
BEACHSIDE CT	DC	23	A4
BEACHVIEW AV	P	19	B5
BEACHVIEW AV	P	23	A5
BEACON AV	SM	29	E3
BEACON ST	MP	38	A5
BEACON ST	SSF	24	B6
BEACON ST	SSF	26	B1
BEACN SHORES DR	RC	33	D3
BEAN HOLLOW RD	SMCO	56	B4
BEAR CK CROSSNG	SMCO	51A	D4
BEAR GLENN	SMCO	41	F6
BEAR GULCH DR	PV	47	C3
BEAR GULCH RD	SMCO	41	F6
BEAR GULCH RD	SMCO	42	C5
BEAR GULCH RD	SMCO	45	E4
BEAR GULCH RD	SMCO	46	A1
BEAR GULCH RD	SMCO	49	B2
BEAR GULCH RD	W	42	C5
BEAR PAW	PV	47	B5
BEATTY AV	BR	22	E4
BEAUMONT BLVD	P	19	B5
BEAUMONT BLVD	P	23	A5
BECKET DR	RC	33	E3
BEECH AV	SBR	26	A3
BEECH AV	SSF	24	B4
BEECH ST	RC	37	A2
BEECH ST	EPA	38	C4
BEECHWOOD DR	DC	19	B1
BEECHWOOD DR	DC	21	D6
BEECHWOOD DR	DC	23	A1
BEECHWOOD DR	SMCO	19	B1
BEECHWOOD DR	SMCO	21	D6
BEECHWOOD DR	SMCO	23	A1
BELAIR WY	RC	36	D5
BEL AIRE CT	H	32	B2
BEL AIRE RD	BLMT	32	B2
BEL AIRE RD	SMCO	32	B2
BELBROOK WY	A	43	A3
BELBURN DR	BLMT	32	F4
BELBURN DR	BLMT	33	A4
BELCREST AV	DC	19	A4
BELCREST AV	DC	23	A4
BELFAST AV	P	27	E1
BELFORD DR	DC	21	C5
BELFORD WY	SM	29	C4
BELHAVEN AV	DC	19	B3
BELHAVEN AV	DC	23	A3
BELL CT	EPA	38	C4
BELL ST	EPA	38	C4
BELLA ST	CLMA	23	E2
BELLAIR WY	MP	43	B3
BELLAIR WY	SMCO	43	B3
BELLA VISTA DR	H	28	D3
BELLE AV	RC	37	D2
BELLE AV	SC	33	C6
BELLE SV	SC	36	C1
BELLE AIR RD	SSF	26	C1
BELLEAU AV	A	37	C4
BELLEMONTI AV	BLMT	32	F3
BELLE ROCHE AV	SMCO	36	C3
BELLE ROCHE CT	SMCO	36	C3
BELLEVILLE BLVD	HMB	34	E4
BELLEVUE AV	B	29	A3
BELLEVUE AV	DC	22	A5

STREET	CITY	PAGE	GRID
BELLEVUE AV	SM	29	B4
BELLFLOWER LN	SC	32	F6
BELLFLOWER LN	SC	35	F1
BELLO CAMPO CT	SMCO	43	C3
BELL VISTA	P	20	E1
BEL MAR AV	DC	21	D5
BELMONT AV	BLMT	33	A3
BELMONT AV	RC	37	A6
BELMONT AV	SC	33	D6
BELMONT AV	SC	36	D1
BELMONT AV	SMCO	36	F6
BELMONT AV	SMCO	37	A6
BELMONT AV	SSF	24	B3
BELMONT DR	DC	21	D4
BELMONT CYN RD	BLMT	32	D4
BELMONT WDS WY	BLMT	32	D5
BELVEDERE AV	HMB	34	E3
BELVEDERE AV	SC	36	D1
BELVEDERE CT	B	28	D3
BENGLOE LN	H	31	F1
BENGLOE LN	H	32	A1
BENITO AV	B	28	E2
BENNETT RD	RC	36	D3
BENNINGTON AV	SBR	25	F4
BENNINGTON CT	SMCO	32	B3
BENNINGTON DR	SMCO	32	B3
BENSON WY	BLMT	32	D5
BEPLER ST	DC	21	F4
BERENDA DR	SSF	23	D5
BERENDA WY	SMCO	43	C6
BERENDOS AV	P	25	B4
BERESFORD AV	A	37	A6
BERESFORD AV	BLMT	32	D4
BERESFORD AV	SMCO	37	A6
BERESFORD CT	SM	32	F2
BERESFORD CT	SM	33	A2
BERGENSEN CT	A	37	A6
BERKELEY AV	MP	36	F3
BERKELEY AV	MP	38	A3
BERKELEY AV	SMCO	37	F4
BERKSHIRE AV	A	37	B4
BERKSHIRE AV	SMCO	37	B4
BERKSHIRE DR	M	26	B6
BERKSHIRE DR	SBR	25	D2
BERMETTA WY	A	37	C4
BERMUDA DR	SM	29	F6
BERNAL AV	B	28	E2
BERNAL AV	SMCO	30	E4
BERNARDO AV	HMB	39	F1
BERNI CT	M	26	C4
BERRYESSA WY	H	32	A2
BERTA CIR	DC	23	C4
BERTOCCHI LN	M	26	B5
BEST CT	SC	36	A2
BETA AV	DC	21	F5
BETTINA AV	BLMT	32	E3
BETTINA AV	SM	32	E3
BETTMAN WY	SSF	23	C6
BETTY LN	A	37	B6
BETTY LN	A	43	B1
BETTY LN	SM	29	E5
BEVERLY AV	M	26	D5
BEVERLY CT	SSF	23	F4
BEVERLY DR	SC	33	B6
BEVERLY DR	SMCO	50	C4
BEVERLY PL	P	19	B5
BEVERLY PL	P	23	A5
BEVERLY ST	DC	23	C5
BEVERLY ST	SM	32	D2
BIDDULPH WY	BLMT	33	B3
BIEBER AV	MP	37	F3
BIG BEND DR	P	27A	C1
BIG PINE RD	SMCO	41	C2
BIG SUR WY	P	27A	B1
BIG TREE LN	SMCO	46	C3
BIG TREE RD	SMCO	46	D3
BIG TREE RD	W	46	D3

COPYRIGHT © 1991 BY Thomas Bros Maps

1991 SAN MATEO COUNTY STREET INDEX

STREET	CITY	PAGE	GRID
BIG TREE WY	SMCO	46	C3
BILLINGSGATE LN	FCTY	33	C2
BILTMORE LN	MP	43	B3
BING ST	SC	33	E6
BINNACLE LN	FCTY	33	E3
BIRCH AV	SC	33	C6
BIRCH AV	SC	36	C1
BIRCH AV	SM	29	E4
BIRCH AV	SSF	23	E3
BIRCH CT	SBR	25	D2
BIRCH LN	P	20	E2
BIRCH ST	RC	36	E2
BIRCH ST	SMCO	27	E6
BIRCH ST	SMCO	30	E1
BIRCHWOOD CT	DC	22	C4
BIRKDALE RD	HMB	39	E2
BISCAYNE AV	FCTY	33	C2
BISHOP LN	SMCO	43	D5
BISHOP RD	BLMT	32	D4
BISMARK ST	DC	21	F6
BLACKBURN AV	MP	37	F5
BLACKBURN TER	P	20	C6
BLACK FOX WY	RC	36	C6
BLACKHAWK LN	SMCO	28	D2
BLACK MTN RD	H	28	F6
BLACK MTN RD	H	29	A6
BLACK MTN RD	H	31	F1
BLACK MTN RD	H	32	A1
BLACK MTN RD	SMCO	28	F6
BLAKE ST	MP	37	E6
BLAKE ST	MP	43	E1
BLAKEWOOD WY	SMCO	46	C2
BLANDFORD BLVD	RC	36	D2
BLENHEIM AV	SMCO	37	B4
BLOMQUIST ST	RC	37	B1
BLONDIN WY	SMCO	23	F6
BLONDIN WY	SSF	23	F6
BLOOM LN	HMB	34	F5
BLOOMFIELD RD	B	29	B2
BLOSSOM CT	DC	21	F6
BLUEBELL CT	M	26	B5
BLUEBELL LN	H	32	A1
BLUE BELLE LN	SC	32	F6
BLUEFISH CT	FCTY	29A	D4
BLUE-JAY CT	EPA	38	C4
BLUE JAY WY	SMCO	41	D4
BLUERIDGE AV	MP	43	C4
BLUERIDGE LN	W	42	D5
BLYTHE ST	FCTY	29A	C6
BLYTHE ST	FCTY	33	C1
BOARDWALK CT	SBR	25	F2
BOARDWALK DR	SBR	25	F2
BOARDWALK PL	RC	33	D2
BOARDWALK PL	SBR	25	F2
BOARDWALK WY	RC	33	D2
BOBSTAY LN	FCTY	33	D2
BODEGA ST	FCTY	33	B2
BOHANNON DR	MP	37	D3
BOLERO WY	DC	22	C4
BOLIVAR LN	PV	47	C2
BOLTON PL	MP	43	D1
BONITA AV	M	26	B5
BONITA AV	P	20	F4
BONITA AV	P	25	B4
BONITA AV	RC	37	A4
BONITA AV	SSF	23	E4
BONITA LN	FCTY	29A	D5
BONITA RD	SMCO	51	C2
BONITA ST	SMCO	30	E5
BONNIE CT	RC	36	F5
BONNIE LN	P	19	B5
BONNIE LN	P	23	A5
BONNIE ST	DC	21	F6
BONSEN CT	SMCO	42	F1
BOOTHBAY AV	FCTY	33	B2
BORDEAUX LN	HMB	34	E2
BORDEN ST	SM	29	F4

STREET	CITY	PAGE	GRID
BOREL AV	SM	29	D6
BOREL AV	SMCO	29	D6
BOREL PL	SM	29	D6
BOROUGHWOOD PL	H	28	F5
BOSTON AV	SM	29	F4
BOTANY CT	FCTY	33	B1
BOULEVARD DR	HMB	34	D3
BOUNTY DR	FCTY	29A	C5
BOURBON CT	SSF	25	D1
BOVET RD	SM	29	D6
BOW DR	SC	36	B3
BOW WY	PV	47	A3
BOWER RD	P	27	E1
BOWFIN ST	FCTY	29A	D5
BOWHILL RD	H	29	B5
BOWSPRIT DR	RC	33	D3
BOWSPRIT LN	FCTY	33	C2
BRADBURY LN	RC	37	A4
BRADFORD DR	SSF	23	D3
BRADFORD ST	RC	36	F2
BRADFORD WY	P	20	F6
BRADFORD WY	P	25	A3
BRADLEY AV	SM	29	E3
BRADLEY CT	SMCO	37	A6
BRADLEY DR	DC	19	B1
BRADLEY DR	DC	21	C6
BRADLEY DR	DC	23	A1
BRADLEY DR	SMCO	21	C6
BRADLEY WY	EPA	38	A4
BRADSHAW TER	RC	36	D4
BRAEMAR DR	H	32	A1
BRAGATO RD	BLMT	33	C4
BRAGATO RD	SMCO	33	C4
BRAMBLE CT	FCTY	29A	D5
BRANDON CT	DC	22	D5
BRANDON CT	H	32	C1
BRANDON WY	MP	43	D2
BRANDT RD	H	28	F6
BRANDT RD	H	29	A6
BRANDY ROCK WY	RC	36	E5
BRANDYWINE RD	SMCO	32	A3
BRANNER DR	MP	43	D4
BRANNER DR	SMCO	43	C4
BRANSON DR	SM	33	A1
BRANSTEN RD	SC	33	D5
BRECON CT	SMCO	36	C2
BREEZE PL	RC	36	D4
BRENT CT	MP	43	B3
BRENTWOOD CT	EPA	38	C4
BRENTWOOD DR	SSF	23	F6
BRENTWOOD DR	SSF	25	F1
BRENTWOOD RD	H	29	B5
BRET HARTE	SMCO	46	C3
BRET HARTE DR	RC	36	D5
BREWER DR	H	29	A4
BREWSTER AV	RC	36	F1
BREWSTER AV	SMCO	36	E3
BRIAR LN	SM	32	E2
BRIARFIELD AV	RC	36	E5
BRIARFIELD WY	BLMT	33	B3
BRIARWOOD DR	SSF	25	E1
BRIARWOOD WY	BLMT	33	B3
BRIDGE CT	BLMT	32	F6
BRIDGE PKWY	RC	33	D3
BRIDGE RD	H	29	B4
BRIDGEPORT DR	SMCO	30A	A4
BRIDGEPORT LN	FCTY	33	C1
BRIDLE WY	H	29	C6
BRIG CT	HMB	34	E2
BRIGGS ST	DC	23	B1
BRIGHTON CT	DC	23	C5
BRIGHTON LN	RC	37	A5
BRIGHTON RD	P	20	F2
BRIGHTON RD	P	25	A2
BRISTOL CT	FCTY	33	B1
BRISTOL WY	RC	36	E5
BRITTAN AV	SC	33	D6
BRITTAN AV	SC	36	D1

STREET	CITY	PAGE	GRID
BRITTANY LN	DC	22	A5
BRITTANY MDWS	A	37	C5
BRITTON AV	A	37	C6
BROAD ACRES RD	A	43	A2
BROADVIEW CT	SM	32	C4
BROADWAY	BLMT	33	B4
BROADWAY	B	28	F2
BROADWAY	M	26	C5
BROADWAY	RC	36	E2
BROADWAY	RC	37	A2
BROADWAY	SMCO	30A	A5
BRODERICK RD	B	26	D6
BROMFIELD RD	H	29	A4
BROMFIELD RD	SM	29	A4
BROMLEY CT	DC	23	C5
BROMLEY DR	SC	36	C2
BROMLEY DR	SMCO	36	C2
BROOKE CT	H	32	B2
BROOK ST	SC	36	C1
BROOKHAVEN CT	P	19	B4
BROOKHAVEN CT	P	23	A4
BROOKLAWN AV	DC	21	C6
BROOKLINE WY	SMCO	36	C5
BROOKS PL	P	27A	B2
BROOKS ST	SM	29	F5
BROOKSIDE DR	PV	47	A4
BROOKSIDE LN	M	26	A5
BROOKVALE RD	H	28	F3
BROOKWOOD RD	W	36	D6
BROOKWOOD RD	W	42	E1
BROSNAN CT	DC	23	D5
BROSNAN CT	SSF	23	F4
BROUGHTON LN	FCTY	33	C1
BROWN ST	DC	22	C4
BROWNING WY	SSF	24	A6
BRUCE ST	P	19	B6
BRUCE ST	P	23	A6
BRUMISS TER	DC	22	A4
BRUNO AV	DC	21	E6
BRUNSWICK CT	SSF	23	C6
BRUNSWICK ST	DC	22	A4
BRUSCO WY	SSF	23	F4
BRYANT ST	DC	23	B1
BRYANT ST	SMCO	23	B1
BRYANT WY	SBR	25	F4
BRYCE AV	SSF	23	E6
BRYCE CT	BLMT	32	D5
BRYCE CANYON WY	P	27A	B1
BUCHANAN CT	EPA	38	C4
BUCK CT	W	42	F1
BUCKEYE	PV	47	B5
BUCKEYE CT	H	29	B6
BUCKEYE ST	RC	37	A3
BUCKINGHAM AV	SMCO	37	B3
BUCKINGHAM CT	H	32	A2
BUCKINGHAM RD	P	20	E2
BUCKINGHAM RD	P	25	A2
BUCKINGHAM WY	H	32	A2
BUCKLAND AV	BLMT	33	B5
BUCKLAND AV	SC	33	B5
BUCKLAND CT	SC	33	B5
BUCKNELL DR	SM	29	C5
BUCKTHORN WY	H	28	F4
BUCKTHORN WY	MP	37	D5
BUDD CT	SM	29A	A5
BUEL AV	P	20	E5
BUENA VISTA	SM	32	E1
BUENA VISTA AV	A	37	A6
BUENA VISTA AV	BLMT	32	E4
BUENA VISTA AV	DC	23	B2
BUENA VISTA AV	SBR	26	B1
BUENA VISTA AV	SMCO	37	A6
BUENA VISTA AV	SMCO	49A	E5
BUENA VISTA LN	SMCO	57	B2
BUENA VISTA RD	SMCO	30	F1
BUENA VISTA RD	SSF	23	D6
BUENA VISTA ST	SMCO	30	E2

STREET	CITY	PAGE	GRID
BUFFALO CT	P	25	C6
BUNKER HILL DR	SMCO	32	B3
BURBANK AV	RC	37	B2
BURBANK AV	SM	32	F3
BURGESS DR	MP	37	E6
BURGOYNE CT	SMCO	32	B4
BURKE LN	FCTY	29A	C3
BURLINGAME AV	B	29	B2
BURLINGVIEW DR	B	28	D3
BURLWAY RD	B	26	F6
BURNHAM CT	SC	36	C2
BURNING TREE CT	HMB	39	F2
BURNING TREE RD	HMB	39	F2
BURNS AV	A	37	D4
BURNS CT	P	20	F3
BURNS CT	P	25	A3
BURREN WY	SSF	25	D1
BURROWS	FCTY	33	C1
BURROWS AV	SBR	25	F3
BURROWS AV	SBR	26	A3
BUSH ST	SC	33	C5
BUSS RD	SMCO	51A	C6
BUTANO CUT OFF	SMCO	56	F2
BUTANO FIRE TR	SMCO	57	C5
BUTANO FIRE TR	SMCO	58	B5
BUTLER AV	SSF	24	C4
BUTLER RD	SSF	24	C4
BUTTERCUP LN	SC	32	F6
BUTTERNUT DR	H	28	D4
BUXTON AV	SSF	23	C4
BYERS DR	MP	38	B5
BYRD LN	FCTY	29A	C6
BYRNE ST	DC	23	C1
BYRON AV	SM	29	F3
BYRON DR	SSF	23	D4
BYRON ST	CLMA	23	E3
C			
C ST	CLMA	23	C1
C ST	MP	37	E6
C ST	RC	36	E1
C ST	SMCO	23	C1
C ST	SSF	23	F5
CABOT CT	SC	36	B2
CABOT CT	SSF	24	D5
CABOT LN	FCTY	29A	C6
CABOT RD	SSF	24	C5
CABRILLO AV	B	28	E1
CABRILLO HWY	HMB	34	E3
CABRILLO HWY	HMB	39	F4
CABRILLO HWY	P	20	D6
CABRILLO HWY	P	25	A4
CABRILLO HWY	P	27	D3
CABRILLO HWY	SMCO	27	D3
CABRILLO HWY	SMCO	30A	B6
CABRILLO HWY	SMCO	40	C4
CABRILLO HWY	SMCO	44	A1
CABRILLO HWY	SMCO	48	B5
CABRILLO HWY	SMCO	48A	B4
CABRILLO HWY	SCMO	56	A3
CABRILLO HWY	SMCO	59A	D3
CABRILLO HWY	SMCO	63	D3
CABRILLO WY	SBR	26	B4
CADILLAC WY	B	28	F1
CADIZ CIR	RC	33	E2
CADIZ CT	P	20	E6
CADIZ CT	P	27	F1
CALAVERAS AV	P	25	B4
CALAVERAS CT	H	32	A2
CALAVERAS WY	SMCO	46	C3
CALGARY ST	DC	22	D4
CALIFORNIA AV	SMCO	30	F5
CALIFORNIA AV	SSF	24	B4
CALIFORNIA DR	B	28	E1
CALIFORNIA DR	B	29	A2
CALIFORNIA DR	M	26	D6
CALIFORNIA ST	RC	36	F2

STREET	CITY	PAGE	GRID
CALIFORNIA WY	RC	36	B5
CALIFORNIA WY	SMCO	36	B6
CALIFORNIA WY	W	36	B5
CALLADO WY	A	43	B2
CALLAN BLVD	DC	23	B4
CALLAN BLVD	SSF	23	C5
CALLIE LN	MP	37	D3
CALVERT AV	SSF	23	D3
CALVIN AV	SMCO	37	B3
CALYPSO LN	SC	35	F1
CAMAHO PL	H	29	B5
CAMARITAS AV	SSF	23	D4
CAMARITAS CIR	SSF	23	D4
CAMBERLY WY	RC	37	A4
CAMBORNE AV	SC	33	A6
CAMBORNE AV	SMCO	33	A6
CAMBRIDGE AV	MP	37	E6
CAMBRIDGE AV	MP	43	E1
CAMBRIDGE LN	SBR	25	E4
CAMBRIDGE RD	B	28	E1
CAMBRIDGE RD	RC	36	D5
CAMBRIDGE ST	BLMT	33	B3
CAMBRIDGE ST	SC	33	B6
CAMDEN AV	BLMT	32	F3
CAMELIA DR	DC	23	B1
CAMELLIA AV	RC	37	A5
CAMELLIA CT	SBR	25	D2
CAMELLIA CT	EPA	38	D5
CAMELLIA DR	EPA	38	D5
CAMELOT CT	DC	23	C5
CAMELOT CT	SC	36	D2
CAMEO CT	DC	23	B4
CAMERON LN	DC	22	A5
CAMERON RD	H	28	F3
CM AL LAGO P LN	A	43	B2
CM A LOS CERROS	A	43	B2
CM A LOS CERROS	SMCO	43	B2
CAMINO ALTO	M	26	C6
CM D LOS ROBLES	A	43	C2
CM D LOS ROBLES	SMCO	43	B2
CAMINO PLAZA	SBR	26	A2
CM POR LS ARBLS	A	43	C2
CAMINO VISTA CT	BLMT	33	A3
CAMPANA AV	DC	19	B2
CAMPANA AV	DC	23	A2
CAMPBELL AV	MP	37	E3
CAMPBELL LN	MP	43	C4
CAMPBELL ST	CLMA	23	D1
CAMPHOR CT	H	28	D5
CAMPHOR WY	EPA	38	C5
CAMPO RD	PV	47	B4
CAMPO BELLO CT	MP	43	C3
CAMPO BELLO LN	MP	43	C3
CMP POMPONIO RD	SMCO	50A	F6
CMP POMPONIO RD	SMCO	51A	A4
CAMPUS DR	DC	23	B3
CAMPUS DR	SM	32	C2
CANADA LN	W	42	D3
CANADA RD	SMCO	32	C6
CANADA RD	SMCO	35	D2
CANADA RD	SMCO	36	A5
CANADA RD	W	36	A5
CANADA RD	W	42	D3
CANADA COVE DR	HMB	39	F3
CANADA VISTA	SMCO	50	C4
CANANEA AV	B	28	C3
CANANEA PL	B	28	C3
CANIS LN	FCTY	29A	B3
CANNERY SQ	DC	23	D1
CANOE CT	RC	33	D1
CANOGA WY	M	26	A4
CANTERBURY AV	DC	23	B5
CANTERBURY RD	H	29	A5
CANVASBACK WY	RC	33	E1
CANYON CT	SSF	25	E1
CANYON DR	DC	22	C4
CANYON DR	P	20	F1

COPYRIGHT © 1991 BY Thomas Bros Maps

1991 SAN MATEO COUNTY STREET INDEX

COPYRIGHT © 1991 BY Thomas Bros Maps

STREET	CITY	PAGE	GRID
CANYON DR	P	25	B1
CANYON DR	PV	47	B4
CANYON LN	RC	36	D4
CANYON LN	SMCO	36	D4
CANYON RD	RC	36	D4
CANYON RD	SMCO	28	D3
CANYON RD	SMCO	36	D4
CANYON RD	SMCO	57	B5
CANYON OAK CT	SM	32	C3
CAPAY CIR	SSF	23	E5
CAPE BRETON CT	P	25	C6
CAPE BRETON DR	P	25	C6
CAPE COD DR	RC	33	F2
CAPE HATTRAS CT	RC	33	D3
CAPISTRANO AV	P	27A	A2
CAPISTRANO RD	SMCO	30A	A5
CAPISTRANO WY	B	28	C2
CAPISTRANO WY	SM	29	D5
CAPISTRANO WY E	SM	29	D5
CAPISTRANO WY W	SM	29	D5
CAPITOL AV	EPA	38	B5
CAPPER CT	SMCO	43	A1
CAPRI LN	FCTY	33	C1
CAPRINO WY	SC	36	B1
CAPSTAN CT	RC	33	D3
CAPUCHINO AV	B	28	E1
CAPUCHINO DR	M	26	B5
CARAVEL LN	FCTY	29A	C5
CARDIFF LN	RC	37	B1
CARDIGAN RD	H	29	A6
CARIBBEAN WY	SM	29	C6
CARINA LN	FCTY	29A	B6
CARLETON AV	DC	19	B1
CARLETON AV	DC	23	A1
CARLETON CT	RC	36	F5
CARLISLE DR	SM	29	E4
CARLMONT DR	BLMT	32	F5
CARLOS AV	B	28	E2
CARLOS AV	RC	37	A4
CARLOS ST	SMCO	30	D2
CARLOW WY	SSF	25	D1
CARLSBAD CT	SSF	23	E6
CARLTON AV	MP	38	A4
CARLTON AV	SBR	26	B3
CARLTON CT	SSF	24	C4
CARLTON RD	H	28	F6
CARLTON RD	H	29	A6
CARMEL AV	DC	19	A2
CARMEL AV	P	20	E1
CARMEL AV	P	25	A1
CARMEL AV	SMCO	30A	B5
CARMEL CIR	SM	29	D5
CARMEL DR	SBR	25	D2
CARMEL LN	SMCO	36	C3
CARMEL WY	SMCO	51	C1
CARMELITA AV	BLMT	32	F4
CARMELITA AV	B	28	F2
CARMELITA DR	SC	33	B6
CARMELO LN	SSF	23	E4
CARNELIAN RD	SSF	24	A4
CAROL AV	B	29	B3
CAROL AV E	B	29	B3
CAROLAN AV	B	28	F1
CAROLAN AV	B	29	A1
CAROLAN AV N	B	28	E1
CAROLE CT	EPA	38	C4
CAROLE WY	RC	36	F4
CAROLINA AV	RC	36	F6
CAROLINA LN	A	37	B5
CAROLINE WY	DC	22	B4
CARRIAGE CT	MP	43	B3
CARSON ST	RC	36	E5
CARTER DR	SSF	23	C6
CARTER ST	DC	22	C4
CARTER WY	MP	43	B3
CARTIER LN	FCTY	29A	C6
CARY AV	SM	29	E3
CASA AV	DC	23	B2
CASA BONA AV	BLMT	32	F4
CASA DE CAMPO	SM	33	A1
CASA DEL MAR DR	HMB	34	D3
CASANOVA DR	SM	33	A1
CASCADE CT	SM	29	D3
CASCADE DR	MP	43	B3
CASEY CT	MP	38	B3
CASEY CT	SM	32	F2
CASEY DR	SSF	23	D5
CASHLEA CT	SSF	23	C5
CASSIA ST	RC	37	A2
CASTANYA WY	SMCO	47	C1
CASTENADA DR	H	28	C1
CASTENADA DR	M	28	C1
CASTILIAN WY	SM	29	C5
CASTILLEJO DR	DC	19	B3
CASTILLEJO DR	DC	23	A3
CASTILLO AV	B	28	E2
CASTLE CT	H	28	E5
CASTLE ST	DC	21	F6
CASTLE WY	MP	43	D1
CASTLE HILL RD	RC	36	D5
CASTLEMONT AV	DC	21	D5
CASTLETON AV	DC	21	C6
CASTLETON WY	SBR	25	D2
CASTOR ST	FCTY	29A	B6
CASTRO CT	B	28	D2
CASTRO CT	P	27A	A
CATALINA AV	P	19	B4
CATALINA AV	P	23	A4
CATALPA AV	SM	29	C3
CATALPA DR	A	37	E4
CATALPA WY	SBR	25	E2
CATAMARAN LN	DC	23	D1
CATAMARAN ST	FCTY	29A	C6
CATHERINE DR	SSF	23	D5
CATHY PL	MP	43	D1
CAVANAUGH ST	SM	29	D2
CAVOUR ST E	DC	21	F6
CAVOUR ST W	DC	21	E6
CAXTON CT	SM	32	D2
CAYMAN LN	FCTY	33	D1
CEBALO LN	A	37	B4
CEDAR AV	SBR	25	F3
CEDAR AV	SBR	26	A3
CEDAR AV	SMCO	57	C3
CEDAR CT	DC	22	C4
CEDAR CT	H	28	F3
CEDAR CT	H	29	A3
CEDAR CT	SMCO	43	B2
CEDAR LN	P	20	F2
CEDAR LN	P	25	A2
CEDAR LN	W	42	D3
CEDAR PL	SSF	24	B4
CEDAR ST	M	26	C4
CEDAR ST	RC	37	A3
CEDAR ST	SC	33	C6
CEDAR ST	SC	36	D1
CEDAR ST	SMCO	27	E6
CEDAR ST	SMCO	30	E1
CEDARWOOD CT	SBR	25	A3
CEDARWOOD DR	SM	32	C3
CEDARWOOD WY	RC	37	A1
CELESTE DR	SM	29	E5
CELESTIAL CT	P	27A	A1
CELESTIAL LN	FCTY	29A	B6
CELIA CT	P	27A	A1
CENTAURUS LN	FCTY	29A	B3
CENTER DR	SSF	23	F6
CENTER ST	M	26	C5
CENTER ST	RC	37	A4
CENTER ST	SC	33	E6
CENTER PARK LN	FCTY	29A	B5
CENTRAL AV	B	29	B3
CENTRAL AV	HMB	34	E5
CENTRAL AV	HMB	39	F1
CENTRAL AV	MP	38	A5
CENTRAL AV	RC	37	A4
CENTRAL AV	SC	36	D1
CENTRAL DR	MP	38	A4
CERES ST	SMCO	30	D3
CERRITO AV	SMCO	36	F6
CERRITO AV	SMCO	37	A6
CERRITO AV	SMCO	42	F1
CERRITO AV	SMCO	43	A1
CERRITO PL	SMCO	42	F1
CERRO DR	DC	23	B2
CERROS MANOR	SMCO	43	B2
CERVANTES RD	PV	47	B2
CERVANTES RD	SMCO	36	C3
CERVANTES WY	P	20	D6
CHABOT DR	SBR	25	D2
CHADBOURNE AV	M	26	C6
CHADWICK CT	M	28	B1
CHALLENGE CT	FCTY	29A	C4
CHAMPS ELYSE BL	HMB	34	D2
CHANNEL CIR	BLMT	33	C2
CHANNEL CT	BLMT	33	C2
CHANNEL DR	RC	33	E2
CHANNING AV	HMB	34	E3
CHANNING LN	P	19	B5
CHANNING LN	P	23	A5
CHANNING RD	B	29	C2
CHANTAL WY	RC	36	F4
CHAPEL LN	MP	38	A4
CHAPEL VIEW DR	SMCO	31	E6
CHAPIN AV	B	29	A3
CHAPIN LN	B	29	A3
CHAPMAN AV	SBR	26	B3
CHAPMAN AV	SSF	24	C4
CHAPMAN RD	SMCO	46	C4
CHARING CRSS RD	SMCO	32	C3
CHARING CRSS WY	P	20	F2
CHARING CRSS WY	P	25	A2
CHARLES LN	SM	29	E5
CHARLESTON AV	SBR	25	E3
CHARLTON ST	SC	33	B6
CHARTER ST	RC	37	B3
CHARTER ST	SMCO	37	B3
CHARTHOUSE LN	FCTY	33	C2
CHATEAU CT	SSF	25	E1
CHATEAU DR	H	28	E5
CHATEAU DR	MP	37	D6
CHATHAM CT	RC	36	D6
CHATHAM CT	SSF	23	C5
CHATHAM RD	B	29	B2
CHATSWORTH LN	RC	37	B1
CHEBEC LN	FCTY	29A	C5
CHELMSFORD RD	H	29	B4
CHELSEA CT	DC	21	F4
CHELSEA WY	RC	37	A5
CHEMICAL WY	RC	37	A1
CHEROKEE CT	PV	47	B3
CHEROKEE WY	PV	47	B3
CHERRY AV	MP	37	E5
CHERRY AV	SBR	26	A3
CHERRY AV	SSF	23	F5
CHERRY AV	SSF	24	A5
CHERRY LN	SC	33	D5
CHERRY ST	SC	33	D5
CHERRYWOOD DR	SM	32	C3
CHERYL CT	SM	32	C3
CHERYL PL	MP	43	D1
CHESAPEAKE AV	FCTY	33	B2
CHESAPEAKE DR	RC	33A	B6
CHESHAM AV	SMCO	33	B6
CHESHAM AV	SMCO	36	B1
CHESHIRE WY	RC	36	E4
CHESS DR	FCTY	29A	B4
CHESTER PL	P	19	B5
CHESTER PL	P	23	A5
CHESTER ST	DC	22	A6
CHESTER ST	MP	38	A4
CHESTER ST	SMCO	23	C1
CHESTER WY	SM	29	A4
CHESTERFIELD AV	HMB	34	E4
CHESTERTON AV	BLMT	33	B3
CHESTERTON AV	RC	36	E5
CHESTERTON PL	SM	29	C4
CHESTNUT AV	SBR	26	A3
CHESTNUT AV	SSF	23	F5
CHESTNUT LN	SM	32	F2
CHESTNUT ST	MP	37	D6
CHESTNUT ST	RC	37	A3
CHESTNUT ST	SC	33	C5
CHESTNUT ST	SC	36	D1
CHEVY ST	BLMT	33	A4
CHEYENNE PT	PV	47	B3
CHICO AV	SMCO	30	D2
CHICO CT	P	20	E6
CHICO CT	P	27	F1
CHICO CT	SSF	23	E5
CHICORY LN	SC	35	F1
CHILCO ST	MP	37	F3
CHILCO ST	MP	38	A3
CHILTERN RD	H	29	B5
CHILTON AV	SC	33	A6
CHILTON LN	SBR	25	C2
CHIN CT	SMCO	36	C5
CHIQUITA ST	SMCO	51	C1
CHRIS LN	SM	32	C3
CHRISTEN AV	DC	23	C5
CHRISTIAN CT	BLMT	32	C5
CHRISTIAN DR	BLMT	32	C5
CHRISTINE LN	M	26	B5
CHRISTOBAL ST	P	23	A6
CHRISTOPHER CT	DC	19	B3
CHRISTOPHER CT	DC	23	A3
CHRISTOPHER WY	MP	37	D3
CHRYSLER DR	MP	37	E2
CHRYSOPOLIS DR	FCTY	29A	C5
CHUKKER CT	SM	29	D6
CHULA VISTA AV	B	28	F2
CHULA VISTA AV	B	29	A2
CHULA VISTA DR	BLMT	33	A5
CHULA VISTA RD	SMCO	27	F6
CHURCH AV	SM	29	F4
CHURCH RD	SM	29	E3
CHURCH ST	HMB	34	F4
CHURCHILL AV	W	42	F1
CHURCHILL DR	H	28	D4
CIERVOS RD	SMCO	51	C2
CIMA WY	PV	47	B4
CINDY WY	P	20	F3
CINDY WY	P	25	A3
CINNABAR RD	W	42	D1
CINNAMON CT	H	28	E4
CIPRIANI BLVD	BLMT	32	E4
CIRCLE CT	SSF	23	F4
CIRCLE DR	SBR	25	F5
CIRCLE DR	EPA	38	C5
CIRCLE LN	MP	37	F4
CIRCLE RD	RC	36	D3
CIRO AV	SM	29A	A6
CIRRUS CT	RC	36	D5
CITATION AV	SBR	26	A1
CITRUS AV	DC	21	E5
CITRUS CT	H	28	E4
CITY HALL LN	B	29	B2
CITYHOMES LN	FCTY	29A	B5
CITY VIEW DR	DC	22	B4
CIVIC LN	BLMT	33	B4
CLAIRE PL	MP	43	D1
CLARA AV	SSF	23	E4
CLAREMONT AV	RC	36	E1
CLAREMONT AV	SSF	24	B3
CLAREMONT CT	M	26	A5
CLAREMONT DR	SBR	25	E3
CLAREMONT PL	MP	37	F6
CLAREMONT PL	MP	43	E1
CLAREMONT ST	SM	29	C3
CLAREMONT WY	MP	37	F6
CLAREMONT WY	MP	43	E1
CLARENCE CT	EPA	38	B3
CLARENDON RD	B	29	B2
CLARENDON RD	P	20	E2
CLARENDON RD	P	25	A2
CLARICE LN	B	28	D1
CLARIDGE DR	P	23	B6
CLARINADA AV	DC	19	B3
CLARINADA AV	DC	23	A3
CLARK AV	CLMA	23	C1
CLARK AV	DC	23	C1
CLARK AV	SBR	26	A3
CLARK AV	SMCO	23	C1
CLARK CT	P	23	B6
CLARK DR	P	23	B4
CLARK DR	SM	29	B4
CLARKE AV	EPA	38	C6
CLAUDIA A	SM	29A	A6
CLAY AV	SSF	23	C4
CLAY DR	A	43	B1
CLAYTON CT	DC	21	F6
CLAYTON DR	MP	43	C3
CLEARFIELD DR	M	26	B6
CLEARVIEW DR	DC	19	B4
CLEARVIEW DR	DC	23	A4
CLEARVIEW WY	SM	32	C2
CLEARVIEW WY	SMCO	32	C3
CLEE ST	BLMT	33	A4
CLELAND PL	MP	38	A5
CLEVELAND AV	SM	29	F5
CLEVELAND CT	RC	36	F3
CLIFDEN DR	SSF	23	C4
CLIFFORD AV	SC	36	C2
CLIFFORD AV	SMCO	36	C2
CLIFFSIDE CT	BLMT	32	F5
CLIFFSIDE DR	DC	21	D5
CLIFTON AV	SC	33	B5
CLIFTON DR	DC	21	C5
CLIFTON RD	P	19	B5
CLIFTON RD	P	23	A5
CLINTON ST	RC	36	F3
CLINTON ST	RC	37	A3
CLINTON, J H AV	SM	29	E3
CLIPPER CT	BLMT	33	B2
CLIPPER DR	BLMT	33	B2
CLIPPER LN	FCTY	29	C5
CLIPPER ST	SM	29	F4
CLIPPER ST	SM	29A	A4
CLIPPER WY	DC	23	D1
CLOISTER WY	DC	22	A5
CLOUD AV	SMCO	43	C2
CLOVELLY LN	B	26	E6
CLOVELLY LN	B	28	E1
CLOVER CIR	SSF	23	F4
CLOVER LN	MP	37	F6
CLOVER LN	SC	36	A1
CLOVERDALE RD	SMCO	56	E1
CLOVERDALE RD	SMCO	57	A5
CLOVERDALE RD	SMCO	57A	B2
CLUB DR	BLMT	32	F6
CLUB DR	BLMT	33	A6
CLUB DR	SC	33	A6
CLUB DR	SMCO	33	A6
CLUB VIEW DR	DC	22	A6
CLYDESDALE DR	H	29	C6
COALMINE VIEW	PV	47	B5
COAST LN	P	20	E5
COBB LN	SMCO	57	B2
COBB ST	SM	29	E4
COBBLE HILL RD	SMCO	32	B4
COBBLESTONE LN	BLMT	33	B3
COBBLESTONE LN	SC	36	C2
COD ST	FCTY	29A	D5
CODO ST	SMCO	30	F5
COGHLAN LN	A	37	B6
COGHLAN LN	A	43	B1
COLBY AV	SMCO	37	F4

1991 SAN MATEO COUNTY STREET INDEX

STREET	CITY	PAGE	GRID
COLBY WY	SBR	25	C1
COLEGROVE CT	SM	32	F2
COLEGROVE ST	SM	32	F2
COLEMAN AV	MP	37	F5
COLEMAN AV	MP	38	A5
COLEMAN AV	SMCO	37	F5
COLEMAN CT	SC	33	B6
COLEMAN CT	SC	36	B1
COLEMAN PL	MP	37	F5
COLEMAN PL	MP	38	A5
COLEPORT LANDNG	RC	33	D1
COLGATE AV	SM	29	C5
COLLEGE AV	MP	37	E6
COLLEGE AV	MP	43	E1
COLLEGE AV	SM	29	C2
COLLEGE AV	SMCO	37	F5
COLLEGE AV	SMCO	43	C3
COLLEGE DR	SBR	25	D2
COLLEGE SN M DR	SM	32	B2
COLLEGE SN M DR	SMCO	32	B2
COLLEGE VIEW WY	BLMT	33	A4
COLLINS AV	CLMA	23	C3
COLMA BLVD	CLMA	23	C2
COLMA CK SER RD	SSF	24	C6
COLONEL WY	HMB	34	F5
COLONIAL PL	SMCO	36	F6
COLONIAL PL	SMCO	37	A6
COLORADOS DR	M	26	B6
COLORADOS DR	M	28	B1
COLTON CT	RC	36	B5
COLTON AV	SC	36	D2
COLUMBA LN	FCTY	29A	B6
COLUMBIA AV	A	37	B4
COLUMBIA AV	SMCO	37	B4
COLUMBIA CIR	RC	33	F3
COLUMBIA DR	SM	29	B6
COLUMBIA ST	SMCO	30	F6
COLUMBIA WY	RC	33	F3
COLUMBUS AV	B	28	E2
COLUMBUSST	SMCO	30A	C5
COLUSA CT	SBR	25	D2
COMERWOOD CT	SSF	23	E6
COMET DR	FCTY	29A	C4
COMMANDER LN	RC	33	D2
COMMERCIAL AV	SSF	23	F4
COMMERCIAL AV	SSF	24	A5
COMMERICAL ST	SC	33	D5
COMMERICAL WY	RC	36	F2
COMMODORE DR	SBR	26	A2
COMMODORE DR W	SBR	25	F2
COMMONS LN	FCTY	29A	B5
COMMONWEALTH DR	MP	37	E3
COMO AV	DC	21	E5
COMPASS CIR	RC	33	D3
COMPASS DR	RC	33	D2
COMPASS LN	FCTY	29A	D6
COMSTOCK CIR	BLMT	32	D5
COMSTOCK RD	SMCO	41	C1
COMUS ST	SMCO	30	D2
CONCAR DR	SM	29	E5
CONCHITA CT	P	19	B6
CONCHITA CT	P	23	A6
CONCORD DR	MP	38	A5
CONCORD WY	B	29	B2
CONCORD WY	SBR	25	E3
CONCOURSE DR	BLMT	33	B2
CONDON CT	SM	32	C3
CONDOR LN	FCTY	29A	D4
CONEJO DR	M	28	B1
CONIFER LN	H	28	F4
CONIL WY	SMCO	47	C1
CONMUR ST	SSF	23	E6
CONMUR ST	SSF	25	E1
CONNECTICUT DR	RC	36	F5
CONNIE AV	SM	29	E5
CONNOLLY WY	EPA	38	C4
CONRAD CT	SSF	23	D4

STREET	CITY	PAGE	GRID
CONSTELLTION CT	RC	33	F3
CONSTITUTION DR	FCTY	29A	C5
CONSTITUTION DR	MP	37	E2
CONSTITUTION WY	SSF	23	F6
CONTINENTAL CT	MP	43	B3
CONTINENTALS WY	BLMT	32	E5
CONVENTION WY	RC	36	F1
COOK ST	CLMA	23	E2
COOKIE CT	SMCO	36	D3
COOLEY AV	EPA	38	B5
COOS CT	FCTY	33	C1
COPELAND ST	P	20	E5
COPLEY AV	RC	36	D2
COQUITO CT	SMCO	47	C1
COQUITO WY	SMCO	47	C1
CORAL LN	FCTY	33	B2
CORAL PL	DC	23	D1
CORAL ST	SMCO	30	D2
CORAL REEF AV	SMCO	30A	A5
CORAL RIDGE CT	P	19	B4
CORAL RIDGE DR	P	19	B4
CORAL RIDGE DR	P	23	A4
CORBITT DR	B	29	A1
CORDILLERAS AV	SC	33	C6
CORDILLERAS AV	SC	36	D1
CORDILLERAS CT	SMCO	36	B3
CORDILLERAS RD	RC	36	C3
CORDILLERAS RD	SMCO	36	C3
CORDOVA CT	PV	47	C3
CORDOVA LN	P	20	E6
COREY WY	SSF	24	C6
CORINNE LN	MP	43	C1
CORK PL	SSF	23	C6
CORK HRBOUR CIR	RC	33	D2
CORLETT WY	H	28	E5
CORNELIA AV	SM	29	C5
CORNELIA DR	H	29	A5
CORNELL AV	SM	29	C5
CORNELL AV	SMCO	30	F5
CORNELL RD	MP	43	E1
CORNISH WY	BLMT	33	B3
CORNWALLIS LN	FCTY	33	C1
CORONA ST	SMCO	30	E5
CORONA DR	P	20	E6
CORONA ST	SMCO	27	E6
CORONA WY	SMCO	47	C1
CORONADO AV	DC	21	D5
CORONADO AV	SC	33	B6
CORONADO AV	SMCO	30A	C6
CORONADO AV	SMCO	34	C1
CORONADO DR	SMCO	30	F1
CORONADO LN	FCTY	29A	C6
CORONADO ST	SMCO	30A	B6
CORONADO WY	B	28	D1
CORONADO WY	SBR	25	C1
CORONET BLVD	BLMT	32	F4
CORRAL WY	HMB	39	F4
CORREAS AV	HMB	34	E5
CORREAS ST	HMB	34	F5
CORRIDO WY	SSF	25	E1
CORSAIR LN	FCTY	29A	C5
CORSICA LN	FCTY	33	C1
CORTE ALEGRA	M	26	B6
CORTE ALEGRA	M	28	B1
CORTE ANNA	M	26	D5
CORTE BALBOA	M	26	D5
CORTE CAMELLIA	M	26	B6
CORTE CAMELLIA	M	28	B1
CORTE COMODA	M	26	D5
CORTE DE FLORES	SM	32	E1
CORTE DEL SOL	M	26	B6
CORTE DORADO	M	26	C6
CORTE MADERA RD	PV	47	B4
CORTE NUEVA	M	26	B6
CORTE PRINCESA	M	26	B6
CORTES AV	SSF	24	B4
CORTEZ AV	B	28	E1
CORTEZ AV	SMCO	30A	C6

STREET	CITY	PAGE	GRID
CORTEZ AV	SMCO	34	C1
CORTEZ AV	SSF	23	F6
CORTEZ LN	FCTY	29A	C5
CORTEZ RD	SMCO	36	C3
CORTO LN	W	42	D2
CORVUS LN	FCTY	29A	B3
COSTA RICA AV	B	29	B3
COSTA RICA AV	SM	29	B3
COTTAGE LN	SC	33	B5
COTTAGE GRV AV	SM	29	E3
COTTON PL	MP	43	D2
COTTON ST	MP	43	D2
COTTONWOOD AV	SSF	23	F4
COTTONWOOD AV	SSF	24	A4
COTTONWOOD CT	H	28	E4
COTTONWOOD DR	DC	21	F5
COTTONWOOD DR	SBR	25	E2
COUNTRY LN	RC	37	A5
COUNTRY LN	SMCO	37	A5
COUNTRY CLUB DR	H	29	A3
COUNTRY CLUB DR	RC	36	D5
COUNTRY CLUB DR	SSF	23	F6
COUNTRYSIDE DR	SM	32	D2
COUNTY RD	P	20	E4
COUNTY RD	SMCO	41	D2
COUNTY ST	DC	21	F6
COUNTY ST	DC	23	C1
COURT E	DC	22	A5
COURTLAND DR	SBR	25	F4
COURTLAND RD	BLMT	33	B5
COURT SAN MARCO	HMB	34	D1
COVE LN	RC	33	D2
COVENTRY CT	SC	36	A2
COVINGTON RD	BLMT	32	F4
COWAN RD	B	26	E5
COWELL LN	A	43	B1
COWPENS WY	SMCO	32	B4
COYOTE HILL	PV	47	B5
COYOTE POINT DR	SM	29	C1
COZZOLINO CT	M	26	B5
CRAGMONT CT	P	19	B6
CRAGMONT CT	P	23	A6
CRAGMONT CT	SM	32	D2
CRAGMONT WY	W	42	D1
CRAIG CT	DC	23	C1
CRAIG RD	H	28	E5
CRANE AV	FCTY	29A	C3
CRANE ST	MP	37	D6
CRANE WY	MP	37	D6
CRANFIELD AV	SC	33	A6
CRANHAM CT	P	27A	A2
CRATER LAKE WY	P	27A	B2
CRAZY PETES RD	SMCO	51	B3
CREEK AV	SMCO	41	C3
CREEK DR	MP	37	F6
CREEK DR	MP	43	E1
CREEK PL	MP	37	E6
CREEK PL	MP	43	E1
CREEK TR	SMCO	41	D2
CREEK PARK DR	PV	47	C3
CREEKRIDGE CT	SM	32	C2
CREEKSIDE DR	HMB	39	F3
CREEKWOOD DR	SMCO	49A	E5
CREEKWOOD WY	H	29	B5
CRENSHAW CT	P	19	B4
CRENSHAW CT	P	23	A4
CRENSHAW DR	DC	23	A4
CRENSHAW DR	P	19	B4
CRENSHAW DR	P	23	A4
CRESCENT AV	B	29	A3
CRESCENT AV	PV	47	B4
CRESCENT AV	SM	29	B3
CRESCENT AV	SMCO	30	E3
CRESCENT ST	SMCO	30	F2
CRESPI DR	P	20	E6
CRESPI DR	P	25	A6
CRESPI DR	P	27A	A1

STREET	CITY	PAGE	GRID
CREST DR	SMCO	36	C4
CREST LN	MP	43	B3
CREST RD	W	42	D1
CRESTA VISTA LN	PV	47	B2
CRESTLINE AV	DC	19	B1
CRESTLINE AV	DC	23	A1
CRESTMOOR CIR	P	19	B5
CRESTMOOR CIR	P	23	A5
CRESTMOOR DR	SBR	25	F4
CRESTON AV	DC	21	C6
CRESTVIEW AV	BLMT	33	A3
CRESTVIEW AV	DC	19	A1
CRESTVIEW AV	DC	21	C6
CRESTVIEW CT	SC	36	B3
CRESTVIEW DR	M	26	A6
CRESTVIEW DR	SC	32	F6
CRESTVIEW DR	SC	35	F1
CRESTVIEW DR	SC	36	A2
CRESTWOOD CT	SM	32	C3
CRESTWOOD DR	DC	21	D5
CRESTWOOD DR	SBR	25	E1
CRESTWOOD DR	SM	32	C3
CRESTWOOD DR	SSF	23	E3
CRINGLE DR	RC	33	D2
CRIPPLERIDGE CT	SM	32	B2
CROCKER AV	DC	22	B5
CROCKER AV	SMCO	37	B3
CROCKER RD	DC	22	A5
CROCKETT LN	H	28	F2
CROCUS CT	SMCO	43	C3
CROFTON WY	SSF	23	C5
CROMPTON RD	RC	36	E5
CROMWELL ROW	SSF	23	B6
CRONER AV	SMCO	43	C2
CROSBY CT	SBR	25	E3
CROSS WY, THE	SMCO	34	D1
CROSSWAY RD	B	29	A2
CROSSWAYS, THE	SMCO	30A	C6
CROWN CIR	SSF	23	D4
CROWN CT	SMCO	32	C4
CROYDON WY	W	42	E1
CRYSTAL CT	FCTY	33	B1
CRYSTAL CT	SBR	26	A4
CRYSTAL DR	H	31	F2
CRYSTAL DR	H	32	A2
CRYSTAL TER	SMCO	28	C3
CRYSTAL SPG AV	SBR	26	A4
CRYSTAL SPG CT	H	29	F1
CRYSTAL SPG RD	H	29	B6
CRYSTAL SPG RD	H	32	A2
CRYSTAL SPG RD	SBR	25	F5
CRYSTAL SPG RD	SM	29	B6
CRYSTAL SPG RD	SMCO	31	F2
CRYSTAL SPG RD	SMCO	32	A2
CRYSTL SPGS TER	H	29	A6
CUARDO AV	M	26	D5
CUESTA AV	SM	32	D1
CUESTA DR	SSF	23	D5
CUESTA REAL	SMCO	50	B5
CULEBRA DR	SMCO	30	E5
CULEBRA RD	H	29	B5
CULLEN DR	P	20	F3
CULLEN DR	P	25	A3
CULVER CT	SM	32	F2
CUMBERLAND CT	FCTY	33	B1
CUMBERLAND RD	B	29	B2
CUNNINGHAM WY	SBR	26	A3
CUPERTINO WY	SM	33	A2
CUPID ROW	SBR	26	B3
CURLEW CT	FCTY	29A	C3
CURRY CT	SC	33	A5
CURTIS AV	SMCO	37	B3
CURTIS CT	SC	33	A5
CURTIS ST	MP	37	D6
CURTIS ST	SM	32	F1
CURTIS ST	SM	33	A1
CURTIS WY	MP	37	D6
CUT ACROSS RD	SMCO	51A	E4

STREET	CITY	PAGE	GRID
CUTTER LN	FCTY	29A	D6
CUTTER ST	FCTY	29A	D6
CUTWATER LN	FCTY	33	C2
CYGNUS LN	FCTY	29A	B6
CYNTHIA ST	CLMA	23	D2
CYPRESS AV	BLMT	33	B4
CYPRESS AV	B	29	B3
CYPRESS AV	HMB	34	E4
CYPRESS AV	SBR	26	B4
CYPRESS AV	SM	29	D3
CYPRESS AV	SMCO	30	D3
CYPRESS AV	SSF	24	B5
CYPRESS CT	DC	22	D5
CYPRESS CT	M	26	B5
CYPRESS CT	SBR	26	B3
CYPRESS CT	SC	36	C2
CYPRESS LN	BR	24	B1
CYPRESS LN	DC	22	D5
CYPRESS ST	EPA	38	D4
CYPRESS ST	RC	37	A4
CYPRESS ST	SMCO	30	F2
CYPRESS CIR DR	SMCO	31	D6
CYPRESS PT RD	HMB	39	E3
D			
D ST	CLMA	23	C1
D ST	MP	37	E5
D ST	RC	36	E1
D ST	SMCO	23	B1
DAFFODILL LN	SC	36	A1
DAIRY LN	BLMT	33	C3
DAISY LN	EPA	38	D5
DAISY ST	SM	29	F4
DAKIN AV	SMCO	43	C2
DAKOTA AV	SM	29	E3
DALE AV	SC	33	B6
DALE AV	SM	29	E4
DALE WY	P	20	D6
DALEHURST AV	SM	32	E2
DALEHURST CT	SM	32	E3
DALEROSE CT	DC	22	C4
DALE VIEW AV	BLMT	33	A2
DALEY CT	M	26	C4
DALEY CT	SBR	25	E3
DALY CT	SSF	23	F4
DAMONTE CT	SSF	24	B3
DANA CT	SSF	23	F6
DANBERRY LN	DC	22	A5
DANBURY LN	RC	37	A4
DANMANN AV	P	20	D6
DAPHNE CT	EPA	38	D5
DAPHNE WY	EPA	38	D6
DARBY PL	SBR	25	F5
DARCY AV	SM	32	F2
DARCY CT	SM	32	F2
DARDENELLE AV	P	25	B4
DARLENE AV	SM	29A	A6
DARLENE ST	SM	29A	A6
DARRELL RD	H	28	E5
DARRELL RD	H	31	F1
DARTMOUTH AV	SC	33	B5
DARTMOUTH RD	MS	29	C5
DARWIN AV	SM	29	F5
DATE ST	SMCO	27	E6
DATE ST	SMCO	30	E1
DAVEY GLEN RD	BLMT	33	A3
DAVID AV	SM	29A	A6
DAVID CT	SM	29A	A6
DAVID RD	B	26	E6
DAVID RD	B	28	E1
DAVIS CT	B	28	D1
DAVIS DR	BLMT	32	E5
DAVIS DR	B	28	D1
DAVIS ST	RC	36	F3
DAVIT LN	RC	33	E2
DAY AV	SM	29A	A6

Copyright © 1991 by Thomas Bros maps

1991 SAN MATEO COUNTY STREET INDEX

STREET	CITY	PAGE	GRID
DAYTON AV	SC	36	C1
DEAN RD	W	42	D2
DEANNA DR	MP	43	B3
DEANNE LN	DC	23	C1
DE ANZA AV	SC	36	C2
DE ANZA BLVD	SM	32	C3
DE ANZA CT	SM	32	C3
DEARBORN PK RD	SMCO	49A	D6
DEARBORN PK RD	SMCO	57	D1
DEBBIE CT	SC	36	C2
DEBBIE LN	BLMT	33	A3
DEBBIE LN	SC	36	C2
DEBBIE PL	SC	36	B2
DE BELL DR	A	37	E5
DECATUR ST	FCTY	29A	C6
DECATUR ST	FCTY	33	C1
DECOTA AV	SMCO	30	E4
DEDALERA DR	SMCO	47	C1
DEER MEADOW LN	PV	47	B2
DEER PARK LN	PV	47	A2
DEER PARK RD	SM	29	D6
DEER PATH DR	SMCO	51	C2
DEGAS RD	PV	47	B2
DE KOVEN AV	BLMT	32	E4
DELAWARE AV	RC	36	F6
DELAWARE ST	SM	29	C2
DEL CENTRO	M	28	B1
DE LEON LN	FCTY	29A	C6
DELFINO WY	MP	43	C2
DELL RD	P	27	F1
DELLBROOK AV	SSF	23	E3
DEL MAR AV	P	19	B5
DEL MAR AV	P	23	A5
DEL MAR AV	SMCO	30	E4
DELMAR CT	RC	37	D2
DELMAR WY	SM	32	E1
DEL MONTE AV	SSF	23	D4
DEL MONTE DR	H	28	D3
DEL MONTE DR	P	19	B4
DEL MONTE DR	P	23	A4
DEL MONTE PL	SM	32	D2
DEL MONTE RD	SMCO	30A	B5
DEL MONTE ST	SMCO	32	D2
DEL NORTE AV	MP	37	F3
DEL NORTE DR	SBR	25	D3
DE LONG ST	DC	21	E4
DEL ORA	RC	36	E3
DEL PASO DR	SSF	23	E5
DEL PRADO DR	DC	19	B2
DEL PRADO DR	DC	23	A2
DELRAY ST	SM	32	D2
DEL REY CT	SMCO	33	B5
DEL ROSA WY	SM	33	A2
DELVIN WY	SSF	25	D1
DEMETER ST	EPA	38	C3
DENALI DR	SM	32	C3
DENARDI WY	SSF	25	E1
DENHAM CT	H	28	F2
DENISE DR	H	28	F6
DENISE DR	H	31	F1
DENISE DR	SMCO	31	F1
DENISE LN	SMCO	37	A6
DENNIS DR	DC	23	C5
DENNIS MARTN RD	W	46	D2
DEODORA DR	A	37	E3
DERBY ST	DC	23	C4
DERECHO ST	SMCO	30	F5
DERRY LN	MP	37	D5
DERRY WY	SSF	23	D6
DE SABLA RD	H	29	C4
DE SABLA RD	SM	29	C4
DE SOLO DR	P	20	D6
DE SOLO DR	P	26	E1
DE SOTO AV	B	28	E2
DE SOTO LN	FCTY	29A	C5
DE SOTO WY	SBR	26	B4
DESVIO CT	P	27A	A2
DESVIO WY	BLMT	33	B5
DETROIT DR	SM	29	F3
DEVEREAUX DR	B	28	E1
DEVON DR	H	29	A4
DEVON WY	RC	36	D4
DEVONSHIRE AV	SMCO	37	B3
DEVONSHIRE BLVD	SC	33	A6
DEVONSHIRE BLVD	SMCO	33	A6
DEVONSHIRE CIR	SMCO	33	A6
DEWEY AV	RC	36	E5
DEWEY DR	FCTY	33	C1
DEWEY ST	SM	29	F5
DEXTER AV	SMCO	37	B4
DEXTER PL	M	26	C5
DIABLO WY	SMCO	36	C5
DIABLO WY	SMCO	51A	D2
DIAMOND AV	SSF	24	B4
DIAMOND ST	SBR	26	B1
DIANNE CT	SSF	25	E1
DIAZ LN	FCTY	29A	C5
DICKENS CT	SC	36	B2
DICKEY ST	RC	36	F3
DILLER ST	RC	36	F2
DINES CT	EPA	38	C4
DIONNE CT	BLMT	32	C4
DIX ST	M	29	E4
DIXON CT	DC	21	E6
DOCKSIDE CIR	RC	33	E2
DOCKSIDE DR	DC	22	A6
DOCKSIDE DR	DC	23	D1
DODGE DR	RC	37	C2
DOELGER BLVD	SMCO	30A	A5
DOHERTY WY	SMCO	37	A6
DOHERTY WY	SMCO	43	A1
DOHERTY RDG RD	SMCO	51A	C5
DOLAN AV	SM	29	E3
DOLLAR AV	SBR	24	B6
DOLLAR AV	SSF	24	B6
DOLLAR AV	SSF	26	B1
DOLORES CT	SM	32	E3
DOLORES ST	SM	32	D1
DOLORES ST	SMCO	30A	B5
DOLORES WY	B	28	C2
DOLORES WY	SSF	23	F4
DOLPHIN CT	HMB	39	F4
DOLPHIN DR	P	19	A6
DOLPHIN ISLE	FCTY	29A	D4
DOLPHINE AV	SMCO	30A	C4
DOLTON AV	SMCO	33	A6
DOLTON AV	SMCO	36	A1
DOMINICA LN	FCTY	33	C1
DOMINGO WY	SMCO	30	F1
DON CT	SMCO	36	D3
DONALDSON AV	P	20	E4
DONDEE WY	P	20	E4
DONEGAL AV	SSF	25	D1
DONNELLY AV	B	29	B2
DONNER AV	SBR	26	A4
DONNER ST	SM	32	F2
DONOHOE ST	MP	38	A4
DONOHOE ST	EPA	38	B5
DORADO LN	FCTY	29A	B6
DORADO WY	SMCO	25	F1
DORADO WY	SSF	23	F6
DORCHESTER DR	DC	21	C5
DORCHESTER RD	SM	29	B4
DORE AV	SM	29	D2
DORIS CT	RC	36	F4
DORIS DR	MP	43	C2
DORY LN	FCTY	33	C2
DORY LN	RC	33	E2
DOS LOMA VIS LN	PV	47	B1
DOUGLAS AV	B	29	A2
DOUGLAS AV	RC	37	B3
DOUGLAS AV	SMCO	37	B3
DOUGLAS CT	SM	32	D3
DOUGLAS WY	A	37	D6
DOUGLAS WY	SSF	23	F3
DOVE LN	FCTY	29A	D4
DOVER CT	DC	23	B4
DOVER CT	SBR	25	F3
DOVER CT	SMCO	33	B6
DOVER CT	SMCO	36	A1
DOVER LN	FCTY	33	C1
DOVER RD	RC	36	D4
DOWNEY CT	SSF	23	D6
DOWNEY WY	H	28	E3
DOYLE ST	MP	37	D6
DRACO LN	FCTY	29A	B6
DRAKE AV	B	28	E2
DRAKE AV	SSF	24	B3
DRAKE CT	FCTY	33	B1
DRAKE CT	SC	36	B2
DRAKE ST	SMCO	30	E1
DRAYTON RD	H	29	A6
DREUSS RD	SMCO	49A	D6
DREUSS RD	SMCO	57	D1
DREW CT	EPA	38	C2
DRIFTWOOD LN	DC	23	D1
DRIFTWOOD TER	HMB	39	F4
DRURY LN	SMCO	36	C4
DRY CREEK LN	W	42	C2
DRYDEN ST	CLMA	23	D2
DUANE ST	RC	36	E2
DUBLIN CT	SSF	23	D6
DUBLIN DR	SSF	23	D6
DUBLIN WY	SM	29	E6
DUBUQUE AV	SSF	24	B5
DUCK CT	FCTY	29A	D4
DUFFERIN AV	B	26	E6
DUFFERIN AV	B	28	E1
DUGGAN CT	SMCO	36	C3
DUGGAN RD	SMCO	36	C3
DUHALLOW WY	SSF	23	C6
DULLES CT	P	27A	A2
DUMBARTON AV	RC	37	B4
DUMBARTON AV	SMCO	37	B4
DUMBARTON AV	EPA	38	B4
DUMONT CT	M	26	A6
DUMONT ST	SM	33	A2
DUNDEE DR	SSF	23	C4
DUNDEE LN	SC	36	B1
DUNKS ST	DC	21	E6
DUNKS ST	SMCO	23	B1
DUNMAN WY	SSF	23	C4
DUNNE CT	SMCO	37	C3
DUNSMUIR WY	MP	37	E3
DURAND DR	SM	33	A2
DURANT CT	P	27A	A2
DURAZNO WY	SMCO	43	C6
DURAZNO WY	SMCO	47	C1
DURHAM ST	MP	38	A4
DURLSTON RD	RC	36	D2
DUSTY TR	SMCO	57	A2
DUVAL DR	SSF	23	D3
DWIGHT AV	HMB	34	E3
DWIGHT RD	B	29	B2

E

STREET	CITY	PAGE	GRID
E ST	BLMT	33	C4
E ST	CLMA	23	B1
E ST	RC	36	E1
EAGLE LN	FCTY	29A	D4
EAGLE HILL TER	RC	36	E3
EAGLE TRACE DR	HMB	39	F2
EARL AV	SBR	25	D3
EAST AV	SBR	26	B3
EAST AV	SMCO	30	D2
EAST CT	SBR	25	F5
EAST LN	B	29	B2
EASTBURN CT	SBR	25	F3
EAST COURT LN	FCTY	29A	B5
EAST CREEK DR	MP	43	E1
EASTGATE DR	DC	21	C4
E GRAND AV OVRC	SSF	24	B5
EASTLAKE AV	DC	21	F5
EASTLAKE AV	P	20	F2
EASTLAKE AV	P	25	A2
EASTLAKE WY	RC	36	C5
EASTMOOR AV	DC	19	B1
EASTMOOR AV	DC	23	A1
EASTMOOR RD	B	28	E1
EASTON AV	SBR	26	A2
EASTON DR	B	28	E2
EASTRIDGE AV	MP	43	C4
EASTRIDGE CIR	P	19	B3
EASTRIDGE CIR	P	23	A4
EASTRIDGE CT	P	19	B3
EASTRIDGE CT	P	23	A3
EASTVIEW WY	RC	36	B5
EASTVIEW WY	W	36	B5
EASTWOOD AV	DC	19	B2
EASTWOOD AV	DC	23	A2
EASTWOOD DR	SM	32	F3
EATON AV	DC	19	A2
EATON AV	RC	36	D2
EATON AV	SC	36	E1
EATON RD	SM	29	C4
EATON VILLA PL	RC	36	C2
EATON VILLA PL	SC	36	C2
EBENER ST	RC	36	F4
EBENER ST	RC	37	A4
EBKEN ST	P	20	E5
ECCLES AV	SSF	24	C4
ECHO AV	SM	29	F4
ECHO DR	SMCO	30	D2
ECHO LN	PV	47	B4
ECHO LN	W	46	C3
EDDINGTON LN	DC	22	A5
EDDYSTONE CT	RC	33	E2
EDEN WY	H	28	E3
EDENBOWER CT	RC	36	C6
EDENBOWER LN	RC	36	D6
EDEN WEST RD	SMCO	57	A5
EDESSA CT	H	28	E3
EDGE RD	A	37	E4
EDGE RD	SMCO	37	E4
EDGECLIFF WY	RC	36	C6
EDGECLIFF WY	SMCO	36	C5
EDGECOURT DR	H	28	E3
EDGEHILL DR	B	28	F2
EDGEHILL DR	B	29	A2
EDGEHILL DR	SC	36	C1
EDGEMAR AV	P	19	B6
EDGEMAR AV	P	23	A6
EDGEMAR ST	DC	22	B4
EDGEMONT DR	DC	19	B2
EDGEMONT DR	DC	23	A2
EDGEWATER BLVD	FCTY	29A	B5
EDGEWATER BLVD	FCTY	33	B1
EDGEWOOD AV	SMCO	23	B1
EDGEWOOD CT	DC	21	F5
EDGEWOOD DR	P	19	B4
EDGEWOOD DR	P	23	A4
EDGEWOOD LN	MP	43	C2
EDGEWOOD RD	RC	36	C3
EDGEWOOD RD	SM	29	A4
EDGEWOOD RD	SMCO	35	F4
EDGEWOOD RD	SMCO	36	C3
EDGEWOOD WY	SSF	23	E4
EDGEWORTH AV	DC	21	E6
EDGEWORTH AV	DC	23	B1
EDGEWORTH AV	SMCO	21	E6
EDINGBURGH ST	SM	29	D6
EDISON AV	SSF	24	B3
EDISON ST	SM	32	F2
EDISON ST	SMCO	27	E6
EDISON ST	SMCO	30	E1
EDISON WY	SMCO	37	C3
EDITH AV	RC	36	D4
EDMOND AV	RC	36	D4
EDMOND DR	SC	36	B3
EDMONDS RD	SMCO	36	A3
EDNA LN	P	19	B5
EDNA LN	P	23	A5
EDNA WY	SM	29	E5
EDWARDS CT	B	26	E6
EDWARDS LN	A	37	C6
EDWARDS RD	B	28	E1
EGRET LN	RC	33	F2
EGRET ST	FCTY	29A	D4
EISENHOWER ST	SM	29	F4
EL ARROYO RD	H	28	F4
EL ARROYO RD	H	29	A4
EL BONITO WY	M	26	C6
EL BONITO WY	M	28	B1
EL CAMINO REAL	A	37	E6
EL CAMINO REAL	BLMT	33	D5
EL CAMINO REAL	B	26	C5
EL CAMINO REAL	B	28	F2
EL CAMINO REAL	B	29	D5
EL CAMINO REAL	CLMA	23	D3
EL CAMINO REAL	MP	37	E6
EL CAMINO REAL	MP	43	E1
EL CAMINO REAL	M	26	C5
EL CAMINO REAL	RC	36	E2
EL CAMINO REAL	RC	37	E6
EL CAMINO REAL	SBR	26	C5
EL CAMINO REAL	SC	33	D5
EL CAMINO REAL	SC	36	E2
EL CAMINO REAL	SM	29	D5
EL CAMINO REAL	SM	32	F1
EL CAMINO REAL	SM	33	D5
EL CAMINO REAL	SSF	23	D3
EL CAMPO DR	SSF	23	E5
EL CAPITAN DR	M	26	B6
EL CENTRO RD	H	29	A4
EL CERRITO AV	H	29	B5
EL CERRITO AV	SM	29	B5
EL CORTEZ AV	SSF	23	F6
ELDER AV	MP	43	C2
ELDER AV	M	26	C5
ELDER CT	MP	43	C2
ELDER CT	SBR	25	E2
ELDER DR	BLMT	32	E5
ELDER LN	P	20	E2
ELDORADO AV	SMCO	30A	A5
ELDORADO CT	SBR	25	E3
EL DORADO DR	DC	23	B2
EL DORADO DR	P	19	B4
EL DORADO DR	P	23	A4
EL DORADO RD	SMCO	30	F1
ELDORADO ST	SM	29	D3
ELEANOR DR	SM	29	E5
ELEANOR DR	W	42	F2
ELENA AV	A	37	C6
ELENA AV	A	43	C1
EL GRANADA BLVD	SMCO	30A	C5
ELIZA CT	FCTY	29A	C5
ELIZABETH LN	MP	37	D6
ELIZABETH ST	SC	33	C6
ELIZABETH WY	A	37	B5
ELK CT	P	25	C6
ELKHORN CT	SM	29	E6
ELK TREE RD	SMCO	46	C3
ELKWOOD DR	SSF	23	D3
ELLENDALE ST	SMCO	30	D3
ELLIOT ST	SM	29A	A6
ELLIOTT DR	MP	38	B5
ELLIS DR	SMCO	21	D6
ELLSWORTH AV	SM	29	C3
ELLSWORTH CT E	SM	29	C3
ELLSWORTH CT W	SM	29	C3
ELM AV	B	29	A3
ELM AV	H	29	A3
ELM AV	SSF	24	A4
ELM CT	P	27A	B1
ELM CT	SSF	24	A4
ELM PL	A	37	E4

COPYRIGHT © 1991 BY Thomas Bros Maps

1991 SAN MATEO COUNTY STREET INDEX

STREET	CITY	PAGE	GRID
ELM ST	MP	38	A5
ELM ST	RC	36	F2
ELM ST	RC	37	A2
ELM ST	SBR	26	A3
ELM ST	SC	33	D6
ELM ST	SC	36	D1
ELM ST	SM	29	C3
ELM ST	SMCO	27	F6
ELM ST	SMCO	30	F1
ELMER ST	BLMT	33	B4
ELMER ST	SMCO	33	B4
ELMWOOD CT	SBR	25	D2
ELMWOOD DR	DC	21	C5
ELMWOOD DR	M	26	A5
ELMWOOD RD	H	28	F3
EL NIDO RD	SMCO	51	C1
EL PARQUE CT	SM	33	B1
EL PASEO	HMB	39	F4
EL PASEO	M	26	C6
EL PORTAL AV	H	29	B4
EL PORTAL AV	SM	29	B4
EL PORTAL WY	DC	21	D4
EL PORTAL WY	SMCO	21	D4
EL PRADO	SMCO	42	F1
EL PRADO	SMCO	43	A1
EL PRADO RD	B	28	D3
EL QUANITO WY	B	28	D3
EL SERENO CTE	SC	36	D1
EL SERENO DR	SC	36	D1
EL SOBRANTE	SM	32	C3
ELSTON CT	SC	33	B6
ELSTON DR	SBR	25	C1
EL VANADA RD	SMCO	36	B3
EL VERANO WY	BLMT	33	A5
ELWOOD ST	RC	36	E2
EMALITA CT	SBR	26	B4
EMARON DR	SBR	25	D2
EMBARCADERO RD	EPA	38	E6
EMERALD AV	SC	36	D2
EMERALD CT	SM	32	D2
EMERALD CT	SSF	23	E4
EMERALD HILL RD	RC	36	D5
EMERALD HILL RD	SMCO	36	D5
EMERALD LAKE PL	SMCO	36	C4
EMILIE AV	A	37	C6
EMILY LN	SSF	23	D6
EMMA LN	MP	38	B5
EMMETT AV	BLMT	33	B4
EMMETT WY	EPA	38	B3
ENCANTO WY	P	20	E6
ENCHANTED WY	SMCO	32	B2
ENCINA AV	A	37	C4
ENCINA AV	RC	37	A4
ENCINA AV	SMCO	37	C4
ENCINA CT	H	28	F3
ENCINA DR	M	28	C1
ENCINA RD	SC	36	C3
ENCINA RD	SMCO	36	C3
ENCINA WY	SMCO	30A	C6
ENCINAL AV	A	37	D5
ENCINAL AV	MP	37	D5
ENCINO RD	A	37	E4
ENCLINE WY	BLMT	32	D4
ENCLINE WY	SMCO	32	D4
ENFIELD WY	H	29	B5
ENGLE RD	SM	29	C3
ENGLISH CT	BLMT	33	B4
ENGLISH CT	M	26	C4
ENGVALL RD	SBR	25	E2
ENSENADA RD	SC	33	B5
ENSENADA WY	SM	32	D1
ENSIGN LN	RC	33	D3
ENTRADA WY	SMCO	37	F4
ENTRADA WY	SMCO	50	B5
ENTRANCE WY	W	42	B3
ERICA DR	SSF	23	D5
ERICA WY	SMCO	43	C6
ERICA WY	SMCO	47	C1
ERICKSON LN	FCTY	29A	C6
ERICSON RD	H	29	C4
ERICSON RD	SM	29	C4
ERIN LN	HMB	34	F4
ERIN PL	SSF	25	D1
ERLIN DR	SC	33	B5
ERRIS CT	SSF	23	C6
ESCALANTE WY	B	28	C2
ESCALERO AV	P	20	E6
ESCALERO AV	P	27	F1
ESCALLE AV	SMCO	30	E4
ESCALONA AV	SMCO	30A	B5
ESCANYO DR	SSF	23	D5
ESCANYO WY	SMCO	47	C1
ESCOBAR RD	PV	47	B1
ESCONDIDO DR	SMCO	50	C5
ESCONDIDO LN	MP	37	C6
ESCONDIDO PL	SMCO	50	C5
ESCONDIDO WY	BLMT	33	A4
ESCONDITA AV	SMCO	30A	A5
ESCUELA DR	DC	23	B2
ESMERALDA AV	SMCO	30	E4
ESMERALDA TER	SMCO	50	C4
ESPINOSA RD	W	46	D2
ESPLANADE DR	P	19	A6
ESSEX CT	SBR	25	F3
ESSEX LN	FCTY	33	C1
ESSEX LN	H	29	B5
ESSEX WY	P	20	C6
ESTA AV	BR	22	F5
ESTATE CT	SC	36	B1
ESTATE CT	SSF	23	F4
ESTATES DR	SBR	25	E3
ESTELLA DR	P	20	F6
ESTELLA DR	P	25	A6
ESTELLE LN	DC	23	C1
ESTHER LN	SMCO	36	D3
ESTON WY	M	28	B1
ESTRADA PL	SMCO	36	C2
ESTRELLA ST	SM	33	A2
ETHEL CT	RC	36	E6
ETHELDORE ST	SMCO	30	E3
EUCALYPTUS AV	H	28	F3
EUCALYPTUS AV	SC	33	C6
EUCALYPTUS AV	SC	36	C1
EUCALYPTUS AV	SSF	23	F4
EUCALYPTUS AV	SSF	24	A4
EUCALYPTUS CT	W	42	C1
EUCALYPTUS WY	SBR	25	E2
EUCLID AV	A	37	A6
EUCLID AV	A	43	A1
EUCLID AV	MP	38	B5
EUCLID AV	RC	36	E4
EUCLID AV	SBR	26	A2
EUCLID AV	EPA	38	B5
EUCLID PL	EPA	38	B4
EUGENIA DR	H	28	D4
EUGENIA LN	W	42	F2
EUREKA DR	P	20	F2
EUREKA DR	P	25	A2
EVA CT	SM	32	F2
EVELYN ST	MP	37	D6
EVERGLADES DR	P	27A	B1
EVERGREEN AV	DC	22	A4
EVERGREEN CT	M	26	B5
EVERGREEN DR	SBR	25	D2
EVERGREEN DR	SSF	23	E3
EVERGREEN ST	MP	43	D2
EVERGREEN ST	SM	29	F3
EVERGREEN WY	M	26	B5
EWELL RD	BLMT	32	F5
EXBOURNE AV	SC	33	B5
EXECUTIVE DR	SSF	24	C4
EXECUTIVE G CIR	RC	33	C3
EXETER AV	SC	33	A5
EXETER DR	SBR	25	B2
EXETER WY	SC	33	A5
F			
F ST	BLMT	33	C4
F ST	CLMA	23	C1
F ST	RC	36	E1
FAGAN DR	H	28	E2
FAIRBANKS AV	SC	36	C1
FAIRFAX AV	A	37	C4
FAIRFAX AV	SM	29	C5
FAIRFAX WY	SSF	23	C5
FAIRFIELD CT	SMCO	32	B3
FAIRFIELD DR	SC	33	D4
FAIRFIELD RD	B	28	F2
FAIRFIELD RD	B	29	A2
FAIRLAWN AV	DC	21	C5
FAIRLAWN CT	DC	21	C5
FAIRMONT AV	SC	36	D2
FAIRMONT DR	DC	21	C5
FAIRMONT DR	SBR	25	E3
FAIRMONT DR	SM	32	C3
FAIR OAKS AV	RC	37	C3
FAIR OAKS AV	SMCO	37	D3
FAIROAKS CT	SM	32	D2
FAIR OAKS LN	A	37	C5
FAIRVIEW AV	A	43	B2
FAIRVIEW AV	DC	19	B1
FAIRVIEW AV	DC	21	D6
FAIRVIEW AV	DC	23	A1
FAIRVIEW AV	RC	36	E4
FAIRVIEW PL	M	26	A5
FAIRWAY CIR	H	28	F3
FAIRWAY CIR	H	29	A3
FAIRWAY DR	BLMT	32	F4
FAIRWAY DR	BLMT	33	A4
FAIRWAY DR	DC	21	D5
FAIRWAY DR	HMB	39	E2
FAIRWAY DR	MP	43	A3
FAIRWAY DR	P	20	E3
FAIRWAY DR	P	25	A3
FAIRWAY DR	SSF	23	E5
FAIRWAY PL	HMB	39	E2
FALDA AV	SM	32	D1
FALK CT	MP	38	B5
FALKIRK LN	H	32	A1
FALLENLEAF DR	H	29	C5
FALLEN LEAF WY	SMCO	36	C6
FALLON AV	SM	29	E3
FAMILY FARM RD	W	46	E1
FANITA WAY	MP	43	D2
FARALLON AV	P	19	B5
FARALLON AV	P	23	A5
FARALLON CT	BLMT	33	C2
FARALLON DR	BLMT	33	C2
FARALLONE AV	SMCO	30	D1
FAR CREEK WY	SMCO	36	C5
FARM LN	H	28	F4
FARM LN	H	29	A4
FARM RD	W	46	F2
FARM HILL BLVD	RC	36	D6
FARMHILL BLVD	W	42	C1
FARMHILL CT	H	28	F4
FARMIN RD	SMCO	57	B2
FARNEE CT	SSF	23	C6
FARRAGUT BLVD	FCTY	29A	C6
FARRAGUT BLVD	FCTY	33	C1
FARRINGDON LN	B	29	A2
FARRINGTON WY	EPA	38	B3
FASHION ISLD BL	SM	29A	A5
FASMAN DR	SBR	25	C1
FASSLER AV	P	20	E5
FASSLER AV	P	25	A6
FATHOM CT	RC	33	D3
FATHOM DR	SM	29A	A4
FAVONIA RD	PV	47	B1
FAWN CT	H	28	E3
FAWN LN	PV	47	B2
FAXON RD	A	37	B6
FAXON RD	A	43	B1
FAY AV	SC	33	B6
FAY AV	SMCO	33	B6
FAY ST	RC	36	F3
FAY ST	RC	37	A3
FELTON AV	SSF	23	D3
FELTON DR	MP	37	D5
FELTON PL	MP	37	D5
FENNWOOD AV	DC	19	A1
FERDINAND AV	SMCO	30A	B5
FERN AV	P	20	F4
FERN AV	P	25	B4
FERN AV	SMCO	57	D3
FERN CT	H	28	E3
FERNANDEZ WY	P	20	E6
FERNDALE AV	SSF	23	E3
FERNDALE WY	SMCO	36	B4
FERN PATH	SMCO	28	D2
FERNSIDE ST	RC	36	E6
FERNWOOD AV	DC	21	C6
FERNWOOD DR	A	37	D5
FERNWOOD DR	M	26	A5
FERNWOOD DR	SBR	25	E2
FERNWOOD DR	SMCO	50	C5
FERNWOOD ST	SM	32	E3
FERNWOOD WY	BLMT	33	A5
FEY DR	SMCO	28	D3
FIELDCREST DR	DC	21	D4
FIESTA AV	SMCO	37	D1
FIESTA CT	SM	29	F6
FIESTA DR	SM	29	E6
FIFTY FIFTY RD	SMCO	57	A2
FILBERT RD	SMCO	41	D3
FILBERT ST	HMB	34	E5
FILLMORE AV	SM	29	F5
FINGER AV	RC	36	E1
FIR AV	SSF	24	A5
FIR CT	H	28	E4
FIR LN	SMCO	57	C4
FIR ST	SC	33	C5
FIR ST	SMCO	30	E1
FIRECREST AV	P	23	B4
FIRETHORN WY	PV	47	C4
FIR VIEW	SMCO	50	C5
FISHER ST	SMCO	23	C1
FIVE POINTS RD	SMCO	51A	F5
FLASHNER LN	BLMT	33	B3
FLEETWOOD CT	SBR	25	C1
FLEETWOOD DR	DC	21	C5
FLEETWOOD DR	SBR	25	E2
FLEETWOOD DR	SC	36	B3
FLEETWOOD DR	SM	29	E4
FLEETWOOD DR	SMCO	21	C1
FLETCHER DR	A	42	F2
FLETCHER DR	A	43	A2
FLEUR PL	A	37	B6
FLEUR PL	A	43	B1
FLINT AV	SM	29A	A6
FLOOD AV	SMCO	37	B3
FLOOD CIR	A	37	E4
FLORENCE LN	MP	43	D1
FLORENCE ST	DC	21	F6
FLORENCE ST	DC	23	E1
FLORENCE ST	RC	37	D3
FLORES DR	P	27	F1
FLORES ST	SM	29	E6
FLORES ST	SM	32	E1
FLORESTA WY	SMCO	43	C6
FLORESTA WY	SMCO	47	C1
FLORIBUNDA AV	B	29	A3
FLORIBUNDA AV	H	28	F3
FLORIBUNDA AV	H	29	A3
FLORIDA AV	SBR	26	B3
FLOURNOY ST	DC	21	F4
FLOWER ST	RC	36	E1
FLYING CLD ISLE	FCTY	29A	C4
FLYING FISH ST	FCTY	29A	D4
FLYING MST ISLE	FCTY	29A	D4
FLYNN AV	RC	37	B3
FOGL CT	A	37	A6
FOLGER CT	BLMT	33	A4
FOLGER DR	BLMT	33	A4
FOLKSTONE AV	SM	29	E4
FOOTHILL DR	P	23	B5
FOOTHILL DR	SM	29	C6
FOOTHILL DR	SM	32	C1
FOOTHILL DR	SMCO	21	D6
FOOTHILL RD	SM	32	C1
FOOTHILL ST	RC	36	E5
FORBES BLVD	SSF	24	C5
FORD ST	DC	21	F6
FORDHAM RD	SM	29	C5
FORDHAM ST	EPA	38	C3
FORESAIL CT	FCTY	29A	C6
FOREST AV	BLMT	32	F4
FOREST LN	SBR	26	A2
FOREST LN	SC	36	C1
FOREST LN	SMCO	37	D5
FOREST RD	SMCO	41	C1
FOREST RD	W	46	D3
FOREST GROVE DR	DC	21	D5
FOREST LAKE DR	P	23	B5
FOREST PARK CT	P	19	B4
FOREST PARK CT	P	23	A4
FOREST PARK DR	P	19	A4
FOREST PARK DR	P	23	A4
FOREST VIEW AV	H	28	E3
FOREST VIEW DR	SSF	23	F4
FOREST VIEW RD	SMCO	35	C6
FOREST VIEW RD	SMCO	41	C1
FORGE RD	SMCO	32	A3
FORRESTAL LN	FCTY	29A	C6
FORREST VIEW RD	W	42	D6
FOSS DR	RC	36	D4
FOSTER ST	SM	29A	A6
FOSTER CTY BLVD	FCTY	29A	C4
FOUNTAIN CIR DR	SMCO	31	E6
FOX CT	RC	37	A4
FOX HILL RD	W	46	D1
FOXHOLLOW LN	DC	22	A5
FOX HOLLOW LN	RC	36	C6
FOX HOLLOW RD	W	42	C3
FOX PLAZA LN	B	29	A3
FOXTAIL	PV	47	B4
FOXWOOD RD	SMCO	51	C1
FRANCEMONT DR	LAH	58	B1
FRANCES AV	P	20	F2
FRANCES AV	P	25	A2
FRANCES LN	RC	36	C2
FRANCES LN	SC	36	C2
FRANCIS AV	BLMT	33	A4
FRANCIS CT	BLMT	33	A4
FRANCISCAN CT	SC	36	C2
FRANCISCAN DR	DC	23	D1
FRANCISCAN RDG	PV	47	B5
FRANCISCO BLVD	P	20	E1
FRANCISCO BLVD	P	25	A1
FRANCISCO DR	B	29	B2
FRANCISCO DR	SSF	23	F6
FRANCISCO DR	SSF	24	A6
FRANCISCO ST	SMCO	30A	C5
FRANKFORT ST	DC	22	B4
FRANKLIN AV	SSF	24	B3
FRANKLIN ST	RC	36	F2
FRANKLIN ST	SM	29	C5
FRANKLIN ST	SMCO	30	E1
FRANKS LN	SMCO	43	C2
FRANZ CT	P	20	F4
FRANZ CT	P	25	A4
FREDRICK AV	A	37	E4
FREDRICK CT	SMCO	37	F4
FREMONT AV	P	19	B6
FREMONT AV	P	23	A6
FREMONT PL	MP	37	D6

COPYRIGHT © 1991 BY Thomas Bros Maps

STREET	CITY	PAGE	GRID
FREMONT PL	MP	43	D1
FREMONT ST	MP	43	D1
FREMONT ST	SM	29	D3
FREMONT ST	SMCO	30	F1
FREMONT WY	SMCO	46	C3
FREMONTIA	PV	47	B5
FRENCH CT	MP	38	B5
FRENCH CREEK PL	SMCO	32	B5
FRENCHMAN CK RD	HMB	34	E2
FRIARS LN	W	46	D2
FRIENDLY CT	RC	37	D2
FRIGATE LN	DC	23	D1
FRONTERA WY	M	28	C1
FULLER ST	RC	36	F2
FULLERTON AV	P	20	F1
FULLERTON AV	P	25	A1
FULTON RD	SM	29	A4
FULTON ST	RC	36	F3
FURLONG ST	BLMT	33	B3
G			
G ST	RC	36	E1
GABARDA WY	SMCO	47	C1
GAILLARDIA WY	EPA	38	C5
GALLEON LN	FCTY	29A	C5
GALLEY LN	FCTY	29A	D6
GALLOWRIDGE CT	SM	32	C2
GALVESTON DR	RC	33A	B6
GALVESTON ST	FCTY	33	B1
GALVEZ DR	P	27	F2
GALWAY DR	SSF	23	D6
GALWAY PL	SSF	23	C6
GAMBETTA ST	DC	21	F5
GARCIA AV	HMB	34	E5
GARCIA RD	M	26	C5
GARDEN AV	SBR	26	B3
GARDEN CT	BLMT	32	F5
GARDEN CT	BLMT	33	A5
GARDEN CT	P	20	E3
GARDEN CT	P	25	A3
GARDEN DR	B	26	D6
GARDEN DR	B	28	D1
GARDEN DR	M	28	D1
GARDEN LN	M	26	D5
GARDEN LN	MP	37	D6
GARDEN LN	MP	43	D1
GARDEN LN	SC	33	B5
GARDEN LN	SM	32	F2
GARDEN LN	SMCO	21	D6
GARDEN ST	RC	36	E1
GARDEN ST	EPA	38	C4
GARDEN GATEWAY	DC	21	E6
GARDEN GATEWAY	SMCO	21	E6
GARDEN GROVE DR	DC	21	C5
GARDENIA CT	EPA	38	C5
GARDENIA WY	EPA	38	C5
GARDN OF DEVOTN	SMCO	31	D6
GARDENSIDE AV	SSF	23	E3
GARDINER AV	SSF	24	C4
GARFIELD ST	SM	32	E1
GARIBALDI CT	DC	21	F6
GARIBALDI ST	DC	21	F6
GARLAND DR	MP	43	D2
GARLAND PL	MP	43	D2
GARNET AV	SC	36	D2
GARVEY WY	SM	29	E5
GARWOOD DR	DC	21	F5
GARWOOD WY	MP	37	D5
GASLIGHT LN	SC	33	B6
GATESHEAD CT	FCTY	33	C1
GATEWAY BLVD	SSF	24	C4
GATEWAY DR	DC	23	A4
GATEWAY DR	P	19	B3
GATEWAY DR	P	23	A4
GAVILAN CT	M	28	C2
GAVILAN WY	M	28	C2
GAYLORD ST	SC	36	C2
GAZOS CREEK RD	SMCO	57A	A4
GAZOS CREEK RD	SMCO	58A	C3
GEDDES CT	SSF	23	C5
GELLERT BLVD	DC	23	C5
GELLERT BLVD	SSF	23	D6
GELLERT BLVD	SSF	25	D1
GELLERT CT	SSF	25	D1
GEMINI LN	FCTY	29A	B5
GENEVA AV	DC	22	D4
GENEVA AV	RC	37	A4
GENEVA AV	SC	33	D6
GENEVA AV	SC	36	D1
GENEVA ST	DC	21	F5
GENEVIEVE AV	P	20	F4
GENEVIEVE AV	P	25	B5
GENEVRA RD	H	29	A3
GEOFFREY DR	SBR	25	C1
GEORGE AV	SM	33	A2
GEORGE ST	SMCO	30	E1
GEORGETOWN AV	SM	29	C5
GEORGETOWN CT	SSF	23	C6
GEORGETOWN ST	EPA	38	C3
GEORGIA AV	SBR	26	B3
GEORGIA LN	PV	47	B4
GERALDINE DR	M	26	B5
GERALDINE WY	BLMT	32	F5
GERALDINE WY	BLMT	33	A5
GERANIUM LN	SC	32	F6
GERANIUM LN	SC	35	F1
GERI LN	H	28	E3
GERI PL	SMCO	36	C4
GERTRUDE CT	EPA	38	B3
GIBBS WY	SSF	23	D4
GIBRALTAR LN	FCTY	33	D2
GILBERT AV	MP	37	F5
GILBERT AV	MP	38	A5
GILBERT CT	SSF	23	C6
GILBRETH RD	B	26	E6
GILLIS DR	SM	33	A2
GILMAN DR	SMCO	21	D6
GILMAN DR	SMCO	23	B1
GINNIVER ST	SM	29	E6
GLACIER AV	P	27A	C1
GLADYS AV	BR	24	C2
GLASGOW DR	P	23	B5
GLASGOW LN	SC	36	B1
GLEN AV	SBR	26	A4
GLEN PKWY	BR	24	C2
GLEN WY	H	28	E3
GLEN WY	EPA	38	B4
GLEN WY	W	36	B6
GLEN AULIN LN	SMCO	28	D3
GLENBROOK AV	DC	19	B2
GLENBROOK AV	DC	23	A2
GLENBROOK DR	H	32	B1
GLENBROOK LN	SBR	25	F4
GLENCOURT WY	P	23	B5
GLENCRAG WY	W	36	B6
GLENDALE AV	SMCO	37	B4
GLENDALE RD	H	29	A4
GLENDALE RD	SM	29	A4
GLENDORA DR	SM	32	C2
GLEN EYRIE RD	SMCO	50	B5
GLENGARRY WY	H	32	A1
GLENLOCK WY	SMCO	36	B4
GLENMERE WY	SMCO	36	C5
GLENN WY	BLMT	33	C4
GLENN WY	RC	36	F5
GLENN WY	SMCO	33	C4
GLENNAN DR	RC	36	D5
GLENROSE AV	DC	21	C6
GLENVIEW DR	SBR	25	E3
GLENWOOD AV	A	37	D5
GLENWOOD AV	DC	21	C5
GLENWOOD AV	RC	36	D4
GLENWOOD AV	W	42	D2
GLENWOOD DR	M	26	A5
GLENWOOD ST	SC	33	C5
GLORIA CT	SM	29	E3
GLORIA WY	EPA	38	B4
GLOUCESTER LN	FCTY	33	C1
GODETIA DR	W	36	C6
GODETIA DR	W	42	B1
GOETHE ST	DC	22	D4
GOLDEN BAY DR	P	19	A4
GOLDEN BAY DR	P	23	A4
GOLDEN GATE AV	HMB	34	E3
GOLDEN HILL DR	PV	47	B2
GOLDEN OAK DR	PV	47	C2
GOLDENRIDGE CT	SM	32	C2
GOLD HUNTER CT	FCTY	29A	C4
GOLF COURSE DR	SMCO	28	D4
GOLF COURSE RD	SMCO	28	E6
GONZAGA ST	EPA	38	C3
GOODMAN RD	P	20	F2
GOODMAN RD	P	25	A2
GOODWIN AV	RC	36	E5
GOODWIN CT	RC	36	E6
GOODWIN DR	SBR	25	C2
GORDON AV	BLMT	33	B3
GORDON AV	SMCO	43	C3
GORDON ST	RC	36	F4
GORDON ST	RC	37	A4
GORDON WY	P	19	B5
GORDON WY	P	23	A5
GOULSON ST	SMCO	56	D1
GOVER LN	SC	36	D1
GOYA RD	PV	47	B1
GRACE AV	EPA	38	B3
GRACE DR	MP	43	D2
GRACELAND AV	SC	36	C2
GRACELAND AV	SMCO	36	C2
GRACELAND LN	SC	36	C2
GRAMERCY DR	SM	29	C4
GRANADA AV	SMCO	30A	C5
GRANADA CT	PV	47	B3
GRANADA DR	B	28	D2
GRANADA DR	P	20	F6
GRANADA DR	P	25	A6
GRANADA DR	P	27A	A1
GRANADA DR	SSF	23	E6
GRANADA DR	SSF	25	E1
GRANADA ST	BLMT	33	B3
GRAND AV	P	20	D6
GRAND AV	P	27	E1
GRAND AV	SSF	23	F4
GRAND AV	SSF	24	A4
GRAND AV E	SSF	24	C5
GRAND BLVD	HMB	34	E4
GRAND BLVD	SM	29	C3
GRAND ST	RC	36	F3
GRAND TETON DR	P	27A	B1
GRANDVIEW AV	DC	19	B2
GRANDVIEW AV	DC	23	A2
GRANDVIEW BLVD	HMB	34	E3
GRANDVIEW DR	SSF	24	D5
GRANDVIEW DR	W	46	D2
GRANELLI AV	HMB	34	E5
GRANGER WY	RC	36	E6
GRANITE CT	SC	36	C2
GRANT PL	SM	29	E4
GRANT PL E	SM	29	E4
GRANT PL W	SM	29	E4
GRANT RD	SMCO	30	F1
GRANT ST	SM	29	E5
GRANT ST	SMCO	30	F1
GRAPE ST	SMCO	30	F1
GRAYSON CT	MP	38	A4
GRAYSTONE DR	SSF	23	D3
GRAYSTONE LN	DC	22	A5
GREBE ST	FCTY	29A	D4
GREEN AV	SBR	26	A2
GREEN AV	SSF	24	C4
GREEN CT	BLMT	32	D4
GREEN ST	EPA	38	C4
GREENBRIAR WY	H	29	B5
GREENBRIER CT	HMB	39	E2
GREENBRIER RD	HMB	39	F2
GREENBRIER RD	SC	36	B2
GREENDALE DR	SSF	23	C6
GREENDALE WY	SMCO	36	C4
GREENFIELD AV	SM	32	F3
GREENFIELD CT	SM	32	F3
GREEN HILLS CT	M	26	B5
GREEN HILLS DR	M	26	C5
GREENOAK CT	SM	32	D2
GREENOAKS DR	A	37	E3
GREENPARK TER	SSF	24	A3
GREEN RIDGE	DC	22	A5
GREEN VIEW DR	DC	22	A5
GREENVIEW LN	H	28	F3
GREENVIEW LN	H	29	A3
GREENWAY DR	P	20	E3
GREENWAY DR	P	25	A3
GREENWAYS DR	SMCO	42	F1
GREENWAYS DR	SMCO	43	A1
GREENWICH LN	FCTY	33	C1
GREENWOOD AV	B	29	B3
GREENWOOD AV	SC	33	D6
GREENWOOD AV	SC	36	C1
GREENWOOD AV	SM	29	B3
GREENWOOD DR	MP	37	E3
GREENWOOD DR	SMCO	37	E3
GREENWOOD DR	SSF	25	F1
GREENWOOD LN	RC	37	B2
GREENWOOD PL	MP	37	E3
GREENWOOD WY	SBR	25	E2
GREER RD	W	42	B2
GREGORY LN	RC	37	B1
GRENADA LN	FCTY	29A	C6
GRENADA LN	FCTY	33	C1
GRESHAM LN	A	37	B4
GREVILLEA CT	H	28	D4
GRIFFEN AV	P	20	F1
GRIFFEN AV	P	25	A2
GROVE AV	B	28	E1
GROVE AV	SSF	24	B3
GROVE CT	PV	47	A3
GROVE DR	PV	47	A3
GROVE ST	HMB	34	E5
GROVELAND ST	PV	47	B4
GRUNDY LN	SBR	26	A2
GRUNION CT	FCTY	29A	D5
GUADALUPE AV	DC	21	E4
GUADALUPE AV	M	26	B4
GUADALUPE RD	SMCO	22	B5
GUADLUPE CYN PY	SMCO	22	A5
GUADLUPE CYN RD	BR	22	D5
GUARDIAN WY	SMCO	50	B5
GUERRERO AV	HMB	34	D1
GUILDFORD AV	SM	29	E5
GUITTARD RD	B	26	E6
GULL AV	FCTY	29A	C4
GUM ST	SM	29	E5
GUNTER LN	RC	33	D3
GUTHRIE WY	SMCO	49A	F5
GUTTENBERG ST	DC	22	B4
GYMKHANA RD	SM	29	D6
GYPSY HILL RD	P	20	F2
GYPSY HILL RD	P	25	A2
H			
HACIENDA AV	SM	29	E6
HACIENDA AV	SM	32	E2
HACIENDA CT	P	19	B6
HACIENDA CT	P	23	A6
HACIENDA WY	M	26	B5
HACIENDAS DR	W	42	D2
HADDOCK ST	FCTY	29A	D5
HADDON DR	SM	29	E5
HAIGHT ST	MP	38	A4
HAINLINE DR	BLMT	33	A3
HALE DR	B	28	D2
HALF MOON LN	SSF	23	C3
HALF MOON BY RD	HMB	34	F4
HALF MOON BY RD	SMCO	31	F6
HALF MOON BY RD	SMCO	32	A5
HALF MOON BY RD	SMCO	34A	A3
HALIBUT ST	FCTY	29A	D5
HALL ST	SC	33	D5
HALLING WY	P	20	D6
HALLMARK CIR	MP	43	B3
HALLMARK DR	BLMT	32	D5
HALSEY AV	RC	37	B3
HALSEY AV	SM	29	F4
HALSEY AV	SMCO	37	B3
HALSEY BLVD	FCTY	29A	C6
HALSEY BLVD	FCTY	33	C1
HALYARD LN	RC	33	C2
HAMILTON AV	MP	37	F3
HAMILTON AV	MP	38	A3
HAMILTON AV	SBR	25	E3
HAMILTON CT	MP	38	B3
HAMILTON CT	P	23	A5
HAMILTON LN	B	26	E6
HAMILTON LN	B	28	E1
HAMILTON ST	RC	36	F2
HAMILTON WY	RC	36	C5
HAMILTON WY	SMCO	36	C5
HAMLET ST	SM	29	F5
HAMPSHIRE AV	DC	23	C5
HAMPSHIRE AV	SMCO	37	B3
HAMPSHIRE CT	DC	23	C5
HAMPTON AV	RC	36	F5
HAMPTON CT	H	32	A2
HAMPTON CT	SBR	25	E3
HAMPTON LN	DC	22	A5
HANCOCK AV	SM	29	F5
HANCOCK ST	RC	37	A3
HANDBURY LN	FCTY	33	C1
HANDLEY TR	SMCO	36	C4
HANOVER ST	DC	22	A4
HANSEN WY	RC	37	A1
HAPPY HOLLOW LN	SMCO	43	D5
HARBOR BLVD	BLMT	33	C4
HARBOR BLVD	RC	33A	B5
HARBOR BLVD	RC	37	B1
HARBOR BLVD	SMCO	33	C4
HARBOR DR	DC	22	A6
HARBOR DR	DC	23	D1
HARBOR WY	SSF	24	C5
HARBR COLONY CT	RC	33	E2
HARBOR SEAL CT	SM	29A	A5
HARBOUR DR	SMCO	30A	A4
HARCOURT WY	H	32	A2
HARCROSS RD	RC	36	E6
HARCROSS RD	W	36	E6
HARDING AV	RC	36	D4
HARDING AV	SM	29	F4
HARDWICK RD	W	36	D6
HARDWICK RD	W	42	E1
HARKINS AV	MP	43	C3
HARKINS AV	SMCO	43	C3
HARKINS RD	SMCO	41	C1
HARKINS FIRE TR	SMCO	41	A1
HARMON DR	MP	37	E3
HARNEY AV	BR	22	F4
HARNEY RD	BR	22	F5
HAROLD RD	BR	24	C2
HARRIS AV E	SSF	24	C5
HARRIS AV W	SSF	24	B5
HARRIS CT	SSF	24	C5
HARRISON AV	RC	36	E3
HARRISON AV	SM	29	F4
HARRISON WY	SMCO	43	C3
HARROW AV	SM	29	E5
HARTE ST	SMCO	30	E1
HARTFORD AV	SC	33	B5

COPYRIGHT © 1991 BY Thomas Bros Maps

1991 SAN MATEO COUNTY STREET INDEX

STREET	CITY	PAGE	GRID
HARVARD AV	MP	37	E6
HARVARD AV	MP	43	E1
HARVARD AV	SMCO	30	F5
HARVARD RD	SM	29	C5
HARVEST DR	RC	36	D6
HARVESTER DR	FCTY	29A	C4
HARVEY WY	P	20	E4
HASKINS DR	BLMT	32	E3
HASKINS WY	SSF	24	D5
HASSLER RD	SMCO	36	A3
HASTINGS AV	RC	36	E5
HASTINGS DR	BLMT	32	F5
HATCH DR	FCTY	29A	B4
HATCH LN	B	29	B2
HATTERAS CT	FCTY	33	B1
HAUSSMAN CT	SSF	23	C5
HAVEN AV	MP	37	D2
HAVEN AV	RC	37	D3
HAVEN AV	SMCO	37	D3
HAVEN AV	SSF	23	F5
HAVEN CT	MP	37	D2
HAVEN DR	DC	22	A6
HAVEN DR	DC	23	D1
HAVENRIDGE CT	SM	32	C3
HAWES CT	RC	37	A4
HAWES ST	RC	36	F4
HAWKSBURY LN	FCTY	33	E3
HAWK VIEW	PV	47	B5
HAWSER LN	HMB	34	E2
HAWTHORNE AV	SBR	25	F3
HAWTHORNE AV	SBR	26	A3
HAWTHORNE DR	A	37	D4
HAWTHORNE DR	SM	29	E4
HAWTHORNE PL	SSF	24	B4
HAWTHORNE ST	SMCO	30	E2
HAWTHORNE WY	M	26	C6
HAWTHORNE WY	M	28	C1
HAYDON CT	BLMT	32	E6
HAYFIELDS RD	PV	46	E3
HAYNE RD	H	28	F5
HAYNE RD	H	29	A5
HAYWARD AV	SM	29	D5
HAYWARD CT	B	28	D2
HAYWARD DR	B	28	D2
HAZEL AV	M	26	C6
HAZEL AV	RC	37	A3
HAZEL AV	SBR	26	A3
HAZEL LN	SMCO	57	D3
HAZELWOOD DR	SSF	23	F6
HAZELWOOD DR	SSF	25	F1
HAZELWOOD WY	EPA	38	B3
HEACOX RD	SMCO	51	B3
HEATH CT	DC	23	B4
HEATHCLIFF DR	P	23	B5
HEATHER CT	P	23	B6
HEATHER DR	A	37	D4
HEATHER DR	SC	36	B1
HEATHER LN	SBR	25	E2
HEATHER LN	SM	32	E2
HEATHER PL	H	31	F1
HEATHER PL	M	26	C4
HEATHER PL	SMCO	23	B1
HEATHER RD	SMCO	23	B1
HEATHER WY	SSF	23	F4
HEDGE RD	MP	37	E3
HEIDI LN	M	28	C1
HELEN DR	M	26	B6
HELEN PL	MP	43	D2
HELENA WY	SMCO	42	F1
HELENA WY	SMCO	43	A1
HELENE CT	SM	29	E3
HELLER ST	RC	37	A3
HELM LN	FCTY	29A	D6
HEMLOCK AV	M	26	D5
HEMLOCK AV	RC	37	A3
HEMLOCK AV	SM	29	F4
HEMLOCK AV	SSF	23	F3

STREET	CITY	PAGE	GRID
HEMLOCK AV	SSF	24	A3
HEMLOCK ST	SC	33	C6
HEMPSTEAD PL	RC	36	F6
HENDERSON AV	MP	37	F3
HENDERSON AV	MP	38	A3
HENDERSON PL	MP	37	F3
HENDERSON PL	MP	38	A3
HENRIK IBSEN RD	SMCO	41	C2
HENRY PL	M	26	C3
HENSLEY AV	SBR	26	A2
HERCULES LN	FCTY	29A	B3
HERITAGE CT	A	37	D4
HERITAGE CT	BLMT	32	D5
HERMAN ST	SBR	26	B1
HERMOSA AV	M	26	C5
HERMOSA AV	P	27	F1
HERMOSA AV	SMCO	34	D1
HERMOSA LN	SSF	23	E5
HERMOSA PL	MP	43	D1
HERMOSA RD	SMCO	30	F1
HERMOSA RD	SMCO	36	B3
HERMOSA ST	SBR	26	B1
HERMOSA WY	MP	43	D2
HERSCHEL ST	SM	29	F4
HESKETH CT	MP	43	C2
HESKETH DR	MP	43	C2
HESS RD	RC	37	A4
HEWITT DR	SC	36	B1
HIAWATHA AV	P	25	B4
HIBBERT CT	P	19	B5
HIBBERT CT	P	23	A5
HIBISCUS CT	EPA	38	D5
HICKEY BLVD	DC	23	C4
HICKEY BLVD	P	23	A5
HICKEY BLVD	SSF	23	C3
HICKORY AV	SBR	25	F3
HICKORY AV	SBR	26	A3
HICKORY LN	SM	32	F2
HICKORY PL	SSF	24	B4
HIDDEN TER	H	28	E3
HIDDEN OAKS DR	MP	43	C2
HIDDEN VLY DR	SMCO	33	B6
HIDDEN VLY LN	W	46	F2
HIGATE DR	DC	19	B3
HIGATE DR	DC	23	A3
HIGGINS WY	P	27	F2
HIGGINS PRMA RD	HMB	34	F6
HIGGINS PRMA RD	SMCO	34	F6
HIGGINS PRMA RD	SMCO	34A	A6
HIGGINS PRMA RD	SMCO	40	C1
HIGH RD	W	42	E1
HIGHCREST LN	SSF	24	A3
HIGH GATE AV	BLMT	32	E3
HIGH GATE LN	H	29	A3
HIGHLAND AV	B	29	B3
HIGHLAND AV	DC	19	A2
HIGHLAND AV	HMB	34	F3
HIGHLAND AV	RC	36	D4
HIGHLAND AV	SC	33	B5
HIGHLAND AV	SM	29	B3
HIGHLAND AV	SMCO	30A	C4
HIGHLAND AV	SSF	24	B3
HIGHLAND DR	SBR	25	B2
HIGHLAND TER	W	42	D2
HIGHLANDS CT	BLMT	32	E5
HIGHVIEW CT	SM	32	E3
HIGHVIEW DR	SM	32	E3
HIGHWAY RD	B	28	E1
HIGHWAY 1	P	19	A6
HIGHWAY 35	DC	19	B1
HILL AV	MP	37	F3
HILL AV	SMCO	36	C2
HILL AV	SSF	23	F5
HILL BLVD S	DC	22	C4
HILL RD	SMCO	56	A2
HILL ST	BLMT	33	B4
HILL ST	DC	23	B1
HILL ST	P	25	A5

STREET	CITY	PAGE	GRID
HILL ST	SMCO	21	E6
HILL ST	SMCO	23	B1
HILL ST	SMCO	30	E2
HILL WY	SC	36	C2
HILLARY LN	SMCO	43	A1
HILLBARN CT	SM	32	F3
HILLBARN CT	SM	33	A3
HILLBROOK DR	PV	47	B3
HILLCREST BLVD	M	26	C6
HILLCREST BLVD	M	28	B1
HILLCREST CIR	SSF	23	E5
HILLCREST DR	BLMT	32	D4
HILLCREST DR	DC	21	E4
HILLCREST DR	RC	36	D4
HILLCREST DR	SMCO	31	E6
HILLCREST DR	SMCO	36	D3
HILLCREST RD	RC	36	D3
HILLCREST RD	SC	33	B5
HILLCREST RD	SM	29	A4
HILLCREST RD	SMCO	36	D3
HILLCREST WY	SMCO	36	C5
HILLER ST	BLMT	33	B3
HILLMAN AV	BLMT	32	F4
HILLMAN AV	BLMT	33	A3
HILLSBOROUGH BL	H	28	F3
HILLSBOROUGH BL	H	29	A4
HILLSBOROUGH BL	SM	29	A4
HILLSDALE AV	DC	21	E4
HILLSDALE BL E	FCTY	29A	B5
HILLSDALE BL E	SM	29A	B5
HILLSDALE BL E	SM	32	F1
HILLSDALE BL W	SM	32	E2
HILLSDALE CT E	SM	33	A1
HILLSDALE PL	SM	32	E2
HILLSDALE WY	SMCO	36	B4
HILLSIDE AV	SMCO	43	B2
HILLSIDE BLVD	DC	21	F5
HILLSIDE BLVD	SMCO	23	F3
HILLSIDE BLVD	SSF	24	B3
HILLSIDE CIR	B	28	E2
HILLSIDE CT	SM	32	E2
HILLSIDE CT	W	42	F1
HILLSIDE DR	B	28	D2
HILLSIDE DR	P	20	F4
HILLSIDE DR	P	25	A4
HILLSIDE DR	W	42	D2
HILLSIDE LN	B	28	C3
HILLSIDE LN	SMCO	28	C3
HILLSIDE RD	RC	36	C4
HILLSIDE RD	SMCO	36	C4
HILLTOP DR	RC	36	D2
HILLTOP RD	SM	29	B3
HILLVIEW AV	RC	36	D3
HILLVIEW CT	B	28	D3
HILLVIEW CT	DC	21	C6
HILLVIEW CT	H	28	E3
HILLVIEW DR	MP	43	C1
HILLVIEW DR	SMCO	31	E6
HILLVIEW PL	MP	43	C1
HILLWAY DR	SMCO	36	C4
HILO WY	P	20	F2
HILO WY	P	25	A1
HILTON AV	SSF	23	D4
HILTON LN	P	20	E2
HILTON LN	P	25	A2
HILTON ST	RC	37	A2
HILTON WY	P	20	E2
HILTON WY	P	25	A2
HIMMEL AV	SMCO	36	F6
HIMMEL AV	SMCO	37	A6
HINCKLEY RD	B	26	E6
HINMAN RD	RC	33A	B4
HINTON RANCH RD	P	20	F6
HINTON RANCH RD	P	25	A6
HOBART AV	SM	29	D6
HOBART ST	MP	43	D2
HOBART HTS RD	W	42	E2

STREET	CITY	PAGE	GRID
HOFFMAN ST	CLMA	23	C1
HOFFMAN ST	DC	22	A6
HOFFMAN ST	DC	23	C1
HOLDEN CT	PV	47	C3
HOLIDAY CT	P	19	A4
HOLIDAY CT	P	23	A4
HOLLAND ST	SM	29A	A6
HOLLAND ST	EPA	38	A4
HOLLY AV	MP	43	D2
HOLLY AV	SBR	25	F3
HOLLY AV	SBR	26	A3
HOLLY AV	SSF	23	E4
HOLLY CT	H	28	E3
HOLLY RD	BLMT	33	B4
HOLLY ST	SC	33	C5
HOLLYBURNE AV	MP	38	A3
HOLLY HILL CT	RC	36	D5
HOMBERG ST	SMCO	36	A1
HOME RD	W	46	E2
HOMEPLACE CT	H	28	F4
HOMER LN	SMCO	43	D4
HOMEWOOD AV	SM	32	D3
HOMEWOOD PL	MP	37	F6
HOMS CT	H	29	C4
HONEYSUCKLE LN	SC	32	F6
HONEYSUCKLE LN	SC	35	F1
HOODS POINT WY	SMCO	32	B4
HOOVER AV	B	28	D2
HOOVER ST	MP	37	D6
HOOVER ST	RC	37	C2
HOPKINS AV	RC	36	F1
HORGAN AV	RC	37	A5
HORIZON WY	P	23	B5
HORNET AV	SSF	26	B1
HORSESHOE CT	H	29	C6
HORSESHOE DR	PV	46	E3
HORSESHOE BEND	PV	47	B5
HOSMER DR	SC	36	B3
HOSMER ST	SM	29A	A6
HOSPITAL PZ	MP	38	A4
HOUNDSRIDGE LN	SM	32	C3
HOWARD AV	B	29	B3
HOWARD AV	SC	33	D6
HOWARD AV	SC	36	D1
HOWARD AV	SM	29	B3
HOWARD CT	SSF	23	C5
HOWARD ST	MP	37	F3
HOWARD ST	MP	38	A3
HOWARD WY	A	37	C6
HOWE ST	SM	29	E3
HOWELLS ST	SMCO	30	E2
HOWLAND ST	RC	36	F1
HOWLAND HILL LN	SMCO	28	D3
HUBBARD AV	SMCO	36	C3
HUCKLEBERRY AV	SMCO	41	C2
HUCKLEBERRY TR	SMCO	41	D2
HUDDART RD	SMCO	41	F1
HUDSON CT	SC	36	B2
HUDSON ST	RC	36	F4
HUDSON ST	RC	37	A4
HUDSON BAY ST	FCTY	33	B2
HULL AV	SMCO	36	F6
HULL AV	SMCO	37	A6
HULL AV	SMCO	42	F1
HULL DR	SC	33	C5
HULL LN	FCTY	29A	D6
HUMBOLDT RD	BR	24	B2
HUMBOLDT ST	B	29	C1
HUMBOLDT ST	SM	29	D3
HUMBOLT CT	P	27A	C2
HUNT DR	B	28	C2
HUNT ST	SMCO	30	F2
HUNTER ST	EPA	38	C3
HUNTINGTON AV	SBR	26	B3
HUNTINGTON AV	SMCO	37	B3
HUNTINGTON AV	SSF	24	A6
HUNTINGTON AV E	SBR	26	B1
HUNTINGTON DR	DC	19	B2

STREET	CITY	PAGE	GRID
HUNTINGTON DR	DC	23	A2
HURLINGAME AV	SMCO	37	B3
HURLINGHAM AV	SM	29	B3
HURON AV	SM	29	D3
HURON AV	SM	29	D2
HYDE CT	DC	23	D5
HYDE ST	RC	36	E1
HYDRA LN	FCTY	29A	B6
I			
IBSEN,HENRIK RD	SMCO	41	C2
IDAHO CT	RC	36	F6
IDAHO ST	SM	29	D3
IDALENE ST	DC	22	C4
IDLEWILD CT	P	23	B5
IDYLLWILD AV	SMCO	37	A6
IDYLLWILD AV	SMCO	43	A1
IDYLLWILD CT	SMCO	37	A6
IDYLLWILD CT	SMCO	43	A1
ILLINOIS ST	CO	23	B5
ILLINOIS ST	EPA	38	C3
IMPERIAL DR	P	23	B5
IMPERIAL WY	SSF	23	C4
INDEPENDENCE DR	MP	37	E2
INDIAN AV	SM	29	C3
INDIAN CROSSING	PV	47	B5
INDIO DR	SSF	23	E5
INDUSTRIAL RD	SC	33	D5
INDUSTRIAL WY	BR	22	E5
INDUSTRIAL WY	B	28	F1
INDUSTRIAL WY	RC	33	E6
INDUSTRIAL WY	RC	36	E1
INGLEWOOD LN	A	37	C5
INGOLD RD	B	26	E6
INNER CIRCLE	RC	36	E3
INNISFREE CIR	DC	23	B3
INNISFREE DR	DC	23	B3
INTREPID LN	RC	33	F3
INVERNESS DR	P	23	B5
INVERNESS DR	SC	33	C5
INVERNESS RD	HMB	39	E2
INVERNESS WY	H	32	A1
INYO CT	SBR	25	D2
INYO PL	SMCO	43	A1
INYO ST	BR	24	B1
IOWA DR	SM	29	C6
IRENE CT	BLMT	32	F3
IRENE CT	BLMT	33	A3
IRIS CT	P	27	F1
IRIS CT	SSF	23	F3
IRIS CT	SM	29	D2
IRIS LN	MP	37	F3
IRIS LN	SC	36	A1
IRIS ST	RC	36	F3
IRISH RIDGE RD	SMCO	40	E6
IROQUOIS TR	PV	47	A3
IRVING AV	A	37	D4
IRVING ST	SM	29	C5
IRVING ST	SMCO	30	E2
IRVING ST	SSF	24	A3
IRVINGTON ST	DC	22	A4
IRWIN CT	H	28	F3
IRWIN DR	H	28	F3
IRWIN PL	M	26	D6
IRWIN ST	BLMT	33	C3
ISABELLA AV	A	37	C6
ISABELLA AV	SMCO	30A	C6
ISABELLA RD	SMCO	30A	C5
ISABELLE AV	SM	29	E6
ISABELLE AV	SM	32	E1
ISLAND DR	RC	33	D2
ISLAND PKWY	BLMT	33	C2
ISLAND PL	RC	33	D2
IVY AV	P	20	F4
IVY AV	P	25	A4
IVY AV	SMCO	41	C2

COPYRIGHT © 1991 BY Thomas Bros Maps

1991 SAN MATEO COUNTY STREET INDEX

COPYRIGHT © 1991 BY Thomas Bros Maps

STREET	CITY	PAGE	GRID
IVY DR	MP	38	A3
IVY ST	SM	29	E5
IVY ST	SMCO	30	E2

J

STREET	CITY	PAGE	GRID
JACARANDA CIR	H	28	E4
JACINTO LN	SSF	23	E5
JACKLING DR	H	28	E3
JACKSON AV	RC	36	F3
JACKSON ST	SM	29	C5
JACQUELINE CT	DC	22	D5
JACQUELINE LN	DC	22	D5
JAIL HOUSE WY	SBR	25	D2
JAMAICA ST	FCTY	33	B1
JAMES AV	A	37	D4
JAMES AV	RC	36	E3
JAMES AV	SMCO	36	D4
JAMES CT	SM	29	E4
JAMES CT	SSF	23	F3
JAMESTON LN	DC	22	A5
JAMIE CT E	SSF	24	D5
JAMIE LN	EPA	38	C4
JANE DR	W	42	D2
J ART YOUNGR FY	FCTY	29A	B4
J ART YOUNGR FY	SM	29	D6
J ART YOUNGR FY	SM	32	C2
JASMINE CT	M	26	C5
JASMINE ST	SM	29	D5
JASMINE WY	EPA	38	D5
JAYNE ST	SMCO	30	F2
JEFFERSON AV	RC	36	F2
JEFFERSON AV	RC	37	A2
JEFFERSON AV	SMCO	36	B6
JEFFERSON AV	W	36	B6
JEFFERSON CT	MP	37	F3
JEFFERSON CT	SM	29	B3
JEFFERSON DR	MP	37	E2
JEFFERSON ST	SSF	24	A3
JENEVEIN AV	SBR	26	A3
JENNIFER CT	DC	22	D5
JENNINGS LN	A	37	C4
JERVIS AV	EPA	38	A4
JETER ST	RC	36	E2
JEWELL PL	H	28	F5
JEWELL PL	H	29	A5
J HART CLNTN DR	SM	29	E3
JIB CT	HMB	34	E2
JIBSTAY LN	FCTY	33	C2
JOANNE DR	SM	29	E5
JOAQUIN DR	SSF	23	D4
JOAQUIN RD	SMCO	51	C2
JODY CT	SM	29	E5
JOHANSEN RD	SMCO	58A	C2
JOHN DALY BLVD	DC	21	C5
JOHN GLENN CIR	DC	23	C5
JOHN PAPAN CT	DC	23	B4
JOHNSON AV	P	19	B6
JOHNSON AV	P	23	A6
JOHNSON LN	MP	37	D6
JOHNSON ST	MP	37	D6
JOHNSON ST	MP	43	D1
JOHNSON ST	RC	36	F3
JOHNSTON SQ	HMB	34	F5
JOHNSTON ST	HMB	34	F5
JONES CT	RC	37	D2
JONES GULCH RD	SMCO	50A	B3
JORDAN ST	SMCO	30	F2
JOSSELYN LN	W	42	B2
JOY AV	BR	24	C2
JOYCE RD	H	32	A2
JUANITA AV	B	28	F1
JUANITA AV	M	26	B5
JUANITA AV	P	20	F4
JUANITA AV	P	25	B4
JUBILEE CT	SMCO	36	F6
JUDITH CT	HMB	34	E3
JUDSON DR	SMCO	50	C4
JUDSON PL	P	27A	B2
JUDSON ST	BLMT	33	C3
JULIA CT	BLMT	33	A3
JULIANA AV	SMCO	30	D3
JULIE LN	SSF	23	C6
JUNE HOLLOW RD	SMCO	30	E2
JUNIPER AV	SBR	25	F3
JUNIPER AV	SBR	26	A3
JUNIPER AV	SSF	24	B4
JUNIPER DR	A	37	E4
JUNIPER ST	SM	32	E2
JUNIPERO AV	RC	36	E4
JUNIPRO SRRA BL	CLMA	23	C3
JUNIPRO SRRA BL	DC	21	E5
JUNIPRO SRRA BL	SBR	25	E2
JUNIPRO SRRA BL	SBR	26	A4
JUNIPRO SRRA BL	SMCO	23	C3
JUNIPRO SRRA BL	SSF	23	C3
JUNIPRO SRRA FY	DC	21	E5
JUNIPRO SRRA FY	DC	23	C3
JUNIPRO SRRA FY	SBR	25	E1
JUNIPRO SRRA FY	SMCO	26	A5
JUNIPRO SRRA FY	SMCO	28	C3
JUNIPRO SRRA FY	SMCO	32	A4
JUNIPRO SRRA FY	SMCO	43	B5
JUNIPRO SRRA FY	SMCO	47	D1
JUNIPRO SRRA FY	SSF	23	C3
JUNO LN	FCTY	29A	B6
JUPITER CT	FCTY	29A	B5

K

STREET	CITY	PAGE	GRID
KAINS AV	SBR	25	F3
KAINS AV	SBR	26	A3
KALMIA ST	SM	29	D5
KAMMERER CT	H	29	A3
KANDLE WY	RC	37	A4
KANOFF AV	SMCO	27	E6
KANOFF AV	SMCO	30	E1
KANSAS ST	RC	36	F5
KAREN CT	B	28	D2
KAREN RD	SMCO	33	C3
KAREN WY	A	43	A2
KATAOKA CT	SMCO	36	C4
KATHERINE AV	RC	36	E3
KATHLEEN CT	P	27A	B1
KATHRYN AV	SMCO	27A	C5
KATHRYNE AV	SM	29	E3
KAUFFMANN CT	SSF	24	D4
KAVANAUGH DR	MP	38	B3
KAVANAUGH DR	EPA	38	B3
KAVANAUGH WY	P	23	B5
KAYNYNE ST	RC	37	B2
KAYNYNE ST	SMCO	37	B2
KEARNEY ST	SSF	24	A3
KEATS AV	SSF	23	D4
KEBET RIDGE RD	SMCO	46	C3
KEDITH ST	BLMT	33	C3
KEEFE CT	SBR	25	F4
KEEL CT	HMB	34	E2
KEEL LN	RC	33	D2
KEELSON CIR	RC	33	E2
KEHOE AV	HMB	34	E3
KEHOE AV	SM	29	E4
KEHOE AV	SM	29A	A4
KEITH AV	P	20	F4
KEITH AV	P	25	B5
KEITH ST	BLMT	33	C3
KELLY AV	HMB	34	E4
KELLY CT	MP	38	B3
KELLY LN	M	28	C1
KELLY ST	HMB	34	F4
KELLY ST	SM	29	F4
KELLY ST	SM	29A	A4
KELMORE ST	SMCO	30	D2
KELTON AV	SC	36	D2
KELTON CT	SM	32	E3
KENDALL CT	P	27A	B1
KENILWORTH RD	H	29	A5
KENMAR WY	B	28	D3
KENMORE WY	W	42	E2
KENNEDY PL	M	26	B6
KENRY WY	SSF	23	D6
KENSINGTON AV	SBR	26	B3
KENSINGTON RD	RC	36	E5
KENT AV	SC	36	A2
KENT CT	DC	23	B3
KENT CT	SBR	25	E4
KENT CT	SM	29	F6
KENT PL	MP	37	E6
KENT RD	P	20	D6
KENT ST	SM	29	F6
KENT WY	SSF	23	C5
KENTFIELD AV	RC	36	F5
KENTFIELD AV	RC	37	A5
KENTON AV	SC	33	B5
KENTUCKY AV	SM	29	C5
KENTUCKY ST	RC	36	F5
KENWOOD AV	SM	32	E3
KENWOOD DR	MP	37	E6
KENWOOD DR	SSF	23	F6
KENWOOD DR	SSF	24	A6
KENWOOD WY	SBR	26	A1
KENWOOD WY	SSF	25	F1
KEONCREST DR	SSF	23	D4
KERRI CT	SMCO	36	F6
KERRI CT	SMCO	37	A6
KESWICK LN	SM	29	E5
KETCH CT	FCTY	29A	D6
KETTERING CT	SM	32	D3
KILCONWAY LN	SSF	23	C6
KILLARNEY LN	B	26	E6
KILLARNEY LN	B	28	E1
KILLDEER CT	FCTY	29A	C4
KILROY WY	A	43	A1
KIMBALL WY	SSF	24	C5
KIMBERLY WY	SM	33	B1
KIMMIE CT	BLMT	32	F4
KINDER LN	H	28	D3
KING CT	SM	32	F2
KING DR	DC	23	B5
KING DR	SSF	23	D5
KING LN	FCTY	33	C1
KING LN	SM	32	F2
KING ST	BLMT	33	C4
KING ST	RC	36	F3
KINGRIDGE DR	SM	32	E3
KINGS LN	SMCO	32	C4
KINGS RD	BR	24	B2
KINGS CANYON WY	P	27A	B1
KINGSFORD LN	RC	37	B1
KINGS MTN RD	SMCO	41	E3
KINGS MTN RD	W	42	A2
KINGSTON AV	SBR	25	F3
KINGSTON RD	BLMT	33	B3
KINGSTON ST	SM	29	D2
KINGSWOOD CIR	H	31	F1
KINGSWOOD CIR	H	32	A1
KINGSWOOD CT	H	32	A1
KINGSWOOD DR	H	32	A1
KIOWA CT	PV	47	B3
KIP LN	B	28	C3
KIPLING AV	SSF	23	D4
KIRKWOOD CT	EPA	38	B3
KIRKWOOD WY	SC	33	B5
KITTIE LN	BLMT	33	A5
KLAMATH AV	SM	29	F4
KLAMATH DR	MP	43	B4
KLAMATH ST	BR	24	C2
KNAPP CT	SM	32	E1
KNIGHTSBRDGE LN	RC	37	B1
KNIGHTWOOD LN	H	28	E3
KNOLL CIR	SSF	23	F5
KNOLL DR	SC	33	C6
KNOLLCREST RD	H	28	F6
KNOLLCREST RD	H	29	A6
KNOLL VISTA	A	43	A3
KNOLL VISTA	SMCO	50	C4
KNOWLES AV	DC	21	E4
KOHALO AV	P	20	F2
KOHALO AV	P	25	A2
KORBEL WY	BLMT	33	A3
KRAMER LN	SMCO	37	B4
KRISTA LN	SC	36	C2
KRISTIE LN	SSF	23	C6
KRISTIN CT	SMCO	32	B2
KYNE RD	SMCO	49A	D6
KYNE RD	SMCO	57	D1

L

STREET	CITY	PAGE	GRID
LABARTHE LN	SC	36	C2
LABURNUM RD	A	37	D4
LA CANADA PATH	SMCO	28	D3
LA CANADA RD	H	29	A5
LA CASA AV	SM	32	F3
LA COUR WY	SMCO	37	A6
LA CROSSE AV	SSF	23	D4
LA CRUZ AV	M	26	C6
LA CUESTA DR	SMCO	28	D3
LA CUESTA DR	SMCO	43	C6
LA CUESTA RD	H	29	A6
LA CUMBRE CT	H	28	F5
LA CUMBRE CT	H	29	A5
LA CUMBRE RD	H	28	F5
LA CUMBRE RD	H	29	A5
LADERA WY	BLMT	32	F5
LADERA WY	BLMT	33	A5
LADERA WY	P	20	E6
LA FAYETTE ST	SM	29	F6
LAGO	SM	29A	B1
LAGO	SM	33	B1
LAGOON DR	RC	33	C3
LAGOON RD	BR	22	F6
LAGOON RD	BR	24	C1
LA GRANADA ST	SMCO	30	F5
LA GRANDE AV	SMCO	30	D4
LAGUNA AV	B	28	F1
LAGUNA CIR	FCTY	33	B1
LAGUNA DR	SMCO	50	C5
LA HONDA LN	SMCO	50	B4
LA HONDA RD	H	28	F5
LA HONDA RD	H	29	A5
LA HONDA RD	SMCO	46	C5
LA HONDA RD	SMCO	48	D4
LA HONDA RD	SMCO	49	B4
LA HONDA RD	SMCO	50	C2
LA HONDA RD	W	42	D6
LA HONDA RD	W	46	C2
LA JOLLA AV	SM	32	E3
LA JUNTA LN	SMCO	50	C4
LAKE BLVD	SMCO	36	C4
LAKE CT	SMCO	36	C4
LAKE DR	SBR	25	D3
LAKE RD	BLMT	32	F5
LAKE RD	SMCO	51	C1
LAKE ST	BR	24	C2
LAKE ST	M	28	C1
LAKE ST	SM	29A	A4
LAKE ST	SMCO	30	D3
LAKE FOREST DR	DC	21	D4
LAKEMEAD WY	RC	36	C5
LAKE MEAD WY	SMCO	36	C5
LAKEMEADOW DR	DC	21	C6
LAKE MERCED BL	DC	21	D5
LAKE MERCED BL	SMCO	21	D5
LAKEMONT DR	DC	21	C4
LAKESHIRE DR	DC	19	B2
LAKESHIRE DR	DC	23	A2
LAKESHORE DR	RC	33	E2
LAKESHORE DR	SMCO	32	B2
LAKESHORE DR	SMCO	42	E6
LAKESIDE AV	P	20	E2
LAKESIDE AV	P	25	A2
LAKESIDE DR	FCTY	29A	B4
LAKEVIEW AV	P	20	E2
LAKEVIEW DR	DC	21	D4
LAKEVIEW DR	H	31	F1
LAKEVIEW DR	H	32	A2
LAKEVIEW DR	W	42	F2
LAKEVIEW LN	P	20	E2
LAKEVIEW LN	P	25	A2
LAKEVIEW WY	RC	36	C5
LAKEVIEW WY	SMCO	36	C5
LAKE VISTA AV	DC	21	D5
LAKEWOOD DR	DC	21	C5
LA LOMA DR	MP	43	B3
LA LOMA LN	SMCO	28	C3
LA MANCHA PL	M	26	C6
LA MANCHA PL	M	28	C1
LA MESA CT	B	28	C3
LA MESA CT	SMCO	43	C6
LA MESA CT	SMCO	47	C1
LA MESA DR	B	28	C3
LA MESA DR	SC	36	B3
LA MESA DR	SMCO	43	C6
LA MESA DR	SMCO	47	C1
LA MESA LN	B	28	C3
LA MESA WY	SMCO	43	C6
LA MIRADA DR	P	20	E6
LA MIRADA DR	P	25	A6
LAMONTE AV	SSF	23	D5
LAMSHIN LN	SC	36	D2
LANCASTER BLVD	SMCO	30	E3
LANCASTER RD	H	29	A6
LANCASTER WY	RC	36	D4
LANDA LN	SMCO	42	F1
LANDFAIR AV	SM	32	F3
LANDING LN	M	26	C4
LANE PL	A	37	D4
LANE ST	BLMT	33	B4
LANG RD	B	29	B1
LANGTON ST	RC	36	D2
LANING DR	W	42	C2
LANSDALE AV	M	26	C5
LANSDALE ST	SM	32	D2
LANYARD DR	RC	33	D3
LA PRENDA	M	26	B6
LA PRENDA	M	28	B1
LA QUESTA WY	W	42	D3
LARCH AV	SSF	23	F3
LARCH AV	SSF	24	A3
LARCH DR	A	37	E4
LARCH LN	P	20	F2
LARCH LN	P	25	A2
LARCHMONT DR	SMCO	19	B1
LARCHMONT DR	SMCO	21	D6
LARGUITA LN	PV	47	A2
LARK AV	RC	36	F4
LARK LN	FCTY	29A	D4
LARKSPUR AV	DC	19	B2
LARKSPUR AV	DC	23	A2
LARKSPUR DR	B	29	A2
LARKSPUR DR	M	26	A6
LARKSPUR DR	EPA	38	C5
LA SALLE DR	SM	29	D6
LA SALLE DR	SM	32	D1
LA SALLE RD	H	28	F6
LA SALLE RD	H	29	A6
LA SANDRA WY	PV	47	A1
LA SELVA	SM	33	A1
LA SENDA RD	H	29	B6
LA SOLANO	M	26	B6
LA SOLANO	M	28	B1
LAS PIEDRAS	SMCO	51	C2
LAS PIEDRAS CT	B	28	C2
LAS PIEDRAS DR	B	28	C2
LAS PULGAS RD	W	36	D6
LASSEN CT	MP	43	B3

1991 SAN MATEO COUNTY STREET INDEX

STREET	CITY	PAGE	GRID
LASSEN CT	SSF	23	F4
LASSEN DR	BLMT	32	D5
LASSEN DR	MP	43	B3
LASSEN DR	SBR	25	D3
LASSEN LN	P	20	F1
LASSEN LN	P	25	A1
LASSEN ST	BR	24	B1
LASSEN ST	SSF	23	E5
LASSEN WY	B	28	D1
LAS SOMBRAS CT	SM	29	A4
LASUEN DR	M	28	C2
LATHAM CT	H	29	A3
LATHAM ST	CLMA	23	E3
LATHROP ST	RC	36	F3
LATHROP ST	RC	37	A3
LAUGHING COW RD	SMCO	41	E4
LAUREL AV	BLMT	33	B4
LAUREL AV	B	29	A2
LAUREL AV	HMB	34	E4
LAUREL AV	MP	38	A5
LAUREL AV	M	26	C5
LAUREL AV	SM	29	D4
LAUREL AV	EPA	38	C3
LAUREL AV	SSF	23	F4
LAUREL CT	BLMT	33	B3
LAUREL LN	P	20	F2
LAUREL LN	P	25	A2
LAUREL PL	A	37	D5
LAUREL PL	MP	37	D5
LAUREL ST	A	37	D5
LAUREL ST	MP	37	E6
LAUREL ST	RC	37	A3
LAUREL ST	SC	33	D6
LAUREL ST	SC	36	D1
LAUREL ST	SMCO	37	D5
LAUREL WY	P	20	C6
LAUREL WY	RC	36	D4
LAUREL CREEK DR	SM	32	E3
LAUREL CREEK RD	BLMT	32	D4
LAURELDALE RD	H	29	B5
LAUREL HILL CT	SMCO	32	A3
LAUREL HILL DR	SMCO	32	A3
LAURELWOOD DR	SM	32	E3
LAUREN AV	P	20	F4
LAUREN AV	P	25	A4
LAURENT RD	H	28	E5
LAUREOLA LN	SC	33	C5
LAURIE LN	SMCO	32	B2
LAURIE MDWS DR	SM	33	A2
LAUSANNE AV	DC	21	F5
LAUSANNE AV	DC	23	D1
LAWLER RANCH RD	SMCO	42	F4
LAWRENCE AV	SSF	24	C5
LAWRENCE RD	SM	29	D3
LAYNE PL	SBR	26	B2
LEAFWOOD CT	SM	32	C3
LEAHY ST	RC	37	A4
LE BLANC CT	HMB	34	D2
LE CONTE AV	SMCO	30	E1
LEE DR	MP	37	D6
LEEWARD LN	FCTY	33	C1
LE HAVRE PL	HMB	34	E2
LEHNING WY	BR	24	B2
LEIGH WY	BLMT	32	E6
LEIX WY	SSF	23	B6
LELAND AV	SMCO	43	D3
LE MANS WY	HMB	34	E2
LEMON AV N	MP	43	C2
LEMON CT	H	28	D4
LEMON ST	MP	43	C2
LEMOORE DR	SC	36	C2
LENNOX AV	MP	37	D5
LENOLT ST	RC	33	E6
LENOLT ST	RC	36	E1
LEO CIR	SSF	24	B4
LEO DR	FCTY	29A	B5
LEON WY	A	37	D6
LEONA ST	SM	32	E3
LERIDA AV	M	26	D5
LERIDA CT	SMCO	47	C1
LERIDA WY	P	20	F6
LERIDA WY	P	25	B6
LERIDA WY	P	27A	A1
LEROY AV	PV	46	E3
LESLIE CT	SC	36	A2
LESLIE DR	SC	36	A2
LESLIE ST	SM	29	E6
LEVEE RD	SM	29	D2
LEWIS AV	M	26	D6
LEWIS AV	SMCO	30A	C5
LEWIS AV	SSF	24	B4
LEWIS LN	P	23	A6
LEWIS FOSTER DR	HMB	34	F3
LEWIS RANCH LN	SC	36	A1
LEXINGTON AV	RC	36	F2
LEXINGTON AV	SMCO	32	A3
LEXINGTON AV	SSF	26	B1
LEXINGTON DR	MP	37	F6
LEXINGTON DR	MP	38	A5
LEXINGTON WY	B	29	B2
LEXINGTON WY	SBR	25	E3
LIBERTY CT	SSF	23	D6
LIBERTY LN	FCTY	33	C1
LIBERTY PARK AV	SMCO	43	C3
LIBRA LN	FCTY	29A	B6
LIBRARY AV	M	26	C5
LIDO CIR	RC	33	E2
LIDO LN	FCTY	29A	C5
LIDO ST	FCTY	29A	C5
LIEBIG ST	DC	22	A4
LIGHT WY	SMCO	37	C3
LIGHTHOUSE LN	DC	23	D1
LIGHTHOUSE RD	HMB	39	F4
LILAC DR	A	37	E3
LILAC LN	EPA	38	B4
LILAC LN	SSF	24	A4
LILLY LN	SC	36	A1
LINARIA WY	SMCO	47	C1
LINCOLN AV	BLMT	32	E4
LINCOLN AV	B	28	F1
LINCOLN AV	DC	19	B2
LINCOLN AV	DC	23	A2
LINCOLN AV	RC	36	F3
LINCOLN AV	SMCO	30	D2
LINCOLN BLVD	P	27A	B2
LINCOLN CIR	M	26	C5
LINCOLN CTR DR	FCTY	29A	C4
LINCOLN LN	P	19	B5
LINCOLN LN	P	23	A5
LINCOLN PL	P	27A	B2
LINCOLN ST	EPA	38	B4
LINCOLN ST	SSF	23	F3
LINCOLN ST	SSF	24	A3
LINDA CT	SM	32	E3
LINDA MAR BLVD	P	20	D6
LINDA MAR BLVD	P	27	F1
LINDA MAR BLVD	P	27A	A2
LINDA VISTA	M	28	B1
LINDA VISTA AV	A	43	B1
LINDA VISTA DR	DC	22	D5
LINDA VISTA RD	SMCO	27	E6
LINDA VISTA RD	SMCO	30	F1
LINDA VISTA ST	SMCO	30	E2
LINDBERGH ST	SM	29	D3
LINDEN AV	A	37	E4
LINDEN AV	B	29	A2
LINDEN AV	M	26	D6
LINDEN AV	SBR	26	B3
LINDEN AV	SSF	24	B6
LINDEN CT	SBR	26	A2
LINDEN LN	SC	33	D5
LINDEN LN	SMCO	32	B2
LINDEN ST	CLMA	23	D2
LINDEN ST	DC	23	C1
LINDEN ST	RC	37	A3
LINDEN WY	SMCO	32	B2
LINDENBROOK CT	W	42	E2
LINDENBROOK RD	W	42	E2
LINFIELD DR	MP	37	F6
LINFIELD PL	MP	37	F6
LINK RD	H	29	A5
LINWOOD WY	SMCO	46	C2
LISA CT	P	27	F2
LISBON ST	CLMA	23	C1
LISBON ST	CLMA	23	E2
LISBON ST	DC	21	F6
LISBON ST	DC	23	C1
LITA LN	EPA	38	C5
LITTLEFIELD AV	SSF	24	C6
LIVE OAK AV	MP	37	D6
LIVE OAK AV	MP	43	D1
LIVE OAK LN	SMCO	28	D3
LIVE OAK LN	SMCO	36	C4
LIVINGSTON AV	P	20	C6
LIVINGSTON AV	P	27	E1
LIVINGSTON PL	SSF	23	F3
LIVNGSTN TER DR	SBR	25	E3
LLANO	SM	33	B1
LLOYDEN DR	A	37	C4
LOBITOS CK RD	SMCO	44	C2
LOBITOS CK CTO	SMCO	44	C3
LOCARNO WY	SC	36	B2
LOCKHAVEN DR	P	23	B6
LOCUST AV	SSF	24	A4
LOCUST ST	RC	37	A3
LOCUST ST	SM	29	D6
LODATO AV	SM	29	E6
LODGE DR	BLMT	32	D5
LODI AV	SM	29	F4
LOGAN LN	A	37	B4
LOG CABN RCH RD	SMCO	50	C6
LOHOMA CT	H	32	C1
LOLA ST	SM	32	E2
LOMA CT	SMCO	36	B2
LOMA RD	SMCO	36	B2
LOMA RD	SC	36	B2
LOMA MAR AV	SMCO	49A	E5
LOMA PRIETA LN	MP	43	C3
LOMA VISTA DR	SMCO	28	C3
LOMA VISTA TER	P	20	F1
LOMA VISTA TER	P	25	A1
LOMBARDI LN	H	29	B5
LOMBARDI LN	M	28	B1
LOMBARDY WY	SMCO	36	C5
LOMITA AV	M	26	B4
LOMITA AV	SBR	26	A4
LOMITA CT	M	26	B4
LOMITAS AV	SSF	23	E5
LOMITAS CT	MP	43	D2
LONDON CT	SBR	25	F4
LONDONDERRY DR	SMCO	32	C3
LONESME PINE RD	RC	36	C6
LONGFELLOW DR	BLMT	32	E3
LONGFORD DR	SSF	23	C4
LONG ISLAND AV	HMB	34	D2
LONG RIDE RD	SMCO	51A	D4
LONGSPUR	PV	47	B5
LONGVIEW CT	H	29	B5
LONGVIEW DR	DC	19	B3
LONGVIEW DR	DC	23	A3
LONGVIEW DR	SBR	25	C2
LOOKOUT RD	H	28	F6
LOON CT	FCTY	29A	D4
LORD IVELSON LN	FCTY	29A	C3
LORD NELSON LN	FCTY	29A	C3
LOREE LN	M	26	C6
LOREE LN	M	28	C1
LORELEI LN	MP	37	E3
LORI CT	BLMT	32	C4
LORI DR	BLMT	32	C4
LORNE LN	SMCO	37	C3
LORRAINE AV	SM	29	E2
LORRY LN	P	23	B6
LORTON AV	B	29	B3
LORYN LN	HMB	34	E3
LOS ALTOS DR	B	28	C3
LOS ALTOS DR	SM	32	B3
LOS ALTOS DR	SMCO	32	B3
LOS ALTOS PL	SMCO	32	B3
LOS BANOS AV	DC	21	E4
LOS BANOS AV	SMCO	30	D4
LOS CERROS RD	SMCO	36	C2
LOS CHARROS LN	PV	47	B3
LOS FLORES AV	SSF	23	E4
LOS GATOS WY	SM	33	A2
LOS MONTES DR	B	28	C3
LOS OLIVOS AV	DC	21	E4
LOS PRADOS	SM	33	B1
LOS ROBLES CT	SMCO	43	B2
LOS ROBLES DR	SMCO	28	D3
LOS TRANCOS CIR	SMCO	51	C1
LOS TRANCOS RD	PV	47	C9
LOS TRANCOS RD	PV	51	C1
LOS TRANCOS RD	SMCO	51	C1
LOS TRANCOS WDS	PV	47	B4
LOS VIENTOS WY	SC	36	A2
LOTUS WY	EPA	38	D5
LOUISE LN	PV	46	E2
LOUISE LN	SM	32	E2
LOUISE ST	MP	43	C2
LOUVAINE DR	SMCO	21	D6
LOUVAINE DR	SMCO	23	B1
LOWE RD	W	42	D3
LOWELL AV	SBR	25	F4
LOWELL ST	DC	22	B4
LOWELL ST	RC	36	E2
LWR DEARBORN PK	SMCO	49A	36
LWR DEARBORN PK	SMCO	57	E1
LOWER LOCK AV	BLMT	32	D4
LOWERY DR	A	37	E4
LOWRIE AV	SSF	24	B6
LOYOLA AV	A	37	B4
LOYOLA AV	SMCO	37	B4
LOYOLA DR	B	28	C1
LOYOLA DR	M	28	C1
LUCERNE AV	RC	37	A4
LUCERO WY	SMCO	43	C6
LUCIA CT	SBR	26	A4
LUCKY AV	SMCO	43	C3
LUDEMAN LN	M	26	B5
LUFF LN	RC	33	D2
LULA BELLE LN	SM	32	E1
LUNDY LN	SMCO	32	B3
LUNDY WY	P	20	F3
LUNDY WY	P	25	A3
LUNETTA AV	P	20	F2
LUNETTA AV	P	25	A2
LUPIN LN	A	37	E3
LUPIN WY	SC	36	C1
LUPINE WY	H	28	E5
LURLINE WY	FCTY	29A	C5
LUX AV	SSF	24	B4
LYALL WY	BLMT	32	F5
LYCETT CIR	DC	23	C5
LYCETT CT	DC	23	C5
LYCETT ST N	DC	23	C5
LYCETT ST S	DC	23	C5
LYDIA CT	H	32	A1
LYME LN	FCTY	33	B2
LYNBROOK DR	P	23	B4
LYNDHURST AV	BLMT	33	B5
LYNDHURST AV	SC	33	B5
LYNDHURST CT	BLMT	33	B4
LYNN WY	W	42	E1
LYNTON AV	SC	33	A6
LYNVALE CT	DC	21	C6
LYNWOOD LN	M	26	A5
LYNX LN	FCTY	29A	B6
LYONRIDGE LN	SM	32	C2
LYONS AV	BLMT	32	F4
LYONS ST	RC	36	F4
M			
MACADAMIA DR	H	28	D3
MACARTHUR AV	SMCO	37	B3
MACARTHUR DR	SMCO	19	B1
MACARTHUR DR	SMCO	21	D6
MACARTHUR DR	SMCO	23	A1
MACDONALD AV	DC	22	E4
MACDONALD ST	RC	36	F5
MADDUX DR	RC	36	F6
MADDUX DR	SMCO	21	D6
MADEIRA DR	P	27A	A2
MADERA AV	MP	38	A4
MADERA AV	SC	33	B6
MADERA LN	SMCO	49	C4
MADERA RD	SMCO	32	D1
MADERA WY	M	28	B1
MADERA WY	SBR	25	C1
MADISON AV	RC	36	F3
MADISON AV	SBR	25	F4
MADISON AV	SM	29	D5
MADISON WY	SMCO	37	F5
MADRID AV	SMCO	30A	A5
MADRID CT	M	26	C5
MADRID CT	P	27A	A2
MADRONA AV	SMCO	30A	A5
MADRONA ST	SC	33	B5
MADRONE AV	SMCO	30	E4
MADRONE AV	SMCO	41	C3
MADRONE AV	SMCO	57	D3
MADRONE AV	SSF	24	C4
MADRONE PL	H	28	F3
MADRONE RD	A	37	E4
MADRONE ST	M	26	C4
MADRONE ST	RC	37	A3
MADRONE TR	SMCO	41	D2
MADRONE WY	P	27A	B2
MAGELLAN AV	SMCO	30A	C6
MAGELLAN AV	SMCO	34	C1
MAGELLAN CT	P	19	B4
MAGELLAN CT	P	23	A4
MAGELLAN DR	P	19	B4
MAGELLAN DR	P	23	A4
MAGELLAN LN	FCTY	29A	C6
MAGNOLIA AV	B	26	D6
MAGNOLIA AV	M	26	D6
MAGNOLIA AV	SBR	26	A3
MAGNOLIA AV	SC	33	C5
MAGNOLIA AV	SMCO	37	D1
MAGNOLIA AV	SSF	24	A5
MAGNOLIA CT	MP	43	D2
MAGNOLIA DR	A	37	D4
MAGNOLIA DR	SM	29	E4
MAGNOLIA ST	HMB	34	E6
MAGNOLIA ST	MP	43	D2
MAHLER RD	B	26	F6
MAHOGANY ROW	SBR	26	A2
MAIDEN LN	SM	33	A3
MAIN DR	SBR	25	F5
MAIN ST	BR	22	E5
MAIN ST	HMB	34	F5
MAIN ST	RC	36	F2
MAIN ST	RC	37	A2
MAIN ST	SM	29	D4
MAIN ST	SMCO	27	D6
MAIN ST	SMCO	30	D1
MAINSAIL CT	FCTY	29A	D6
MAITLAND RD	P	20	E4
MAJILLA AV	B	29	A2
MAJORCA WY	SC	36	B2
MALABAR CT	SC	32	F6
MALAGA ST	SMCO	30A	C6
MALAVEAR CT	P	27A	A1
MALAVEAR DR	P	27A	A1
MALCOLM AV	BLMT	33	A3

1991 SAN MATEO COUNTY STREET INDEX

COPYRIGHT © 1991 BY Thomas Bros Maps

STREET	CITY	PAGE	GRID
MALCOLM RD	B	26	E6
MALLARD ST	FCTY	29A	C4
MALLET CT	MP	43	D1
MALONEY LN	MP	37	D6
MALORY CT	SMCO	37	A6
MALTA LN	FCTY	33	C1
MANDARIN DR	SSF	23	C3
MANDARIN WY	A	43	A2
MANDELA CT	EPA	38	C4
MANHATTAN AV	EPA	38	B5
MANILA WY	SMCO	21	D6
MANOR CT	DC	21	D4
MANOR CT	RC	36	E2
MANOR DR	H	28	F2
MANOR DR	P	19	B5
MANOR DR	P	23	B6
MANOR DR	SC	33	B6
MANOR DR	SSF	23	F6
MANOR DR	SSF	24	A6
MANOR DR	SSF	25	F1
MANOR DR W	P	19	A5
MANOR PL	MP	37	E6
MANOR PZ	P	19	A5
MANOR PZ	P	23	A5
MANSFIELD DR	SSF	23	C4
MANSION CT	MP	43	B3
MANUELLA AV	W	42	C3
MANZANITA AV	BLMT	33	A4
MANZANITA AV	DC	19	B3
MANZANITA AV	DC	23	A3
MANZANITA AV	SC	33	C5
MANZANITA AV	SMCO	43	B2
MANZANITA AV	SSF	24	A5
MANZANITA CT	M	28	C1
MANZANITA DR	M	28	C1
MANZANITA DR	P	27A	A1
MANZANITA RD	A	37	E4
MANZANITA ST	RC	37	A3
MANZANITA WY	W	42	D4
MAPACHE CT	PV	46	F1
MAPACHE DR	PV	46	F2
MAPACHE DR	PV	47	A1
MAPLE AV	A	37	C5
MAPLE AV	B	29	A2
MAPLE AV	SBR	26	A3
MAPLE AV	SSF	24	B5
MAPLE AV	SSF	26	A1
MAPLE AV S	SSF	24	A6
MAPLE PL	M	26	C6
MAPLE PL	M	28	C1
MAPLE ST	RC	36	F3
MAPLE ST	RC	37	A3
MAPLE ST	SM	29	D5
MAPLE WY	SC	36	C2
MAPLE WY	W	36	B5
MAPLE LEAF WY	A	37	E5
MARBLY AV	DC	23	B4
MARBURGER AV	BLMT	32	E4
MARCELLA WY	M	28	D1
MARCIE CIR	SSF	23	F4
MARCO WY	SSF	24	C6
MARCO POLO WY	B	28	D1
MARCUSSEN DR	MP	37	E5
MARGARET AV	BR	24	B2
MARGARET CT	SM	33	A2
MARGARITA AV	B	28	C3
MARGATE ST	DC	23	C4
MARGO LN	H	28	E2
MARIALINDA CT	H	28	E3
MARIANI CT	SMCO	36	C5
MARIANNA LN	A	37	C4
MARIE CT	HMB	34	E3
MARIGOLD LN	SC	35	F1
MARIN DR	B	29	B2
MARINA BLVD	BR	24	D2
MARINA BLVD	SSF	24	D4
MARINA CT	SM	29A	A6
MARINA DR	RC	33	D3
MARINA WY	P	20	E3
MARINA WY	P	25	A3
MARINA VISTA	SM	29A	B4
MARINE BLVD	SMCO	30	D4
MARINE RD	SMCO	41	D2
MARINER WY	DC	22	A6
MARINERS ISL BL	SM	29A	A4
MARINE VIEW AV	BLMT	33	B3
MARINE WRLD PKY	RC	33	C3
MARION DR	SMCO	42	F1
MARIPOSA AV	DC	19	B2
MARIPOSA AV	DC	23	A2
MARIPOSA CT	B	28	C2
MARIPOSA DR	B	28	C2
MARIPOSA DR	SSF	23	E6
MARIPOSA ST	BR	24	B1
MARIPOSA WK	P	25	B4
MARISMA	SM	33	B1
MARITIME AV	SMCO	30	D2
MARKET PL	MP	37	F3
MARKET ST E	DC	21	F6
MARKET ST E	DC	23	C1
MARKET ST W	DC	21	E6
MARKET ST W	DC	23	C1
MARKET ST W	SMCO	23	B1
MARKHAM AV	SBR	25	F4
MARKHAM AV	SMCO	37	B4
MARLBOROUGH AV	SMCO	37	B4
MARLBOROUGH RD	H	28	F6
MARLBOROUGH RD	H	29	A6
MARLBOROUGH RD	H	31	F1
MARLIN AV	FCTY	29A	D4
MARLIN CT	RC	33	D2
MARLIN DR	RC	33	E2
MARMONA CT	MP	37	F5
MARMONA CT	MP	38	A5
MARMONA DR	MP	37	F5
MARMONA DR	MP	38	A5
MARQUETTE LN	FCTY	29A	C6
MARQUITA AV	B	28	F1
MARSEILLE PL	HMB	34	E2
MARSH DR	FCTY	29A	B3
MARSH RD	A	37	D4
MARSH RD	RC	37	D4
MARSH RD	SMCO	37	D4
MARSHALL AV	SM	32	E3
MARSHALL CT	RC	37	A2
MARSHALL ST	RC	36	F2
MARSHALL ST	RC	37	A2
MARSHALL WY	DC	22	A6
MARSTEN AV	BLMT	32	D4
MARSTEN RD	B	26	F6
MARSTEN RD	B	28	F1
MARTIN CT	DC	22	D5
MARTIN DR	SM	33	A1
MARTIN LN	W	42	C3
MARTIN PL	SBR	26	B3
MARTIN ST	DC	22	D5
MARTINEZ DR	B	28	D2
MARTINEZ RD	W	46	D3
MARTINIQUE DR	RC	33	E2
MARTINIQUE LN	FCTY	33	C1
MARVA OAKS DR	W	42	B1
MARVILLA CIR	P	20	E6
MARVILLA PL	P	20	E6
MAR VISTA DR	DC	22	B5
MARY CT	DC	22	D5
MARYANN LN	DC	23	C5
MARYLAND PL	SBR	26	B3
MARYLAND ST	RC	36	F6
MARY LU LN	SM	32	E1
MARYMONT AV	A	43	A1
MASON DR	P	20	F6
MASON DR	P	25	B6
MASON LN	SM	32	D2
MASONIC AV	HMB	34	E5
MASONIC WY	BLMT	33	B3
MASSACHUSETT AV	RC	36	F6
MASSON AV	SBR	26	B2
MASTHEAD LN	FCTY	33	E3
MASTICK AV	SBR	26	B3
MATEO AV	DC	21	E6
MATEO AV	M	26	C5
MATSONIA DR	FCTY	29A	C4
MATT TR	SMCO	57	B3
MAUSOLEUM DR	SMCO	31	E6
MAXINE AV	SM	29	F4
MAXWELL LN	RC	36	D2
MAY BROWN AV	MP	43	D1
MAYBURY PL	W	36	E6
MAYFAIR AV	DC	21	C6
MAYFAIR AV	SSF	23	F5
MAYFAIR AV	SSF	24	A5
MAYFAIR AV N	DC	21	D5
MAYFAIR AV S	DC	19	A1
MAYFAIR AV S	DC	21	D5
MAYFAIR AV S	DC	23	A1
MAYFAIR DR	DC	21	E5
MAYFIELD AV	DC	19	B2
MAYFIELD AV	DC	23	A2
MAYFLOWER LN	SC	32	F6
MAYFLOWER LN	SC	35	F1
MAYWOOD AV	DC	19	B1
MAYWOOD AV	DC	23	A1
MAYWOOD DR	BLMT	32	F5
MAYWOOD DR	BLMT	33	A5
MAYWOOD DR	SBR	25	D2
MAYWOOD LN	MP	43	D1
MAYWOOD WY	SSF	23	F6
MAYWOOD WY	SSF	25	F1
MC AKER CT	SM	29	E6
MCARTHUR AV	SM	29	C6
MCBAIN AV	A	37	D6
MCCORMICK LN	A	37	C4
MCCORMICK LN	SMCO	37	C4
MCCREERY DR	H	28	E3
MCCUE AV	SC	33	D5
MCDONALD WY	B	28	D1
MCDONELL DR	SSF	23	D4
MCEVOY ST	RC	37	A4
MCGARVEY AV	RC	36	E5
MCKENDRY DR	MP	37	F5
MCKENDRY DR	MP	38	A5
MCKENDRY PL	MP	37	F5
MCKENDRY PL	MP	38	A5
MCKENZIE CT	H	29	A4
MCKINLEY ST	RC	36	F4
MCKINLEY ST	SM	29	F5
MCKINNEY AV	P	19	B6
MCKINNEY AV	P	23	A6
MCLAIN RD	BR	24	C2
MCLELLAN AV	SM	32	F1
MCLELLAN AV	SM	33	A1
MCNULTY WY	RC	36	D5
MEADOW CT	SM	32	F1
MEADOW CT	SM	33	A1
MEADOW LN	A	43	A3
MEADOW LN	B	26	E6
MEADOW LN	B	28	E1
MEADOW LN	RC	37	B3
MEADOW LN	W	46	E2
MEADOW RD	W	46	E3
MEADOW GLEN AV	M	26	C5
MEADOWOOD DR	PV	47	A2
MEADOW PARK CIR	BLMT	32	D5
MEADOWSWEET LN	SC	32	F6
MEADOW VIEW PL	SM	29	F4
MEATH DR	SSF	23	C6
MEDFORD AV	RC	36	E5
MEDINA DR	SBR	25	C1
MEDIO AV	SMCO	30A	C6
MEDIO AV	SMCO	34	C1
MEDITERRNEAN LN	RC	33	E2
MEDWAY RD	W	46	D3
MEFFERD AV	SM	29	D2
MELANIE LN	A	42	F2
MELBOURNE ST	FCTY	33	C1
MELENDY DR	SC	36	B1
MELISSA CT	SM	29	C6
MELLO ST	EPA	38	B4
MELROSE CT	H	29	B6
MELROSE CT	P	23	A5
MELROSE PL	RC	36	D2
MELVIN HENRY CT	SMCO	42	F1
MEMORIAL DR	SSF	23	F5
MEMORY LN	SBR	26	A3
MENALTO AV	MP	38	A5
MENALTO AV	EPA	38	A5
MENDOCINO CT	SBR	25	D2
MENDOCINO ST	BR	24	B1
MENDOCINO WY	RC	33	E2
MENHADEN CT	FCTY	29A	D5
MENLO AV	DC	19	A2
MENLO AV	DC	23	A2
MENLO AV	MP	37	D6
MENLO OAKS DR	MP	37	F4
MENLO OAKS DR	SMCO	37	F4
MERCAT PL	H	32	A1
MERCED DR	SBR	25	D3
MERCEDES LN	A	37	C5
MERION DR	SBR	25	D1
MERION RD	HMB	39	E2
MERNER RD	H	29	B6
MERRILL ST	MP	37	E6
MERRY MOPPET LN	BLMT	32	F5
MESA CT	A	43	A2
MESA LN	SC	36	B2
MESA VERDE WY	SC	36	B2
METRO CENTER BL	FCTY	29A	B5
METZGAR ST	HMB	34	E5
MEYN RD	SMCO	44	B3
MEZES AV	BLMT	32	F3
MICHAEL CT	SC	36	C2
MICHAEL DR	RC	37	D2
MICHAEL DR	SM	32	E2
MICHAEL LN	M	26	B5
MICHAELS WY	A	37	D6
MICHAELS WY	MP	37	D6
MICHELE CT	SSF	24	D5
MICHELLE LN	DC	23	C5
MICHIGAN AV	EPA	38	C3
MIDDLE AV	MP	37	E6
MIDDLE AV	MP	43	D2
MIDDLE CT	MP	43	D2
MIDDLE CT	SBR	25	F5
MIDDLE RD	BLMT	33	B3
MIDDLEFIELD RD	A	37	D4
MIDDLEFIELD RD	MP	37	D4
MIDDLEFIELD RD	RC	36	F1
MIDDLEFIELD RD	RC	37	B3
MIDDLEFIELD RD	SMCO	37	B3
MIDDLE GATE	A	37	C5
MIDDLESEX RD	BLMT	33	B3
MIDDLETON RD	SMCO	51A	C5
MIDFIELD WY	RC	36	D4
MIDGLEN WY	W	36	B6
MIDLAND WY	SMCO	36	C4
MIDVALE AV	SM	32	F3
MIDVALE DR	DC	19	B2
MIDVALE DR	DC	23	A2
MIDWAY AV	SM	29	B4
MIDWAY AV	SMCO	21	D6
MIDWAY CT	DC	22	D5
MIDWAY DR	DC	22	D5
MIDWAY RD	SMCO	46	D3
MIELKE DR	MP	37	E6
MILAGRA CT	P	19	B6
MILAGRA CT	P	23	A6
MILAGRA DR	P	19	B6
MILAGRA DR	P	23	A6
MILANO WY	SC	36	C2
MILFORD AV	H	29	B4
MILL ST	HMB	34	F4
MILLBRAE AV	M	26	C6
MILLBRAE AV	M	28	B1
MILLBRAE CIR	M	26	C6
MILLBRAE CIR	M	28	C1
MILLER AV	BLMT	32	F3
MILLER AV	P	19	B6
MILLER AV	P	23	A6
MILLER AV	SSF	23	F4
MILLER AV	SSF	24	A4
MILLER CT	SMCO	37	A6
MILLIE AV	MP	37	D6
MILLS AV	A	43	B2
MILLS AV	BLMT	32	F3
MILLS AV	B	28	E1
MILLS AV	SBR	26	B2
MILLS AV	SMCO	43	B2
MILLS CT	MP	37	D5
MILLS ST	MP	37	D5
MILLS WY	RC	37	B2
MILLS CYN CT	B	28	D2
MILLWOOD DR	M	26	B5
MILTON AV	SBR	26	B3
MILTON LN	P	19	B5
MILTON LN	P	23	A5
MILTON ST	CLMA	23	E3
MILTON ST	SMCO	36	F6
MILTON ST	SMCO	37	A6
MIMOSA WY	SMCO	43	C6
MIMOSA WY	SMCO	47	B1
MINA LN	P	23	B5
MINERVA AV	P	20	F4
MINERVA AV	P	25	B4
MINOCA RD	PV	47	C2
MINORCA WY	M	26	C6
MIO CORTE	M	26	C6
MIO CORTE	M	28	C1
MIRA ST	FCTY	29A	B6
MIRA WY	SMCO	43	C6
MIRA WY	SMCO	47	C1
MIRADA DR	DC	23	B2
MIRADA RD	HMB	34	C1
MIRADA RD	SMCO	30A	C6
MIRADA RD	SMCO	34	C1
MIRADOR TER	P	20	F1
MIRADOR TER	P	25	A1
MIRAMAR	SM	29A	A2
MIRAMAR DR	HMB	34	D1
MIRAMAR DR	SMCO	34	D1
MIRAMAR TER	BLMT	33	B4
MIRAMONTE CT	SC	33	B5
MIRAMONTES AV	HMB	34	E5
MIRAMONTES RD	W	42	C3
MIRAMONTES ST	HMB	34	F5
MIRAMONTS PT RD	HMB	39	F3
MIRANDA CT	H	29	A6
MIRANDA CT	H	32	A1
MIRANDA CT	P	20	F6
MIRANDA CT	P	25	A6
MIRASOL CT	H	32	A1
MIRA VISTA CT	DC	22	C4
MIRA VISTA WY	SSF	25	E1
MIRIAM ST	DC	21	E5
MISSION AV	SM	29	C5
MISSION CIR	DC	21	F4
MISSION DR	EPA	38	C5
MISSION RD	CLMA	23	D3
MISSION RD	SSF	23	D3
MISSION ST	DC	21	F6
MISSION HLLS DR	DC	22	B4
MISSION TR RD	W	42	C2
MISTY LN	BLMT	33	A4
MITCHELL AV	SSF	24	C5
MITCHELL WY	RC	36	E6
MITTEN RD	B	26	E5
MIZZEN LN	HMB	34	E2
MOANA WY	P	20	F2

1991 SAN MATEO COUNTY STREET INDEX

STREET	CITY	PAGE	GRID
MOANA WY	P	25	A2
MODOC AV	MP	37	F3
MODOC PL	P	25	B4
MOHICAN WY	RC	36	C5
MOLITOR RD	BLMT	33	B4
MOLONEY CT	SMCO	36	D3
MOLTKE ST E	DC	21	F6
MOLTKE ST W	DC	21	E6
MONGINI CT	SM	29	E6
MONO ST	BR	24	B2
MONROE AV	BLMT	32	F3
MONROE AV	SM	29	D3
MONROE ST	RC	36	F2
MONROE ST	RC	37	A2
MONSERAT AV	BLMT	32	E4
MONTALVO RD	SMCO	36	B3
MONTANA LN	SMCO	43	B2
MONTANA ST	SMCO	30	D2
MONTARA BLVD	SMCO	30	E1
MONTARA CT	PV	47	B3
MONTCLAIR AV	DC	21	C6
MONTEBELLO DR	DC	19	B4
MONTEBELLO DR	DC	23	A3
MONTECITO AV	P	20	E2
MONTECITO AV	SMCO	30A	B4
MONTECITO RD	W	46	E2
MONTECITO WY	B	28	C2
MONTE CORVNO WY	B	28	D1
MONTE CRESTA CT	BLMT	32	E4
MONTE CRESTA DR	BLMT	32	E4
MONTE DIABLO AV	SM	29	D3
MONTEGO LN	FCTY	33	B2
MONTEGO LN	SMCO	42	F1
MONTEGO LN	SMCO	43	A1
MONTELENA CT	W	42	C5
MONTEREY AV	FCTY	33	C1
MONTEREY AV	SMCO	30	D4
MONTEREY AV	SMCO	43	B2
MONTEREY CT	SBR	25	D3
MONTEREY DR	DC	19	B2
MONTEREY DR	DC	23	A2
MONTEREY DR	SBR	25	D3
MONTEREY RD	P	19	A5
MONTEREY RD	P	23	A5
MONTEREY ST	BR	24	C1
MONTEREY ST	M	26	C4
MONTEREY ST	SM	32	D2
MONTERO AV	B	28	E2
MONTE ROSA DR	MP	43	C3
MONTE VERDE DR	P	27	F2
MONTE VISTA AV	A	43	B1
MONTEVISTA LN	DC	23	C4
MONTE VISTA LN	HMB	34	F5
MONTE VISTA RD	SC	33	D4
MONTE VISTA RD	SMCO	30	F1
MONTEZUMA DR	P	20	D6
MONTEZUMA DR	P	27	E1
MONTGOMERY AV	SBR	26	B1
MONTGOMERY AV	SMCO	36	F5
MONTGOMERY AV	SMCO	37	A5
MONTGOMERY LN	SC	33	D5
MONTGOMERY ST	SC	33	D5
MONTICELLO CT	W	36	B6
MONTICELLO RD	SMCO	32	A3
MONTROSE AV	DC	19	B1
MONTROSE AV	DC	21	D6
MONTROSE AV	DC	23	A1
MONTWOOD CIR	SMCO	37	A6
MONTWOOD CIR	SMCO	43	A1
MOON GATE CT	P	19	B4
MOON GATE CT	P	23	A4
MOONSAIL LN	FCTY	29A	D5
MOORE CT	SBR	25	E3
MOORE RD	W	42	E2
MOORING LN	DC	23	D1
MORELAND DR	SBR	25	D2
MOREY DR	MP	37	E6
MOREY DR	MP	43	E1
MORIS POINT RD	P	20	E3
MORIS POINT RD	P	25	A3
MORNINGSIDE AV	SSF	23	E3
MORNINGSIDE DR	DC	19	A1
MORNINGSIDE DR	M	26	B6
MORO AV	SMCO	30A	C6
MORRELL AV	B	29	A2
MORRIS ST	SMCO	30	F2
MORRO CT	FCTY	33	B1
MORRO VISTA LN	SMCO	43	B6
MORSE BLVD	SC	33	D6
MORSE LN	SMCO	46	B2
MORSHEAD RD	SMCO	46	D4
MORTON DR	DC	23	B4
MOSELEY RD	H	28	F5
MOSSWOOD LN	SBR	26	A5
MOSSWOOD RD	H	28	E6
MOSSWOOD WY	A	37	E3
MOSSWOOD WY	SSF	23	F6
MOSSWOOD WY	SSF	25	F1
MOSSWOOD WY	SSF	26	A1
MOULTON AV	SC	33	B6
MOULTON DR	A	37	D5
MOULTON DR	SBR	25	B2
MOUNDS RD	SM	29	C4
MOUNTAIN RD	SSF	24	A4
MTN HOME CT	W	42	D4
MTN HOME RD	W	42	D5
MOUNTAIN MDW DR	SMCO	46	A1
MOUNTAIN VIEW	DC	22	F5
MOUNTAIN VW AV	BLMT	33	B3
MOUNTAIN VW PL	SMCO	32	B3
MOUNTAIN VW WY	SMCO	36	B4
MTN WOOD LN	W	42	D4
MOUNT VERNON LN	A	37	C4
MUIR WY	BLMT	32	D5
MUIR WY	P	27A	B1
MUIRFIELD CIR	SBR	25	C1
MUIRFIELD RD	HMB	39	E2
MUIRWOOD DR	DC	21	F5
MULBERRY AV	SSF	23	F5
MULBERRY AV	SSF	24	A5
MULBERRY CT	BLMT	32	F5
MULBERRY DR	SM	32	C3
MULBERRY LN	A	43	B2
MULLER CT	RC	36	E6
MULLET CT	FCTY	29A	D5
MULLINS CT	M	28	B1
MULRYAN CT	SM	32	F2
MURCHISON DR	M	26	D6
MURCHISON DR	M	28	D1
MURPHY CT	SM	32	C1
MURPHY DR	SM	29	C6
MURPHY DR	SM	32	C1
MURRAY CT	RC	37	A4
MURRAY CT	SM	32	F2
MYRNA LN	SSF	23	C6
MYRTLE AV	SSF	23	F5
MYRTLE AV	SSF	24	A5
MYRTLE RD	B	29	B2
MYRTLE ST	RC	36	E3
MYRTLE ST	EPA	38	C5
MYSTIC LN	FCTY	33	C1
N			
NADINA AV	M	26	D5
NADINA ST	SM	29	D5
NANCY WY	MP	43	C2
NANETTE DR	SC	36	B1
NANTUCKET DR	RC	33	F3
NANTUCKET ST	FCTY	33	B2
NAOMI AV	P	20	F4
NAOMI AV	P	25	A4
NAOMI CT	RC	36	F4
NARANJA WY	PV	47	A2
NASH AV	MP	37	F5
NASH DR	SM	29	F3
NASSAU DR	SMCO	42	F1
NASSAU DR	SMCO	43	A1
NATAGUA AV	P	25	B4
NATHHORST AV	PV	47	B4
NATIVE SONS RD	SMCO	57	B1
NATIVE SOGWP RD	SMCO	45	A1
NAUGHTON AV	BLMT	32	D4
NAVAJO PL	PV	47	A2
NAVARRA AV	SMCO	30A	B5
NAVARRE DR	P	20	D6
NAVARRE DR	P	27	E1
NEAL AV	SC	36	C2
NEEDLERIDGE CT	SM	32	C2
NELSON AV	P	19	B5
NELSON AV	P	23	A5
NELSON CT	DC	23	C5
NEPTUNE CT	SM	29A	A4
NEPTUNE DR	RC	33	D3
NEPTUNE LN	FCTY	29A	B6
NERLI LN	B	28	F1
NUECHATEL AV	B	29	A2
NEUMAN LN	W	42	D2
NEVADA AV	SM	29	C6
NEVADA AV	SMCO	30	D3
NEVADA ST	RC	36	E3
NEWBRIDGE AV	SM	29	E3
NEWBRIDGE ST	MP	37	F3
NEWBRIDGE ST	MP	38	A3
NEW BRUNSWCK DR	SMCO	32	B4
NEWCASTLE CT	RC	37	A5
NEWCASTLE DR	RC	37	A5
NEWELL RD	EPA	38	C6
NEWHALL RD	B	28	F2
NEWHALL RD	H	28	F2
NEWLANDS AV	BLMT	32	E4
NEWLANDS AV	B	29	B3
NEWLANDS AV	SM	32	E4
NEWMAN DR	SSF	23	D5
NEW PLACE RD	H	28	F4
NEWPORT AV	SMCO	30	D4
NEWPORT CIR	RC	33	D2
NEWPORT CT	FCTY	33	B1
NEWPORT ST	SMCO	32	A3
NEWTON DR	SMCO	28	D2
NEW YEARS CK RD	SMCO	59A	E6
NIAGARA AV	SMCO	30	D2
NIANTIC AV	DC	21	E5
NIANTIC DR	FCTY	29A	C4
NILES AV	SBR	26	A4
NIMITZ AV	A	37	A6
NIMITZ AV	RC	37	A5
NIMITZ AV	SMCO	37	A6
NIMITZ DR	SMCO	21	D6
NIMITZ LN	FCTY	33	C1
NINA LN	FCTY	29A	C4
NINER CT	SMCO	36	B4
NOB HILL RD	RC	36	D5
NOE AV	SM	29	F4
NOEL DR	MP	37	E5
NOEL RD	W	42	B4
NOOR AV	SSF	26	A1
NORA WY	A	37	B4
NORA WY	SSF	23	B4
NORBURT LN	SC	36	C2
NORFOLK DR	P	23	B5
NORFOLK ST	SM	29	D3
NORFOLK ST	SM	29A	A6
NORFOLK ST	SM	33	A1
NORIEGA WY	P	27	F1
NORMA LN	FCTY	29A	B3
NORMAN ST	RC	36	F4
NORMANDY CT	H	29	C5
NORMANDY CT	SC	36	A2
NORMANDY LN	A	37	C5
NORMANDY LN	W	36	E6
NORTE AV	MP	37	F3
NORTH CT	BLMT	33	A3
NORTH CT	SBR	25	F5
NORTH PZ	MP	37	F4
NORTH RD	BLMT	33	A3
NORTH ST	B	29	B2
NORTH ST	SMCO	56	E1
NORTHAM AV	SC	33	B5
NORTHAVEN DR	DC	19	B3
NORTHAVEN DR	DC	23	A3
NORTH CANAL ST	SSF	24	A5
NORTHCREST DR	SSF	24	A3
NORTH GATE	A	37	B5
NORTHGATE AV	DC	21	C5
NORTHGATE CT	DC	21	D5
NORTHGATE DR	W	42	F1
NORTH HILL DR	BR	22	E6
NORTHRIDGE DR	DC	19	A2
NORTHRIDGE LN	W	36	E6
NORTHRIDGE LN	W	42	E1
NORTHSIDE AV	SMCO	37	B3
NORTHUMBRLND AV	RC	37	B3
NORTHUMBRLND AV	SMCO	37	B3
NORTH VIEW WY	SMCO	36	C4
NORTHWOOD DR	SC	33	C5
NORTHWOOD DR	SSF	23	F6
NORTHWOOD DR	SSF	25	E1
NORTON ST	SM	29	E3
NORWICH DR	SSF	23	C4
NORWOOD AV	DC	23	C4
NOTRE DAME AV	BLMT	33	A4
NOTRE DAME AV	SM	29	C5
NOTRE DAME AV	EPA	38	C3
NOTRE DAME PL	BLMT	33	A4
NOTTINGHAM AV	RC	37	B3
NOTTINGHAM AV	SMCO	37	B3
NOTTINGHAM LN	FCTY	33	D2
NOVA LN	MP	38	A5
NUEVA AV	RC	37	A4
NYLA AV	SSF	23	D5
O			
OAK AV	HMB	34	E4
OAK AV	MP	38	A4
OAK AV	MP	43	D3
OAK AV	RC	36	F3
OAK AV	RC	37	A3
OAK AV	SBR	26	A3
OAK AV	SMCO	30	E3
OAK AV	SSF	23	F4
OAK CT	BLMT	32	E3
OAK CT	DC	22	C4
OAK CT	MP	38	B5
OAK DR	A	37	C3
OAK DR	SMCO	37	C3
OAK LN	MP	37	D6
OAK LN	MP	43	D1
OAK ST	M	26	C4
OAK ST	SC	33	C5
OAK ST	SM	29	D5
OAK CREEK LN	SC	36	C2
OAKCREST AV	SSF	23	E4
OAKDALE AV	EPA	38	B4
OAKDALE RD	H	28	E3
OAKDALE ST	RC	36	E2
OAKDELL DR	MP	43	D2
OAKFIELD AV	RC	37	A5
OAKFIELD LN	MP	43	D3
OAKFORD RD	W	36	E6
OAK FOREST CT	PV	47	C5
OAK GROVE AV	A	37	E5
OAK GROVE AV	B	29	A2
OAK GROVE AV	MP	37	D6
OAK GROVE PZ	MP	37	C6
OAKHAVEN WY	W	42	E2
OAKHILL CT	SM	32	C3
OAKHILL DR	W	42	C4
OAK HILL LN	SMCO	28	D3
OAKHURST AV	SC	36	D1
OAKHURST PL	MP	37	E3
OAK KNOLL DR	BLMT	32	F4
OAK KNOLL DR	RC	36	D3
OAK KNOLL DR	SMCO	36	D4
OAK KNOLL LN	MP	43	C3
OAKLAND AV	MP	37	F4
OAKLAWN DR	DC	21	D5
OAKLEY AV	SC	33	A6
OAKLEY AV	SMCO	33	A6
OAKLEY AV	SMCO	43	B3
OAKMONT DR	DC	21	C6
OAKMONT DR	SBR	25	C1
OAKMONT DR	SSF	23	C6
OAK PARK WY	SMCO	36	B5
OAKRIDGE AV	DC	22	C4
OAKRIDGE DR	DC	22	C4
OAKRIDGE DR	RC	36	D4
OAK RIM DR	H	31	F2
OAK RIM DR	H	32	A2
OAKS DR	H	28	E3
OAKSIDE AV	SMCO	37	C3
OAKTREE PL	H	28	E3
OAK VALLEY RD	SM	29	B6
OAKVIEW DR	SC	36	C2
OAKVIEW WY	SMCO	36	D4
OAKWOOD BLVD	A	37	B4
OAKWOOD BLVD	RC	37	B4
OAKWOOD BLVD E	RC	37	B4
OAKWOOD BLVD W	RC	37	B4
OAKWOOD CT	P	27	F3
OAKWOOD DR	M	26	A5
OAKWOOD DR	RC	37	B4
OAKWOOD DR	SM	32	C3
OAKWOOD DR	EPA	38	B4
OAKWOOD PL	MP	37	F3
OBISPO RD	SMCO	30A	B6
OBRIEN DR	MP	38	A3
OCCIDENTAL AV	B	29	A3
OCCIDENTAL AV	SM	29	A3
OCCIDENTAL WY	SMCO	36	C5
OCEAN AV	HMB	34	E5
OCEAN VIEW DR	SMCO	31	E6
OCEANA BLVD	P	19	A6
OCEANA BLVD	P	20	E1
OCEANA BLVD	P	25	A1
OCEANA GROVE AV	DC	19	B1
OCEANA GROVE AV	DC	23	A1
OCEANSIDE DR	DC	19	A2
OCEANSIDE DR	DC	23	A3
OCEAN VIEW	HMB	39	F4
OCEAN VIEW AV	SM	29	E3
O'CONNOR ST	MP	38	A5
O'CONNOR ST	EPA	38	C5
O'CONNOR ST W	MP	38	A5
ODDSTAD BLVD	P	25	C6
ODDSTAD BLVD	P	27A	B2
ODDSTAD DR	RC	37	A1
ODDSTAD WY	P	20	E5
ODELL PL	A	37	C5
ODESSA CT	RC	37	D2
OFARRELL ST	SM	29	D6
OGDEN DR	B	26	D6
OGDEN DR	B	28	D1
OHIO AV	RC	36	F6
OHLONE	PV	47	B5
OHLONE WY	SMCO	51A	E4
OKEEFE ST	MP	38	A5
OKEEFE ST E	EPA	38	B5
OLCESE CT	DC	23	B2
OLD BAYSHORE HY	M	26	D4
OLD BAYSHORE HY	SMCO	26	C2
OLD COUNTY RD	BLMT	33	B3
OLD COUNTY RD	BR	24	C1
OLD COUNTY RD	SC	33	D6
OLD COUNTY RD	SMCO	33	B3
OLD LA HONDA RD	SMCO	46	D5

1991 SAN MATEO COUNTY STREET INDEX

STREET	CITY	PAGE	GRID
OLD LA HONDA RD	W	46	E2
OLD PAGE MLL RD	SMCO	51	D5
OLD PAGE MLL RD	SMCO	51A	C3
OLD RANCH RD	SMCO	41	C2
OLD SPANISH TR	SMCO	51	C2
OLD STAGE RD	SMCO	48A	D2
OLD STGCOACH RD	SMCO	36	B3
OLIVE AV	SSF	24	B4
OLIVE CT	SBR	26	A3
OLIVE CT	SM	29	E3
OLIVE LN	P	20	F2
OLIVE LN	P	25	A2
OLIVE ST	MP	43	D2
OLIVE ST	SC	33	D6
OLIVE HILL LN	W	42	B2
OLIVER CT	MP	43	B3
OLIVER ST	DC	22	A4
OLIVER ST	RC	36	F4
OLIVET PKWY	CLMA	23	C2
OLMSTEAD CT	SSF	23	C6
OLYMPIAN WY	P	20	C6
OLYMPIAN WY	P	27	E1
OLYMPIC AV	MP	43	C4
OLYMPIC AV	SM	32	F2
OLYMPIC AV	SM	33	A2
OLYMPIC CT	SBR	25	D1
OLYMPIC DR	SBR	25	D1
OLYMPIC DR	SSF	23	D6
OLYMPIC DR	SSF	25	D1
OLYMPIC WY	DC	21	C5
ONEILL DR	SM	33	A2
ONEILL AV	BLMT	33	C3
ONEONTA AV	P	20	F4
ONEONTA AV	P	25	A4
ONEONTA SIERRA	P	25	A4
ONTARIO ST	SM	29	E3
OPAL AV	RC	36	D3
ORACLE PKWY	RC	33	C2
ORANGE AV	MP	43	C2
ORANGE AV	SC	33	C6
ORANGE AV	SC	36	D1
ORANGE AV	SMCO	43	C2
ORANGE AV	SSF	23	F5
ORANGE AV W	SSF	24	A5
ORANGE CT	DC	21	F6
ORANGE CT	H	28	E4
ORANGE ST	DC	21	F6
ORANGE ST	DC	22	A6
ORCHARD AV	RC	37	A4
ORCHARD HILL LN	W	46	E3
ORCHARD HILLS	A	43	A1
OREGON AV	RC	36	E5
OREGON AV	SM	29	C6
ORIENTE ST	DC	22	D4
ORINDA AV	P	20	F4
ORINDA AV	P	25	A4
ORINDA DR	SM	33	A2
ORISKANY DR	SMCO	32	B3
ORION LN	FCTY	29A	B6
ORREY WY	SSF	25	D1
ORTEGA CT	P	20	E6
ORVAL AV	SMCO	30	D4
OSBORN AV	SMCO	37	A6
OSO ST	SM	32	F2
OSO ST	SM	33	A2
OTAY AV	SM	32	F2
OTAY AV	SM	33	A2
OTIS AV	W	42	D2
OTTAWA ST	SM	29	D2
OTTILIA ST	DC	22	D4
OUTER CIRCLE	RC	36	D3
OUTRIGGER LN	FCTY	29A	D6
OVERLAND DR	SM	32	C3
OVERLOOK CT	SM	32	D3
OVIEDO CT	P	27	F1
OXFORD AV	SM	29	F5
OXFORD LN	SBR	25	F5

STREET	CITY	PAGE	GRID
OXFORD RD	B	28	E1
OXFORD ST	RC	36	F4
OXFORD ST	RC	37	A4
OXFORD WY	BLMT	33	B3
OYSTER CT	FCTY	33	C1
OYSTER PT BLVD	SSF	24	C4
P			
PABLO CT	HMB	34	F5
PACIFIC AV	P	20	E2
PACIFIC AV	P	25	A2
PACIFIC AV	SBR	26	A1
PACIFIC AV	SMCO	37	B3
PACIFIC BLVD	SM	29	E6
PACIFIC BLVD	SM	32	F2
PACIFIC BLVD	SM	33	A2
PACIFIC HTS BL	SBR	25	C2
PACIFICO AV	DC	19	B3
PACIFICO AV	DC	23	A3
PACIFIC VIEW DR	SMCO	31	E6
PACIFIC VIEW LN	SMCO	57	B1
PADDINGTON CT	BLMT	32	E5
PAGE ST	RC	37	C2
PAGE MILL RD	SMCO	51	E4
PALISADES DR	DC	19	A1
PALISADES DR	DC	21	C6
PALM AV	BLMT	33	B4
PALM AV	M	26	C5
PALM AV	RC	36	F5
PALM AV	RC	37	A4
PALM AV	SC	33	B6
PALM AV	SM	29	E6
PALM AV	SM	32	E1
PALM AV	SSF	23	F4
PALM AV	SSF	24	A4
PALM CT	MP	43	C2
PALM CT	SBR	25	D2
PALM DR	B	28	F2
PALM DR	B	29	A2
PALM PL	SM	29	E6
PALM PL	SM	32	E1
PALMA ST	SMCO	30A	C6
PALM BEACH AV	SMCO	30A	A5
PALM CIRCLE RD	W	36	B6
PALMCREST DR	DC	21	D5
PALMDALE AV	DC	19	B1
PALMDALE AV	DC	21	D6
PALMDALE AV	DC	23	A1
PALMER AV	BLMT	32	E4
PALMER LN	PV	47	B3
PALMETTO AV	P	19	A6
PALMETTO AV	P	20	E1
PALMETTO AV	P	23	A4
PALMETTO CT	P	19	B4
PALMETTO CT	P	23	A4
PALMITO DR	M	26	B4
PALO ALTO WY	SMCO	43	D3
PALOMA AV	BLMT	33	B4
PALOMA AV	B	28	F2
PALOMA AV	B	29	A2
PALOMA AV	P	20	E1
PALOMA AV	P	25	A1
PALOMA AV	SMCO	30A	B5
PALOMA RD	PV	47	A2
PALOMAR CT	SBR	26	A4
PALOMAR DR	DC	19	B2
PALOMAR DR	DC	23	A2
PALOMAR DR	SMCO	36	C3
PALOS VERDES CT	SM	32	C2
PALOS VERDES DR	SM	32	C2
PALOS VERDES WY	SSF	23	C6
PALOU DR	P	27	F2
PALO VERDE AV	EPA	38	B4
PAMELA CT	DC	19	B1
PAMELA CT	DC	23	A1
PANORAMA CT	H	28	D4
PARADISE CT	H	32	B2

STREET	CITY	PAGE	GRID
PARADISE DR	P	19	B4
PARADISE DR	P	23	A4
PARADISE WY	SMCO	36	C5
PARAMOUNT DR	M	26	B5
PARK AV	B	29	A2
PARK AV	SBR	25	F3
PARK AV	SBR	26	A3
PARK AV	SMCO	30	E4
PARK BLVD	M	26	B4
PARK DR	A	37	B5
PARK LN	A	37	C6
PARK LN	A	43	C1
PARK LN	MP	37	F4
PARK LN	SC	36	D1
PARK LN	SM	29	B4
PARK LN	BR	24	B1
PARK PL	M	26	B4
PARK RD	B	29	B3
PARK RD	SMCO	36	C4
PARK RD	SMCO	37	C3
PARK ST	RC	37	A4
PARK ST	SMCO	30	F2
PARK WY	SMCO	30	E4
PARK WY	SMCO	50	C4
PARK WY	SSF	23	F4
PARK WY	SSF	24	A4
PARKDALE WY	RC	36	E5
PARKER AV	A	37	A6
PARKER AV	A	43	A1
PARKGROVE DR	SSF	24	A3
PARK MANOR DR	DC	21	C6
PK PACIFICA AV	P	27A	B2
PARK PLAZA DR	DC	21	D6
PARK PLAZA DR	SMCO	21	D6
PARKRIDGE CIR	SSF	24	A3
PARKRIDGE CT	BLMT	32	F6
PARKROSE AV	DC	23	B4
PARKSIDE AV	DC	21	D4
PARKSIDE AV	H	28	F3
PARKSIDE AV	H	29	A3
PARKSIDE WY	SM	32	E1
PARKVIEW AV N	DC	21	E5
PARKVIEW CIR	P	23	B4
PARKVIEW CT	P	23	B4
PARKVIEW CT	SBR	26	A4
PARKVIEW DR	SBR	26	A4
PARKVIEW WY	SM	32	D2
PARKWAY LN W	FCTY	29A	B5
PARKWOOD DR	A	37	F4
PARKWOOD DR	DC	21	D5
PARKWOOD DR	SM	32	C3
PARKWOOD DR	SMCO	37	F4
PARKWOOD WY	RC	37	A5
PARMA ST	DC	21	F6
PARNELL AV	DC	23	C4
PARROTT CT	SM	32	C3
PARROTT DR	H	29	B6
PARROTT DR	H	32	B1
PARTOTT DR	SM	29	C5
PARROTT DR	SM	32	B2
PARROTT DR	SMCO	32	C2
PARTITION RD	W	42	B4
PARTRIDGE AV	DC	22	D5
PARTRIDGE AV	MP	37	E6
PARTRIDGE AV	MP	43	E1
PARTRIDGE LN	DC	22	B4
PASADENA DR	SM	33	A2
PASEITO TER	P	20	E1
PASEITO TER	P	25	A2
PASO DEL ARROYO	PV	47	C3
PASS RD	SM	29A	A5
PATRICIA AV	SM	29	E4
PATRICIA DR	A	37	B5
PATRICIA PL	MP	43	D1
PATRICK WY	HMB	34	F4
PATROL CT	W	42	A3
PATROL RD	W	42	A2

STREET	CITY	PAGE	GRID
PATTERSON AV	SMCO	43	B2
PATTON PL	H	28	D3
PAUL AV	BR	24	B2
PAUL ST	DC	21	F6
PAUL ROBESON CT	EPA	38	C4
PAULSON CT	SM	29	E6
PAULSON CT	SM	32	E1
PAVO LN	FCTY	29A	B6
PEACHWOOD CT	SBR	26	A2
PEAK LN	PV	47	B2
PEAR CT	H	28	E4
PEARL AV	SC	36	D2
PEARL AV	SMCO	30	E3
PEARL ST	SMCO	30	D2
PEBBLE DR	SC	36	B3
PEBBLEWOOD WY	SM	33	B2
PECAN CT	RC	36	F5
PECK AV	SM	29	E3
PECKS LN	SSF	24	B4
PECORA WY	SMCO	47	C1
PEGASUS LN	FCTY	29A	B5
PEGGY LN	SMCO	37	E3
PELICAN CIR	HMB	39	F4
PELICAN CT	FCTY	29A	D4
PELICAN LN	RC	33	D2
PEMBROKE CT	HMB	39	E2
PEMBROKE PL	MP	43	D2
PENHURST AV	DC	23	B4
PENHURST CT	DC	23	B4
PENINSULA AV	B	29	B3
PENINSULA WY	SMCO	37	F4
PENNANT CT	RC	33	D3
PENNSYLVANIA AV	RC	36	F2
PENNSYLVANIA AV	RC	37	A2
PENOBSCOT DR	RC	33A	B6
PENSACOLA ST	FCTY	33	B1
PEORIA ST	DC	22	A5
PEPPER AV	B	29	A3
PEPPER AV	H	29	A3
PEPPER DR	SBR	25	F3
PEPPER LN	SCR	33	B5
PEPPER TREE CT	RC	36	D6
PERALTA AV	SMCO	30A	A5
PERALTA RD	P	20	E6
PERALTA RD	P	27	F1
PERCHERON PL	H	29	C6
PEREZ DR	P	27	F2
PERIMETER RD N	MP	38	A4
PERIMETER RD S	MP	37	F4
PERIMETER RD W	MP	37	F4
PERITA DR	DC	19	B2
PERITA DR	DC	23	A3
PERRY AV	P	19	B6
PERRY AV	P	23	A6
PERRY AV	SMCO	43	D3
PERRY ST	RC	36	F2
PERSEUS LN	FCTY	29A	B6
PERSHING AV	SM	29	F4
PERSIMMON CT	H	28	D4
PESCADERO CK RD	SMCO	48A	B6
PESCADERO CK RD	SMCO	49A	B6
PESCADERO CK RD	SMCO	50	C6
PESCADERO CK RD	SMCO	50A	B3
PESCADERO CK RD	SMCO	56	C1
PESCADERO CK RD	SMCO	57	A1
PETER ST	DC	21	F6
PETRINI CT	M	28	B1
PETRINI WY	M	28	B1
PHELPS RD	SC	33	B5
PHILIP RD	DC	23	C3
PHILLIP RD	W	42	D6
PHOENIX LN	FCTY	29A	B3
PHYLLIS CT	BLMT	33	A3
PICARDO AV	P	25	B6
PICARDO CT	P	27A	B1
PICCADILLY CT	SC	36	B1
PICCADILLY PL	SBR	25	F2
PICO AV	SM	32	D1

STREET	CITY	PAGE	GRID
PICO BLVD	RC	33	D4
PICO TER	P	20	F1
PICO TER	P	25	A1
PIEDMONT AV	P	20	F4
PIEDMONT AV	P	25	A4
PIEDMONT AV	SBR	25	F4
PIEDMONT AV	RC	36	D4
PIERCE RD	MP	37	F3
PIERCE RD	MP	38	A3
PIERCE ST	DC	23	B1
PIERCE ST	SM	29	F5
PIERCE ST	SMCO	23	B1
PIER POINT LN	RC	33	D2
PIGEON POINT RD	SMCO	56A	C3
PIKES LN	SM	32	F1
PIKES LN	SM	33	A1
PILARCITOS AV	HMB	34	E4
PILARCITOS CT	H	31	F2
PILARCITOS RD	SMCO	27A	F3
PILARCITOS RD	SMCO	28	A4
PILARCTOS CK RD	SMCO	31	D6
PILGRIM DR	FCTY	29A	C4
PINE AV	HMB	34	E4
PINE AV	SC	33	B6
PINE AV	SMCO	30	E3
PINE CT	H	28	E5
PINE LN	SMCO	57	D4
PINE ST	MP	37	E5
PINE ST	M	26	C4
PINE ST	RC	37	A3
PINE ST	SBR	26	B2
PINE TER	SSF	24	B4
PINECREST DR	SBR	25	D2
PINECREST TER	SM	29	B3
PINEHAVEN DR	DC	21	C6
PINEHAVEN WY	P	20	F3
PINEHAVEN WY	P	25	A3
PINEHILL RD	H	28	F5
PINEHURST CT	M	26	A5
PINEHURST LN	HMB	39	F2
PINEHURST WY	SBR	26	A1
PINEHURST WY	SSF	23	F6
PINEHURST WY	SSF	25	F1
PINE KNOLL DR	BLMT	32	F3
PINE KNOLL DR	BLMT	33	A3
PINE RIDGE DR	SMCO	31	E6
PINE RIDGE WY	PV	47	C2
PINEVIEW LN	MP	43	C2
PINEWOOD CT	SM	32	C3
PINON AV	B	28	D1
PINON AV	M	28	D1
PINON DR	PV	47	A1
PINRAIL LN	FCTY	33	D1
PINTA LN	FCTY	29A	C4
PINTO WY	W	42	A3
PIONEER CT	SM	29	E6
PIO PICO WY	P	27A	C1
PIRATE COVE	DC	22	A6
PISA CT	SSF	23	F6
PISCES LN	FCTY	29A	A6
PITCAIRN DR	FCTY	33	C1
PIXIE LN	SC	35	F1
PIZARRO LN	FCTY	29A	C6
PLACER WY	BR	24	B2
PLACITAS AV	A	37	C4
PLACITAS AV	SMCO	37	C4
PLAID PL	H	31	F1
PLATEAU DR	BLMT	32	D4
PLAYA	SM	33	B1
PLAY BOWL DR	SMCO	50	B5
PLAZA LN	B	26	D6
PLAZA LN	FCTY	29A	B5
PLAZA ALHAMBRA	SMCO	30A	B6
PLAZA ALHMBR ST	SMCO	30A	B6
PLAZA CABRILLO	SMCO	30A	C6
PLEASANT ST	FCTY	33	B2
PLEASANT HL RD	RC	36	D5

STREET	CITY	PAGE	GRID
PLOVER ST	FCTY	29A	C4
PLUMAS AV	MP	37	F3
PLUMAS CT	SBR	25	D2
PLUMAS ST	BR	24	C1
PLUMWOOD PL	SBR	26	A2
PLYMOUTH AV	SC	33	B6
PLYMOUTH CIR	DC	23	C5
PLYMOUTH LN	FCTY	33	C1
PLYMOUTH WY	B	29	B2
PLYMOUTH WY	SBR	25	E3
POBLAR AV	M	26	D5
POETT RD	H	29	B4
POINSETTIA AV	SM	32	F2
POINSETTIA AV	SM	33	A1
POINTE PACIFIC	DC	22	A5
POINT REYES WY	P	27A	B1
PT SAN BRUNO BL	SSF	24	D4
POLARIS AV	FCTY	29A	B6
POLARIS WY	DC	22	B4
POLHEMUS AV	A	37	B6
POLHEMUS RD	SM	32	B3
POLHEMUS RD	SMCO	32	B3
POLITZER DR	MP	43	C2
POLK AV	SM	29	F4
POLLUX CT	FCTY	29A	B6
POLO CT	SM	29	D6
POLYNESIA DR	FCTY	29A	C5
POMEROY CT	SSF	23	C5
POMPANO CIR	FCTY	29A	D5
POMPONIO	PV	47	B5
POMPONIO CK RD	SMCO	48A	E1
POMPONIO CK RD	SMCO	49A	C1
PONCE AV	BLMT	32	E4
PONCETTA DR	DC	21	E4
PONDEROSA RD	SMCO	23	E6
PONDEROSA RD	SSF	23	E6
POPE RD	SMCO	50	B6
POPE ST	DC	22	B4
POPE ST	MP	38	A5
POPLAR AV	M	26	C5
POPLAR AV	P	27A	B1
POPLAR AV	RC	36	F4
POPLAR AV	RC	37	A3
POPLAR AV	SBR	26	B3
POPLAR AV	SM	29	D2
POPLAR AV	EPA	38	B4
POPLAR CT	DC	22	C4
POPLAR ST	HMB	34	E5
POPPY AV	MP	43	D2
POPPY DR	B	28	D2
POPPY LN	SC	32	F6
POPPY LN	SC	35	F1
PORT DR	SM	29A	A3
PORTAL LN	FCTY	29A	B5
PORTIFINO CIR	RC	33	F3
PORTIFINO CT	SC	36	B1
PORTIFINO DR	SC	36	B1
PORTMAN DR	RC	33	E1
PORTO FINO LN	FCTY	29A	B5
PORTOLA AV	DC	19	B3
PORTOLA AV	DC	23	A3
PORTOLA AV	HMB	39	E2
PORTOLA AV	SMCO	30	E2
PORTOLA AV	SSF	24	A6
PORTOLA AV	SSF	23	F6
PORTOLA DR	SM	32	E1
PORTOLA RD	W	42	E6
PORTOLA RD	PV	46	E2
PORTOLA RD	PV	47	A3
PORTOLA RD	SMCO	27A	E1
PORTOLA RD	SMCO	46	E2
PORTOLA RD	W	46	E2
PORTOLA WY	SBR	26	B4
PORTOLA GRN CIR	PV	47	B4
PORTOLA HTS RD	SMCO	51A	F2
PORTLA ST PK RD	SMCO	51A	B5
PORTO MARINO DR	SC	36	B2

STREET	CITY	PAGE	GRID
PORTO MARINO LN	SC	36	B1
PORTO MARINO WY	SC	36	B2
PORTO ROSA WY	SC	36	B1
PORTROYAL AV	FCTY	33	B2
PORTSMOUTH LN	FCTY	33	C1
PORTSMOUTH WY	SM	29	F6
PORT WALK PL	RC	33	D2
POSSUM LN	PV	46	F3
POSSUM LN	PV	47	A3
POTOMAC WY	SM	29	F6
POTTER AV	HMB	34	E5
POWELL ST	SM	29	E3
POWHATAN PL	SMCO	32	B4
PRADO CT	PV	47	B4
PRADO SECOYA	A	43	C1
PRAGUE ST	SM	29	D2
PRAIRIE CK DR	P	27A	C1
PRECITA AV	SMCO	30	D5
PRESCOTT LN	FCTY	33	C1
PRESIDIO AV	SMCO	30A	A5
PRESTON RD	W	46	E1
PRICE AV	RC	36	F1
PRICE ST	DC	21	F6
PRIMROSE LN	SC	33	B5
PRIMROSE RD	B	29	A2
PRINCETON AV	SMCO	30	F6
PRINCETON DR	SBR	25	E3
PRINCETON RD	MP	43	E1
PRINCETON RD	SM	29	C6
PRINDLE RD	BLMT	32	F4
PRIOR LN	A	37	D4
PRIVET DR	H	28	D4
PRODUCE AV	SSF	24	B5
PROMONTRY PT LN	FCTY	29A	A6
PROSPECT ROW	SM	29	B3
PROSPECT ST	BLMT	33	B5
PROSPECT ST	SC	33	C6
PROSPECT ST	SMCO	43	C3
PROSPECT ST	W	42	D3
PROSPECT WY	SMCO	30A	A5
PROVIDENT DR	H	28	E4
PROWSHEAD LN	FCTY	33	D1
PUEBLO ST	DC	22	D4
PUFFIN CT	FCTY	29A	C3
PULGAS AV	EPA	38	C5
PULLMAN AV	BLMT	32	F4
PULLMAN AV	HMB	34	D1
PULLMAN RD	H	28	F5
PURDUE AV	EPA	38	C3
PURISIMA RD	SMCO	41	B1
PURISIMA ST	HMB	34	F5
PURISIMA WY	HMB	34	D1
PURISIMA WY	SMCO	30A	D6
PURISIMA WY	SMCO	34	D1
PURISIMA CK RD	SMCO	40	D3
PURISIMA CK RD	SMCO	41	C3
PYROLA LN	SC	35	F1

Q

STREET	CITY	PAGE	GRID
QUADRANT LN	FCTY	33	E3
QUAIL	PV	47	B4
QUAIL LN	SMCO	35	A4
QUAIL LN	SC	36	A2
QUAIL HOLLOW	W	42	C2
QUAIL MDWS CT	W	42	E3
QUAIL MDWS DR	W	42	E3
QUAIL POINT CIR	SBR	25	E2
QUARRY RD	SMCO	33	C4
QUARTZ ST	HMB	34	E3
QUARTZ ST	RC	36	E3
QUAY LN	RC	33	D3
QUEBEC ST	SM	29	E2
QUEEN ANNE CT	M	26	B5
QUEENS AV	SM	29	F5
QUEENS CT	A	43	B1
QUEENS LN	SMCO	32	C4
QUESADA WY	B	28	D1
QUINCE ST	SM	29	D6

R

STREET	CITY	PAGE	GRID
RADBURN DR	SSF	23	D6
RADFORD LN	FCTY	33	C1
RADIO RD	SMCO	22	B6
RAILROAD AV	HMB	34	E5
RAILROAD AV	SM	29	E5
RAILROAD AV	SMCO	21	E6
RAILROAD AV	SMCO	39	F5
RAILROAD AV	SMCO	44	A2
RAILROAD AV	SSF	24	A5
RAINBOW DR	SMCO	32	B2
RAINIER AV	P	25	C6
RAINIER AV	P	27A	C1
RAINIER AV	SSF	23	F6
RALMAR AV	EPA	38	B6
RALSTON AV	BLMT	32	D5
RALSTON AV	BLMT	33	B4
RALSTON AV	B	29	A3
RALSTON AV	HMB	34	E4
RALSTON AV	H	28	F4
RALSTON AV	H	29	A3
RALSTON AV	SMCO	32	C5
RALSTON CT	H	28	E5
RALSTON RD	A	37	B5
RALSTON RD	SMCO	45	C6
RALSTON RD	SMCO	49	C1
RAM LN	FCTY	29A	B6
RAMBLEWOOD WY	SM	33	B2
RAMONA AV	P	20	F4
RAMONA AV	P	25	A4
RAMONA AV	SSF	23	F6
RAMONA AV	SSF	24	A6
RAMONA RD	SMCO	51	C2
RAMONA ST	SM	29	C3
RAMOSO RD	PV	47	A1
RAMPART WY	DC	22	B5
RANCH RD	W	46	C2
RANCH RD S	SMCO	57	B4
RANCH RD W	SMCO	57	A2
RANCHO AV	SMCO	37	D1
RAND ST	SM	29	E3
RANDALL CT	P	23	B4
RANDALL CT	SMCO	19	B1
RANDALL CT	SMCO	23	A1
RANDALL PL	MP	43	D2
RANDALL RD	SMCO	32	C3
RANDOLF PL	P	27A	B2
RANDOLPH AV	SSF	24	B3
RANDY CT	SMCO	36	F6
RANELAGH RD	H	29	C4
RANGER CIR	FCTY	29A	C4
RAPLEY RD	SMCO	46	D4
RAPLEY RD	W	46	D4
RAPLEY TR	PV	51	A2
RAVENS COURT RD	H	29	B4
RAVENSWOOD AV	A	37	E6
RAVENSWOOD AV	MP	37	E6
RAVENWOOD WY	SSF	25	F1
RAVILLA CT	DC	22	A4
RAVINE DR	W	42	D1
RAY CT	B	28	D1
RAY DR	B	28	D1
RAYMOND CT	SC	36	C2
RAYMUNDO DR	W	36	B6
RAYMUNDO DR	W	42	A1
RAYNOR PL	SMCO	57	B2
READ AV	BLMT	32	F4
REBECCA LN	A	37	E5
REBECCA LN	SMCO	37	E5
RECREATION AV	MP	38	A4
RECREATION DR	SMCO	50	C5
RECREATION WY	RC	36	E5
REDINGTON RD	H	28	E3
REDLAND RD	SMCO	46	C2

STREET	CITY	PAGE	GRID
RED LEAF CT	DC	22	C4
RED OAK WY	RC	36	D5
REDONDO AV	SMCO	30	D4
REDONDO RD	SMCO	50	B5
REDONDO BCH RD	HMB	39	E2
REDWOOD AV	MP	37	F4
REDWOOD AV	RC	36	F3
REDWOOD AV	RC	37	A3
REDWOOD AV	SBR	26	A3
REDWOOD AV	SMCO	57	D3
REDWOOD AV	SSF	24	A5
REDWOOD DR	H	29	C5
REDWOOD DR	SMCO	49A	E5
REDWOOD DR	SMCO	50	B5
REDWOOD LN	SMCO	50	B4
REDWOOD TER	SMCO	41	D1
REDWOOD WY	A	37	C4
REDWOOD WY	M	26	A5
REDWOOD WY	P	27A	A1
REDWOOD SHORES	RC	33	D3
REEF DR	FCTY	29A	A4
REEF DR	SM	29A	A4
REEF POINT RD	SMCO	30	D3
REESE ST	RC	36	F4
REFLECTN CIR DR	SMCO	31	D6
REGAL CT	MP	38	A4
REGAN DR	SM	33	A2
REGENT CT	RC	36	F4
REGENT CT	RC	37	A4
REGENT CT	SC	36	A2
REGENT ST	RC	36	F4
REGENT ST	SMCO	30	F5
REGINA WY	P	20	E6
REGINA WY	P	25	A6
REGINA WY	P	27	F1
REGULUS ST	FCTY	29A	B6
REICHLING AV	P	20	F4
REICHLING AV	P	25	A4
REID AV	SBR	26	A2
REIDS ROOST	SMCO	41	F6
REINA DL MAR AV	P	20	F4
REINA DL MAR AV	P	25	A4
REINER ST	SMCO	23	C1
REMILLARD DR	H	28	F5
RENATO CT	RC	37	B4
REPOSO WY	BLMT	32	D4
RESERVOIR RD	A	43	A3
RESERVOIR RD	H	29	B5
RESERVOIR RD	SMCO	27	F6
RESERVOIR RD	SMCO	48A	B6
RESERVOIR RD	SMCO	56	B1
RESERVOIR HL DR	DC	22	A5
RESIDENT LN	MP	38	A4
RESSA RD	P	20	F2
RESSA RD	P	25	A2
RESTON CT	SSF	23	C5
RESTWOOD DR	SSF	23	E3
RETIRO ST	SMCO	30	E5
REVERE WY	SMCO	36	C5
REX ST	SM	29	F5
REYNA PL	MP	43	D1
REYNOLDS CT	H	28	E2
REYNOLDS ST	DC	22	C4
RHINE ST	DC	21	F4
RHINETTE AV	B	28	F2
RHUS RD	SMCO	51A	E5
RHUS ST	SM	29	D6
RIBBON ST	FCTY	29A	D4
RICE ST	DC	21	F4
RICHLAND CT	SC	36	D1
RICHMOND DR	M	26	C5
RICHMOND RD	H	29	B4
RICKOVER LN	FCTY	33	C1
RIDER TR	SMCO	45	F3
RIDGE CT	SSF	23	F3
RIDGE CT	W	42	D2
RIDGE RD	BLMT	33	A3
RIDGE RD	SC	36	C2

STREET	CITY	PAGE	GRID
RIDGE RD	SMCO	41	D3
RIDGECREST TER	SM	32	C3
RIDGEFIELD AV	DC	19	B3
RIDGEFIELD AV	DC	23	A3
RIDGEVIEW CT	SSF	23	F3
RIDGEVIEW DR	A	42	F2
RIDGEVIEW DR	A	43	A2
RIDGEWAY AV	SBR	25	E4
RIDGEWAY DR	P	20	F3
RIDGEWAY DR	P	25	A3
RIDGEWAY RD	H	29	B6
RIDGEWAY RD	W	42	D1
RIDGEWOOD CT	BLMT	32	F5
RIDGEWOOD DR	M	26	A5
RIFLE RANGE RD	P	25	B3
RIGEL LN	FCTY	29A	B5
RILEY AV	RC	37	A4
RINCONADA CIR	BLMT	32	D5
RINCONADA CIR	SMCO	32	D5
RINGWOOD AV	A	37	F4
RINGWOOD AV	MP	37	F3
RINGWOOD AV	SMCO	37	F4
RIO CT	B	28	D1
RIO VERDE ST	DC	22	D4
RIO VISTA DR	P	27	F2
RISEL AV	DC	22	A4
RITTENHOUSE AV	A	37	C4
RIVERA DR	B	28	C2
RIVER OAKS RD	HMB	39	E2
RIVERSIDE DR	SBR	25	D2
RIVERTON DR	M	26	A6
RIVERTON DR	M	28	B1
RIVERTON DR	SC	33	C5
RIVIERA CIR	RC	33	E2
RIVIERA CT	SBR	25	D1
RIVIERA RD	SMCO	27	F6
RIVIERA RD	SMCO	30	F1
RIX LN	W	46	E2
RIZAL DR	H	32	A1
ROAN PL	W	42	A3
ROBERT AV	BLMT	32	C4
ROBERT PL	M	26	C5
ROBERTA DR	SM	29	F5
ROBERTA DR	W	42	D4
ROBERT PEARY LN	FCTY	29A	C6
ROBERTS DR	MP	43	C1
ROBERTS RD	P	20	E5
ROBERTS WY	H	28	F6
ROBERTSON WY	RC	36	B5
ROBESON,PAUL CT	EPA	38	C4
ROBIN CT	EPA	38	C4
ROBIN LN	M	26	A5
ROBIN RD	H	28	F5
ROBIN WY	MP	37	F5
ROBIN WY	MP	38	A5
ROBIN WY	SC	36	C2
ROBINSON DR	DC	22	C4
ROBIN WHIPLE WY	BLMT	33	A4
ROBINWOOD LN	H	28	F6
ROBLAR AV	H	29	B4
ROBLAR AV	M	26	D5
ROBLE AV	MP	37	D6
ROBLE AV	MP	43	D1
ROBLE AV	RC	37	A4
ROBLE PL	SMCO	50	C4
ROBLE RD	M	28	C1
ROBLEDA DR	A	37	B5
ROBLES DR	W	42	D4
ROCCA AV	SSF	24	A4
ROCCA CT	SSF	24	A4
ROCHESTER ST	SM	29	E2
ROCKAWAY BCH AV	P	20	D4
ROCKAWAY BCH AV	P	25	A5
ROCKFORD AV	DC	19	A4
ROCKFORD AV	DC	23	A3
ROCK HARBOR LN	FCTY	33	B2
ROCKRIDGE AV	DC	19	B2

COPYRIGHT © 1991 BY Thomas Bros Maps

1991 SAN MATEO COUNTY STREET INDEX

1991 SAN MATEO COUNTY STREET INDEX

STREET	CITY	PAGE	GRID
SEA PORT BLVD	RC	37	B1
SEA RANCH AV	SMCO	30	F5
SEARS RANCH RD	SMCO	50	B4
SEARSVILLE CT	H	32	A2
SEA SHELL CIR	HMB	39	F4
SEASHORE DR	DC	22	A6
SEASHORE DR	DC	23	D1
SEASIDE DR	P	20	E3
SEASIDE DR	P	25	A3
SEASIDE SCHL RD	SMCO	48	D4
SEA SPRAY LN	FCTY	29A	B6
SEAVIEW DR	DC	19	A1
SEBASTIAN DR	B	28	C1
SEBASTIAN DR	M	28	C1
SECLUDED AV	SMCO	37	D1
SEKI CT	SMCO	36	C5
SELBY LN	A	37	B6
SELBY LN	SMCO	37	B6
SELBY LN E	SMCO	37	B4
SELBY LN W	SMCO	37	A6
SEM LN	BLMT	33	C3
SEMERIA AV	BLMT	32	F4
SEMICIRCULAR RD	SMCO	37	C4
SEMINOLE WY	RC	36	C5
SENECA LN	SMCO	32	A3
SEQUOIA AV	B	28	D1
SEQUOIA AV	M	26	C6
SEQUOIA AV	SBR	25	E2
SEQUOIA AV	SM	32	D1
SEQUOIA AV	SMCO	27A	A3
SEQUOIA AV	SMCO	36	F6
SEQUOIA AV	SMCO	37	A6
SEQUOIA AV	SSF	23	E4
SEQUOIA CT	SC	33	A5
SEQUOIA DR	SMCO	46	C5
SEQUOIA DR	SMCO	50	B5
SEQUOIA WY	BLMT	32	E4
SEQUOIA WY	P	27A	B2
SEQUOIA WY	SMCO	37	A6
SEQUOIA WY	SMCO	46	C3
SERANA CT	SSF	23	E5
SERENA DR	P	20	E6
SERENITY CIR DR	SMCO	31	E6
SERENITY VLY DR	SMCO	57	B2
SERRA AV	M	26	D5
SERRA CT	SBR	26	A4
SERRA CT	SM	29	D3
SERRA DR	P	27	F2
SERRA DR	SSF	23	D4
SERRAMONTE BLVD	CLMA	23	C2
SERRAMONTE BLVD	DC	23	B3
SERRANO DR	A	37	B5
SERRAVISTA AV	DC	23	C4
SEVERN LN	H	29	B4
SEVIER AV	MP	38	A4
SEVILLA AV	SMCO	30A	A5
SEVILLE CT	M	26	B5
SEVILLE DR	P	20	E6
SEVILLE DR	P	27	F1
SEVILLE WY	SM	29	C5
SEVILLE WY	SSF	25	E1
SEXTANT CT	SM	29A	A4
SEYMOUR LN	MP	43	C2
SEYMOUR ST	HMB	34	E6
SHAD CT	FCTY	29A	D4
SHADOW BROOK LN	W	42	E5
SHADY LN	H	28	F6
SHADY LN	H	29	A6
SHAFTER ST	SM	29	D6
SHAKESPEARE ST	DC	21	F4
SHAMROCK CT	M	26	C5
SHAMROCK CT	SSF	23	B5
SHAMROCK RCH RD	SMCO	27	E2
SHANNON DR	SSF	25	C1
SHANNON WY	RC	33	E2
SHARON AV	BLMT	32	F4
SHARON AV	H	28	F2
SHARON CT	MP	43	C3
SHARON PL	SM	29	E3
SHARON RD	MP	43	C3
SHARON RD	SMCO	43	C3
SHARON WY	P	19	A6
SHARON WY	P	20	E1
SHARON OAKS DR	MP	43	C3
SHARON PARK DR	MP	43	B3
SHARP PARK RD	P	20	F2
SHARP PARK RD	P	25	A3
SHARP PARK RD	SBR	25	A3
SHASTA CT	SSF	23	E6
SHASTA DR	SM	32	C2
SHASTA LN	MP	43	B4
SHASTA LN	P	19	B5
SHASTA LN	P	23	A5
SHASTA ST	RC	37	A3
SHAW CT	RC	36	E4
SHAW RD	SSF	24	B6
SHEARER DR	A	37	B4
SHEARWATER PKWY	RC	33	E1
SHEARWATER ISLE	FCTY	29A	C4
SHEFFIELD DR	DC	21	E4
SHEFFIELD LN	RC	37	B1
SHEILA CT	P	27A	A1
SHELBOURNE AV	DC	19	B2
SHELBOURNE AV	DC	23	A2
SHELBURNE PL	SMCO	32	B4
SHELDEN RD	SMCO	50	B6
SHELDON AV	SC	33	B5
SHELDON WY	H	28	E2
SHELFORD AV	SC	33	B5
SHELL BLVD	FCTY	29A	B5
SHELL PKWY	RC	33	D1
SHELL ST	P	20	E1
SHELTER LN	DC	23	D1
SHELTER COVE DR	SMCO	30A	A5
SHELTER COVE RD	P	20	C6
SHELTERCREEK LN	SBR	25	F3
SHENANDOAH WY	P	27A	C1
SHEPARD WY	RC	36	D5
SHERATON PL	SMCO	32	B4
SHERBORNE DR	BLMT	32	E6
SHERIDAN DR	MP	37	E3
SHERIDAN DR	SMCO	37	F3
SHERIDAN PL	P	27A	B2
SHERIDAN WY	W	42	E1
SHERMAN AV	B	28	E2
SHERMAN AV	MP	43	C2
SHERMAN AV	SMCO	43	C2
SHERMAN RD	SMCO	30	F1
SHERWOOD CT	H	29	C4
SHERWOOD CT	M	28	B1
SHERWOOD DR	SBR	25	D2
SHERWOOD DR	SC	36	C2
SHERWOOD WY	MP	37	E6
SHERWOOD WY	SSF	25	F1
SHERYL DR	SBR	25	C2
SHIPLEY AV	DC	23	C5
SHIRLEY RD	BLMT	32	F3
SHIRLEY WY	MP	38	A5
SHOAL DR	DC	23	D1
SHOAL DR	SM	29A	A4
SHOOTNG STR ISL	FCTY	29A	D5
SHOPPE LN	MP	37	F4
SHOREBIRD CIR	RC	33	D2
SHORELINE CT	BR	24	D3
SHORELINE CT	SSF	24	D3
SHORELINE DR	BLMT	33	C3
SHORELINE DR	SM	29A	A5
SHORELINE DR	SM	33	C3
SHORESIDE DR	P	20	D6
SHOREVIEW AV	P	19	A6
SHOREVIEW AV	P	20	E1
SHOREVIEW AV	SM	29	F4
SHOREWAY DR	BLMT	33	C3
SHOREWAY RD	RC	33	C3
SHOREWAY RD	SC	33	D4
SHORT ST	P	23	A5
SHORT ST	PV	46	E3
SHOSHONE PL	PV	47	A3
SHRATTON AV	SC	33	A6
SHRATTON AV	SMCO	33	A6
SIERRA AV	P	20	F4
SIERRA DR	H	29	B5
SIERRA DR	MP	43	B3
SIERRA DR	SMCO	43	B3
SIERRA LN	PV	47	B2
SIERRA ST	RC	36	F4
SIERRA ST	SMCO	30	D2
SIERRA TER	P	20	F1
SIERRA TER	P	25	A1
SRA MORENA RD	SMCO	41	D4
SIERRA POINT PY	BR	22	F6
SIERRA POINT PY	BR	24	D1
SIERRA POINT RD	BR	24	C2
SIESTA CT	SMCO	47	C1
SILK TREE CT	H	28	E5
SILVA AV	M	26	C5
SILVER AV	HMB	34	F3
SILVER AV	RC	36	F4
SILVER HILL RD	RC	36	D6
SILVIA CT	P	27	F1
SIMPSON DR	DC	23	B4
SIOUX WY	PV	47	B3
SISKIYOU CT	SBR	25	C3
SISKIYOU DR	MP	43	B4
SISKIYOU PL	MP	43	B4
SKIFF CIR	RC	33	D2
SKIPJACK LN	FCTY	33	E3
SKY CT	SM	32	E2
SKYFARM DR	H	28	E4
SKYLAWN DR	SMCO	31	E6
SKYLINE BLVD	B	28	C2
SKYLINE BLVD	DC	23	B4
SKYLINE BLVD	M	28	C2
SKYLINE BLVD	P	23	B4
SKYLINE BLVD	P	25	C1
SKYLINE BLVD	SBR	25	E4
SKYLINE BLVD	SMCO	25	C1
SKYLINE BLVD	SMCO	26	A6
SKYLINE BLVD	SMCO	28	C2
SKYLINE BLVD	SMCO	31	E1
SKYLINE BLVD	SMCO	32	A6
SKYLINE BLVD	SMCO	34A	F1
SKYLINE BLVD	SMCO	35	A4
SKYLINE BLVD	SMCO	41	E5
SKYLINE BLVD	SMCO	45	F1
SKYLINE BLVD	SMCO	46	B2
SKYLINE BLVD	SMCO	50	F1
SKYLINE BLVD	SMCO	51	B4
SKYLINE BLVD	W	46	E5
SKYLINE DR	DC	19	A1
SKYLINE DR	DC	21	C6
SKYLINE DR	DC	23	A4
SKYLINE DR	SMCO	46	C3
SKYLINE FRWY	DC	19	B1
SKYLINE FRWY	DC	23	A1
SKYLINE FRNT RD	H	28	D4
SKYLONDA DR	SMCO	46	C3
SKYMONT CT	BLMT	32	D4
SKYMONT DR	BLMT	32	D4
SKYPARK CIR	SSF	24	A3
SKYVIEW DR	SMCO	28	C4
SKYWAY RD	SC	33	D5
SKYWOOD WY	W	46	C2
SLATE CREEK RD	SMCO	51A	B5
SLEEPY HOLLW AV	SMCO	37	D1
SLEEPY HOLLW LN	M	26	A6
SLOOP CT	FCTY	29A	D6
SMOKE TREE LN	W	42	C4
SNEATH LN	SBR	25	F1
SNEATH LN	SBR	26	A1
SNECKNER CT	SMCO	43	D4
SNOWDEN AV	A	37	C4
SOFICON WY	W	42	D5
SOHO CIR	BLMT	32	E5
SOLANA CT	BLMT	33	A5
SOLANA DR	BLMT	33	A5
SOLANA RD	PV	47	A2
SOLANO AV	SMCO	30A	B5
SOLANO DR	P	27	F2
SOLANO ST	BR	24	B1
SOMERSET CT	BLMT	32	F6
SOMERSET CT	SC	36	B2
SOMERSET DR	BLMT	32	E6
SOMERSET LN	A	43	C1
SOMERSET LN	FCTY	33	C1
SOMERSET PL	W	42	C1
SOMERSET ST	RC	36	E2
SONJA RD	SSF	24	A4
SONOMA AV	MP	36	F3
SONOMA CT	SBR	25	D2
SONOMA PL	MP	37	F3
SONORA AV	SMCO	30A	A5
SONORA AV	SSF	23	F6
SONORA AV	SSF	24	A6
SONORA DR	SM	29	C5
SORICH RD	SMCO	51A	D3
SORREL LN	SC	32	F6
SOUTH BLVD	SM	29	E5
SOUTH PL	RC	36	E3
SOUTH PZ	MP	37	F4
SOUTH RD	BLMT	33	B4
SOUTH ST	B	29	B2
SOUTHAMPTON WY	SM	29	F6
SOUTH CANCAL ST	SSF	24	B5
SOUTHCLIFF AV	SSF	23	D5
SOUTHDALE AV	DC	19	B2
SOUTHDALE AV	DC	23	A2
SOUTHDALE WY	W	36	B6
SOUTHDOWN CT	H	29	A6
SOUTHDOWN CT	H	32	A1
SOUTHDOWN RD	H	29	A6
SOUTHDOWN RD	H	32	A1
SOUTH GATE	RC	36	E3
SOUTH GATE AV	A	37	C5
SOUTHGATE AV	DC	19	B1
SOUTHGATE AV	DC	21	D5
SOUTHGATE AV	DC	23	A2
SOUTHGATE DR	W	42	E2
SOUTH HILL BLVD	DC	22	B4
SOUTH HILL DR	BR	22	D6
SOUTH HILL DR	BR	24	A1
SOUTH HILL DR	SMCO	22	D6
SOUTH HILL DR	SMCO	24	A1
SOUTHMOOR DR	P	23	B6
SOUTHPORT DR	RC	33	F2
SOUTHRIDGE CT	SM	32	C2
SOUTHRIDGE WY	DC	22	C4
S SN FRNCSCO DR	SSF	24	A3
SOUTHVIEW CT	BLMT	33	A4
SOUTH VIEW WY	W	36	C6
SOUTHWOOD AV	SM	32	E3
SOUTHWOOD CTR	SSF	23	F5
SOUTHWOOD DR	SSF	23	F5
SOVEREIGN WY	RC	33	F3
SPAR DR	RC	33	D3
SPAR DR	SM	29A	A4
SPARROW CT	EPA	38	C5
SPEERS AV	SM	29	F5
SPENCER LN	A	37	C5
SPINDRIFT WY	HMB	34	E3
SPINNAKER CT	FCTY	29A	D6
SPINNAKER LN	HMB	34	E2
SPINNAKER PL	RC	33	D2
SPINNAKER ST	FCTY	29A	D6
SPIROS WY	SMCO	43	B2
SPRAGUE LN	FCTY	29A	C6
SPRING LN	BLMT	33	B4
SPRING ST	RC	37	B2
SPRING ST	SC	33	C5
SPRING ST	SMCO	30	D3
SPRING ST	SMCO	37	C3
SPRINGDALE DR	P	23	A4
SPRINGDALE WY	SMCO	36	B4
SPRINGFIELD DR	M	26	A6
SPRINGFIELD DR	SC	33	C5
SPRINGFIELD WY	SM	29	F6
SPRING VLY LN	M	28	B1
SPRING VLY WY	SC	33	B5
SPRINGWOOD WY	P	27	F3
SPRINGWOOD WY	SSF	25	F1
SPRUANCE LN	FCTY	29A	C6
SPRUCE AV	MP	37	D5
SPRUCE AV	SSF	23	F6
SPRUCE AV	SSF	24	A6
SPRUCE AV N	SSF	24	B3
SPRUCE CT	P	20	F6
SPRUCE CT	P	27A	A1
SPRUCE LN	SMCO	57	C4
SPRUCE ST	HMB	34	E5
SPRUCE ST	M	26	C4
SPRUCE ST	RC	37	A3
SPURWAY DR	SM	29	D6
SPYGLASS DR	SBR	25	B1
SPYGLASS DR	SM	32	D3
STACEY CT	H	28	F3
STADLER DR	W	46	C2
STAFFORD ST	DC	23	C5
STAFFORD ST	RC	36	E1
STAG AV	SMCO	32	C4
STAGE RD	SMCO	48	D4
STAGE RD	SMCO	48A	D2
STAGE RD	SMCO	56	D1
STAMBAUGH ST	RC	37	A2
STAMFORD CT	SSF	23	B6
STANCHION LN	FCTY	33	E3
STANDISH CT	P	27	F1
STANDISH RD	P	27	F1
STANDISH ST	RC	36	F1
STANFORD AV	MP	43	C2
STANFORD AV	SM	29	F5
STANFORD AV	SMCO	30	F6
STANFORD AV	SMCO	37	B3
STANFORD AV	SMCO	43	D3
STANFORD CT	MP	43	D2
STANFORD LN	SC	36	D1
STANISLAUS CT	SBR	25	C3
STANLEY AV	P	20	D6
STANLEY RD	B	29	C2
STANLEY ST	RC	36	D3
STANTON RD	B	26	E6
STAR WY	B	28	F1
STARBOARD DR	RC	33	D2
STARBOARD DR	SM	29A	A3
STARFISH CT	HMB	39	F4
STARFISH LN	RC	33	D3
STAR HILL RD	SMCO	41	C6
STAR HILL RD	SMCO	44	F6
STAR HILL RD	SMCO	45	C2
STAR HILL RD	SMCO	48	C1
STARLITE DR	SMCO	32	B2
STARLITE ST	SSF	24	A5
STARWOOD DR	SMCO	46	B3
STATE ST	SM	29	C3
STATE HWY 92	HMB	34	F4
STATION AV	DC	21	E6
STATION LN	A	37	C4
STAYSAIL CT	FCTY	29A	D6
STEIN CT	SSF	23	C5
STEIN AM RHN CT	RC	37	B1
STEPHEN RD	SM	32	E2
STERLING AV	P	20	D6
STERLING AV	SMCO	43	B3
STERLING WY	RC	36	E5
STERLING VW AV	BLMT	33	A2
STERN LN	A	43	B1
STERN LN	FCTY	29A	D6
STETSON ST	SMCO	30	D2

COPYRIGHT © 1991 BY Thomas Bros Maps

1991 SAN MATEO COUNTY STREET INDEX

SAN MATEO

INDEX

COPYRIGHT © 1991 BY Thomas Bros Maps

1991 SAN MATEO COUNTY STREET INDEX

STREET	CITY	PAGE	GRID
UPLAND AV	SC	33	C6
UPLAND RD	RC	36	D4
UPLAND RD	SMCO	36	D4
UPLANDS DR	H	29	C5
UPPER LAKE RD	W	46	E2
UPPER LOCK AV	BLMT	32	D4
UPTON ST	RC	36	E4
UPTON ST	SMCO	36	E4
URSA LN	FCTY	29A	B6
URSULA AV	P	20	F4
URSULA AV	P	25	B4
URSULA WY	EPA	38	B3
UTAH AV	SSF	24	C6
UTAH WY	RC	36	D4
V			
VAILWOOD PL	SM	33	B2
VAILWOOD WY	SM	33	B2
VALDEFLORES DR	SMCO	28	D3
VALDEZ AV	BLMT	33	A5
VALDEZ AV	HMB	34	E5
VALDEZ WY	P	27A	A2
VALDIVIA CT	B	28	D2
VALDIVIA WY	B	28	D2
VALE ST	DC	21	E6
VALENCIA AV	SMCO	30A	B5
VALENCIA CT	PV	47	C3
VALENCIA DR	M	28	B1
VALENCIA DR	SSF	23	E6
VALENCIA DR	SSF	25	E1
VALENCIA ST	HMB	34	D1
VALENCIA WY	P	20	F6
VALENCIA WY	P	25	A6
VALERGA DR	BLMT	32	F5
VALERGA DR	BLMT	33	A5
VALLECITO LN	P	25	B4
VALLECITOS RD	SMCO	27	F6
VALLECITOS RD	SMCO	30	F1
VALLEJO CT	M	28	B2
VALLEJO DR	M	28	B1
VALLEJO ST	SMCO	30A	B5
VALLEJO TER	P	20	F1
VALLEJO TER	P	25	A1
VALLEMAR ST	SMCO	30	D2
VALLE VISTA RD	SMCO	27	F6
VALLEY CT	W	42	F3
VALLEY DR	BR	22	D6
VALLEY DR	SMCO	24	B1
VALLEY RD	A	43	A3
VALLEY RD	SC	33	C5
VALLEY ST	DC	21	F6
VALLEY ST	DC	23	C1
VALLEY ST	SMCO	21	F6
VALLEY ST	SMCO	23	C1
VALLEY OAK	PV	47	B5
VALLEY VIEW AV	BLMT	32	F3
VALLEY VIEW AV	BLMT	33	A4
VALLEY VIEW CT	SMCO	32	B3
VALLEYVIEW WY	SSF	25	E1
VALLEYWOOD CT	P	27	F2
VALLEYWOOD DR	SBR	25	D3
VALMAR PL	SC	36	C2
VALOTA RD	RC	36	F5
VALOTA RD	RC	37	A5
VALPARAISO AV	A	43	C2
VALPARAISO AV	MP	37	D6
VALPARAISO AV	MP	43	C2
VALPARAISO AV	SMCO	43	B3
VALVERDE DR	SSF	23	E6
VALVERDE DR	SSF	25	E1
VALVERDE RD	SMCO	30	F1
VAN BUREN RD	MP	37	F3
VAN BUREN ST	SM	29	F4
VANCE LN	EPA	38	C4
VANCOUVER AV	B	28	E2
VANNESSA DR	SM	29	E5
VANNIERDR	BLMT	33	A3
VAQUERO WY	SMCO	36	C4
VARIAN ST	SC	33	E6
VARIAN ST	SC	36	E1
VASCO DA GAMA	FCTY	29A	C6
VASILAKOS CT	SMCO	43	B2
VASILAKOS WY	SMCO	43	B2
VASQUES DR	HMB	34	F5
VASSAR ST	SMCO	30	F6
VEGA CIR	FCTY	29A	B6
VEGA CT	P	20	F6
VEGA CT	P	25	B6
VENDOME AV	DC	21	F4
VENDOME AV	HMB	34	E3
VENICE BLVD	HMB	34	D3
VENTURA AV	SM	32	D2
VENTURA AV	SMCO	50	B4
VENTURA CT	P	27A	B2
VENTURA ST	HMB	34	D1
VENTURA ST	SMCO	30A	C6
VENUS CT	FCTY	29A	B5
VERA AV	RC	36	F3
VERA CT	RC	36	F3
VERA ST	RC	36	E4
VERANO CT	H	29	C6
VERANO CT	SM	29	C6
VERANO DR	DC	19	B2
VERANO DR	DC	23	A2
VERANO DR	SSF	23	E5
VERBALEE LN	H	29	B6
VERBENA DR	EPA	38	C5
VERDE AV	HMB	39	E3
VERDE RD	SMCO	40	A6
VERDE RD	SMCO	44	B2
VERDUCCI CT	DC	23	C5
VERDUCCI DR	DC	23	C5
VERDUN AV	SM	32	D2
VERITAS WK	P	25	B4
VERMONT AV	SMCO	30	E3
VERMONT WY	SBR	25	E3
VERNAL WY	SMCO	36	C5
VERNON TER	SM	29	C6
VERNON WY	B	29	B2
VERONA AV	P	20	F4
VERONA AV	P	25	A4
VERONICA CT	EPA	38	C4
VERONICA PL	PV	47	B4
VERSAILLES DR	MP	37	D6
VERPERO AV	P	25	B4
VETERANS BLVD	RC	36	F1
VETERANS BLVD	RC	37	A1
VIA CANON	M	26	C6
VIA CANON	M	28	C1
VIA DELIZIA	H	29	B6
VIA LAGUNA	SM	29A	A2
VIA PORTOLA	P	20	F5
VIA VISTA	SM	29A	A2
VICTORIA AV	M	26	C6
VICTORIA DR	A	37	D5
VICTORIA DR	DC	23	B4
VICTORIA DR	MP	37	D5
VICTORIA RD	B	29	C2
VICTORIA WY	P	20	F6
VICTORIA WY	P	25	A6
VICTORIA MANOR	SC	36	C2
VICTOR PARK LN	H	29	A5
VICTORY AV	SSF	24	A6
VIEW AV	SMCO	30	D3
VIEW TR	M	28	C1
VIEW WY	P	27A	A1
VIEWCREST CIR	SSF	24	A3
VIEW HAVEN RD	H	29	A6
VIEWMONT TER	SSF	23	F4
VIEWRIDGE DR	SM	32	D3
VILLA AV	BLMT	32	F4
VILLA AV	CLMA	23	C2
VILLA CT	SSF	23	E4
VILLA LN	M	28	C1
VILLA ST	CLMA	23	D2
VILLA ST	DC	23	C1
VILLA ST	SMCO	23	C1
VILLA TER	SM	29	C3
VILLAGE CT	BLMT	32	F5
VILLAGE DR	BLMT	32	F5
VILLAGE DR	BLMT	33	A5
VILLAGE LN	DC	21	D6
VILLAGE LN	SMCO	21	D6
VILLAGE WY	SSF	24	B5
VILLA VISTA	SMCO	36	D4
VINE CT	SM	29	F3
VINE ST	BLMT	33	B5
VINE ST	MP	43	C3
VINE ST	SC	33	B5
VINEYARD DR	RC	36	D6
VINEYARD HLL RD	W	42	D5
VINTAGE PARK DR	FCTY	29A	B4
VIOLET LN	SC	32	F6
VIOLET LN	SC	35	F1
VIRGINIA AV	BLMT	33	B3
VIRGINIA AV	RC	36	F5
VIRGINIA AV	SM	29	C5
VIRGINIA AV	SMCO	30	D3
VIRGINIA LN	A	37	D4
VIRGO LN	FCTY	29A	B6
VISITACION AV	BR	24	B2
VISTA AV	SC	33	C6
VISTA AV	SM	33	A2
VISTA AV E	DC	21	F5
VISTA CIR	SMCO	34A	E1
VISTA CT	SBR	26	B4
VISTA CT	SMCO	36	D4
VISTA CT	SSF	25	D1
VISTA DR	RC	36	D4
VISTA DR	SMCO	34A	E1
VISTA DR	SMCO	36	D4
VISTA LN	SMCO	28	D2
VISTA RD	H	29	B6
VISTA CAY	SM	29A	A2
VISTA DL GRANDE	SC	33	B6
VISTA DEL MAR	SM	29A	A2
VISTA DE SOL	SM	29A	A2
VISTA GRANDE	M	26	B6
VISTA GRANDE	M	28	B1
VISTA GRANDE AV	DC	21	E5
VISTA GRAND LWR	M	28	B1
VISTA MAR AV	P	19	B6
VISTA MAR AV	P	23	A6
VIS MONTARA CIR	P	27	F1
VISTA VERDE WY	SMCO	51	C3
VOELKER DR	SM	32	E2
VOLANS LN	FCTY	29A	B3
VUE DE MAR AV	SMCO	30	E3
VUELTA WY	SMCO	50	B5
W			
WAKEFIELD AV	DC	23	B5
WAKEFIELD CT	BLMT	32	E5
WAKEFIELD DR	BLMT	32	E5
WALLEA DR	MP	43	D1
WALNUT AV	A	37	C5
WALNUT AV	B	28	F2
WALNUT AV	B	29	A2
WALNUT AV	SSF	24	B4
WALNUT ST	RC	36	F2
WALNUT ST	RC	37	A2
WALNUT ST	SBR	26	B2
WALNUT ST	SC	33	D6
WALNUT ST	SC	36	D1
WALSH RD	A	43	A3
WALSH RD	MP	43	A3
WALTERMIRE ST	BLMT	33	B4
WALTHAM CROSS	BLMT	32	D5
WALTON ST	SC	33	C5
WARD CT	DC	23	B3
WARD RD	SMCO	51A	F6
WARD RD	SMCO	59	C3
WARD WY	SMCO	42	F1
WARE RD	SMCO	41	C1
WAREHOUSE RD	MP	37	F4
WARM CANYON WY	H	28	F5
WARMWOOD WY	H	28	E5
WARNER RANGE AV	MP	43	C4
WARREN RD	SM	29	A4
WARREN ST	RC	36	F2
WARRINGTON AV	SMCO	37	B3
WARWICK ST	DC	23	C5
WARWICK ST	RC	36	E1
WARWICK ST	SC	36	E1
WASHINGTON AV	RC	36	E5
WASHINGTON BLVD	HMB	34	D1
WASHINGTON BLVD	SMCO	34	D1
WASHINGTON ST	DC	21	E6
WASHINGTON ST	DC	23	B1
WASHINGTON ST	SC	33	E6
WASHINGTON ST	SM	29	F5
WASHINGTON ST	SMCO	23	B1
WATER LN	SMCO	48A	C6
WATER LN	SMCO	56	C1
WATERBURY LN	FCTY	33	C1
WATERFORD CT	RC	33	D1
WATERFORD ST	P	19	B5
WATERFORD ST	P	23	A5
WATERLOO CT	BLMT	32	E6
WATERMAN AV	SMCO	57	B1
WATERS PARK BL	SM	29A	A6
WATERSIDE CIR	RC	33	E2
WATKINS AV	A	37	D4
WATTIS WY	SSF	24	C6
WAVE AV	HMB	34	D3
WAVE AV	SMCO	30	E3
WAVECREST DR	DC	19	A2
WAVECREST DR	DC	23	A2
WAVECREST RD	HMB	34	F6
WAVECREST RD	HMB	39	E1
WAVERLY AV	SMCO	37	B4
WAVERLY CT	MP	37	E6
WAVERLY CT	SSF	25	E1
WAVERLY PL	H	29	C4
WAVERLY PL	P	23	B5
WAVERLY ST	MP	37	E6
WAVERLY WY	DC	22	B4
WAYNE CT	RC	37	D3
WAYNE CT E	RC	37	D3
WAYSIDE RD	PV	46	E3
WEDGEWOOD DR	H	31	F2
WEDGEWOOD DR	H	32	A1
WEEKS ST	EPA	38	C4
WEEPINGRIDGE CT	SM	32	C2
WEILAND ST	DC	22	D4
WELLER RANCH RD	P	27A	B3
WELLER RANCH RD	SMCO	27A	B2
WELLESLEY AV	SM	29	F5
WELLESLEY CRES	RC	36	E2
WELLINGTON AV	DC	21	F5
WELLINGTON DR	SC	33	B5
WELLS ST	RC	37	A4
WEMBERLY DR	BLMT	32	D5
WEMBLEY CT	RC	37	A5
WEMBLEY DR	DC	23	B4
WENDY WY	SMCO	43	C2
WENTWORTH DR	SBR	25	D1
WENTWORTH DR	SSF	25	D1
WERNER AV	DC	21	E6
WERTH AV	MP	43	D1
WESSEX WY	BLMT	33	B3
WESSEX WY	RC	36	E4
WESSEX WY	SC	33	B5
WESSIX CT	DC	23	C5
WEST LN	B	29	B2
WESTBOROUGH BL	SBR	25	C1
WESTBOROUGH BL	SMCO	23	E5
WESTBOROUGH BL	SSF	23	C6
WESTBRAE DR	DC	19	A2
WESTBROOK AV	DC	21	C5
WESTCHESTER CT	SSF	23	D5
WESTCLIFF CT	P	19	B4
WESTCLIFF CT	P	23	A4
WESTDALE AV	DC	21	D4
WESTFIELD AV	DC	19	B1
WESTFIELD AV	DC	23	A1
WESTFIELD DR	MP	43	D1
WESTGATE ST	RC	36	D3
WESTGATE ST	SMCO	36	D3
WESTHAVEN DR	DC	21	D5
WESTHILL DR	BR	22	D6
WESTHILL PL	SMCO	22	C6
WESTLAKE AV	DC	21	E5
WESTLAWN AV	DC	21	D4
WESTLINE DR	DC	19	A3
WESTLINE DR	DC	23	A3
WESTLINE DR	P	19	A4
WESTMINSTER AV	EPA	38	A4
WESTMONT DR	DC	21	C5
WESTMOOR AV	DC	19	A1
WESTMOOR AV	DC	23	A1
WESTMOOR RD	B	28	E1
WESTMORELAND AV	RC	37	B3
WESTMORELAND AV	SM	29	B4
WESTMORELAND AV	SMCO	37	B3
WESTON DR	DC	21	C5
WESTPARK DR	DC	21	D4
WEST POINT AV	SMCO	30	F6
WESTPOINT PL	SMCO	32	A3
WESTPORT DR	P	20	F3
WESTPORT DR	P	25	A3
WESTRIDGE AV	DC	19	A1
WESTRIDGE AV	DC	21	C6
WESTRIDGE DR	PV	47	A3
WESTSIDE AV	SMCO	37	B3
WESTVIEW DR	SSF	23	E4
WESTWOOD CT	SM	32	C3
WESTWOOD ST	RC	36	E5
WEXFORD AV	SSF	25	D1
WHARF ROW	RC	33	D1
WHARFSIDE RD	SM	29A	A5
WHEELER AV	RC	37	A4
WHEEL HOUSE LN	FCTY	29A	D6
WHEEL HOUSE LN	FCTY	33	D1
WHIPPLE AV	RC	36	D3
WHISKEY HILL RD	W	42	E4
WHITAKER WY	MP	43	C2
WHITE ST	SMCO	21	D6
WHITE WY	SBR	26	A2
WHITECLIFF CT	SM	32	C3
WHITECLIFF WY	SBR	25	F3
WHITECLIFF WY	SM	32	C3
WHITEHALL LN	RC	37	A5
WHITEHORN WY	B	28	F1
WHITE HORSE CYN	SMCO	59A	A1
WHITE HSE CK RD	SMCO	57A	C6
WHITE HSE CK RD	SMCO	59A	B2
WHITE OAK CT	MP	43	D3
WHITE OAK DR	MP	43	D3
WHITE OAK WY	SC	36	D1
WHITE PLAINS CT	SMCO	32	B4
WHITHERIDGE RD	SMCO	32	F6
WHITMAN CT	SC	36	B2
WHITMAN WY	SBR	25	F3
WHITNEY CT	MP	43	B3
WHITNEY DR	MP	43	B3
WHITTIER ST	DC	22	A4
WHITWELL RD	H	29	A5
WHY WORRY LN	W	42	C4
WICHAM PL	H	29	B4
WICKLOW DR	SSF	23	C4
WIDEVIEW CT	SMCO	36	C4
WIDGEON ST	FCTY	29A	C4
WIENKE WY	SMCO	30	A3
WILBURN AV	A	37	C4

COPYRIGHT © 1991 BY Thomas Bros Maps

1991 SAN MATEO COUNTY STREET INDEX

STREET	CITY	PAGE	GRID
WILDWOOD AV	DC	21	C5
WILDWOOD AV	SC	36	C2
WILDWOOD AV	SMCO	21	C5
WILDWOOD CT	SMCO	21	D6
WILDWOOD DR	SSF	23	F6
WILDWOOD DR	SSF	25	F1
WILDWOOD DR	SM	29	B6
WILDWOOD LN	SMCO	43	D4
WILDWOOD WY	W	36	E6
WILDWOOD WY	W	42	E1
WILLARD LN	H	29	A5
WILLBOROUGH PL	B	29	A2
WILLIAM AV	BR	24	C2
WILLIAM AV	SMCO	37	B4
WILLIAM CT	MP	43	C2
WILLIAM LNDG DR	FCTY	33	C2
WILLIAMS AV	BLMT	33	A3
WILLIAMS AV	SBR	26	A3
WILLIAMS CT	SSF	23	D5
WILLIAMS LN	SC	33	B5
WILLIAMS PL	SM	29	C3
WILLIAMSBURG CT	SSF	23	D6
WILLITS ST	DC	21	E5
WILLOW AV	B	28	F2
WILLOW AV	B	29	A2
WILLOW AV	HMB	34	E4
WILLOW AV	H	29	A2
WILLOW AV	M	26	C6
WILLOW AV	SSF	23	E4
WILLOW CT	H	28	F3
WILLOW DR	P	27	F2
WILLOW LN	BLMT	33	A4
WILLOW PL	MP	37	F6
WILLOW RD	H	28	F3
WILLOW RD	MP	37	F6
WILLOW RD	MP	38	A5
WILLOW ST	RC	37	B2
WILLOW ST	SMCO	37	B2
WILLOW WY	SBR	25	D2
WILLOWBROOK DR	PV	47	A4
WILLOW GLEN	SC	33	B6
WILLOW SPG RD	SMCO	57	A2
WILMINGTON RD	SM	29	C6
WILMINGTON RD	SM	32	C1
WILMINGTON WY	SMCO	36	C6
WLMGTN ACRS CT	SMCO	36	C6
WILMS AV	SSF	23	F6
WILMS AV	SSF	24	A6
WILSHIRE AV	DC	21	D4
WILSHIRE AV	SM	32	E3
WILSHIRE CT	DC	21	D4
WILSHIRE CT	SC	36	C1
WILSON ST	DC	21	F4
WILSON ST	RC	36	F2
WINCHESTER CT	FCTY	33	B2
WINCHESTER DR	A	37	C5
WINCHESTER DR	B	29	B2
WINCHESTER ST	DC	22	A4
WINDCREST LN	SSF	24	A3
WINDEMERE RD	H	31	F2
WINDEMERE RD	H	32	A2
WINDERMERE AV	MP	37	F4
WINDERMERE AV	MP	38	A4
WINDING WY	BLMT	32	F3
WINDING WY	BLMT	33	A3
WINDING WY	SMCO	36	B1
WINDING WY	W	42	D4
WINDJAMMER CIR	FCTY	29A	C6
WINDJAMMER PL	DC	23	D1
WINDLASS LN	FCTY	33	D1
WINDSOR CT	SBR	25	E3
WINDSOR CT	SC	33	B6
WINDSOR DR	DC	21	D5
WINDSOR DR	H	28	F2
WINDSOR DR	MP	43	D1
WINDSOR DR	SC	33	B6
WINDSOR DR	SC	36	B1
WINDSOR DR	SMCO	33	B6
WINDSOR DR	SMCO	36	B1
WINDSOR WY	MP	43	D1
WINDSOR WY	RC	36	E5
WINDWARD WY	SM	29A	A2
WINGATE AV	SMCO	36	B1
WINGED FOOT RD	HMB	39	F2
WINKLEBLECK ST	RC	36	F2
WINONA AV	P	20	F4
WINONA AV	P	25	A4
WINSLOW ST	RC	36	F1
WINTERCREEK	PV	47	B5
WINWAY	SM	32	E2
WINWAY CIR	SM	32	F2
WINWOOD AV	P	19	B5
WINWOOD AV	P	23	A5
WISNOM AV	SM	29	C3
WISTERIA DR	EPA	38	D5
WISTERIA WY	A	37	E4
WOLFE DR	SM	29	E5
WONDERCOLOR LN	SSF	24	B6
WONG WY	SBR	25	F2
WOOD LN	MP	43	C2
WOODBERRY AV	SM	32	C3
WOODBRIDGE CIR	SM	33	B2
WOOD CREEK CT	SMCO	32	B4
WOODCREST CT	H	29	A6
WOODFERN	PV	47	B5
WOODGATE CT	H	28	D3
WOODGATE DR	MP	43	A3
WOODHILL DR	RC	36	D6
WOODHILL DR	RC	42	D1
WOODHILL DR	W	42	D1
WOODHUE CT	SMCO	36	C3
WOODLAND AV	DC	19	B2
WOODLAND AV	DC	23	A2
WOODLAND AV	MP	38	B5
WOODLAND AV	SC	33	D5
WOODLAND AV	SC	36	D1
WOODLAND AV	EPA	38	B5
WOODLAND CT	MP	38	A6
WOODLAND DR	H	29	C6
WOODLAND DR	SM	29	C6
WOODLAND PL	SMCO	36	C4
WOODLAND WY	RC	36	C5
WOODLAND WY	SMCO	36	C5
WOODLAND VISTA	SMCO	50	C5
WOODLAWN AV	P	20	F4
WOODLAWN AV	P	25	A4
WOODLEAF AV	RC	36	D6
WOODLEAF AV	RC	42	D1
WOODRIDGE CT	RC	36	D6
WOODRIDGE CT	RC	42	D1
WOODRIDGE RD	H	29	A6
WOODROW PL	P	27A	B2
WOODROW ST	DC	21	E5
WOODROW ST	RC	36	F3
WOODROW ST	RC	37	A3
WOODSIDE AV	DC	19	B3
WOODSIDE AV	DC	23	A3
WOODSIDE CT	SSF	23	F4
WOODSIDE DR	W	36	E6
WOODSIDE DR	W	42	E2
WOODSIDE RD	RC	36	F6
WOODSIDE RD	RC	37	A4
WOODSIDE RD	W	36	F6
WOODSIDE RD	W	42	C3
WOODSIDE WY	SM	29	C3
WOODSIDE WY	W	36	B6
WOODSTOCK PL	RC	36	E2
WOODSTOCK RD	H	29	B4
WOODSWORTH AV	RC	36	D2
WOODVIEW LN	W	46	F3
WOODVIEW LN	W	47	A3
WOOSTER AV	BLMT	32	E4
WOOSTER AV	SM	32	E4
WREN CT	SSF	23	D6
WRIGHT CT	SSF	23	D6
WURR RD	SMCO	49A	F5
WURR RD	SMCO	50A	A5
WYANDOTTE AV	DC	21	F5
WYANDOTTE AV	DC	23	D1
WYCOMBE AV	SC	33	A5
WYLVALE AV	SMCO	30	D3
WYNDHAM DR	PV	46	F2
X			
XAVIER ST	EPA	38	C3
Y			
YACHT LN	DC	23	D1
YALE AV	SMCO	30	F5
YALE DR	SM	29	C6
YALE RD	MP	43	E1
YANEZ CT	SMCO	36	C5
YARBOROUGH LN	RC	37	B1
YARNALL PL	RC	37	D2
YAWL CT	FCTY	29A	D6
YELLOWSTONE DR	SSF	23	E6
YELLOWSTONE WY	P	27A	B2
YEW ST	SM	29	C6
YOLO CT	SBR	25	D2
YORK AV	SM	29	D3
YORK ST	SSF	23	B5
YORKSHIRE CT	SBR	25	E4
YORKSHIRE LN	SMCO	36	D2
YORKSHIRE WY	BLMT	33	B3
YORKTOWN RD	SMCO	32	B3
YOSEMITE DR	BLMT	32	D5
YOSEMITE DR	P	27A	B1
YOSEMITE DR	SSF	23	E6
YOUNG AV	HMB	34	D2
YOUNG ST	SM	29	E4
YSABEL DR	SBR	25	B2
YUBA CT	SBR	25	D2
Z			
ZAMORA DR	P	20	F6
ZAMORA DR	P	25	A6
ZAMORA DR	P	27A	A1
ZAMORA DR	SSF	23	E6
ZAMORA DR	SSF	25	E1
ZAPATA WY	PV	47	A2
ZITA DR	SSF	23	D4
ZITA MANOR	DC	23	B1
ZUMWALT LN	FCTY	33	C1
NUMERICAL STREETS			
1ST AV	DC	21	F6
1ST AV	DC	23	C1
1ST AV	SBR	26	B2
1ST AV	SM	29	D4
1ST AV	SMCO	34	C1
1ST AV	SMCO	37	B3
1ST LN	SSF	24	A5
1ST ST	MP	37	E5
1ST ST	SMCO	27	D6
1ST ST	SMCO	30	E1
1ST ST	SSF	23	F5
1ST ST W	SBR	26	A1
2ND AV	DC	21	F6
2ND AV	DC	23	C1
2ND AV	RC	37	C3
2ND AV	SBR	26	B2
2ND AV	SM	29	E3
2ND AV	SMCO	34	C1
2ND AV	SMCO	37	C3
2ND LN	SSF	23	F4
2ND LN	SSF	24	A5
2ND ST	SMCO	27	D6
2ND ST	SMCO	30	D1
2ND ST	SSF	23	F5
2ND ST W	SBR	26	A1
3RD AV	DC	21	F6
3RD AV	DC	23	C1
3RD AV	FCTY	29A	A3
3RD AV	HMB	34	E5
3RD AV	RC	37	C2
3RD AV	SBR	26	B2
3RD AV	SM	29	C4
3RD AV	SMCO	30A	C6
3RD AV	SMCO	34	C1
3RD AV	SMCO	37	C3
3RD LN	SSF	23	F4
3RD LN	SSF	24	B5
3RD ST	MP	37	E5
3RD ST	SMCO	27	D6
3RD ST	SMCO	30	D1
3RD ST W	SBR	25	F2
3RD ST W	SBR	26	A2
4TH AV	RC	37	C2
4TH AV	SBR	26	B2
4TH AV	SM	29	D4
4TH AV	SMCO	30A	C6
4TH AV	SMCO	34	C1
4TH AV	SMCO	37	C3
4TH LN	SSF	23	F4
4TH LN	SSF	24	A4
4TH ST	MP	37	E6
4TH ST	SMCO	30	E1
5TH AV	A	37	B4
5TH AV	BLMT	33	B4
5TH AV	RC	37	C2
5TH AV	SBR	26	B2
5TH AV	SM	29	D4
5TH AV	SMCO	30A	D6
5TH AV	SMCO	34	D1
5TH AV	SMCO	37	C3
5TH ST	SMCO	30	D1
6TH AV	BLMT	33	B4
6TH AV	RC	37	C3
6TH AV	SBR	26	B2
6TH AV	SM	29	D4
6TH AV	SMCO	30A	D6
6TH AV	SMCO	34	D1
6TH AV	SMCO	37	C3
6TH LN	SSF	24	B4
6TH ST	SMCO	30	D1
7TH AV	RC	37	C3
7TH AV	SBR	26	B2
7TH AV	SM	29	D4
7TH AV	SMCO	37	C3
7TH LN	SSF	24	B4
7TH ST	SMCO	30	D1
8TH AV	RC	37	C3
8TH AV	SM	29	D4
8TH AV	SMCO	37	C4
8TH LN	SSF	24	B4
8TH ST	SMCO	30	D1
9TH AV	SM	29	D5
9TH AV	SMCO	37	C4
9TH LN	SSF	24	B4
9TH ST	SMCO	30	D1
10TH AV	RC	37	D3
10TH AV	SM	29	E4
10TH AV	SMCO	37	C3
10TH ST	SMCO	30	D1
11TH AV	SM	29	D5
11TH AV	SMCO	37	C3
11TH ST	SMCO	30	D1
12TH AV	SM	29	D5
12TH AV	SMCO	37	D3
12TH ST	SMCO	30	D1
13TH AV	SM	29	D5
13TH AV	SMCO	30	D2
14TH AV	SM	29	D5
14TH AV	SMCO	37	D4
14TH ST	SMCO	30	D2
15TH AV	RC	37	D4
15TH AV	SM	29	D5
15TH AV	SMCO	37	D4
15TH ST	SMCO	30	D2
16TH AV	RC	37	D2
16TH AV	SM	29	E5
16TH AV	SMCO	37	D3
16TH ST	SMCO	30	D2
17TH AV	A	37	D4
17TH AV	RC	37	D3
17TH AV	SM	29	E5
17TH AV	SMCO	37	D4
18TH AV	RC	37	D2
18TH AV	SMCO	37	D3
18TH ST	SM	29	E6
19TH AV	SM	29	E5
20TH AV	SM	29	E6
21ST AV	SM	29	E6
22ND AV	SM	29	D6
22ND AV	SM	32	E1
23RD AV	SM	29	E6
23RD AV	SM	32	E1
24TH AV	SM	29	E6
24TH AV	SM	32	E1
25TH AV	SM	29	E6
25TH AV	SM	32	E1
26TH AV	SM	32	E1
26TH PL	SM	32	E1
27TH AV	SM	32	E1
28TH AV	SM	32	E2
29TH AV	SM	32	E2
30TH AV	SM	32	E2
31ST AV	SM	32	F2
36TH AV	SM	32	F3
37TH AV	SM	32	F2
38TH AV	SM	32	F3
38TH AV	SM	33	A2
39TH AV	SM	32	F3
39TH AV	SM	33	A2
40TH AV	SM	32	F3
40TH AV	SM	33	A2
41ST AV	SM	32	F3
41ST AV	SM	33	A2
41ST PL	SM	33	A2
42ND AV	SM	32	E3
42ND AV	SM	33	A3
43RD AV	SM	32	F3
43RD AV	SM	33	A3
44TH AV	SM	32	F3
44TH AV	SM	33	A3
87TH ST	DC	21	D6
87TH ST	SMCO	21	E6
88TH ST	DC	21	D6
88TH ST	SMCO	21	D6
89TH ST	DC	21	D6
89TH ST	SMCO	21	D6
90TH ST	DC	21	E6
90TH ST	SMCO	21	E6
91ST ST	DC	21	D6
91ST ST	SMCO	21	D6
92ND ST	DC	23	B1
92ND ST	SMCO	21	E6
92ND ST	SMCO	23	B1

COPYRIGHT © 1991 BY Thomas Bros Maps

1991 SAN MATEO COUNTY POINTS OF INTEREST

PAGE	GRID	NAME	ADDRESS	CITY	PHONE
		AIRPORTS (SEE TRANSPORTATION)			
		BUILDINGS			
26	D6	AIRPORT EXECUTIVE	1813 EL CAMINO REAL	BURLINGAME	692 1592
29	B1	ANZA PACIFIC CORP	433 AIRPORT BLVD	BURLINGAME	342 5711
29	D6	BOREL PLACE	1611 BOREL PL	SAN MATEO	341 7497
36	F2	COUNTY GOVERNMENT CTR	MIDDLEFIELD RD	REDWOOD CITY	364 5600
36	F2	COUNTY OFFICE BUILDING	590 HAMILTON	REDWOOD CITY	364 5600
29	B3	FIVE TWENTY EL CAMINO	520 S EL CAMINO REAL	SAN MATEO	342 9495
26	E6	FOURTEEN NINETY-NINE B	1499 BAYSHORE HWY	BURLINGAME	697 0121
36	F2	HALL OF JUSTICE	401 MARSHALL ST	REDWOOD CITY	364 5600
32	E1	HILLSDALE EXECUTIVE CN	2555 FLORES ST	SAN MATEO	349 2109
29	D4	MEDICAL ARTS BLDG CO	205 E 3RD AV	SAN MATEO	343 7501
23	E4	SAN MATEO COUNTY COURT	1050 MISSION RD	S SN FRANCSCO	873 1800
36	F2	SAN MATEO CO GOVT CTR	MIDDLEFIELD RD	REDWOOD CITY	364 5600
29	A1	SEABREEZE PLAZA III	ANZA BLVD	BURLINGAME	348 7600
36	F3	VETERANS MEMORIAL BLDG	1455 MADISON AV	REDWOOD CITY	366 9913
21	F5	WAR MEMORIAL BUILDING	6655 MISSION ST	DALY CITY	755 9846
		CEMETERIES & MEMORIAL PARKS			
34	F4	CATHOLIC	MAIN ST & HWY 92	HALF MOON BAY	
23	B3	CHINESE	CALLAN BLVD	DALY CITY	992 4581
23	D2	CYPRESS LAWN MEM PARK	MISSION RD	COLMA	755 0580
23	C2	ETERNAL HOME	EL CAMINO REAL	COLMA	755 5236
25	F1	GOLDEN GATE NATIONAL	SNEATH LN	SAN BRUNO	761 1646
23	C2	GREEK ORTHODOX MEM PK	EL CAMINO REAL	COLMA	755 6939
23	C2	GREENLAWN MEMORIAL PK	EL CAMINO REAL	COLMA	755 7622
23	D2	HILLS OF ETERNITY	EL CAMINO REAL	COLMA	756 3633
23	D3	HOLY CROSS	MISSION RD	COLMA	756 2060
23	D2	HOME OF PEACE	EL CAMINO REAL	COLMA	755 4700
34	F4	I O O F	MAIN ST & HWY 92	HALF MOON BAY	
23	C2	ITALIAN	EL CAMINO REAL	COLMA	755 1511
23	C1	JAPANESE	EL CAMINO REAL	COLMA	755 3747
23	D1	OLIVET MEMORIAL PARK	1601 HILLSIDE BLVD	COLMA	755 0322
29	B6	ST JOHNS	PARROTT DR	SAN MATEO	
23	D2	SALEM MEMORIAL PARK	EL CAMINO REAL	COLMA	755 5296
23	D1	SERBIAN	1801 HILLSIDE BLVD	COLMA	755 2453
31	E6	SKYLAWN MEMORIAL PARK	SKYLINE BLVD	SAN MATEO	349 4411
23	C2	WOODLAWN MEMORIAL PARK	JUNIPERO SERRA BLVD	COLMA	755 1727
		CHAMBERS OF COMMERCE			
33	B4	BELMONT CITY	1365 5TH AV	BELMONT	595 8696
24	C1	BRISBANE	44 VISITACION AV	BRISBANE	467 7283
29	B2	BURLINGAME	290 CALIFORNIA DR	BURLINGAME	344 1735
21	E6	DALY CITY GREATER	244 92ND ST	DALY CITY	755 8526
29A	C4	FOSTER CITY	1125 HILLSIDE BLVD	FOSTER CITY	573 7600
34	F5	HALF MOON BAY	225 S CABRILLO HWY	HALF MOON BAY	726 5202
37	D6	MENLO PARK	1100 MERRILL ST	MENLO PARK	325 2818
26	C5	MILLBRAE	485 BROADWAY	MILLBRAE	697 7324
25	A2	PACIFICA	220 PALOMA AV	PACIFICA	355 4122
37	A2	REDWOOD CITY	1675 BROADWAY	REDWOOD CITY	364 1722
26	B2	SAN BRUNO	618 SAN MATEO AV	SAN BRUNO	588 0180
36	D1	SAN CARLOS	1560 LAUREL ST	SAN CARLOS	593 1068
29	E6	SAN MATEO	2031 PIONEER CT	SAN MATEO	341 5679
24	B5	SOUTH SAN FRANCISCO	435 GRAND AV	S SN FRANCSCO	588 1911
29	B1	UNITED STATES	500 AIRPORT BLVD	BURLINGAME	348 4011
		CITY HALLS			
37	C5	ATHERTON	91 ASHFIELD RD	ATHERTON	325 4457
33	B4	BELMONT	1365 5TH AV	BELMONT	573 2790
24	C1	BRISBANE	44 VISITACION AV	BRISBANE	467 1515
29	A2	BURLINGAME	501 PRIMROSE RD	BURLINGAME	342 8931
23	C2	COLMA	235 EL CAMINO REAL	COLMA	997 8300
21	E6	DALY CITY	90TH ST	DALY CITY	991 8000
29A	C5	FOSTER CITY	610 FOSTER CITY BLVD	FOSTER CITY	349 1200
34	F5	HALF MOON BAY	501 MAIN ST	HALF MOON BAY	726 5566
29	A2	HILLSBOROUGH	1600 FLORIBUNDA AV	HILLSBOROUGH	343 2795
37	E6	MENLO PARK	701 LAUREL ST	MENLO PARK	858 3360
26	C5	MILLBRAE	621 MAGNOLIA AV	MILLBRAE	692 6890
20	E1	PACIFICA	170 SANTA MARIA AV	PACIFICA	875 7300

PAGE	GRID	NAME	ADDRESS	CITY	PHONE
47	A3	PORTOLA VALLEY	765 PORTOLA RD	PORTOLA VLY	851 1700
36	F2	REDWOOD CITY	MIDDLEFIELD & JEFFRSON	REDWOOD CITY	369 6251
26	B3	SAN BRUNO	567 EL CAMINO REAL	SAN BRUNO	877 8897
33	C5	SAN CARLOS	666 ELM ST	SAN CARLOS	593 8011
29	D6	SAN MATEO	330 W 20TH AV	SAN MATEO	574 6760
24	B5	SOUTH SAN FRANCISCO	400 GRAND AV	S SN FRANCSCO	877 8500
42	D3	WOODSIDE TOWN HALL	3195 WOODSIDE RD	WOODSIDE	851 7764
		COLLEGES			
36	C6	CANADA COLLEGE	4200 FARM HILL BLVD	REDWOOD CITY	306 3100
33	A4	COLLEGE OF NOTRE DAME	1500 RALSTON AV	BELMONT	593 1601
32	C2	COLLEGE OF SAN MATEO	1700 W HILLSDALE BLVD	SAN MATEO	574 6161
37	C5	MENLO COLLEGE	EL CAMINO REAL	ATHERTON	323 6141
25	C2	SKYLINE COLLEGE	3300 COLLEGE DR	SAN BRUNO	355 7000
		GOLF COURSES & COUNTRY CLUBS			
32	F1	BAY MEADOWS	BAY MEADOWS RACE TRACK	SAN MATEO	341 7204
28	F3	BURLINGAME COUNTRY CLB	80 NEW PLACE RD	HILLSBOROUGH	343 1843
23	E5	CALIF GOLF CLUB OF S F	844 W ORANGE AV	S SN FRANCSCO	588 9021
28	D5	CRYSTAL SPGS GOLF CLUB	6650 SKYLINE BLVD	BURLINGAME	342 4188
23	E1	CYPRESS HILLS	HILLSIDE BLVD	COLMA	992 5155
36	C6	EMERALD HILLS	WILMINGTON & JEFFERSON	REDWOOD CITY	368 7820
26	B5	GREEN HILLS C C	LUDEMAN LN	MILLBRAE	583 0882
39	E2	HALF MOON BAY G LINKS	CABRILLO HWY	HALF MOON BAY	726 4438
21	E5	LAKE MERCED GOLF & C C	2300 JUNIPERO SERRA BL	DALY CITY	755 2720
42	E1	MENLO COUNTRY CLUB	WOODSIDE RD	WOODSIDE	366 9910
21	B4	OLYMPIC COUNTRY CLUB	SKYLINE BLVD	DALY CITY	587 4800
32	C1	PENINSULA GOLF & C C	710 MADERA DR	SAN MATEO	573 5511
21	D4	SAN FRANCISCO GOLF CLB	JUNIPERO SERRA BL	DALY CITY	585 0480
29	D1	SAN MATEO MUNICIPAL	COYOTE POINT DR	SAN MATEO	347 1461
43	A4	SHARON HTS GOLF & C C	2900 SAND HILL RD	MENLO PARK	854 6422
20	E3	SHARP PARK	CABRILLO HWY	PACIFICA	355 2862
		HOSPITALS			
		*EMERGENCY SERVICES	AVAILABLE		
37	A2	*KAISER-PERMANENTE	1150 VETERANS BLVD	REDWOOD CITY	780 2000
23	E4	*KAISER-PERMANENTE	1200 EL CAMINO REAL	S SN FRANCSCO	876 1700
29	C4	*MILLS MEMORIAL	100 S SAN MATEO DR	SAN MATEO	696 4400
26	D6	*PENINSULA	1783 EL CAMINO REAL	BURLINGAME	872 5400
30	E3	*ST CATHERINE	ETHELDORE AT MARINE BL	MOSS BEACH	728 5521
32	F2	SAN MATEO CO GENERAL	222 W 39TH AV	SAN MATEO	573 2222
23	B2	*SETON MEDICAL CENTER	1900 SULLIVAN AV	DALY CITY	992 4000
43	E2	*STANFORD UNIV MED CTR	300 PASTEUR DR	PALO ALTO	497 2300
36	D3	*SEQUOIA	WHIPPLE & ALA D L PLGS	REDWOOD CITY	369 5811
		HOTELS			
26	F6	AMFAC HOTEL	1380 OLD BAYSHORE HWY	BURLINGAME	347 5444
26	E5	CLARION HOTEL	401 E MILLBRAE AV	MILLBRAE	692 6363
29	F5	DUNFEY SAN MATEO HOTEL	1770 S AMPHLETT BLVD	SAN MATEO	573 7661
29	A1	EMBASSY SUITES	150 ANZA BLVD	BURLINGAME	342 4600
24	C6	GROSVENOR AIRPORT INN	380 S AIRPORT BLVD	S SN FRANCSCO	873 3200
29A	B4	HOLIDAY INN	1221 CHESS DR	FOSTER CITY	570 5700
29	B1	HOLIDAY INN-CROWN PZ	600 AIRPORT BLVD	BURLINGAME	340 8500
24	B6	HOLIDAY INN-SF AIRPORT	245 S AIRPORT BLVD	S SN FRANCSCO	589 7200
29	A1	HOTEL IBIS	835 AIRPORT BLVD	BURLINGAME	344 5500
33	C3	HOTEL SOFITEL	223 TWIN DOLPHIN DR	REDWOOD CITY	598 9000
26	F6	HYATT REGENCY SF AIRPT	1333 OLD BAYSHORE HWY	BURLINGAME	347 1234
24	B6	RADISSON INN	275 S AIRPORT BLVD	S SN FRANCSCO	873 3550
26	F6	RAMADA INN	1250 BAYSHORE HWY	BURLINGAME	347 2381
29A	B5	RESIDENCE INN	2000 WINDWARD WY	SAN MATEO	574 4700
26	C4	S F INTERNTL AIRPORT	S F INTERNTL AIRPORT	S SN FRANCSCO	589 0770
26	E5	S F AIRPORT MARRIOTT	1800 BAYSHORE HWY	MILLBRAE	692 9100
28	F1	SHERATON INN	1177 AIRPORT BLVD	BURLINGAME	342 9200
37	E6	STANFORD PARK HOTEL	100 EL CAMINO REAL	MENLO PARK	322 1234
33	A2	VILLA HOTEL	4000 S EL CAMINO REAL	SAN MATEO	341 0966
26	E5	WESTIN-SF AIRPORT	1 OLD BAYSHORE	MILLBRAE	692 3500
		LIBRARIES			
37	C5	ATHERTON	2 STATION LN	ATHERTON	328 2422
22	D4	BAYSHORE	2960 GENEVA AV	DALY CITY	991 8074
32	F5	BELMONT	1110 ALAMEDA D L PLGAS	BELMONT	591 8286

COPYRIGHT © 1991 BY Thomas Bros Maps

COPYRIGHT © 1991 BY Thomas Bros Maps

PAGE	GRID	NAME	ADDRESS	CITY	PHONE
24	C1	BRISBANE	250 VISITACION AV	BRISBANE	467 2060
29	A2	BURLINGAME	480 PRIMROSE RD	BURLINGAME	342 1036
28	E2	BURLINGAME BRANCH	1800 EASTON DR	BURLINGAME	343 1794
38	B4	EAST PALO ALTO BRANCH	2415 UNIVERSITY AV E	E PALO ALTO	321 7712
37	B3	FAIR OAKS BRANCH	2600 MIDDLEFIELD RD	REDWOOD CITY	780 7261
29A	C5	FOSTER CITY	600 FOSTER CITY BLVD	FOSTER CITY	574 4842
24	B5	GRAND AVENUE	306 WALNUT AV	S SN FRANCSCO	877 8530
34	F5	HALF MOON BAY	620 CORREAS AV	HALF MOON BAY	726 2316
32	E2	HILLSDALE BRANCH	205 W HILLSDALE BLVD	SAN MATEO	377 4688
21	F4	JOHN D DALY	6351 MISSION ST	DALY CITY	991 8073
29	F5	MARINA BRANCH	1530 SUSAN CT	SAN MATEO	377 4686
37	E6	MENLO PARK	ALMA & RAVENSWOOD AV	MENLO PARK	858 3460
26	C5	MILLBRAE	1 LIBRARY AV	MILLBRAE	697 7607
20	E2	PACIFICA BRANCH	HILTON WY&PALMETTO AV	PACIFICA	355 5196
46	F3	PORTOLA VALLEY BRANCH	765 PORTOLA RD	PORTOLA VLY	851 0560
36	F2	REDWOOD CITY	1044 MIDDLEFIELD RD	REDWOOD CITY	780 7018
26	B3	SAN BRUNO	701 ANGUS AV W	SAN BRUNO	877 8878
33	C5	SAN CARLOS	655 CHESTNUT ST	SAN CARLOS	591 0341
27A	B2	SANCHEZ	1111 TERRA NOVA BLVD	PACIFICA	359 3397
29	C4	SAN MATEO	55 W 3RD AV	SAN MATEO	377 4680
32	C5	SAN MATEO COUNTY	25 TOWER RD	BELMONT	573 2058
36	E4	SCHABERG, H W BRANCH	2140 EUCLID AV	REDWOOD CITY	780 7010
23	B4	SERRAMONTE MAIN BRANCH	40 WEMBLEY DR	DALY CITY	991 8023
21	D5	WESTLAKE BRANCH	275 SOUTHGATE AV	DALY CITY	991 8071
23	E5	WEST ORANGE	840 W ORANGE AV	S SN FRANCSCO	877 8525
42	D3	WOODSIDE	3140 WOODSIDE RD	WOODSIDE	851 0147
		MOTELS			
29	D6	COMFORT INN	1390 EL CAMINO	MILLBRAE	952 3200
24	C5	COMFORT SUITES	121 E GRAND AV	S SN FRANCSCO	589 7766
26	A2	COURTYARD BY MARRIOTT	1050 BAYHILL DR	SAN BRUNO	952 3333
29	A1	DAYS INN	777 AIRPORT BLVD	BURLINGAME	342 7772
26	C4	EL RANCHO INN	1100 EL CAMINO REAL	MILLBRAE	588 2912
34	D2	HALF MOON BAY LODGE	2400 S CABRILLO HWY	HALF MOON BAY	726 9000
29A	A6	TRAVELODGE LOS PRADOS	2940 S NORFOLK ST	SAN MATEO	341 3300
29	B1	VAGABOND INN	1640 BAYSHORE FWY	BURLINGAME	692 4040
		PARKS			
59A	C6	ANO NUEVO STATE PARK	NEW YEARS CREEK RD	SAN MATEO CO	879 0227
29A	A5	AQUATIC	ROBERTA DR	SAN MATEO	
33	B5	ARGUELLO	WELLINGTON AV	SAN CARLOS	
37	E1	BAYFRONT PARK	MARSH RD	MENLO PARK	858 3470
22	D5	BAYSHORE PARK	45 MIDWAY ST	DALY CITY	
22	D5	BAYSHORE HEIGHTS PARK	400 MARTIN ST	DALY CITY	
29	D2	BAYSIDE	MONTE DIABLO AV	SAN MATEO	
32	D1	BERESFORD	2720 ALAMEDA D LS PLGS	SAN MATEO	574 6745
37	E6	BURGESS	LAUREL & MIELKE DR	MENLO PARK	322 3261
33	D6	BURTON	BRITTAN AV	SAN CARLOS	593 3139
57	E5	BUTANO STATE	CLOVERDALE RD	PESCADERO	879 0173
29	D4	CENTRAL	50 E 5TH AV	SAN MATEO	574 6975
29	C1	COYOTE POINT COUNTY	1701 COYOTE POINT DR	SAN MATEO	573 2592
28	C2	CUERNAVACA	HUNT & ALCAZAR DR	BURLINGAME	
21	F5	EDGEWOOD	EDGEWOOD CT	DALY CITY	
36	A4	EDGEWOOD COUNTY	EDGEWOOD RD	REDWOOD CITY	363 4000
23	A4	FAIRMONT	649 PARKVIEW CIR	PACIFICA	355 9875
25	A3	FAIRWAY	CINDY WY	PACIFICA	
30	E5	FITZGERALD MARINE RES	BEACH WY	MOSS BEACH	728 3584
37	E3	FLOOD COUNTY	BAY RD	MENLO PARK	363 4022
22	A4	FRANKFORT	FRANKFORT ST	DALY CITY	
27A	C2	FRONTIERLAND	YOSEMITE DR	PACIFICA	
56A	F6	GAZOS CK ANGLNG ACCESS	CABRILLO HWY	SAN MATEO CO	
23	B4	GELLERT PARK	50 WEMBLEY DR	DALY CITY	
25	C4	GOLDEN GATE NATL REC	CABRILLO HWY	PACIFICA	
27	D4	GRAYWHALE CV STATE BCH	CABRILLO HWY	PACIFICA	
34	D4	HALF MOON BAY BEACH	95 KELLY AV	HALF MOON BAY	726 6238
32	E6	HALLMARK PARK	HALLMARK DR	BELMONT	
36	F3	HAWES	OAK AV & JOHNSON ST	REDWOOD CITY	
32	E2	HILLSDALE PARK E & W	HILLSDALE BLVD	SAN MATEO	
21	F6	HILLSIDE PARK	222 LAUSANNE AV	DALY CITY	
41	E2	HUDDART COUNTY	KINGS MOUNTAIN RD	WOODSIDE	851 0326
26	A4	JUNIPERO SERRA COUNTY	CRYSTAL SPRINGS AV	SAN BRUNO	589 5708
37	E3	KELLY PARK	100 TERMINAL AV	MENLO PARK	322 4578
29	C3	KING PARK	725 MONTE DIABLO AV	SAN MATEO	574 6755
29A	A6	LAKESHORE	1550 MARINA CT	SAN MATEO	574 6777

PAGE	GRID	NAME	ADDRESS	CITY	PHONE
33	C5	LAUREOLA	25 LAUREOLA LN	SAN CARLOS	592 9921
22	A4	LINCOLN	901 BRUNSWICK ST	DALY CITY	239 9413
19	A3	LONGVIEW	LONGVIEW DR	DALY CITY	
21	E5	MARCHBANK	PARKVIEW AV	DALY CITY	
27	E4	MCKNEE RANCH STATE PK	CABRILLO HWY	MONTARA	
50A	A4	MEMORIAL COUNTY	PESCADERO RD	PESCADERO	879 0212
23	B6	MILAGRA RIDGE REC AREA	CABRILLO HWY	PACIFICA	
36	E4	MORTON	1120 ROOSEVELT AV	REDWOOD CITY	369 9222
21	B5	MUSSEL ROCK PARK	SKYLINE FWY	DALY CITY	
37	D6	NEALON	802 MIDDLE AV	MENLO PARK	324 3511
19	C2	NORTHRIDGE	NORTHRIDGE DR	DALY CITY	
27A	A1	ODDSTAD PARK	CRESPI DR	PACIFICA	355 9837
23	F5	ORANGE MEMORIAL	ORANGE AV	S SN FRANCSCO	877 8572
21	C6	PALISADES	PALISADES DR	DALY CITY	
50A	D5	PESCADERO CREEK	ALPINE RD	SAN MATEO CO	
48A	A5	PESCADERO STATE BEACH	CABRILLO HWY	PESCADERO	
22	B4	POLARIS	POLARIS WY	DALY CITY	
48A	B1	POMPONIO STATE BEACH	CABRILLO HWY	SAN MATEO CO	
51A	D6	PORTOLA STATE	PORTOLA STATE PARK RD	LA HONDA	948 9098
28	E1	RAY	BALBOA WY	BURLINGAME	
29	B1	ROBERT E WOOLEY	AIRPORT BLVD	BURLINGAME	
50	A6	SAM MCDONALD COUNTY	SAN GREGORIO RD	LA HONDA	747 0403
26	B4	SAN BRUNO	CRYSTAL SPGS & OAK AVS	SAN BRUNO	583 5295
22	B5	SAN BRUNO MOUNTAIN CO	RADIO RD	SAN MATEO CO	
27	F1	SANCHEZ ADOBE COUNTY	LINDA MAR BLVD	PACIFICA	359 1881
25	D5	S F BAY DISCOVERY SITE	RIDGE RD	PACIFICA	
29A	F5	SF BAY NATL WILDLF REF	HARBOR BLVD	REDWOOD CITY	
35	C4	SN FRANCISCO GAME RES	CANADA RD	SAN MATEO CO	
48	B4	SAN GREGORIO STATE BCH	CABRILLO HWY	SAN GREGORIO	
29A	C3	SAN MATEO FISHING PIER	ARTHUR YOUNGER FWY	FOSTER CITY	
27A	B3	SAN PEDRO VALLEY CO	600 ODDSTAD BLVD	PACIFICA	355 8289
25	B3	SHARP PARK	SHARP PARK RD	PACIFICA	
29	E3	SHOREVIEW	950 OCEAN VIEW AV	SAN MATEO	574 6738
36	E2	STAFFORD	HOPKINS AV & LOWELL ST	REDWOOD CITY	
36	D6	STULSAFT	RECREATION WY	REDWOOD CITY	
33	B4	TWIN PINES PARK	RALSTON AV	BELMONT	
29	B2	WASHINGTON	850 BURLINGAME AV	BURLINGAME	344 6386
21	D5	WESTLAKE	149 LAKE MERCED BLVD	DALY CITY	755 9807
23	A2	WESTMOOR	123 EDGEMONT DR	DALY CITY	756 9828
23	B6	WESTVIEW	SKYLINE BLVD	PACIFICA	
27	F1	WHITE FIELD	LINDA MAR BLVD	PACIFICA	
38	A5	WILLOW OAKS	500 WILLOW RD	MENLO PARK	325 1245
42	C6	WUNDERLICH COUNTY	4040 WOODSIDE RD	WOODSIDE	851 7570
		POINTS OF INTEREST			
43	E1	ALLIED ARTS GUILD	ARBOR RD & CREEK DR	MENLO PARK	325 3259
29	F6	BAY MEADOWS RACE TRACK	EL CAMINO REAL	SAN MATEO	574 7223
22	D4	COW PALACE	GENEVA & RIO VERDE	DALY CITY	334 4852
29	D1	COYOTE POINT MUSEUM	COYOTE POINT DR	SAN MATEO	342 7755
32	B5	CRYSTAL SPGS RESERVOIR	SKYLINE BLVD	SAN MATEO CO	
35	E4	FILOLI CENTER	CANADA RD	WOODSIDE	364 2880
41	E5	METHUSELAH REDWOOD	SKYLINE BLVD	SAN MATEO CO	
24	E3	OYSTER POINT MARINA	END OF OYSTER POINT BL	S SN FRANCSCO	871 4057
33A	A6	PETE'S HARBOR	FOOT OF WHIPPLE AV	REDWOOD CITY	366 0922
56A	C4	PIGEON PT LIGHTHOUSE	PIGEON POINT RD	SAN MATEO CO	
30	E6	PILLAR PT BREAKWATER	CABRILLO HWY	HALF MOON BAY	
33A	B4	PORT OF REDWOOD CITY	775 HARBOR BLVD	REDWOOD CITY	365 1613
35	D2	PULGAS WATER TEMPLE	CANADA RD	SAN MATEO CO	
33A	B6	REDWOOD CTY MUN MARINA	HARBOR BLVD	REDWOOD CITY	369 6988
37	A1	REDWOOD MARINA	FOOT OF MAPLE ST	REDWOOD CITY	
27	F1	SANCHEZ ADOBE MUSEUM	LINDA MAR BL & ADOBE	PACIFICA	359 1462
29	E6	SAN MATEO COUNTY FAIR	2495 S DELAWARE ST	SAN MATEO	345 3541
36	F2	SAN MATEO CO GOV'T CTR	MIDDLEFIELD&JEFFERSON	REDWOOD CITY	364 5600
32	C2	SAN MATEO CO HIST MUS	1700 W HILLSDALE BLVD	SAN MATEO	574 6441
33A	B6	STANFORD CREW HDQRTRS	MUNICIPAL MARINA	REDWOOD CITY	
43	B5	STANFORD LINEAR AC CTR	2575 SAND HILL RD	MENLO PARK	854 3300
42	B3	WOODSIDE COUNTRY STORE	471 KINGS MOUNTAIN RD	WOODSIDE	851 7615
		POST OFFICES			
26	D4	AIRPORT BRANCH	SF INTERNAT'L AIRPORT	SAN MATEO CO	742 1431
33	B3	BELMONT	640 MASONIC WY	BELMONT	591 9471
24	C1	BRISBANE	250 OLD COUNTY RD	BRISBANE	467 8171
28	F2	BROADWAY STATION	1141 CAPUCHINO AV	BURLINGAME	343 7861
29	B2	BURLINGAME	220 PARK RD	BURLINGAME	342 7694

1991 SAN MATEO COUNTY POINTS OF INTEREST

PAGE	GRID	NAME	ADDRESS	CITY	PHONE
26	E6	BURLINGAME ANNEX	820 STANTON RD	BURLINGAME	697 9588
23	F5	CHESTNUT STATION	36 CHESTNUT AV	S SN FRANCSCO	583 0376
21	E6	COLMA	7373 MISSION ST	DALY CITY	755 1868
21	E6	DALY CITY	1100 SULLIVAN AV	DALY CITY	756 2303
36	F2	DOWNTOWN STATION	855 JEFFERSON AV	REDWOOD CITY	369 5228
30A	B6	EL GRANADA	20 AVENUE PORTOLA	EL GRANADA	726 5000
29A	C3	FOSTER CITY	1050 SHELL BLVD	FOSTER CITY	349 5529
34	F5	HALF MOON BAY	500 STONE PINE RD	HALF MOON BAY	726 5517
24	B5	LINDEN AVENUE STATION	322 LINDEN AV	S SN FRANCSCO	589 2242
49A	E5	LOMA MAR	8150 PESCADERO CK RD	LOMA MAR	879 0401
37	D3	MENLO PARK	3875 BOHANNON DR	MENLO PARK	323 0038
26	C5	MILLBRAE	501 BROADWAY	MILLBRAE	697 2506
30	D1	MONTARA	215 7TH ST	MONTARA	728 5251
30	D3	MOSS BEACH	2315 CARLOS ST	MOSS BEACH	728 3151
19	A5	PACIFICA	50 W MANOR DR	PACIFICA	355 4000
56	F1	PESCADERO	2020 PESCADERO RD	PESCADERO	879 0214
36	F2	REDWOOD CITY	1100 BROADWAY	REDWOOD CITY	368 4181
29	D4	ST MATTHEWS STATION	210 S ELLSWORTH AV	SAN MATEO	343 5618
33	D5	SAN CARLOS	809 LAUREL ST	SAN CARLOS	591 5321
48	D4	SAN GREGORIO	9615 STAGE RD	SAN GREGORIO	726 1045
29	E5	SAN MATEO	1630 S DELAWARE ST	SAN MATEO	349 2301
24	B6	SOUTH SAN FRANCISCO	381 S AIRPORT BLVD	S SN FRANCSCO	588 2855
37	D6	STATION A	690 ROBERTS RD	MENLO PARK	321 7681
20	E6	STATION A	1231 LINDA MAR SHP CTR	PACIFICA	359 2661
36	F5	STATION A	364 WOODSIDE PLAZA	REDWOOD CITY	368 3605
32	E1	STATION A	135 W 25TH AV	SAN MATEO	345 2611
26	A2	USPS WESTERN REGION HQ	850 CHERRY AV	SAN BRUNO	742 4710
22	A4	VISTA GRANDE STATION	6025 MISSION ST	DALY CITY	334 7884
21	D5	WESTLAKE STATION	199 SOUTHGATE AV	DALY CITY	756 1842
43	C3	WEST MENLO PARK BRANCH	2120 AVY AV	MENLO PARK	854 5752
42	D3	WOODSIDE BRANCH	2995 WOODSIDE RD #200	WOODSIDE	851 8711
		SCHOOLS - PRIVATE ELEMENTARY			
24	A4	ALL SOULS	479 MILLER AV	S SN FRANCSCO	583 3562
27	F1	ALMA HEIGHTS CHRISTIAN	1295 SEVILLE DR	PACIFICA	359 0555
32	D1	BELMONT OAKS ACADEMY	2200 CARLMONT DR	BELMONT	593 6175
28	E2	CARDEN	2109 BROADWAY	BURLINGAME	348 2131
32	D1	CAREY	2101 ALMDA D LS PULGS	SAN MATEO	345 8205
25	A1	GOOD SHEPHERD	909 OCEANA BLVD	PACIFICA	359 4544
25	D3	HIGHLANDS CHRISTIAN	1900 MONTEREY DR	SAN BRUNO	873 4090
23	C1	HOLY ANGELS	20 REINER ST	COLMA	755 0220
32	F5	IMMACULATE HEART MARY	1000 ALAMDA D L PULGAS	BELMONT	593 4265
23	F4	MATER DOLOROSA	1040 MILLER AV	S SN FRANCSCO	588 8175
37	D5	NATIVITY	1250 LAUREL ST	MENLO PARK	325 7304
33	A4	NOTRE DAME ELEMENTARY	1500 RALSTON AV	BELMONT	591 2209
28	E2	OUR LADY OF ANGELS	1328 CABRILLO AV	BURLINGAME	343 9200
21	C5	OUR LADY OF MERCY	7 ELMWOOD DR	DALY CITY	756 3395
36	E2	OUT LADY OF MT CARMEL	301 GRAND ST	REDWOOD CITY	366 6127
21	F4	OUR LADY PERPETUAL HLP	80 WELLINGTON AV	DALY CITY	755 4438
37	A2	PENINSULA CHRISTIAN	1305 MIDDLEFIELD	REDWOOD CITY	366 3842
37	F4	PENINSULA SCHOOL, LTD	920 PENINSULA WY	MENLO PARK	325 1584
43	C3	PHILLIPS BROOKS	2245 AVY AV	MENLO PARK	854 4545
36	E3	REDEEMER LUTHERAN	468 GRAND ST	REDWOOD CITY	366 3466
24	A4	ROGER WILLIAMS	600 GRAND AV	S SN FRANCSCO	877 3955
29	B3	ST CATHERINE OF SIENA	1300 BAYSWATER AV	BURLINGAME	344 7176
33	C6	ST CHARLES	850 TAMARACK AV	SAN CARLOS	593 1629
26	C5	ST DUNSTAN	1150 MAGNOLIA AV	MILLBRAE	697 8119
32	E1	ST GREGORY	2701 HACIENDA AV	SAN MATEO	573 0111
37	C6	ST JOSEPH	50 EMILIE AV	ATHERTON	322 9913
29	D5	ST MATTHEW	900 S EL CAMINO REAL	SAN MATEO	343 1373
29	C4	ST MATTHEWS EPISCOPAL	EL CAMINO REAL&BALDWIN	SAN MATEO	342 5436
37	A5	ST PIUS	1100 WOODSIDE RD	REDWOOD CITY	368 8327
43	D1	ST RAYMOND	1211 ARBOR RD	MENLO PARK	322 2312
26	A3	ST ROBERT	349 OAK AV	SAN BRUNO	583 5065
29	E3	ST TIMOTHY	1515 DOLAN AV	SAN MATEO	342 6567
23	F6	ST VERONICA	434 ALIDA WY	S SN FRANCSCO	589 3909
43	C6	WOODLAND	360 LA CUESTA DR	SAN MATEO CO	854 9065
		SCHOOLS - PRIVATE MIDDLE			
37	D6	MENLO	1000 EL CAMINO REAL	ATHERTON	323 6141
23	B3	SN FRANCISCO CHRISTIAN	699 SERRAMONTE BL	DALY CITY	991 4551

PAGE	GRID	NAME	ADDRESS	CITY	PHONE
		SCHOOLS - PRIVATE HIGH			
29	B5	CRYSTL SPGS & UPLANDS	400 UPLANDS DR	HILLSBOROUGH	342 4175
25	D3	HIGHLANDS CHRISTIAN	1900 MONTEREY DR	SAN BRUNO	873 4090
37	D6	MENLO	1000 EL CAMINO REAL	ATHERTON	323 6141
28	D2	MERCY HIGH SCHOOL	2750 ADELINE DR	BURLINGAME	343 3631
33	A4	NOTRE DAME HIGH SCHOOL	1540 RALSTON AV	BELMONT	595 1913
37	C6	SACRED HEART	150 VALPARAISO AV	ATHERTON	322 1929
23	B3	SN FRANCISCO CHRISTIAN	699 SERRAMONTE BL	DALY CITY	991 4551
29	D6	SERRA HIGH SCHOOL	451 W 20TH AV	SAN MATEO	345 8207
47	B4	WOODSIDE PRIORY	302 PORTOLA RD	PORTOLA VLY	851 8221
		SCHOOLS - PUBLIC ELEMENTARY			
26	A3	ALLEN	875 W ANGUS AV	SAN BRUNO	589 5900
34	F5	ALVIN S HATCH	MIRAMONTES ST	HALF MOON BAY	726 9007
33	B5	ARUNDEL	PHELPS & ARUNDEL RD	SAN CARLOS	593 3126
29A	D4	AUDUBON	841 GULL AV	FOSTER CITY	349 9922
22	D4	BAYSHORE	155 ORIENTE ST	DALY CITY	467 0442
29	C5	BAYWOOD	600 ALAMEDA D L PULGAS	SAN MATEO	349 9922
26	B3	BELLE AIR	450 3RD AV	SAN BRUNO	589 5900
37	F3	BELLE HAVEN	415 IVY DR	MENLO PARK	329 2898
38	C5	BRENTWOOD OAKS	2086 CLARKE AV	E PALO ALTO	329 2875
24	C2	BRISBANE	500 SAN BRUNO AV	BRISBANE	467 0120
36	C1	BRITTAN ACRES	BELLE & TAMARACK AV	SAN CARLOS	593 7891
23	D4	BURI BURI	120 EL CAMPO DR	S SN FRANCSCO	877 8776
20	E6	CABRILLO	601 CRESPI DR	PACIFICA	355 0414
33	B3	CENTRAL	525 MIDDLE RD	BELMONT	593 1085
23	A3	CHRISTOPHER COLUMBUS	60 CHRISTOPHER CT	DALY CITY	991 1206
36	C2	CLIFFORD	CLIFFORD AV& SCENIC DR	REDWOOD CITY	366 8011
36	D5	CLOUD	3790 RED OAK WY	REDWOOD CITY	369 2264
21	F6	COLMA	444 E MARKET ST	DALY CITY	991 1211
38	C3	COSTANO	2695 FORDHAM ST	E PALO ALTO	329 2830
25	E3	CRESTMOOR	2322 CRESTMOOR DR	SAN BRUNO	589 5900
23	B2	DANIEL WEBSTER	425 EL DORADO DR	DALY CITY	991 1222
26	B4	EL CRYSTAL	201 N BALBOA WY	SAN BRUNO	589 5900
30A	C6	EL GRANADA	SANTIAGO ST	EL GRANADA	726 5577
37	D4	ENCINAL	195 ENCINAL AV	ATHERTON	326 5164
23	A4	FAIRMONT	290 EDGEWOOD DR	PACIFICA	359 5473
37	B3	FAIR OAKS	2950 FAIR OAKS AV	REDWOOD CITY	368 3953
30	E1	FARALLONE VIEW	LE CONTE AV & KANOFF	MONTARA	728 3351
37	E3	FLOOD	320 SHERIDAN DR	MENLO PARK	329 2890
36	F5	FORD	2498 MASSACHUSTTS AV	REDWOOD CITY	368 2981
29A	B6	FOSTER CITY	461 BEACH PARK BLVD	FOSTER CITY	349 9922
32	D5	FOX	3100 ST JAMES RD	BELMONT	593 1627
25	D1	FOXRIDGE	2525 WEXFORD AV	S SN FRANCSCO	877 8773
28	D1	FRANKLIN	2385 TROUSDALE DR	BURLINGAME	697 5911
23	A4	FRANKLIN D ROOSEVELT	1200 SKYLINE DR	DALY CITY	991 1230
21	D6	GARDEN VILLAGE	208 GARDEN LN	DALY CITY	991 1233
37	C4	GARFIELD	MIDDLEFIELD&SEMICIRCLR	REDWOOD CITY	369 3759
33	A2	GEORGE HALL	130 SAN MIGUEL WY	SAN MATEO	349 9922
22	B4	GEORGE WASHINGTON	251 WHITTIER ST	DALY CITY	991 1236
36	E3	GILL	555 AVENIDA DEL ORA	REDWOOD CITY	365 8320
26	B5	GREEN HILLS	401 LUDEMAN LN	MILLBRAE	588 6485
36	F3	HAWES	909 ROOSEVELT AV	REDWOOD CITY	366 3122
36	B1	HEATHER	2757 MELENDY DR	SAN CARLOS	591 0797
32	A3	HIGHLANDS	2320 NEWPORT ST	SAN MATEO	349 9922
24	A3	HILLSIDE	1400 HILLSIDE BLVD	S SN FRANCSCO	877 8801
43	C2	HILLVIEW	1100 ELDER AV	MENLO PARK	326 4341
37	B2	HOOVER	701 CHARTER ST	REDWOOD CITY	366 6236
29	E3	HORRALL	949 OCEAN VIEW AV	SAN MATEO	349 9922
21	F6	JOHN F KENNEDY	785 PRICE ST	DALY CITY	991 1239
25	E4	JOHN MUIR	130 CAMBRIDGE LN	SAN BRUNO	589 5900
23	B4	JUNIPERO SERRA	151 VICTORIA DR	DALY CITY	877 8853
41	C4	KINGS MOUNTAIN	SWETT RD	WOODSIDE	851 1298
50	B4	LA HONDA	SEARS RANCH RD	LA HONDA	747 0051
43	B2	LAS LOMITAS	299 ALAMEDA D L PULGAS	ATHERTON	854 5900
32	E2	LAUREL	316 36TH AV	SAN MATEO	349 9922
37	E4	LAUREL	95 EDGE RD	ATHERTON	324 0186
28	E1	LINCOLN	1801 DEVEREUX DR	BURLINGAME	697 8230
27	F2	LINDA MAR	830 ROSITA RD	PACIFICA	359 2400
26	C4	LOMITA PARK	200 SANTA HELENA AV	MILLBRAE	588 5852
23	F5	LOS CERRITOS	210 W ORANGE AV	S SN FRANCSCO	877 8841
23	B1	MARGARET PAULINE BROWN	305 EASTMOOR AV	DALY CITY	991 1243
21	C6	MARJORIE TOBIAS	725 SOUTHGATE AV	DALY CITY	991 1246

COPYRIGHT © 1991 BY Thomas Bros Maps

1991 SAN MATEO COUNTY POINTS OF INTEREST

PAGE	GRID	NAME	ADDRESS	CITY	PHONE
24	B4	MARTIN	35 SCHOOL ST	S SN FRANCSCO	877 3955
32	D1	MEADOW HEIGHTS	2619 DOLORES ST	SAN MATEO	349 9922
26	A5	MEADOWS	1101 HELEN DR	MILLBRAE	583 7590
38	A5	MENLO OAKS	475 POPE ST	MENLO PARK	329 2828
29	A2	MCKINLEY	701 PALOMA AV	BURLINGAME	344 9313
25	D1	MONTE VERDE	2551 ST CLOUD DR	SAN BRUNO	877 8838
33	B3	NESBIT	500 BIDDULPH WY	BELMONT	591 0741
28	F4	NORTH HILLSBOROUGH	545 EUCALYPTUS AV	HILLSBOROUGH	347 4175
29	D3	NORTH SHOREVIEW	1301 CYPRESS AV	SAN MATEO	349 9922
43	D3	OAK KNOLL	1895 OAK KNOLL LN	MENLO PARK	854 4433
27A	C1	ODDSTAD	930 ODDSTAD BLVD	PACIFICA	355 3638
36	E6	ORION	3150 GRANGER WY	REDWOOD CITY	363 0611
47	A3	ORMONDALE	200 SHAWNEE PASS	PORTOLA VLY	851 7230
27A	B1	ORTEGA	1283 TERRA NOVA BLVD	PACIFICA	359 3941
25	C2	PACIFIC HEIGHTS	3791 PACIFIC HTS BLVD	SAN BRUNO	355 6900
23	A5	PACIFIC MANOR	411 OCEANA BLVD	PACIFICA	355 3730
22	B4	PANORAMA	25 BELLEVUE AV	DALY CITY	586 6595
29	B4	PARK	161 CLARK DR	SAN MATEO	349 9922
29	F4	PARKSIDE	1685 EISENHOWER ST	SAN MATEO	349 9922
56	E1	PESCADERO	620 NORTH ST	PESCADERO	879 0332
23	F6	PONDEROSA	295 PONDEROSA RD	S SN FRANCSCO	877 8825
25	D3	PORTOLA	300 AMADOR AV	SAN BRUNO	871 7133
25	E2	ROLLINGWOOD	2500 COTTONWOOD DR	SAN BRUNO	589 5900
36	E4	ROOSEVELT	2223 VERA AV	REDWOOD CITY	369 5597
37	A5	SELBY LANE	170 SELBY LN	ATHERTON	368 3996
23	D5	SERRA VISTA	257 LONGFORD DR	S SN FRANCSCO	877 8823
20	E1	SHARP PARK	1427 PALMETTO AV	PACIFICA	355 7400
23	C5	SKYLINE	55 CHRISTEN AV	DALY CITY	877 8846
29	B4	SOUTH HILLSBOROUGH	303 EL CERRITO AV	HILLSBOROUGH	344 0303
26	D6	SPRING VALLEY	817 MURCHISON DR	MILLBRAE	697 5681
24	A4	SPRUCE	501 SPRUCE AV	S SN FRANCSCO	877 8780
29	E4	SUNNYBRAE	1031 S DELAWARE ST	SAN MATEO	349 9922
23	E3	SUNSHINE GARDENS	1200 MILLER AV	S SN FRANCSCO	877 8784
37	C3	TAFT	903 10TH AV	REDWOOD CITY	369 2589
23	A2	THOMAS EDISON	1267 SOUTHGATE AV	DALY CITY	991 1250
25	A4	VALLEMAR	377 REINA DEL MAR	PACIFICA	359 2444
29	B2	WASHINGTON	801 HOWARD AV	BURLINGAME	344 2941
28	F6	WEST HILLSBOROUGH	376 BARBARA WY	HILLSBOROUGH	344 9870
21	D4	WESTLAKE	80 FIELDCREST DR	DALY CITY	991 1252
23	B6	WESTVIEW	367 GLENCOURT WY	PACIFICA	355 6441
36	D1	WHITE OAKS	CEDAR & WHITE OAK WY	SAN CARLOS	593 7801
38	A5	WILLOW OAKS	620 WILLOW RD	MENLO PARK	329 2850
21	E5	WOODROW WILSON	43 MIRIAM ST	DALY CITY	991 1255
42	D3	WOODSIDE	3195 WOODSIDE RD	WOODSIDE	851 1571

SCHOOLS - PUBLIC INTERMEDIATE

PAGE	GRID	NAME	ADDRESS	CITY	PHONE
32	E2	ABBOTT MIDDLE	600 36TH AV	SAN MATEO	349 9922
23	D4	ALTA LOMA	116 ROMNEY AV	S SN FRANCSCO	877 8797
29	F4	BAYSIDE MIDDLE	2025 KEHOE AV	SAN MATEO	349 9922
21	D6	BENJAMIN FRANKLIN INT	700 STEWART AV	COLMA	991 1202
29	D6	BOREL MIDDLE	425 BARNESON AV	SAN MATEO	349 9922
29A	D5	BOWDITCH MIDDLE	1450 TARPON ST	FOSTER CITY	349 9922
28	D1	BURLINGAME INT	1715 QUESADA WY	BURLINGAME	697 2424
33	C6	CENTRAL INTERMEDIATE	828 CHESTNUT ST	SAN CARLOS	591 7197
47	B5	CORTE MADERA	4575 ALPINE RD	PORTOLA VLY	851 0409
28	F4	CROCKER INTERMEDIATE	2600 RALSTON AV	HILLSBOROUGH	342 6331
23	A2	FERNANDO RIVERA INT	1255 SOUTHGATE AV	DALY CITY	991 1225
22	D5	GARNET ROBERTSON INT	1 MARTIN ST	DALY CITY	467 5443
36	E5	KENNEDY INTERMEDIATE	2521 GOODWIN AV	REDWOOD CITY	365 4611
43	C3	LA ENTRADA	2200 SHARON RD	MENLO PARK	854 3962
24	B1	LIPMAN INTERMEDIATE	1 SOLANO ST	BRISBANE	467 9541
34	F5	MANUEL F CUNHA INT	KELLY AV & CHURCH ST	HALF MOON BAY	726 9011
36	F3	MCKINLEY INTERMEDIATE	400 DUANE ST	REDWOOD CITY	366 3827
38	C5	MCNAIR INTERMEDIATE	2033 PULGAS AV	E PALO ALTO	329 2888
26	A4	PARKSIDE INTERMEDIATE	1801 NILES AV	SAN BRUNO	589 5900
23	F4	PARKWAY	825 PARKWAY	S SN FRANCSCO	877 8788
32	E5	RALSTON INTERMEDIATE	2675 RALSTON AV	BELMONT	591 5385
38	B4	RAVENSWOOD MIDDLE	2450 RALMAR AV	E PALO ALTO	329 6700
26	C6	TAYLOR INTERMEDIATE	850 TAYLOR BLVD	MILLBRAE	697 4096
21	F6	THOMAS R POLLICITA MID	550 E MARKET ST	DALY CITY	991 1216
23	C6	WESTBOROUGH	2570 WESTBOROUGH BLVD	S SN FRANCSCO	877 8848

SCHOOLS - PUBLIC HIGH

PAGE	GRID	NAME	ADDRESS	CITY	PHONE
29	C6	ARAGON	900 ALAMEDA D L PULGAS	SAN MATEO	342 7980
24	A4	BADEN CONTINUATION	825 SOUTHWOOD DR	S SN FRANCSCO	877 8770
29	B2	BURLINGAME	CAROLAN & OAK GROVE AV	BURLINGAME	342 8971
26	B4	CAPUCHINO	1501 MAGNOLIA DR	SAN BRUNO	583 9977
33	A5	CARLMONT	1400 ALAMEDA D LS PLGS	BELMONT	595 0210
23	E3	EL CAMINO	1320 MISSION RD	S SN FRANCSCO	877 8806
34	F3	HALF MOON BAY	LEWIS FOSTER DR	HALF MOON BAY	726 4441
32	D2	HILLSDALE	31ST AV & DEL MONTE ST	SAN MATEO	574 7230
21	E6	JEFFERSON	6996 MISSION ST	DALY CITY	992 4050
37	E5	MENLO-ATHERTON	555 MIDDLEFIELD RD	ATHERTON	322 5311
26	D6	MILLS	400 MURCHISON DR	MILLBRAE	697 3344
25	A1	OCEANA	401 PALOMA AV	PACIFICA	355 4131
25	F4	PENINSULA CONTINUATION	300 PIEDMONT	SAN BRUNO	583 3016
56	F2	PESCADERO	350 BUTANO CUTOFF RD	PESCADERO	879 0274
36	E1	REDWOOD CONTINUATION	1968 OLD COUNTY RD	REDWOOD CITY	369 1411
29	C2	SAN MATEO	506 DELAWARE ST	SAN MATEO	348 8050
36	E2	SEQUOIA	1201 BREWSTER AV	REDWOOD CITY	367 9780
23	F5	SOUTH SAN FRANCISCO	400 B ST	S SN FRANCSCO	877 8754
25	B6	TERRA NOVA	1450 TERRA NOVA BLVD	PACIFICA	359 3961
23	A1	WESTMOOR	131 WESTMOOR AV	DALY CITY	756 3434
42	F1	WOODSIDE	199 CHURCHILL AV	WOODSIDE	367 9750

SHOPPING CENTERS

PAGE	GRID	NAME	ADDRESS	CITY	PHONE
32	E1	HILLSDALE	60 HILLSDALE MALL	SAN MATEO	345 8222
29A	B4	ISLAND SHOPPING CENTER	FASHION ISLAND RD	SAN MATEO	570 5300
23	B3	SERRAMONTE CENTER	3 SERRAMONTE CENTER	DALY CITY	992 8686
26	A1	TANFORAN PARK	EL CAMINO REAL	SAN BRUNO	873 2000
21	D5	WESTLAKE	285 LAKE MERCED BLVD	DALY CITY	756 2161

TRANSPORTATION

PAGE	GRID	NAME	ADDRESS	CITY	PHONE
37	C4	CALTRAIN	FAIR OAKS LN & STATION	ATHERTON	
33	B4	CALTRAIN	EL CM REAL&RALSTON AV	BELMONT	
28	F1	CALTRAIN	BROADWAY & CALIFORNIA	BURLINGAME	
29	B2	CALTRAIN	BURLINGAME & CALIFRNIA	BURLINGAME	
37	D6	CALTRAIN	STA CRUZ AV&MERRILL ST	MENLO PARK	
26	D6	CALTRAIN	E MILLBRAE & CALIFRNIA	MILLBRAE	
36	F2	CALTRAIN	JAMES AV & FRANKLN AV	REDWOOD CITY	
26	B3	CALTRAIN	HUNTNGTN AV & SYLVN AV	SAN BRUNO	
33	D5	CALTRAIN	EL CM REAL & SN CARLOS	SAN CARLOS	
29	D4	CALTRAIN	2ND AV & RAILROAD AV	SAN MATEO	
29	E5	CALTRAIN	16TH AV & S 'B' ST	SAN MATEO	
32	F1	CALTRAIN	E HLSDLE BL&EL CM REAL	SAN MATEO	
24	B5	CALTRAIN	DUBUQUE AV & GRAND AV	S SN FRANCSCO	
30	E4	HALF MOON BAY AIRPORT	CABRILLO HWY	MOSS BEACH	573 3701
32	C5	PARK & RIDE	HWY 92 & RALSTON AV	BELMONT	
24	C1	PARK & RIDE	OLD BAYSHRE & TUNNL RD	BRISBANE	
23	C1	PARK & RIDE	3501 JUNIPER SERRA RD	COLMA	
21	E4	PARK & RIDE	DALY CITY BART STATION	DALY CITY	
23	B3	PARK & RIDE	SERRAMONTE SHOPPNG CTR	DALY CITY	
37	D6	PARK & RIDE	MENLO PK CALTRAIN STN	MENLO PARK	
26	D6	PARK & RIDE	MURCHISN DR&EL CM REAL	MILLBRAE	
19	A5	PARK & RIDE	PACIFIC MANOR SHOP CTR	PACIFICA	
20	D6	PARK & RIDE	CRESPI DR & HWY 1	PACIFICA	
20	E6	PARK & RIDE	LINDA MAR BL & HWY 1	PACIFICA	
43	F1	PARK & RIDE	STANFORD SHOPPING CTR	PALO ALTO	
36	F1	PARK & RIDE	VETERANS BL&WHIPPLE AV	REDWOOD CITY	
36	F2	PARK & RIDE	REDWD CTY CALTRAIN STN	REDWOOD CITY	
26	A1	PARK & RIDE	TANFORAN SHOPPING CTR	SAN BRUNO	
33	C5	PARK & RIDE	SN CARLOS CALTRAIN STN	SAN CARLOS	
29	D4	PARK & RIDE	FIRST AV & 'B' ST	SAN MATEO	
29	F6	PARK & RIDE	HWY 92 & FWY 101	SAN MATEO	
32	F2	PARK & RIDE	HILLSDALE SHOPPING CTR	SAN MATEO	
23	E5	PARK & RIDE	ARROYO DR & EL CM REAL	S SN FRANCSCO	
24	B4	PARK & RIDE	AIRPORT BL & LINDEN AV	S SN FRANCSCO	
33	D4	SAN CARLOS AIRPORT	BAYSHORE FWY	SAN CARLOS	573 3700
26	E4	SAN FRANCISCO INTERNTL	1799 BAYSHORE HWY	SAN BRUNO	876 2222

WINERIES

PAGE	GRID	NAME	ADDRESS	CITY	PHONE
34A	B3	OBESTER WINERY	12341 SAN MATEO RD	HALF MOON BAY	726 9463

COPYRIGHT © 1991 BY Thomas Bros Maps

COPYRIGHT © 1991 BY Thomas Bros Maps

1991 SAN MATEO COUNTY REGIONAL TRANSIT INFORMATION

For the location of park and ride lots, see the Points of Interest Index in this atlas, page 83 and look under the heading *"Transportation"*.

The transit information for this page is provided by the **San Mateo County Transit District (SamTrans).** For a SamTrans Route Map showing all of San Mateo County's public transportation routes, call the Telephone Information Center phone number listed below or send your request to: SamTrans, 1250 San Carlos Av., P.O. Box 3006, San Carlos, CA 94070-1306.

Park and Ride Facilities

Seven Park and Ride lots provided by SamTrans and Caltrans are located throughout the county to encourage public transit use and ridesharing. SamTrans is planning to build additional park and ride lots in San Mateo County in the next few years.

Free Personalized Trip Planning, Maps, Timetables

Your public transit itinerary can be planned for you by telephone any weekday from 6 a.m. to 10 p.m. and on weekends and holidays from 8 a.m. to 5 p.m. When the operator answers, just have paper, pencil and the following information ready:

- Your departure point (address or nearest intersection)
- Your destination (address or nearest intersection)
- Day and time you wish to travel

The toll-free **Telephone Information Center** phone number is:

1-800-660-4BUS (1-800-660-4287)

Hearing Impaired (TTY) 508-6448

San Francisco International Airport -

Transbay Terminal Courtesy Phone .... Lift Receiver
BART/Daly City Courtesy Phone .... Lift Receiver
Redwood City SamTrans Depot .... Lift Receiver

The SamTrans Information Specialists also have information on Peninsula CalTrain schedules and can provide basic information on neighboring Bay Area transit systems.

Fares

Pay your bus fare when boarding. Exact change is required. Time-saving monthly and weekly passes, in various denominations, are available from more than 90 pass sales agencies, including all Safeway Stores (monthly passes only), throughout the Peninsula.

Buses

SamTrans operates more than 75 Express and Local routes along the San Francisco Peninsula, serving residential areas, major business parks, shopping centers, recreational areas and more. Buses also serve major transportation hubs along the Peninsula, San Francisco International Airport, CalTrain Stations and Bay Area Rapid Transit stations.

Fourteen routes have buses equipped with wheelchair access lifts and SamTrans is cooperating with the cities in San Mateo County to make major bus stops accessible.

Special Services

SamTrans offers special express service to and from Candlestick Park for all San Francisco Forty-Niners and Giants home games. Special service is also provided to: Ano Nuevo State Reserve, Half Moon Bay Pumpkin Festival, Pacifica Fog Fest, Examiner Bay to Breakers race and the Foster City Fourth of July celebration.

CalTrain Information

For information regarding fares, tickets, schedules or train / bus connections or any questions and / or comments concerning CalTrain service, please call:

The Peninsula Commute Service

Hotline .... (415) 557-8661
Toll free (Voice or TDD) 1-800-558-8661

Monday through Friday, 7 a.m. to 7 p.m.; Saturday, 8 a.m. to 5 p.m.; Sunday, 8 a.m. to 3 p.m.

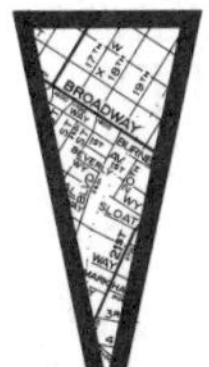

SANTA CLARA COUNTY
1991 *Thomas Guide*®
TABLE OF CONTENTS

Copyright, © 1991 by THOMAS BROS. MAPS.
Design, maps, index and text of this publication are copyrighted. It is unlawful to copy or reproduce any part thereof for personal use or resale.

Corporate Office & Showroom
17731 Cowan, Irvine, CA 92714 (714) 863-1984; toll-free, 1-800-899-MAPS
Retail Stores
603 W. 7th St., Los Angeles, CA 90017 (213) 627-4018
550 Jackson St., San Francisco, CA 94133 (415) 981-7520

GOLDEN GATE COMBINATION	TBM 4025	***$33.95***
SANTA CLARA-SAN MATEO COMBINATION	TBM 4036	***$21.95***
SANTA CLARA	TBM 3037	***$12.95***
ALAMEDA-SANTA CLARA COMBINATION	TBM 4037	***$21.95***

B HOW TO USE THE THOMAS GUIDE PAGE AND GRID SYSTEM

Finding Your Destination

- Use the Street Index to find the page number and grid location of a street name.
- Use the Cities and Communities or Points of Interest Index to find the page number and grid of a specific destination.

Planning Your Route

- Use the Key Maps or the Foldout Map to go from city to city, or to find what page your destination is on.
- Follow a street page to page by using the "See Map" page number in the border of each page.

COMO USAR EL SISTEMA DE PAGINA Y CUADRADO DEL THOMAS GUIDE

Encontrando Su Destinación

- Se puede usar el Indice de Calle para encontrar el número de página y locación del cuadrado del nombre de la calle.
- Se puede usar los Indices de las Ciudades y las Comunidades, o de Puntos de Interés para encontrar el número de página y el cuadrado de la destinación específica.

Planeando Su Ruta

- Se puede usar el Mapa Clave o el Mapa Doblado para viajar de ciudad a ciudad, o para encontrar la página de su destinación.
- Se puede usar el número de página con las palabras "See Map" se encuentran al borde de cada página para seguir una calle de página a página.

LIST OF ABBREVIATIONS

AL	ALLEY
AR	ARROYO
ARR	ARROYO
AV	AVENUE
AVD	AVENIDA
AVD D LS	AVENIDA DE LOS
BCH	BEACH
BL	BOULEVARD
BLVD	BOULEVARD
CEM	CEMETERY
CIR	CIRCLE
CK	CREEK
CL	CALLE
CL DL	CALLE DEL
CL D LS	CALLE DE LAS CALLE DE LOS
CL EL	CALLE EL
CLJ	CALLEJON
CL LA	CALLE LA
CL LS	CALLE LAS CALLE LOS
CM	CAMINO
CM D	CAMINO DE
CM D LA	CAMINO DE LA
CM D LS	CAMINO DE LAS CAMINO DE LOS
CMTO	CAMINITO
CN	CANAL
COM	COMMON
CR	CRESCENT
CRES	CRESCENT
CSWY	CAUSEWAY
CT	COURT
CTE	CORTE
CTO	CUT OFF
CTR	CENTER
CV	COVE
CY	CANYON
CYN	CANYON
D	DE
DL	DEL
DR	DRIVE
DS	DOS
E	EAST
EST	ESTATE
EXPWY	EXPRESSWAY
EXT	EXTENSION
FRWY	FREEWAY
FRW	FREEWAY
FY	FREEWAY
GN	GLEN
GRDS	GROUNDS
GRN	GREEN
GRV	GROVE
HTS	HEIGHTS
HWY	HIGHWAY
HY	HIGHWAY
JCT	JUNCTION
KPN	KEY PENINSULA NORTH
KPS	KEY PENINSULA SOUTH
L	LA
LN	LANE
LP	LOOP
LS	LAS, LOS
MDW	MEADOW
MHP	MOBILE HOME PARK
MNR	MANOR
MT	MOUNT
MTN	MOUNTAIN
MTWY	MOTORWAY
MTY	MOTORWAY
N	NORTH
PAS	PASEO
PAS DE	PASEO DE
PAS DL	PASEO DEL
PAS D LS	PASEO DE LAS PASEO DE LOS
PGD	PLAYGROUND
PK	PARK
PK	PEAK
PKWY	PARKWAY
PL	PLACE
PT	POINT
PY	PARKWAY
PZ	PLAZA
RCH	RANCH
RCHO	RANCHO
RD	ROAD
RDG	RIDGE
RES	RESERVOIR
RIV	RIVER
RV	RIVER
RO	RANCHO
S	SOUTH
SN	SAN
SPG	SPRING
SPGS	SPRINGS
SQ	SQUARE
SRA	SIERRA
ST	SAINT
ST	STREET
STA	SANTA
STA	STATION
TER	TERRACE
THTR	THEATER
TK TR	TRUCK TRAIL
TR	TRAIL
VIA D	VIA DE
VIA D LS	VIA DE LAS VIA DE LOS
VIA DL	VIA DEL
VIS	VISTA
VLG	VILLAGE
VLY	VALLEY
VW	VIEW
W	WEST
WK	WALK
WY	WAY

LEGEND

COPYRIGHT © 1991 BY Thomas Bros Maps

CALTRAIN
STA
MLRS BART
CC
CH
CTH
FS
HOSP
LIB
PO
MALL
4
2
3
3
J1
(PROP)
200
100W
100E
JR HS
HS
HS
CEM

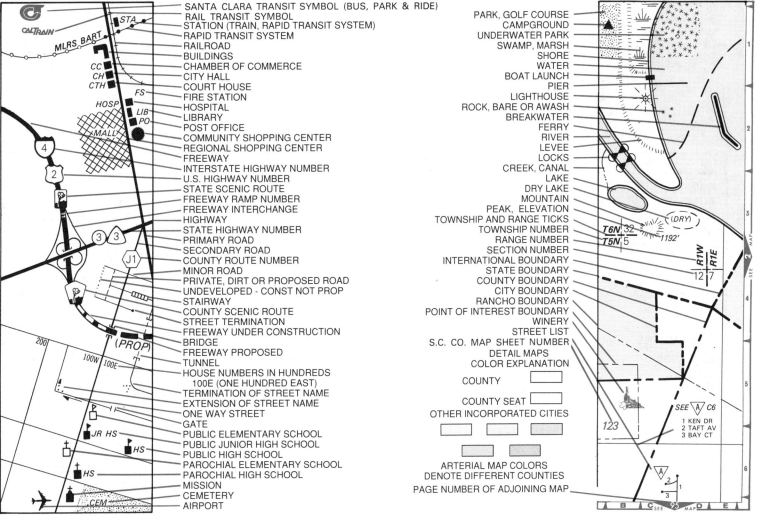

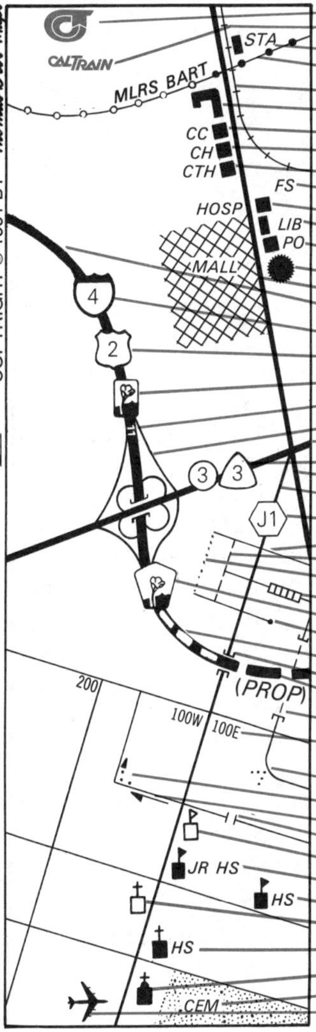

- SANTA CLARA TRANSIT SYMBOL (BUS, PARK & RIDE)
- RAIL TRANSIT SYMBOL
- STATION (TRAIN, RAPID TRANSIT SYSTEM)
- RAPID TRANSIT SYSTEM
- RAILROAD
- BUILDINGS
- CHAMBER OF COMMERCE
- CITY HALL
- COURT HOUSE
- FIRE STATION
- HOSPITAL
- LIBRARY
- POST OFFICE
- COMMUNITY SHOPPING CENTER
- REGIONAL SHOPPING CENTER
- FREEWAY
- INTERSTATE HIGHWAY NUMBER
- U.S. HIGHWAY NUMBER
- STATE SCENIC ROUTE
- FREEWAY RAMP NUMBER
- FREEWAY INTERCHANGE
- HIGHWAY
- STATE HIGHWAY NUMBER
- PRIMARY ROAD
- SECONDARY ROAD
- COUNTY ROUTE NUMBER
- MINOR ROAD
- PRIVATE, DIRT OR PROPOSED ROAD
- UNDEVELOPED - CONST NOT PROP
- STAIRWAY
- COUNTY SCENIC ROUTE
- STREET TERMINATION
- FREEWAY UNDER CONSTRUCTION
- BRIDGE
- FREEWAY PROPOSED
- TUNNEL
- HOUSE NUMBERS IN HUNDREDS 100E (ONE HUNDRED EAST)
- TERMINATION OF STREET NAME
- EXTENSION OF STREET NAME
- ONE WAY STREET
- GATE
- PUBLIC ELEMENTARY SCHOOL
- PUBLIC JUNIOR HIGH SCHOOL
- PUBLIC HIGH SCHOOL
- PAROCHIAL ELEMENTARY SCHOOL
- PAROCHIAL HIGH SCHOOL
- MISSION
- CEMETERY
- AIRPORT

- PARK, GOLF COURSE
- CAMPGROUND
- UNDERWATER PARK
- SWAMP, MARSH
- SHORE
- WATER
- BOAT LAUNCH
- PIER
- LIGHTHOUSE
- ROCK, BARE OR AWASH
- BREAKWATER
- FERRY
- RIVER
- LEVEE
- LOCKS
- CREEK, CANAL
- LAKE
- DRY LAKE
- MOUNTAIN
- PEAK, ELEVATION
- TOWNSHIP AND RANGE TICKS
- TOWNSHIP NUMBER
- RANGE NUMBER
- SECTION NUMBER
- INTERNATIONAL BOUNDARY
- STATE BOUNDARY
- COUNTY BOUNDARY
- CITY BOUNDARY
- RANCHO BOUNDARY
- POINT OF INTEREST BOUNDARY
- WINERY
- STREET LIST
- S.C. CO. MAP SHEET NUMBER
- DETAIL MAPS

COLOR EXPLANATION

COUNTY

COUNTY SEAT

OTHER INCORPORATED CITIES

ARTERIAL MAP COLORS DENOTE DIFFERENT COUNTIES

PAGE NUMBER OF ADJOINING MAP

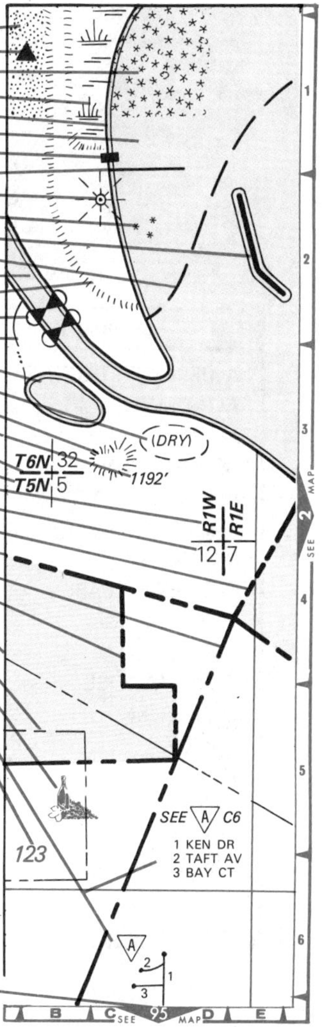

1
2
3
4
5
6
(DRY)
T6N
T5N
32
5
1192'
R1W
R1E
12
7
MAP
2
SEE
123
SEE
A
C6
1 KEN DR
2 TAFT AV
3 BAY CT
A
2
1
3
B
C
SEE
95
MAP
D
E

0
¼
½
¾
1
2
MILES
KILOMETERS
0
.1
.2
.5
1
2

SCALE OF MULTIPLE MAP PAGES
1 INCH TO 1 MILE

SCALE OF SINGLE MAP PAGES
1 INCH TO ½ MILE

0
¼
½
¾
1
2
MILES
KILOMETERS
0
.1
.2
.5
1
2

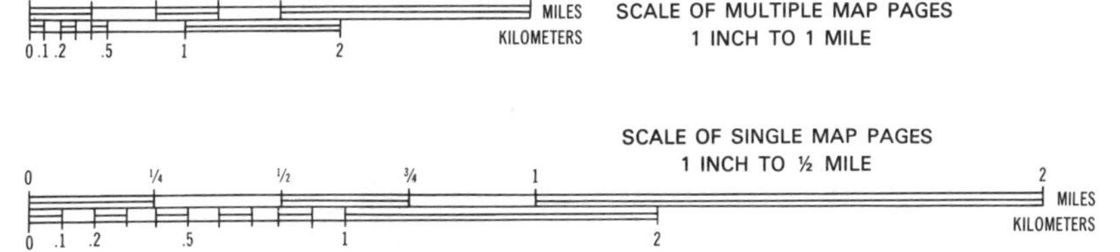

MAJOR DEPARTMENT STORES

BK	BULLOCKS
EC	EMPORIUM CAPWELL
IM	I MAGININ
MA	MACYS
ME	MERVYNS
MW	MONTGOMERY WARD
NW	NEIMAN MARCUS
N	NORDSTROM
P	JC PENNEY
SF	SAKS FIFTH AVENUE
S	SEARS

MALL
P
MW
S

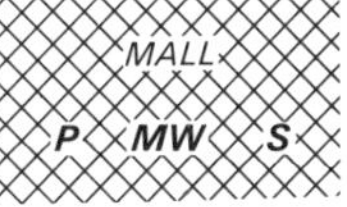

1991 SANTA CLARA COUNTY CITIES AND COMMUNITIES INDEX

ESTIMATED POPULATION INCORPORATED CITIES	1,358,585
ESTIMATED POPULATION UNINCORPORATED AREAS	104,915
ESTIMATED TOTAL POPULATION	1,463,500

COMMUNITY NAME	ABBR.	ZIP CODE	ESTIMATED POPULATION	PAGE
ALDERCROFT HEIGHTS		95030		73
ALUM ROCK		95127		56
ALVISO		95002		46
BELL STATION		95020		82D
BERRYESSA		95132		55
CAMBRIAN VILLAGE		95124		66
* CAMPBELL	C	95008	34,850	66
CHEMEKETA PARK		95030		73
COYOTE		95013		72B
* CUPERTINO	CPTO	95014	40,600	59
EAST SAN JOSE		95127		56
EVERGREEN		95121		63
* GILROY	G	95020	30,000	83
HOLY CITY		95026		78G
IDYLWILD		95030		73
* LOS ALTOS	LA	94022	27,600	51
* LOS ALTOS HILLS	LAH	94022	8,175	51
* LOS GATOS	LG	95030	28,200	70
MADRONE		95037		79

COMMUNITY NAME	ABBR.	ZIP CODE	ESTIMATED POPULATION	PAGE
* MILPITAS	MPTS	95035	48,100	47
MONTA VISTA		95014		59
* MONTE SERENO	MS	95030	3,460	70
* MORGAN HILL	MH	95037	25,200	79
* MOUNTAIN VIEW	MVW	94040	65,000	52
NEW ALMADEN		95042		76
* PALO ALTO	PA	94301	57,400	44
PARADISE VALLEY		95037		80K
RANCHO RINCONADA		95014		60
REDWOOD ESTATES		95044		78G
RUCKER		95020		82
* SAN JOSE	SJ	95103	749,800	61
SAN MARTIN		95046		81
* SANTA CLARA	SCL	95050	92,200	60
- -SANTA CLARA COUNTY	SCCO		1,463,500	
SAN TOMAS		95008		65
* SARATOGA	S	95070	30,700	64
STANFORD		94305		43
* SUNNYVALE	SVL	94086	117,300	53

*INDICATES INCORPORATED CITY

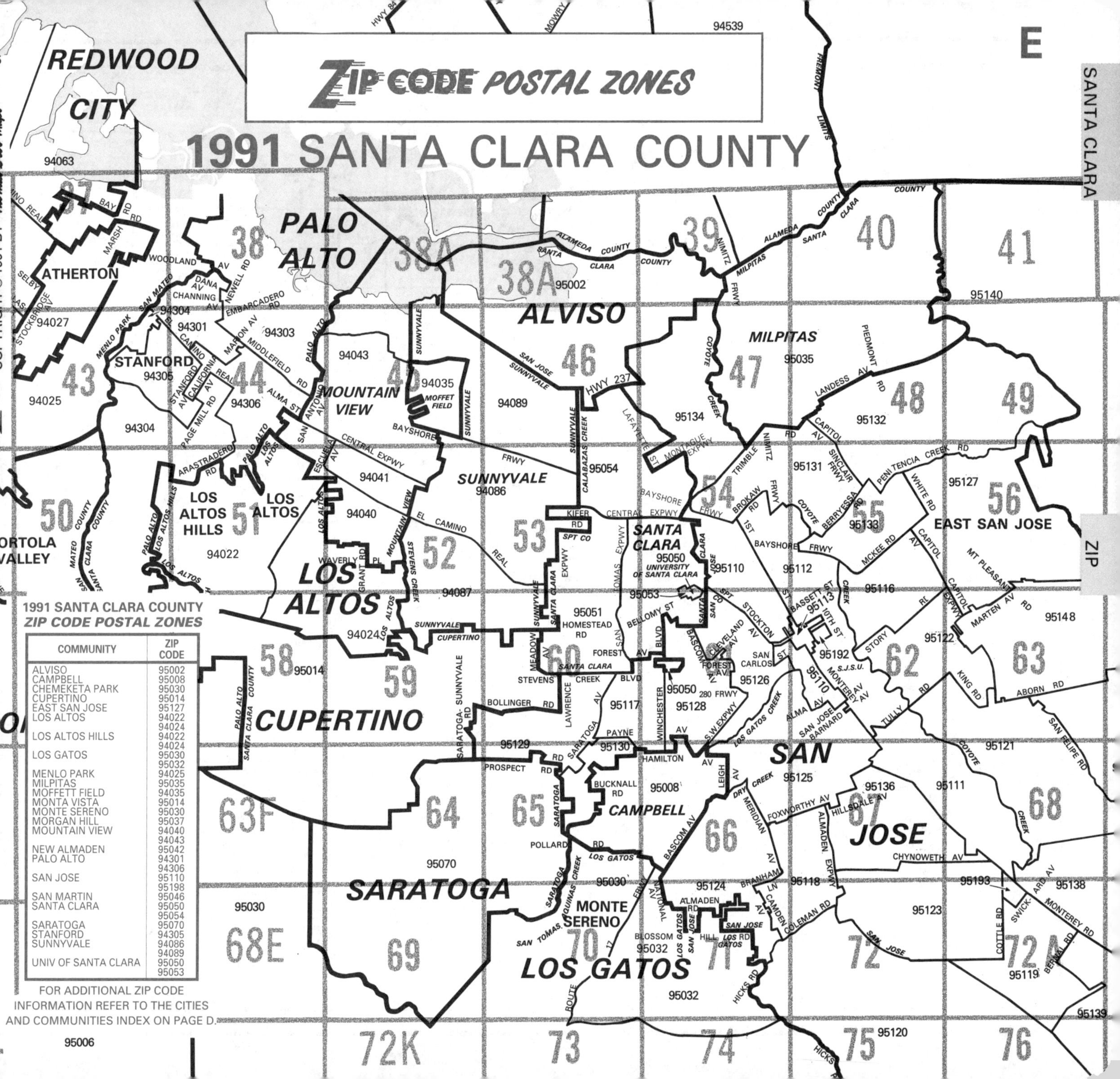

COMMUNITY	ZIP CODE
ALVISO	95002
CAMPBELL	95008
CHEMEKETA PARK	95030
CUPERTINO	95014
EAST SAN JOSE	95127
LOS ALTOS	94022
	94024
LOS ALTOS HILLS	94022
	94024
LOS GATOS	95030
	95032
MENLO PARK	94025
MILPITAS	95035
MOFFETT FIELD	94035
MONTA VISTA	95014
MONTE SERENO	95030
MORGAN HILL	95037
MOUNTAIN VIEW	94040
	94043
NEW ALMADEN	95042
PALO ALTO	94301
	94306
SAN JOSE	95110
	95198
SAN MARTIN	95046
SANTA CLARA	95050
	95054
SARATOGA	95070
STANFORD	94305
SUNNYVALE	94086
	94089
UNIV OF SANTA CLARA	95050
	95053

FOR ADDITIONAL ZIP CODE INFORMATION REFER TO THE CITIES AND COMMUNITIES INDEX ON PAGE D.

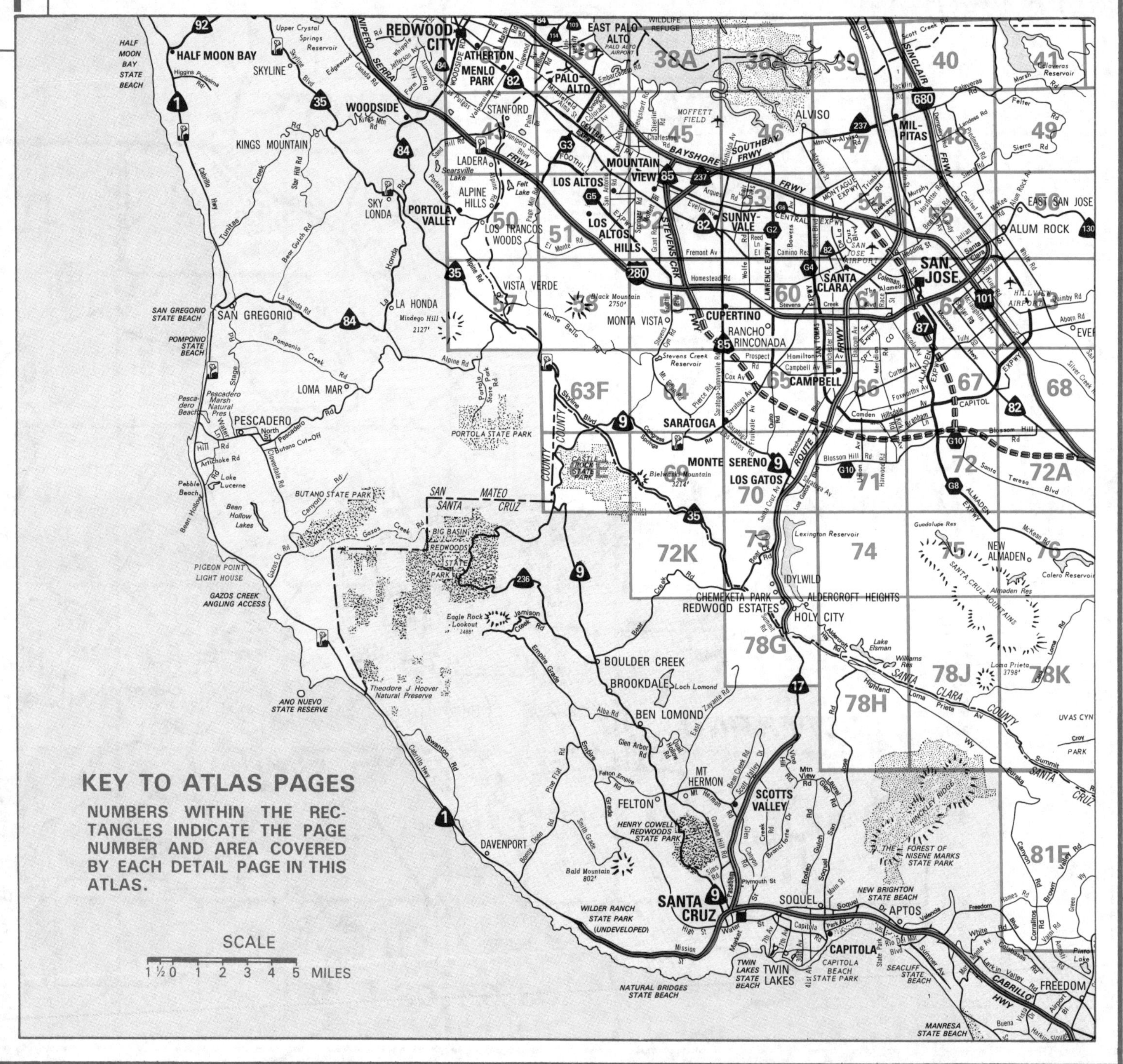

COPYRIGHT © 1991 BY Thomas Bros Maps

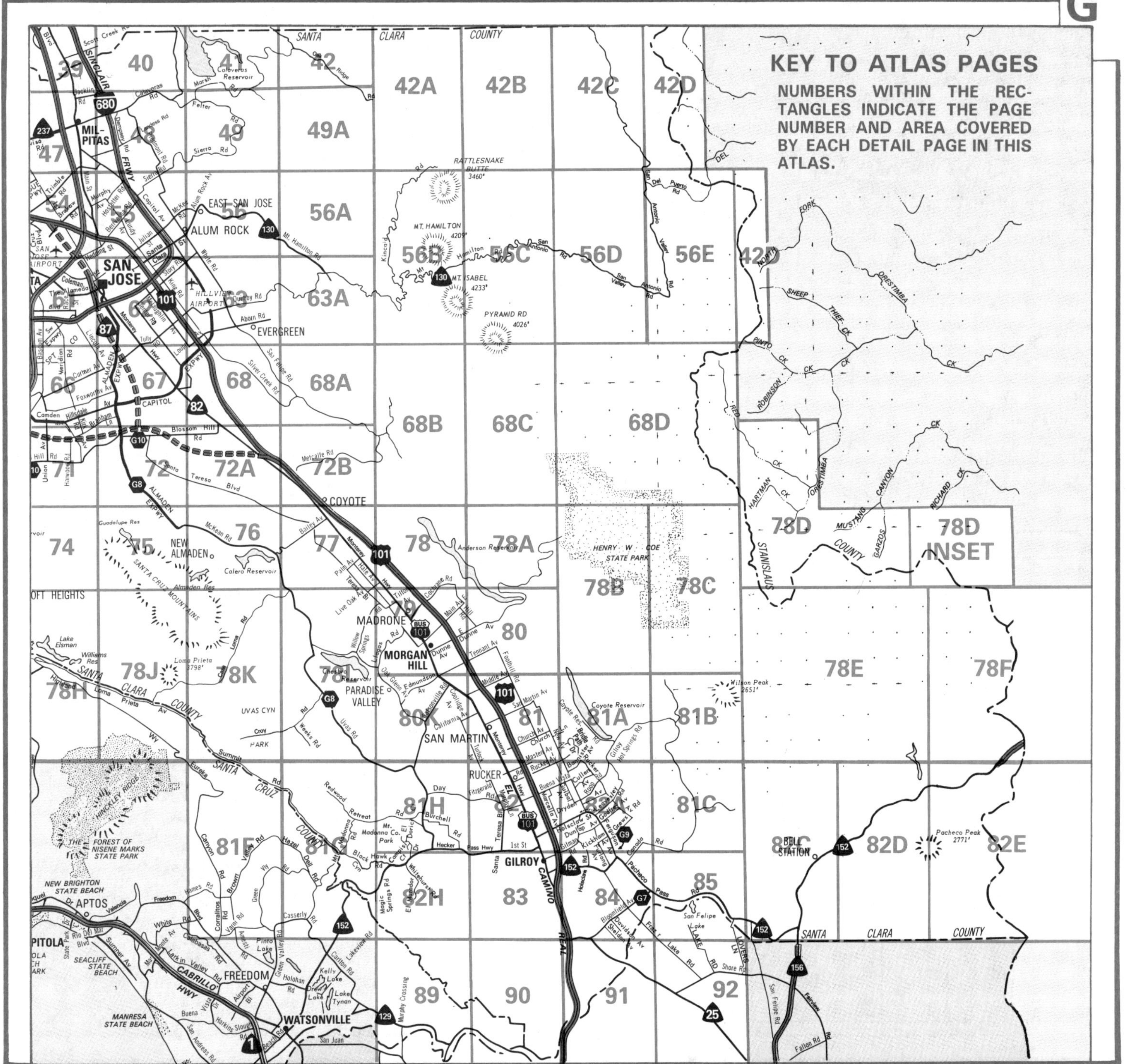

COPYRIGHT © 1991 BY Thomas Bros. Maps

CROSS-REFERENCE INDEX

COUNTY SHEET	ATLAS PAGE
1	38
2	38A
3	38A
4	38A
5	39
6	40
7	40
8	41
9	42
10	42A
11	42B
12	42B
13	42C
14	42D
15	43
16	44
17	45
18	45
19	46
20	47
21	48
22	48
23	49
24	49A
25	42A
26	42B
27	42B
28	42C
29	42D
30	43
31	44
32	45
33	45
34	46
35	47
36	48
37	48
38	49
39	49A
40	42A
41	42B
42	42B
43	42C
44	42D
45	50
46	51
47	52
48	52
49	53
50	54
51	55
52	55
53	56
54	56A
55	56B
56	56C
57	56C
58	56D

COUNTY SHEET	ATLAS PAGE
59	56E
60	42D
61	50
62	51
63	52
64	52
65	53
66	54
67	55
68	55
69	56
70	56A
71	56B
72	56C
73	56C
74	56D
75	56E
76	42D
77	57
78	58
79	59
80	59
81	60
82	61
83	62
84	62
85	63
86	63A
87	56B
88	56C
89	56C
90	56D
91	56E
92	42D
93	57
94	63F
95	64
96	64
97	65
98	66
99	67
100	67
101	68
102	68A
103	56B
104	56C
105	56C
106	56D
107	56E
108	42D
109	63F
110	64
111	64
112	65
113	66
114	67
115	67
116	68

COUNTY SHEET	ATLAS PAGE
117	68A
118	68B
119	68C
120	68C
121	68D
122	68D
123	68E
124	69
125	69
126	70
127	71
128	72
129	72
130	72A
131	72B
132	68B
133	68C
134	68C
135	68D
136	68D
137	69
138	69
139	70
140	71
141	72
142	72
143	72A
144	72B
145	68B
146	68C
147	68C
148	68D
149	68D
150	78D
151	72K
152	73
153	74
154	75
155	75
156	76
157	77
158	78
159	78A
160	78A
161	78B
162	78C
163	78D
164	78D

COUNTY SHEET	ATLAS PAGE
165	72K
166	73
167	74
168	75
169	75
170	76
171	77
172	78
173	78A
174	78A
175	78B
176	78C
177	78D
178	78D
179	78D
180	78D
181	78G
182	78H
183	78J
184	78K
185	78K
186	78L
187	79
188	80
189	80
190	78B
191	78C
192	78E
193	78E
194	78E
195	78F
196	78F
197	78H
198	78J
199	78K
200	78K
201	78L
202	80K
203	80
204	80
205	81A
206	78C
207	78E

COUNTY SHEET	ATLAS PAGE
208	78E
209	78E
210	78F
211	78F
212	78K
213	78K
214	78L
215	80K
216	81
217	81
218	81A
219	81B
220	78E
221	78E
222	78E
223	78F
224	78F
225	81F
226	81G
227	81H
228	82
229	82
230	82A
231	81C
232	82C
233	82D
234	82D
235	82E
236	82E
237	81G
238	81H
239	82
240	82
241	82A

COUNTY SHEET	ATLAS PAGE
242	81C
243	82C
244	82D
245	82D
246	82E
247	82E
248	81G
249	82H
250	82H
251	83
252	84
253	85
254	82C
255	82D
256	82D
257	82E
258	82E
259	82H
260	83
261	83
262	84
263	85
264	82C
265	82D
266	82D
267	82E
268	82E
269	89
270	90
271	90
272	91
278	90
279	90
280	91

COPYRIGHT © 1991 BY Thomas Bros Maps

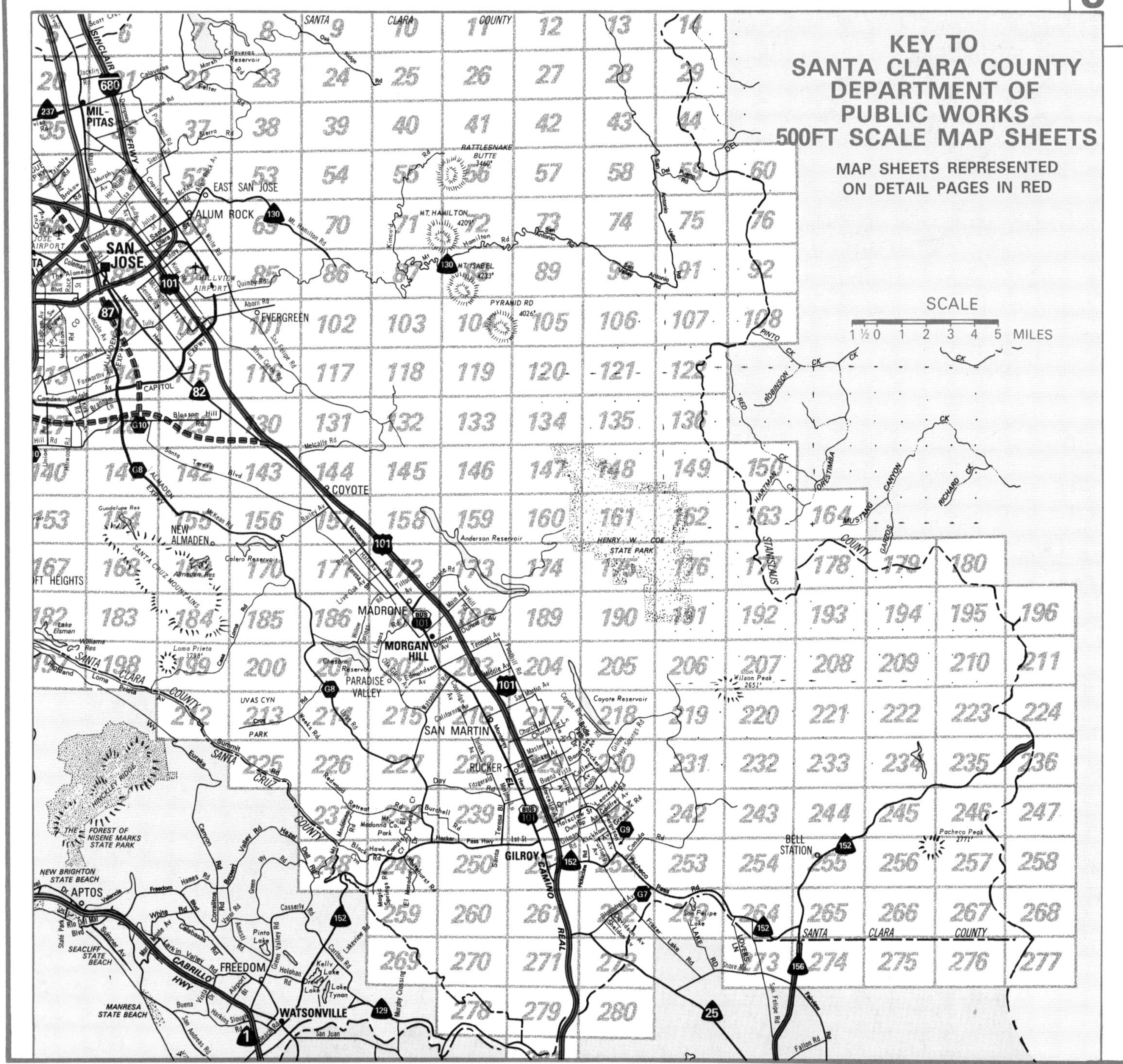

COPYRIGHT © 1991 BY Thomas Bros Maps

SANTA CLARA

SEE 54 MAP SEE 55 MAP

Thomas Bros. Maps

DOWNTOWN SAN JOSE

PARKS & CIVIC CENTER

POINTS OF INTEREST

No.	Point of Interest	Grid
18	CENTER FOR THE PERFORMING ARTS	D6
1	CHAMBER OF COMMERCE	D5
2	CITY HALL	D3
7	CIVIC AUDITORIUM	D6
3	CIVIC CENTER	D3
14	CONVENTION & VISITORS BUREAU	D6
4	COUNTY COURTHOUSE	D5
15	FAIRMONT HOTEL	D6
5	HOLIDAY INN	D6
6	LIBRARY	D6
19	MUSEUM OF ART	D5
8	PERALTA ADOBE	D6
9	ROSICRUCIAN MUSEUM & PLANETARIUM	A5
16	SAINTE CLAIRE HOTEL	D6
10	SAN JOSE BIBLE COLLEGE	F6
17	SAN JOSE CONVENTION CENTER	D6
11	SAN JOSE HOSPITAL	E4
12	SAN JOSE INTERNATIONAL AIRPORT	A1
13	SAN JOSE STATE UNIVERSITY	E5

COPYRIGHT © 1991 BY Thomas Bros Maps

SEE 54 MAP

SEE 55 MAP

SEE 61 MAP

DOWNTOWN

SEE 62 MAP

SEE 61 MAP SEE 62 MAP

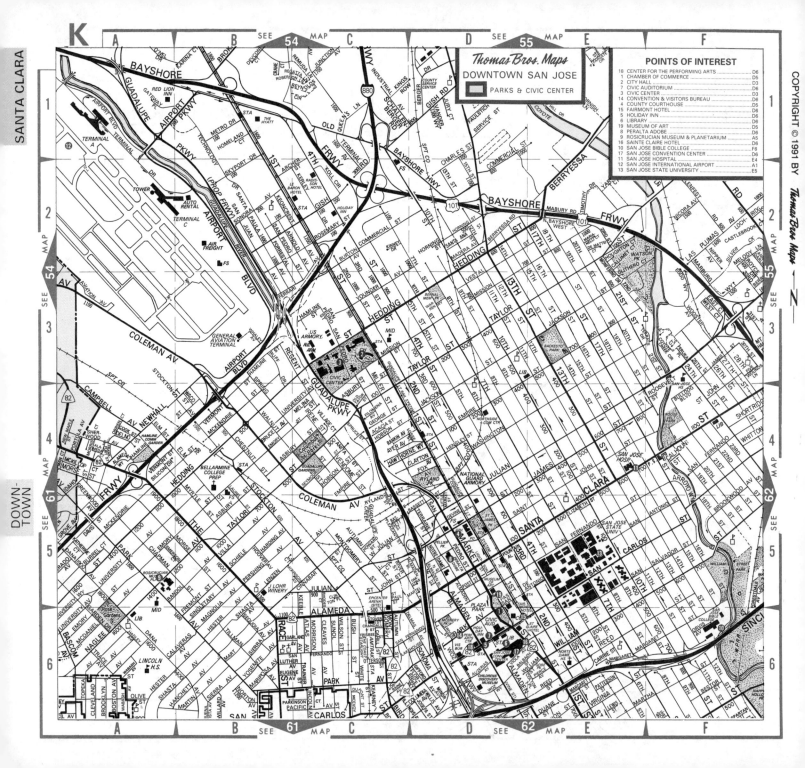

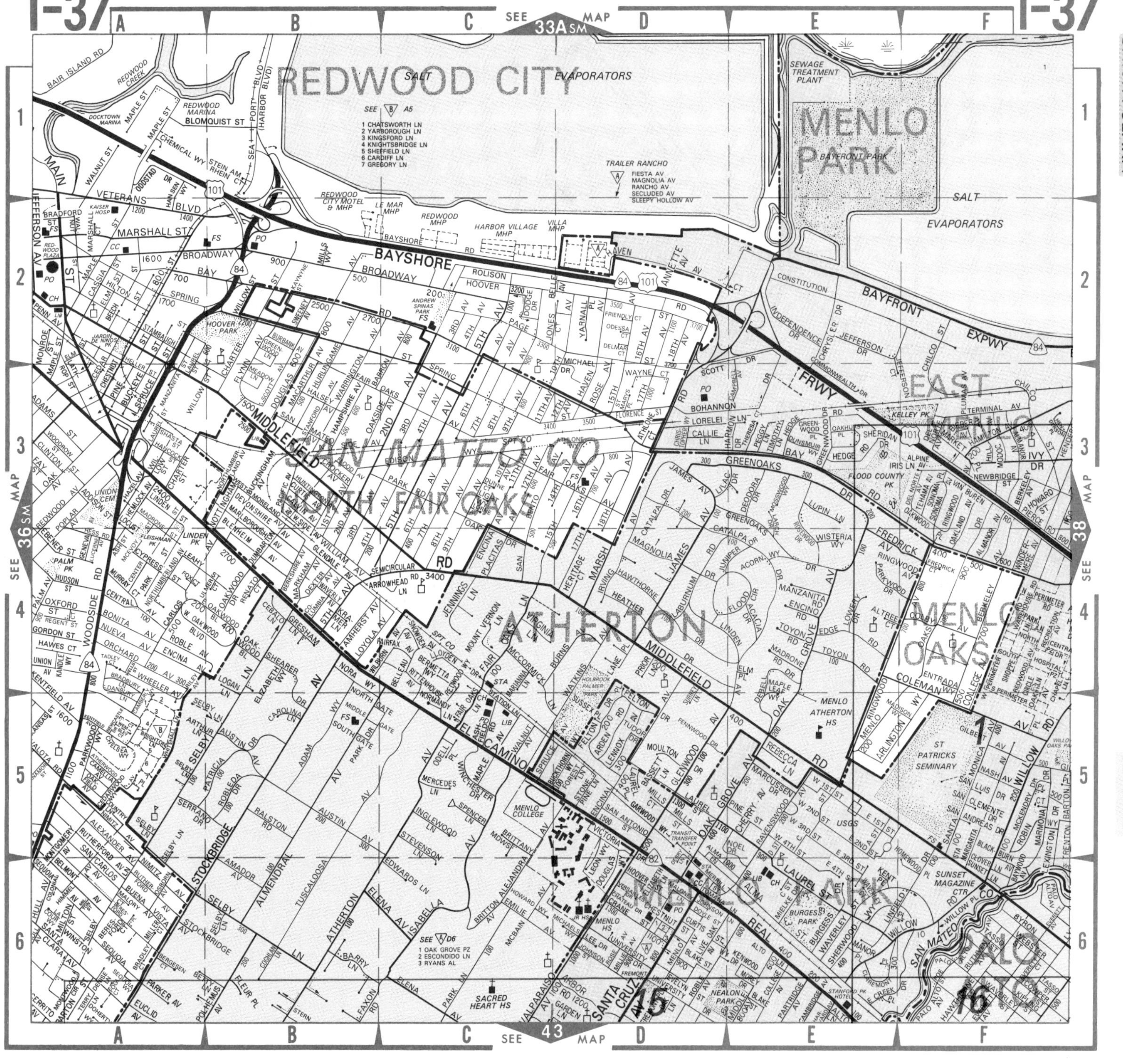
SEE 33A SM MAP
REDWOOD CITY
SALT EVAPORATORS
MENLO PARK
BAYFRONT PARK
SEWAGE TREATMENT PLANT
TRAILER RANCHO
SEE B A5
1 CHATSWORTH LN
2 YARBOROUGH LN
3 KINGSFORD LN
4 KNIGHTSBRIDGE LN
5 SHEFFIELD LN
6 CARDIFF LN
7 GREGORY LN
FIESTA AV
MAGNOLIA AV
RANCHO AV
SECLUDED AV
SLEEPY HOLLOW AV
SAN MATEO CO
NORTH FAIR OAKS
ATHERTON
EAST MENLO
MENLO OAKS
MENLO PARK
PALO ALTO
SANTA CLARA
DETAIL
SEE 36 SM MAP
SEE 38 MAP
SEE 43 MAP
SEE A D6
1 OAK GROVE PZ
2 ESCONDIDO LN
3 RYANS AL
MENLO COLLEGE
MENLO ATHERTON HS
ST PATRICKS SEMINARY
SUNSET MAGAZINE CTR
SACRED HEART HS
MENLO HS
BAYSHORE
MIDDLEFIELD
EL CAMINO REAL
WOODSIDE RD
BAYFRONT EXPWY
FLOOD COUNTY PK
HOOVER PARK
MARSH RD
FREDRICK AV
WILLOW RD

SANTA CLARA

DETAIL

SEE MAP 105AL

SAN FRANCISCO BAY

MENLO PARK

EAST MENLO PARK

EAST PALO ALTO

PALO ALTO

RAVENSWOOD OPEN SPACE PRESERVE

SAN FRANCISCO BAY NATIONAL WILDLIFE REFUGE

SALT EVAPORATORS

RAVENSWOOD SLOUGH

TO DUMBARTON BRIDGE (TOLL $1.00 WEST ONLY)

BAYFRONT EXPWY

COOLEY LANDING

SAN FRANCISQUITO CREEK

SAN MATEO CO
SANTA CLARA CO

ALAMEDA CO
SAN MATEO CO

PALO ALTO AIRPORT

PALO ALTO MUNICIPAL GOLF COURSE

BAYLANDS ATHLETIC CENTER

BYXBEE REC AREA

BAYLANDS NATURE INTERPRETIVE CENTER

BOAT LAUNCH

PALO ALTO YACHT HARBOR

SAND POINT

HOOKS POINT

BAYSHORE FRWY

SEE MAP 37

SEE MAP 38A

SEE MAP 44

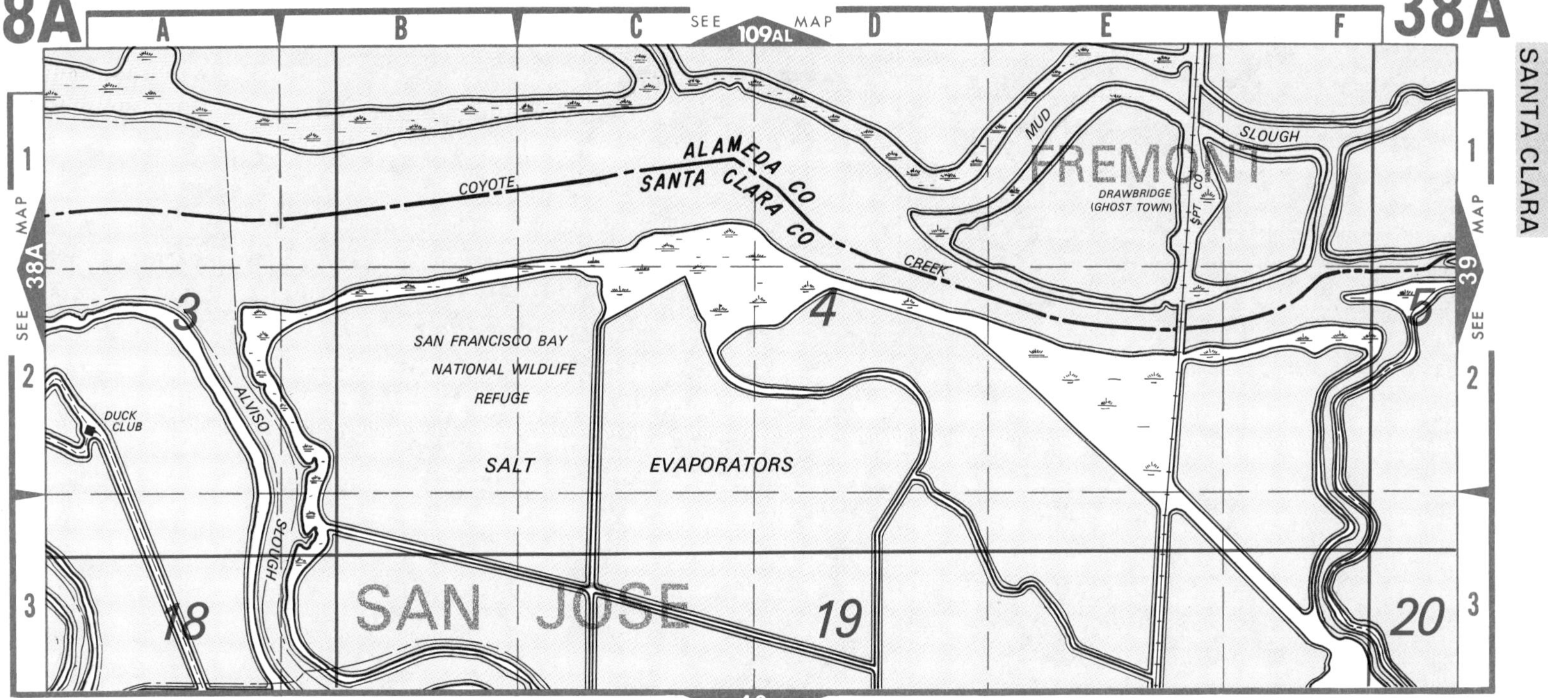
38A
SEE MAP 109AL
A
B
C
D
E
F
1
2
3
SEE MAP 38A
SEE MAP 39
FREMONT
MUD
SLOUGH
DRAWBRIDGE
(GHOST TOWN)
SPT CO
ALAMEDA CO
SANTA CLARA CO
COYOTE
CREEK
3
4
5
SAN FRANCISCO BAY
NATIONAL WILDLIFE
REFUGE
DUCK
CLUB
ALVISO
SLOUGH
SALT
EVAPORATORS
SAN JOSE
18
19
20
SEE MAP 46

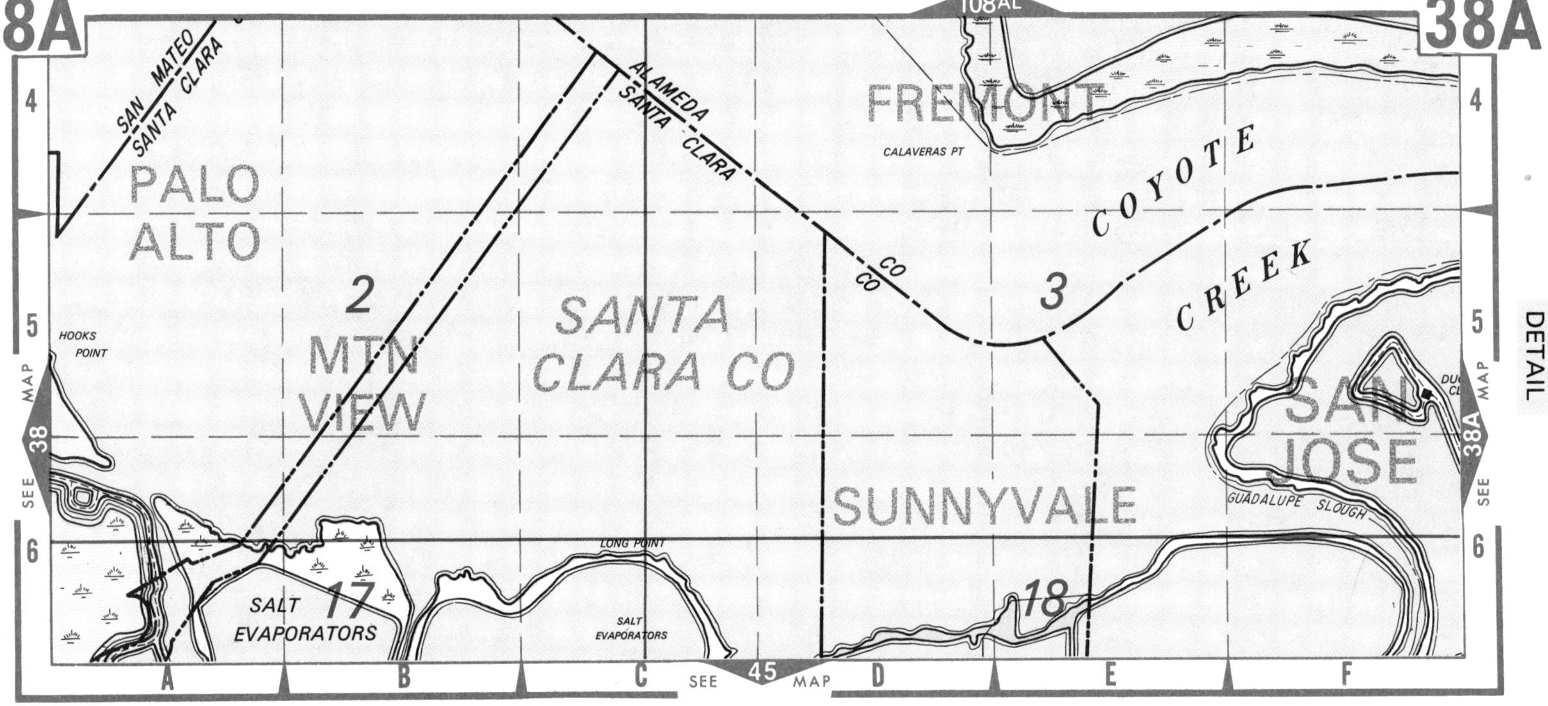
SEE MAP 108AL
A
B
C
D
E
F
4
5
6
SEE MAP 38
SEE MAP 38A
SAN MATEO
SANTA CLARA
ALAMEDA
SANTA CLARA
FREMONT
CALAVERAS PT
PALO
ALTO
2
MTN
VIEW
SANTA
CLARA CO
CO
CO
3
COYOTE
CREEK
HOOKS
POINT
SUNNYVALE
SAN
JOSE
DUCK
CLUB
GUADALUPE SLOUGH
LONG POINT
SALT
EVAPORATORS
17
18
SEE MAP 45

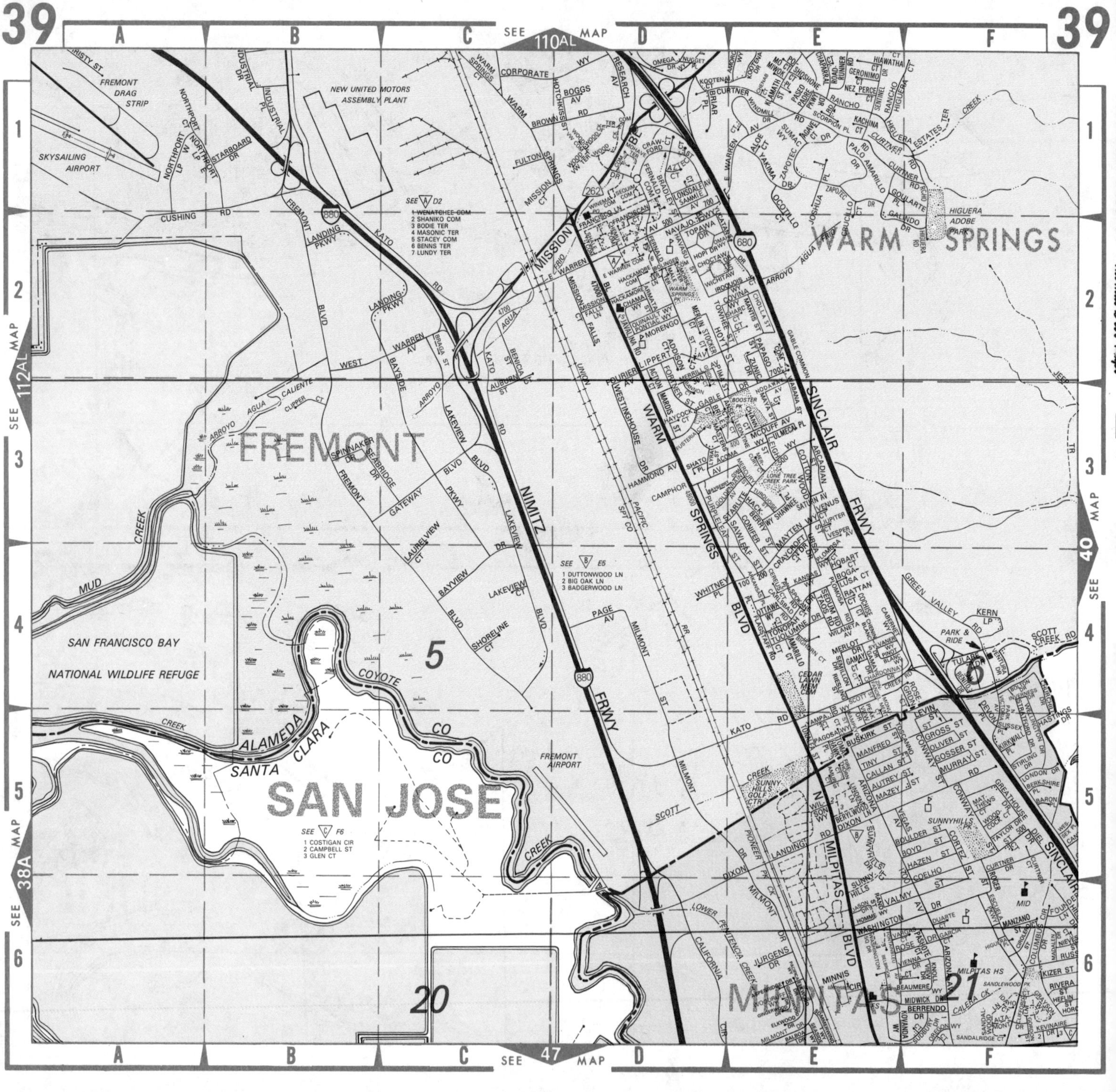

SEE 110AL MAP

SANTA CLARA

DETAIL

SEE 112AL MAP

SEE 40 MAP

SEE 38A MAP

FREMONT

WARM SPRINGS

SAN JOSE

MILPITAS

FREMONT DRAG STRIP

SKYSAILING AIRPORT

NEW UNITED MOTORS ASSEMBLY PLANT

SAN FRANCISCO BAY NATIONAL WILDLIFE REFUGE

FREMONT AIRPORT

HIGUERA ADOBE PARK

SUNNY HILLS GOLF CTR

CEDAR LAWN MEM CEM

LONE TREE CREEK PARK

SUNNYHILLS PK

MILPITAS HS

PARK & RIDE

NIMITZ FRWY

SINCLAIR FRWY

MISSION BLVD

WARM SPRINGS BLVD

MILPITAS BLVD

FREMONT BLVD

LAKEVIEW BLVD

BAYSIDE BLVD

KATO RD

CUSHING RD

SCOTT CREEK RD

MUD CREEK

COYOTE CREEK

ARROYO AGUA CALIENTE

ALAMEDA CREEK

SANTA CLARA CO

SEE A D2
1 WENATCHEE COM
2 SHANIKO COM
3 BODIE TER
4 MASONIC TER
5 STACEY COM
6 BENNS TER
7 LUNDY TER

SEE B E5
1 DUTTONWOOD LN
2 BIG OAK LN
3 BADGERWOOD LN

SEE C F6
1 COSTIGAN CIR
2 CAMPBELL ST
3 GLEN CT

5

6

20

21

SEE 47 MAP

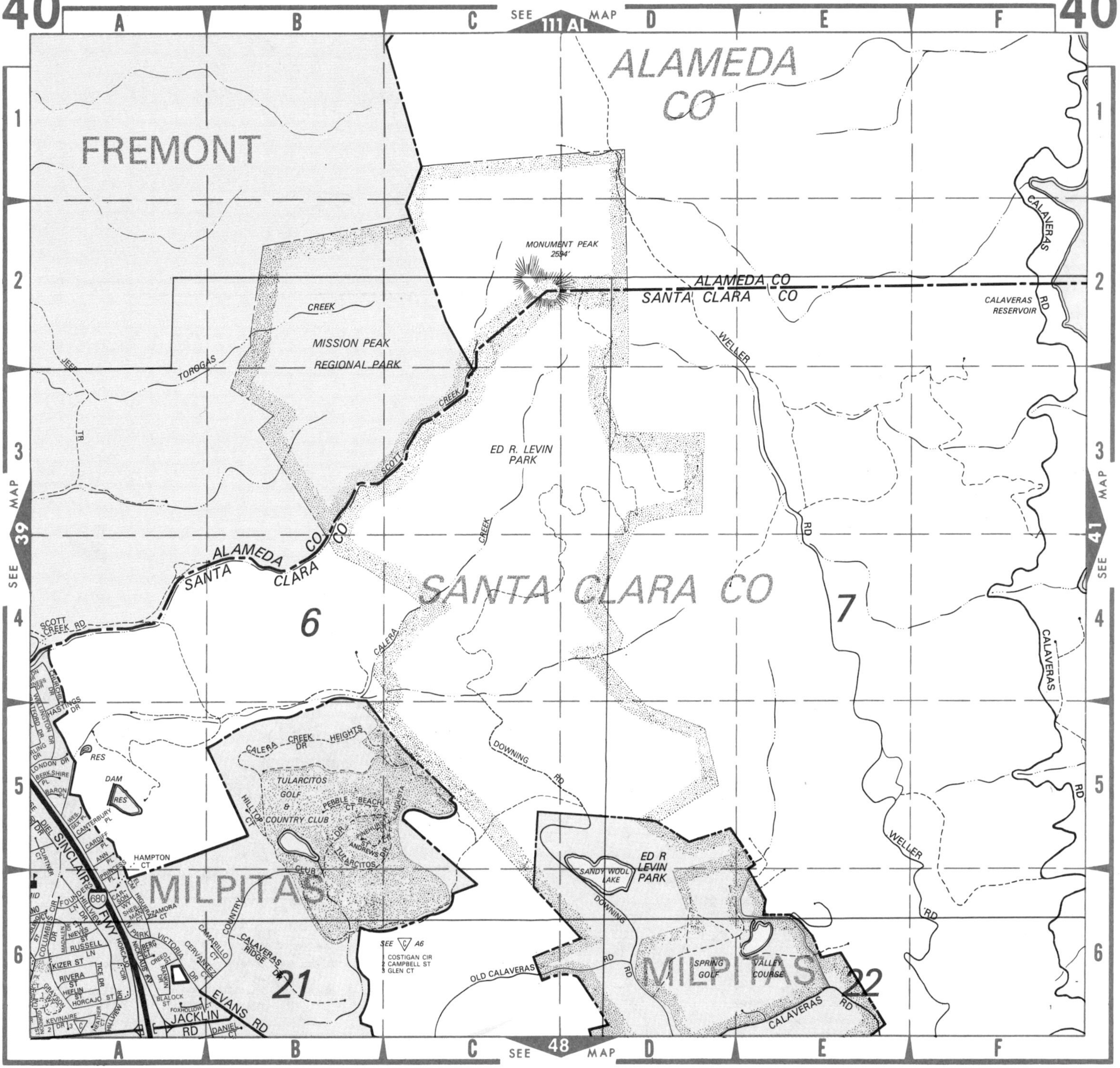

SEE 111 AL MAP

SEE 39 MAP

SEE 41 MAP

SEE 48 MAP

SANTA CLARA

DETAIL

COPYRIGHT © 1991 BY Thomas Bros Maps

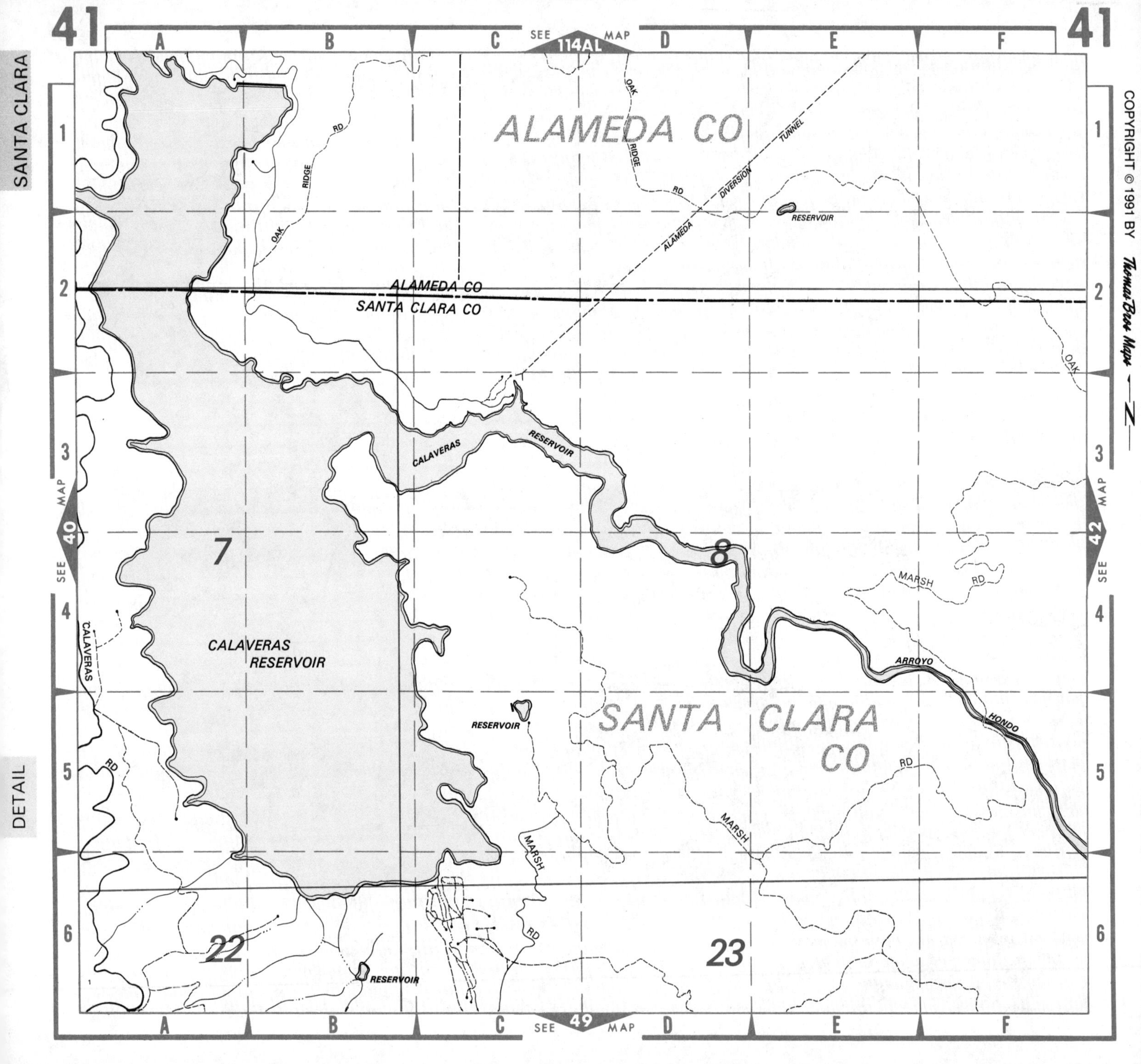

COPYRIGHT © 1991 BY Thomas Bros Maps

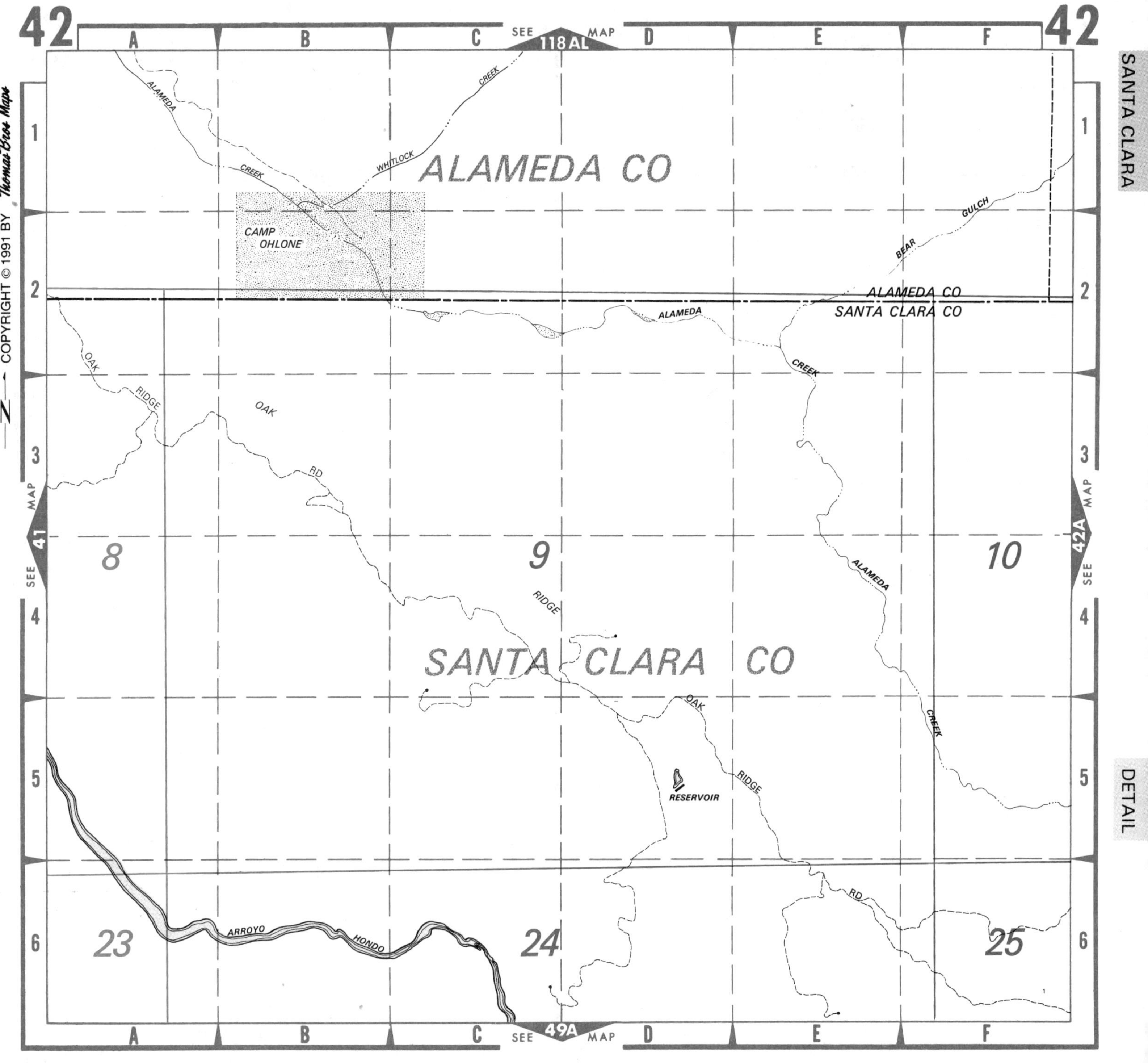

COPYRIGHT © 1991 BY Thomas Bros Maps

42

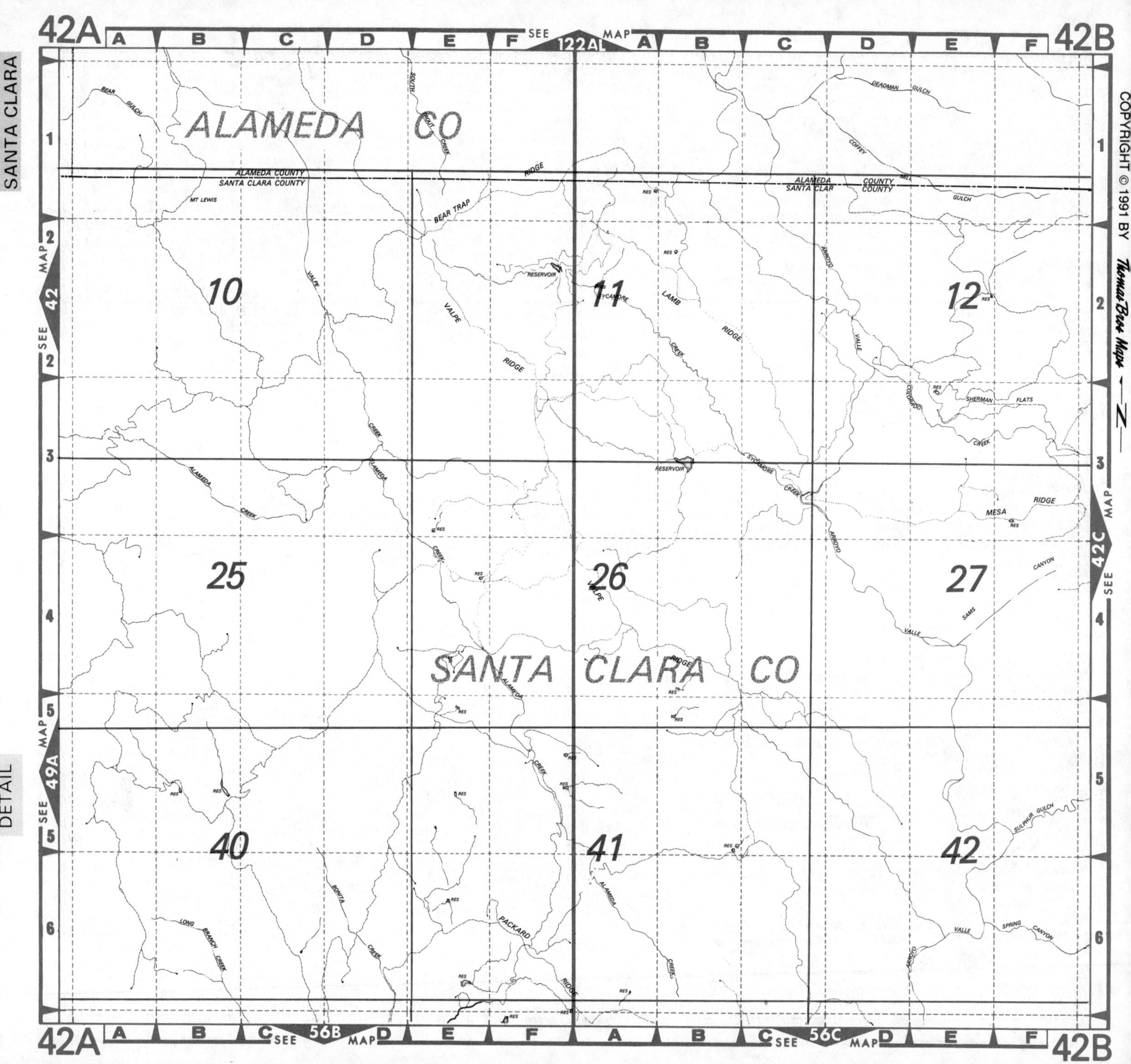
42A
42B
SEE 122A MAP
SEE 42 MAP
SEE 42C MAP
SEE 49A MAP
SEE 56B MAP
SEE 56C MAP
SANTA CLARA
DETAIL
ALAMEDA CO
SANTA CLARA CO
ALAMEDA COUNTY
SANTA CLARA COUNTY
MT LEWIS
BEAR GULCH
SOUTH TROUT CREEK
BEAR TRAP
RIDGE
DEADMAN GULCH
COFFEY MILL GULCH
RESERVOIR
VALPE RIDGE
SYCAMORE CREEK
LAMB RIDGE
CREEK
ARROYO VALLE
COLORADO CREEK
SHERMAN FLATS
ALAMEDA CREEK
MESA RIDGE
SAMS CANYON
SULPHUR GULCH
VALLE SPRING CANYON
LONG BRANCH CREEK
BONITA CREEK
PACKARD RIDGE
RES
10
11
12
25
26
27
40
41
42
COPYRIGHT © 1991 BY Thomas Bros Maps

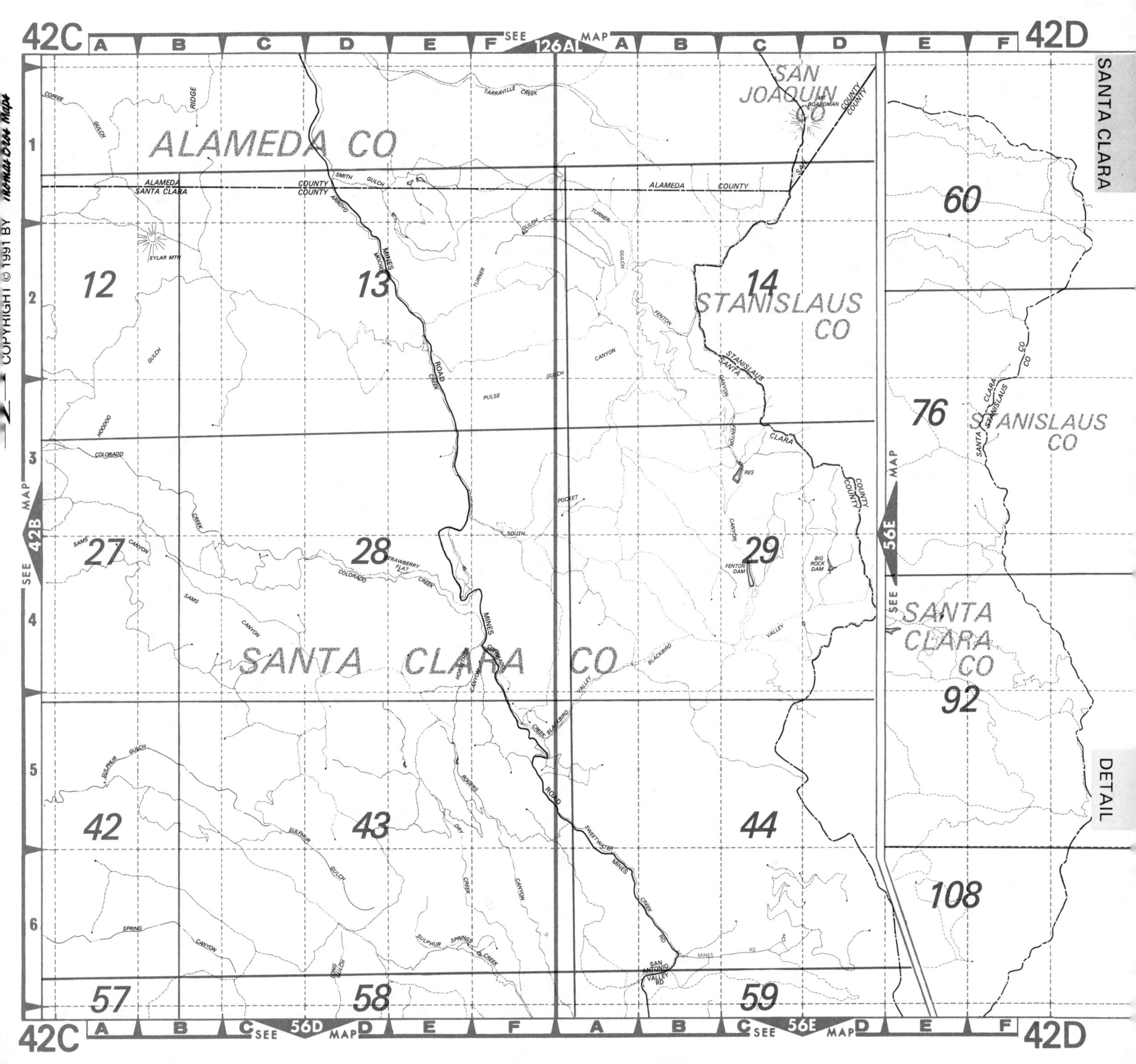

COPYRIGHT © 1991 BY Thomas Bros Maps

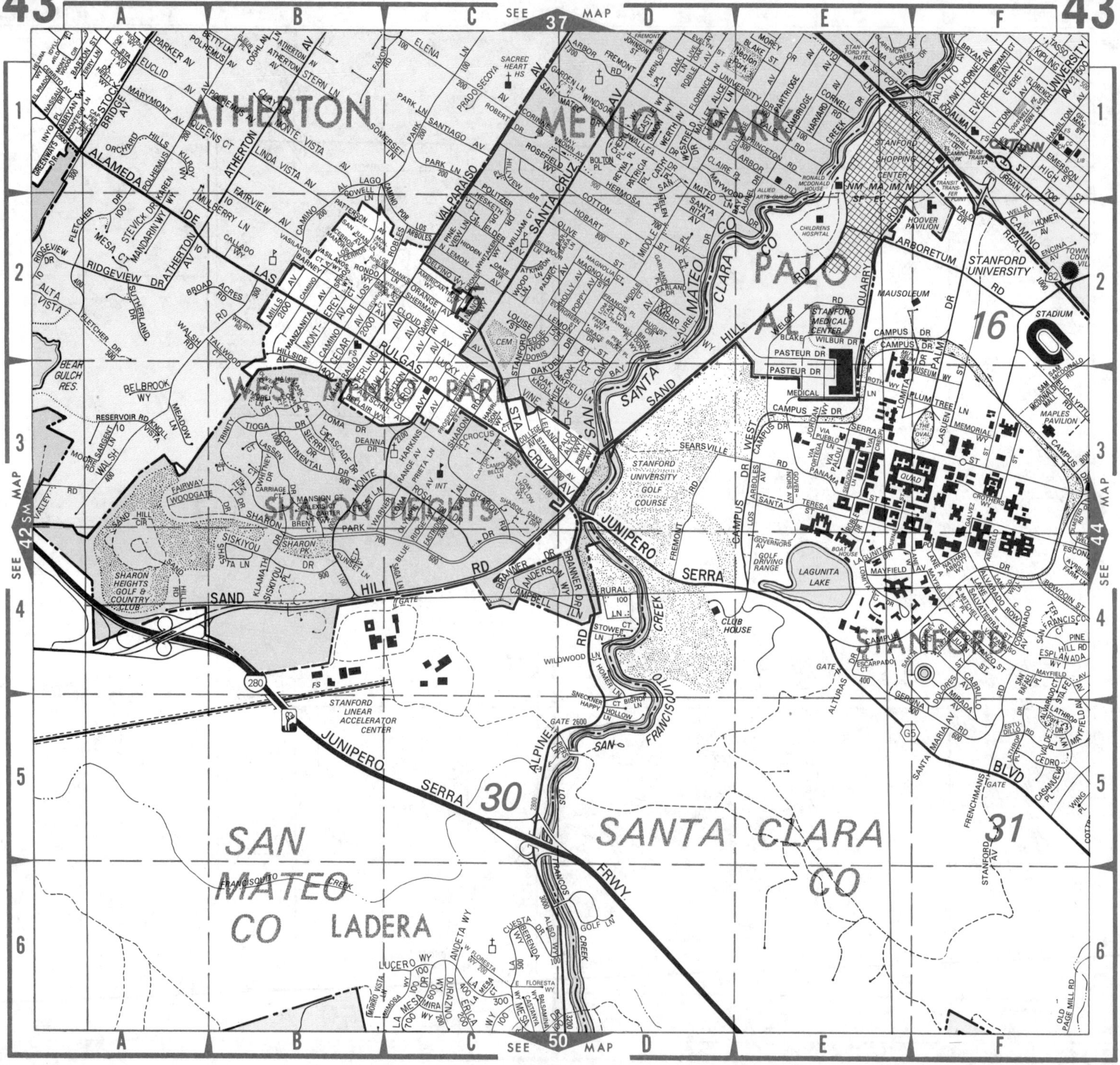

ATHERTON

MENLO PARK

WEST MENLO PARK

SHARON HEIGHTS

PALO ALTO

STANFORD UNIVERSITY

STANFORD

STANFORD SHOPPING CENTER

STANFORD MEDICAL CENTER

STANFORD UNIVERSITY GOLF COURSE

STANFORD LINEAR ACCELERATOR CENTER

SHARON HEIGHTS GOLF & COUNTRY CLUB

BEAR GULCH RES.

LAGUNITA LAKE

HOOVER PAVILION

MAPLES PAVILION

CHILDRENS HOSPITAL

MAUSOLEUM

STADIUM

QUAD

CLUB HOUSE

GOLF DRIVING RANGE

SAN FRANCISQUITO CREEK

SAND HILL RD

JUNIPERO SERRA FRWY

JUNIPERO SERRA BLVD

ALAMEDA DE LAS PULGAS

EL CAMINO REAL

SANTA CRUZ AV

VALPARAISO AV

UNIVERSITY AV

ALPINE RD

LADERA

SAN MATEO CO

SANTA CLARA CO

16

30

31

280

82

G5

1 2 3 4 5 6

SEE 42 SM MAP

SEE 44 MAP

COPYRIGHT © 1991 BY Thomas Bros Maps

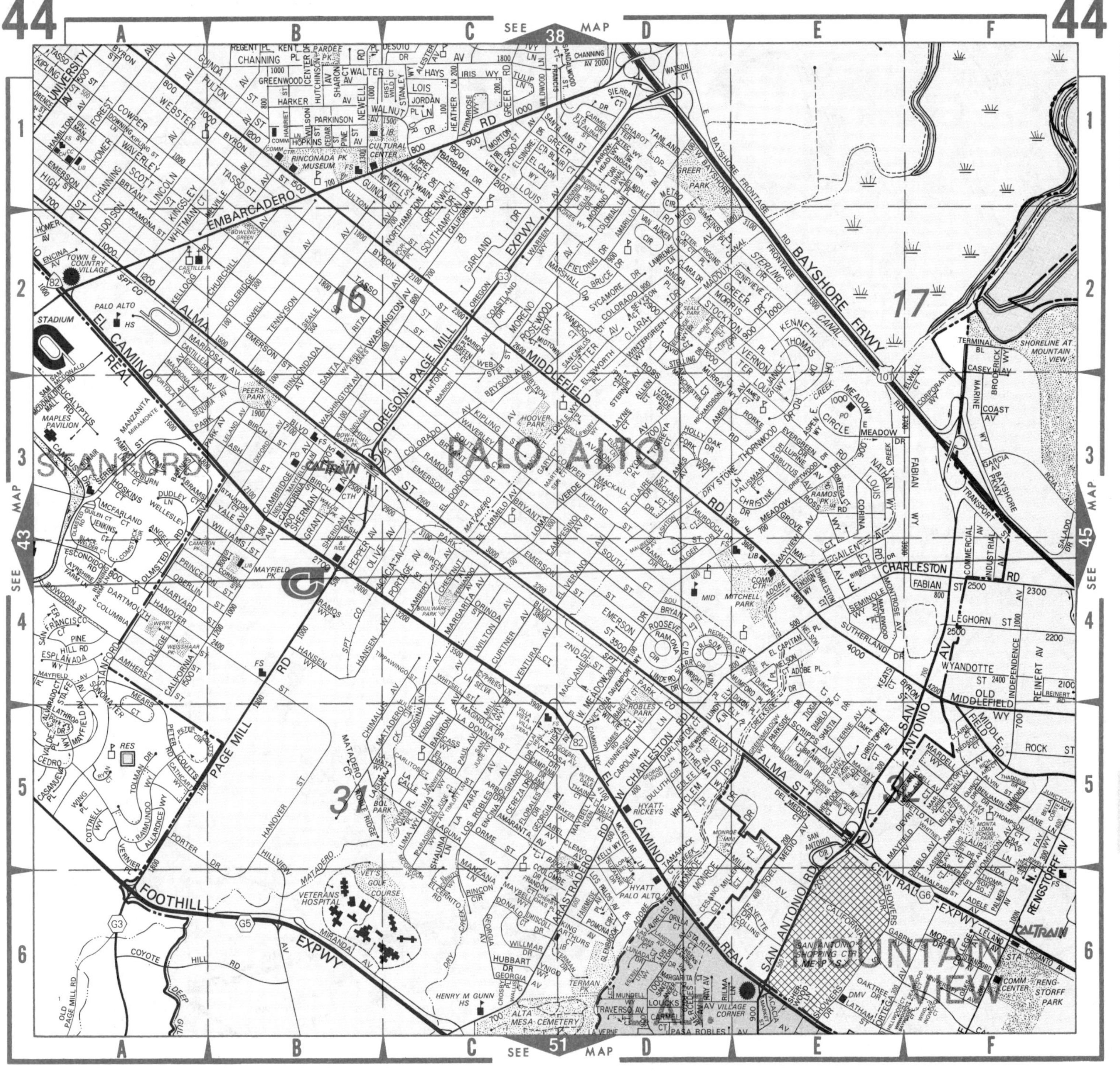
44
SEE MAP 38
SEE MAP 51
SEE MAP 43
SEE MAP 45
A
B
C
D
E
F
1
2
3
4
5
6
PALO ALTO
STANFORD
MOUNTAIN VIEW
16
17
31
32
EL CAMINO REAL
ALMA ST
MIDDLEFIELD RD
OREGON-PAGE MILL EXPWY
PAGE MILL RD
EMBARCADERO RD
BAYSHORE FRWY
CHARLESTON RD
SAN ANTONIO RD
CENTRAL EXPWY
FOOTHILL EXPWY
MITCHELL PARK
SHORELINE AT MOUNTAIN VIEW
VETERANS HOSPITAL
ALTA MESA CEMETERY
HENRY M GUNN HS
SAN ANTONIO SHOPPING CTR
RENGSTORFF PARK
TOWN & COUNTRY VILLAGE
STADIUM
CALTRAIN
DETAIL
COPYRIGHT © 1991 BY Thomas Bros Maps

SEE 38A MAP

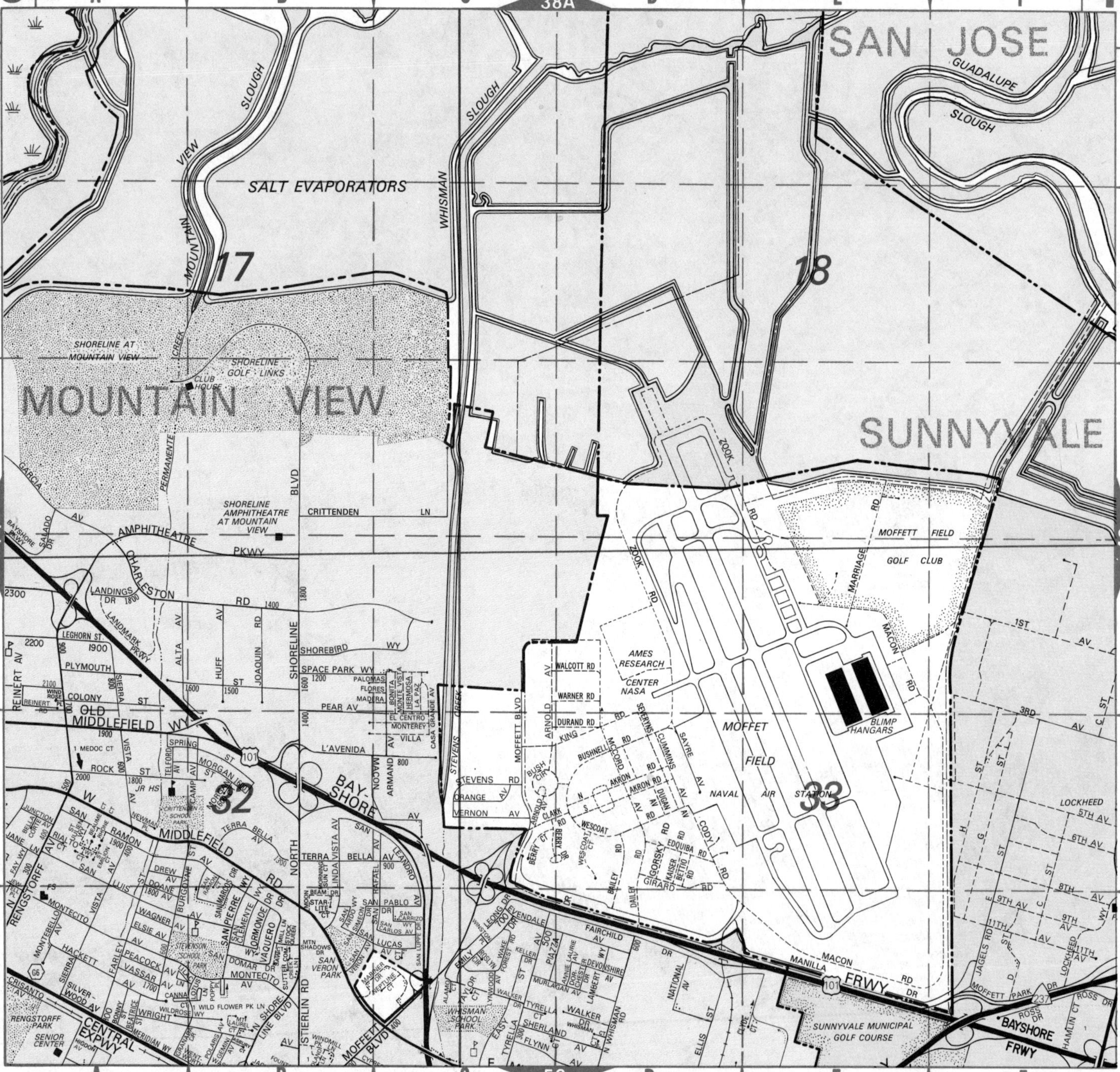
SAN JOSE
GUADALUPE
SLOUGH
SLOUGH
MOUNTAIN VIEW SLOUGH
WHISMAN SLOUGH
SALT EVAPORATORS
17
18
SHORELINE AT MOUNTAIN VIEW
SHORELINE GOLF LINKS
CLUB HOUSE
MOUNTAIN VIEW
SUNNYVALE
PERMANENTE CREEK
SHORELINE AMPHITHEATRE AT MOUNTAIN VIEW
CRITTENDEN LN
AMPHITHEATRE PKWY
CHARLESTON RD
LANDINGS DR
LANDMARK PKWY
GARCIA AV
SALADO DR
BAYSHORE PKWY
SHORELINE BLVD
SHOREBIRD WY
SPACE PARK WY
ALTA AV
HUFF AV
JOAQUIN RD
LEGHORN ST
PLYMOUTH
COLONY ST
REINERT AV
OLD MIDDLEFIELD WY
PEAR AV
L'AVENIDA
SPRING ST
ROCK ST
MORGAN
JR HS
CRITTENDEN SCHOOL PARK
32
MIDDLEFIELD RD
SAN RAMON
SAN LUIS
TERRA BELLA AV
NORTH
LEANDRO
BAYSHORE
101
MONTECITO
WAGNER
PEACOCK
VASSAR
STEVENSON SCHOOL PARK
RENGSTORFF PARK
SENIOR CENTER
CENTRAL EXPWY
RENGSTORFF
CRISANTO AV
SAN VERON PARK
STIERLIN RD
MOFFETT BLVD
STEVENS CREEK
STEVENS RD
ORANGE AV
VERNON AV
MOFFETT BLVD
WALCOTT RD
WARNER RD
DURAND RD
AMES RESEARCH CENTER NASA
MOFFET FIELD
NAVAL AIR STATION
33
BLIMP HANGARS
ZOOK RD
MARRIAGE RD
MACON RD
MOFFETT FIELD GOLF CLUB
1ST AV
3RD AV
5TH AV
6TH AV
8TH AV
9TH AV
11TH AV
LOCKHEED
JAGELS RD
MOFFETT PARK DR
237
BAYSHORE FRWY
HAMLIN CT
ROSS DR
MANILLA DR
MACON RD
FRWY
SUNNYVALE MUNICIPAL GOLF COURSE
WHISMAN SCHOOL PARK
FAIRCHILD
EVENDALE
NATIONAL AV
ELLIS ST
WALKER
FLYNN AV
N WHISMAN RD

SEE 44 MAP

SEE 46 MAP

SEE 52 MAP

SANTA CLARA

DETAIL

COPYRIGHT © 1991 BY Thomas Bros Maps

SEE 38A MAP

COPYRIGHT © 1991 BY Thomas Bros Maps

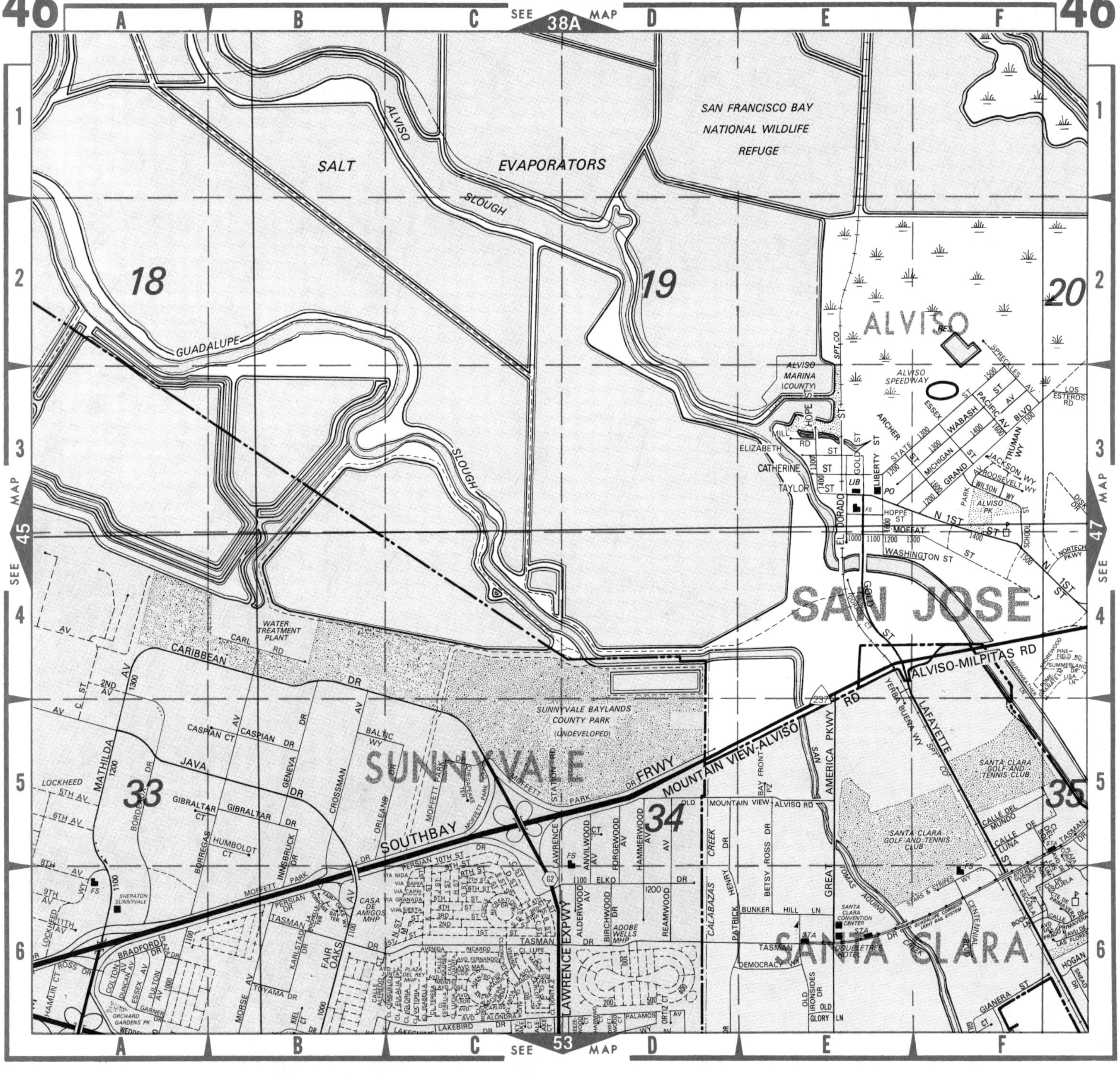

SANTA CLARA

SAN FRANCISCO BAY NATIONAL WILDLIFE REFUGE

SALT EVAPORATORS

ALVISO SLOUGH

GUADALUPE SLOUGH

ALVISO

ALVISO MARINA (COUNTY)

ALVISO SPEEDWAY

SAN JOSE

WATER TREATMENT PLANT

SUNNYVALE BAYLANDS COUNTY PARK (UNDEVELOPED)

SUNNYVALE

ALVISO-MILPITAS RD

MOUNTAIN VIEW-ALVISO RD

SOUTHBAY FRWY

LAWRENCE EXPWY

SANTA CLARA GOLF AND TENNIS CLUB

SANTA CLARA CONVENTION CENTER

DOUBLETREE HOTEL

SANTA CLARA

SHERATON SUNNYVALE

ORCHARD GARDENS PK

ALVISO PK

DETAIL

SEE 45 MAP

SEE 47 MAP

SEE 53 MAP

SEE 39 MAP

A B C D E F

1 2 3 4 5 6

SEE 46 MAP

SEE 48 MAP

DETAIL

SAN JOSE

MILPITAS

SANTA CLARA

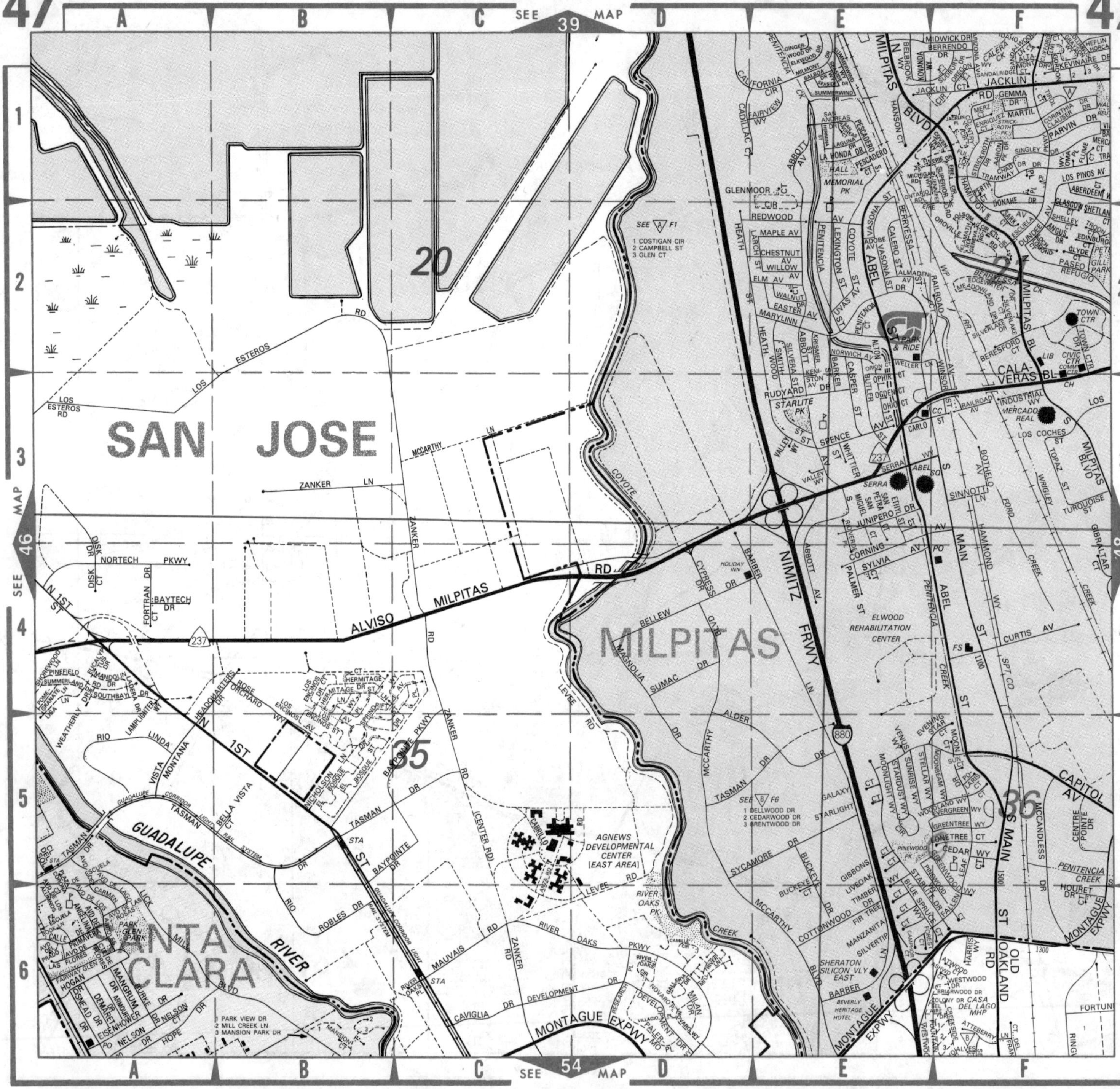

20

21

35

36

LOS ESTEROS RD

ZANKER RD

ZANKER LN

MCCARTHY LN

NORTECH PKWY

DISK DR

DISK CT

FORTRAN DR

BAYTECH DR

N 1ST ST

ALVISO MILPITAS RD

237

RIO LINDA

VISTA MONTANA

BELLA VISTA

HEADQUARTERS DR

ROSE ORCHARD WY

LOS ENCINOS AV

HERMITAGE CT

NICHOLSON LN

EL BOSQUE ST

BAYPOINTE PKWY

BAYPOINTE DR

TASMAN DR

GUADALUPE CORRIDOR LIGHT RAIL SYSTEM

GUADALUPE RIVER

STA

RIO ROBLES DR

MAUVAIS

RIVER OAKS PKWY

RIVER OAKS PK

(CENTER RD)

AGNEWS DEVELOPMENTAL CENTER (EAST AREA)

CABRILLO

LEVEE RD

CAVIGLIA DR

DEVELOPMENT DR

RESEARCH PL

MONTAGUE EXPWY

MILAN DR

VILLAGIO

PALERMO

LICK MILL BLVD

PARK GLEN

CORRIDOR

HOPE DR

NELSON

EISENHOWER

DEMARET DR

ARMOUR

MANGRUM

HOGAN DR

SNEAD

FAIRWAY GLEN

LAS FLORES

PRIMAVERA

CALLE

ESCUELA

AVD DE LOS ARBOLES

CARMEN

1 PARK VIEW DR
2 MILL CREEK LN
3 MANSION PARK DR

COYOTE CREEK

SEE A F1
1 COSTIGAN CIR
2 CAMPBELL ST
3 GLEN CT

SEE B F6
1 DELLWOOD DR
2 CEDARWOOD DR
3 BRENTWOOD DR

NIMITZ FRWY

880

BARBER LN

CYPRESS DR

HOLIDAY INN

BELLEW DR

GATE

MAGNOLIA

SUMAC DR

ALDER DR

MCCARTHY BLVD

TASMAN DR

GALAXY

STARLIGHT

SYCAMORE DR

BUCKEYE CT

COTTONWOOD DR

GIBBONS

LIVEOAK

TIMBER

FIR TREE

MANZANITA

SILVERTIP

SHERATON SILICON VLY EAST

BEVERLY HERITAGE HOTEL

BARBER LN

CALIFORNIA CIR

FAIRVIEW WY

CADILLAC CT

GLENMOOR

REDWOOD

MAPLE AV

CHESTNUT AV

WILLOW

ELM AV

WALNUT

EASTER AV

MARYLINN

HEATH

SMITH

SILVERA

ABBOTT AV

RUDYARD

STARLITE PK

SPENCE

VALLEY WY

WHITTIER

PENITENCIA

LEXINGTON ST

COYOTE

VASONA ST

UVAS AV

CALERO ST

ALMADEN

BERRYESSA

ABEL ST

SAN ANDREAS

PESCADERO

LA HONDA DR

HALL MEMORIAL PK

MILPITAS BLVD

HANSON CT

BELBROOK

JACKLIN RD

GEMMA DR

PARVIN DR

LOS PINOS AV

ABERDEEN WY

GLASGOW

SHETLAND

HAMILTON

DUNDEE

ESCUELA

SHELLEY

TROON

EDINBURGH

GLYDE

PASEO REFUGIO

SINGLEY

DONAHE DR

TOWN CTR

CIVIC CTR

LIB

COMM CTR

CH

CALAVERAS BL

INDUSTRIAL WY

MERCADO REAL

LOS COCHES ST

TOPAZ ST

TURQUOISE ST

RAILROAD AV

CARLO ST

SERRA WY

ABEL SQ

SINNOTT LN

BOTHELO AV

WRIGLEY

FORD

JUNIPERO DR

CORNING AV

SYLVIA AV

PALMER ST

PO

ELWOOD REHABILITATION CENTER

MAIN ST

HAMMOND WY

CREEK

CURTIS AV

FS

SPT CO

GIBRALTAR CT

PARK & RIDE

WELLER LN

NORWICH AV

ORION CT

OPHIR CT

BUTLER

OGDEN CT

OHIO CT

BERESFORD CT

CAPITOL AV

S MAIN ST

MCCANDLESS DR

CENTRE POINTE DR

PENITENCIA CREEK

HOURET DR

MONTAGUE EXPWY

OLD OAKLAND RD

EVENING STAR

MOONLIGHT WY

STARDUST WY

SUNRISE WY

STELLAR WY

WOODLAND WY

EVERGREEN WY

GREENTREE WY

LONETREE CT

CEDAR WY

PINEWOOD

STARLITE

BILLIE SPRUCE

FALLEN LEAF

HARRIS WY

ATWOOD

WESTWOOD

BRIARWOOD DR

COLONY DR

CASA DEL LAGO MHP

ATTEBERRY LN

FORTUNE

RINGWOOD

SEE 54 MAP

COPYRIGHT © 1991 BY Thomas Bros Maps

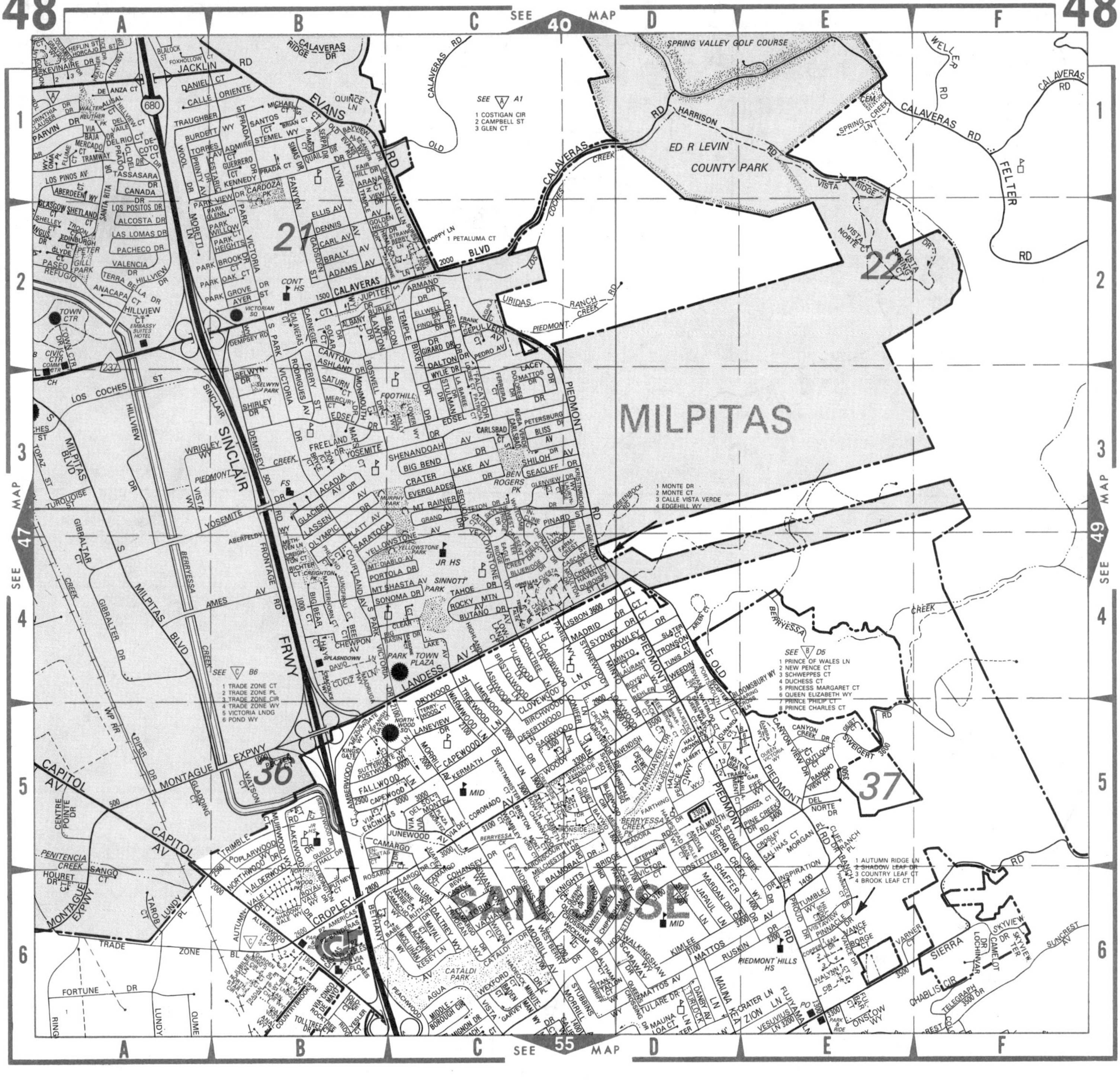

COPYRIGHT © 1991 BY Thomas Bros Maps

MILPITAS

SAN JOSE

ED R LEVIN COUNTY PARK

SPRING VALLEY GOLF COURSE

SEE A A1
1 COSTIGAN CIR
2 CAMPBELL ST
3 GLEN CT

1 PETALUMA CT

1 MONTE DR
2 MONTE CT
3 CALLE VISTA VERDE
4 EDGEHILL WY

SEE C B6
1 TRADE ZONE CT
2 TRADE ZONE PL
3 TRADE ZONE CIR
4 TRADE ZONE WY
5 VICTORIA LNDG
6 POND WY

SEE B D5
1 PRINCE OF WALES LN
2 NEW PENCE CT
3 SCHWEPPES CT
4 DUCHESS CT
5 PRINCESS MARGARET CT
6 QUEEN ELIZABETH WY
7 PRINCE PHILIP CT
8 PRINCE CHARLES CT

1 AUTUMN RIDGE LN
2 SHADOW LEAF DR
3 COUNTRY LEAF CT
4 BROOK LEAF CT

SEE 47 MAP

SEE 49 MAP

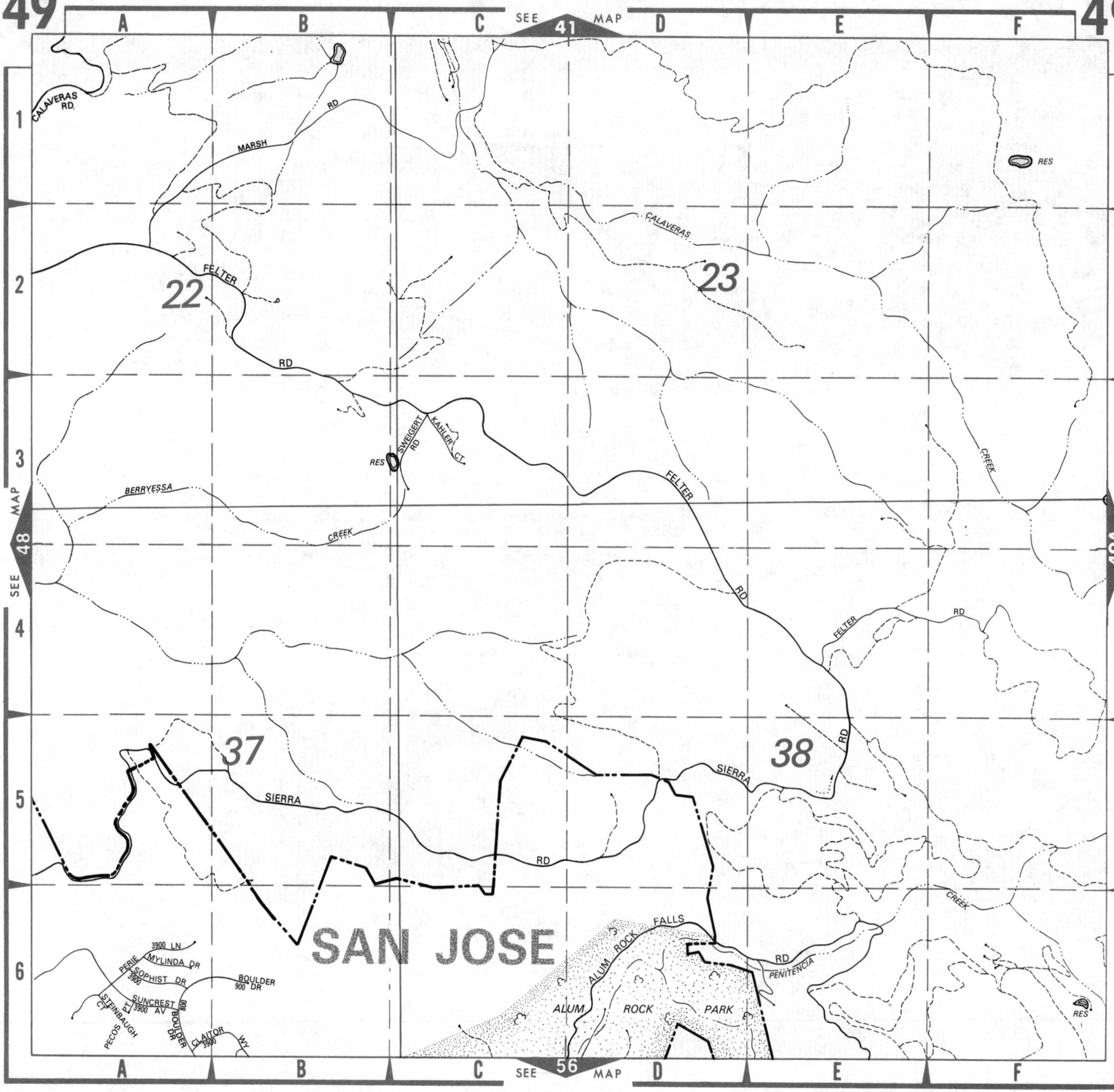

SEE MAP 41
SEE MAP 48
SEE MAP 49A
SEE MAP 56
SANTA CLARA
DETAIL
COPYRIGHT © 1991 BY Thomas Bros Maps
CALAVERAS RD
MARSH RD
FELTER RD
22
23
37
38
CALAVERAS
RES
SWEIGERT RD
KAHLER CT
BERRYESSA CREEK
CREEK
SIERRA RD
SAN JOSE
ALUM ROCK FALLS RD
PENITENCIA CREEK
ALUM ROCK PARK
3900 LN
MYLINDA DR
PERIE
SOPHIST DR
BOULDER 900 DR
SUNCREST 3900 AV
STEINBAUGH CT
PECOS PL
BOULDER DR
CLAITOR WY

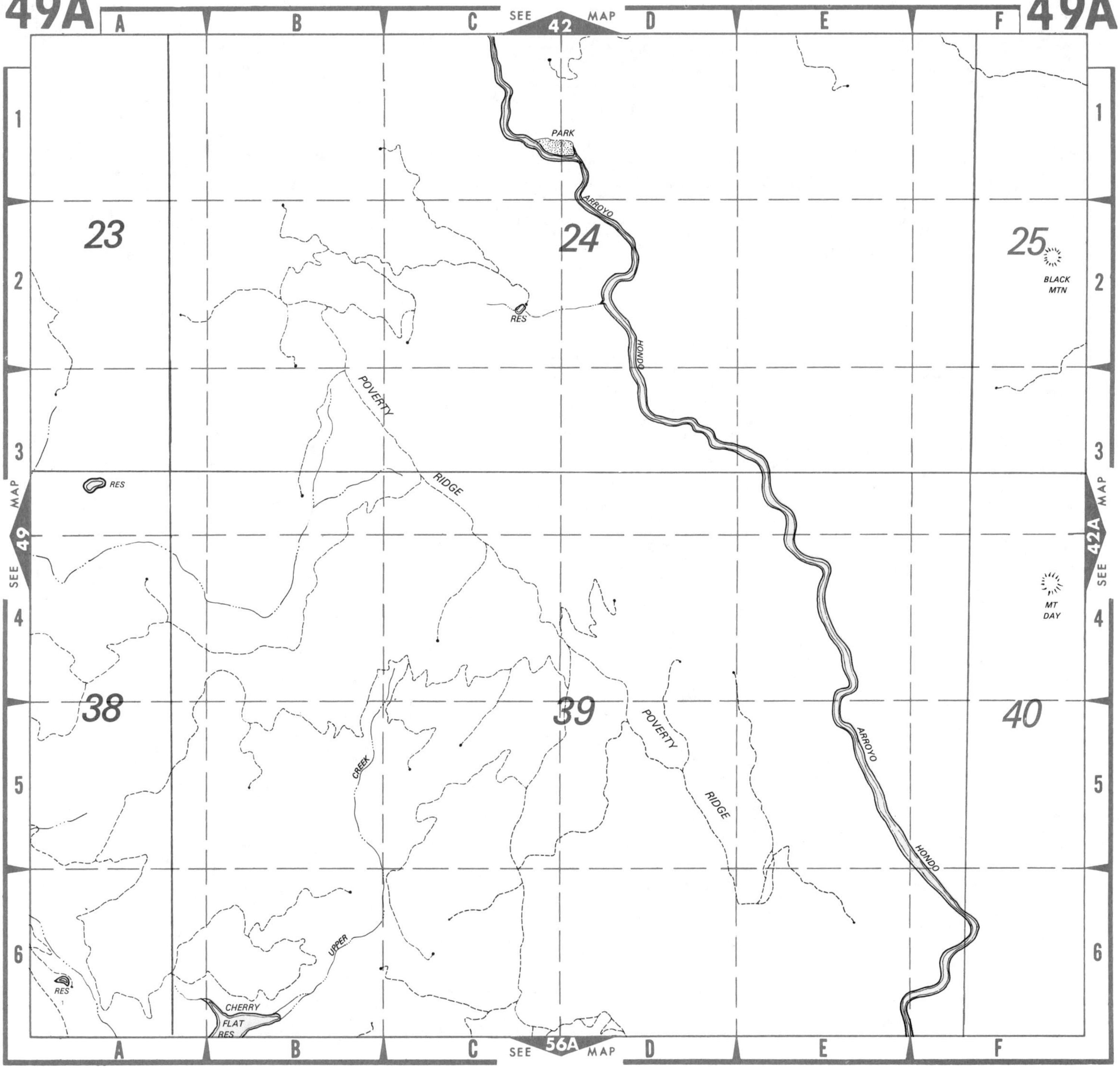

49A

COPYRIGHT © 1991 BY Thomas Bros Maps

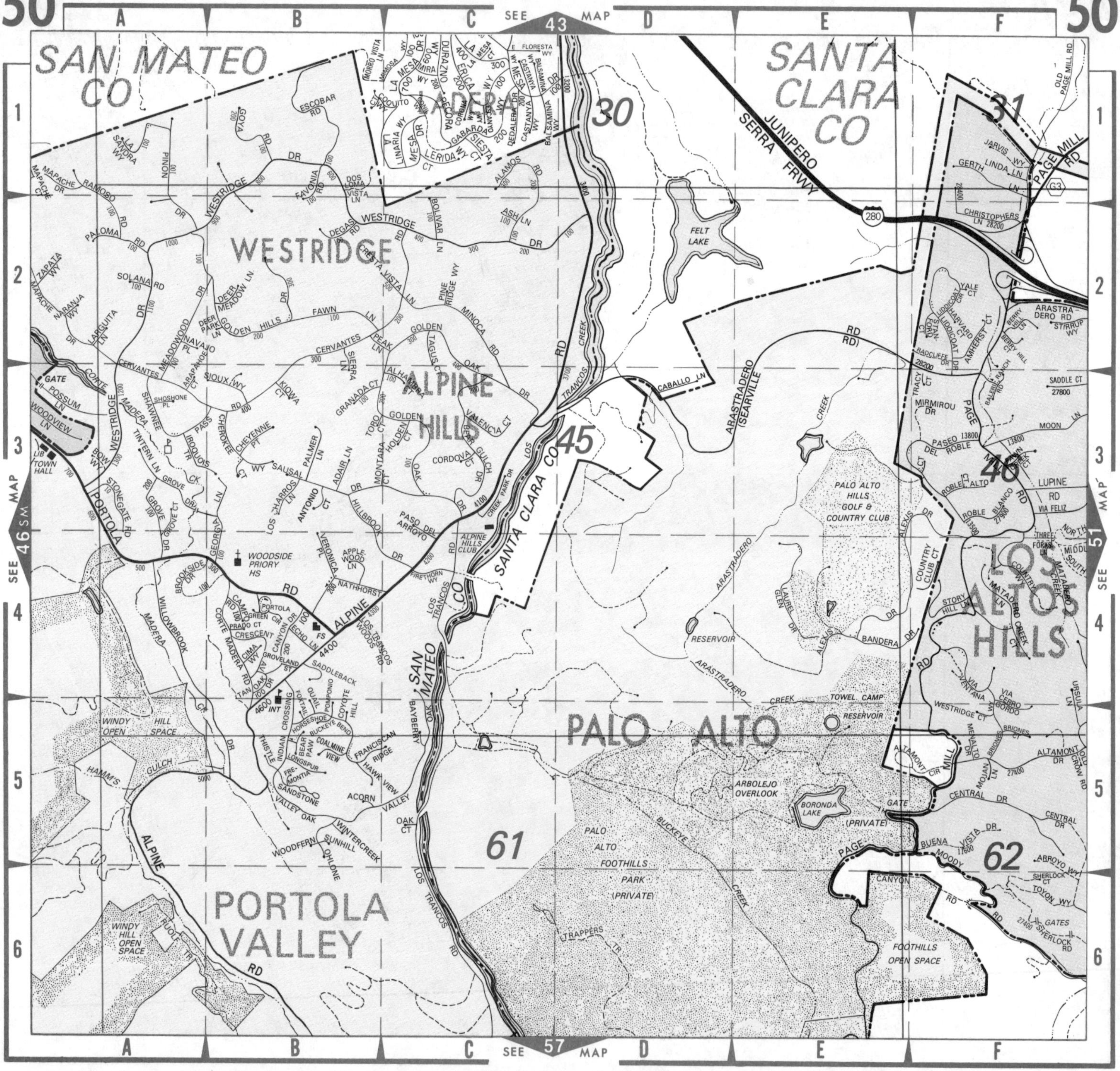

SAN MATEO CO

SANTA CLARA CO

LADERA

WESTRIDGE

ALPINE HILLS

PALO ALTO

LOS ALTOS HILLS

PORTOLA VALLEY

30 31 45 46 61 62

JUNIPERO SERRA FRWY

280

PAGE MILL RD

OLD PAGE MILL RD

G3

FELT LAKE

WESTRIDGE DR

ALPINE RD

PORTOLA RD

ARASTRADERO RD

LOS TRANCOS RD

SANTA CLARA CO

SAN MATEO CO

LOS TRANCOS CREEK

PALO ALTO HILLS GOLF & COUNTRY CLUB

RESERVOIR

TOWEL CAMP RESERVOIR

ARBOLEJO OVERLOOK

BORONDA LAKE

GATE (PRIVATE)

PALO ALTO FOOTHILLS PARK (PRIVATE)

BUCKEYE CREEK

TRAPPERS TR

FOOTHILLS OPEN SPACE

WINDY HILL OPEN SPACE

HAMM'S GULCH

WOODSIDE PRIORY HS

ALPINE HILLS CLUB

LIB TOWN HALL

FS

INT

CENTRAL DR

BUENA VISTA DR

MOODY RD

PAGE MILL RD

CANYON RD

ALTAMONT CIR

MATADERO CREEK

LUPINE RD

VIA FELIZ

MOON LN

SADDLE CT

PASEO DEL ROBLE

ROBLE ALTO

ROBLE BLANCO

ALEXIS DR

BANDERA DR

LAUREL GLEN DR

COUNTRY CLUB CT

STORY HILL LN

MIRMIROU DR

TRACY CT

CABALLO LN

ARASTRADERO (SEARSVILLE) RD

GOLDEN OAK DR

MINOCA RD

PINE RIDGE WY

CERVANTES RD

GOLDEN HILLS DR

FAWN LN

PEAK LN

SIERRA LN

GRANADA CT

KIOWA CT

SIOUX WY

CHEROKEE CT

IROQUOIS TR

SHAWNEE PASS

MEADOWOOD DR

NAVAJO PL

ARAPAHOE CT

DEER MEADOW LN

DEER PARK LN

SOLANA RD

PALOMA RD

RAMOSO RD

MAPACHE DR

ZAPATA WY

NARANJA WY

LARGUITA LN

ESCOBAR RD

GOYA RD

LA SANDRA WY

PINON DR

FAVONIA RD

DOS LOMA VISTA LN

BOLIVAR LN

ALAMOS RD

ASH LN

DEGAS RD

CRESTA VISTA LN

GATE

POSSUM LN

WOODVIEW LN

CORTE MADERA

BOW WY

STONEGATE RD

GROVE DR

TINTERN LN

CHEYENNE PT

SAUSAL DR

PALMER LN

LOS CHARROS LN

ANTONIO CT

ADAIR LN

MONTARA CT

HILLBROOK DR

PASO DEL ARROYO

VERONICA PL

APPLEWOOD LN

NATHHORST

FIRETHORN WY

TORO CT

HOLDEN CT

CORDOVA CT

BEAR GULCH DR

VALENCIA CT

TAGUS CT

ALHAMBRA

BROOKSIDE DR

WILLOWBROOK

MADERA

CAMPO RD

PORTOLA

GREEN OAK DR

PRADO CT

CRESCENT

CANYON DR

ECHO LN

CIMA WY

GROVELAND ST

SADDLEBACK

TAN OAK

INDIAN CROSSING

FOXTAIL

QUAIL

POMPONIO

COYOTE HILL

HORSESHOE BEND

BUCKEYE

BEAR PAW

COALMINE VIEW

FRANCISCAN RIDGE

HAWK VIEW

LONGSPUR

FREMONTIA

THISTLE

SANDSTONE

VALLEY OAK

ACORN

WINTERCREEK

SUNHILL

OHLONE

WOODFERN

BAYBERRY

OAK CT

LOS TRANCOS WOODS RD

VIA VENTANA

VIA CERRO GORDO

WESTRIDGE CT

MENALTO DR

BRIONES CT

MOHAN LN

ALTAMONT DR

OLD CROW RD

URSULA LN

ARROYO WY

SHERLOCK CT

TOYON WY

SHERLOCK RD

GATES

JARVIS WY

LINDA LN

GERTH LN

CHRISTOPHERS LN

YALE CT

HARVARD CT

LIDDICOAT CIR

LIDDICOAT DR

STANFORD CT

AMHERST CT

RADCLIFFE DR

BERRY HILL CT

ARASTRADERO RD

STIRRUP WY

BALERIE RANCH RD

THREE FORKS LN

NORTH

MIDDLE

SOUTH

COUNTRY WY

SEE 46 SM MAP

SEE 51 MAP

SEE MAP 44
SEE MAP 58
SEE MAP 50
SEE MAP 52
SANTA CLARA
DETAIL
PALO ALTO
31
MOUNTAIN VIEW
32
46
47
62
63
LOS ALTOS
LOS ALTOS HILLS
A
B
C
D
E
F
1
2
3
4
5
6
JUNIPERO SERRA FRWY
280
FOOTHILL EXPWY
EL CAMINO REAL
G3
G5
82
PAGE MILL RD
ARASTRADERO RD
DEER CREEK
FOOTHILL COLLEGE
ALTA MESA CEMETERY
HENRY M GUNN HS
PINEWOOD HS
LOS ALTOS HS
JR HS
ESTHER CLARK PARK
VILLAGE CORNER
FREMONT RD
PURISSIMA RD
MORA DR
EL MONTE AV
SAN ANTONIO RD
SPRINGER RD
MIRANDA AV
ARBOR AV
MOODY RD
ALTAMONT RD
BLACK MOUNTAIN RD
ROBLEDA RD
LOS ALTOS COUNTRY CLUB

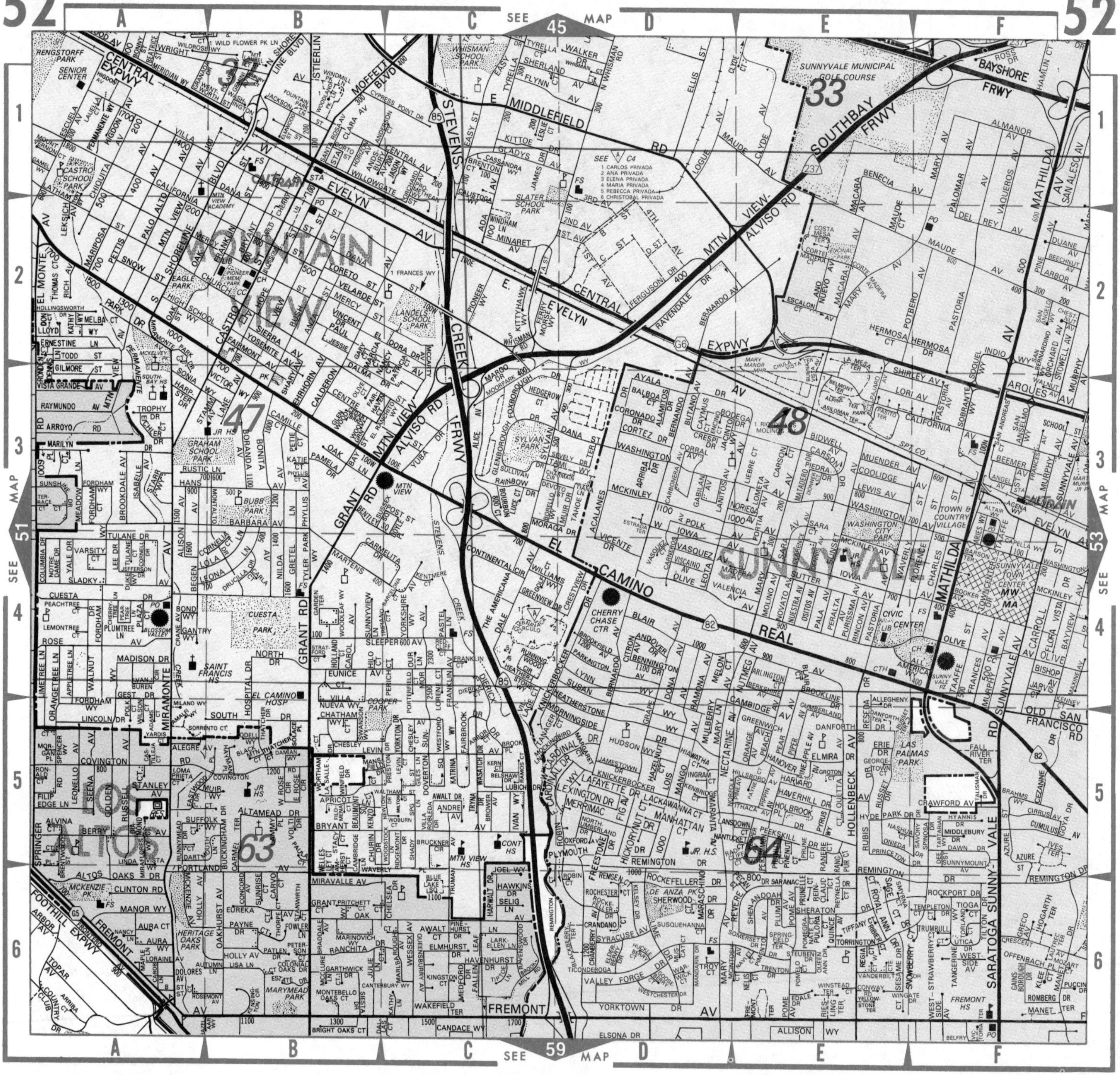

SEE 45 MAP
SEE 59 MAP
SEE 51 MAP
SEE 53 MAP
A
B
C
D
E
F
1
2
3
4
5
6
MOUNTAIN VIEW
SUNNYVALE
LOS ALTOS
37
33
47
48
63
64
CENTRAL EXPWY
SOUTHBAY FRWY
BAYSHORE FRWY
STEVENS CREEK FRWY
EL CAMINO REAL
MTN VIEW ALVISO RD
E MIDDLEFIELD RD
EVELYN AV
CENTRAL EXPWY
FOOTHILL EXPWY
GRANT RD
MATHILDA AV
SARATOGA SUNNYVALE RD
FREMONT AV
SUNNYVALE MUNICIPAL GOLF COURSE
RENGSTORFF PARK
WHISMAN SCHOOL PARK
SLATER SCHOOL PARK
LANDELS SCHOOL PARK
GRAHAM SCHOOL PARK
CUESTA PARK
SYLVAN PARK
WASHINGTON CITY PARK
LAS PALMAS PARK
HERITAGE OAKS PARK
MARYMEAD PARK
COOPER PARK
BUBB PARK
MTN VIEW
CHERRY CHASE CTR
SUNNYVALE TOWN CENTER
CIVIC CENTER
EL CAMINO HOSP
SAINT FRANCIS HS
MTN VIEW HS
FREMONT HS
CONT HS
SEE C4
1 CARLOS PRIVADA
2 ANA PRIVADA
3 ELENA PRIVADA
4 MARIA PRIVADA
5 REBECCA PRIVADA
6 CHRISTOBAL PRIVADA
COPYRIGHT © 1991 BY Thomas Bros Maps

COPYRIGHT © 1991 BY Thomas Bros. Maps

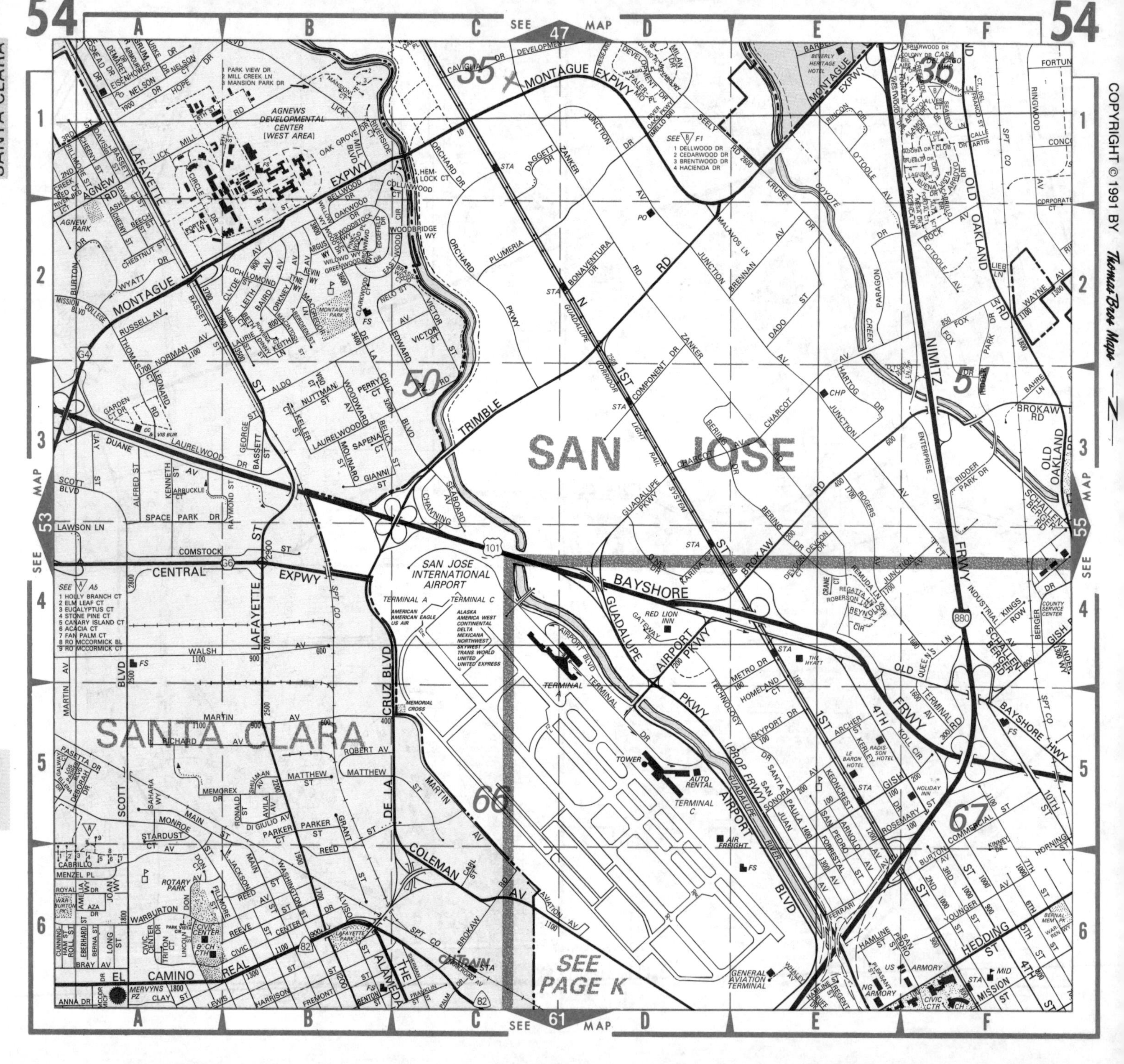

COPYRIGHT © 1991 BY Thomas Bros Maps

55

COPYRIGHT © 1991 BY Thomas Bros Maps

SEE 49 MAP
SEE 55 MAP
SEE 56A MAP
SEE 63 MAP
SEE A A6
1 BETTEN CT
2 MERVYNS WY

SAN JOSE
EAST SAN JOSE
ALUM ROCK
SAN JOSE
ALUM ROCK PARK
SAN JOSE COUNTRY CLUB
PENITENCIA CREEK RD
ALUM ROCK FALLS RD
MT HAMILTON RD
CLAYTON RD
ALUM ROCK AV
STORY RD
WHITE RD
CAPITOL EXPWY
MT PLEASANT
LO BUES PLAZA
FLINT CREEK
BABB CREEK
AGUAGUE
ARROYO

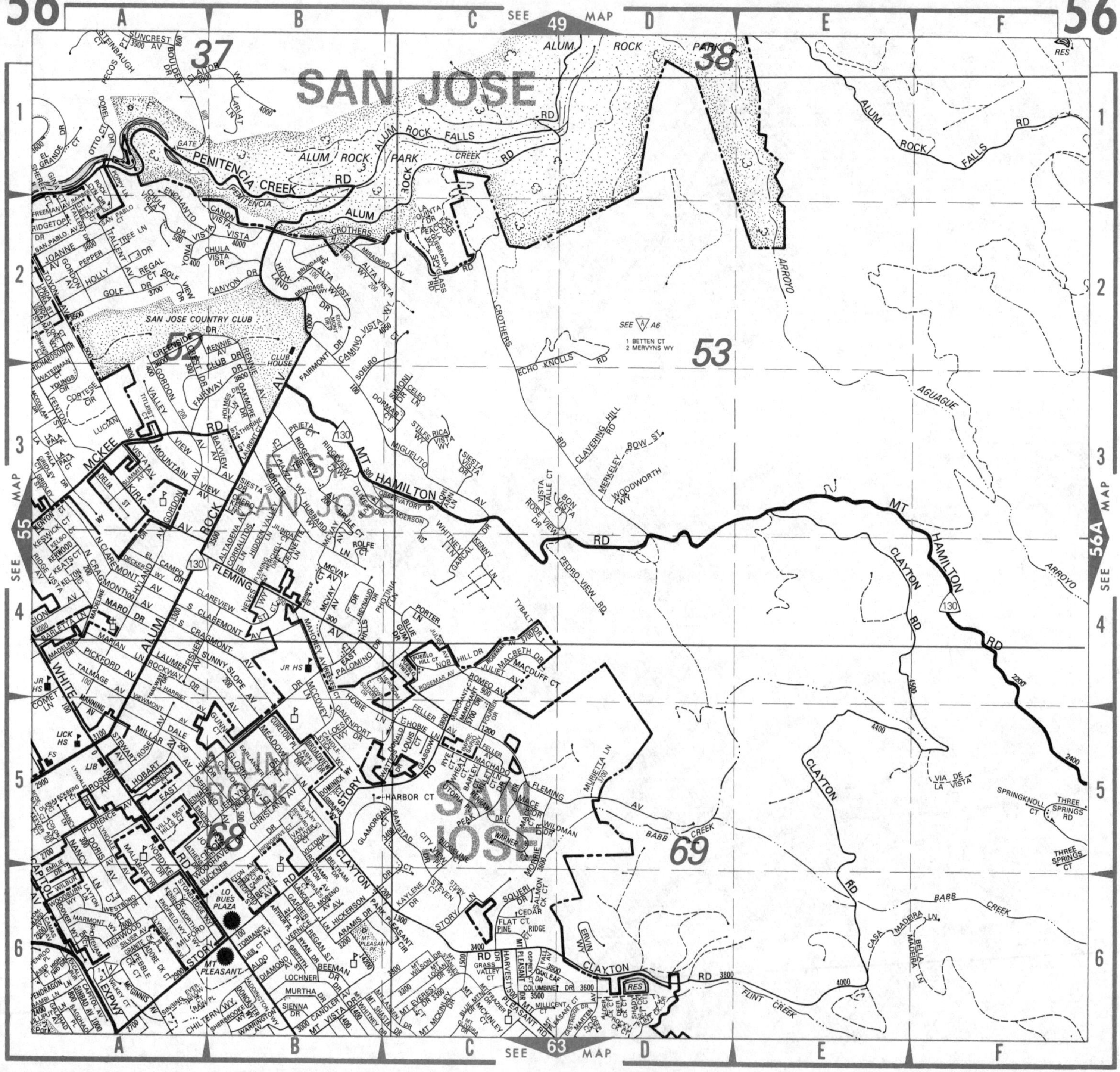

COPYRIGHT © 1991 BY Thomas Bros Maps

DETAIL

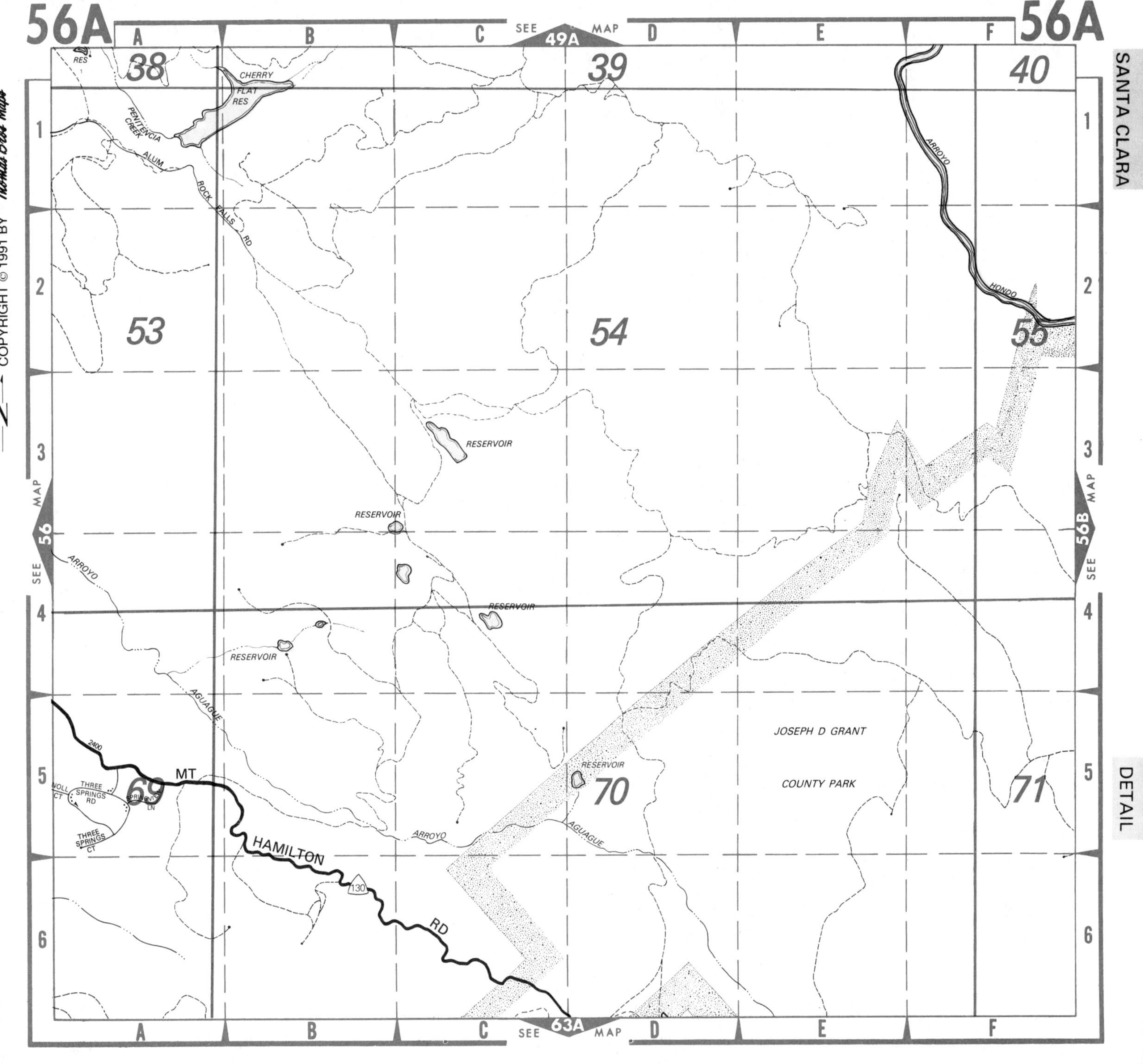

COPYRIGHT © 1991 BY Thomas Bros Maps

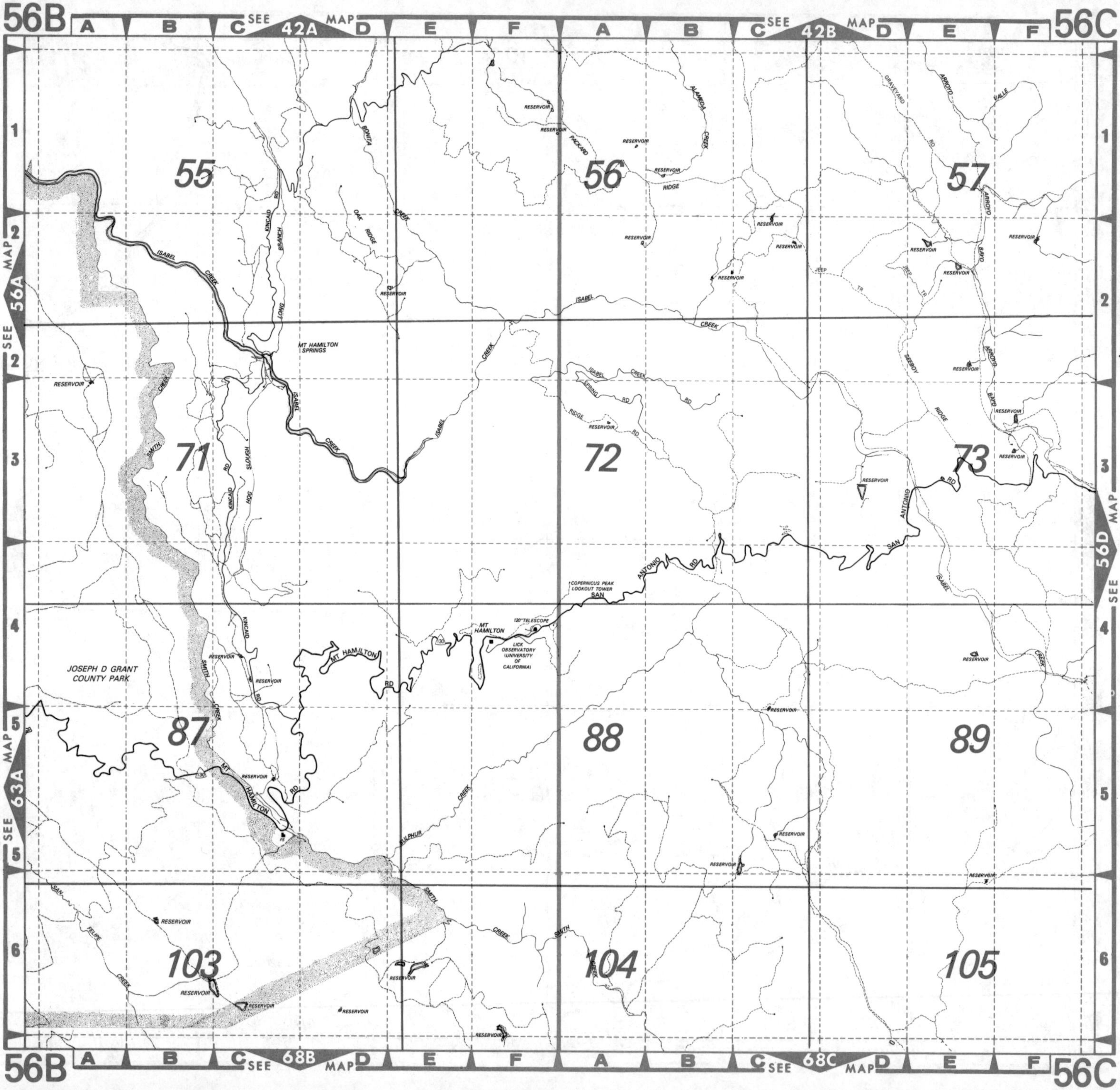

SANTA CLARA

COPYRIGHT © 1991 BY Thomas Bros Maps

SEE 56A MAP

SEE 56D MAP

SEE 63A MAP

DETAIL

55 56 57 71 72 73 87 88 89 103 104 105

ISABEL CREEK
KINCAID RD
LONG BRANCH
OAK RIDGE
BONITA CREEK
PACKARD RIDGE
ALAMEDA CREEK
GRAVEYARD RD
ARROYO VALLE
ARROYO BAYO
JEEP TR
MT HAMILTON SPRINGS
ISABEL SPRING RD
RIDGE RD
SMITH CREEK
HOG SLOUGH
SEEBOY RIDGE
SAN ANTONIO RD
COPERNICUS PEAK LOOKOUT TOWER
120" TELESCOPE
MT HAMILTON
LICK OBSERVATORY (UNIVERSITY OF CALIFORNIA)
MT HAMILTON RD
JOSEPH D GRANT COUNTY PARK
SULPHUR CREEK
SAN FELIPE CREEK
RESERVOIR

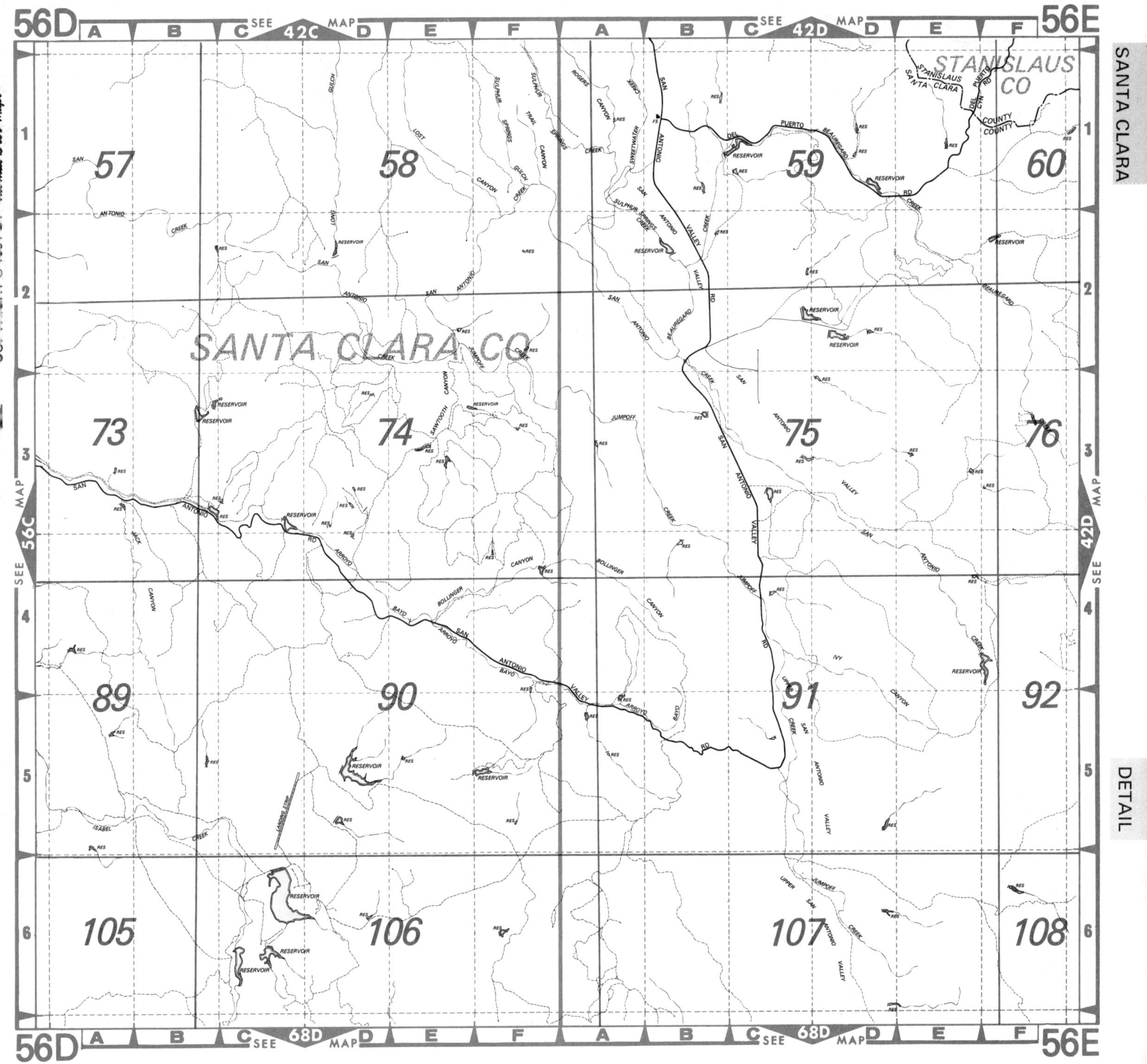
56D
A
B
C SEE 42C MAP D
E
F
A
B
C SEE 42D MAP D
E
F
56E
SANTA CLARA
STANISLAUS CO
SANTA CLARA CO
57
58
59
60
73
74
75
76
89
90
91
92
105
106
107
108
SEE 56C MAP
SEE 42D MAP
SAN ANTONIO VALLEY RD
DEL PUERTO CYN RD
BEAUREGARD
RESERVOIR
RES
LANDING STRIP
SAN ANTONIO CREEK
ARROYO BAYO
JUMPOFF CREEK
BOLLINGER CANYON
IVY CANYON
ISABEL CREEK
JACK CANYON
SWEETWATER CREEK
SULPHUR SPRINGS CREEK
UPPER SAN ANTONIO CREEK
56D
A
B
C SEE 68D MAP D
E
F
A
B
C SEE 68D MAP D
E
F
56E
DETAIL

SANTA CLARA

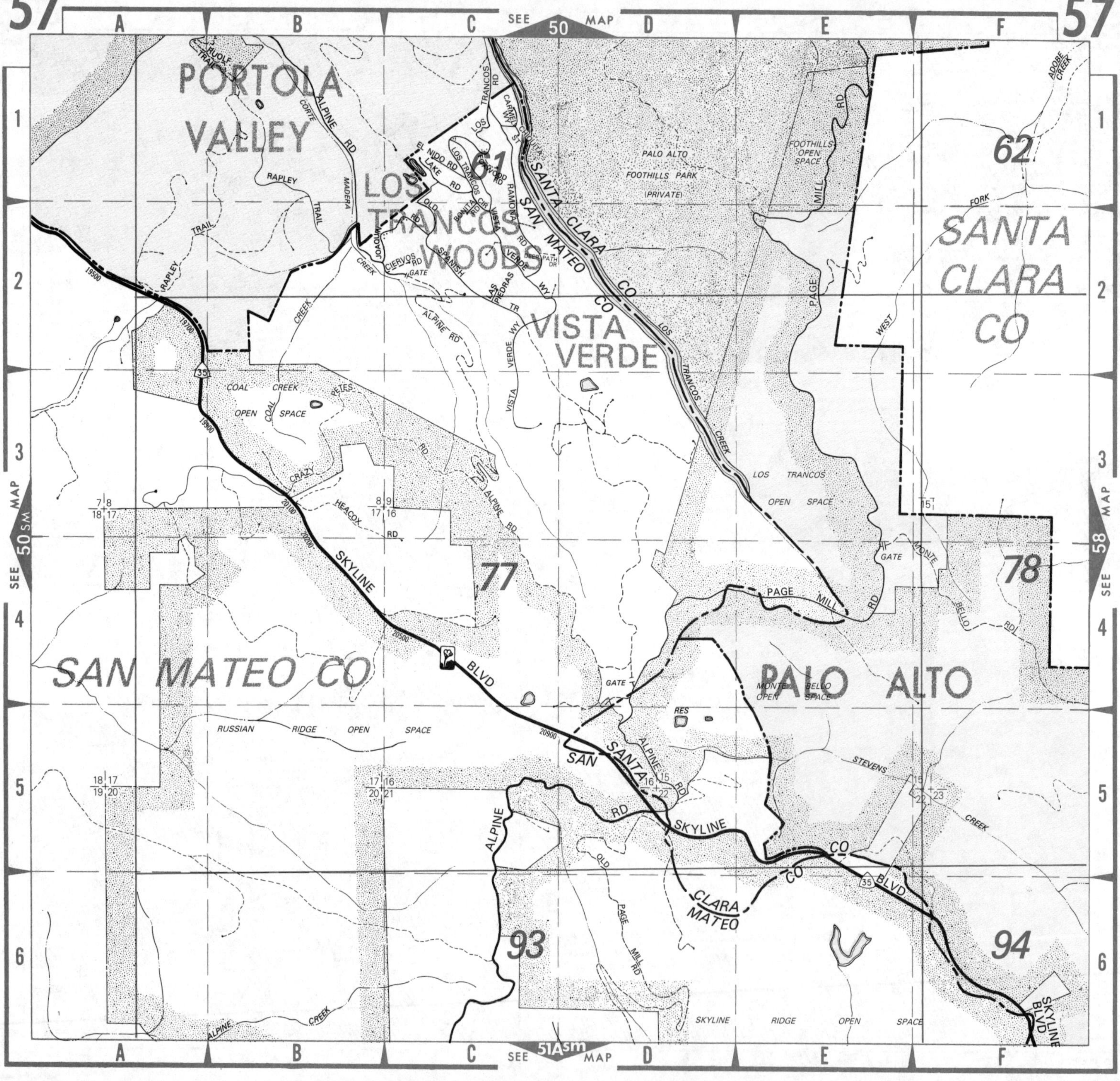

DETAIL

PORTOLA VALLEY

LOS TRANCOS WOODS

VISTA VERDE

SANTA CLARA CO

SAN MATEO CO

PALO ALTO

PALO ALTO FOOTHILLS PARK (PRIVATE)

FOOTHILLS OPEN SPACE

COAL CREEK OPEN SPACE

LOS TRANCOS OPEN SPACE

MONTE BELLO OPEN SPACE

RUSSIAN RIDGE OPEN SPACE

SKYLINE RIDGE OPEN SPACE

WOLF TRAIL

ALPINE RD

CORTE MADERA TRAIL

RAPLEY TRAIL

EL NIDO RD

LAKE RD

LOS TRANCOS RD

LOS TRANCOS CIR

OLD SPANISH TR

BONITA RD

VISTA VERDE WY

RAMONA RD

ARROYO

CIERVOS RD

CARMEL WY

ST

CREEK

GATE

LAS PIEDRAS TR

PATH DR

SAN MATEO SANTA CLARA CO

LOS TRANCOS CREEK

PAGE MILL RD

WEST FORK

ADOBE CREEK

PETES

CRAZY

HEACOX RD

SKYLINE BLVD

MONTE BELLO RD

RES

STEVENS CREEK

OLD PAGE MILL RD

ALPINE CREEK

35

19500 19700 19900 20100 20200 20500 20900

61 62 77 78 93 94

1 2 3 4 5 6

SEE 50SM MAP

SEE 58 MAP

SEE 51 MAP

SEE 57 MAP

SEE 59 MAP

SEE 63F MAP

SEE MAP 52

SEE MAP 58

SEE MAP 60

SEE MAP 64

A B C D E F

1 2 3 4 5 6

LOS ALTOS

SUNNYVALE

CUPERTINO

MONTA VISTA

LOS ALTOS COUNTRY CLUB

ST JOSEPHS SEMINARY

MARYKNOLL SEMINARY

RANCHO SAN ANTONIO COUNTY PARK

RANCHO SAN ANTONIO OPEN SPACE

CEMENT PLANT

HOMESTEAD HS

HOMESTEAD SQ

DE ANZA COLLEGE

CUPERTINO CROSS-ROADS

MCCLELLAN RANCH PARK

BLACKBERRY FARM GOLF COURSE

DEEP CLIFF GOLF COURSE

STEVENS CREEK COUNTY PARK

MONTA VISTA HS

JUNIPERO SERRA FRWY

FOOTHILL EXPWY

STEVENS CREEK BLVD

DE ANZA BLVD

SARATOGA SUNNYVALE RD

1 ENGLISH OAK WY
2 BYERLY CT
3 SWAN OAK LN
4 WEEPING OAK CT
5 AMADOR OAK CT
6 MAJESTIC OAK WY
7 BERKSHIRE CT
8 WESTMINSTER CT

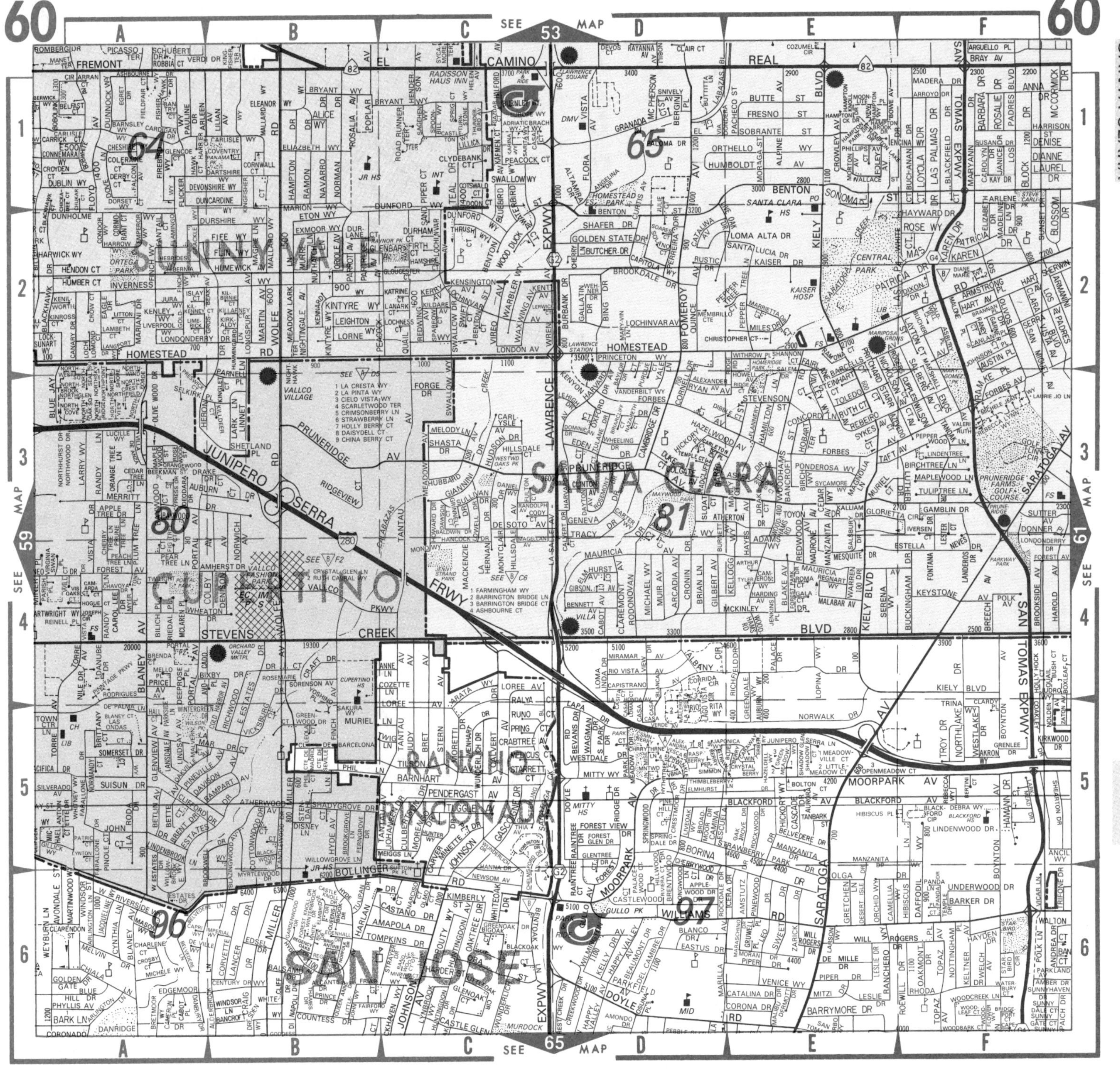

COPYRIGHT © 1991 BY Thomas Bros. Maps

SEE 54 MAP

A B C D E F

1 2 3 4 5 6

SANTA CLARA

SAN JOSE

SAN JOSE INTERNATIONAL AIRPORT

GENERAL AVIATION TERMINAL

UNIVERSITY OF SANTA CLARA

SANTA CLARA CATHOLIC CEM

MISSION CITY MEMORIAL PARK CEM

PRUNERIDGE FARMS GOLF COURSE

CARMELITE MONASTERY

VALLEY FAIR

TOWN & COUNTRY VILLAGE

WINCHESTER MYSTERY HOUSE

ROSICRUCIAN MUS & PLAN

BELLARMINE COLLEGE PREP

J LOHR WINERY

CALTRAIN STA

SAN JOSE CITY COLLEGE

SANTA CLARA VALLEY MEDICAL CTR

SAN JOSE CLUB

EL CAMINO REAL

STEVENS CREEK BLVD

SAN CARLOS

ROUTE 17 FRWY

SINCLAIR FRWY

SW EXPWY

THE ALAMEDA

COLEMAN AV

BASCOM AV

WINCHESTER BLVD

SEE PAGE K

SEE 60 MAP

SEE 62 MAP

SEE 66 MAP

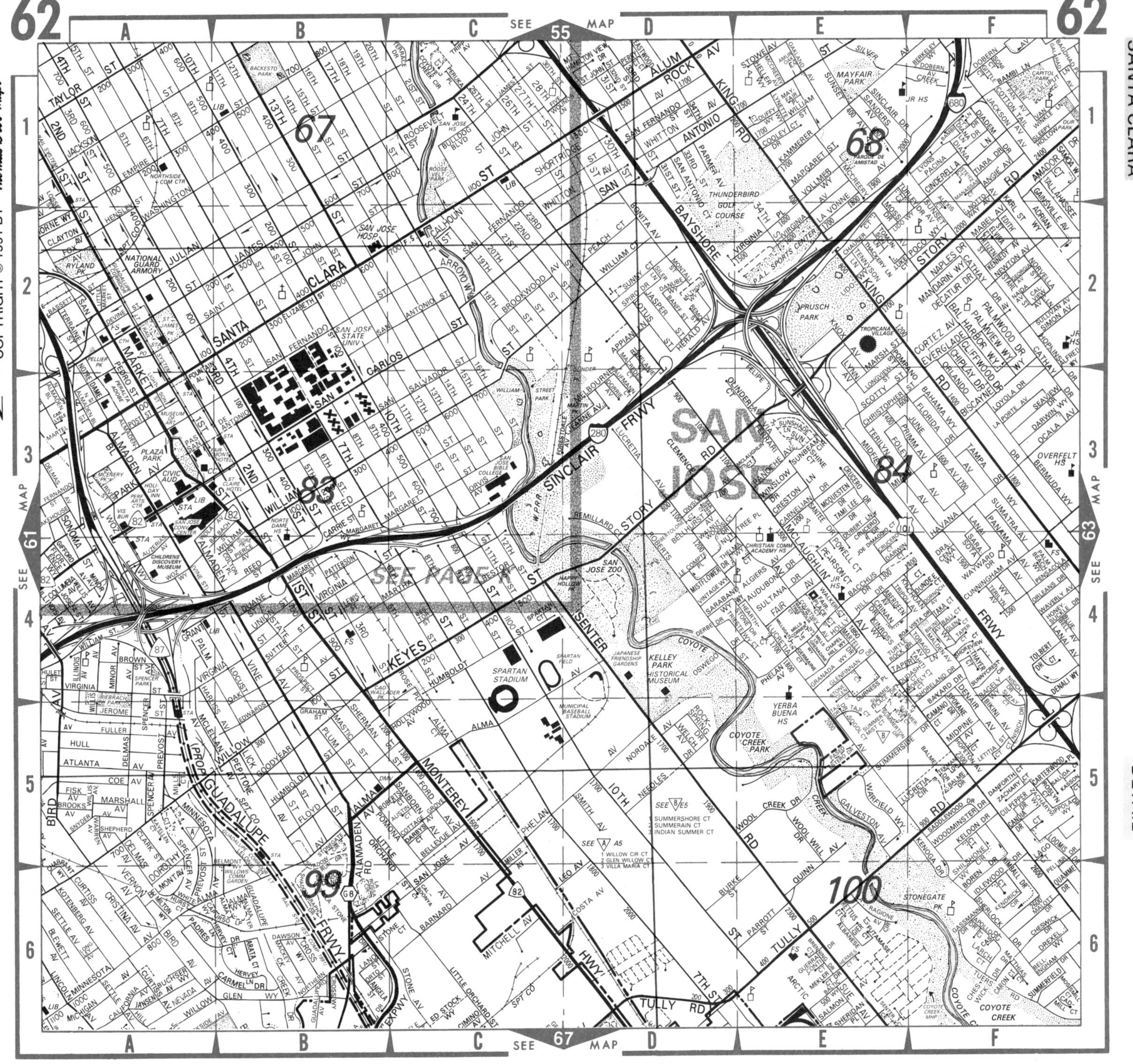

SEE MAP 55
SAN JOSE
SANTA CLARA
DETAIL
SEE MAP 61
SEE MAP 63
SEE MAP 67
SEE PAGE K
SAN JOSE STATE UNIV
THUNDERBIRD GOLF COURSE
MAYFAIR PARK
PRUSCH PARK
SPARTAN STADIUM
MUNICIPAL BASEBALL STADIUM
KELLEY PARK
HISTORICAL MUSEUM
JAPANESE FRIENDSHIP GARDENS
SAN JOSE ZOO
HAPPY HOLLOW PK
COYOTE CREEK PARK
YERBA BUENA HS
STONEGATE PK
SINCLAIR FRWY
BAYSHORE FRWY
GUADALUPE FRWY
ALUM ROCK AV
SANTA CLARA ST
STORY RD
TULLY RD
KING RD
MONTEREY HWY
SEE B E5
1 SUMMERSHORE CT
2 SUMMERAIN CT
3 INDIAN SUMMER CT
SEE A A5
1 WILLOW CIR CT
2 GLEN WILLOW CT
3 VILLA MARIA CT

SEE 56 MAP

A B C D E F

SANTA CLARA

1 2 3 4 5 6

SEE 62 MAP

SEE 63A MAP

SAN JOSE

EVERGREEN

LAKE CUNNINGHAM

RAGING WATERS

REID-HILLVIEW AIRPORT

EASTRIDGE SHOPPING CENTER

PLEASANT HILLS GOLF COURSE

CYPRESS GREENS GOLF COURSE

MIRASSOU VINEYARDS

FOWLER CREEK PARK

GROESBECK HILL PARK

ABORN SQUARE

OVERFELT HS

MT PLEASANT HS

SILVER CREEK HS

SEE H F5

1 HERITAGE OAKS DR
2 HERITAGE OAKS CT
3 HERITAGE POINT CT

SEE F C5

1 MELNIKOFF DR
2 KLAUS DR
3 JUERGEN DR

SEE C D5

1 RENICK CT
2 WYCLIFFE CT
3 FERRUM CT
4 TRUETT CT
5 MARIST CT
6 WEYERS CT
7 CASALS CT
8 DAWES CT
9 BRANDEIS CT
10 CHESAPEAKE CIR
11 MURMAN CT

SEE G E5

1 SCOTCH HEATHER CT
2 TRUFFLE CT
3 PERIVALE CT
4 DUNWICH CT

1 EVERMONT CT
2 EVERWOOD CT

1 CANYON RIDGE DR
2 SOUTHAMPTON CT
3 SHADYHOLLOW CT
4 SUMMIT RIDGE CT

SEE A A5

1 LA BOHEME WY
2 PURITANI CT
3 PURITANI WY
4 LAKME WY
5 LAKME CT
6 TANNHAUSER WY
7 TANNHAUSER CT
8 TOSCA WY
9 TOSCA CT
10 TURANDOT CT
11 FAUST CT
12 SALOME CT
13 FRENI CT
14 FEDORA CT
15 CARMEN CT
16 MOFFO CT
17 SUZUKI CT

SEE B D6

1 ANNANDALE PL
2 DALMUIR CT
3 WALLYFORD CT

SEE D C6

1 TURNHOUSE LN
2 BOSWALL CT
3 HALBREATH CT
4 POLTONHALL CT

A B C D E F

SEE 68 MAP

DETAIL

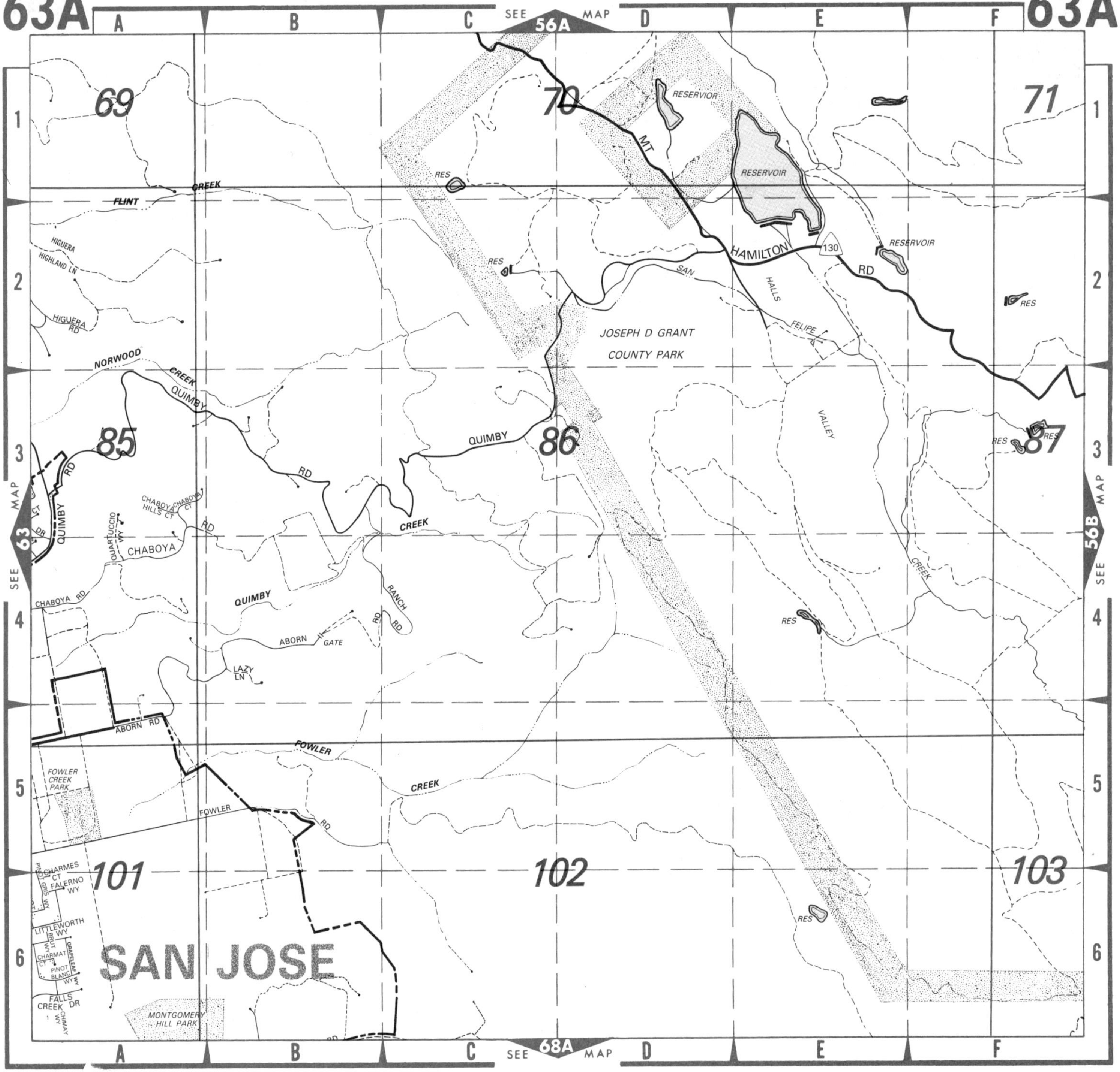

SEE 56A MAP

63A

A B C D E F

1 2 3 4 5 6

69 70 71

RESERVIOR

RESERVOIR

RES

FLINT CREEK

MT HAMILTON RD 130

RESERVOIR

HIGUERA HIGHLAND LN

HIGUERA RD

SAN FELIPE

HALLS VALLEY

JOSEPH D GRANT COUNTY PARK

NORWOOD CREEK

QUIMBY RD

85 86 87

RES

QUIMBY RD

CHABOYA HILLS CT

CHABOYA CT

QUARTUCCIO WY

CHABOYA RD

CHABOYA

CREEK

RANCH RD

CHABOYA RD

QUIMBY

ABORN GATE

LAZY LN

ABORN RD

FOWLER CREEK PARK

FOWLER

CREEK

FOWLER RD

101 102 103

CHARMES CT

PINOT GRIS WY

FALERNO WY

LITTLEWORTH WY

BRUT WY

GRAPELEAF WY

CHARMAT CT

PINOT BLANC WY

FALLS CREEK DR

CHIMAY WY

SAN JOSE

MONTGOMERY HILL PARK

RD

SEE 63 MAP

SEE 56B MAP

SEE 68A MAP

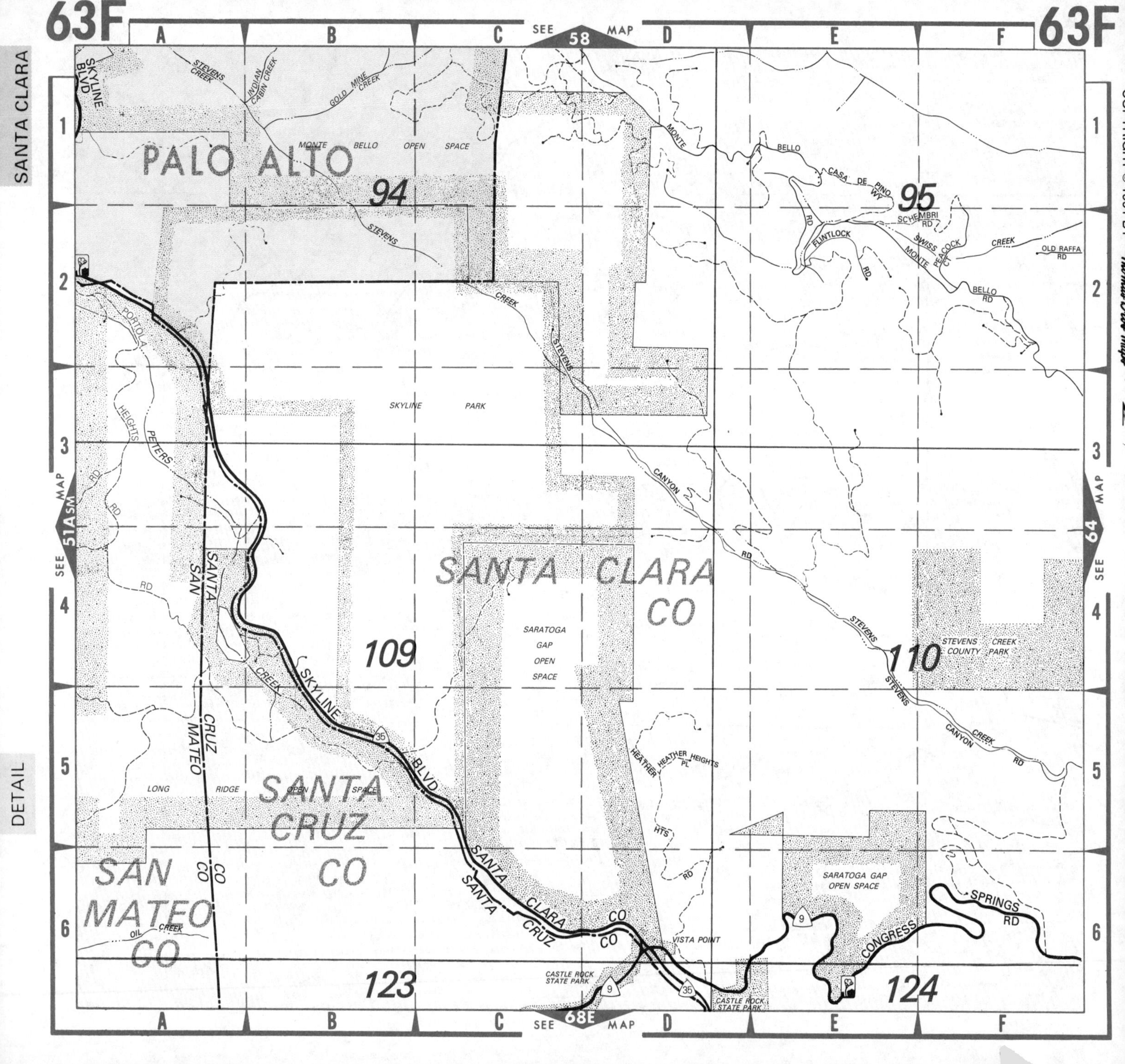
SEE MAP 58
SANTA CLARA
DETAIL
SEE MAP 51ASM
SEE MAP 64
SEE MAP 68E
PALO ALTO
94
95
109
110
123
124
SANTA CLARA CO
SANTA CRUZ CO
SAN MATEO CO
SKYLINE BLVD
STEVENS CREEK
INDIAN CABIN CREEK
GOLD MINE CREEK
MONTE BELLO OPEN SPACE
MONTE BELLO RD
CASA DE PINO WY
SCHEMBRI RD
FLINTLOCK RD
SWISS PEACOCK CT
OLD RAFFA RD
SKYLINE PARK
PORTOLA HEIGHTS RD
PETERS RD
STEVENS CANYON RD
SARATOGA GAP OPEN SPACE
STEVENS CREEK COUNTY PARK
STEVENS CANYON CREEK RD
HEATHER HEIGHTS PL
HEATHER HTS RD
LONG RIDGE OPEN SPACE
OIL CREEK
VISTA POINT
CASTLE ROCK STATE PARK
CONGRESS SPRINGS RD
35
9

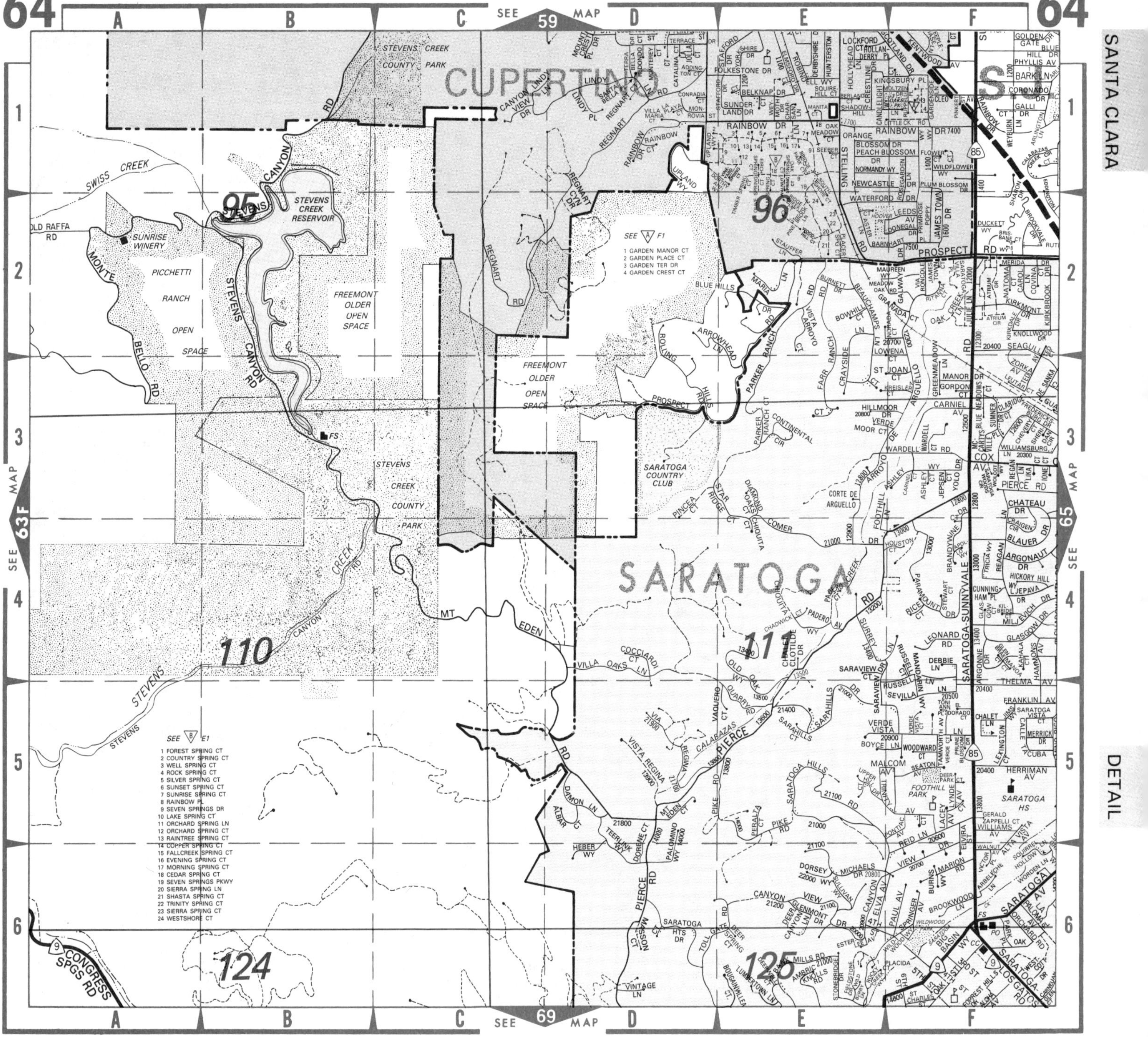

SEE 59 MAP

SANTA CLARA

DETAIL

CUPERTINO

SARATOGA

STEVENS CREEK COUNTY PARK

STEVENS CREEK RESERVOIR

PICCHETTI RANCH OPEN SPACE

SUNRISE WINERY

FREEMONT OLDER OPEN SPACE

SARATOGA COUNTRY CLUB

FOOTHILL PARK

SARATOGA HS

SEE A F1

1 GARDEN MANOR CT
2 GARDEN PLACE CT
3 GARDEN TER DR
4 GARDEN CREST CT

SEE B E1

1 FOREST SPRING CT
2 COUNTRY SPRING CT
3 WELL SPRING CT
4 ROCK SPRING CT
5 SILVER SPRING CT
6 SUNSET SPRING CT
7 SUNRISE SPRING CT
8 RAINBOW PL
9 SEVEN SPRINGS DR
10 LAKE SPRING CT
11 ORCHARD SPRING LN
12 ORCHARD SPRING CT
13 RAINTREE SPRING CT
14 COPPER SPRING CT
15 FALLCREEK SPRING CT
16 EVENING SPRING CT
17 MORNING SPRING CT
18 CEDAR SPRING CT
19 SEVEN SPRINGS PKWY
20 SIERRA SPRING LN
21 SHASTA SPRING CT
22 TRINITY SPRING CT
23 SIERRA SPRING CT
24 WESTSHORE CT

SEE 63F MAP

SEE 65 MAP

SEE 69 MAP

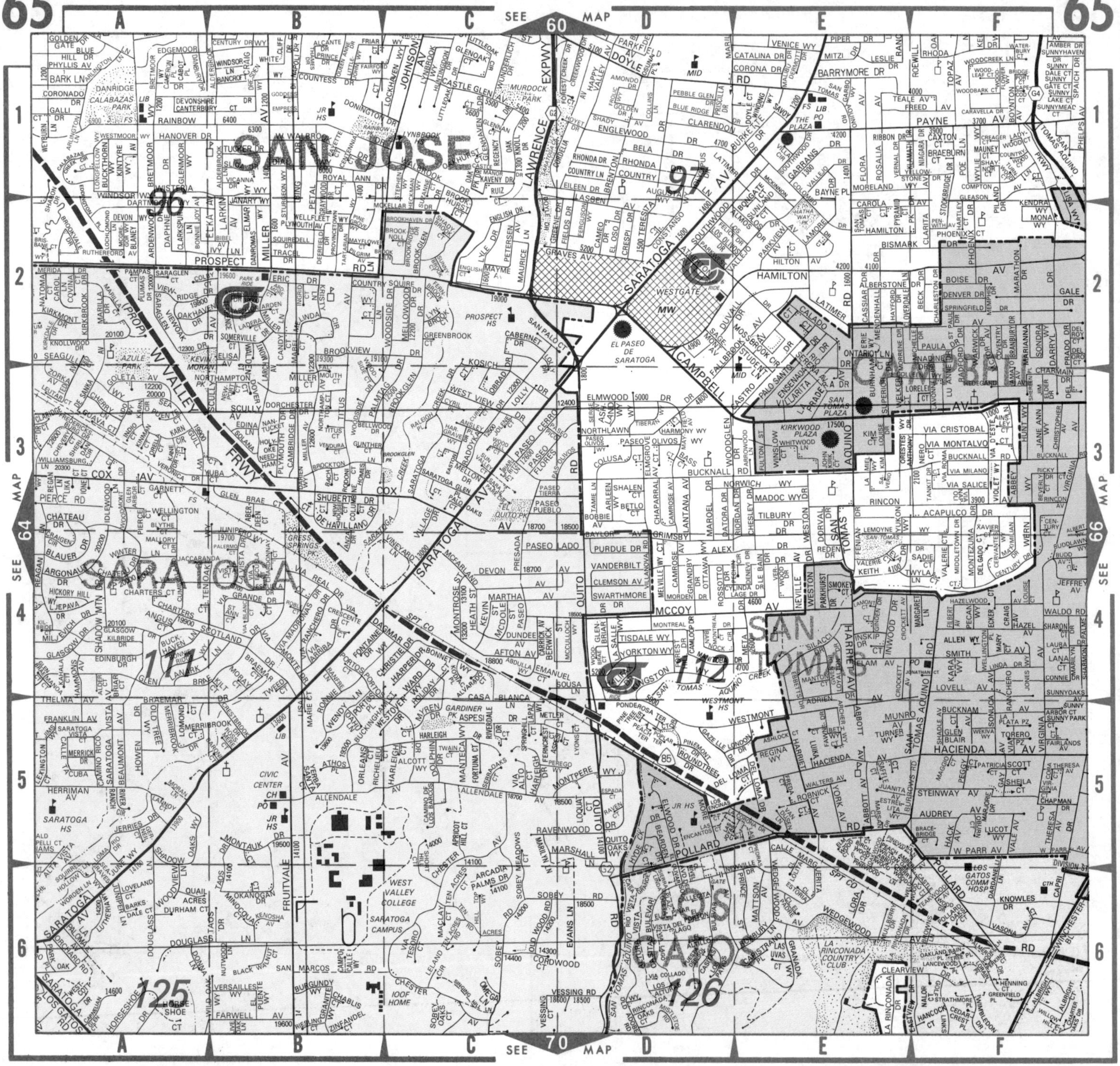

A B C D E F

SEE MAP 60

SEE MAP 64

SEE MAP 66

SEE MAP 70

1 2 3 4 5 6

SAN JOSE

SARATOGA

CAMBRIAN

SAN TOMAS

LOS GATOS

96 97 111 112 125 126

LAWRENCE EXPWY

SARATOGA AV

CAMPBELL AV

W VALLEY FRWY

SAN TOMAS AQUINO RD

QUITO RD

PROSPECT RD

COX AV

WESTGATE

EL PASEO DE SARATOGA

PROSPECT HS

WESTMONT HS

SARATOGA HS

WEST VALLEY COLLEGE SARATOGA CAMPUS

CIVIC CENTER

IOOF HOME

LA RINCONADA COUNTRY CLUB

LOS GATOS COMM HOSP

CALABAZAS PARK

AZULE PARK

GARDINER PK

CONGRESS SPRINGS PK

SPT CO

COPYRIGHT © 1991 BY Thomas Bros. Maps

SEE 62 MAP
SEE 66 MAP
SEE 68 MAP
SEE 72 MAP

A B C D E F

1 2 3 4 5 6

SAN JOSE

99 100 114 115 128 129

COUNTY FAIRGROUNDS

OAK HILL CEMETERY

COYOTE CREEK PARK

RIVER GLEN PARK

RAOUL WALLENBERG PARK

WILLOW GLEN

WILLOW GLEN HS

ANDREW HILL HS

GUNDERSON HS

SEVEN TREES

SEE A F2
1 GROTH PL
2 GROTH DR
3 GROTH CT
4 SIEBER WY
5 SIEBER CT
6 SIEBER PL
7 SHOFNER PL
8 LEAFWOOD LN
9 CARPENTIER WY

1 HEATHER RIDGE CT
2 PHEASANT RIDGE WY
3 MOUNTAIN SPRINGS DR
4 ELK RIDGE WY

SEE B E4
1 MEADOWSIDE CT
2 GOLDEN LEAF CT
3 SHADOW WOOD CT

1 PINTO RIV CT
2 DURANGO RIV CT
3 JOSEPH SPECIALE CT

1 CLAYCOMB CT
2 ODYSSEY CT
3 ILLIAD CT
4 ROBERTSVILLE CT
5 MARLENE CT
6 NORMA JEAN WY

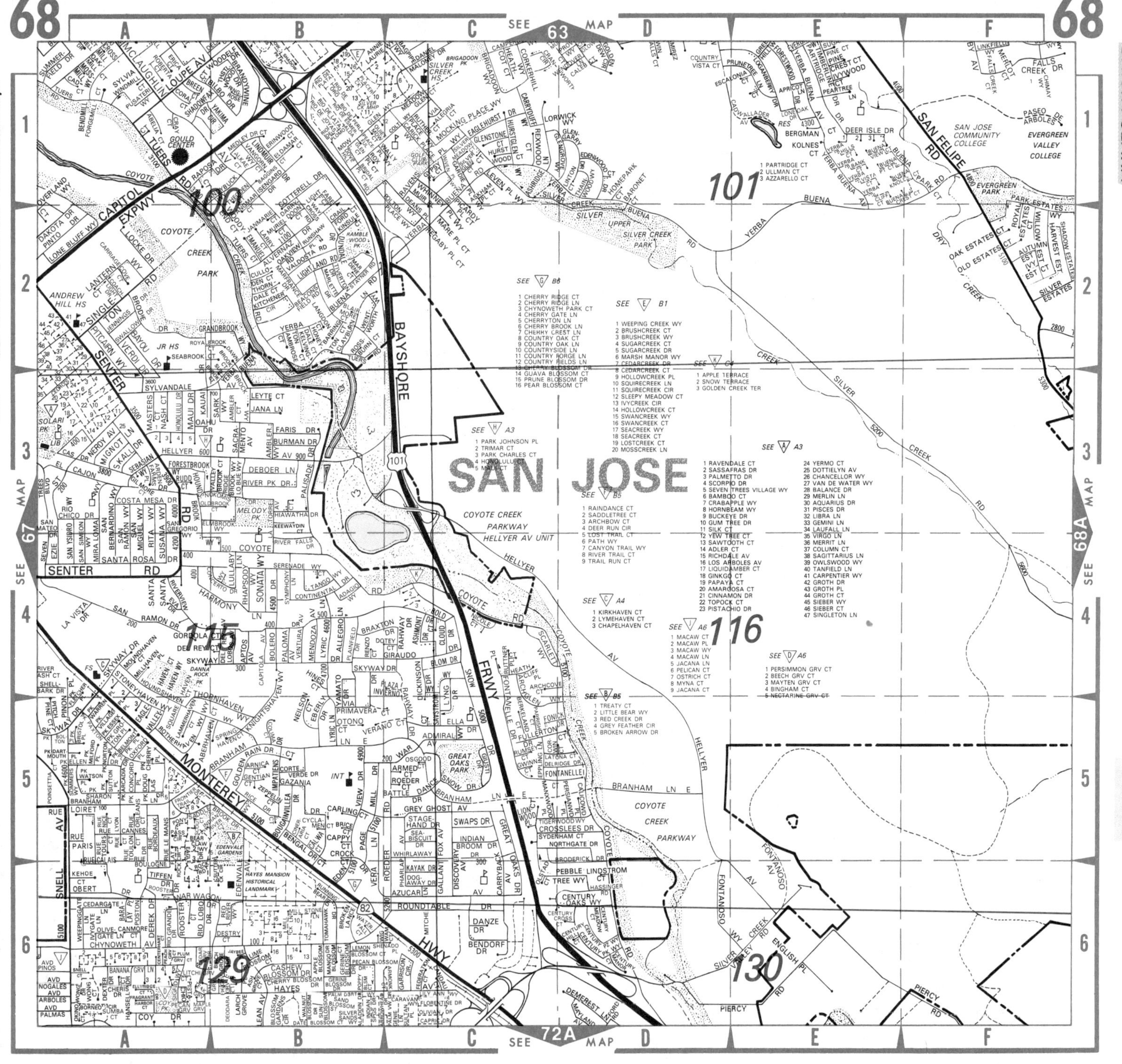

68
SANTA CLARA
DETAIL
SEE 63 MAP
SEE 72A MAP
SEE 67 MAP
SEE 68A MAP
A
B
C
D
E
F
1
2
3
4
5
6
SAN JOSE
100
101
115
116
129
130
COYOTE CREEK PARK
COYOTE CREEK PARKWAY HELLYER AV UNIT
COYOTE CREEK PARKWAY
UPPER SILVER CREEK PARK
SAN JOSE COMMUNITY COLLEGE
EVERGREEN VALLEY COLLEGE
GOULD CENTER
ANDREW HILL HS
JR HS
SILVER CREEK HS
GREAT OAKS PARK
HAYES MANSION HISTORICAL LANDMARK
EDENVALE GARDENS
BAYSHORE FRWY
MONTEREY HWY
CAPITOL EXPWY
SENTER RD
SAN FELIPE RD
SILVER CREEK
SEE G B6
1 CHERRY RIDGE CT
2 CHERRY RIDGE LN
3 CHYNOWETH PARK CT
4 CHERRY GATE LN
5 CHERRYTON LN
6 CHERRY BROOK LN
7 CHERRY CREST LN
8 COUNTRY OAK CT
9 COUNTRY OAK LN
10 COUNTRYSIDE LN
11 COUNTRY FORGE LN
12 COUNTRY FIELDS LN
13 CHERRY BLOSSOM DR
14 GUAVA BLOSSOM CT
15 PRUNE BLOSSOM DR
16 PEAR BLOSSOM CT
SEE E B1
1 WEEPING CREEK WY
2 BRUSHCREEK CT
3 BRUSHCREEK WY
4 SUGARCREEK CT
5 SUGARCREEK DR
6 MARSH MANOR WY
7 CEDARCREEK DR
8 CEDARCREEK CT
9 HOLLOWCREEK PL
10 SQUIRECREEK LN
11 SQUIRECREEK CIR
12 SLEEPY MEADOW CT
13 IVYCREEK CIR
14 HOLLOWCREEK CT
15 SWANCREEK WY
16 SWANCREEK CT
17 SEACREEK WY
18 SEACREEK CT
19 LOSTCREEK CT
20 MOSSCREEK LN
SEE K C4
1 APPLE TERRACE
2 SNOW TERRACE
3 GOLDEN CREEK TER
SEE H A3
1 PARK JOHNSON PL
2 TRIMAR CT
3 PARK CHARLES CT
4 HONOLULU CT
5 MAUI CT
SEE A A3
1 RAVENDALE CT
2 SASSAFRAS DR
3 PALMETTO DR
4 SCORPIO DR
5 SEVEN TREES VILLAGE WY
6 BAMBOO CT
7 CRABAPPLE WY
8 HORNBEAM WY
9 BUCKEYE DR
10 GUM TREE DR
11 SILK CT
12 YEW TREE CT
13 SAWTOOTH CT
14 ADLER CT
15 RICHDALE AV
16 LOS ARBOLES AV
17 LIQUIDAMBER CT
18 GINKGO CT
19 PAPAYA CT
20 AMARGOSA CT
21 CINNAMON DR
22 TOPOCK CT
23 PISTACHIO DR
24 YERMO CT
25 DOTTIELYN AV
26 CHANCELLOR WY
27 VAN DE WATER WY
28 BALANCE DR
29 MERLIN LN
30 AQUARIUS DR
31 PISCES DR
32 LIBRA LN
33 GEMINI LN
34 LAUFALL LN
35 VIRGO LN
36 MERRIT LN
37 COLUMN CT
38 SAGITTARIUS LN
39 OWLSWOOD WY
40 TANFIELD LN
41 CARPENTIER WY
42 GROTH DR
43 GROTH PL
44 GROTH CT
45 SIEBER WY
46 SIEBER CT
47 SINGLETON LN
SEE F B5
1 RAINDANCE CT
2 SADDLETREE CT
3 ARCHBOW CT
4 DEER RUN CIR
5 LOST TRAIL CT
6 PATH WY
7 CANYON TRAIL WY
8 RIVER TRAIL CT
9 TRAIL RUN CT
SEE C A4
1 KIRKHAVEN CT
2 LYMEHAVEN CT
3 CHAPELHAVEN CT
SEE J A6
1 MACAW CT
2 MACAW PL
3 MACAW WY
4 MACAW LN
5 JACANA LN
6 PELICAN CT
7 OSTRICH CT
8 MYNA CT
9 JACANA CT
SEE D A6
1 PERSIMMON GRV CT
2 BEECH GRV CT
3 MAYTEN GRV CT
4 BINGHAM CT
5 NECTARINE GRV CT
SEE B B5
1 TREATY CT
2 LITTLE BEAR WY
3 RED CREEK DR
4 GREY FEATHER CIR
5 BROKEN ARROW DR

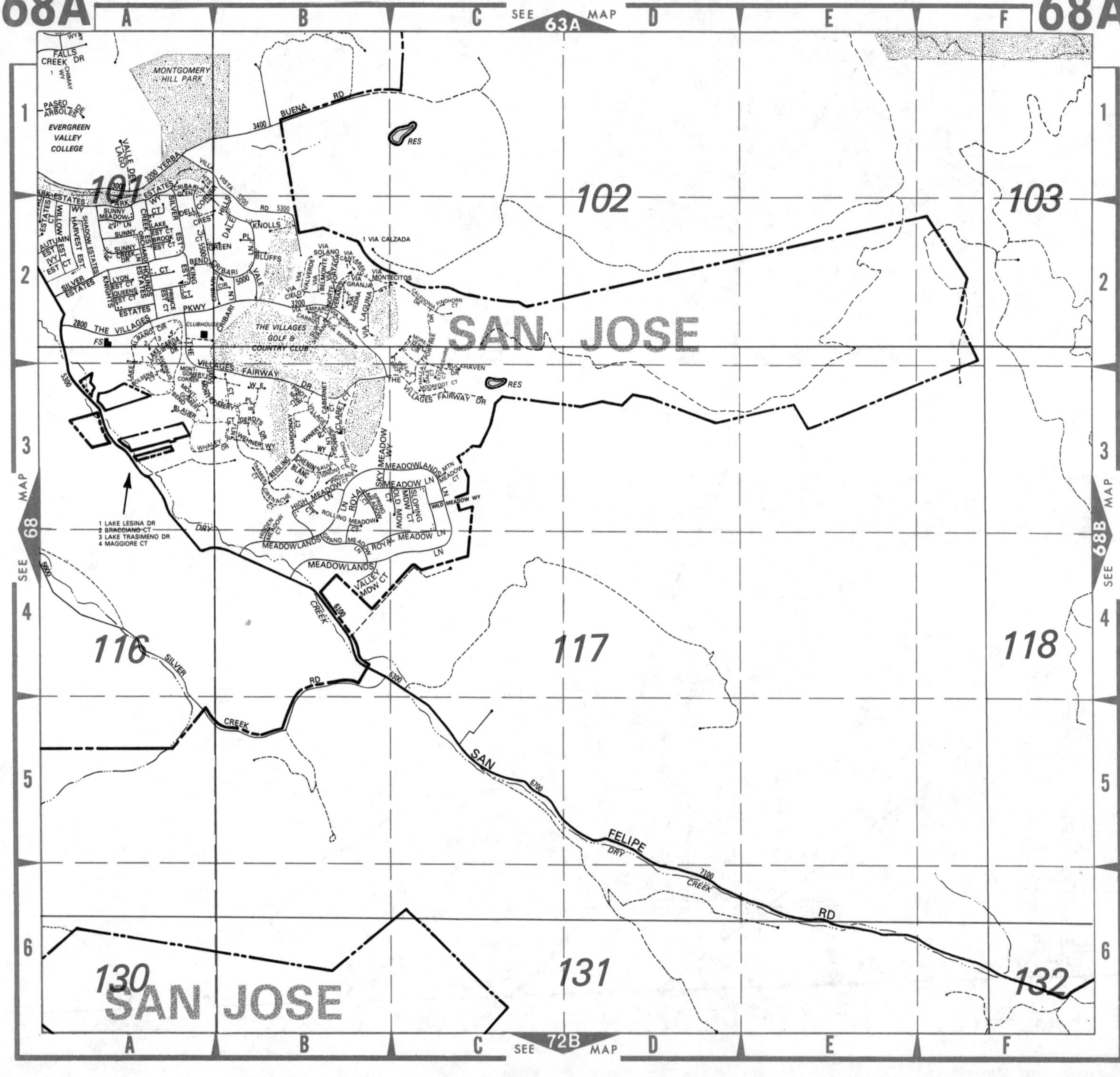
A
B
C
D
E
F
SEE 63A MAP
SEE 72B MAP
SEE 68 MAP
SEE 68B MAP
1
2
3
4
5
6
101
102
103
116
117
118
130
131
132
SAN JOSE
SAN JOSE
MONTGOMERY HILL PARK
EVERGREEN VALLEY COLLEGE
PASEO DE ARBOLES
FALLS CREEK DR
BUENA RD
3400
RES
RES
1 VIA CALZADA
VALLE DEL LAGO
3200 YERBA
VILLA VISTA
5200
RD 5300
KNOLLS
BLUFFS
VIA MONTECITOS
CALEDONIA
FINDHORN CT
THE VILLAGES GOLF & COUNTRY CLUB
CLUBHOUSE
FS
2800 THE VILLAGES PKWY
THE VILLAGES FAIRWAY DR
BUCKHAVEN
MOORFOOT CT
LAKE GARDA DR
ALBANO CIR
MONTGOMERY
BLAUER
WHALEY DR
WEHNER WY
CHARDONAY
CABERNET
REISLING
CHENIN BLANC LN
SKY MEADOW WY
MEADOWLANDS
HIGH MEADOW CT
ROLLING MEADOW
ROYAL MEADOW LN
WILD MEADOW WY
SLOPING MDW CT
OLD MDW CT
VALLEY MDW CT
GRAND MEADOW LN
1 LAKE LESINA DR
2 BRACCIANO CT
3 LAKE TRASIMENO DR
4 MAGGIORE CT
DRY CREEK
6100
6300
SILVER CREEK RD
SAN FELIPE RD
6700
7100
DRY CREEK
5300
5500

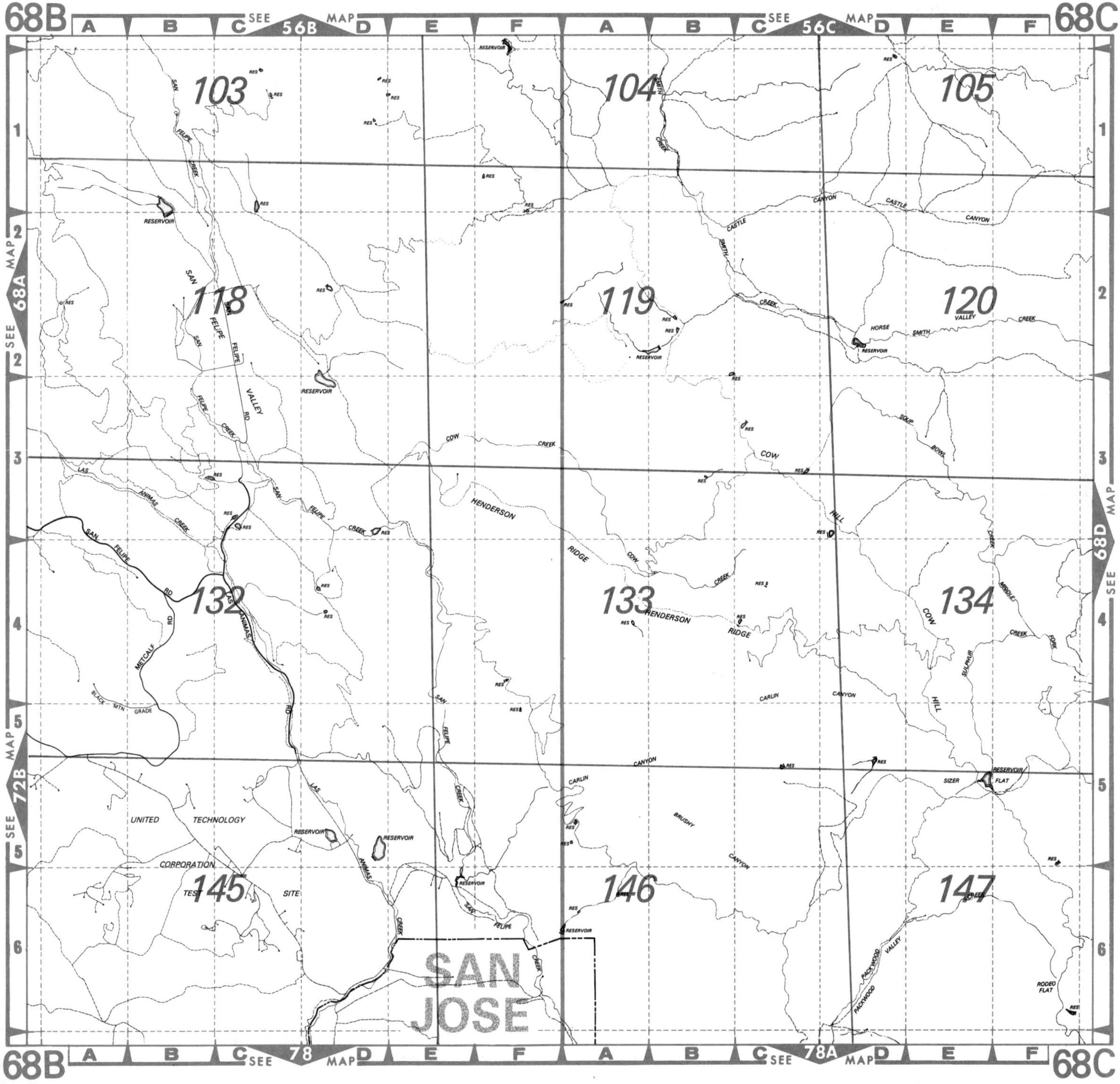

SANTA CLARA

DETAIL

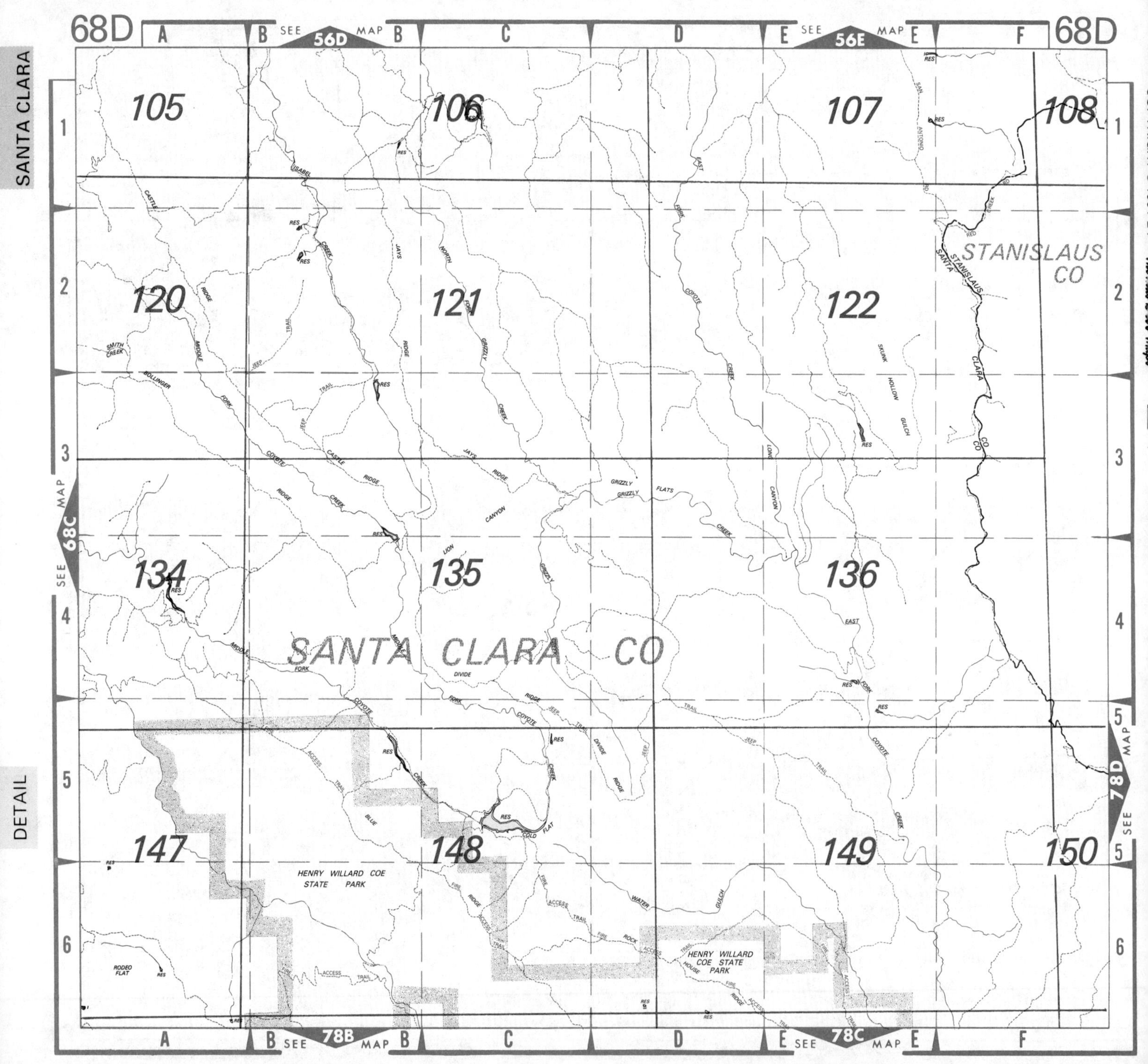

68D
SEE 56D MAP
SEE 56E MAP
SANTA CLARA
DETAIL
SEE 68C MAP
SEE 78D MAP
SEE 78B MAP
SEE 78C MAP
105
106
107
108
120
121
122
134
135
136
147
148
149
150
STANISLAUS CO
SANTA CLARA CO
HENRY WILLARD COE STATE PARK
HENRY WILLARD COE STATE HOUSE PARK

SEE 63F MAP

68E

SEE 59SM MAP

SEE 69 MAP

COPYRIGHT © 1991 BY Thomas Bros. Maps

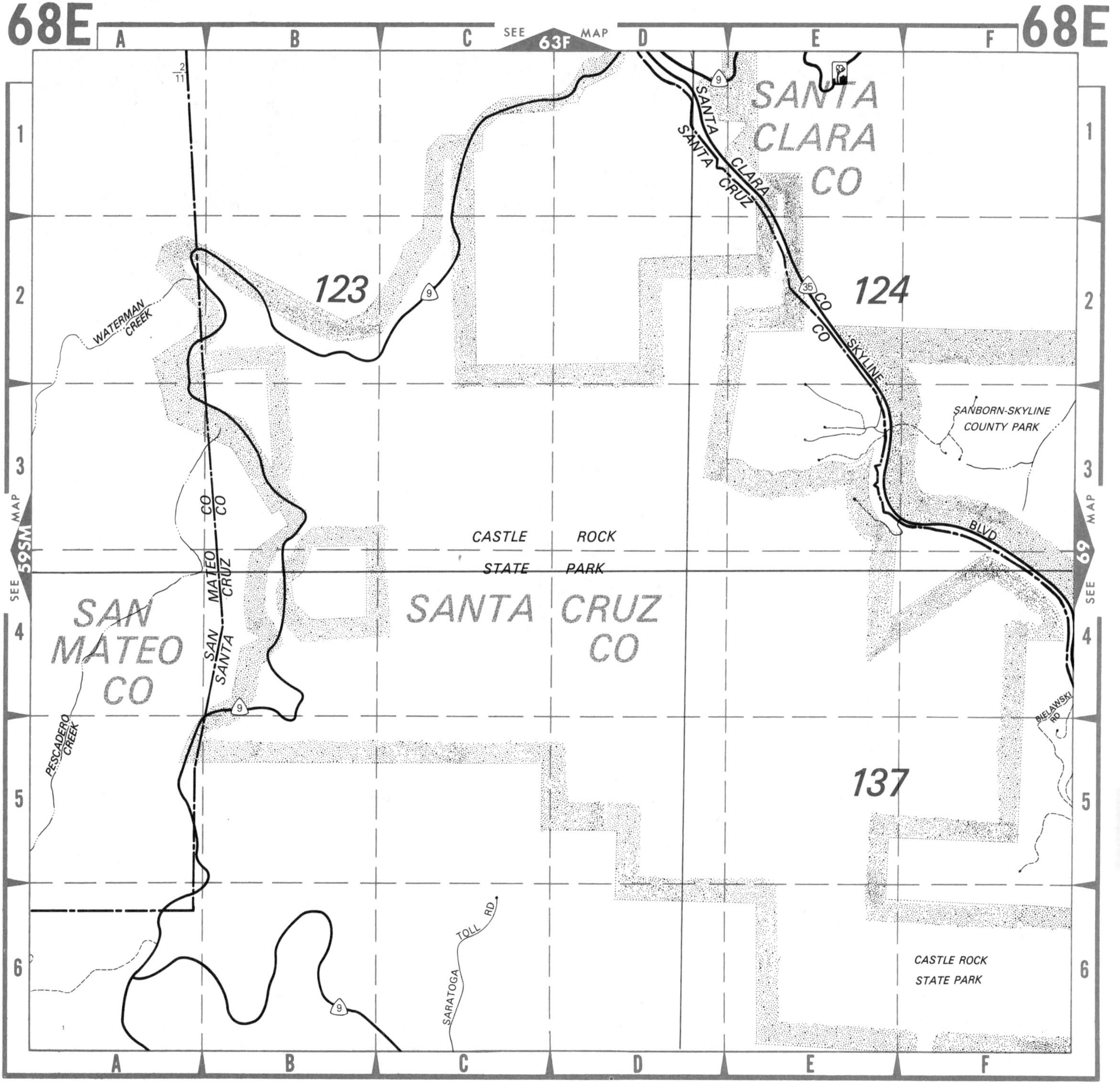

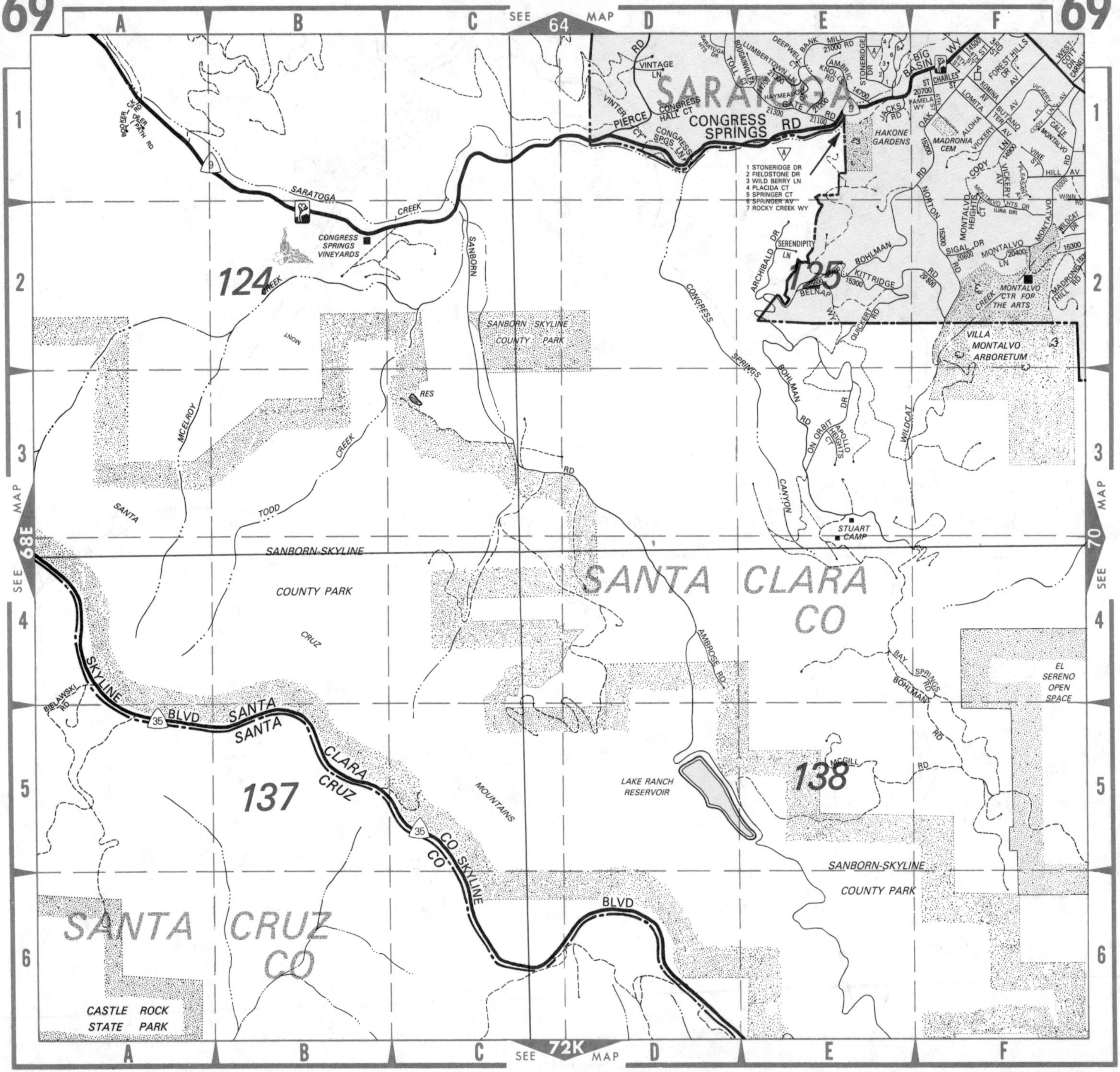

SEE 64 MAP

SEE 68E MAP

SEE 70 MAP

SEE 72K MAP

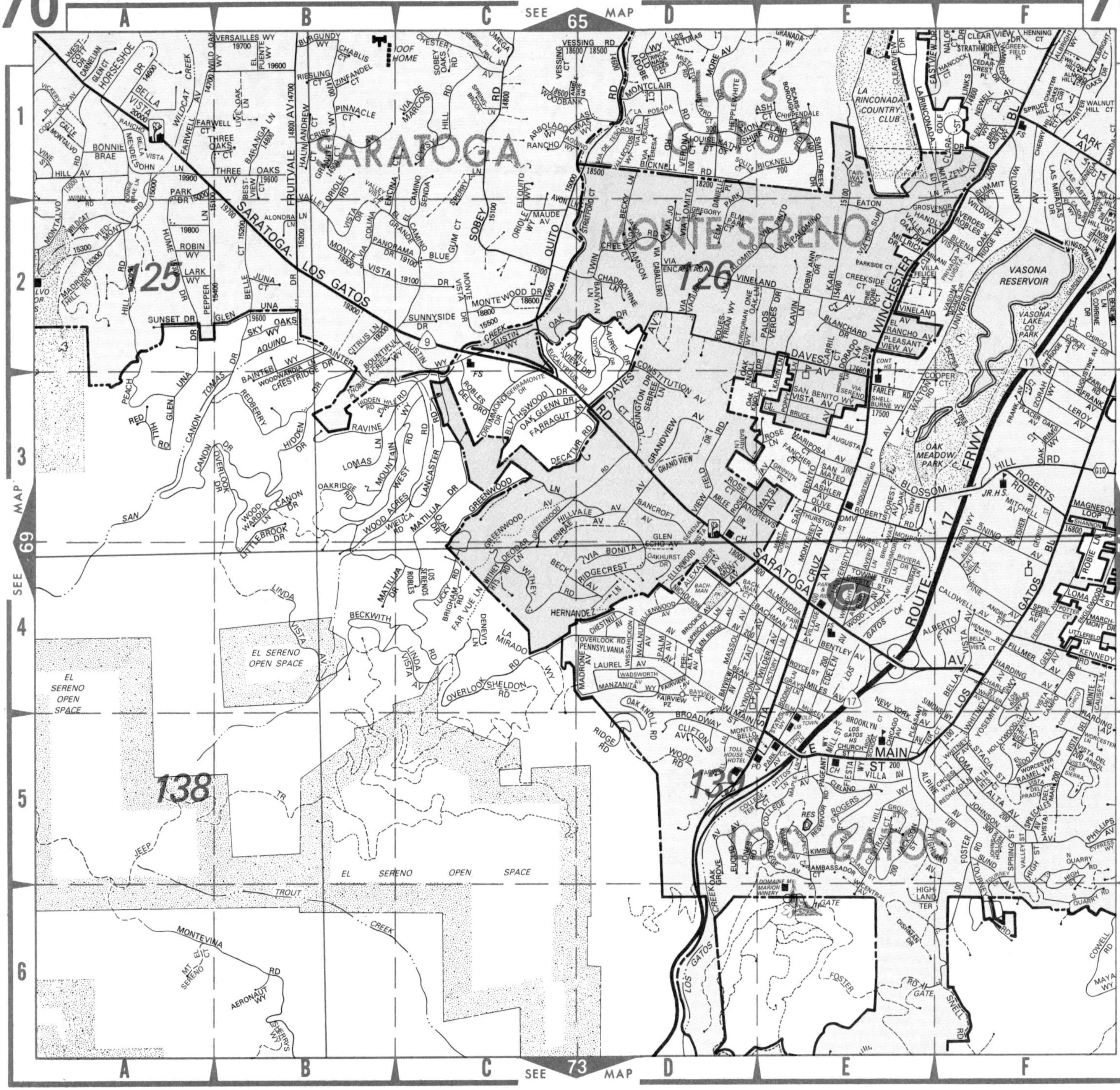

SEE 65 MAP

SANTA CLARA

SARATOGA

LOS GATOS

MONTE SERENO

125

126

138

139

VASONA RESERVOIR

VASONA LAKE CO PARK

OAK MEADOW PARK

LA RINCONADA COUNTRY CLUB

EL SERENO OPEN SPACE

SEE 69 MAP

SEE 71 MAP

DETAIL

COPYRIGHT © 1991 BY Thomas Bros. Maps

SEE 73 MAP

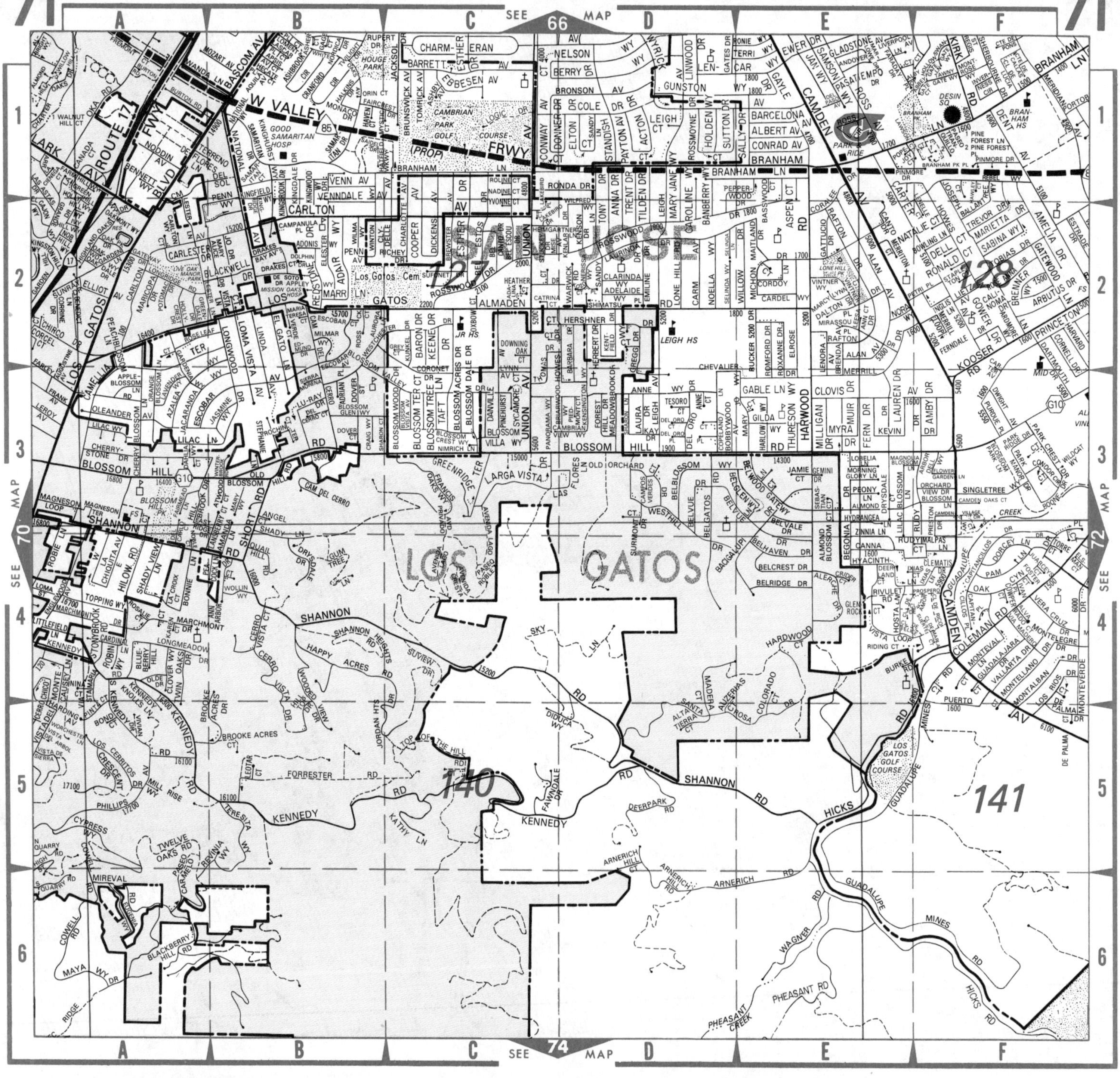

SEE 66 MAP

SEE 70 MAP

SEE 72 MAP

SEE 74 MAP

A B C D E F

1 2 3 4 5 6

SAN JOSE

LOS GATOS

127 128 140 141

W VALLEY FRWY 85
ROUTE 17 FWY
BASCOM AV
BRANHAM LN
CAMDEN AV
LOS GATOS ALMADEN RD
BLOSSOM HILL RD
UNION AV
SHANNON RD
KENNEDY RD
HICKS RD
GUADALUPE MINES RD
CAMDEN AV
HARWOOD RD
LEIGH AV
MERIDIAN AV
CARLTON AV
NATIONAL AV
SHORT RD
BLACKWELL DR
CHERRY AV
LOS GATOS BLVD
LARGA VISTA
OLD ORCHARD
BELWOOD GATEWY
ALMOND BLOSSOM LN
GUADALUPE MINES RD
SKY LN
DIDUCA WY
ARNERICH RD
WAGNER RD
PHEASANT RD
PHEASANT CREEK
COWELL RD
MAYA WY
RIDGE DR
BLACKBERRY HILL RD
MIREVAL RD
TWELVE OAKS RD
KATHY LN
TERESITA WY
PHILLIPS AV
FORRESTER RD
TOP OF THE HILL
JORDAN HTS DR
HAPPY ACRES RD
SHANNON HEIGHTS
CERRO VISTA CT
WOODED VIEW DR
DEERPARK RD
FAWNDALE DR
HARDWOOD CT
COLORADO CT
MADERA CT
BELCREST DR
BELRIDGE DR
BELHAVEN DR
PUERTO
DE PALMA
MONTEVERDE
LOS RIOS
VERA CRUZ
MONTELEGRE
SINGLETREE
PARK CREST DR
DWIGHT AV
PRINCETON
KOOSER RD
DARTMOUTH DR
AMELIA DR
ARBUTUS DR
GATEWOOD DR

GOOD SAMARITAN HOSP
CAMBRIAN PARK GOLF COURSE (PROP)
HOUGE PARK
Los Gatos Cem.
MISSION OAKS HOSP
JR HS
LEIGH HS
BRANHAM HS
DESIN SQ
PARK RIDE
MID
LOS GATOS GOLF COURSE
BLOSSOM HILL PK

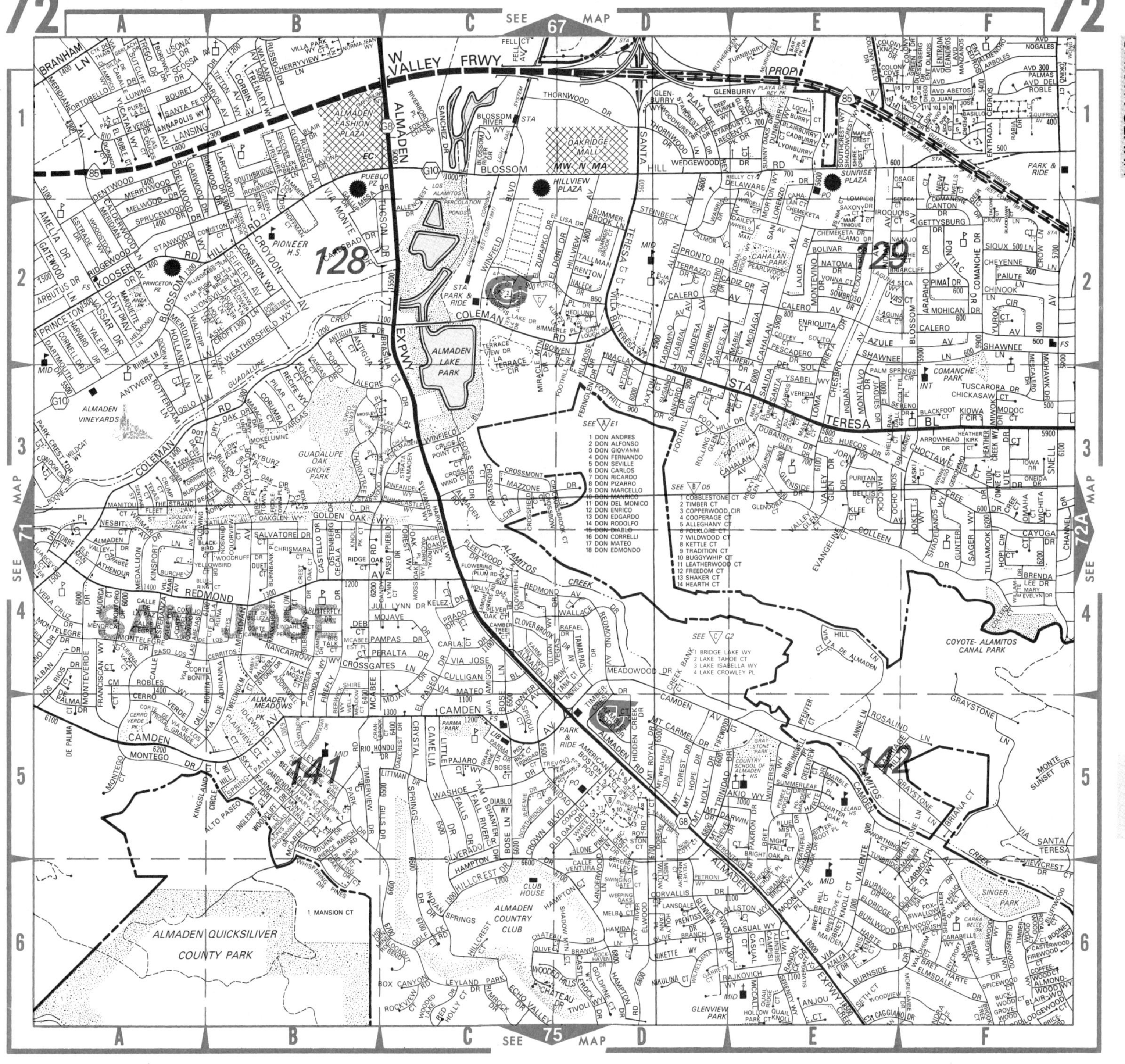
SEE 67 MAP
SANTA CLARA
DETAIL
SEE 71 MAP
SEE 72A MAP
SEE 75 MAP
W VALLEY FRWY
ALMADEN FASHION PLAZA
OAKRIDGE MALL
HILLVIEW PLAZA
SUNRISE PLAZA
PUEBLO PZ
PRINCETON PZ
PIONEER H.S.
ALMADEN LAKE PARK
ALMADEN EXPWY
BLOSSOM HILL RD
SANTA TERESA BL
COLEMAN RD
CAMDEN AV
ALMADEN VINEYARDS
GUADALUPE OAK GROVE PARK
COMANCHE PARK
SAN JOSE
ALMADEN MEADOWS
COYOTE-ALAMITOS CANAL PARK
ALMADEN COUNTRY CLUB
CLUB HOUSE
ALMADEN QUICKSILIVER COUNTY PARK
SINGER PARK
GLENVIEW PARK
LELAND HS
COUNTRY SCHOOL OF ALMADEN HS
PARK & RIDE
1 MANSION CT
128
129
141
142
SEE A E1
1 DON ANDRES
2 DON ALFONSO
3 DON GIOVANNI
4 DON FERNANDO
5 DON SEVILLE
6 DON CARLOS
7 DON RICARDO
8 DON PIZARRO
9 DON MARCELLO
10 DON MANRICO
11 DON DEL MONICO
12 DON ENRICO
13 DON EDGARDO
14 DON RODOLFO
15 DON DIABLO
16 DON CORRELLI
17 DON MATEO
18 DON EDMONDO
SEE B D5
1 COBBLESTONE CT
2 TIMBER CT
3 COPPERWOOD CIR
4 COOPERAGE CT
5 ALLEGHANY CT
6 FOLKLORE CT
7 WILDWOOD CT
8 KETTLE CT
9 TRADITION CT
10 BUGGYWHIP CT
11 LEATHERWOOD CT
12 FREEDOM CT
13 SHAKER CT
14 HEARTH CT
SEE C C2
1 BRIDGE LAKE WY
2 LAKE TAHOE CT
3 LAKE ISABELLA WY
4 LAKE CROWLEY PL
A B C D E F
1 2 3 4 5 6

SEE 68 MAP

A B C D E F

1 2 3 4 5 6

SEE D D1
1 JANUARY DR
2 FEBRUARY DR
3 MARCH DR
4 APRIL DR
5 MAY DR
6 JUNE DR
7 JULY DR
8 SUMMER PL
9 AUGUST DR
10 SEPTEMBER DR
11 OCTOBER DR

SEE C C1
1 BAGDAD WY
2 CARAVAN WY
3 INDIAN SPGS DR
4 PALM DESERT WY
5 OMAR DR
6 POPPY BLOSSOM CT
7 PECAN BLOSSOM DR
8 GARRISON CIR
9 FEDERATION CT
10 LANDAU CT

SEE B D3
1 PURPLE SAGE CT
2 PURPLE KNOLL CT
3 PURPLE GLEN DR
4 PURPLE CLIFF CT
5 PURPLE VALE CT

SAN JOSE

OAK RIDGE GOLF COURSE

SANTA TERESA COMM HOSP

PLAZA DE SANTA TERESA

SANTA TERESA GOLF COURSE

COUNTY OF SANTA CLARA GIRLS RANCH

SANTA TERESA COUNTY PARK

IBM RESEARCH LABORATORY

COYOTE CREEK PARK

LOS PASEOS PARK

CALERO PARK

LA COLINA PK

OAK GROVE HS

SANTA TERESA HS

SANTA TERESA VILLAGE

MONTEREY HWY

SOUTH VALLEY FRWY

STA TERESA BLVD

BLOSSOM HILL RD

HARRY RD

BERNAL RD

SAN JOSE

SEE 72 MAP

SEE 72B MAP

DETAIL

SEE 76 MAP

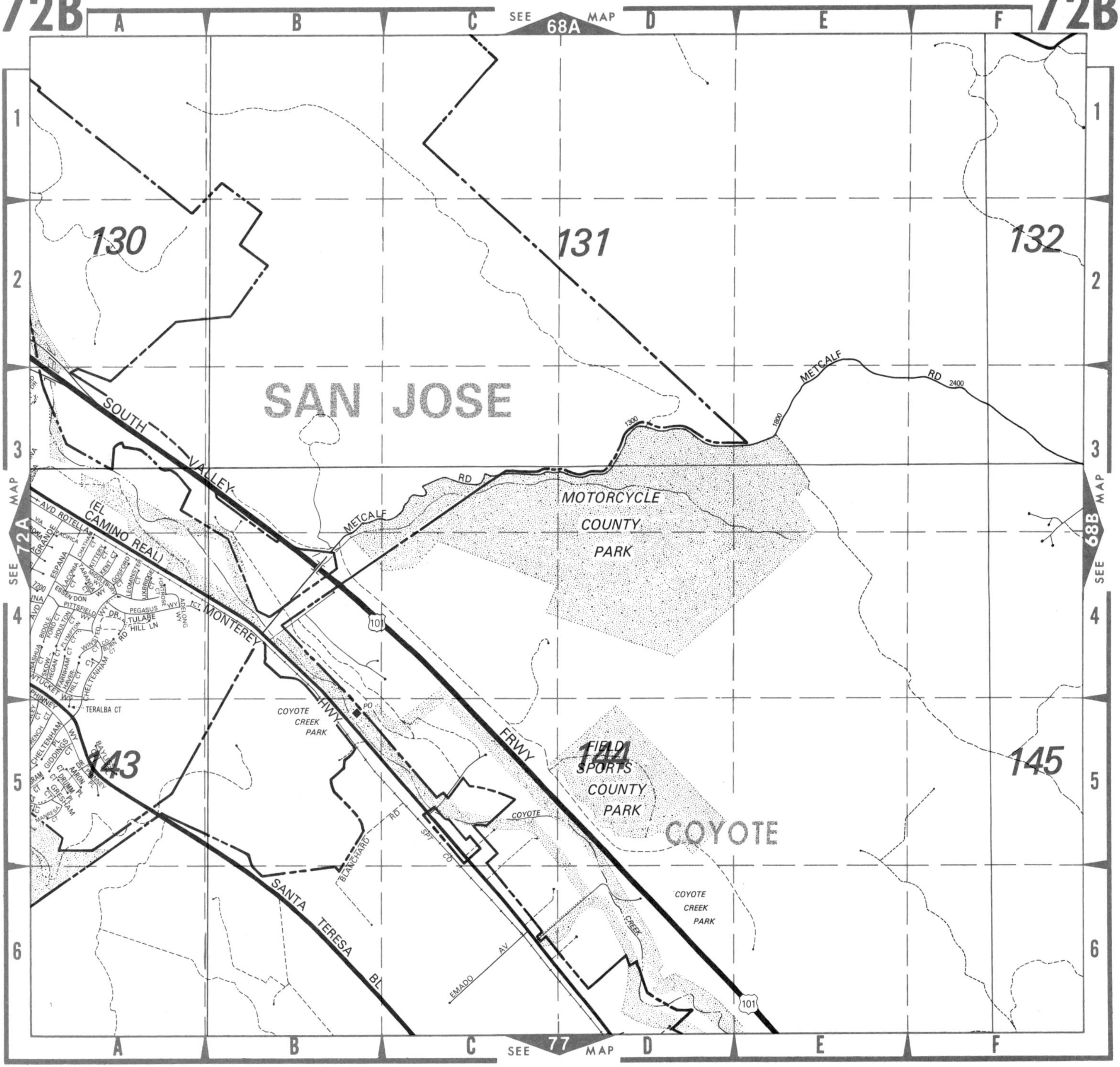

SEE 68A MAP

SAN JOSE

130

131

132

143

144

145

SOUTH VALLEY FRWY

METCALF RD

MOTORCYCLE COUNTY PARK

(EL CAMINO REAL)

MONTEREY HWY

COYOTE CREEK PARK

FIELD SPORTS COUNTY PARK

COYOTE

COYOTE CREEK PARK

SANTA TERESA BL

BLANCHARD RD

EMADO AV

SPT CO

101

SEE 72A MAP

SEE 68B MAP

SEE 77 MAP

DETAIL

72K

SEE 69 MAP
SEE 73 MAP
COPYRIGHT © 1991 BY Thomas Bros. Maps

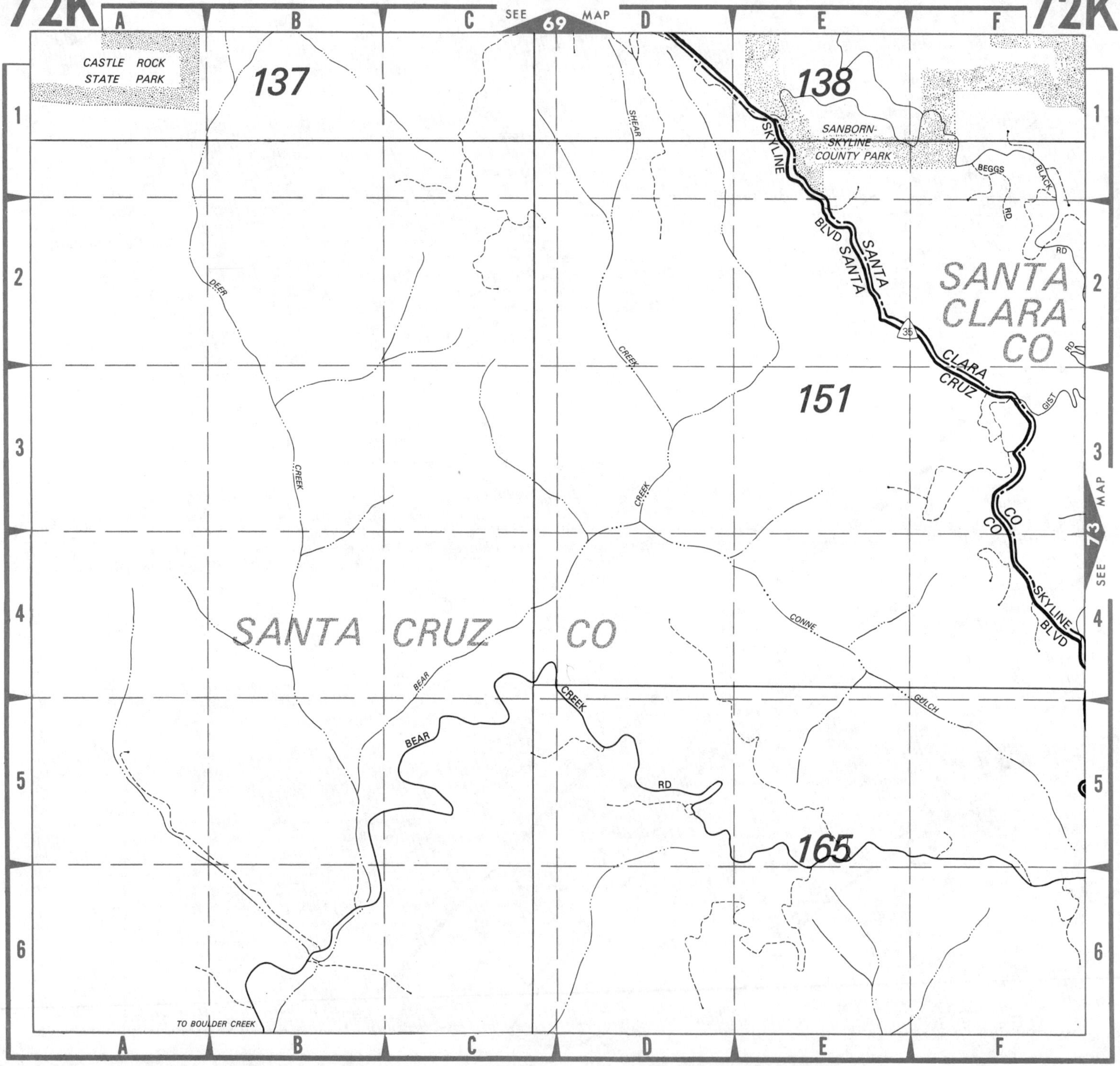

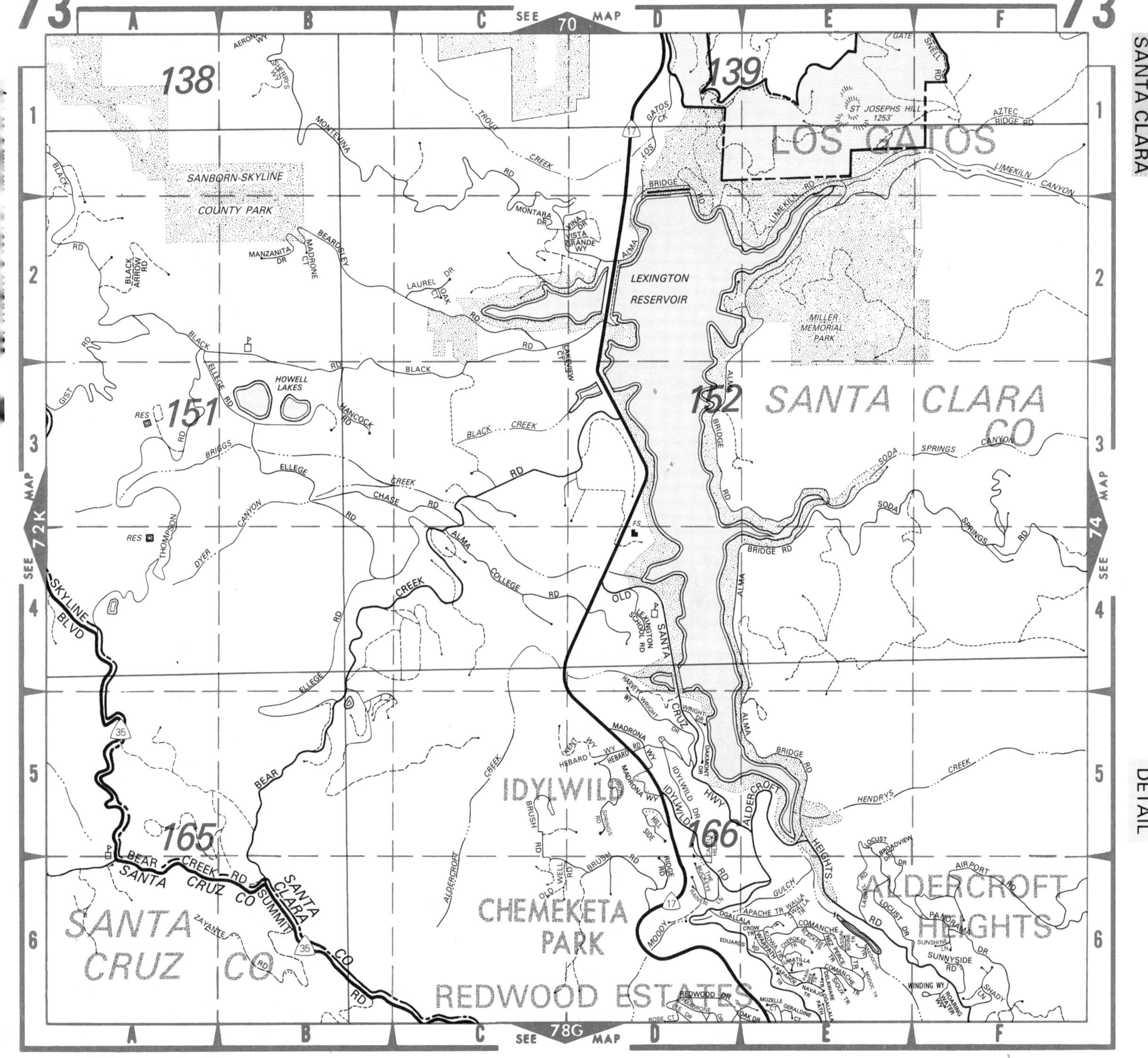

SEE 70 MAP
SEE 78G MAP
SEE 72K MAP
SEE 74 MAP
SANTA CLARA
DETAIL
138
139
151
152
165
166
SANBORN-SKYLINE COUNTY PARK
LOS GATOS
ST JOSEPHS HILL 1253'
LEXINGTON RESERVOIR
MILLER MEMORIAL PARK
HOWELL LAKES
SANTA CLARA CO
SANTA CRUZ CO
IDYLWILD
CHEMEKETA PARK
REDWOOD ESTATES
ALDERCROFT HEIGHTS
SKYLINE BLVD
SANTA CLARA SUMMIT RD
SANTA CRUZ CO
BEAR CREEK RD
ALMA BRIDGE RD
LIMEKILN CANYON
SODA SPRINGS CANYON
SODA SPRINGS RD
BLACK RD
ELLEGE RD
HANCOCK RD
BRIGGS
CHASE RD
ALMA COLLEGE RD
OLD SANTA CRUZ HWY
LEXINGTON SCHOOL RD
MONTEVINA RD
TROUT CREEK
BEARDSLEY
MADRONE CT
MANZANITA DR
BLACK ARROW RD
LAUREL DR
OAK CT
MONTARA DR
VINA DR
VISTA GRANDE WY
LAKEVIEW CT
BLACK CREEK
DYER CANYON
THOMPSON
GIST
AERON WY
SHERRYS WY
AZTEC RIDGE RD
SNELL RD
GATE
LOS GATOS CK
HENDRYS CREEK
ALDERCROFT HEIGHTS
ALDERCROFT
MADRONA RD
MADRONA WY
HEBARD RD
HEBARD WY
KENT WY
HARVEY WY
WRIGHT DR
OAKMONT DR
IDYLWILD DR
HILL SIDE
BRUSH RD
SPRINGS RD
WELL RD
OLD
RIDGE RD
MOODY
RAINIERI LN
THE BUCKEYE
GULCH
APACHE TR
WALLA WALLA TR
OGALLALA
CROW TR
COMANCHE TR
CHEROKEE TR
EDUARDS
UMATILLA TR
ARAPAHOE TR
NAVAJO TR
DELAWARE TR
SIOUX TR
NEZ PERCE TR
MODOC TR
LOCUST DR
BROADVIEW DR
AIRPORT RD
PANORAMA DR
SUNSHINE LN
SUNNYSIDE RD
SHADY LN
WINDING WY
ROARING WATER WY
REDWOOD DR
MADRONE DR
MOZELLE CT
GERALDINE CT
OAK DR
BOSE CT
ZAYANTE
RES
FS
17
35

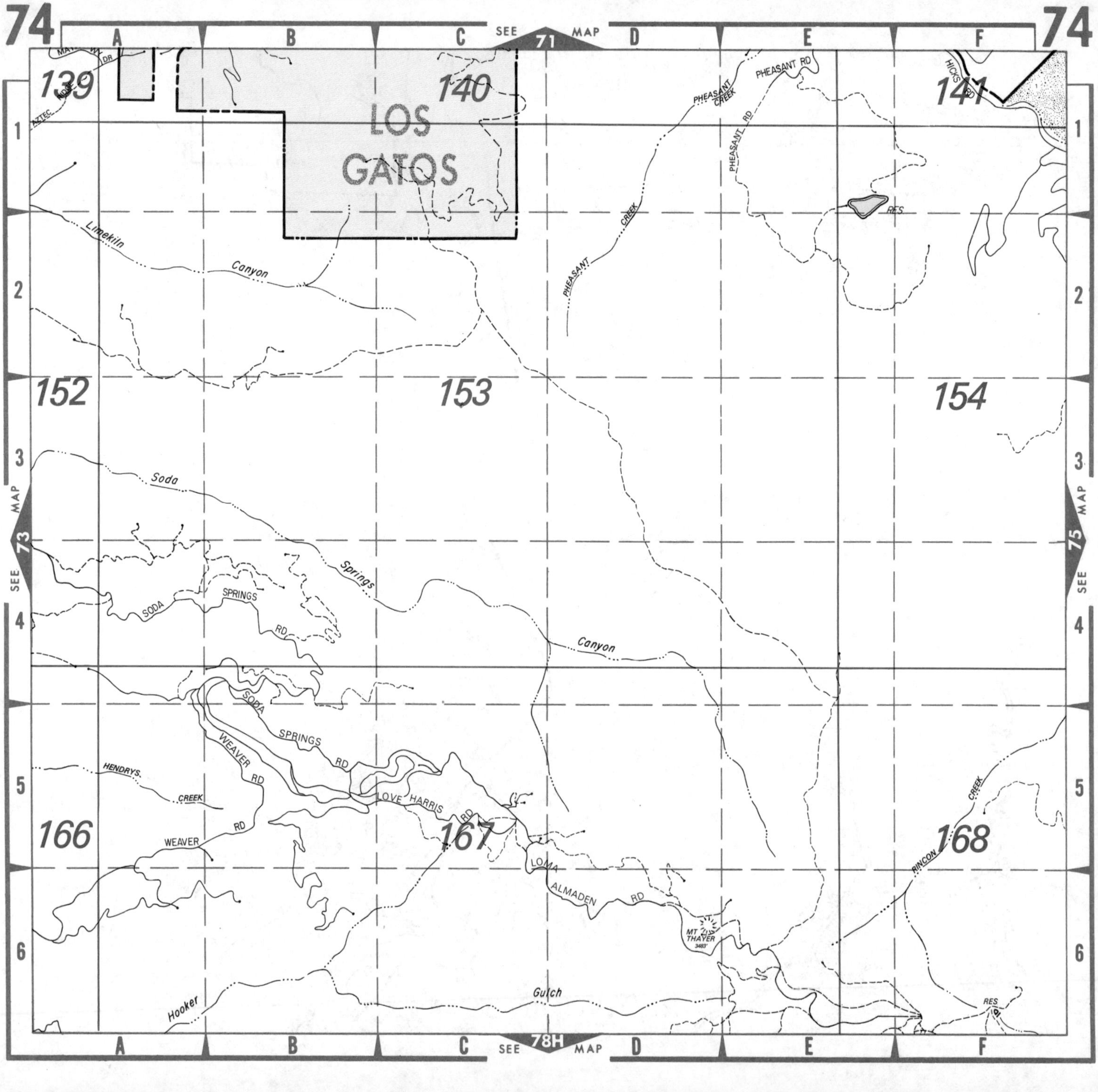

SEE 71 MAP

SANTA CLARA

DETAIL

SEE 73 MAP

SEE 75 MAP

SEE 78H MAP

A B C D E F

1 2 3 4 5 6

139 140 141 152 153 154 166 167 168

LOS GATOS

AZTEC RIDGE DR

HICKS RD

PHEASANT CREEK

PHEASANT RD

RES

Limekiln Canyon

Soda Springs Canyon

SODA SPRINGS RD

WEAVER RD

HENDRYS CREEK

LOVE HARRIS RD

LOMA ALMADEN RD

MT THAYER 3483'

RINCON CREEK

Hooker Gulch

74

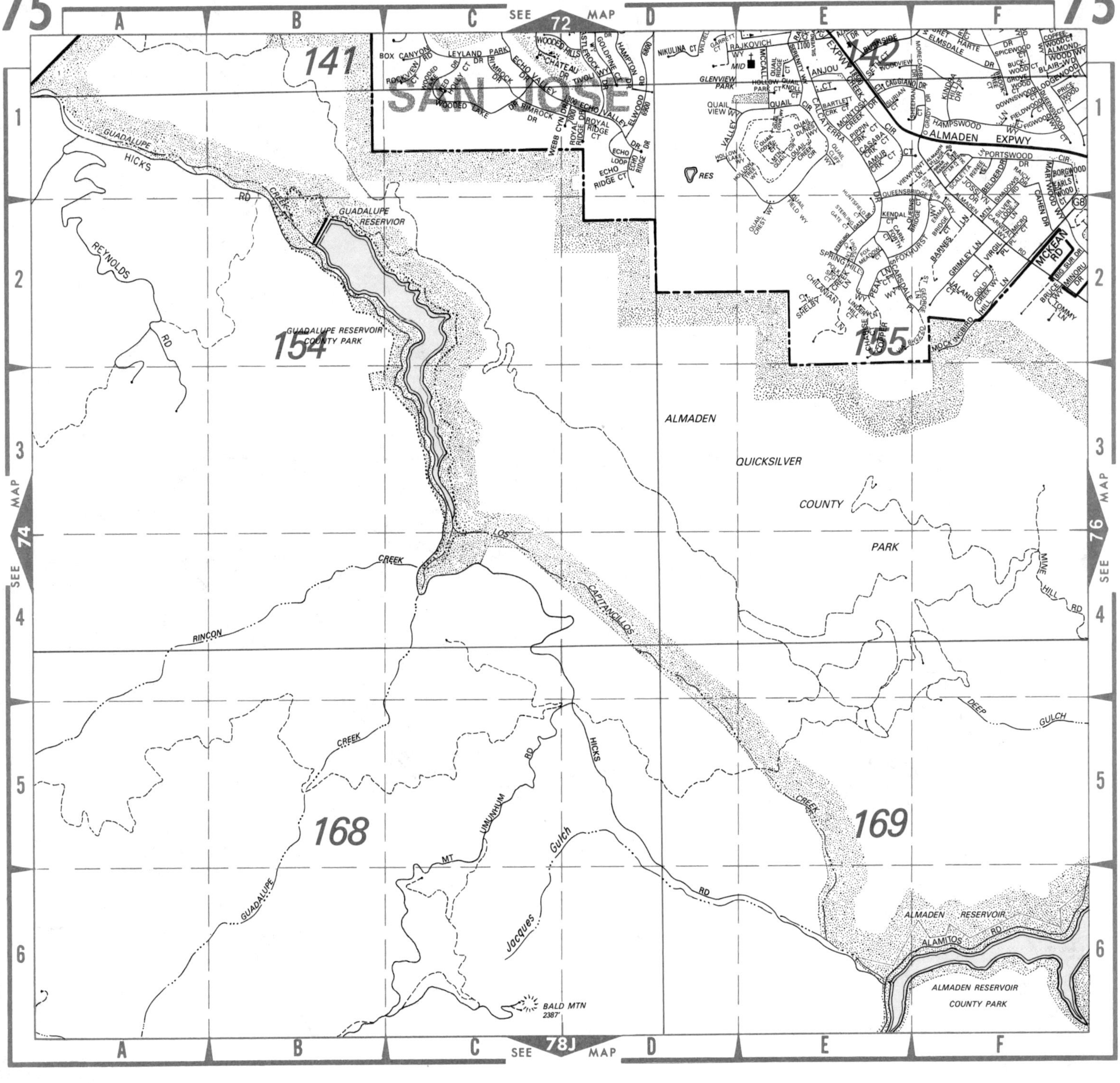

SANTA CLARA
SAN JOSE
141
142
154
155
168
169
GUADALUPE RESERVIOR
GUADALUPE RESERVOIR COUNTY PARK
ALMADEN QUICKSILVER COUNTY PARK
ALMADEN RESERVOIR
ALMADEN RESERVOIR COUNTY PARK
ALMADEN EXPWY
HICKS RD
REYNOLDS RD
GUADALUPE CREEK
LOS CAPITANCILLOS CREEK
RINCON CREEK
MT UMUNHUM RD
Jacques Gulch
DEEP GULCH
MINE HILL RD
ALAMITOS RD
MCKEAN RD
BALD MTN 2387'
SEE MAP 74
SEE MAP 76
DETAIL

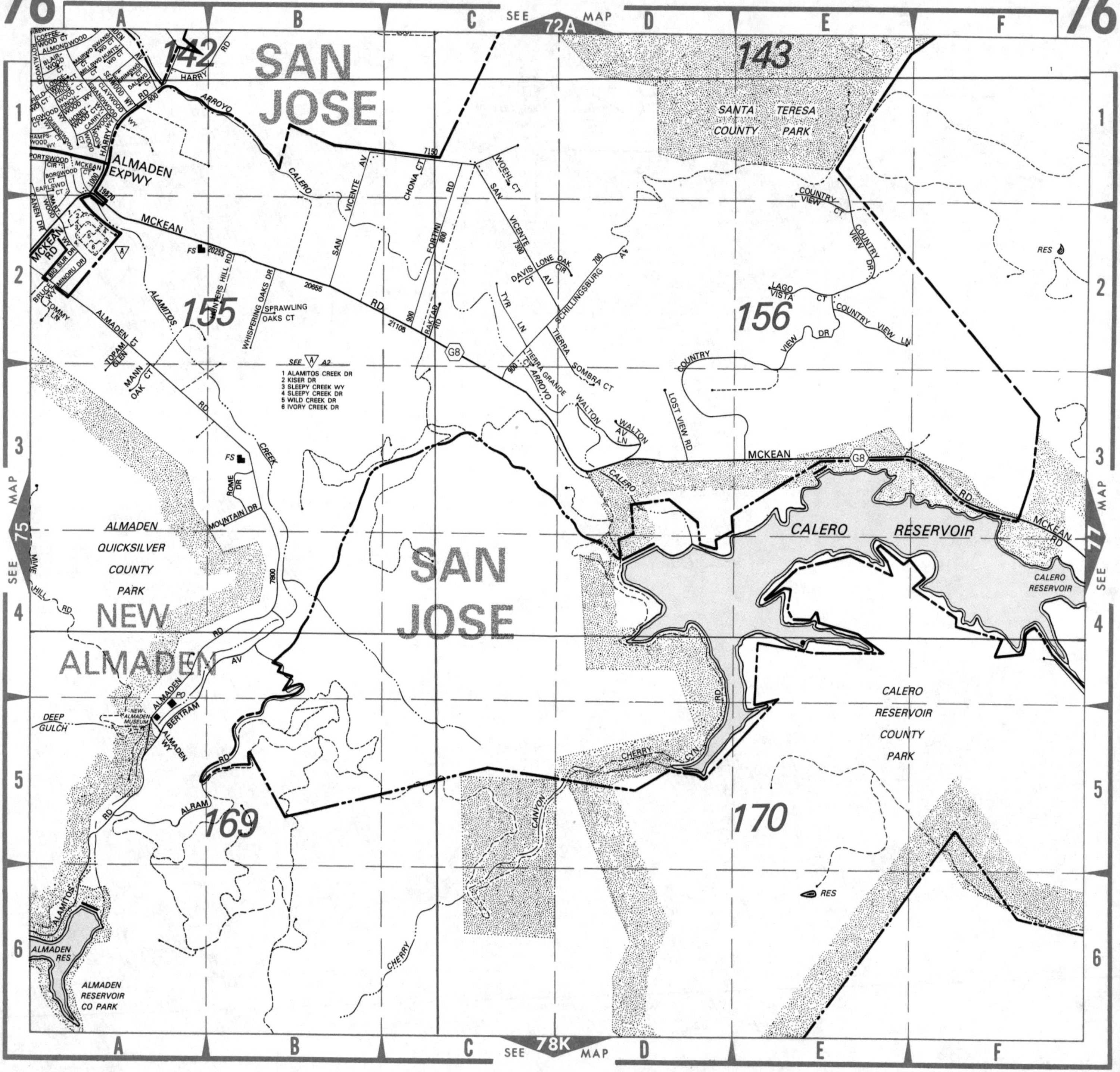

SEE 72A MAP
SEE 75 MAP
SEE 77 MAP
SEE 78K MAP

A B C D E F

1 2 3 4 5 6

SAN JOSE

142 143 155 156 169 170

SANTA TERESA COUNTY PARK

ALMADEN EXPWY

MCKEAN RD

HARRY RD

ARROYO CALERO

SAN VICENTE AV

CHONA CT

FORTINI RD

WOEHL CT

SAN VICENTE AV

COUNTRY VIEW CT

COUNTRY VIEW DR

COUNTRY VIEW LN

LAGO VISTA CT

SCHILLINGSBURG AV

DAVIS CT

LONE OAK CIR

TYR LN

TIERRA SOMBRA CT

TIERRA GRANDE CT

ARROYO

WALTON AV

WALTON LN

LOST VIEW RD

HUNTERS HILL RD

WHISPERING OAKS DR

SPRAWLING OAKS CT

BAKTAR RD

ALAMITOS CREEK

ALMADEN RD

TOPAM GLEN CT

MANN OAK CT

ROMIE DR

MOUNTAIN DR

SEE A A2
1 ALAMITOS CREEK DR
2 KISER DR
3 SLEEPY CREEK WY
4 SLEEPY CREEK DR
5 WILD CREEK DR
6 IVORY CREEK DR

G8

FS

MCKEAN RD

CALERO RESERVOIR

CALERO RESERVOIR

CALERO RESERVOIR COUNTY PARK

RES

ALMADEN QUICKSILVER COUNTY PARK

NEW ALMADEN

MINE HILL RD

DEEP GULCH

NEW ALMADEN MUSEUM

ALMADEN WY

BERTRAM

PO

ALMADEN RD

ALRAM RD

CHERRY CYN RD

CANYON

CHERRY

ALAMITOS

ALMADEN RES

ALMADEN RESERVOIR CO PARK

TOMMY LN

BRUCE WY

BIG SUR DR

MINORU DR

PORTSWOOD CIR

BORGWOOD CT

EARLSWOOD CT

CAMEN DR

COFFEEWOOD CT

ALMONDWOOD

BLAIRWOOD

FINCHWOOD CT

CLAYWOOD

FIGWOOD

RAMPSWOOD

HONEYWOOD

CARRYWOOD

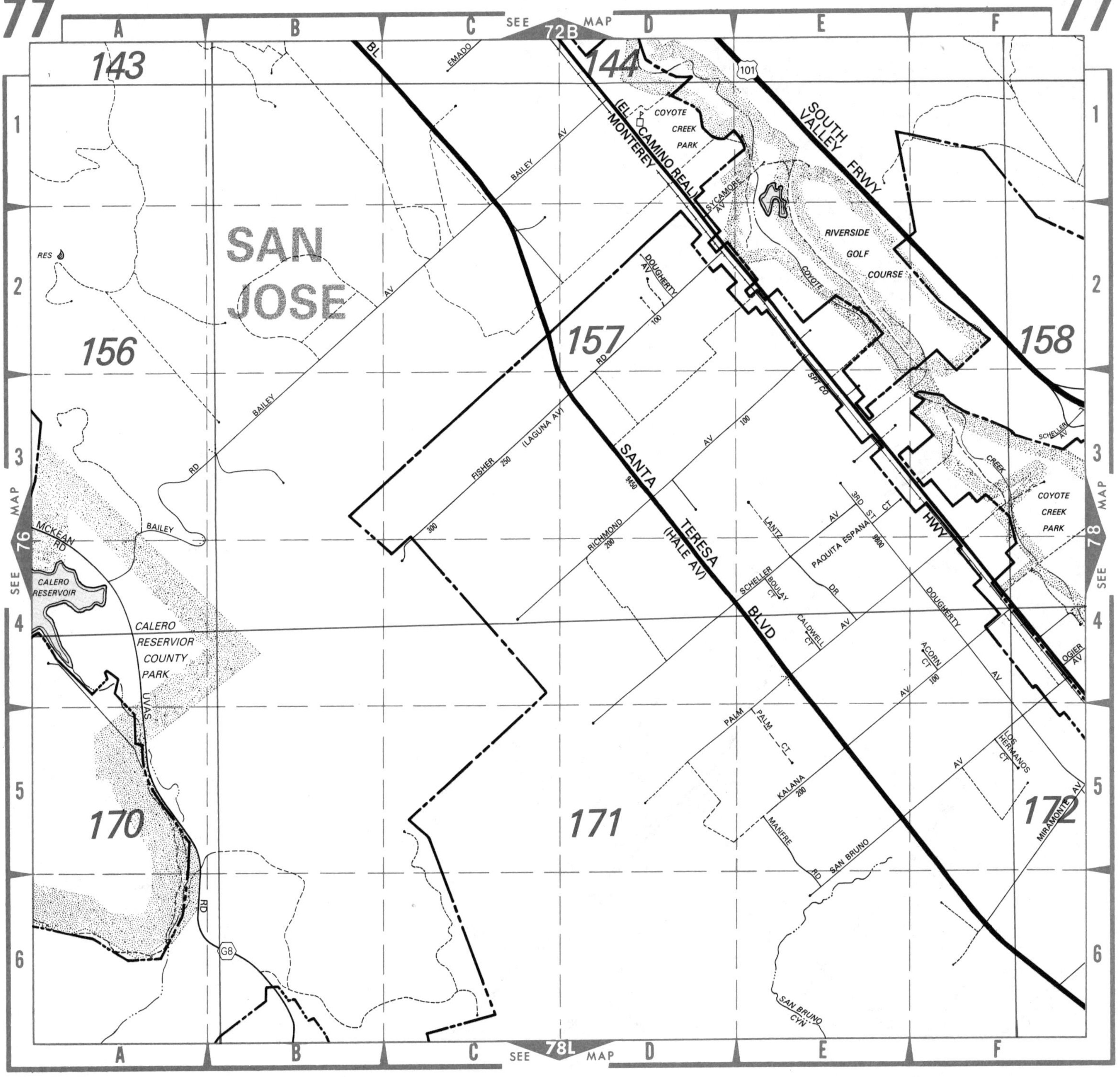

SEE 72B MAP

SANTA CLARA

SAN JOSE

143 144 156 157 158 170 171 172

SOUTH VALLEY FRWY

MONTEREY (EL CAMINO REAL) HWY

COYOTE CREEK PARK

RIVERSIDE GOLF COURSE

CALERO RESERVOIR

CALERO RESERVIOR COUNTY PARK

SANTA TERESA BLVD (HALE AV)

BAILEY AV

FISHER (LAGUNA AV)

UVAS RD

McKEAN RD

SAN BRUNO CYN

SEE 76 MAP

SEE 78 MAP

SEE 78L MAP

DETAIL

COPYRIGHT © 1991 BY Thomas Bros. Maps

78

SEE 68B MAP 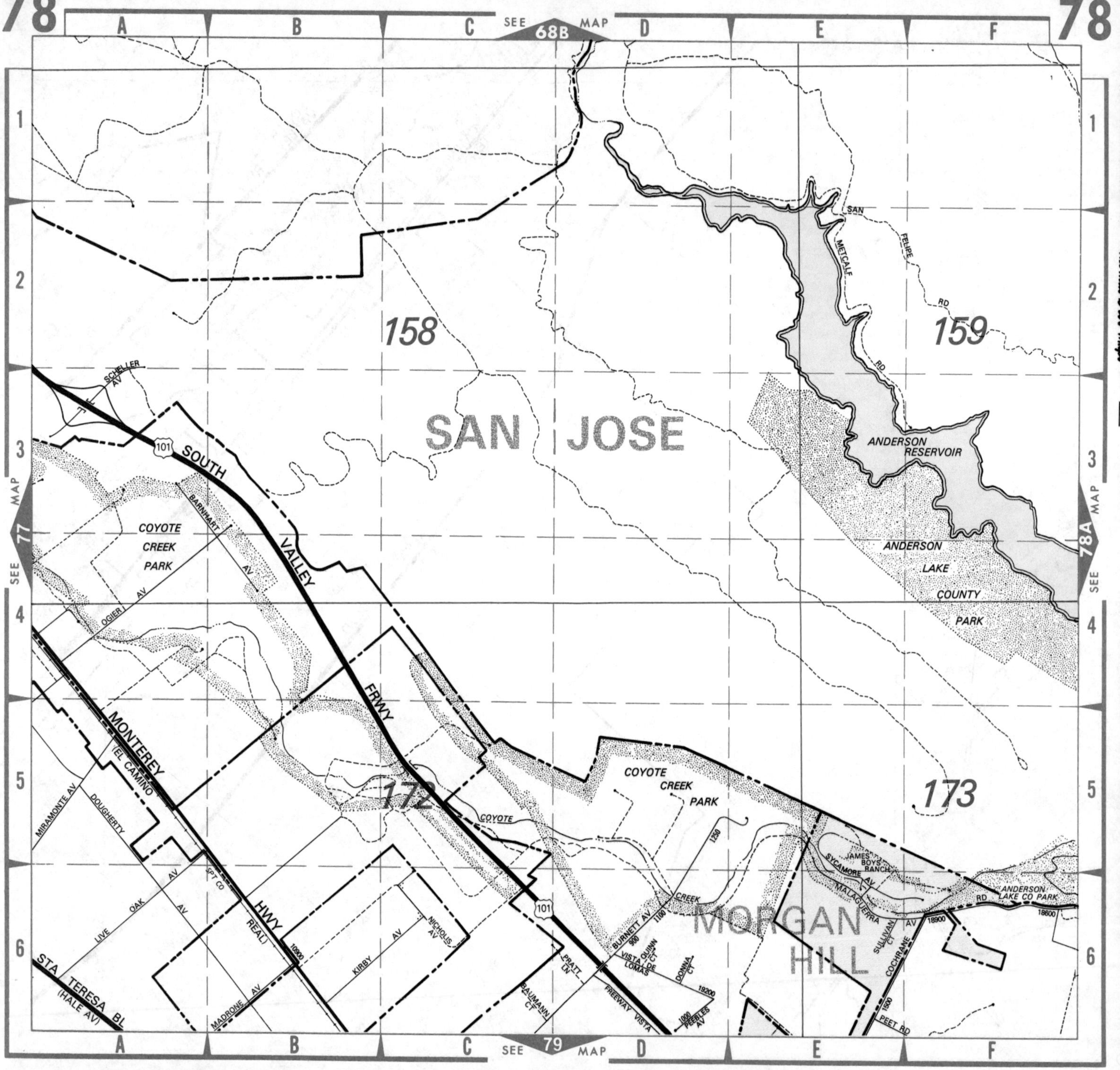
SEE 77 MAP
SEE 78A MAP
SEE 79 MAP

A B C D E F

1 2 3 4 5 6

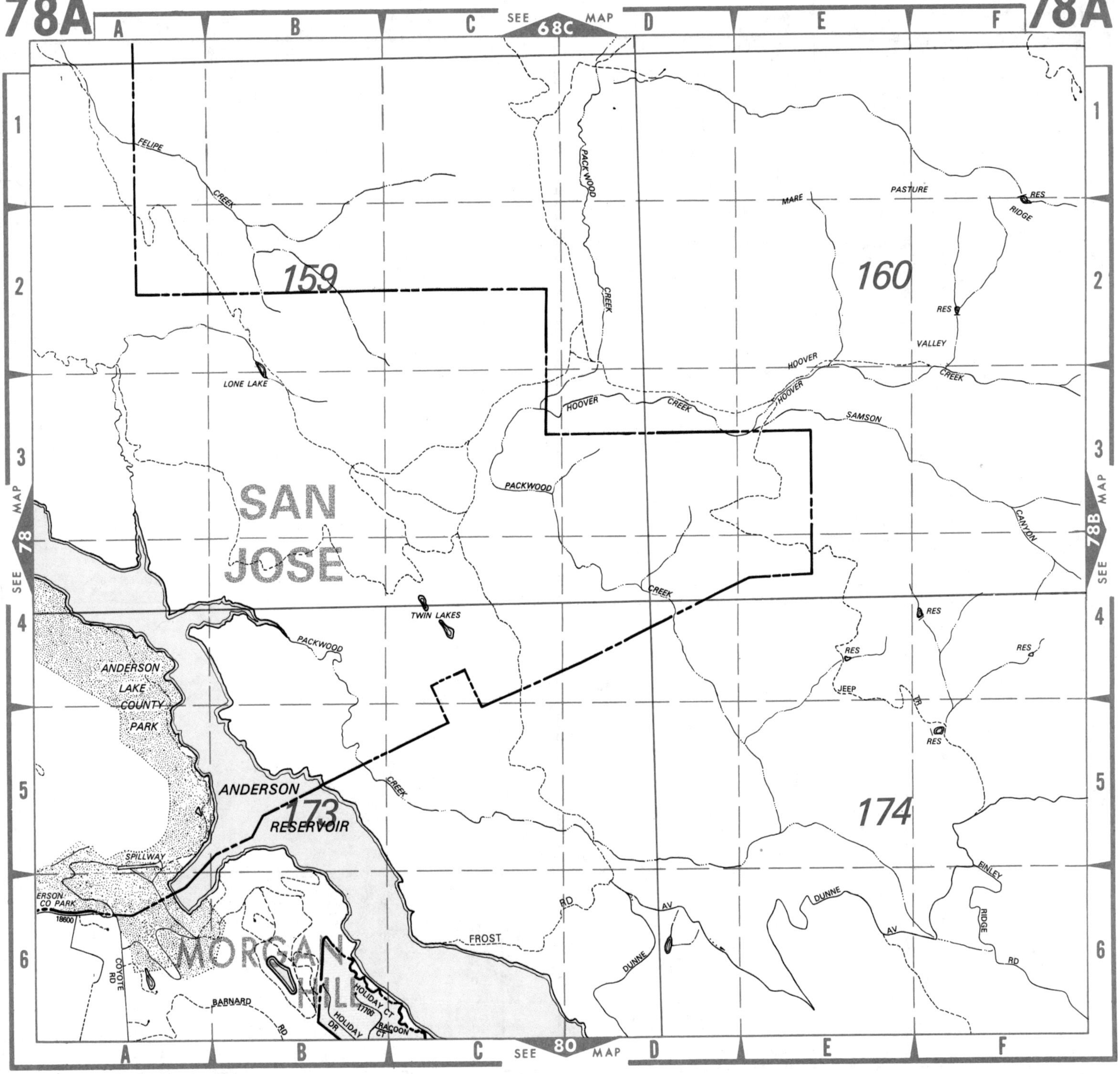

SEE MAP 68C
SEE MAP 78
SEE MAP 78B
SEE MAP 80

A B C D E F

1 2 3 4 5 6

FELIPE CREEK
PACKWOOD CREEK
MARE
PASTURE
RES
RIDGE
159
160
RES
VALLEY
HOOVER
CREEK
LONE LAKE
HOOVER CREEK
HOOVER
SAMSON
PACKWOOD
SAN JOSE
CANYON
CREEK
TWIN LAKES
RES
PACKWOOD
ANDERSON LAKE COUNTY PARK
RES
RES
JEEP TR
RES
CREEK
ANDERSON RESERVOIR
173
174
SPILLWAY
FINLEY
ERSON CO PARK
18600
RD
DUNNE
AV
RIDGE
FROST
AV
DUNNE
RD
COYOTE RD
MORGAN HILL
BARNARD
RD
HOLIDAY CT
17700
HOLIDAY DR
RACOON CT

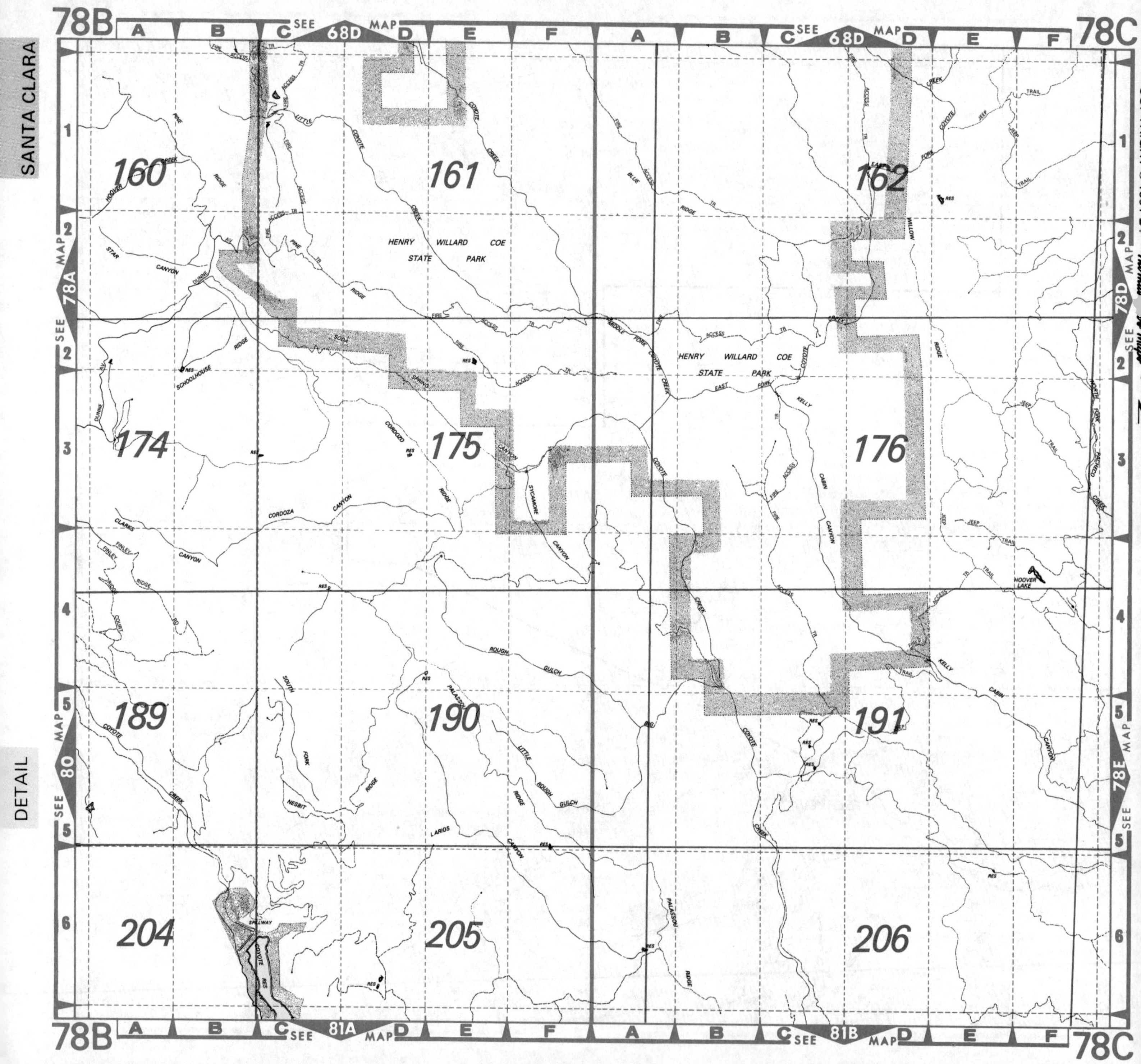
78B
78C
SANTA CLARA
DETAIL
SEE 68D MAP
SEE 81A MAP
SEE 81B MAP
SEE 78A MAP
SEE 78D MAP
SEE 80 MAP
SEE 78E MAP
160
161
162
174
175
176
189
190
191
204
205
206
HENRY WILLARD COE STATE PARK
COYOTE CREEK
LITTLE COYOTE CREEK
PINE RIDGE
HOOVER
STAR CANYON
DUNNE AV
SCHOOLHOUSE RIDGE
SODA SPRING CANYON
CORDOZO RIDGE
CORDOZA CANYON
SYCAMORE CANYON
CLARKS CANYON
FINLEY RIDGE
COURT
MIDDLE FORK COYOTE CREEK
EAST FORK
KELLY CABIN CANYON
BLUE RIDGE
FIRE ACCESS TR
WILLOW RIDGE
JEEP TRAIL
NORTH FORK PACHECO CREEK
HOOVER LAKE
ROUGH GULCH
LITTLE ROUGH GULCH
SOUTH FORK
NESBIT RIDGE
PALASSOU RIDGE
LARIOS CANYON
BIG
SPILLWAY
COYOTE RES
RES

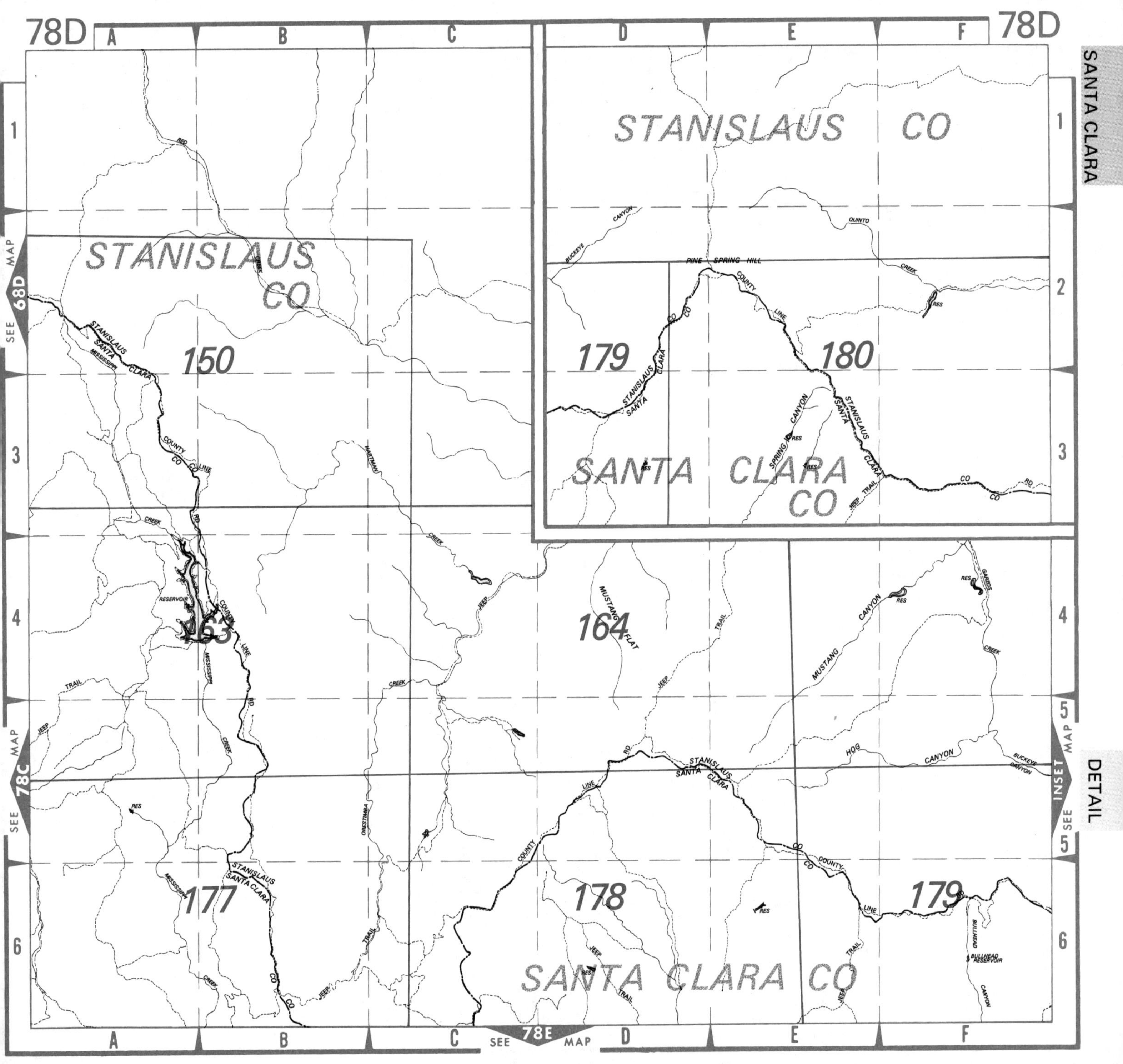
78D
78D
SANTA CLARA
STANISLAUS CO
STANISLAUS CO
150
163
164
177
178
179
179
180
SANTA CLARA CO
SANTA CLARA CO
PINE SPRING HILL
COUNTY LINE
QUINTO CREEK
BUCKEYE CANYON
SPRING CANYON
MUSTANG FLAT
MUSTANG CANYON
HOG CANYON
BULLHEAD RESERVOIR
BULLHEAD CANYON
ORESTIMBA
HARTMAN
MISSISSIPPI CREEK
RESERVOIR
JEEP TRAIL
RED CREEK
SEE 68D MAP
SEE 78C MAP
SEE 78E MAP
SEE INSET MAP
DETAIL

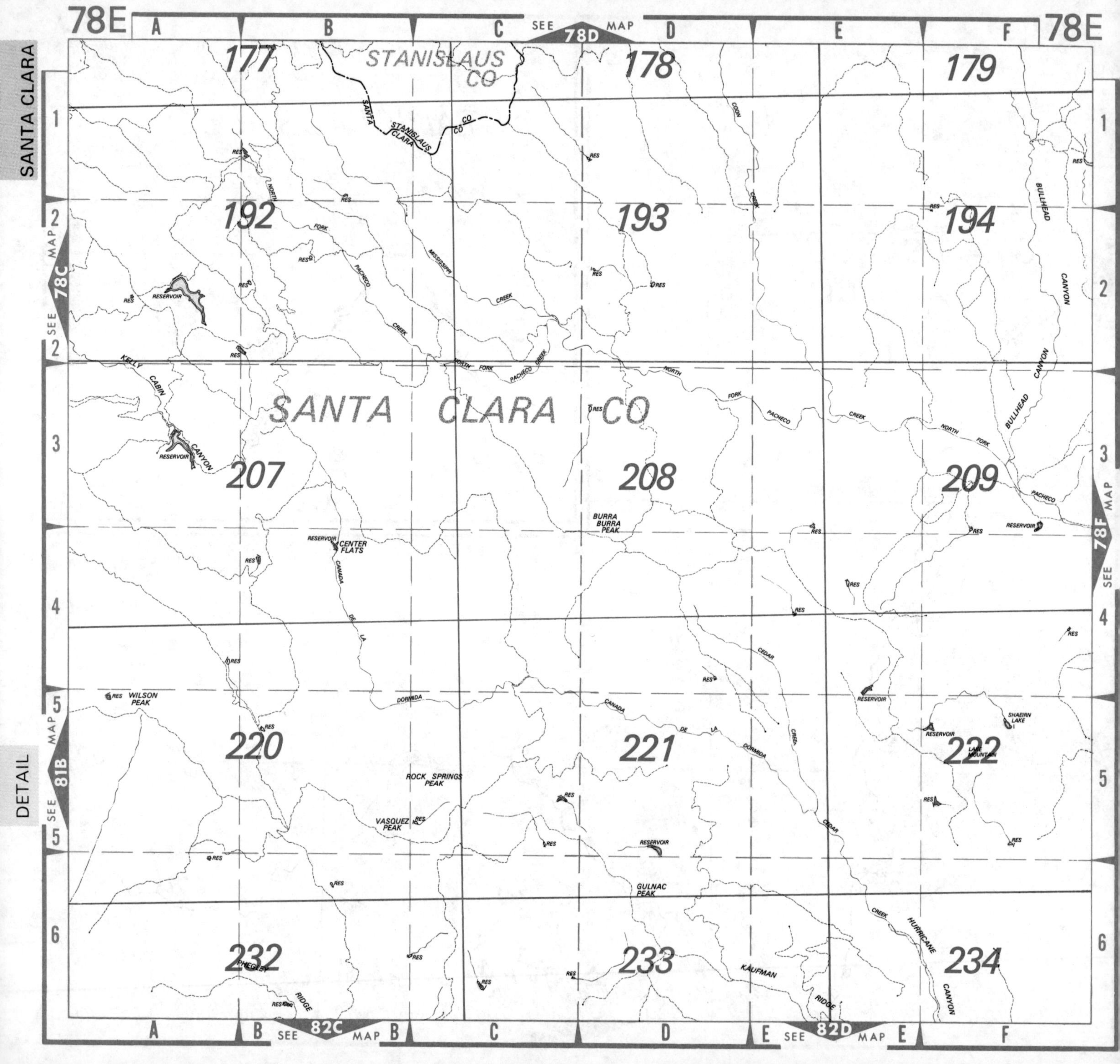
78E
SEE 78D MAP
SANTA CLARA
SEE 78C MAP
SEE 78F MAP
DETAIL
SEE 81B MAP
SEE 82C MAP
SEE 82D MAP
STANISLAUS CO
SANTA CLARA CO
177
178
179
192
193
194
207
208
209
220
221
222
232
233
234
NORTH FORK PACHECO CREEK
MISSISSIPPI CREEK
KELLY CABIN CANYON
BULLHEAD CANYON
COON CREEK
RESERVOIR
BURRA BURRA PEAK
CENTER FLATS
CANADA DE LA DORMIDA
CEDAR CREEK
WILSON PEAK
ROCK SPRINGS PEAK
VASQUEZ PEAK
SHAEIRN LAKE
LAKE MOUNTAIN
GULNAC PEAK
KAUFMAN RIDGE
HURRICANE CANYON
PHEGLEY RIDGE

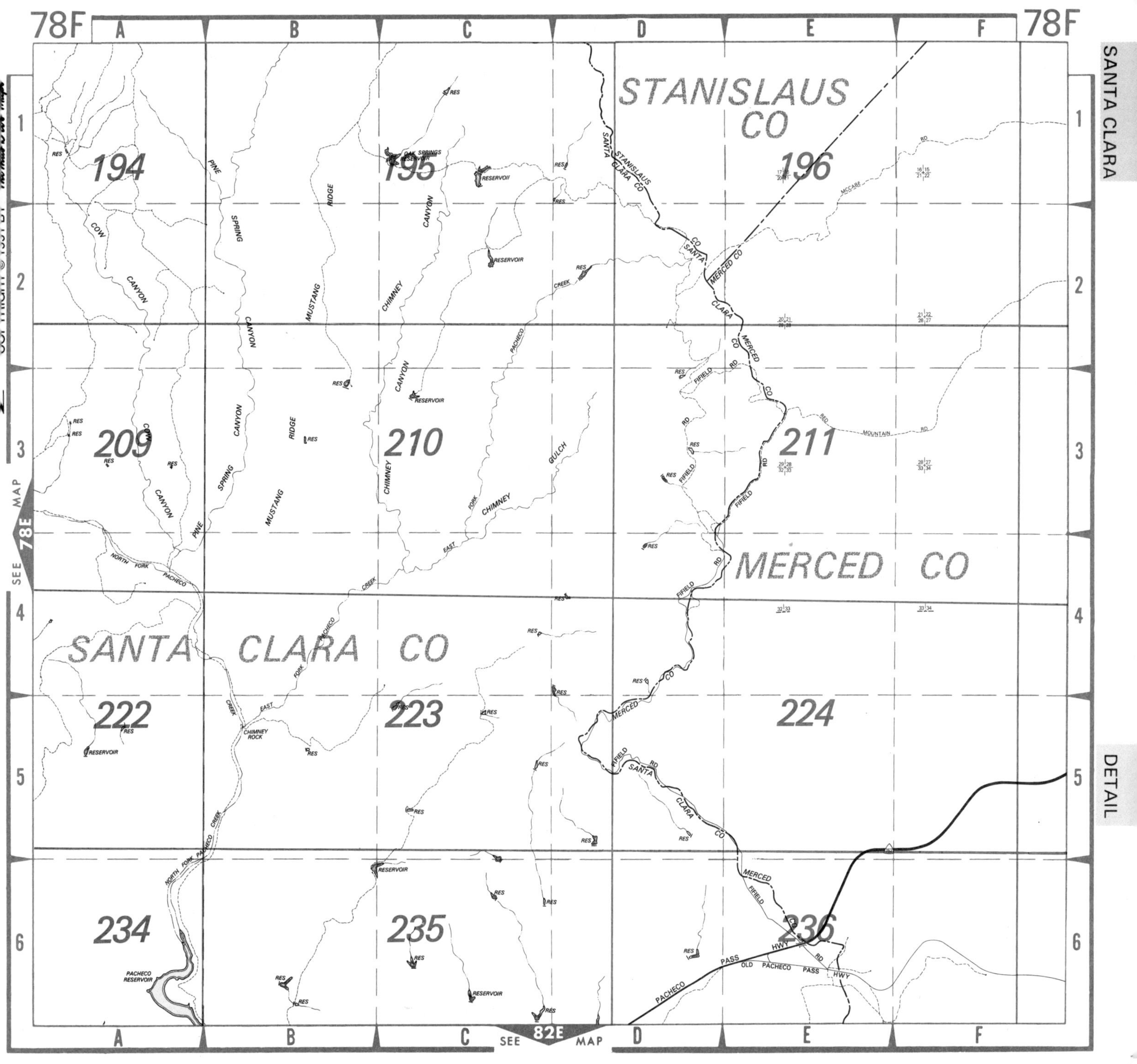
78F
A
B
C
D
E
F
SANTA CLARA
DETAIL
STANISLAUS CO
MERCED CO
SANTA CLARA CO
194
195
196
209
210
211
222
223
224
234
235
236
COW CANYON
PINE SPRING CANYON
MUSTANG RIDGE
CHIMNEY CANYON
OAK SPRINGS RESERVOIR
RESERVOIR
RES
PACHECO CREEK
EAST FORK CHIMNEY GULCH
NORTH FORK PACHECO
EAST FORK PACHECO CREEK
CHIMNEY ROCK
FIFIELD RD
RED MOUNTAIN RD
MCCABE RD
PACHECO RESERVOIR
PACHECO PASS HWY
OLD PACHECO PASS HWY
SEE 78E MAP
SEE 82E MAP
1
2
3
4
5
6

SEE MAP 73

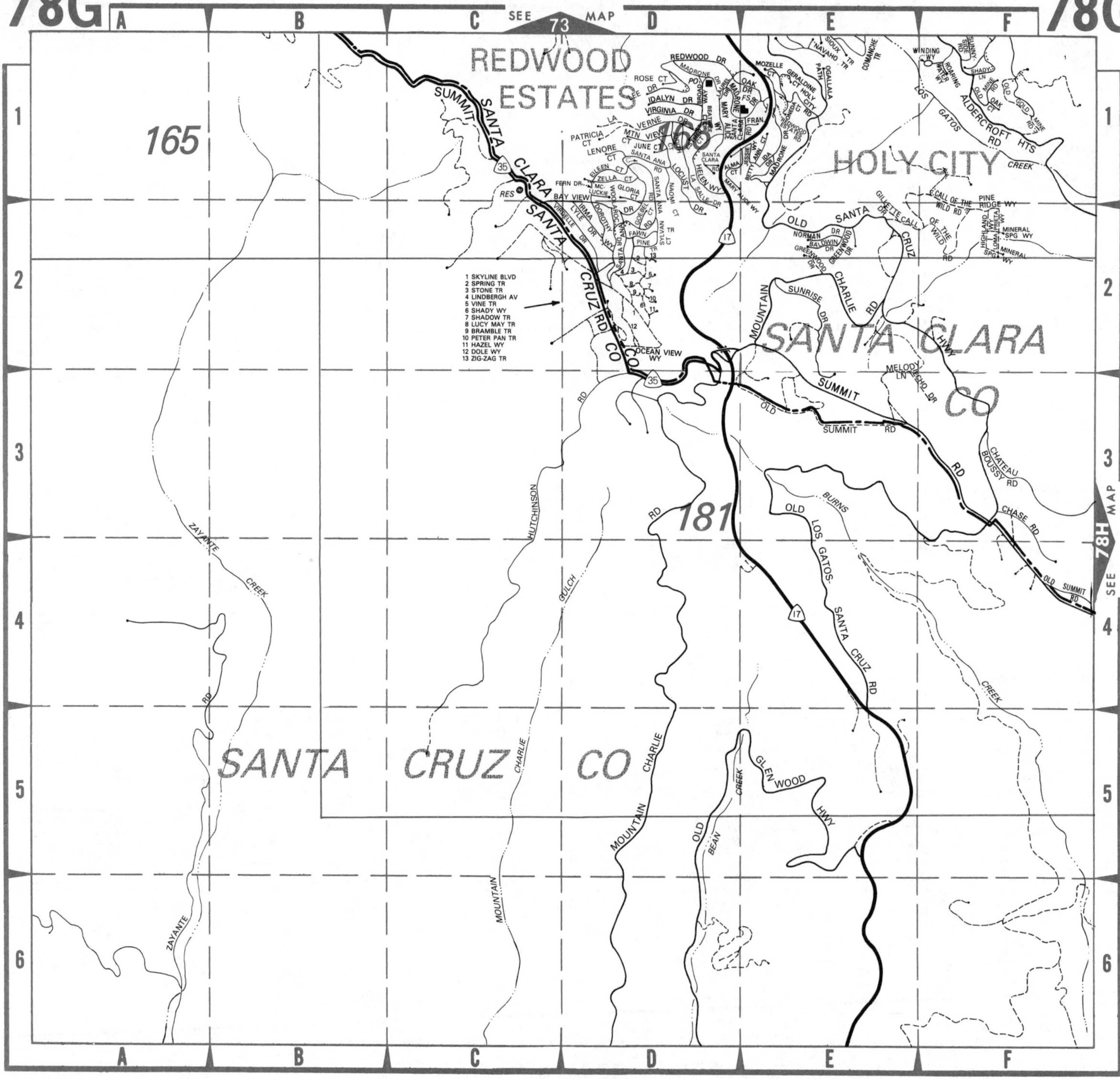

78G

SANTA CLARA

DETAIL

REDWOOD ESTATES

HOLY CITY

SANTA CLARA CO

SANTA CRUZ CO

165

166

181

1 SKYLINE BLVD
2 SPRING TR
3 STONE TR
4 LINDBERGH AV
5 VINE TR
6 SHADY WY
7 SHADOW TR
8 LUCY MAY TR
9 BRAMBLE TR
10 PETER PAN TR
11 HAZEL WY
12 DOLE WY
13 ZIG-ZAG TR

SUMMIT RD
SANTA CLARA SANTA CRUZ CO
OLD SANTA CRUZ HWY
MOUNTAIN CHARLIE RD
OLD LOS GATOS-SANTA CRUZ RD
OLD SUMMIT RD
CHATEAU BOUSSY RD
CHASE RD
GLENWOOD HWY
OLD BEAN CREEK
ZAYANTE CREEK
ZAYANTE RD
HUTCHINSON RD
GULCH
LOS GATOS CREEK
ALDERCROFT HTS
SUNRISE DR
MELODY LN
ECHO DR
OCEAN VIEW WY
BAY VIEW

SEE MAP 78H

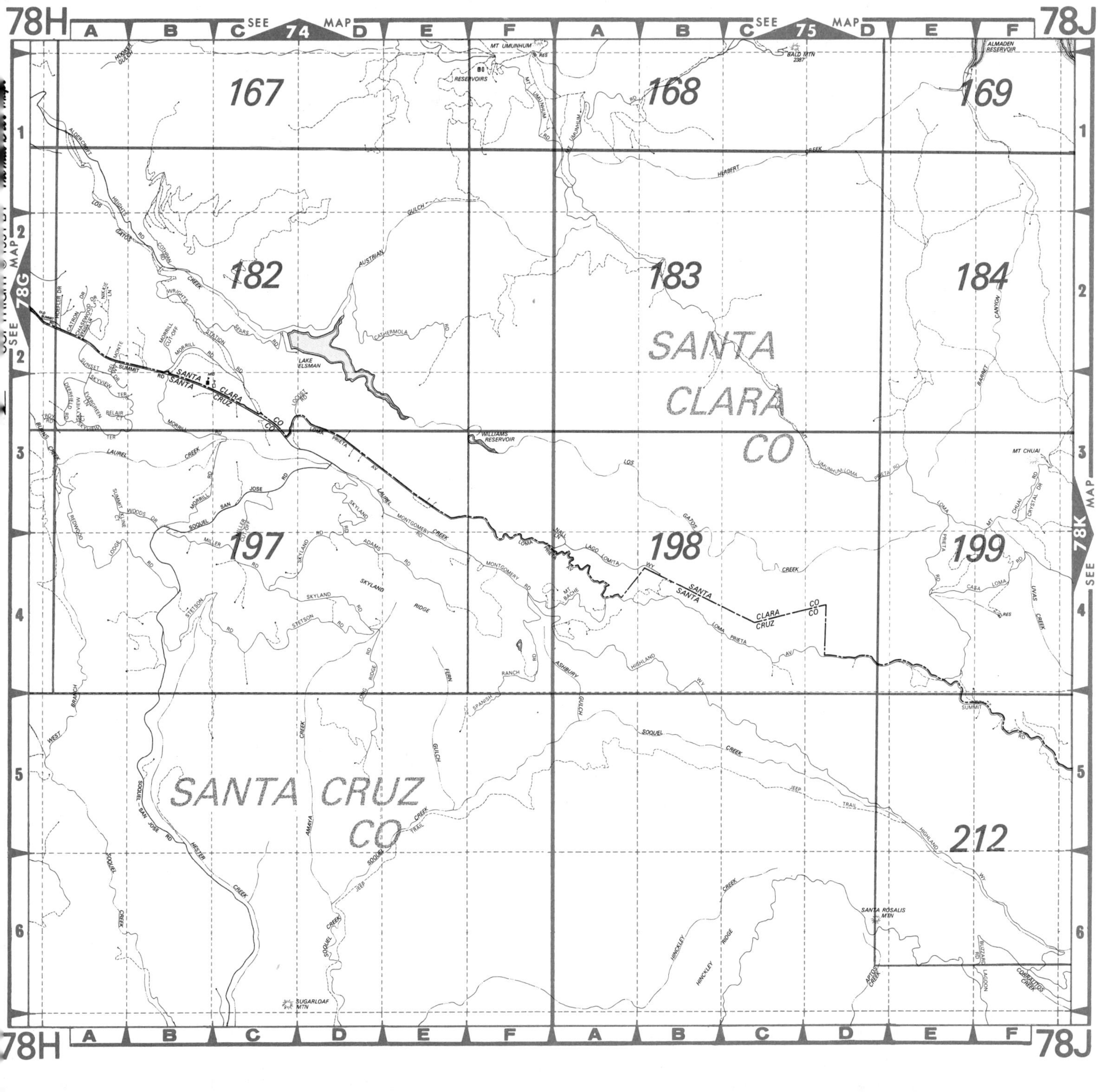

78H SEE MAP 74 · SEE MAP 75 · 78J

A B C D E F A B C D E F

SANTA CLARA DETAIL

SEE MAP 78G · SEE MAP 78K

167 168 169

182 183 184

197 198 199

212

SANTA CLARA CO

SANTA CRUZ CO

MT UMUNHUM
BALD MTN 2387
ALMADEN RESERVOIR
LAKE ELSMAN
WILLIAMS RESERVOIR
MT CHUAL
MT BACHE
SANTA ROSALIS MTN
SUGARLOAF MTN

78H A B C D E F A B C D E F 78J

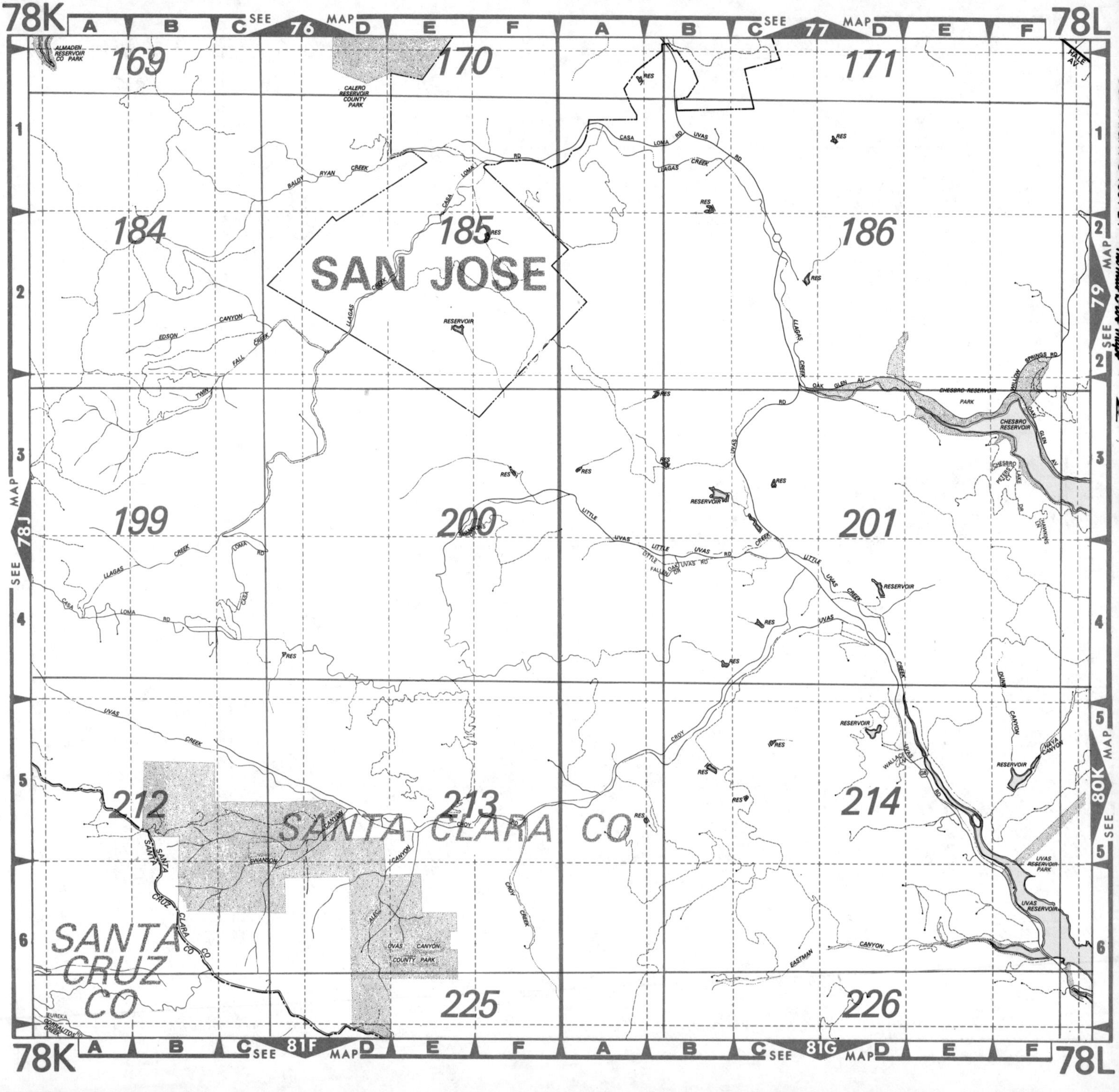

SANTA CLARA

DETAIL

169 170 171

184 185 186

SAN JOSE

199 200 201

212 213 214

225 226

SANTA CLARA CO

SANTA CRUZ CO

ALMADEN RESERVOIR CO PARK

CALERO RESERVOIR COUNTY PARK

CHESBRO RESERVOIR PARK

CHESBRO RESERVOIR

UVAS RESERVOIR PARK

UVAS RESERVOIR

UVAS CANYON COUNTY PARK

CASA LOMA RD

UVAS RD

LLAGAS CREEK

BALDY RYAN CREEK

EDSON CANYON

TWIN FALL CREEK

OAK GLEN AV

WILLOW SPRINGS RD

LITTLE UVAS CREEK

LITTLE UVAS RD

UVAS CREEK

CROY RD

CROY CREEK

SWANSON CANYON

ALEC CANYON

EASTMAN CANYON

DUNNE CANYON

HAYA CANYON

WALLACE LN

HALE AV

EUREKA

CORRALITOS CREEK

SEE 78J MAP

SEE 79 MAP

SEE 80K MAP

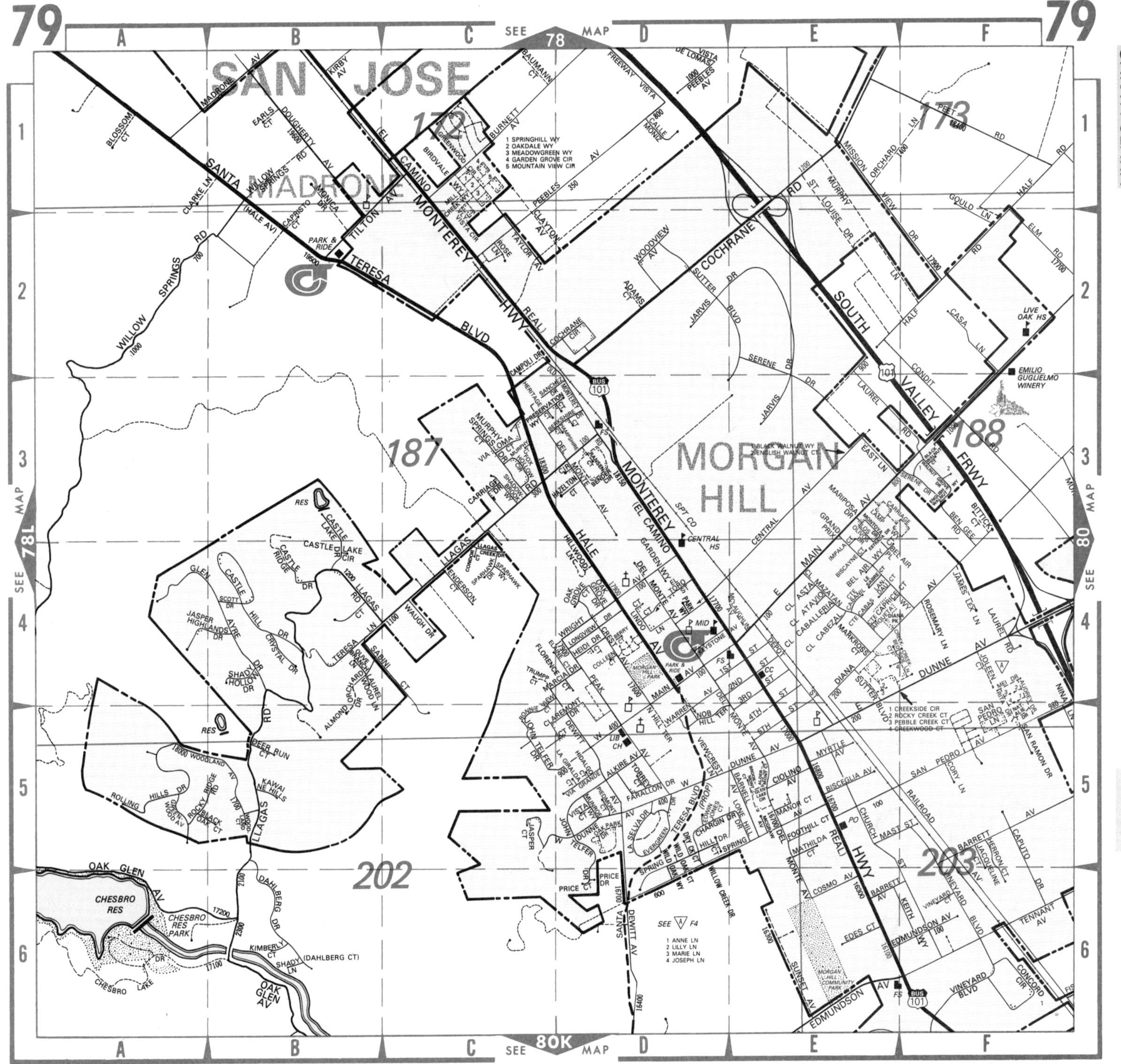
SEE 78 MAP
SEE 78L MAP
SEE 80 MAP
SEE 80K MAP
SAN JOSE
MADRONE
MORGAN HILL
172
173
187
188
202
203
1 SPRINGHILL WY
2 OAKDALE WY
3 MEADOWGREEN WY
4 GARDEN GROVE CIR
5 MOUNTAIN VIEW CIR
1 BLACK WALNUT WY
2 ENGLISH WALNUT CT
1 CREEKSIDE CIR
2 ROCKY CREEK CT
3 PEBBLE CREEK CT
4 CREEKWOOD CT
SEE A F4
1 ANNE LN
2 LILLY LN
3 MARIE LN
4 JOSEPH LN
MONTEREY HWY
SOUTH VALLEY FRWY
COCHRANE RD
SANTA TERESA BLVD
WILLOW SPRINGS RD
LLAGAS RD
HALE AV
DUNNE AV
MAIN AV
CENTRAL AV
SAN PEDRO AV
EDMUNDSON AV
VINEYARD BLVD
MONTEREY (EL CAMINO REAL) HWY
PARK & RIDE
LIVE OAK HS
EMILIO GUGLIELMO WINERY
CENTRAL HS
CHESBRO RES
CHESBRO RES PARK
OAK GLEN AV
MORGAN HILL COMMUNITY PARK
MORGAN HILL PARK
SPT CO
A
B
C
D
E
F
1
2
3
4
5
6

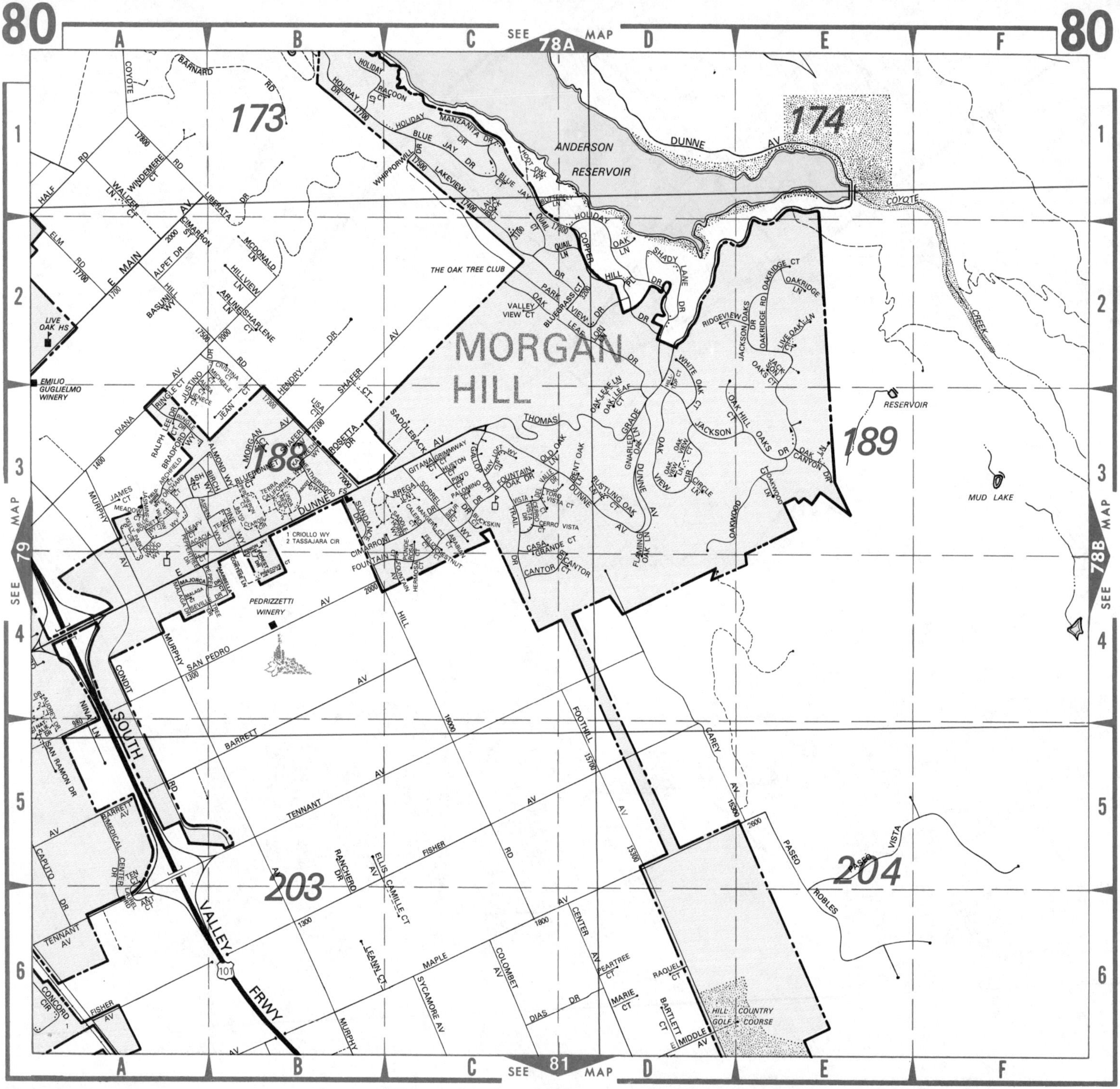

SEE 78A MAP

SEE 79 MAP

SEE 78B MAP

SEE 81 MAP

COPYRIGHT © 1991 BY Thomas Bros. Maps

SEE 79 MAP

SEE 78L MAP

SEE 81 MAP

SEE 81H MAP

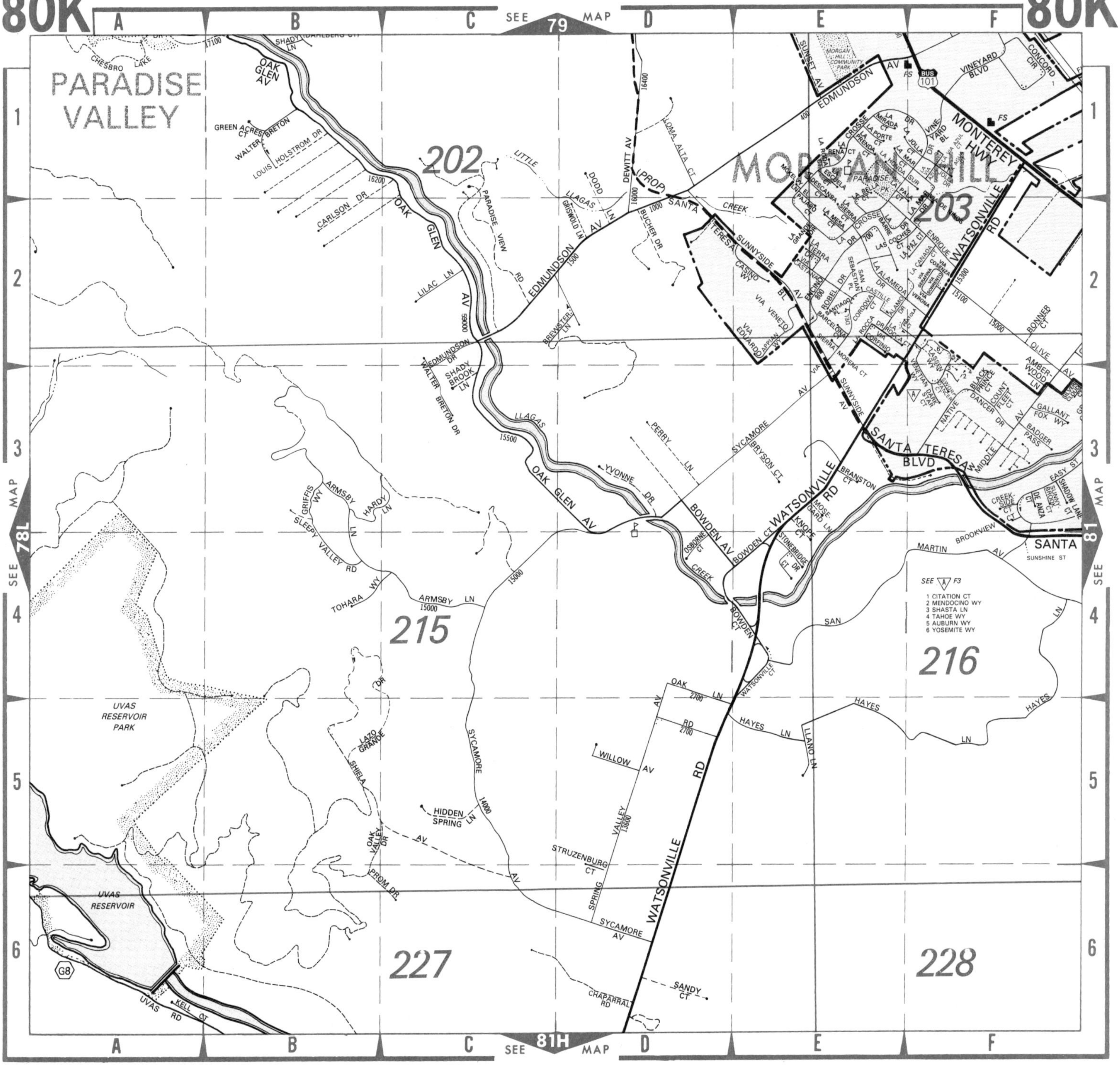

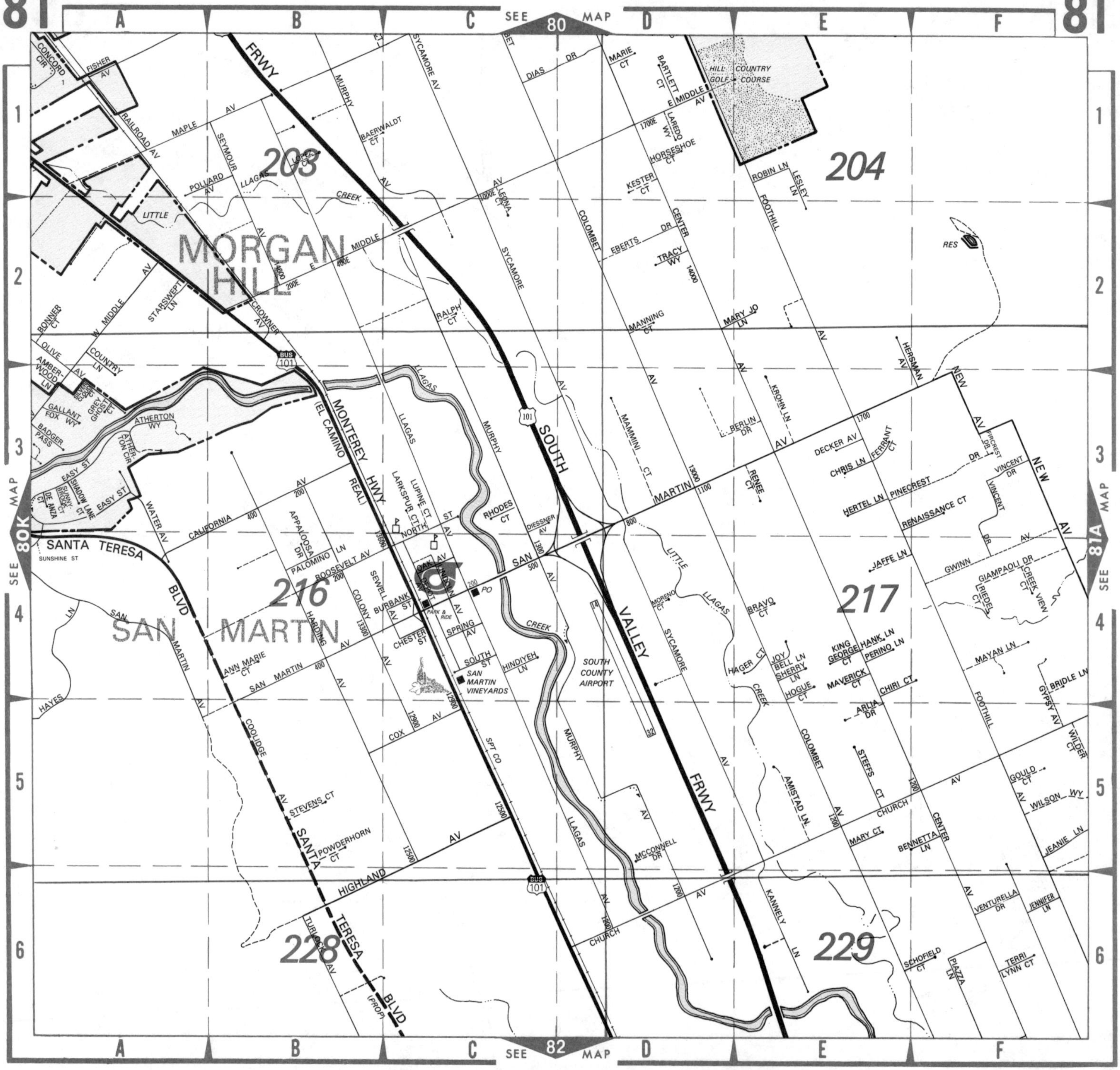

SEE 80K MAP
SEE 81A MAP

MORGAN HILL

SAN MARTIN

203 204 216 217 228 229

SOUTH VALLEY FRWY

MONTEREY HWY

SANTA TERESA BLVD

SAN MARTIN AV

SOUTH COUNTY AIRPORT

HILL COUNTRY GOLF COURSE

SAN MARTIN VINEYARDS

SANTA CLARA DETAIL

SEE 78B MAP
SANTA CLARA
204
205
217
218
229
230
COYOTE RESERVOIR
COYOTE LAKE COUNTY PARK
COYOTE RESERVOIR RD
COYOTE CREEK
SHEEP RIDGE
DEXTER
GILROY HOT SPRINGS RD
FITZGERALD RD
ROOP RD
BLUE OAKS RD
GWINN AV
GIAMPAOLI DR
BRIDLE LN
GYPSY AV
CHURCH AV
DE PAUL CIR
CHURCH AV
WILDER CT
NEW AV
WILSON WY
JEANIE LN
CHURCH LN
HOWELL LN
BRIDLE PATH
BRIDLE PATH CT
ALESSI CT
JENNIFER LN
FOOTHILL AV
GUIBAL AV
ASHCROFT CT
RUCKER AV
DUTCHESS CT
BUTCH DR
SEE 81 MAP
SEE 81B MAP 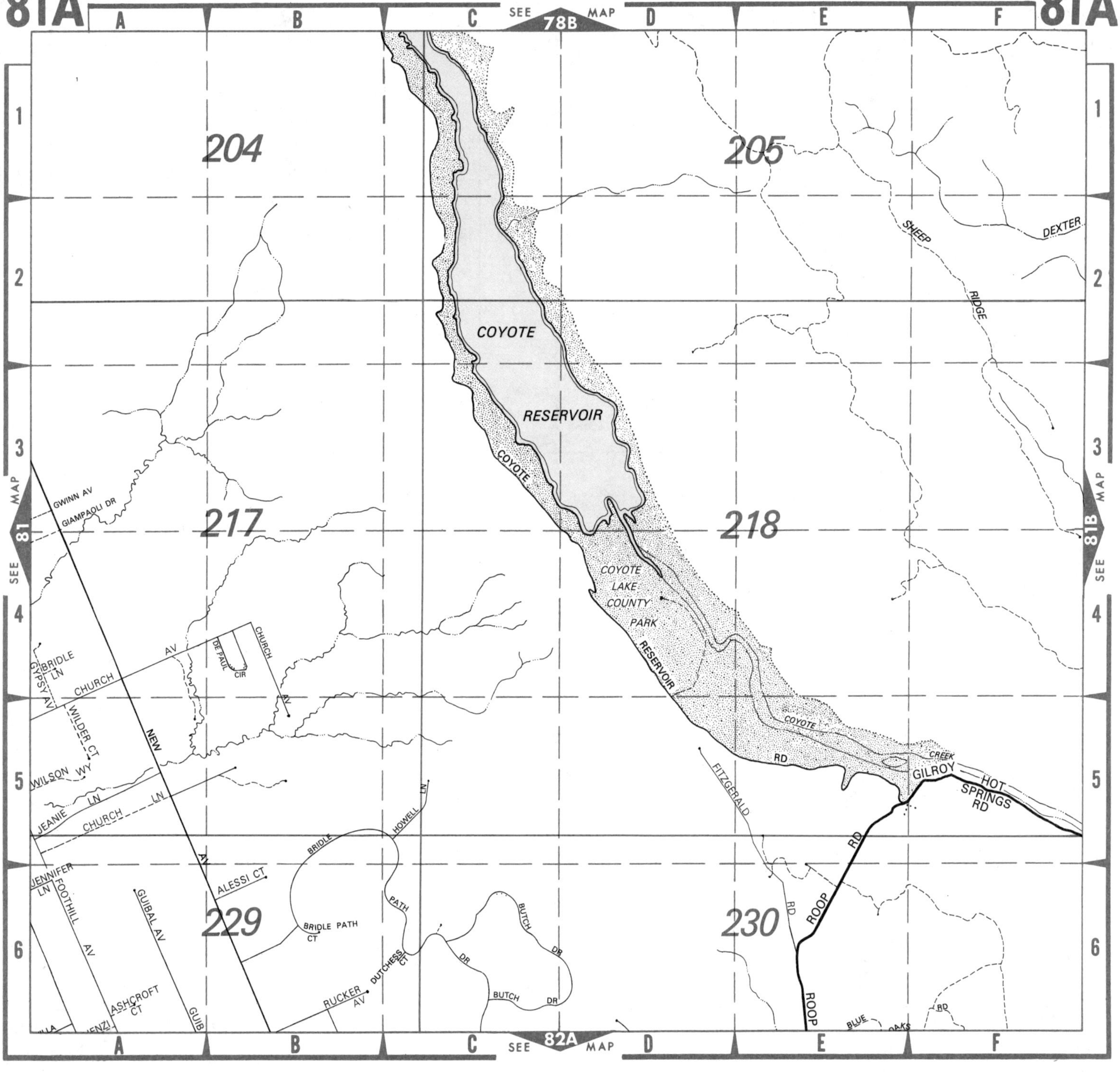
SEE 82A MAP
DETAIL

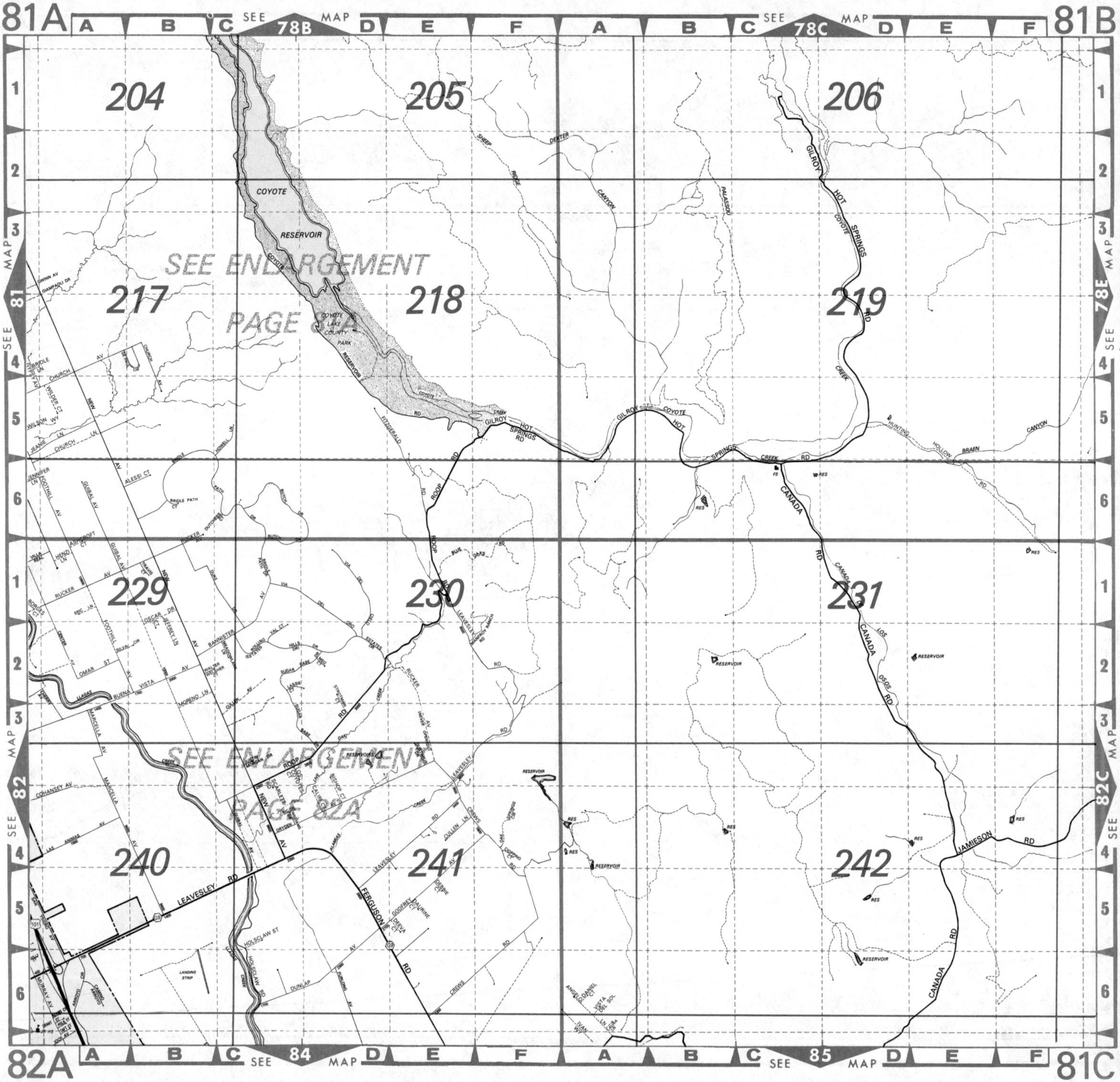

81A SEE 78B MAP
SEE 78C MAP 81B

SANTA CLARA

204 205 206

217 218 219

229 230 231

240 241 242

SEE ENLARGEMENT PAGE 81A

SEE ENLARGEMENT PAGE 82A

COYOTE RESERVOIR

COYOTE LAKE COUNTY PARK

GILROY HOT SPRINGS RD

COYOTE CREEK

CANADA RD

LOS OSOS RD

JAMIESON RD

ROOP RD

LEAVESLEY RD

FERGUSON RD

NEW AV

HUNTING HOLLOW

BRAEN CANYON RD

SHEEP RIDGE

DEXTER CANYON

RESERVOIR

LANDING STRIP

DETAIL

SEE 81 MAP
SEE 82 MAP
SEE 78E MAP
SEE 82C MAP
82A SEE 84 MAP
SEE 85 MAP 81C

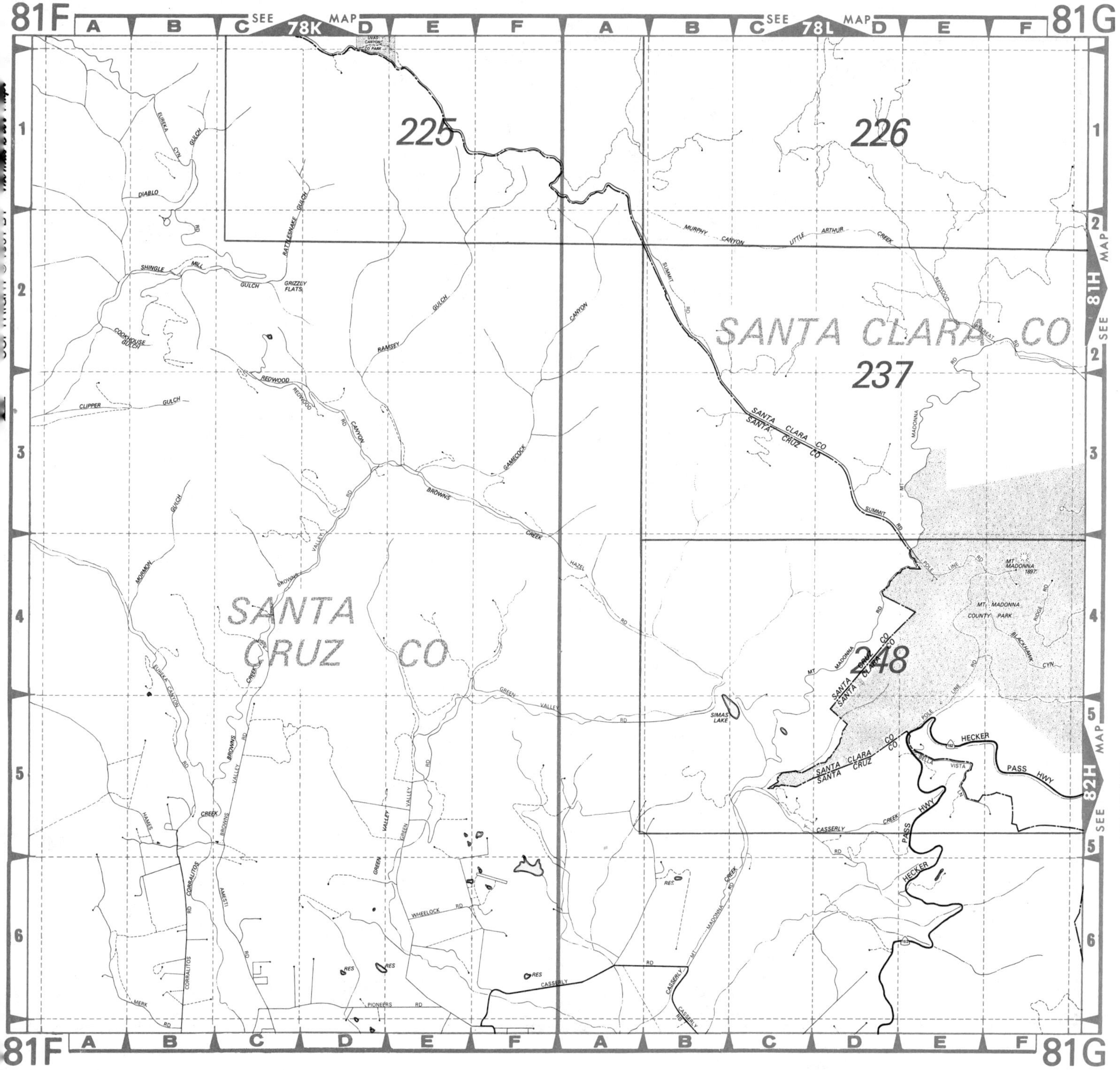
81F
81G
SEE 78K MAP
SEE 78L MAP
SEE 81H MAP
SEE 82H MAP
A
B
C
D
E
F
1
2
3
4
5
6
225
226
237
248
SANTA CLARA CO
SANTA CRUZ CO
UVAS CANYON CO PARK
EUREKA CYN
GULCH
DIABLO
RD
SHINGLE MILL GULCH
GRIZZLY FLATS
RATTLESNAKE GULCH
COOKHOUSE GULCH
CLIPPER GULCH
REDWOOD
REDWOOD RD
CANYON
RAMSEY
GULCH
CANYON
GAMECOCK
BROWNS
CREEK
BROWNS VALLEY RD
HAZEL
RD
MORMON GULCH
EUREKA CANYON RD
CREEK
GREEN VALLEY RD
SIMAS LAKE
MURPHY CANYON
LITTLE ARTHUR CREEK
SUMMIT RD
REDWOOD
RETREAT RD
SANTA CLARA CO
SANTA CRUZ CO
MADONNA
MT
SUMMIT RD
POLE LINE RD
MT MADONNA 1897
MT MADONNA COUNTY PARK
RIDGE RD
BLACKHAWK CYN
RD
MT MADONNA RD
HECKER PASS HWY
BELLA VISTA
CASSERLY CREEK
RD
HECKER PASS HWY
152
HAMES RD
CORRALITOS RD
AMESTI RD
BROWNS VALLEY RD
GREEN VALLEY
VALLEY
RES
WHEELOCK RD
RES
CASSERLY RD
PIONEERS RD
MERK RD
CASSERLY RD
MT MADONNA RD
CREEK

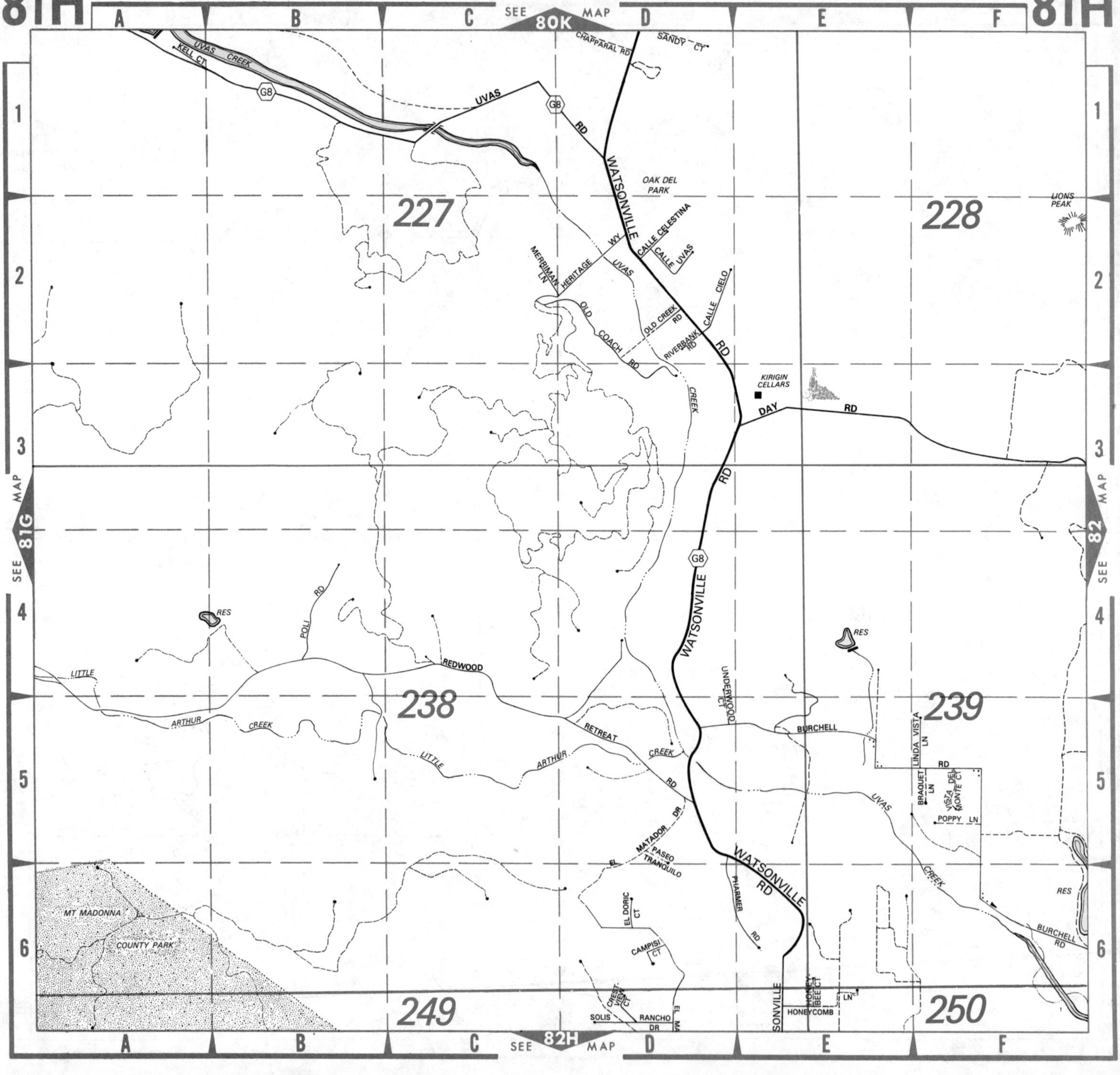

SEE 80K MAP

SEE 81G MAP

SEE 82 MAP

SEE 82H MAP

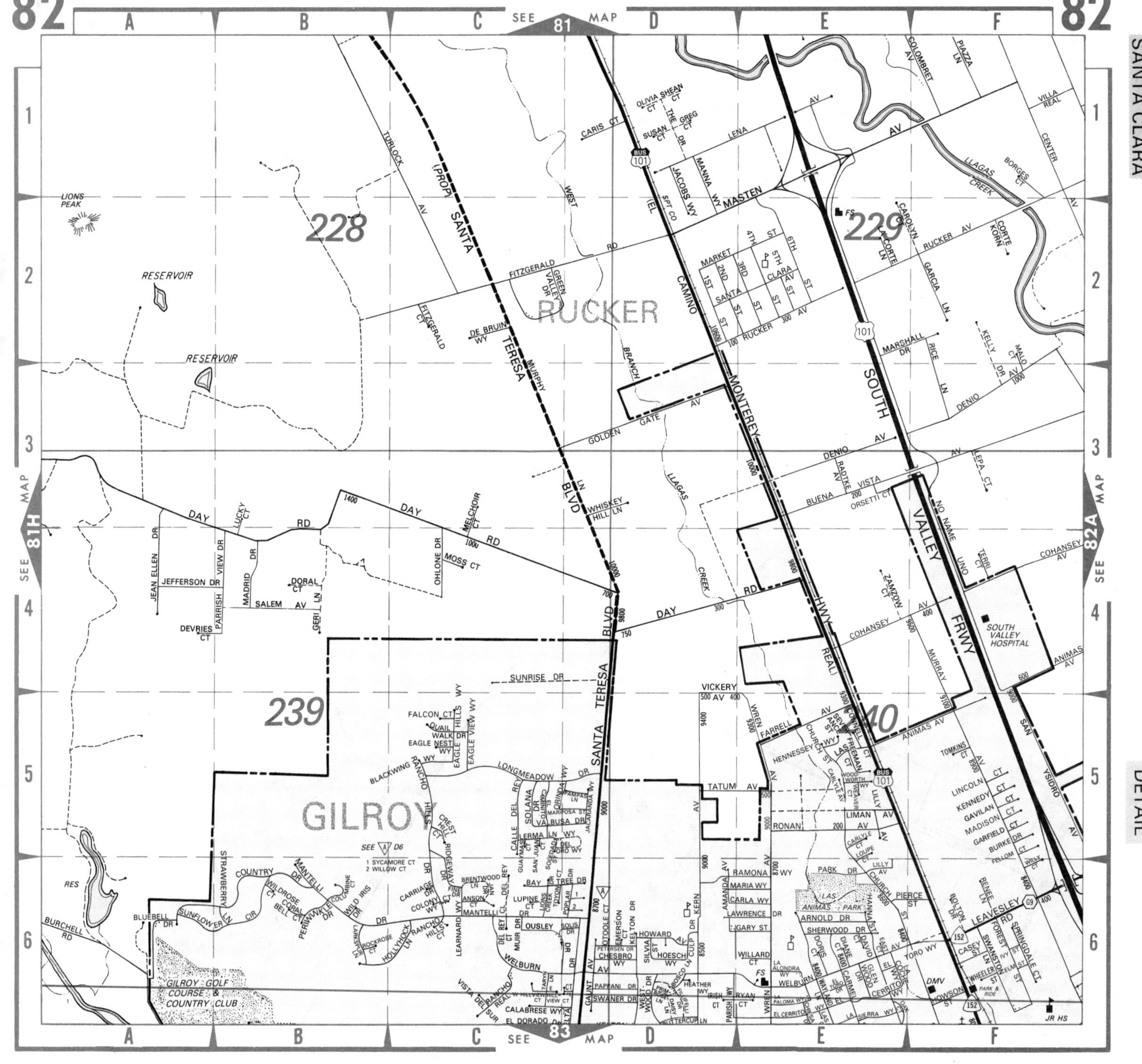
SEE MAP 81
SEE MAP 83
SEE MAP 81H
SEE MAP 82A
A
B
C
D
E
F
1
2
3
4
5
6
228
229
239
240
RUCKER
GILROY
LIONS PEAK
RESERVOIR
RESERVOIR
RES
TURLOCK AV
(PROP) SANTA TERESA BLVD
FITZGERALD RD
FITZGERALD CT
DE BRUIN WY
MURPHY LN
WEST BRANCH
GREEN VALLEY DR
GOLDEN GATE AV
WHISKEY HILL LN
LLAGAS CREEK
CAMINO REAL
MONTEREY HWY
SOUTH VALLEY FRWY
CARIS CT
OLIVIA CT
SHEAN CT
SUSAN CT
THE DR
GREG CT
LENA AV
JACOBS WY
MANNA WY
MASTEN AV
SPT CO
MARKET ST
1ST ST
2ND ST
3RD ST
4TH ST
5TH ST
6TH ST
SANTA CLARA AV
RUCKER AV
COLOMBRET AV
PLAZA LN
VILLA REAL
CENTER AV
BORGES CT
LLAGAS CREEK
CAROLYN LN
LA CORTE LN
CORTE KORN
GARCIA LN
MARSHALL DR
RICE LN
KELLY DR
MALO CT
DENIO AV
FS
DAY RD
LUCKY CT
JEAN ELLEN DR
JEFFERSON DR
PARRISH VIEW DR
MADRID DR
DORAL CT
SALEM AV
GERI LN
DEVRIES CT
MELCHOIR CT
OHLONE DR
MOSS CT
RADTKE AV
BUENA VISTA AV
ORSETTI CT
LEPA CT
NO NAME UNO
TERRI CT
COHANSEY AV
ZAMZOW CT
MURRAY AV
SOUTH VALLEY HOSPITAL
ANIMAS AV
SAN YSIDRO AV
SUNRISE DR
VICKERY AV
WREN AV
FARRELL AV
HENNESSEY WY
CHURCH ST
SEVEN ANCE
LAS ANIMAS
FREEMAN ST
CONNELL ST
CARLYLE AV
WOODWORTH ST
TATUM AV
LILLY
LIMAN AV
RONAN AV
TOMKINS CT
LINCOLN CT
KENNEDY CT
GAVILAN CT
MADISON CT
GARFIELD CT
BURKE CT
FELLOM CT
WILLY CT
FALCON CT
QUAIL HILLS WY
WALK DR
EAGLE NEST WY
EAGLE VIEW WY
BLACKWING WY
RANCHO HILLS DR
LONGMEADOW DR
CREST HILL
RIDGEWAY
CALLE DEL REY
SOLANA
ORINDA WY
JACARANDA WY
VALBUSA DR
LERMA LN
SEE A D6
1 SYCAMORE CT
2 WILLOW CT
STRAWBERRY LN
COUNTRY DR
MANTELLI DR
WILDROSE CT
COBALT CT
BELL CT
PERIWINKLE DR
COLUMBINE CT
WILD IRIS DR
SUNFLOWER CIR
BLUEBELL DR
CARRIAGE DR
COLONY CT
BRENTWOOD LN
ANSON CT
MANTELLI DR
BAY TREE DR
LUPINE CT
HOLLYHOCK LN
ROCKROSE CT
LEARNARD WY
OUSLEY
MUIR DR
WELBURN AV
GAUNT AV
OTOOLE CT
EMERSON CT
KELTON DR
CHESBRO WY
SILVIA ST
HOWARD AV
HOESCH WY
KERN AV
CULP DR
AMANDA AV
RAMONA WY
MARIA WY
CARLA WY
LAWRENCE DR
GARY ST
WILLARD CT
PARK DR
LAS ANIMAS PARK
ARNOLD DR
SHERWOOD DR
HANNA ST
PIERCE ST
TORO WY
LA ALONDRA WY
DORIS CT
DIANE CT
DAVID CT
CARMEL
GLEN WOOD DR
CERRITOS WY
DMV
HOWSON ST
BOLTON DR
RENEE CT
LEAVESLEY RD
FOREST ST
SWANSTON LN
CASEY ST
IVY ST
SPRINGDALE CT
WHEELER ST
ELM ST
PARK & RIDE
JR HS
PAPPANI DR
SWANER DR
HEATHER WY
IRISH CT
PARISH WY
RYAN CT
LA PALOMA WY
EL CERRITO WY
LA SIERRA WY
BUTTERCUP LN
CALABRESE WY
EL DORADO
VISTA DEL SUR
RANCHO REAL
BURCHELL RD
GILROY GOLF COURSE & COUNTRY CLUB

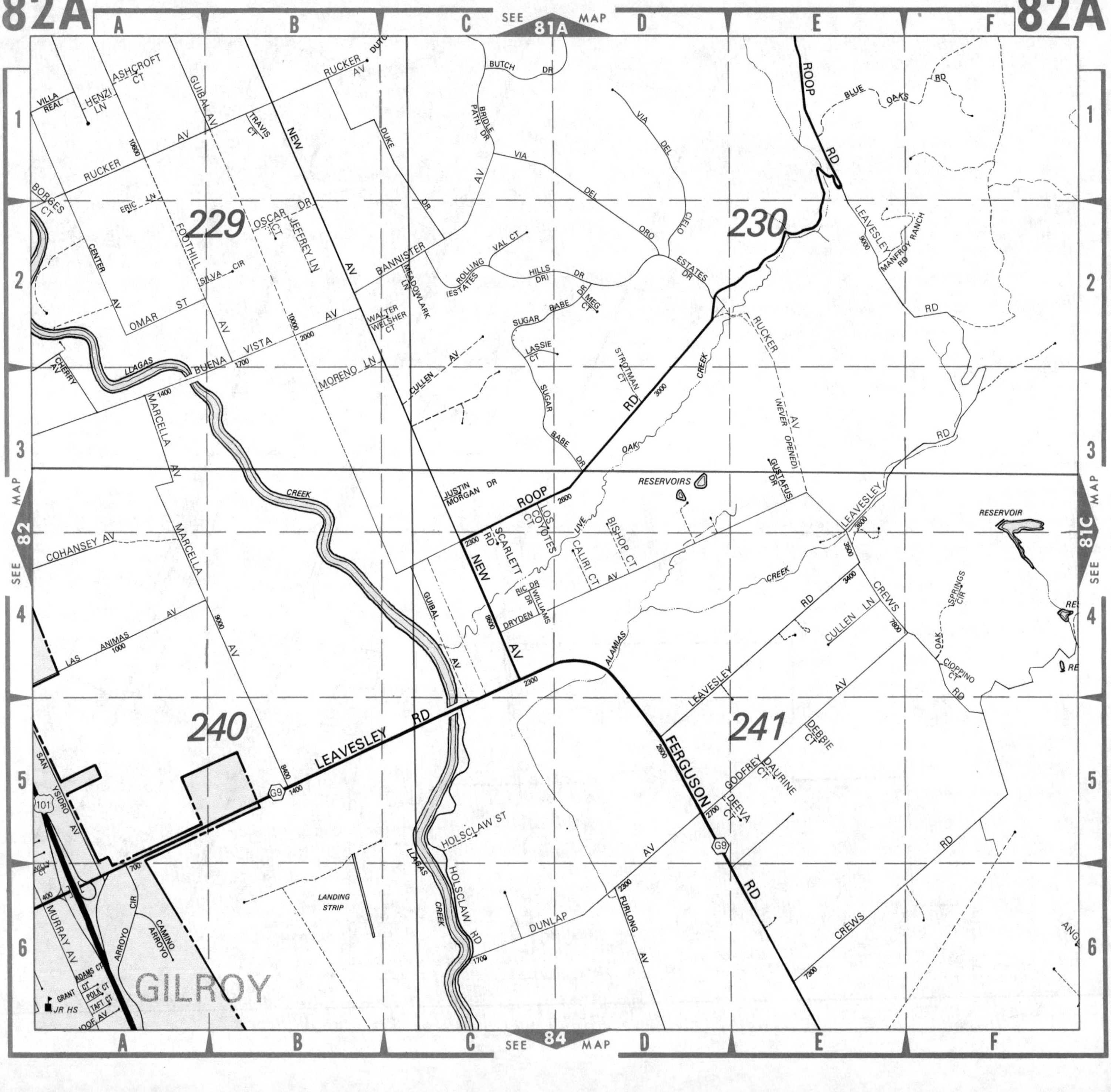
SEE 81A MAP
SEE 82 MAP
SEE 81C MAP
SEE 84 MAP
SANTA CLARA
DETAIL
A
B
C
D
E
F
1
2
3
4
5
6
229
230
240
241
GILROY
VILLA REAL
HENZI LN
ASHCROFT CT
GUIBAL AV
TRAVIS CT
RUCKER AV
DUTCH
NEW AV
DUKE DR
BUTCH DR
BRIDLE PATH DR
VIA DEL ORO
VIA DEL CIELO
ROOP RD
BLUE OAKS RD
BORGES CT
ERIC LN
FOOTHILL AV
OSCAR DR
OSCAR CT
JEFFREY LN
BANNISTER DR
MEADOWLARK LN
ROLLING HILLS DR
ESTATES
VAL CT
ESTATES DR
LEAVESLEY RD
MANFROY RANCH RD
CENTER AV
SILVA CIR
OMAR ST
WALTER CT
WELSHER CT
SUGAR BABE DR
MEG CT
LASSIE CT
STROTMAN CT
BUENA VISTA AV
LLAGAS CREEK
CHERRY AV
MORENO LN
CULLEN AV
RUCKER AV (NEVER OPENED)
MARCELLA AV
CREEK
OAK CREEK
GUSTAFUS DR
RESERVOIRS
RESERVOIR
JUSTIN MORGAN DR
ROOP RD
LOS COYOTES CT
SCARLETT RD
SCARLETT CT
LIVE OAK
BISHOP CT
CALIRI CT
COHANSEY AV
RIC DR
WILLIAMS DR
DRYDEN
LAS ANIMAS AV
GUIBAL AV
CULLEN LN
CREWS RD
SPRINGS CIR
OAK CIOPPINO CT
ALAMIAS
FERGUSON RD
DEBBIE CT
DAURINE CT
GODFREY CT
DEEVA CT
SAN YSIDRO AV
HOLSCLAW ST
HOLSCLAW RD
LANDING STRIP
MURRAY AV
ARROYO CIR
CAMINO ARROYO
ADAMS CT
POLK CT
TAFT CT
GRANT
JR HS
HOOF AV
DUNLAP AV
FURLONG AV
CREWS RD
101
G9
1000
2000
1700
1400
9000
8400
8600
2300
2600
3000
3400
3500
3600
7800
2700
2900
700
400
1700
7300

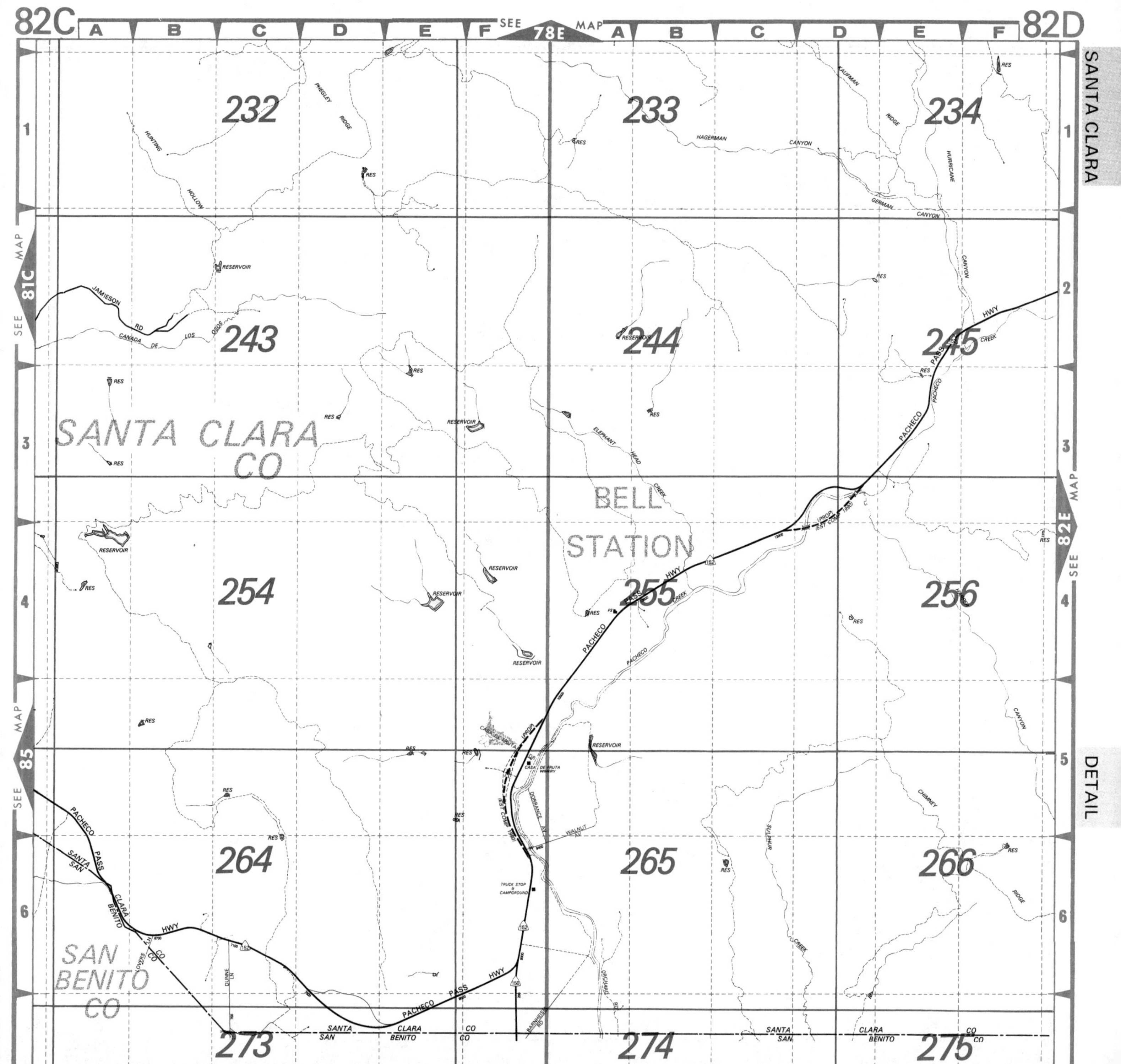

82C
82D
SEE MAP 78E
SEE MAP 81C
SEE MAP 85
SEE MAP 82E
SANTA CLARA
DETAIL
232
233
234
243
244
245
254
255
256
264
265
266
273
274
275
HUNTING HOLLOW
PHEGLEY RIDGE
HAGERMAN CANYON
KAUFMAN RIDGE
HURRICANE
GERMAN CANYON
CANYON
JAMIESON RD
CANADA DE LOS OSOS
RESERVOIR
RES
SANTA CLARA CO
ELEPHANT HEAD CREEK
BELL STATION
PACHECO PASS HWY
PACHECO CREEK
CREEK
CASA DE FRUTA
CASA DE FRUTA WINERY
DORRANCE AV
WALNUT AV
TRUCK STOP & CAMPGROUND
CHIMNEY CANYON
RIDGE
SULPHUR CREEK
DUNNE LN
LOVERS LN
ORCHARD RD
BARNHEISEL RD
SANTA CLARA CO
SAN BENITO CO
SAN BENITO CO
152
156

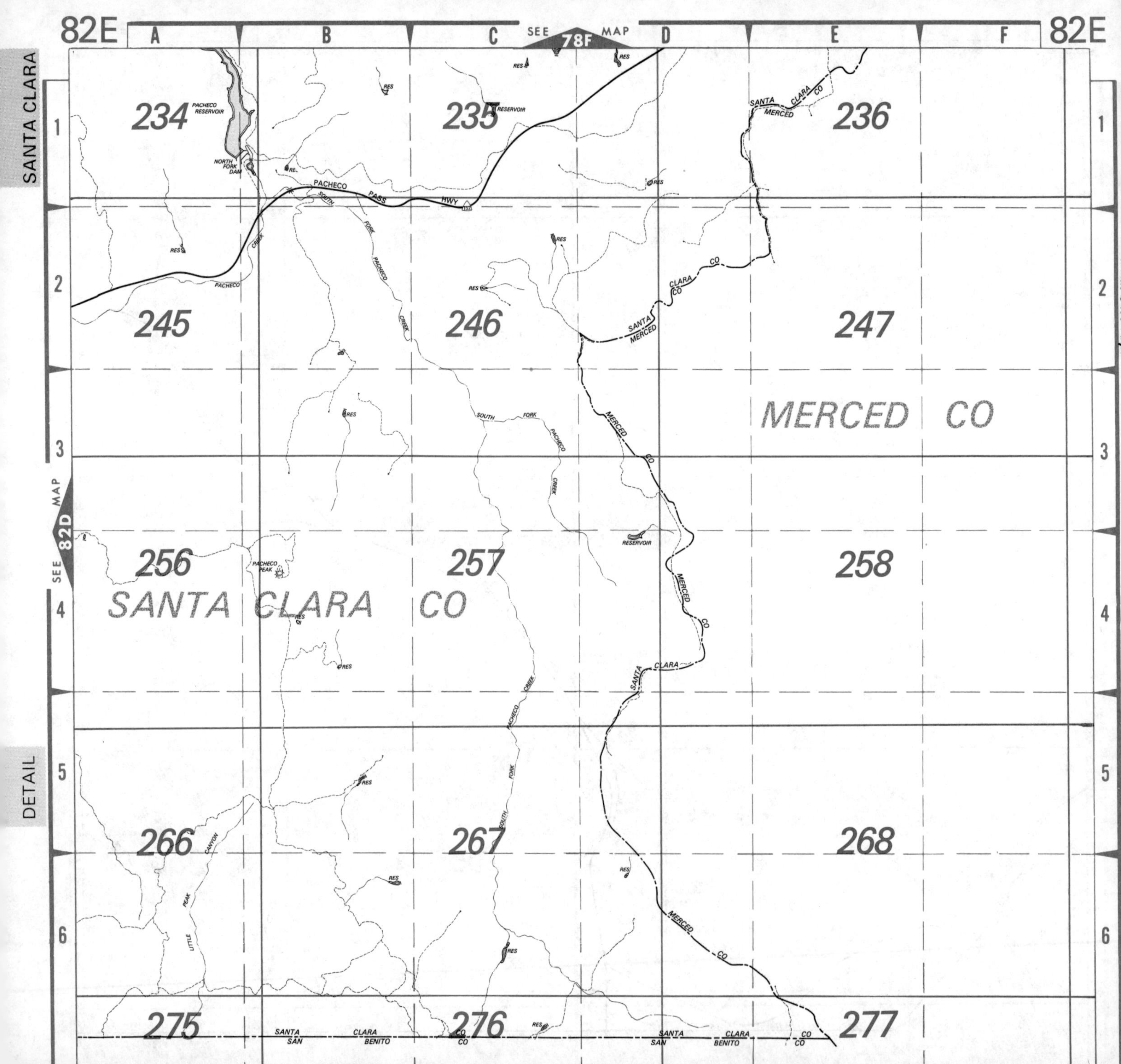

SEE MAP 78F
SEE MAP 82D
SANTA CLARA
DETAIL
A
B
C
D
E
F
1
2
3
4
5
6
234
235
236
245
246
247
256
257
258
266
267
268
275
276
277
PACHECO RESERVOIR
NORTH FORK DAM
PACHECO PASS HWY
152
SOUTH FORK PACHECO CREEK
PACHECO CREEK
PACHECO PEAK
RESERVOIR
RES
SANTA CLARA CO
MERCED CO
SANTA CLARA CO
SANTA MERCED
LITTLE PEAK CANYON
SANTA CLARA CO
SAN BENITO CO

82E

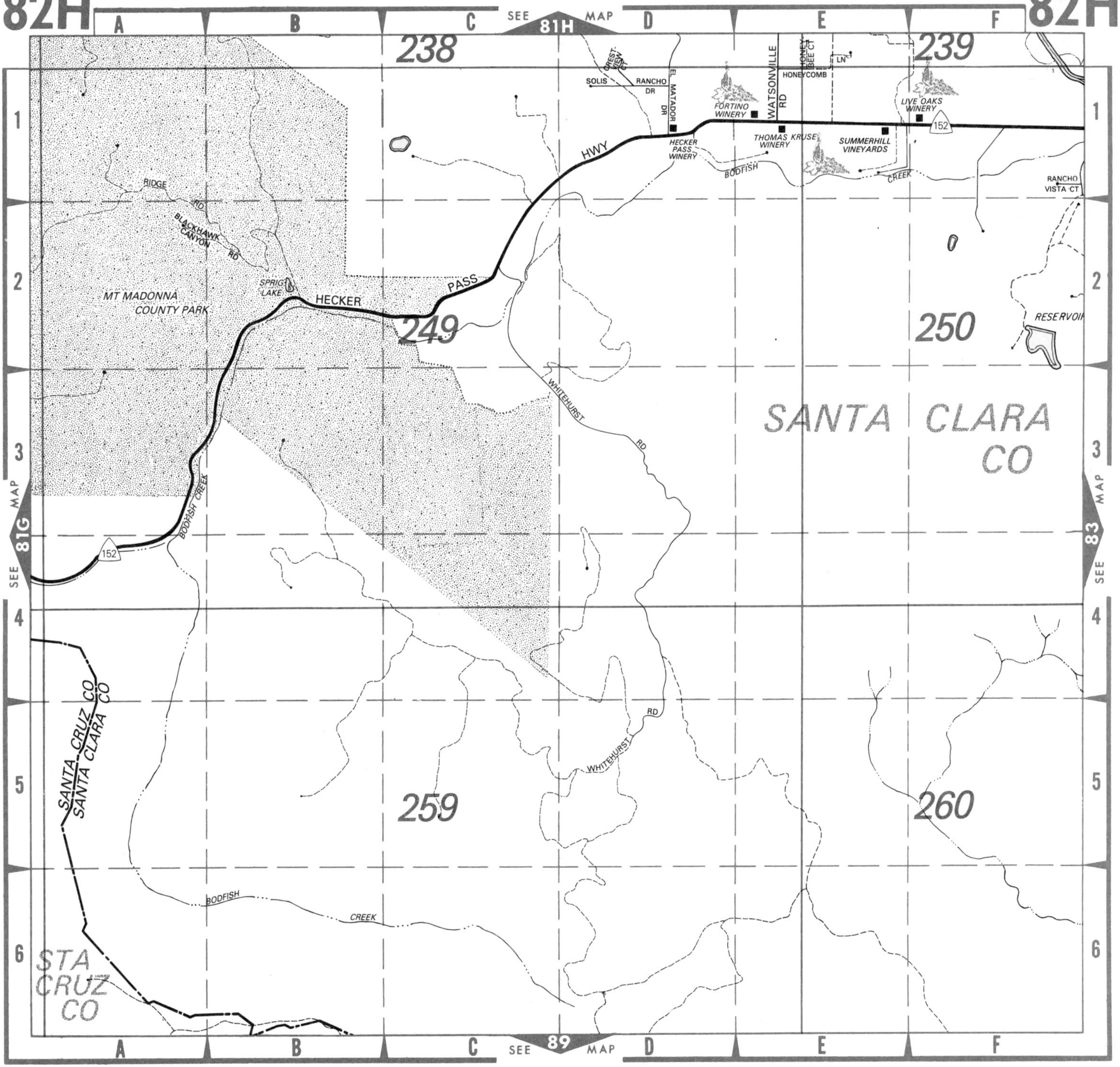

SEE 81H MAP

SEE 81G MAP

SEE 83 MAP

SEE 89 MAP

COPYRIGHT © 1997 BY Thomas Bros. Maps

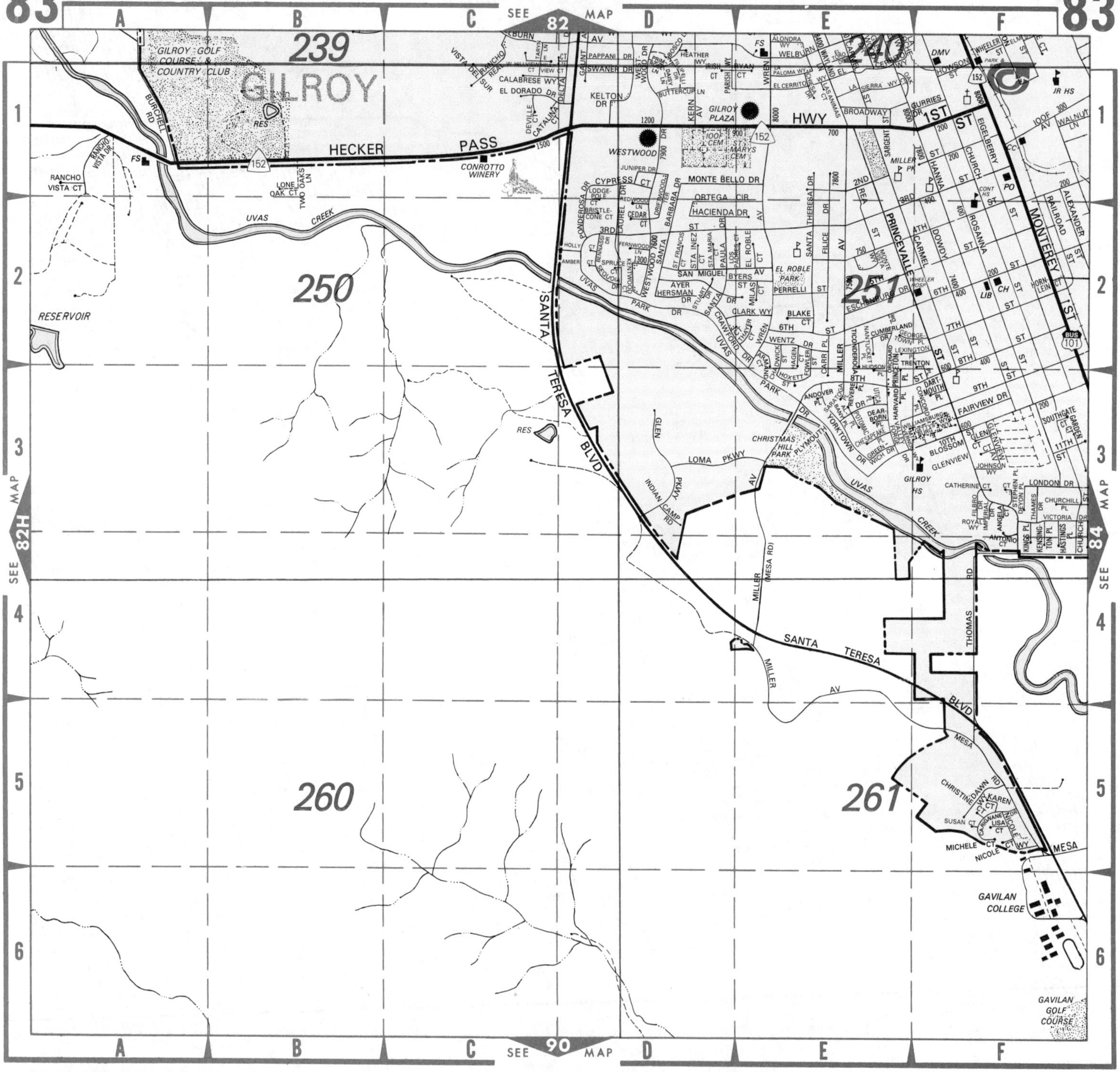
SEE 82 MAP
SEE 84 MAP
SEE 82H MAP
SEE 90 MAP
A
B
C
D
E
F
1
2
3
4
5
6
239
240
250
251
260
261
GILROY
GILROY GOLF COURSE & COUNTRY CLUB
HECKER PASS HWY
152
CONROTTO WINERY
BURCHELL RD
RANCHO VISTA DR
RANCHO VISTA CT
LONE OAK CT
TWO OAKS LN
UVAS CREEK
RESERVOIR
RES
WESTWOOD
GILROY PLAZA
IOOF CEM
ST MARYS CEM
1ST ST
BROADWAY
MONTEREY ST
101
SANTA TERESA BLVD
UVAS PARK DR
CHRISTMAS HILL PARK
GLEN LOMA PKWY
INDIAN CAMP RD
MILLER AV
(MESA RD)
THOMAS RD
MESA RD
PRINCEVALLE ST
MONTE BELLO DR
ORTEGA CIR
HACIENDA DR
SAN MIGUEL
ELROBLE PARK
MILLER PK
GILROY HS
JR HS
FAIRVIEW DR
GLENVIEW
BLOSSOM
9TH
10TH
11TH
LONDON DR
CHURCHILL PL
VICTORIA
HASTINGS
CHRISTINE DR
DAWN RD
KAREN CT
MICHELE CT
NICOLE WY
GAVILAN COLLEGE
GAVILAN GOLF COURSE

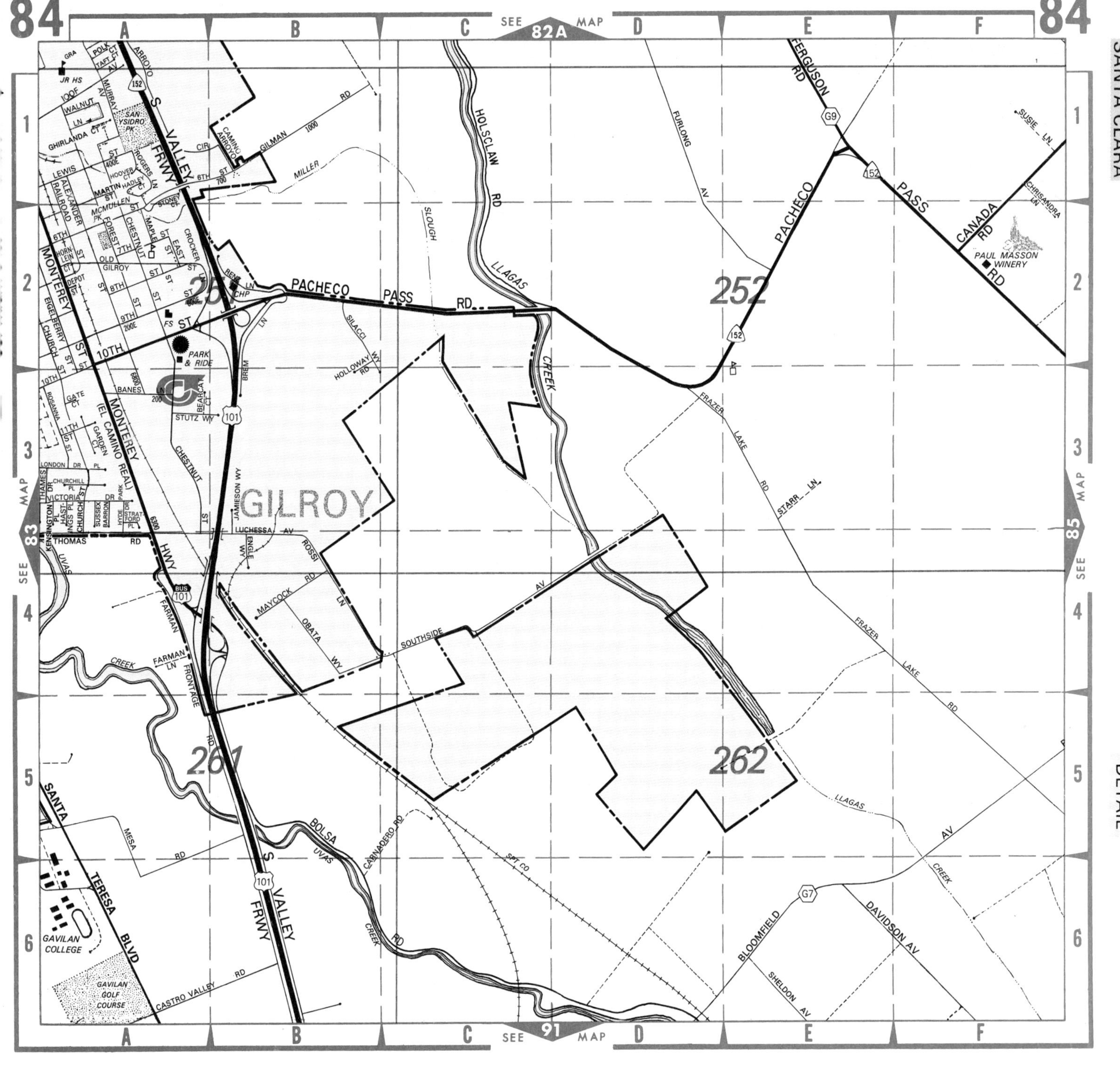
SEE MAP 82A
SEE MAP 83
SEE MAP 85
SEE MAP 91
SANTA CLARA
DETAIL
GILROY
252
261
262
PACHECO PASS RD
S VALLEY FRWY
HOLSCLAW RD
FURLONG AV
FERGUSON RD
PACHECO PASS
CANADA RD
PAUL MASSON WINERY
SUSIE LN
CHRISANDRA LN
GILMAN RD
MILLER SLOUGH
LLAGAS CREEK
FRAZER LAKE RD
STARR LN
SILACCI WY
HOLLOWAY RD
BREM LN
LUCHESSA AV
ROSSI LN
MAYCOCK RD
OBATA WY
SOUTHSIDE AV
FARMAN LN
FRONTAGE RD
MONTEREY (EL CAMINO REAL) HWY
THOMAS RD
10TH ST
PARK & RIDE
BANES LN
STUTZ WY
CHESTNUT ST
JAMIESON WY
ENGLE WY
UVAS CREEK
BOLSA RD
CARNADERO RD
SPT CO
MESA RD
SANTA TERESA BLVD
GAVILAN COLLEGE
GAVILAN GOLF COURSE
CASTRO VALLEY RD
BLOOMFIELD AV
SHELDON AV
DAVIDSON AV
LLAGAS CREEK
ARROYO
CAMINO ARROYO
6TH ST
STONEY CT
MARTIN ST
LEWIS
ALEXANDER
RAILROAD
McMULLEN
FOREST ST
7TH ST
8TH ST
9TH ST
OLD GILROY ST
EIGELBERRY
CHURCH ST
DEPOT ST
MAPLE
CROCKER
EAST ST
REN LN
CHP
FS
WALNUT LN
GHIRLANDA CT
SAN YSIDRO PK
JR HS
IOOF AV
MURRAY AV
POLK
TAFT CT
HOOVER CT
HADLEY CT
ROGERS LN
CIR
GATE CT
ROSANNA
11TH ST
GARDEN CT
LONDON DR
PL
CHURCHILL PL
THAMES DR
VICTORIA DR
KENSINGTON
HASTINGS PL
SUSSEX
BARRON
PARK
HYDE DR
STRATFORD PL
BEARCAT CT
BUS 101
101
152
G9
G7
1000
700
400E
200E
600E
6000
6300
200
A B C D E F
1 2 3 4 5 6

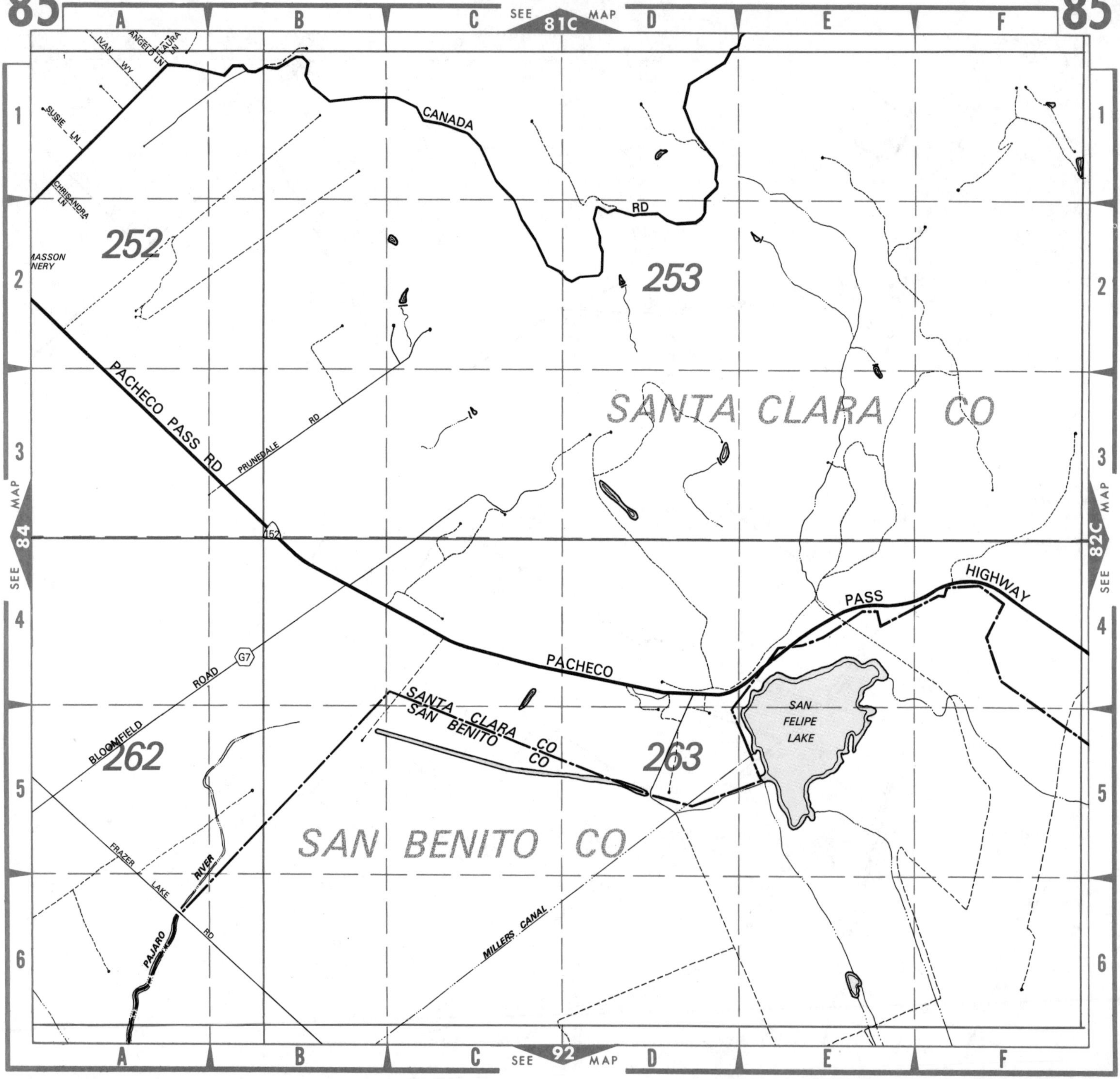

SEE 81C MAP

SEE 84 MAP
SEE 82C MAP
SEE 92 MAP

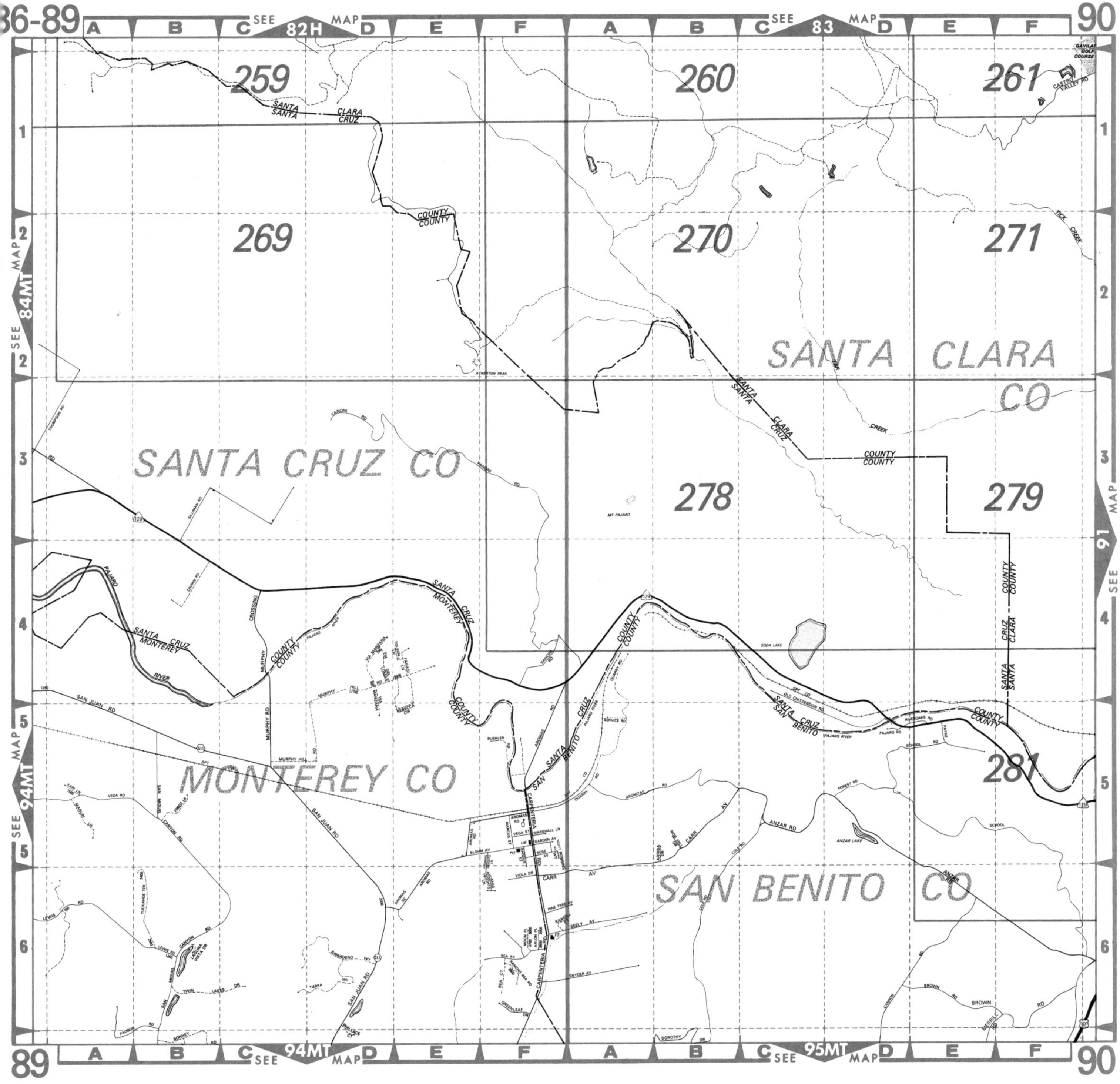

SEE 82H MAP
SEE 83 MAP
SEE 84MT MAP
SEE 91 MAP
SEE 94MT MAP
SEE 95MT MAP

SANTA CLARA

DETAIL

259 260 261
269 270 271
278 279
281

SANTA CRUZ CO

SANTA CLARA CO

MONTEREY CO

SAN BENITO CO

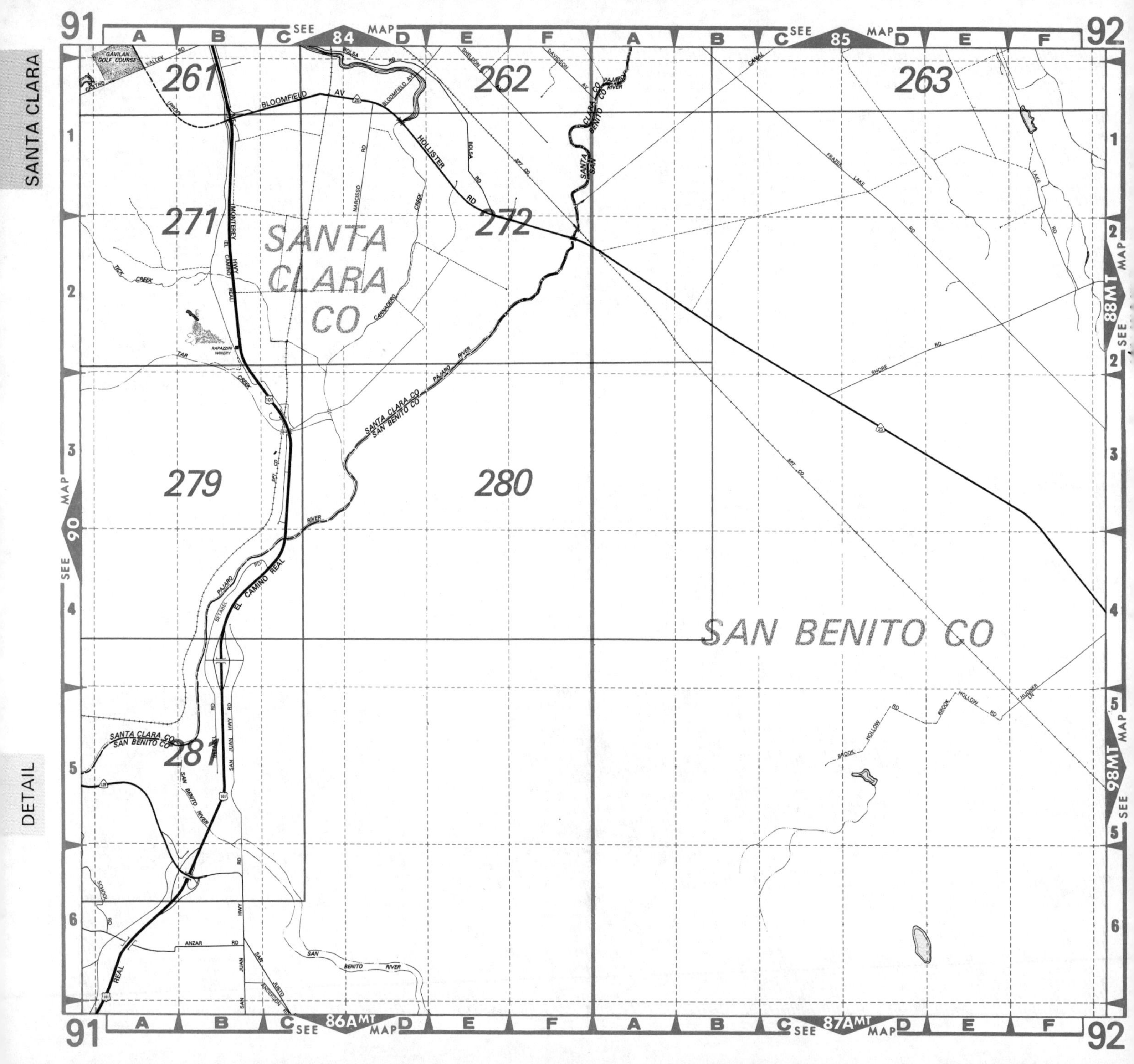

91
92
SANTA CLARA
DETAIL
SEE MAP 84
SEE MAP 85
SEE MAP 90
SEE 88MT MAP
SEE 98MT MAP
SEE 86AMT MAP
SEE 87AMT MAP
GAVILAN GOLF COURSE
261
262
263
271
272
279
280
281
SANTA CLARA CO
SAN BENITO CO
BLOOMFIELD AV
HOLLISTER RD
MONTEREY HWY
EL CAMINO REAL
PAJARO RIVER
FRAZER LAKE RD
SHORE RD
BROOK HOLLOW RD
HUDNER LN
SAN BENITO RIVER
ANZAR RD
SAN JUAN HWY
RAPAZZINI WINERY

STREET	CITY	PAGE	GRID
A			
A ST	LA	52	A6
A ST	LA	59	A1
A ST	MVW	52	C2
A ST	SVL	46	C6
AARON CT	SJ	72A	F5
AARON PL	SJ	72A	F5
AARON PARK DR	MPTS	47	F1
ABBEY CT	SJ	65	F3
ABBEY LN	C	65	F3
ABBEY LN	SJ	65	F3
ABBEYFIELD CT	SJ	72	B4
ABBEYGATE CT	SJ	71	F1
ABBOTT AV	C	65	E5
ABBOTT AV	MPTS	47	E2
ABBOTT AV	SCCO	65	E5
ABBOTT AV S	MPTS	47	E4
ABBY WOOD CT	LG	65	E5
ABDON AV	SJ	55	F3
ABDON AV	SCCO	55	F3
ABDULLA WY	S	65	C4
ABED CT	SJ	56	A6
ABEL AV	PA	44	D5
ABEL ST	MPTS	47	F4
ABELIA CT	SJ	68	A1
ABERDEEN CT	MPTS	48	A1
ABERDEEN CT	SJ	62	E4
ABERDEEN CT	S	65	B3
ABERDEEN DR	SVL	59	D1
ABERDEEN ST	SCL	54	B2
ABERDEEN WY	MPTS	48	A1
ABERFELDY WY	MPTS	48	B3
ABERFORD DR	SJ	55	C2
ABERHAVEN CT	SJ	68	A5
ABINANTE LN	SJ	66	D5
ABINGTON CT	SJ	55	C4
ABORN CT	SJ	63	D5
ABORN RD	SJ	63	C5
ABORN RD	SCCO	63	C5
ABORN RD	SCCO	63A	B4
ABORN SQ LP RD	SJ	63	B5
ABRA CT	SJ	72A	F5
ABRAMS CT	SCCO	44	A3
ACACIA AV	LA	44	E6
ACACIA AV	LA	51	E1
ACACIA AV	PA	44	C4
ACACIA AV	SVL	53	B3
ACACIA CT	SCL	54	A4
ACACIA LN	SJ	72A	F3
ACACIA ST	SJ	61	F2
ACACIA WY	MH	80	A3
ACADIA AV	MPTS	48	B3
ACADIA CT	CPTO	59	F3
ACALANES DR	SVL	52	D3
ACAPULCO DR	SJ	65	F3
ACORN CT	SJ	61	B6
ACORN CT	SCCO	77	F4
ACORN LN	LA	51	E2
ACORN WY	SJ	61	B6
ACTON CT	SCCO	71	D1
ACTON DR	SCCO	71	D1
ADA AV	MVW	52	C2
ADA AV	SCCO	52	C2
ADA DR	LG	65	E6
ADAGIO WY	SJ	68	B4
ADAIR WY	SJ	71	B2
ADALINA CT	SJ	71	C2
ADAMO CT	SJ	67	D5
ADAMO DR	SJ	67	C6
ADAMS AV	MPTS	48	B2
ADAMS AV	MH	79	D2
ADAMS CT	G	82A	A6
ADAMS CT	MVW	52	A5
ADAMS CT	SJ	55	E1
ADAMS DR	SJ	55	D1
ADAMS WY	SCL	60	E4
ADAMSWOOD DR	SJ	63	D4
ADDIEWELL PL	SJ	72	B4
ADDINGTON CT	CPTO	59	D6
ADDINGTON CT	CPTO	64	D1
ADDISON AV	PA	38	B6
ADDISON AV	PA	44	A2
ADDISON PL	SCL	53	E5
ADELAIDE WY	SJ	71	D2
ADELE AV	MVW	44	F6
ADELE PL	SJ	66	E3
ADELE PL	SCCO	66	E3
ADELHEID CT	CPTO	59	C5
ADELONG WY	SJ	72B	A4
ADENTRO ARENA	SVL	46	C6

STREET	CITY	PAGE	GRID
ADLER AV	C	66	A4
ADLER CT	SJ	68	D4
ADMIRAL PL	SJ	55	C3
ADMIRE CT	CPTO	48	B1
ADOBE AV	MPTS	47	E2
ADOBE CT	SJ	67	B5
ADOBE DR	SJ	54	F1
ADOBE LN	LAH	51	C6
ADOBE PL	PA	44	E4
ADOBE CREEK CT	SJ	56	A6
ADOBE CK LDG RD	LAH	51	B6
ADOBE RIVER CT	SJ	67	D5
ADOLFO DR	SJ	55	B2
ADONIS CT	SVL	53	B4
ADONIS WY	SJ	71	B2
ADONNA CT	LAH	51	B4
ADRA AV	SJ	61	A5
ADRA AV	SCCO	61	A5
ADRAGNA CT	SJ	67	F5
ADRIAN PL	LG	71	B3
ADRIAN WY	SJ	62	F2
ADRIAN WY	SJ	63	A2
ADRIANA AV	SCCO	59	D4
ADRIATIC WY	SCL	60	C1
ADRIEN DR	C	65	E4
AERONAUT WY	SCCO	70	B6
AETNA WY	SJ	63	A6
AFTON AV	S	65	C4
AFTON CT	SJ	72	D3
AFUERA ARENA	SVL	46	C6
AGATE CT	SCL	53	D4
AGATE DR	SCL	53	D4
AGATHA WY	SJ	67	D4
AGENA WY	SVL	52	F3
AGNES WY	PA	44	D2
AGNEW RD	SCL	53	F3
AGNEW RD	SCL	54	A1
AGUACATE CT	SJ	55	E2
AGUA VISTA DR	SJ	48	C6
AGUA VISTA DR	SJ	55	C1
AGUILA TER	SVL	59	F1
AGUILAR CT	MPTS	48	C2
AHWANEE AV	SVL	53	C2
AHWANEE AV	SVL	53	A1
AHWANEE TER N	SVL	53	C2
AHWANEE TER S	SVL	53	C2
AIDA AV	SJ	63	B5
AIELLO DR	SJ	67	E2
AIKINS WY	SJ	63	F4
AINSLEY CT	SJ	65	F3
AINSWORTH DR	CPTO	59	C3
AINSWORTH DR	SCCO	59	C3
AINTREE DR	SJ	72A	D4
AIRES LN	SJ	67	F3
AIRPORT BLVD	SJ	54	E5
AIRPORT PKWY	SJ	54	D4
AIRPORT RD	SCCO	73	F6
AITKEN AV	MVW	51	E2
AJAX DR	SVL	53	B4
AKINO CT	SJ	63	C4
AKIO WY	SJ	72	E5
AKLAN CT	SJ	72A	D4
AKRON RD N	SCCO	45	D5
AKRON RD S	SCCO	45	D5
AKRON WY	SJ	60	F5
ALADDIN DR	SJ	68	B6
ALADDIN DR	SJ	72A	B1
ALAMEDA CT	SJ	61	C2
ALAMEDA WY	SJ	61	D2
ALAMEDA, THE	SJ	61	F3
ALAMEDA, THE	SCL	54	C6
ALAMEDA, THE	SCL	61	C1
ALAMITOS DR	SVL	52	D3
ALAMITOS RD	SCCO	75	F6
ALAMITOS RD	SCCO	76	A6
ALAMITOS CK DR	SJ	76	B3
ALAMO CT	MVW	45	C6
ALAMO DR	MH	80K	E2
ALAMO DR	SJ	54	F1
ALAMO DR	SJ	72	E2
ALAMO WY	CPTO	59	D5
ALAN AV	SJ	71	E2
ALANNAH CT	PA	38	C6
ALBA CT	LA	51	D2
ALBA CT	SCCO	55	F2
ALBANESE CIR	SJ	62	E6
ALBANY CIR	SJ	60	D4
ALBANY CT	MPTS	48	B2
ALBANY DR	SJ	60	E4
ALBANY PL	G	83	E3
ALBAR CT	S	64	D5
ALBATROSS CT	C	66	B2

STREET	CITY	PAGE	GRID
ALBATROSS DR	SVL	59	F2
ALBEMAR CT	SJ	63	D5
ALBERSTONE DR	SJ	65	E2
ALBERT AV	SJ	71	E1
ALBERT CT	LG	70	F3
ALBERT DR	LG	70	F3
ALBERT WY	C	65	F3
ALBERT WY	C	66	A3
ALBERTA AV	SJ	67	A1
ALBERTA AV	SCCO	59	F2
ALBERTA AV	SVL	59	F2
ALBERTA CT	SCL	53	F5
ALBERTO WY	LG	70	F4
ALBERTSWORTH LN	LAH	58	E2
ALBION CT	SJ	67	D4
ALBION CT	SVL	59	C1
ALBION DR	SJ	67	D5
ALBION LN	SVL	59	C1
ALBRIGHT CT	LG	65	F6
ALBRIGHT CT	LG	66	A6
ALBRIGHT CT	LG	70	F1
ALBRIGHT CT	LG	71	A1
ALBRIGHT WY	LG	65	F6
ALBRIGHT WY	LG	66	A6
ALBRIGHT WY	LG	70	F1
ALBRIGHT WY	LG	71	A1
ALBY CT	SJ	66	F6
ALBY CT	SJ	71	E1
ALCALDE RD	CPTO	59	C5
ALCALDE RD	SCCO	59	C5
ALCALDE ST	SCL	53	F1
ALCANTE DR	SJ	60	B6
ALCANTE DR	SJ	65	B1
ALCAZAR AV	CPTO	59	D5
ALCAZAR AV	SCCO	59	D5
ALCAZAR DR	SJ	72	E2
ALCOSTA DR	MPTS	48	A2
ALCOTT WY	S	65	C5
ALDEAN AV	MVW	44	F5
ALDEN WY	SJ	61	A4
ALDER CT	SJ	68	D4
ALDER CT	S	65	A4
ALDER DR	MPTS	47	D5
ALDERBROOK LN	CPTO	60	B6
ALDERBROOK LN	SJ	60	B6
ALDERBROOK LN	SJ	65	B1
ALDERBROOK WY	SCCO	60	B5
ALDER CREEK CT	SJ	63	D1
ALDRCRFT HTS RD	SCCO	73	E6
ALDRCRFT HTS RD	SCCO	78G	F1
ALDRCRFT HTS RD	SCCO	78H	A1
ALDERMONT CT	MH	79	E5
ALDERNEY CT	SCCO	59	C3
ALDER SPRING WY	SJ	72A	F4
ALDERWOOD AV	SVL	46	D6
ALDERWOOD DR	SJ	48	B6
ALDO AV	SCL	54	B3
ALDO CT	SJ	56	B6
ALDRICH WY	SJ	63	B5
ALDWORTH DR	SJ	63	E3
ALEGRE AV	LA	52	A5
ALEJANDRO DR	LAH	51	B2
ALERCHE DR	LG	71	E4
ALESSI CT	SCCO	81A	B6
ALESTER AV	PA	38	C6
ALESTER AV	PA	44	C1
ALEX DR	SJ	65	E4
ALEXANDER AV	LG	70	D4
ALEXANDER AV	MS	70	D4
ALEXANDER AV	SJ	55	E5
ALEXANDER AV	SCL	60	D3
ALEXANDER CT	LA	59	C1
ALEXANDER CT	SJ	55	F5
ALEXANDER PL	LAH	51	C2
ALEXANDER ST	G	84	A1
ALEXANDER ST	SCCO	84	A1
ALEXANDER WY	LA	59	C1
ALEXANDER WY	MPTS	48	B1
ALEXANDRIA LN	SJ	60	D5
ALEXIAN DR	SJ	55	E5
ALEXIS CT	SJ	62	F1
ALEXIS DR	LAH	50	E3
ALEXIS DR	PA	50	E4
ALFORD AV	LA	59	C2
ALFRED ST	SCL	54	A3
ALFRED WY	SJ	62	F2
ALFRED WY	SJ	63	A2
ALGER DR	PA	44	D4
ALGIERS AV	SJ	62	E4
ALHAMBRA AV	CPTO	59	D4
ALHAMBRA DR	SCL	53	E4
ALICANTE LN	LAH	51	C2
ALICE AV	C	66	B3

STREET	CITY	PAGE	GRID
ALICE AV	MVW	52	C3
ALICE DR	SCL	61	A1
ALICE WY	SVL	60	B1
ALICIA CT	CPTO	59	B5
ALICIA WY	LA	51	E2
ALISA CT	SCCO	80	A3
ALISAL AV	SJ	66	F4
ALISAL AV	SJ	67	A4
ALISAL AV	SCCO	66	F4
ALISAL CT	MPTS	48	A1
ALISON AV	MVW	52	A4
ALKAE CT	SJ	68	B1
ALKIRE AV	MH	79	D5
ALL AMERICA WY	SVL	52	F4
ALLARDICE WY	SCCO	52	A5
ALLEGAN CIR	SJ	72A	B3
ALLEGHANY CT	SJ	72	D3
ALLEGHENY DR	SVL	52	E4
ALLEGRO LN	SJ	68	B4
ALLEN AV	SJ	72	D2
ALLEN AV	SCCO	72	D2
ALLEN CT	PA	44	D3
ALLEN CT	SCL	60	D3
ALLEN WY	C	65	F4
ALLEN WY	SCL	60	D3
ALLENCREST DR	SJ	72	B2
ALLENCREST DR	SCCO	72	B2
ALLENDALE AV	S	65	B5
ALLENTOWN CT	SJ	67	B2
ALLENWOOD CT	SJ	63	D4
ALLENWOOD DR	SJ	63	D4
ALLISON WY	SJ	48	B6
ALLISON WY	SVL	52	E6
ALLISON WY	SVL	59	E1
ALLSTON CT	SJ	72	D6
ALLSTON WY	SJ	72	D6
ALMA AV	SJ	62	C5
ALMA CT	LA	51	D2
ALMA CT	SJ	62	C5
ALMA CT	SCCO	78G	E1
ALMA LP	SJ	62	B6
ALMA ST	MVW	44	E5
ALMA ST	PA	43	F1
ALMA ST	PA	44	A2
ALMA ST	SJ	62	C5
ALMA TER	SJ	62	B6
ALMA WY	SJ	62	B6
ALMA BRIDGE RD	SCCO	73	D1
ALMA COLLEGE RD	SCCO	73	C4
ALMADEN AV	MPTS	47	E2
ALMADEN AV	SJ	62	B4
ALMADEN AV	CPTO	59	D5
ALMADEN AV	SCCO	62	B4
ALMADEN AV	SVL	53	C2
ALMADEN BLVD	SJ	62	A3
ALMADEN BLVD N	SJ	61	F3
ALMADEN BLVD N	SJ	62	A3
ALMADEN CT	LAH	51	A5
ALMADEN EXPWY	SJ	67	B2
ALMADEN EXPWY	SJ	75	F1
ALMADEN EXPWY	SCCO	67	B2
ALMADEN EXPWY	SCCO	76	A1
ALMADEN RD	SJ	62	B6
ALMADEN RD	SJ	67	B2
ALMADEN RD	SJ	72	C4
ALMADEN RD	SJ	75	F2
ALMADEN RD	SCCO	67	B2
ALMADEN RD	SCCO	75	F2
ALMADEN RD	SCCO	76	A2
ALMADEN RD	SCCO	78L	B1
ALMADEN WY	SCCO	76	A5
ALMADEN VLY RD	SJ	72	A4
ALMADEN VLGE RD	SJ	75	F1
ALMA JO CT	MS	70	D2
ALMANOR AV	SVL	52	F1
ALMANOR CT	SJ	55	D1
ALMANSA CT	SJ	55	E2
ALMARIDA DR	C	66	B1
ALMENDRA AV	LG	70	E4
ALMENDRA LN	LA	51	E2
ALMERIA DR	SJ	72	D2
ALMOND AV	LA	51	E2
ALMOND DR	SJ	63	C3
ALMOND WY	MH	80	A3
ALMOND BLOSM CT	LG	71	E4
ALMOND BLOSM LN	LG	71	E3
ALMOND BLOSM LN	SJ	71	E3
ALMOND GROVE CT	SJ	68	A6
ALMOND HILL CT	LG	70	F1
ALMOND ORCHD DR	MH	79	B4
ALMONDWOOD WY	SJ	72A	A6
ALMONDWOOD WY	SJ	75	F1
ALOHA AV	S	64	F6

STREET	CITY	PAGE	GRID
ALOHA AV	S	69	F1
ALOHA DR	SJ	67	E4
ALONDRA LN	S	70	B2
ALONSO DR	SJ	61	D6
ALONSO DR	SJ	66	D1
ALPET DR	SCCO	80	A2
ALPHA CT	C	66	A4
ALPINE AV	LG	70	E5
ALPINE AV	SJ	55	F4
ALPINE AV	SCL	60	E1
ALPINE DR	CPTO	59	C4
ALPINE TER	SVL	52	E3
ALRAM RD	SCCO	76	A5
ALRIC CT	SJ	72A	C4
ALRIC DR	SJ	72A	C4
ALRIDGE DR	SVL	52	E6
ALRIDGE DR	SVL	59	E1
ALTA AV	MVW	45	A4
ALTA AV	SCCO	45	A4
ALTA CT	SJ	54	F2
ALTA LN N	LAH	51	C4
ALTA LN S	LAH	51	C4
ALTADENA AV	SCCO	56	B4
ALTADENA DR	LAH	51	C2
ALTA GLEN CT	SJ	66	E2
ALTA GLEN DR	SJ	66	E2
ALTA HEIGHTS CT	LG	70	F5
ALTAIR WY	SVL	52	F3
ALTAMEAD DR	LA	52	B5
ALTA MESA AV	PA	44	D5
ALTA MIRA DR	SCL	60	D1
ALTAMIRA PL	SJ	66	D5
ALTAMONT AV	SJ	66	F4
ALTAMONT AV	SJ	67	A4
ALTAMONT CIR	LAH	50	E5
ALTAMONT CT	LAH	51	B6
ALTAMONT CT	SVL	53	B2
ALTAMONT DR	LAH	51	A5
ALTAMONT DR	MPTS	39	F6
ALTAMONT DR	MPTS	47	F1
ALTAMONT RD	LAH	50	A5
ALTAMONT RD	LAH	51	B6
ALTA TIERRA CT	LG	71	D5
ALTA TIERRA RD	LAH	51	C4
ALTA VISTA AV	LA	51	D3
ALTA VISTA AV	S	64	F6
ALTA VISTA AV	S	65	A6
ALTA VISTA WY	SCCO	56	B2
ALTHAM CT	SJ	48	D6
ALTHOFF WY	SJ	62	D2
ALTIPLANO WY	SJ	72A	D4
ALTO CT	SJ	63	D2
ALTON ST	MPTS	47	E2
ALTO PASEO CT	SJ	72	B5
ALTOS OAKS DR	LA	52	A6
ALTO VERDE LN	LAH	51	C3
ALTURAS AV	SVL	53	A1
ALTURAS DR	SCCO	43	E5
ALTURA VISTA	LG	65	D6
ALUM ROCK AV	SJ	55	E6
ALUM ROCK AV	SJ	56	B4
ALUM ROCK AV	SJ	62	D1
ALUM ROCK AV	SCCO	56	B4
ALUM ROCK RD	SJ	56	B2
ALUM RCK FLS RD	SJ	49	D6
ALUM RCK FLS RD	SJ	56	F1
ALUM RCK FLS RD	SCCO	49	D6
ALUM RCK FLS RD	SCCO	56	F1
ALUM RCK FLS RD	SCCO	56A	A1
ALVARADO AV	LA	51	E2
ALVARADO AV	SVL	53	B2
ALVARADO CT	SJ	71	F4
ALVARADO CT	SCCO	43	F5
ALVARADO CT	SCCO	44	A5
ALVARADO CT	S	65	C4
ALVARADO DR	SCL	53	F5
ALVARADO ROW	SCCO	43	F4
ALVERNAZ DR	SJ	68	B2
ALVES CT	SJ	54	F1
ALVES DR	CPTO	59	E4
ALVESWOOD CIR	SJ	48	B6
ALVIENA DR	SCCO	55	F4
ALVIN AV	SJ	63	A5
ALVIN ST	MVW	44	F5
ALVINA CT	LA	52	A5
ALVISO ST	SCL	54	B6
ALVISO ST	SCL	61	C2
ALVISO-MLPTS RD	MPTS	47	B4
ALVISO-MLPTS RD	SJ	46	F4
ALVISO-MLPTS RD	SJ	47	B4
ALVISO-MLPTS RD	SCCO	46	F4
ALVISO-MLPTS RD	SCCO	47	B4

STREET	CITY	PAGE	GRID
ALWOOD CT	SJ	63	D3
AMADOR AV	LA	51	F4
AMADOR AV	SVL	53	C2
AMADOR CT	SJ	62	F1
AMADOR CT	SJ	63	A1
AMADOR DR	SJ	62	F1
AMADOR DR	SJ	63	A1
AMADOR OAK CT	CPTO	59	B4
AMALFI WY	MVW	52	A5
AMANDA AV	G	82	D6
AMANDA DR	SJ	67	D5
AMANDA LN	LG	71	B4
AMANDA LN	SCCO	71	B4
AMAPOLA DR	SJ	60	B6
AMARANTA AV	PA	44	C5
AMARANTA CT	PA	44	C5
AMARGOSA CT	SJ	68	D4
AMARILLO AV	PA	44	D2
AMARYL CT	SJ	55	D2
AMARYL DR	SJ	55	D2
AMATO AV	SCCO	65	F3
AMBASSADOR CT	LG	70	E5
AMBER CT	G	83	D2
AMBER DR	SJ	61	A6
AMBER DR	SJ	66	A1
AMBER LN	LA	51	E5
AMBERGROVE DR	SJ	55	B3
AMBER OAK CT	LG	65	E5
AMBERSTONE DR	SJ	65	E2
AMBERWOOD CT	SJ	48	B5
AMBERWOOD LN	SJ	48	B5
AMBERWOOD LN	SCCO	80K	F2
AMBLER CT	SJ	68	B3
AMBLER WY	SJ	68	B3
AMBLESIDE LN	S	70	C1
AMBOY DR	SJ	67	D5
AMBRA WY	MPTS	48	E5
AMBRIC KNOLS RD	SCCO	69	E1
AMBRIC KNOLS RD	S	64	E6
AMBRIC KNOLS RD	S	69	E1
AMBROSE CT	SJ	68	B2
AMBROSE RD	SCCO	69	D4
AMBUM AV	SJ	63	E3
AMBY DR	SJ	71	F3
AMELIA CT	CPTO	59	C4
AMELIA DR	SJ	71	F2
AMELIA DR	SJ	72	A2
AMELIA WY	SCL	53	F6
AMERICA AV	SVL	53	A3
AMERICAN CT	SJ	72	D5
AMERICUS DR	SJ	63	E3
AMES AV	MPTS	48	B4
AMES AV	PA	44	D3
AMES CT	PA	44	E3
AMESBURY WY	SJ	63	B1
AMETHYST CT	SJ	67	C6
AMETHYST DR	SCL	53	D4
AMHERST CT	LAH	50	F2
AMHERST CT	MVW	52	B5
AMHERST DR	CPTO	60	B4
AMHERST LN	SJ	61	A6
AMHERST ST	PA	44	A4
AMIGOS CT	SCCO	51	E5
AMISTAD CT	CPTO	59	B5
AMISTAD LN	SCCO	81	E5
AMONDO DR	SJ	60	D6
AMONDO DR	SJ	65	D1
AMOS WY	SJ	63	E6
AMPHITHEATRE PY	MVW	45	A3
AMSTEL CT	SJ	55	E5
AMSTUTZ DR	SJ	60	E6
AMULET DR	CPTO	59	D3
AMULET PL	CPTO	59	D3
AMUR CT	MPTS	39	E5
AMUR CREEK CT	SJ	75	E1
AMUR OAK LN	SJ	55	E6
AMUR OAK LN	SJ	62	E1
ANACAPA CT	MPTS	48	A2
ANACAPA DR	LAH	51	B3
ANACONDA WY	SVL	59	D1
ANA PRIVADA	MVW	52	D1
ANCHOR WY	SJ	48	B6
ANCIL WY	SJ	60	F6
ANCIL WY	SJ	61	A5
ANCORA CT	LA	59	B3
ANCRUM CT	SJ	63	C5
ANDALUSIA WY	SJ	66	F4
ANDERSON CT	MVW	52	C1
ANDERSON DR	LA	51	F4
ANDERSON RD	SCCO	56	C4
ANDORA DR	SJ	63	C2
ANDOVER DR	SVL	52	D4

1991 SANTA CLARA COUNTY STREET INDEX

STREET	CITY	PAGE	GRID
ANDOVER LN	SJ	66	E6
ANDOVER LN	SJ	71	E1
ANDOVER PL	G	83	E3
ANDOVER WY	LA	59	A2
ANDRE AV	MVW	52	C5
ANDRE CT	LG	70	F4
ANDREA CT	SJ	60	F6
ANDREA CT	SJ	61	A6
ANDREA DR	SJ	60	F6
ANDREA DR	SJ	61	A6
ANDREA PL	SCL	53	E6
ANDREW CT	S	70	B1
ANDREWS AV	SJ	66	D6
ANDREWS ST	LG	70	E3
ANDREWS ST	MS	70	E3
ANDSBURY AV	MVW	52	C1
ANFIELD CT	SJ	67	C5
ANGEL AV	SVL	52	F3
ANGEL CT	LG	71	B3
ANGELA CT	G	83	F3
ANGELA CT	LA	51	E3
ANGELA CT	SJ	66	C5
ANGELA DR	LA	51	E3
ANGELA ST	SJ	62	B6
ANGELA ST	SJ	67	B1
ANGELINA DR	SCL	60	D1
ANGELL CT	SCCO	44	A3
ANGELLA AV	SVL	59	E1
ANGELO LN	SCCO	81C	A6
ANGIE AV	SJ	62	F1
ANGMAR CT	SJ	68	B1
ANGUS CT	S	65	A4
ANGUS DR	MPTS	47	F2
ANITA AV	SCCO	51	E5
ANITA ST	SJ	61	F2
ANJOU CREEK CIR	SJ	75	E1
ANJOU CREEK CT	SJ	75	E1
ANN PL	MPTS	40	A5
ANNA AV	MVW	44	F5
ANNA DR	SJ	71	D2
ANNA DR	SCL	53	F6
ANNA DR	SCL	54	A6
ANNA DR	SCL	60	F1
ANNA DR	SCL	61	A1
ANNANDALE PL	SJ	63	E5
ANNAPOLIS WY	SJ	72	B1
ANN ARBOR AV	CPTO	59	E4
ANN ARBOR AV	SCCO	59	E4
ANN ARBOR CT	CPTO	59	E4
ANN ARBOR CT	LG	71	B4
ANN ARBOR DR	LG	71	B4
ANNDARLING DR	SJ	55	D6
ANNE CT	SJ	71	D3
ANNE LN	MH	79	D6
ANNE LN	SCCO	60	B4
ANNE WY	LG	71	C3
ANNE WY	SJ	71	C3
ANNE MARIE CT	SJ	48	C6
ANNERLY CT	SJ	63	C5
ANNETTE LN	LA	59	C2
ANNETTE WY	CPTO	59	F6
ANNIE LN	SCCO	72	E5
ANNIE LAURIE AV	MVW	45	D6
ANNIE LAURIE WY	SJ	68	B1
ANN MARIE CT	SCCO	81	B4
ANNONA AV	SJ	63	A4
ANO NUEVO AV	SVL	52	E2
ANSDELL WY	SJ	72A	B3
ANSHEN CT	SVL	53	B5
ANSLEY PL	S	65	C3
ANSON AV	CPTO	59	E3
ANSON CT	G	82	C6
ANT CT	SCCO	80	A6
ANTELOPE DR	SJ	55	B4
ANTERO CT	SJ	55	B4
ANTHONY CT	MVW	51	F2
ANTHONY DR	SJ	65	E3
ANTHONY PL	CPTO	59	C4
ANTIGUA CT	SJ	72	B2
ANTIGUA DR	SJ	72	B2
ANTIGUA WY	SJ	72	B2
ANTOINETTE DR	CPTO	59	F5
ANTOINETTE DR	CPTO	60	A5
ANTON CT	PA	44	C3
ANTON WY	CPTO	59	E4
ANTONACCI CT	SJ	63	D2
ANTONIO CT	G	83	F3
ANTONIO LN	SJ	66	A1
ANTONIO LN	SCCO	66	A1
ANTWERP LN	SJ	72	A3
ANVIL CT	SJ	55	D4
ANVILWOOD AV	SVL	46	D5

STREET	CITY	PAGE	GRID
ANVILWOOD CT	SVL	46	D5
ANZA DR	S	65	B4
ANZA RD	SJ	47	C6
ANZA ST	MVW	52	B2
APACHE CT	SJ	72	E2
APACHE TR	SCCO	73	E6
APOLLO CT	SJ	62	F6
APOLLO DR	SJ	62	F6
APOLLO WY	S	64	F4
APOLLO WY	SVL	53	D3
APOLLO HTS CT	SCCO	69	E3
APPALOOSA DR	SCCO	81	B3
APPALOOSA WY	LAH	51	A5
APPERSON RDG CT	SJ	63	E5
APPERSON RDG DR	SJ	65	E5
APPIAN LN	SJ	62	D3
APPIAN WY	MH	80K	E2
APPLE TER	SJ	68	D3
APPLE BLOSSM DR	SJ	68	B6
APPLEBLOSSOM LN	SCCO	71	A3
APPLEGATE CT	SJ	72A	D4
APPLETON DR	SJ	61	A6
APPLE TREE DR	CPTO	60	A3
APPLETREE LN	MVW	51	F4
APPLETREE LN	MVW	52	A4
APPLE VALLEY DR	SJ	67	C3
APPLEWOOD DR	SJ	60	D6
APPLEY WY	SJ	71	B2
APRICOT AV	C	66	C3
APRICOT LN	LG	70	D4
APRICOT LN	MVW	52	B5
APRICOT LN	SJ	68	E1
APRICOT HILL CT	S	65	C5
APRIL DR	SJ	72A	D1
APRIL WY	C	66	D2
APRILSONG CT	SJ	55	C3
APSIS AV	SJ	66	B6
APSIS AV	SJ	71	B1
APSIS CT	SJ	66	B6
APSIS CT	SJ	71	B1
APTOS AV	SJ	68	B4
APTOS BEACH CT	SJ	72A	F4
AQUARIUS DR	SJ	68	E3
AQUILA AV	SJ	66	B6
AQUILA AV	SJ	71	B1
AQUINO WY	S	70	C1
ARABIAN CT	MH	80	C3
ARABIAN CT	SJ	72A	A3
ARABIAN ST	SJ	72A	A3
ARAGON CT	SJ	66	E4
ARAGON WY	SJ	66	E4
ARAM AV	C	66	C1
ARAM AV	SJ	66	C1
ARAMIS DR	SJ	56	B6
ARANA CT	MPTS	48	B1
ARAPAHO DR	SJ	72	F2
ARAPAHOE TR	SCCO	73	E6
ARASTRADERO RD	LAH	50	E3
ARASTRADERO RD	LAH	50	F2
ARASTRADERO RD	PA	44	D6
ARASTRADERO RD	PA	50	E3
ARASTRADERO RD	PA	51	B2
ARASTRADERO RD	SCCO	50	E3
ARASTRADERO RD	SCCO	51	B2
ARATA CT	SJ	62	B6
ARATA WY	SCCO	60	C4
ARAUJO ST	SJ	55	B3
ARBELECHE LN	S	64	F6
ARBOL DR	PA	44	C5
ARBOLADO WY	S	70	C1
ARBOLEDA DR	LA	51	F4
ARBOR AV	SCCO	51	F6
ARBOR AV	SCCO	52	A6
ARBOR AV	SCCO	59	A1
ARBOR AV	SVL	52	F2
ARBOR AV	SVL	53	A2
ARBOR CT	MVW	52	C5
ARBOR DR	SJ	67	B1
ARBOR DELL WY	SJ	71	F3
ARBORETUM DR	LA	59	B3
ARBORETUM RD	SCCO	59	B3
ARBORETUM RD	PA	43	E2
ARBORETUM RD	SCCO	43	E2
ARBOR PARK CT	SJ	61	E6
ARBOR PARK DR	SJ	61	E6
ARBOR VALLEY DR	SJ	72A	E4
ARBOR VALLEY PL	SJ	72A	E4
ARBOR VISTA WY	SJ	61	F6
ARBUCKLE AV	SJ	66	D6
ARBUCKLE CT	SCL	54	A3
ARBUELO WY	LA	51	E2
ARBUTUS AV	PA	44	E3

STREET	CITY	PAGE	GRID
ARBUTUS AV	SVL	53	A4
ARBUTUS DR	SJ	71	F2
ARBUTUS DR	SJ	72	A2
ARC RD	C	66	C2
ARCADIA AV	SCL	60	D4
ARCADIA DR	SJ	61	A4
ARCADIA PL	PA	38	B6
ARCADIA PLMS DR	S	65	C6
ARCHBOW CT	SJ	68	D3
ARCHBURY CT	SJ	63	E4
ARCHCOVE CT	SJ	68	C4
ARCHER CT	C	65	E5
ARCHER ST	SJ	46	E3
ARCHER ST	SJ	54	E5
ARCHER WY	C	65	E5
ARCHGLEN WY	SJ	68	C4
ARCHIBALD DR	SCCO	69	E2
ARCHSHIRE CT	SJ	63	E4
ARCHWOOD CIR	SJ	63	D4
ARCO CT	SJ	72A	A1
ARCOLA CT	SJ	63	D5
ARCTIC AV	SJ	67	E1
ARDEN CT	S	65	B2
ARDEN WY	SJ	63	A2
ARDEN FARMS PL	SJ	68	A3
ARDENWOOD DR	SJ	65	A2
ARDILLA CT	SJ	66	C1
ARDIS AV	SJ	61	A5
ARDIS AV	SCCO	61	A4
ARDIS DR	SJ	67	B2
ARDMORE CT	S	65	B2
ARDMORE WY	SJ	71	F2
ARDSLEY CT	SJ	72	B3
AREQUIPA CT	SJ	72A	E3
ARGONAUT DR	S	64	F4
ARGONAUT DR	S	65	A4
ARGONNE DR	S	64	F4
ARGUELLO PL	SCL	53	F6
ARGUELLO PL	SCL	60	F1
ARGUELLO ST	SCCO	43	F4
ARGUS WY	SCL	54	B2
ARGYLE CT	SJ	48	D5
ARIC LN	LAH	51	B2
ARIEL CT	SJ	72A	A2
ARIEL DR	SJ	72A	A2
ARIES WY	SVL	52	F3
ARIZONA AV	MPTS	39	E5
ARIZONA AV	MPTS	47	F1
ARLEE DR	MS	70	D3
ARLEEN AV	SVL	60	A1
ARLEEN WY	SJ	65	D3
ARLEN CT	SJ	48	D4
ARLENE DR	SCL	60	F1
ARLETTA AV	SCCO	61	C5
ARLIA DR	SCCO	81	E4
ARLINE LN	SCCO	80	B2
ARLINGTON CT	SVL	52	E4
ARLINGTON DR	CPTO	60	A6
ARLINGTON LN	SJ	60	A6
ARLINGTON LN	SJ	64	F1
ARLINGTON LN	SJ	65	A1
ARMAND AV	MVW	45	C5
ARMAND CT	G	83	E2
ARMAND DR	MPTS	48	C2
ARMANINI AV	SCL	60	F2
ARMANINI AV	SCL	61	A2
ARMDALE CT	SJ	63	C5
ARMED CT	SJ	68	C5
ARMONK CT	SJ	68	C6
ARMOUR DR	SCL	47	A6
ARMOUR DR	SCL	54	A1
ARMSBY LN	SCCO	80K	B3
ARMSTEAD CT	SJ	63	B5
ARMSTRONG PL	SCL	60	F2
ARNERICH RD	SCCO	71	D6
ARNERICH HLL CT	SCCO	71	D5
ARNERICH HLL RD	SCCO	71	D6
ARNICA CT	SJ	68	B5
ARNOLD AV	SJ	54	E6
ARNOLD AV	SCCO	45	C5
ARNOLD DR	G	82	E6
ARNOLD WY	SJ	61	C6
ARNOLD WY	SJ	66	C1
ARNOTT WY	C	66	D3
ARPEGGIO AV	SJ	67	E5
ARQUEADO DR	SJ	63	D3
ARQUES AV	SVL	52	F3
ARQUES AV	SVL	53	B3
ARRAN CT	SVL	59	F1
ARRAN CT	SVL	60	A1
ARRIBA CT	SCCO	51	F6
ARRIBA CT	SCCO	52	A6
ARRIBA CT	SCCO	58	F1

STREET	CITY	PAGE	GRID
ARRIBA CT	SCCO	59	A1
ARRIBA DR	SVL	52	D3
ARROBA WY	SJ	66	F5
ARROW LN	SJ	66	E1
ARROWHEAD DR	SJ	68	C6
ARROWHEAD DR	SJ	72	F3
ARROWHEAD DR	SJ	72A	B1
ARROWHEAD LN	SCCO	64	E2
ARROWHEAD WY	PA	44	D1
ARROWOOD CT	LA	51	F5
ARROWOOD LN	SJ	65	E3
ARROW ROCK PL	SVL	59	D1
ARROYO CIR	G	82A	A6
ARROYO CIR	G	84	A1
ARROYO DR	SJ	54	F1
ARROYO DR	SCL	60	F1
ARROYO RD	LA	51	F3
ARROYO RD	LA	52	A3
ARROYO WY	LAH	51	A5
ARROYO WY	SJ	62	C2
ARR DE ARGUELLO	S	64	E3
ARROYO DE ORO	SJ	55	D6
ARR DE PLATINA	SJ	55	D6
ARROYO GRAND WY	LG	70	F2
ARROYO GRAND WY	LG	71	A2
ARROYO OAKS	SCCO	58	E2
ARROYO SECO DR	C	66	D3
ARROYO SECO DR	SCCO	66	D3
ARTHUR AV	SJ	56	B6
ARTHUR CT	LA	59	B1
ARTHUR CT	SCL	60	E4
ARTHUR PL	SJ	56	B6
ARUNDEL CT	SJ	67	D5
ASBURY CT	MVW	45	B6
ASBURY PL	SCL	60	F2
ASBURY ST	SJ	61	F1
ASCENSION DR	LAH	51	B3
ASCENSION DR	S	65	B2
ASCOT CT	MH	80	B3
ASCHAUER CT	SJ	55	B4
ASCOT LN	SJ	67	F2
ASH CT	C	66	C2
ASH CT	LG	70	E1
ASH CT	MH	80	A3
ASH ST	PA	44	B3
ASH ST	SCL	54	A1
ASHBOURNE DR	SVL	60	A1
ASHBROOK CIR	SJ	66	B6
ASHBROOK CIR	SJ	71	B1
ASHBURTON DR	SJ	72A	B3
ASHBY AV	SJ	71	C1
ASHBY DR	PA	38	B6
ASHBY LN	LA	51	D2
ASHCROFT CT	SCCO	82A	A1
ASHCROFT LN	SJ	72	B2
ASHCROFT WY	SVL	59	C2
ASHDALE DR	SCCO	56	B5
ASHEBORO CT	SJ	55	B2
ASHER CT	SJ	66	B6
ASHER CT	SJ	71	B1
ASHFIELD CT	SJ	72	B5
ASHFORD CT	SJ	55	B4
ASHGLEN WY	SJ	55	D4
ASH GROVE CT	SJ	68	B6
ASHLAND DR	MPTS	48	B2
ASHLAND WY	SJ	65	D3
ASHLER AV	LG	70	E3
ASHLEY CT	S	64	F3
ASHLEY PL	MVW	51	F2
ASHLEY WY	S	64	F3
ASHLOCK CT	C	65	E5
ASHMEADE CT	SJ	66	D2
ASHMONT DR	SJ	68	C4
ASHRIDGE LN	SJ	68	C1
ASHTON AV	PA	44	D3
ASHTON CT	PA	44	D3
ASHTON CT	S	65	B2
ASHWOOD CT	SJ	47	F6
ASHWOOD LN	SJ	48	C4
ASHWORTH WY	SJ	63	E3
ASILOMAR TER	SVL	52	E3
ASKAM LN	LA	59	C2
ASKHAM PLACE CT	SJ	68	C1
ASPEN CT	SJ	71	E2
ASPEN DR	SCL	60	E3
ASPEN DR	SCCO	59	B2
ASPEN WY	MH	80	A3
ASPEN WY	PA	44	E3
ASPEN WY	SCCO	59	B2
ASPENRIDGE DR	MPTS	39	E6
ASPESI CT	S	65	C5
ASPESI DR	S	65	C5
ASSINBOINE TR	SCCO	73	E6

STREET	CITY	PAGE	GRID
ASSUNTA WY	SJ	66	D5
ASTER AV	SVL	53	C4
ASTER CT	CPTO	64	E2
ASTER CT	SVL	53	B4
ASTER LN	CPTO	64	E1
ASTORIA DR	SVL	59	D1
ASTRAHAN LN	SJ	63	D2
ASTRO CT	SJ	55	B2
ATHENE DR	SCCO	56	A5
ATHENOUR CT	SJ	72	A4
ATHERTON AV	SJ	65	D2
ATHERTON CIR	SCCO	81	A3
ATHERTON CT	LAH	51	C4
ATHERTON DR	SCL	60	E3
ATHERTON WY	SCCO	81	A3
ATHERWOOD AV	CPTO	60	B5
ATHOS PL	S	65	B5
ATLANTA AV	SJ	61	F5
ATLANTA AV	SJ	62	A5
ATLANTIC CT	SCL	53	F2
ATLAS AV	SJ	61	E3
ATRIUM CIR	S	64	F2
ATRIUM DR	S	64	F2
ATTEBERRY LN	SJ	47	F6
ATTEBERRY LN	SJ	54	F1
ATWOOD CT	LG	71	B3
ATWOOD CT	SJ	47	F6
ATWOOD DR	SJ	63	B5
AUBURN CT	CPTO	60	B3
AUBURN DR	CPTO	60	B3
AUBURN LN	CPTO	59	C3
AUBURN WY	MH	80K	F2
AUBURN WY	SJ	60	E4
AUDREY AV	C	65	F5
AUDREY DR	MH	79	F4
AUDUBON DR	SJ	62	E4
AUGUST DR	SJ	72A	D1
AUGUST LN	CPTO	59	E5
AUGUSTA CT	LG	70	E3
AUGUSTA CT	MPTS	40	C5
AUGUSTA CT	SCL	53	E5
AUGUSTA PL	SCL	53	E5
AUGUSTA WY	SJ	65	D1
AUGUSTINE AV	LG	70	F3
AUGUSTINE AV	LG	71	A3
AUGUSTINE DR	SCL	53	E3
AULIN DR	SJ	67	B4
AURA CT	LA	52	A6
AURA WY	LA	52	A6
AURELIAN LN	SJ	66	D1
AURORA AV	SJ	60	E5
AURORA LN	LG	71	B2
AUSTIN AV	LA	59	B1
AUSTIN CT	SJ	62	C5
AUSTIN PL	SCL	60	F2
AUSTIN WY	MS	70	C2
AUSTIN WY	SCCO	70	C2
AUSTIN WY	S	70	C2
AUSTWICK CT	SJ	72A	E4
AUTOMATION PKWY	SJ	55	B2
AUTREY ST	MPTS	39	E5
AUTUMN LN	LA	52	A6
AUTUMN LN	SJ	72A	D1
AUTUMN ST	SJ	61	F3
AUTUMN ESTATES	SJ	68	F2
AUTUMN GOLD DR	SJ	55	B2
AUTUMN RIDGE LN	SJ	48	E5
AUTUMNSONG WY	SJ	55	B3
AUTUMNTREE CT	SJ	55	B2
AUTUMNVALE DR	SJ	48	B6
AUTUMNWOOD CT	SJ	63	E4
AUZERAIS AV	SJ	61	E4
AUZERAIS AV	SJ	62	A4
AUZERAIS CT	LG	71	D4
AVALANI AV	SJ	55	D5
AVALON CT	PA	44	D3
AVALON DR	LA	51	E3
AVALON DR	MVW	51	E3
AVALON DR	SJ	67	A4
AVATI CT	SJ	55	B3
AVENIDA LN	CPTO	59	B5
AVENIDA ABETOS	SJ	72	F1
AVD ALMENDROS	SJ	72	E1
AVENIDA ALONDRA	SVL	46	C6
AVENIDA ARBOLES	SJ	68	A6
AVENIDA ARBOLES	SJ	72	F1
AVENIDA ARBOLES	SJ	72A	A1
AVENIDA CARLOS	SVL	46	C6
AVENIDA CRESTA	LG	71	C4
AVD DE ANGELINA	SCL	47	A6
AVD DE CARMEN	SCL	47	A5
AVD DE COBRE	SJ	55	D6

STREET	CITY	PAGE	GRID
AVD D GUADALUPE	SCL	46	F6
AVENIDA DE LAGO	SCL	47	A6
AVD D LS FLORES	SCL	47	A6
AVD D LS ALUMNS	SCL	46	F6
AVD D LS ARBOLS	SCL	47	A6
AVD D LOS ROSAS	SCL	47	A6
AVD DEL PRADO	SCL	46	F6
AVD DEL PRADO	SCL	47	A6
AVD DEL ROBLE	SJ	72	F1
AVENIDA DEL SOL	LG	65	D5
AVENIDA ESPANA	SJ	72A	F4
AVENIDA FELIPE	SVL	46	C6
AVD FERNANDO	SVL	46	C6
AVENIDA GRANDE	SJ	72A	F4
AVENIDA GRANDE	SVL	46	C6
AVENIDA JOSE	SVL	46	C6
AVENIDA LAGO	LG	71	C3
AVD LA JUNTA	SVL	46	C6
AVENIDA LEON	SVL	46	C6
AVENIDA MANUELO	SVL	46	C6
AVD MANZANOS	SJ	67	F6
AVD MANZANOS	SJ	72	F1
AVENIDA MARCOS	SVL	46	C6
AVENIDA MONTEZ	SVL	46	C6
AVENIDA NOGALES	SJ	68	A6
AVENIDA NOGALES	SJ	72	F1
AVENIDA PALMAS	SJ	68	A6
AVENIDA PALMAS	SJ	72	F1
AVENIDA PINOS	SJ	67	F6
AVENIDA PINOS	SJ	68	A6
AVENIDA PRIVADO	LG	71	C4
AVENIDA RICARDO	SVL	46	C6
AVENIDA ROTELLA	SJ	72A	F4
AVENIDA ROTELLA	SJ	72B	A3
AVENUE A	SCCO	55	F5
AVENUE B	SCCO	55	F5
AVENUE C	SCCO	55	F5
AVERNUS CT	SJ	68A	A2
AVERY CT	SJ	67	D6
AVERY LN	LG	70	E4
AVIATION AV	SJ	54	C6
AVILA AV	SCL	54	B5
AVILA CT	LAH	51	A3
AVIS DR	SJ	61	E6
AVOCADO PL	CPTO	60	A4
AVON CT	SJ	67	E4
AVON LN	MS	70	C1
AVON LN	S	70	C1
AVON WY	LA	51	F6
AVONDALE ST	CPTO	59	F6
AVONDALE ST	CPTO	60	A6
AVONDALE ST	SJ	59	F6
AVONDALE ST	SJ	60	A6
AVOSET TER	SVL	59	F1
AWALT CT	LA	52	C6
AWALT DR	MVW	52	C5
AYALA DR	SVL	52	D3
AYER AV	SJ	61	F2
AYER DR	G	83	D2
AYER ST	MPTS	48	B2
AYRSHIRE DR	SJ	72	B1
AYRSHIRE FRM LN	SCCO	44	A4
AZA DR	SCL	54	A6
AZALEA DR	SJ	72	E6
AZALEA DR	SVL	53	B4
AZALEA LN	SJ	67	D4
AZALEA WY	LA	51	F3
AZALEA WY	SCCO	71	A3
AZARA PL	SVL	53	A4
AZEVEDO CT	SCL	60	F3
AZTEC AV	SJ	67	E4
AZTEC WY	PA	44	D1
AZTEC RIDGE DR	SCCO	71	A6
AZUCAR AV	SJ	68	C6
AZULE AV	SJ	72	E2
AZURE ST	SVL	52	F5
AZZARELLO CT	SJ	68	E1

B

STREET	CITY	PAGE	GRID
B ST	LA	52	A6
B ST	LAH	59	A1
B ST	MVW	52	D2
B ST S	SVL	46	C6
BABCHUK LN	SJ	63	C5
BABERO AV	SJ	66	F5
BABE RUTH CT	SJ	48	C6
BABE RUTH DR	SJ	48	C6
BACCHUS DR	SJ	62	E4
BACH CT	S	65	B3
BACHMAN AV	LG	70	E4
BACHMAN CT	LG	70	D4

COPYRIGHT © 1991 BY Thomas Bros. Maps

STREET	CITY	PAGE	GRID
BACHMANN CT	SJ	66	E4
BACIGALUPI DR	LG	71	D4
BADEN CT	SJ	48	C6
BADGER PASS	MH	80K	F3
BADGERWOOD LN	MPTS	39	D4
BAERWALDT CT	SCCO	81	B1
BAGDAD WY	SJ	72A	B5
BAGHDAD PL	SJ	55	F6
BAGHDAD PL	SJ	56	A6
BAGHDAD PL	SJ	62	F1
BAGHDAD PL	SJ	63	A1
BAGELY WY	SJ	62	F4
BAGGINS CT	SJ	68	B1
BAGPIPE WY	SJ	63	C6
BAGSHAW CT	SJ	72A	B3
BAGUIO CT	SJ	72A	D4
BAGWORTH CT	SJ	63	C5
BAHAMA WY	SJ	62	F3
BAHIA AV	SJ	67	E4
BAHIA CT	SJ	72A	E4
BAHL ST	CPTO	59	C3
BAHRE LN	SJ	54	F3
BAHRE LN	SJ	55	A3
BAILEY AV	MVW	45	B6
BAILEY AV	MVW	52	B1
BAILEY AV	SJ	61	C4
BAILEY AV	SJ	77	B2
BAILEY AV	SCCO	45	B6
BAILEY AV	SCCO	52	B1
BAILEY AV	SCCO	61	C4
BAILEY AV	SCCO	77	B2
BAILEY RD	SJ	77	A3
BAILEY RD	SCCO	45	D5
BAINBRIDGE CT	SVL	59	D1
BAINTER AV	SCCO	70	B2
BAINTER AV	S	70	B2
BAINTER WY	SCCO	70	B2
BAINTREE PL	LG	65	F6
BAIRD AV	SCL	54	B2
BAKER AV	PA	44	D5
BAKER CT	SCCO	59	D1
BAKER LN	LAH	51	B3
BAKER PL	SJ	55	B3
BALANCE DR	SJ	68	E3
BALARDO WY	SJ	63	E4
BALBACH ST	SJ	62	A4
BALBOA AV	SJ	55	D6
BALBOA CT	SVL	52	D3
BALBOA DR	MPTS	39	E6
BALBOA DR	MPTS	47	E1
BALBOA RD	CPTO	59	B6
BALCOM RD	SCCO	63	F2
BALD EAGLE WY	SJ	67	B6
BALDERSTONE DR	SJ	72	B4
BALDWIN AV	SCCO	81A	B5
BALDWIN DR	SCL	60	C3
BALDWIN DR	SCCO	78G	E2
BALERI RANCH RD	LAH	50	F3
BALFOUR DR	SJ	67	F1
BALFOUR DR	SCCO	67	F1
BALGRAY CT	SJ	63	C5
BAL HARBOR WY	SJ	62	F4
BALI CT	SJ	62	F4
BALLANTREE WY	SJ	71	F2
BALLARD CT	SJ	55	C3
BALME DR	SJ	62	F5
BALMORAL DR	SJ	48	C6
BALSA AV	SJ	66	E5
BALSAM AV	SVL	53	B2
BALSAMO DR	SJ	60	B6
BALTIC WY	SJ	62	E6
BALTIC WY	SJ	67	E1
BALTIC WY	SVL	46	B5
BALUSTROL CT	CPTO	59	C5
BAMBI LN	SJ	55	F6
BAMBI LN	SJ	62	F1
BAMBI LN	SJ	63	A1
BAMBOO CT	SJ	68	D3
BAMBOO DR	SVL	53	B4
BAN CT	SJ	60	F6
BAN CT	SJ	61	A6
BANANA GROVE LN	SJ	68	A6
BANBERRY WY	SJ	71	D2
BANCROFT AV	MS	70	D3
BANCROFT ST	SCL	60	E3
BANCROFT WY	SJ	60	B6
BANCROFT WY	SJ	65	B1
BANDERA DR	PA	50	E4
BANDLEY DR	CPTO	59	F4
BANES LN	G	84	A3
BANES LN	SCCO	84	A3
BANFF DR	SVL	59	D3

STREET	CITY	PAGE	GRID
BANFF ST	SJ	62	D2
BANFF SPRING CT	SJ	72A	E4
BANFF SPRING WY	SJ	72A	E4
BANGOR AV	SJ	72A	A2
BANKHEAD WY	SJ	63	C6
BANK MILL RD	S	69	E1
BANNER CT	SJ	72A	B3
BANNER DR	SJ	72A	A3
BANNISTER AV	SCCO	82A	B2
BANNOCK CIR	SJ	65	D4
BANTA CT	SJ	67	D5
BANTRY CT	SVL	60	A1
BANYAN LN	MS	70	D2
BARALAY PL	SJ	68	A6
BARANGA LN	S	70	B1
BARBANO AV	C	66	C3
BARBARA AV	MVW	52	B3
BARBARA DR	LG	71	D2
BARBARA DR	PA	44	C1
BARBARA DR	SCL	60	F1
BARBARA LN	CPTO	59	E4
BARBARA WY	SJ	67	B3
BARBEE CT	SCCO	56	A1
BARBER LN	MPTS	47	E4
BARBER LN	MPTS	47	E6
BARBERRY CT	SJ	63	A6
BARBERRY LN	SJ	63	B6
BARCELLS AV	SCL	60	E3
BARCELONA AV	SJ	71	E1
BARCELONA CT	MH	80K	E2
BARCELONA CT	MVW	52	C4
BARCLAY CT	PA	44	D5
BARCLAY CT	SJ	72A	B3
BARD ST	SCCO	55	F2
BARDEN WY	SJ	61	D6
BAREOAK CT	SJ	63	E3
BARK LN	SJ	59	F6
BARK LN	SJ	60	A6
BARK LN	SJ	64	F1
BARK LN	SJ	65	A1
BARKER DR	SJ	60	F6
BARKER ST	MPTS	47	E2
BARKLEY AV	SCL	53	E6
BARKSDALE CT	S	65	A6
BARKWOOD WY	SJ	66	B1
BARLETTA LN	SJ	55	F4
BARLETTA LN	SJ	56	A4
BARLEY CT	SJ	56	C5
BARLEY HILL RD	LAH	51	D5
BARLOW AV	SJ	62	F2
BARLOW AV	SJ	63	A2
BARNALL AV	MH	79	E5
BARNARD AV	SJ	62	C6
BARNARD RD	SCCO	78A	B6
BARNARD RD	SCCO	80	A1
BARNES CT	SCCO	44	A3
BARNES LN	SCCO	75	F2
BARNHART AV	SCCO	60	C5
BARNHART AV	SCCO	78	A3
BARNHART CT	SCCO	60	C5
BARNHART PL	CPTO	64	F2
BARNHEISEL RD	SCCO	82C	F6
BARNSDALE CT	SJ	72	B5
BARNSLEY WY	SVL	60	A1
BARNSWELL WY	SJ	72A	D1
BARON DR	SJ	71	C2
BARON PL	MPTS	39	F5
BARON PL	MPTS	40	A5
BARONET CT	SJ	68	D1
BARONI AV	SJ	67	E4
BARONI AV	SCCO	67	E4
BARONI CT	S	65	B5
BARONI GREEN DR	SJ	67	E4
BARONS COURT WY	SJ	48	C5
BARRANCA DR	CPTO	59	D3
BARRETT AV	MH	79	F5
BARRETT AV	MH	80	A5
BARRETT AV	SJ	66	C6
BARRETT AV	SCCO	80	B5
BARRINGTON CT	SJ	68	B2
BARRON AV	PA	44	C5
BARRON PL	G	84	A3
BARRON PARK CT	SJ	67	E6
BARRON PARK DR	SJ	67	E6
BARRON PARK DR	SJ	72	E1
BARROW CT	SJ	63	B5
BARRY LN	MS	70	D3
BARRYMORE DR	SJ	65	E1
BARRYMORE DR	SCCO	60	E6
BARSON TER	SVL	52	F4
BARSTOW CT	SVL	53	C2
BARTLETT AV	SVL	53	B3

STREET	CITY	PAGE	GRID
BARTLETT CT	SCCO	80	D6
BARTLETT CK CT	SJ	75	E1
BARTO ST	SCL	60	E3
BARTON CT	LAH	51	D3
BARTON DR	SVL	59	C2
BASALT CT	SJ	55	D3
BASCH AV	SJ	55	D6
BASCOM AV	C	66	C3
BASCOM AV	SJ	61	C4
BASCOM AV	SJ	66	B6
BASCOM AV	SCCO	61	C5
BASCOM AV	SCCO	66	C3
BASCOM AV	SCCO	71	B1
BASCOM CT	C	66	B6
BASILE AV	SCCO	61	D5
BASIN CT	SJ	67	E1
BASS CT	SJ	65	D3
BASSETT LN	LAH	51	C6
BASSETT ST	SJ	61	F2
BASSETT ST	SJ	62	A2
BASSETT ST	SCL	46	F6
BASSETT ST	SCL	54	A1
BASSWOOD CT	SJ	71	E2
BASUNI WY	SCCO	80	A2
BATAAN CT	SJ	55	E4
BATEMAN WY	SJ	63	F4
BATES CT	SJ	63	E4
BATHGATE LN	SJ	63	C6
BATHURST WY	SJ	72A	D3
BATON ROUGE CT	SJ	55	E3
BATON ROUGE DR	SJ	55	E3
BATON ROUGE DR	SJ	55	E4
BATTAGLIA CIR	SJ	55	C2
BATTERSEA CT	SJ	48	D5
BATTLE DANCE DR	SJ	68	C5
BAUMAN CT	SCCO	79	C1
BAUMANN CT	SCCO	78	C6
BAUTISTA CT	PA	44	D2
BAVA CT	SJ	72A	B3
BAXLEY CT	CPTO	59	D6
BAXTER AV	CPTO	59	C3
BAXTER AV	SCCO	59	C3
BAY ST	MVW	52	B3
BAY ST	SJ	72A	A2
BAY ST	SCCO	52	B3
BAYARD DR	SJ	62	F4
BAYBERRY LN	SJ	63	D4
BAY FRONT PZ	SCL	46	E5
BAYHAVEN DR	SJ	63	A3
BAY LAUREL LN	SJ	55	F1
BAYLEAF CT	SJ	66	C1
BAYLISS CT	SJ	72B	A5
BAYLISS DR	SJ	72A	F5
BAYLISS DR	SJ	72B	A5
BAYLISS PL	SJ	72B	A5
BAYLOR AV	S	65	D3
BAYLOR DR	SCL	60	D3
BAYNE PL	SJ	65	E1
BAYO CLAROS CIR	MH	80	B3
BAYOU DR	SJ	68	A2
BAYOU DR	SCCO	68	A2
BAYO VISTA	SJ	55	F1
BAYPOINTE DR	SJ	47	B5
BAYPOINTE PKWY	SJ	47	B5
BAY RIDGE CT	SJ	72	B5
BAYSHORE FRWY	MVW	44	E2
BAYSHORE FRWY	MVW	45	B5
BAYSHORE FRWY	PA	38	C5
BAYSHORE FRWY	PA	44	E2
BAYSHORE FRWY	SJ	54	D4
BAYSHORE FRWY	SJ	55	A5
BAYSHORE FRWY	SJ	62	D2
BAYSHORE FRWY	SJ	63	A6
BAYSHORE FRWY	SJ	68	C2
BAYSHORE FRWY	SCL	53	A1
BAYSHORE FRWY	SCL	54	D4
BAYSHORE FRWY	SCCO	62	D2
BAYSHORE FRWY	SCCO	68	C2
BAYSHORE FRWY	SVL	45	B5
BAYSHORE FRWY	SVL	53	A1
BAYSHORE PKWY	MVW	45	A3
BAYSHORE PKWY	PA	44	F3
BAYSHORE RD	PA	38	C5
BAYSHR FRNT RD	PA	44	D1
BAYSIDE CT	SJ	55	E4
BAYSLAND CT	SJ	55	B3
BAYSMILL CT	SJ	63	A6
BAY SPRINGS RD	SCCO	69	E4
BAYTECH DR	SJ	47	B4
BAYTON DR	SJ	72A	D1
BAY TREE DR	G	82	C6
BAY TREE LN	LA	51	D5
BAYVIEW AV	LG	70	D4

STREET	CITY	PAGE	GRID
BAYVIEW AV	SCCO	56	B3
BAYVIEW AV	SVL	52	F4
BAYVIEW AV	SVL	53	A4
BAYVIEW CT	LG	70	D4
BAY VIEW DR	SCCO	78G	D1
BAYVIEW PARK DR	MPTS	48	B1
BAYWOOD AV	C	61	B6
BAYWOOD AV	SJ	61	B6
BAYWOOD CT	CPTO	60	A3
BAYWOOD CT	MVW	44	F6
BAYWOOD CT	MVW	51	F1
BAYWOOD DR	CPTO	60	A3
BAYWOOD SQ	SJ	48	D5
BEACON DR	MPTS	48	C2
BEACON LN	SJ	66	F5
BEACONSFIELD RD	SJ	68	B2
BEAL CT	SJ	72A	C4
BEAN AV	LG	70	D4
BEAR CLAW WY	SJ	68	A5
BEAR CREEK RD	SCCO	73	B5
BEARDEN DR	C	65	D5
BEARDON DR	CPTO	59	F4
BEARDON DR	SCCO	59	F4
BEARDSLEY RD	SCCO	75	B2
BEAR VALLEY LN	SJ	55	D3
BEATRICE CIR	SCCO	78G	D1
BEATRICE CT	SJ	61	D6
BEATRICE LN	LAH	51	C3
BEATRICE ST	MVW	45	A6
BEATRICE ST	MVW	52	A1
BEATTIE CT	SJ	72	B3
BEAUCHAMPS CT	S	64	E2
BEAUCHAMPS LN	S	64	E2
BEAULIEU CT	SJ	66	D1
BEAUME CT	MVW	45	A5
BEAUMERE WY	MPTS	39	F6
BEAUMONT AV	S	65	A5
BEAUMONT DR	SJ	60	D6
BEAUMONT SQ	MVW	52	B5
BEAVEN DR	CPTO	59	D3
BEAVER LN	LAH	51	B2
BEAVER CREEK WY	SJ	55	D3
BEAVERTON CT	SVL	59	E1
BECK AV	MS	70	C4
BECK DR	SJ	65	F2
BECKER LN	LA	51	D2
BECKET DR	SJ	63	A6
BECKHAM DR	SJ	72A	C4
BECKLEY DR	SJ	63	F6
BECKWITH RD	SCCO	70	B4
BECKY LN	LAH	51	C6
BECKY LN	MS	70	D2
BEDAL LN	C	66	A5
BEDFORD AV	SVL	59	C2
BEDFORD CT	SVL	59	C1
BEDFORD ST	SCCO	56	B6
BEDIVERE DR	SJ	55	F3
BEE CT	MPTS	48	B4
BEEBE CIR	SJ	63	F6
BEECH ST	SCL	54	A2
BEECHER CT	SJ	63	B5
BEECH GROVE CT	SJ	68	E4
BEECHMONT AV	SJ	67	C5
BEECHNUT AV	SVL	52	F2
BEECHNUT AV	SVL	53	A2
BEECHVALE CT	SJ	72A	D4
BEECHWOOD AV	SJ	61	B4
BEECHWOOD DR	LA	59	B2
BEECHWOOD DR	SCCO	59	B2
BEEGUM WY	SJ	72A	B1
BEEKMAN PL	CPTO	60	A3
BEEMAN DR	SJ	56	B6
BEEMER AV	SVL	52	F3
BEGEN AV	MVW	52	A4
BEGGS RD	SCCO	72K	F1
BEGONIA DR	SJ	71	E4
BEGONIA LN	SJ	67	D4
BEGONIA WY	SVL	53	A4
BEHLER DR	SJ	48	D4
BELA DR	SJ	65	D1
BEL AIR AV	SJ	61	C3
BEL AIR CT	MH	79	E4
BEL AIR PL	MH	79	E4
BEL AIR WY	MH	79	E4
BEL AIRE CT	CPTO	59	D6
BEL AIRE DR	SJ	54	F1
BEL AYRE DR	SCL	61	A4
BELBLOSSOM WY	LG	71	D3
BELBROOK CT	SJ	72	B5
BELBROOK PL	MPTS	39	E6
BELBROOK WY	MPTS	39	E6
BELBROOK WY	MPTS	47	E1
BEL CANTO DR	SJ	71	C2

STREET	CITY	PAGE	GRID
BELCREST DR	LG	71	E4
BELDEN CT	LA	51	E2
BELDEN DR	LA	51	E1
BELDEN DR	SJ	72A	B1
BELDER DR	SJ	75	F1
BEL ESCOU DR	SJ	71	C2
BEL ESCOU DR	SCCO	71	C2
BEL ESTOS DR	SJ	71	C2
BEL ESTOS DR	SCCO	71	C2
BELFAIR CT	SVL	52	E6
BELFAIR CT	SVL	59	E1
BELFAST CT	SVL	59	F1
BELFAST CT	SVL	60	A1
BELFAST DR	SJ	63	A1
BELFORD DR	SJ	55	D2
BELFRY WY	SVL	59	F1
BELGATOS RD	LG	71	D3
BELGLEN LN	LG	71	D3
BELGLEN WY	LG	71	D3
BELGRAVIAN CT	SJ	63	D6
BELGROVE CIR	SJ	63	F4
BELGROVE CT	SJ	63	F4
BELHAVEN DR	LG	71	E4
BELICK ST	SCL	54	B3
BELKNAP CT	CPTO	64	E1
BELKNAP DR	CPTO	64	E1
BELL AV	SCCO	55	F3
BELLA CORTE	MVW	45	A5
BELLADONNA CT	SVL	53	A5
BELLA LADERA DR	LAH	51	E5
BELLA MADEIR LN	SCCO	56	F6
BELLARMINE CT	SCL	53	D5
BELLA VISTA	S	70	A1
BELLA VISTA AV	LG	70	F4
BELLA VISTA AV	SCL	53	D6
BELLA VISTA CT	LG	70	F4
BELLA VISTA CT	SCL	53	D6
BELLA VISTA CT	SJ	47	B5
BELLE CT	S	70	B2
BELLEROSE DR	SJ	61	C4
BELLEROSE DR	SCCO	61	C4
BELLEVILLE WY	SCCO	59	D2
BELLEVILLE WY	SVL	59	D2
BELLEVUE AV	CPTO	59	C4
BELLEVUE AV	SJ	62	C5
BELLEVUE CT	LA	51	E4
BELLEW DR	MPTS	47	D4
BELLFLOWER AV	SVL	53	A5
BELLFLOWER CT	SCCO	56	A2
BELLHURST AV	SJ	62	D3
BELLINGHAM CT	SJ	63	A6
BELLINGHAM DR	SJ	62	F6
BELLINGHAM DR	SJ	63	A6
BELLINGHAM WY	SVL	59	D1
BELLINI CT	SJ	55	D1
BELLIS CT	SJ	72	E3
BELLO AV	SJ	66	F3
BELLOMO AV	SVL	53	B6
BELLOMY ST	SCL	61	B2
BELLVIEW CT	PA	44	C1
BELLWOOD CT	LA	59	B1
BELLWOOD DR	SCL	54	B2
BELLWOOD DR	S	65	B3
BELMONT AV	LG	70	D4
BELMONT AV	MS	70	D4
BELMONT AV	SJ	62	A6
BELMONT DR	SJ	62	B6
BELMONT TER	SVL	52	E3
BELMONT WY	SJ	62	B6
BELNAP DR	S	69	E2
BELRIDGE DR	LG	71	E4
BELSHAW DR	MVW	52	C5
BELTHORN CT	SJ	55	C3
BELTRAMI DR	SJ	56	B6
BELVALE DR	LG	71	E3
BELVEDERE DR	SJ	60	E5
BELVEDERE DR	SCCO	60	E5
BELVEDERE LN	SJ	60	A6
BELVOIR DR	SCCO	59	A1
BELVUE DR	LG	71	D3
BELWOOD CT	LG	71	E3
BELWOOD LN	LG	71	E3
BELWOOD GATEWAY	LG	71	E3
BENBOW AV	SJ	72A	B2
BEND AV	SJ	67	C5
BEND DR	SVL	59	E1
BENDER CIR	MH	79	D3
BENDIGO DR	LA	59	B1
BENDMILL WY	SJ	68	A1
BENDORF DR	SJ	68	C6
BENECIA AV	SVL	52	E1
BENEDICT LN	LG	70	F2

STREET	CITY	PAGE	GRID
BENEDICT LN	LG	71	A2
BENEFIT CT	SJ	55	E5
BENETTI CT	CPTO	59	D3
BENGAL CT	SJ	68	B5
BENGAL DR	SJ	68	B5
BEN GEE RD	SCCO	79	F3
BEN HUR CT	SJ	66	D4
BENJAMIN AV	SJ	66	C5
BENJAMIN CT	SJ	66	C5
BENJAMIN DR	MVW	44	F5
BEN LOMOND DR	PA	44	E5
BEN LOMOND WY	SJ	63	C6
BENNASSI DR	G	83	D2
BENNETT AV	SCL	60	C4
BENNETT WY	SJ	67	A2
BENNETT WY	SCCO	71	A1
BENNETTA LN	SCCO	81	F5
BENNIGHOF CT	SJ	63	C6
BENNINGTON DR	SVL	52	D4
BENNY CT	SJ	55	B4
BEN ROE DR	LA	59	C1
BENSON LN	SJ	66	F4
BENT DR	C	66	D3
BENTLEY AV	LG	70	E4
BENTLEY CT	LAH	51	D4
BENTLEY DR	SJ	48	C6
BENTLEY SQ	MVW	52	B3
BENTOAK CT	SJ	60	C6
BENT OAK LN	MH	80	D3
BENTOAK LN	SJ	60	C6
BENTON CT	SVL	60	C2
BENTON ST	SCL	54	B6
BENTON ST	SCL	60	E1
BENTON ST	SCL	61	B1
BENTON ST	SVL	60	C2
BENVENUE AV	LA	51	F4
BENZO DR	SJ	72A	B4
BERCAW LN	SJ	66	D6
BERCAW LN	SCCO	66	D6
BERESFORD CT	MPTS	47	F2
BERG CT	MPTS	40	A6
BERGER DR	SJ	54	F4
BERGIN PL	SCL	60	D1
BERGMAN CT	SJ	68	E1
BERING DR	SJ	54	E3
BERINGER CT	SJ	66	D1
BERKELAND CT	SJ	68	C5
BERKELEY CT	SCCO	59	C3
BERKELEY WY	SJ	55	E6
BERKELEY WY	SJ	62	F1
BERKSFORD WY	SJ	63	B1
BERKSHIRE AV	SVL	52	E4
BERKSHIRE CT	CPTO	59	C4
BERKSHIRE CT	MH	79	D3
BERKSHIRE DR	MH	79	D3
BERKSHIRE DR	SJ	67	B4
BERKSHIRE DR	SCCO	58	F2
BERKSHIRE PL	MPTS	39	F5
BERKSHIRE PL	MPTS	40	A5
BERLAND CT	CPTO	64	E1
BERLIN DR	SCCO	81	E3
BERMUDA CT	SVL	53	B5
BERMUDA WY	SJ	62	F3
BERN CT	SJ	55	A4
BERNA ST	SCL	53	F6
BERNA ST	SCL	54	A6
BERNAL AV	SVL	53	B2
BERNAL RD	SJ	72A	E5
BERNAL RD	SCCO	72A	D5
BERNAL WY	SJ	72A	F3
BERNARDO AV	CPTO	59	D2
BERNARDO AV	MVW	52	D2
BERNARDO AV	SCCO	52	D4
BERNARDO AV	SCCO	59	D2
BERNARDO AV	SVL	52	D4
BERNARDO AV	SVL	59	D2
BERNICE WY	SJ	66	D6
BERONA WY	SJ	63	A2
BERRENDO DR	MPTS	39	F6
BERRENOO DR	MPTS	47	E1
BERRY AV	LA	52	A5
BERRY CT	MH	79	D4
BERRY CT	SCCO	45	C5
BERRY DR	SCCO	45	D5
BERRY WY	SCL	53	D5
BERRY WY	SJ	66	D6
BERRY WY	SCCO	66	D6
BERRY WY	SCCO	71	D1
BERRYESSA RD	SJ	55	B5
BERRYESSA ST	MPTS	47	E2
BERRY HILL CT	LAH	50	F2
BERRY HILL LN	LAH	50	F2

STREET	CITY	PAGE	GRID
BERRYWOOD DR	SJ	55	D6
BERTINI CT	SJ	60	F5
BERTLAND CT	SJ	55	C3
BERTOLONE CT	SJ	62	D3
BERTRAM AV	SCCO	76	A5
BERWICK ST	S	65	C4
BERWICK WY	SCCO	59	F1
BERWICK WY	SCCO	60	A1
BERWICK WY	SVL	59	F1
BERWICK WY	SVL	60	A1
BERWICKSHIRE WY	SJ	72	B5
BERYLWOOD LN	MPTS	39	E5
BESS CT	SJ	66	C1
BEST CT	SJ	55	C3
BESTOR ST	SJ	62	C4
BESTVIEW CT	S	70	B2
BESWICK DR	SJ	72A	C1
BETA CT	C	66	A4
BETH CT	SCL	54	B2
BETH DR	SJ	67	F2
BETH WY	C	65	E5
BETHANY AV	SJ	48	B6
BETHANY CT	SJ	48	B6
BETHEL AV	SCCO	56	B6
BETLIN AV	SJ	60	A5
BETLO AV	MVW	44	F5
BETLO CT	SJ	65	D3
BETSY WY	SJ	55	E3
BETSY ROSS DR	SCL	46	E6
BETTE AV	CPTO	60	A5
BETTE CT	SJ	60	A5
BETTEN CT	SJ	56	A6
BETTIO RD	SCCO	45	D5
BETTY CT	SCL	53	E6
BETTY CT	SVL	53	A5
BETTY LN	SCCO	52	E2
BETTY ANN CT	SCCO	78G	E1
BEVANS DR	SJ	60	D5
BEVANS DR	SCCO	60	D5
BEVERLY BLVD	SJ	55	D6
BEVERLY CT	C	65	F3
BEVERLY CT	C	66	A3
BEVERLY LN	LA	51	E3
BEVIL CT	SJ	72A	C4
BEWCASTLE CT	SJ	48	C6
BEXLEY LANDING	SJ	48	B6
BIANCHI WY	CPTO	59	E4
BIARRITZ CIR	LA	51	E2
BIARRITZ CT	S	65	C3
BIARRITZ LN	S	65	C3
BIBBITS DR	PA	44	E4
BIBEL AV	SJ	65	B2
BICKLEY CT	SJ	67	C6
BICKNELL RD	LG	70	D1
BIDDLEFORD CT	SJ	72A	F4
BIDWELL AV	SVL	52	E3
BIEBER DR	SJ	72A	B1
BIEN CT	SJ	63	D3
BIEN WY	SJ	63	D3
BIG BASIN DR	MPTS	48	C4
BIG BASIN WY	S	64	F6
BIG BASIN WY	S	69	F1
BIG BEAR CT	MPTS	48	B4
BIG BEND DR	MPTS	48	C3
BIGELOW CT	SJ	72A	C3
BIGGS CT	SJ	67	D5
BIGOAK CT	SJ	60	C6
BIGOAK DR	SJ	60	C6
BIG OAK LN	MPTS	39	D4
BIG SUR DR	SJ	75	F1
BIG SUR DR	SJ	76	A2
BIG TALK CT	SJ	72	B4
BIG WOOD DR	SJ	55	F4
BIKINI AV	SJ	62	F4
BILBO CT	SJ	68	B1
BILBO DR	SJ	68	B1
BILICH PL	CPTO	60	A4
BIMBER CT	SJ	63	D3
BIMMERLE PL	SJ	72	C2
BING DR	SJ	65	B1
BING DR	SCL	60	D2
BINGHAM CT	SJ	68	E4
BIRCH AV	SCCO	66	E2
BIRCH AV	SVL	53	B3
BIRCH DR	C	66	C2
BIRCH LN	SCCO	55	F5
BIRCH ST	PA	44	C4
BIRCH WY	MH	80	A5
BIRCH WY	SJ	72A	F3
BIRCH WY	SCL	60	E3
BIRCH GROVE DR	SJ	68	B6
BIRCH HILL WY	LAH	51	C4

STREET	CITY	PAGE	GRID
BIRCH SPRING CT	CPTO	64	E1
BIRCHTREE LN	SCL	60	F3
BIRCHWOOD CT	LA	51	F4
BIRCH WOOD CT	LG	65	E5
BIRCHWOOD DR	SVL	46	D6
BIRCHWOOD LN	SJ	48	C5
BIRD AV	LG	70	E4
BIRD AV	SJ	61	F4
BIRD AV	SJ	62	A5
BIRD AV	SJ	67	B1
BIRDVALE WY	MH	79	C1
BIRKENSHAW PL	SJ	67	D5
BIRMINGHAM DR	SJ	67	E6
BISCAYNE CT	MH	79	E4
BISCAYNE WY	SJ	62	F3
BISCEGLIA AV	MH	79	E5
BISHOP AV	SVL	52	F4
BISHOP AV	SVL	53	A4
BISHOP CT	SCCO	82A	D3
BISMARK DR	C	65	F2
BISMARK DR	SJ	65	F2
BISON CT	SJ	72A	D4
BITTERN DR	SVL	59	F2
BITTERNUT CT	SJ	55	C3
BITTER OAK ST	CPTO	59	C3
BITTERROOT PL	SJ	72	E5
BITTICK CT	SCCO	79	F3
BIXBY DR	CPTO	60	A4
BIXBY DR	MPTS	48	C2
BIXBY WY	SCCO	56	B3
BLACK RD	SCCO	73	B2
BLACK ARROW RD	SCCO	73	A2
BLACKBERRY TER	SVL	52	D6
BLACKBERY HL RD	LG	71	A6
BLACKBERY HL RD	SCCO	71	B6
BLACKBIRD CT	SJ	72	A4
BLACKFEET TR	SCCO	73	E6
BLACKFIELD CT	SCL	60	F1
BLACKFIELD DR	SCL	60	F1
BLACKFIELD WY	MVW	51	F2
BLACKFOOT CT	SJ	72	F3
BLACKFORD AV	SJ	60	E5
BLACKFORD AV	SJ	61	D6
BLACKFORD AV	SJ	66	D1
BLACKFORD AV	SCCO	61	D6
BLACKFORD AV	SCCO	66	D1
BLACKFORD CIR	SJ	60	F5
BLACKFORD LN	C	66	D1
BLACKFORD LN	SCCO	66	D1
BLACKHAWK CT	SJ	72	F2
BLACKHAWK CT	SVL	59	F2
BLACKHAWK CT	SVL	60	A2
BLACKHAWK DR	SVL	59	F2
BLACKHAWK DR	SVL	60	A2
BLACKHAWK CY RD	SCCO	82H	A2
BLACKLOCK CT	SJ	72A	B3
BLACKMORE CT	SJ	48	C6
BLACK MTN CT	LA	52	B5
BLACK MTN RD	LAH	51	A4
BLACK MTN GRADE	SCCO	68B	A4
BLACK OAK CT	MH	79	B5
BLACK OAK LN	SJ	72	C4
BLACKOAK WY	SJ	60	C6
BLACK PRINCE CT	MH	80K	F3
BLACK RIVER CT	SJ	67	C5
BLACKSTONE AV	SJ	67	A4
BLACKSTONE AV	SCCO	67	A4
BLACK WALNUT CT	MH	79	F3
BLACK WALNUT CT	S	65	B6
BLACK WALNUT WY	MH	79	E3
BLACKWELDER CT	SCCO	44	A4
BLACKWELL DR	LG	71	B2
BLACKWING WY	G	82	B5
BLACKWOOD DR	CPTO	60	B5
BLAIR AV	SCCO	52	D4
BLAIR AV	SVL	52	D4
BLAIR CT	PA	44	D1
BLAIR CT	SVL	52	E4
BLAIR DR	SJ	72	B1
BLAIRBETH DR	SJ	72A	D4
BLAIRBURRY WY	SJ	72	E1
BLAIRMORE CT	SJ	68	B2
BLAIRWOOD CT	SJ	72A	A6
BLAIRWOOD CT	SJ	75	F1
BLAISDELL CT	SJ	61	A5
BLAKE AV	SCL	60	E4
BLAKE CT	G	83	E2
BLAKE WILBUR DR	PA	43	E2
BLALOCK ST	MPTS	40	A6
BLALOCK ST	MPTS	48	A1
BLANCHARD DR	MS	70	E2
BLANCHARD RD	SJ	72B	B5

STREET	CITY	PAGE	GRID
BLANCHARD RD	SCCO	72B	B5
BLANCHARD WY	SVL	59	E1
BLANCO DR	SJ	60	D6
BLAND AV	C	66	A2
BLANDING AV	SJ	63	D6
BLANDOR WY	LAH	58	D2
BLANEY AV	CPTO	60	A6
BLANEY AV	SJ	65	A2
BLANEY CT	CPTO	60	A5
BLAUER CT	SJ	68A	A3
BLAUER DR	S	64	F4
BLAUER DR	S	65	A4
BLAUER LN	SJ	68A	A3
BLAZINGWOOD AV	CPTO	60	B6
BLAZINGWOOD DR	SVL	53	C1
BLENHEIM LN	SJ	63	D5
BLEWETT AV	SJ	61	F6
BLEWETT AV	SJ	62	A6
BLINN CT	LA	51	F3
BLISS AV	MPTS	48	C3
BLISS CT	SJ	67	D4
BLOCK DR	SCL	60	F1
BLOCK DR	SCL	61	A1
BLOM DR	SJ	68	C4
BLOOMFIELD AV	SCCO	84	E6
BLOOMFIELD AV	SCCO	91	C1
BLOOMFIELD DR	SJ	66	F6
BLOOMFIELD RD	SCCO	85	A5
BLOOMSBURY WY	SJ	48	D4
BLOSSOM AV	SJ	72	F2
BLOSSOM CT	SCCO	79	A1
BLOSSOM DR	SCL	60	F2
BLOSSOM DR	SCL	61	A2
BLOSSOM LN	CPTO	59	F5
BLOSSOM LN	MVW	52	B2
BLOSSOM ACRS DR	SJ	71	C3
BLOSSOM CRST WY	SJ	71	C3
BLOSSOM DALE DR	SJ	71	C3
BLSSM GRDNS CIR	SJ	68	B6
BLSSM GRDNS CIR	SJ	72A	B1
BLOSSOM GLEN CT	G	83	F3
BLOSSOM GLEN WY	LG	71	B3
BLOSSOM GLEN WY	SJ	71	B3
BLOSSOM HILL RD	LG	70	F3
BLOSSOM HILL RD	SJ	71	D3
BLOSSOM HILL RD	SJ	72	C1
BLOSSOM HILL RD	SJ	72A	B2
BLOSSOM HILL RD	SCCO	71	D3
BLOSSOM HILL RD	SCCO	72	C1
BLOSSOM PARK LN	SJ	71	F3
BLOSSOM RIV DR	SJ	72	C1
BLOSSOM RIV WY	SJ	72	C1
BLOSSOM TER CT	SJ	71	C3
BLOSSOM TREE LN	SJ	71	C3
BLOSSOM VLY DR	SJ	71	C3
BLOSSOMVIEW DR	SJ	67	A6
BLOSSOM VLLA WY	LG	71	C3
BLOSSOM VIS AV	SJ	71	C3
BLOSSOM WOOD DR	SJ	71	C3
BLUEBELL AV	SJ	63	A4
BLUEBELL DR	G	82	A6
BLUEBELL WY	SVL	53	B4
BLUEBERRY TER	SJ	60	E5
BLUEBERRY HILL	LG	71	A4
BLUEBIRD AV	SCL	60	C2
BLUEBIRD CT	SVL	59	F1
BLUEBIRD DR	SJ	61	B6
BLUEBIRD DR	SJ	66	B1
BLUEBONNET CT	MH	80	B3
BLUE BONNET DR	SVL	53	B5
BLUEBONNET WY	MH	80	A3
BLUE CREEK CT	SJ	63	E5
BLUE DOLPHIN DR	SJ	67	E4
BLUEFIELD CT	SJ	67	E5
BLUEFIELD DR	SJ	67	E5
BLUE GRASS CT	MH	80	D2
BLUEGRASS LN	SJ	72	A2
BLUE GUM CT	S	70	C2
BLUE GUM DR	SCCO	56	C4
BLUE HILL DR	SJ	59	F6
BLUE HILL DR	SJ	60	A6
BLUE HILL DR	SJ	64	F1
BLUE HILL DR	SJ	65	A1
BLUE HILLS DR	SCCO	64	E2
BLUEJACKET WY	SJ	55	C3
BLUE JAY CT	MH	80	C1
BLUE JAY DR	CPTO	59	F3
BLUE JAY DR	CPTO	60	A3
BLUE JAY DR	MH	80	C1
BLUE JAY DR	SJ	67	C3
BLUE JAY DR	SVL	59	F3
BLUE JAY DR	SVL	60	A3
BLUE LAGOON DR	SCL	53	F2

STREET	CITY	PAGE	GRID
BLUELAKE SQ	MVW	52	C6
BLUE MEADOWS CT	S	64	F3
BLUE MIST PL	SJ	72	E5
BLUE MTN DR	SJ	56	C6
BLUE MTN DR	SJ	63	C1
BLUE OAK CT	SJ	63	E3
BLUE OAK LN	SCCO	51	D2
BLUE OAKS RD	SCCO	81A	E6
BLUE OAKS RD	SCCO	82A	E1
BLUERIDGE DR	MPTS	48	C4
BLUE RIDGE DR	SJ	65	D1
BLUERING CT	SJ	72	A4
BLUE ROCK CT	SJ	55	D3
BLUE SAGE DR	SVL	53	B5
BLUE SPRUCE CT	MPTS	47	E6
BLUE SPRUCE WY	MPTS	47	E6
BLUESTONE CT	SJ	63	A2
BLUEWATER CT	SJ	63	B2
BLUEWOOD CIR	SJ	48	D5
BLUFFWOOD CT	SJ	72	F6
BLUFFWOOD CT	SJ	72A	A6
BLYTHE AV	SVL	53	B2
BLYTHE CT	S	65	A3
BLYTHE CT	SVL	53	B2
BLYTHSWOOD DR	SCCO	70	C3
BOA VISTA DR	SJ	62	E4
BOBBIE AV	SJ	65	D3
BOBBYWOOD AV	SCCO	71	D3
BOBOLINK CIR	SVL	59	F1
BOBOLINK CIR	SVL	60	A1
BOBOLINK DR	SJ	67	B3
BOBWHITE AV	SVL	59	F1
BOBWHITE AV	SVL	60	A1
BOB WHITE PL	SJ	55	B3
BODEGA DR	SVL	52	D3
BODEGA WY	SJ	72A	C3
BODIE CT	SJ	72A	B1
BOEGER LN	SJ	63	D2
BOHANNON DR	SCL	61	A3
BOHLMAN RD	S	69	E2
BOISE CT	SVL	59	E1
BOISE DR	C	65	F2
BOISE DR	SJ	65	F2
BOLADO DR	SJ	72A	E4
BOLD CT	SJ	68	F4
BOLD DR	SJ	68	F4
BOLERO DR	SJ	68	B4
BOLIVAR DR	SJ	72	E2
BOLLINGER RD	CPTO	59	F5
BOLLINGER RD	SJ	59	F5
BOLLINGER RD	SJ	60	C6
BOLLINGER RD	SCCO	60	C6
BOLSA RD	G	84	B5
BOLSA RD	SCCO	84	B5
BOLSA RD	SCCO	91	E1
BOLSENA CT	SJ	68A	A3
BOLTON CT	SJ	60	E5
BOLTON DR	G	82	F6
BOLTON DR	MPTS	39	F4
BONACCORSO PL	SJ	55	E3
BONAIR	SCCO	44	A3
BONAIR CT	SJ	61	A6
BONANZA CT	SVL	59	E1
BONAVENTURA DR	SJ	54	D2
BONBON DR	SJ	63	C3
BONCHEFF DR	SJ	55	E3
BOND CT	LG	71	A5
BOND WY	MVW	52	A4
BONGATE CT	SJ	65	E1
BONITA	MVW	45	C4
BONITA AV	MVW	52	B3
BONITA AV	SJ	62	D2
BONITA AV	SCL	53	D5
BONITA AV	SCCO	62	D2
BONITA CT	SCL	53	D5
BONNER CT	SCCO	80K	F2
BONNER CT	SCCO	81	A2
BONNET CT	SJ	55	D1
BONNET WY	S	65	C4
BONNEVILLE WY	SVL	59	D1
BONNIE DR	SCL	53	E5
BONNIE LN	LG	71	A4
BONNIE LN	SCCO	71	A4
BONNIEBRAE LN	S	70	A1
BONNIEBRAE WY	S	70	A1
BONNIE JOY AV	SJ	65	A2
BONNIE RIDGE WY	S	65	A4
BONNIE VIEW CT	MH	79	C4
BONNY DR	CPTO	59	E5
BONNY ST	MVW	45	A6
BON VISTA CT	SJ	56	D3
BOOK LN	SCL	46	F6
BOOKER AV	SVL	52	F4

STREET	CITY	PAGE	GRID
BOOKER CREEK RD	SCCO	69	A1
BOOKSIN AV	SJ	66	F3
BOOKSIN AV	SJ	67	A4
BOOKSIN AV	SCCO	66	F4
BOOKSIN AV	SCCO	67	A4
BOONE DR	SJ	71	F3
BOONE LN	LG	70	E4
BOONEWOOD CT	SJ	72	F6
BOONEWOOD CT	SJ	72A	A6
BORANDA AV	MVW	52	B3
BORAX DR	SCL	53	D4
BORCHERS DR	SJ	66	D5
BORDEAUX DR	SVL	46	A5
BORDENRAE CT	SJ	61	A5
BORDER RD	SCCO	51	F5
BORDER HILL DR	SCCO	51	F5
BORDWELL DR	SJ	67	A6
BORDWELL DR	SJ	72	A1
BORELLO DR	SJ	66	C2
BORELLO WY	MVW	52	D3
BOREN DR	SJ	62	F5
BORGE CT	SJ	48	E6
BORGES CT	SCCO	82	F1
BORGES CT	SCCO	82A	A1
BORGWOOD CT	SJ	75	F1
BORGWOOD CT	SJ	76	A1
BORINA DR	SJ	60	D5
BORNEO CIR	SJ	68	A6
BORNEO CIR	SJ	72A	A1
BORREGAS AV	SVL	46	A5
BORREGAS AV	SVL	53	A2
BOSCO LN	G	82	D6
BOSE CT	SJ	72	C5
BOSE LN	SJ	72	C5
BOSTON AV	SJ	61	D4
BOSTON AV	SCCO	61	D4
BOSTON POST CT	SJ	72	D5
BOSWALL CT	SJ	63	C6
BOTHELL CIR	SJ	72A	B4
BOTHELO AV	MPTS	47	F3
BOTTLE BRUSH LN	SJ	72	B2
BOUGAINVILEA CT	S	69	E1
BOUGAINVILEA DR	SJ	68	B5
BOULAY CT	SCCO	77	E4
BOULDER BLVD	SJ	72A	C1
BOULDER DR	SJ	56	A1
BOULDER ST	MPTS	39	F5
BOUNTIFUL ACRES	S	70	B2
BOURBON CT	MVW	52	C3
BOURET DR	SJ	67	A6
BOURET DR	SJ	72	A1
BOURGEOIS WY	SJ	67	F2
BOURNEMOUTH CT	SJ	67	C4
BOUVERON CT	SJ	63	D5
BOWDEN AV	SCCO	80K	D3
BOWDEN CT	SCCO	80K	E4
BOWDOIN ST	PA	44	A4
BOWDOIN ST	SCCO	43	F4
BOWDOIN ST	SCCO	44	A4
BOWE AV	SCL	60	E1
BOWEN AV	SJ	72	D2
BOWEN CT	SJ	72	D2
BOWERS AV	SCL	53	E4
BOWERS AV	SCL	60	E1
BOWHILL CT	S	64	E2
BOWLING LN	SJ	71	F2
BOWLING GRN DR	SJ	63	A5
BOX CANYON RD	SJ	75	C1
BOXLEAF CT	SJ	60	F4
BOXLEAF CT	SJ	61	A4
BOXWOOD DR	SJ	61	B2
BOYCE AV	PA	38	B6
BOYCE LN	S	64	E5
BOYD CT	SJ	72A	B3
BOYD ST	MPTS	39	F5
BOYNTON AV	SJ	60	F6
BOYNTON AV	SJ	65	F1
BOYSEA DR	SJ	67	A6
BOYSOL CT	SJ	48	D4
BRACCIANO CT	SJ	68	A4
BRACE AV	SJ	61	F6
BRACE AV	SJ	66	F1
BRACEBRIDGE CT	C	65	F5
BRACH WY	SCL	60	C1
BRACKETT AV	SJ	63	D3
BRADBURY DR	SJ	63	B5
BRADDALE AV	LA	52	B6
BRADDOCK CT	SJ	66	D2
BRADEN CT	SJ	63	E3
BRADFORD WY	SJ	66	E6
BRADFORD WY	SCCO	80	A3
BRADFORD WY	SVL	46	A6

STREET	CITY	PAGE	GRID
BRADLEY AV	SJ	61	C5
BRADLEY AV	SCCO	61	C5
BRADSHAW DR	SJ	63	D4
BRADWELL CT	SJ	72A	E2
BRADY CT	SCL	53	E6
BRAEBRIDGE RD	SJ	55	B3
BRAEBURN CT	SJ	65	F1
BRAEMAR CT	S	65	B4
BRAEMAR DR	S	65	A5
BRAEMER CT	SJ	55	D2
BRAHMS AV	SJ	63	B5
BRAHMS CT	SJ	63	B4
BRAHMS WY	SVL	52	F5
BRALY AV	MPTS	48	B2
BRAMBLE TR	SCCO	78G	C2
BRANBURY DR	C	65	F2
BRANBURY WY	SJ	55	C3
BRANDEIS CT	SJ	63	E1
BRANDY LN	SJ	55	E1
BRANDYBUCK WY	SJ	68	B1
BRANDYWINE CT	S	64	F4
BRANDYWINE DR	SJ	68	B1
BRANDYWINE DR	S	64	F4
BRANHAM LN	SJ	66	F6
BRANHAM LN	SJ	67	B6
BRANHAM LN	SJ	68	A5
BRANHAM LN	SJ	71	E1
BRANHAM LN	SJ	72	A1
BRANHAM LN	SCCO	66	F6
BRANHAM LN	SCCO	71	C1
BRANHAM LN	SCCO	72	A1
BRANHAM LN E	SJ	68	B5
BRANHAM PARK CT	SJ	71	F1
BRANHAM PARK PL	SJ	71	F1
BRANNAN PL	SCL	60	F2
BRANSTON CT	SCCO	80K	E3
BRANTLEY DR	SJ	55	C3
BRAQUET LN	SCCO	81H	F5
BRASILIA WY	SJ	72	B2
BRASSWOOD CT	SCL	54	C2
BRATER CT	SJ	55	C3
BRAVO CT	SCCO	81	E4
BRAXTON DR	SJ	68	B4
BRAY AV	SCL	53	F6
BRAY AV	SCL	60	F1
BRAY AV	SCL	61	A1
BRAY ST	SCL	54	A6
BREECH AV	SCL	60	F4
BREEN CT	SJ	68	A1
BREEZEWOOD CT	SVL	53	D1
BREEZYGLEN CT	SJ	55	E4
BREGA LN	MH	80	C3
BREM LN	G	84	B3
BREMERTON DR	SVL	59	E1
BRENDA AV	SJ	71	E2
BRENDA CT	CPTO	60	A4
BRENDA LEE DR	SJ	72	F4
BRENDA LEE DR	SJ	72A	A4
BRENDEL DR	LAH	51	C5
BRENFORD DR	SJ	63	A1
BRENNAN AV	SJ	54	E2
BRENNER WY	SJ	71	F2
BRENNING DR	SJ	62	E6
BRENT DR	CPTO	60	A5
BRENTON AV	SJ	65	D1
BRENTON CT	MVW	52	C1
BRENTWOOD CT	LA	51	F5
BRENTWOOD CT	LA	52	A5
BRENTWOOD DR	SJ	47	E5
BRENTWOOD DR	SJ	54	F1
BRENTWOOD DR	SJ	60	D6
BRENTWOOD LN	G	82	C6
BRENTWOOD PL	LA	51	F5
BRENTWOOD PL	LA	52	A5
BRENTWOOD ST	LA	51	F5
BRENTWOOD ST	LA	52	A6
BRET AV	SCCO	60	C5
BRET COVE CT	SJ	72	E6
BRET HARTE CT	SCL	61	A4
BRET HARTE DR	SJ	72	E6
BRET HARTE ST	PA	44	C1
BRET HILL CT	SJ	72	E6
BRET KNOLL CT	SJ	72	E6
BRETMOOR WY	SJ	60	A6
BRETMOOR WY	SJ	65	A1
BREWER AV	CPTO	59	E3
BREWSTER AV	SJ	71	C2
BREWSTER AV	SCCO	71	C2
BREWSTER LN	SCCO	80K	C2
BRIAN CT	MPTS	48	B1
BRIAN CT	SJ	72A	C3
BRIAN LN	SCL	60	D4

1991 SANTA CLARA COUNTY STREET INDEX

STREET	CITY	PAGE	GRID
BRIANA CT	SJ	72	F5
BRIAR CT	S	65	A4
BRIARBERRY CT	SJ	55	B3
BRIARBROOK CT	SJ	48	D5
BRIARBUSH CT	SJ	55	B3
BRIARCLIFF CT	SCL	60	D3
BRIARCLIFF DR	SJ	72	F2
BRIARCREEK CT	SJ	55	B3
BRIARCREST CT	SJ	55	B3
BRIARCREST DR	SJ	55	B3
BRIARGLEN DR	SJ	67	B5
BRIARLEAF CIR	SJ	55	B4
BRIAR MDWS CT	SJ	55	B3
BRIARPOINT DR	SJ	55	B4
BRIAR RANCH LN	SJ	75	F1
BRIARTREE DR	SJ	55	B4
BRIARWOOD CT	LA	51	F5
BRIARWOOD DR	SJ	47	F6
BRIARWOOD DR	SJ	66	E3
BRIARWOOD DR	SCL	53	D6
BRIARWOOD WY	LG	71	D3
BRIARWOOD WY	PA	44	E5
BRIARWOOD WY	SCCO	66	C4
BRICE CT	SJ	68	B5
BRIDAL PLACE CT	SJ	68	B1
BRIDGE CT	SJ	75	F2
BRIDGECASTLE CT	SJ	63	C5
BRIDGE PARK CT	CPTO	64	E1
BRIDGEPORT CT	SJ	65	F1
BRIDGEPRT LK WY	SJ	72	C2
BRIDGET DR	SJ	67	D4
BRIDGEWOOD WY	SVL	53	D1
BRIDGTON CT	LA	51	D3
BRIDLE LN	SCCO	81A	A4
BRIDLE WY	SJ	72A	A2
BRIDLE PATH CT	SCCO	81A	B6
BRIDLE PATH DR	SCCO	81A	B5
BRIDLE PLACE CT	LG	70	E4
BRIGADOON WY	SJ	63	C6
BRIGANTINE DR	SJ	60	B6
BRIGGS CT	SJ	72A	F5
BRIGHAM RD	SCCO	70	C4
BRIGHTEN AV	SJ	66	D5
BRIGHT OAK PL	SJ	72	E5
BRIGHT OAKS CT	LA	59	B1
BRIGHTON PL	MVW	51	F2
BRIGHTSIDE CT	SJ	63	A1
BRIGHTWOOD CT	SJ	63	D3
BRIGHTWOOD DR	SJ	63	D3
BRILL CT	SJ	55	E5
BRINDOS CT	SJ	72A	B1
BRIONES CT	LAH	50	F5
BRIONES WY	LAH	50	F5
BRISBANE CT	SJ	64	F2
BRISBANE CT	SJ	65	A2
BRISBANE WY	SJ	64	F2
BRISBANE WY	SJ	65	A2
BRISTLECONE CT	G	83	D2
BRISTOL DR	SJ	63	A1
BRISTOLWOOD LN	SJ	48	C4
BRITT CT	SJ	63	C4
BRITT WY	SJ	63	C4
BRITTANY CT	CPTO	60	A5
BRITTON AV	SJ	61	E6
BRITTON AV	SJ	66	E1
BRITTON AV	SVL	53	B3
BRITWELL CT	SJ	67	D5
BRIXTON CT	SJ	48	C5
BROADACRES DR	SJ	72	B5
BROADLEAF LN	SJ	61	C3
BROADMOOR DR	SJ	60	D5
BROADVIEW DR	SCCO	56	B5
BROADVIEW DR	SCCO	73	F5
BROADWAY	G	83	E1
BROADWAY	LG	70	D5
BROADWAY	SJ	61	F6
BROADWAY	SCCO	78G	D1
BROADWAY CT	SJ	61	F5
BROCASTLE WY	LG	70	F1
BROCK WY	SJ	68	B3
BROCKENHURST DR	SJ	72A	D5
BROCKHAMPTON LN	SJ	67	C5
BROCKTON LN	S	65	B3
BRODERICK DR	SJ	68	D5
BRODERICK WY	MVW	44	F3
BRODIE DR	SJ	68	A2
BROKAW RD	SJ	55	A3
BROKAW RD	SCL	54	E4
BROKEN ARROW DR	SJ	68	D5
BROKEN LANCE CT	SJ	68	B6
BROKEN OAK CT	SJ	63	E3
BROMLEY CRSS DR	SJ	72A	E4
BRONSON AV	SCCO	71	D1
BROOK EST CT	SJ	68A	A2
BROOK LN	S	65	B2
BROOK PL	MVW	52	C5
BROOKDALE AV	MVW	52	A3
BROOKDALE DR	SJ	66	F1
BROOKDALE DR	SCL	60	D2
BROOKDALE DR	SCCO	60	D2
BROOKE ACRES CT	LG	71	B5
BROOKE ACRES DR	LG	71	B5
BROOKFIELD AV	SVL	52	D4
BROOK GLEN CT	S	65	B3
BROOK GLEN DR	SJ	65	C2
BROOK GLEN DR	S	65	C3
BROOKGROVE LN	CPTO	60	B5
BROOKHAVEN DR	S	65	C2
BROOKHURST CT	SJ	65	C2
BROOKINGS LN	SVL	59	C1
BROOK LEAF CT	SJ	48	E6
BROOKLINE DR	SVL	52	E4
BROOKLYN AV	LG	70	E5
BROOKLYN AV	SJ	61	D4
BROOKLYN AV	SCCO	61	D4
BROOKMERE DR	SJ	72A	C4
BROOKMILL RD	LA	52	C6
BROOKMILL RD	LA	59	C1
BROOKMONT CT	MH	79	E5
BROOKNOLL CT	S	65	C2
BROOKRIDGE DR	S	65	C2
BROOKS AV	LG	70	D4
BROOKS AV	SJ	61	F5
BROOKS AV	SJ	62	A5
BROOKSIDE AV	SCL	60	F4
BROOKSIDE AV	SCL	61	A4
BROOKSIDE AV	SCCO	61	A4
BROOKTREE CT	SJ	75	F1
BROOKTREE WY	SJ	72	F6
BROOKVALE DR	SJ	65	A2
BROOKVIEW CT	MH	80K	F3
BROOKVIEW DR	S	65	B2
BROOKWELL DR	CPTO	60	A6
BROOKWOOD AV	SJ	62	C2
BROOKWOOD LN	S	64	F6
BROWER AV	MVW	52	C5
BROWN AV	SCL	53	E5
BROWN AV	SCCO	67	F3
BROWN CT	SCL	53	E5
BROWN ST	SJ	62	A4
BROWNHILL CT	SJ	63	E5
BROWNING DR	SJ	66	D6
BROWNING DR	SCCO	66	B6
BROWNS LN	LG	65	F6
BROWNSTONE CT	SJ	63	A2
BROWNVIEW DR	SJ	72	B5
BROWNWOOD WY	SCL	54	C2
BRUCE AV	LG	70	E3
BRUCE AV	MS	70	E3
BRUCE AV	SJ	61	E2
BRUCE CT	MS	70	E3
BRUCE CT	SCL	53	E5
BRUCE DR	PA	44	D2
BRUCE WY	SCCO	75	F2
BRUCE WY	SCCO	76	A2
BRUCITO AV	LA	59	B1
BRUCKNER CIR	MVW	52	C5
BRULE CT	SCCO	56	B3
BRUNDAGE WY	SCCO	56	B2
BRUNNHILDE WY	SJ	63	A5
BRUNSWICK AV	SJ	66	C6
BRUNSWICK AV	SJ	71	C1
BRUSH RD	SCCO	73	C5
BRUSHCREEK CT	SJ	68	D2
BRUSHCREEK WY	SJ	68	D2
BRUSHGLEN WY	SJ	55	E4
BRUT WY	SJ	63	E6
BRYAN AV	SJ	67	B5
BRYAN AV	SVL	53	A4
BRYANT AV	MVW	52	B5
BRYANT AV	SCCO	52	B5
BRYANT CT	PA	43	F1
BRYANT ST	MVW	52	B2
BRYANT ST	PA	43	F1
BRYANT ST	PA	44	D4
BRYANT WY	SVL	60	C1
BRYCE CT	MPTS	48	B3
BRYCE DR	SJ	72	D1
BRYSON AV	PA	44	C3
BRYSON CT	SCCO	80K	E3
BUBB RD	CPTO	59	D6
BUBB RD	CPTO	64	E1
BUBB RD	SJ	64	E1
BUBB RD	SCCO	59	D6
BUBB RD	SCCO	64	E1
BUBBLINGWELL PL	SJ	72	E5
BUCHANAN CT	SCL	60	F1
BUCHANAN DR	SCL	60	F1
BUCHER AV	SCL	60	F2
BUCHER DR	SCCO	80K	D2
BUCHSER WY	SJ	62	A6
BUCKEYE CT	MPTS	47	E6
BUCKEYE CT	SVL	53	B5
BUCKEYE DR	MPTS	47	E5
BUCKEYE DR	SJ	68	D3
BUCKEYE DR	SVL	53	B5
BUCKHAVEN DR	SJ	68A	C3
BUCKHAVEN LN	S	65	A4
BUCKHILL CT	SJ	63	C3
BUCKINGHAM CT	S	65	B5
BUCKINGHAM DR	LA	52	B5
BUCKINGHAM DR	SJ	67	B5
BUCKINGHAM DR	SCL	60	F4
BUCKINGHAM DR	SCCO	67	B5
BUCKINGHM PK DR	SJ	67	E5
BUCKLEY ST	SCL	53	C6
BUCKNALL RD	C	65	F3
BUCKNALL RD	C	66	A3
BUCKNALL RD	SJ	65	F3
BUCKNALL RD	S	65	D3
BUCKNAM AV	C	65	F5
BUCKNAM AV	SCCO	65	F5
BUCKNAM CT	C	65	F5
BUCKNER DR	SJ	56	B6
BUCKNER DR	SCCO	56	B6
BUCKSKIN CT	MH	80	C3
BUCKTHORN WY	SJ	65	A1
BUCKWOOD CT	SJ	75	F1
BUDD AV	C	65	F4
BUDD AV	C	66	A4
BUDD CT	C	65	F4
BUDD CT	C	66	A4
BUDDLAWN WY	C	65	F4
BUDDLAWN WY	C	66	A4
BUENA CREST CT	SJ	68	E1
BUENA KNOLL CT	SJ	68	E1
BUENA LUNA CT	SJ	66	C2
BUENA MONTE DR	SCCO	72A	A5
BUENA PARK CT	SJ	68	E1
BUENA POINT CT	SJ	68	E1
BUENA VIEW CT	SJ	68	E1
BUENA VISTA AV	LG	70	F2
BUENA VISTA AV	SJ	61	D4
BUENA VISTA AV	SCCO	61	D5
BUENA VISTA AV	SCCO	82	E3
BUENA VISTA AV	SCCO	82A	A3
BUENA VISTA AV	SVL	52	E3
BUENA VISTA DR	LAH	50	F5
BUENA VISTA DR	SJ	54	F1
BUFKIN CT	SJ	72A	A2
BUFKIN DR	SJ	72A	A3
BUGATTI CT	SJ	67	F6
BUGGYWHIP CT	SJ	72	D4
BULLDOG BLVD	SJ	62	C1
BULLION CIR	SJ	72	B3
BULLION CT	SJ	72	B3
BULLION PL	SJ	72	B3
BUNCE CT	SJ	55	E1
BUNDY AV	SJ	61	A5
BUNDY AV	SCCO	61	A4
BUNKER CT	SJ	63	B5
BUNKER HILL CT	SJ	72	D5
BUNKER HILL LN	SCL	46	E6
BURBANK DR	SCL	60	D2
BURBANK ST	SCCO	81	B4
BURCHELL AV	SJ	72	A4
BURCHELL CT	SJ	72	A4
BURCHELL RD	G	83	A1
BURCHELL RD	SCCO	81H	E5
BURCHELL RD	SCCO	82	A6
BURDETT WY	CPTO	48	A1
BURDETTE DR	SJ	63	A4
BURDICK WY	SJ	63	C4
BURGOYNE ST	MVW	45	A6
BURGUNDY CT	SJ	55	E1
BURGUNDY DR	SJ	55	E1
BURGUNDY WY	S	70	B1
BURKE DR	G	82	F5
BURKE DR	SCL	47	A6
BURKE DR	SCL	54	A1
BURKE LN	LAH	51	D4
BURKE RD	LAH	51	D4
BURKE RD	LG	71	E4
BURKE ST	SJ	62	E6
BURKETTE DR	SJ	65	E1
BURL CT	SJ	63	E6
BURL WY	SJ	63	E6
BURLEY DR	MPTS	48	B2
BURLINGAME WY	SJ	63	D6
BURLINGTON ST	SJ	72A	C2
BURLWOOD DR	SJ	72	E6
BURMAN DR	SJ	68	B3
BURNBANK PL	SJ	72	B4
BURNETT AV	MH	79	C1
BURNETT AV	SCL	60	D3
BURNETT AV	SCCO	78	D6
BURNETT AV	SCCO	79	C1
BURNETT DR	S	64	E2
BURNHAM CT	C	65	E3
BURNHAM DR	SJ	55	D1
BURNHAM WY	PA	44	D1
BURNING HLLS PL	SJ	72A	E4
BURNING TREE CT	SJ	72A	E4
BURNING TREE DR	SJ	72A	E4
BURNLEY WY	SCL	60	C1
BURNLEY WY	SVL	60	C1
BURNS AV	SCCO	59	C1
BURNS AV	SVL	59	C1
BURNS LN	S	64	F6
BURNSIDE DR	SJ	72	E6
BURNTWOOD AV	SVL	53	D1
BURNTWOOD CT	SVL	53	D1
BURREL CT	SJ	61	D3
BURROWS RD	C	65	F5
BURTON AV	SJ	54	F6
BURTON DR	SCL	53	F2
BURTON DR	SCL	54	A2
BURTON RD	SCCO	66	A6
BURTON RD	SCCO	71	A1
BUSH CIR	SCCO	45	C5
BUSH ST	MVW	52	B2
BUSH ST	SJ	61	F3
BUSHNELL RD	SCCO	45	D5
BUSINESS CIR	SJ	61	C4
BUSKIRK ST	MPTS	39	E5
BUTANO AV	SVL	52	D3
BUTANO CT	SJ	72	E3
BUTANO DR	MPTS	48	C4
BUTANO TER	S	69	F1
BUTCH DR	SCCO	81A	C6
BUTCHER DR	SCL	60	D2
BUTLER ST	MPTS	47	E3
BUTTE CT	SVL	59	D1
BUTTE ST	SCL	60	E1
BUTTERCUP LN	G	83	D1
BUTTERFLY DR	SJ	72	B4
BUTTERFLY LN	SCCO	80	C1
BUTTITTA LN	SCL	60	D1
BUTTONWOOD CT	SJ	63	E2
BYERLEY AV	SJ	67	A2
BYERLY CT	CPTO	59	B3
BYERS ST	G	83	E2
BYRD LN	LAH	51	A4
BYRNE AV	CPTO	59	D5
BYRNE AV	SCCO	59	D5
BYRNE PARK LN	LAH	51	A5
BYRON DR	SJ	66	C5
BYRON ST	PA	37	F6
BYRON ST	PA	38	A6
BYRON ST	PA	44	C3
C			
C ST	MVW	52	D2
C ST	SVL	46	A4
C ST	SVL	46	C6
C ST S	SVL	46	C6
CABALLO CT	SJ	55	E1
CABALLO LN	SCCO	50	D3
CABANA DR	SCCO	66	D3
CABERNET CT	SJ	68A	B3
CABERNET DR	S	65	C2
CABOT AV	SCL	60	D4
CABOT PL	SJ	60	A6
CABOT PL	SJ	65	A1
CABRAL AV	SJ	72	D2
CABRILLO AV	SJ	55	C1
CABRILLO AV	SCL	53	F6
CABRILLO AV	SCCO	43	F4
CABRILLO CT	SCL	53	E5
CABRILLO DR	SJ	54	F2
CABRILLO RD	SJ	47	C5
CABRILLO WY	SCL	54	A6
CACTUS DR	SJ	72A	B1
CADBURRY CT	SJ	72	E1
CADET PL	SJ	55	D3
CADILLAC CT	MPTS	47	D1
CADILLAC DR	SJ	66	B1
CADIZ DR	SJ	72	D2
CADMILL CT	SJ	62	F6
CADMILL CT	SJ	67	F1
CADMILL CT	SJ	68	A1
CADWALLADER AV	SJ	63	E6
CADWALLADER AV	SJ	68	E1
CADWALLADER LP	SJ	63	D5
CADWELL CT	SJ	72A	D1
CAGGIANO CT	SJ	75	E1
CAGGIANO DR	SJ	75	E1
CAHALAN AV	SJ	72	E2
CAHALAN CT	SJ	72	E2
CAHEN DR	SJ	75	F2
CAHILL ST	SJ	61	F3
CAIRO CT	SCCO	56	B6
CALABAZAS BLVD	SCL	53	D5
CALABAZAS BLVD	SCL	60	D1
CALABAZAS CT	SCL	60	D1
CALBAZAS CK CIR	SJ	65	A1
CALABRESE WY	G	83	C1
CALADO AV	C	65	E2
CALADO CT	C	65	E2
CALAVERAS AV	SJ	61	D3
CALAVERAS BLVD	MPTS	47	F3
CALAVERAS BLVD	MPTS	48	B2
CALAVERAS CT	MPTS	48	B2
CALAVERAS RD	MPTS	40	E6
CALAVERAS RD	MPTS	48	C1
CALAVERAS RD	SCCO	40	F4
CALAVERAS RD	SCCO	41	A4
CALAVERAS RD	SCCO	49	A1
CALAVERAS RIDGE	MPTS	40	B6
CALAVERAS RIDGE	MPTS	48	B1
CALBOONYA CT	SJ	62	C6
CALBORO DR	SJ	61	A6
CALCATERRA CT	SJ	75	E1
CALCATERRA DR	SJ	75	E1
CALCATERRA PL	PA	44	E5
CALDERON AV	MVW	52	B3
CALDERWOOD LN	SJ	72	A2
CALDWELL AV	LG	70	F4
CALDWELL CT	SCCO	77	E4
CALDWELL CT	SVL	59	C1
CALDWELL PL	SCL	60	F2
CALEB CT	SJ	63	D6
CALEDONIA DR	SJ	68A	C2
CALERO AV	SJ	72	E2
CALERO AV	SJ	72A	A2
CALERO CT	MH	80	C3
CALERO ST	MPTS	47	E2
CALERO HILLS CT	SJ	72A	F4
CALFHILL CT	LG	70	F4
CALGARY CT	SCCO	56	B5
CALGARY DR	SVL	59	D3
CALHOUN ST	SJ	62	C2
CALI AV	CPTO	59	F4
CALI AV	CPTO	60	A4
CALICO AV	SJ	66	C6
CALICO AV	SCCO	66	C6
CALICO CT	SVL	53	B5
CALIDA DR	SJ	67	D5
CALIENTE DR	SVL	53	B2
CALIENTE WY	SJ	55	C1
CALIFORNIA AV	PA	44	C2
CALIFORNIA AV	SJ	62	A6
CALIFORNIA AV	SJ	67	A1
CALIFORNIA AV	SCL	61	A2
CALIFORNIA AV	SCCO	81	A3
CALIFORNIA AV	SVL	52	F3
CALIFORNIA AV	SVL	53	A3
CALIFORNIA CIR	MPTS	39	D6
CALIFORNIA CIR	MPTS	47	D1
CALIFORNIA ST	C	66	A3
CALIFORNIA ST	MVW	44	E6
CALIFORNIA ST	MVW	51	F1
CALIFORNIA ST	MVW	52	A1
CALIFORNIA ST	SVL	53	B3
CALIF OAK WY	CPTO	59	B4
CALINOMA DR	SJ	71	F2
CALIRI CT	SCCO	82A	D4
CALISTOGA DR	SJ	66	D4
CALISTOGA WY	MVW	52	C1
CALLA DR	SVL	53	B5
CALLAN ST	MPTS	39	E5
CALLE ALEGRE	SJ	72	A4
CALLE ALFREDO	SVL	46	B5
CALLE ALICIA	SVL	46	C6
CALLE ALMADEN	SJ	72	B3
CALLE ANITA	SVL	46	C6
CALLE ARTIS	SJ	54	F1
CALLE ASTA	MH	79	E4
CALLE ATAVIO	MH	79	E4
CALLE BONITA	SJ	72	A5
CL CABALLERIA	MH	79	E4
CALLE CABEZAL	MH	79	E4
CALLE CARLOTTA	SVL	46	C6
CALLE CELESTINA	SCCO	81H	D2
CALLE CIELO	SCCO	81H	D2
CALLECITA	LG	65	D6
CALLECITA ST	SJ	66	F2
CALLECITA ST	SCCO	66	F2
CALLE CONCHITA	SVL	46	C6
CALLE CONSUELO	SVL	46	C6
CALLE DE AIDA	SJ	66	F6
CALLE DE AMOR	SJ	71	F4
CALLE DE ARROYO	SJ	67	A6
CL DE BARCELONA	CPTO	60	B5
CL DE BARCELONA	SCCO	60	B5
CL DE ESCUELA	SCL	46	F6
CALLE DE FARRAR	SJ	67	A6
CALLE DE FELICE	SJ	71	F4
CALLE DE GILDA	SJ	67	A6
CALLE DE GILDA	SJ	72	A1
CL DE GUADALUPE	SJ	55	E6
CALLE DE LA PAZ	SJ	72	A6
CL D LS ESTRLLA	SJ	63	C5
CL DE LS FLORES	SJ	63	C5
CALLE DL CONEJO	SJ	72	A4
CALLE DEL MUNDO	SCL	46	F5
CL DEL PRADO CT	MPTS	48	A1
CALLE DEL REY	G	82	C6
CALLE DEL SOL	LAH	51	C4
CALLE DEL SOL	SCL	46	F5
CALLE DE LUCIA	SJ	71	F1
CALLE DE LUNA	SCL	46	F5
CALLE DE PLATA	SJ	55	D6
CL DE PRIMAVERA	SCL	46	F6
CL DE PROSPERO	SJ	71	F4
CALLE DE RICO	SJ	71	F4
CL DE STUARDA	SJ	66	F6
CL DE STUARDA	SJ	67	A6
CALLE DE SUERTE	SJ	71	F4
CALLE DE TOSCA	SJ	67	A6
CALLE DE VERDE	SJ	67	C5
CALLE DOLORES	SVL	46	C6
CALLE DORITA	SVL	46	C6
CALLE EL PADRE	SCCO	65	E5
CALLE ENRIQUE	MH	80K	F2
CALLE ESPERANZA	SJ	72	A4
CALLE ESTORIA	SCCO	65	E6
CALLE ESTRELLA	SVL	46	C6
CALLE EULALIA	SVL	46	C6
CALLE GLORIA	SVL	46	C6
CALLE ISABELLA	SVL	46	C6
CALLE JUANITA	SVL	46	C6
CALLE LOLITA	SCCO	65	E6
CALLE LUCIA	SVL	46	C6
CALLE LUPE	SVL	46	C6
CL MARGUERITA	LG	65	E5
CALLE MARIA	SVL	46	C6
CALLE MAZATAN	MH	79	E4
CL MESA ALTA	MPTS	48	C4
CALLE MONIZ	SCCO	79	D1
CALLE MONTALVO	S	70	A1
CALLE NIVEL	LG	65	D5
CALLE ORIENTE	MPTS	48	A1
CALLE ROSITA	SVL	46	C6
CALLE TACUBA	S	64	F5
CALLE TACUBA	S	65	A5
CALLE TERESA	SVL	46	C6
CALLE UVAS	SCCO	81H	D2
CALLE VENTURA	SJ	72	D6
CALLE VICTORIA	SVL	46	C6
CL VISTA VERDE	MPTS	48	D3
CALL OF WILD RD	SCCO	78G	F1
CALMA CT	SJ	66	C2
CALMOR AV	SJ	72	D2
CALMOR CT	SJ	72	D2
CALOOSA CT	SJ	55	B3
CALPELLA DR	SJ	67	D6
CALPINE DR	SJ	72A	B1
CALRA CK HTS DR	MPTS	40	B5
CALUMET CT	SJ	55	B6
CALVARY WY	SJ	67	B4
CALVELLI CT	SJ	66	B6
CALVERT CT	SCL	60	D4
CALVERT DR	SJ	60	C5
CALVERT DR	SCL	60	D4
CALVERT DR	SCCO	60	C5
CALVIEW AV	SJ	62	F2
CALVIEW AV	SJ	63	A2
CALVIEW LN	SJ	62	F2
CALVIEW LN	SJ	63	A2
CALVIN AV	SJ	66	C6
CALVIN AV	SCCO	66	C6
CALWA CT	SJ	68	B5

STREET	CITY	PAGE	GRID
CALYPSO CT	SJ	63	A1
CALZAR DR	SJ	66	F5
CAMACHO WY	SJ	48	C6
CAMANO CT	SJ	62	F5
CAMARDA CT	CPTO	60	A4
CAMARGO CT	SJ	48	C6
CAMARGO DR	SJ	48	B5
CAMARGO DR	SJ	55	C1
CAMARILLO CT	MPTS	40	B6
CAMAS AV	SJ	55	F6
CAMAS AV	SJ	56	A6
CAMBERLEY LN	CPTO	59	B5
CAMBER TREE CT	SJ	72	C4
CAMBRIAN DR	SCCO	66	C4
CAMBRIANNA DR	SJ	66	D5
CAMBRIAN VW WY	LG	71	D3
CAMBRIDGE AV	PA	44	B3
CAMBRIDGE AV	SVL	52	E5
CAMBRIDGE DR	SJ	67	B4
CAMBRIDGE DR	SCL	60	D3
CAMBRIDGE DR	S	65	B3
CAMBRIDGE LN	MVW	52	B5
CAMDEN AV	C	66	B5
CAMDEN AV	SJ	66	D6
CAMDEN AV	SJ	71	E1
CAMDEN AV	SJ	72	C5
CAMDEN AV	SJ	72A	A6
CAMDEN AV	SCCO	66	B5
CAMDEN AV	SCCO	72	D5
CAMDEN OAKS CT	SJ	71	F3
CAMDEN VLG CIR	SJ	71	F3
CAMDEN VLG CT	SJ	71	F3
CAMDEN VLG WY	SJ	71	F3
CAMELFORD WY	SJ	55	F4
CAMELIA DR	SJ	72	C5
CAMELLIA TER	SCCO	71	A3
CAMELLIA WY	LA	51	F3
CAMELLIA WY	SJ	60	E6
CAMELOT DR	SCCO	48	F6
CAMEO CT	C	66	D3
CAMEO DR	SJ	65	D2
CAMEO DR	C	66	D3
CAMERON PL	SJ	60	A6
CAMERON PL	SJ	65	A1
CAMERON WY	SCL	60	E4
CAMILLE CIR	SJ	47	D6
CAMILLE CT	MVW	52	B3
CAMILLE CT	SCCO	80	C6
CAMINA ESCUELA	SJ	60	D5
CAMINO DR	SCL	61	C2
CAMINO ALTA	SCCO	56	B2
CAMINO ARROYO	G	82A	A6
CAMINO ARROYO	G	84	B1
CAMINO CERRADO	SJ	66	C2
CM DEL CERRO	LG	71	B3
CM DEL CERRO	SCCO	71	B3
CM D LOS BARCOS	S	65	C5
CAMINO DEL REY	SJ	55	C1
CAMINO DEL SOL	LG	71	A1
CAMINO DEL SOL	SCCO	71	B1
CAMINO ECCO	SJ	63	A5
CAMINO HERMOSO	LAH	58	E2
CAMINO HERMOSO	SCCO	58	E2
CAMINO MEDIO	LAH	51	B3
CAMINO MONDE	SJ	66	E1
CAMINO PABLO	SJ	61	F6
CAMINO PABLO	SJ	66	F1
CAMINO RAMON	SJ	61	E6
CAMINO RAMON	SJ	66	E1
CAMINO RICARDO	SJ	61	F6
CAMINO RICARDO	SJ	66	F1
CAMINO RICO	S	65	A5
CM ROBLES CT	SJ	72	A4
CM ROBLES WY	SJ	72	A4
CAMINO VERDE DR	SJ	72A	C3
CAMINO VISTA DR	CPTO	59	C4
CAMINO VISTA WY	SCCO	56	B2
CAMLOOP DR	SJ	65	D4
CAMP AV	MVW	45	B5
CAMPANA DR	PA	44	C5
CAMPANULA PL	LG	71	B2
CAMPBELL AV	C	65	D2
CAMPBELL AV	C	66	A3
CAMPBELL AV	LA	51	F5
CAMPBELL AV	SJ	61	C1
CAMPBELL AV	SJ	65	D2
CAMPBELL AV	SJ	72A	D2
CAMPBELL AV	SCL	61	C1
CAMPBELL AV	SCCO	66	D3
CAMPBELL ST	MPTS	39	B5
CAMPBELL ST	MPTS	40	C6
CAMPBELL ST	MPTS	47	D2
CAMPBELL ST	MPTS	48	C1
CAMPERDOWN CT	SJ	63	D6
CAMPERDOWN WY	SJ	63	C6
CAMPESINO AV	PA	44	D3
CAMPHOR CT	MPTS	47	E6
CAMPISI CT	SJ	72	E6
CAMPISI CT	SCCO	81H	D6
CAMPISI WY	C	66	C2
CAMPO CALLE WY	S	65	B6
CAMPOLI DR	SCCO	79	C2
CAMPOS VERDES	LG	71	D3
CAMPO VISTA LN	LAH	51	C3
CAMPUS DR	SCCO	43	E4
CAMPUS DR	SCCO	44	A3
CAMPUS DR N	SCCO	43	E3
CAMPUS DR S	SCCO	43	E3
CAMPUS DR W	SCCO	43	E3
CAMROSE AV	SJ	65	D4
CANADA DR	MPTS	48	A1
CANADA RD	SCCO	81B	C6
CANADA RD	SCCO	81C	D2
CANADA RD	SCCO	84	F2
CANADA RD	SCCO	85	C1
CANAL WY	SJ	48	B6
CANARIO WY	LAH	51	B3
CANARY DR	SVL	60	A3
CANARY LN	SJ	66	A1
CANARY ISLND CT	SCL	53	D3
CANARY ISLND CT	SCL	54	A4
CANDACE WY	LA	59	C1
CANDIA DR	SJ	62	F5
CANDLELIGHT WY	CPTO	64	E1
CANDLER AV	SJ	56	B6
CANDLER AV	SJ	63	B1
CANDLESTICK WY	SJ	56	B5
CANDLEWOOD AV	SVL	53	D1
CANDLEWOOD CT	CPTO	60	B5
CANDLEWOOD CT	SVL	53	D1
CANDLEWOOD DR	CPTO	60	B5
CANDY CT	S	65	B2
CANDY LN	S	65	B2
CANDY LYNN CT	SJ	72	C4
CANEN DR	SJ	75	F1
CANEN DR	SJ	76	A2
CANFIELD CT	SJ	67	C5
CANMORE CT	SJ	68	A6
CANNA CT	MVW	45	A6
CANNA LN	SCCO	71	F4
CANOAS GARDN AV	SJ	67	C2
CANOAS GARDN AV	SCCO	67	C2
CANON DR	SCCO	70	B3
CANONGATE CT	SJ	63	C6
CANON VISTA	SJ	56	B2
CANON VISTA	SCCO	56	B2
CANTATA WY	LAH	51	D5
CANTATA WY	SCCO	51	D5
CANTERBURY CT	SJ	65	B1
CANTERBURY PL	MPTS	40	A5
CANTERBURY WY	LA	52	C6
CANTO DR	SJ	71	E2
CANTON DR	MPTS	48	B2
CANTON DR	SJ	72	F2
CANTOR CT	MH	80	C4
CANTOR DR	MH	80	C4
CANYON DR	SCCO	56	B2
CANYON RD	PA	50	E6
CANYON RD	SCCO	50	E6
CANYON CREEK DR	SJ	48	E5
CANYON RIDGE DR	SJ	63	F4
CANYON RIVER CT	SJ	67	D5
CANYON RIVER CT	SCCO	67	D5
CANYON TRAIL WY	SJ	68	D4
CANYON VIEW CT	SJ	48	E5
CANYON VIEW DR	CPTO	64	C1
CANYON VIEW DR	SJ	48	E5
CANYON VIEW DR	S	64	F6
CANYON VISTA CT	CPTO	59	C6
CANYON VISTA DR	CPTO	59	C6
CAPAY CT	SJ	67	A6
CAPAY DR	SJ	67	A6
CAPE ANITA PL	SJ	55	D3
CAPE ANN PL	SJ	55	D4
CAPE ASTON CT	SJ	55	C4
CAPE BLANCO CT	SVL	59	F1
CAPE BRETON PL	SJ	55	D4
CAPE BUFFALO DR	SJ	55	C4
CP CANAVERAL PL	SJ	55	C4
CAPE COD CT	SJ	65	F1
CAPE COLONY DR	SJ	55	C4
CAPE CORAL DR	SJ	55	C4
CAPE DIAMOND DR	SJ	55	C4
CP FLATTERY PL	SJ	55	C4
CP HATTERAS WY	SJ	55	B4
CAPE HILDA PL	SJ	55	C4
CAPE HORN CT	SJ	55	C4
CAPE HORN DR	SJ	55	C4
CAPE HORN PL	SJ	55	C4
CAPE JASMINE PL	SJ	55	C4
CAPE JESSUP DR	SJ	55	C4
CAPE KENNEDY DR	SJ	55	C4
CAPELAW CT	SJ	63	F6
CAPELLA WY	SVL	52	F3
CAPE MARY PL	SJ	55	D3
CAPE MAY PL	SJ	55	B5
CAPE MISTY DR	SJ	55	C4
CAPE MORRIS PL	SJ	55	C4
CAPE POINT PL	SJ	55	C4
CAPE TOWN PL	SJ	55	C4
CAPE TRINITY PL	SJ	55	D4
CAPE VERDE PL	SJ	55	C4
CAPE VINCENT PL	SJ	55	B4
CAPEWOOD CT	SJ	48	B5
CAPEWOOD LN	SJ	48	C5
CAPE YORK PL	SJ	55	C4
CAPISTRANO AV	SJ	60	D4
CAPISTRANO DR	SCL	53	D5
CAPISTRANO PL	LG	65	E6
CAPISTRANO WY	LA	59	B2
CAPITANCILOS DR	SJ	71	F4
CAPITANCILOS PL	SJ	71	F4
CAPITOL AV	MPTS	47	F5
CAPITOL AV	MPTS	48	A5
CAPITOL AV	SJ	55	D3
CAPITOL AV	SJ	56	A6
CAPITOL AV	SCCO	55	D3
CAPITOL AV	SCCO	56	A6
CAPITOL CT	SJ	63	A1
CAPITOL EXPWY	SJ	55	F6
CAPITOL EXPWY	SJ	63	C6
CAPITOL EXPWY	SJ	67	F4
CAPITOL EXPWY	SJ	68	A2
CAPITOL EXPWY	SCCO	67	C4
CAPITOLA AV	SJ	68	B4
CAPITOLA WY	SCL	60	D2
CAPITOL REEF CT	SJ	67	D5
CAPITOL VLG CIR	SJ	67	E4
CAPPY CT	SJ	68	B5
CAPRI DR	C	65	F6
CAPRI DR	LG	65	F6
CAPRI DR	LG	66	A5
CAPRI WY	SJ	60	A6
CAPRIC DR	SJ	68	C6
CAPRIC DR	SJ	72A	C1
CAPRICE CT	MH	79	E4
CAPRICORN CT	SJ	67	F3
CAPRISTO CT	SCCO	79	B1
CAPUTO DR	MH	79	F5
CAPURSO WY	SJ	62	B6
CARACAS CT	SJ	63	A3
CARADO CT	LAH	51	C2
CARASTON WY	SJ	63	C4
CARAVAN WY	SJ	68	C6
CARAVAN WY	SJ	72A	B5
CARAVELLA DR	SJ	65	F1
CARAWAY CT	SJ	60	E5
CARBONERA AV	SCCO	52	D3
CARBONERA AV	SVL	52	D3
CARDEL WY	SJ	71	E2
CARDIFF CT	SJ	61	A6
CARDIFF CT	SJ	66	A1
CARDIFF PL	MPTS	40	A5
CARDIGAN DR	SVL	60	A1
CARDIN AV	SJ	66	F5
CARDIN AV	SJ	67	A5
CARDINAL DR E	SVL	52	D5
CARDINAL DR W	SVL	52	D5
CARDINAL LN	LG	71	A4
CARDINAL LN	SJ	67	A4
CARDINAL WY	PA	44	D1
CARDINGTON DR	SJ	48	B6
CARDONA WY	SJ	55	C3
CARDOZA CT	SJ	48	E5
CARERA CT	SJ	72A	B1
CAREY AV	SCCO	80	D5
CARIBBEAN DR	SVL	46	A4
CARIBE WY	SJ	55	E5
CARIBOU CT	SVL	59	E1
CARICK PL WY	SJ	68	C1
CARIGNANE DR	G	83	F5
CARILLO LN	LAH	51	B2
CARIS CT	SCCO	82	D1
CARL AV	MPTS	48	B2
CARL RD	SVL	46	B4
CARL ST	SCL	54	C6
CARLA CT	MVW	52	B4
CARLA CT	SJ	72	C4
CARLA DR	SJ	72	C4
CARLA WY	G	82	E6
CARLESTER DR	LG	71	B2
CARLETON PL	SCL	60	E3
CARLING CT	SJ	68	B5
CARLISLE WY	SVL	59	F1
CARLISLE WY	SVL	60	A1
CARLITA CT	SCCO	59	D3
CARLITOS CT	PA	44	C5
CARLO ST	MPTS	47	E3
CARLO SCIMEC DR	SJ	55	D1
CARLOS PRIVADA	MVW	52	D1
CARLOTTA CT	SJ	67	D4
CARLOW CT	SVL	59	F1
CARLSBAD CT	MPTS	48	C3
CARLSBAD DR	SJ	72	B2
CARLSBAD ST	MPTS	48	C3
CARLSEN WY	SJ	67	B5
CARLSON CIR	PA	44	D4
CARLSON CT	PA	44	E4
CARLSON DR	SCCO	80K	B2
CARLTON AV	LG	71	A2
CARLTON AV	SJ	71	B2
CARLTON AV	SCCO	71	B1
CARLTON CT	LG	71	A2
CARLTON WY	LG	71	A2
CARLYLE AV	G	82	E5
CARLYLE CT	G	82	E5
CARLYLE ST	SJ	61	F3
CARLYN AV	C	66	A3
CARLYN CT	SVL	53	A4
CARLYSLE AV	SCL	60	C3
CARLYSLE ST	SJ	61	F3
CARM AV	SJ	71	D2
CARMEL AV	LA	51	D1
CARMEL AV	SVL	53	B2
CARMEL CT	LA	44	D6
CARMEL CT	LA	51	D1
CARMEL DR	PA	44	D1
CARMEL DR	SJ	62	B6
CARMEL DR	SJ	67	B1
CARMEL ST	G	82	E6
CARMEL ST	G	83	F2
CARMEL TER	LA	52	B5
CARMEL WY	SCL	61	A1
CARMELITA DR	MVW	52	B4
CARMEN CT	SJ	63	B5
CARMEN RD	CPTO	59	C4
CARMINE WY	SJ	55	B2
CARMONA CT	CPTO	59	D4
CARNABY CT	SJ	67	D5
CARNADERO RD	SCCO	84	B6
CARNATION CT	LA	51	E5
CARNATION WY	SCL	54	B3
CARNAVON WY	SJ	55	A2
CARNEGIE DR	MPTS	48	B2
CARNELIAN DR	SJ	62	E3
CARNELIAN GN CT	S	70	A1
CARNEROS AV	SVL	52	D4
CARNFORTH CT	SJ	75	E2
CARNIEL AV	S	64	F3
CARNIEL CT	S	64	F3
CARNIVAL WY	SJ	75	F2
CARNOT DR	SJ	66	D1
CARNOUSTIE CT	CPTO	59	C5
CAROB LN	LA	52	A6
CAROBWOOD CT	SJ	48	C4
CAROBWOOD LN	SJ	48	C4
CAROL AV	MVW	52	B4
CAROL AV	SCCO	52	B4
CAROL DR	SCCO	67	C2
CAROL LN	S	65	A2
CAROLA AV	SJ	65	E2
CAROLA CT	SJ	65	E1
CAROL LEAF CT	SJ	63	E4
CAROLINA AV	SVL	53	B2
CAROLINA LN	PA	44	D5
CAROLINE DR	CPTO	59	D3
CAROLINE WY	SJ	71	D2
CAROL LEE DR	CPTO	60	A4
CAROLYN AV	SJ	61	F6
CAROLYN CT	SCCO	82	F2
CAROLYN DR	SCL	60	F1
CARON CT	SJ	62	F6
CARPENTER PL	SCL	53	D4
CARPENTIER WY	SJ	67	E3
CARPENTIER WY	SJ	68	C3
CARR PL	G	83	E2
CARRABELLE WY	SJ	72	F6
CARRIAGE CIR	CPTO	59	E6
CARRIAGE CT	LA	51	D2
CARRIAGE DR	G	82	C6
CARRIAGE DR	MH	79	C3
CARRIAGE DR	SCL	61	A2
CARRIAGE CV CT	SJ	68	A2
CARRIAGE HIL DR	SCCO	72	E5
CARRIAGE LMP WY	MH	79	E3
CARRICK CT	SVL	59	F1
CARRICK CT	SVL	60	A1
CARRICK ST	S	65	C4
CARRIE ST	SJ	62	B4
CARRIE LEE WY	SJ	67	B5
CARRIL CT	MS	70	E2
CARRINGTON CIR	LAH	51	A5
CARRINGTON CIR	SJ	67	A4
CARRINGTON CT	SJ	67	A4
CARROLL ST	SVL	52	F4
CARROLL ST	SVL	53	A4
CARRYBACK AV	SJ	68	C6
CARRYDUFF WY	SJ	68	C1
CARRYWOOD WY	SJ	76	A1
CARSON CT	MVW	52	E3
CARSON DR	SVL	52	E3
CARSON WY	MPTS	40	A6
CARSON WY	SJ	66	D5
CARTA BLANCA ST	CPTO	59	C3
CARTAGO CT	SJ	55	D6
CARTER AV	SJ	71	F3
CARTER WY	SCL	60	D3
CARTERWOOD PL	SJ	62	F5
CARTWRIGHT WY	CPTO	59	F4
CARVER DR	SCCO	60	C6
CARVER PL	MVW	51	F2
CARVER ST	SJ	55	F3
CARVER ST	SCCO	55	F3
CARVO CT	LA	52	B6
CAS DR	SJ	67	F3
CAS DR	SJ	68	A3
CASA CT	SCL	60	C1
CASA LN	SCCO	79	F2
CASABA CREEK CT	SJ	75	E1
CASA BLANCA AV	SJ	60	D5
CASA BLANCA LN	S	65	C4
CASA BONITA CT	LA	51	F4
CASA D FRUTA DR	SCCO	82C	F5
CASA DE PINO WY	SCCO	63F	E1
CASA DE PONSELE	SJ	67	A6
CASA GRANDE	LG	65	D6
CASA GRANDE AV	MVW	45	C5
CASA GRANDE CT	MH	80	C3
CASA GRANDE CT	SJ	66	B5
CASA GRANDE WY	SJ	67	B5
CASALINO CT	SJ	63	D2
CASA LOMA CT	SJ	60	D5
CASA LOMA RD	SJ	78J	E4
CASA LOMA RD	SCCO	78K	E1
CASA LOMA RD	SCCO	78L	A1
CASALS CT	SJ	63	E1
CASA MADEIRA LN	SCCO	56	E6
CASA MIA DR	SJ	66	C5
CASA MIA WY	LAH	51	E6
CASANUEVA PL	SCCO	43	F5
CASANUEVA PL	SCCO	44	A5
CASA VERDE AV	SJ	60	D5
CASA VIEW DR	SJ	60	D5
CASCADE DR	SJ	60	E5
CASCADE DR	SVL	59	F1
CASCADE ST	MPTS	48	D4
CASCADE TER	SVL	59	F1
CASCO CT	SJ	62	F6
CASEY AVE	MVW	44	F2
CASEY ST	G	82	F6
CASEY WY	SJ	63	D6
CASHDAN CT	SCL	53	D4
CASHEW BLOSM DR	SJ	68	B6
CASHMERE CT	SVL	59	F1
CASHMERE TER	SVL	59	F1
CASINO WY	MH	80K	E2
CASITA CT	LA	51	E2
CASITA CT	SJ	60	D5
CASITA WY	LA	51	F1
CASITAS BULEVAR	LG	65	D6
CASPER ST	MPTS	47	E3
CASPIAN CT	SVL	46	A5
CASPIAN DR	SVL	46	B5
CASPIAN SEA DR	SJ	61	D6
CASPIAN SEA DR	SJ	66	D1
CASS PL	CPTO	59	C4
CASS WY	PA	44	C5
CASSADAY CT	SJ	67	D4
CASSANDRA WY	MVW	52	C1
CASSATT WY	SCCO	67	B2
CASSIA WY	SVL	53	C5
CASSIAR DR	C	65	E2
CASSIAR DR	SJ	65	E2
CASSLAND CT	SJ	55	B3
CASSWELL CT	SJ	72A	D1
CASSWOOD CT	SJ	72A	A6
CASTANO DR	SJ	60	B6
CASTANO CORTE	LA	51	E2
CASTELLO DR	SJ	72	B4
CASTELLO WY	SCL	53	D4
CASTERWOOD CT	SJ	72	F6
CASTERWOOD CT	SJ	72A	A6
CASTILE CT	SJ	66	E4
CASTILLEJA AV	PA	44	A2
CASTILLEJA CT	LA	52	A5
CASTILLON WY	SJ	72A	D3
CASTINE AV	CPTO	59	E3
CASTLE DR	SJ	67	B4
CASTLE LN	LA	51	F3
CASTLEBRIDGE DR	SJ	55	A2
CASTLEBROOK CT	SJ	55	D5
CASTLEBURY DR	SJ	55	A2
CASTLECREST DR	SJ	55	A2
CASTLEGATE DR	SJ	48	D6
CASTLE GLEN AV	SJ	60	C6
CASTLE GLEN AV	SJ	65	C1
CASTLE GLEN AV	SCCO	60	C6
CASTLE GLEN AV	SCCO	65	C1
CASTLE HILL DR	MH	79	B4
CASTLE HILL WY	SCCO	73	D5
CASTLEKNOLL DR	SJ	60	B6
CASTLE LAKE CIR	MH	79	B4
CASTLE LAKE DR	MH	79	B3
CASTLE MANOR DR	SJ	65	C1
CASTLEMONT AV	SJ	61	B6
CASTLEMONT AV	SJ	66	B1
CASTLE RIDGE DR	MH	79	B4
CASTLEROCK CT	SVL	59	F1
CASTLEROCK DR	SJ	72	D6
CASTLEROCK TER	SVL	59	F1
CASTLETON CT	SJ	63	C4
CASTLETON DR	SJ	63	C4
CASTLETON ST	CPTO	59	D6
CASTLETON TER	SVL	60	C1
CASTLETON WY	SVL	60	C1
CASTLETREE CT	SJ	55	B2
CASTLEWOOD CT	SJ	60	D6
CASTLEWOOD DR	LG	65	F6
CASTLEWOOD DR	SJ	60	D6
CASTRO CT	C	65	E3
CASTRO DR	C	65	E3
CASTRO DR	SJ	65	E3
CASTRO PL	SCL	53	F6
CASTRO ST	MVW	52	B2
CASTRO VLY RD	SCCO	84	A6
CASTRO VLY RD	SCCO	91	A1
CASUAL CT	SJ	72	E6
CASUAL WY	SJ	72	E6
CATALA CT	SCL	61	A2
CATALDI DR	SJ	48	C6
CATALINA AV	SCL	60	D2
CATALINA CT	CPTO	59	D6
CATALINA CT	G	83	D1
CATALINA CT	LA	51	E1
CATALINA DR	SJ	60	E6
CATALINA DR	SJ	65	E1
CATALINA WY	LA	51	E1
CATALONIA WY	SJ	66	E4
CATALPA LN	C	66	B3
CATAMARAN ST	SJ	72A	D4
CATHARINE CT	LAH	51	C3
CATHAY DR	SJ	63	A3
CATHCART WY	SCCO	44	A5
CATHEDRAL DR	SVL	59	E1
CATHERINE CT	G	83	F3
CATHERINE ST	SJ	46	E3
CATHERINE ST	SCL	61	A1
CATHERMOLA RD	SCCO	78H	E2
CATHY DR	SJ	62	F3
CATKIN CT	SJ	61	C5
CATRINA CT	SJ	71	C2
CATRON DR	SCCO	78H	A2
CAUSEY LN	LG	70	F4
CAVALIER CT	LA	51	D1
CAVALIER CT	SJ	66	D4
CAVALIER CT	SCCO	66	D4
CAVENDISH DR	SJ	48	D5
CAVIGLIA DR	SJ	47	C6
CAVIGLIA DR	SJ	54	C1
CAXTON CT	SJ	65	F1
CAYMAN PL	SJ	55	E2
CAYMAN WY	SJ	55	E2
CAYMUS CT	SVL	52	D3
CAYUGA CT	SJ	72	F4

1991 SANTA CLARA COUNTY STREET INDEX

1991 SANTA CLARA COUNTY STREET INDEX

STREET	CITY	PAGE	GRID
CLEARVIEW DR	SCCO	65	F6
CLEARVIEW DR	SCCO	70	E1
CLEARWATER CT	SVL	59	F1
CLEARWOOD CT	CPTO	59	D4
CLEAVES AV	SJ	61	E3
CLELAND AV	S	70	E5
CLEMATIS DR	SJ	71	F4
CLEMATIS DR	SVL	53	C5
CLEMENCE AV	SJ	62	D3
CLEMENCE AV	SCCO	62	D3
CLEMENCE CT	SJ	62	E4
CLEMO AV	PA	44	D5
CLEMSON AV	S	65	D4
CLEO AV	CPTO	64	F1
CLEO AV	SJ	64	F1
CLEVELAND AV	SJ	61	C4
CLEVELAND AV	SCCO	61	C4
CLIFDEN WY	CPTO	59	F5
CLIFDEN WY	CPTO	60	A5
CLIFF DR	SJ	48	E5
CLIFFORD CT	CPTO	60	A5
CLIFFORD DR	CPTO	60	A5
CLIFFORD LN	MPTS	39	F6
CLIFFORD LN	MPTS	47	F1
CLIFFORD ST	SCL	61	A1
CLIFFWOOD DR	SJ	62	F2
CLIFTON AV	C	61	B6
CLIFTON AV	LG	70	D5
CLIFTON AV	SJ	61	B6
CLIFTON AV	SCCO	61	D4
CLIFTON CT	PA	44	D2
CLINTON AV	SCL	60	D3
CLINTON PL	SJ	61	F3
CLINTON RD	LA	52	A6
CLINTONIA AV	SJ	61	F5
CLIPPER CT	SJ	55	E1
CLISE CT	SJ	72A	B3
CLOGSTON CT	SJ	55	E4
CLOUD DR	SJ	68	C4
CLOVE DR	SCCO	61	C5
CLOVER AV	C	61	B6
CLOVER AV	SJ	61	B6
CLOVER WY	LG	71	A4
CLOVERBROOK DR	SJ	72	C4
CLOVERCREST DR	SJ	72	B2
CLOVERDALE CT	SVL	59	D2
CLOVERDALE LN	SJ	65	E2
CLOVERHILL DR	SJ	72	C4
CLOVERLY CT	SCCO	59	D3
CLOVER OAK DR	SJ	63	E3
CLOVEWOOD LN	SJ	48	C5
CLOVIS AV	SJ	71	E3
CLUB DR	SJ	54	F1
CLUB DR	SCCO	56	B2
CLUBHOUSE LN	CPTO	59	C5
CLUB VIEW TER	SCCO	51	F6
CLYDA AV	SJ	62	F1
CLYDA AV	SCCO	62	F1
CLYDA DR	SJ	55	F6
CLYDE AV	MVW	52	E1
CLYDE AV	SCL	54	B2
CLYDE CT	MPTS	47	F2
CLYDE CT	MVW	45	E6
CLYDEBANK CT	SVL	60	C1
CLYDELLE AV	SJ	71	C2
CLYDELLE AV	SCCO	71	C2
CLYDESDALE AV	SJ	72A	A3
COACH CT	SJ	72	D5
COACHELLA AV	SVL	53	C2
COACHLIGHT DR	SJ	68	A2
COAKLEY DR	SJ	60	F5
COAKLEY DR	SJ	61	A6
COALBROOK DR	SJ	61	D6
COALBROOK DR	SJ	66	D1
COAST AV	MVW	44	F3
COASTLAND AV	SJ	67	B1
COASTLAND DR	PA	44	C2
COBALT WY	SVL	53	D3
COBBERT DR	SJ	63	E3
COBBLESTONE CT	SJ	72	D3
COBURN CT	SJ	72B	A4
COCCIARDI CT	S	64	D4
COCHRANE CIR	MH	79	D2
COCHRANE RD	MH	79	D2
COCHRANE RD	SCCO	78	E6
COCHRANE RD	SCCO	79	D2
COCONUT DR	SJ	63	D3
CODY CT	SCL	60	C3
CODY LN	LA	51	E3
CODY LN	S	69	F1
CODY WY	SJ	66	D4
COE AV	SJ	61	F5
COE AV	SJ	62	A5
COELHO CT	MPTS	39	F5
COELHO ST	MPTS	39	F5
COEUR DALENE WY	SVL	59	D1
COFFEEWOOD CT	SJ	72	F6
COFFEEWOOD CT	SJ	72A	A6
COFFEY CT	SJ	72	E2
COHANSEY AV	SCCO	82	E4
COHANSEY AV	SCCO	82A	A4
COHANSEY DR	SJ	48	C6
COHASSET WY	SJ	72A	C2
COIT DR	SJ	66	D4
COLBY AV	CPTO	60	B4
COLBY CT	S	65	A2
COLD HARBOR AV	CPTO	60	A5
COLDWATER DR	SJ	63	C2
COLE DR	SCCO	71	D1
COLEMAN AV	SJ	54	C6
COLEMAN AV	SJ	61	F2
COLEMAN AV	SCL	54	C6
COLEMAN RD	SJ	71	F4
COLEMAN RD	SJ	72	A3
COLEMAN RD	SCCO	71	F4
COLEMAN RD	SCCO	72	A3
COLEMAN RD	SJ	72	C2
COLERAINE CT	SVL	60	A1
COLERIDGE AV	PA	44	B2
COLETTE DR	SJ	55	E1
COLFAX CT	SCL	53	D6
COLFAX DR	SJ	72A	A2
COLGATE AV	SCL	60	D3
COLIBRI CT	SJ	72A	E3
COLINA DR	LAH	51	E6
COLINTON WY	SVL	59	D1
COLLEEN CT	MH	79	D4
COLLEEN CT	SJ	72	F4
COLLEEN DR	LA	59	B2
COLLEEN DR	SJ	72	E3
COLLEEN DR	SJ	72A	A4
COLLEEN WY	C	65	E3
COLLEGE AV	LG	70	E5
COLLEGE AV	PA	44	A4
COLLEGE AV	SCL	61	C2
COLLEGE CT	LA	51	E4
COLLEGE DR	SJ	61	D6
COLLEGE ST	MVW	44	F6
COLLEGE TER CT	LG	70	D5
COLLINGSWRTH ST	CPTO	59	D6
COLLINGWOOD AV	SJ	66	F2
COLLINS CT	MVW	44	E6
COLLINS LN	SJ	65	D1
COLLINWOOD CT	SCL	54	C2
COLLOMIA CT	SJ	68	B5
COLMERY CT	SJ	66	F6
COLMERY LN	SJ	66	F6
COLOMBET AV	SCCO	80	C6
COLOMBET AV	SCCO	81	D2
COLOMBET AV	SCCO	82	F1
COLOMBO DR	SJ	65	E2
COLONADE SQ	SJ	55	F5
COLONADE SQ	SJ	56	A5
COLONIAL LN	PA	44	D2
COLONIAL LN	SJ	55	F1
COLONIAL WY	SJ	66	B2
COLONIAL OKS DR	LA	52	B6
COLONY AV	SCCO	81	B4
COLONY CT	G	82	C6
COLONY DR	SJ	54	F1
COLONY ST	SCCO	45	A4
COLONY WY	G	82	C6
COLONY COVE DR	SJ	67	E6
COLONY COVE DR	SJ	72	E1
COLONY CREST DR	SJ	67	E6
COLONY FIELD DR	SJ	67	E6
COLONY FIELD DR	SJ	72	E1
COLONY GREEN DR	SJ	67	F6
COLONY GREEN DR	SJ	72	F1
COLONY HILLS LN	CPTO	59	E6
COLONY KNOLL DR	SJ	67	E6
COLONY KNOLL DR	SJ	72	E1
COLORADO AV	PA	44	D2
COLORADO CT	LG	71	E4
COLORADO PL	PA	44	D2
COLORVIEW CT	SJ	72	B4
COLT WY	SJ	68	B1
COLTER PL	SJ	72	E3
COLTON AV	SVL	46	A6
COLTON AV	SVL	53	A1
COLTON PL	SJ	62	B4
COLTWOOD CT	SJ	63	D2
COLTWOOD DR	SJ	63	D2
COLUMBIA AV	SVL	53	A3
COLUMBIA AV	SJ	61	F4
COLUMBIA AV	SJ	62	A4
COLUMBIA DR	MVW	51	F4
COLUMBIA DR	MVW	52	A4
COLUMBIA ST	PA	44	A4
COLUMBIA RIV CT	SJ	67	C5
COLUMBINE AV	SVL	53	C5
COLUMBINE CT	G	82	B6
COLUMBINE CT	S	65	B3
COLUMBINE DR	SJ	56	C6
COLUMBUS AV	CPTO	59	D6
COLUMBUS CIR	MPTS	39	F6
COLUMBUS CIR	MPTS	40	A6
COLUMBUS DR	MPTS	39	F6
COLUMBUS DR	MPTS	40	A6
COLUMBUS PL	SCL	53	E6
COLUMN CT	SJ	68	E4
COLUSA AV	SVL	53	C2
COLUSA WY	SCCO	65	D3
COLUSA WY	SJ	65	D3
COLVILLE DR	SJ	72A	A2
COMANCHE CT	SJ	72	F1
COMANCHE DR	SJ	72	F2
COMANCHE TR	SCCO	73	E6
COMANCHE TR	SCCO	78G	E1
COMER DR	S	64	E4
COMET LN	SJ	55	F4
COMMERCE DR	SJ	55	A1
COMMERCIAL AV	MVW	44	F4
COMMERCIAL AV	PA	44	F4
COMMERCIAL ST	SJ	54	F5
COMMERCIAL ST	SJ	55	A5
COMMERCIAL ST	SVL	53	B4
COMMODORE DR	SJ	55	D3
COMMUNITY LN	PA	44	B1
COMO LN	SJ	66	F5
COMPONENT DR	SJ	54	D3
COMPTON LN	SJ	65	F1
COMPTON LN	SCCO	65	F1
COMSTOCK CIR	SCCO	44	A4
COMSTOCK LN	SJ	66	E4
COMSTOCK ST	SCL	54	B4
COMSTOCK WY	SJ	66	E4
COMSTOCK QN CT	MVW	45	B6
CONCANNON CT	SCL	61	A3
CONCEPCION RD	LAH	51	C4
CONCERTO DR	SJ	68	B4
CONCERTO WY	SJ	68	B4
CONCORD AV	LA	52	B6
CONCORD AV	SJ	61	E5
CONCORD CIR	MH	79	F6
CONCORD DR	SJ	72A	C1
CONCORD LN	SCL	60	E3
CONCORD PL	G	83	F3
CONCOURSE DR	SJ	55	A1
CONDENSA ST	SCL	53	F4
CONDIT RD	MH	80	A4
CONDIT RD	SCCO	79	F2
CONDIT RD	SCCO	80	A4
CONDON CT	SCL	61	A2
CONDOR CIR	SJ	71	F3
CONDOR CT	SJ	71	F3
CONDOR CT	SCCO	79	C4
CONDOR WY	SVL	60	A2
CONEJO CT	LAH	51	B2
CONEJO DR	SJ	72A	D4
CONESTOGA WY	SJ	72A	A3
CONGRESS PL	CPTO	59	E4
CONGRSS HALL CT	S	69	D1
CONGRESS SPG LN	S	69	D1
CONGRESS SPG RD	SCCO	63F	E6
CONGRESS SPG RD	SCCO	64	A6
CONGRESS SPG RD	SCCO	69	D1
CONGRESS SPG RD	S	69	D1
CONIFER CT	SJ	48	D5
CONIFER LN	SJ	48	D5
CONISTON CT	SJ	72	B2
CONISTON WY	SJ	72	B2
CONLIN CT	SJ	72A	A3
CONNELL CT	G	82	E5
CONNEMARA WY	SVL	59	F1
CONNEMARA WY	SVL	60	A1
CONNIE DR	C	65	F4
CONNIE DR	C	66	A4
CONRAD AV	SJ	71	E1
CONRADIA CT	CPTO	64	D1
CONSTANCE DR	SJ	60	F5
CONSTANCE DR	SJ	61	A5
CONSTANSO CT	SJ	65	D2
CONSTANSO WY	SJ	65	D2
CONSTANZO ST	SCCO	43	F4
CONSTITUTION AV	MS	70	D3
CONSTITUTION CT	SJ	66	E3
CONSTITUTION DR	SJ	66	E3
CONSUELO AV	SCL	61	A3
CONTESSA CT	SJ	72A	A4
CONTI CT	SJ	62	E6
CONTINENTAL CIR	MVW	52	C4
CONTINENTAL CIR	S	64	E3
CONTINENTAL DR	SJ	68	B4
CONVENTRY DR	C	65	F2
CONWAY AV	SCCO	71	C1
CONWAY CT	SCCO	71	C1
CONWAY RD	SVL	52	E6
CONWAY ST	MPTS	39	F5
COOK ST	SJ	61	D1
COOKSEY LN	SCCO	43	F4
COOLEY CT	SJ	62	E1
COOLIDGE AV	SJ	61	F6
COOLIDGE AV	SJ	66	F1
COOLIDGE AV	SCCO	81	B4
COOLIDGE AV	SVL	52	E3
COOLIDGE DR	SCL	53	F6
COOPER AV	SCCO	71	C2
COOPER RD	LG	70	F2
COOPER DR	SCL	53	D5
COOPERAGE CT	SJ	72	D3
COOPER RIVER DR	SJ	61	D6
COOPER RIVER DR	SJ	66	D1
COPAL CT	SCCO	55	F2
COPCO LN	SJ	72A	B2
COPELAND CT	SJ	71	D3
COPELAND PL	SJ	71	D3
COPELAND LN	SJ	71	D3
COPPER RD	SCL	53	D4
COPPER HILL CT	SCCO	80	D2
COPPER HILL DR	MH	80	D2
COPPER HILL DR	SCCO	80	D2
COPPER LEAF DR	SJ	48	E6
COPPER PEAK LN	SJ	75	E2
COPPER SPG CT	CPTO	64	A6
COPPERWOOD CIR	SJ	72	D3
CORA CT	C	65	F5
CORA CT	C	66	A5
CORAL CT	LA	51	F3
CORAL CT	SJ	68	A1
CORAL BELL CT	G	82	B6
CORAL CANYON DR	SJ	72A	C1
CORALEE DR	SJ	71	E2
CORAL GABLS CIR	SJ	72A	E4
CORAL SANDS DR	SJ	67	E4
CORALTREE PL	SJ	55	B1
CORALWOOD WY	SJ	72	E2
CORBETTA LN	LAH	51	B5
CORBIN AV	SJ	72	B1
CORBY DR	SJ	63	E5
CORCEL CT	LG	70	F2
CORCEL CT	LG	71	A2
CORD CT	SJ	63	D4
CORDA DR	SJ	63	B5
CORDELIA AV	SJ	60	D6
CORDELIA AV	SJ	65	D1
CORDILLERAS AV	SVL	59	E1
CORDOBA WY	SJ	66	E4
CORDOVA CT	MH	80K	E2
CORDOVA RD	CPTO	59	C5
CORDOY LN	SJ	71	E2
CORDWOOD CT	S	65	C6
CORIE CT	SJ	55	A3
CORINA WY	PA	44	E3
CORINNE DR	SCCO	70	F2
CORINTHIA DR	MPTS	47	F1
CORKERHILL WY	SJ	63	C6
CORK OAK WY	PA	44	D3
CORKTREE LN	SJ	48	C4
CORKWOOD CT	SJ	67	F5
CORLISS WY	C	66	A3
CORLISTA DR	SJ	61	D6
CORMORANT CT	SVL	60	A2
CORNELIA CT	MVW	52	B4
CORNELL DR	MVW	52	A4
CORNELL DR	SJ	71	F2
CORNELL DR	SJ	72	A2
CORNELL DR	SCL	60	D3
CORNELL ST	PA	44	B4
CORNFLOWER CT	SVL	53	C5
CORNING AV	MPTS	47	E4
CORNING DR	SJ	66	F5
CORNISH LN	SJ	55	B4
CORNWALL CT	SVL	60	B1
CORNWALL DR	SJ	63	A1
CORONA DR	SJ	65	E1
CORONACH AV	SVL	59	D2
CORONADO AV	LA	51	E2
CORONADO AV	SCCO	43	F4
CORONADO DR	SJ	64	F1
CORONADO DR	SJ	65	A1
CORONADO DR	SCL	53	E4
CORONADO DR	SVL	52	D3
CORONET DR	SJ	71	C3
CORPORATE CT	SJ	55	A2
CORPORATION WY	PA	44	F3
CORRAL AV	SVL	52	D3
CORRALES DR	SJ	67	C5
CORRALITOS LN	SCCO	56	B4
CORRIDA CIR	SJ	60	D4
CORRINE DR	LG	70	F2
CORRINE DR	LG	71	A2
CORTA VIA	SCCO	59	A1
CORTE ARQUETA	MH	79	E4
CORTE BONITA	SJ	72	A4
CORTE CABANIL	MH	79	E4
CORTE CABAS	MH	79	E4
CORTE CAMULA	SJ	72	B4
CORTE DE ARBOL	SJ	66	F5
CORTE DE ARBOL	SJ	67	A5
CTE DE ARGUELLO	S	64	E3
CTE DE AVELLANO	SJ	67	C5
CTE DE BELLEZA	SJ	72	B4
CORTE DE BLANCO	SJ	67	C5
CORTE DE BOLEYN	SJ	67	A6
CORTE DE CALLAS	SJ	71	F1
CTE DE CERVATO	SJ	67	C5
CORTE DE FLORES	SJ	66	F5
CORTE DE FLORES	SJ	67	A5
CORTE DE FLORES	SCL	67	A6
CTE DE LA REINA	SJ	72	A4
CORTE DL CONJEO	SJ	72	A4
CORTE DE MADRID	SCCO	60	B5
CORTE DE MEDEA	SJ	66	F6
CORTE DE MOFFO	SJ	67	A6
CORTE DE PLATA	SJ	67	C5
CORTE DE PONS	SJ	71	F1
CORTE DE ROSA	SJ	72	A5
CTE DE SEVILLE	SCCO	60	B5
CTE DE TEBALDI	SJ	66	F6
CORTE DE THAIS	SJ	67	A6
CORTE DE THAIS	SJ	72	A1
CORTE KORN	SCCO	82	F2
CORTE MADERA AV	SVL	52	E2
CORTE MADERA CT	SVL	52	E2
CORTE MADERA LN	CPTO	59	D4
CORTE MADERA LN	LAH	51	C3
CORTESE CIR	SJ	55	F3
CORTESE CIR	SJ	56	A3
CORTESE LN	SCCO	80	B4
CORTE VERDE DR	SJ	68	B5
CORTEZ AV	SJ	62	F2
CORTEZ AV	SJ	67	E4
CORTEZ DR	SCL	53	E4
CORTEZ DR	SVL	52	D3
CORTEZ LN	LAH	51	A5
CORTEZ ST	MPTS	39	F5
CORTINA DR	SJ	55	D1
CORTO ST	MVW	52	B1
CORUMBA CT	SJ	72	B3
CORVALLIS CT	SJ	72	D6
CORVALLIS DR	SJ	72	D6
CORVALLIS DR	SVL	59	E1
CORVETTE DR	SJ	60	B6
CORVIN DR	SCL	53	D4
CORVIN DR	SVL	53	D4
CORWIN CT	SJ	68	C5
CORY AV	SJ	61	B3
CORY CT	CPTO	59	E5
CORY LN	MH	79	F5
CORY RD	SCCO	53	B4
CORY RD	SVL	53	B4
COSMO AV	MH	79	E6
COSTA AV	SCCO	62	C6
COSTA MESA DR	SJ	68	A3
COSTA MESA TER	SVL	52	E2
COSTELLO CT	SCCO	51	E5
COSTELLO DR	SCCO	51	E5
COSTIGAN CIR	MPTS	39	B5
COSTIGAN CIR	MPTS	40	C6
COSTIGAN CIR	MPTS	47	D2
COSTIGAN CIR	MPTS	48	C1
COT CT	SJ	61	A5
COTHRAN RD	SCCO	78H	B2
COTSWALD CT	SVL	60	C1
COTTAGE GRV AV	SJ	62	C5
COTTERELL DR	SJ	68	B1
COTTLE AV	SJ	66	F2
COTTLE AV	SJ	67	A3
COTTLE RD	SJ	72A	C2
COTTLE RD	SCCO	72A	C3
COTTON CT	SJ	72A	B3
COTTON TAIL AV	SJ	62	F1
COTTONWOOD CT	CPTO	60	B5
COTTONWOOD CT	SCL	60	E3
COTTONWOOD DR	CPTO	60	B5
COTTONWOOD DR	MPTS	47	E6
COTTRELL WY	SCCO	44	A5
COTY WY	SJ	67	E4
COULOMBE DR	PA	44	C6
COUNTESS CT	SJ	60	B6
COUNTESS CT	SJ	65	B1
COUNTESS DR	SJ	60	B6
COUNTESS DR	SJ	65	B1
COUNT FLEET CT	MH	80K	F3
COUNTRY DR	G	82	B6
COUNTRY LN	SJ	65	D1
COUNTRY LN	SCCO	65	D1
COUNTRY LN	SCCO	81	A2
COUNTRY WY	LAH	50	F4
COUNTRY CLUB CT	PA	50	F4
COUNTRY CLUB DR	MPTS	40	B6
COUNTRY CLUB DR	SCCO	51	F6
COUNTRY CLUB DR	SCCO	52	A6
COUNTRY CLUB DR	SCCO	58	F1
COUNTRY CLUB DR	SCCO	59	A1
CNTRY FIELDS LN	SJ	68	C2
CNTRY FORGE LN	SJ	68	C2
COUNTRY LEAF CT	SJ	48	E6
COUNTRY OAK CT	SJ	68	C2
COUNTRY OAK LN	SJ	68	C2
COUNTRYSIDE LN	SJ	68	C2
COUNTRY SPG CT	CPTO	64	A5
CNTRY SQUIRE CT	S	65	B2
CNTRY SQUIRE DR	S	65	B2
CNTRY SQUIRE LN	S	65	B2
CNTRY SQUIRE WY	S	65	B2
COUNTRY VIEW CT	SCCO	76	E1
COUNTRY VIEW DR	SCCO	76	E2
COUNTRY VIEW LN	SCCO	76	E2
COUNTRY VIS CT	SJ	63	D6
COUNTRY WK CIR	SJ	48	C5
COUNTRYBROOK	SJ	48	B6
COUNTRYWOOD CT	SJ	65	F1
COURTLAND AV	MPTS	48	B4
COURTNEY AV	SJ	62	E4
COURTNEY AV	SCCO	62	E4
COURTYARD DR	SJ	67	A6
COVE CT	SJ	63	C2
COVENTRY CIR	MPTS	47	F1
COVENTRY CT	SVL	60	B1
COVENTRY DR	C	65	F2
COVENTRY DR	SJ	63	A2
COVENTRY WY	MPTS	47	F1
COVEWOOD CT	SJ	63	D4
COVINA AV	SJ	72A	A2
COVINA CT	S	65	A2
COVINGTON CT	LA	52	A5
COVINGTON CT	SJ	67	F4
COVINGTON RD	LA	51	E4
COVINGTON RD	LA	52	B5
COWDEN PL	LAH	51	B4
COWELL LN	SCCO	43	F4
COWELL RD	LG	71	A6
COWELL RD	SCCO	71	A6
COWPER CT	PA	44	D4
COWPER CT	SJ	71	F4
COWPER ST	PA	37	F6
COWPER ST	PA	38	A6
COWPER ST	PA	44	D3
COX AV	SJ	65	B3
COX AV	SCCO	81	C5
COX AV	S	64	F3
COX AV	S	65	A3
COY DR	SJ	72A	A1
COYNE CT	SJ	63	A3
COYOTE CK CIR	SJ	55	C6
COYOTE CK CIR	SJ	62	C1
COYOTE CK CT	SJ	55	C6
COYOTE CK CT	SJ	62	C1
COYOTE CK PL	SJ	55	C6
COYOTE CK PL	SJ	62	C1
COYOTE RD	SJ	68	B4
COYOTE RD	SCCO	68	C4
COYOTE RD	SCCO	78A	A6
COYOTE RD	SCCO	80	A1
COYOTE ST	MPTS	47	E2
COYOTE HILL RD	PA	44	A6
COYOTE HILL RD	SCCO	44	A6
COYOTE RESER RD	SCCO	81A	C3
COZETTE LN	SCCO	60	B4
COZUMEL CIR	SCL	53	E6
COZY CT	SJ	72A	A3
COZY DR	SJ	72A	A3

1991 SANTA CLARA COUNTY STREET INDEX

STREET	CITY	PAGE	GRID
CRABAPPLE WY	SJ	68	D3
CRABTREE AV	SCCO	60	C5
CRACOLICE WY	MPTS	48	B4
CRAFT DR	CPTO	60	B5
CRAGMONT AV	SCCO	56	A4
CRAGMONT AV S	SCCO	56	B4
CRAGWOOD LN	SJ	63	B2
CRAIG AV	C	65	F4
CRAIG AV	SJ	65	F4
CRAIG CT	CPTO	59	F5
CRAIG CT	MVW	44	F5
CRAIG DR	SJ	60	B6
CRAIG DR	SJ	65	B1
CRAIG WY	LG	71	B3
CRAIGEN CIR	S	64	F4
CRAIGEN CIR	S	65	A4
CRAILFORD CT	SJ	68	B2
CRAMER CIR	SJ	67	E1
CRANBERRY AV	SVL	52	D6
CRANBERRY CIR	CPTO	59	E6
CRANBERRY DR	CPTO	59	E6
CRANBROOK CT	SJ	72	B5
CRANDALL ST	SJ	61	F3
CRANDANO CT	SVL	52	D6
CRANE AV	MVW	52	A4
CRANE CT	SJ	54	E4
CRANFORD CIR	SJ	66	B6
CRANFORD CIR	SJ	71	B1
CRANWORTH CIR	SJ	63	C6
CRATER LN	SJ	48	E6
CRATER LAKE AV	MPTS	48	C3
CRATER LAKE CT	SVL	59	F2
CRAVENS CT	SJ	55	E5
CRAWFORD AV	SCCO	52	F5
CRAWFORD AV	SVL	52	F5
CRAWFORD CT	G	83	E2
CRAWFORD DR	G	83	D2
CRAY CT	SJ	68	A1
CRAYSIDE LN	S	64	E3
CREAGER CT	SJ	65	F1
CREE CT	SJ	72	F3
CREE DR	SJ	72	F3
CREED ST	MPTS	40	A6
CREEDEN WY	LA	51	E2
CREEDEN WY	MVW	51	E2
CREEK DR	SJ	62	B6
CREEK DR	SJ	67	B1
CREEK BANK CT	SJ	72	D4
CREEKBED CT	MH	79	E4
CREEK BED CT	SCL	53	F1
CREEK EST CT	SJ	68A	A2
CREEK ESTATES	SJ	68A	A2
CREEKFIELD DR	SJ	67	C3
CREEKLAND CIR	SJ	55	C4
CREEKLINE DR	CPTO	59	E6
CREEKMORE WY	SJ	63	F3
CREEKSIDE CIR	MH	79	F5
CREEKSIDE CT	CPTO	59	D4
CREEKSIDE CT	MH	80K	F3
CREEKSIDE CT	MS	70	E2
CREEKSIDE DR	PA	44	E5
CREEKSIDE DR	SJ	48	C5
CREEKSIDE DR	SJ	54	F1
CREEKSIDE LN	MH	79	E4
CREEKSIDE WY	C	66	C2
CREEKSTONE CIR	SJ	55	C4
CREEKVIEW CT	SJ	72	E5
CREEK VIEW CT	SCCO	81	F4
CREEKVIEW DR	MH	79	E4
CREEKWOOD CT	MH	79	F5
CREEKWOOD DR	SJ	60	D6
CREEKWOOD DR	SJ	65	D1
CREIGHTON CT	MPTS	48	B4
CREIGHTON PL	SCL	53	D5
CRENSHAW CT	SJ	72	D5
CRESCENDO AV	SJ	67	E5
CRESCENT AV	SCCO	52	F6
CRESCENT AV	SVL	52	F6
CRESCENT AV	SVL	53	A6
CRESCENT DR	LG	71	A5
CRESCENT DR	PA	38	B5
CRESCENT DR	SJ	61	F6
CRESCENT LN	LAH	51	C5
CRESCENT RD	CPTO	59	C4
CRESCENT TER	SVL	53	A6
CRESENT TER	MPTS	48	C4
CRESPI DR	SJ	65	D2
CRESPI DR	SVL	52	D3
CREST AV	MH	79	D4
CREST DR	SCCO	56	A2
CRESTA VISTA WY	SJ	72A	C3
CRESTBROOK DR	S	65	B5
CRESTFIELD DR	SJ	67	A4
CRESTHAVEN LN	SJ	67	A6
CRESTHAVEN ST	MPTS	48	D4
CREST HILL CT	G	82	C5
CRESTLINE DR	CPTO	64	E1
CRESTMONT DR	SJ	66	E3
CRESTMOOR CT	SJ	60	D5
CRESTMOOR DR	SJ	60	D5
CRESTOAK CT	SJ	72	B4
CRESTON DR	CPTO	59	C3
CRESTON DR	SCCO	59	C3
CRESTON LN	SJ	62	E3
CRESTPOINT DR	SJ	55	B4
CRESTRIDGE DR	SCCO	58	E1
CRESTRIDGE DR	SCCO	70	B3
CRESTVIEW CT	SCCO	82H	D1
CRESTVIEW DR	MVW	52	D4
CRESTVIEW DR	SJ	61	A4
CRESTVIEW DR	SCL	61	A4
CRESTVIEW DR	SCCO	59	A1
CRESTWOOD CT	SVL	53	D1
CRESTWOOD DR	SJ	67	B4
CREWE CT	SJ	48	D5
CREWS RD	SCCO	82A	E4
CRIBARI CIR	SJ	68A	B2
CRIBARI CT	SJ	68A	A2
CRIBARI LN	SJ	68A	B2
CRIBARI PL	SJ	68A	B2
CRIBARI BEND	SJ	68A	A2
CRIBARI BLUFFS	SJ	68A	B2
CRIBARI CORNER	SJ	68A	A1
CRIBARI CREST	SJ	68A	A2
CRIBARI DALE	SJ	68A	B2
CRIBARI DELL	SJ	68A	A2
CRIBARI GLEN	SJ	68A	A1
CRIBARI GREEN	SJ	68A	A2
CRIBARI HEIGHTS	SJ	68A	A1
CRIBARI HILLS	SJ	68A	B1
CRIBARI KNOLLS	SJ	68A	B2
CRIBARI VALE	SJ	68A	B2
CRICKET HILL RD	CPTO	59	B4
CRIDER CT	LG	71	E4
CRIMSON DR	SJ	72	B4
CRIMSONBERRY LN	CPTO	60	B3
CRIMSONBERRY LN	SJ	60	D5
CRINAN DR	SJ	62	E4
CRIOLLO WY	MH	80	B3
CRISANTO AV	MVW	44	F6
CRISANTO AV	MVW	45	A6
CRISANTO AV	MVW	52	A1
CRISP AV	S	70	B1
CRIST DR	LA	59	C2
CRISTICH LN	C	66	B4
CRISTINA AV	SJ	62	A6
CRISTINA CT	SCCO	80	B2
CRISTOBL PRIVDA	MVW	52	D2
CRISTO REY DR	LA	59	B3
CRISTO REY DR	SCCO	59	B3
CRISTO REY PL	LA	59	B3
CRITTENDEN LN	MVW	45	B3
CROCKER CT	SJ	68	B5
CROCKER DR	SJ	68	B5
CROCKER LN	G	84	A2
CROCKER WY	SCL	53	D5
CROCKETT AV	C	65	E4
CROCKETT AV	SJ	65	E4
CROCKETT AV	SCCO	65	E4
CROCUS CT	SVL	53	C5
CROCUS DR	SJ	67	D5
CROFT DR	SJ	63	D5
CROMART CT	SVL	59	F1
CRONIN DR	SCL	60	D4
CRONWELL DR	C	66	D2
CRONWELL DR	SCCO	66	D2
CROOKED CK DR	LA	59	A2
CROPLEY AV	SJ	48	B6
CROPLEY CT	SJ	48	D5
CROSBY CT	SJ	60	A6
CROSBY CT	SCL	53	E6
CROSBY PL	PA	44	C6
CROSLEY CT	SJ	48	E5
CROSS WY	LG	70	F5
CROSS WY	SJ	62	B6
CROSS WY	SJ	67	B1
CROSSBOW CT	SJ	72	C3
CROSSBROOK CT	SJ	72	D3
CROSSFIELD CT	SJ	72	C3
CROSSGATES LN	SJ	72	C4
CROSSLEES DR	SJ	68	D5
CROSSMAN AV	SVL	46	B5
CROSSMILL CT	SJ	63	A6
CROSSMONT CIR	SJ	72	C3
CROSSMONT CT	SJ	72	C3
CROSSPOINT CT	SJ	72	C3
CROSS SPGS CT	SJ	72	C3
CROSS SPGS DR	SJ	72	C3
CROSSVIEW CIR	SJ	72	C3
CROSSVIEW CT	SJ	72	C3
CROSSWIND CT	SJ	72	C3
CROTHERS WY	SCCO	43	F3
CROTHERS RD	SJ	56	B2
CROTHERS RD	SCCO	56	C2
CROW CT	SJ	72A	A2
CROW CT	SVL	60	A2
CROW LN	SJ	72	F2
CROW TR	SCCO	73	E6
CROWDER AV	SJ	66	E6
CROWLEY AV	SCL	60	E1
CROWN BLVD	SJ	72	D5
CROWNER AV	SCCO	81	B2
CROY RD	SCCO	78K	E5
CROY RD	SCCO	78L	B4
CROYDEN CT	SVL	59	F1
CROYDEN CT	SVL	60	A1
CROYDON AV	SJ	72	B2
CRUCERO CT	SJ	62	E4
CRUCERO DR	SJ	62	E3
CRUMP CT	SJ	72	A3
CRYSTAL DR	MH	79	B4
CRYSTAL DR	SCL	53	D5
CRYSTAL DR	SCCO	78J	F3
CRYSTALBERY TER	SJ	60	E5
CRYSTAL CK DR	SJ	55	E2
CRYSTAL GLEN LN	SCL	60	B4
CRYSTAL SPGS CT	SJ	72	C6
CRYSTAL SPGS DR	SJ	72	C5
CRYSTAL SPGS WY	SJ	72A	B1
CUCIZ LN	MPTS	48	B4
CUEN CT	SJ	67	C4
CUERNAVACA CIR	MVW	52	C4
CUERNAVACA CT	SJ	72	A4
CUESTA CT	SJ	63	D2
CUESTA DR	LA	51	E4
CUESTA DR	MPTS	48	C4
CUESTA DR	MVW	52	B4
CUESTA DR	SJ	63	D2
CULBERTSON DR	SCCO	60	C5
CULLEN AV	SCCO	82A	C2
CULLEN LN	SCCO	82A	E4
CULLIGAN BLVD	SJ	72	C4
CULLODEN CT	SJ	68	B2
CULP DR	G	82	D6
CULPEPPER DR	SJ	62	F5
CULVERT DR	SJ	72A	A4
CUMBERLAND AV	SVL	52	E5
CUMBERLAND DR	G	83	F2
CUMBERLAND DR	S	65	A4
CUMBERLAND PL	SJ	67	B3
CUMBRA VISTA CT	LAH	51	B4
CUMMINS AV	SCCO	45	D5
CUMULUS AV	SVL	52	F5
CUMULUS AV	SVL	53	A5
CUNARD CT	SJ	48	D5
CUNNINGHAM AV	SJ	62	F4
CUNNINGHAM AV	SJ	63	A3
CUNNINGHAM AV	SCCO	63	A3
CUNNINGHAM CT	SJ	63	B2
CUNNINGHAM PL	S	64	F4
CUNNINGHAM ST	SCL	53	F6
CUNNINGHAM ST	SCL	54	A6
CUPERTINO RD	CPTO	59	C4
CUPPLES CT	SCL	60	F3
CURCI DR	SJ	61	E6
CURETON PL	SCCO	56	B5
CURIE CT	SJ	72A	B5
CURIE DR	SJ	72A	A4
CURLING CT	SJ	63	C6
CURRENT DR	SJ	72A	A3
CURRY CT	S	65	C3
CURTIS AV	MPTS	47	F4
CURTIS AV	SCL	60	D2
CURTISS AV	SJ	61	F6
CURTISS AV	SJ	62	A6
CURTISS AV	SJ	67	A1
CURTNER AV	C	66	B4
CURTNER AV	PA	44	C4
CURTNER AV	SJ	66	F3
CURTNER AV	SJ	67	A3
CURTNER AV	SCCO	66	B4
CURTNER AV	SCCO	67	B2
CURTNER CT	MPTS	39	F5
CURTNER CT	MPTS	40	A5
CURTNER DR	MPTS	39	F5
CURTNER GLEN CT	SCCO	66	C4
CUSTER DR	SJ	66	E4
CUTFORTH CT	SJ	55	D1
CYCLAMEN CT	SJ	68	B5
CYLINDA DR	SJ	65	E4
CYNTHIA AV	SCCO	60	C5
CYNTHIA LN	SJ	60	A6
CYNTHIA WY	LA	59	C2
CYPRESS AL	SCL	61	C2
CYPRESS AV	SJ	61	A5
CYPRESS AV	SCL	61	A3
CYPRESS AV	SCCO	61	A5
CYPRESS AV	SVL	53	B2
CYPRESS CT	CPTO	60	A3
CYPRESS CT	G	83	D1
CYPRESS CT	LA	51	D3
CYPRESS DR	CPTO	60	A3
CYPRESS DR	LA	51	D3
CYPRESS DR	MPTS	47	D4
CYPRESS LN	C	66	C2
CYPRESS LN	PA	44	C4
CYPRESS LN	SJ	72A	F3
CYPRESS WY	LG	70	F5
CYPRESS WY	LG	71	A5
CYPRESS PK CT	SJ	67	E5
CYPRESS PT CT	SJ	72A	F4
CYPRESS PT DR	MVW	52	B1
CYPRESS RIDGE	CCO	63	E2
CYRIL PL	S	65	C3
CYRUS AV	SJ	66	E5
D			
D ST	MVW	52	D2
D ST	SVL	46	C6
D ST S	SVL	46	C6
DADE CT	SJ	72A	C4
DADIS WY	SJ	67	F1
DADO ST	SJ	54	E2
DAFFODIL CT	MH	80	A3
DAFFODIL CT	SVL	53	B5
DAFFODIL WY	SJ	60	F6
DAGGETT DR	SJ	54	C1
DAGMAR CT	SJ	67	D4
DAGMAR DR	S	65	C4
DAHILL CT	SJ	63	D6
DAHLBERG CT	SCCO	79	B6
DAHLBERG DR	SCCO	79	B6
DAHLIA CT	SVL	53	C5
DAHLIA DR	SVL	53	C5
DAHLIA WY	LG	71	A3
DAILEY AV	SJ	72	E2
DAILEY RD	SCCO	45	D5
DAIMILER CT	SJ	67	F6
DAISY CT	SVL	53	C5
DAISY LN	G	82	D6
DAISYDELL CT	CPTO	60	B3
DAISYDELL CT	SJ	60	D5
DAKAN CT	SJ	67	C4
DAKE AV	PA	44	E5
DAKOTA DR	SJ	67	F2
DAKOTA DR	SJ	68	A2
DAL BON CT	SJ	72A	F3
DALE AV	MVW	52	F4
DALE AV	SJ	66	F2
DALE DR	SCCO	56	A5
DALEHURST AV	LA	59	C1
DALEWOOD CT	SJ	76	A1
DALLAS CT	LA	52	C6
DALLAS CT	LA	59	C1
DALLAS CT	SCL	53	E6
DALLAS DR	SCCO	66	B4
DALMA DR	MVW	52	B3
DALMENY CT	SJ	72	F6
DALMUIR CT	SJ	63	E5
DALTON DR	MPTS	48	C2
DALTON DR	SJ	71	E2
DALTON PL	SJ	71	E2
DALTREY WY	SJ	48	C6
DAMASCUS CT	SJ	66	E3
DAMEY DR	SJ	55	E5
DAMIAN WY	LA	52	B5
D'AMICO DR	SJ	63	D5
DAMON LN	S	64	E5
DAMSEN DR	SJ	55	E5
DANA AV	PA	38	B6
DANA AV	SJ	61	D3
DANA ST	MVW	52	B2
DANBURY DR	SJ	60	A6
DANBURY DR	SJ	65	A1
DANBY AV	SJ	48	D6
DANDERHALL WY	SJ	63	C6
DANDINI CIR	SJ	61	D6
DANFORTH CT	SJ	62	F5
DANFORTH DR	SVL	52	E5
DANFORTH TER	SVL	52	E5
DANIEL CT	MPTS	48	B5
DANIEL CT	SCCO	81C	A6
DANIEL WY	SJ	61	B6
DANIEL WY	SCL	60	C3
DANIELLE PL	MS	70	D1
DAN MALONEY DR	SJ	63	C6
DANRIDGE DR	SJ	65	A1
DANRIDGE LN	SJ	60	A6
DANROMAS WY	SJ	65	B2
DANUBE DR	CPTO	60	A4
DANUBE WY	SJ	62	D2
DANVILLE DR	LG	71	C3
DANWOOD CT	SJ	63	D4
DANZE DR	SJ	68	C6
DAPHNE DR	SJ	65	A2
DARBY CT	SJ	62	C5
DARDANELLI LN	LG	65	F6
DARKNELL CT	SJ	63	E2
DARKNELL WY	SJ	63	E2
DARK STAR CT	MH	80K	F3
DARLENE AV	SJ	66	F3
DARLING LN	LAH	51	D4
DARLINGTON CT	PA	44	D5
DARNELL CT	SJ	55	D4
DARREL	SCCO	73	D5
DARRINGTON CT	SVL	59	D2
DARRYDOON CT	SJ	68	B1
DARRYL CT	SJ	65	F1
DARRYL DR	C	65	F2
DARRYL DR	C	66	A2
DARRYL DR	SJ	65	F2
DARRYL DR	SJ	66	A2
DARTMOOR WY	SJ	65	A1
DARTMOUTH DR	SJ	71	F3
DARTMOUTH DR	SJ	72	A3
DARTMOUTH LN	LA	52	B5
DARTMOUTH PL	G	83	F3
DARTMOUTH ST	PA	44	A4
DARTSHIRE CT	SVL	60	B1
DARTSHIRE WY	SVL	60	B1
DARWIN CT	SJ	62	E4
DARWIN WY	SJ	62	F3
DARWIN WY	SJ	63	A3
DASH CT	SJ	72	A3
DASHWOOD AV	SJ	63	D6
DATE BLOSSOM CT	SJ	72A	B1
DATORO DR	SJ	65	D3
DAUPHINE PL	LA	51	E2
DAURINE CT	SCCO	82A	E5
DAVENPORT CT	SVL	59	F2
DAVENPORT DR	SJ	56	B5
DAVENPORT WY	PA	44	D4
DAVES AV	MS	70	B3
DAVID AV	C	66	B1
DAVID AV	PA	44	D2
DAVID AV	SJ	66	B1
DAVID AV	SCCO	66	B1
DAVID CT	G	82	E6
DAVID CT	PA	44	D2
DAVID LN	MPTS	48	B4
DAVIDSON AV	SCCO	84	E6
DAVIDWOOD WY	SJ	63	D4
DAVIS CT	SCCO	76	C2
DAVIS ST	SJ	61	C2
DAVIS ST	SCL	54	A2
DAVISON AV	CPTO	60	B5
DAWES CT	SJ	63	E1
DAWN DR	SVL	52	F5
DAWN LN	LAH	51	B4
DAWN WY	G	83	F5
DAWNBROOK CT	SJ	68	B2
DAWNRIDGE DR	LAH	51	E6
DAWNVIEW CT	SJ	67	C6
DAWSON AV	SJ	62	B6
DAWSON DR	LAH	58	E1
DAWSON DR	SOL	60	C4
DAY CT	SCL	53	E6
DAY RD	SCCO	81H	E3
DAY RD	SCCO	82	A3
DAYLIGHT WY	SJ	67	B2
DAYO CT	SJ	63	D5
DAYTON AV	SCL	60	D3
DAYTONA DR	SJ	63	A3
DEAN AV	SJ	67	A1
DEAN CT	CPTO	59	C4
DEANA CT	MH	79	B4
DEANS PLACE WY	SJ	68	C1
DE ANZA AV	SJ	67	E4
DE ANZA BLVD N	CPTO	59	F4
DE ANZA BLVD S	CPTO	59	F5
DE ANZA CIR N	CPTO	59	C6
DE ANZA CIR S	CPTO	59	C6
DE ANZA CT	MPTS	48	A1
DE ANZA CT	MH	80K	F3
DE ANZA LN	LA	51	E4
DE ANZA WY	SJ	66	E1
DEARBORN PL	G	83	E3
DEARWELL WY	SJ	72A	E2
DEARWOOD CT	MVW	44	F6
DEARWOOD CT	MVW	51	F1
DEB CT	SJ	72	B4
DEBBIE CT	SCCO	82A	E5
DEBBIE LN	S	64	F4
DE BELL RD	LAH	51	C2
DEBOER LN	SJ	68	B3
DEBORAH DR	SCL	53	F5
DEBORAH DR	SCL	54	A5
DEBRA WY	SJ	60	F5
DEBRA WY	SJ	61	A5
DE BRUIN WY	SCCO	82	C2
DECATUR DR	SJ	62	F2
DECATUR RD	SCCO	70	D3
DECKER AV	SCCO	81	E3
DECKER WY	SCCO	56	A4
DECLARATION CT	SJ	55	F5
DECLARATION DR	SJ	55	F5
DECLARATION WY	SJ	55	F5
DECORAH LN	SCCO	66	D3
DECOTO CT	MPTS	48	A1
DEE ST	SVL	52	F5
DEEDHAM CT	SJ	63	F3
DEEDHAM DR	SJ	63	E4
DEEP CLIFF	CPTO	59	C5
DEEP PURPLE WY	SJ	72	D1
DEEPROSE PL	CPTO	60	A4
DEEPWELL CT	S	69	E1
DEEPWELL LN	LA	51	D5
DEER CT	SJ	72	F1
DEER CANYON LN	S	64	E6
DEER CREEK CT	SJ	63	D1
DEER CREEK RD	PA	51	A1
DEER CREEK RD	SCCO	51	A1
DEERCROSS LN	SJ	66	C4
DEERFIELD DR	LAH	51	D4
DEERFIELD DR	SJ	65	B2
DEER ISLE DR	SJ	68	E1
DEERLAND CT	SJ	71	D4
DEERPARK CT	S	64	F5
DEERPARK RD	SCCO	71	D5
DEER PATH DR	LAH	57	C2
DEER PATH RD	SCCO	69	A1
DEER RUN CIR	SJ	68	D3
DEER RUN CT	MH	79	B5
DEER SPRING CT	S	64	E6
DEER SPRINGS WY	LAH	51	A6
DEERWOOD DR	SJ	63	D4
DEEVA CT	SCCO	82A	E5
DE FLORES LN	SCCO	71	B1
DE FOE DR	CPTO	59	F5
DEGAS CT	CPTO	59	B5
DE GUIGNE DR	SVL	53	C3
DEHAVILLAND CT	S	65	B3
DEHAVILLAND DR	S	65	B3
DE LA CRUZ BLVD	SJ	54	B5
DE LA CRUZ BLVD	SCL	54	B5
DE LA CRUZ BLVD	SCCO	54	B2
DE LA FARGE DR	CPTO	59	F6
DELAND AV	SJ	61	E5
DELANO CT	SJ	63	B6
DE LA PENA AV	SCL	61	A2
DELAWARE AV	SJ	72	E1
DELAWARE TR	SCCO	73	E6
DELBARR CT	SJ	67	B2
DELBERT WY	SJ	61	E5
DEL CAMBRE DR	SJ	60	D6
DEL CANTO DR	SJ	72A	C3
DEL CARLO CT	LG	71	A3
DEL CENTRO WY	LA	51	F4
DEL CERRO CT	LG	71	B3
DEL FRANCO CT	SJ	54	F1
DEL FRANCO ST	SJ	54	F1
DELGADO CT	SJ	65	F4
DELIA ST	SJ	56	A3
DELIA ST	SCCO	56	A3
DELL AV	C	66	B4
DELL AV	MVW	44	F5
DELL AV	PA	44	F5
DELL CT	SJ	71	F2
DEL LOMA CT	SJ	65	E5
DEL LOMA DR	SJ	65	E5
DELLWOOD DR	SJ	47	E5
DELLWOOD DR	SJ	54	F1
DELLWOOD WY	SJ	72	A1

1991 SANTA CLARA COUNTY STREET INDEX

STREET	CITY	PAGE	GRID
DEL MAR AV	SJ	61	C6
DELMAS AV	SJ	61	F4
DELMAS AV	SJ	62	A5
DEL MEDIO AV	MVW	44	E6
DEL MEDIO CT	MVW	44	E5
DEL MONTE AV	LA	51	D1
DEL MONTE AV	MH	79	D3
DEL MONTE AV	SCL	53	D5
DEL MONTE CIR	MH	79	D3
DELMONTE PL	SJ	61	A6
DELNA MANOR LN	SJ	61	C6
DELNO ST	SJ	61	D2
DEL NORTE AV	SVL	53	A1
DEL NORTE DR	SJ	48	E5
DE LOACH CT	SJ	66	D1
DEL ORO CT	C	65	F2
DEL ORO CT	C	66	A2
DEL ORO CT	SJ	71	D3
DEL ORO DR	SJ	71	D3
DEL ORO PL	SJ	71	D3
DEL ORO WY	G	82	D5
DEL PASO AV	SJ	71	E1
DELPHI CIR	LA	51	E1
DELPHI CT	LA	51	E1
DEL PRADO DR	C	65	F3
DEL PRADO DR	C	66	A2
DEL PUERTO RD	SCCO	56E	C1
DEL REY AV	SJ	68	B4
DEL REY AV	SVL	52	F2
DEL REY CT	G	82	C6
DEL REY CT	SJ	68	A4
DELRIDGE DR	SJ	68	C5
DEL RIO CT	MPTS	48	A1
DEL RIO DR	SJ	72A	E4
DEL ROBLES CT	SJ	72A	D3
DEL ROY CT	C	65	F2
DEL ROY CT	C	66	A2
DELSON CT	LAH	51	A4
DELTA CT	G	83	C1
DELTA DR	G	82	D6
DELTA DR	G	83	D1
DELTA RD	SJ	63	E6
DELUCA DR	SJ	55	B2
DEL VAILE CT	MPTS	48	A1
DELYNN WY	SJ	67	B3
DEMARET DR	SCL	47	A6
DEMARET DR	SCL	54	A1
DE MARIETTA AV	SJ	66	D1
DE MARIETTA CT	SJ	66	D1
DE MATTEI CT	SJ	55	B5
DEMEREST LN	SJ	68	D6
DEMEREST LN	SJ	72A	D1
DE MILLE DR	SJ	60	E6
DEMOCRACY WY	SCL	46	E6
DEMPSEY RD	MPTS	48	B3
DEMPSEY WY	MPTS	48	B2
DEMPSTER AV	CPTO	59	D4
DENAIR AV	SJ	62	F5
DENALI WY	SJ	63	A4
DENEVI DR	SJ	65	E4
DENEVI LN	SCCO	70	C4
DENISE DR	SCL	60	F1
DENISE DR	SCL	61	A1
DENISE WY	SJ	67	B3
DENISON AV	CPTO	60	B4
DENNIS AV	MPTS	48	B2
DENNIS AV	SVL	52	E4
DENNIS CT	SCCO	56	B6
DENNIS DR	PA	44	D1
DENNIS LN	MVW	51	F3
DENNIS LN	MVW	52	A3
DENNYWOOD CT	SJ	63	D3
DENO AV	SCCO	82	E3
DENSMORE CT	SJ	63	E3
DENSMORE DR	SJ	63	E3
DENT AV	SJ	71	F2
DENT AV	SJ	72	A2
DENT AV	SCCO	71	F1
DENTON WY	SJ	63	C6
DENTWOOD DR	SJ	72	A1
DENVER DR	C	65	F2
DEODAR LN	MS	70	C3
DEODAR WY	SVL	53	A4
DEODARA DR	CPTO	60	A3
DEODARA DR	SCCO	59	B2
DEODARA GRVE CT	SJ	68	B6
DEODORA DR	LA	59	C3
DE PALMA CT	SJ	71	F5
DE PALMA DR	SJ	71	F4
DE PALMA LN	CPTO	60	A5
DE PAUL CIR	SCCO	81A	B4
DE PAUL PL	SCL	53	D5

STREET	CITY	PAGE	GRID
DEPOT AV	SCCO	81	C4
DEPOT ST	G	84	A2
DEPOT ST	MH	79	E4
DERBE DR	SJ	62	D4
DERBY CT	SVL	60	A1
DERBYSHIRE DR	CPTO	59	E6
DERBYSHIRE DR	CPTO	64	E1
DEREK DR	SJ	68	A6
DERMOTT DR	SJ	60	E6
DERMOTT DR	SJ	65	E1
DEROCHE CT	SVL	59	D1
DE ROSE WY	SJ	66	D1
DE SANKA AV	S	64	F3
DE SANKA AV	S	65	A3
DESCANSA CT	MH	80K	E1
DESDEMONA CT	SJ	63	A5
DESERT FLAME DR	SJ	72	B4
DESERT ISLE DR	SJ	60	E6
DESERT SANDS WY	SJ	72A	B1
DESERTWOOD LN	SJ	48	C5
DESIN DR	SJ	67	B6
DES MOINES PL	SJ	55	E3
DE SOTO AV	SCL	60	C3
DE SOTO DR	LG	72	B2
DE SOTO DR	PA	38	C6
DE SOTO DR	PA	44	C1
DE SOTO DR	SJ	71	B2
DESTRY CT	SJ	68	B6
DE TRACY ST	SJ	66	B2
DETROIT CT	SJ	55	E3
DEVCON CT	SJ	54	E4
DEVCON DR	SJ	54	E4
DEVELOPMENT DR	SJ	47	D6
DEVELOPMENT DR	SJ	54	D1
DEVERON CT	SJ	68A	C2
DEVILLE CT	G	83	C1
DE VILLE WY	SJ	60	A6
DEVIN DR	SCCO	63	E2
DEVINE ST	SJ	61	F2
DEVINE ST	SJ	62	A2
DEVLIN CT	SJ	55	A5
DEVON AV	SCCO	65	C4
DEVON AV	S	65	C4
DEVON PL	MPTS	39	F4
DEVON WY	SJ	65	A2
DEVON PARK CT	SJ	67	E6
DEVONSHIRE AV	MVW	45	D6
DEVONSHIRE DR	SJ	65	B1
DEVONSHIRE WY	SVL	60	B1
DEVOS CT	SCL	53	D6
DEVOTO ST	MVW	52	C3
DEVRI CT	MVW	44	F5
DEVRIES CT	SCCO	82	A4
DEWEY WY	SJ	72A	A4
DE WITT AV	MH	79	D5
DE WITT AV	SCCO	79	D6
DE WITT AV	SCCO	80K	D1
DEXTER DR	CPTO	59	E3
DEXTER DR	SJ	68	A6
DEYON PL	G	83	F3
DEZAHARA WY	LAH	51	B5
DIABLO AV	MVW	44	F6
DIABLO CT	PA	44	E5
DIABLO WY	SJ	72	C5
DIADEM DR	SJ	62	F1
DIAL WY	SJ	65	B1
DIAMENTE CT	SJ	55	D5
DIAMOND AV	SCCO	56	B6
DIAMOND CT	LA	52	A5
DIAMOND CT	SCCO	52	A5
DIAMOND HEAD DR	SJ	67	E4
DIAMOND OAKS CT	S	64	E3
DIANA AV	MH	79	E4
DIANA AV	SJ	62	F1
DIANA AV	SCCO	79	E4
DIANA LN	SJ	62	F1
DIANE CT	G	82	E6
DIANE MARIE WY	SCL	60	F2
DIANNE DR	LAH	51	D4
DIANNE DR	SCL	60	F1
DIANNE DR	SCL	61	A1
DIAS DR	SJ	63	D2
DIAS DR	SCCO	80	C6
DIBBLE CT	SCL	60	E3
DICKENS AV	SCCO	71	C2
DICKINSON DR	SJ	68	C4
DICKINSON WY	SJ	68	C4
DIDION CT	SJ	72A	B4
DIDION WY	SJ	72A	B4
DIDUCA WY	SCCO	71	C5
DIEL DR	MPTS	39	F5
DIEL DR	MPTS	40	A6

STREET	CITY	PAGE	GRID
DIERICX CT	MVW	52	C4
DIERICX DR	MVW	52	C4
DIERICX DR	SCCO	52	C4
DIESSNER AV	SCCO	81	C3
DI FIORE DR	SJ	61	D6
DI GIULIO AV	SCL	54	B5
DILLARD CT	SJ	61	C6
DILLION CT	SJ	55	D3
DILLON AV	C	66	B3
DILLWOOD CT	SJ	67	C3
DINA CT	SJ	63	A5
DINA LN	SJ	63	A5
DI NAPOLI DR	SJ	60	B6
DI NAPOLI DR	SJ	65	B1
DINKEL CT	SJ	67	B6
DINNY ST	SCL	54	B2
DIONNE WY	SJ	55	C4
DIOR TER	LA	51	E2
DIPPER CIR	SJ	61	B5
DI SALVO AV	SJ	61	C4
DI SALVO AV	SCCO	61	C4
DISCOVERY AV	SJ	68	C6
DISHMAN DR	LG	70	E6
DISK CT	SJ	47	A4
DISK DR	SJ	46	F3
DISK DR	SJ	47	A4
DISNEY LN	CPTO	60	B5
DISTEL CIR	LA	51	E1
DISTEL DR	LA	51	E2
DITTOS LN	LG	70	E5
DIVISION ST	C	66	A6
DIX WY	SCCO	67	B1
DIXIE DR	SJ	65	A4
DIXON DR	SCL	60	F2
DIXON PL	PA	44	E5
DIXON RD	MPTS	39	E5
DIXON WY	LA	51	D1
DIXON LANDNG RD	MPTS	39	E5
DOANE AV	MVW	45	A6
DOBBIN DR	SJ	55	C5
DOBERN AV	SJ	55	F6
DOBERN AV	SJ	62	F1
DODD LN	SCCO	80K	D1
DOGAWAY DR	SJ	68	C6
DOGWOOD CT	SJ	66	C1
DOGWOOD DR	SJ	72A	F3
DOGWOOD WY	MH	80	A4
DOLE LN	SCCO	78G	C2
DOLLAR MTN DR	SJ	55	F4
DOLORES AV	LA	52	A6
DOLORES AV	SCL	61	A3
DOLORES AV	SCCO	59	D5
DOLORES DR	MPTS	48	C2
DOLORES DR	MPTS	48	C3
DOLORES DR	SCCO	66	E1
DOLORES ST	SCCO	43	F4
DOLPHIN DR	SJ	71	B2
DOLPHIN DR	S	65	C5
DOMA DR	SJ	61	A5
DOMA DR	SCCO	61	A5
DOME AV	SCL	61	B3
DOMINICAN DR	SCL	60	D3
DOMINICK CT	SJ	56	B5
DOMINICK WY	SJ	56	B5
DOMINION AV	SVL	59	D2
DON AV	SJ	66	E5
DON AV	SCL	54	A6
DON CT	MVW	51	F2
DON CT	MVW	52	A2
DON CT	SCL	54	A6
DONA AV	SVL	52	D4
DONAHE DR	MPTS	47	F2
DONAHE PL	MPTS	47	F2
DONALD CT	SJ	56	C5
DONALD DR	PA	44	C6
DON ALFONSO CT	SJ	72	D3
DON ALFONSO WY	SJ	72	D3
DON ANDRES CT	SJ	72	D3
DON ANDRES WY	SJ	72	D3
DON BASILLO CT	SJ	72	E1
DON BASILLO WY	SJ	72	E1
DON CARLOS CT	SJ	72	D3
DONCASTER WY	SJ	56	B6
DONCASTER WY	SJ	63	B1
DON CORRELLI CT	SJ	72	D4
DON CORRELLI WY	SJ	72	D4
DON DEL MONC CT	SJ	72	D3
DONDERO WY	SJ	72A	D3
DON DIABLO CT	SJ	72	D4
DON DIEGO CT	SJ	72	E1
DON EDGARDO CT	SJ	72	E1
DON EDMONDO CT	SJ	72	D4
DONEGAL DR	CPTO	64	F2

STREET	CITY	PAGE	GRID
DONELSON PL	LAH	51	C3
DON ENRICO	SJ	72	D3
DON FERNANDO WY	SJ	72	E1
DON GIOVANNI CT	SJ	72	D3
DONINGTON DR	SJ	65	B1
DONIZETTI CT	SJ	55	D1
DON JOSE WY	SJ	72	E1
DON JUAN CIR	SJ	72	F1
DON KIRK ST	LA	59	B1
DON MANRICO CT	SJ	72	E1
DON MARCELLO CT	SJ	72	D3
DON MARCO CT	SJ	72	E1
DON MATEO CT	SJ	72	D4
DONNA CT	SCCO	78	D6
DONNA LN	SJ	66	E6
DONNA LN	S	65	A6
DONNER CT	SVL	52	E3
DONNER DR	SCCO	71	D1
DONNER PL	SCL	60	F3
DONNER PL	SCL	61	A3
DONNORA CT	SJ	55	E1
DON OCTAVIO CT	SJ	72	E1
DONOHUE CT	SJ	55	B2
DONOHUE DR	SJ	55	B2
DONOVAN AV	SCL	53	E6
DONOVAN CT	SJ	66	D2
DON PEDRO CT	SJ	72	E1
DON PIZARRO CT	SJ	72	D3
DON RICARDO CT	SJ	72	D3
DON RODOLFO CT	SJ	72	D3
DON SCALA CT	SJ	72	F1
DON SEVILLE CT	SJ	72	D3
DOON CT	SVL	60	C1
DOORN LN	SJ	72	A2
DORADO LN	MS	70	E2
DORAL CT	SCCO	82	B4
DORALEE WY	SJ	67	B3
DORCEY LN	SJ	71	F4
DORCHESTER DR	MVW	45	D6
DORCHESTER DR	S	65	B3
DORCHESTER LN	SJ	72	B2
DORCICH ST	SCL	61	A4
DOREL DR	SJ	56	A1
DORENE CT	S	64	D6
DORENE PL	SJ	72	D5
DORI LN	LAH	51	C5
DORIAN CT	SCCO	55	F2
DORIS AV	SCCO	56	A5
DORIS CT	G	82	E6
DORIS CT	SCCO	56	A5
DORMAR CT	SCCO	56	C3
DORN CT	SJ	72A	C3
DORNOCH AV	SJ	62	F4
DOROTHY AV	SJ	62	A6
DOROTHY WY	SCCO	78G	D2
DORRANCE AV	SCCO	82C	F5
DORRANCE CT	SJ	66	E3
DORRANCE DR	SJ	66	E3
DORRIE AV	SJ	62	D3
DORRIE AV	SCCO	62	D3
DORSET WY	SVL	60	A1
DORSEY WY	S	64	E6
DORTHY ANN WY	CPTO	64	D1
DORVAL DR	SJ	65	E4
DOS PALOS CT	CPTO	59	D3
DOT AV	C	66	A3
DOT CT	SJ	72	A3
DOTEY CT	SJ	68	C4
DOTTIELYN AV	SJ	68	E3
DOUD DR	LA	51	F3
DOUGHERTY AV	SJ	78	A5
DOUGHERTY AV	SJ	79	B1
DOUGHERTY AV	SCCO	77	F4
DOUGHERTY AV	SCCO	78	A5
DOUGHERTY AV	SCCO	79	B1
DOUGLANE AV	SCL	61	A4
DOUGLAS ST	SCCO	61	E4
DOUGLASS LN	S	65	A6
DOVE LN	SVL	60	A1
DOVE HILL RD	SJ	68	B1
DOVELA WY	SJ	66	F5
DOVE OAK CT	CPTO	59	C4
DOVER CT	LA	51	D5
DOVER CT	LG	71	B3
DOVER CT	S	65	B3
DOVER ST	LG	71	B3
DOVER WY	C	66	D2
DOVER WY	SCCO	55	F6
DOVER WY	SCCO	56	A6
DOVERTON SQ	MVW	52	C5
DOW DR	SJ	67	C4
DOWDY ST	G	83	F2
DOWNING AV	SJ	61	C6

STREET	CITY	PAGE	GRID
DOWNING AV	SJ	66	C1
DOWNING CT	SCL	53	E6
DOWNING LN	PA	44	A1
DOWNING RD	MPTS	40	C5
DOWNING RD	SCCO	40	C5
DOWNING OAK CT	LG	71	C2
DOWNS DR	SJ	72A	F5
DOWNSGLEN WY	SJ	55	E4
DOWNSWICK DR	SJ	67	B5
DOWNSWOOD CT	SJ	75	F1
DOXEY CT	SJ	55	C2
DOXEY DR	SJ	55	C2
DOYLE CT	SJ	65	E1
DOYLE DR	SJ	65	C1
DOYLE PL	MVW	52	C3
DOYLE RD	SJ	60	D5
DOYLE RD	SJ	65	D1
DOYLE RD	SCCO	60	D6
DRACENA LN	LA	51	E3
DRACENA WY	SJ	62	F4
DRAGONFLY CT	SJ	55	D4
DRAGONFLY WY	SJ	55	D4
DRAKE CT	CPTO	60	B3
DRAKE CT	SCL	60	E3
DRAKE DR	CPTO	60	B3
DRAKE ST	SJ	61	F5
DRAKES CT	LG	71	B2
DRAKES BAY AV	LG	71	B2
DREA RD	CPTO	59	C6
DRESDEN WY	SJ	60	B6
DRESDEN WY	SJ	65	B1
DREW AV	MVW	45	A5
DREXEL WY	SJ	62	F6
DRIFTER DR	SJ	72A	A3
DRIFTWOOD CT	SVL	46	D6
DRIFTWOOD CT	SVL	53	D1
DRIFTWOOD DR	PA	44	E3
DRIFTWOOD DR	SJ	66	B1
DRIFTWOOD TER	G	83	D1
DRISCOLL CT	PA	44	C6
DRUCILLA DR	MVW	52	B4
DRUMHEAD CT	SJ	55	B2
DRUMM CT	SJ	72A	F5
DRUMM PL	SJ	72A	F5
DRUMMOND DR	SCCO	70	C3
DRY BED CT	SCL	53	F3
DRY CREEK CT	SJ	66	C3
DRY CREEK RD	SJ	66	E3
DRY CREEK RD	SCCO	66	C4
DRY CREEK WY	SJ	66	E3
DRYDEN AV	CPTO	59	D6
DRYDEN AV	SCCO	82A	C4
DRYDEN DR	SJ	55	B3
DRY OAK CT	SJ	72	B3
DRY OAK DR	SJ	72	B3
DRY OAK PL	SJ	72	B3
DRYSDALE CT	SJ	71	E3
DRYSDALE DR	SJ	71	E3
DRYSDALE DR	SCCO	72	B4
DRYSDALE DR	SVL	59	D1
DRYTOWN PL	SJ	72	B3
DRYWOOD LN	SJ	48	C4
DRY YARD DR	SJ	61	A5
DUANE AV	SCL	53	F3
DUANE AV	SCL	54	A3
DUANE AV	SVL	52	F2
DUANE AV	SVL	53	B2
DUANE CT	SVL	53	C2
DUANE ST	SJ	62	B4
DUARTE CT	MPTS	39	F6
DUBANSKI DR	SJ	72	E3
DUBERT LN	SJ	62	E4
DUBLIN DR	SJ	63	A1
DUBLIN WY	SVL	59	F1
DUBLIN WY	SVL	60	A1
DUBOIS ST	MPTS	48	D4
DUBON AV	CPTO	59	C5
DUCHESS CT	SJ	48	E4
DUCKETT WY	SJ	64	F2
DUDASH CT	SJ	62	F4
DUDLEY AV	SJ	61	B5
DUDLEY AV	SCCO	61	B5
DUDLEY LN	SCCO	44	A3
DUENA ST	SCCO	43	E4
DUESENBERG DR	SJ	67	F6
DUESENBERG DR	SJ	72	F1
DUET CT	SJ	72	B4
DUFF CT	SVL	53	B5
DUFFY CT	SJ	62	E1
DUFFY WY	SJ	62	E1
DUGGAN DR	SJ	66	F6
DUKE CT	SCL	60	D3

STREET	CITY	PAGE	GRID
DUKE DR	SCCO	82A	C1
DUKE WY	MVW	52	A4
DUKE WY	SJ	66	F2
DULCEY DR	SJ	67	E5
DULUTH CIR	PA	44	D5
DUMAS DR	CPTO	59	F6
DUMBARTON AV	SJ	66	E4
DUMONT CIR	SJ	63	A1
DUMONT CT	SJ	63	A1
DUNBAR DR	CPTO	59	F3
DUNBAR DR	SCCO	59	F3
DUNCAN AV	SVL	46	A6
DUNCAN AV	SVL	53	A1
DUNCAN PL	PA	44	E4
DUNCAN ST	SJ	55	F3
DUNCAN ST	SCCO	55	F3
DUNCANVILLE CT	C	66	C3
DUNCARDINE WY	SVL	60	B1
DUNDALE DR	SJ	68	B2
DUNDEE AV	MPTS	47	F2
DUNDEE AV	S	65	C4
DUNDEE CT	SJ	62	F4
DUNDEE DR	SCL	53	E5
DUNDONALD CT	SJ	63	C6
DUNFORD WY	SCL	60	C2
DUNFORD WY	SVL	60	C2
DUNHOLME WY	SVL	59	F2
DUNHOLME WY	SVL	60	A2
DUNIGAN CT	SJ	72A	B1
DUNLAP AV	SCCO	82A	C6
DUNN AV	SJ	72A	A3
DUNNE AV	SCCO	78A	D6
DUNNE AV E	MH	79	F4
DUNNE AV E	MH	80	A4
DUNNE AV E	SCCO	80	A3
DUNNE AV W	MH	79	D5
DUNNE LN	SCCO	82C	C6
DUNNOCK WY	SVL	60	A1
DUNRAVEN CT	SJ	67	D6
DUNSBURRY CT	SJ	72	E1
DUNSBURRY WY	SJ	72	E1
DUNSTER DR	C	66	B2
DUNWELL CT	SJ	72A	E2
DUNWICH CT	SJ	63	E1
DUPONT ST	SCCO	61	F4
DURAND RD	SCCO	45	D5
DURANGO CT	SJ	72	A1
DURANGO RIV CT	SJ	67	D6
DURANT AV	SJ	67	F2
DURHAM CT	S	65	A6
DURHAM CT	SVL	60	C2
DURLANE CT	SVL	60	B2
DURNESS PL	SJ	62	E4
DURSHIRE WY	SVL	60	B2
DU SAULT DR	SJ	72A	D4
DUSTIN CT	SJ	72A	B1
DUTCHESS CT	SCCO	81A	B6
DUTTONWOOD LN	MPTS	39	D4
DUVAL WY	LAH	51	C5
DUVALL CT	SVL	59	F1
DUVALL DR	SJ	65	E2
DWIGHT AV	SJ	71	F3
DWIGHT AV	SVL	53	B4
DWYER AV	SJ	72	C5
DWYER CT	SJ	72	C5
DYMOND CT	PA	44	C3
E			
E ST	SVL	46	C6
EAGLE DR	SVL	60	A2
EAGLEHAVEN CT	SJ	68	A5
EAGLE HILLS WY	G	82	C5
EAGLEHURST DR	SJ	68	C1
EAGLE LAKE DR	SJ	67	C5
EAGLE NEST WY	G	82	C5
EAGLE RIDGE WY	MPTS	48	C4
EAGLE ROCK RD	SJ	68	A5
EAGLES LN	SJ	72A	A1
EAGLE VIEW WY	G	82	C5
EAGLEWOOD AV	SVL	53	A2
EARL AV	SCCO	61	E4
EARL DR	SCL	53	D5
EARLANDER CT	SCCO	56	B5
EARLANDER ST	SCCO	56	B5
EARLINGTON CT	SVL	59	D2
EARLS CT	SCCO	79	B1
EARLSWOOD CT	SJ	75	F1
EARLSWOOD CT	SJ	76	A1
EASINGTON WY	SJ	61	D6
EASINGTON WY	SJ	66	D1
EAST CT	G	82	E6

1991 SANTA CLARA COUNTY STREET INDEX

STREET	CITY	PAGE	GRID
EAST CT	SJ	55	C6
EAST LN	SCCO	79	E3
EAST ST	G	84	A2
EASTBROOK AV	LAH	51	E6
EASTBROOK AV	SCCO	51	E6
EASTBROOK AV	SCCO	58	F1
EASTBROOK AV	SCCO	59	A2
EASTBROOK CT	SCCO	58	F2
EASTBROOK CT	SCCO	59	A2
EASTER AV	MPTS	47	E2
EASTGATE AV	SJ	55	D6
EAST HILLS CT	SCCO	56	B4
EAST HILLS DR	SJ	56	B4
EAST HILLS DR	SCCO	56	B4
EAST LAKE DR	SJ	61	D6
EAST LAKE DR	SJ	66	D1
EASTON CT	SJ	55	E4
EASTON CT	S	65	C3
EASTON DR	SJ	55	E4
EASTON DR	S	65	C3
EASTON LN	SJ	55	E4
EASTON PL	SJ	55	E4
EASTON TER	SJ	55	E4
EASTON WY	SJ	55	E4
EAST PARR AV	SCCO	65	F6
EASTRIDGE BLVD	SCCO	63	B4
EASTRIDGE DR	LG	71	A3
EASTRIDGE DR	SJ	63	D1
EASTRIDGE LN	SJ	63	B3
EASTRIDGE LP	SJ	63	B4
EASTRIDGE WY	SJ	63	B4
EASTSIDE DR	SJ	55	F4
EASTUS DR	SJ	60	D6
EAST VALLEY CT	SCCO	63	D1
EASTVIEW DR	LG	65	F6
EASTVIEW DR	LG	70	F1
EASTWOOD CIR	SCL	54	B2
EASTWOOD CT	LA	52	A5
EASTWOOD CT	SJ	55	D6
EASTWOOD CT	SJ	62	D1
EASTWOOD DR	LA	52	B5
EASTWOOD PL	LA	52	A5
EASY ST	MH	80K	F3
EASY ST	MH	81	A3
EASY ST	MVW	45	C6
EASY ST	MVW	52	C1
EASY ST	SCCO	52	C1
EATON LN	MS	70	E2
EATON LN	SJ	72A	E1
EBANO CT	SJ	63	A6
EBBESEN AV	SJ	66	C6
EBBESEN AV	SJ	71	C1
EBBETTS DR	C	65	E4
EBERHARD ST	SCL	53	F6
EBERHARD ST	SCL	54	A6
EBERLY DR	SJ	68	B5
EBERTS DR	SCCO	81	D2
EBONY WY	SJ	63	E3
ECHO AV	C	66	A4
ECHO DR	LA	51	F5
ECHO DR	SCCO	78G	F3
ECHO LP	SJ	75	D1
ECHO NOLLS	SCCO	56	C2
ECHO RIDGE CT	SJ	75	D1
ECHO RIDGE DR	SJ	75	D1
ECHO VALLEY DR	SJ	75	D1
ECKBERG CT	SJ	55	F5
ECKBERG CT	SJ	56	A5
EDALE DR	SVL	52	E6
EDDINGTON PL	SJ	65	A1
EDELEN AV	LG	70	E4
EDELWEISS DR	SJ	67	D5
EDEN AV	C	66	A2
EDEN AV	SJ	61	A6
EDEN AV	SJ	66	A2
EDEN AV N	SVL	53	B2
EDEN AV S	SVL	53	B2
EDEN AV W	SVL	53	B2
EDEN CT	SCL	60	D3
EDEN DR	SCL	60	D3
EDENBANK CT	SJ	63	D5
EDENBANK DR	SJ	63	D5
EDENBURY LN	SJ	67	C5
EDENHALL DR	SJ	60	B6
EDEN PARK PL	SJ	72A	E1
EDENVALE AV	SJ	68	B6
EDEN VIEW DR	SJ	68	B6
EDENWOOD CT	SJ	68	D1
EDENWOOD DR	SJ	68	D1
EDES CT	MH	79	E6
EDGAR CT	SJ	67	B6
EDGE LN	LA	51	F5

STREET	CITY	PAGE	GRID
EDGE LN	LA	52	A5
EDGEBANK DR	SJ	63	B4
EDGEBROOK CT	SJ	72	B5
EDGECLIFF LN	SCCO	51	D6
EDGECLIFF PL	SCCO	51	C6
EDGECREST DR	SJ	63	A4
EDGEDALE CT	SJ	63	B4
EDGEFIELD CT	SJ	63	B4
EDGEFIELD DR	SCL	54	B2
EDGEFORT CT	SJ	63	A4
EDGEGATE DR	SJ	63	B4
EDGEHILL WY	MPTS	48	D3
EDGEHILL WY	MPTS	48	C4
EDGEMONT DR	SCCO	56	B2
EDGEMOOR WY	SJ	60	A6
EDGEMOOR WY	SJ	65	A1
EDGERTON RD	LAH	51	A4
EDGESTONE CIR	SJ	63	A4
EDGEVIEW CT	SJ	63	B4
EDGEVIEW DR	SJ	63	B4
EDGEWATER DR	MPTS	47	F2
EDGEWATER DR	SJ	67	E4
EDGEWOOD DR	PA	38	B6
EDGEWOOD LN	LA	51	E4
EDGEWOOD WY	SJ	66	F2
EDINA LN	S	65	B3
EDINBURGH DR	S	65	A4
EDINBURGH CT	MPTS	47	A2
EDISON DR	SCCO	55	F4
EDITH AV	LA	51	E3
EDITH RD	LAH	51	D3
EDITH ST	SJ	62	F1
EDLEE AV	PA	44	D5
EDMOND CT	SJ	66	F3
EDMONDS CT	SVL	59	D2
EDMONDS WY	SVL	59	D2
EDMONTON AV	SVL	59	D2
EDMUND DR	LG	71	B2
EDMUNDSON AV	MH	79	E6
EDMUNDSON AV	SCCO	80K	C2
EDNA AV	SCCO	56	A5
EDNA CT	LA	51	E3
EDNAMARY WY	MVW	51	F2
EDQUIBA RD	SCCO	45	D5
EDSEL DR	MPTS	48	B3
EDSEL DR	SJ	60	B6
ED STOCK WY	SJ	67	C1
EDUARDS RD	SCCO	73	D6
EDUCATION PK DR	SJ	55	D4
EDWARD AV	SCL	54	C2
EDWARD WY	CPTO	59	D6
EDWARDS AV	SJ	62	B5
EDWIN JONES CT	MH	79	D5
EGGO WY	SJ	55	C6
EGRET DR	SVL	60	A1
EHRHORN AV	MVW	52	B3
EICHLER CT	MVW	52	A3
EICHLER DR	MVW	52	A3
EIGELBERRY ST	G	83	F1
EILEEN CT	SCCO	78G	D1
EILEEN DR	SJ	65	D1
EISENHOWER DR	SJ	61	C6
EISENHOWER DR	SJ	66	C1
EISENHOWER DR	SCL	47	A6
EISENHOWER DR	SCL	54	A1
EL ABRA CT	SJ	61	F6
ELAINE CT	MH	79	D4
ELAINE DR	SJ	66	D6
EL ALTILLO	LG	65	D6
ELAM AV	C	65	E4
ELAM AV	SCCO	65	E4
EL BOSQUE DR	SJ	47	B5
EL BOSQUE ST	SJ	47	B5
ELBRIDGE WY	PA	44	D2
EL CAJON DR	SJ	67	F3
EL CAJON DR	SJ	68	A3
EL CAJON WY	LG	70	F2
EL CAJON WY	LG	71	A2
EL CAJON WY	PA	44	C1
EL CAMINITO	G	82	C5
EL CAMINITO	SCCO	58	E2
EL CAMINITO AV	C	66	B3
EL CAMINITO RD	LAH	58	E2
EL CAMINO WY	PA	44	D5
EL CM GRANDE	S	70	C2
EL CM HIGUERA	SCCO	40	A6
EL CAMINO REAL	G	82	D1
EL CAMINO REAL	G	84	A3
EL CAMINO REAL	LA	44	D5
EL CAMINO REAL	MH	79	D3
EL CAMINO REAL	MVW	51	F1
EL CAMINO REAL	MVW	52	D4

STREET	CITY	PAGE	GRID
EL CAMINO REAL	PA	43	F2
EL CAMINO REAL	PA	44	D5
EL CAMINO REAL	SJ	72B	A3
EL CAMINO REAL	SJ	77	D1
EL CAMINO REAL	SCL	53	C6
EL CAMINO REAL	SCL	54	B6
EL CAMINO REAL	SCL	60	E1
EL CAMINO REAL	SCL	61	B1
EL CAMINO REAL	SCCO	53	C6
EL CAMINO REAL	SCCO	60	E1
EL CAMINO REAL	SCCO	78	A5
EL CAMINO REAL	SCCO	81	B3
EL CAMINO REAL	SCCO	82	D1
EL CAMINO REAL	SVL	52	D4
EL CAMINO REAL	SVL	53	C6
EL CAMINO REAL	SVL	60	E1
EL CAMINO SENDA	S	70	C1
EL CAMPO DR	SCCO	56	A4
EL CAPITAN AV	SCL	53	F5
EL CAPITAN PL	PA	44	E4
EL CARMELO AV	PA	44	C3
EL CENTRO	MVW	45	C4
EL CENTRO ST	PA	44	C5
EL CERRITO RD	CPTO	59	B5
EL CERRITO RD	PA	44	C6
EL CERRITO WY	G	82	F6
EL CERRITO WY	PA	44	C6
EL CODO WY	SJ	66	F4
EL CORAL CT	SJ	67	B5
EL CORAL WY	SJ	66	B5
ELDAMAR CT	SJ	68	B1
ELDEN DR	SJ	66	C4
ELDER CT	SJ	72A	A4
ELDERBERRY DR	SVL	52	D6
ELDERBERRY WY	SJ	66	E2
ELDERWOOD CT	CPTO	59	E6
EL DORA DR	MVW	52	C2
EL DORADO AV	PA	44	C3
EL DORADO AV	SJ	61	C3
EL DORADO AV	SJ	67	E4
EL DORADO CT	SJ	46	E3
EL DORADO CT	S	64	F5
ELDORADO DR	G	83	D1
EL DORADO ST	SJ	46	E3
EL DORI DR	SJ	72	C2
EL DORIC CT	SCCO	81H	D6
ELDRIDGE DR	SJ	72	E6
ELEANOR AV	LA	51	E3
ELEANOR WY	SVL	60	B1
ELECTRA AV	SJ	67	A5
ELENA RD	CPTO	59	B5
ELENA RD	LAH	51	B5
ELENA WY	LG	70	F1
ELENA PRIVADA	MVW	52	D1
ELENDA DR	SCCO	59	F4
EL ESCARPADO CT	SCCO	43	E4
ELESTER DR	SJ	71	B2
EL GATO LN	SCCO	71	B2
ELGIN LN	SJ	66	F5
EL GRANDE CT	SJ	55	F1
EL GRANDE CT	SJ	56	A1
EL GRANDE DR	SJ	55	F1
ELISA AV	S	65	B2
ELISE CT	LAH	58	D1
ELIZABETH DR	SJ	61	E6
ELIZABETH DR	SCL	60	F2
ELIZABETH ST	SJ	46	E3
ELIZABETH ST	SJ	62	B2
ELIZABETH WY	SVL	60	B1
ELJA WY	SJ	72	D2
ELK LN	SJ	55	D3
ELKA AV	MVW	44	F5
ELKA AV	SJ	65	B2
ELK CREEK PL	SJ	55	F4
ELK RIDGE CT	SJ	67	D3
ELK RIDGE WY	SJ	67	D3
ELKHORN CT	SJ	66	F3
ELKINS WY	SJ	63	C6
ELKO DR	SVL	46	D6
ELKWOOD DR	MPTS	39	E6
ELKWOOD DR	MPTS	47	E1
ELLA CT	SJ	68	C5
ELLA DR	SJ	68	C5
ELLEGE RD	SCCO	73	B4
ELLEN AV	SJ	67	A1
ELLENA DR	SCL	53	F5
ELLENWOOD AV	LG	70	D4
ELLENWOOD AV	MS	70	D4
ELLENWOOD AV W	MS	70	D4
ELLERBROOK WY	SJ	72A	C3
ELLERY ST	SJ	55	F3
ELLIOT AV	LG	71	A2
ELLIOTT CT	SCL	53	F5

STREET	CITY	PAGE	GRID
ELLIOTT ST	SJ	61	D4
ELLIOTT ST	SCL	53	E5
ELLIOTT ST	SCCO	61	D4
ELLIS AV	MPTS	48	B2
ELLIS AV	SJ	67	A1
ELLIS AV	SCCO	80	B5
ELLIS ST	MVW	45	D6
ELLIS ST	MVW	52	D1
ELLISA DR	SJ	72	C2
ELLMAR OAKS CT	SJ	67	E4
ELLMAR OAKS DR	SJ	67	E4
ELLMAR OAKS LP	SJ	67	E4
ELLSWORTH PL	PA	44	D3
ELLWELL DR	MPTS	48	C2
ELLYRIDGE CT	SJ	72A	A1
ELLYRIDGE DR	SJ	72A	A1
ELM AV	MPTS	47	E2
ELM CT	CPTO	59	E5
ELM CT	MPTS	47	E2
ELM CT	SVL	53	A4
ELM RD	MH	79	F2
ELM RD	SCCO	79	F2
ELM ST	G	82	F6
ELM ST	LG	70	E5
ELM ST	SJ	61	D2
ELMAR WY	SJ	65	B2
EL MARCERO CT	SJ	72A	E5
EL MATADOR DR	SCCO	81H	D5
EL MATADOR DR	SCCO	82H	D1
ELMBROOK WY	SJ	68	A3
ELMBRIDGE DR	SJ	60	B6
ELMDALE PL	PA	44	D1
ELMGATE CT	SJ	63	E5
ELMGROVE CT	SJ	65	D3
ELMGROVE LN	SJ	65	D3
ELMGROVE LN	SCCO	65	D3
ELMHURST AV	SCL	60	D4
ELMHURST CT	SCL	60	D4
ELMHURST DR	LA	52	C6
ELMHURST DR	SJ	60	E5
ELMIRA DR	SVL	52	E5
ELM LEAF CT	SCL	55	E3
ELM LEAF CT	SCL	54	A4
EL MOLINO WY	SJ	72A	C4
EL MONTE AV	LA	51	E4
EL MONTE AV	MVW	51	F3
EL MONTE AV	SCCO	51	C6
EL MONTE AV	SCCO	58	C1
EL MONTE AV N	LA	51	F3
EL MONTE CT	LA	51	F3
EL MONTE RD	LAH	51	C6
EL MONTE RD	LAH	58	C1
EL MONTE WY	SJ	63	B2
EL MORO DR	C	66	D3
ELM PARK	MS	70	D2
ELM PARK CT	MS	70	D2
ELMSDALE DR	SJ	72	F6
ELMSFORD CT	CPTO	59	E6
ELMSFORD CT	CPTO	64	E1
ELMSFORD DR	CPTO	59	E6
ELMSFORD DR	CPTO	64	E1
ELMTREE CT	SJ	55	B1
ELMWOOD CT	LG	65	E5
ELMWOOD DR	SJ	65	D3
ELMWOOD ST	MVW	52	B1
EL NIDO AV	LG	70	F5
ELNORA CT	LA	59	C1
ELODIE WY	SJ	55	E5
ELOISE CIR	SCCO	58	F2
EL OLIVAR	LG	65	D6
EL OSO DR	LG	65	D2
EL PAJARO CT	MH	80K	E1
EL PASEO	C	66	C3
EL PASEO DR	SJ	72	C4
EL PAS D LS PAS	SCCO	63	F3
EL PATIO CT	C	66	C2
EL PATIO DR	C	66	C2
EL PINAR	LG	65	D6
EL PORTAL WY	SJ	72A	C3
EL PORTON	LG	65	D6
EL PRADO CT	SJ	72	C4
EL PRADO DR	SJ	72	C4
EL PRADO WY	CPTO	59	B5
EL PUENTE WY	S	70	B1
EL QUITO WY	S	70	C2
EL RANCHITO WY	MVW	52	C3
EL RANCHITO WY	SCCO	52	C3
EL RANCHO AV	MS	70	F2
EL RO VERDE CT	SJ	55	E6
EL RO VERDE DR	SCCO	55	D5
EL RIO DR	SJ	67	B2
EL ROBLE CT	G	83	E2
EL ROBLE CT	SJ	72	A1

STREET	CITY	PAGE	GRID
ELROSE AV	SJ	71	E2
EL SERENO AV	LA	59	C2
EL SERENO CT	LA	59	C2
EL SERENO DR	SJ	72	E3
ELSIE AV	MVW	45	A6
ELSINORE CT	PA	44	C1
ELSINORE DR	PA	44	C1
ELSMAN CT	SJ	72	A4
EL SOBRANTE ST	SCL	60	E1
EL SOLYO AV	C	66	C3
EL SOMBROSO DR	SJ	72	E2
ELSONA CT	SVL	59	D1
ELSONA DR	SVL	52	D6
ELSONA DR	SVL	59	D1
ELTON CT	SCCO	71	D1
ELTON DR	SCCO	71	D1
EL TORO CT	MH	79	D4
EL TORO CT	SJ	72	E3
EL TORO DR	G	82	E6
EL TORO ST	MH	79	D4
EL TORO WY	G	82	E6
ELVA AV	S	64	F6
EL VERANO AV	PA	44	D4
ELVIRA CT	SJ	62	F2
ELVIRA ST	S	64	F6
ELVIS DR	SJ	72A	A4
EL VISTA WY	SJ	63	D3
ELWELL CT	PA	44	F3
ELWOOD CT	SJ	72	D5
ELWOOD DR	C	65	D5
ELWOOD RD	SJ	72	D6
ELWOOD RD	SCCO	72	D6
ELY CT	SJ	72A	B1
ELY PL	PA	44	E5
EL ZUPARKO DR	SJ	72	C2
EMADO AV	SCCO	72B	C6
EMANUEL CT	SJ	68	B2
EMANUEL CT	S	65	C4
EMBARCADERO RD	PA	38	D6
EMBARCADERO RD	PA	44	B2
EMBARCADERO WY	PA	38	E6
EMBEE DR	SJ	72A	B2
EMERALD WY	SJ	61	A6
EMERLD HLLS CIR	SJ	55	C2
EMERALD HLLS LN	LAH	51	D6
EMERICK AV	SCCO	56	A5
EMERSON AV	SCCO	66	B6
EMERSON CT	G	82	D6
EMERSON CT	SJ	61	D3
EMERSON ST	PA	43	F1
EMERSON ST	PA	44	B2
EMIG CT	SCL	53	D6
EMILIE DR	SCCO	55	F5
EMILIE DR	SCCO	56	A6
EMILINE DR	LG	71	D2
EMILINE DR	SJ	71	D2
EMILY DR	MVW	45	C6
EMLYN CT	SJ	72A	B3
EMMA CT	SJ	75	F2
EMMETT CT	SCL	53	D5
EMMETT PL	SCL	53	D5
EMMONS DR	MVW	44	F5
EMORY AV	C	66	A4
EMORY ST	SJ	61	D2
EMPEROR WY	SVL	60	E2
EMPEY WY	SCCO	61	C6
EMPIRE AV	CPTO	59	D4
EMPIRE ST	SJ	55	B6
EMPIRE ST	SJ	61	F2
EMPIRE ST	SJ	62	A1
EMPORIUM WY	SJ	72	B1
EMPRESS CT	SJ	65	B1
EMRICK AV	SCCO	56	A5
ENBORG LN	SCCO	61	C5
ENCHANTO VISTA	SCCO	56	A1
ENCINA AV	PA	43	F2
ENCINA AV	PA	44	A2
ENCINA CT	S	70	B2
ENCINA WY	SCL	60	F1
ENCINA GRAND DR	PA	44	C5
ENCINAL CT	LAH	58	E2
ENCINAL DR	SJ	72A	D3
ENCINITAS CT	SJ	48	B5
ENCINO CT	SVL	52	D3
ENCINO DR	MH	80K	E2
ENCINO DR	SCCO	80K	E2
ENDERBY WY	SVL	59	D1
ENDERSON CT	SCCO	79	C4
ENDFIELD WY	SCCO	56	A6
ENDICOTT BLVD	SJ	72A	C1
ENDICOTT DR	SJ	63	A2
ENDICOTT DR	SVL	59	F2

STREET	CITY	PAGE	GRID
ENDMOOR CT	SJ	72A	D4
ENDMOOR DR	SJ	72A	D4
ENESCO AV	SJ	63	B5
ENGLE WY	G	84	B4
ENGLERT CT	SJ	55	D5
ENGLEWOOD AV	LG	70	F4
ENGLEWOOD AV	LG	71	A4
ENGLEWOOD AV	SCCO	70	F4
ENGLEWOOD AV	SCCO	71	A4
ENGLEWOOD DR	SJ	65	D1
ENGLISH CT	SJ	65	C2
ENGLISH DR	SJ	65	C2
ENGLISH DR	SCCO	65	C2
ENGLISH PL	SCCO	68	E6
ENGLISH OAK WY	CPTO	59	B3
ENGLSH WALNT CT	MH	79	F3
ENGLISH WLNT WY	MH	79	F3
ENNING AV	SJ	72A	A1
ENOCHS ST	SCL	53	C3
ENOS CT	SCL	60	F3
ENRIGHT AV	SCL	61	A2
ENRIQUEZ CT	MPTS	47	F1
ENRIQUITA CT	SJ	72	E2
ENSALMO AV	SJ	66	F5
ENSENADA DR	C	65	E3
ENSENADA WY	LA	59	B1
ENSIGN WY	PA	44	E4
ENSIGN WY	SJ	55	C3
ENTERPRISE DR	SJ	54	F3
ENTRADA PL	SCCO	58	F1
ENTRADA CEDROS	SJ	72	F1
ENTRADA OLENDRS	SJ	67	F6
ENTRADA OLENDRS	SJ	72	F1
ENTRADA OLMOS	SJ	67	F6
ENTRADA OLMOS	SJ	72	F1
ENTRANCE DR	SJ	55	B3
EPPLING LN	SJ	68	C5
EQUESTRIAN WY	MS	70	D2
ERIC DR	S	65	B2
ERIC LN	SCCO	82	A2
ERICA CT	SJ	68	A1
ERICA DR	SVL	53	B5
ERIE CIR	MPTS	47	F1
ERIE CT	MPTS	47	F1
ERIE CT	SCL	53	F2
ERIE DR	MPTS	47	F1
ERIE DR	SVL	52	E5
ERIE PL	MPTS	47	F1
ERIE WY	C	65	E2
ERIN WY	CPTO	59	E5
ERIN WY	SCCO	66	B5
ERINBROOK PL	SJ	55	C4
ERINWOOD CT	SJ	68	B1
ERNESTINE LN	MVW	52	A2
ERSRINE CT	SJ	72A	B2
ERSTWILD CT	PA	44	C1
ERVIN WY	SCCO	56	D6
ESBERG RD	SCCO	58	F1
ESBERG RD	SCCO	59	A1
ESCALON AV	SVL	52	E2
ESCALON CT	SVL	52	E2
ESCALONIA CT	SJ	68	E1
ESCAZU CT	SJ	55	E6
ESCHENBURG DR	G	83	F2
ESCOBAR AV	LG	71	B2
ESCOBAR AV	SCCO	71	B3
ESCOBAR CT	LG	71	B2
ESCOBITA AV	PA	44	A2
ESCONDIDO CT	SJ	72A	D3
ESCONDIDO RD	SCCO	43	A4
ESCOVER LN	SJ	72	B1
ESCUELA AV	MVW	51	F1
ESCUELA AV	MVW	52	A1
ESCUELA DR	MPTS	47	F2
ESCUELA PKWY	MPTS	39	F6
ESCUELA PKWY	MPTS	47	F2
ESCUELA PL	MPTS	47	F2
ESMERALDA CT	SJ	55	D5
ESPADA CT	S	65	D5
ESPERANZA DR	LAH	51	B3
ESPLANADA WY	SCCO	43	F4
ESPLANADA WY	SCCO	44	A4
ESQUIRE PL	CPTO	59	E3
ESSENDON WY	SJ	72B	A4
ESSEX AV	SVL	46	A6
ESSEX AV	SVL	53	A1
ESSEX ST	SJ	46	F3
ESSEX WY	SJ	66	A2
ESSEX WY	SCCO	66	A2
ESTACADA DR	LAH	51	C2
ESTACADA WY	LAH	51	C2
ESTATE DR	LA	52	B6

COPYRIGHT © 1991 BY Thomas Bros Maps

1991 SANTA CLARA COUNTY STREET INDEX

STREET	CITY	PAGE	GRID
ESTATES CT	SJ	63	B1
ESTATES DR	SCCO	60	A5
ESTATES DR	SCCO	82A	C2
ESTATES DR E	CPTO	60	A5
ESTATES DR E	SCCO	60	A5
ESTATES DR W	SCCO	60	A5
ESTATE VIEW CT	SJ	63	D1
ESTATE VIEW WY	SJ	63	D1
ESTEBAN WY	SJ	72A	D3
ESTELLA DR	SCL	60	E4
ESTELLE AV	SJ	66	F5
ESTELLE AV	SJ	67	A5
ESTERLEE	S	64	E6
ESTHER AV	C	66	B2
ESTHER CT	SCCO	78G	D1
ESTHER CT	SJ	66	C6
ESTHER DR	SJ	71	C2
ESTHER DR	SCCO	66	C6
ESTHER DR	SCCO	71	C2
ESTONIA CT	SJ	72	E2
ESTRADA DR	MH	79	E4
ESTRADA TER	SVL	52	D3
ESTRADE DR	SJ	72	A2
ESTRALITA PL	LAH	51	B4
ESTRELLITA WY	C	65	E5
ESTRELLITA WY	LA	44	D6
ESTUDILLO RD	SCCO	45	F5
ETHAN CT	SJ	67	C4
ETHYL CT	MPTS	47	E3
ETHYL ST	MPTS	47	E3
ETON AV	SCCO	56	B6
ETON WY	SVL	60	B2
ETTERSBERG DR	SJ	72A	B2
EUCALYPTUS CT	SCL	53	D3
EUCALYPTUS DR	SJ	47	A4
EUCALYPTUS DR	SCCO	70	D3
EUCALYPTUS LN	LAH	51	C2
EUCALYPTUS RD	SCCO	43	F3
EUCALYPTUS RD	SCCO	44	A3
EUCLID AV	LG	70	D5
EUGENE AV	SJ	61	E4
EUGENE CT	SVL	59	D2
EUGENIA WY	LA	59	C2
EUGENIA WY	SCCO	71	A6
EULALIE DR	SJ	63	A6
EUNICE AV	MVW	52	C4
EUNICE AV	SCCO	52	C4
EUREKA AV	LA	52	B6
EUREKA CT	LA	52	B6
EUREKA CT	SVL	53	A2
EUROPE WY	SCL	60	C1
EVA AV	LA	59	B1
EVA CT	SJ	65	E4
EVA DR	SJ	68	A4
EVANDALE AV	MVW	45	D6
EVANGELINE CT	SJ	72	E4
EVANGELINE DR	SJ	72	E3
EVANS LN	SJ	67	B2
EVANS LN	SCCO	67	B2
EVANS LN	S	65	D6
EVANS RD	MPTS	40	B6
EVANS RD	MPTS	48	B1
EVCO CT	SJ	55	F3
EVELYN AV	SJ	63	A3
EVELYN AV	SCCO	52	C2
EVELYN AV	SVL	52	F3
EVELYN AV	SVL	53	A3
EVELYN AV E	MVW	52	C2
EVELYN TER	SVL	53	C4
EVELYN TER E	SVL	53	C4
EVELYN TER W	SVL	53	B4
EVEMARIE AV	LA	59	C1
EVENING SPG CT	CPTO	64	A6
EVENING STAR CT	MPTS	47	E5
EVERDALE CT	SJ	63	C4
EVERDALE DR	SJ	63	C4
EVERETT AV	C	66	B3
EVERETT AV	PA	37	F6
EVERETT AV	PA	38	A6
EVERETT AV	PA	43	F1
EVERETT AV	SJ	66	F2
EVERETT CT	PA	37	F6
EVERETT CT	PA	38	A6
EVERETT CT	PA	43	F1
EVERGLADE AV	SJ	62	F2
EVERGLADES DR	MPTS	48	C3
EVERGLOW CT	SJ	56	A6
EVERGLOW CT	SJ	63	A1
EVERGREEN DR	MH	79	D6
EVERGREEN DR	PA	44	E3
EVERGREEN WY	MPTS	47	F5
EVERGREEN WY	SJ	63	E6

STREET	CITY	PAGE	GRID
EVERMONT CT	SJ	63	B2
EVERSOLE DR	SJ	55	E3
EVERWOOD CT	SJ	63	B2
EVORA DR	SJ	66	D4
EVULICH CT	CPTO	59	D6
EWER DR	SJ	66	E6
EWER DR	SJ	71	E1
EXCALIBUR DR	SJ	55	F6
EXCALIBUR DR	SJ	56	A6
EXETER CT	SVL	59	F2
EXMOOR WY	SVL	60	B2
EZIE ST	SJ	67	F4
EZIE ST	SJ	68	A4
F			
F ST	SVL	46	C6
FABER PL	PA	38	E6
FABIAN DR	SJ	66	E4
FABIAN ST	PA	44	F4
FABIAN WY	PA	44	F3
FABLED OAK CT	SJ	63	E3
FAHRNER CT	SJ	63	E6
FAIR AV	SCCO	62	E4
FAIR LN	LG	70	E4
FAIRBANKS AV	C	66	B5
FAIRBROOK CT	SJ	55	D2
FAIRBROOK DR	MVW	52	C5
FAIRCHILD DR	MVW	45	D6
FAIRCLIFF CT	SJ	67	A4
FAIRCREST DR	SJ	71	B1
FAIRDELL DR	SJ	66	F4
FAIRFAX AV	SJ	63	C4
FAIRFAX CT	SJ	63	C4
FAIRFIELD AV	SCL	61	A2
FAIRFIELD CT	PA	44	E5
FAIRFORD WY	SJ	60	B6
FAIRGLEN DR	SJ	66	F3
FAIRGROVE CT	SJ	66	F4
FAIRHAVEN CT	MVW	52	B3
FAIRHAVEN CT	SJ	67	A5
FAIRHAVEN CT	SCCO	52	B3
FAIRHAVEN DR	SJ	67	A5
FAIR HILL DR	MPTS	48	B1
FAIRHILL LN	SJ	66	F3
FAIRLANDS AV	C	65	F5
FAIRLANDS AV	C	66	A5
FAIRLANDS CT	C	65	F5
FAIRLANDS CT	C	66	A5
FAIRLANE AV	SCL	60	E3
FAIRLAWN AV	SJ	66	F4
FAIRLAWN CT	SJ	66	F3
FAIRMEAD LN	LG	71	A3
FAIRMEDE AV	PA	44	D6
FAIRMONT AV	MVW	52	B2
FAIRMONT CT	SJ	63	D2
FAIRMONT DR	SJ	63	D2
FAIRMONT DR	SCCO	56	B2
FAIROAK CT	SJ	66	F4
FAIR OAKS AV	SVL	46	B6
FAIR OAKS AV	SVL	53	A3
FAIR OAKS ST	MVW	44	F6
FAIR OAKS ST	MVW	51	F1
FAIROAKS WY	SVL	46	B6
FAIRORCHARD AV	SJ	66	F4
FAIRPLACE CT	SJ	62	E4
FAIRVALLEY CT	SJ	66	F3
FAIRVIEW AV	LG	70	D4
FAIRVIEW AV	SJ	67	A2
FAIRVIEW DR	G	83	F3
FAIRVIEW LN	SCL	53	F5
FAIRVIEW PZ	LG	70	D5
FAIRVIEW WY	MPTS	47	E1
FAIRWAY CIR	MS	70	E1
FAIRWAY DR	SCCO	51	F6
FAIRWAY DR	SCCO	56	B3
FAIRWAY DR	SCCO	58	F1
FAIRWY ENTRN DR	SJ	55	B3
FAIRWAY GLEN DR	SCL	47	A6
FAIRWAY GLEN LN	SJ	72A	E4
FAIRWAY GRN CIR	SJ	55	B3
FAIRWEATHER LN	SJ	61	D6
FAIRWEATHER LN	SJ	66	D1
FAIRWOOD AV	SJ	66	F3
FAIRWOOD AV	SVL	53	D2
FAIRWOODS CT	CPTO	59	E5
FAITH CT	SJ	55	F3
FALCATO DR	MPTS	48	C3
FALCON AV	SVL	60	A1
FALCON CT	G	82	C5
FALCON CT	SVL	60	A1
FALERNO WY	SJ	63	E6

STREET	CITY	PAGE	GRID
FALKIRK CT	SVL	59	F2
FALL AV	SJ	56	C6
FALL CT	CPTO	59	E5
FALLBROOK AV	SJ	65	E3
FALLCREEK SPG CT	CPTO	64	A6
FALLEN LEAF DR	MPTS	47	F6
FALLENLEAF LN	CPTO	59	F6
FALLEN LEAF LN	LA	52	C6
FALLENLEAF LN	LA	59	C2
FALLENLEAF LN	SJ	59	F6
FALLEN OAK CT	SJ	63	D5
FALLEN OAK DR	SCCO	78L	B4
FALLINGTREE DR	SJ	55	B1
FALLING WATR CT	SCL	53	F2
FALLON AV	SCL	61	A2
FALL RIVER DR	SJ	72	C5
FALL RIVER TER	SVL	52	F5
FALLS CREEK CT	SJ	63	F6
FALLS CREEK DR	SJ	63	F6
FALLWOOD LN	SJ	48	B5
FALMOUTH CT	S	65	B3
FALMOUTH ST	SJ	48	D5
FALON WY	SJ	72A	B2
FAN ST	SJ	55	B4
FANCHER CT	LG	70	E3
FAN PALM CT	SCL	54	A4
FANTAIL CT	SVL	60	A2
FANWOOD CT	SJ	55	C4
FANYON ST	MPTS	48	B1
FARADAY CIR	SJ	71	E1
FARADAY CT	SJ	66	E6
FARADAY CT	SJ	71	E1
FARADAY CT	SCCO	66	E6
FARADAY DR	SJ	66	E6
FARADAY DR	SJ	71	E1
FARADAY PL	SJ	71	E1
FARALLON AV	MH	79	D5
FARALLONE DR	CPTO	59	F5
FARALLONE DR	CPTO	60	A5
FARAONE CT	SJ	67	D5
FARAONE DR	SJ	67	D5
FARGATE CIR	SJ	55	B4
FARGHER DR	SCL	53	E6
FARGO DR	CPTO	59	F3
FARGO DR	SCCO	59	F3
FARIS DR	SJ	68	B3
FARLEY RD	LG	70	F3
FARLEY RD	LG	71	A3
FARLEY RD	SCCO	71	A3
FARLEY ST	MVW	45	A6
FARM DR	SJ	67	C4
FARM RD	LA	59	B2
FARM WY	SJ	72	C4
FARMAN LN	SCCO	84	A4
FARMAN FRTG RD	SCCO	84	A4
FARMCREST ST	MPTS	48	D4
FARM HILL WY	LG	71	A1
FARM HILL WY	SJ	72	D4
FARNDON AV	LA	59	C2
FARNHAM CT	SJ	72B	A4
FARR CT	SJ	66	F1
FARRAGUT LN	SCCO	70	C3
FARRAGUT WY	SCCO	55	C3
FARRELL AV	SCCO	82	E5
FARRINGDON CT	SJ	63	B1
FARRINGDON DR	SJ	63	B1
FARR RANCH CT	S	64	E3
FARR RANCH RD	S	64	E2
FARTHING WY	SJ	48	D5
FAR VUE LN	SCCO	70	C4
FARWELL AV	S	65	B6
FARWELL AV	S	70	A1
FARWELL CT	S	70	B1
FARWELL LN	LG	70	D5
FATJO PL	SCL	53	F6
FAULSTICH CT	SJ	55	A4
FAUST CT	SJ	63	B5
FAWN CT	C	65	E5
FAWN DR	C	65	E5
FAWN DR	SJ	66	D6
FAWN TR	SCCO	78G	D2
FAWN CREEK CT	LAH	50	F3
FAWNDALE DR	SCCO	71	C5
FAWNWOOD CT	SJ	63	D4
FAY DR	SJ	66	E5
FAY WY	MVW	44	F5
FAY WY	MVW	45	A5
FAYE PARK DR	SJ	67	D5
FAYETTE DR	MVW	44	E6
FEBRUARY DR	SJ	72A	D1
FEDERATION CT	SJ	68	C6
FEDERATION CT	SJ	72A	B5
FEDORA CT	SJ	63	B5

STREET	CITY	PAGE	GRID
FEHREN DR	SJ	67	E3
FEHREN DR	SCCO	67	E3
FELDER DR	SJ	72A	B4
FELDSPAR DR	SJ	67	E1
FELIPE AV	SJ	62	E2
FELIPE AV	SCCO	62	E2
FELIX WY	SCCO	67	B1
FELIZ CT	MH	80	C3
FELL AV	SJ	67	C6
FELL CT	SJ	67	C6
FELLER AV	SJ	56	C5
FELLOM CT	G	82	F5
FELTER RD	SCCO	49	B2
FELTON WY	CPTO	59	F5
FENIAN DR	SJ	65	E4
FENLEY AV	SJ	61	A5
FENLEY AV	SCCO	61	A5
FENTON ST	SJ	55	F2
FENTON ST	SCCO	55	F2
FENWAY CT	CPTO	59	E4
FENWICK WY	SJ	63	C5
FERGUSON DR	MVW	52	D2
FERGUSON DR	SVL	52	D2
FERGUSON RD	SCCO	82A	D5
FERGUSON RD	SCCO	84	E1
FERGUSON WY	SJ	65	D2
FERN DR	SJ	71	E3
FERN DR	SCCO	78G	D1
FERNANDEZ CT	SCL	61	A3
FERNANDO AV	PA	44	C4
FERNBROOK CT	S	65	C2
FERNCREST CT	S	65	C5
FERNDALE AV	SVL	53	A1
FERNDALE CT	SJ	55	D4
FERNDALE DR	SJ	71	F2
FERNDALE WY	SJ	55	D4
FERNE AV	PA	44	E5
FERNE CT	PA	44	E5
FERNGLEN DR	SJ	72	D3
FERNGROVE DR	CPTO	60	B5
FERNHILL DR	LAH	58	E2
FERN HOLLOW CT	SJ	55	B3
FERNISH DR	SJ	63	D1
FERNLEAF DR	SVL	53	C5
FERN PINE CT	SJ	55	C4
FERN RIDGE CT	SVL	59	F2
FERNSIDE SQ	SJ	48	D5
FERNWOOD AV	SJ	61	B4
FERNWOOD CIR	SVL	53	A2
FERNWOOD CIR N	SVL	53	A2
FERNWOOD CIR S	SVL	53	A2
FERNWOOD CIR W	SVL	53	A2
FERNWOOD CT	S	65	C2
FERNWOOD LN	G	83	D2
FERRANT CT	SCCO	81	E3
FERRARI AV	SJ	54	E6
FERREIRA CT	MPTS	48	C3
FERREL CT	SJ	55	D1
FERRIS AV	LG	70	F4
FERRUM CT	SJ	63	E1
FERRY MORSE WY	MVW	52	C2
FESTIVAL CT	CPTO	59	E5
FESTIVAL DR	CPTO	59	E5
FETZER DR	SJ	66	D2
FEVER DR	SJ	72A	A3
FEWTRELL DR	C	66	D3
FEWTRELL DR	SCCO	66	D3
FIDDLERS GREEN	SJ	61	F6
FIDDLETOWN PL	SJ	72	B3
FIELDCREST DR	MPTS	48	C4
FIELDCREST DR	SJ	72A	C4
FIELDFAIR CT	SVL	60	A1
FIELDFAIR WY	SVL	60	A1
FIELDGATE CT	SJ	63	E4
FIELDING DR	PA	44	D2
FIELDS DR	SJ	65	D2
FIELDSHIRE WY	MH	80	A3
FIELDSTONE DR	S	64	E6
FIELDSTONE DR	S	69	D1
FIELDWOOD CT	SJ	75	F1
FIELDWOOD CT	SJ	76	A1
FIESTA LN	CPTO	59	E5
FIESTA WY	LG	70	E5
FIFE AV	PA	38	B6
FIFE WY	SJ	48	E5
FIFE WY	SVL	60	B2
FIFEWOOD CT	SJ	72	D5
FIG AV	SVL	52	D5
FIG GROVE CT	SJ	68	A6
FIG TREE CT	CPTO	60	A4
FIGWOOD CT	SJ	75	F1
FIGWOOD CT	SJ	76	A1
FIJI DR	SJ	55	E2

STREET	CITY	PAGE	GRID
FILBERT AV	C	65	F4
FILBRO DR	G	83	F3
FILICE DR	G	83	E2
FILIP RD	LA	51	F5
FILIP RD	LA	52	A5
FILLIPELLI DR	G	82	D6
FILLMER AV	LG	70	F4
FILLMORE ST	SCL	53	F1
FILLMORE ST	SCL	54	A6
FILOMENA AV	SJ	61	F1
FILOMENA CT	MVW	52	B5
FINCH AV	CPTO	60	B5
FINCH AV	SCCO	60	B5
FINCH DR	SJ	61	A6
FINCH DR	SJ	66	A1
FINCH WY	SVL	60	A2
FINCHWELL CT	SJ	72A	D2
FINCHWOOD WY	SJ	76	A1
FINDHORN CT	SJ	68A	C2
FINDLEY DR	MPTS	48	C2
FINE DR	G	82	C6
FINLEY RIDGE CT	SCCO	78B	A4
FINLEY RIDGE RD	SCCO	78A	F6
FINLEY RIDGE RD	SCCO	78B	A4
FINN LN	LAH	51	D6
FIR AV	SVL	53	B2
FIR LN	SCCO	59	B2
FIRCREST DR	SCCO	81	F3
FIREBIRD WY	SVL	60	A1
FIREFLY DR	SJ	72	B4
FIRESIDE DR	SJ	61	B6
FIRESIDE DR	SJ	66	B1
FIRESIDE DR	SCCO	61	B6
FIRESIDE DR	SCCO	66	B1
FIRETHORN CT	MPTS	39	E5
FIRETHORN ST	MPTS	39	E5
FIRETHORNE DR	CPTO	59	F2
FIREWOOD CT	SJ	72	F6
FIREWOOD CT	SJ	72A	A6
FIRLOCH AV	SVL	53	A4
FIRTH CT	SVL	60	C2
FIRTH WY	SJ	63	C6
FIR TREE CT	MPTS	47	E6
FIRWOOD DR	CPTO	59	B4
FISHBURNE AV	SJ	72	D2
FISHER AV	LG	70	F3
FISHER AV	SCCO	56	A4
FISHER AV	SCCO	80	B5
FISHER RD	SCCO	77	C3
FISHER HAWK DR	SVL	60	A1
FISK AV	SJ	61	F5
FISK AV	SJ	62	A5
FITCHVILLE AV	SJ	61	D6
FITCHVILLE AV	SJ	66	D1
FITZGERALD CT	SCCO	82	C2
FITZGERALD DR	CPTO	59	D4
FITZGERALD RD	SCCO	81A	D5
FITZGERALD RD	SCCO	82	C2
FIVE WOUNDS LN	SJ	62	C1
FLAGG AV	SCCO	61	C5
FLAGLER ST	SJ	55	F3
FLAGSTAD CT	SJ	63	A5
FLAGSTONE DR	SJ	55	D2
FLAMEWOOD AV	SVL	53	D2
FLAMINGO DR	C	66	D3
FLAMINGO WY	SVL	60	A1
FLAMING OAK LN	MH	80	D3
FLANDERS DR	SJ	55	E2
FLANIGAN DR	SJ	63	A5
FLANNERY ST	SCL	60	E3
FLATER DR	SJ	63	C5
FLAT ROCK CIR	SJ	68	A5
FLAX MOSS CT	SJ	72	B4
FLAXWOOD ST	SJ	72	C3
FLEDERMAUS CT	SJ	63	A5
FLEET ST	SJ	72	A3
FLEETWOOD DR	SJ	72	C4
FLEMING AV	SJ	56	C5
FLEMING AV	SCCO	56	B4
FLEMING CT	SCCO	56	B4
FLEUR DE LIS CT	SJ	55	E1
FLICKER WY	SVL	60	A2
FLICKINGER AV	SJ	55	B1
FLICKINGER CT	SJ	55	B1
FLICKINGER PL	SJ	55	B1
FLICKINGER WY	SJ	55	B1
FLIN WY	SVL	60	B2
FLINT AV	SJ	63	D2
FLINT CT	SJ	63	D2
FLINTBURY CT	SJ	63	C2
FLINT CREEK CT	SJ	63	D1
FLINT CREEK DR	SJ	63	D1

STREET	CITY	PAGE	GRID
FLINT CREEK WY	SJ	63	D1
FLINTCREST CT	SJ	63	C2
FLINTCREST DR	SJ	63	C2
FLINTDALE DR	SJ	63	C2
FLINTFIELD DR	SJ	63	D1
FLINTHAVEN DR	SJ	63	C2
FLINTHILL CT	SJ	63	D1
FLINTLOCK RD	SCCO	63F	E2
FLINTMONT CT	SJ	63	C2
FLINTMONT DR	SJ	63	C2
FLINTMORE CT	SJ	63	D1
FLINTRIDGE DR	LG	70	F2
FLINTSHIRE ST	CPTO	59	D6
FLINTSIDE CT	SJ	63	D2
FLINTVIEW CT	SJ	63	D3
FLINTWELL CT	SJ	72A	D1
FLINTWELL WY	SJ	72A	D2
FLINTWICK CT	SJ	63	D1
FLINTWOOD CT	SJ	63	D3
FLOOD DR	SJ	66	D4
FLORA AV	SJ	65	E1
FLORALES DR	PA	44	C5
FLORA VISTA AV	SCL	53	D6
FLORA VISTA AV	SCL	60	D1
FLORA VISTA AV	SCCO	59	E4
FLORA VISTA DR	SVL	52	F4
FLORA VISTA DR	SVL	53	A4
FLORENCE AV	SJ	56	A5
FLORENCE AV	SCCO	55	F5
FLORENCE AV	SCCO	56	A5
FLORENCE CT	MH	79	C4
FLORENCE CT	SJ	56	A5
FLORENCE DR	CPTO	59	D3
FLORENCE ST	PA	44	A1
FLORENCE ST	SVL	52	F4
FLORENCE WY	C	66	B5
FLORENCE WY	SJ	61	F4
FLORENCE WY	SJ	62	A4
FLORENCE ST	PA	43	F1
FLORENTINE DR	SJ	68	C6
FLORENTINE DR	SJ	72A	C1
FLORES	MVW	45	B4
FLORESTA DR	SJ	63	D2
FLORIDA AV	SJ	62	F3
FLORY DR	SJ	62	F5
FLORY DR	SJ	63	A5
FLOWER CT	CPTO	64	F1
FLOWER ST	SJ	65	E4
FLOWER GARDN LN	SJ	71	F3
FLWRING PEAR DR	CPTO	59	F2
FLWRING PLUM RD	SJ	72	C4
FLOWERS LN	PA	44	D3
FLOYD AV	SVL	60	A1
FLOYD ST	SJ	62	B5
FLUME CT	MPTS	47	F1
FLYNN AV	MVW	52	C1
FOLEY AV	SJ	62	E3
FOLEY AV	SCL	60	E1
FOLKESTONE DR	CPTO	59	E6
FOLKESTONE DR	CPTO	64	E1
FOLKLORE CT	SJ	72	D3
FOLSOM CIR	MPTS	47	F2
FOLSOM CT	MPTS	47	F2
FOLSOM DR	MPTS	47	F2
FOLSOM PL	MPTS	47	F2
FONICK DR	SJ	68	C5
FONTAINBLEU AV	MPTS	39	E6
FONTAINBLEU CT	MPTS	39	F6
FONTAINBLEU TER	LA	51	E2
FONTAINE DR	S	65	B4
FONTAINE RD	SJ	63	A5
FONTANA DR	SCL	60	F4
FONTANELLE CT	SJ	68	C5
FONTANELLE DR	SJ	68	C5
FONTANELLE PL	SJ	68	C4
FONTANOSO AV	SJ	68	E6
FONTANOSO WY	SJ	68	D6
FONTENBLEU	SVL	59	D1
FOOTE AV	C	66	C3
FOOTHILL AV	SCCO	80	D4
FOOTHILL AV	SCCO	81	E1
FOOTHILL AV	SCCO	81A	A6
FOOTHILL AV	SCCO	82A	A2
FOOTHILL BLVD	CPTO	59	C5
FOOTHILL BLVD	SCCO	59	C5
FOOTHILL CT	MH	79	E5
FOOTHILL CT	SJ	72	D3
FOOTHILL DR	SJ	72	D3
FOOTHILL EXPWY	LA	51	D2
FOOTHILL EXPWY	LA	59	B1
FOOTHILL EXPWY	PA	44	A6
FOOTHILL EXPWY	PA	51	D2

1991 SANTA CLARA COUNTY STREET INDEX

1991 SANTA CLARA COUNTY STREET INDEX

STREET	CITY	PAGE	GRID
GLACIER DR	SJ	67	A6
GLADDING CT	MPTS	48	A5
GLADE DR	SCL	53	D5
GLADIOLA DR	SVL	53	B5
GLADSTONE AV	SJ	66	E6
GLADSTONE AV	SJ	71	E1
GLADYS AV	MVW	52	C1
GLADYS WY	SJ	66	D4
GLAMORGAN CT	SJ	56	C5
GLASGOW CT	MPTS	47	F2
GLASGOW CT	SJ	56	C5
GLASGOW CT	S	64	F4
GLASGOW DR	S	65	A4
GLAUSER DR	SJ	55	E3
GLEASON AV	SJ	65	F1
GLEASON AV	SCCO	65	F1
GLEN AV	SCCO	78L	F3
GLEN CT	MPTS	39	B5
GLEN CT	MPTS	40	C6
GLEN CT	MPTS	47	D2
GLEN CT	MPTS	48	C1
GLEN DR	SJ	66	E2
GLEN DR	SCCO	66	E2
GLEN PARKWAY	G	83	D3
GLEN PL	CPTO	59	E4
GLENA CT	SJ	62	F4
GLEN ALDEN CT	SJ	63	C3
GLEN ALMA WY	SJ	63	C3
GLEN ALTO CT	SJ	63	D4
GLEN ALTO DR	LA	51	F4
GLEN AMADOR CT	SJ	63	C4
GLEN ANGUS WY	SJ	63	C3
GLEN ARBOR CT	S	65	A3
GLEN ASCOT WY	SJ	63	C3
GLEN AYRE DR	MH	79	B4
GLENBAR AV	SVL	60	C2
GLENBLAIR WY	C	65	F5
GLENBOROUGH DR	MVW	52	C3
GLEN BRAE CT	S	64	F4
GLENBRAE DR	SJ	65	D4
GLEN BRAE DR	S	64	F4
GLEN BRAE DR	S	65	A4
GLENBRAE LN	SJ	72	B1
GLEN BROOK AV	SJ	61	E6
GLENBROOK DR	PA	44	D6
GLENBURRY WY	SJ	72	D1
GLENCO DR	SCCO	59	E4
GLENCOE CT	SVL	60	A1
GLEN COMO WY	SJ	63	C3
GLEN COTSWLD CT	SJ	63	C3
GLEN CRAIG CT	SJ	63	C3
GLENCREST CT	SJ	66	F6
GLENCREST DR	SJ	66	F6
GLENCREST DR	SJ	67	A6
GLENCREST WY	SJ	66	F6
GLEN CROW CT	SJ	63	C3
GLENDALE AV	SVL	53	B1
GLENDALE DR	SJ	72A	C2
GLEN DARBY CT	SJ	63	C3
GLEN DECKER CT	SJ	63	C3
GLEN DELL DR	SJ	66	F1
GLENDENNING AV	SCL	61	A3
GLEN DONEGAL DR	SJ	63	C3
GLEN DOON CT	SJ	63	B3
GLENDORA CT	SJ	72	E3
GLEN DUFF WY	SJ	63	C3
GLEN DUNDEE CT	SJ	63	C3
GLEN DUNDEE WY	SJ	63	C3
GLEN ECHO AV	MS	70	D3
GLEN ECHO AV	SJ	61	E6
GLEN ECHO AV	SJ	66	E1
GLENEDEN WY	SJ	61	B6
GLEN ELK CT	SJ	63	C3
GLEN ELLEN WY	SJ	66	F2
GLEN ELM CT	SJ	63	C3
GLEN EVANS CT	SJ	63	C3
GLEN EXETER WY	SJ	63	C3
GLEN EYRIE AV	SJ	61	E6
GLEN EYRIE AV	SJ	66	E1
GLEN FALL CT	SJ	63	C3
GLEN FARM CT	SJ	63	C3
GLEN FENTON WY	SJ	63	C4
GLEN FERGSN CIR	SJ	63	C3
GLENFIELD DR	SJ	66	F4
GLENFINNAN CT	SJ	62	E4
GLENFINNAN DR	SJ	62	E4
GLEN FIRTH DR	SJ	55	E3
GLENFORD PK CT	SJ	67	E5
GLEN FOX CT	SJ	63	C3
GLEN FROST CT	SJ	63	C3
GLENGARRY DR	SJ	68	D1
GLENGROVE WY	SJ	68	C1
GLEN HAIG WY	SJ	63	C3
GLEN HANCOCK CT	SJ	63	C3
GN HANLEIGH DR	SJ	63	B3
GLEN HARBOR DR	SJ	72A	B3
GLEN HARDY CT	SJ	63	C3
GLEN HARWICK CT	SJ	63	C3
GLEN HASTNGS CT	SJ	63	C3
GLEN HAVEN CT	SJ	65	C1
GLEN HAVEN DR	SJ	65	C1
GLEN HAWKINS CT	SJ	63	C3
GLEN HEATHER DR	SJ	55	E3
GLEN HEDGE CT	SJ	63	C3
GLENHURST DR	SJ	66	F5
GLEN IAN CT	SJ	63	C3
GLEN KEATS CT	SJ	63	C3
GLENKIRK CT	SJ	66	E3
GLENKIRK DR	SJ	66	E3
GLEN LAKE CIR	MH	79	E5
GLEN LOMAN WY	SJ	63	B3
GLEN MEAD CT	SJ	55	E3
GLEN MEADOW CT	SJ	66	F1
GLENMONT DR	SJ	67	C5
GLENMONT DR	S	64	F6
GLENMOOR CIR	MPTS	47	D1
GLENMOOR CT	MPTS	47	D1
GLENMOOR WY	SJ	65	A1
GLENN AV	C	66	A4
GLENN AV	SJ	61	F6
GLENN AV	SJ	66	F1
GLENNAN CT	SJ	65	C1
GLENOAK CT	SJ	65	C1
GLENPARK DR	SJ	67	C5
GLEN PINE DR	SJ	66	F1
GLEN RIDGE AV	LG	70	D4
GLENRIDGE DR	SJ	67	C5
GLENRIO DR	SJ	63	D5
GLENROCK CT	SJ	71	E4
GLENROY DR	SJ	66	F5
GLEN SHARON WY	SJ	63	C3
GLENSIDE DR	SJ	72	E3
GLENSTONE CT	SJ	68	C1
GLENTREE CT	SJ	60	D5
GLENTREE DR	SJ	60	D5
GLEN UNA AV	SJ	67	A1
GLEN UNA DR	SCCO	70	B2
GLEN UNA DR	S	70	B2
GLEN UNA DR	SJ	70	B2
GLENVIEW AV	CPTO	60	A5
GLENVIEW CT	G	83	F3
GLENVIEW CT	MPTS	48	C3
GLENVIEW DR	G	83	F3
GLENVIEW DR	MPTS	48	C3
GLENVIEW DR	SJ	72	D6
GLENVILLE DR	SJ	66	F6
GLEN WILLOW CT	SJ	62	D5
GLENWOOD AV	SJ	66	F1
GLENWOOD CT	MVW	52	B3
GLENWOOD RD	G	82	E6
GLIDER DR	SJ	72A	A4
GLITHERO CT	SJ	55	B6
GLORIA AV	SCCO	56	B5
GLORIA CT	SCCO	78G	D1
GLORIETTA CIR	SCL	60	E3
GLOUCESTER CT	SVL	60	C2
GLOUCHESTER CT	SJ	67	E6
GLOWING CT	SJ	72	A4
GNARLED OAK LN	MH	80	D3
GOBLE LN	SJ	67	D2
GODDESS CT	SJ	65	B1
GODFREY AV	SCCO	82A	E5
GOEBEL AV	PA	44	D5
GOEBEL CT	SCCO	78G	D2
GOLD ST	SJ	46	E3
GOLD CREEK CT	SJ	75	F2
GOLD CREEK WY	SJ	75	F2
GOLDEN DR	SJ	65	D1
GOLDEN WY	LA	52	A5
GOLDEN WY	MVW	52	A5
GOLDEN ACRE CT	SJ	67	B5
GOLDEN ASPEN WY	CPTO	59	F2
GOLDEN CK TER	SJ	68	D3
GOLDEN DEW CIR	SJ	63	D6
GOLDEN GATE AV	SCCO	82	D3
GOLDEN GATE DR	SJ	59	F6
GOLDEN GATE DR	SJ	60	A6
GOLDEN GATE DR	SJ	64	F1
GOLDEN GATE DR	SJ	65	A1
GOLDEN HILL CT	LAH	51	C4
GOLDEN HILLS DR	MPTS	48	B2
GOLDEN LAKE RD	SJ	55	B2
GOLDEN LEAF CT	SJ	67	E5
GOLDEN MDW SQ	SJ	66	A1
GOLDEN OAK CT	SVL	53	A5
GOLDEN OAK DR	SVL	53	A5
GOLDEN OAK WY	SJ	72	B3
GOLDEN RAIN CT	SJ	68	B5
GOLDEN RAIN DR	SJ	68	B5
GOLDENROD CT	SVL	53	B5
GOLDEN STATE DR	SCL	60	D2
GOLDENTREE DR	SJ	55	B1
GOLDFIELD DR	SJ	72A	A1
GOLDFINCH WY	SVL	60	A2
GOLDPINE CT	SJ	75	D1
GOLDPINE WY	SJ	72	D6
GOLDRIDGE CT	SJ	63	D5
GOLD RUN WY	SJ	67	F4
GOLDRUSH CT	SJ	55	B2
GOLD VIEW DR	SCCO	56	A2
GOLDWOOD CT	SJ	63	D3
GOLETA AV	S	65	A3
GOLETA CT	S	65	A3
GOLF CT	MVW	52	C4
GOLF DR	SJ	55	F3
GOLF DR	SCCO	55	F3
GOLF DR	SCCO	56	A2
GOLF LN	SCCO	43	D6
GOLF COURSE LN	SJ	72A	E4
GOLF CREEK DR	SJ	72	C6
GOLF LINKS CIR	SCL	60	F3
GOLF LINKS CIR	SCL	61	A3
GOLF LINKS DR	LG	65	E6
GOLF LINKS DR	LG	70	F1
GOLF LINKS DR	SCCO	70	F1
GOLZIO CT	SJ	55	D3
GOMES CT	C	66	B2
GOMES DR	SJ	55	D1
GONDOLA WY	SJ	72	B4
GONZAGA PL	SCL	53	D5
GOODFELLOW WY	SVL	53	C5
GOODWIN AV	SJ	61	D6
GOODY LN	SJ	55	A3
GOODYEAR ST	SJ	62	B5
GOOSEBERRY CT	SVL	52	D6
GORDOLA CT	SJ	68	A4
GORDON AV	SCL	53	D4
GORDON AV	SCCO	55	F2
GORDON AV	SCCO	56	A4
GORDON CT	S	64	F3
GORDON ST	MPTS	39	F6
GORDON ST	MPTS	47	F1
GORDON WY	LA	51	E3
GORDY DR	SJ	55	B3
GORSKY RD	SCCO	45	D5
GOSFORD CT	SJ	72B	A4
GOSSER ST	MPTS	39	F5
GOULARTE WY	SJ	55	E6
GOULD CT	SCCO	81	F5
GOULD LN	SCCO	79	E1
GOVERNORS AV	SCCO	43	E3
GOWER DR	SJ	71	F2
GOYA DR	SVL	52	F5
GOYA DR	SVL	53	A5
GRACE AV	SCCO	66	D2
GRACE CT	SCCO	66	D2
GRACKLE WY	SYL	60	A2
GRADELL PL	SJ	63	D2
GRAFTON WY	SJ	63	E3
GRAHAM LN	SCL	53	F6
GRAHAM ST	SJ	62	B5
GRAMERCY CT	SCCO	55	E5
GRAMERCY PL	SJ	55	E5
GRANADA AV	CPTO	59	D4
GRANADA AV	SCL	60	D1
GRANADA CT	SCL	60	D1
GRANADA CT	S	64	E2
GRANADA DR	MVW	45	A6
GRANADA ST	CPTO	59	D4
GRANADA WY	LG	65	E6
GRANADA WY	LG	70	E1
GRANADA WY	SJ	62	E4
GRAND AV	SJ	61	E4
GRAND AV	SCCO	61	E4
GRAND AV	CPTO	59	D4
GRAND BLVD	SJ	46	F3
GRANDBROOK WY	SJ	68	B2
GRANDBY DR	SJ	65	D4
GRAND COULEE AV	SVL	59	E2
GRAND FIR AV	SVL	53	A5
GRANDIN CT	SJ	72A	A2
GRAND MEADOW LN	SCCO	68A	B4
GRANDPARK CIR	SJ	67	E5
GRAND PRIX WY	MH	79	E4
GRAND TETON DR	MPTS	48	C3
GRANDVIEW AV	MS	70	D3
GRANDVIEW DR	MS	70	D3
GRANDVIEW DR	SJ	55	E3
GRANDWELL WY	SJ	72A	D1
GRANDWOOD WY	SJ	76	A1
GRANGER AV	LA	59	B1
GRANGER TER	SVL	59	F2
GRANITE CT	S	70	B1
GRANITE LN	SJ	55	D4
GRANITE WY	SJ	55	D4
GRANITE WY	S	70	B1
GRANITE CK PL	SJ	56	A6
GRANITE ROCK WY	SJ	67	E3
GRANT AV	PA	44	B3
GRANT CT	G	82A	A6
GRANT CT	LA	52	B6
GRANT RD	LA	52	B4
GRANT RD	LA	59	C2
GRANT RD	MVW	52	C5
GRANT RD	SCCO	52	B4
GRANT RD	SCCO	59	C2
GRANT ST	C	66	B2
GRANT ST	SJ	62	A4
GRANT ST	SCL	54	B5
GRANT PARK LN	LA	59	C2
GRANVILLE CT	SJ	72A	F5
GRAPE AV	SVL	52	D5
GRAPELEAF WY	SJ	63	F6
GRAPEVINE WY	SJ	72	C5
GRAPNEL PL	CPTO	59	E3
GRASS VALLEY CT	SJ	56	C6
GRAVES AV	SJ	65	D2
GRAYS LN	LG	70	E4
GRAYSON WY	MPTS	39	F6
GRAYSON WY	MPTS	40	A6
GRAYSON WY	MPTS	47	F1
GRAYSON WY	MPTS	48	A1
GRAYSTONE LN	SCCO	72	E5
GRAYWOOD DR	SJ	65	B2
GRT AMERICA PKY	SCL	46	E6
GRT AMERICA PKY	SCL	53	E1
GREATHOUSE DR	MPTS	39	F5
GREAT OAKS BLVD	SJ	72A	E3
GREAT OAKS DR	SJ	68	C5
GRECIA CT	SJ	55	D5
GRECO AV	SVL	56	F6
GREEN CT	PA	44	C2
GREEN ACRES CT	SCCO	80K	B1
GREENBANK CT	SJ	72	B1
GREENBAY CT	SJ	66	C1
GREENBRIAR AV	SJ	61	B6
GREENBRIAR AV	SJ	66	B1
GREENBRIAR CT	SJ	66	B1
GREENBROOK CT	S	65	C2
GREEN CREEK DR	SJ	66	D3
GREENDALE DR	LG	71	A2
GREENDALE WY	SJ	60	E5
GREENE DR	SJ	65	C2
GREENFIELD PL	LG	65	F6
GREENFIELD PL	LG	70	F1
GREENFORD CT	SJ	63	E5
GREENGATE DR	SJ	55	C1
GREEN GLEN CT	SJ	61	E6
GREEN HILL WY	LG	71	A2
GREEN HILL WY	SJ	63	E6
GREEN HILLS CT	LAH	51	C6
GREENLAKE DR	SVL	53	B1
GREENLAND WY	SJ	63	E5
GREENLEAF DR	CPTO	59	F3
GREENLEAF DR	SCCO	59	F3
GREENLEAF LN	SJ	63	D6
GREENLEE DR	SJ	60	F5
GREENLEE DR	SJ	61	A5
GREENMEADOW LN	S	64	F3
GREENMEADOW WY	PA	44	E5
GREENMEADOW WY	SJ	65	E5
GREENMOOR DR	SJ	67	B5
GREENOAK DR	SJ	60	C6
GREEN OAK LN	LA	59	B1
GREENPARK WY	SJ	67	E5
GREENRIDGE TER	LG	71	C3
GREENROCK RD	MPTS	48	D3
GREENSBORO CT	SJ	55	B2
GREENSIDE DR	SCCO	56	A2
GREENSTONE CT	SJ	63	A2
GREENTREE CIR	MPTS	47	F5
GREENTREE WY	MPTS	47	F5
GREENTREE WY	SJ	61	B6
GREENTREE WY	SJ	66	B1
GREEN VALLEY DR	SCCO	82	F2
GREENVIEW CT	SCCO	51	F6
GREENVIEW DR	MVW	52	C4
GREENWICH AV	SVL	52	E5
GREENWICH CT	SJ	66	D1
GREENWICH DR	G	83	F3
GREENWICH DR	PA	44	C2
GREENWOOD AV	MS	70	C3
GREENWOOD AV	MH	79	A5
GREENWOOD AV	PA	38	B6
GREENWOOD AV	PA	44	B1
GREENWOOD AV	SJ	61	D2
GREENWOOD CIR	MH	79	C1
GREENWOOD CT	CPTO	60	B5
GREENWOOD DR	CPTO	60	B5
GREENWOOD DR	SCL	54	B2
GREENWOOD DR	SCCO	78G	E2
GREENWOOD LN	MS	70	C3
GREENWOOD LN	SCCO	70	C3
GREENWOOD RD	MS	70	C3
GREENWOOD WY	MPTS	47	F5
GREER RD	PA	38	C6
GREER RD	PA	44	E2
GREER RD	PA	58	C6
GREG CT	SCCO	82	D1
GREGG CT	LG	71	D2
GREGG DR	SJ	71	D3
GREGORY PL	MS	70	D2
GREGORY ST	SJ	61	F5
GREMLIN CT	SJ	67	F3
GRENACHE CT	SJ	68A	B3
GRENADINE WY	SJ	62	E4
GRENOLA DR	SCCO	59	E3
GRESHAM AV	SVL	53	A2
GRESHAM CT	SJ	72A	F5
GRESHAM CT	SVL	53	B2
GRETCHEN LN	SJ	60	E6
GRETEL LN	MVW	52	B4
GREY CT	SJ	71	B2
GREY FEATHR CIR	SJ	68	D5
GREY GHOST AV	SJ	68	C5
GREY GHOST CT	MH	81	A3
GREYLANDS DR	SJ	66	D2
GRIDLEY CT	SJ	55	F3
GRIDLEY ST	SJ	55	F3
GRIDLEY ST	SJ	56	A3
GRIDLEY ST	SCCO	55	F2
GRIFFIS WY	SCCO	80K	B3
GRIFFITH LN	C	66	B4
GRIFFITH PL	LG	70	E3
GRIFFITH ST	SCCO	56	B6
GRIMLEY LN	SCCO	75	F2
GRIMMWAY CT	MH	80	C3
GRIMSBY CT	SJ	65	D3
GRIMSBY DR	SJ	65	D3
GRIMSWOOD CT	SJ	76	A1
GRINNELL CT	SCL	60	C3
GRISWOLD LN	SCCO	80K	D2
GRIZILO DR	SJ	66	E5
GROESBCK HLL RD	SJ	63	E2
GRONWALL CT	SCOO	51	F6
GRONWALL LN	SCCO	51	F6
GROSBEAK AV	SVL	60	B2
GROSS ST	MPTS	39	F5
GROSSMONT DR	SJ	55	F1
GROSVENOR CT	MS	70	E2
GROSVENOR DR	SJ	48	D5
GROTH CT	SJ	67	E3
GROTH CT	SJ	68	E4
GROTH DR	SJ	67	E3
GROTH DR	SJ	68	E4
GROTH PL	SJ	67	E3
GROTH PL	SJ	68	E4
GROTON CT	SVL	52	E5
GROUSE WY	SJ	55	D4
GROVE AV	PA	44	E3
GROVE CT	PA	44	E3
GROVE ST	SCCO	70	F5
GROVETREE CT	SJ	55	B2
GROVEWOOD CT	SJ	75	F1
GRUBER CT	SJ	72A	F4
GRUWELL PL	SJ	60	E6
GUADALAJARA CT	SJ	71	F4
GUADALAJARA DR	SJ	71	F4
GUADALUPE AV	SJ	62	B6
GUADALUPE AV	SJ	67	B1
GUADALUPE AV	SCCO	62	B6
GUADALUPE AV	SCCO	67	B1
GUADALUPE DR	LA	51	D2
GUADALUPE PKWY	SJ	54	D5
GUADALUPE PKWY	SJ	61	F1
GUADALUP MNS CT	SJ	71	F5
GUADALUP MNS RD	SJ	71	F5
GUADALUP MNS RD	SCCO	71	F6
GUANACASTE CT	SCCO	55	D5
GUANDABERT LN	SJ	67	D6
GUANDABERT LN	SCCO	67	C6
GUAVA CT	S	65	A3
GUAVA BLOSSM DR	SJ	68	C3
GUAYMAS CT	G	82	C5
GUERRA CT	SJ	62	E6
GUERRA DR	SJ	62	E6
GUERRERO CT	MPTS	48	B1
GUIBAL AV	SCCO	81A	A6
GUIBAL AV	SCCO	82A	A1
GUIFRIDA CT	SJ	72	F1
GUIFRIDA CT	SJ	72A	A1
GUILDFORD PL	SJ	63	E6
GUILDHALL DR	SJ	48	B5
GUINDA ST	PA	38	A6
GUINDA ST	PA	44	B1
GULLO AV	SJ	60	D6
GULLO AV	SCCO	60	D6
GULUZZO DR	SJ	63	D2
GUMDROP DR	SJ	63	D3
GUM TREE DR	SJ	68	D3
GUM TREE LN	LG	71	B4
GUNAR DR	SJ	66	D4
GUNDERSEN DR	SJ	66	E3
GUNN CT	SJ	56	B5
GUNSTON WY	SJ	71	D1
GUNTER WY	SJ	72	F4
GUNTHER CT	S	65	B3
GURNEY CT	SJ	55	E1
GURRIES DR	G	82	F6
GURRIES DR	G	83	F1
GUSTAFUS DR	SCCO	82A	E3
GWEN DR	C	65	E4
GWINN AV	SCCO	81	F4
GWINN AV	SCCO	81A	A3
GWINN CT	SJ	68	C5
GYPSEY HILL RD	S	70	C1
GYPSY AV	SCCO	81A	A4
GYPSY PLACE CT	SJ	68	C1
H			
H ST	SVL	46	C6
HABBITTS CT	SJ	67	E1
HACIENDA AV	C	65	F5
HACIENDA AV	C	66	A5
HACIENDA AV	SJ	65	E5
HACIENDA AV	SCCO	65	F5
HACIENDA CT	C	65	E5
HACIENDA CT	LA	51	D2
HACIENDA DR	G	83	E1
HACIENDA DR	SJ	54	F1
HACIENDA WY	LA	51	D2
HACK AV	C	65	F5
HACKETT AV	MVW	45	A6
HADEOCK CT	SJ	48	C6
HADLEY AV	SJ	61	D3
HADLEY CT	G	84	A1
HAGA DR	SJ	67	F2
HAGA DR	SCCO	67	F3
HAGA WY	SCCO	67	F3
HAGEN CT	G	83	E2
HAGER CT	SCCO	81	E4
HAIG ST	SCL	54	B2
HAINES AV	SJ	67	D5
HAINES PL	SCL	53	D6
HALBREATH CT	SJ	63	C6
HALE AV	MH	79	D3
HALE AV	SCCO	79	A1
HALE PL	CPTO	59	E3
HALE ST	PA	38	A6
HALEY CT	SJ	72A	A4
HALF RD	MH	79	F2
HALF RD	SCCO	79	F2
HALF CROWN LN	SJ	48	D5
HALF MOON CT	SJ	67	F2
HALFORD AV	SCL	53	C6
HALFORD AV	SCL	60	C1
HALF PENCE CT	SJ	48	D5
HALF PENCE WY	SJ	48	D5
HALGRIM CT	SJ	55	E1
HALIFAX DR	SJ	65	D4
HALKINS DR	SJ	71	B1
HALL CT	CPTO	60	A5
HALLADALE CT	SJ	68A	C3
HALLBROOK DR	SJ	66	F6
HALLBROOK DR	SJ	67	A6
HALLCREST DR	SJ	66	F6
HALLCREST DR	SJ	67	A6
HALLECK DR	SJ	72	D2
HALLMARK LN	SJ	66	E6
HALSEY AV	SCCO	61	C4
HAMANN DR	SJ	60	F5
HAMIDA CT	SJ	72	D6
HAMILTON AV	C	65	E2
HAMILTON AV	C	66	B2

STREET	CITY	PAGE	GRID
HOGUE CT	CPTO	60	A4
HOGUE CT	SCCO	81	E4
HOITING DR	SJ	63	E3
HOKETT WY	SJ	72	F3
HOLBROOK PL	SVL	52	E5
HOLDEN CT	SCCO	71	D1
HOLDEN WY	SCCO	71	D1
HOLDERMAN DR	SJ	63	D2
HOLGATE AV	SJ	72A	B3
HOLIDAY CT	MH	80	B1
HOLIDAY CT	S	65	C4
HOLIDAY DR	MH	80	B1
HOLIDAY DR	SCCO	80	C1
HOLIDAY DR	S	65	C4
HOLIN ST	SJ	55	B4
HOLISTER AV	SVL	52	E2
HOLLAND CT	MVW	52	B4
HOLLAND CT	SJ	72	B3
HOLLAND LN	SJ	72	A2
HOLLANDERRY PL	CPTO	59	F6
HOLLANDERRY PL	CPTO	64	F1
HOLLENBECK AV	SCCO	52	E5
HOLLENBECK AV	SCCO	59	E2
HOLLENBECK AV	SVL	52	E5
HOLLENBECK AV	SVL	59	E2
HOLLERAN CT	SJ	48	D5
HOLLIDALE CT	LA	59	C2
HOLLINGSWRTH DR	MVW	51	F2
HOLLINGSWRTH DR	MVW	52	A2
HOLLIS AV	C	66	A4
HOLLOWAY RD	G	84	B2
HOLLOWCREEK CT	SJ	68	D3
HOLLOWCREEK PL	SJ	68	D3
HOLLOWGATE LN	SJ	71	F1
HOLLOW LAKE WY	SJ	75	D1
HOLLOW PARK CT	SJ	75	E1
HOLLOW TREE WY	SJ	75	E1
HOLLY AV	LA	52	A6
HOLLY CT	G	83	D2
HOLLY DR	SCCO	55	F2
HOLLY DR	SCCO	56	A2
HOLLY LN	SJ	67	D4
HOLLY WY	MPTS	48	C3
HOLLY ANN PL	SJ	72	D6
HOLLY BERRY CT	CPTO	60	B3
HOLLY BERRY CT	SJ	60	D5
HOLLY BRANCH CT	SCL	53	D3
HOLLY BRANCH CT	SCL	54	A4
HOLLYCREST DR	LG	71	A2
HOLLYHEAD LN	SJ	59	E6
HOLLYHEAD LN	SJ	64	E1
HOLLY HILL DR	SJ	62	E4
HOLLY HILL WY	LG	70	F2
HOLLY HILL WY	LG	71	A2
HOLLY HOCK CT	SJ	60	F4
HOLLY HOCK CT	SJ	61	A4
HOLLYHOCK LN	G	82	C6
HOLLYLEAF LN	SJ	72	A2
HOLLY OAK CIR	SJ	72	C4
HOLLY OAK DR	CPTO	59	E5
HOLLY OAK DR	PA	44	D3
HOLLYTREE LN	CPTO	59	F3
HOLLYWOOD AV	LG	70	F5
HOLLYWOOD AV	SJ	62	C5
HOLMES AV	SCCO	66	B6
HOLMES DR	SCCO	56	B3
HOLMES LN	SCCO	56	B3
HOLSCLAW RD	SCCO	82A	C6
HOLSCLAW RD	SCCO	84	C1
HOLSCLAW ST	SCCO	82A	C5
HOLSTON RIV CT	SJ	67	D5
HOLT AV	LA	59	C2
HOLY CITY RD	SCCO	78G	E1
HOLYCON CIR	SJ	67	F5
HOLYOKE CT	S	65	B3
HOME ST W	SJ	61	F4
HOME CREST DR	SJ	63	B2
HOME GATE DR	SJ	63	B2
HOMELAND CT	SJ	54	E5
HOMEPARK CT	SJ	68	D1
HOMER AV	PA	38	A6
HOMER AV	PA	43	F2
HOMER AV	PA	44	A1
HOMER AV	PA	44	C2
HOMERITE DR	SJ	66	D6
HOMERITE DR	SCCO	66	D6
HOMES DR	S	65	B3
HOMESTEAD CT	CPTO	59	C2
HOMESTEAD RD	CPTO	59	D2
HOMESTEAD RD	CPTO	60	A2
HOMESTEAD RD	LA	59	D2
HOMESTEAD RD	SJ	72A	D2
HOMESTEAD RD	SCL	60	D2
HOMESTEAD RD	SCL	61	A2
HOMESTEAD RD	SCCO	59	D2
HOMESTEAD RD	SCCO	60	D2
HOMESTEAD RD	SVL	59	D2
HOMESTEAD RD	SVL	60	A2
HOMEWOOD DR	SJ	61	B3
HOMME WY	MPTS	39	E6
HONEYBEE CT	SCCO	82H	E1
HONEYCOMB LN	SCCO	82H	E1
HONEYDALE CT	SJ	68	B2
HONEYSUCKLE DR	SJ	65	A4
HONEY SUCKLE LN	SJ	67	D4
HONEYSUCKLE PL	LA	59	C3
HONEYWOOD CT	SJ	76	A1
HONFLEUR CT	SVL	59	D2
HONFLEUR DR	SVL	59	D2
HONG KONG DR	SJ	55	A2
HONOLULU CT	SJ	68	C3
HONOLULU DR	SJ	68	A3
HONOLULU DR	SCCO	68	A3
HOOD CT	SCL	53	D6
HOO HOO CT	CPTO	59	C4
HOOKE LN	LG	65	F6
HOOPER LN	LAH	58	E1
HOOSHANG CT	CPTO	59	E5
HOOT OWL WY	SCCO	80	C1
HOOVER AV	SJ	61	E3
HOOVER CT	G	84	A1
HOOVER CT	SCL	53	F6
HOOVER DR	SCL	53	F6
HOPE DR	SCL	47	A6
HOPE DR	SCL	54	A1
HOPE ST	MVW	52	B2
HOPE ST	SJ	46	E3
HOPE ST	SCCO	67	E2
HOPE TER	SVL	59	F2
HOPETON AV	SJ	62	F5
HOPETON CT	SJ	62	F5
HOPI CIR	SJ	72	F4
HOPI CIR	SJ	72A	A4
HOPI CT	SJ	72	F4
HOPKINS AV	PA	44	B1
HOPKINS DR	SJ	62	F2
HOPKINS DR	SJ	63	A2
HOPPE ST	AVSO	46	E3
HORACE AV	SJ	66	C4
HORCAJO CIR	MPTS	40	A6
HORCAJO ST	MPTS	40	A6
HORCAJO ST	MPTS	48	A1
HORIZON AV	MVW	52	B1
HORNBEAM WY	SJ	68	D3
HORNBLOWER CT	SJ	67	D5
HORNING ST	SJ	54	F6
HORNING ST	SJ	55	A5
HORNLEIN CT	G	84	A2
HORSESHOE CT	LAH	51	A2
HORSESHOE CT	SCCO	81	D2
HORSESHOE CT	S	65	A6
HORSESHOE DR	S	65	A6
HORSESHOE DR	S	70	A1
HORSESHOE LN	LAH	51	A2
HORSESHOE LN	SCCO	51	A2
HORWEDEL DR	SJ	63	D5
HOSKINS CT	SCCO	44	A3
HOSPITAL DR	MVW	52	B5
HOSPITAL PKWY	SJ	72A	C3
HOSTA LN	SJ	71	E4
HOSTETTER RD	SJ	48	D5
HOSTETTER RD	SCCO	55	B2
HOUGHTON CT	SJ	55	B2
HOULTON CT	SJ	72A	F4
HOUNDSBROOK WY	SJ	68	A3
HOUNDS ESTATES	SJ	68A	A2
HOUNDSHAVEN WY	SJ	68	A4
HOUNSLOW DR	SJ	55	C2
HOURET CT	MPTS	47	F6
HOURET DR	MPTS	47	F6
HOUSTON CT	S	64	F4
HOWARD AV	G	82	D6
HOWARD DR	SCL	60	C4
HOWARD ST	SJ	61	F2
HOWDEN CT	SJ	72A	F3
HOWELL AV	SCL	60	E3
HOWELL LN	SCCO	81A	C5
HOWEN DR	S	65	A5
HOWES CT	LG	71	D2
HOWES DR	LG	71	D2
HOWES LN	SJ	71	F2
HOWSON ST	G	82	F6
HOXETT ST	G	83	F2
HOYET DR	SJ	65	D1
HUBBARD AV	SCL	60	C3
HUBBARD WY	SCCO	56	B3
HUBBART DR	PA	44	C6
HUBBELL WY	LG	70	E4
HUCKLEBERRY CT	SVL	52	D6
HUDDERSFIELD CT	SJ	61	E6
HUDSON DR	SJ	66	E4
HUDSON DR	SCL	60	C3
HUDSON PL	G	83	F2
HUDSON WY	SVL	52	D5
HUERTO CT	SJ	66	C1
HUERTO DR	SJ	66	C1
HUFF AV	MVW	45	B4
HUFF AV	SJ	61	B5
HUGO LN	SJ	67	A5
HULA DR	SJ	67	E4
HULET ST	SJ	61	F4
HULET ST	SJ	62	A4
HULL AV	SJ	61	F5
HULL AV	SJ	62	A5
HULME CT	SCCO	44	A3
HUMBER CT	SVL	59	F2
HUMBERSIDE CT	SJ	63	E5
HUMBOLDT AV	SCL	60	E1
HUMBOLDT CT	SVL	46	B5
HUMBOLDT ST	SJ	62	B5
HUME DR	S	70	A2
HUMEWICK AV	SVL	60	B2
HUMMEL CT	SJ	63	C4
HUMMINGBIRD DR	SJ	67	B3
HUMMINGBIRD LN	SVL	60	B3
HUNKEN DR	SJ	67	F1
HUNT WY	C	65	F3
HUNTER WY	SCCO	60	C5
HUNTERS HILL RD	SCCO	76	B2
HUNTERSTON PL	CPTO	59	E6
HUNTERSTON PL	CPTO	64	E1
HUNTINGDON AV	SJ	60	C6
HUNTINGDON DR	SJ	60	C6
HUNTINGDON DR	SJ	65	C1
HUNTING HLLW RD	SCCO	81B	D5
HUNTINGTON LN	LA	59	A1
HUNTRIDGE LN	CPTO	59	E5
HUNTSFIELD CT	SJ	75	E2
HUNTSWOOD CT	SJ	76	A1
HURAN CT	SJ	63	A4
HURAN DR	SJ	63	A3
HURLINGHAM WY	SJ	63	B1
HURLSTONE LN	SJ	72	F5
HURST AV	SCCO	66	E3
HURSTGLEN WY	SJ	68	C1
HURSTWOOD CT	SJ	68	C1
HUSTED AV	SJ	66	F4
HUSTED AV	SJ	67	A3
HUSTON CT	MH	80	C3
HUTCHINSON AV	PA	44	B1
HUTTON CT	SJ	72A	B3
HUTTON CT	SVL	59	F2
HUXLEY CT	SJ	66	D2
HYACINTH LN	SJ	71	E4
HYANNIS DR	SVL	52	F5
HYANNISPORT DR	CPTO	59	D5
HYDE AV	CPTO	60	B5
HYDE CT	C	65	D5
HYDE DR	C	65	D5
HYDE PARK DR	G	84	A3
HYDE PARK DR	SJ	67	E6
HYDE PARK DR	SVL	52	E5
HYDRANGEA CT	SVL	53	B5
HYDRANGEA LN	SJ	71	E3
HYLAND AV	SCCO	56	A4
I			
I ST	SVL	46	C6
IBERIS CT	SVL	53	C5
ICEFIELD CT	SCL	53	E4
IDA DR	SCCO	78G	E1
IDA WY	SJ	66	C5
IDAHO CT	MPTS	39	F6
IDAHO CT	MPTS	47	F1
IDAHO ST	SJ	61	D2
IDAHO ST	SCL	61	C2
IDALYN DR	SCCO	78G	D1
IDLEBROOK CT	SJ	72	B5
IDLEWILD CT	SJ	72	B5
IDLEWOOD CT	SJ	62	F6
IDLEWOOD DR	SJ	62	F6
IDLEWOOD LN	S	65	A3
IDYLWILD DR	SCCO	73	D5
IDYLWILD RD	SCCO	73	D5
IGNEOUS CT	SJ	55	B4
ILIKAI AV	SJ	66	F6
ILIKAI AV	SJ	67	A6
ILIMA CT	PA	44	C5
ILIMA WY	PA	44	C5
ILLIAD CT	SJ	67	C6
ILLINOIS AV	SJ	61	F4
ILLINOIS AV	SJ	62	A4
ILLSLEY CT	SJ	67	F5
IMPALA CT	MH	79	E3
IMPALA DR	SJ	66	A2
IMPATIENS DR	SJ	68	B5
IMPERIAL AV	CPTO	59	D5
IMPERIAL DR	G	83	F3
IMPERIAL WY	SJ	60	B6
IMPRESARIO WY	SJ	56	C5
IMWALLE CT	SJ	55	C3
INCA CT	SCCO	71	A6
INCLINE CT	MPTS	48	C3
INCLINE WY	SJ	72A	E5
INDEPENDENCE AV	MVW	44	F4
INDEPENDENCE DR	SJ	67	F2
INDIAN AV	SJ	72	E2
INDIAN DR	PA	44	D1
INDIAN BROOM DR	SJ	68	C5
INDIAN CAMP RD	G	83	D3
INDIAN CREEK CT	SJ	63	D1
INDIAN RIVER CT	SJ	68	A5
INDIAN RIVER DR	SJ	68	A5
INDIAN SPGS CT	SJ	72	C6
INDIAN SPGS DR	SJ	72A	B5
INDIAN SUMMR CT	SJ	62	D5
INDIAN VLY CT	SJ	72A	F4
INDIAN WELLS CT	SJ	72A	E4
INDIGO DR	SJ	67	D5
INDIO CT	S	65	A3
INDIO WY	SVL	52	F2
INDUS CT	SJ	55	E2
INDUSTRIAL AV	MVW	44	F4
INDUSTRIAL AV	PA	44	F4
INDUSTRIAL AV	SJ	54	F4
INDUSTRIAL RD	LG	70	E3
INDUSTRIAL ST	C	66	B4
INDUSTRIAL WY	MPTS	47	F3
INEZ WY	SCCO	61	A5
INGALLS CT	SJ	67	E1
INGERSOLL CT	SJ	63	E4
INGERSOLL DR	SJ	63	E4
INGLESIDE CT	SJ	72	B5
INGLEWOOD DR	SCL	54	C1
INGLIS LN	SJ	71	F2
INGRAM CT	SJ	72A	F5
INGRAM CT	SVL	52	D5
INGRID CT	S	65	B2
INMAN WY	SJ	63	A3
INNERWICK LN	SJ	63	C6
INNSBRUCK DR	SVL	46	B6
INSKIP DR	C	65	E4
INSPIRATION CT	SJ	48	E6
INSPIRATION DR	SJ	48	E6
INTERBAY DR	SJ	63	A3
INTERDALE WY	PA	44	D5
INTERNTIONL CIR	SJ	72A	C3
INVERNESS AV	SCL	61	A1
INVERNESS CIR	SJ	71	F1
INVERNESS DR	MPTS	39	F4
INVERNESS WY	SVL	59	F2
INVERNESS WY	SVL	60	A2
INVICTA WY	SJ	67	A5
INWOOD CT	C	65	E4
INWOOD DR	C	65	E4
ION CT	C	66	B4
IONE CT	S	64	F3
IONE CT	S	65	A3
IONE DR	SJ	55	D1
IOOF AV	G	82A	A6
IOOF AV	G	84	A1
IOWA AV	SVL	52	E4
IOWA DR	SJ	72	F3
IRAZU CT	SCCO	55	E5
IRENE ST	SJ	61	E1
IRIS AV	SVL	53	A5
IRIS CT	SJ	61	F6
IRIS CT	SJ	66	F1
IRIS CT	SJ	67	A1
IRIS WY	PA	38	C6
IRIS WY	PA	44	C1
IRIS BLOSSOM CT	SJ	72A	B1
IRISH CT	G	83	E1
IRLANDA WY	SJ	66	E5
IRMA LYLE DR	SCCO	78G	D2
IRONBRIDGE WY	SJ	72	B1
IRONSIDE CT	SJ	48	D5
IRON SPRING RD	SCCO	73	D5
IRONSTONE CT	SJ	55	D2
IRONWOOD DR	SJ	67	B3
IRONWOOD TER	SVL	53	A5
IROQUOIS CT	SJ	72	E2
IRVEN CT	PA	44	D5
IRVING AV	SJ	61	D5
IRVING AV	SCCO	61	D5
IRWINDALE DR	SJ	63	B5
ISABEL DR	SCCO	66	E1
ISABEL CREEK RD	SCCO	56C	A2
ISABELLA ST	SCL	61	B2
ISABELLE AV	MVW	52	A3
ISADORA DR	SJ	48	D5
ISDLIO CT	SJ	72A	A1
ISENGARD CT	SJ	68	B1
ISENGARD DR	SJ	68	B1
ISHIMATSU PL	SJ	71	D2
ISLAND DR	PA	38	B6
ISLAY CT	SVL	60	A2
ITHACA DR	SVL	52	E5
IVALYNN CIR	SJ	48	E6
IVALYNN CT	SJ	48	E6
IVALYNN PL	SJ	48	E6
IVAN PL	SJ	71	F4
IVAN WY	MVW	52	C5
IVAN WY	SCCO	81C	A6
IVAN WY	SCCO	85	A1
IVANHOE CT	SJ	67	E6
IVEGILL CT	SJ	72A	E4
IVERSEN CT	SCL	60	F3
IVES TER	SVL	52	F5
IVES TER	SVL	53	A5
IVORY CREEK DR	SJ	76	B3
IVY LN	PA	38	C6
IVY LN	PA	44	C1
IVY LN	SJ	65	B2
IVY ST	G	82	F6
IVYCREEK CIR	SJ	68	D3
IVY ESTATES CT	SJ	68A	A2
IVYGATE LN	SJ	68	A6
IVY HILL WY	LG	70	F2
IVY HILL WY	LG	71	A2
IVY MILLS LN	SJ	62	E4
IVYWOOD CT	SJ	63	E6
IVYWOOD CT	SJ	68	E1
IXIAS CT	SJ	71	F4
IXIAS LN	SJ	71	F4
IZORAH WY	LG	70	F3
J			
J ST	SVL	45	F4
J ST	SVL	46	C6
JABIL LN	LAH	58	D1
JACANA CT	SJ	68	D4
JACANA LN	SJ	68	D4
JACARANDA WY	G	82	D5
JACARANDA WY	SCCO	71	A3
JACARANDA WY	SVL	53	B4
JACCARANDA CT	S	65	A4
JACINTO RD	CPTO	59	B5
JACINTO WY	SVL	52	D3
JACKIE DR	SJ	67	F2
JACKLIN CIR	MPTS	47	E1
JACKLIN CT	MPTS	47	E1
JACKLIN PL	MPTS	47	F1
JACKLIN RD	MPTS	40	A6
JACKLIN RD	MPTS	47	F1
JACKLIN RD	MPTS	48	A1
JACKPINE CT	SVL	53	A5
JACKS RD	S	69	E1
JACKSOL DR	SJ	66	C6
JACKSOL DR	SJ	71	C1
JACKSON AV	SJ	55	E5
JACKSON AV	SJ	62	F1
JACKSON AV	SVL	53	A3
JACKSON CT	SCL	54	B6
JACKSON DR	PA	38	C6
JACKSON ST	LG	70	E5
JACKSON ST	MVW	52	B1
JACKSON ST	SJ	55	B6
JACKSON ST	SJ	61	F1
JACKSON ST	SJ	62	A1
JACKSON ST	SCL	54	B6
JACKSON ST	SCL	61	B1
JACKSON WY	SJ	46	F3
JACKSON OAKS CT	MH	80	E3
JACKSON OAKS DR	MH	80	E2
JACOB AV	SJ	66	F6
JACOB AV	SJ	67	A5
JACOBS WY	SCCO	82	D1
JACQUELINE CT	MH	79	F5
JACQUELINE WY	SJ	60	A6
JACQUES DR	SJ	72	E3
JADE AV	SJ	61	A6
JADE LAKE CT	SVL	53	C1
JAFFE LN	SCCO	81	E4
JAGELS RD	SCCO	45	F6
JAGELS RD	SVL	45	F6
JAGGERS DR	SJ	72A	D4
JAI DR	SJ	72A	C4
JALAND CT	SJ	75	F2
JAMAICA WY	SJ	63	A4
JAMES CT	SCL	53	D6
JAMES CT	SCCO	80	A3
JAMES DR	MVW	52	C1
JAMES PL	SCCO	66	E3
JAMES RD	PA	44	D5
JAMES ST	SJ	55	D6
JAMES LEX LN	MH	79	F4
JAMES TOWN CT	S	64	F2
JAMES TOWN DR	CPTO	64	F2
JAMESTOWN DR	SVL	52	D5
JAMIE CT	LG	71	E3
JAMIESON RD	SCCO	81C	E4
JAMIESON RD	SCCO	82C	A2
JAMIESON WY	G	84	A3
JAMISON PL	SCL	53	D5
JAN DR	G	82	C6
JAN WY	SJ	66	E6
JAN WY	SJ	71	E1
JAN WY	SCCO	66	E6
JANA LN	SJ	68	B3
JANARY WY	SJ	65	B2
JANE LN	MVW	44	F5
JANE LN	MVW	45	A5
JANE ANN WY	C	65	F3
JANE ANN WY	C	66	A3
JANELLE DR	SJ	63	E5
JANET AV	SJ	66	D6
JANICE AV	CPTO	59	C4
JANICE DR	SCL	60	F1
JANICE WY	PA	44	E3
JANIS WY	SJ	67	A3
JANKU CT	SJ	55	F2
JANMARIE CT	SJ	68	B2
JANOR CT	MS	70	D2
JANSEN AV	SJ	62	A6
JANSEN AV	SJ	67	A1
JANUARY DR	SJ	72A	D1
JAPAUL LN	SJ	48	D6
JAPONICA WY	SJ	60	D5
JARDIN DR	LA	51	E2
JARDIN DR	MVW	51	E2
JARVIS AV	SJ	67	A5
JARVIS AV	SJ	72	A1
JARVIS CT	SJ	67	A5
JARVIS CT	SVL	52	F4
JARVIS CT	SVL	53	A4
JARVIS DR	MH	79	D2
JARVIS PL	SJ	67	A6
JARVIS WY	LAH	50	F1
JASMINE CT	MPTS	48	C2
JASMINE DR	SVL	53	B5
JASMINE WY	MH	80	A3
JASMINE WY	SJ	60	F5
JASMINE WY	SCCO	71	B3
JASMINE WY	SCOO	80	A3
JASON CT	SJ	72A	B3
JASON DR	MPTS	39	E6
JASON WY	MVW	52	C1
JASPER CT	MH	79	C5
JASPER DR	SVL	59	D2
JASPER ST	SJ	62	D2
JASPER HLNDS DR	MH	79	A4
JAVA DR	SVL	46	A5
JAY ST	LA	51	F2
JAY ST	SCL	54	A3
JAYBEE PL	SJ	68	B6
JEAN CT	SCCO	80	B3
JEAN ELLEN DR	SCCO	82	A4
JEANETTE CT	CPTO	59	E6
JEANETTE LN	SCCO	56	B4
JEANIE LN	SCCO	81	F5
JEANIE LN	SCCO	81A	A5
JEANNE AV	SJ	62	D3
JEFFERS WY	C	66	B3
JEFFERSON CT	SJ	55	E3
JEFFERSON DR	MVW	52	A4
JEFFERSON DR	PA	38	C6
JEFFERSON DR	SCCO	82	A4
JEFFERSON ST	SCL	61	B1
JEFFERY AV	SJ	67	A4
JEFFERY AV	SCCO	67	A4
JEFFERY CT	SCL	53	E6

STREET	CITY	PAGE	GRID
JEFFREY AV	C	65	F4
JEFFREY AV	C	66	A4
JEFFREY LN	SCCO	82A	B2
JENECE CT	SCCO	80	A3
JENKINS AV	SJ	67	A4
JENKINS CT	SCCO	44	A3
JENKINS PL	SCL	60	E4
JENNIFER LN	SCCO	81	F6
JENNIFER LN	SCCO	81A	A6
JENNIFER WY	SJ	66	C6
JENNIFER WY	MPTS	47	F1
JENNINGS DR	SJ	68	A2
JENNY LIND CT	SJ	72	B3
JENVEY AV	SJ	66	F3
JENVEY AV	SJ	67	A3
JEPSEN CT	S	64	F3
JERABEK CT	SJ	67	D4
JERALD AV	SCL	53	E6
JEREMIE CT	SJ	72	C5
JEREMIE DR	SJ	72	C5
JERICHO LN	SJ	61	A6
JERILYN CT	SCCO	56	B5
JERILYN DR	SCCO	56	B5
JEROME ST	SJ	61	F5
JEROME ST	SJ	62	A5
JERRIES DR	S	65	A5
JESSE JAMES DR	SJ	72A	A3
JESSICA LN	LAH	58	E1
JESSICA WY	SJ	63	B5
JESSIE CT	SJ	66	C5
JESSIE LN	MVW	52	B2
JESSIE WY	SCCO	78G	E1
JEWELL DR	SJ	66	C5
JEWELL PL	MVW	44	F6
JEWELL PL	MVW	45	A6
JILINDA CT	SCCO	56	B3
JILL AV	SJ	61	B4
JIM DR	SJ	55	E3
JIM ELDER DR	C	65	F3
JIMS WY	S	64	F5
JIMS WY	S	65	A5
JO DR	LG	71	B2
JOAN WY	SCL	54	A6
JOANDRA CT	SCCO	51	F6
JOANNE AV	SJ	56	A2
JOANNE AV	SCCO	55	F2
JOANNE AV	SCCO	56	A2
JOAQUIN RD	MVW	45	B4
JOE DIMAGGIO CT	SJ	62	E4
JOEL WY	LA	52	C5
JOHANNA AV	SVL	53	B2
JOHANSEN DR	SCCO	60	C5
JOHN DR	CPTO	60	A5
JOHN ST	SJ	55	D6
JOHN WY	CPTO	59	F5
JOHN KIRK CT	C	65	E3
JOHN MISE CT	SJ	60	D5
J MONTGOMERY DR	SJ	63	A2
JOHNSON AV	LG	70	F5
JOHNSON AV	SJ	60	C6
JOHNSON AV	SJ	65	C1
JOHNSON AV	SCCO	60	C5
JOHNSON AV	S	65	C1
JOHNSON PL	SCL	60	F2
JOHNSON WY	G	83	F3
JOHNSTON AV	SJ	67	B1
JOHNSON HOLLOW	LG	70	F5
JOHN TELFER DR	MH	79	C5
JOLEEN CT	MH	79	F4
JOLENE CT	S	65	C3
JOLLY CT	LA	59	B1
JOLLYMAN DR	CPTO	59	F6
JOLLYMAN LN	SCCO	59	E5
JONATHAN AV	SJ	67	B1
JONATHAN CT	C	65	F4
JONATHAN ST	SCL	61	B2
JONES AV	SCL	53	D6
JONES LN	LA	59	C2
JONES RD	LG	70	D5
JONES WY	C	65	F4
JONESBORO CT	SJ	55	B2
JONESPORT AV	SJ	55	C3
JONESPORT CT	SJ	55	C3
JONQUIL DR	SJ	67	E5
JOPLIN DR	SJ	67	B6
JORDAN AV	LA	51	E1
JORDAN PL	PA	44	C1
JORDAN WY	SCCO	43	E3
JORDAN HGTS DR	LG	71	B5
JORN CT	SJ	72	E3
JOSEFA LN	LAH	51	C5
JOSEFA ST	SJ	61	F4

STREET	CITY	PAGE	GRID
JOSEFA ST	SJ	62	A4
JOSE FIGUERS AV	SJ	55	E6
JOSEPH AV	SJ	66	C5
JOSEPH AV	SCCO	66	C5
JOSEPH CIR	CPTO	60	A4
JOSEPH LN	MH	79	D6
JOSEPH LN	SJ	71	F2
JOSEPHINE AV	SJ	66	D4
JOSEPH SPECL DR	SJ	67	D6
JOSHUA WY	SVL	53	B4
JOSINA AV	PA	44	C5
JOSSLYN DR	SJ	75	F1
JOY BELL LN	SCCO	81	E4
JOYCE CT	SCCO	56	A5
JOYERIN CT	SJ	55	B3
JOYNER CT	SJ	55	B3
JUANITA AV	SJ	67	A1
JUANITA DR	SCL	61	A3
JUANITA DR	SCCO	61	A3
JUANITA WY	LA	51	D2
JUANITA WY	SCCO	65	E5
JUARCEYS CT	SJ	71	F4
JUAREZ AV	LA	59	B1
JUAREZ CT	SJ	48	C5
JUBILEE LN	SJ	48	B6
JUDITH CT	SCCO	78G	D1
JUDITH ST	SJ	72A	A1
JUDKINS CT	SJ	63	C4
JUDRO WY	SJ	60	F4
JUDRO WY	SJ	61	A4
JUDSON DR	MVW	51	F2
JUDY AV	CPTO	60	C5
JUDY AV	SCCO	60	C5
JUERGEN DR	SJ	63	F1
JULIAN ST	SJ	55	C6
JULIAN ST	SJ	61	E3
JULIAN ST	SJ	62	A2
JULIAN ST W	SJ	61	F2
JULIANA CT	SCL	61	B3
JULIE CT	PA	44	C5
JULIE CT	SCL	60	D1
JULIE LN	LA	52	B6
JULIE LN	LA	59	C1
JULIE LN	S	64	F2
JULIET AV	SJ	56	C4
JULIET AV	SCCO	56	C4
JULIETTA LN	LAH	51	B6
JULIETTE LN	SCL	53	F2
JULI LYNN DR	SJ	72	B4
JULIO AV	SJ	66	E5
JULY DR	SJ	72A	D1
JUNA CT	S	70	B2
JUNCTION AV	MVW	44	F5
JUNCTION AV	MVW	45	A5
JUNCTION AV	SJ	54	D2
JUNCTION CT	SJ	54	F4
JUNE AV	SJ	62	F3
JUNE CT	SCCO	78G	D1
JUNE DR	SJ	72A	D1
JUNE WY	S	65	A6
JUNEBERRY CT	SJ	67	F4
JUNESONG WY	SJ	55	C3
JUNEWOOD AV	SJ	48	C5
JUNGFRAU CT	MPTS	48	B4
JUNIPER CT	SVL	53	B4
JUNIPER DR	G	83	D1
JUNIPER LN	S	65	A6
JUNIPERO DR	MPTS	47	E3
JUNIPERO WY	S	65	B4
JUNIPRO SRRA BL	SCCO	43	D3
JUNIPRO SRRA FY	CPTO	59	E3
JUNIPRO SRRA FY	CPTO	60	B3
JUNIPRO SRRA FY	LA	59	E3
JUNIPRO SRRA FY	LAH	50	E1
JUNIPRO SRRA FY	LAH	51	A2
JUNIPRO SRRA FY	LAH	58	E1
JUNIPRO SRRA FY	PA	50	E1
JUNIPRO SRRA FY	SCR	60	B3
JUNIPRO SRRA FY	SJ	60	B3
JUNIPRO SRRA FY	SCCO	43	B5
JUNIPRO SRRA FY	SCCO	50	E1
JUNIPRO SRRA FY	SCCO	51	A2
JUNIPRO SRRA FY	SCCO	58	E1
JUNIPRO SRRA FY	SCCO	59	E3
JUNIPRO SRRA FY	SCCO	60	B3
JUNIPRO SRRA FY	SVL	59	E3
JUNIPRO SRRA LN	SJ	60	E5
JUPITER CT	MPTS	48	B2
JUPITER DR	MPTS	48	B2
JUPITER WY	MPTS	48	B2
JURA WY	SVL	60	A2
JURGENS DR	MPTS	39	E6

STREET	CITY	PAGE	GRID
JURY CT	SJ	55	A4
JUSTINE DR	SJ	66	E6
JUSTIN MORGN DR	SCCO	82A	C3
JUSTINO DR	SCCO	80	A3
JUSTO CT	C	66	B4
K			
K ST	SVL	46	C6
KAHALA CT	S	64	F4
KAHLER CT	SCCO	49	C3
KAISER DR	SCL	60	E2
KAISER RD	SCCO	45	D5
KALANA AV	SJ	77	E5
KALANA AV	SCCO	77	E5
KALISPELL CT	SVL	59	D2
KALLIAM DR	SCL	60	E3
KAMIAH WY	SVL	59	D2
KAMMERER AV	SJ	55	E6
KAMMERER AV	SJ	62	E1
KAMSACK CT	SVL	59	D2
KAMSACK DR	SVL	59	D2
KAMSON WY	C	66	A2
KANDICE CT	SJ	72A	A1
KANE CT	S	65	A3
KANE CT	SJ	63	A6
KANE DR	S	65	A3
KANEKO DR	SJ	72A	D4
KANNELY LN	SCCO	81	E5
KARA WY	C	65	F4
KARAMEOS CT	SVL	59	D3
KARAMEOS DR	SVL	59	D3
KAREN CT	G	83	F5
KAREN CT	LG	71	A4
KAREN CT	SJ	66	E5
KAREN DR	SCL	60	F2
KAREN WY	MVW	51	F2
KARIE ANN WY	SJ	67	B4
KARINA CT	SJ	54	D4
KARINA WY	SCL	60	C1
KARL AV	MS	70	E2
KARL ST	SJ	62	F2
KARL ST	SJ	63	A2
KARLSTAD DR	SVL	46	B6
KARMEN CT	SCL	60	C1
KARN CIR	S	65	A3
KARO CT	SVL	53	B5
KASKI CT	SJ	72	F3
KASSON CT	SJ	62	F5
KATHERINE CT	SJ	61	C3
KATHLEEN ST	SJ	66	D5
KATHY CT	LG	70	D1
KATHY LN	LA	52	C6
KATHY LN	LG	71	C5
KATHY WY	MVW	51	F2
KATHY WY	MVW	52	A2
KATIE CT	MVW	52	B3
KATON CT	SVL	53	B5
KATRINA WY	MVW	52	C5
KATRINE CT	SVL	60	C2
KATYBETH WY	MH	80	B3
KAUAI DR	SJ	68	A3
KAUFMANN CT	SJ	62	D3
KAUFMANN CT	SCCO	62	D3
KAVENY DR	SJ	65	C1
KAVIN LN	LG	70	E2
KAVIN LN	MS	70	E2
KAWAII NE HILLS	MH	79	B5
KAWALKER LN	SJ	55	E2
KAY DR	LA	59	B2
KAY DR	SJ	71	D3
KAY DR	SCL	60	F1
KAYAK DR	SJ	68	C6
KAYBE CT	SJ	72A	F5
KAYELLEN CT	SJ	62	A5
KAYLA CT	SJ	66	D4
KAYLENE CT	SJ	56	C5
KAYLENE DR	SJ	56	C6
KEARNEY AV	SCL	53	E5
KEARNEY ST	SJ	61	F4
KEATON LOOP	SJ	63	D5
KEATS CT	PA	44	E4
KEATS CT	SCCO	55	F4
KEATS CT	SCCO	56	A4
KEEBLE AV	SJ	61	E3
KEELER CT	SJ	72A	F5
KEENAN WY	SJ	66	D1
KEENE DR	SJ	71	C2
KEESLING AV	SJ	66	E2
KEESLING AV	SCCO	66	D2
KEEVER CT	SJ	55	F5
KEEVER CT	SJ	56	A5
KEEWAYDIN CT	SJ	68	B3

STREET	CITY	PAGE	GRID
KEHOE CT	SJ	68	A6
KEITH DR	SJ	65	E4
KEITH LN	SCL	54	B2
KEITH WY	MH	79	F6
KELDON CT	SJ	62	F5
KELDON DR	SJ	62	F5
KELEZ CT	SJ	72	C4
KELEZ DR	SJ	72	C4
KELL CT	SCCO	80	A6
KELL CT	SCCO	81H	A1
KELL WY	SJ	67	B4
KELLER CT	SCL	54	B3
KELLER DR	MVW	45	C6
KELLER ST	SCL	54	B3
KELLOGG AV	PA	44	A2
KELLOGG WY	SCL	60	E4
KELLY DR	SJ	60	D6
KELLY DR	SCCO	82	F2
KELLY WY	PA	44	D5
KELLY PARK CIR	MH	80	A3
KELOWAY CT	SVL	59	D1
KELSEY DR	SVL	52	D6
KELSO CT	SCCO	55	F4
KELSO CT	SCCO	56	A4
KELTNER AV	SJ	60	F6
KELTON CT	SCCO	55	F4
KELTON CT	SCCO	56	A4
KELTON DR	G	82	D6
KELTON DR	G	83	D1
KELVINGTON CT	SJ	68	B2
KEN CIR	C	66	A2
KENBAR RD	SCCO	58	F2
KENBRIDGE CT	SVL	52	D5
KENBROOK CIR	SJ	67	E3
KENDAL CT	SJ	75	E2
KENDALL AV	PA	44	C5
KENDLE ST	CPTO	59	C4
KENDRA WY	SJ	65	B5
KENDRICK CIR	SJ	62	F6
KENESTA WY	SJ	63	A4
KENHILL DR	SJ	67	E3
KENILWORTH CT	SVL	60	A2
KENILWORTH WY	SCCO	56	A6
KENISTON AV	MPTS	47	E3
KENLAND DR	SJ	67	E3
KENLAR DR	SJ	71	D2
KENLEY WY	SVL	60	A2
KENMAR CT	SJ	55	D2
KENMORE AV	SVL	53	A4
KENMORE CT	CPTO	59	E6
KENNARD WY	SVL	60	B2
KENNEDY AV	C	66	B3
KENNEDY AV	SJ	62	F2
KENNEDY CT	G	82	F5
KENNEDY DR	MPTS	48	B1
KENNEDY RD	LG	70	F4
KENNEDY RD	LG	71	A5
KENNEDY RD	SCCO	70	F4
KENNEDY RD	SCCO	71	B5
KENNEDY RD S	LG	71	A5
KENNEDY KNLS LN	LG	71	A5
KENNETH AV	C	66	A4
KENNETH DR	PA	44	E2
KENNETH ST	C	66	A4
KENNETH ST	SCL	54	A3
KENNETH ST	SCCO	66	A4
KENNEWICK DR	CPTO	59	E2
KENNEWICK DR	SVL	59	E2
KENNEY CT	SVL	52	F4
KENNEY CT	SVL	53	A4
KENNY LN	SCCO	56	C4
KENOGA DR	SJ	62	F5
KENOSHA AV	S	65	B6
KENPARK CT	SJ	66	D4
KENRAE AV	MS	70	D3
KENSINGTON AV	LA	59	B1
KENSINGTON AV	SCL	60	C2
KENSINGTON AV	SVL	60	C2
KENSINGTON CIR	LA	52	B6
KENSINGTON CIR	LA	59	B1
KENSINGTON PL	G	83	F4
KENSINGTON WY	LG	71	D3
KENSINGTON WY	SJ	71	D3
KENSINGTN PK CT	SJ	67	E5
KENSON DR	SJ	71	D2
KENT AV	SVL	60	C2
KENT CT	SJ	72B	A4
KENT DR	LA	59	A2
KENT DR	SCCO	59	A2
KENT PL	PA	38	B6
KENT PL	PA	44	B1
KENT WY	SCCO	73	D5
KENTFIELD DR	SJ	71	D2

STREET	CITY	PAGE	GRID
KENTMERE CT	MVW	52	C4
KENTON CT	SJ	67	C4
KENTON LN	SJ	67	C4
KENTRIDGE DR	SCCO	55	F4
KENTWOOD AV	CPTO	59	F6
KENTWOOD AV	CPTO	64	F1
KENTWOOD AV	SJ	59	F6
KENTWOOD AV	SJ	64	F1
KENTWOOD CT	G	83	D2
KENTWORTH WY	SCL	53	E4
KENWOOD AV	SJ	61	B3
KENYON CT	SCCO	55	F3
KENYON CT	SCCO	56	A3
KENYON DR	SCL	60	D3
KENZO CT	MVW	52	B5
KEONCREST AV	SJ	54	E5
KEPPLER CT	SJ	63	C4
KEPPLER DR	SJ	63	C4
KERLEY DR	SJ	54	E5
KERMATH DR	SJ	48	C5
KERN AV	G	82	D5
KERN AV	SJ	63	A6
KERN AV	SCCO	82	D5
KERN AV	SVL	53	C3
KERN CT	MVW	52	C5
KERRY AV	SVL	60	C2
KERRY DR	SJ	61	A4
KERRY DR	SCL	61	A4
KERRYSHIRE LN	SCL	53	E4
KERSTEN DR	SJ	66	E6
KERWOOD WY	SCCO	55	F4
KERWOOD WY	SCCO	56	A4
KESEY LN	SJ	48	C6
KESTER CT	SCCO	81	D1
KESTER DR	CPTO	59	C6
KESWICK CT	SCCO	55	F4
KESWICK CT	SCCO	56	A4
KETCH PL	SJ	55	C3
KETCHUM DR	SJ	55	E4
KETCHUM WY	SJ	55	E6
KETCHUM WY	SJ	62	E1
KETTLE CT	SJ	72	D4
KETTMANN RD	SJ	63	D6
KETTMANN RD	SCCO	63	D6
KEVENAIRE DR	MPTS	48	A1
KEVIN DR	SJ	71	E3
KEVIN ST	S	65	C4
KEVIN WY	SCL	54	B2
KEVINAIRE DR	MPTS	39	F6
KEVINAIRE DR	MPTS	40	A6
KEW GARDENS CT	SJ	72	A3
KEYES ST	SJ	62	C4
KEYMAR DR	SJ	72A	A1
KEYSTONE AV	MH	79	D4
KEYSTONE AV	SCL	60	F4
KEYSTONE CT	SJ	55	D2
KIEL CT	SVL	53	B1
KIELY BLVD	SJ	60	F4
KIELY BLVD	SCL	60	E4
KIELY BLVD	SCCO	60	E4
KIFER CT	SVL	53	B4
KIFER RD	SJ	54	A4
KIFER RD	SCL	53	E4
KIFER RD	SVL	53	B4
KILBIRNIE CT	SVL	60	B2
KILBRIDE CT	S	64	F4
KILBRIDE DR	S	65	A4
KILCHOAN CT	SJ	62	F4
KILCHOAN WY	SJ	62	F4
KILDARE AV	SVL	60	C2
KILKENNEY CT	SVL	60	A2
KILLARNEY CT	SVL	60	B2
KILLDEER CT	SVL	60	B3
KILLEAN CT	SVL	59	F2
KILMER AV	SCCO	66	B6
KILO AV	SJ	66	E5
KILT CT	S	65	B4
KIM CT	C	65	E3
KIM ST	CPTO	59	F5
KIMBALL DR	SJ	62	F5
KIMBER CT	SJ	66	D5
KIMBERLIN PL	SCL	53	D4
KIMBERLY CT	SJ	67	A5
KIMBERLY CT	SCCO	79	B6
KIMBERLY DR	SJ	67	B5
KIMBERLY DR	SVL	59	D3
KIMBERLY ST	SJ	60	C6
KIMBLE AV	LG	70	E5
KIMLEE DR	SJ	48	D6
KIM LOUISE DR	C	65	E3
KIM LOUISE DR	SJ	65	E3
KIMPTON CT	SJ	55	A5

STREET	CITY	PAGE	GRID
KINCAID RD	SCCO	56B	C3
KINDRA HILL DR	SJ	75	F1
KINER AV	SJ	66	F4
KINER AV	SJ	67	A4
KING CT	SJ	63	B5
KING CT	SCL	53	D5
KING EST CT	SJ	68A	A2
KING ESTATES	SJ	68A	A2
KING RD	SJ	55	D6
KING RD	SJ	62	D1
KING RD	SJ	63	A4
KING RD	SCCO	45	D5
KING ARTHURS CT	PA	44	D6
KINGBROOK DR	SJ	71	B2
KINGDALE DR	SJ	71	B1
KINGFIELD WY	SJ	71	B2
KINGFISHER DR	SJ	67	B3
KINGFISHER TER	SVL	53	B6
KINGFISHER TER	SVL	60	B1
KINGFISHER WY	SVL	60	B2
KING GEORGE CT	SCCO	81	E4
KINGHURST WY	SJ	71	B1
KINGLET CT	SVL	60	B3
KINGMAN AV	SJ	61	D5
KINGMAN AV	SCCO	61	C5
KINGRIDGE DR	SJ	71	B1
KINGS CT	C	66	A2
KINGS LN	PA	38	B6
KINGTON PL	SCL	53	D6
KINS PL	G	83	F4
KINGS ROW	SJ	54	F4
KINGSBURY CT	CPTO	64	F1
KINGSBURY PL	CPTO	64	F1
KINGS CROSS WY	SJ	67	E6
KINGSGATE CT	SJ	48	B5
KINGSGATE DR	SVL	59	E2
KINGSLAND CT	SJ	72	A5
KINGSLEY AV	PA	44	A2
KINGSLEY WY	LAH	51	C2
KINGSPARK DR	SJ	67	F5
KINGS RIVER CT	SJ	67	D6
KINGSTON CT	LA	52	C6
KINGSTON WY	SJ	65	D4
KINGSTON WY	SJ	72A	C2
KINGSTON HL WY	LG	70	F2
KINGSTON HL WY	LG	71	A2
KINGSTON HL WY	SCCO	70	F2
KINGSWOOD WY	LA	51	D2
KINGWOOD DR	SCL	53	F5
KINGWOOD WY	SJ	71	B1
KINMAN CT	S	65	A3
KINNEY DR	SJ	54	F5
KINROSS CT	SVL	60	A2
KINROSS WY	SJ	62	E4
KINSPORT LN	SJ	72	A4
KINST CT	CPTO	59	C5
KINSULE CT	SJ	68	B2
KINTYRE WY	SJ	65	A1
KINTYRE WY	SVL	60	B2
KIOWA CIR	SJ	72	F3
KIOWA TR	SCCO	73	E6
KIPERASH CT	SJ	55	E2
KIPERASH DR	SJ	55	E2
KIPLING CT	SJ	67	B6
KIPLING ST	PA	37	F6
KIPLING ST	PA	38	A6
KIPLING ST	PA	58	A6
KIPLING ST	PA	43	F1
KIPLING ST	PA	44	D3
KIRBY AV	SCCO	78	B6
KIRBY PL	PA	38	B6
KIRBY WY	SJ	66	D4
KIRBYHILL WY	SVL	59	F2
KIRCHER CT	LA	59	C1
KIRK AV	SCCO	56	A3
KIRK AV	SVL	53	A2
KIRK CT	SJ	66	F6
KIRK RD	SJ	66	E5
KIRK RD	SCCO	66	E5
KIRK RD	SCCO	71	F1
KIRKALDY CT	SVL	60	B2
KIRKBROOK DR	S	65	A2
KIRKDALE DR	S	64	F2
KIRKDALE DR	S	65	A2
KIRK GLEN DR	SJ	55	E3
KIRKHAVEN CT	SJ	68	D4
KIRKLAND AV	SJ	67	B1
KIRKLAND DR	SVL	59	F2
KIRKLYN DR	SJ	66	E3
KIRKMONT DR	SJ	66	D3
KIRKMONT DR	S	64	F2
KIRKMONT DR	S	65	A2

1991 SANTA CLARA COUNTY STREET INDEX

STREET	CITY	PAGE	GRID
KIRKORIAN WY	MS	70	D2
KIRKSIDE CT	SJ	61	E6
KIRKWALL PL	MPTS	39	F5
KIRKWOOD DR	SJ	60	F5
KIRKWOOD DR	SJ	61	A5
KIRKWOOD DR	SCCO	61	A5
KIRWIN LN	CPTO	59	E5
KISER DR	SJ	76	B3
KISSELL CT	SJ	67	F2
KIT CARSON CT	SCL	61	A4
KITCHENER CIR	SJ	68	B2
KITCHENER DR	SVL	59	E2
KITIMAT PL	SVL	59	D1
KITSAP CT	SCL	53	D4
KITTERY CT	SJ	72B	A4
KITTOE DR	MVW	52	C1
KITTREDGE RD	S	69	F2
KITTYHAWK WY	MVW	52	C2
KIZER ST	MPTS	39	F6
KIZER ST	MPTS	40	A6
KLAMATH AV	SCL	53	C6
KLAMATH DR	SJ	65	F1
KLAMATH DR	SVL	59	E2
KLAMATH RD	MPTS	47	F2
KLAUS DR	SJ	63	F1
KLEE CT	SJ	72	E3
KLEE CT	SVL	52	F6
KLEE CT	SVL	53	A6
KLEIN CT	SJ	63	E2
KLEIN RD	SJ	63	E2
KLEIN RD	SCCO	63	E2
KLUNE CT	SCL	55	F1
KNICKERBOCKR DR	SVL	52	D5
KNICKERSON DR	SJ	63	E4
KNIGHTS BRDG CT	SJ	48	C6
KNIGHTSBRIDG LN	SCL	53	E1
KNIGHTS BRDG RD	SJ	48	C6
KNIGHTS ESTATES	SJ	68A	A2
KNIGHTSHAVEN WY	SJ	68	B5
KNIGHTSWOOD WY	SJ	63	E4
KNOLL DR	SCCO	51	F5
KNOLLFIELD WY	SJ	67	C5
KNOLLGLEN WY	SJ	67	B5
KNOLL PARK CT	SJ	72	B4
KNOLLVIEW DR	MPTS	39	F6
KNOLLWELL WY	SJ	72A	D2
KNOLLWOOD AV	SJ	66	F4
KNOLLWOOD DR	S	64	F2
KNOLLWOOD DR	S	65	A2
KNOLLWOOD LN	LA	59	B2
KNOPF CT	SCCO	80K	E3
KNOWLES AV	SCL	61	B3
KNOWLES DR	LG	65	F6
KNOWLES DR	LG	66	A6
KNOWLTON DR	SVL	59	E2
KNOX AV	SJ	62	E2
KOA CT	SVL	59	B5
KOBARA LN	SJ	66	D5
KOCH LN	SJ	66	F4
KOCH LN	SJ	67	A4
KOCHER DR	SCCO	66	E3
KODIAC PL	S	65	C4
KODIAK CT	SJ	72A	F4
KODIAK CT	SVL	59	F2
KOHLER RD	SJ	63	D2
KOHNER CT	SCL	61	A3
KOLL CIR	SJ	54	E5
KOLLMAR DR	SJ	63	A1
KOLNES CT	SJ	68	E1
KOMINA AV	S	69	F1
KONA CT	SJ	72A	D3
KONA PL	SJ	72A	D3
KOOSER RD	SJ	71	F3
KOOSER RD	SJ	72	A2
KOREMATSU CT	SJ	72	B5
KORHUMMEL WY	SJ	72A	D4
KOSICH CT	S	65	C2
KOSICH DR	S	65	C2
KOTAKE CT	SJ	55	F3
KOTENBERG AV	SJ	61	F6
KOTENBERG AV	SJ	62	A6
KOVANDA WY	MPTS	39	F6
KOVANDA WY	MPTS	47	E1
KOZERA DR	SJ	67	D6
KOZO CT	SJ	71	D2
KOZO PL	SJ	71	D2
KREBS CT	SJ	55	B4
KREISLER CT	S	64	F3
KRING DR	SJ	67	A4
KRING WY	LA	59	C3
KRISINRIDGE CT	MPTS	48	D3
KRISMER ST	MPTS	47	E2
KRISTA CT	CPTO	59	B5
KRISTE LN	LAH	51	B5
KRISTEN CT	SJ	72	E6
KRISTY LN	S	65	B2
KROHN LN	SCCO	81	E3
KRUSE DR	SJ	54	E1
KRZICH PL	CPTO	59	E6
KUEHNIS DR	C	66	D2
KUMQUAT DR	SJ	61	A5
KUNKEL DR	SJ	71	C2
KURTZ LN	SJ	72	C2
KUYKENDALL PL	SJ	63	E3
KYBURZ PL	SJ	72	B3
KYLE CT	SVL	59	E1
KYLE ST	SJ	55	E2
KYRA CIR	SJ	63	B5

L

STREET	CITY	PAGE	GRID
L ST	SVL	46	C6
LA AGUA CT	MH	80K	F1
LA ALAMEDA	MH	80K	E2
LA ALONDRA WY	G	82	E6
LA BARBERA DR	SJ	61	D6
LA BAREE DR	MPTS	48	C3
LA BAREE DR	MH	80K	E2
LA BARRANCA RD	LAH	51	B4
LA BELLA AV	SVL	59	F1
LA BELLA CT	MH	80K	E1
LA BOHEME WY	SJ	63	B4
LABURNUM DR	SVL	53	B5
LA CALLE	PA	44	C5
LA CANADA CT	LG	71	A1
LA CANADA CT	MH	80K	F2
LACEY AV	S	64	F5
LACEY DR	MPTS	48	C2
LACHINE DR	SVL	59	E2
LA CHIQUITA AV	SCCO	71	A4
LA CIENEGA CT	LG	70	F1
LA CIENEGA CT	LG	71	A1
LACKAWANNA CT	SVL	52	D5
LA COCHE WY	G	82	E6
LA CON CT	SJ	66	C4
LACONIA CT	SJ	72B	A4
LA CONNER DR	SVL	59	F2
LA CORONA CT	C	65	E5
LA CORONA DR	C	65	E5
LA CORTE LN	SCCO	82	E2
LA CRESTA CT	LAH	51	B3
LA CRESTA DR	LAH	51	B3
LA CRESTA WY	CPTO	60	B3
LA CROIX CT	LG	71	A4
LA CROSSE CT	SVL	59	E2
LA CROSSE DR	MPTS	48	C2
LA CROSSE DR	MH	80K	E1
LA CROSSE DR	SVL	59	E2
LACSA CT	SJ	55	E5
LA CUESTA DR	SCCO	51	E5
LADDIE CT	SJ	63	C6
LADDIE WY	SJ	63	C6
LADERA CT	S	65	B2
LADERA DR	SJ	47	A4
LADIS CT	SVL	53	B5
LADNER DR	SJ	72A	A1
LA DONNA ST	PA	44	C5
LADYMUIR CT	SJ	55	B2
LADYWOOD CT	SJ	65	F1
LA ESCUELA CT	MH	80K	E1
LAFAYETTE DR	SVL	52	D5
LAFAYETTE ST	SCL	46	F5
LAFAYETTE ST	SCL	54	B4
LAFAYETTE ST	SCL	61	B1
LAFAYETTE WY	SCL	61	C2
LAFERN CT	SJ	72	B5
LA FIESTA PL	SJ	60	D5
LAGE DR	SJ	65	E4
LA GIRALDA CT	MH	79	D5
LAGO CT	SJ	62	F5
LAGO CT	SJ	63	A6
LAGO LOMITA WY	SCCO	78J	A4
LAGOON WY	SJ	48	B6
LAGO VISTA CIR	SJ	60	D5
LAGO VISTA CT	SCCO	76	E2
LA GRANDE DR	MH	80K	E2
LA GRANDE DR	SVL	59	F2
LAGUNA AV	PA	44	C5
LAGUNA CT	PA	44	B5
LAGUNA CT	SCL	53	D6
LAGUNA DR	MPTS	47	E1
LAGUNA DR	SJ	54	F1
LAGUNA OAKS PL	PA	44	C5
LAGUNA SECA CT	SJ	72	E2
LAGUNA SECA WY	SJ	72	E2
LAGUNITA DR	SCCO	43	E4
LAHAINA WY	SJ	67	A6
LA HERRAN DR	SCL	60	C4
LA HERRAN DR	SCCO	60	C4
LA HONDA AV	SJ	60	D4
LA HONDA CT	MH	80K	E1
LA HONDA DR	MPTS	47	E1
LA HONDA DR	MH	80K	E1
LA HONDA SUR	MH	80K	F1
LAINE AV	SCL	53	F6
LA JENNIFER WY	PA	44	C5
LA JOLLA AV	SJ	66	E5
LA JOLLA CT	CPTO	59	D6
LA JOLLA CT	MH	80K	F1
LA JOLLA DR	MH	80K	F1
LAKE ALBANO CIR	SJ	68A	A3
LAKE ALMANOR DR	SJ	72	C2
LAKEBIRD CT	SJ	71	C2
LAKEBIRD DR	SJ	71	C1
LAKEBIRD DR	SVL	46	C6
LAKEBIRD DR	SVL	53	C1
LAKEBIRD PL	SJ	71	C1
LAKECHIME DR	SVL	55	C1
LAKE CROWLEY PL	SJ	72	C2
LAKEDALE WY	SVL	53	C1
LAKE ESTATES CT	SJ	68A	A2
LAKEFAIR DR	SVL	53	B1
LAKE GARDA DR	SJ	68A	A2
LAKEHAVEN DR	SVL	53	C1
LAKEHAVEN TER	SVL	53	B1
LAKEHOUSE AV	SJ	61	F3
LAKEHOUSE AV	SJ	62	A3
LK ISABELLA WY	SJ	72	C2
LAKEKNOLL DR	SVL	53	C1
LAKE LESINA DR	SJ	68	A3
LAKEMUIR DR	SVL	53	C1
LAKEPARK DR	SJ	55	A2
LK STA CLARA DR	SCL	53	F2
LAKESHIRE CT	SJ	61	E6
LAKESHORE CIR	SJ	55	A1
LAKESHORE DR	SCL	53	F1
LAKESIDE DR	SVL	53	D3
LAKE SPRING CT	CPTO	64	A5
LAKE TAHOE CT	SJ	72	C2
LK TRASIMENO DR	SJ	68	A4
LAKETREE CT	SJ	55	B2
LAKE VIEW CT	MH	80	C1
LAKEVIEW CT	SCCO	75	C2
LAKE VIEW DR	MH	80	C1
LAKEWAY	SVL	53	D2
LAKEWOOD CT	SJ	48	B5
LAKEWOOD DR	SJ	48	B5
LAKEWOOD DR	SVL	53	C1
LAKME CT	SJ	63	B5
LAKME WY	SJ	63	B5
LA LANNE CT	LAH	51	D2
LA LOMA CT	LAH	51	C6
LA LOMA CT	LAH	58	D1
LA LOMA DR	LAH	51	C6
LA LOMA DR	LAH	58	C1
LALOR DR	SJ	72	E2
LAMA WY	SJ	66	F5
LA MAISON DR	SJ	61	B5
LA MAR CT	CPTO	60	B5
LA MAR CT	MH	80K	E1
LA MAR DR	CPTO	60	B5
LA MAR DR	MH	80K	F2
LA MATA WY	PA	44	C5
LAMBERT AV	PA	44	C4
LAMBERT LN	SJ	67	A3
LAMBERT WY	MVW	45	D6
LAMBETH CT	SJ	48	C5
LAMBETH CT	SVL	60	A2
LA MESA CT	MH	80K	E2
LA MESA LN	SJ	66	E6
LA MESA TER	SVL	52	E2
LA MIEL WY	SJ	65	E3
LA MIRADA CT	MH	80K	E1
LA MIRADA DR	SJ	66	F4
LA MIRADO RD	SCCO	70	C4
LA MIRADO WY	SCCO	70	C4
LAMMERHAVEN CT	SJ	68	A5
LAMMY PL	LA	52	B5
LAMOND CT	SJ	63	D5
LAMONT CT	C	65	E4
LAMONT CT	SVL	59	D3
LAMORE CT	SJ	65	E2
LAMORE DR	SJ	65	E2
LAMPLIGHTER SQ	CPTO	59	B4
LAMPLIGHTER WY	SJ	47	A5
LANA CT	C	65	F4
LANA CT	C	66	A4
LANAI AV	SJ	62	F4
LANAI AV	SJ	63	A4
LANAI DR	SJ	62	F4
LANARK CT	SVL	60	C2
LANARK LN	S	65	A4
LANCASTER CT	SCL	53	E1
LANCASTER DR	SJ	66	E6
LANCASTER RD	SCCO	70	C3
LANCELOT LN	SJ	56	B6
LANCELOT LN	SCCO	56	B6
LANCER DR	CPTO	60	B6
LANCER DR	SJ	60	B6
LANCEWOOD PL	LG	65	E6
LANDAU CT	MH	79	E4
LANDAU CT	SJ	68	C6
LANDAU CT	SJ	72A	B5
LANDELL CT	LA	59	C1
LANDEROS DR	SCL	60	F4
LANDERWOOD LN	SJ	72	D6
LANDESS AV	MPTS	48	C4
LANDINGS DR	MVW	45	A4
LANDMARK PKWY	MVW	45	A4
LANDSLIDE CT	SCL	53	E4
LANE AV	MVW	52	B3
LANE A	SCCO	43	F4
LANE B	SCCO	43	F4
LANE C	SCCO	43	F4
LANE W	SCCO	43	F4
LANEVIEW DR	SJ	48	C5
LANEWOOD CT	SJ	67	B3
LANEWOOD DR	SJ	67	B3
LANFAIR CIR	SJ	67	D4
LANFAIR CT	SJ	67	D4
LANFAIR DR	SJ	67	D4
LANGOON CT	SJ	68	B2
LANGPORT DR	SVL	60	A2
LANGPORT WY	SVL	60	A2
LANGTON AV	LA	44	D6
LANHAM CT	SJ	63	C4
LANIER LN	SJ	63	A6
LANITOS AV	SCCO	52	E3
LANITOS AV	SVL	52	E3
LANNING CT	SJ	55	E4
LANNING WY	SJ	55	E4
LANNOY CT	S	65	A5
LANO ST	SJ	62	B6
LANSBERRY CT	LG	71	A4
LANSBERRY CT	SCCO	71	A4
LANSDALE AV	CPTO	60	A5
LANSDALE CT	SJ	72	D6
LANSDOWN CT	SVL	52	E5
LANSFORD AV	SJ	66	F3
LANSFORD AV	SJ	67	A4
LANSING AV	SJ	72	A1
LANTANA AV	SJ	65	D3
LANTANA DR	SVL	53	B5
LANTERN CT	SJ	68	A2
LANTERN WY	SJ	68	A2
LANTIS LN	LA	59	C1
LANTZ AV	SJ	66	C5
LANTZ DR	SCCO	77	E3
LAPA DR	SJ	60	D5
LA PALA CT	MH	80K	F1
LA PALA CT	SJ	55	F3
LA PALA DR	SJ	55	F3
LA PALA DR	SJ	56	A3
LA PALA PL	SJ	55	F3
LA PALOMA AV	S	64	F6
LA PALOMA AV	S	65	A6
LA PALOMA DR	CPTO	59	D6
LA PALOMA RD	LAH	51	C4
LA PALOMA WY	G	82	E6
LA PARA AV	PA	44	C5
LA PAZ	C	66	C3
LA PAZ	MVW	45	C4
LA PAZ CT	MH	80K	F2
LA PAZ CT	SJ	72	A1
LAPAZ WY	S	65	C5
LAPETITE WY	SJ	55	E3
LA PINTA WY	CPTO	60	B3
LA PLATA PZ	C	65	F5
LA PLAYA CT	CPTO	64	D1
LA PORTE AV	SJ	62	F3
LA PORTE AV	SJ	63	A3
LA PORTE CT	MH	80K	E3
LA PRADERA DR	C	65	E3
LA PRENDA CT	MH	80K	E1
LA PRENDA RD	LA	51	F4
LAPRIDGE LN	SJ	66	B6
LA QUEBRADA WY	SJ	56	B2
LA QUINTA DR	SJ	56	C2
LARABEE CT	SJ	72	A4
LA RAGIONE AV	SJ	62	E6
LARCH CT	SJ	62	F6
LARCH ST	MPTS	47	E2
LARCH GROVE PL	SJ	68	B6
LARCH GROVE PL	SJ	72A	B1
LARCHMONT AV	S	65	B3
LARCHMONT CT	SJ	72A	C3
LARCHMONT DR	SJ	72A	C3
LARCHWOOD DR	SJ	72	B1
LAREDO WY	SCCO	81	D1
LA RENA CT	MH	80K	E1
LA RENA LN	LAH	51	D5
LARGA VISTA DR	LG	71	C3
LARGO DR	SJ	48	C6
LA RHEE DR	SJ	66	E5
LARIAT LN	SJ	56	A1
LA RINCONADA DR	MS	70	E1
LA RINCONADA DR	SCCO	65	F6
LA RINCONADA DR	SCCO	70	E1
LARIOS CT	SJ	72	E3
LARIOS WY	SJ	72	E3
LARISSA CT	SJ	67	C6
LARK AV	LG	70	F1
LARK AV	LG	71	A2
LARK LN	SVL	60	B3
LARK WY	S	70	A2
LARKELLEN LN	LA	52	D6
LARKIN AV	SJ	65	B2
LARKMEAD CT	SJ	60	F5
LARKMEAD CT	SJ	61	A5
LARKMEAD DR	SJ	60	F5
LARKSPUR AV	SVL	53	B5
LARKSPUR CT	SCCO	81	C3
LARKSPUR DR	SJ	66	F4
LARKSPUR DR	SJ	67	A4
LARKSPUR LN	G	82	B6
LARNEL PL	LA	59	A1
LA ROCCA CT	MH	80K	E2
LA ROCCA DR	MH	80K	E2
LA ROCHELLE TER	SVL	46	B6
LA RODA CT	CPTO	60	A5
LA RODA CT	MH	80K	E1
LA RODA DR	CPTO	60	A5
LA ROSSA CIR	SJ	62	B6
LA ROSSA CT	SJ	62	B6
LARRY CT	SJ	68	B2
LARRY WY	CPTO	59	F3
LARRY WY	CPTO	60	A3
LARSEN CT	SCL	53	E6
LARSEN PL	SCL	53	E6
LARSENS LANDING	LA	44	D6
LARSON WY	SJ	60	E6
LA SALLE AV	SCL	60	C4
LA SALLE DR	MVW	52	B5
LA SALLE DR	SCCO	78G	D1
LA SALLE DR	SVL	59	D2
LA SALLE WY	SJ	65	D4
LAS ANIMAS AV	SCCO	82	F5
LAS ANIMAS AV	SCCO	82A	D1
LAS ANIMAS CT	G	82	E6
LAS ANIMAS CT	G	83	E1
LAS ANIMAS RD	SCCO	68B	C4
LAS ANIMAS WY	SJ	72	E3
LAS ASTAS DR	LG	70	F1
LAS ASTAS DR	LG	71	A1
LAS CAMPANAS CT	LA	59	B3
LASCAR CT	SJ	66	B6
LASCAR CT	SJ	71	B1
LASCAR PL	SJ	66	B6
LASCAR PL	SJ	71	B1
LAS CASAS D L P	SJ	55	D4
LAS COCHES CT	MH	80K	E2
LAS COLINAS LN	SJ	72A	E3
LAS CRUCES CT	SJ	72	A1
LA SELVA DR	MH	79	D5
LA SELVA DR	PA	44	C4
LAS ENCINAS CT	C	65	D5
LAS FLORES CT	LA	44	D6
LAS FLORES LN	LG	71	D3
LA SIERRA CT	MH	80K	E2
LA SIERRA WY	G	82	E6
LAS JOYAS CT	C	65	D5
LAS LOMAS DR	MPTS	48	A2
LAS MIRADAS DR	LG	70	F2
LAS ONDAS CT	CPTO	60	A5
LAS ONDAS WY	CPTO	60	A5
LAS PALMAS DR	SCL	60	F2
LAS PIEDRAS CT	C	65	E5
LAS PLUMAS AV	SJ	55	C6
LASSEN AV	MPTS	48	B3
LASSEN AV	MVW	44	F6
LASSEN AV	SJ	65	D1
LASSEN ST	LA	51	E4
LASSEN WY	MH	80K	F2
LASSENPARK CIR	SJ	67	E5
LASSIE CT	SCCO	82A	C2
LASTRETO AV	SVL	53	A3
LASUEN ST	SCCO	43	F3
LAS UVAS CT	LG	65	E1
LASWELL AV	SJ	61	C5
LASWELL AV	SCOO	61	C5
LA TERRACE CIR	SJ	72	C2
LATHAM ST	MVW	44	E6
LATHAM ST	MVW	51	F1
LATHAM ST	MVW	52	A1
LATHROP CT	SJ	72A	B1
LATHROP DR	SJ	72A	A2
LATHROP DR	SCCO	43	F5
LATHROP DR	SCCO	44	A5
LATHROP PL	SCCO	43	F5
LA TIERRA DR	MH	80K	E2
LATIMER AV	C	66	A2
LATIMER AV	SJ	65	E2
LATIMER AV	C	65	E2
LATIMER CIR	C	66	A2
LATONA CT	SJ	68	C5
LA TORRE AV	SJ	68	B3
LAUELLA CT	MVW	52	A1
LAUFALL LN	SJ	68	E3
LAUMER AV	SCCO	56	A4
LAURA CT	C	65	F4
LAURA CT	C	66	A4
LAURA DR	C	65	F4
LAURA DR	C	66	A4
LAURA DR	SJ	71	D3
LAURA LN	SCCO	81C	A6
LAURA LN	MVW	44	F5
LAURA LN	PA	38	D6
LAURA LN	SCCO	85	A1
LAURAL AV	SJ	72A	F3
LAURANT WY	SJ	48	D4
LAUREL AV	LG	70	D4
LAUREL DR	G	83	D2
LAUREL DR	SCL	60	F1
LAUREL DR	SCL	61	A1
LAUREL DR	SCCO	70	D2
LAUREL DR	SCCO	73	C2
LAUREL DR	SCCO	78G	D1
LAUREL LN	LAH	51	C4
LAUREL RD	MH	79	F4
LAUREL RD	MH	80	A5
LAUREL RD	SCCO	73	E6
LAUREL RD	SCCO	79	E3
LAUREL RD	SCCO	80	A5
LAUREL ST	SJ	61	E2
LAURELDALE LN	SJ	67	C5
LAURELEI AV	SJ	61	C3
LAURELES DR	LA	44	D6
LAURELGLEN CT	SJ	67	B5
LAUREL GLEN DR	PA	50	E4
LAURELWOOD DR	SJ	66	E3
LAUREL WOOD LN	MH	79	B4
LAURELWOOD RD	SCL	54	B3
LAUREN DR	SJ	71	E3
LAURENTIAN WY	SVL	59	D3
LAURETTA DR	CPTO	59	E4
LAURIE AV	SJ	67	A2
LAURIE AV	SCL	54	B2
LAURIE JO LN	SCL	60	F3
LAURINDA DR	SJ	71	D2
LAURYNRIDGE CT	MPTS	48	D3
LAUSANNE CT	SJ	55	D2
LAUSETT AV	SJ	55	E6
LAUTREC TER	SVL	52	F6
LAUTREC TER	SVL	53	A6
LAVA DR	SJ	55	D4
LAVA WY	SJ	55	D4
LAVA ROCK CT	MH	80	C1
LAVEILLE CT	SJ	55	A3
LAVENDER DR	SVL	53	B5
LAVENDER LN	SCCO	71	A3
LAVENIDA	MVW	45	B5
LAVER CT	LA	59	B2
LA VERNE DR	SCCO	78G	D1
LA VERNE WY	LA	51	D1
LA VIA AZUL	MH	80K	F1
LA VIA AZUL CT	MH	80K	F1
LA VIDA REAL	LAH	51	B5
LAVINA CT	SCCO	59	E3
LA VISTA CT	S	65	B4
LA VISTA DR	SCCO	68	A4
LA VISTA DR	S	65	B4
LAVONA DR	SJ	72	B1
LA VONNE AV	SJ	62	E2
LA VONNE DR	C	65	F3

COPYRIGHT © 1991 BY Thomas Bros Maps

1991 SANTA CLARA COUNTY STREET INDEX

STREET	CITY	PAGE	GRID
LA VONNE DR	SJ	65	F3
LAWNDALE AV	C	66	B2
LAWRENCE CT	SCL	53	D6
LAWRENCE DR	G	82	D6
LAWRENCE EXPWY	SJ	60	C3
LAWRENCE EXPWY	SJ	65	C1
LAWRENCE EXPWY	SCL	53	C6
LAWRENCE EXPWY	SCL	60	C3
LAWRENCE EXPWY	SCCO	46	D6
LAWRENCE EXPWY	S	65	C1
LAWRENCE EXPWY	SVL	53	C6
LAWRENCE EXPWY	SVL	60	C3
LAWRENCE LN	PA	44	D2
LAWRENCE RD	SCL	53	D6
LAWRENCE STA RD	SVL	46	C5
LAWRENCE STA RD	SVL	53	C4
LAWSON CT	SJ	71	E1
LAWSON LN	SCL	53	F4
LAWSON LN	SCL	54	A4
LAWTHER CT	SJ	63	F5
LAWTON AV	SJ	61	D6
LAWTON DR	MPTS	48	B2
LAYNE CT	PA	44	D3
LAYTON CT	SCL	60	F2
LAYTON ST	SCL	60	F2
LAYTON WY	SCCO	56	A6
LAZANEO DR	CPTO	59	F4
LAZO GRANDE DR	SCCO	80K	B5
LAZY LN	SCCO	63A	B4
LAZY OAK CT	CPTO	59	C4
LAZY RIVER WY	SJ	72	D6
LEAF CT	LA	51	D2
LEAFWOOD LN	SJ	67	E3
LEAFY CT	MH	80	A3
LEAN AV	SJ	68	B6
LEAN AV	SJ	72A	B2
LEANDER DR	LAH	51	C4
LEANN CT	SCCO	80	B6
LEARNARD WY	G	82	C6
LEATHERWOOD CT	SJ	72	D4
LEAVESLEY PL	CPTO	59	D6
LEAVESLEY RD	G	82	F6
LEAVESLEY RD	G	82A	B5
LEAVESLEY RD	SCCO	82A	E1
LE BAIN DR	SJ	65	E4
LEBANON AV	CPTO	59	B5
LEBANON DR	CPTO	59	B5
LE COMPTE PL	SJ	62	D4
LEDERER CIR	SJ	55	B3
LEDGEWOOD DR	SJ	66	E5
LEE DR	MVW	52	A4
LEE DR	SCCO	73	D6
LEE DR	SCCO	78G	D1
LEE ST	LA	51	E4
LEEDS AV	CPTO	64	F2
LEESA ANN CT	SJ	71	E2
LEEWARD CT	SJ	63	A1
LEEWARD DR	SJ	63	A2
LEFONT DR	SJ	55	A3
LEGHORN ST	MVW	44	F4
LEGHORN ST	MVW	45	A4
LEGHORN ST	PA	44	F4
LEHIGH DR	SCL	60	C3
LEIGH AV	C	66	D3
LEIGH AV	SJ	61	D5
LEIGH AV	SJ	66	D6
LEIGH AV	SJ	71	D3
LEIGH AV	SCCO	61	D5
LEIGH AV	SCCO	66	D3
LEIGH AV	SCCO	71	D2
LEIGH CT	SCCO	71	D1
LEIGH-ANN PL	SCCO	66	D3
LEIGHTON WY	SVL	60	B2
LEISURE CT	SJ	55	E1
LEITH AV	SCL	54	B2
LEKSICH AV	MVW	51	F2
LEKSICH AV	MVW	52	A2
LELAND AV	MVW	44	F6
LELAND AV	PA	44	B3
LELAND AV	SJ	61	D5
LELAND AV	SCCO	61	D5
LELAND CIR	S	65	C6
LELONG ST	SJ	62	B5
LEMON BLOSSM CT	SJ	68	B6
LEMONTREE CT	MVW	51	F4
LEMONTREE CT	MVW	52	A4
LEMON TREE RD	SJ	72	C4
LEMONWOOD CT	SJ	72A	A6
LEMOYNE WY	SJ	65	E3
LENA AV	SCCO	82	D1
LENA DR	SJ	66	E5
LENARK CT	SJ	55	E1

STREET	CITY	PAGE	GRID
LENARK DR	SJ	55	E1
LENCAR WY	SJ	66	E6
LENCAR WY	SJ	71	E1
LENDRUM AV	SJ	55	F6
LENELLE CT	SJ	71	E1
LENFEST RD	SJ	55	C5
LENN DR	SJ	66	E2
LENNON WY	SJ	66	F2
LENNON WY	SJ	67	A2
LENNOX CT	SVL	59	E1
LENNOX WY	SVL	59	E1
LENOR WY	C	61	B6
LENOR WY	C	66	B1
LENORA AV	SJ	71	E2
LENORE CT	SCCO	78G	D1
LENOX WY	LAH	51	D4
LENRAY LN	SCCO	66	D6
LENWOOD WY	SJ	72	D6
LENZEN AV	SJ	61	E3
LENZEN CT	SJ	61	E3
LEO AV	SJ	62	D6
LEO DR	SJ	60	E6
LEOLA CT	CPTO	60	B5
LEOMINSTER CT	SJ	72B	A4
LEON DR	SJ	61	D6
LEON DR	SCCO	61	D6
LEONA CT	SJ	61	F5
LEONA CT	SCCO	81	C1
LEONA LN	MVW	52	B4
LEONARD CT	SCL	54	A3
LEONARD RD	S	64	F4
LEONELLO AV	LA	51	F5
LEONELLO AV	LA	52	A5
LEONG CT	CPTO	59	E6
LEONG DR	MVW	45	C6
LEOTA AV	SCCO	52	D4
LEOTA AV	SVL	52	D4
LEOTAR CT	LG	71	B5
LEPA CT	SCCO	82	F3
LERIDA AV	LA	51	E4
LERMA LN	G	82	C5
LERMA WY	G	82	C5
LEROY AV	LG	70	F3
LEROY AV	LG	71	A3
LERWICK CT	SVL	60	C2
LE SABRE CT	MH	79	E4
LESHER CT	SJ	66	F2
LESLEY LN	SCCO	81	E1
LESLIE CT	MVW	52	C1
LESLIE DR	SJ	60	E6
LESTER AV	SJ	61	F6
LESTER CT	SCL	60	F3
LESTER LN	LG	71	A2
LESTER LN	SCCO	71	A2
LETITIA CT	SJ	62	F5
LETITIA ST	SJ	62	F5
LEUTAR CT	S	64	F3
LEVEE RD	SJ	47	C4
LEVEN PLACE WY	SJ	68	C1
LEVIN AV	LA	52	C5
LEVIN AV	MVW	52	B5
LEVIN AV	SCCO	52	C5
LEVIN CT	MVW	52	C5
LEVIN ST	MPTS	39	F5
LEWIS AV	SVL	52	E3
LEWIS RD	SJ	67	E2
LEWIS ST	G	84	A1
LEWIS ST	SJ	62	B4
LEWIS ST	SCL	54	B6
LEWIS ST	SCL	61	B1
LEWISTON CT	SVL	59	E1
LEWISTON DR	SJ	67	C4
LEWISTON DR	SVL	59	E2
LEXANN AV	SJ	63	B6
LEXFORD AV	SJ	66	D5
LEXINGTON AV	SJ	72A	C2
LEXINGTON CT	S	65	A5
LEXINGTON DR	MS	70	D3
LEXINGTON DR	SJ	66	A1
LEXINGTON DR	SCCO	66	A1
LEXINGTON DR	SVL	52	D5
LEXINGTON PL	G	83	F2
LEXINGTON ST	MPTS	47	E2
LEXINGTON ST	SCL	61	B1
LEXNGTN SCHL RD	SCCO	73	D4
LEYLAND PARK CT	SJ	72	B5
LEYLAND PARK DR	SJ	72	C6
LEYTE CT	SJ	68	B3
LIBERATA DR	SCCO	80	B1
LIBERIA CIR	SJ	55	E6
LIBERTY CT	CPTO	59	D5
LIBERTY ST	SJ	46	E3

STREET	CITY	PAGE	GRID
LIBERTY ST	SCL	61	A2
LIBERTY OAK LN	CPTO	59	C4
LIBRA LN	SJ	68	A2
LICK AV	SJ	62	B5
LICK MILL BLVD	SCL	47	A6
LICK MILL BLVD	SCL	54	B1
LICK MILL RD	SCL	54	A1
LIDA DR	MVW	44	F6
LIDDICOAT CIR	LAH	50	F2
LIDDICOAT DR	LAH	50	F2
LIDO WY	SJ	62	E2
LIDO WY	S	65	A3
LIEB CT	SJ	56	B6
LIEB LN	SCCO	54	F2
LIEBELT CT	SJ	61	E6
LIEBRE CT	SVL	52	E3
LIETZ AV	SJ	71	F2
LIGHTFARE CT	SJ	68	B1
LIGHTLAND RD	SJ	68	B2
LIGHTSON ST	SJ	62	A3
LIKA CT	S	64	F3
LIKA CT	S	65	A5
LILAC CT	CPTO	59	E5
LILAC LN	LA	51	D5
LILAC LN	MVW	45	A6
LILAC LN	SJ	67	D4
LILAC LN	SCCO	71	A3
LILAC LN	SCCO	80K	C2
LILAC WY	CPTO	59	E5
LILAC WY	LG	71	A3
LILAC BLOSSOM LN	SJ	71	E3
LILIAN AV	SVL	60	B1
LILLIAN WY	SJ	72	C4
LILLICK DR	SCL	60	C1
LILLICK DR	SVL	60	C1
LILLIPUT LN	SJ	55	F6
LILLIPUT LN	SJ	56	A6
LILLIPUT LN	SJ	62	F1
LILLIPUT LN	SJ	63	A1
LILLY AV	G	82	E5
LILLY LN	MH	79	D6
LILY AV	CPTO	59	E5
LILY AV	SVL	53	C5
LILY CT	CPTO	59	E5
LILY ANN WY	SJ	68	C6
LILY ANN WY	SJ	72A	C1
LILY BLOSSOM CT	SJ	72A	B1
LIMA CT	SJ	61	D6
LIMA CT	SJ	66	D1
LIMAN AV	G	82	E5
LIMAN AV	SCCO	82	E5
LIME DR	SVL	52	D6
LIME BLOSSOM CT	SJ	68	B6
LIMEKILN RD	SCCO	73	E2
LIMERICK CT	SVL	60	A2
LIMETREE LN	MVW	51	F4
LIMETREE LN	MVW	52	A4
LIMEWELL CT	SCCO	72A	D2
LIMEWOOD DR	SJ	48	C4
LINBURN CT	SJ	63	C5
LINCOLN AV	LA	51	D4
LINCOLN AV	PA	38	B6
LINCOLN AV	PA	44	A1
LINCOLN AV	SJ	61	E5
LINCOLN AV	SJ	62	A6
LINCOLN AV	SJ	66	F1
LINCOLN AV	SJ	67	A2
LINCOLN AV	SCCO	61	E5
LINCOLN AV	SCCO	81	C4
LINCOLN AV	SVL	53	A4
LINCOLN CT	G	82	F5
LINCOLN CT	SJ	67	A2
LINCOLN DR	MVW	52	A5
LINCOLN ST	SCL	54	A6
LINCOLN ST	SCL	61	B1
LINCOLNSHIRE WY	SJ	61	F6
LINCOLN VLG DR	SJ	67	B3
LINDA AV	LG	71	B2
LINDA AV	SCCO	71	B3
LINDA DR	C	65	F4
LINDA LN	LAH	50	F1
LINDA ANN CT	CPTO	59	C3
LINDA FLORA ST	SCCO	55	F2
LINDA FLORA ST	SCCO	56	A2
LINDAHL CT	SJ	72	B4
LINDAIRE AV	SJ	61	C6
LINDAIRE AV	SCCO	61	C6
LINDA MESA DR	MH	80	B3
LINDA VISTA AV	MVW	45	B5
LINDA VISTA AV	SCCO	45	B6
LINDA VISTA AV	SCCO	70	C4
LINDA VISTA DR	CPTO	59	D5
LINDA VISTA LN	SCCO	81H	F5

STREET	CITY	PAGE	GRID
LINDA VISTA PL	CPTO	59	D5
LINDA VISTA ST	SCCO	55	F2
LINDA VISTA ST	SCCO	56	A2
LINDA VISTA WY	LA	52	A5
LINDBERGH AV	SJ	61	C6
LINDBERGH AV	SCCO	78G	C2
LINDEN AV	LA	51	D2
LINDEN AV	SVL	53	B6
LINDEN DR	SJ	61	C2
LINDEN DR	SCL	61	C2
LINDEN LN	MPTS	39	E5
LINDENBROOK LN	CPTO	60	A5
LINDENBROOK LN	SCCO	60	A5
LINDENOAKS DR	SJ	61	A5
LINDENOAKS DR	SCCO	61	A5
LINDENTREE LN	SCL	60	F3
LINDENWOOD DR	SJ	60	F5
LINDENWOOD DR	SJ	61	A5
LINDER HILL CT	SJ	75	E2
LINDER HILL LN	SJ	75	E2
LINDERO DR	PA	44	D4
LINDMUIR DR	SJ	68	B1
LINDO CT	MH	79	D4
LINDO LN	MH	79	D4
LINDSAY AV	CPTO	60	A5
LINDSAY WY	SJ	67	B5
LINDSAY ANN TER	SJ	55	B2
LINDSTROM CT	SJ	68	D5
LINDY LN	CPTO	59	D6
LINDY LN	CPTO	64	D1
LINDY PL	CPTO	64	D1
LINKFIELD WY	SJ	63	F6
LINKHORNE CT	SJ	55	D5
LINKSHEAD CT	SJ	63	D4
LINNET LN	SVL	60	B3
LINTON CT	SJ	68	D1
LINWELL CT	SJ	72A	D2
LINWOOD DR	SJ	66	D6
LINWOOD DR	SJ	71	D1
LIONS CREEK DR	G	82	C6
LIONWOOD PL	SJ	68	C5
LIQUIDAMBAR WY	SVL	53	B4
LIQUIDAMBER CT	SJ	68	D4
LIRA DR	S	69	F2
LISA CT	G	83	F5
LISA CT	SCCO	80	B3
LISA LN	LA	52	B6
LISA LN	LA	59	B1
LISA LN	SJ	46	F4
LISA LN	SJ	47	A5
LISA WY	C	65	F1
LISA MARIE CT	S	65	B5
LISBON CT	SJ	48	D4
LISBON DR	SJ	48	D4
LISKA LN	SJ	72A	D3
LISMORE CT	SJ	63	F6
LITCHFIELD PL	SCL	53	D3
LITCHI GROVE CT	SJ	68	A6
LITTLE AV	SJ	72A	D2
LITTLE BEAR WY	SJ	68	D4
LITTLE BOY LN	SCCO	63	E3
LITTLEBROOK DR	SCCO	70	B4
LITTLE CREEK RD	CPTO	64	F1
LITTLE FALLS DR	SJ	72	C5
LITTLEFIELD LN	SCCO	70	F4
LITTLEFIELD LN	SCCO	71	A4
LITTLEJOHN WY	SJ	60	B6
LITTLE MARKT ST	SJ	62	A2
LITTLEMEADOW CT	SJ	60	E5
LITTLEOAK CIR	SJ	65	C1
LITTLEOAK DR	SJ	60	C6
LITTLEOAK DR	SJ	65	C1
LITTL ORCHRD AV	SJ	62	C6
LITTL ORCHRD AV	SCCO	67	D1
LITTL ORCHRD ST	SJ	62	C6
LITTLE RIVER CT	SCCO	67	D6
LITTLE ROCK CT	SJ	55	E3
LITTLE ROCK DR	SJ	55	E3
LITTLETON DR	SJ	55	B4
LITTLE UVAS RD	SCCO	78L	A3
LITTLE WOOD LN	SJ	55	F4
LITTLEWORTH WY	SJ	63	F6
LITTMAN DR	SJ	72	B5
LITTON CT	SVL	60	A2
LIVE OAK AV	SCCO	78	A6
LIVEOAK CT	MPTS	47	E6
LIVE OAK CT	MH	80	E2
LIVE OAK DR	SCL	60	D2
LIVE OAK LN	LA	51	D2
LIVE OAK LN	MH	80	E2
LIVE OAK LN	S	70	B1
LIVEOAK WY	SJ	60	D5
LIVERPOOL AV	SJ	66	E6

STREET	CITY	PAGE	GRID
LIVERPOOL WY	SVL	60	A2
LIVINGSTON AV	SJ	66	F3
LIVINGSTON ST	SJ	67	A3
LIZZIE LN	SJ	67	B5
LJEPAVA DR	S	65	A4
LLAGAS AV	MH	79	C4
LLAGAS RD	MH	79	C4
LLAGAS RD	SCCO	81	C3
LLAGAS CK DR	SCCO	79	C4
LLANO LN	SCCO	80K	E5
LLEWELLYN AV	C	66	A3
LLOYD WY	MVW	51	F2
LLOYD WY	MVW	52	A2
LOBELIA LN	SJ	71	E3
LOBOS AV	SJ	68	B4
LO BUE WY	SJ	68	B3
LOCHBURRY CT	SJ	72	E1
LOCHINVAR	SCCO	48	F6
LOCHINVAR AV	SCL	60	C2
LOCHINVAR AV	SVL	60	C2
LOCH LOMOND CT	MPTS	47	F2
LOCH LOMOND CT	SVL	59	F2
LOCH LOMOND CT	SVL	60	A2
LOCH LOMOND LN	SJ	65	A2
LOCH LOMOND ST	SCL	54	B2
LOCHNER DR	SJ	56	B6
LOCHNER DR	SJ	63	B1
LOCHNESS CT	SVL	60	C2
LOCH NESS WY	SJ	63	C6
LOCHRIDGE DR	SJ	55	D5
LOCKE DR	SJ	68	A2
LOCKFORD CT	CPTO	59	F6
LOCKFORD CT	CPTO	64	F1
LOCKHART LN	LA	51	D3
LOCKHAVEN CT	LA	59	B2
LOCKHAVEN DR	LA	59	B2
LOCKHAVEN WY	SJ	60	C6
LOCKHEED WY	SVL	46	A6
LOCKSLEY PK DR	SJ	48	D6
LOCKSUNART WY	SVL	59	F2
LOCKSUNART WY	SVL	60	A2
LOCKWOOD DR	CPTO	59	C5
LOCKWOOD DR	SJ	48	D4
LOCKWOOD DR	SJ	48	D5
LOCUST DR	SCCO	73	E6
LOCUST DR	SCCO	78G	D1
LOCUST RD	SCCO	78H	C3
LOCUST ST	SJ	62	B4
LOCUST ST	SCL	61	C2
LODESTONE DR	SJ	55	D2
LODGE CT	SJ	63	A5
LODGEPOLE CT	G	83	D1
LODGEWOOD CT	SJ	75	F1
LODGEWOOD CT	SJ	76	A1
LODI LN	SJ	66	E4
LOES WY	SJ	56	B5
LOGAN CT	SVL	59	E2
LOGAN ST	SCCO	63	D5
LOGANBERRY DR	SJ	68	E1
LOGIC DR	SJ	71	C1
LOGSDEN WY	SJ	63	A1
LOGUE AV	MVW	52	D1
LOIS AV	SVL	52	D5
LOIS LN	PA	38	C6
LOIS LN	PA	44	C1
LOIS ST	MVW	44	F5
LOIS WY	SCCO	66	C5
LOLA LN	MVW	52	B4
LOLLIE CT	SJ	66	E6
LOLLY CT	S	65	C3
LOLLY DR	S	65	C3
LOMA CT	SJ	54	F1
LOMA PARKWAY	G	83	D3
LOMA ST	SCCO	70	F4
LOMA ST	SCCO	71	A4
LOMA ALMADEN RD	SCCO	74	C5
LOMA ALTA AV	LG	70	F5
LOMA ALTA CT	SCCO	80K	D1
LOMA ALTA DR	SCL	60	E2
LOMA LINDA DR	SJ	60	D5
LOMAPARK CT	SJ	66	D3
LOMAPARK DR	SJ	66	E3
LOMA PRIETA CT	LA	52	B5
LOMA PRIETA DR	SJ	72	E3
LOMA PRIETA RD	SCCO	78J	E3
LOMA PRIETA WY	SCCO	78G	F2
LOMA RIO DR	S	65	A5
LOMAS LN	SCCO	70	B3
LOMA VERDE AV	PA	44	C3
LOMA VERDE DR	SJ	66	B1
LOMA VERDE PL	PA	44	D3
LOMA VISTA AV	SCCO	71	B3

STREET	CITY	PAGE	GRID
LOMA VISTA CT	LG	71	B2
LOMA VISTA LN	SCL	53	E1
LOMBARD AV	SJ	55	F6
LOMENT CT	SJ	66	B6
LOMENT CT	SJ	71	B1
LOMENT PL	SJ	66	B6
LOMENT PL	SJ	71	B1
LOMER WY	MPTS	48	C3
LOMETA AV	SVL	52	E3
LOMITA AV	SCCO	59	D4
LOMITA AV	S	69	F1
LOMITA CT	SCCO	43	E4
LOMITA DR	SCCO	43	E4
LOMITA ST	SCCO	59	D4
LOMITA LINDA CT	LAH	58	E1
LOMOND CT	S	65	A5
LOMPICO DR	SJ	72	E2
LONARDO AV	SJ	67	A5
LONDON AV	SVL	60	C2
LONDON DR	G	83	F3
LONDON DR	MPTS	39	F5
LONDON DR	MPTS	40	A5
LONDON DR	SJ	65	D5
LONDON PL	G	83	F3
LONDON PL	G	84	A3
LONDONDERRY DR	SJ	61	A4
LONDONDERRY DR	SCL	60	F4
LONDONDERRY DR	SCL	61	A4
LONDONDERRY DR	SVL	60	A2
LONDONDERRY PL	SCL	61	A4
LONDON PARK CT	SJ	67	E4
LONE BLUFF WY	SJ	67	F1
LONE BLUFF WY	SJ	68	A2
LONE HILL DR	MH	79	E5
LONE HILL RD	SJ	71	D2
LONE OAK CIR	SCCO	76	C2
LONE OAK CT	SCCO	83	B1
LONE OAK DR	SJ	68	E1
LONE OAK LN	LAH	58	E2
LONE PINE LN	SJ	72	D5
LONETREE CT	MPTS	47	F5
LONG CT	SJ	72A	B3
LONG ST	SCL	54	A6
LONGACRE CT	SJ	63	B5
LONGBRANCH CT	SJ	61	D6
LONGBRANCH CT	SJ	66	D1
LONGDALE DR	SJ	66	E5
LONGDEN CIR	LAH	59	A2
LONGDOWN RD	CPTO	59	B4
LONGFELLOW AV	SCCO	66	B6
LONGFELLOW CT	SJ	65	A1
LONGFELLOW WY	SJ	65	A1
LONGFORD DR	SJ	55	C1
LONGLEY AV	SJ	61	F6
LONGLEY AV	SJ	62	A6
LONGMEADOW DR	G	82	C5
LONGMEADOW DR	LG	71	A4
LONG OAK LN	CPTO	59	C4
LONGRIDGE RD	LG	71	A2
LONGSHORE DR	SJ	61	C6
LONGSPUR AV	SVL	60	B2
LONGVIEW DR	MH	79	D4
LONGVIEW ST	SJ	62	E3
LONGWOOD DR	SCCO	71	B3
LONGWOOD LN	SJ	60	D6
LONNA LN	CPTO	59	F5
LONUS ST	SJ	61	F5
LOO LN	SJ	55	B2
LOOKOUT BEND	SJ	72	C6
LOOMIS CT	SJ	62	F5
LOOMIS CT	SJ	63	A5
LOOMIS DR	SJ	62	F5
LOOP DR N	SJ	61	E6
LOOP RD	SJ	72A	C6
LOPEZ CT	SCCO	81	B1
LOPINA WY	SJ	60	E4
LOQUAT CT	S	65	D5
LORA DR	LG	65	E6
LORABELLE CT	PA	44	D5
LORAIN PL	LG	65	F6
LORAINE AV	LA	52	A6
LOREE AV	SCCO	60	C5
LORELEI CT	C	65	F3
LORENE CT	SCCO	52	C4
LORENZEN DR	SJ	66	E4
LORETO ST	MVW	52	B2
LORETTA DR	SJ	71	D1
LORI AV	SVL	52	E3
LORI LN	MH	80	D2
LORI ANN LN	SCCO	56	C3
LORNE WY	SVL	60	B2
LORRAINE AV	SJ	61	F4

1991 SANTA CLARA COUNTY STREET INDEX

STREET	CITY	PAGE	GRID
LORWICK WY	SJ	68	C1
LOS ALMOS DR	SJ	65	E2
LOS ALONDRAS CT	LAH	51	B4
LOS ALTOS AV	LA	44	D6
LOS ALTOS AV	LA	51	D3
LOS ALTOS CT	LA	51	D3
LOS ALTOS CT	SJ	63	D6
LOS ALTOS DR	SJ	63	D6
LOS ALTOS SQ	LA	51	E1
LOS ALTURAS	LG	65	D6
LOS ARBOLES AV	SJ	68	D4
LOS ARBOLES AV	SCCO	43	E3
LOS ARBOLES AV	SCCO	59	F1
LOS ARBOLES AV	SVL	59	F1
LOS CERRITOS DR	LG	71	A5
LOS COCHES AV	SCCO	61	C4
LOS COCHES ST	MPTS	47	F3
LOS COCHES ST	MPTS	48	A3
LOS COYOTES CT	SCCO	82A	C3
LOS ENCANTOS CT	C	65	D5
LOS ENCINOS AV	SJ	47	B4
LOS ENCINOS CT	SJ	47	B4
LOS ENCINOS DR	SJ	47	B4
LOS ENCINOS ST	SJ	47	B5
LOS ESTEROS RD	SJ	47	A3
LOS FELICE DR	SJ	65	E2
LOS GARCIAS DR	SJ	55	F1
LOS GATOS BLVD	LG	70	F4
LOS GATOS BLVD	LG	71	A3
LOS GATOS BLVD	SCCO	71	A3
LOS GATOS ALMDN	LG	71	C2
LOS GATOS ALMDN	SJ	71	C2
LOS GATOS ALMDN	SCCO	71	C2
LOS GATOS ALMDN	SCCO	73	D5
LOS GATOS ALMDN	SCCO	78G	F2
LOS HERMANOS CT	SCCO	77	F5
LOS HUECOS DR	SJ	72	E3
LOS NINOS WY	LA	51	E2
LOS OLIVOS DR	MH	79	E3
LOS OLIVOS DR	SJ	65	E2
LOS OLIVOS DR	SCL	60	F3
LOS OLIVOS DR	SCL	61	A3
LOS PADRES BLVD	SJ	61	A3
LOS PADRES BLVD	SCL	53	F6
LOS PADRES BLVD	SCL	54	A5
LOS PADRES BLVD	SCL	60	F2
LOS PADRES BLVD	SCL	61	A3
LOS PADRES CT	G	83	E2
LOS PAJAROS CT	LA	51	E4
LOS PALMOS WY	SJ	72A	C3
LOS PALOS AV	PA	44	D6
LOS PALOS CIR	PA	44	D6
LOS PALOS PL	PA	44	D6
LOS PALOS WY	SJ	67	B5
LOS PATIOS	LG	65	D6
LOS PINOS AV	MPTS	48	A1
LOS PINOS WY	SJ	72A	C3
LOS POSITOS DR	MPTS	48	A2
LOS RIOS CT	SJ	71	F4
LOS RIOS DR	SJ	71	F4
LOS ROBLES AV	PA	44	C5
LOS ROBLES WY	LG	70	F4
LOSSE CT	SJ	61	F2
LOSSE ST	SJ	62	A2
LOS SERENS RBLS	SCCO	70	C4
LOSTCREEK CT	SJ	68	D3
LOST LAKE LN	C	66	B5
LOST RANCH RD	SCCO	72A	C6
LOS TRANCOS WDS	PA	50	A6
LOST TRAIL CT	SJ	68	D4
LOST VIEW RD	SCCO	76	D3
LOTUS LN	MVW	45	B6
LOTUS ST	SJ	62	D2
LOTUS LAKE CT	SVL	53	C1
LOUCKS AV	LA	44	D6
LOUCKS AV	LA	51	D1
LOUIS CT	SJ	56	C5
LOUIS RD	PA	44	E3
LOUISA CT	PA	38	C6
LOUISA CT	PA	58	C6
LOUISE AV	MVW	52	C2
LOUISE AV	SJ	67	A1
LOUISE CT	C	65	F4
LOUISE CT	LG	70	D1
LOUISE CT	MPTS	48	C3
LOUISE DR	SVL	59	E2
LOUISE LN	LA	59	C2
LOUIS HOLSTM DR	SCCO	80K	B1
LOUMENA LN	SJ	67	F2
LOUPE AV	SJ	63	A6
LOUPE AV	SJ	68	A1
LOUPE CT	G	82	E5

STREET	CITY	PAGE	GRID
LOVE HARRIS RD	SCCO	74	C5
LOVELAND CT	S	65	A6
LOVELL AV	C	65	F4
LOVELL PL	SCL	53	D6
LOVERBROOK DR	SJ	72	C4
LOVERS LN	SCCO	82C	B6
LOVEWOOD WY	SJ	63	D4
LOVOI WY	SJ	67	A2
LOWELL AV	PA	44	B2
LOWELL CT	SVL	59	E2
LOWELL DR	SCL	60	C4
LOWELL LN	LAH	51	C2
LOWELL LN	PA	51	C2
LOWELL LN	SJ	67	A4
LOWELL WY	C	66	B3
LOWENA CT	S	64	E2
LOWLAND CT	MPTS	48	C4
LOWNEY WY	SJ	55	B2
LOWRY DR	SJ	67	A4
LOYALTON DR	C	65	E4
LOYE WY	SJ	63	D3
LOYOLA CT	SCL	60	F1
LOYOLA DR	SJ	62	F3
LOYOLA DR	SCL	60	F1
LOYOLA DR	SCCO	58	F2
LOYOLA DR	SCCO	59	A1
LU ANNE DR	C	65	F3
LUBEC ST	CPTO	59	C3
LUBICH DR	MVW	52	C5
LUBY DR	SJ	55	D5
LUCAS CT	SJ	63	F4
LUCAS DR	SJ	63	F4
LUCE CT	MVW	52	C3
LUCENA CT	SJ	55	C1
LUCENA DR	SJ	55	C1
LUCERNE DR	SVL	53	B3
LUCERNE WY	SJ	63	A2
LUCERO LN	LAH	51	A5
LUCHESSA AV	SCCO	84	B3
LUCHESSI DR	SJ	67	B6
LUCIAN AV	SJ	55	F3
LUCIAN AV	SJ	56	A3
LUCILLE AV	CPTO	59	F3
LUCILLE AV	CPTO	60	A3
LUCILLE AV	SCCO	59	F3
LUCILLE AV	SCCO	60	A3
LUCILLE WY	CPTO	60	A3
LUCKY CT	SCCO	82	B3
LUCKY RD	MS	70	C4
LUCKY RD	SCCO	70	C4
LUCKY OAK ST	CPTO	59	C3
LUCOT WY	C	65	F5
LUCRETIA AV	SJ	62	E4
LUCRETIA AV	SCCO	62	E4
LUCRETIA CIR	SJ	62	F5
LUCRETIA CT	SJ	62	E4
LUCY MAY TR	SCCO	78G	C2
LUDLOW CT	SJ	63	C5
LUFKIN CT	SJ	63	F3
LUGANO WY	SJ	55	D1
LUIKA PL	C	65	E5
LUJOSO CT	SJ	66	C1
LUKE CT	SJ	62	E2
LULLABY LN	SJ	68	B4
LUMBERTOWN LN	S	69	E1
LUNADA CT	LA	44	D3
LUNADA DR	LA	44	D6
LUNAR CT	CPTO	59	E6
LUNDER CT	SJ	55	C3
LUNDY AV	SJ	55	A1
LUNDY AV	SCCO	55	B3
LUNDY LN	LG	70	E5
LUNDY LN	PA	44	D5
LUNDY LN	SCCO	59	A1
LUNDY PL	SJ	48	A6
LUNETA CT	SJ	67	D4
LUNETA DR	SJ	67	D4
LUNING DR	SJ	67	A6
LUNING DR	SJ	72	A1
LUPINE AV	PA	44	E3
LUPINE CT	G	82	C6
LUPINE CT	SJ	67	A5
LUPINE CT	SCCO	81	C3
LUPINE DR	SVL	53	B5
LUPINE RD	LAH	50	F3
LUPINE RD	LAH	51	A3
LUPTON AV	SJ	66	F1
LU-RAY DR	LG	71	B3
LUSARDI DR	SJ	63	D5
LUSTERLEAF DR	SVL	53	B5
LUTHER	SJ	61	E4
LUTHER AV	SJ	66	E5

STREET	CITY	PAGE	GRID
LUTHER DR	SCL	60	F3
LUTHERIA WY	S	65	A6
LUX CT	SJ	67	D4
LUZ AV	SJ	55	E6
LYELL ST	LA	51	E4
LYLE CT	SCL	53	E6
LYLE DR	SJ	61	F6
LYLE DR	SJ	65	C2
LYLE LN	SJ	66	C5
LYMEHAVEN CT	SJ	68	D4
LYNBROOK CT	S	65	C2
LYNBROOK WY	SJ	60	C6
LYNBROOK WY	SJ	65	C1
LYNCH ST	SJ	54	E2
LYNDALE AV	SCCO	56	A6
LYNDE AV	S	64	F5
LYNDE CT	S	64	F5
LYNDON AV	LG	70	D4
LYNETTE WY	SJ	62	E1
LYNFIELD LN	SJ	67	C5
LYNG DR	SJ	68	C5
LYNHURST CT	SJ	67	B5
LYNHURST WY	SJ	67	B5
LYNN AV	LG	71	C3
LYNN AV	MPTS	48	B1
LYNN AV	SJ	62	E2
LYNN WY	SVL	52	D4
LYNNHAVEN DR	SJ	61	D6
LYNN OAKS DR	SJ	61	A6
LYNTON CT	CPTO	59	F5
LYNTON CT	CPTO	60	A5
LYNVIEW DR	SJ	63	D4
LYNWOOD AV	MVW	45	C6
LYNWOOD AV	SJ	61	C3
LYNWOOD TER	MPTS	48	C4
LYNX CT	SJ	67	C4
LYNX DR	SJ	67	C4
LYNXWOOD CT	SVL	53	B5
LYONBURRY PL	SJ	72	E1
LYONCROSS WY	SJ	72A	A2
LYON ESTATES CT	SJ	68A	A2
LYONS CT	SJ	62	F1
LYONS CT	S	65	D5
LYONS DR	SJ	62	F1
LYONSVILLE LN	SJ	72	A2
LYRELAKE CT	SVL	53	C1
LYRIC LN	SJ	68	B4
LYTER WY	SJ	63	D5
LYTTON AV	PA	38	A6
LYTTON AV	PA	43	F1
M			
M ST	SVL	46	C6
MABEL AV	SJ	62	F2
MABEL CT	S	65	B2
MABIE CT	SJ	72	E2
MABURY CT	SJ	55	E3
MABURY RD	SJ	55	E3
MABURY RD	SCCO	55	C5
MACADAM CT	SJ	72A	A2
MACADAMIA GR CT	SJ	68	A6
MACARA AV	SVL	52	E2
MACARTHUR AV	SJ	61	C5
MACARTHUR AV	SCCO	61	C5
MACAW CT	SJ	68	D4
MACAW LN	SJ	68	D4
MACAW PL	SJ	68	D4
MACAW WY	SJ	68	D4
MACBETH DR	SJ	56	C4
MACDONALD AV	SJ	55	D6
MAC DUEE CT	SJ	63	C6
MAC DUEE WY	SJ	63	C6
MACDUFF CT	SJ	56	C4
MACE CT	SJ	56	C5
MACE DR	SJ	56	C5
MACGREGOR LN	SCL	54	B2
MACHADO AV	SCL	53	D5
MACHADO LN	SJ	56	C5
MACHADO LN	SCCO	56	C5
MACINTOSH ST	SCL	54	B2
MACKALL WY	PA	44	D3
MACKAY DR	PA	44	E5
MACKENZIE DR	SCL	60	C4
MACKENZIE DR	SVL	59	D2
MACKEY AV	SJ	62	B6
MACKEY AV	SJ	67	B1
MACKLIN CT	SJ	55	E3
MACLANE ST	PA	44	D4
MACLAY CT	SJ	72	D2
MACLAY CT	S	65	C6
MACLAY DR	SJ	72	D2
MACON AV	MVW	45	C5

STREET	CITY	PAGE	GRID
MACON AV	SJ	61	A6
MACON RD	SCCO	45	E4
MACOUFF CT	SJ	56	C4
MACREDES AV	SCCO	62	D3
MADALEN DR	MPTS	39	F6
MADALEN DR	MPTS	40	A6
MADDEN AV	SJ	55	E5
MADDUX DR	PA	44	D2
MADELAINE CT	LA	59	A2
MADELINE DR	SCCO	55	F4
MADELINE DR	SCCO	56	A4
MADELINE LN	SCL	60	F2
MADERA	MVW	45	B4
MADERA AV	SJ	55	A5
MADERA AV	SVL	52	E4
MADERA CT	LG	71	D4
MADERA DR	CPTO	59	D3
MADERA DR	SCL	53	F6
MADERA DR	SCL	60	F1
MADERA RD	CPTO	59	B5
MADISON CT	G	82	F5
MADISON CT	SJ	72A	A3
MADISON DR	MVW	52	A5
MADISON DR	SJ	72A	A3
MADISON ST	SCL	61	B1
MADISON WY	PA	38	C6
MADOC WY	SJ	65	E3
MADONNA DR	SJ	61	A6
MADONNA WY	LA	51	E5
MADRID CT	SJ	48	D4
MADRID DR	SJ	48	D4
MADRID DR	SCCO	82	B4
MADRID RD	SCCO	59	D5
MADRONA AV	PA	44	A2
MADRONA AV	SJ	66	F3
MADRONA AV	SJ	67	A2
MADRONA WY	SCCO	73	D5
MADRONE AV	LG	70	D4
MADRONE AV	SJ	78	B6
MADRONE AV	SJ	79	A1
MADRONE AV	SCL	60	E4
MADRONE AV	SCCO	78	B6
MADRONE AV	SCCO	79	A1
MADRONE AV	SVL	53	A2
MADRONE CT	SCCO	75	B2
MADRONE DR	SCCO	73	D6
MADRONE DR	SCCO	78G	E1
MADRONE HILL RD	S	69	F2
MADRONE HILL RD	S	70	A2
MADRUGA WY	MPTS	48	B4
MAGDALENA AV	LAH	58	E1
MAGDALENA AV	SCCO	51	F6
MAGDALENA CIR	SCL	53	C6
MAGDALENA CT	SCCO	51	F6
MAGDALENA RD	LAH	58	D1
MAGELLAN AV	SJ	55	D6
MAGELLAN AV	SCL	60	C4
MAGGIO CT	C	65	F5
MAGGIORE CT	SJ	68	A4
MAGIC SANDS WY	SJ	72A	B1
MAGLIOCCO DR	SJ	61	B5
MAGNESON LOOP	LG	70	F3
MAGNESON LOOP	LG	71	A3
MAGNESON TER	LG	71	A3
MAGNOLIA AV	SJ	61	E3
MAGNOLIA DR	MPTS	47	D4
MAGNOLIA DR	PA	44	C5
MAGNOLIA LN	SCL	60	E3
MAGNLIA BLSM LN	SJ	71	F4
MAGNLIA TREE CT	SJ	62	E4
MAGNUM DR	SJ	63	E5
MAGPIE LN	SVL	60	B2
MAHAN DR	SJ	72A	A4
MAHOGANY LN	SVL	53	B5
MAHONEY AV	SJ	56	B4
MAHONEY AV	SCCO	56	B4
MAIDEN LN	SJ	72	E6
MAIN AV E	MH	79	E4
MAIN AV E	SCCO	80	A2
MAIN AV W	MH	79	D4
MAIN ENTRNCE DR	SJ	55	A3
MAIN ST	LA	51	D3
MAIN ST	SCL	54	B6
MAIN ST	SCL	61	B1
MAIN ST E	LG	70	E5
MAIN ST S	MPTS	47	F4
MAIN ST W	LG	70	D4
MAIRWOOD CT	SJ	72A	A6
MAITLAND DR	SJ	71	E2
MAJESTIC CT	SJ	48	D5
MAJESTIC WY	SJ	48	D5
MAJESTIC OAK WY	CPTO	59	B4
MAJORCA CT	SJ	72	A4

STREET	CITY	PAGE	GRID
MAJORCA DR	MH	80	A4
MAKATI CIR	SJ	72A	C1
MALABAR AV	SCL	60	E4
MALABAR DR	SJ	56	A6
MALAGA CT	MH	80	A4
MALAGA DR	MH	80	A4
MALAGA DR	SJ	66	E4
MALAGUERRA AV	MH	78	E6
MALAGUERRA AV	SCCO	78	E6
MALARIN AV	SCL	61	A2
MALAVOS LN	SCCO	54	D2
MALCOM	S	64	F5
MALDEN AV	SJ	62	F4
MALERO PL	SJ	60	D5
MALIBU DR	SJ	60	E6
MALIBU DR	SJ	65	E1
MALLARD WY	SVL	60	B2
MALLORY CT	S	65	A4
MALO CT	SCCO	82	F2
MALONE PL	SCL	60	F2
MALONE RD	SJ	67	A2
MALORY DR	SJ	72A	B4
MALOTT DR	SJ	62	F5
MALPAS DR	SJ	71	F4
MALTON CT	SJ	63	E5
MALVERN CT	CPTO	60	A5
MALVINI DR	SJ	67	A5
MAMMINI CT	SCCO	81	D3
MAMMOTH DR	SJ	55	E5
MANASSAS CT	SJ	62	F2
MANCHESTER AV	C	66	D2
MANCHESTER AV	SCCO	66	D2
MANCHESTER CT	PA	44	D3
MANCHESTER DR	SCL	61	C2
MANCUSO ST	SJ	72	B4
MANDA DR	SJ	66	E5
MANDARIN DR	SVL	52	D6
MANDARIN WY	SJ	62	F2
MANDARIN WY	S	64	F4
MANDEL CT	SJ	55	B3
MANDOLI DR	LAH	51	B2
MANDOLI DR	PA	51	B2
MANDOLIN DR	SJ	47	A4
MANET DR	SVL	52	F6
MANET DR	SVL	53	A6
MANET TER	SVL	53	A6
MANET TER	SVL	60	A1
MANFRE RD	SCCO	77	E5
MANFRED ST	MPTS	39	E5
MANFROY RNCH RD	SCCO	82A	E2
MANGIN WY	SCCO	63	E1
MANGO AV	SVL	52	D5
MANGO BLOSSM CT	SJ	68	B6
MANGO GROVE CT	SJ	68	A6
MANGROVE AV	SVL	53	B6
MANGRUM DR	SCL	47	A6
MANHATTAN CT	SVL	52	D5
MANHATTAN PL	SCL	53	E5
MANICHETTI CT	SJ	72A	A2
MANILA DR	SJ	72A	C4
MANILA WY	SJ	72A	D4
MANITA CT	CPTO	64	E1
MANITOBA DR	SJ	65	D4
MANITOBA DR	SVL	59	E2
MANITOU CT	SJ	72	A3
MANLEY CT	SJ	72A	F5
MANLY CT	SCL	60	E3
MANN DR	CPTO	59	D4
MANNA WY	SCCO	82	D1
MANNING AV	SJ	56	A5
MANNING AV	SCCO	56	A5
MANNING CT	SCCO	81	D2
MANN OAK CT	SCCO	76	A3
MANOA CT	S	64	F4
MANOR CT	MH	79	E5
MANOR DR	SJ	67	B3
MANOR DR	S	64	F3
MANOR WY	LA	52	A6
MANORWOOD CT	SJ	60	C6
MANRESA CT	SJ	72A	F5
MANRESA CT	LA	51	D4
MANRESA LN	LA	51	D4
MANRESA WY	LA	51	D4
MANSFIELD DR	MVW	52	B5
MANSFIELD DR	SJ	61	D5
MANSION CT	SJ	72	B6
MANSION CT	SCL	54	B1
MANSION PARK DR	SCL	54	B1
MANTECA CT	SJ	72	E3
MANTECA WY	S	65	C5
MANTELLI DR	G	82	C6
MANTIS DR	SJ	63	E3

STREET	CITY	PAGE	GRID
MANTON CT	SCCO	65	E4
MANTON DR	SJ	72A	B1
MANUELA AV	PA	51	C1
MANUELA CT	PA	51	C1
MANUELA WY	PA	51	C2
MANUELLA RD	LAH	51	C3
MANX AV	C	66	A4
MANXWOOD PL	SJ	68	C5
MANZANA LN	PA	44	C6
MANZANITA AV	PA	44	A3
MANZANITA AV	SCL	60	E4
MANZANITA AV	SVL	53	A2
MANZANITA CT	MPTS	47	E6
MANZANITA DR	MH	80	C1
MANZANITA DR	SJ	60	E5
MANZANITA DR	SCCO	73	B2
MANZANITA WY	LG	70	D4
MANZANO CT	MPTS	39	F6
MANZANO ST	MPTS	39	F6
MANZANO WY	SVL	53	D1
MAPLE AV	C	66	C3
MAPLE AV	MPTS	47	E2
MAPLE AV	SCCO	80	C6
MAPLE AV	SCCO	81	A1
MAPLE LN	LA	52	A6
MAPLE LN	LG	70	E5
MAPLE ST	G	84	A2
MAPLE ST	PA	38	B6
MAPLE ST	SVL	53	A2
MAPLECREST CT	SJ	72	E1
MAPLE GROVE CT	SJ	68	A6
MAPLE LEAF CT	SJ	63	C6
MAPLETREE PL	CPTO	59	F2
MAPLEWOOD AV	PA	44	E4
MAPLEWOOD AV	SJ	61	A5
MAPLEWOOD AV	SCL	61	A5
MAPLEWOOD AV	SCCO	61	A5
MAPLEWOOD LN	SCL	60	F3
MAPLEWOOD PL	PA	44	D4
MAPLEWOOD ST	CPTO	60	A3
MARACAIBO CT	SJ	72	B3
MARANTA AV	SVL	52	D5
MARASCHINO DR	SCCO	60	E6
MARASCHINO DR	SVL	52	D6
MARATHON DR	C	65	F2
MARBELLA CT	MH	80	B4
MARBLE CT	SJ	72	E5
MARBURG WY	SJ	55	C6
MARCELLA AV	SCCO	82A	A3
MARCELYN AV	MVW	44	F5
MARCH DR	SJ	72A	D1
MARCHANT CT	SJ	56	C5
MARCHANT DR	SJ	56	C5
MARCHESE CT	SCL	55	D4
MARCHESE WY	SCL	53	D4
MARCHMONT CT	LG	71	A4
MARCHMONT DR	LG	71	A4
MARCHMONT DR	SCCO	71	A4
MARCIA AV	SJ	66	F3
MARCIA AV	SJ	67	A3
MARCIA CT	MVW	52	B2
MARCIA DR	MH	79	C4
MARCO DR	SJ	55	B3
MARCO WY	SJ	55	B3
MARCONI WY	SJ	66	E2
MARCROSS DR	SJ	55	B2
MARCY CT	CPTO	59	E4
MARCY LYNN CT	SJ	71	E2
MARDAN DR	SJ	48	D6
MARDELL LN	SJ	61	D6
MARDELL WY	MVW	44	F5
MARDEN AV	S	64	F6
MARDEN AV	S	65	A6
MARDENE CT	SJ	68	B2
MAREE CT	SJ	72	F3
MARENGO LN	SJ	55	E1
MARE PLACE CT	SJ	68	C2
MARFRANCE DR	SJ	68	B2
MARGARET CT	SVL	52	D5
MARGARET LN	C	65	F4
MARGARET ST	SJ	62	B3
MARGARET WY	SJ	62	B3
MARGARITA AV	PA	44	C4
MARGARITA CT	LA	44	D6
MARGATE AV	SJ	61	A5
MARGE WY	SCCO	61	A5
MARGO CT	SCCO	52	C3
MARGOT PL	SJ	66	E3
MARIA CT	SCL	61	B2
MARIA LN	S	64	E2
MARIA LN	SVL	53	B6
MARIA ST	SCL	61	B2

1991 SANTA CLARA COUNTY STREET INDEX

STREET	CITY	PAGE	GRID
MARIA WY	G	82	D6
MARIA WY	SJ	66	A1
MARIA WY	SCCO	66	A1
MARIAN LN	SCCO	56	A4
MARIANELLI CT	SJ	55	B5
MARIANI AV	CPTO	59	F3
MARIANI DR	SVL	60	A2
MARIANNA LN	SJ	61	D5
MARIANNA WY	C	65	F2
MARIA PRIVADA	MVW	52	D1
MARIA ROSA WY	CPTO	59	D6
MARIA TERESA CT	LG	71	B2
MARICH WY	LA	51	E1
MARICH WY	MVW	51	F2
MARICOPA DR	LG	71	A2
MARIE CT	SCCO	80	D6
MARIE LN	MH	79	D6
MARIE LN	S	64	E2
MARIETTA CT	SCL	60	E2
MARIETTA DR	SJ	71	F2
MARIETTA DR	SCL	60	E2
MARIGOLD CT	SJ	55	D5
MARIGOLD CT	SVL	53	C5
MARILLA AV	SJ	60	D6
MARILLA AV	SJ	65	E1
MARILLA CT	S	65	A2
MARILLA DR	S	65	A2
MARILYN CT	MVW	51	F3
MARILYN CT	MVW	52	A3
MARILYN DR	C	65	F5
MARILYN DR	C	66	A5
MARILYN DR	MVW	51	F3
MARILYN DR	MVW	52	A3
MARILYN LN	S	65	C5
MARILYN PL	MVW	51	F3
MARILYN PL	MVW	52	A3
MARINA WY	SCCO	66	E2
MARINE WY	MVW	44	F3
MARINER DR	SCCO	45	B6
MARINOVICH WY	LA	52	B6
MARION AV	PA	44	C3
MARION PL	PA	44	C2
MARION RD	S	64	F6
MARION WY	SVL	60	B1
MARIPOSA AV	LA	51	D2
MARIPOSA AV	LG	70	E3
MARIPOSA AV	MVW	52	A2
MARIPOSA AV	PA	44	A2
MARIPOSA AV	SJ	61	E4
MARIPOSA CT	LG	70	E3
MARIPOSA DR	MH	79	E3
MARIPOSA ST	G	82	C5
MARIST CT	SJ	63	E1
MARJORIE CT	MVW	44	F5
MARJORIE DR	C	65	F5
MARK AV	SJ	66	F5
MARK AV	SCL	53	E6
MARKET ST	LA	51	E1
MARKET ST	SJ	62	A3
MARKET ST	SCL	61	B2
MARKET ST	SCCO	82	D2
MARKHAM AV	SJ	67	A3
MARKINGDON AV	SJ	63	B1
MARKROSS CT	MH	79	E4
MARKS AV	SJ	67	A5
MARK TWAIN CT	SJ	61	A4
MARK TWAIN CT	SCL	61	A4
MARK TWAIN ST	PA	44	C1
MARKWOOD CT	SJ	63	D4
MARLA CT	SJ	71	F4
MARLBAROUGH AV	LA	52	C6
MARLBAROUGH CT	LA	52	C6
MARLBORO CT	SJ	61	D6
MARLENE CT	SJ	67	C6
MARLETTE DR	SJ	68	B2
MARLINTON CT	SJ	72	F5
MARLOWE DR	SJ	66	E6
MARLOWE DR	SJ	71	E1
MARLOWE ST	PA	38	B6
MARLYN WY	SJ	66	F2
MARLYN WY	SJ	67	A2
MARMON CT	SCL	53	F5
MARMONT WY	SCCO	56	A6
MARO DR	SCCO	56	A4
MAROEL DR	SJ	65	D3
MARQUES AV	SJ	66	F3
MARQUETTE DR	SJ	72	A2
MARQUETTE ST	SCL	53	C5
MARR LN	SJ	71	B2
MARRIAGE RD	SCCO	45	E4
MARS CT	MPTS	48	B3
MARSAN CT	C	65	E5
MARSH RD	SCCO	41	C6
MARSH RD	SCCO	49	B1
MARSH ST	SJ	62	E3
MARSHA WY	SJ	67	A3
MARSHALL AV	SJ	62	A5
MARSHALL AV	SVL	53	A4
MARSHALL CT	LA	59	C2
MARSHALL CT	SCL	60	F3
MARSHALL DR	PA	44	D2
MARSHALL DR	SCCO	82	E2
MARSHALL LN	S	65	D5
MARSHGLEN CT	SJ	55	D4
MARSH MANOR WY	SJ	68	D2
MARSHWELL WY	SJ	72A	E2
MARSTON WY	SJ	63	F4
MARTEL ST	SJ	61	F3
MARTEL ST	SJ	62	A3
MARTELLO DR	SJ	62	E4
MARTEN AV	SJ	56	D6
MARTEN AV	SJ	63	C2
MARTENS AV	MVW	52	C4
MARTHA AV	SCCO	65	C4
MARTHA AV	S	65	C4
MARTHA ST	SJ	62	C4
MARTI WY	SJ	67	E4
MARTIL WY	MPTS	47	F1
MARTIN AV	PA	38	B6
MARTIN AV	PA	58	B6
MARTIN AV	SJ	61	D4
MARTIN AV	SCL	53	F5
MARTIN AV	SCL	54	B5
MARTIN AV	SVL	60	B2
MARTIN ST	G	84	A1
MARTINIQUE CT	SJ	72	E2
MARTIN JUE ST	SJ	55	B4
MARTINSEN CT	PA	44	C3
MARTINVALE LN	SJ	72A	E4
MARTINWOOD WY	CPTO	59	F6
MARTINWOOD WY	CPTO	60	A6
MARTINWOOD WY	SJ	59	F6
MARTINWOOD WY	SJ	60	A6
MARTWOOD WY	SJ	75	F1
MARTWOOD WY	SJ	76	A1
MARVIN AV	LA	51	E3
MARY AV	CPTO	59	E2
MARY AV	SCCO	59	D1
MARY AV	SVL	52	E4
MARY AV	SVL	59	E2
MARY CT	C	65	F4
MARY CT	SCCO	81	E5
MARY WY	LG	71	B3
MARY ALICE DR	LG	71	B2
MARY ALICE DR	SCCO	78G	D1
MARYANN DR	SCL	60	F1
MARY CAROLNE CT	SJ	55	E2
MARY CAROLNE DR	SJ	55	E3
MARY EVELYN DR	SJ	72	F4
MARY EVELYN DR	SJ	72A	A4
MARY JANE WY	SJ	71	D2
MARY JANE WY	SCCO	71	D1
MARY JO CT	SJ	71	E3
MARY JO LN	SCCO	81	E2
MARY JO WY	SJ	71	E3
MARY LEE WY	SJ	67	B5
MARYLINN DR	MPTS	47	E2
MARYMEADE LN	LA	59	B1
MARYMONTE CT	SJ	72	B5
MARY-VIN LN	SCL	60	D2
MASON WY	SJ	60	A6
MASONIC DR	SCCO	67	C2
MASONWOOD ST	SJ	63	D4
MASSACHUSETTS	SJ	67	D6
MASSAR AV	SJ	55	F6
MASSOL AV	LG	70	D4
MASSON CT	S	64	D6
MAST ST	MH	79	F5
MASTEN AV	SCCO	82	D1
MASTERS CT	SJ	68	A3
MASTIC ST	SJ	62	B5
MASUDA LANDING	SJ	48	B6
MAT AV	SJ	72A	A2
MATADERO AV	SCCO	44	C5
MATADERO CT	PA	44	B5
MATADERO DR	SVL	52	E3
MATADERO CK CT	LAH	50	F4
MATADERO CK LN	LAH	50	F4
MATHER DR	SJ	55	E5
MATHEW ST	SCL	54	B5
MATHILDA AV	SCCO	52	F1
MATHILDA AV	SVL	46	A5
MATHILDA AV	SVL	52	F4
MATHILDA AV	SVL	53	A1
MATHILDA CT	MH	79	E5
MATILIJA DR	SCCO	70	C4
MATISSE CT	SVL	52	F6
MATOS CT	SCL	61	A2
MATSON DR	SJ	66	F5
MATTERHORN CT	MPTS	48	B4
MATTERHORN DR	SJ	55	D1
MATTHEW CT	SJ	72A	C4
MATTHEWS CT	MPTS	39	F5
MATTHIAS CT	SJ	62	F6
MATTHIAS DR	SJ	62	F6
MATTOS AV	SJ	48	D6
MATTOS DR	MPTS	48	C3
MATTS CT	LA	51	E5
MATTSON AV	LG	65	E6
MATZLEY CT	SJ	66	E5
MATZLEY DR	SJ	66	E5
MAUDE AV	MVW	52	E1
MAUDE AV	SCCO	52	F2
MAUDE AV	S	70	C2
MAUDE AV	SVL	52	F2
MAUDE AV	SVL	53	A2
MAUDE CT	SVL	52	E2
MAUI CT	SJ	68	C3
MAUI DR	SJ	68	A3
MAUNA KEA LN	SJ	48	D6
MAUNA KEA LN	SJ	55	D1
MAUNA LOA CT	SJ	55	D1
MAUNEY CT	SJ	65	F1
MAUREEN AV	PA	44	D4
MAUREEN WY	S	64	F2
MAURER LN	LAH	51	C3
MAURICE LN	SJ	65	C2
MAURICIA AV	SCL	60	D4
MAUVAIS RD	SJ	47	C6
MAVERICK CT	SCCO	81	E4
MAXEY CT	SJ	55	E1
MAXEY DR	SJ	55	E1
MAXIMILIAN DR	SJ	65	F4
MAXINE AV	SJ	66	F3
MAXINE AV	SJ	67	A3
MAXINE AV	SVL	52	F4
MAXINE AV	SVL	53	A4
MAXINE DR	CPTO	59	D3
MAY DR	SJ	72A	D1
MAY LN	LA	51	E1
MAY LN	SJ	66	C6
MAYA WY	SCCO	71	A6
MAYALL CT	SJ	48	C6
MAYAN LN	SCCO	81	F4
MAYBELL AV	PA	44	D5
MAYBELL WY	PA	44	C6
MAYBURY SQ	SJ	55	E3
MAYELLEN AV	SJ	61	D5
MAYER CT	LA	51	F3
MAYETTE AV	SJ	67	A3
MAYFAIR CT	SJ	62	E1
MAYFIELD AV	MVW	44	F6
MAYFIELD AV	SJ	65	D3
MAYFIELD AV	SCCO	43	E4
MAYFIELD AV	SCCO	44	A5
MAYFIELD CT	SJ	65	D3
MAYFLOWER CT	MVW	51	F2
MAYFLOWER CT	SJ	65	B2
MAYGLEN CT	SJ	55	E3
MAYGLEN WY	SJ	55	E3
MAYHEW CT	SJ	63	A5
MAYHEW DR	SJ	63	A5
MAYKIRK CT	SJ	66	E3
MAYKIRK RD	SJ	66	E3
MAYLAND AV	SJ	68	D6
MAYLAND AV	SJ	72A	D1
MAYLAND CT	SJ	72A	D1
MAYME AV	SJ	65	C2
MAYNARD CT	LA	51	E2
MAYNARD WY	LA	51	E2
MAYO DR	SJ	72A	C4
MAYO WY	SJ	72A	C4
MAYOCK RD	G	84	B4
MAYS AV	MS	70	E3
MAYSONG CT	SJ	55	C3
MAYTEN GROVE CT	SJ	68	E4
MAYTEN TREE CT	SVL	53	B5
MAYVIEW AV	PA	44	E4
MAYWOOD AV	SJ	61	C6
MAYWOOD AV	SCCO	61	C6
MAYWOOD CT	LA	51	F5
MAZEY ST	MPTS	39	E5
MAZZAGLIA AV	SJ	67	A3
MAZZONE DR	SJ	72	C3
MCABEE RD	SJ	72	B5
MCABEE RD	SCCO	72	B5
MCABEE EST PL	SJ	72	B4
MCALISTER DR	SJ	61	C4
MCARDLE DR	SJ	72	E1
MCAULEY CT	PA	38	B6
MCBAIN AV	C	66	C2
MCBAIN AV	SCCO	66	D2
MCBAIN CT	C	66	D3
MCCABE RD	SCCO	78F	E1
MCCALL DR	SJ	72	E6
MCCALL DR	SJ	75	E1
MCCAMISH AV	SJ	72A	B3
MCCANDLESS DR	MPTS	47	F5
MCCARTHY BLVD	MPTS	47	E6
MCCARTHY LN	SJ	47	C3
MCCARTY AV	MVW	52	C2
MCCARTYSVILL PL	S	64	F3
MCCHERRY AV	SCCO	62	E1
MCCLELLAN RD	CPTO	59	C5
MCCLELLAN RD	SCCO	59	D5
MCCLUHAN WY	SJ	48	C6
MCCLURE LN	LA	52	B6
MCCOLLAM DR	SJ	55	F3
MCCONNELL DR	SCCO	81	D5
MCCOPPIN PK CT	SJ	66	B6
MCCORD AV	SCCO	45	D5
MCCORMICK DR	SCL	53	F6
MCCORMICK DR	SCL	54	A6
MCCORMICK DR	SCL	60	F1
MCCORMICK DR	SCL	61	A1
MCCOVEY LN	SJ	56	B5
MCCOY AV	SJ	65	D4
MCCOY AV	SCCO	65	D4
MCCOY AV	S	65	D4
MCCREERY AV	SJ	55	E6
MCCREERY AV	SJ	62	E2
MCCREERY CT	SJ	62	E2
MCCULLOCH ST	S	65	D4
MCDANIEL AV	SJ	61	D3
MCDOLE AV	S	65	C4
MCDONALD LN	SCCO	80	B2
MCEVOY ST	SJ	61	F4
MCEVOY ST	SCCO	61	F4
MCFARLAND AV	S	65	C4
MCFARLAND CT	SCCO	44	A3
MCGILL RD	SCCO	69	E5
MCGILVRA CT	SJ	72A	B2
MCGINNESS AV	SCCO	56	A6
MCGINNESS AV	SJ	63	B2
MC GLINCEY LN	C	66	B4
MCGRAW AV	MH	79	E5
MCGREGOR WY	PA	44	C5
MCGREGOR WY	SJ	65	A2
MCINTOSH AV	SVL	52	E6
MCINTOSH CT	SVL	52	E6
MCINTOSH CK DR	SJ	75	E1
MCKAY DR	SJ	55	A2
MCKAY DR	SCCO	55	A2
MCKEAN CT	SJ	76	A1
MCKEAN RD	SJ	76	E3
MCKEAN RD	SJ	77	A4
MCKEAN RD	SCCO	76	E3
MCKEE RD	SJ	56	A3
MCKEE RD	SJ	55	D5
MCKEE RD	SCCO	55	D5
MCKEE RD	SCCO	56	A3
MCKELLAR DR	SJ	65	C1
MCKELLAR LN	PA	44	D5
MCKELVY LN	MH	80K	E1
MCKENDRIE ST	SJ	61	D2
MCKENZIE AV	LA	52	A6
MCKILLOP CT	SCL	61	C2
MCKINLEY AV	SJ	61	D6
MCKINLEY AV	SCCO	61	D6
MCKINLEY AV	SVL	52	D3
MCKINLEY AV	SVL	53	A4
MCKINLEY DR	SCL	60	E4
MCKINNON CT	SCCO	65	E1
MCKINNON DR	SJ	65	E1
MCKLINTOCK LN	CPTO	59	C5
MCLAREN PL	CPTO	60	A4
MCLAUGHLIN AV	MH	79	E4
MCLAUGHLIN AV	SJ	62	E4
MCLAUGHLIN AV	SJ	63	A6
MCLAUGHLIN AV	SJ	68	B1
MCLAUGHLIN AV	SCCO	62	E4
MCLAUGHLIN AV	SCCO	63	A6
MCLAUGHLIN AV	SCCO	68	A1
MCLAUGHLIN CT	SJ	62	E3
MCLEAN AV	SJ	68	B3
MCLEAN CT	SJ	68	B3
MCLELLAN AV	SJ	62	A5
MCMURDIE DR	C	66	A5
MCPHERSON ST	SCL	60	D1
MCQUESTEN DR	SJ	62	E3
MCVAY AV	SCCO	56	B4
MCVAY CT	SCCO	56	B4
MEAD AV	SCL	53	E4
MEADOW AV	SCL	60	C3
MEADOW CIR E	PA	44	E3
MEADOW CT	MH	80	A3
MEADOW DR E	PA	44	E3
MEADOW DR W	PA	44	D5
MEADOW LN	LA	51	D1
MEADOW LN	MVW	52	A3
MEADOW LN	SCCO	56	B5
MEADOW PL	CPTO	59	C5
MEADOWBROOK DR	LG	71	D3
MEADOWBROOK DR	SCL	53	E5
MEADOW CREEK DR	SJ	67	D5
MEADOW DALE CT	SJ	67	D5
MEADOWGATE WY	SJ	48	B5
MEADOW GLEN CT	SJ	68	C1
MEADOW GLEN WY	SJ	68	B1
MEADOWGREEN WY	MH	79	C1
MEADOWHURST CT	SJ	67	C5
MEADOWLAKE DR	SVL	53	C1
MEADOWLAND DR	MPTS	47	F2
MEADOWLANDS LN	SCCO	68A	B4
MEADOWLARK AV	SJ	61	B3
MEADOW LARK LN	SCCO	82A	C2
MEADOW LARK LN	SVL	60	B2
MEADOWMONT DR	SJ	55	D4
MEADOW OAK RD	S	64	F2
MEADOWOOD DR	SJ	72	D4
MEADOW RDGE CIR	SJ	55	B3
MEADOWSIDE CT	SJ	67	E5
MEADOWVIEW LN	CPTO	59	D4
MEADOWVILLE CT	SJ	60	E5
MEADWELL CT	SJ	72A	E1
MEANDER DR	SJ	72	A3
MEARS CT	SCCO	44	A4
MEDALLION DR	SJ	72	A4
MEDFORD DR	LA	52	C6
MEDIA WY	SJ	66	F4
MEDICAL LN	PA	43	E3
MEDICAL CTR DR	MH	80	A5
MEDICUS CT	SCCO	60	C5
MEDINA CT	CPTO	59	B5
MEDINA LN	CPTO	59	B5
MEDLEY CT	SJ	68	B1
MEDLEY DR	SJ	68	B1
MEDOC CT	MVW	45	A5
MEDWIN CT	SJ	63	C5
MEG CT	SCCO	82A	D2
MEG DR	SJ	67	D5
MEI DR	MH	79	F4
MEIGGS LN	SCCO	60	C5
MEKLER CT	SJ	62	E6
MEKLER DR	SJ	62	E6
MELANNIE CT	SJ	62	D3
MELBA CT	MVW	52	A2
MELBA CT	SJ	72	D6
MELBOURNE BLVD	SJ	62	C3
MELCHESTER DR	SJ	48	C5
MELCHOIR CT	SCCO	82	D3
MELINA ST	SJ	61	E1
MELINDA CIR	S	65	B2
MELISSA CT	CPTO	59	B5
MELLISA CT	SJ	63	A5
MELLO DR	SJ	54	D1
MELLO PL	CPTO	60	A4
MELLON DR	S	65	C3
MELLOWOOD DR	S	65	C2
MELNIKOFF DR	SJ	63	F1
MELODY LN	LAH	51	A4
MELODY LN	SJ	55	C6
MELODY LN	SCL	60	C3
MELODY LN	SCCO	78G	F2
MELON CT	SVL	52	D4
MELROSE AV	SJ	55	D6
MELVILLE AV	PA	44	B2
MELVILLE WY	SJ	65	D4
MELVIN DR	SJ	60	A6
MELWOOD DR	SJ	72	A2
MEMBRILLO CTE	SCL	60	D2
MEMOREX DR	SCL	54	A5
MEMORIAL WY	SCCO	43	F3
MEMORY LN	C	66	C3
MEMPHIS DR	C	65	F2
MENALTO DR	LAH	50	F5
MENAUL CT	SJ	72A	F4
MENDELSOHN LN	S	70	A1
MENDENHALL DR	C	65	E2
MENDENHALL DR	SJ	65	E2
MENDOCINO CT	MH	80K	F2
MENDOTA WY	SJ	63	A3
MENDOZA AV	SJ	68	B4
MENHART DR	SCCO	60	C5
MENKER AV	SJ	61	D5
MENLO DR	SJ	72	D4
MENORCA CT	SJ	72	A4
MENZEL PL	SCL	53	F6
MENZEL PL	SCL	54	A6
MERCADO CT	MPTS	48	A1
MERCED CT	SCL	53	E6
MERCEDES AV	LA	44	D6
MERCEDES AV	LA	51	D1
MERCEDES RD	CPTO	59	B5
MERCER AV	SJ	66	F2
MERCURY CT	MPTS	48	B3
MERCURY DR	SVL	53	D3
MERCY ST	MVW	52	B2
MEREDITH AV	SJ	61	F6
MERIDA DR	S	65	A2
MERIDIAN AV	SJ	61	E5
MERIDIAN AV	SJ	66	F6
MERIDIAN AV	SJ	72	A2
MERIDIAN AV	SCCO	61	E5
MERIDIAN AV	SCCO	66	E3
MERIDIAN WY	MVW	52	A1
MERIDIAN WY	SJ	61	E5
MERKLEY ROW ST	SCCO	56	D3
MERLE AV	SJ	61	F6
MERLIN LN	SJ	68	E3
MERLOT CT	SJ	63	F6
MERRIBROOK CT	S	65	B5
MERRIBROOK DR	S	65	A5
MERRICK DR	S	64	F5
MERRICK DR	S	65	A5
MERRILL DR	SJ	71	E3
MERRILL LOOP	SJ	71	F2
MERRIMAC DR	SVL	52	D5
MERRIMAC DR	SJ	66	A2
MERRIMAN LN	SCCO	81H	D2
MERRIMAN RD	CPTO	59	C5
MERRIT LN	SJ	68	E4
MERRITON CT	SJ	71	E2
MERRITT DR	CPTO	60	B3
MERRITT RD	LA	51	E3
MERRIVALE W SQ	SJ	66	A1
MERRIWEATHER LN	SJ	46	F4
MERRY LN	SJ	66	B2
MERRYWOOD DR	SJ	72	A1
MERVYNS WY	SCCO	56	A6
MERZ CT	MPTS	47	F1
MESA AV	PA	51	C1
MESA CT	PA	51	C1
MESA DR	SJ	54	F2
MESA DR	SJ	72	B2
MESA RD	G	83	F5
MESA RD	SCCO	83	E4
MESA OAK CT	SVL	53	B5
MESA VERDE DR	MPTS	48	C3
MESCALARO DR	SJ	72	F3
MESITA WY	SJ	66	D5
MESQUITE DR	SCL	60	E4
MESQUITE PL	SVL	53	B5
MESSINA DR	SJ	48	D5
META DR	SJ	65	E4
METCALF RD	SJ	72B	B3
METCALF RD	SJ	78	E2
METCALF RD	SCCO	68B	B4
METCALF RD	SCCO	72B	E3
METEOR DR	CPTO	59	D3
METEOR PL	CPTO	59	E3
METHILHAVEN CT	SJ	63	C6
METHILHAVEN LN	SJ	63	C6
METHVEN LN	MPTS	48	B4
METLER CT	S	65	C5
METRO CIR	PA	44	D1
METRO DR	SJ	54	E4
MEYER CIR	SJ	63	C5
MEYERHOLZ ST	CPTO	59	D3
MIA CIR	SJ	67	F5
MIAMI DR	SJ	62	F3
MICHAEL CT	CPTO	59	F5
MICHAEL CT	CPTO	60	A5
MICHAEL CT	MPTS	48	B1
MICHAEL DR	C	66	C3
MICHAEL LN	MS	70	E3
MICHAEL ST	MPTS	48	B1
MICHAEL WY	SCL	60	D4
MICHAELS DR	S	64	E6
MICH BLUFF DR	SJ	55	C3
MICHELANGELO DR	SVL	53	A6
MICHELE CT	G	83	F5
MICHELE WY	SJ	60	A6
MICHELE JEAN WY	SCL	60	F3

1991 SANTA CLARA COUNTY STREET INDEX

1991 SANTA CLARA COUNTY STREET INDEX

STREET	CITY	PAGE	GRID
MOUNT DIABLO AV	MPTS	48	B4
MOUNT DIABLO DR	SJ	63	B1
MOUNT EDEN CT	S	64	D5
MOUNT EDEN RD	SCCO	64	C4
MOUNT EDEN RD	S	64	C4
MT EL SERENO CT	SCCO	70	A6
MT EVEREST CT	SJ	56	C6
MT EVEREST CT	SJ	63	C1
MT EVEREST DR	SJ	56	C6
MT EVEREST DR	SJ	63	C1
MOUNTFORD DR	SJ	72A	B4
MOUNT FOREST DR	SJ	72	D5
MT FRAZIER DR	SJ	56	C6
MT FRAZIER DR	SJ	63	C1
MT HAMILTON AV	LA	51	D3
MT HAMILTON CT	LA	51	D3
MT HAMILTON RD	SCCO	56	F4
MT HAMILTON RD	SCCO	56B	C5
MT HAMILTON RD	SCCO	63A	D1
MT HAMLTN VW DR	SJ	55	D6
MT HAMLTN VW DR	SJ	62	D1
MOUNT HERMAN DR	SJ	63	B1
MOUNT HOLLY DR	SJ	72	D5
MOUNT HOOD WY	SJ	63	B1
MOUNT HOPE DR	SJ	72	D5
MOUNT ISABEL CT	SJ	63	E4
MOUNT ISABEL DR	SJ	63	E4
MOUNT KENYA DR	SJ	63	D1
MOUNT LASSEN DR	SJ	56	C6
MOUNT LASSEN DR	SJ	63	C1
MT LAUREL CT	MVW	45	B6
MOUNT LENEVE DR	SJ	72	D5
MOUNT LOGAN DR	SJ	56	C6
MOUNT LOGAN DR	SJ	63	C1
MT MADONNA DR	SJ	63	C1
MT MADONNA RD	SCCO	81G	E3
MT MCKINLEY CT	SJ	56	C6
MT MCKINLEY CT	SJ	63	C1
MT MCKINLEY DR	SJ	56	C6
MT MCKINLEY DR	SJ	63	C1
MT OLIVEIRA DR	SJ	56	C6
MT OLIVEIRA DR	SJ	63	C1
MOUNT OSO DR	SJ	63	E4
MOUNT PAKRON CT	SJ	72	E5
MOUNT PAKRON DR	SJ	72	E5
MT PALOMAR DR	SJ	63	B1
MT PLEASANT CT	SJ	63	D1
MT PLEASANT RD	SJ	56	D6
MT PLEASANT RD	SJ	63	D1
MT PLEASANT RD	SCCO	63	D1
MT PRIETA DR	SJ	63	C1
MT RAINIER AV	MPTS	48	C3
MT RAINIER DR	SJ	63	C1
MOUNT ROYAL DR	SJ	72	D5
MT RUSHMORE DR	SJ	63	C1
MT ST HELENA DR	SJ	63	C1
MOUNT SHASTA AV	MPTS	48	B4
MOUNT SHASTA DR	SJ	56	C6
MOUNT SHASTA DR	SJ	63	C1
MT STANLEY WY	SJ	56	C6
MT UMUNHUM RD	SCCO	75	C5
MT UMUNHUM RD	SCCO	78H	F1
MT UMUNHUM RD	SCCO	78J	A1
MT UMHM-LM PRTA	SCCO	78J	D3
MOUNT VERNON CT	MVW	51	F1
MOUNT VERNON CT	MVW	52	A1
MOUNT VERNON DR	SJ	66	E2
MOUNT VERNON WY	G	83	E3
MOUNT VISTA DR	SJ	56	B6
MOUNT VISTA DR	SJ	63	B1
MOUNT VISTA DR	SCCO	63	B1
MT WLLINGTON DR	SJ	72	D5
MT WHITNEY DR	SJ	56	C6
MT WHITNEY DR	SJ	63	C1
MOUNT WILSON DR	SJ	56	C6
MOUNT ZION AV	SJ	63	C1
MOZART AV	SJ	63	B4
MOZART AV E	SCCO	66	B6
MOZART AV W	LG	66	A6
MOZART CT	SVL	52	F6
MOZART CT	SVL	53	A6
MOZART WY	LG	66	A6
MUELLER AV	SJ	55	E5
MUENCH CT	SJ	55	B3
MUENDER AV	SVL	52	E3
MUIR AV	SCL	60	D4
MUIR DR	G	82	C6
MUIR DR	MVW	52	D3
MUIR DR	SJ	71	E3
MUIR WY	LA	52	B5
MUIRDRUM PL	SJ	63	D3
MUIRFIELD CT	SJ	55	F5

STREET	CITY	PAGE	GRID
MUIRFIELD DR	SJ	55	F6
MUIRHOUSE PL	SJ	67	E6
MUIRHOUSE PL	SJ	72	E1
MUIR PLACE CT	SJ	68	C1
MUIRWOOD CT	SJ	48	B5
MUIRWOOD WY	SJ	48	B5
MULBERRY CIR	SJ	66	E3
MULBERRY DR	LG	65	E6
MULBERRY LN	LAH	51	C3
MULBERRY LN	SJ	66	E3
MULBERRY LN	SVL	52	D5
MULCASTER CT	SJ	67	C5
MULLEN AV	LG	70	E4
MUMFORD PL	PA	44	E4
MUNDELL CT	LA	44	D6
MUNDELL WY	LA	44	D6
MUNRO AV	C	65	E5
MUNROE WY	MH	79	D5
MURDOCH CT	PA	44	D3
MURDOCH DR	PA	44	D3
MURGUIA AV	SCL	61	A2
MURIEL CT	SJ	68	B2
MURIEL CT	SCL	60	E3
MURIEL LN	SCCO	60	B5
MURIETTA LN	LAH	51	B6
MURIETTA LN	LAH	58	B1
MURIETTA LN	SJ	56	D5
MURILLO AV	SJ	63	E2
MURLAGAN AV	MVW	45	D6
MURMAN CT	SJ	63	E2
MURPHY AV	SJ	55	A3
MURPHY AV	SCCO	80	A4
MURPHY AV	SCCO	81	B1
MURPHY AV	SVL	52	F4
MURPHY AV	SVL	53	A3
MURPHY CT	MH	79	C3
MURPHY LN	MH	79	E1
MURPHY SPGS CT	MH	79	C3
MURPHY SPGS DR	MH	79	C3
MURRAY AV	G	82	F5
MURRAY AV	G	82A	A6
MURRAY AV	SCCO	82	F5
MURRAY ST	MPTS	39	F5
MURRAY WY	PA	44	D3
MURRE LN	SVL	60	B2
MURTHA DR	SJ	56	B6
MURTHA DR	SJ	63	A1
MUSCAT CT	SVL	52	D6
MUSCAT DR	SJ	72A	E4
MUSETTA CT	SJ	63	A5
MUSEUM WY	SCCO	43	F3
MUSTANG ST	SJ	72A	A2
MUSTO AV	SJ	72A	C1
MYER PL	CPTO	60	A4
MYERSLY CT	SJ	63	E3
MYLES CT	SJ	61	A5
MYLINDA DR	SJ	49	A6
MYNA CT	SJ	68	D4
MYRA DR	SJ	71	E3
MYREN CT	S	65	C5
MYREN DR	S	65	C5
MYRTLE AV	MH	79	E5
MYRTLE AV	SJ	67	A5
MYRTLE DR	SVL	53	C5
MYRTLE ST	SJ	61	D2
MYRTLE GROVE LN	SJ	68	A6
MYRTLEWOOD DR	CPTO	60	B6
MYSTIC CT	SJ	71	B1
N			
N ST	SVL	46	C6
NADINE CT	SCCO	71	C1
NADINE DR	C	65	E2
NAGLEE AV	SJ	61	D3
NAIDA AV	SJ	62	F2
NAIDA AV	SJ	63	A2
NAKOOCHE TR	SCCO	73	E6
NALL LN	SCCO	78H	F3
NALOR CT	LG	65	F6
NALOR CT	LG	70	F1
NANCARROW WY	SJ	72	B4
NANCY CT	CPTO	59	F5
NANCY CT	MVW	52	C2
NANCY CT	SCCO	56	A6
NANCY LN	LA	52	A6
NANCY LN	SCCO	56	A5
NANDELL LN	SCCO	51	F6
NANDELL LN	SCCO	58	F1
NANDINA WY	SVL	53	C5
NANTUCKET CT	SJ	61	E6
NANTUCKET CT	S	65	B3

STREET	CITY	PAGE	GRID
NANTUCKET CT	SVL	52	E5
NANTUCKET PL	G	83	F2
NAOMI CT	SJ	67	D4
NAOMI CT	SCCO	78G	D1
NAPA CT	SJ	63	D3
NAPA DR	SJ	63	D3
NAPA RIVER CT	SJ	67	D5
NAPLES DR	SJ	62	F2
NARCISO CT	SJ	60	C6
NARCISSO RD	SCCO	91	D2
NARVAEZ AV	SJ	67	D5
NARVAEZ AV	SCCO	67	D4
NASH CT	SJ	68	A3
NASH RD	LA	51	E5
NASHUA CT	SJ	72A	F4
NASHUA CT	SVL	52	E5
NASHVILLE DR	SJ	55	E3
NASSAU DR	SJ	63	A3
NATALIE AV	SCL	53	E6
NATALIE CT	SJ	71	E2
NATALIE DR	MH	79	F5
NATALYE RD	MS	70	F1
NATHAN WY	PA	44	E3
NATHN ABBOTT WY	SCCO	43	F4
NATHANSON AV	CPTO	59	E3
NATIONAL AV	LG	71	B1
NATIONAL AV	MVW	45	D6
NATIONAL AV	MVW	52	D1
NATIONAL AV	SCCO	71	B1
NATIONAL WY	SJ	71	B1
NATIVE DANCR DR	MH	80K	F3
NATOMA CT	S	65	A2
NATOMA DR	SJ	72	E2
NATOMA RD	LAH	51	A4
NATURE CT	SJ	72A	C3
NATURE DR	SJ	72A	C3
NAUTILUS CT	SJ	61	C6
NAVAJO CT	SJ	72	E2
NAVAJO LN	LA	51	E3
NAVAJO TR	SCCO	73	E6
NAVAJO TR	SCCO	78G	E1
NAVARRO DR	SVL	60	B1
NAVLET CT	SVL	52	E6
NAVY DR	SVL	53	B2
NAVY PL	SCCO	55	C4
NAZARENE WY	SJ	61	A6
NAZARETH CT	SCL	60	D3
NEAL AV	SJ	61	B5
NECTARINE AV	SVL	52	D5
NECTARNE GRV CT	SJ	68	E4
NEDSON CT	MVW	44	F5
NEEDHAM LN	S	65	B3
NEEDLES DR	SJ	62	D5
NEET AV	SJ	61	B6
NEILSON CT	SJ	68	B5
NELA LN	LA	51	E1
NELIS CT	SVL	52	E6
NELLO DR	C	66	A4
NELO ST	SCL	54	C2
NELSON CT	PA	44	E4
NELSON CT	SCL	47	A6
NELSON CT	SCL	54	A1
NELSON CT	SCCO	66	C6
NELSON CT	SCCO	71	D1
NELSON DR	PA	44	E4
NELSON DR	SCL	47	A6
NELSON DR	SCL	54	A1
NELSON WY	SJ	66	D6
NELSON WY	SCCO	66	D6
NELSON WY	SCCO	71	D1
NELSON WY	SVL	59	E1
NEPO CT	SJ	72A	C4
NEPO DR	SJ	72A	C4
NEPTUNE CT	SJ	72	B5
NEPTUNE CT	SCCO	45	C6
NERDY AV	SJ	68	A3
NERISSA WY	LG	71	D2
NERISSA WY	SJ	71	D2
NERO CT	SJ	65	F3
NESBIT CT	SJ	72	A3
NESTA DR	SJ	66	F5
NESTA DR	SJ	67	A5
NESTON WY	LA	59	C2
NESTORITA WY	SJ	66	D5
NETTLE PL	SVL	53	B5
NEVADA AV	PA	44	B3
NEVADA AV	SJ	62	A6
NEVADA AV	SJ	66	F1
NEVADA AV	SJ	67	A1
NEVADA PL	SJ	67	A1
NEVES CT	SCL	60	F4
NEVES WY	SJ	56	B4
NEVILLE AV	SJ	65	E4

STREET	CITY	PAGE	GRID
NEVIN WY	SJ	61	E6
NEW AV	SCCO	81	F3
NEW AV	SCCO	81A	A5
NEW AV	SCCO	82A	B2
NEW CT	SJ	72	F1
NEWARK WY	SJ	66	D5
NEW BEDFORD CT	SJ	55	B2
NEWBERRY CT	PA	44	D5
NEWBERRY DR	SJ	67	B4
NEW BRIDGE DR	LAH	51	C4
NEW BRUNSWICK	SVL	59	E2
NEWCASTLE DR	CPTO	64	F1
NEWCASTLE DR	LA	59	C2
NEW COMPTON CT	SJ	67	E6
NEW COMPTON DR	SJ	67	E5
NEW DORSET CT	SJ	67	E5
NEWELL AV	LG	70	F1
NEWELL CT	LG	70	F1
NEWELL PL	PA	38	B6
NEWELL PL	PA	44	B1
NEWELL RD	PA	38	C6
NEWELL RD	PA	44	B1
NEW ENGLAND CT	SJ	67	D6
NEWFOUNDLAND DR	SVL	59	E1
NEWHALL ST	SJ	54	E6
NEWHALL ST	SJ	61	D1
NEWHALL ST	SCL	61	D1
NEWHALL ST	SCCO	61	A2
NEW HAMPTON WY	SCL	60	E1
NEW HAVEN CT	CPTO	59	D5
NEWHOUSE CT	S	65	B4
NEW IRELAND CT	SJ	67	E5
NEW JERSEY AV	SJ	66	D6
NEW JERSEY AV	SCCO	66	D6
NEWMAN PL	MVW	45	A5
NEW MAPLE ST	SCL	61	C1
NEW MAYFIELD LN	PA	44	B3
NEW PENCE CT	SJ	48	E4
NEWPORT AV	SJ	66	F1
NEWPORT AV	SJ	67	A2
NEWPORT CT	S	65	B3
NEW RAMSEY CT	SJ	67	E6
NEW RIVER DR	SJ	72A	E4
NEWSOM AV	SCCO	60	C6
NEWTON AV	SJ	62	F2
NEWTON AV	SJ	63	A2
NEWTON DR	MVW	52	C5
NEW TRIER AV	SJ	67	D6
NEWVILLE DR	LG	65	E5
NEW WORLD DR	SJ	67	D6
NEW YORK AV	LG	70	E5
NEZ PERCE TR	SCCO	73	E6
NIAGARA DR	SJ	65	F1
NIBLICK AV	SCCO	51	F6
NIBLICK AV	SCCO	58	F1
NICHOLAS DR	SJ	66	C5
NICHOLIS AV	SJ	78	C6
NICHOLLS AV	SCCO	78	B5
NICHOLSON AV	LG	70	D4
NICHOLSON AV	SCL	60	E3
NICHOLSON AV	SCCO	70	D4
NICHOLSON LN	SJ	47	B5
NICKEL AV	SJ	63	A5
NICKLAUS AV	MPTS	40	A6
NICOLE CT	G	83	F5
NICOLE CT	SJ	68	C4
NICOLE LN	LAH	51	E5
NICOLE WY	G	83	F5
NICORA AV	SJ	55	C5
NIDO DR	C	66	B4
NIEMAN CT	SJ	63	D6
NIEMAN BLVD	SJ	63	C5
NIEMEYER CT	SJ	55	C2
NIEVES CT	MPTS	40	A6
NIEVES ST	MPTS	40	A6
NIGHTFALL CT	SJ	72	E5
NIGHTHAWK TER	SVL	60	B2
NIGHTINGALE AV	SVL	60	B2
NIGHTINGALE CT	LA	59	B1
NIGHTINGALE DR	SJ	67	B3
NIKETTE WY	SJ	72	D6
NIKKIE LN	SCCO	78H	A2
NIKULINA CT	SJ	72	D6
NILDA AV	MVW	52	B4
NILE DR	CPTO	60	A4
NIMITZ FRWY	MPTS	39	C3
NIMITZ FRWY	MPTS	47	E4
NIMITZ FRWY	SJ	54	F2
NIMITZ FRWY	SCCO	54	F2
NIMRICH LN	SJ	71	C3
NINA CT	LG	71	A4
NINA LN	SCCO	80	A4
NINA PL	LAH	51	B2

STREET	CITY	PAGE	GRID
NINO AV	LG	70	F3
NINO WY	LG	70	F3
NIPPER AV	SJ	55	C6
NISICH CT	SJ	62	F5
NISICH DR	SJ	62	F5
NISQUALLY DR	SVL	59	E2
NITA AV	MVW	44	F5
NOB HILL DR	SJ	56	C4
NOB HILL DR	SCCO	56	C4
NOB HILL TER	MH	79	D5
NOB HILL WY	LG	70	F2
NOB HILL WY	LG	71	A2
NOBILI AV	SCL	53	D5
NOBLE AV	SJ	55	F1
NOBLE CT	LG	71	A4
NOBLE LN	SJ	55	F1
NOBLE LN	SCCO	55	F1
NOBLE FIR	CPTO	59	E5
NOBU DR	SJ	55	B2
NODDIN AV	SCCO	71	A1
NOEL AV	CPTO	59	D3
NOEL DR	LA	59	B2
NOELLA WY	SJ	71	D2
NOKOMIS DR	SJ	68	B3
NOLA DR	SJ	66	F3
NOLDEN AV	SJ	60	F5
NOLDEN AV	SJ	61	A5
NOMARK CT	SJ	66	F2
NOMARK DR	SJ	66	F2
NOME CT	SVL	59	E2
NO NAME UNO	G	82	F3
NOONAN CT	CPTO	59	D5
NOONWOOD CT	SJ	76	A1
NORA WY	SJ	71	E2
NORADA CT	S	64	E2
NORANDA DR	SVL	59	E3
NORBERT CT	SJ	63	E3
NORCLIFFE CT	SJ	67	B5
NORCOTT CT	SJ	72	D5
NORCREST CT	SJ	63	E3
NORCREST DR	SJ	63	E3
NORCROSS CT	SJ	63	E3
NORCROSS DR	SJ	63	E3
NORD LN	SJ	66	F4
NORDALE AV	SJ	62	D5
NORDICA CT	SJ	66	B6
NORDICA CT	SJ	71	B1
NORDYKE DR	SJ	56	A5
NOREEN DR	SJ	66	E6
NORELIUS CT	SJ	72	A3
NORFOLK DR	SJ	60	B6
NORFOLK PINE AV	SVL	52	D5
NORIEGA AV	SVL	52	E3
NORIN CT	SCCO	66	B4
NORITA CT	SJ	55	E4
NORLAND DR	SVL	59	E2
NORMA JEAN CT	SJ	67	C6
NORMA JEAN WY	SJ	72	B2
NORMAN AV	SCL	54	A2
NORMAN AV	SCCO	66	D2
NORMAN DR	SVL	60	B1
NORMAN DR	SCCO	78G	E2
NORMANDALE DR	SJ	67	A5
NORMANDY CT	CPTO	60	A5
NORMANDY DR	SCCO	66	B5
NORMANDY LN	LAH	51	D5
NORMANDY WY	CPTO	64	F1
NORMANDY WY	SCL	61	B2
NORMINGTON WY	SJ	67	C5
NORSEMAN DR	SJ	55	D4
NORSTAD ST	SJ	61	C6
NORTECH PKWY	SJ	46	F4
NORTECH PKWY	SJ	47	A4
NORTE VERANO	SJ	68A	B2
NORTH DR	MVW	52	B4
NORTH ST	SCCO	81	C3
NORTHAMPTON CT	S	65	B3
NORTHAMPTON DR	PA	44	C2
NORTHAMPTON DR	SJ	66	E3
NORTHAMPTON DR	S	65	A3
N BAYSHORE W	SJ	55	B5
NORTHBROOK SQ	CPTO	60	A3
NORTHCOVE SQ	CPTO	60	A3
NORTH CREEK DR	SJ	72A	F5
NORTHCREST LN	SCCO	58	D1
NORTHCREST SQ	CPTO	60	A3
NORTHDALE CT	SJ	72A	A4
NORTHERN RD	SJ	62	B6
NORTHERN RD	SJ	67	B1
NORTHERN RD	SCCO	62	B6
NORTHFIELD SQ	CPTO	60	A3
NORTHFORDE DR	CPTO	60	A3

STREET	CITY	PAGE	GRID
NORTH FORK LN	LAH	51	A3
NORTHGATE DR	SJ	68	C5
NORTHGLEN SQ	CPTO	60	A3
NORTHGROVE LN	SJ	55	D3
NORTHGROVE WY	SJ	55	D3
NORTH HILL TER	MH	79	D5
NORTHHURST DR	CPTO	60	A3
NORTHLAKE DR	SJ	60	F5
NORTHLAWN DR	SJ	65	D3
NORTH LOOP DR	SJ	66	E1
NORTHOAK SQ	CPTO	60	A3
NORTHPOINT WY	CPTO	60	A3
NORTHRIDGE DR	SJ	72	C5
NORTHRIDGE SQ	CPTO	60	A3
NORTHRUP ST	SJ	61	E5
NORTHRUP ST	SCCO	61	E5
NORTHSEAL SQ	CPTO	60	A3
NORTHSHORE SQ	CPTO	60	A3
NORTH SKY SQ	CPTO	60	A3
NORTH STAR CIR	SJ	48	B6
NORTH STAR PL	SJ	48	B6
NORTHUMBRLND DR	SVL	52	D5
NORTHVIEW SQ	CPTO	60	A3
NORTHWEST SQ	CPTO	60	A3
NORTHWESTERN PY	SCL	53	F4
NORTHWIND SQ	CPTO	60	A2
NORTHWOOD DR	CPTO	60	A3
NORTHWOOD DR	SJ	48	B6
NORTON AV	SJ	61	E4
NORTON RD	S	69	F2
NORTREE ST	SJ	63	E3
NORVAL WY	SJ	67	A2
NORVELLA ST	SJ	62	F2
NORVELLA ST	SJ	63	A2
NORWALK DR	SJ	60	E5
NORWICH AV	CPTO	60	B4
NORWICH AV	MPTS	47	E2
NORWICH WY	SJ	65	D3
NORWOOD AV	SJ	63	D3
NOTRE DAME DR	MVW	51	F4
NOTRE DAME DR	MVW	52	A4
NOTRE DAME DR	SCL	53	D5
NOTRE DAME ST	SJ	61	F3
NOTRE DAME ST	SJ	62	A3
NOTTINGHAM PL	SJ	60	F6
NOTTINGHAM WY	C	66	D2
NOTTINGHAM WY	LA	59	A1
NOTTING HILL DR	SJ	55	B4
NOTTOWAY AV	SJ	62	F2
NOVAK DR	SJ	55	F3
NOVA SCOTIA ST	SJ	66	C6
NOVA SCOTIA ST	SCCO	66	C6
NOVARO PL	SJ	47	D6
NOVARO WY	SJ	47	D6
NOVATO AV	SVL	52	E4
NOVEMBER DR	CPTO	59	E6
NOYO DR	SJ	72A	B2
NOYO RIVER CT	SJ	67	D5
NUBE CT	SJ	63	D3
NUESTRA AV	SVL	52	E4
NUEVA DR	SJ	72A	D4
NUGGET CT	SJ	63	B1
NUNES DR	SJ	55	B2
NUTHATCH LN	SVL	60	B2
NUTMEG AV	SVL	52	E4
NUTMEG CT	SJ	55	C2
NUTTAL OAK CT	SVL	53	B5
NUTTMAN ST	SCL	54	B3
NUT TREE PL	SJ	62	D4
NUTWOOD LN	S	65	A6
O			
OAHU LN	S	65	B5
OAK AV	LA	52	B6
OAK AV	SCCO	81	C4
OAK PARK CIR	LAH	51	D6
OAK PARK CT	LAH	51	D6
OAK CT	G	82	F6
OAK CT	SCCO	73	C2
OAK CT	SCCO	78G	F1
OAK CT	SVL	53	A3
OAK DR	MS	70	C2
OAK DR	SJ	72A	F3
OAK DR	SCCO	70	C2
OAK DR	SCCO	73	D6
OAK DR	SCCO	78G	D1
OAK LN	MVW	52	B3
OAK LN	SCCO	80	D2
OAK LN	SCCO	80K	D4
OAK PL	S	64	F6
OAK PL	S	65	A6

STREET	CITY	PAGE	GRID
OAK ST	LA	51	D3
OAK ST	MVW	52	A2
OAK ST	SJ	62	B5
OAK ST	S	64	F6
OAK ST	S	69	F1
OAKBERRY WY	SJ	72A	C3
OAKBERRY WY	SJ	55	C3
OAKBLUFF CT	SJ	55	C3
OAKBRIDGE DR	SJ	63	B6
OAK BROOK CIR	SJ	72A	E4
OAK CANYON CT	SJ	71	F4
OAK CANYON DR	MH	80	E3
OAK CANYON DR	SJ	71	F4
OAK CANYON LN	MH	80	E3
OAK CANYON PL	SJ	71	F4
OAK CREEK LN	S	64	F2
OAK CREEK WY	SVL	53	D1
OAKCREST CT	CPTO	59	C3
OAKCREST DR	SJ	72	C5
OAK DALE DR	LG	71	A2
OAKDALE WY	MH	79	C1
OAKDELL PL	CPTO	59	D4
OAKDELL PL	SJ	61	A6
OAK ESTATES CT	SJ	68	F2
OAK FLAT RD	SJ	55	B1
OAK FOREST WY	SJ	72	C4
OAKGATE WY	SJ	63	E4
OAK GLEN AV	SCCO	78L	D3
OAK GLEN AV	SCCO	79	A6
OAK GLEN AV	SCCO	80K	B1
OAKGLEN WY	SJ	72	B3
OAK GLENN DR	SCCO	70	C3
OAK GROVE AV	LG	70	D6
OAK GROVE CT	MH	79	D4
OAK GROVE DR	MH	79	D4
OAK GROVE DR	SJ	60	E5
OAK GROVE DR	SCL	54	B1
OAKHAVEN DR	S	65	B2
OAK HILL AV	PA	51	C1
OAK HILL CT	MH	80	D3
OAK HILL WY	LG	70	E5
OAKHURST AV	LA	52	B6
OAKHURST CT	SJ	65	C1
OAKHURST DR	MS	70	D4
OAK KNOLL CT	LG	70	D3
OAK KNOLL DR	MS	70	D3
OAK KNOLL DR	SJ	65	C1
OAK KNOLL RD	LG	70	D5
OAKLAND AV	SJ	55	E6
OAKLAND AV	SJ	62	E1
OAKLAND PL	LG	65	E6
OAKLEAF CT	CPTO	59	D4
OAK LEAF CT	MH	80	D3
OAK LEAF DR	MH	80	D2
OAKLEAF DR	SJ	56	C6
OAK LEAF LN	MH	80	D3
OAKLEAF PL	CPTO	59	D4
OAKLEY DR	LA	59	C1
OAKMEAD PKWY	SVL	53	D2
OAK MEADOW CT	CPTO	64	E1
OAK MEADOW DR	LG	70	E3
OAKMEAD VLGE CT	SCL	53	E4
OAKMEAD VLGE DR	SCL	53	E3
OAKMILL CT	SJ	63	A6
OAKMONT DR	SJ	60	F6
OAKMONT DR	SCCO	73	D5
OAKMONT PL	SJ	60	F6
OAKMONT WY	LG	71	A2
OAKMORE DR	SCCO	56	B3
OAKNOLL CT	CPTO	59	D4
OAK PARK DR	LG	71	A2
OAK PARK DR	MH	79	D5
OAK PARK DR	SJ	65	C1
OAK PARK LN	SJ	66	C4
OAKRIDGE CT	MH	80	E2
OAKRIDGE DR	SCCO	58	F1
OAKRIDGE LN	MH	80	E2
OAKRIDGE RD	MH	80	E2
OAK RIDGE RD	SCCO	41	D1
OAK RIDGE RD	SCCO	42	A2
OAKRIDGE RD	SCCO	70	B3
OAK RIDGE WY	LG	70	F2
OAK RIM CT	LG	70	F3
OAK RIM WY	LG	70	F3
OAK SPRING CT	CPTO	64	E1
OAK SPRINGS CIR	SCCO	82A	F4
OAKTON CT	SJ	63	B2
OAKTREE DR	MVW	44	E6
OAKTREE DR	MVW	51	E1
OAKTREE DR	SJ	60	C6
OAK VALLEY DR	SCCO	80K	B5
OAK VIEW CIR	MH	80	D3

STREET	CITY	PAGE	GRID
OAK VIEW CT	MH	80	D4
OAKVIEW LN	MH	80	D3
OAKVIEW LN	CPTO	59	D4
OAKVIEW RD	SJ	68	B2
OAKVILLE AV	CPTO	60	A5
OAKWOOD AV	SJ	66	E6
OAKWOOD CT	LA	51	F5
OAKWOOD CT	MH	80	D3
OAK WOOD DR	LG	65	E5
OAKWOOD DR	SCL	54	B2
OAKWOOD LN	MH	80	E3
OAKWOOD WY	LG	71	A2
OASIS CT	CPTO	59	C4
OASIS DR	SJ	72A	C1
OBATA WY	G	84	B4
OBERLIN ST	PA	44	A4
OBERLIN WY	SJ	72A	C4
OBERT DR	SJ	68	A6
OBRAD DR	S	65	C3
OBRIEN CT	SJ	61	D2
OBRINE LN	PA	38	D6
OBSERVATORY DR	SCCO	56	C3
OBSIDIAN CT	CPTO	59	E6
OBURN CT	C	65	F5
OCALA AV	SJ	62	F3
OCALA AV	SJ	63	B2
OCALA CT	SJ	63	B2
OCCIDENTAL CT	SJ	72A	B1
OCEAN VIEW WY	SCCO	78G	D2
OCHO RIOS DR	SJ	72	E3
OCONNOR DR	SJ	61	C4
OCTAVIO	SJ	72	F1
OCTAVIUS DR	SCL	53	F3
OCTOBER DR	SJ	72A	D1
OCTOBER WY	CPTO	59	E5
ODELL WY	LA	52	B5
ODYSSEY CT	SJ	67	C6
OELLA CT	SJ	66	F6
OFFENBACH PL	SVL	52	F6
OGALLALA PATH	SCCO	73	E6
OGALLALA PATH	SCCO	78G	E1
OGALLALA WARPTH	SCCO	73	D6
OGDEN CT	MPTS	47	E3
OGIER AV	SCCO	78	A4
O'GRADY DR	SJ	75	F1
OHARA CT	SJ	55	D4
O'HIGGINS DR	SJ	66	D1
OHIO CT	MPTS	47	E3
OHLONE DR	SJ	55	D2
OHLONE DR	SCCO	82	C4
OJAI DR	MS	70	C3
OJAI DR	SCCO	70	C3
OJO DE AGUA CT	SJ	55	E5
OKA CT	LG	66	A6
OKA CT	LG	71	A1
OKA LN	C	66	A6
OKA RD	LG	66	A6
OKA RD	LG	71	A1
OKANOGAN CT	S	65	B6
OKANOGAN DR	S	65	B6
OKEEFE LN	LAH	51	D5
OKEEFE LN	LA	51	D5
OKINO CT	SJ	67	F6
OKINO CT	SJ	68	A6
OKINO CT	SJ	72	F1
OKINO CT	SJ	72A	A1
OLCOTT ST	SCL	53	F3
OLD ABBEY PL	SJ	55	C2
OLD ADOBE RD	LG	65	D6
OLD ADOBE RD	LG	70	D1
OLD ADOBE RD	PA	51	B1
OLD ADOBE WY	LG	65	D6
OLD ADOBE WY	LG	70	D1
OLD ALMADEN RD	SJ	67	B4
OLD ALTOS RD	LAH	51	D3
OLD BAYSHORE HY	SJ	54	F4
OLD BLSM HIL RD	LG	71	B3
OLDBRIDGE RD	SJ	55	B3
OLDBROOK CT	SJ	68	A3
OLD CALAVRAS RD	SCCO	40	C6
OLD CALAVRAS RD	SCCO	48	C1
OLD CALAVRAS RD	MPTS	48	C1
OLD COACH RD	SCCO	81H	D2
OLD OREEK DR	SJ	72	F6
OLD CREEK RD	SCCO	81H	D2
OLD CREST PL	SJ	55	C2
OLD CROW RD	LAH	51	A5
OLDE DR	LG	71	A4
OLD ELM CT	SJ	55	C2
OLD ESTATES CT	SJ	68	F2
OLD EVANS RD	MPTS	48	B1
OLDFIELD WY	SJ	63	F6

STREET	CITY	PAGE	GRID
OLD FORGE LN	SJ	55	C2
OLD GATE CT	SJ	55	C2
OLD GILROY ST	G	84	A2
OLD GLENWOOD HWY	SCCO	78G	E5
OLD GLORY LN	SCL	53	E1
OLD GOLD MNE RD	SCCO	78G	F1
OLDHAM WY	SJ	67	F1
OLDHAM WY	SCCO	67	F1
OLD IRONSDES DR	SCL	46	E6
OLD IRONSDES DR	SCL	53	E1
OLD LS GATOS-SC	SCCO	78G	E3
OLD MANOR PL	SJ	55	C2
OLD MEADOW CT	SJ	63A	C3
OLD MIDDLFLD WY	MVW	44	F4
OLD MIDDLFLD WY	MVW	45	A5
OLD MILL CT	SJ	72	D5
OLD MINE RD	SCCO	78G	F1
OLD MONTEREY RD	MH	79	D3
OLD MTNV-ALV RD	SCL	46	D5
OLD MTNV-ALV RD	SVL	46	D5
OLD OAK CT	LA	51	D3
OLD OAK DR	SJ	72	D5
OLD OAK LN	MH	80	C3
OLD OAK WY	S	64	E4
OLD OAKLAND RD	SJ	47	F6
OLD OAKLAND RD	SJ	54	F1
OLD OAKLAND RD	SJ	55	A4
OLD OAKLAND RD	SCCO	54	F1
OLD OAKLAND RD	SCCO	55	A3
OLD ORCHARD CT	LG	71	D3
OLD ORCHARD DR	LG	71	D3
OLD ORCHARD RD	C	66	A4
OLD PAGE MLL RD	SCCO	43	F6
OLD PAGE MLL RD	SCCO	44	A6
OLD PAGE MLL RD	SCCO	51	A1
OLD PARK PL	SJ	55	C2
OLD PIEDMONT RD	SJ	48	D4
OLD PIEDMONT RD	SCCO	48	D4
OLD POST WY	SJ	55	C2
OLD RAFFA RD	SCCO	64	A2
OLD RANCH LN	SCCO	58	E1
OLD RANCH RD	SCCO	58	E1
OLD RIDGE CT	SJ	55	C2
OLD ROSE PL	SJ	55	C2
OLD SAN FRAN RD	SCCO	52	F4
OLD SAN FRAN RD	SVL	52	F4
OLD SAN FRAN RD	SVL	53	A5
OLD STA CRUZ HY	SCCO	73	D5
OLD STA CRUZ HY	SCCO	78G	E2
OLD SNAKEY RD	LAH	51	B6
OLD STONE PL	SJ	55	C2
OLD STONE WY	SJ	55	C2
OLD SUMMIT RD	SCCO	78G	F4
OLD SUMMIT RD	SCCO	78H	A2
OLD TAYLOR ST	CPTO	61	F1
OLD TAYLOR ST	SJ	61	F1
OLD TOWN CT	SJ	59	D5
OLD TRACE CT	PA	51	C1
OLD TRACE LN	LAH	51	B2
OLD TRACE LN	PA	51	B2
OLD TRACE RD	PA	51	C1
OLDTREE CT	SJ	55	B1
OLD TREE WY	S	65	A5
OLDWELL CT	SCCO	72A	D2
OLD WELL RD	SCCO	73	C6
OLD WILLOW PL	SJ	61	F6
OLD WILLOW PL	SJ	66	F1
OLD WOOD RD	S	65	C6
OLDWOOD CT	SJ	63	E4
OLEANDER AV	SCCO	71	A3
OLEANDER CT	SVL	53	C5
OLENA CT	SJ	55	F5
OLENA CT	SJ	56	A5
OLGA DR	SJ	60	E6
OLGA DR	SCCO	60	E6
OLIN ST	SJ	61	B4
OLIN ST	SCCO	61	B4
OLINDER CT	SJ	62	E3
OLIVE AV	LG	70	E3
OLIVE AV	PA	44	B4
OLIVE AV	SCCO	59	D6
OLIVE AV	SCCO	80K	F2
OLIVE AV	SCCO	81	A2
OLIVE AV	SVL	52	F4
OLIVE AV	SVL	53	A4
OLIVE CT	MVW	52	B3
OLIVE DR	SCCO	56	B3
OLIVE PL	SCCO	56	B3
OLIVE ST	SJ	61	D4
OLIVE ST	SCCO	61	D4
OLIVE BRANCH CT	SJ	72	C6
OLIVE BRANCH LN	MH	79	B6
OLIVE BRANCH LN	SJ	72	C6

STREET	CITY	PAGE	GRID
OLIVE BRANCH RD	SJ	72	D6
OLIVE BRANCH RD	SCCO	75	D1
OLIVEGATE LN	SJ	68	A6
OLIVER ST	MPTS	39	F5
OLIVE SPRING CT	CPTO	64	E1
OLIVESTONE WY	SJ	55	C2
OLIVE TREE CT	LAH	58	D2
OLIVETREE DR	SJ	55	B1
OLIVE TREE LN	LAH	58	D2
OLIVETTI CT	SJ	63	F3
OLIVEWOOD DR	SVL	60	A3
OLIVEWOOD PL	SJ	63	E4
OLIVIA CT	SCCO	82	D1
OLIVIAN DR	SJ	68	C6
OLMO CT	SJ	60	C6
OLMSTED RD	SCCO	44	A4
OLSEN DR	SJ	60	F5
OLSEN DR	SJ	61	A5
OLSTAD CT	SJ	68	C6
OLYMPIA AV	SJ	66	B5
OLYMPIA AV	SCCO	66	B5
OLYMPIC DR	MPTS	48	B4
OLYMPUS CT	SVL	59	D3
OLYMPUS DR	SJ	65	D1
OLMSTEAD RD	SCCO	43	F3
OMAHA CT	SJ	72	F3
OMAHA CT	SJ	72A	A3
OMAR DR	SJ	72A	B5
OMAR ST	SCCO	82A	A2
OMEGA CT	SJ	55	E2
OMEGA LN	S	65	C6
OMEGA LN	S	70	C1
OMIRA DR	SJ	72A	B1
ONEIDA DR	SJ	72	F3
ONEIDA DR	SJ	72A	A3
ONEIDA DR	SVL	52	E5
O'NEL DR	SJ	54	D4
ONE OAK LN	MS	70	D2
ONEONTA DR	LAH	51	D6
ON ORBIT DR	SCCO	69	E3
ONSLOW WY	SJ	48	E6
ONTARIO CT	SVL	59	E2
ONTARIO DR	CPTO	59	E2
ONTARIO DR	SJ	66	D4
ONTARIO DR	SVL	59	E2
ONTARIO LN	C	65	E2
ONTARIO RD	MPTS	47	E1
ONYX CT	SJ	61	A5
OPAL DR	SJ	61	A5
OPENMEADOW CT	SJ	60	E5
OPHELIA AV	SJ	63	B5
OPHELIA CT	SJ	63	B5
OPHIR CT	MPTS	47	E3
ORA ST	SJ	60	C6
ORACLE OAK PL	SVL	53	B5
ORANGE AV	CPTO	59	D5
ORANGE AV	LA	51	D4
ORANGE AV	SCCO	45	C5
ORANGE AV	SCCO	59	D5
ORANGE AV	SVL	52	E5
ORANGE ST	SJ	55	F3
ORANGE BLOSM DR	CPTO	64	F1
ORANGE BLOSM LN	SCCO	71	A3
ORANGEBRICK WY	SJ	72	E6
ORANGE GROVE DR	SJ	66	D5
ORANGESTONE WY	SJ	55	C2
ORANGE TREE LN	CPTO	60	A3
ORANGETREE LN	MVW	52	A4
ORANGEWOOD DR	SJ	63	B6
ORANGEWOOD ST	CPTO	60	A3
ORCHARD AV	MVW	52	C1
ORCHARD AV	SCCO	52	C1
ORCHARD AV	SVL	52	F2
ORCHARD AV	SVL	53	A2
ORCHARD CT	MH	80	A3
ORCHARD DR	G	83	F2
ORCHARD DR	SJ	54	C1
ORCHARD LN	SCCO	79	E1
ORCHARD PKWY	SJ	54	C2
ORCHARD RD	CPTO	59	D4
ORCHARD RD	SCCO	82D	A6
ORCHARD RD	S	64	F6
ORCHARD RD	S	65	A6
ORCHARD ST	LG	70	E5
ORCHARD CITY DR	C	66	B3
ORCHARD HILL LN	LAH	51	C3
ORCHARD PARK DR	SJ	72A	A1
ORCHARD SPG CT	CPTO	64	A6
ORCHARD SPG LN	CPTO	64	A5
ORCHARD VIEW DR	SJ	71	F3
ORCHID DR	SVL	53	C5
ORCHID PL	LA	51	E4
ORCHID WY	SJ	60	E6

STREET	CITY	PAGE	GRID
OREGON AV	PA	44	C2
OREGON CT	MPTS	39	F6
OREGON CT	MPTS	47	F1
OREGON WY	MPTS	39	F6
OREGON WY	MPTS	47	F1
OR-PAGE MLL EXP	PA	44	C3
ORELLA CT	S	65	A3
ORESTES WY	SJ	65	E3
ORI AV	SJ	61	B5
ORICK CT	SJ	72A	A1
ORILLA CT	LA	44	D6
ORILLIA CT	SVL	59	E2
ORIN CT	SJ	71	B1
ORINDA DR	SJ	63	D6
ORINDA WY	G	82	C5
ORIOLE AV	SVL	60	B2
ORIOLE DR	SJ	61	A6
ORIOLE DR	SJ	66	B1
ORIOLE RD	S	70	B1
ORIOLE WY	S	70	C2
ORION CT	MPTS	47	E2
ORION LN	CPTO	59	E6
ORION PL	CPTO	59	E6
ORKNEY AV	SCL	54	B2
ORLANDO DR	SJ	62	F3
ORLANDO DR	SJ	63	A3
ORLEANS CT	S	65	B5
ORLEANS DR	SJ	63	A4
ORLEANS DR	SVL	46	B5
ORLINE CT	CPTO	59	E5
ORME ST	PA	44	C5
ORMONDE DR	MVW	45	B6
ORMONDE WY	MVW	45	B6
ORMSBY DR	SVL	59	E2
ORNELLAS DR	MPTS	48	C4
ORNIDA ST	PA	44	C4
ORO WY	MVW	45	B4
OROGRANDE PL	CPTO	59	E6
OROLETTE PL	SJ	55	B2
ORONSAY CT	SJ	72A	D4
ORONSAY WY	SJ	72A	D4
OROPEZA CT	SJ	55	A5
OROSI CT	SCCO	55	E5
OROSI WY	SCCO	55	E5
OROVILLE RD	MPTS	47	F2
ORR CT	LA	59	C1
ORSETTI CT	SCCO	82	E3
ORTEGA AV	MVW	44	E6
ORTEGA AV	MVW	51	E1
ORTEGA CIR	G	83	E2
ORTEGA CT	PA	44	E3
ORTEGA DR	LAH	51	B2
ORTHELLO WY	SCL	60	E1
ORTIZ CT	SVL	53	D1
ORTIZ CT	SVL	46	D6
ORTO ST	SJ	62	B6
ORTO ST	SJ	67	B1
ORVIS AV	SJ	62	C3
OSAGE AV	LA	51	E3
OSAGE CT	SJ	72	E1
OSBORNE AV	SCL	61	A3
OSBORNE CT	SCCO	80K	D4
OSCAR CT	SCCO	82A	B2
OSCAR DR	SCCO	82A	B2
OSGOOD CT	SJ	68	C5
OSITOS AV	SVL	52	E4
OSLO LN	SJ	72	A3
OSPREY CT	SJ	56	C6
OSTENBERG DR	SJ	72	B4
OSTRICH CT	SJ	68	D4
OSUNA PL	SJ	65	D1
OSWALD PL	SCL	53	F6
OSWEGO DR	SJ	62	D4
OTHELLO AV	SJ	63	B5
OTIS WY	LA	51	F3
OTONO CT	SJ	68	B5
OTOOLE AV	SJ	54	E1
OTOOLE AV	SCCO	54	E1
OTOOLE CT	G	82	D6
OTOOLE LN	SJ	54	E3
OTOOLE WY	SJ	54	E3
OTTAWA CT	SVL	59	E2
OTTAWA WY	SJ	65	D4
OTTERSON CT	PA	44	D2
OTTERSON ST	SJ	61	F4
OTTO CT	SJ	56	A1
OUR LN	MVW	52	C4
OUR LADYS WY	SCL	53	E2
OUSLEY DR	G	82	C6
OUTLOOK CT	SJ	48	E5
OUTLOOK DR	SCCO	51	F5
OVERBROOK DR	SJ	67	A5

STREET	CITY	PAGE	GRID
OVERLAND CT	SJ	67	F2
OVERLAND CT	SJ	68	A2
OVERLAND WY	SJ	67	F2
OVERLAND WY	SJ	68	A2
OVERLOOK DR	SCCO	70	B3
OVERLOOK RD	LG	70	D4
OVERLOOK RD	SCCO	70	C4
OWEN ST	SCL	53	F4
OWEN ST	SCL	54	A3
OWENS LAKE DR	SJ	72	C2
OWEN SOUND DR	SVL	59	E2
OWLSWOOD WY	SJ	68	E4
OWSLEY AV	SJ	62	D3
OXBOW CT	SJ	71	C2
OXBOW CT	SVL	59	E1
OXFORD AV	PA	44	B3
OXFORD AV	SVL	52	C5
OXFORD CT	SCL	60	D3
OXFORD DR	LA	59	B2
OXFORD DR	SCL	60	D3
OXFORD LN	SJ	61	A6
OXFORD LN	SJ	66	A1
OXTON DR	SJ	63	A6
OYAMA DR	SJ	55	A3
OYAMA PL	SJ	55	A3
OYSTER BAY DR	SJ	67	C5
P			
PACER LN	SCCO	67	E1
PACHECO DR	MPTS	48	A2
PACHECO DR	SJ	55	D4
PACHECO ST	SCL	60	E1
PACHECO PASS HY	SCCO	82C	A5
PACHECO PASS HY	SCCO	82D	A4
PACHECO PASS HY	SCCO	85	C4
PACHECO PASS RD	G	84	B2
PACHECO PASS RD	SCCO	84	B2
PACIFIC AV	SJ	46	F3
PACIFIC AV	SCCO	61	E4
PACIFIC DR	SCL	53	D5
PACIFICA DR	CPTO	59	F5
PACIFICA DR	CPTO	60	A5
PACIFICA DR	SJ	54	F1
PACIFICA WY	MPTS	39	E6
PACINA DR	SJ	62	F1
PACO DR	LA	51	F3
PADDINGTON WY	SJ	56	B6
PADDINGTON WY	SJ	63	B1
PADDON CIR	SJ	72A	B2
PADERO AV	S	64	E4
PADERO CT	S	64	E4
PADILLA WY	SJ	63	D3
PADRE CT	LAH	51	C6
PADRES CT	SJ	62	B6
PADRES DR	SJ	62	A6
PAGANINI AV	SJ	63	B4
PAGE ST	C	66	C3
PAGE ST	SJ	61	E4
PAGE ST	SCCO	61	E4
PAGEANT WY	LG	70	E5
PAGE MILL DR	SJ	68	B5
PAGE MILL RD	LAH	50	F4
PAGE MILL RD	PA	44	B5
PAGE MILL RD	PA	50	F4
PAGE MILL RD	PA	57	E4
PAGE MILL RD	SCCO	44	B5
PAGE MILL RD	SCCO	50	F4
PAGE MILL RD	SCCO	51	A1
PAGODA TREE CT	SVL	53	B5
PAINTBRUSH DR	SVL	53	C6
PAINTED ROCK DR	SCL	53	E4
PAIUTE LN	SJ	72	F2
PAJARO AV	SVL	52	E2
PAJARO CT	SJ	72	C5
PAJARO CT	SVL	52	E3
PAJARO WY	SJ	72	C5
PALA AV	SCCO	55	F5
PALA AV	SVL	52	E4
PALACE DR	SJ	60	E4
PALACEWOOD CT	SJ	60	D6
PALACIO ESPD CT	SCCO	55	D6
PALACIO ROYL CR	SCCO	55	D6
PALACIO VERD CT	SCCO	55	D5
PALADIN DR	SJ	66	E6
PALAMOS AV	SVL	46	D6
PALAMOS AV	SVL	55	D1
PALERMO CT	S	65	B4
PALERMO PL	SJ	47	D6
PALISADE DR	SJ	68	B3
PALM AV	CPTO	59	C5
PALM AV	LA	51	E4

1991 SANTA CLARA COUNTY STREET INDEX

STREET	CITY	PAGE	GRID
PFEIFLE AV	SCCO	67	F3
PHALANX CT	SJ	56	C5
PHANTOM AV	C	66	D2
PHANTOM AV	SCCO	66	D2
PHARLAP AV	SJ	68	C6
PHAR LAP DR	CPTO	59	D4
PHARMER RD	SCCO	81H	E6
PHEASANT RD	SCCO	71	E6
PHEASANT RDG WY	SJ	67	D3
PHELAN AV	SJ	62	C5
PHELAN CT	SJ	62	E4
PHELAND CT	MPTS	48	B4
PHELPS AV	SJ	61	A6
PHELPS AV	SJ	65	F1
PHELPS AV	SJ	66	A1
PHELPS AV	SCCO	65	F1
PHELPS AV	SCCO	61	A1
PHIL CT	CPTO	60	B5
PHIL LN	SCCO	60	B5
PHILIP CT	SJ	63	A6
PHILLIPS AV	LG	70	F5
PHILLIPS AV	LG	71	A5
PHILLIPS AV	SCL	60	E1
PHILLIPS CT	SCL	60	E1
PHILLIPS RD	PA	38	C6
PHINNEY PL	SJ	72B	A5
PHINNEY WY	SJ	72A	F4
PHOENIX CT	SJ	65	F2
PHOENIX DR	C	65	F2
PHOENIX DR	SJ	65	F2
PHOTINIA LN	SCCO	56	C4
PHYLLIS AV	MVW	52	B3
PHYLLIS AV	SJ	59	F6
PHYLLIS AV	SJ	60	A6
PHYLLIS AV	SJ	64	F1
PHYLLIS AV	SJ	65	A1
PHYLLIS CT	MVW	52	B3
PIAZZA CT	SCCO	56	B3
PIAZZA DR	MVW	45	D6
PIAZZA LN	SCCO	81	F6
PIAZZA LN	SCCO	82	F1
PIAZZA WY	SCCO	56	B3
PICADILLY DR	SJ	67	B4
PICADILLY DR	SCCO	67	B4
PICADILLY PL	C	66	D2
PICARDY PL CT	SJ	68	C2
PICASSO DR	SVL	53	A6
PICASSO TER	SVL	53	A6
PICASSO TER	SVL	60	A1
PICKFORD AV	SCCO	56	A4
PICO LN	LA	51	E1
PIEDMONT CT	LA	71	D3
PIEDMONT CT	MH	79	D5
PIEDMONT RD	MPTS	48	D3
PIEDMONT RD	SJ	48	D4
PIEDMONT RD	SJ	55	E1
PIEDMONT RD	SCCO	48	D3
PIEDMONT RD	SCCO	55	E1
PIEDMONT RD	S	70	A2
PIEDRA DR	SVL	52	E3
PIERCE AV	SJ	62	B4
PIERCE CT	S	65	A3
PIERCE RD	S	64	F3
PIERCE RD	S	65	A3
PIERCE RD	S	69	D1
PIERCE ST	G	82	F6
PIERCE ST	SCL	61	A1
PIERCE RANCH RD	SJ	72	B5
PIERCY RD	SJ	68	D6
PIERCY RD	SJ	72A	E1
PIERCY RD	SCCO	68	F6
PIERCY RD	SCCO	72A	E1
PIERINO AV	SVL	53	A5
PIERS CT	PA	44	D2
PIETRO DR	SJ	55	B3
PIETZ CT	SJ	72	D3
PIKE RD	S	64	E5
PILAND DR	SJ	65	F2
PILAR CT	SJ	72	B3
PILGRIM AV	MVW	51	F2
PILGRIM AV	SJ	65	B2
PILINUT CT	SVL	52	E5
PILOT KNOB DR	SCL	53	E4
PILOT KNOB PL	SCL	53	E4
PIMA DR	SJ	72	F2
PIMENTO AV	SVL	52	E6
PINARD ST	MPTS	48	C3
PINCEA CT	S	64	D3
PINE	C	66	B3
PINE AV	LG	70	F4
PINE AV	SJ	66	F2
PINE AV	SJ	67	A1

STREET	CITY	PAGE	GRID
PINE AV	SVL	52	F2
PINE AV	SVL	53	A2
PINE LN	LA	51	D2
PINE ST	PA	44	B1
PINE TR	SCCO	78G	D2
PINE WY	MH	80	B3
PINEAPPLE AV	SVL	52	E5
PINE BROOK CT	CPTO	64	E2
PINE BROOK LN	CPTO	64	E2
PINE CONE CT	MS	70	E2
PINECONE CT	MH	80	B4
PINE CREEK DR	SJ	48	E5
PINECREST CT	SJ	63	E6
PINECREST DR	SCCO	59	B2
PINECREST DR	SCCO	81	E3
PINEDALE CT	SJ	72A	F4
PINEFIELD RD	SJ	46	F4
PINEFIELD RD	SJ	47	A4
PINE FOREST LN	SJ	71	F1
PINE FOREST PL	SJ	71	F1
PINEGATE WY	SJ	63	E4
PINE GLEN CT	SJ	66	F1
PINE GROVE WY	SJ	65	B2
PINE HILL CT	SJ	60	D5
PINE HILL RD	SCCO	43	F4
PINE HILL RD	SCCO	44	A4
PINE HOLLOW CIR	SJ	55	D4
PINEHURST AV	LG	71	C3
PINEHURST CT	MPTS	40	B5
PINEHURST DR	LA	52	C6
PINEHURST DR	SJ	67	A5
PINEHURST SQ	SJ	66	A1
PINELAND AV	SJ	72A	A3
PINEMONT DR	SJ	65	D5
PINENUT CT	SVL	52	E5
PINE RIDGE CT	SJ	56	C6
PINE RIDGE WY	SJ	56	C6
PINE RIDGE WY	SCCO	78G	F1
PINE SPRING CT	SJ	63	C6
PINETREE CT	SJ	55	B2
PINETREE TER	SJ	65	D5
PINEVIEW DR	SJ	61	A4
PINEVIEW DR	SCL	61	A4
PINEVILLE AV	CPTO	60	A5
PINEWELL CT	SJ	72A	D1
PINEWOOD CT	LG	65	E5
PINEWOOD CT	MPTS	47	E5
PINEWOOD DR	SJ	60	E6
PINE WOOD LN	LG	65	E5
PINEWOOD PL	SCL	54	B2
PINEWOOD WY	MPTS	47	E5
PINION WY	MH	80	B3
PINKERT ST	CPTO	64	F1
PINKERTON CT	SJ	63	D3
PINKERTON DR	SJ	63	D3
PINKSTONE CT	SJ	63	A2
PINMORE DR	SJ	71	E1
PINNACLE CT	SJ	48	E6
PINNACLE CT	S	70	B1
PINNACLE DR	SJ	48	E6
PINNTAGE PKWY	CPTO	60	A4
PIN OAK CT	SJ	63	E3
PIN OAK DR	SVL	53	B5
PINOLE CT	CPTO	60	A5
PINON CT	SVL	53	B5
PINON PL	SJ	67	F5
PINON PL	SJ	68	A5
PINOT CT	SJ	72A	E4
PINOTAGE CT	SJ	68A	B3
PINOT BLANC WY	SJ	63	F6
PINOT GRIS WY	SJ	63	E6
PINOT NOIR CT	SJ	68A	B3
PINTA CT	LG	71	A5
PINTAIL CT	SJ	67	B6
PINTO CT	MH	80	C3
PINTO DR	SJ	67	F2
PINTO DR	SJ	68	A2
PINTO RIVER CT	SJ	67	D6
PIONEER AV	SCCO	61	C5
PIONEER WY	MVW	52	C2
PIPER AV	SVL	52	E5
PIPER DR	MPTS	48	A5
PIPER DR	SJ	60	E6
PIPER DR	SJ	65	E1
PIPER DR	SCCO	65	E1
PIPPIN AV	SVL	52	E5
PIPPIN CREEK CT	SJ	75	E1
PISCES DR	SJ	68	E3
PISMO CT	SJ	72A	B4
PISTACHIO DR	SJ	68	D4
PISTCHIO GRV CT	SJ	68	A6
PITCAIRN WY	SJ	68	A2

STREET	CITY	PAGE	GRID
PITCAIRN WY	SCCO	68	A2
PITCH PINE CT	SJ	67	F5
PITCH PINE CT	SJ	68	A5
PITMAN AV	PA	38	B6
PITNER CT	SJ	63	D4
PITTSFIELD WY	SJ	72B	A4
PIXANNE CT	SJ	63	B2
PLACERCREEK CT	SJ	68	B1
PLACER OAKS AV	LG	70	F3
PLACER SPG CT	CPTO	64	E2
PLACIDA CT	S	64	E6
PLACIDA CT	S	69	D1
PLAINFIELD DR	SJ	68	B4
PLAINVIEW CT	SJ	72	B5
PLANETREE PL	SVL	53	B5
PLATEAU AV	SCCO	51	F6
PLATEAU AV	SCCO	58	F1
PLATINUM CT	SJ	55	D6
PLATT AV	MPTS	48	B3
PLATT CT	MPTS	48	B3
PLATTE RIVER CT	SJ	67	F1
PLAYA DEL REY	SJ	72	E1
PLAZA CT	MVW	52	A4
PLAZA DR	SJ	61	F5
PLAZA DR	SVL	46	A6
PLAZA AMERICAS	SJ	48	B6
PLAZA BANDERAS	SJ	48	B6
PLAZA CASITAS	SJ	48	B6
PLAZA CLAVELES	SJ	48	B6
PLAZA CORONA	SCL	46	F5
PZ DE GUADALUPE	SJ	55	E6
PLAZA ESCUELA	SCL	46	F6
PLAZA INVIERNO	SJ	68	C4
PLAZA LA POSADA	LG	70	D1
PLAZA MONTEZ	SJ	48	C5
PLAZOLETA	LG	65	D6
PLEASANT AV	S	69	F2
PLEASANT ST	LG	70	E5
PLEASANT ST	SJ	54	E6
PLEASANT ST	SJ	61	F2
PLEASANT ST	SJ	62	A3
PLEASANT WY	LA	51	D1
PLEASNT ACRE DR	SCCO	63	E2
PLEASNT CRST CT	SJ	63	D1
PLEASNT CRST DR	SJ	63	D1
PLEASNT ECHO DR	SJ	63	D1
PLEASANT GRV CT	SJ	67	D1
PLEASANT GRV CT	SCCO	67	D1
PLEASANT HLS CT	SJ	72A	E4
PLEASNT KNLL DR	SJ	63	D1
PLEASANT RDG AV	SCCO	55	F5
PLEASANT ROW CT	SJ	63	D1
PLEASANT VW AV	MS	70	F2
PLEASANT VIS DR	SCCO	63	E1
PLUM AV	SVL	52	E6
PLUM ST	SJ	62	B5
PLUMAS DR	S	65	A2
PLUMAS DR	SJ	63	A6
PLUM BLOSSOM DR	CPTO	64	F1
PLUMERIA DR	SJ	54	C2
PLUM GROVE CT	SJ	68	A6
PLUMMER AV	SJ	66	F3
PLUMMER AV	SJ	67	A3
PLUMSTEAD CT	SJ	63	C5
PLUMSTEAD WY	SJ	65	C5
PLUM TREE LN	CPTO	60	A4
PLUM TREE LN	SCCO	43	F3
PLUMTREE LN	MVW	52	A4
PLYMOUTH AV	SJ	65	B2
PLYMOUTH DR	G	83	E3
PLYMOUTH DR	S	65	B3
PLYMOUTH DR	SVL	52	D5
PLYMOUTH ST	MVW	45	A4
PLYMRTON CT	SJ	72B	A4
POAS CIR	SJ	55	E5
POAS CT	SJ	55	E5
POCATELLO AV	SVL	59	D3
POCATELLO CT	SJ	67	F2
POCATELLO DR	SJ	67	F2
POCO WY	SJ	62	F2
POE LN	SJ	65	F1
POE ST	PA	57	F6
POE ST	PA	37	F6
POETT LN	SCL	53	F5
POINCIANA DR	SCL	53	C6
POINCIANA DR	SVL	53	C6
POINSETTIA CT	SJ	67	F5
POINSETTIA CT	SJ	68	A5
POINT CREEK CT	SJ	55	E3
POINT CREEK DR	SJ	55	E3
POINTDEXTER CT	SJ	55	E2
POINT DUNES CT	SJ	72A	E4
POINTE CLARE CT	SVL	59	E1

STREET	CITY	PAGE	GRID
POINTE CLARE DR	SVL	59	E1
POKER FLAT PL	SJ	72	B3
POLARIS AV	MVW	45	B6
POLARIS AV	MVW	52	B1
POLARIS CT	MPTS	47	F5
POLE LINE RD	SCCO	81G	E4
POLI RD	CO	81H	B4
POLK AV	SCL	60	F4
POLK AV	SVL	52	D3
POLK CT	G	82A	A6
POLK CT	MVW	52	A5
POLK LN	SCCO	61	A6
POLK SPRING CT	SJ	75	E2
POLLARD AV	SCCO	81	A1
POLLARD CT	C	65	D5
POLLARD RD	C	65	D5
POLLARD RD	LG	65	F6
POLLARD RD	S	65	D5
POLLARD OAKS CT	LG	65	F6
POLLEN CT	SJ	55	C3
POLTONHALL CT	SJ	63	C6
POLTON PLACE WY	SJ	68	C1
POLVADERO DR	SJ	72A	E4
POMANDER PL	SJ	72	E5
POME AV	SVL	52	E6
POMEGRANATE CT	SVL	52	E6
POMEGRANATE LN	SJ	46	F4
POMEGRANATE LN	SJ	47	A4
POMELO CT	SVL	52	E6
POMEROY AV	SJ	63	C5
POMEROY AV	SCL	53	D6
POMEROY AV	SCL	60	D2
POMEROY CT	SJ	63	C6
POMONA AV	PA	44	D6
POMONA AV	SJ	62	C5
POMPANO ST	SJ	62	E2
POMPEY DR	SJ	66	B2
PONCE CT	SJ	72	B3
PONCE DR	PA	44	E5
POND WY	SJ	48	B6
PONDEROSA AV	SVL	53	B6
PONDEROSA CT	MH	80	C3
PONDEROSA DR	G	83	D2
PONDEROSA TER	SJ	65	D5
PONDEROSA WY	SCL	60	E3
PONSELLE CT	SJ	63	A5
PONTIAC AV	S	64	F5
PONTIAC AV	S	64	F5
PONTIAC DR	SJ	72	F2
PONTIUS CT	SJ	72A	A2
PONY PASS CIR	SJ	68	A5
POPE CT	C	66	B5
POPEJOY CT	SJ	71	E1
POPLAR AV	C	66	C3
POPLAR AV	SVL	53	B6
POPLAR AV	SVL	60	B1
POPLAR CT	SVL	53	B6
POPLAR DR	G	82	D6
POPLAR DR	SJ	63	A2
POPLAR ST	SCL	61	B2
POPLAR TER	SJ	65	D5
POPLAR GROVE SQ	CPTO	59	B4
POPLARWOOD WY	SJ	48	B5
POPPY CT	MPTS	48	C2
POPPY CT	SVL	53	C6
POPPY DR	CPTO	59	C4
POPPY LN	MPTS	48	C2
POPPY LN	MS	70	E3
POPPY LN	SCCO	56	A2
POPPY LN	SCCO	81H	F5
POPPY PL	MVW	45	B6
POPPY WY	CPTO	64	F1
POPPY BLOSSM CT	SJ	68	B6
POPPY BLOSSM CT	SJ	72A	B5
POPPY BLOSSM DR	SJ	72A	B5
POPULUS PL	SVL	53	B6
PORGY PL	SJ	66	C1
PORPISE BAY TER	SVL	46	B6
PORT WY	SJ	55	D3
PORTAGE AV	PA	44	C4
PORTAGE MTN DR	SJ	66	D1
PORTAL AV	CPTO	60	A4
PORTAL CT	SJ	54	F2
PORTAL PL	PA	44	C2
PORTAL PZ	CPTO	60	A4
PORTAL WY	SJ	63	D2
PORTER DR	PA	44	A5
PORTER LN	SCCO	56	B3
PORTERFIELD CT	MVW	52	C4
PORTIA AV	SVL	52	E3
PORTLAND AV	LA	52	B5
PORTO ALEGRE CT	SJ	72	B2
PORTO ALEGRE DR	SJ	72	B2

STREET	CITY	PAGE	GRID
PORTO ALEGRE PL	SJ	72	B2
PORTOBELLO DR	SJ	72	A1
PORTOLA AV	LA	51	E1
PORTOLA AV	PA	44	A3
PORTOLA AV	SJ	61	C2
PORTOLA AV	SCL	61	C2
PORTOLA CT	LA	51	E1
PORTOLA DR	MPTS	48	B4
PORTOLA RD	CPTO	59	C6
PORTOS CT	S	65	B4
PORTOS DR	S	65	B4
PORTOS PL	S	65	B5
PORTREE DR	SJ	68A	C2
PORT ROWAN DR	SJ	72A	F3
PORTSMOUTH CT	SJ	48	D4
PORTSWOOD CIR	SJ	75	F1
PORTSWOOD CIR	SJ	76	A1
PORTSWOOD DR	SJ	75	F1
POST ST	MVW	52	C3
POST ST	SJ	61	F3
POST ST	SJ	62	A3
POSTGATE CT	SJ	63	C6
POST OAK CIR	SJ	72	B3
POSTON DR	SJ	68	A6
POSTWOOD DR	SJ	48	B5
POTOMAC	SJ	67	D6
POTOMAC DR	LG	71	A2
POTOMAC PL	G	83	E3
POTRERO AV	SVL	52	E2
POTRERO DR	SJ	66	D5
POTTER CT	SCCO	70	F4
POTTRS HTCH CIR	CPTO	59	B4
POTTS DR	SCCO	67	F3
POTTS WY	SCCO	67	F2
POUGHKEEPSIE RD	SJ	72A	C1
POWDERBORN CT	SJ	67	D5
POWDERHORN CT	SCCO	81	B5
POWELL CT	SJ	62	E4
POWER CT	SJ	55	A5
PRADA CT	MPTS	48	B1
PRADA DR	MPTS	48	B1
PRADO LN	SJ	63	D2
PRADO VISTA DR	CPTO	59	C4
PRAGUE CT	SJ	72A	D4
PRAGUE DR	SJ	72A	D4
PRAIRIE LN	SJ	55	F4
PRAIRIE VIEW CT	SJ	55	F4
PRAIRIEWOOD CT	SJ	55	F4
PRATOLA CT	MH	80K	F2
PRATT LN	SCCO	78	D6
PRELUDE DR	SJ	55	B3
PRENTISS DR	SJ	72	D6
PRESCOTT AV	SJ	66	D6
PRESCOTT AV	SVL	53	D1
PRESERVATION CT	MH	79	C3
PRESERVATION WY	MH	79	C3
PRESIDIO DR	CPTO	59	D5
PRESTON CT	MVW	52	C5
PRESTON DR	MVW	52	C5
PRESTON DR	SJ	71	F4
PRESWICK CT	SVL	60	A3
PRETORIA CT	SJ	55	E2
PREVOST CT	SJ	62	A5
PREVOST ST	SJ	62	A5
PRICE AV	CPTO	60	A4
PRICE CT	MH	79	D6
PRICE CT	PA	44	D3
PRICE DR	MH	79	D6
PRICE WY	SJ	66	D4
PRICEWOOD CT	SJ	75	F1
PRICEWOOD CT	SJ	76	A1
PRICILLA CT	MVW	51	F2
PRIDE CT	SJ	55	E2
PRIDE ST	SJ	55	E2
PRIETA CT	SCCO	56	B3
PRIMERA CT	SJ	63	D2
PRIMM AV	SJ	62	E3
PRIMO CT	SJ	55	B2
PRIMROSE AV	SVL	53	B6
PRIMROSE LN	G	82	D6
PRIMROSE WY	CPTO	64	F2
PRIMROSE WY	PA	44	C1
PRINCE DR	SJ	60	B6
PRINCE DR	SJ	65	B1
PRINCE ST	LG	65	E6
PRINCE ALBRT CT	SJ	48	D5
PRINCE CHRLS CT	SJ	48	E5
PRINCE EDWRD WY	SVL	59	F2
PRINCE EST CT	SJ	68A	A2
PRNCE GEORGE DR	SJ	55	A2
PRNCE OF WLS LN	SJ	48	E4
PRINCE PHILP CT	SJ	48	E5

STREET	CITY	PAGE	GRID
PRINCE ROYAL PL	SJ	67	E5
PRINCESS PL	MPTS	40	A6
PRINCSS ANNE DR	SJ	61	D6
PRINCSS ELNA CT	LAH	51	E6
PRINCSS MARG CT	SJ	48	E4
PRINCETON CT	SCL	60	D2
PRINCETON DR	SJ	71	F2
PRINCETON DR	SJ	72	A2
PRINCETON DR	SVL	52	E5
PRINCETON PL	G	83	E2
PRINCETON ST	PA	44	A4
PRINCETON WY	SCL	60	D2
PRINCEVALLE ST	G	83	E2
PRING CT	SCCO	60	C5
PRINTY AV	MPTS	48	A1
PRISCILLA DR	SJ	60	D6
PRISCILLA DR	SJ	65	D1
PRISCILLA LN	LAH	51	D6
PRITCHARD CT	SCL	60	E2
PRITCHETT CT	LA	52	B6
PRITCHETT WY	LA	52	B6
PRIVADA LUISITA	LG	70	F2
PRIVET CT	SVL	53	B5
PROM DR	SCCO	80K	C6
PROMETHEAN WY	MVW	52	C1
PRONTO DR	SJ	72	D2
PROSPECT AV	LAH	51	D6
PROSPECT AV	LG	70	E5
PROSPECT AV	SCCO	58	D1
PROSPECT CT	LG	70	E5
PROSPECT RD	CPTO	64	F2
PROSPECT RD	SJ	64	F2
PROSPECT RD	SJ	65	B2
PROSPECT RD	SCCO	64	F2
PROSPECT RD	SCCO	65	B2
PROSPECT ST	SJ	62	B4
PROSPER AV	SJ	67	C5
PROUD DR	SJ	48	E6
PROUTY WY	SJ	60	C6
PROVANMILL WY	SJ	63	D6
PROVIDENCE CT	CPTO	59	D5
PROVINCETOWN DR	SJ	65	B2
PROVO CT	SJ	55	E3
PRUNE CT	SVL	52	E5
PRUNE WY	SJ	61	A5
PRUNE BLOSSM DR	SJ	68	C3
PRUNE BLOSSM DR	S	68	F5
PRUNEDALE RD	SCCO	85	B3
PRUNELLE CT	SVL	52	E6
PRUNERIDGE AV	CPTO	60	B3
PRUNERIDGE AV	SJ	61	A3
PRUNERIDGE AV	SCL	60	F3
PRUNERIDGE AV	SCL	61	B3
PRUNETREE CT	SJ	68	E1
PRUNE TREE LN	CPTO	60	A4
PRUNETREE LN	SJ	68	E1
PUCCINI AV	SJ	63	B5
PUCCINI DR	SVL	53	A6
PUEBLA CT	SJ	72	A1
PUEBLO DR	SJ	54	F1
PUEBLO HILL CT	SJ	56	C4
PUEBLO VISTA	SCCO	56	C4
PUENTE CT	S	65	A3
PUERTO GOLFO CT	SJ	55	E5
PUERTO LIMON CT	SJ	55	E6
PUERTO VLRTA DR	SJ	71	F4
PUESTA DEL SOL	LG	65	D6
PUFFIN CT	C	66	B2
PUGET SOUND WY	SJ	55	C4
PULLMAN WY	SJ	67	E2
PULORA CT	SVL	52	E6
PUMPHERSTON CT	SJ	63	C5
PUMPHERSTON WY	SJ	63	C5
PUMPKIN CT	CPTO	59	D6
PUMPKIN DR	CPTO	59	D6
PURDUE CT	SCL	60	D3
PURDUE DR	S	65	D4
PURDUE PL	SJ	71	F3
PURE CT	SJ	67	E6
PURISSIMA AV	SVL	52	E4
PURISSIMA RD	LAH	51	B4
PURITAN CT	SJ	72	E3
PURITANI CT	SJ	63	B4
PURITANI WY	SJ	63	B4
PURPLE CLIFF CT	SJ	72A	D3
PURPLE GLEN DR	SJ	72A	D3
PURPLE HILLS DR	SJ	72A	D4
PURPLE KNOLL CT	SJ	72A	D3
PURPLE SAGE CT	SJ	72A	D3
PURPLE VALE CT	SJ	72A	D3
PUSATERI WY	SJ	68	A1
PUTNEY CT	SJ	48	B6

STREET	CITY	PAGE	GRID
PUTTER WY	SCCO	58	E1
PYLE CT	SCL	53	F5
PYRAMID CT	SJ	65	E2
PYRUS WY	SVL	52	E5

Q

STREET	CITY	PAGE	GRID
QUADROS LN	SJ	55	C3
QUAIL AV	SVL	60	C2
QUAIL CT	MH	80	D2
QUAIL DR	MPTS	48	B1
QUAIL LN	LAH	51	C3
QUAIL LN	MH	80	D2
QUAIL ACRES	S	65	A6
QUAIL BUSH CT	SJ	60	F4
QUAIL BUSH CT	SJ	61	A4
QUAIL CANYON CT	SCCO	63	F2
QUAIL CANYON RD	SCCO	63	F2
QUAIL CLIFF WY	SJ	75	E1
QUAIL COVE CT	SJ	75	E1
QUAIL COVE WY	SJ	75	E1
QUAIL CREEK CIR	SJ	75	E1
QUAIL CREST WY	SJ	75	E2
QUAIL DUNES WY	SJ	75	E1
QUAIL FIELD WY	SJ	75	E1
QUAIL HILL RD	LG	71	B4
QUAIL HOLLOW DR	SJ	66	C1
QUAIL KNOLL CT	SJ	72	E6
QUAIL KNOLL CT	SJ	75	E1
QUAIL MEADOW RD	SCCO	59	A2
QUAIL RIDGE CT	SJ	75	E1
QUAIL RUN CT	SJ	67	B6
QUAIL VIEW WY	SJ	75	D1
QUAIL WALK DR	G	82	C5
QUAMME DR	SJ	62	F5
QUANTICO CT	SJ	61	C6
QUARRY RD	LG	70	F6
QUARRY RD	PA	43	E2
QUARRY RD	S	64	E5
QUARRY RD N	LG	70	F5
QUARRY RD N	LG	71	A5
QUARRY RD S	LG	70	F6
QUARRY RD S	LG	71	A6
QUARTUCCIO WY	SCCO	63A	A4
QUARTZ WY	SJ	67	A5
QUEBEC CT	SVL	59	E2
QUEBEC WY	SJ	66	D4
QUEEN ANN DR	SVL	52	E6
QUEEN ANNE DR	SJ	60	B6
QUEEN ANNE DR	SJ	65	B1
QN CHARLOTTE DR	SVL	59	F2
QN ELIZABETH WY	SJ	48	E4
QUEEN MARY CT	SJ	48	D5
QUEEN MARY WY	SJ	48	D5
QUEENS CT	C	66	A2
QUEENS LN	SJ	54	F4
QUEENSBRIDGE CT	SJ	75	E2
QUEENSBRIDGE WY	SJ	75	F1
QUEENSBROOK DR	SJ	60	B6
QUEENSBURY AV	LA	52	C6
QUEENSBURY AV	LA	59	C1
QUEENS CRSSG DR	SJ	48	D6
QUEENS EST CT	SJ	68A	A2
QUEENS OAK CT	CPTO	59	C4
QUEENSTOWN CT	SVL	59	F2
QUEENSTOWN DR	SJ	48	D6
QUEENSWOOD CT	SJ	75	F1
QUEENSWOOD CT	SJ	76	A1
QUEENSWOOD WY	SJ	72	F6
QUEENSWOOD WY	SJ	75	F1
QUEENSWOOD WY	SJ	76	A1
QN VICTORIA WY	SJ	48	E5
QUERCUS CT	SVL	53	C6
QUESADA DR	SJ	63	D3
QUETTA AV	SVL	52	E5
QUETTA CT	SVL	52	E5
QUICKERT RD	S	69	E2
QUICKSILVER DR	SJ	67	C6
QUIET CIR	SJ	48	D5
QUIET MEADOW CT	SJ	68	B1
QUILEN CT	SCCO	44	A3
QUIMBY RD	SJ	63	B4
QUIMBY RD	SCCO	63	F3
QUIMBY RD	SCCO	63A	A3
QUINCE AV	SCL	60	D2
QUINCE AV	SVL	52	E6
QUINCE LN	MPTS	48	B1
QUINCY DR	MVW	44	F5
QUINCY DR	SJ	55	E1
QUINLAN LN	SJ	67	A5
QUINN AV	SJ	62	E6
QUINN AV	SCL	53	E5
QUINN CT	SCL	53	F5
QUINN CT	SCCO	78	D6
QUINNHILL AV	SCCO	51	E5
QUINTERNO CT	CPTO	59	C4
QUINTINIA DR	SVL	53	B6
QUINTO WY	SJ	66	E5
QUITO RD	LG	70	C2
QUITO RD	MS	70	C2
QUITO RD	SJ	65	D6
QUITO RD	SCCO	65	D6
QUITO RD	SCCO	70	C2
QUITO RD	S	70	C2
QUITO OAKS WY	S	65	D5
QUME DR	SJ	55	A1

R

STREET	CITY	PAGE	GRID
RABIA DR	SJ	72	F1
RACE LN	SJ	61	E5
RACE ST	SJ	61	E5
RACE ST	SCCO	61	E5
RACHEL CT	SJ	72A	A2
RACOON CT	MH	80	B1
RADCLIFF CT	SVL	52	D5
RADCLIFF DR	SJ	61	A6
RADCLIFF WY	SVL	52	E5
RADCLIFFE DR	LAH	50	F2
RADCLIFFE DR	SCL	60	D3
RADFORD DR	C	65	F3
RADIANT DR	SJ	72A	A4
RADIO AV	SJ	67	A2
RADKO DR	SJ	72A	D4
RADOYKA DR	S	65	C3
RADTKE AV	SCCO	82	E3
RAE LN	CPTO	59	C5
RAE LN	SCCO	59	C5
RAEBURN CT	SJ	67	C5
RAFAEL DR	SJ	72	D4
RAFTON DR	SJ	71	E2
RAGGIO AV	SCL	53	F6
RAHWAY DR	SJ	68	C4
RAICH DR	SJ	75	F1
RAILROAD AV	MPTS	47	F2
RAILROAD AV	MH	79	F5
RAILROAD AV	SCL	54	C6
RAILROAD AV	SCCO	79	F5
RAILROAD AV	SCCO	81	A1
RAILROAD CT	MPTS	47	F2
RAILROAD ST	G	84	A1
RAILWAY AV	C	66	B3
RAIMUNDO WY	SCCO	43	F5
RAIMUNDO WY	SCCO	44	A5
RAINBOW CT	CPTO	64	D1
RAINBOW DR	CPTO	64	D1
RAINBOW DR	MVW	52	C3
RAINBOW DR	SJ	64	F1
RAINBOW DR	SJ	65	A1
RAINBOW DR	SCCO	65	A1
RAINBOW PL	CPTO	64	A5
RAINDANCE CT	SJ	68	D3
RAINERI LN	SCCO	73	D6
RAINFIELD DR	SJ	55	E4
RAINTREE CT	SJ	60	D6
RAINTREE DR	SJ	60	D5
RAINTREE SPG CT	CPTO	64	A6
RAINVIEW DR	SJ	55	E4
RAINWELL CT	SJ	55	E4
RAINWELL DR	SJ	55	E4
RAINWOOD CT	SJ	63	D3
RAJKOVICH WY	SJ	72	D6
RAKTAD RD	SCCO	76	C2
RALEIGH DR	SJ	66	E4
RALEIGH PL	S	65	C3
RALEIGH RD	SJ	72A	C2
RALENE CT	SJ	55	B1
RALENE PL	SJ	55	B1
RALPH CT	SCCO	81	C2
RALPH LEE CT	MH	80	A3
RALPH LEE DR	SCCO	80	A3
RALSTON CT	SJ	63	C5
RALSTON CT	SCL	53	E6
RALSTON DR	SJ	63	C5
RALT CT	SJ	72A	B1
RALYA CT	SCCO	60	C5
RAMA DR	SJ	66	E5
RAMBLEWOOD DR	SJ	72	D5
RAMBO CT	SCL	53	F1
RAMBOW DR	PA	44	D4
RAMEL WY	LG	70	F5
RAMIREZ CT	SJ	63	D6
RAMISH DR	SJ	55	C2
RAMITA CT	SJ	66	C2
RAMKE PL	SCL	60	F3
RAMON DR	LA	51	F3
RAMON DR	SVL	60	B1
RAMONA AV	CPTO	59	C4
RAMONA AV	SJ	61	F5
RAMONA AV	SVL	52	D5
RAMONA CIR	PA	44	D4
RAMONA CT	SJ	61	F5
RAMONA CT	SCL	60	E2
RAMONA ST	PA	44	C3
RAMONA WY	G	82	E6
RAMOS CT	MPTS	48	B1
RAMOS CT	MVW	52	C5
RAMOS WY	PA	44	B4
RAMPART AV	CPTO	60	B5
RAMSGATE WY	SJ	63	B1
RAMSTAD DR	SJ	56	C5
RAMSTAD DR	SCCO	56	B5
RAMSTREE DR	SJ	55	B1
RANCH CT	SJ	48	E5
RANCH PL	SJ	48	E5
RANCH RD	SCCO	63A	C4
RANCHERO DR	SCCO	80	B5
RANCHERO WY	SJ	60	E6
RANCHITA CT	LA	52	B6
RANCHITA DR	LA	52	B6
RANCHO DR	SJ	67	F3
RANCHO PL	CPTO	59	C5
RO BELLA VISTA	S	70	A1
RO DEEP CLIF DR	CPTO	59	C6
RANCHO HILLS CT	G	82	C6
RANCHO HILLS DR	G	82	C5
RO LAS CIMAS WY	S	70	C1
RANCHO MANOR CT	SJ	67	F3
RO MANUELLA LN	LAH	51	C2
RO MCCORMICK BL	SCL	53	D3
RO MCCORMICK BL	SCL	54	A4
RO MCCORMICK CT	SCL	53	D3
RO MCCORMICK CT	SCL	54	A4
RANCHO REAL	G	82	C6
RO VENTURA ST	CPTO	59	C5
RANCHO VIEW CT	SJ	48	E5
RANCHO VISTA CT	SCCO	83	A1
RANCHO VISTA DR	SCCO	83	A1
RAND ST	MPTS	39	E6
RANDALL CT	SJ	72	E3
RANDERS CT	PA	44	D2
RANDLESWOOD CT	SJ	60	C6
RANDOL AV	SJ	61	D3
RANDOL CREEK DR	SJ	72	E6
RANDOLPH AV	SCL	60	C3
RANDOLPH DR	SJ	61	D5
RANDOLPH PKWY	LA	59	C1
RANDY LN	CPTO	60	A4
RANERE CT	SCCO	52	E5
RANEY CT	SCL	60	F2
RANFRE LN	S	65	B4
RANGER CT	MH	80	C3
RANGPUR CT	SCCO	52	E5
RANIER ST	SJ	61	E4
RANKIN AV	SJ	61	F2
RANKIN DR	MPTS	40	A6
RANSEN CT	MH	79	D3
RANSON DR	SJ	55	D4
RANWICK CT	SJ	67	B5
RAPOSA CT	SJ	68	A1
RAPOSA DR	SJ	68	A1
RAQUEL CT	LA	51	D2
RAQUEL CT	SJ	61	D6
RAQUEL CT	SCCO	80	D6
RAQUEL LN	LA	51	D2
RARITAN PL	SJ	63	E2
RASMUS CIR	SJ	63	E4
RASPBERRY PL	SJ	60	D5
RATHMANN DR	SJ	63	E3
RATTAN TER	SVL	55	B6
RAVEN CT	S	65	D5
RAVENDALE CT	SJ	68	D3
RAVENDALE DR	MVW	52	D2
RAVENSBURY AV	SCCO	58	E2
RAVENSCOURT AV	C	66	C1
RAVENSCOURT AV	SJ	66	C1
RAVENS PLACE WY	SJ	68	C1
RAVENSWOOD DR	LA	52	C6
RAVENSWOOD WY	SJ	63	E4
RAVENWOOD DR	S	65	D5
RAVINE CT	SJ	55	D4
RAVINE DR	SJ	55	D4
RAVINE RD	SCCO	70	B3
RAVIZZA AV	SCL	53	E6
RAWLINGS DR	SJ	67	C5
RAY AV	LA	44	D6
RAY AV	LA	51	D1
RAYANNA AV	SCL	53	D6
RAYANNA AV	SCL	60	D1
RAYBAL CT	SJ	72A	B4
RAYMOND AV	SCCO	61	D5
RAYMOND ST	SCL	54	A3
RAYMUNDO AV	LA	51	F3
RAYMUNDO AV	LA	52	A3
REA ST	G	83	F1
REALM DR	SJ	72A	E4
REAMWOOD AV	SVL	46	D6
REBECCA LN	LAH	58	E1
REBECCA WY	SJ	60	F5
REBECCA LYNN WY	SCL	60	F3
REBECCA PRIVADA	MVW	52	D2
REBEIRO AV	SCL	60	E3
REBEL CT	SJ	71	F1
REBEL WY	SJ	71	F1
RECIFE WY	SJ	72	B3
RECREATION DR	SVL	46	C6
REDBERRY DR	SCCO	70	B3
REDBIRD DR	SJ	67	B3
REDBUD CTR	SJ	66	C1
REDBUSH TER	SJ	61	C3
REDCLIFF CT	SCCO	52	C4
REDCLIFF DR	SJ	67	B4
RED CREEK DR	SJ	68	D4
RED CREEK RD	SCCO	68E	E2
REDDING RD	C	66	B5
REDDING RD	SJ	66	B5
REDEN DR	SJ	65	E4
REDFIELD CT	SJ	63	B6
RED FIR CT	CPTO	59	E5
REDGLEN CT	SJ	63	E5
REDHEAD LN	LG	70	F5
RED HILL RD	SCCO	70	A3
RED HOLLY CT	SJ	75	C1
REDMOND AV	SJ	72	A4
REDMOND AV	SCCO	72	A4
REDMOND CT	SJ	72	C4
RED MOUNTAIN RD	SCCO	78F	E3
RED OAK DR	SVL	53	B4
RED OAK DR E	SVL	53	B4
RED OAK DR W	SVL	53	B4
REDOAKS DR	SJ	61	B6
REDOAKS DR	SJ	66	B1
REDONDO CT	CPTO	59	D6
REDONDO DR	SJ	67	A2
REDONDO RD	CPTO	59	C5
RED PINE CT	SJ	66	F1
RED RIVER WY	SJ	68	B6
REDROCK CT	SVL	53	D1
REDSTONE DR	SJ	71	B2
REDWING AV	SVL	60	C2
REDWOOD AV	MPTS	47	E2
REDWOOD AV	SJ	61	B4
REDWOOD AV	SCL	60	E4
REDWOOD AV	SVL	53	C6
REDWOOD CIR	PA	44	D4
REDWOOD DR	SJ	72A	F3
REDWOOD DR	LA	59	C3
REDWOOD DR	SCCO	73	D6
REDWOOD DR	SCCO	78G	D1
REDWOOD LN	G	83	D1
REDWOOD EST RD	SCCO	78G	E1
RDWOOD RETRT RD	SCCO	81G	E2
RDWOOD RETRT RD	SCCO	81H	C4
REECE WY	SJ	55	E3
REED AV	SVL	53	B5
REED ST	SJ	62	B3
REED ST	SCL	54	B6
REED TER	SVL	53	C5
REEDHURST AV	SJ	67	A6
REEVE ST	SCL	54	B6
REEVES CT	SCCO	56	B4
REFREDI CT	CPTO	59	D4
REGABY PLACE CT	SJ	68	C2
REGAL CT	SCCO	56	A2
REGAL LN	S	65	A4
REGALO CT	SJ	66	C2
REGAN LN	S	64	F4
REGAN LN	S	65	A3
REGAN ST	SCCO	56	B6
REGAS DR	C	66	C4
REGAS DR	SJ	66	C4
REGATTA LN	SJ	54	E4
REGENCY DR	SJ	65	C1
REGENCY PL	SJ	65	C1
REGENCY KNLL DR	SJ	60	B6
REGENCY OAKS DR	SJ	60	B6
REGENT DR	LA	59	A2
REGENT PL	PA	38	B6
REGENT PL	PA	44	B1
REGENT ST	SJ	54	E6
REGENT ST	SJ	61	E1
REGENT PARK DR	SJ	72	D1
REGIA CT	SVL	52	E6
REGINA CT	SCL	53	F1
REGINA WY	C	65	E5
REGINA WY	SJ	65	E5
REGIS CT	SCL	53	D5
REGNART CT	CPTO	64	D1
REGNART RD	CPTO	64	D1
REGNART RD	SCCO	64	D1
REGNART WY	SCL	60	E4
REGNART CYN DR	CPTO	64	D1
REID LN	S	64	F5
REINCLAUD CT	SVL	52	E6
REINELL PL	CPTO	59	F4
REINERT AV	MVW	44	F4
REINERT AV	MVW	45	A4
REINERT RD	MVW	45	A4
REINOSO CT	SJ	67	C4
REISLING WY	SJ	68A	B3
REMBRANDT DR	SVL	53	A6
REMILLARD CT	SJ	62	D3
REMINGTON CT	SJ	63	D4
REMINGTON CT	SVL	52	D6
REMINGTON DR	SVL	52	E5
REMINGTON DR	SVL	53	A6
REMINGTON WY	SJ	63	D4
REMO CT	SCL	53	F1
REMO ST	SJ	62	D2
REMSEN CT	SVL	52	D6
REMUDA LN	SJ	54	E4
RENAISSANCE CT	SCCO	81	F3
RENEE CT	SCCO	81	E3
RENEE CT	SJ	75	F1
RENEE LN	G	82	F6
RENETTA CT	LA	51	E5
RENFIELD WY	SJ	63	C5
RENFREW CT	SJ	55	B2
RENGSTORFF AV	MVW	45	A6
RENGSTORFF AV N	MVW	44	F6
RENGSTORFF AV S	MVW	51	F1
RENICK CT	SJ	63	E1
RENNIE AV	SCCO	56	B2
RENO DR	SJ	63	D2
RENO DR	SCCO	63	D2
RENOIR CT	SVL	53	A6
RENOVA DR	SCCO	61	C5
RENRAW DR	SJ	56	C5
RENTON CT	SJ	72	D2
RENZ LN	G	84	B2
RENZO CT	SJ	68	B4
REPOSA CT	SJ	68	A1
REPOSA DR	SJ	68	A1
REPUBLIC AV	SJ	55	F5
REPUBLIC CT	SJ	55	F5
REPUBLIC PL	SJ	55	F5
REQUA CT	SJ	63	E3
RESEARCH PL	SJ	47	D6
RESEDA DR	SVL	52	E5
RESERVOIR RD	LG	70	E5
RESULTS WY	CPTO	59	D5
RETTUS CT	SJ	62	E6
REVA CT	SCCO	56	B5
REVELSTOKE WY	SVL	59	F2
REVERE AV	SJ	67	A4
REVERE AV	SCCO	67	A4
REVERE DR	SVL	52	E6
REVERE PL	G	83	F3
REVEY AV	SJ	61	C4
REVEY AV	SCCO	61	C4
REVINIA WY	LG	71	A5
REX CIR	C	66	B2
REXFORD WY	SJ	61	D5
REXFORD WY	SCCO	61	D5
REXWOOD CT	SJ	68	C1
REYNAUD DR	SCCO	56	C4
REYNELLA CT	SVL	52	E6
REYNOLDS CIR	SJ	54	E4
REYNOLDS RD	SCCO	75	A2
RHAPSODY WY	SJ	68	B4
RHINE LN	SJ	72	A3
RHINECASTLE WY	SJ	72	B3
RHINECLIFF WY	SJ	61	D6
RHINECLIFF WY	SJ	66	D1
RHODA DR	LAH	51	B3
RHODA DR	SJ	60	F6
RHODA DR	SJ	65	F1
RHODES CT	SCCO	81	C3
RHODES CT	SJ	61	F3
RHODES DR	PA	38	C6
RHODESIA WY	SJ	66	D1
RHONDA DR	SJ	65	D1
RHONE CT	MVW	45	A5
RHUS RIDGE RD	LAH	51	C6
RHUS RIDGE RD	LAH	58	C1
RIALTO CT	MVW	45	A5
RIBSON DR	SJ	65	E1
RIBCHESTER CT	SJ	72A	A2
RIBIER CT	SVL	52	E6
RIBISI CIR	SJ	55	C3
RIBISI WY	SJ	55	C3
RIC DR	SCCO	82A	C4
RICARDO RD	CPTO	59	C6
RICA VISTA WY	SCCO	56	C3
RICE CT	SJ	68	B5
RICE CT	S	64	F4
RICE DR	SJ	68	B5
RICE LN	SCCO	82	F2
RICE WY	SJ	68	B5
RICH AV	MVW	51	F2
RICH AV	MVW	52	A2
RICHARD AV	SCL	54	B5
RICHARD CT	MVW	44	F5
RICHARDS AV	SJ	66	E1
RICHARDSON AV	LA	59	B1
RICHARDSON CT	PA	44	D3
RICHARDSON DR	SJ	56	A2
RICHDALE AV	SJ	68	D4
RICHDALE AV	SCCO	68	A3
RICHELIEU CT	LA	51	E2
RICHELIEU CT	S	65	B5
RICHELIEU PL	SVL	59	F2
RICHEY DR	SCCO	71	C2
RICHFIELD DR	SJ	60	E4
RICHGROVE CT	SJ	63	E3
RICHLAND AV	SJ	67	B4
RICHLEE DR	C	66	D2
RICHMOND AV	SJ	61	D5
RICHMOND AV	SCCO	77	D3
RICHTER CT	MPTS	48	B4
RICHWOOD CT	CPTO	60	B4
RICHWOOD DR	CPTO	60	B5
RICKENBACKER ST	SJ	61	C6
RICKY CT	C	65	F3
RICKY CT	C	66	A3
RICKY DR	C	65	F3
RICKY DR	C	66	A3
RIDDER PARK DR	SJ	54	F3
RIDDLE RD	SJ	61	A5
RIDGE CT	SCL	60	E3
RIDGE RD	LG	70	D5
RIDGE RD	SCL	60	E3
RIDGE RD	SCCO	56C	A2
RIDGE RD	SCCO	70	D5
RIDGE RD	SCCO	73	D5
RIDGE RD	SCCO	81G	F4
RIDGE RD	SCCO	82H	A1
RIDGEBROOK WY	SJ	68	B3
RIDGECLIFF CT	SJ	55	B1
RIDGE CREEK CT	CPTO	64	E2
RIDGECREST AV	MS	70	D4
RIDGEFARM DR	SJ	72A	A2
RIDGEGATE DR	SJ	55	E3
RIDGEGLEN WY	SJ	55	E4
RIDGELEY DR	C	66	D2
RIDGELEY DR	SCCO	66	D2
RIDGELINE CT	SJ	56	C5
RIDGEMONT DR	MPTS	48	D3
RIDGEMONT DR	MVW	52	C5
RIDGEMONT DR	SJ	63	B2
RIDGE OAK CT	SJ	72	B4
RIDGETREE WY	SJ	55	B1
RIDGETOP DR	SJ	55	F2
RIDGETOP DR	SCCO	55	F2
RIDGETOP DR	SCCO	56	A2
RIDGEVIEW AV	SCCO	56	B3
RIDGEVIEW CT	CPTO	60	B3
RIDGEVIEW CT	MH	80	D2
RIDGEVIEW CT	SCCO	56	B3
RIDGEVIEW TER	SCCO	56	B3
RIDGEVIEW WY	SCCO	56	B3
RIDGE VISTA AV	SJ	55	F3
RIDGE VISTA AV	SCCO	55	F4
RIDGE VISTA AV	SCCO	56	A4
RIDGEWAY DR	CPTO	59	B4
RIDGEWAY DR	G	82	C5
RIDGEWOOD DR	SJ	72	A2
RIDGEWOOD LN	LAH	51	B6
RIDING CT	SJ	71	E4
RIDLEY WY	SJ	61	E6
RIDLEY WY	SJ	66	E1
RIEDAL PL	CPTO	60	A4
RIEDEL CT	SCCO	81	F4
RIEDEL CT	SJ	63	D5

STREET	CITY	PAGE	GRID
RIEDEL DR	SJ	63	D5
RIELLY CT	SJ	72	E1
RIESLING CT	S	70	B1
RIESLING TER	SVL	52	E6
RIESLING TER	SVL	59	E1
RIGOLETTO DR	SJ	63	A5
RILMA LN	LA	44	D6
RILMA LN	LA	51	D1
RIMROCK DR	SJ	75	C1
RIMWOOD DR	SJ	72	B1
RINCON AV	C	65	F3
RINCON AV	C	66	A3
RINCON AV	SJ	65	F3
RINCON AV	SCCO	65	F3
RINCON AV	SVL	52	E4
RINCON CIR	PA	44	C6
RINCON CIR	SJ	54	E1
RINCONADA AV	PA	44	B3
RINCONADA CT	LA	51	E3
RINCONADA DR	SJ	67	B3
RINCNADA OKS CT	LG	65	D6
RINCNADA OKS CT	LG	70	D1
RINEHART DR	SJ	55	E4
RINGLE CT	SCCO	80	A3
RINGLE DR	SCCO	80	A3
RINGROSE CT	SJ	68	B1
RINGWOOD AV	SJ	54	F1
RINGWOOD AV	SJ	55	A1
RINGWOOD CT	SJ	55	A2
RIO BARRANCA CT	SJ	55	E5
RIO BRAVO DR	SJ	63	D2
RIO CHICO DR	SJ	67	F3
RIO CHICO DR	SJ	68	A3
RIO D ESMERALDA	SJ	68	B1
RIO DE JOYAS	SJ	68	B1
RIO DE LATA	SJ	68	B1
RIO D LS MLINOS	SVL	52	E3
RIO DE ORO	SJ	63	B6
RIO DE ORO	SJ	68	B1
RIO DE PERLA	SJ	68	B1
RIO DE PLATA	SJ	68	B1
RIO DE PLOMO	SJ	68	B1
RIO GRANDE DR	SJ	68	A6
RIO GUACIMAL CT	SJ	55	E5
RIO HONDO DR	SJ	72	B5
RIO LINDA	SJ	47	A5
RIO LOBO DR	SJ	68	A6
RIORDAN DR	SJ	65	D3
RIO RITA WY	SJ	60	D5
RIO ROBLES	SJ	47	B6
RIO SERENA AV	C	65	E2
RIO SERENA AV	SJ	65	E2
RIO VERDE DR	SJ	72	A1
RIO VERDE PL	MPTS	47	E3
RIO VISTA	LG	65	D6
RIO VISTA AV	SJ	60	D4
RIPLEY DR	SJ	55	D5
RITA CT	SCL	61	A3
RITA DR	MH	79	F4
RITANNA CT	S	64	F2
RITZ CT	SJ	63	F3
RIVER ST	SJ	61	F3
RIVER ST	SJ	62	A3
RIVERA ST	MPTS	39	F6
RIVERA ST	MPTS	40	A6
RIVER ASH CT	SJ	67	F4
RIVER ASH CT	SJ	68	A4
RIVERBANK RD	SCCO	81H	D2
RIVER BED CT	SCL	53	F2
RIVER BIRCH CT	SJ	55	C4
RIVERBORO PL	SJ	72	C1
RIVERCREST CT	CPTO	59	D4
RIVERDALE CT	S	65	C5
RIVERDALE DR	S	65	C5
RIVER FALLS DR	SJ	68	B3
RIVERMONT CT	SJ	55	F6
RIVER OAKS CIR	SJ	47	D6
RIVER OAKS PKWY	SJ	47	C6
RIVER OAKS PKWY	SJ	54	D1
RIVER OAKS PL	SJ	47	C6
RIVER PARK DR	SJ	68	B3
RIVER RANCH CIR	S	65	A5
RIVERRUN DR	SJ	55	E5
RIVERRUN DR	SCCO	55	E5
RIVERSIDE CT	SCL	54	B1
RIVERSIDE DR	CPTO	59	C6
RIVERSIDE DR	LA	51	F5
RIVERSIDE DR	SJ	61	F5
RIVERSIDE WY W	SJ	60	A6
RIVER TRAIL CT	SJ	68	D4
RIVER VIEW DR	SJ	68	B4
RIVIERA CT	SJ	60	D6
RIVIERA DR	LA	51	F3
RIVIERA DR	LG	70	E4
RIVIERA RD	CPTO	59	C5
RIVIERA RD	SCCO	59	C5
RIVOIR DR	SJ	66	F6
RIVULET RD	SJ	71	E4
RIXFORD LN	LA	51	F5
RIZAL CT	SJ	72A	C4
ROADING DR	SJ	72A	A2
ROAD RUNNER TER	SVL	60	C1
ROAN ST	SJ	72A	A2
ROARING WTR WY	SCCO	73	F6
ROARING WTR WY	SCCO	78G	F1
ROBALO CT	SJ	55	E1
ROBB DR	SJ	67	A6
ROBB RD	PA	51	C2
ROBBIA CT	SVL	53	A6
ROBBIA DR	SVL	53	A6
ROBERSON LN	SJ	54	E4
ROBERT AV	SCL	54	B5
ROBERTA CT	SJ	68	A1
ROBT FOWLER WY	SCCO	63	B2
ROBERTS CT	SJ	62	C5
ROBERTS RD	LG	70	F3
ROBERTS RD W	LG	70	E3
ROBERTS ST	SJ	62	D4
ROBERTSON CT	SJ	67	C6
ROBERTSON RD	SCL	53	E5
ROBIE LN	SCCO	70	F4
ROBIE LN	SCCO	71	A4
ROBIN CT	SVL	52	D5
ROBIN DR	SCCO	61	A2
ROBIN DR	SJ	66	D5
ROBIN DR	SCL	61	A2
ROBIN LN	C	66	A4
ROBIN WY	LG	71	A4
ROBIN WY	S	70	A2
ROBIN WY	SVL	52	D5
ROBIN ANN DR	MS	70	E2
ROBINDELL WY	CPTO	59	E6
ROBINDELL WY	CPTO	64	E1
ROBIN HOOD CT	LA	59	A2
ROBINHOOD DR	LA	59	A2
ROBINSON AV	SCL	53	F6
ROBLAR LN	SCL	53	E2
ROBLE CT	S	65	B4
ROBLE DR	MH	80K	E2
ROBLE DR	SCCO	43	E3
ROBLE DR	SVL	53	C6
ROBLE ALTO	LAH	50	F3
ROBLE ALTO CT	LAH	50	F3
ROBLE BLANCO	LAH	50	F3
ROBLEDA CT	LAH	51	D3
ROBLEDA RD	LAH	51	C4
ROBLE LADERA RD	LAH	51	B3
ROBLE RIDGE	PA	44	B5
ROBLES DEL ORO	SCCO	70	C3
ROBLE VENENO LN	LAH	51	C3
ROBNICK CT	C	65	E5
ROBSHEAL DR	SJ	66	F2
ROBWAY AV	C	66	D2
ROCHELLE DR	SJ	66	D4
ROCHESTER CT	SVL	52	D6
ROCHESTER RD	SJ	72A	C1
ROCHIN CT	LG	71	B3
ROCHIN CT	SCCO	71	B3
ROCKLIN CT	SJ	55	B3
ROCHIN TER	LG	71	B3
ROCHIN TER	SCCO	71	B3
ROCK AV	SCCO	54	F2
ROCK ST	MVW	44	F5
ROCK ST	MVW	45	A5
ROCK ST	SCCO	45	A5
ROCK CANYON CIR	SJ	56	A1
ROCKDALE DR	SJ	60	D6
ROCKDALE DR	SCCO	60	D6
ROCKEFELLER DR	SVL	52	D6
ROCKHAVEN DR	SJ	72	C6
ROCKHURST CT	SCL	53	D5
ROCKNG HORSE CT	SJ	72A	A4
ROCKPOINT LN	LA	51	E5
ROCKPORT AV	SJ	55	E1
ROCKPORT DR	SVL	52	F6
ROCKRIDGE WY	SCL	53	F5
ROCK RIVER CT	SJ	67	F1
ROCKROSE AV	SVL	53	C6
ROCKROSE CT	G	82	B6
ROCK SPRING CT	CPTO	64	A5
ROCKSPRING DR	SJ	62	D5
ROCKTON AV	SJ	72A	E3
ROCKTON PL	SJ	72A	F3
ROCKTREE CT	SJ	55	B1
ROCKVIEW CT	SJ	75	C1
ROCKWAY DR	SJ	56	A4
ROCKWOOD DR	SJ	60	E5
ROCKY CREEK CT	MH	79	F5
ROCKY CREEK CT	SJ	63	D1
ROCKY CREEK WY	S	64	E6
ROCKY CREEK WY	S	69	D2
ROCKY GLEN CT	SJ	72	E3
ROCKY MTN AV	MPTS	48	C4
ROCKY MTN DR	SJ	63	C1
ROCKY RIDGE RD	MH	79	A5
ROCKY WATER LN	SJ	63	C5
RODECK WY	C	66	C2
RODEO CT	SJ	67	F2
RODEO DR	SJ	67	F2
RODEO PL	SJ	67	F2
RODNEY DR	SJ	67	B5
RODONI CT	S	65	B3
RODONOVAN CT	SCL	60	D4
RODONOVAN DR	SCL	60	D4
RODRIGUES AV	CPTO	59	F5
RODRIGUES AV	CPTO	60	A4
RODRIGUES AV	MPTS	48	B2
ROEDER CT	SJ	68	C5
ROEDER RD	SJ	68	C5
ROEHAMPTON AV	SCCO	56	B6
ROENOKE WY	SJ	61	D6
ROEWILL DR	SJ	60	F6
ROEWILL DR	SJ	65	F1
ROGER ST	MPTS	39	F6
ROGERS AV	SJ	54	E4
ROGERS CT	SCL	60	F2
ROGERS LN	G	84	A1
ROGERS ST	LG	70	E5
ROHN WY	SJ	72A	B2
ROJO PL	SJ	66	C2
ROLFE CT	SCCO	56	B4
ROLINE CT	SCCO	71	C1
ROLL ST	SCL	53	F6
ROLL ST	SCL	54	A6
ROLLINGDELL CT	CPTO	59	F6
ROLLINGDELL DR	CPTO	59	F6
ROLLINGDELL DR	SJ	59	F6
ROLLING GLEN CT	SJ	72	D3
ROLLING HLS DR	MH	79	A5
ROLLING HLS DR	SCCO	82A	C2
ROLLING HLS RD	SCCO	64	D3
ROLLING MDW CT	SJ	68A	C3
ROLLING OAKS CT	SJ	72	B6
ROLLING OAKS DR	SJ	72	B6
ROLLINGSIDE DR	SJ	63	E3
ROLLINGWOOD CT	SJ	63	F3
ROLLY RD	SCCO	58	F2
ROMA CT	SCL	60	E4
ROMBERG DR	SVL	52	F6
ROME DR	SCCO	76	B3
ROMEO AV	SCCO	56	C4
ROMEO AV	SJ	56	C4
ROMERO ST	SJ	66	C1
ROMFORD DR	SJ	71	E3
RONALD AV	C	66	A4
RONALD CT	LA	51	F5
RONALD CT	LA	52	A5
RONALD CT	SJ	71	F2
RONALD ST	SCL	54	B5
RONALD WY	CPTO	59	D6
RONAN AV	G	82	E5
RONCO DR	SJ	55	D2
RONDA DR	SCCO	71	D1
RONDEAU DR	SJ	66	E6
RONDEN CT	MVW	52	A3
RONIE WY	SJ	66	E6
RONIE WY	SJ	71	E1
RONNIE WY	S	65	B5
ROOP RD	SCCO	81A	E6
ROOP RD	SCCO	82A	C3
ROOP RD	SCCO	82A	E1
ROOSEVELT AV	SCCO	81	B4
ROOSEVELT AV	SVL	53	A3
ROOSEVELT CIR	PA	44	D4
ROOSEVELT CIR	SCL	53	F5
ROOSEVELT CT	SCL	53	F5
ROOSEVELT ST	SJ	62	C1
ROOSEVELT WY	SJ	46	F3
ROOSTER CT	SJ	68	A6
ROOSTER DR	SJ	68	A6
RORKE WY	PA	44	E3
ROSA AV	SVL	53	B6
ROSA CT	SVL	53	B6
ROSALIA AV	SJ	65	E1
ROSALIA AV	SVL	60	B1
ROSALIE CT	LG	71	A4
ROSALIE DR	SCL	60	F1
ROSALIND LN	SCCO	72	E5
ROSALINDA CT	SJ	63	A5
ROSANNA ST	G	83	F2
ROSARIO AV	CPTO	59	D6
ROSARIO CT	SJ	48	B6
ROSARIO DR	SJ	48	B6
ROSE AV	LA	52	A4
ROSE AV	LG	70	D3
ROSE AV	MS	70	D3
ROSE AV	MVW	51	F4
ROSE AV	MVW	52	A4
ROSE AV	SJ	55	F5
ROSE AV	SJ	56	A5
ROSE AV	SCCO	56	A5
ROSE CIR E	LA	52	B5
ROSE CIR W	LA	52	B5
ROSE CT	C	66	A3
ROSE CT	MS	70	D3
ROSE CT	SCL	60	F2
ROSE CT	SCCO	73	D6
ROSE CT	SCCO	78G	D1
ROSE DR	MPTS	39	F6
ROSE LN	LA	51	F4
ROSE LN	LG	70	E3
ROSE PL	SJ	62	C4
ROSE WY	SCL	60	F2
ROSE ANNA DR	SJ	71	F2
ROSEBAY CT	SJ	55	F5
ROSEBAY CT	SJ	56	A5
ROSE BLOSSOM DR	CPTO	59	E5
ROSEBRIAR WY	SJ	55	B3
ROSEBUD CT	SJ	61	D6
ROSEDALE DR	SJ	61	A5
ROSEGARDEN LN	CPTO	64	F2
ROSELEAF CT	SCCO	71	A2
ROSEMAR AV	SJ	56	C4
ROSEMAR AV	SCCO	56	C4
ROSEMARIE CT	CPTO	60	B4
ROSEMARY LN	C	66	B2
ROSEMARY LN	MH	79	F4
ROSEMARY WY	SJ	66	B2
ROSEMARY ST	SJ	54	F5
ROSEMONT AV	LA	52	B6
ROSEMONT CT	LA	52	B6
ROSEMONT DR	SCL	60	D3
ROSENBAUM AV	SJ	67	E4
ROSENCRANS WY	SJ	72A	F4
ROSE ORCHARD WY	SJ	47	B4
ROSETTA DR	SCCO	80	B3
ROSETTE CT	SVL	53	B6
ROSETTE TER	SVL	53	B6
ROSE VIEW DR	SJ	56	C3
ROSEWELL CT	SCCO	72A	D1
ROSEWELL WY	SJ	72A	D1
ROSEWOOD AV	SJ	61	A5
ROSEWOOD AV	SCCO	61	A5
ROSEWOOD CT	LA	51	F5
ROSEWOOD DR	PA	44	C2
ROSEWOOD ST	CPTO	60	A3
ROSITA AV	LA	51	E4
ROSITA AV	SCL	61	A3
ROSITA CT	SCL	61	A3
ROSLYN CIR	MVW	45	C6
ROSLYN CT	SJ	62	F5
ROSS AV	SJ	66	E5
ROSS AV	SJ	71	E1
ROSS AV	SCCO	71	E1
ROSS CIR	SCCO	71	E1
ROSS CT	C	66	B3
ROSS CT	PA	44	D3
ROSS DR	S	45	F6
ROSS RD	PA	44	E3
ROSSBURN CT	SJ	68	B2
ROSS CREEK CT	LG	71	B2
ROSSI LN	G	84	B4
ROSSMERE CT	S	65	B5
ROSSMORE CT	SJ	63	C4
ROSSMORE LN	SJ	63	D4
ROSSMORE WY	SJ	63	C4
ROSSMOYNE DR	SCCO	71	D1
ROSSOTTO DR	SJ	65	D4
ROSS PARK CT	SJ	67	A5
ROSS PARK DR	SJ	67	A5
ROSSWAY CT	LA	59	B1
ROSSWOOD DR	SJ	71	D2
ROSWELL CT	MPTS	48	B3
ROSWELL DR	MPTS	48	B3
ROTH WY	PA	43	E3
ROTHE DR	SCCO	82	D1
ROTHERHAVEN WY	SJ	68	A5
ROTHLAND CT	SJ	55	B3
ROTHROCK DR	SJ	55	E5
ROTTERDAM LN	SJ	72	A3
ROUGH&READY RD	SJ	55	E3
ROUNDLEAF CT	SJ	55	B2
ROUNDTABLE DR	SJ	68	C6
ROUNDTREE CT	SJ	65	D5
ROUNDTREE DR	SJ	65	D5
ROUSE CT	SJ	72A	F4
ROUSSEAU DR	SVL	53	A6
ROUTE 17 FRWY	C	66	A6
ROUTE 17 FRWY	LG	70	F4
ROUTE 17 FRWY	LG	71	A1
ROUTE 17 FRWY	SJ	61	C6
ROWENA CT	SCL	54	B2
ROWLEY DR	SJ	48	D4
ROXANNE DR	SJ	71	E3
ROXBURY CT	SCL	61	B2
ROXBURY LN	LG	65	E6
ROXBURY ST	SCL	61	B2
ROX PLACE CT	SJ	68	B1
ROY AV	SJ	67	A3
ROYAL AV	SJ	61	F4
ROYAL DR	SCL	53	F6
ROYAL DR	SCL	54	A6
ROYAL WY	G	83	F3
ROYAL ACORN PL	SJ	72	C3
ROYAL ACRES CT	SJ	67	B5
ROYAL ANN CT	SJ	65	B1
ROYAL ANN CT	SVL	52	E6
ROYAL ANN DR	SJ	65	B1
ROYAL ANN DR	SVL	52	E6
ROYALBROOK CT	SJ	68	A2
ROYAL CREST DR	SJ	55	B3
ROYALE PARK CT	SJ	67	E5
ROYALE PARK DR	SJ	67	E5
ROYAL ESTATE CT	SJ	68	F1
ROYAL FOREST CT	SJ	67	E5
ROYAL GARDEN PL	SJ	67	E5
ROYAL GATE PL	SJ	67	E5
ROYAL GLEN CT	SJ	55	E3
ROYAL GLEN DR	SJ	55	E3
ROYAL GROVE CT	SJ	67	E5
ROYAL MEADOW LN	SJ	63A	B3
ROYAL OAK CT	SJ	72A	B3
ROYAL OAK WY	CPTO	59	C4
ROYAL RIDGE CT	SJ	75	D1
ROYAL RIDGE DR	SJ	75	D1
ROYALRIDGE WY	SCL	53	E2
ROYALTREE CIR	SJ	55	B1
ROYALVALE WY	SJ	48	B6
ROYALWOOD CT	SJ	76	A1
ROYALWOOD WY	SJ	72	F6
ROYALWOOD WY	SJ	72A	A6
ROYCE DR	SJ	55	C6
ROYCE ST	LG	70	E4
ROYCOTT WY	SJ	66	F2
ROYCOTT WY	SJ	67	A2
ROYSTON CT	ST	72	D5
RUBION CT	SJ	63	C1
RUBION DR	SJ	63	C1
RUBIS DR	SVL	52	E5
RUBY AV	SJ	63	E2
RUBY AV	SCCO	63	E2
RUBY CT	SJ	63	E3
RUCKER AV	SCCO	82	E2
RUCKER AV	SCCO	82A	A1
RUCKER DR	CPTO	59	D6
RUCKER DR	SJ	71	E3
RUDD CT	SJ	68	A3
RUDY CT	SJ	71	E4
RUDY DR	SJ	71	F3
RUDYARD DR	MPTS	47	E3
RUE AVATI	SJ	55	B3
RUE BORDEAUX	SJ	68	A5
RUE BOULOGNE	SJ	68	A5
RUE CALAIS	SJ	68	A6
RUE CANNES	SJ	68	A5
RUE FERRARI	SJ	72A	E2
RUE LE MANS	SJ	68	A5
RUE LOIRET	SJ	68	A5
RUE LYON	SJ	68	A5
RUE LYON CT	SJ	68	A5
RUE MONTAGNE	C	66	C3
RUE NICE CT	SJ	68	A5
RUE ORLEANS CT	SJ	68	A5
RUE PARIS	SJ	68	A5
RUE TOULON CT	SJ	68	A5
RUE TOURS CT	SJ	68	A5
RUFF DR	SJ	54	E6
RUFF DR	SJ	61	E1
RUGBY CT	SJ	72	B3
RUGE DR	SJ	55	D2
RUIZ CT	SJ	65	C1
RUMFORD DR	CPTO	59	E4
RUMSEY CT	SJ	68	C5
RUNNING BEAR DR	SJ	68	B6
RUNNING FARM LN	SCCO	44	A4
RUNNING WATR CT	SCL	53	F1
RUNNINGWOOD CIR	MVW	52	C4
RUNNYMEAD CT	LA	52	A5
RUNNYMEAD DR	LA	52	A5
RUNNYMEDE DR	SJ	61	A6
RUNNYMEDE DR	SJ	66	A1
RUNO CT	SCCO	60	C5
RUNSHAW PL	SJ	68	B2
RUPERT DR	SJ	66	B6
RUPERT DR	SJ	71	B1
RUPPELL PL	CPTO	64	F1
RUSHMORE LN	LG	70	E4
RUSKIN DR	SJ	48	D6
RUSSELL AV	LA	52	A5
RUSSELL AV	SCL	54	A2
RUSSELL CT	S	64	F4
RUSSELL LN	MPTS	40	A6
RUSSELL LN	S	64	F4
RUSSET DR	SVL	52	E5
RUSSETT TER	SVL	52	E5
RUSSO DR	SJ	72	B1
RUSTIC AV	SJ	66	D5
RUSTIC DR	SJ	66	D5
RUSTIC DR	SCL	60	D2
RUSTIC LN	MVW	52	A3
RUSTIC RANCH CT	SJ	75	F1
RUSTLING OAK CT	MH	80	D3
RUSTLING OAK LN	MH	80	D3
RUTH AV	MVW	44	F5
RUTH CT	SCL	60	E3
RUTH DR	SJ	67	B3
RUTH CABRAL WY	SCL	60	B4
RUTHELMA AV	PA	44	D5
RUTHELMA WY	PA	44	D5
RUTHERFORD AV	SJ	65	A2
RUTHERGLEN PL	SJ	67	D6
RUTHER PLACE CT	SJ	68	C1
RUTHER PLACE WY	SJ	68	C1
RUTHVEN AV	PA	37	F6
RUTLAND AV	SJ	61	D5
RUTLAND AV	SCCO	61	D5
RUTLEDGE PL	SCL	53	D4
RUTTNER CT	SJ	68	C4
RUTTNER PL	SJ	68	C4
RYAN AV	SCL	60	D3
RYAN CT	G	84	E1
RYAN CT	PA	44	A5
RYAN DR	SCCO	56	B6
RYCROFT CT	SJ	72	F6
RYDER ST	SCL	53	D3
RYE CT	SJ	56	C5
RYEGATE CT	SJ	55	D5
RYLAND ST	SJ	61	F2
RYMAR CT	SJ	55	D3
RYMAR DR	SJ	55	D3
RYMAR LN	SJ	55	D3
RYMAR PL	SJ	55	D3
RYMAR TER	SJ	55	D3
RYMAR WY	SJ	55	D3
S			
SABAL DR	SJ	55	D1
SABINA WY	SJ	71	F2
SABINI CT	SCCO	79	C4
SACRAMENTO AV	SJ	68	B3
SADDLE CT	LAH	51	A3
SADDLEBACK DR	MH	80	C3
SADDLE BROOK DR	SJ	68	A5
SADDLEHORN WY	MH	80	C3
SADDLE MTN DR	LAH	51	A3
SADDLE TREE CT	SJ	68	D3
SADDLEWOOD DR	SJ	62	F5
SADIE CT	SJ	65	F4
SAFARI DR	SJ	72A	A3
SAFFARIAN CT	SJ	63	C6
SAFFLE CT	C	65	E5
SAGE CT	CPTO	59	E6
SAGE CT	SVL	52	E6
SAGE HEN CT	SJ	67	B6
SAGE HEN WY	SVL	60	C1
SAGELAND DR	SJ	55	B3
SAGEMILL CT	SJ	63	A6
SAGEMONT AV	SJ	65	D2
SAGE OAK WY	SJ	72	C4
SAGER WY	SJ	72	F4
SAGEWELL WY	SJ	72A	D2
SAGEWOOD LN	SJ	48	C5
SAGITTARIUS LN	SJ	68	E4

1991 SANTA CLARA COUNTY STREET INDEX

STREET	CITY	PAGE	GRID
SCOTTSDALE DR	SJ	63	C5
SCOTTSFIELD DR	SJ	67	C5
SCOTTSVILLE CT	SJ	55	D5
SCOTTY ST	SJ	62	E3
SCOUT CT	SJ	68	A5
SCRIPPS AV	PA	44	E5
SCRIPPS CT	PA	44	E5
SCULLY AV	SJ	65	A3
SCULLY AV	S	65	B3
SEABEE PL	SCCO	55	C4
SEABISCUIT DR	SJ	68	C5
SEABOARD AV	SJ	54	C3
SEABROOK CT	SJ	68	A2
SEABURY DR	SJ	67	D5
SEACLIFF DR	MPTS	48	C3
SEACLIFF WY	SJ	63	A4
SEACREEK CT	SJ	68	D3
SEACREEK WY	SJ	68	D3
SEAFIELD CT	SJ	63	C5
SEAGRAVES WY	S	65	A6
SEA GULL CT	S	65	A3
SEA GULL WY	S	64	F2
SEA GULL WY	S	65	A2
SEALE AV	PA	44	B2
SEAMAN PL	SJ	55	C3
SEAN CIR	SJ	72A	A1
SEAN CT	SJ	72A	A1
SEAN LN	SJ	72A	B1
SEARCY DR	SJ	67	A6
SEAREEL LN	SJ	54	F1
SEARLES AV	SJ	66	F1
SEARLES AV	SJ	67	A1
SEARS RD	SCCO	78H	C2
SEARSVILLE RD	SCCO	43	D3
SEASIDE DR	MPTS	47	E1
SEASIDE WY	MPTS	39	E6
SEASIDE WY	MPTS	47	E1
SEATON AV	S	64	F5
SEAVIEW DR	SJ	62	F3
SEAVIEW DR	SJ	63	A3
SEAWELL CT	SJ	72A	E2
SEAWOOD WY	SJ	76	A1
SEBASIAN WY	SJ	68	A3
SEBASTIAN CT	LG	71	E3
SEBASTN BORELLO	SJ	63	D5
SEBREE LN	MS	70	D3
SEDLAK CT	SJ	63	C4
SEEBECK CT	SJ	48	D5
SEEBER CT	CPTO	64	E1
SEELEY RD	SJ	54	E1
SEENA AV	LA	52	A5
SEGO CT	SJ	55	B4
SEGOVIA CT	SJ	55	E2
SEIFERT AV	SJ	72	B2
SELBY LN	SCCO	55	F2
SELIG LN	LA	52	C6
SELINDA LN	SJ	71	D2
SELKIRK PL	SVL	60	A3
SELMAC AV	SJ	67	D5
SELO DR	SVL	59	F1
SELVA DR	SJ	63	D2
SELWYN DR	MPTS	48	B3
SEMICONDUCTR DR	SCL	53	C4
SEMINOLE WY	PA	44	E4
SEMINOLE WY	SJ	63	A4
SENATE WY	CPTO	59	E4
SENECA CT	SJ	72	E2
SENECA ST	PA	38	A6
SENNA CT	SVL	53	C5
SENTER RD	SJ	62	D4
SENTER RD	SJ	67	F1
SENTER RD	SJ	68	A4
SENTER RD	SCCO	62	D4
SENTER RD	SCCO	67	F1
SENTER RD	SCCO	68	A4
SENTER CREEK CT	SJ	67	E1
SENTINEL ST	SJ	72	A3
SEPTEMBER CT	CPTO	59	E5
SEPTEMBER DR	CPTO	59	E5
SEPTEMBER DR	SJ	72A	D1
SEPTEMBERSNG CT	SJ	55	C3
SEPULVEDA AV	MPTS	48	C2
SEPULVEDA CT	MPTS	48	C2
SEQUESTER CT	SJ	55	D2
SEQUOIA AV	PA	44	A3
SEQUOIA AV	SJ	61	E3
SEQUOIA DR	G	83	D2
SEQUOIA DR	MPTS	48	C3
SEQUOIA DR	SCCO	59	B2
SEQUOIA DR	SVL	53	B5
SEQUOIA LN	SCCO	43	E3
SEQUOIA WY	SCCO	59	B2

STREET	CITY	PAGE	GRID
SERENA WY	SCL	60	E4
SERENADE CT	SJ	68	B4
SERENADE WY	SJ	68	B4
SERENA VISTA CT	MS	70	D3
SERENDIPITY LN	SCCO	69	E2
SERENE DR	MH	79	F3
SERENE WY	SCCO	72A	A6
SERENE VLY CT	SJ	72	D6
SERENITY CT	SJ	72	E6
SERENITY WY	SJ	72	E6
SERENITY WY	SJ	75	E1
SERENO VISTA WY	SCCO	55	D4
SERGE AV	SJ	65	D3
SERPA DR	MPTS	48	B1
SERPA DR	SJ	63	C5
SERRA AV	SCL	60	F2
SERRA ST	SCCO	43	E3
SERRA ST	SCCO	44	A3
SERRA WY	MPTS	47	E3
SERRAMONTE DR	SCCO	70	C3
SERRANO AV	SCCO	56	B5
SERRAOAKS CT	S	65	C5
SERVICE ST	SJ	55	A4
SESAME CT	SJ	63	B2
SESAME CT	SVL	52	E6
SESAME DR	SVL	52	E6
SESSIONS CT	SJ	68	E1
SESSIONS DR	SJ	72A	F3
SETAREH CT	SJ	61	F6
SETAREH CT	SJ	66	F1
SETH CT	SJ	75	E1
SETTLE AV	SJ	61	F6
SETTLE AV	SJ	62	A6
SETTLE AV	SJ	67	A1
SEVELY DR	MVW	52	C3
SEVEN ACRES LN	LAH	51	C3
SEVEN SPGS DR	CPTO	64	A5
SEVEN SPGS PKY	CPTO	64	A5
SEVEN TREES BL	SJ	67	F4
SEVEN TREES BL	SJ	68	A4
SEVEN TR VLG WY	SJ	68	D3
SEVERAGE CT	SJ	67	D5
SEVERAGE DR	SJ	67	D5
SEVERANCE CT	SJ	67	D6
SEVERANCE DR	SJ	67	D6
SEVERANCE ST	G	82	E5
SEVERYNS AV	SCCO	45	D4
SEVILLA DR	LA	51	E2
SEVILLA LN	S	64	F5
SEVILLE DR	MH	80	A4
SEVILLE WY	SJ	55	C3
SEVYSON CT	PA	44	D2
SEWARD CT	SCCO	56	B5
SEWELL AV	SCCO	81	C4
SEYFERTH WY	SJ	67	B4
SEYMOUR AV	SCCO	81	B1
SEYMOUR ST	SJ	61	E2
SHADELANDS DR	SJ	72	F4
SHADE TREE LN	SJ	55	B1
SHADLE AV	C	65	F5
SHADOW CT	SJ	60	E5
SHADOW TR	SCCO	78G	C2
SHADOW BROOK DR	SJ	72	E5
SHADOWBROOK WY	MH	79	C3
SHADOW CREEK DR	SJ	67	D4
SHADOW CREEK PL	SCCO	59	A1
SHADOWCREST WY	SJ	72	E1
SHADOW DANCE DR	SJ	62	B6
SHADOW ESTATES	SJ	68A	A2
SHADOWFAX DR	SJ	68	A1
SHADOW GLEN	SJ	60	E5
SHADOWGRAPH DR	SJ	62	B6
SHADOWHILL LN	CPTO	64	F1
SHADOWHURST CT	SJ	67	D5
SHADOW LANE CT	MH	80K	F3
SHADOW LEAF DR	SJ	48	E5
SHADOW MTN CT	SJ	72	D6
SHADOW MTN DR	S	65	A4
SHADOW OAKS WY	S	65	A5
SHADOW PK PL	SJ	63	B6
SHADOW RUN DR	SJ	62	B5
SHADOW SPGS PL	SJ	63	B6
SHADOWTREE DR	SJ	55	B1
SHADOWVALE WY	SJ	48	B6
SHADOW WOOD CT	SJ	67	E5
SHADY AV	SJ	65	D1
SHADY LN	LG	71	B3
SHADY LN	SCCO	73	F6
SHADY LN	SCCO	79	B6
SHADY WY	SCCO	78G	C2
SHADYBROOK CT	S	65	C2
SHADY BROOK LN	SCCO	80K	C2

STREET	CITY	PAGE	GRID
SHADY CREEK CT	SJ	63	D1
SHADY DALE AV	C	66	D3
SHADY DALE LN	C	66	D3
SHADY GLEN AV	SCL	61	C2
SHADYGROVE CT	CPTO	60	B5
SHADYGROVE DR	CPTO	60	B5
SHADYGROVE DR	SCCO	60	B5
SHADY HOLLOW CT	SJ	63	F4
SHADY HOLLOW DR	MH	79	B4
SHADY LANE DR	SCCO	80	D2
SHADY OAK LN	CPTO	59	F2
SHADY OAKS CT	LAH	51	B2
SHADY SPRING LN	MVW	52	C5
SHADY VIEW LN	SCCO	71	A4
SHAFER AV	SCCO	80	B3
SHAFER CT	SCCO	80	B3
SHAFER DR	SCL	60	D2
SHAFFER DR	SJ	48	D6
SHAKER CT	SJ	72	D4
SHALEN CT	SJ	65	D3
SHAMROCK AV	SCL	53	E6
SHAMROCK DR	SJ	66	C5
SHAMROCK DR	SCCO	66	B5
SHANDWICK CT	SJ	67	B4
SHANG CT	SJ	55	F4
SHANGHAI CIR	SJ	55	A3
SHANGHAI CT	SJ	55	A3
SHANNON CT	CPTO	59	E5
SHANNON CT	SCL	60	E2
SHANNON RD	LG	70	F4
SHANNON RD	LG	71	B4
SHANNON RD	SCCO	70	F4
SHANNON RD	SCCO	71	D5
SHANNON RD	SCCO	78G	E4
SHANNON HTS RD	LG	71	B4
SHANNONS DR	SCCO	78K	E3
SHARMON PLMS LN	C	65	F5
SHARMON PLMS LN	C	66	A5
SHARON CT	C	65	F4
SHARON CT	C	66	A4
SHARON CT	LG	71	B3
SHARON CT	PA	38	B6
SHARON CT	PA	44	B1
SHARON DR	SJ	64	F2
SHARON DR	SJ	65	A1
SHARON DR	SCCO	65	A1
SHARON LN	SJ	71	D3
SHARP AV	C	66	B5
SHARP CT	C	66	B5
SHARY AV	MVW	52	B3
SHASTA AV	SJ	61	D4
SHASTA DR	PA	44	E5
SHASTA DR	SCL	60	C3
SHASTA LN	MH	80K	F2
SHASTA ST	LA	51	D3
SHASTA FIR DR	SVL	53	B5
SHASTA FIR WY	SVL	53	B5
SHASTA SPG CT	CPTO	64	A6
SHATTUCK DR	CPTO	59	D6
SHAUNA LN	PA	44	C5
SHAW DR	SJ	66	F5
SHAW DR	SJ	67	A5
SHAWCROFT DR	SJ	72A	A3
SHAWN DR	SJ	67	B6
SHAWNEE LN	SJ	72	F3
SHAWNEE LN	SJ	72A	A2
SHAYNOR CT	SJ	65	F1
SHEA CT	SJ	72A	F4
SHEAN CT	SCCO	82	D1
SHEARTON DR	SJ	60	F5
SHEARTON DR	SJ	61	A5
SHEARWATER DR	SJ	72	F6
SHEEHAN CT	SJ	75	E1
SHEFFIELD AV	C	66	D2
SHEFFIELD CT	C	66	D2
SHEILA AV	SCCO	80K	C5
SHEILA CT	C	65	F5
SHELBY LN	LA	51	E4
SHELBY CREEK CT	SJ	75	E2
SHELBY CREEK LN	SJ	75	E2
SHELDON AV	SCCO	84	B4
SHELDON RD	SCCO	70	C5
SHELLBACK PL	SJ	55	C3
SHELLBARK DR	SJ	67	F4
SHELLBARK DR	SJ	68	A4
SHELLBURNE WY	LG	70	E3
SHELLEY AV	C	66	B5
SHELLEY AV	SCCO	66	B5
SHELLEY CT	MPTS	47	F2
SHELLY AV	SJ	66	B5
SHELLY CT	SJ	72	E3
SHELLY DR	CPTO	59	F5
SHELTON WY	SJ	61	E6

STREET	CITY	PAGE	GRID
SHELTON WY	SJ	66	E1
SHENADO PL	SJ	68	B6
SHENANDOAH AV	MPTS	48	C3
SHENANDOAH DR	SJ	67	B2
SHENANDOAH DR	SVL	52	E6
SHEPHERD AV	SJ	62	A5
SHERATON DR	SCL	53	F5
SHERATON DR	SVL	52	E6
SHERBOURNE DR	SJ	71	F1
SHERBROOKE WY	SJ	56	B6
SHERBROOKE WY	SJ	63	B1
SHEREE CT	SJ	56	A1
SHEREE CT	SCCO	55	F1
SHEREEN PL	C	65	F3
SHERIDAN AV	PA	44	B4
SHERIDAN CIR	S	65	A3
SHERIDAN PL	SJ	62	E6
SHERIDAN PL	SJ	67	E1
SHERIDAN ST	LA	51	D4
SHERLAND AV	MVW	45	D6
SHERLAND AV	MVW	52	D1
SHERLAND CT	MVW	45	D6
SHERLAND CT	MVW	52	B1
SHERLOCK CT	LAH	50	F6
SHERLOCK DR	SJ	62	F6
SHERLOCK RD	LAH	50	F6
SHERLOCK RD	LAH	51	A6
SHERMAN AV	PA	44	B3
SHERMAN CT	MPTS	40	A6
SHERMAN CT	SJ	72A	D1
SHERMAN ST	LA	51	D4
SHERMAN ST	SJ	62	B5
SHERMAN ST	SCL	54	C6
SHERMAN ST	SCL	61	C1
SHERMAN OAKS DR	SJ	61	D6
SHERMAN OAKS DR	SCCO	61	D6
SHERRY CT	SJ	72A	E4
SHERRY LN	SCCO	81	E4
SHERRYS WY	SCCO	70	B6
SHERWIN AV	SCL	60	F2
SHERWIN AV	SCL	61	A2
SHERWOOD AV	SJ	61	C1
SHERWOOD AV	SCL	61	C1
SHERWOOD CT	SVL	52	D6
SHERWOOD DR	G	82	E6
SHERWOOD DR	SVL	52	D6
SHERWOOD LN	LA	51	E1
SHETLAND CT	MPTS	48	A2
SHETLAND CT	SJ	55	E2
SHETLAND PL	SVL	60	B3
SHIBLEY AV	SJ	66	F3
SHIBLEY AV	SJ	67	A3
SHILLING CT	SJ	48	D5
SHILOH AV	MPTS	48	C3
SHILSHONE CIR	SJ	62	F6
SHILSHONE WY	SJ	62	F6
SHIRE CT	LG	70	D1
SHIRECREST CT	SJ	72	E1
SHIRLEY AV	SCCO	58	F1
SHIRLEY AV	SVL	52	F2
SHIRLEY DR	MPTS	48	B3
SHIRLYNN CT	LA	51	E4
SHOFNER PL	SJ	67	E3
SHOLES CT	LAH	51	C3
SHONA CT	SJ	66	F6
SHOOTNG STR TER	SVL	53	B6
SHOREBIRD WY	MVW	45	B4
SHOREHAM CT	SCCO	56	A6
SHORELAND DR	SJ	62	F5
SHORELINE BL N	MVW	45	B6
SHORELINE BL S	MVW	52	A2
SHORESIDE CT	SCL	53	F2
SHOREVIEW CT	SJ	62	F4
SHOREWOOD LN	SJ	46	F4
SHOREWOOD LN	SJ	47	A4
SHORT RD	LG	71	B4
SHORT HILL CT	S	65	C5
SHORTRIDGE AV	SJ	55	D6
SHORTRIDGE AV	SJ	62	D1
SHOSHONE CT	SJ	55	F4
SHOSHONE DR	SJ	55	F4
SHOWERS DR	LA	51	E1
SHOWERS DR	MVW	44	E6
SHOWERS DR	MVW	51	E1
SHREEN CT	SJ	66	F6
SHRIVER CT	SJ	55	E1
SHRIVER DR	SJ	55	E1
SHUBERT CT	S	65	B3
SHUBERT DR	S	65	B3
SHULMAN AV	SCL	54	B5
SHUMAKER WY	SJ	55	C2
SIBELIUS AV	SJ	63	B4
SIDLAW CT	SJ	67	D5

STREET	CITY	PAGE	GRID
SIEBER CT	SJ	67	E3
SIEBER CT	SJ	68	E4
SIEBER PL	SJ	67	E3
SIEBER WY	SJ	67	E3
SIEBER WY	SJ	68	E4
SIENNA DR	SJ	56	B6
SIENNA DR	SJ	63	B1
SIERRA AV	MVW	52	B2
SIERRA AV	SJ	61	E4
SIERRA CT	PA	44	D1
SIERRA CT	SJ	55	D2
SIERRA RD	SJ	48	F6
SIERRA RD	SJ	49	B5
SIERRA RD	SJ	55	D1
SIERRA RD	SCCO	48	F6
SIERRA RD	SCCO	49	B5
SIERRA CREEK WY	SJ	48	D5
SRA GRANDE CT	SJ	55	F5
SRA GRANDE WY	SJ	55	F5
SIERRA LINDA	LG	65	D6
SIERRA MAR DR	SJ	67	B4
SRA MEADOW CT	SJ	55	F5
SRA MEADOW DR	SJ	55	F5
SIERRA MESA DR	SJ	55	F5
SIERRA MONTE WY	SJ	55	F6
SIERRA MORENA	LG	71	B3
SRA MORENA CT	MH	80K	E2
SRA SERENA CT	SJ	55	F6
SIERRA SPG CT	CPTO	64	A6
SIERRA SPG LN	CPTO	64	A6
SRA VENTURA DR	LA	59	B2
SIERRA VLG CT	SJ	55	D1
SIERRA VLG PL	SJ	55	D1
SIERRA VLG WY	SJ	55	D1
SIERRAVILLE AV	SJ	55	D1
SIERRA VISTA AV	MVW	45	A4
SIERRA VISTA AV	MVW	45	A6
SIERRA VISTA CT	SJ	55	F5
SIERRA VISTA PL	SJ	55	F5
SIERRA WOOD DR	SJ	48	B5
SIESTA DR	LA	52	B6
SIESTA DR	LA	59	B1
SIESTA DR	SCCO	56	B3
SIETA CT	SJ	67	A4
SIGAL DR	S	69	F2
SIGRID WY	SJ	68	A6
SIGRID WY	SJ	72A	A1
SILACCI DR	C	65	E4
SILACCI WY	G	84	B2
SILBERMAN DR	SJ	72	B4
SILBURY CT	SJ	63	E5
SILENCE DR	SJ	63	D1
SILENT HILLS LN	LAH	51	B6
SILER LN	SJ	62	D2
SILICON DR	SJ	61	D2
SILICON VLY RD	SJ	72A	F2
SILK CT	SJ	68	D3
SILKOAK WY	SVL	53	C5
SILVA AV	MVW	44	E5
SILVA AV	PA	44	E5
SILVA AV	SJ	67	B6
SILVA CIR	SCCO	82	B2
SILVA CT	PA	44	E5
SILVER AV	SJ	56	A6
SILVERA LN	SJ	67	C6
SILVERA ST	MPTS	47	E2
SILVERADO AV	CPTO	59	F5
SILVERADO AV	CPTO	60	A5
SILVERADO DR	SJ	72	C5
SILVERBERRY DR	SJ	67	F5
SILVER CLOUD CT	MH	81	A3
SILVER CREEK CT	SJ	68	C1
SILVER CREEK RD	SJ	63	B6
SILVER CREEK RD	SJ	68	C1
SILVER CREEK RD	SCCO	63	B6
SILVER CREEK RD	SCCO	68	D2
SILVER CREEK RD	SCCO	68A	A4
SILVR CK VLY RD	SJ	68	D6
SILVERCREST DR	SJ	66	F6
SILVER ESTATES	SJ	68	F2
SILVER ESTATES	SJ	68A	A2
SILVERGATE CT	SJ	72	E6
SILVER GLEN CT	SJ	68	C1
SILVERIA CT	SCL	53	F1
SILVERLAKE CT	MPTS	47	F2
SILVERLAKE DR	MPTS	47	F2
SILVERLAKE DR	SVL	53	C1
SILVERLAND CT	SJ	63	E5
SILVERLAND DR	SJ	63	E5
SILVER LEAF RD	SJ	72A	E2
SILVER LODE LN	SJ	75	F2
SILVER MDW CT	SJ	68	C1

STREET	CITY	PAGE	GRID
SILVER MINE DR	SJ	75	F2
SILVER OAK CT	CPTO	59	C4
SILVER OAK CT	SJ	72	C4
SILVER OAK LN	CPTO	59	C4
SILVER OAK WY	CPTO	59	C4
SILVER PINE CT	SVL	53	C5
SILVER SAGE	SJ	72A	C1
SILVER SANDS WY	SJ	68	B6
SILVER SPG CT	CPTO	64	E1
SILVER SPGS WY	SJ	72A	B1
SILVERSTONE PL	SJ	63	A1
SILVERTIP CT	MPTS	47	E6
SILVER TIP WY	SVL	53	C5
SILVERTREE DR	SJ	55	B2
SILVERWOOD AV	MVW	45	A6
SILVERWOOD DR	SJ	66	E6
SILVIA CT	LA	51	F3
SILVIA ST	G	82	D6
SIMAS DR	MPTS	48	B1
SIMBERLAN DR	SJ	63	E4
SIMKINS CT	PA	44	D2
SIMON AV	SJ	62	F2
SIMON AV	SJ	63	A2
SIMON LN	LAH	51	A4
SIMONI DR	SCCO	56	C3
SIMONS WY	LG	70	E4
SIMONSON CT	SJ	63	A5
SIMONSON WY	SJ	63	A5
SIMPSON WY	SJ	66	F2
SINBAD AV	SJ	56	A6
SINBAD AV	SJ	63	A1
SINCLAIR DR	SJ	62	E1
SINCLAIR FRWY	MPTS	39	F5
SINCLAIR FRWY	MPTS	48	B3
SINCLAIR FRWY	SJ	55	D4
SINCLAIR FRWY	SJ	61	D5
SINCLAIR FRWY	SJ	62	D3
SINCLAR FRTG RD	MPTS	48	B3
SINGING HILL LN	S	65	C6
SINGING HILL LN	S	70	C1
SINGING RAIN PL	SJ	56	A6
SINGING RAIN PL	SJ	63	A1
SINGLETARY AV	SJ	61	D3
SINGLETON LN	SJ	68	E3
SINGLETON RD	SJ	68	A2
SINGLETON RD	SCCO	67	F3
SINGLETON RD	SCCO	68	A2
SINGLETREE WY	SJ	71	F3
SINGLEY DR	MPTS	47	F1
SINNOTT LN	MPTS	47	F3
SIOUX LN	LA	51	E3
SIOUX LN	SJ	72	F2
SIOUX TR	SCCO	73	E6
SIPPOLA WY	SJ	62	F5
SITKA TER	SVL	53	C5
SKALL DR	SJ	68	A3
SKOWHEGAN CT	SJ	72A	F4
SKY LN	SCCO	71	C4
SKYFARM CT	SJ	72	B5
SKYFARM DR	SJ	72	B5
SKYLAKE CT	SVL	53	C1
SKYLARK DR	SJ	67	B3
SKYLARK DR	SCCO	67	B3
SKYLINE BLVD	PA	57	B4
SKYLINE BLVD	SCCO	57	B4
SKYLINE BLVD	SCCO	63F	B5
SKYLINE BLVD	SCCO	68E	E2
SKYLINE BLVD	SCCO	69	A4
SKYLINE BLVD	SCCO	73	A4
SKYLINE DR	MPTS	48	C3
SKYMEADOW WY	SJ	63A	B3
SKY OAKS WY	SCCO	70	B2
SKYPORT DR	SJ	54	E5
SKYVIEW DR	SCCO	48	F6
SKYVIEW TER	SCCO	48	F6
SKYWAY DR	SJ	67	F5
SKYWAY DR	SJ	68	B4
SLADKY AV	MVW	51	F4
SLADKY AV	MVW	52	A4
SLATER CT	SJ	48	D4
SLEEPER AV	MVW	52	B4
SLEEPY CK DR	SJ	76	B3
SLEEPY CK WY	SJ	76	B3
SLEEPY HOLLW LN	SJ	62	F1
SLEEPY HOLLW LN	SJ	63	A1
SLEEPY MDW CT	SJ	68	D3
SLEEPY VLY RD	SCCO	80K	B4
SLIDA DR	SJ	65	B1
SLOAT CT	SCL	60	D3
SLOPEVIEW DR	SJ	63	F3
SLOPING MDW CT	SJ	63A	C3
SMITH AV	C	65	F4

1991 SANTA CLARA COUNTY STREET INDEX

STREET	CITY	PAGE	GRID
SMITH AV	SJ	62	D5
SMITH CREEK RD	LG	70	E1
SMITHERS DR	SJ	63	C4
SMITHWOOD ST	MPTS	47	E2
SMOKE RIVER CT	SJ	67	D5
SMOKETREE CT	SJ	67	F5
SMOKE TREE WY	SVL	53	C5
SMOKEY CT	C	65	E4
SMYRNA CT	SVL	52	E6
SNEAD DR	SCL	46	F6
SNEAD DR	SCL	47	A6
SNEAD DR	SCL	53	F1
SNEAD DR	SCL	54	A1
SNELL AV	SJ	68	A6
SNELL AV	SJ	67	F4
SNELL AV	SJ	72	F3
SNELL AV	SJ	72A	A3
SNELL AV	SCCO	67	E4
SNELL AV	SCCO	72	F3
SNELL AV	SCCO	72A	A3
SNELL CT	LAH	51	C2
SNELL CT	SJ	67	F6
SNELL CT	SJ	68	A6
SNELL LN	LAH	51	B2
SNELL RD	LG	70	F6
SNELL RD	SJ	68	A6
SNELL RD	SCCO	68	A6
SNELL RD	SCCO	70	F6
SNELL RD	SCCO	73	F1
SNIVELY AV	SCL	60	D1
SNOW DR	SJ	68	C4
SNOW ST	MVW	52	A2
SNOW TER	SJ	68	D3
SNOWBANK CT	SJ	63	F6
SNOWBERRY CT	SJ	72A	C3
SNOWBERRY CT	SVL	52	F6
SNYDER AV	SJ	61	F5
SNYDER AV	SJ	62	A5
SOARES CT	SCL	60	D2
SOBEY RD	S	65	C6
SOBEY RD	S	70	C2
SOBEY MDWS CT	S	65	C6
SOBEY OAKS CT	S	65	C6
SOBEY OAKS RD	S	70	C1
SOBRANTE WY	SVL	52	F3
SOBRATO CT	C	66	A4
SOBRATO DR	C	66	A4
SOBRATO LN	C	66	A4
SOBRATO WY	C	66	A4
SOCORRO AV	SVL	53	D1
SODA SPRINGS RD	SCCO	73	F3
SODA SPRINGS RD	SCCO	74	A4
SOELRO CT	SCCO	56	B3
SOGOL CT	SJ	62	E5
SOGOL DR	SJ	62	E4
SOLA ST	CPTO	59	E5
SOLACE PL	MVW	52	B5
SOLANA CT	MVW	51	F2
SOLANA DR	G	82	C5
SOLANA DR	LA	51	F3
SOLANA DR	MVW	51	F2
SOLANA DR	PA	44	C5
SOLANA DR	S	65	B3
SOLANO CT	SCL	60	D2
SOLANO DR	SJ	72A	C3
SOLAR CT	MPTS	48	B2
SOLEDAD ST	G	82	C5
SOLIS DR	G	82	D6
SOLIS RANCHO DR	SCCO	82H	D1
SOLITA CT	LG	70	D1
SOLITO CT	SJ	72	E2
SOLOMON CT	SJ	72A	C4
SOLTERO DR	SJ	72	D2
SOMERSET CT	CPTO	60	A5
SOMERSET CT	LA	59	B2
SOMERSET DR	CPTO	60	A5
SOMERSET DR	SVL	52	E6
SOMERSET LN	SJ	55	E1
SOMERSET PL	PA	38	B6
SOMERSET PK CIR	SJ	55	D1
SOMERSWORTH DR	SJ	66	D4
SOMERVILLE CT	S	65	B2
SOMERVILLE DR	S	65	B2
SONATA WY	SJ	68	B4
SONDRA WY	C	65	F2
SONDRA WY	C	66	A2
SONG CT	SJ	55	C4
SONI CT	SJ	62	F1
SONIA WY	MVW	52	A3
SONOMA DR	MPTS	48	B4
SONOMA PL	SCL	60	E1
SONOMA ST	SJ	61	F4

STREET	CITY	PAGE	GRID
SONOMA ST	SJ	62	A4
SONOMA TER	SCCO	44	A4
SONORA AV	SCCO	54	E5
SONORA CT	SVL	53	C4
SONUCA AV	C	65	F5
SOPHIST DR	SJ	49	A6
SOQUEL WY	SVL	52	F2
SORCI DR	SJ	66	F5
SORENSON AV	CPTO	60	B4
SORGEPARK PL	SJ	55	F4
SORREL AV	SJ	72A	A3
SORREL WY	MH	80	C3
SORRENTO CT	MVW	52	A5
SORRENTO WY	SJ	72A	C3
SOTO CT	SJ	63	A5
SOUSA LN	S	65	D4
SOUTH CT	PA	44	D4
SOUTH DR	MVW	52	B5
SOUTH DR	SCL	53	F5
SOUTH ST	SCCO	81	C4
SOUTHAMPTON CT	SJ	63	F4
SOUTHAMPTON DR	PA	44	C2
SOUTHBAY DR	SJ	47	A4
SOUTH BAY FRWY	SVL	46	C5
SOUTH BREEZE CT	SJ	72A	E2
SOUTHBRIDGE CT	SJ	72	B1
SOUTHBRIDGE PL	SJ	72	B1
SOUTHBROOK CT	SJ	72A	E2
SOUTHBROOK DR	SJ	72A	E2
SOUTHCREEK CT	SJ	72A	E2
SOUTHCREST WY	SJ	72	E1
SOUTHFIELD CT	SJ	72A	E2
SOUTH FORK LN	LAH	51	A4
SOUTH GARDEN CT	SJ	72A	E2
SOUTHGATE CT	G	84	A3
SOUTHGATE CT	SJ	72A	E2
SOUTHGROVE DR	SJ	55	D3
SOUTHGROVE LN	SJ	55	D3
SOUTHLAKE CT	SJ	72A	E2
SOUTHLAKE DR	SJ	72A	E2
SOUTH LITE CT	SJ	72A	E2
SOUTHMAR CT	SJ	72A	E2
SOUTHMONT CT	SJ	72A	E2
SOUTHOAKS CT	SJ	72A	E2
SOUTH PARK DR	SJ	60	D5
SOUTH PARK LN	SCL	53	F5
SOUTHPINE CT	SJ	72A	E2
SOUTHPINE DR	SJ	72A	E2
SOUTHPORT CT	SJ	72A	E2
SOUTHRIDGE CT	SJ	72A	E2
SOUTHSEA CT	SJ	72A	E2
SOUTHSHORE CT	CPTO	64	E1
SOUTHSIDE AV	G	84	C4
SOUTHSIDE DR	SJ	67	F2
SOUTHSIDE DR	SCCO	67	E3
SOUTHSUN CT	SJ	72A	E2
SOUTH SURF CT	SJ	72A	E2
SOUTH TER CT	SJ	72A	E2
SOUTH VALLEY FY	MH	79	E2
SOUTH VALLEY FY	MH	81	C3
SOUTH VALLEY FY	SJ	72A	D1
SOUTH VALLEY FY	SCCO	72B	A3
SOUTH VALLEY FY	SCCO	77	E1
SOUTH VALLEY FY	SCCO	78	B4
SOUTH VALLEY FY	SCCO	79	E2
SOUTH VALLEY FY	SCCO	80	A5
SOUTH VALLEY FY	SCCO	82	E3
SOUTH VALLEY FY	SCCO	84	B5
SOUTHVIEW CT	SJ	72A	E2
SOUTHVIEW DR	SJ	72A	E2
SOUTHWEST EXPWY	SJ	66	C1
SOUTHWICK CT	SJ	67	D6
SOUTHWIND DR	SJ	72A	E2
SOUTHWOOD AV	SVL	53	A4
SOUTHWOOD DR	PA	38	B6
SOUTHWOOD DR	SJ	65	D2
SPACE PARK DR	SCL	54	A3
SPACE PARK WY	MVW	45	B4
SPADAFORE AV	SJ	67	B3
SPADAFORE CT	SJ	67	B3
SPAGNOLI CT	LA	51	D2
SPAICH DR	SJ	65	F1
SPAICH DR	SJ	66	A1
SPALDING AV	SCCO	51	E6
SPALDING AV	SCCO	58	E1
SPALDING AV	SVL	53	A6
SPANISHGATE CT	SJ	48	B5
SPANISH OAK CT	CPTO	59	C4
SPAR AV	SCCO	61	B5
SPARGUR DR	LA	51	F2
SPARGUR DR	MVW	51	F2
SPARHAWK DR	SCCO	79	C4

STREET	CITY	PAGE	GRID
SPARHAWK WY	SCCO	79	C4
SPARKLING WY	SJ	66	E2
SPARROW CT	SVL	60	C2
SPARTAN CT	SJ	62	C4
SPEAK LN	SJ	67	B6
SPECIALE WY	SJ	67	B4
SPENCE AV	MPTS	47	E3
SPENCER AV	LG	70	F4
SPENCER AV	SJ	61	F3
SPENCER AV	SJ	62	A5
SPENCER CT	LA	52	A5
SPENCER CT	MVW	51	F5
SPENCER WY	LA	52	A5
SPENCER WY	MVW	51	F5
SPENO DR	SJ	66	A1
SPERRY LN	S	70	C2
SPICEWOOD CT	SJ	72	F6
SPINDRIFT AV	SJ	47	B5
SPINDRIFT DR	SJ	47	B5
SPINDRIFT LN	SJ	47	B5
SPINDRIFT PL	SJ	47	C4
SPINDRIFT ST	SJ	47	B5
SPINDRIFT WY	SJ	47	B5
SPINNAKER DR	SJ	72A	A1
SPINNAKER WKWY	SJ	72A	A1
SPINOSA DR	SVL	52	F5
SPIRO DR	SJ	62	D2
SPODE WY	SJ	72A	C3
SPOKANE DR	SJ	62	F5
SPONSON CT	SJ	72A	C4
SPONSON LN	SJ	72A	C4
SPOONBILL WY	SVL	60	C1
SPOONWOOD CT	SJ	67	F4
SPOSITO CIR	SJ	67	E5
SPRAWLNG OKS CT	SCCO	76	B2
SPRECKLES AV	LG	70	F5
SPRECKLES AV	SJ	46	F2
SPRIERING DR	C	66	B5
SPRIG CT	SVL	60	C1
SPRING AV	MH	79	D5
SPRING AV	SCCO	81	C4
SPRING DR	SJ	72A	D1
SPRING RD	SCCO	56C	A3
SPRING ST	LG	70	F5
SPRING ST	MVW	45	A5
SPRING ST	SJ	61	E1
SPRING TR	SCCO	78G	C2
SPRINGBROOK AV	SJ	63	F3
SPRINGBROOK CT	SJ	63	F3
SPRINGBROOK LN	S	70	C1
SPRING CREEK LN	SCCO	48	E1
SPRINGDALE CT	G	82	F6
SPRINGDALE DR	SJ	60	D5
SPRINGER AV	S	64	F6
SPRINGER AV	S	69	D2
SPRINGER CT	S	69	D2
SPRINGER RD	LA	51	F5
SPRINGER RD	LA	52	A5
SPRINGER RD	MVW	51	F5
SPRINGER RD	MVW	52	A5
SPRINGER TER	LA	51	F3
SPRINGER WY	SJ	72A	C3
SPRINGFIELD DR	C	65	F2
SPRINGFIELD DR	SJ	65	F2
SPRINGFIELD TER	SVL	52	E6
SPRINGFIELD WY	SJ	67	F2
SPRING GARDN DR	SJ	55	F4
SPRING GROVE DR	SJ	61	E6
SPRINGHAVEN CT	SJ	68	B5
SPRING HILL CT	MH	79	D5
SPRINGHILL CT	S	65	C5
SPRINGHILL DR	LAH	51	C2
SPRING HILL DR	MH	79	D5
SPRINGHILL WY	MH	79	C1
SPRING HILL WY	SJ	75	E2
SPRINGKNOLL CT	SCCO	56	F5
SPRING MDW CT	SJ	68A	C3
SPRINGPARK CIR	SJ	67	E5
SPRINGPATH LN	SJ	72	B5
SPRINGS RD	SCCO	79	B1
SPRINGSONG DR	SJ	55	C3
SPRING VLY AV	SCCO	80K	D6
SPRING VLY LN	MPTS	48	B1
SPRINGVIEW LN	SCCO	56A	A5
SPRING WOOD DR	SJ	60	D5
SPROUL CT	SJ	72	C5
SPRUANCE CT	SJ	66	C1
SPRUANCE ST	SJ	66	C1
SPRUCE	SJ	72A	F3
SPRUCE CT	G	83	D2
SPRUCE DR	SVL	53	C5
SPRUCE ST	SJ	61	F2
SPRUCEGATE CT	SJ	63	E4

STREET	CITY	PAGE	GRID
SPRUCE HILL CT	LG	70	F1
SPRUCEMONT PL	SJ	72A	F5
SPRUCE ROCK ST	SJ	63	D6
SPRUCEWOOD DR	SJ	72	A2
SPUR CT	MH	80	C3
SPYGLASS CT	SJ	55	B3
SPYGLASS HLL RD	SJ	56	C2
SQUAREHAVEN CT	SJ	68	A5
SQUERI DR	SJ	56	C6
SQUIRECREEK CIR	SJ	68	D3
SQUIRECREEK LN	SJ	68	D3
SQUIREDELL DR	SJ	65	B2
SQUIREHILL CT	CPTO	64	E1
SQUIREWOOD WY	CPTO	59	E6
SQUIREWOOD WY	CPTO	64	E1
SQUIRREL HLW LN	S	65	A6
STAATS WY	SCL	53	F6
STACIA DR	SJ	66	E5
STACIA ST	LG	70	F5
STACY CT	MVW	52	B5
STAFFORD DR	CPTO	59	E6
STAFFORD DR	CPTO	64	E1
STAFFORD ST	SCL	61	A1
STAGEHAND DR	SJ	68	C5
STAGHORN CT	SJ	63	B6
STAGHORN LN	SJ	63	B6
STAGI CT	LA	51	E5
STAGI LN	LA	51	E5
STAGIA LN	SCCO	78H	A2
STAHL ST	SJ	62	F2
STALLION WY	SJ	63	B6
STAMM AV	MVW	52	B3
STANDER DR	SJ	63	E4
STANDING OAK CT	CPTO	59	B5
STANDISH DR	SJ	71	D1
STANDISH DR	SCCO	66	D6
STANDISH DR	SCCO	71	D1
STANDRIDGE CT	SJ	72A	C4
STANFIELD DR	C	66	C4
STANFIELD DR	SJ	66	C4
STANFORD AV	MVW	44	F6
STANFORD AV	PA	44	A4
STANFORD AV	SCCO	43	F6
STANFORD AV	SCCO	44	A4
STANFORO CT	LAH	50	F2
STANFORD PL	CPTO	59	F6
STANFORD PL	SCL	53	D5
STANHOPE CT	SJ	63	B6
STANHOPE DR	SJ	63	B6
STANISLAUS CT	SJ	55	D4
STANISLAUS DR	SJ	55	D4
STANLEY AV	LA	52	A5
STANLEY AV	SCL	61	B2
STANLEY CT	SJ	72A	C3
STANLEY WY	PA	44	C1
STANLTON CT	SJ	63	C2
STANWICH RD	SJ	55	B1
STANWIRTH CT	LA	52	B6
STANWOOD DR	SJ	72	A2
STAPLES AV	SCCO	55	F3
STAPLETON CT	SJ	71	F2
STARBIRD CIR	SJ	60	F6
STARBRIGHT DR	SJ	66	C6
STARBUSH DR	SVL	53	C5
STAR BUSH LN	SJ	72	A2
STARCREST DR	SJ	72	D1
STARDUST CT	SCL	54	A5
STARDUST LN	LA	51	F3
STARDUST LN	SJ	72	D1
STARDUST WY	MPTS	47	E5
STARFISH CT	SJ	63	C2
STARFLOWER CT	SVL	53	B6
STARK WY	SJ	67	A5
STARLIGHT CT	SJ	61	A5
STARLING DR	CPTO	59	C3
STARLITE CT	MPTS	47	E5
STARLITE CT	MVW	45	B6
STARLITE DR	MPTS	47	E5
STARLITE LN	LA	51	E5
STARR CT	SCL	60	E3
STARR LN	SCCO	84	E3
STARR WY	MVW	52	A3
STARRETT CT	SCCO	60	C5
STAR RIDGE CT	S	64	E3
STARR KING CIR	PA	44	D4
STARS&STRIPE WY	SCL	46	F6
STARSWEPT LN	SCCO	81	A2
STARWOOD CT	SJ	72	C3
STARWOOD DR	SJ	72	C3
STARWOOD PL	SJ	72	C3
STARVIEW DR	SJ	66	B6
STATE ST	LA	51	D3
STATE ST	SJ	46	E3

STREET	CITY	PAGE	GRID
STATE ST	SJ	62	B4
STATION WY	LG	70	E5
STAUFFER LN	CPTO	64	E2
STAUNTON CT	PA	44	B3
STAYNER RD	SJ	68	B2
STEBBINS AV	SCL	53	E5
STEEPLECHASE LN	CPTO	59	F6
STEEPLECHASE LN	SJ	59	F6
STEEPLECHASE LN	SJ	64	F1
STEFFS CT	SCCO	81	E5
STEINBAUGH CT	SJ	49	A6
STEINBECK DR	SCCO	72	D2
STEINHART CT	SCL	60	E3
STEINWAY AV	C	65	F5
STEITZ CT	SJ	62	F1
STELLA CT	SJ	72A	B3
STELLA RD	CPTO	59	B6
STELLAR WY	MPTS	47	E5
STELLING DR	PA	44	D2
STELLING RD	CPTO	64	E1
STELLING RD	SCCO	64	E1
STELLING RD N	CPTO	59	E4
STELLING RD N	SCCO	59	E4
STELLING RD S	CPTO	59	E5
STELLING RD S	SCCO	59	E5
STEMEL CT	MPTS	48	B1
STEMEL WY	MPTS	48	B1
STEMPLE CT	SJ	63	B5
STENDER WY	SCL	53	F3
STENDHAL LN	CPTO	60	B5
STEPHAN CT	G	83	F3
STEPHANIE CT	SJ	48	D5
STEPHANIE LN	LG	71	B3
STEPHANIE LN	SCCO	71	B3
STEPHEN CT	G	83	F3
STEPHEN WY	SJ	65	C1
STEPHENS LN	SJ	63	D4
STERLING BLVD	SCCO	60	C5
STERLNG GATE CT	SJ	75	E2
STERLNG GATE DR	SJ	75	E2
STERLNG OAKS DR	SJ	72	B3
STERN AV	PA	44	D3
STERN AV	SJ	60	C5
STEUBEN DR	SVL	52	E6
STEVAL PL	SJ	67	C4
STEVEN CT	SJ	56	C6
STEVENS CT	C	66	A5
STEVENS CT	SJ	63	D4
STEVENS CT	SCCO	81	B5
STEVENS FRWY	MVW	52	C1
STEVENS FRWY	SVL	59	D2
STEVENS LN	SJ	63	D4
STEVENS PL	LA	59	C2
STEVENS RD	SCCO	45	C5
STEVENS CYN RD	CPTO	59	B6
STEVENS CYN RD	SCCO	63F	C2
STEVENS CYN RD	SCCO	64	B2
STEVENS CYN RD	S	64	B2
STEVENS CK BLVD	CPTO	59	E4
STEVENS CK BLVD	CPTO	60	B4
STEVENS CK BLVD	SJ	61	B4
STEVENS CK BLVD	SCL	60	B4
STEVENS CK BLVD	SCL	61	B4
STEVENS CK BLVD	SCCO	59	E4
STEVENS CK BLVD	SCCO	60	B4
STEVENS CK FRWY	MVW	52	C1
STEVENSON ST	SCL	60	E3
STEWART AV	SJ	56	A5
STEWART AV	SCCO	56	A5
STEWART CT	S	64	F4
STEWART CT	SVL	53	C3
STEWART DR	G	83	D2
STEWART DR	SVL	53	B3
STIERLIN RD	MVW	45	B6
STIERLIN RD	MVW	52	B1
STIERLIN RD	SCCO	45	B5
STILFS WY	SCCO	56	C3
STILLWATER LN	SJ	72A	F5
STIMSON WY	SJ	63	F6
STIRLING DR	MPTS	39	F5
STIRRUP WY	LAH	50	F2
STIRRUP WY	LAH	51	A2
STOCKBRIDGE DR	SJ	65	F1
STOCKLMEIR CT	CPTO	59	C4
STOCKTON AV	SJ	61	E2
STOCKTON PL	PA	44	D2
STOESSER CT	SJ	75	F1
STOKES AV	CPTO	59	D3
STOKES ST	C	66	C1
STOKES ST	SJ	61	E6
STOKES ST	SJ	66	C1
STOKES ST	SCCO	61	E6

STREET	CITY	PAGE	GRID
STONE AV	SJ	62	C6
STONE AV	SJ	67	C1
STONE CT	SJ	62	B6
STONE LN	PA	44	D3
STONE TR	SCCO	78G	C2
STONEBRIDGE	SCCO	59	B4
STONEBRIDGE CT	SCCO	80K	E4
STONEBRIDGE DR	SCCO	80K	E4
STONEBROOK CT	LAH	51	D6
STONEBROOK DR	LAH	51	D6
STONEBROOK DR	SCCO	51	D6
STONEBROOK DR	SCCO	58	D1
STONE CANYON DR	SJ	67	F4
STONE CREEK DR	SJ	48	D5
STONECREST WY	SJ	55	E2
STONEGATE CIR	SJ	62	B5
STONEHAVEN DR	LA	59	B2
STONEHEDGE CT	SCCO	56	A6
STONEHEDGE WY	SCCO	56	A6
STONEHURST DR	SCCO	66	C4
STONEMAG WY	SJ	56	A2
STONE PINE CT	SCL	53	D3
STONE PINE CT	SCL	54	A4
STONE RANCH DR	SCCO	81	F4
STONERIDGE DR	S	69	D1
STONESHIRE CT	SJ	68A	C3
STONEWOOD LN	SJ	48	D4
STONEY CT	G	84	A2
STONEYHAVEN WY	SJ	68	A4
STONYBROOK RD	LG	71	A4
STONYDALE DR	CPTO	59	C4
STONYLAKE CT	SVL	53	C1
STORY CT	SJ	56	C6
STORY LN	SJ	56	C6
STORY RD	SJ	56	A6
STORY RD	SJ	62	D3
STORY RD	SJ	63	A1
STORY RD	SCCO	62	E3
STORY HILL LN	LAH	50	F4
STOVER ST	SJ	61	F3
STOWE AV	SJ	55	E6
STOWE AV	SJ	62	E1
STOWELL AV	SVL	52	F2
STOWELL AV	SVL	53	A2
STOWELL AV	SVL	59	E2
STRATA ALMADEN	SJ	72	B3
STRATFORD CT	MS	70	C2
STRATFORD CT	MVW	52	B4
STRATFORD DR	MPTS	39	F5
STRATFORD DR	SJ	66	B6
STRATFORD DR	SCCO	66	B6
STRATFORD PL	G	84	A3
STRATFORD PL	LA	51	D3
STRATFORD PK CT	SJ	67	E5
STRATHMORE PL	LG	65	E6
STRATHMORE PL	LG	70	F1
STRATTON PL	SJ	55	C2
STRAUSS AV	SJ	55	D1
STRAWBERRY CT	SVL	52	F6
STRAWBERRY LN	CPTO	60	B3
STRAWBERRY LN	G	82	A6
STRAWBERRY LN	MPTS	48	C2
STRAWBERRY LN	SJ	60	D5
STRAWBERY PK DR	SJ	60	E5
STRAWFLOWER LN	SJ	72	B2
STRAYER DR	SJ	60	B6
STRELOW CT	SJ	72	B4
STRICKROTH DR	MPTS	47	F1
STROTMAN CT	SCCO	82A	D2
STROUD PL	SJ	67	F2
STRUZENBURG CT	SCCO	80K	D5
STUART CT	LA	51	E2
STUART DR	G	83	D2
STUBBINS WY	SJ	48	D6
STUCKEY DR	SJ	71	C2
STUDEBAKER CIR	SJ	67	F6
STUDENT LN	SJ	65	E2
STULMAN DR	MPTS	48	C3
STURGEON WY	SJ	65	B2
STURLA DR	SJ	63	C4
STUTZ WY	G	86	A3
STUTZ WY	SJ	63	D4
SUDBURY CT	MPTS	39	F6
SUDBURY CT	MPTS	47	F1
SUDBURY DR	MPTS	39	F6
SUDBURY DR	MPTS	47	F1
SUE AV	SJ	62	E6
SUE AV	SJ	67	E1
SUENO DR	SJ	63	D2
SUFFOLK CT	LA	52	A5
SUFFOLK DR	SJ	63	A1
SUFFOLK WY	LA	52	A5

STREET	CITY	PAGE	GRID
SUFONET DR	SJ	71	C2
SUGAR BABE DR	SCCO	82A	C2
SUGARCREEK CT	SJ	68	D2
SUGARCREEK DR	SJ	68	D2
SUGAR MAPLE DR	SJ	67	F4
SUGARPINE AV	SVL	53	C6
SUGAR PINE CT	SJ	63	E6
SUGAR PLUM DR	SJ	63	D3
SUISSE DR	SJ	72A	A3
SUISUN AV	SJ	63	D6
SUISUN DR	CPTO	60	A5
SULLIVAN AV	SJ	62	F2
SULLIVAN AV	SJ	63	A2
SULLIVAN CT	MH	78	E6
SULLIVAN DR	MVW	52	C3
SULLIVAN DR	SCL	60	C3
SULLIVAN WY	S	64	E3
SULPHUR SPG CT	SJ	63	E4
SULTAN PL	SJ	68	C6
SULTAN PL	SJ	72A	C1
SULTANA DR	SJ	62	E4
SULU CT	SJ	72A	D4
SUMAC DR	G	84	A3
SUMAC DR	MPTS	47	D4
SUMAC DR	SVL	53	C6
SUMATRA AV	SJ	62	F3
SUMBA CT	SJ	68	A6
SUMBA CT	SJ	72A	A1
SUMMER CT	SJ	55	F6
SUMMER DR	SJ	72A	D1
SUMMER PL	SJ	72A	D1
SUMMER ST	SJ	55	F6
SUMMERAIN CT	SJ	62	D5
SUMMERBROOK CT	SJ	72	D2
SUMMERBROOK LN	SJ	72	D2
SUMMERCREEK DR	SJ	67	C4
SUMMERDALE DR	SJ	55	E2
SUMMERDAYS CT	SJ	55	D2
SUMMEREVE CT	SJ	62	E5
SUMMERFIELD DR	SJ	63	A6
SUMMERGARDEN CT	SJ	55	E2
SUMMERHEIGHTS DR	SJ	55	D2
SUMMERHILL AV	SCCO	51	E5
SUMMERHILL CT	SJ	63	F4
SUMMERHILL CT	SCCO	51	E5
SUMMERLAND DR	SJ	46	F4
SUMMERLAND DR	SJ	47	A4
SUMMERLEAF DR	SJ	72	E5
SUMMERMIST CT	SJ	62	E5
SUMMERPARK CT	SJ	55	D2
SUMMERPLACE DR	SJ	62	E5
SUMMERSHORE CT	SJ	62	D5
SUMMERSIDE DR	SJ	62	E5
SUMMERSONG CT	SJ	55	E2
SUMMERTON DR	SJ	62	E5
SUMMERTREE CT	SJ	55	D2
SUMMERVIEW DR	SJ	55	D2
SUMMERWIND CT	SJ	55	D2
SUMMERWIND DR	MPTS	47	E1
SUMMERWIND WY	MPTS	39	E6
SUMMERWIND WY	MPTS	47	E1
SUMMERWINGS CT	SJ	55	D2
SUMMERWOOD CT	SJ	55	D2
SUMMIT AV	SCCO	56	A3
SUMMIT RD	SCCO	78G	E3
SUMMIT RD	SCCO	81G	B2
SUMMIT WY	LG	70	F1
SUMMIT RIDGE CT	SJ	63	F4
SUMMIT WOOD RD	LAH	51	C6
SUMNER DR	S	64	F3
SUN CT	MPTS	47	F5
SUN LN	SJ	48	D6
SUNBEAM CIR	SJ	62	E3
SUNBERRY DR	C	66	A2
SUN BLOSSOM DR	SJ	72A	B1
SUNBROOK CT	SJ	68	B3
SUNBURST DR	SJ	67	E2
SUNCREST AV	SJ	48	F6
SUNCREST AV	SJ	49	A6
SUNCREST AV	SJ	55	F1
SUND AV	LG	70	F5
SUNDANCE DR	MH	80	B3
SUNDERLAND DR	CPTO	64	E1
SUNDOWN LN	SJ	63	B1
SUNDOWN CYN WY	LAH	58	E2
SUNFLOWER CIR	G	82	A6
SUNFLOWER LN	SJ	72	B2
SUN GLORY LN	SJ	66	C5
SUNHILLS DR	SCCO	58	F2
SUNKEN GDNS TER	SVL	53	B6
SUNKIST CT	LA	51	E2
SUNKIST LN	LA	51	E3

STREET	CITY	PAGE	GRID
SUNLAND CT	SJ	65	E2
SUNLITE DR	SCL	61	A2
SUNMOR AV	MVW	52	C5
SUNNY CT	SJ	62	D2
SUNNYARBOR CT	C	65	F5
SUNNYBROOK CT	C	66	A4
SUNNYBROOK CT	MH	80K	F3
SUNNYBROOK CT	S	65	C2
SUNNYBROOK DR	C	66	A3
SUNNY CREEK DR	SJ	68A	A2
SUNNYCREST CIR	SJ	62	F4
SUNNYDALE CT	SJ	65	F1
SUNNYDALE CT	SJ	66	A1
SUNNYGATE CT	SJ	65	F1
SUNNYGATE CT	SJ	66	A1
SUNNYGLEN DR	SJ	63	A2
SUNNYHAVEN DR	SJ	60	F6
SUNNYHAVEN DR	SJ	66	A1
SUNNYHILLS CT	MPTS	39	E6
SUNNYHILLS DR	MPTS	39	E5
SUNNYLAKE CT	SJ	65	F1
SUNNYLAKE CT	SJ	66	A1
SUNNYMEAD CT	SJ	65	F1
SUNNYMEAD CT	SJ	66	A1
SUNNY MEADOW LN	SJ	68A	A2
SUNNY MEADOW PL	SJ	68A	A2
SUNNYMOUNT AV	SVL	52	F5
SUNNYOAKS AV	C	65	F4
SUNNYOAKS AV	C	66	A4
SUNNYOAKS AV	SCCO	66	A4
SUNNYOAKS DR	SJ	72	E1
SUNNY ORCHRD LN	SJ	68A	A2
SUNNYPARK CT	C	65	F5
SUNNYSIDE AV	C	66	B3
SUNNYSIDE AV	MH	80K	E2
SUNNYSIDE AV	SCCO	80K	E2
SUNNYSIDE DR	S	70	C2
SUNNYSIDE DR	SCCO	73	F6
SUNNYSIDE RD	SCCO	78G	F1
SUNNYSLOPE AV	SCCO	56	B4
SUNNYVALE AV	SYL	52	F4
SUNNYVALE AV	SVL	53	A3
SUNNYVIEW LN	MVW	52	B4
SUNNY VISTA DR	SJ	61	B3
SUNOL ST	SJ	61	F4
SUNOL ST	SCCO	61	F4
SUNPARK CT	SJ	67	E5
SUNPARK LN	SJ	67	E5
SUNPARK PL	SJ	67	E5
SUNRAY DR	LG	70	F2
SUNRAY DR	LG	71	A2
SUNRISE CT	LA	52	B6
SUNRISE DR	CPTO	59	F4
SUNRISE DR	SJ	66	B6
SUNRISE DR	SCCO	78G	E2
SUNRISE DR	SCCO	82	C4
SUNRISE WY	MPTS	47	E5
SUNRISE FARM RD	LAH	51	A5
SUNRISE SPG CT	CPTO	64	A5
SUNSET AV	SJ	55	E6
SUNSET AV	SJ	62	F1
SUNSET AV	SCCO	79	E6
SUNSET AV	SVL	52	E4
SUNSET CT	SJ	55	E6
SUNSET DR	SCL	60	F2
SUNSET DR	SCL	61	A2
SUNSET DR	SCCO	70	A2
SUNSET DR E	LAH	51	D4
SUNSET DR W	LAH	51	D4
SUNSET GLEN DR	SJ	72	E3
SUNSET SPG CT	CPTO	64	A5
SUNSET VIEW PL	SJ	55	E6
SUNSHADE LN	SJ	62	E3
SUNSHADOW LN	SJ	63	B1
SUNSHINE CT	LA	51	F3
SUNSHINE CT	LA	52	A3
SUNSHINE CT	SJ	62	E3
SUNSHINE DR	LA	51	F3
SUNSHINE DR	LA	52	A3
SUNSHINE LN	SCCO	73	F6
SUNSHINE ST	MH	80K	F4
SUNSHINE ST	MH	81	A4
SUNSPRING CIR	SJ	72A	D1
SUNTREE CT	SVL	53	C6
SUN VALLEY CT	S	65	C3
SUNWOOD DR	SJ	67	F2
SUNWOOD MDWS PL	SJ	72A	F4
SUPERIOR DR	C	65	E3
SUPERIOR RD	MPTS	47	F1
SUPREME DR	SJ	63	B2
SURBER DR	SJ	72A	B3
SURF CT	SCCO	55	F2

STREET	CITY	PAGE	GRID
SURIAN CT	SJ	75	E1
SURMONT CT	LG	71	D3
SURMONT DR	LG	71	D4
SURREY CIR	CPTO	59	B4
SURREY CT	MPTS	48	C2
SURREY LN	S	64	E4
SURREY PL	LA	51	D2
SURREY PL	SJ	66	C4
SUR VERANO	SJ	68A	B2
SUSAN CT	G	83	F5
SUSAN CT	SJ	72	D3
SUSAN CT	SCCO	82	D1
SUSAN DR	SCL	60	F1
SUSAN WY	SVL	52	D4
SUSIE LN	SCCO	85	A1
SUSQUEHANNA CT	SVL	52	D6
SUSSEX DR	SJ	63	A1
SUSSEX PL	G	84	A3
SUSSEX PL	MPTS	39	F5
SUSSEX SQ	MVW	52	B3
SUSSEX PARK CT	SJ	67	D6
SUTCLIFF AV	SJ	67	A6
SUTCLIFF AV	SJ	72	A1
SUTHERLAND AV	CPTO	59	D6
SUTHERLAND DR	PA	44	E4
SUTRO DR	SJ	66	D4
SUTTER AV	PA	44	D2
SUTTER AV	SCL	60	F3
SUTTER AV	SCL	61	A3
SUTTER AV	SVL	52	E4
SUTTER BLVD	MH	79	D2
SUTTER BLVD	MH	79	E4
SUTTER ST	SJ	62	B4
SUTTER CK CIR	SJ	68	A6
SUTTER CREEK LN	MVW	45	B6
SUTTERGATE CT	SJ	48	B5
SUTTERGATE WY	SJ	48	B5
SUTTON DR	SCCO	71	D1
SUTTON PARK PL	CPTO	60	C5
SUVIEW DR	LG	71	C4
SUZANNE CT	PA	44	D6
SUZANNE CT	SJ	65	C1
SUZANNE DR	PA	44	D6
SUZAY CT	SJ	62	F5
SUZUKI CT	SJ	63	B5
SWALLOW DR	SJ	68	A2
SWALLOW DR	SVL	60	C2
SWALLOW WY	CPTO	60	C3
SWALLOW WY	SCL	60	C1
SWANCREEK CT	SJ	68	D3
SWANCREEK WY	SJ	68	D3
SWANER DR	G	82	D6
SWANGATE WY	SJ	71	F1
SWAN OAK LN	CPTO	59	B3
SWANSEA CT	SJ	48	D4
SWANSON WY	MVW	52	B5
SWANSTON LN	G	82	F6
SWANSTON WY	SJ	48	C6
SWANSWOOD CT	SJ	72A	A6
SWAPS DR	SJ	68	C5
SWARTHMORE DR	S	65	D4
SWEET DR	SJ	60	E6
SWEETBAY DR	SVL	53	C5
SWEETBERRY CT	SJ	67	F4
SWEETBRIAR DR	C	66	C4
SWEETBRIAR DR	SCCO	66	C4
SWEETBRIAR DR	SJ	66	E3
SWEETGUM CT	SJ	55	C3
SWEETLEAF CT	SJ	63	E3
SWEET OAK ST	CPTO	59	C3
SWEETWATER WY	SJ	55	B4
SWEIGERT RD	SJ	48	E5
SWEIGERT RD	SCCO	48	E5
SWEIGERT RD	SCCO	49	C3
SWENSEN CT	SJ	55	C3
SWICKARD AV	SJ	72A	D2
SWICKARD AV	SCCO	72A	D2
SWIFT AV	SJ	63	B3
SWIFT CT	SVL	60	C2
SWINDON CT	SJ	63	E5
SWINGNG GATE CT	SJ	72	D6
SWORD DANCER CT	MH	80K	F3
SYCAMORE AV	MH	80K	E3
SYCAMORE AV	SCCO	77	D1
SYCAMORE AV	SCCO	78	E5
SYCAMORE AV	SCCO	80	C6
SYCAMORE AV	SCCO	81	C2
SYCAMORE CT	G	82	B6
SYCAMORE CT	LA	59	C3
SYCAMORE CT	LG	71	C3
SYCAMORE DR	MPTS	47	D5
SYCAMORE DR	PA	44	D2
SYCAMORE GN	SJ	66	E3

STREET	CITY	PAGE	GRID
SYCAMORE ST	SJ	62	A4
SYCAMORE TER	SVL	53	C6
SYCAMORE TER	SVL	60	C1
SYCAMORE WY	SCL	60	E3
SYDENHAM CT	SJ	68	D5
SYDNEY CT	SJ	48	D4
SYDNEY DR	SJ	48	D4
SYDNEY DR	SVL	59	F1
SYDNOR DR	SCCO	66	C4
SYKES CT	SCL	60	E3
SYLVAN AV	MVW	52	C3
SYLVAN AV	SJ	61	B4
SYLVAN AV	SCCO	61	B4
SYLVAN CT	SCCO	78G	D2
SYLVAN DR	SJ	63	C2
SYLVANDALE AV	SJ	67	F3
SYLVANDALE AV	SJ	68	B3
SYLVANDALE AV	SCCO	67	F3
SYLVANDALE AV	SCCO	68	B3
SYLVANDALE WY	SCCO	67	F3
SYLVANER WY	SJ	72	C3
SYLVIA AV	MPTS	47	E4
SYLVIA CT	MPTS	47	E4
SYLVIA DR	SJ	63	A6
SYLVIAN WY	LA	51	E2
SYMPHONY LN	SJ	68	B4
SYRACUSE AV	SVL	52	D6
T			
TAAFFE RD	LAH	51	B5
TAAFFE ST	SVL	52	F3
TACONIC CT	SJ	72	F2
TAFFY CT	SJ	63	C3
TAFFY DR	SJ	63	C3
TAFT AV	SCL	60	F3
TAFT CT	G	82A	A6
TAFT CT	SCL	60	E3
TAFT DR	SJ	71	C3
TAGLIO CT	SJ	72	F6
TAHITI CT	SJ	62	F4
TAHOE DR	MPTS	48	C4
TAHOE TER	MVW	52	D3
TAHOE WY	MH	80K	F2
TAHOE WY	SJ	67	A4
TAHOE WY	SCL	53	C4
TAIDA ST	SJ	55	B4
TAINAN CT	SJ	55	A3
TAINAN DR	SJ	55	A3
TAINAN PL	SJ	55	A3
TAIPEI DR	SJ	55	A1
TAIT AV	LG	70	D4
TAJI CT	SJ	62	E5
TAJI DR	SJ	62	E5
TAKA CT	SJ	62	F4
TALATHY WY	SJ	63	E6
TALESFORE CT	SJ	55	C3
TALIA AV	SCL	61	A3
TALISMAN CT	PA	44	E3
TALISMAN DR	PA	44	E3
TALISMAN DR	SCCO	52	F5
TALISMAN DR	SVL	52	F5
TALLAHASSEE DR	SJ	62	F2
TALLAHASSEE DR	SJ	63	A2
TALLENT AV	SCCO	56	A2
TALLENT DR	SCCO	55	F1
TALLENT DR	SCCO	56	A5
TALLMAN CT	SJ	72	D2
TALMAGE AV	SCCO	56	A4
TAMALPAIS AV	SJ	72	D4
TAMALPAIS ST	MVW	44	F6
TAMARACK AV	SJ	61	C3
TAMARACK LN	SVL	53	C6
TAMARACK CT	PA	44	D5
TAMARACK LN	SCL	53	C6
TAMARIND CT	SCCO	59	E3
TAMI WY	MVW	52	C3
TAMIE LN	SJ	65	D3
TAMIE LN	SCCO	65	D3
TAMI LEE DR	SJ	62	E4
TAM O SHANTR DR	SJ	72	C5
TAMPA CT	SJ	63	A4
TAMPA WY	SJ	62	F4
TAMPA WY	SJ	63	A4
TAMPICO WY	SJ	67	A6
TAMPICO WY	SJ	72	A1
TAMSON CT	MS	70	D2
TAMWORTH AV	S	64	F5
TANAGER CT	SVL	52	C5
TANAKA DR	SJ	55	B3
TANBARK ST	SJ	60	E5
TANDERA AV	SJ	72	D2
TANFIELD LN	SJ	68	E4

STREET	CITY	PAGE	GRID
TANGERINE WY	SVL	52	F6
TANGLEWOOD DR	SJ	63	B2
TANGLEWOOD LN	LAH	51	A6
TANGO WY	SJ	68	B4
TANKERLAND CT	SJ	63	D6
TANKIT CT	SJ	65	F3
TANKIT DR	SJ	65	F3
TANLAND DR	PA	44	D1
TANNAHILL DR	SJ	72	D5
TANNERY WY	SCL	53	E3
TANNHAUSER CT	SJ	63	A5
TANNHAUSER WY	SJ	63	A5
TANOAK DR	SCL	60	F3
TANTALLON CT	SJ	48	D6
TANTAU AV	CPTO	60	B5
TANTAU AV	SCCO	60	B5
TAORMINO AV	SJ	72	D2
TAOS DR	S	65	B6
TAPER AV	SJ	66	D5
TAPER AV	SCL	53	E6
TAPER CT	SJ	62	F4
TAPER LN	SCCO	62	E4
TAPROOT CT	SJ	55	B4
TARANGA CT	SJ	72B	A4
TAROB CT	MPTS	48	A6
TARRYTOWN CT	SJ	67	D5
TARTAN DR	SCL	53	E5
TARTARIAN WY	SJ	65	B2
TARTARIAN WY	SVL	52	F5
TARYN LN	G	83	D1
TASHMAN DR	SVL	46	C6
TASMAN CT	SVL	46	B6
TASMAN DR	MPTS	47	D5
TASMAN DR	SJ	47	A5
TASMAN DR	SCL	46	E5
TASMAN DR	SVL	46	B6
TASSAJARA CIR	MH	80	B3
TASSASARA DR	MPTS	48	A1
TASSO ST	PA	37	F6
TASSO ST	PA	38	A6
TASSO ST	PA	43	F1
TASSO ST	PA	44	B2
TATRA CT	SJ	67	D6
TATRA DR	SJ	67	D6
TATUM AV	SCCO	82	D5
TAUBEH CT	SJ	67	E4
TAWNYGATE WY	SJ	71	F1
TAYLOR AV	SCCO	79	C1
TAYLOR AV	SVL	53	A3
TAYLOR CT	MVW	45	C6
TAYLOR DR	MPTS	39	F5
TAYLOR ST	SJ	46	E3
TAYLOR ST	SJ	55	A6
TAYLOR ST	SJ	61	F1
TAYLOR ST	SJ	62	A1
TEABERRY CT	SJ	72A	C3
TEAK CT	MH	80	B3
TEAK GROVE CT	SJ	68	A6
TEAKWOOD AV	LG	65	F6
TEAKWOOD CT	LG	65	F6
TEAKWOOD DR	SJ	66	B1
TEAL DR	SCL	60	C1
TEAL DR	SVL	60	C1
TEALE AV	SJ	65	E1
TEAL RIDGE CT	SJ	67	D3
TEATREE CT	SJ	61	C5
TECHNOLOGY DR	SJ	54	D4
TED AV	S	64	F3
TED AV	S	65	A3
TED CT	S	65	A2
TEDDINGTON DR	SJ	63	E5
TEERLINK WY	S	64	D6
TEHAMA AV	SJ	63	A3
TEKMAN DR	SJ	62	F5
TELEFORD AV	MVW	45	A5
TELEGRAPH DR	SJ	48	F6
TELEGRAPH DR	SJ	55	F1
TELFER AV	SJ	66	F1
TELFER AV	SJ	67	A1
TEMPELTON CT	SVL	52	F6
TEMPELTON DR	SVL	52	F6
TEMPLE CT	SCL	60	D3
TEMPLE DR	MPTS	48	B1
TEMPLE DR	MPTS	48	C2
TEMPLE DR	SJ	60	F6
TEMPLEBAR WY	LA	51	D2
TEMPLETON PL	LAH	51	D3
TEN CT	MH	80	A5
TEN CT	SCCO	80	A5
TEN ACRES CT	S	65	C6
TEN ACRES RD	S	65	C6
TENAKA PL	SVL	59	F2

STREET	CITY	PAGE	GRID
TENAYA DR	SJ	67	A4
TENLEY CT	SJ	63	D5
TENLEY DR	SJ	63	D5
TENNANT AV	MH	79	F6
TENNANT AV	SJ	72A	E2
TENNANT AV	SCCO	72A	E2
TENNANT AV	SCCO	80	A6
TENNESSEE LN	PA	44	D5
TENNYSON AV	PA	44	B2
TENNYSON LN	SJ	62	E2
TEN OAK CT	S	65	A4
TEN OAK WY	S	65	A4
TEOLA WY	SJ	63	C6
TEPA WY	LAH	51	C6
TERALBA CT	SJ	72B	A5
TERESA LN	MH	79	B4
TERESI CT	SJ	61	A5
TERESI LN	LA	51	F4
TERESITA DR	SJ	65	D2
TERESITA WY	LG	71	B5
TERFIDIA LN	MPTS	48	C2
TERILYN AV	SJ	62	F4
TERMAN DR	PA	44	D6
TERMINAL AV	SJ	54	F5
TERMINAL BLVD	MVW	44	F2
TERMINAL DR	SJ	54	D5
TERRA ALTA CT	MPTS	48	C4
TERRA ALTA DR	MPTS	48	C4
TERRA BELLA AV	MVW	45	B5
TERRA BELLA AV	SJ	67	B2
TERRA BELLA DR	CPTO	59	D6
TERRA BELLA DR	MPTS	48	A2
TERRACE CT	LA	51	F3
TERRACE CT	LA	52	A3
TERRACE CT	LG	70	E5
TERRACE DR	CPTO	59	D6
TERRACE DR	SJ	55	C6
TERRACE DR	SJ	62	C1
TERRACE DR	SCCO	59	A1
TERRACE LAKE DR	SJ	72	C2
TERRACE VIEW DR	SJ	72	C2
TERRA CALIF WY	MH	80	B3
TERRA COTTA CT	SJ	63	E5
TERRA COTTA DR	SJ	63	E5
TERRAINE ST	SJ	61	F2
TERRAINE ST	SJ	62	A2
TERRA NOBLE WY	SJ	55	F1
TERRAZZO CT	SJ	72	D2
TERRAZZO DR	SJ	72	D2
TERRELL ST	SJ	67	C5
TERRENCE AV	S	65	B2
TERNO D FLRS LN	LG	71	A1
TERRI CT	SCCO	82	F4
TERRI WY	SJ	66	E6
TERRI WY	SJ	71	E1
TERRIER CT	SJ	72A	B3
TERRI LYNN CT	SCCO	81	F6
TERRY WY	CPTO	59	F5
TERRY WY	SCCO	58	F2
TERRYWOOD CT	SJ	48	C5
TERSINI CT	SJ	55	B3
TERSTINA PL	SCL	53	C6
TESORO CT	SJ	71	D3
TEVIS PL	PA	38	B6
TEXAS CT	SJ	72	A3
THACKERAY LN	SJ	62	E2
THADDEUS DR	MVW	44	F5
THAIN AV	PA	44	D5
THAINWOOD WY	SJ	68	D1
THAMES DR	G	83	F3
THAMES DR	SJ	60	B6
THAMES DR	SJ	65	B1
THAMES LN	LA	51	D1
THAMES PARK CT	SJ	67	E4
THATCHER CT	LA	52	B5
THATCHER DR	LA	52	B5
THAYER CT	G	83	E2
THAYER CT	SJ	62	F4
THE ALAMEDA	SJ	61	F3
THE ALAMEDA	SCL	54	C6
THE ALAMEDA	SCL	61	C1
THE AMERICANA	MVW	52	C4
THE BUCKEYE	SCCO	73	D6
THE DALLES AV	SVL	59	D2
THELMA AV	S	64	F4
THELMA AV	S	65	A4
THELMA WY	SJ	62	D4
THENDARA WY	LAH	51	B2
THEO DR	SJ	55	A3
THEODEN CT	SJ	68	B1
THERESA AV	C	65	F5
THERESA AV	C	66	A5

1991 SANTA CLARA COUNTY STREET INDEX

STREET	CITY	PAGE	GRID
THERESA AV	SCCO	65	F5
THERESA LN	SJ	66	C5
THE STRAND AV	SJ	72	A3
THETA CT	SJ	72A	B4
THE VLGS FRW DR	SJ	68A	A2
THE VILLAGES PY	SJ	68A	A2
THE WOODS DR	SJ	67	F4
THIMBLEBERRY LN	SJ	60	D5
THIMBLEHALL LN	SJ	63	C6
THISTLE CT	SVL	53	C6
THISTLE DR	SJ	67	D5
THISTLEWOOD CT	SJ	68	B1
THOBURN CT	SCCO	44	A3
THOMAS CT	MVW	51	F2
THOMAS DR	LG	71	C2
THOMAS DR	PA	44	E2
THOMAS RD	G	83	F4
THOMAS RD	G	84	A4
THOMAS RD	SCL	54	A2
THOMAS RD	SCCO	83	F4
THOMAS GRADE	MH	80	C3
THOMPSON AV	MVW	44	F6
THOMPSON AV	SJ	67	A5
THOMPSON CT	MVW	44	F5
THOMPSON PL	SCL	53	F6
THOMPSON PL	SVL	53	B3
THOMPSON RD	SCCO	73	A3
THOMPSON SQ	MVW	44	F6
THOMPSON CK CT	SJ	63	E6
THORNAPPLE DR	SVL	53	C5
THORNBRIAR DR	SJ	55	B4
THORNCREST DR	SJ	55	B4
THORNDALE CT	SJ	68	B2
THORNHAVEN WY	SJ	68	A5
THORNLEAF WY	SJ	55	B4
THORNMILL WY	SJ	63	A6
THORNTON WY	SJ	61	C6
THORNTON WY	SCCO	61	C6
THORNTREE CT	SJ	72	B3
THORNTREE DR	SJ	72	B3
THORNTREE PL	SJ	72	B3
THORN VALLEY CT	SJ	55	B4
THORNMOOD DR	PA	44	E3
THORNWOOD DR	SJ	72	D1
THORP PL	SCCO	70	B3
THORP PL	S	70	B3
THORPE CT	LA	52	B6
THORSEN CT	SCCO	58	F2
THORSEN CT	SCCO	59	A2
THOUSAND OAK CT	SJ	67	C5
THOUSAND OAK DR	SJ	67	B5
THOUSND PNES CT	SJ	63	D5
THRASHER LN	SJ	67	A4
THREADNEEDLE WY	SJ	63	C6
THREE FORKS LN	LAH	51	A3
THREE OAKS CT	S	70	B1
THREE OAKS WY	S	70	B1
THREE SPGS CT	SCCO	56	F5
THREE SPGS CT	SCCO	56A	A5
THREE SPGS RD	SCCO	56	F5
THREE SPGS RD	SCCO	56A	A5
THRIFT PL	SJ	63	E3
THRING CT	SJ	55	F4
THRUSH CT	SCL	60	C2
THRUSH DR	SJ	67	B3
THRUSH WY	SCL	60	C2
THUNDERBIRD AV	SCL	60	C1
THUNDERBIRD AV	SVL	60	C1
THUNDERBIRD WY	SCCO	66	D3
THURESON WY	SJ	71	E3
THURMAN DR	SJ	63	E4
THURSTON AV	LA	59	B1
THURSTON ST	LG	70	E3
TIA PL	SJ	55	C3
TIANA LN	MVW	52	D3
TIANI CT	SJ	55	C4
TIARA DR	SJ	62	F1
TIBERAN WY	SJ	65	D3
TICE DR	MPTS	40	A6
TICONDEROGA DR	SVL	52	D6
TICONDEROGA PL	G	83	F2
TIERRA BUENA DR	SJ	63	A5
TIERRA GRNDE CT	SCCO	76	C2
TIERRA SOMBR CT	SCCO	76	D2
TIFFANY CT	SVL	52	E6
TIFFANY WY	SJ	66	F4
TIFFIN DR	SJ	68	A6
TIFTON WY	SJ	67	B6
TIFTON WY	SJ	71	A1
TIGARA CT	SJ	67	C4
TIGERWOOD WY	SJ	68	C5
TILBURY DR	SJ	65	E3
TILDEN DR	SJ	71	D2
TILLAMOOK DR	SJ	72	F4
TILLMAN AV	SJ	61	E3
TILSON AV	CPTO	60	C5
TILSON AV	SCCO	60	C5
TILTON AV	MH	79	B2
TILTON AV	SCCO	79	B2
TILTON CT	SJ	62	F5
TILTON CT	SJ	63	A5
TILTON DR	SVL	52	F6
TIMBER CT	SJ	72	D3
TIMBER WY	MPTS	47	E6
TIMBER COVE	C	66	B4
TIMBER CREEK DR	SJ	55	B2
TIMBER CREST DR	SJ	72	D4
TIMBERLAKE AV	SJ	63	D3
TIMBERLAKE CT	SJ	63	D3
TIMBERLINE CT	SJ	63	D6
TIMBERLINE DR	SJ	63	D6
TIMBERPINE AV	SVL	53	C5
TIMBERPINE CT	SVL	53	C5
TIMBER SPG CT	CPTO	64	E1
TIMBERVIEW CT	SJ	72	B5
TIMBERVIEW DR	SJ	72	B5
TIMBERWOOD CT	SJ	72A	A6
TIMLOTT CT	PA	44	C5
TIMLOTT LN	PA	44	C5
TIMOR CT	SJ	55	F2
TIMOTHY DR	SJ	55	B5
TINY ST	MPTS	39	E5
TIOGA CT	PA	44	E5
TIOGA CT	SVL	52	F6
TIOGA WY	SJ	66	D4
TIPPAWINGO ST	PA	44	C4
TIPTOE LN	CPTO	59	F6
TIPTOE LN	LA	52	C6
TIROL CT	MPTS	47	F1
TIROS WY	SVL	53	D3
TISCH WY	SJ	61	B5
TISDALE WY	SJ	65	D4
TITAN WY	SVL	53	D3
TITLEIST CT	SJ	56	A3
TITUS AV	SCCO	65	B3
TITUS AV	S	65	B3
TITUS CT	S	65	B3
TIVERTON DR	SJ	68	B2
TIVOLI WY	SJ	72	D6
TOANO CT	SJ	55	C2
TOBAGO AV	SJ	62	F4
TOBIAS DR	SJ	71	F2
TOBIN DR	SJ	48	C6
TODD LN	LAH	51	C3
TODD ST	MVW	51	F2
TODD ST	MVW	52	A2
TODD WY	SJ	66	D6
TOFT ST	MVW	52	A1
TOFTS DR	SJ	55	C3
TOHARA WY	SCCO	80K	B4
TOIYABE CT	SJ	55	D3
TOIYABE WY	SJ	55	D3
TOKAY CT	SJ	63	C1
TOKAY WY	SJ	63	C1
TOLBERT CT	SJ	63	A4
TOLBERT DR	SJ	63	A4
TOLEDO AV	SCL	60	E3
TOLIN CT	SJ	72A	F5
TOLL GATE RD	S	64	D6
TOLL GATE RD	S	69	E1
TOLLIVER DR	SJ	63	D5
TOLLTREE DR	SJ	55	B1
TOLMAN DR	SCCO	44	A5
TOLWORTH DR	C	66	C1
TOLWORTH DR	SJ	61	C6
TOLWORTH DR	SJ	66	C1
TOLWORTH DR	SCCO	66	C1
TOMAHAWK DR	SJ	68	B6
TOMAS CT	MVW	52	A2
TOMASINA CT	SJ	66	C5
TOMI LEA ST	LA	51	D2
TOMKINS CT	G	82	F5
TOMLIN WY	SJ	55	E5
TOMLINSON LN	SJ	62	E2
TOMMY LN	SCCO	75	F2
TOMMY LN	SCCO	76	A2
TOMPKINS DR	SJ	60	B6
TOMRICK AV	SJ	66	C6
TOMRICK AV	SJ	71	C1
TONGA CT	SJ	55	E2
TONI CT	CPTO	60	A4
TONI ANN PL	S	64	F5
TONINO DR	SJ	67	C6
TONITA WY	CPTO	59	F5
TONOPAH DR	SJ	72A	A2
TONY DR	SJ	71	D2
TOPAM GLEN CT	SCCO	76	A2
TOPAR AV	SCCO	51	F6
TOPAR AV	SCCO	52	A6
TOPAR AV	SCCO	59	A1
TOPAZ AV	SJ	60	F6
TOPAZ AV	SJ	65	F1
TOPAZ ST	MPTS	47	F3
TOPEKA AV	SJ	61	C4
TOPEKA AV	SCCO	61	C4
TOPOCK CT	SJ	68	D4
TOP OF HILL CT	SCCO	71	C5
TOP OF HILL RD	LG	71	C5
TOP OF HILL RD	SCCO	71	C5
TOPPING WY	SCCO	71	A4
TORELLO LN	LAH	51	C3
TORERO PZ	C	65	F5
TORLAND CT	SVL	52	F6
TORO VISTA CT	MH	80	C3
TORRANCE AV	SJ	56	B6
TORRANCE AV	SVL	53	D1
TORRE AV	CPTO	59	F5
TORRE CT	SJ	71	F4
TORRES AV	MPTS	48	A1
TORREY CT	MH	79	D5
TORREYA AV	SVL	53	C5
TORREYA CT	PA	44	D3
TORRINGTON CT	SJ	72	A3
TORRINGTON DR	SVL	52	E6
TORTOLA WY	SJ	55	E4
TORWOOD CT	LA	51	D2
TORWOOD LN	LA	51	D2
TORYGLEN WY	SJ	63	C6
TOSCA CT	SJ	63	B5
TOSCA WY	SJ	63	B5
TOSCANO ST	MPTS	39	F5
TOTTENHAM CT	SJ	67	E6
TOURNEY DR	SJ	55	C2
TOURNEY LP	LG	70	F5
TOURNEY RD	LG	70	F6
TOURNEY RD	SCCO	70	F6
TOVAR DR	SJ	72A	B3
TOWERS LN	SJ	63	B6
TOWLE PL	PA	44	D3
TOWLE WY	PA	44	D3
TOWNE TER	LG	70	E4
TOWN & CNTRY LN	SCL	61	A2
TOWN CENTER DR	MPTS	47	F2
TOWN CENTER DR	MPTS	48	A2
TOWNCENTER DR	SVL	52	F4
TOWN CENTER LN	CPTO	59	F5
TOWN CLUB DR	SJ	66	F5
TOWNSEND AV	SJ	55	A4
TOWNSEND AV	SCL	53	D6
TOWNSEND PK CIR	SJ	55	B3
TOWNSQUARE DR	SJ	56	B4
TOY LN	SJ	63	D6
TOYAMA DR	SVL	46	B6
TOYAMA DR	SVL	53	B1
TOYON AV	LA	51	D2
TOYON AV	SJ	55	F2
TOYON AV	SJ	56	A2
TOYON AV	SCCO	56	A2
TOYON AV	SVL	53	C5
TOYON CT	G	82	D6
TOYON CT	SCCO	55	F2
TOYON DR	SCL	60	E3
TOYON DR	SCCO	70	D2
TOYON PL	PA	44	D3
TOYON WY	LAH	50	F6
TOYON WY	LAH	51	A6
TOYONITA RD	LAH	58	E2
TOYONITA RD	SCCO	58	E2
TRACE AV	SJ	61	D3
TRACEL DR	SJ	65	B2
TRACY CT	LAH	50	F3
TRACY DR	SCL	60	D3
TRACY WY	SCCO	81	D2
TRADAN DR	SJ	48	B6
TRADEWINDS CT	SJ	72A	A1
TRADEWINDS DR	SJ	72A	A1
TRADEWINDS WKWY	SJ	72A	A1
TRADE ZONE BL	SJ	48	A6
TRADE ZONE CIR	SJ	48	B4
TRADE ZONE CT	SJ	48	B4
TRADE ZONE PL	SJ	48	B4
TRADE ZONE WY	SJ	48	B5
TRADITION CT	SJ	72	D4
TRAFALGAR PL	SJ	48	D5
TRAIL DR	MH	80	C3
TRAIL RUN CT	SJ	68	D4
TRAILWAY DR	SJ	56	A4
TRAMIER CT	SJ	68A	B3
TRAMWAY DR	MPTS	47	F1
TRAMWAY DR	MPTS	48	A1
TRAMWAY PL	MPTS	47	F1
TRANSPORT ST	PA	44	F3
TRAUGHBER ST	MPTS	48	A1
TRAVERSO AV	LA	44	D6
TRAVERSO AV	LA	51	D1
TRAVERSO CT	LA	44	D6
TRAVERSO CT	LA	51	D1
TRAVIS CT	SCCO	82A	B1
TREADWAY DR	SJ	55	D4
TREATY CT	SJ	68	D4
TREBOL LN	SJ	63	D3
TREE TOP CT	SJ	72A	B2
TREEWOOD LN	SJ	48	C4
TREGO DR	SJ	67	A6
TREGO DR	SJ	72	A1
TRELLIS PL	SJ	63	E5
TRENARY WY	SJ	72	B1
TRENT DR	SJ	71	D2
TRENTON DR	SJ	66	D5
TRENTON DR	SCCO	52	E6
TRENTON DR	SVL	52	E6
TRENTON PL	G	83	F2
TRENTS FERRY CT	SJ	55	D5
TREVINO TER	SJ	72	D5
TREVOR DR	SJ	71	F2
TRIANON WY	LA	51	E2
TRIBOROUGH LN	SJ	61	D6
TRIBOROUGH LN	SJ	66	D1
TRICIA WY	S	64	F4
TRIESTE CT	SJ	62	E4
TRIESTE WY	SJ	62	D4
TRIFONE DR	SJ	60	F6
TRIFONE DR	SJ	61	A6
TRIMAR CT	SJ	68	C3
TRIMBLE CT	SJ	48	B5
TRIMBLE RD	SJ	48	B5
TRIMBLE RD	SJ	54	C3
TRINA WY	SJ	60	F5
TRINIDAD CT	SJ	72	D5
TRINIDAD DR	SJ	72	D5
TRINITY AV	S	64	F5
TRINITY CT	S	64	F5
TRINITY PL	SJ	66	C5
TRINITY RIV CT	SJ	67	F1
TRINITY SPG CT	CPTO	64	A6
TRIPIANO CT	MVW	52	C4
TRIPOLI AV	SJ	62	F4
TRIPOLI CT	LAH	51	A5
TRIPP AV	SJ	55	C6
TRIPP AV	SJ	62	C1
TRISTAN AV	SJ	55	F3
TRITON CT	SCL	54	A6
TRONA WY	SJ	66	F4
TRONSON CT	SJ	48	D4
TROON CT	MPTS	48	A2
TROPHY DR	MVW	52	A3
TROY CT	SVL	52	D6
TROY DR	SJ	60	F5
TRUCKEE CT	SJ	67	F4
TRUCKEE LN	SJ	67	F4
TRUDEAN WY	SJ	48	C6
TRUETT CT	SJ	63	E1
TRUFFLE CT	SJ	63	E1
TRUMAN AV	LA	52	C6
TRUMAN AV	LA	59	C1
TRUMAN AV	MVW	52	C6
TRUMAN AV	SCCO	59	C1
TRUMAN WY	SJ	46	F3
TRUMBULL CT	SVL	52	F6
TRUMPP CT	MH	79	C4
TRYNA DR	MVW	52	C5
TUBAC LN	SJ	72	B2
TUBBY ST	C	66	B2
TUBMAN CT	SCCO	67	B2
TUCKER DR	SJ	65	B1
TUCSON AV	SVL	53	D1
TUCSON DR	SJ	72	B2
TUDOR CT	SJ	63	A1
TUERS CT	SJ	68	A1
TUERS RD	SJ	62	F6
TUERS RD	SJ	67	F1
TUERS RD	SJ	68	A1
TUERS RD	SCCO	68	A1
TUGGLE AV	SCCO	60	C5
TULA CT	CPTO	59	E5
TULA LN	CPTO	59	E5
TULANE CT	MVW	52	A4
TULANE CT	SCL	60	D3
TULANE DR	MVW	51	F4
TULANE DR	MYW	52	A3
TULANE DR	SCL	60	D3
TULARCITOS DR	MPTS	40	B5
TULARE DR	SJ	48	D6
TULARE HILL DR	SJ	72B	A4
TULARE HILL LN	SJ	72B	A4
TULARE HILL RD	SJ	72B	A4
TULIP CT	SVL	53	C6
TULIP DR	SVL	53	C6
TULIP LN	PA	38	C6
TULIP LN	PA	44	C1
TULIP RD	SJ	61	B3
TULIPAN DR	SJ	60	B6
TULIP BLOSSM CT	SJ	72A	B1
TULIPTREE LN	SCL	60	F3
TULIPWOOD LN	SJ	48	C4
TULITA CT	SCCO	59	E3
TULLY CT	SJ	63	F3
TULLY RD	SJ	62	E6
TULLY RD	SJ	63	B4
TULLY RD	SJ	67	D1
TULLY RD	SCCO	62	E6
TULLY RD	SCCO	67	D1
TUMBLE WY	SJ	48	E6
TUNBRIDGE WY	SJ	72	E5
TUNIS AV	SJ	48	D4
TUOLOMNE CT	SJ	72	F3
TURANDOT CT	SJ	63	B5
TURLEY CT	SJ	62	F1
TURLEY DR	SJ	62	F1
TURLOCK AV	SCCO	81	B6
TURLOCK AV	SCCO	82	C1
TURLOCK LN	SJ	48	D6
TURNBERRY PL	SJ	67	E6
TURNER CT	SJ	72A	F5
TURNER DR	SCCO	61	C5
TURNER WY	C	65	E5
TURNHOUSE LN	SJ	63	C6
TURNSTONE WY	SVL	60	C1
TURNWOOD CT	SJ	65	F1
TURQUESA CT	SJ	55	D5
TURQUOISE ST	MPTS	48	A3
TURRETT DR	SJ	55	C2
TURRIFF WY	SJ	48	D6
TURTLE CREEK CT	SJ	67	C1
TURTLEROCK DR	SJ	62	E4
TUSCANY PL	CPTO	59	E6
TUSCARORA CT	SJ	72A	A3
TUSCARORA DR	SJ	72	F3
TUSCARORA DR	SJ	72A	A3
TUSTIN DR	SJ	63	B5
TWAIN CT	S	65	C5
TWEED CT	S	65	B5
TWEEDHOLM CT	SJ	72	B4
TWEEDSMUIR CT	SJ	63	D6
TWELVE ACRES DR	LA	51	D2
TWELVE OAKS RD	LG	71	A5
TWIG LN	SCCO	60	B5
TWILIGHT CT	CPTO	60	A4
TWILIGHT DR	SJ	66	B6
TWILIGHT DR	SJ	71	B1
TWIN BROOK CT	SJ	61	E6
TWIN BROOK DR	SJ	61	E6
TWIN CREEKS RD	MS	70	D2
TWIN FALLS CT	SJ	63	D6
TWIN LAKE DR	SVL	53	C1
TWIN OAKS DR	LG	71	A5
TWIN OAKS LN	SJ	63	B2
TWO OAKS LN	SCCO	83	B1
TWYLA CT	SJ	65	F4
TWYLA LN	SJ	65	F4
TYBALT DR	SJ	56	C4
TYHURST CT	SJ	72A	A1
TYHURST WKWY	SJ	72A	A1
TYLER AV	SCL	61	A4
TYLER CT	SCL	60	E4
TYLER PARK WY	MVW	52	B4
TYMN WY	SJ	63	A3
TYNDALL ST	LA	51	E4
TYNE WY	SCL	54	B2
TYR LN	SCCO	76	C2
TYRELLA AV	MVW	45	C6
TYRELLA AV	MVW	52	C1
TYRELLA CT	MVW	45	C6
U			
ULMAN CT	SJ	68	E1
ULSTER DR	SJ	55	C2
UMATILLA TR	SCCO	73	E6
UMBARGER RD	SJ	63	A6
UMBARGER RD	SJ	67	E2
UMBARGER RD	SCCO	67	E2
UNDAJON DR	SJ	55	D4
UNDERWOOD CT	SCCO	81H	D4
UNDERWOOD DR	SJ	60	F6
UNION AV	C	66	C3
UNION AV	LG	71	C3
UNION AV	SJ	66	C4
UNION AV	SJ	71	C2
UNION AV	SCCO	66	C4
UNION AV	SCCO	71	C2
UNION PL	C	66	C3
UNION ST	SJ	62	B4
UNITED PL	CPTO	59	E4
UNIVERSITY AV	LA	51	E4
UNIVERSITY AV	LG	70	E4
UNIVERSITY AV	MVW	44	F6
UNIVERSITY AV	MVW	51	F1
UNIVERSITY AV	PA	38	A6
UNIVERSITY AV	PA	43	F1
UNIVERSITY AV	PA	44	A1
UNIVERSITY AV	SJ	61	E1
UNIVERSITY ST	SCL	61	B2
UNIVERSITY TER	LA	51	D4
UNIVERSITY WY	SJ	61	C3
UNIVERSITY WY	CPTO	59	D4
UPHALL CT	SJ	63	C6
UPLAND WY	SCCO	64	D1
UPPER HILL CT	S	64	E5
UPPER HILL DR	S	64	E5
UPTON CT	SJ	67	D5
UPTON WY	SJ	67	C5
URANIUM RD	SVL	53	E4
URBAN LN	PA	43	F1
URIDIAS RCH RD	MPTS	48	C2
URLIN CT	SJ	72A	B3
URNA AV	SJ	66	E5
URSULA LN	LAH	51	A4
URZI CT	SJ	63	D5
URZI DR	SJ	63	E5
USONA DR	SJ	67	A6
USONA DR	SJ	72	A1
UTE CT	SJ	72	F3
UTE DR	SJ	72	F3
UTICA CT	SJ	72A	C4
UTICA CT	SVL	52	F6
UTICA DR	SVL	52	F6
UTICA LN	SJ	72A	C4
UTICA PL	G	83	E3
UTOPIA PL	SJ	56	C5
UVAS AV	MPTS	47	E2
UVAS CT	SJ	72	E2
UVAS RD	SJ	77	A4
UVAS RD	SCCO	78L	B1
UVAS RD	SCCO	80K	A6
UVAS RD	SCCO	81H	C1
UVAS PARK DR	G	83	E3
UXBRIDGE CT	SJ	72B	A4
V			
VAI AV	CPTO	59	E6
VAL CT	SCCO	82A	C2
VALBUSA DR	G	82	C5
VALCARTIER DR	SVL	59	F2
VALDEZ PL	SCCO	43	F5
VALDEZ PL	SCCO	44	A5
VALDOSTA RD	SJ	68	B2
VALE AV	C	65	F5
VALE CT	SJ	72A	B3
VALE DR	SJ	72A	B3
VALELAKE CT	SVL	53	C1
VALENCIA AV	SVL	52	E4
VALENCIA CT	SJ	66	F3
VALENCIA DR	LA	51	E2
VALENCIA DR	MPTS	48	A2
VALERIAN CT	SVL	53	C6
VALERIAN WY	SVL	53	C6
VALERIE CT	SJ	65	F4
VALERIE DR	SJ	65	E4
VALERI RUTH CT	SCL	60	F3
VALHALLA CT	SJ	48	C6
VALHALLA DR	SJ	48	C6
VALLA DR	SJ	66	E5
VALLCO PKWY	CPTO	60	B4
VALLECITO RD	CPTO	59	C5
VALLECITO RD	SCCO	59	D5
VALLECITOS WY	LG	70	D2
VALLE DEL LAGO	SJ	68A	A1
VALLEJO DR	SJ	65	E2
VALLEY CT	SCL	60	E3
VALLEY ST	LA	51	E3
VALLEY ST	LG	70	F5
VALLEY WY	MPTS	47	E3

1991 SANTA CLARA COUNTY STREET INDEX

STREET	CITY	PAGE	GRID
VALLEY WY	SCL	60	E3
VALLEYBROOK CT	SJ	68	B3
VALLEY CREST CT	SJ	55	B4
VALLEY CREST DR	SJ	55	B4
VALLEY FORGE DR	G	83	F3
VALLEY FORGE DR	SVL	52	D6
VALLEY FORGE WY	SJ	66	A1
VALLEY GLEN CT	SJ	72	E3
VALLEY GLEN DR	SJ	72	E3
VALLEY GREEN DR	CPTO	59	E3
VALLEYHAVEN WY	SJ	68	A5
VALLEY HTS DR	SJ	55	E3
VALLEY MDW CT	SJ	68A	B4
VALLEY OAK DR	MS	70	E2
VALLEY PARK CIR	SJ	72A	F4
VLY QUAIL CIR	SJ	75	D1
VALLEY RIDGE LN	SCCO	63	E1
VALLEY SQ LN	SJ	66	A1
VALLEY VIEW AV	SCCO	56	A3
VALLEY VIEW CT	MH	80	C2
VALLEY VIEW CT	SCCO	51	E5
VALLEY VIEW DR	SCCO	51	F5
VALLEYVISTA CIR	MH	79	C2
VALLEY VISTA CT	S	70	B1
VALLEY VISTA DR	S	70	B2
VALLEYWOOD CT	SJ	63	E4
VALMAINE CT	SJ	63	F6
VALMY ST	MPTS	39	F6
VALPARAISO ST	SCCO	43	F4
VALPICO DR	SJ	66	E4
VALROY CT	SJ	72A	B4
VALROY DR	SJ	72A	B4
VAN AUKEN CIR	PA	44	D2
VAN BUREN CIR	MVW	52	A5
VAN BUREN ST	LA	51	D1
VANCE CT	SJ	48	E6
VANCE DR	SJ	48	E6
VAN COTT CT	SJ	55	F5
VANCOUVER CT	SCCO	56	B5
VANDELL WY	C	66	A5
VANDER WY	SJ	55	A4
VANDERBILT CT E	SVL	52	E6
VANDERBILT CT W	SVL	52	E6
VANDERBILT DR	SJ	65	D4
VANDERBILT DR	SCCO	52	E6
VANDERBILT DR	SVL	52	E6
VANDERBILT WY	SCL	60	D3
VAN DE WATER WY	SJ	68	E3
VAN DUSEN LN	C	65	E5
VAN DYCK CT	SVL	53	B6
VAN DYCK DR	SVL	53	A6
VANESSA DR	SJ	66	D1
VANGORN CT	SJ	68	B1
VANGORN WY	SJ	68	B1
VANNA CT	SJ	55	A3
VANPORT CT	SJ	63	B5
VANPORT DR	SJ	63	B5
VAN SANSUL AV	SJ	61	B6
VAN WINKLE LN	SJ	62	F1
VAN WINKLE LN	SJ	63	A1
VAQUERO CT	S	64	E5
VAQUERO DR	MVW	45	B6
VAQUEROS AV	SVL	52	F1
VARDEN AV	SJ	66	D5
VARGAS CT	MPTS	39	F6
VARGAS CT	SJ	72	B3
VARGAS DR	SJ	72	B3
VARGAS PL	SCL	53	F6
VARIAN CT	SJ	72A	D4
VARIAN WY	CPTO	59	C4
VARNER CT	SJ	48	E6
VARSITY CT	MVW	52	A4
VASONA AV	LG	65	F6
VASONA AV	LG	66	A6
VASONA CT	LG	65	F6
VASONA ST	MPTS	47	E2
VASONA OAKS DR	LG	70	F2
VASQUEZ AV	SVL	52	D4
VASQUEZ CT	SVL	52	D3
VASSAR AV	MVW	45	A6
VASSAR DR	SJ	72	A2
VAUGHN AV	SCCO	61	C4
VAUXHALL CIR	SJ	67	F6
VEGAS AV	MPTS	39	F5
VEGAS DR	SJ	72	C4
VELARDE ST	MVW	52	B2
VELASCO DR	SJ	72	E1
VELVET LAKE DR	SVL	53	C2
VELVET MEADW CT	SJ	72	D6
VENADO CT	SJ	72A	B2
VENADO WY	SJ	72A	B1
VENDOME ST	SJ	61	F2
VENDURA CT	S	65	B3
VENECIA DR	SJ	55	E4
VENETIAN WY	MH	80K	F2
VENICE WY	SJ	60	E6
VENICE WY	SJ	65	E1
VENN AV	SJ	71	B1
VENNDALE AV	SJ	71	B2
VENTURA AV	CPTO	59	C5
VENTURA AV	PA	44	C4
VENTURA AV	SJ	68	B4
VENTURA AV	SCCO	59	C5
VENTURA CT	PA	44	C4
VENTURA PL	SCL	53	E5
VENTURELLA DR	SCCO	81	F6
VENUS WY	MPTS	47	E5
VERA LN	SJ	68	B6
VERA CRUZ AV	LA	51	E2
VERA CRUZ DR	SJ	71	F4
VERANO CT	SJ	68	B5
VERANO DR	LA	51	F2
VERANO DR	MVW	51	F2
VERBENA WY	SJ	60	D5
VERDANT WY	SJ	61	D6
VERDE CT	LG	71	B2
VERDE CT	S	64	F5
VERDE MOOR CT	S	64	E3
VERDES ROBLES	LG	70	F2
VERDE VISTA CT	S	64	F5
VERDE VISTA LN	S	64	E5
VERDI DR	SJ	68	A2
VERDI DR	SVL	53	A6
VERDOSA DR	PA	44	C5
VEREDA CT	SJ	72	E3
VERMILION CT	SJ	63	E5
VERMONT ST	SJ	61	D1
VERNA DR	SCCO	55	E3
VERNAL CT	LA	51	D1
VERNAL DR	SJ	65	E1
VERNICE AV	SJ	56	B6
VERNIE CT	CPTO	59	E5
VERNIER PL	SCCO	44	A5
VERNON AV	SJ	62	A6
VERNON AV	SCCO	45	C5
VERNON TER	PA	44	E2
VERONA CT	LG	70	D1
VERONICA DR	S	65	A3
VERONICA PL	SJ	66	C5
VERSAILLES WY	S	70	B1
VERWOOD DR	SJ	65	E4
VESCA WY	SJ	60	D5
VESSING CT	S	65	C6
VESSING CT	S	70	C1
VESSING RD	S	65	D6
VESSING RD	S	70	D1
VESTAL ST	SJ	55	A6
VESUVIUS LN	SJ	48	E6
VESUVIUS LN	SJ	55	E1
VIA ALEGRIA CT	SJ	68	C1
VIA ALMADEN	SJ	72	B3
VIA ALTO CT	S	65	C5
VIA AMIGOS	SJ	72	C5
VIA AMPARO	SJ	68A	B2
VIA ANACAPA	SJ	72A	F3
VIA ARRIBA CT	S	65	B4
VIA ARRIBA DR	S	65	B4
VIA BAHIA	SVL	46	C6
VIA BAJA DR	MPTS	48	A1
VIA BARRANCA	SJ	72A	F4
VIA BELLA	SJ	72A	F4
VIA BELMONTE	SJ	68A	B2
VIA BLANC CT	S	65	B4
VIA BLANCA	SJ	72A	F3
VIA BREZZO	SJ	75	E2
VIA CABALLERO	MS	70	D2
VIA CALZADA	SJ	68A	B2
VIA CAMINO CT	CPTO	59	C3
VIA CAMPINA	SJ	72A	F3
VIA CANCION	SJ	66	C2
VIA CANTARES	SJ	68A	B2
VIA CAPRI	SVL	46	C6
VIA CARMELA	SJ	72A	F4
VIA CARMEN	SJ	66	C5
VIA CARRIZO	SJ	68A	B2
VIA CASTANA	MH	80K	E2
VIA CASTANA	SCCO	80K	E2
VIA CERRO GORDO	LAH	50	F4
VIA CIELO	SJ	68A	B2
VIA CINCO D MYO	SJ	48	B6
VIA CINCO D MYO	SJ	55	B1
VIA CODORNIZ	SJ	66	C1
VIA COLINA	SJ	72A	F4
VIA COLINA	S	70	B2
VIA COLLADO	LG	65	D6
VIA CONTENTA	SJ	66	C2
VIA CORDURA	SJ	72A	F3
VIA CORFINIO	MH	80K	E2
VIA CORITA	LAH	51	A4
VIA CORONA	SJ	72A	F3
VIA CORTA	SCCO	72A	A5
VIA COSENZA	MH	80K	F2
VIA CRECENTE CT	S	65	B4
VIA CRESPI	SCCO	43	E3
VIA CRISTOBAL	SJ	65	F3
VIA DE ADRIANNA	SJ	72	B4
VIA DE CABALLE	SJ	67	A6
VIA DE CABALLE	SJ	72	A1
VIA D GUADALUPE	SJ	55	E6
VIA D LAS ABEJA	SJ	72	A4
VIA DE LA VISTA	SCCO	56	F5
VIA DL CASTILLE	MH	80K	E2
VIA DEL CIELO	SCCO	82A	D2
VIA DL CORONADO	SJ	48	C5
VIA DL LOS GRND	SJ	72	A5
VIA D LOS REYES	SJ	72	A4
VIA DEL MAR	SJ	66	C6
VIA DEL ORO	SJ	72A	E3
VIA DEL ORO	SCCO	82A	D2
VIA DEL POZO	LA	44	D6
VIA DEL RIO	SJ	72A	F3
VIA DEL SOL	SJ	48	C5
VIA DEL SUR	MS	70	E2
VIA DE MARCOS	S	70	C1
VIA DE NINOS	MH	80K	F2
VIADER CT	SCL	61	A2
VIA DESTE	SJ	65	F3
VIA DE TESOROS	LG	70	D2
VIA DONDERA	SCL	60	D1
VIA EDUARDO	MH	80K	E2
VIA EL CAPITAN	SJ	66	D5
VIA ENCANTADA	MS	70	D2
VIA ENCINITAS	SJ	48	B5
VIA ESCALERA	LA	59	B3
VIA ESCUELA CT	S	65	B4
VIA ESCUELA DR	S	65	B4
VIA FELIZ	LAH	50	F3
VIA FERRARI	SJ	62	E3
VIA FLORES	SJ	48	B6
VIA GRANADA	SVL	46	C6
VIA GRANDE	MH	79	D5
VIA GRANDE CT	S	65	B4
VIA GRANDE DR	S	65	B4
VIA GRANJA	SJ	68A	B2
VIA HUERTA	LA	59	B2
VIA HUERTA	SCCO	59	B2
VIA JOSE	SJ	72	C4
VIA LAGO	LG	65	D6
VIA LAGUNA	SJ	68A	B2
VIA LA POSADA	LG	70	D1
VIA LOMA CT	MH	79	C3
VIA LOMAS	SJ	72A	F4
VIA LOMITA	MS	70	D2
VIA MADERO	SJ	71	F4
VIA MADEROS	LA	59	B3
VIA MADRONAS CT	S	65	B4
VIA MADRONAS DR	S	65	B4
VIA MARIA	SJ	72A	F4
VIA MATEO	SJ	72	C5
VIA MESA	SJ	72A	F3
VIA MILANO	SJ	65	F3
VIA MIMOSA	SJ	68A	B2
VIA MONTALVO	SJ	65	F3
VIA MONTE DR	S	65	B4
VIA MONTE DR	SJ	72	B1
VIA MONTECITOS	SJ	68A	B2
VIA MONTEZ	SJ	48	C5
VIA NAPOLI	SJ	65	F3
VIA NIDA	SVL	46	C6
VIA ORTEGA	SCCO	43	E3
VIA PACIFICA	SJ	72A	F3
VIA PALOMINO	MS	70	D2
VIA PALOU	SCCO	43	E3
VIA PIEDRA	SJ	68A	B2
VIA PINTO	MS	70	E2
VIA PISA	SJ	61	D5
VIA PORTADA	SJ	68A	B2
VIA PRADERA	SJ	72A	F4
VIA PRIMAVERA	SJ	68	B5
VIA PRIMAVRA CT	SJ	68	B5
VIA PUEBLO	SCCO	43	E3
VIA RAMADA	SJ	72A	F4
VIA RANCHERO	C	65	F5
VIA RANCHERO CT	S	65	B4
VIA RANCHERO DR	S	65	B4
VIA REAL DR	S	65	B4
VIA REGINA	S	64	D5
VIA ROMA	SJ	65	F3
VIA ROMERA	SJ	72A	F4
VIA RONCOLE	S	64	F2
VIA SALICE	SJ	65	F3
VIA SANTA MARIA	LG	71	A5
VIA STA TERESA	SCCO	72A	A6
VIA SENDERO	SJ	68A	B2
VIA SERAFINA	MH	80K	F2
VIA SERENA	SJ	72A	F4
VIA SERENO	MS	70	E3
VIA SIESTA	SVL	46	C6
VIA SOLANO	SJ	68A	B2
VIA SORRENTO	MH	80K	F2
VIA TERESA	LG	70	D1
VIA TESORO CT	C	65	C6
VIA VALIENTE	SJ	72	E6
VIA VALVERDE	SJ	68A	B2
VIA VAQUERO	MS	70	D2
VIA VENETO	MH	80K	E2
VIA VENTANA	LAH	50	F4
VIA VERONA	MH	80K	F2
VIA VICA	SJ	59	F6
VIA VISTA	SJ	72A	F4
VICANNA DR	SJ	65	B1
VICAR LN	SJ	60	F6
VICAR LN	SJ	61	A6
VICENTE DR	SVL	52	D3
VICEROY CT	CPTO	59	C4
VICEROY WY	SJ	55	E2
VICKERY AV	SCCO	82	D4
VICKERY AV	S	69	F2
VICKERY AV	S	70	A1
VICKERY PL	S	70	A1
VICKSBURG CT	CPTO	60	B5
VICKSBURG DR	CPTO	60	B5
VICTOR AV	C	65	F3
VICTOR AV	SJ	65	F3
VICTOR AV	SCCO	65	F3
VICTOR CT	SJ	48	D6
VICTOR CT	SCL	54	C2
VICTOR PL	S	64	F6
VICTOR ST	SCL	54	C2
VICTOR WY	MVW	52	B3
VICTORIA AV	SCL	53	D6
VICTORIA CT	LA	59	C2
VICTORIA CT	SCCO	56	B5
VICTORIA DR	G	83	F3
VICTORIA PL	PA	44	D5
VICTORIA TER	SVL	52	F6
VICTORIA TER	SVL	59	F1
VICTORIA LNDING	SJ	48	B6
VICTORIA PK DR	SJ	67	E5
VICTORY AV	MVW	44	F5
VICTORY LN	LG	70	E4
VIDA LEON CT	SCCO	55	D5
VIENNA DR	MPTS	39	F6
VIENNA DR	SVL	46	C6
VIERRA CT	SJ	66	F2
VIETENHEIMER	C	66	B4
VIEW DR	MPTS	48	B1
VIEW ST	LA	51	D3
VIEW ST	MVW	52	B2
VIEWCREST CT	SCCO	72	F6
VIEWCREST CT	SCCO	72A	A6
VIEWCREST DR	SCCO	72	F6
VIEWCREST DR	SCCO	72A	A6
VIEWCREST LN	MH	79	D5
VIEWFIELD RD	MS	70	D3
VIEWMONT AV	SCCO	56	A5
VIEWOAK DR	S	65	A2
VIEW OAKS WY	SCCO	72A	A5
VIEWPARK CIR	SJ	67	E4
VIEWPOINT LN	SJ	75	E1
VIEWRIDGE DR	S	65	A2
VILLA	MVW	45	C5
VILLA AV	LG	70	E5
VILLA AV	SJ	61	E3
VILLA CIR	C	65	E1
VILLA DR	SCCO	51	F6
VILLA ST	MVW	52	A1
VILLA DE ANZA	CPTO	60	A3
VILLA E HLLS CT	SJ	56	A5
VILLA FELICE CT	LG	70	E2
VILLAGE CT	MVW	52	C5
VILLAGE CT	SJ	61	F1
VILLAGE DR	S	65	C3
VILLAGE LN	LG	70	E4
VLG HERMOSA LN	SJ	68A	B3
VILLAGETREE DR	SJ	55	B2
VILLAGEWOOD WY	SJ	72	F6
VILLAGIO PL	SJ	47	D6
VILLA GLEN WY	SJ	67	C4
VILLA MARIA CT	SJ	62	D5
VILLA MONTEREY	SJ	67	E2
VILLANOVA CT	SCL	53	D5
VILLANOVA RD	SJ	65	D4
VILLANOVA RD	SCCO	65	D4
VILLANUEVA CT	MVW	52	B4
VILLANUEVA WY	MVW	52	B4
VILLA OAKS LN	S	64	D4
VILLA PARK CT	SJ	67	B6
VILLA PARK LN	SJ	67	B6
VILLA PARK WY	SJ	67	B6
VILLA REAL	PA	44	C5
VILLA REAL	SCCO	82	F1
VILLA REAL	SCCO	82A	A1
VILLARITA DR	C	65	E3
VILLARITA DR	SJ	65	E3
VILLA ROBLDA DR	MVW	52	C5
VILLA STONE DR	SJ	62	B6
VILLA STONE DR	SJ	67	B1
VILLA TERESA WY	SJ	72	D2
VILLA VERA	PA	44	C5
VILLA VISTA	PA	44	C5
VILLA VISTA RD	SJ	68A	A1
VILMAR AV	SJ	72	A4
VINA AV	SCCO	73	D2
VINCENT CT	SJ	72A	B3
VINCENT DR	MVW	52	B2
VINCENT DR	SCL	53	D5
VINCENT DR	SCCO	81	F3
VINCI PARK WY	SJ	55	C3
VINE AV	SCCO	63	F5
VINE AV	SVL	53	A4
VINE ST	SJ	62	A4
VINE ST	S	69	F1
VINE ST	S	70	A1
VINE TR	SCCO	78G	C2
VINEDALE SQ	SJ	48	D5
VINEDO LN	LAH	51	B5
VINELAND AV	LG	70	E2
VINELAND AV	MS	70	E2
VINELAND AV	SCCO	70	E2
VINELAND CT	MS	70	E2
VINEMAPLE AV	SVL	53	C5
VINEYARD BL	MH	79	F6
VINEYARD BL	MH	80K	F1
VINEYARD BL	MH	79	F6
VINEYARD CT	LA	59	C3
VINEYARD CT	MH	79	F6
VINEYARD DR	LA	59	C3
VINEYARD DR	SJ	72A	E4
VINEYARD LN	S	65	C4
VINEYARD SPG CT	CPTO	64	E1
VINTAGE LN	S	64	D6
VINTAGE LN	S	69	D1
VINTAGE WY	SJ	62	D4
VINTAGE ACRS WY	SJ	63	E5
VINTAGE CRST DR	SJ	63	E4
VINTAGE HLLS CT	SJ	63	E4
VINTAGE OAKS CT	SJ	63	E5
VINTNER CT	S	69	D1
VINTNER WY	SJ	71	E2
VINYARD CT	LG	70	D1
VIOLA AV	SJ	62	A3
VIOLA PL	LA	51	E4
VIOLET WY	SJ	65	F3
VIRDELLE DR	SCCO	78G	D2
VIREO AV	SVL	60	C2
VIRGIL PL	SJ	75	F2
VIRGINIA AV	C	65	F5
VIRGINIA AV	C	66	A4
VIRGINIA AV	SJ	62	E2
VIRGINIA CT	C	65	F5
VIRGINIA CT	C	66	A5
VIRGINIA DR	SCCO	78G	D1
VIRGINIA PL	SJ	62	D2
VIRGINIA ST	SJ	61	F4
VIRGINIA ST	SJ	62	B4
VIRGINA SWAN PL	CPTO	59	F4
VIRGO LN	SJ	68	E4
VISCAINO AV	SVL	52	D4
VISCAINO CT	LAH	51	B3
VISCAINO DR	LAH	51	B3
VISCAINO PL	LAH	51	B3
VISCAINO RD	LAH	51	B3
VISCAINO WY	SJ	72A	C4
VISO CT	SCL	54	B3
VISTA AV	MS	70	E3
VISTA AV	PA	44	C5
VISTA AV	SCCO	56	A3
VISTA CT	CPTO	59	F4
VISTA CT	MH	79	C5
VISTA DR	CPTO	59	F4
VISTA DR	CPTO	60	A4
VISTA LN	LS	71	B2
VISTA LN	SCCO	71	B2
VISTA LOOP	SJ	71	E4
VISTA WY	MPTS	48	A3
VISTA ARROYO CT	S	64	E2
VISTA CREEK DR	SJ	55	E2
VIS DE ALMADEN	SCCO	72	E4
VIS D ALMADN CT	SCCO	72	E4
VISTA DEL ARBOL	LG	70	F5
VISTA DEL ARBOL	LG	71	A5
VISTA DEL CAMPO	LG	70	F5
VISTA DEL LAGO	LG	65	D6
VISTA DEL MAR	LG	70	F5
VISTA DEL MAR	SJ	55	F1
VISTA DEL MONTE	LG	70	F5
VISTA DEL MONTE	LG	71	A5
VIS DL MONTE CT	SCCO	81H	F5
VISTA DE LOMAS	SCOO	78	D6
VISTA DE LOMAS	SCCO	79	D1
VISTA DEL PRADO	LG	70	F5
VISTA DEL SOL	SJ	55	F5
VISTA DEL SOL	SCCO	81C	A6
VISTA DEL SUR	G	82	C6
VISTA DEL SUR	G	83	C1
VISTA DEL VALLE	MH	80	C3
VISTA DEL VALLE	SJ	55	F1
VISTA DL VAL CT	LAH	51	B5
VISTA DL VAL CT	MH	80	C3
VISTA DE SIERRA	LG	70	F5
VISTA DE SIERRA	LG	71	A5
VISTAGLEN CT	SJ	63	A2
VISTAGLEN DR	SJ	63	A2
VISTA GRANDE AV	LA	52	A3
VISTA GRANDE WY	SCCO	73	D2
VISTA KNOLL BL	CPTO	59	C3
VISTA LOMA	SCCO	72A	A5
VISTA LOOP	SJ	71	E4
VISTAMONT DR	SJ	67	B4
VISTA MONTANA	SJ	47	A5
VISTA NORTE CT	SCCO	48	E2
VISTA OAK	SJ	55	F1
VISTA OAKS CT	CPTO	60	A4
VISTAPARK DR	SJ	67	E4
VISTA REGINA	S	64	D5
VISTA RIDGE DR	MPTS	48	E1
VISTA SERENA	LAH	51	D5
VISTA SPRING CT	MPTS	48	E2
VISTA VALLE CT	SJ	56	C3
VISTA VERDE DR	SJ	63	D2
VISTAVIEW DR	SJ	48	E6
VIVIAN DR	LG	71	A5
VIVIAN LN	SJ	66	D5
VOGUE CT	LAH	51	B4
VOLLMER WY	SJ	62	E1
VOLTI DR	LA	52	B5
VONNA CT	SJ	72	E2
VOORHEES DR	LAH	51	D5
VOSS AV	CPTO	59	B5
VOSS PARK LN	SJ	55	C3
W			
WABASH AV	SJ	61	D4
WABASH AV	SCCO	61	D4
WABASH ST	SJ	46	F3
WACO ST	SJ	61	D1
WADDINGTON AV	SVL	53	A2
WADE AV	SCL	53	E6
WADSWORTH AV	LG	70	D4
WAGMAN DR	SJ	60	D5
WAGMAN DR	SCCO	60	D5
WAGNER AV	MVW	45	A6
WAGNER RD	SCCO	71	E6
WAIMEA CT	SJ	67	A6
WAINWRIGHT AV	SJ	61	C4
WAINWRIGHT DR	SJ	66	C1
WAINWRIGHT DR	SJ	61	C6
WAITE AV	SVL	53	A2
WAKEFIELD TER	LA	52	C6
WAKEFIELD TER	LA	59	B1
WAKE FOREST RD	MVW	45	C6
WALBROOK DR	SJ	65	C1
WALBROOK DR	S	65	C1
WALBROOK DR W	SJ	65	B1
WALCOTT RD	SCCO	45	D4
WALDEN CT	S	65	B2
WALDEN SQ	SJ	66	E3
WALDHEIM CT	SJ	72	F6
WALDO RD	C	65	F4
WALDO RD	C	66	A4
WALGLEN CT	SJ	67	C5
WALGROVE WY	SJ	61	B6

1991 SANTA CLARA COUNTY STREET INDEX

STREET	CITY	PAGE	GRID
WILTON DR	C	66	A4
WIMBLEDON DR	LG	65	F6
WIMBLEDON DR	LG	70	F1
WIMBLEDON PL	LA	59	B2
WINCHESTER BLVD	C	66	B2
WINCHESTER BLVD	LG	65	F6
WINCHESTER BLVD	LG	66	A5
WINCHESTER BLVD	LG	70	E2
WINCHESTER BLVD	MS	70	E2
WINCHESTER BLVD	SJ	61	B6
WINCHESTER BLVD	SJ	66	B2
WINCHESTER BLVD	SCL	61	B3
WINCHESTER BLVD	SCCO	61	B6
WINCHESTER BL N	SCL	61	B2
WINDELL CT	SJ	72	E2
WINDEMERE CT	SCCO	80	A1
WINDHAM LN	MVW	52	C2
WINDIMER DR	LA	59	B2
WINDING WY	SJ	65	E1
WINDING WY	SCCO	51	E6
WINDING WY	SCCO	58	E1
WINDING WY	SCCO	73	F6
WINDING WY	SCCO	78G	F1
WINDING CK CT	SJ	63	D1
WINDINGWOOD CT	MVW	44	F6
WINDINGWOOD CT	MVW	51	F1
WINDMILL CT	SJ	68	A1
WINDMILL PK LN	MVW	52	B1
WINDSOR CT	LAH	51	A5
WINDSOR LN	SJ	60	B6
WINDSOR LN	SJ	65	B1
WINDSOR ST	CPTO	59	F6
WINDSOR ST	CPTO	60	A6
WINDSOR ST	SJ	59	F6
WINDSOR ST	SJ	60	B6
WINDSOR WY	SJ	65	A1
WINDSOR PK DR	SJ	67	E5
WINE BARREL WY	SJ	66	B5
WINE CASK WY	SJ	66	C5
WINE CORK WY	SJ	66	B5
WINE GROWER WY	SJ	66	B5
WINE MAKER WY	SJ	66	B5
WINERY CT	SJ	68A	B3
WINFIELD BLVD	SJ	72	C2
WINFIELD DR	MVW	52	B5
WING PL	SCCO	43	F5
WING PL	SCCO	44	A5
WINGATE DR	SVL	52	F6
WINGHAM PL	SJ	63	E6
WINN RD	S	70	A1
WINNEBAGO CT	SJ	72	F3
WINONA DR	SJ	66	F2
WINSLOW CT	C	65	E3
WINSLOW DR	SJ	62	E3
WINSOR ST	MPTS	47	F2
WINSTEAD CT	SYL	52	E6
WINSTEAD TER	SVL	52	E6
WINSTED CT	SJ	72B	A4
WINSTON CT	SJ	55	C4
WINSTON PL	MVW	45	C6
WINSTON ST	SJ	55	C4
WINSTON WY	CPTO	59	C4
WINTER LN	SJ	72A	D1
WINTER LN	S	65	A4
WINTERBERRY WY	SJ	60	E5
WINTERBROOK DR	SJ	60	B6
WINTERBROOK RD	LG	71	B3
WINTERGATE LN	SJ	67	F6
WINTERGREEN DR	CPTO	60	A5
WINTERGREEN WY	PA	44	D2
WINTER PARK WY	SJ	63	A3
WINTERSET WY	SJ	72	E5
WINTERSONG CT	SJ	55	C3
WINTON WY	LAH	58	E2
WINTON WY	SJ	71	B2
WINTON WY	SCCO	71	B2
WINWOOD CT	MVW	51	F1
WINWOOD WY	SJ	63	D4
WISSAHICKON AV	LG	70	D4
WISTARIA CT	LA	59	C2
WISTARIA LN	LA	59	C2
WISTARIA WY	SCL	61	C2
WISTERIA WY	SJ	65	A1
WITHEY RD	MS	70	C4
WITHEY HTS RD	MS	70	C4
WITHROW PL	SCL	60	E2
WIVEN PL WY	SJ	68	C1
WIZARD CT	SJ	55	C2
WOBURN CT	MVW	52	C5
WOEHL CT	SCCO	76	C1
WOLCOT WY	S	64	F3
WOLCOT WY	S	65	A3
WOLFBERRY CT	SJ	67	F4
WOLFE RD	CPTO	60	B4
WOLFE RD	SCCO	60	B2
WOLFE RD	SVL	53	B6
WOLFE RD	SVL	60	B2
WOLLETT CT	SJ	56	B1
WOLLIN WY	LG	71	B4
WONDERAMA DR	SJ	63	B2
WONG CT	SJ	68	A6
WONG CT	SJ	72A	A1
WONG DR	SJ	67	F6
WONG DR	SJ	68	A6
WONG DR	SJ	72	F1
WONG DR	SJ	72A	A1
WOOD RD	LG	70	D5
WOOD ACRES RD	SCCO	70	C3
WOODALE CT	SJ	63	B1
WOODARD RD	SJ	66	C6
WOODARD RD	SCCO	66	B6
WOODBANK WY	S	70	D1
WOODBARK CT	SJ	65	F1
WOODBINE WY	SJ	61	A6
WOODBRAE CT	SJ	65	D4
WOODBRIDGE WY	SCL	54	C2
WOODBURN WY	SCCO	55	F6
WOODBURN WY	SCCO	56	A6
WOODBURY DR	CPTO	59	D4
WOODCLIFF CT	SJ	72	B5
WOODCLIFF DR	SJ	72	B5
WOODCOCK CT	MPTS	39	F5
WOODCREEK LN	SJ	65	F1
WOODCREST DR	SJ	67	B4
WOOD DELL CT	S	65	C3
WOOD DUCK AV	SCL	60	C2
WOOD DUCK CT	SCL	60	C2
WOODED GLEN DR	LA	59	A2
WOODED HILLS DR	SJ	72	C6
WOODED LAKE DR	SJ	75	C1
WOODED VIEW DR	LG	71	B4
WOODELF DR	SJ	68	A1
WOODFLOWER WY	SJ	65	F1
WOODFORD DR	SJ	66	E6
WOODGATE CT	SJ	66	F5
WOODGLEN DR	SJ	65	D3
WOODGREEN LN	MVW	52	B3
WOODGROVE LN	SJ	67	C5
WOODGROVE SQ	SJ	66	A1
WOODHAMS RD	SCL	60	E4
WOODHAVEN DR	SCCO	56	B6
WOODHILL CT	CPTO	64	E2
WOODHURST LN	SJ	72	D1
WOODING CT	SJ	66	C1
WOODLAND AV	LG	70	E4
WOODLAND AV	MH	79	A5
WOODLAND AV	SJ	61	B3
WOODLAND AV	SOL	61	B3
WOODLAND CT	MPTS	47	E5
WOODLAND CT	MH	79	B5
WOODLAND WY	MPTS	47	E5
WOODLAND PK LN	MVW	52	B1
WOODLARK WY	CPTO	59	E6
WOODLAWN AV	SJ	61	B6
WOODLAWN AV	SJ	66	B1
WOODLEAF CT	SJ	65	F1
WOODLEAF WY	MVW	52	B4
WOODLEY DR	SJ	63	F3
WOODMAN CT	SJ	63	A6
WOODMINSTER DR	SJ	62	F5
WOODMONT DR	SJ	63	B2
WOODMONT DR	SJ	67	B4
WOODMONT DR	S	65	A5
WOODMOOR DR	SJ	63	B2
WOODRIDGE CT	CPTO	59	C5
WOODRIDGE WY	SJ	63	B2
WOODRUFF DR	SJ	72	B4
WOODRUFF WY	MPTS	39	E6
WOODS CT	SJ	63	D4
WOODS LN	LA	59	B2
WOODS WY	SJ	63	D4
WOODSIDE CT	SJ	63	D5
WOODSIDE CT	S	65	B2
WOODSIDE DR	S	65	B3
WOODSIDE LN	SJ	63	D5
WOODSON CT	SJ	67	A5
WOODSTOCK LN	LA	51	E4
WOODSTOCK LN	MVW	52	C5
WOODSTOCK WY	SJ	71	F1
WOODSTOCK WY	SCL	54	B2
WOODSTOCK WY	SCCO	72	A1
WOODTHRUSH CT	SJ	72	F6
WOODTREE CT	SJ	63	D5
WOODVIEW AV	MH	79	D2
WOODVIEW LN	S	65	A6
WOODVIEW PL	SJ	75	E1
WOODVIEW TER	LA	59	B2
WOODWARD AV	SCL	54	B3
WOODWARD CT	S	64	F5
WOODWARDIA LN	SCCO	70	B3
WOODWORTH WY	G	82	E5
WOODWORTH WY	SCCO	56	D3
WOODY CT	SJ	48	C5
WESSEX PL	MPTS	39	F5
WOODY LN	SJ	48	C5
WOODYEND CT	SJ	68	B1
WOOL AV	SCCO	67	F3
WOOL DR	MPTS	48	A1
WOOLAROC DR	SCCO	78G	D1
WOOL CREEK DR	SJ	62	E5
WOOL WILL DR	SJ	62	E5
WOOSLEY DR	SJ	72A	C4
WOOSTER AV	SJ	55	C6
WOOSTER ST	SJ	62	C1
WORCESTER LN	LG	70	F5
WORCESTER LN	LG	71	A5
WORCESTER LOOP	LG	70	F5
WORDEN LN	S	65	A6
WORLEY AV	SVL	53	B2
WORTH WY	SCCO	56	A6
WORTHAM CT	MVW	52	B5
WORTHING CT	SJ	72	E5
WOZ WY	SJ	62	A4
WRAIGHT AV	LG	70	E4
WREN AV	G	82	E6
WREN AV	SCCO	82	E6
WREN AV	SVL	60	C2
WREN DR	SJ	67	B3
WREN WY	C	65	F3
WREN WY	SJ	65	F3
WRIGHT AV	MH	79	D4
WRIGHT AV	MVW	45	A6
WRIGHT AV	MVW	52	B1
WRIGHT AV	SCCO	52	B1
WRIGHT AV	SVL	59	D3
WRIGHT CT	SVL	59	D1
WRIGHT DR	SCCO	73	D5
WRIGHT PL	PA	44	D4
WRIGHT TER	SVL	59	D1
WRIGHT WY	LAH	51	A4
WRIGHTS STA RD	SCCO	78H	B2
WRIGLEY WY	MPTS	48	A3
WUNDERLICH DR	SJ	60	C6
WUNDERLICH DR	SCCO	60	C6
WYANDOTTE DR	SJ	72A	B2
WYANDOTTE ST	MYW	44	F4
WYATT DR	SCL	54	A2
WYCLIFFE CT	SJ	65	E1
WYLIE DR	MPTS	48	C3
WYLIE WY	SJ	65	F1
WYMAN WY	SJ	55	D3
WYOMA PL	MPTS	47	F1
WYRICK AV	SJ	66	D6
WYRICK AV	SJ	71	E1
WYRICK AV	SCCO	66	D6
WYRICK AV	SCCO	71	D1

X

STREET	CITY	PAGE	GRID
XAVIER CT	SJ	65	F3
XAVIER CT	SCL	53	D5

Y

STREET	CITY	PAGE	GRID
YAKIMA CIR	SK	68	B1
YALE CT	LAH	50	F2
YALE DR	MVW	51	F4
YALE DR	MVW	52	A4
YALE DR	SJ	72	A2
YALE LN	SCL	60	D3
YALE ST	PA	44	B3
YAMADA DR	SJ	55	B3
YAMATO DR	SJ	68	B4
YANCY DR	SJ	63	D4
YANKEE POINT CT	SJ	55	B2
YARD CT	SJ	55	B5
YARDIS CT	MVW	52	A5
YARMOUTH CT	SJ	72	F6
YARMOUTH WY	SJ	72	F6
YARWOOD CT	SJ	61	C5
YELLOWBIRD CT	SJ	72	B4
YELLOWLEAF CT	SJ	63	D5
YELLOWSTONE AV	MPTS	48	B4
YELLOWSTONE DR	SJ	65	F1
YELLOWSTONE TER	SVL	52	E6
YERBA BANK CT	SJ	68	E1
YERBA BUENA AV	LA	51	D2
YERBA BUENA AV	SJ	63	E6
YERBA BUENA AV	SJ	68	E1
YERBA BUENA CT	SJ	63	E6
YERBA BUENA PL	LA	51	D2
YERBA BUENA RD	SJ	60	F1
YERBA BUENA RD	SJ	68	B2
YERBA BUENA RD	SJ	68	F1
YERBA BUENA RD	SJ	68A	A1
YERBA BUENA RD	SCCO	68	E2
YERBA BUENA RD	SCCO	68A	A1
YERBA BUENA WY	SCL	46	E4
YERBA CLIFF CT	SJ	68	E1
YERBA HILLS CT	SJ	68	E1
YERBA SANTA AV	LA	51	D2
YERBA SANTA CT	S	65	B5
YERBA VISTA CT	SJ	68	E1
YERMO CT	SJ	68	E3
YESLER CT	SJ	55	B1
YEW TREE CT	SJ	68	D4
YNIGO WY	PA	44	C6
YOLANDA CT	SJ	67	B5
YOLO CT	SJ	67	D4
YOLO DR	SJ	67	D5
YOLO DR	S	64	F3
YONA VISTA	SCCO	56	A2
YORK AV	C	65	E5
YORK ST	SJ	66	E5
YORKSHIRE CT	CPTO	64	E1
YORKSHIRE DR	CPTO	59	E6
YORKSHIRE DR	CPTO	64	E1
YORKSHIRE DR	LA	59	A2
YORKSHIRE WY	MVW	52	C4
YORKTON DR	MVW	52	B5
YORKTON WY	SJ	65	D4
YORKTOWN DR	G	83	E3
YORKTOWN DR	SVL	52	D6
YORKTOWN DR	SVL	59	D1
YOSEMITE AV	MVW	52	B2
YOSEMITE AV	SJ	61	E4
YOSEMITE DR	MPTS	48	B3
YOSEMITE WY	LG	70	F5
YOSEMITE WY	MH	80K	F2
YOSHINO PL	CPTO	60	B4
YOUNG CT	SCCO	51	F6
YOUNGER AV	SJ	54	F6
YOUNGS CIR	SJ	56	A3
YOUNGS CT	SJ	56	A3
YUBA AV	SJ	61	A6
YUBA AV	SJ	66	A1
YUBA CT	S	65	A3
YUBA DR	MVW	52	C3
YUBA DR	SCCO	52	C3
YUCATAN WY	SJ	72	A1
YUCCA AV	SJ	66	F5
YUKON DR	SVL	59	F1
YUKON TER	SVL	59	F1
YUKON WY	SJ	65	E3
YUMA AV	SVL	53	D2
YUMA DR	SJ	67	F2
YUROK CIR	SJ	72	F2
YUROK CT	SJ	72	F2
YVETTE CT	SJ	67	B6
YVONNE CT	SCCO	71	C2
YVONNE DR	SCCO	80K	D3

Z

STREET	CITY	PAGE	GRID
ZACHARY CT	SJ	62	F5
ZACHARY WY	SJ	62	F5
ZAMORA CT	MPTS	40	A6
ZAMZOW CT	SCCO	82	E4
ZANKER LN	SJ	47	B3
ZANKER RD	SJ	47	C3
ZANKER RD	SJ	54	D2
ZARICK DR	SJ	60	E6
ZATON AV	SJ	60	F5
ZATON AV	SJ	61	A5
ZATON AV	SCCO	61	A5
ZEKA DR	SJ	55	A3
ZELLA CT	SCCO	78G	D1
ZENA AV	MS	70	F1
ZEPHYR CT	SJ	63	B1
ZEPPELIN CT	SJ	68	B5
ZIG ZAG TR	SCCO	78G	C2
ZILEMAN CT	SJ	72A	B2
ZILEMAN DR	SJ	72A	B2
ZINFANDEL CT	S	70	B1
ZINFANDEL WY	SJ	72	B3
ZINNIA LN	SJ	71	E4
ZION CT	MPTS	48	B3
ZION LN	SJ	48	E6
ZION LN	SJ	55	E1
ZIRCON CT	SJ	67	C6
ZISCH DR	SJ	67	A5
ZOOK RD	SCCO	45	E3
ZORIA CIR	SJ	55	C2
ZORKA AV	S	64	F3
ZORKA AV	S	65	A3
ZUNI CT	SJ	55	C2
ZURICH CT	SJ	55	E2
ZURICH TER	SVL	59	F1

NUMERICAL STREETS

STREET	CITY	PAGE	GRID
1ST AV	MVW	52	D2
1ST AV	SVL	45	F4
1ST ST	C	66	B3
1ST ST	G	83	F1
1ST ST	LA	51	D3
1ST ST	MH	79	D4
1ST ST	SJ	54	E5
1ST ST	SJ	61	F1
1ST ST	SJ	62	B4
1ST ST	SCCO	82	D2
1ST ST	SVL	46	C6
1ST ST N	SJ	46	F4
1ST ST N	SJ	47	A4
1ST ST N	SJ	47	B5
1ST ST N	SJ	54	D3
2ND AV	MVW	52	D2
2ND AV	SVL	46	A4
2ND ST	C	66	B3
2ND ST	G	83	E1
2ND ST	LA	51	D3
2ND ST	MH	79	E4
2ND ST	PA	44	D4
2ND ST	SJ	54	F6
2ND ST	SJ	61	F1
2ND ST	SJ	62	B3
2ND ST	SCL	53	F1
2ND ST	SCL	54	A1
2ND ST	SCCO	82	D2
2ND ST	SVL	46	C6
3RD AV	MVW	52	D2
3RD AV	SCCO	77	E4
3RD ST	G	83	F1
3RD ST	LA	51	D3
3RD ST	MH	79	E4
3RD ST	SJ	54	F6
3RD ST	SJ	61	F1
3RD ST	SJ	62	B4
3RD ST	SCL	53	F1
3RD ST	SCCO	77	E4
3RD ST	SCCO	82	E2
3RD ST	SCCO	83	D2
3RD ST	S	64	F6
3RD ST	S	69	F1
3RD ST	SVL	46	C6
3RD ST E	SVL	46	C6
4TH AV	MVW	52	D2
4TH ST	C	66	B3
4TH ST	G	83	F2
4TH ST	LA	51	E3
4TH ST	MH	79	E5
4TH ST	SJ	54	F6
4TH ST	SJ	55	A6
4TH ST	SJ	61	F1
4TH ST	SJ	62	B3
4TH ST	SCCO	82	E2
4TH ST	S	64	F6
4TH ST	S	69	F1
4TH ST	SVL	46	C6
4TH ST E	SVL	46	C6
5TH AV	SVL	46	A5
5TH ST	G	83	F2
5TH ST	MH	79	E5
5TH ST	SJ	54	F6
5TH ST	SJ	55	A6
5TH ST	SJ	61	F1
5TH ST	SJ	62	B3
5TH ST	SCCO	82	E2
5TH ST	S	64	F6
5TH ST	S	69	F1
5TH ST	SVL	46	C6
6TH AV	SVL	46	A5
6TH ST	G	83	F2
6TH ST	SJ	54	F6
6TH ST	SJ	55	A6
6TH ST	SJ	62	B3
6TH ST	SCCO	82	E2
6TH ST	S	64	F6
6TH ST	S	69	F1
6TH ST	SVL	46	C6
7TH ST	G	83	F2
7TH ST	SJ	54	F6
7TH ST	SJ	55	A6
7TH ST	SJ	62	D6
7TH ST	SJ	67	D1
7TH ST	SCCO	62	D6
7TH ST	SCCO	67	D1
7TH ST	SVL	46	C6
8TH AV	SVL	46	A5
8TH ST	G	83	F2
8TH ST	SJ	55	A6
8TH ST	SJ	62	B3
8TH ST	SVL	46	C6
9TH AV	SVL	46	A6
9TH ST	G	83	F2
9TH ST	SJ	55	A6
9TH ST	SJ	62	B3
9TH ST	SVL	46	C5
10TH ST	G	83	F3
10TH ST	SJ	55	A5
10TH ST	SJ	62	C3
10TH ST	SVL	46	C5
11TH AV	SVL	46	A6
11TH ST	G	84	A3
11TH ST	SJ	55	A6
11TH ST	SJ	62	C3
12TH ST	SJ	55	A6
12TH ST	SJ	62	C3
13TH ST	SJ	55	A6
13TH ST	SJ	62	C3
14TH ST	SJ	55	A6
14TH ST	SJ	62	C3
15TH ST	SJ	55	B6
15TH ST	SJ	62	C3
16TH ST	SJ	55	B6
16TH ST	SJ	62	C3
17TH ST	SJ	55	B5
17TH ST	SJ	62	B1
18TH ST	SJ	55	B5
18TH ST	SJ	62	C2
19TH ST	SJ	55	B6
19TH ST	SJ	62	C2
20TH ST	SJ	55	B6
20TH ST	SJ	62	C2
20TH ST	SCCO	62	C2
21ST ST	SJ	55	B6
21ST ST	SJ	62	C2
21ST ST	SCCO	62	C2
22ND ST	SJ	55	B6
22ND ST	SJ	62	C2
22ND ST	SCCO	62	C2
23RD ST	SJ	55	B5
23RD ST	SJ	62	C2
23RD ST	SCCO	62	C2
24TH ST	SJ	62	C1
25TH ST	SJ	62	C1
26TH ST	SJ	55	C6
26TH ST	SJ	62	C1
27TH ST	SJ	55	C6
27TH ST	SJ	62	C1
28TH ST	SJ	55	C6
28TH ST	SJ	62	C1
30TH ST	SJ	62	D1
31ST ST	SJ	55	C6
31ST ST	SJ	62	C2
32ND ST	SJ	55	D6
33RD ST	SJ	55	C6
33RD ST	SJ	62	D1
34TH ST	SJ	55	D6
34TH ST	SJ	62	E2

PAGE	GRID	NAME	ADDRESS	CITY	PHONE
		AIRPORTS (SEE TRANSPORTATION)			
		BUILDINGS			
54	C6	AIRPORT PARK OFFICE	1400 COLEMAN AV	SANTA CLARA	244 7211
62	A2	ANGLO BANK	1 N MARKET ST	SAN JOSE	
61	F1	BANK OF AMERICA	777 N 1ST ST	SAN JOSE	277 7237
62	A2	BRUNO	447 N 1ST ST	SAN JOSE	
54	B5	BUILDERS EXCHANGE	400 REED ST	SANTA CLARA	249 4000
62	A3	BURRELL	246 S 1ST ST	SAN JOSE	
61	E3	CAMPISI	919 THE ALAMEDA	SAN JOSE	
62	A3	CENTRAL BLOCK	14 E SAN FERNANDO ST	SAN JOSE	
62	A3	CIVIC AUDITORIUM	145 W SAN CARLOS ST	SAN JOSE	277 5277
54	6F	CIVIC CENTER	888 N 1ST ST	SAN JOSE	297 7794
62	A3	CLAYTON & CO	38 W SANTA CLARA ST	SAN JOSE	
62	A3	COMMERCIAL	28 N 1ST ST	SAN JOSE	
62	A2	COMMUNITY BANK	111 W ST JOHN ST	SAN JOSE	286 9101
62	A2	COURT HOUSE S C CO	191 N 1ST ST	SAN JOSE	299 1121
61	F1	COURT HOUSE S J	200 W HEDDING ST	SAN JOSE	299 2271
59	F5	CUPERTINO TOWN CENTER	20380 TOWN CENTER LN	CUPERTINO	255 6010
62	A2	DAVIS OFFICE BLDG	210 S 1ST ST	SAN JOSE	
62	A3	EL PASEO	40 S 1ST ST	SAN JOSE	
62	A3	EMPIRE	510 N 1ST ST	SAN JOSE	
60	E4	FAIRVIEW	2858 STEVENS CREEK BL	SAN JOSE	
54	A6	FERNMAR	1659 SCOTT BLVD	SANTA CLARA	248 5481
62	A3	GREAT WESTERN FINANCE	111 N MARKET ST	SAN JOSE	
61	F1	HALL OF RECORDS CO	70 W HEDDING ST	SAN JOSE	299 2483
66	E2	HAMILTON OFFICE CENTER	1777 HAMILTON AV	SAN JOSE	269 1700
62	A4	INSURANCE CENTER	491 ALMADEN AV	SAN JOSE	
62	A3	LABOR TEMPLE	45 SANTA TERESA ST	SAN JOSE	
51	D3	LOS ALTOS	199 1ST ST	LOS ALTOS	
62	A3	MEDICAL ARTS	48 E SANTA CLARA ST	SAN JOSE	
62	A5	MEDICAL CENTER	123 S 3RD ST	SAN JOSE	
62	B2	MEDICAL SCIENCE	25 N 14TH ST	SAN JOSE	286 3998
62	B2	MEDICO-DENTAL	6TH & SANTA CLARA STS	SAN JOSE	
62	A2	MURDOCK DAVID DEVLP CO	111 W ST JOHN ST	SAN JOSE	
62	A3	NEW CENTURY BLOCK	66 E SANTA CLARA ST	SAN JOSE	
62	A3	PADRE THEATRE	141 S 1ST ST	SAN JOSE	
62	A3	PARK CENTER	476 PARK AV	SAN JOSE	
62	B2	PHYSICIANS & SURGEONS	626-636 E STA CLARA ST	SAN JOSE	
62	A3	PORTER	57 E SANTA CLARA ST	SAN JOSE	
62	A3	PROFESSIONAL	82 N 2ND ST	SAN JOSE	
61	E4	PROFESSIONAL	220 MERIDIAN AV	SAN JOSE	
61	F1	PROFESSIONAL CENTER	586 N 1ST ST	SAN JOSE	
62	A3	REALTY	19 N 2ND ST	SAN JOSE	
62	A3	SAINTE CLAIRE	311 S 1ST ST	SAN JOSE	
46	E6	STA CLARA CONV CENTER	5001 GREAT AMERICAN PY	SANTA CLARA	
62	A3	SANTA CLARA CO FRE INS	60 N 2ND ST	SAN JOSE	
67	A1	SECURITY	1116 TELFER AV	SAN JOSE	293 8359
62	A3	SHERMAN CLAY	85 S 1ST ST	SAN JOSE	
62	A3	SPRING	85 W SANTA CLARA ST	SAN JOSE	
61	A4	STEVENS CREEK REALTY	3275 STEVENS CREEK BL	SAN JOSE	249 4660
61	F1	SWENSON	777 N 1ST ST	SAN JOSE	294 8070
54	E5	TEAMSTERS	1452 N 4TH ST	SAN JOSE	998 0550
62	A2	TERRACE	481 N 1ST ST	SAN JOSE	
51	D3	THIRD & MAIN	200 3RD ST	LOS ALTOS	
66	C2	TOWERS EXECUTIVE SUITE	1901 S BASCOM AV	CAMPBELL	371 0811
62	A3	TWOHY	210 S 1ST ST	SAN JOSE	
62	A5	VICTORY	45 N 1ST ST	SAN JOSE	
62	A3	VINE ST PROFESSIONAL	260 VINE ST	SAN JOSE	
65	D2	WESTGATE OFFICE PLAZA	4960 HAMILTON AV	SAN JOSE	
65	F6	WEST VALLEY COURT BLDG	14205 CAPRI DR	LOS GATOS	
		CEMETERIES			
51	C1	ALTA MESA	695 ARASTRADERO RD	PALO ALTO	493 1041
55	F5	CALVARY CATHOLIC	2655 MADDEN AV	SAN JOSE	258 2940
59	B3	GATE OF HEAVEN CATH	22555 CRISTO REY DR	LOS ALTOS	738 2121
71	B2	LOS GATOS	2255 LS GATOS ALMD RD	LOS GATOS	356 4151
69	F1	MADRONIA	14766 OAK ST	SARATOGA	867 3717
83	B1	MASON & ODD FELLOWS	HECKER PASS HWY	GILROY	842 2948
61	A3	MISSION CITY	WINCHESTER BLVD	SANTA CLARA	984 3090
67	D1	OAK HILL	300 CURTNER AV	SAN JOSE	297 2447
83	E1	ST MARYS CATHOLIC	HECKER PASS HWY	GILROY	847 5151
61	B2	SANTA CLARA MISSION	490 LINCOLN ST	SANTA CLARA	296 4656
		CHAMBERS OF COMMERCE & VISITORS BUREAUS			
66	B3	CAMPBELL	328 E CAMPBELL AV	CAMPBELL	378 6252
62	A3	CONV & VISITORS BUREAU	333 W SAN CARLOS	SAN JOSE	295 9600
59	E4	CUPERTINO	21380 STEVENS CREEK	CUPERTINO	252 7054
83	F1	GILROY	7780 MONTEREY ST	GILROY	842 6437
51	D4	LOS ALTOS	321 UNIVERSITY AV	LOS ALTOS	948 1455
70	E5	LOS GATOS	5 MONTEBELLO WY	LOS GATOS	354 9300
47	E2	MILPITAS	1 N MAIN ST	MILPITAS	262 2613
79	E4	MORGAN HILL	17320 MONTEREY WY	MORGAN HILL	779 9444
52	B2	MOUNTAIN VIEW	580 CASTRO ST	MOUNTAIN VIEW	968 8378
44	A1	PALO ALTO	325 FOREST AV	PALO ALTO	324 3121
62	A3	SAN JOSE	1 PASEO DE SN ANTONIO	SAN JOSE	998 7000
54	A3	SANTA CLARA CC	2200 LAURELWOOD RD	SANTA CLARA	970 9825
54	A3	SANTA CLARA VIS BUREAU	2200 LAURELWOOD RD	SANTA CLARA	296 7111
64	F6	SARATOGA	20460 SARATOGA-LS GATS	SARATOGA	867 0753
52	F4	SUNNYVALE	499 MURPHY AV	SUNNYVALE	736 4971
66	C2	US CHAMBER OF COMMERCE	1901 S BASCOM AV	CAMPBELL	371 6000
		CITY HALLS			
66	B3	CAMPBELL	75 N CENTRAL AV	CAMPBELL	378 8141
60	A5	CUPERTINO	10300 TORRE AV	CUPERTINO	252 4505
83	F2	GILROY	7390 ROSANNA ST	GILROY	842 3191
51	E3	LOS ALTOS	1 N SAN ANTONIO RD	LOS ALTOS	948 1491
51	C3	LOS ALTOS HILLS	26379 W FREMONT RD	LOS ALTOS HLS	941 7222
70	E5	LOS GATOS	110 E MAIN ST	LOS GATOS	354 6801
47	F2	MILPITAS	455 E CALAVERAS BLVD	MILPITAS	942 2374
70	D3	MONTE SERENO	18041 SARATOGA-LS GATS	MONTE SERENO	354 6834
79	D5	MORGAN HILL	17555 PEAK AV	MORGAN HILL	779 7259
52	B2	MOUNTAIN VIEW	540 CASTRO ST	MOUNTAIN VIEW	966 6300
43	F1	PALO ALTO	250 HAMILTON AV	PALO ALTO	329 2311
61	F1	SAN JOSE	801 N 1ST ST	SAN JOSE	277 4000
54	A6	SANTA CLARA	1500 WARBURTON AV	SANTA CLARA	984 3000
65	B5	SARATOGA	13777 FRUITVALE AV	SARATOGA	867 5438
52	E4	SUNNYVALE	456 W OLIVE AV	SUNNYVALE	738 5411
		COLLEGES & UNIVERSITIES			
59	E4	DE ANZA	21250 STEVENS CREEK BL	CUPERTINO	996 4760
68	F1	EVERGREEN VALLEY	3095 YERBA BUENA RD	SAN JOSE	274 7900
51	D5	FOOTHILL	12345 S EL MONTE AV	LOS ALTOS HLS	960 4600
84	A6	GAVILAN	5055 SANTA TERESA BLVD	GILROY	847 1400
61	E4	LINCOLN UNIVERSITY	1050 PARK AV	SAN JOSE	298 3311
53	E2	MISSION COLLEGE	3000 MISSION COLLGE BL	SANTA CLARA	988 2200
61	D5	SAN JOSE CITY COLLEGE	2100 MOORPARK AV	SAN JOSE	298 2181
68	F1	SAN JOSE COMMUNITY COL	4750 SAN FELIPE RD	SAN JOSE	274 6700
62	B3	SAN JOSE STATE	125 S 7TH ST	SAN JOSE	924 1000
43	E3	STANFORD	JUNIPERO SERRA BLVD	PALO ALTO	497 2300
61	C1	UNIV OF SANTA CLARA	820 ALVISO ST	SANTA CLARA	984 4242
65	B6	WEST VALLEY-SARATOGA	14000 FRUITVALE AV	SARATOGA	867 2200
		GOLF COURSES			
72	C6	ALMADEN COUNTRY CLUB	6663 HAMPTON DR	SAN JOSE	268 4653
59	C4	BLACKBERRY FARM	22100 STEVENS CREEK BL	CUPERTINO	253 9200
77	B3	CALERO HILLS	400 BAILEY AV	SAN JOSE	463 0609
71	C1	CAMBRIAN GOLF CLUB	15211 BRANHAM LN	SAN JOSE	377 3363
63	C2	CYPRESS GREENS	2050 S WHITE RD	SAN JOSE	238 3485
59	C6	DEEP CLIFF	22222 MCCLELLAN RD	CUPERTINO	253 5357
84	A6	GAVILAN	5055 SANTA THERESA BL	GILROY	847 9926
82	B6	GILROY GOLF & CNTRY CL	2695 HECKER PASS HWY	GILROY	842 2501
81	D1	HILL COUNTRY	15060 FOOTHILL RD	MORGAN HILL	779 4136
65	E6	LA RINCONADA CNTRY CLB	14595 CLEARVIEW DR	LOS GATOS	356 3144
58	F1	LOS ALTOS GOLF & C CLB	1560 COUNTRY CLUB DR	LOS ALTOS	948 1024
71	E5	LOS GATOS	14000 GUADALUPE MINES	SAN JOSE	268 1232
45	E3	MOFFETT FIELD GOLF CLB		MOFFETT FIELD	966 5332
72A	B2	OAK RIDGE GOLF CLUB	225 COTTLE RD	SAN JOSE	227 6557
50	E3	PALO ALTO HILLS G & CC	3000 ALEXIS DR	PALO ALTO	948 1800
38	D5	PALO ALTO MUNICIPAL	1875 EMBARCADERO RD	PALO ALTO	325 6326
63	C2	PLEASANT HILLS G & CC	2050 S WHITE RD	SAN JOSE	238 3485
60	F3	PRUNERIDGE FARMS	400 N SARATOGA AV	SANTA CLARA	248 4424
77	E2	RIVERSIDE	MONTEREY RD	COYOTE	463 0622
56	A2	SAN JOSE COUNTRY CLUB	15571 ALUM ROCK AV	SAN JOSE	258 4901
55	A3	SAN JOSE MUNICIPAL	1560 OAKLAND RD	SAN JOSE	287 5100
46	F6	SCL GOLF & TENNIS CLUB	2501 TALLUTO WY	SANTA CLARA	748 7000
72A	E5	SANTA TERESA	260 BERNAL RD	SAN JOSE	225 2650
64	D3	SARATOGA COUNTRY CLUB	21990 PROSPECT RD	SARATOGA	253 5494
45	B3	SHORELINE GOLF LINKS	2600 N SHORELINE BLVD	MOUNTAIN VIEW	969 2041
40	D6	SPRING VALLEY	E CALAVERAS BLVD	MILPITAS	262 1722
43	D3	STANFORD UNIVERSITY	CAMPUS	STANFORD	497 2300
53	B6	SUNKEN GARDENS	1010 S WOLFE RD	SUNNYVALE	739 6588
52	E1	SUNNYVALE MUNICIPAL	605 MACARA AV	SUNNYVALE	738 3666
80	C2	THE OAK TREE CLUB	17140 PARKVIEW DR	MORGAN HILL	779 3171
68A	B2	THE VILLAGES	5000 CRIBARI LN	SAN JOSE	274 3220
62	D1	THUNDERBIRD GOLF & CC	221 S KING RD	SAN JOSE	259 3355
40	B5	TULARCITOS GOLF & CC	1200 COUNTRY CLUB DR	MILPITAS	262 8813
44	B6	VETS	3801 MIRANDA AV	PALO ALTO	495 8250
		HOSPITALS			
		*EMERGENCY SERVICES	AVAILABLE		
47	D5	AGNEWS DEVLP CTR-EAST	MAUVAIS RD	SANTA CLARA	432 8500
54	B1	AGNEWS DEVLP CTR-WEST	MONTAGUE RD	SANTA CLARA	432 8500
55	E5	*ALEXIAN BROS	225 N JACKSON AV	SAN JOSE	259 5000
43	E2	*CHILDRNS HOS STANFORD	520 SAND HILL RD	PALO ALTO	327 4800
65	F6	*COM LS GATOS-SARATOGA	815 POLLARD RD	LOS GATOS	553 6211
52	B4	*EL CAMINO	2500 GRANT RD	MOUNTAIN VIEW	940 7000
71	B1	*GOOD SAMARITAN	2425 SAMARITAN DR	SAN JOSE	559 2011
60	E2	*KAISER MEDICAL CENTER	900 KIELY BLVD	SANTA CLARA	985 4000
71	B2	*MISSION OAKS	15891 LOS GATOS-ALMADN	LOS GATOS	356 4111
61	C4	*O'CONNOR HOSPITAL	2105 FOREST AV	SAN JOSE	947 2500
62	B2	*SAN JOSE	675 E SANTA CLARA ST	SAN JOSE	998 3212
61	C5	*STA CLARA VLY MED CTR	751 S BASCOM AV	SAN JOSE	299 5100
72A	C3	*STA TERESA COMMUNITY	250 HOSPITAL PKWY	SAN JOSE	972 7000
82	F4	*SOUTH VALLEY HOSP	94 NO NAME UNO	GILROY	848 2000
43	E2	*STANFORD UNIV MED CTR	300 PASTEUR DR	PALO ALTO	723 5222
44	B6	VETERANS ADMINISTRATN	3801 MIRANDA AV	PALO ALTO	493 5000
83	E2	*WHEELER HOSPITAL	651 6TH ST	GILROY	842 5621
		HOTELS			
47	E6	BEVERLY HERITAGE	1820 BARBER LN	MILPITAS	943 9080
46	E6	DOUBLETREE HOTEL	5101 GREAT AMERICAN PY	SANTA CLARA	986 0700
53	E2	EMBASSY SUITES	2885 LAKESIDE DR	SANTA CLARA	496 6400
48	A2	EMBASSY SUITES HOTEL	901 E CALAVERAS BLVD	MILPITAS	942 0400
62	A3	FAIRMONT HOTEL	170 S MARKET ST	SAN JOSE	998 1900
47	D4	HOLIDAY INN MILPITAS	777 BELLEW DR	MILPITAS	945 0800
62	A3	HOLIDAY INN-PK CTR PZ	282 ALMADEN BLVD	SAN JOSE	998 0400
53	D2	HOLIDAY INN SUNNYVALE	1217 WILDWOOD AV	SUNNYVALE	245 5330
44	D5	HYATT HOUSE-RICKEYS	4219 EL CAMINO REAL	PALO ALTO	493 8000
44	D5	HYATT - PALO ALTO	4290 EL CAMINO REAL	PALO ALTO	493 0800

PAGE	GRID	NAME	ADDRESS	CITY	PHONE
54	E4	HYATT - SAN JOSE	1740 N 1ST ST	SAN JOSE	298 0300
54	E5	LE BARON HOTEL	1350 N 1ST ST	SAN JOSE	288 9200
53	E2	QUALITY SUITES	3100 LAKESIDE DR	SANTA CLARA	
53	C6	RADISSON HAUS INN	1085 E EL CAMINO REAL	SUNNYVALE	247 0800
54	E5	RADISSON HOTEL	1471 N 4TH ST	SAN JOSE	298 0100
54	D4	RED LION INN	2050 GATEWAY PL	SAN JOSE	279 0600
66	C5	RESIDENCE INN	2761 S BASCOM AV	SAN JOSE	559 1551
53	C2	RESIDENCE INN	1080 STEWART DR	SUNNYVALE	720 8893
53	D2	RESIDENCE INN	750 LAKEWAY DR	SUNNYVALE	720 1000
62	B3	SAINTE CLAIRE	302 S MARKET ST	SAN JOSE	295 2000
53	E2	SANTA CLARA MARRIOTT	GREAT AMERICA PKWY	SANTA CLARA	988 1500
47	E6	SHERATON SILICON VLY E	1801 BARBER LN	MILPITAS	943 0600
46	A6	SHERATON SUNNYVALE INN	1100 MATHILDA AV	SUNNYVALE	745 6000
53	D2	SUNNYVALE HILTON	1250 LAKESIDE DR	SUNNYVALE	738 4888
70	D5	TOLL HOUSE HOTEL	140 S SANTA CRUZ AV	LOS GATOS	395 7070
		LIBRARIES			
72	C5	ALMADEN BRANCH	6455 CAMDEN AV	SAN JOSE	268 7600
55	F5	ALUM ROCK	75 S WHITE RD	SAN JOSE	251 1280
46	E3	ALVISO BRANCH	1060 TAYLOR ST	ALVISO	263 3626
55	E2	BERRYESSA	3311 NOBLE AV	SAN JOSE	272 3554
62	A4	BIBLIOTECA LATINO AMER	690 LOCUST ST	SAN JOSE	294 1237
65	A1	CALABAZAS BRANCH	1230 BLANEY AV	SAN JOSE	996 1535
66	E5	CAMBRIAN BRANCH	1780 HILLSDALE AV	SAN JOSE	269 5062
66	B3	CAMPBELL	77 HARRISON AV	CAMPBELL	378 8122
44	B1	CHILDRENS LIBRARY	1276 HARRIET AV	PALO ALTO	329 2134
44	B4	COLLEGE TERRACE	2300 WELLESLEY ST	PALO ALTO	329 2298
54	F4	COUNTY CENTRAL	1095 N 7TH ST	SAN JOSE	295 2326
59	F4	CUPERTINO	10400 TORRE AV	CUPERTINO	253 6212
44	A1	DOWNTOWN BRANCH	270 FOREST AV	PALO ALTO	329 2641
62	C1	EAST SAN JOSE CARNEGIE	1102 E SANTA CLARA ST	SAN JOSE	998 2069
55	D5	EDUCATIONAL PARK	1776 EDUCATIONAL PK DR	SAN JOSE	272 3662
62	B1	EMPIRE BRANCH	491 E EMPIRE ST	SAN JOSE	286 5627
63	D5	EVERGREEN BRANCH	2635 ABORN RD	SAN JOSE	238 4433
83	F2	GILROY	7387 ROSANNA ST	GILROY	842 8207
63	A2	HILLVIEW BRANCH	2255 OCALA AV	SAN JOSE	272 3100
51	E3	LOS ALTOS	13 S SAN ANTONIO RD	LOS ALTOS	948 7683
70	E5	LOS GATOS	110 E MAIN ST	LOS GATOS	354 6891
48	A2	MILPITAS COMMUNITY	40 N MILPITAS BLVD	MILPITAS	262 1171
61	B1	MISSION BRANCH	LEXINGTON & MAIN STS	SANTA CLARA	984 3154
44	E4	MITCHELL PARK	3700 MIDDLEFIELD RD	PALO ALTO	329 2586
79	D5	MORGAN HILL	17575 PEAK AV	MORGAN HILL	779 3196
52	B2	MOUNTAIN VIEW	585 FRANKLIN ST	MOUNTAIN VIEW	968 6595
44	B1	PALO ALTO	1213 NEWELL RD	PALO ALTO	329 2436
67	C5	PEARL AV BRANCH	4270 PEARL AV	SAN JOSE	265 7833
61	D3	ROSEGARDEN BRANCH	1580 NAGLEE AV	SAN JOSE	998 1511
62	A3	SAN JOSE MAIN BRANCH	180 W SAN CARLOS ST	SAN JOSE	277 5700
60	E2	SANTA CLARA CENTRAL	2635 HOMESTEAD RD	SANTA CLARA	984 3097
72A	C3	SANTA TERESA	290 INTERNATIONAL CIR	SAN JOSE	281 1878
65	B5	SARATOGA COMMUNITY	13650 SARATOGA AV	SARATOGA	867 6126
68	A3	SEVENTREES BRANCH	3597 CAS DR	SAN JOSE	629 4535
65	E1	WEST VALLEY BRANCH	1245 SN TOMAS AQUINO	SAN JOSE	244 4747
62	A6	WILLOW GLEN BRANCH	1157 MINNESOTA AV	SAN JOSE	998 2022
59	B2	WOODLAND	1975 GRANT RD	LOS ALTOS	969 6030
		MOBILE HOME PARKS			
46	D6	ADOBE WELLS	1220 TASMAN DR	SUNNYVALE	734 8424
46	C6	CASA DE AMIGOS	1085 TASMAN DR	SUNNYVALE	734 3379
67	E3	CALIFORNIA-HAWAIIAN	3637 SNELL AV	SAN JOSE	227 0330
54	F1	CASA DE LAGO	OAKLAND RD	SAN JOSE	262 1323
67	D4	COLONIAL	3300 NARVAEZ AV	SAN JOSE	269 4404
67	E1	COYOTE CREEK	2580 SENTER RD	SAN JOSE	279 0925
53	B2	FAIROAKS	580 AHWANEE AV	SUNNYVALE	736 6672
52	E2	MARY MANOR	125 N MARY AV	SUNNYVALE	245 4700
67	C2	MILL POND	2320 CANOAS GARDEN AV	SAN JOSE	267 9790
53	B2	MOBILAND	780 N FAIR OAKS AV	SUNNYVALE	773 1210
67	D4	MOUNTAIN SHADOWS	633 SHADOW CREEK DR	SAN JOSE	269 9090
67	D3	MOUNTAIN SPRINGS	625 HILLSDALE AV	SAN JOSE	226 7611
46	C6	PLAZA DEL REY	1225 VIENNA DR	SUNNYVALE	
63	B6	SILVER CK MOBILE ESTS	1520 E CAPITOL EXPWY	SAN JOSE	274 5455
72A	D1	VLG OF THE 4 SEASONS	200 FORD RD	SAN JOSE	225 7255
61	A5	WINCHESTER RANCH	500 CHARLES CALI DR	SAN JOSE	249 7661
63	B6	WOODBRIDGE	3051 TOWERS LN	SAN JOSE	274 7500
		MOTELS			
47	E3	BROOKSIDE INN	400 VALLEY WY	MILPITAS	943 1466
66	C3	CAMPBELL INN	675 E CAMPBELL	CAMPBELL	374 4300
80	A5	COUNTRY INN	16525 CONDIT RD	MORGAN HILL	779 0447
44	C4	CREEKSIDE INN	3400 EL CAMINO REAL	PALO ALTO	493 2411
53	E1	DAYS INN	4200 GREAT AMERICAN PY	SANTA CLARA	980 1525
43	F2	HOLIDAY INN	625 EL CAMINO REAL	PALO ALTO	328 2800
64	F6	HOLIDAY INN	1217 WILDWOOD WY	SUNNYVALE	245 5330
54	E5	HOLIDAY INN-AIRPORT	1355 N 4TH ST	SAN JOSE	287 5340
54	E4	HOWARD JOHNSONS	1755 N 1ST ST	SAN JOSE	287 7535
60	B4	HOWARD JOHNSONS	5405 STEVENS CK BLVD	SANTA CLARA	257 8600
70	F4	LOS GATOS LODGE	50 SARATOGA AV	LOS GATOS	354 3300
53	A5	MAPLE TREE INN	711 E EL CAMINO REAL	SUNNYVALE	720 9700
53	E6	MARIANIS	2500 EL CAMINO REAL	SANTA CLARA	243 1431
67	D1	PEPPER TREE INN	2112 MONTEREY HWY	SAN JOSE	294 1480
54	B3	RAMADA INN	2151 LAURELWOOD RD	SANTA CLARA	988 8411
54	C3	SANDMAN	2585 SEABOARD AV	SAN JOSE	263 8800
54	E5	SAN JOSE LODGE	1440 N 1ST ST	SAN JOSE	293 6745
44	B3	STANFORD TERRACE INN	531 STANFORD AV	PALO ALTO	857 0333
45	F6	SUNDOWNER INN	504 ROSS DR	SUNNYVALE	734 9900
53	A1	SUNNYVALE INN	940 WEDDELL DR	SUNNYVALE	734 3742
54	D2	VAGABOND INN	1488 N 1ST STREET	SAN JOSE	294 8138
52	D4	WOODFIN SUITES	635 E EL CAMINO REAL	SUNNYVALE	738 1700

PAGE	GRID	NAME	ADDRESS	CITY	PHONE
		PARKS			
72	C2	ALMADEN LAKE	COLEMAN RD	SAN JOSE	
72	B6	ALMADEN QUICKSILVER CO		STA CLARA CO	268 3883
75	F6	ALMADEN RESERVOIR CO	ALAMITOS RD	STA CLARA CO	
56	B1	ALUM ROCK	16240 ALUM ROCK AV	SAN JOSE	277 4661
61	A3	ALVAREZ	2280 ROSITA AV	SANTA CLARA	
46	E3	ALVISO MARINA	1195 HOPE ST	ALVISO	263 1608
78	F6	ANDERSON LAKE CO	59 BURNETT AV	MORGAN HILL	779 3634
55	B6	BACKESTO	13TH & EMPIRE STS	SAN JOSE	
62	A4	BIEBRACH	WILLIS & VIRGINIA	SAN JOSE	
44	C4	BOULWARE	ASH ST & FERNANDO AV	PALO ALTO	
44	B3	BOWDEN	ALMA ST & CALIFORNIA	PALO ALTO	
53	E6	BOWERS	2582 CABRILLO AV	SANTA CLARA	
53	E4	BRACHER	2700 CHROMITE DR	SANTA CLARA	
53	A5	BRALY	704 DAFFODIL CT	SUNNYVALE	732 4891
44	D5	BRIONES	PARK AV	PALO ALTO	
76	E4	CALERO RESERVOIR CO	23201 MCKEAN RD	SAN JOSE	268 3883
44	A3	CAMERON	STANFORD & WILLIAMS	PALO ALTO	
60	E2	CENTRAL	969 KIELY BLVD	SANTA CLARA	
79	A6	CHESBRO RESERVOIR PARK	OAK GLEN AV	MORGAN HILL	
83	E3	CHRISTMAS HILL	MESA RD & S MILLER AV	GILROY	
61	B1	CITY PLAZA	LEXINGTON & MAIN STS	SANTA CLARA	
54	A6	CIVIC CENTER	LINCOLN & EL CM REAL	SANTA CLARA	
51	C2	CLARK, ESTHER	LOWELL AV	PALO ALTO	
78B	D2	COE, HENRY W STATE	DUNNE AV	MORGAN HILL	779 2728
61	E2	COLUMBUS	1600 WALNUT ST	SAN JOSE	
72B	B5	COYOTE CREEK	MONTEREY HWY	SAN JOSE	
68	C3	COYOTE-HELLYER COUNTY	985 HELLYER AV	SAN JOSE	225 0225
81A	D4	COYOTE LAKE	COYOTE RESERVOIR RD	GILROY	842 7800
52	D6	DE ANZA	1150 LIME DR	SUNNYVALE	736 9280
43	F1	EL CAMINO	EL CAMINO REAL	PALO ALTO	
68	F1	EVERGREEN PK	YERBA BUENA RD	SAN JOSE	
53	B2	FAIR OAKS	540 N FAIR OAKS AV	SUNNYVALE	739 1603
48	C3	FOOTHILL	ROSWELL DR	MILPITAS	
60	F2	GOMEZ, MARY	651 BUCHER AV	SANTA CLARA	243 5583
63A	D2	GRANT, J D COUNTY PK	1060 MT HAMILTON RD	STA CLARA CO	274 6121
75	B2	GUADALUPE RES REC AREA	HICKS RD	STA CLARA CO	
60	D6	GULLO PK	WILLIAMS RD	SAN JOSE	
62	D4	HAPPY HOLLOW	1300 SENTER RD	SAN JOSE	292 8188
60	E3	HOMERIDGE	2985 STEVENSON ST	SANTA CLARA	
60	D1	HOMESTEAD	3445 BENTON ST	SANTA CLARA	
44	C3	HOOVER	2901 COWPER AV	PALO ALTO	
62	D4	KELLEY	KEYES ST & SENTER RD	SAN JOSE	297 0778
66	F4	KIRK PK	BRIARWOOD DR	SAN JOSE	
54	B6	LAFAYETTE	EL CM REAL & LAFAYETTE	SANTA CLARA	
63	B3	LAKE CUNNINGHAM	TULLY & WHITE RD	STA CLARA CO	277 4319
53	C1	LAKEWOOD	834 LAKECHIME DR	SUNNYVALE	734 2310
82	E6	LAS ANIMAS	END OF HANNA ST	GILROY	
40	D6	LEVIN, ED R COUNTY	3100 CALAVERAS RD	MILPITAS	262 6980
73	D2	LEXINGTON	ALMA BRIDGE RD	STA CLARA CO	355 2729
66	B5	LOS GATOS CREEK	DELL AV & SN TOMAS EXP	CAMPBELL	358 3741
53	D6	MACADO	3360 CABRILLO AV	SANTA CLARA	
44	B4	MAYFIELD	WILLIAMS ST	PALO ALTO	
60	D3	MAYWOOD	3330 PRUNERIDGE AV	SANTA CLARA	
62	A3	MCENERY PK	SAN FERNANDO & RIVER	SAN JOSE	
84	A2	MC MULLEN	GILMAN RD	GILROY	
59	E4	MEMORIAL	STEVENS CK BL & ANTON	CUPERTINO	
83	E1	MILLER	PRINCEVALLE ST	GILROY	
44	E4	MITCHELL	600 E MEADOW DR	PALO ALTO	
79	D4	MORGAN HILL	HALE AV	MORGAN HILL	
79	E6	MORGAN HILL COMMUNITY	EDMUNDSON AV	MORGAN HILL	
44	F6	MOUNTAIN VIEW REC CTR	RENGSTORFF AV	MOUNTAIN VIEW	
82H	A2	MT MADONNA COUNTY PK	HECKER PASS HWY	GILROY	842 2341
70	E3	OAK MEADOW	BLOSSOM HILL RD	LOS GATOS	
53	A1	ORCHARD GARDENS	238 GARNER DR	SUNNYVALE	734 1038
60	A2	ORTEGA	636 HARROW WY	SUNNYVALE	739 6320
50	D6	PALO ALTO FOOTHILLS	PAGE MILL RD	PALO ALTO	
38	E5	PALO ALTO YACHT HARBOR	2500 EMBARCADERO RD	PALO ALTO	856 1343
38	B6	PARDEE	851 CENTER ST	PALO ALTO	
44	B3	PEERS	1899 PARK BLVD	PALO ALTO	
55	E2	PENITENCIA COUNTY PARK	PENITENCIA CREEK RD	SAN JOSE	356 2729
47	E5	PINEWOOD	GREENWOOD & PINEWOOD	MILPITAS	
53	C5	PONDEROSA	HENDERSON AV	SUNNYVALE	244 0805
44	E3	RAMOS	800 E MEADOW DR	PALO ALTO	
59	A3	RANCHO SAN ANTONIO	CRISTO REY DR	STA CLARA CO	867 3654
60	C2	RAYNOR	1565 QUAIL AV	SUNNYVALE	739 0744
48	A1	REUTHER, WALTER	JACKLIN RD	MILPITAS	
44	B1	RINCONDADA	777 EMBARCADERO RD	PALO ALTO	
44	D4	ROBLES	4116 PARK BLVD	PALO ALTO	
61	D3	ROSE GARDENS	GARDEN DR & NAGLEE AV	SAN JOSE	
61	F2	RYLAND	FOX AV & 1ST ST	SAN JOSE	
62	A2	ST JAMES	1ST & ST JAMES STS	SAN JOSE	
69	B4	SANBORN-SKYLINE CO	16055 SANBORN RD	COUNTY	867 3654
72A	D5	SANTA TERESA CO	BERNAL RD	SAN JOSE	268 3883
69	C1	SARATOGA SPRINGS	CONGRESS SPRINGS RD	SARATOGA	867 3016
44	D2	SEALE	3100 STOCKTON PL	PALO ALTO	
59	E2	SERRA	730 THE DALLES AV	SUNNYVALE	736 4229
45	A3	SHORELINE AT MTN VIEW		MOUNTAIN VIEW	
51	D4	SHOUP	400 UNIVERSITY AV	LOS ALTOS	
62	A4	SPENCER PK	SPENCER AV	SAN JOSE	
47	E3	STARLIGHT	ABBOTT AV & RUDYARD DR	MILPITAS	
60	F1	STEVE CARLI	1045 LOS PADRES BLVD	SANTA CLARA	
64	C3	STEVENS CREEK COUNTY	11401 STEVENS CYN RD	CUPERTINO	867 3654
39	F5	SUNNYHILLS	CONWAY ST	MILPITAS	
63F	B2	UPPER STEVENS CREEK	SKYLINE BLVD	PALO ALTO	
78K	D6	UVAS CANYON COUNTY	8515 CROY RD	MORGAN HILL	779 9232
80K	A4	UVAS RESERVOIR	UVAS RD	STA CLARA CO	
70	F2	VASONA LAKE COUNTY	298 GARDEN HILL DR	LOS GATOS	356 2729

PAGE	GRID	NAME	ADDRESS	CITY	PHONE
69	F2	VILLA MONTALVO ARBORET	15400 MONTALVO RD	SARATOGA	867 0190
68	C5	WAR ADMIRAL	SNOW DR	SAN JOSE	
53	F6	WARBURTON	2250 ROYAL DR	SANTA CLARA	241 6465
52	E3	WASHINGTON	880 W WASHINGTON AV	SUNNYVALE	732 3479
61	B2	WASHINGTON	POPLAR ST	SANTA CLARA	
44	A4	WEISSHAAR	DARTMOUTH ST	PALO ALTO	
44	A4	WERRY	DARTMOUTH ST	PALO ALTO	
60	C3	WESTWOOD OAKS	460 LA HERRAN DR	SANTA CLARA	
62	C3	WILLIAM STREET	16TH & WILLIAM STS	SAN JOSE	
48	C4	YELLOWSTONE	1400 YELLOWSTONE AV	MILPITAS	
		POINTS OF INTEREST			
75	E1	ALMADEN TROUT FARM	20420 ALMADEN RD	SAN JOSE	268 6711
56	B1	ALUM ROCK PARK	ALUM ROCK FALLS RD	SAN JOSE	259 5477
45	D5	AMES RESEARCH CENTER	MOFFETT FIELD	MOUNTAIN VIEW	965 5585
62	A3	AUDITORIUM, SAN JOSE	145 W SAN CARLOS ST	SAN JOSE	277 5277
38	E5	BAYLANDS NTR INTR CTR	2775 EMBARCADERO RD	PALO ALTO	329 2506
62	A4	CHILDRNS DISCOVERY MUS	180 WOZ WY	SAN JOSE	298 5437
61	C1	DE SAISSET GALLERY	UNIV OF SANTA CLARA	SANTA CLARA	554 4528
59	E4	FLINT CENTER	21250 STEVENS CREEK BL	CUPERTINO	257 9555
44	A4	FRENCHMANS TOWER	OFF PAGE MILL RD	PALO ALTO	
53	E1	GREAT AMERICA THEME PK	1 GREAT AMERICA PKWY	SANTA CLARA	988 1776
69	E1	HAKONE GARDENS	21000 BIG BASIN WY	SARATOGA	867 3438
62	D4	HAPPY HOLLOW PARK	1300 SENTER RD	SAN JOSE	295 8383
43	F3	HOOVER TOWER	STANFORD UNIVERSITY	STANFORD	
62	D4	JAPANESE FRIENDSHP GDN	1300 SENTER RD	SAN JOSE	295 8383
56B	F4	LICK OBSERVATORY	MT HAMILTON RD	MT HAMILTON	274 5062
61	B1	MSN STA CLARA DE ASIS	820 ALVISO ST	SANTA CLARA	554 4023
69	F2	MONTALVO CTR F T ARTS	MONTALVO RD	SARATOGA	867 3586
61	D3	MUNICIPAL ROSE GARDEN	GARDEN DR & NAGLEE AV	SAN JOSE	277 4661
61	E1	NATIONAL GUARD ARMORY	155 W HEDDING ST	SAN JOSE	294 6953
45	E3	NAVAL AIR STATION	MOFFETT FIELD	MOUNTAIN VIEW	966 0111
76	A5	NEW ALMADEN MUSEUM	21570 ALMADEN RD	NEW ALMADEN	268 7869
70	E4	OLD TOWN	50 UNIVERSITY AV	LOS GATOS	354 6596
55	D5	OVERFELT GARDENS	MCKEE RD & EDUCATNL PK	SAN JOSE	277 4661
62	A3	PERALTA ADOBE	ST JOHN & SAN PEDRO ST	SAN JOSE	287 2290
62	A3	PERFORMING ARTS CENTER	W SN CARLOS & ALAMEDA	SAN JOSE	288 7461
63	B3	RAGING WATERS	2333 S WHITE RD	SAN JOSE	270 8000
61	D3	ROSICRUCN MUS/PLANETRM	1342 NAGLEE AV	SAN JOSE	287 2807
62	A3	SN JOSE CONVENTION CTR	100 W SAN CARLOS ST	SAN JOSE	277 5277
62	D4	SAN JOSE HIST MUSEUM	635 PHELAN AV	SAN JOSE	287 2290
62	A3	SAN JOSE MUSEUM OF ART	110 S MARKET ST	SAN JOSE	294 2787
62	C4	SAN JOSE ZOO	1300 SENTER RD	SAN JOSE	292 8188
67	E1	STA CLARA FAIRGROUNDS	344 TULLY RD	SAN JOSE	295 3050
45	B3	SHORELINE AMPHITHEATRE	AMPHITHEATRE PKWY	MOUNTAIN VIEW	
48	B4	SPLASHDOWN	1200 S DEMPSEY RD	MILPITAS	942 5581
43	E3	STANFORD UNIVERSITY	JUNIPERO SERRA BLVD	PALO ALTO	321 2300
66	B3	THE FACTORY	93 S CENTRAL AV	CAMPBELL	374 4650
69	F2	VILLA MONTALVO ARBORET	15400 MONTALVO RD	SARATOGA	867 0190
61	B5	WINCHESTER MYSTERY HSE	525 S WINCHESTER BLVD	SAN JOSE	247 2000
		POST OFFICES			
54	A1	AGNEW STATION	4601 LAFAYETTE ST	SANTA CLARA	988 2626
72	D5	ALMADEN VALLEY STATION	6525 CROWN BLVD	SAN JOSE	268 0444
46	E3	ALVISO STATION	1160 TAYLOR ST	SAN JOSE	262 4258
55	B2	BAYSIDE STATION	1750 LUNDY AV	SAN JOSE	437 6868
55	E1	BERRYESSA STATION	1315 PIEDMONT RD	SAN JOSE	259 3050
72	E2	BLOSSOM HILL STATION	5706 CAHALAN AV	SAN JOSE	225 8020
52	A4	BLOSSOM VALLEY STATION	1776 MIRAMONTE AV	MOUNTAIN VIEW	964 2475
66	E5	CAMBRIAN PARK STATION	1769 HILLSDALE AV	SAN JOSE	267 0770
66	B2	CAMPBELL	90 E LATIMER AV	CAMPBELL	378 2153
72B	B5	COYOTE	MONTEREY RD	COYOTE	463 0666
59	E4	CUPERTINO	20850 STEVENS CK BLVD	CUPERTINO	252 6798
44	E3	EAST MEADOW STATION	1035 E MEADOW CIR	PALO ALTO	494 7191
38	D6	EAST PALO ALTO	2197 E BAYSHORE RD	PALO ALTO	326 8560
52	F6	ENCINAL STATION	526 W FREMONT AV	SUNNYVALE	245 0617
83	F1	GILROY	100 4TH ST	GILROY	842 2550
63	A4	HILLVIEW STATION	2450 ALVIN AV	SAN JOSE	238 1854
51	D3	LOS ALTOS	100 1ST ST	LOS ALTOS	948 6000
70	E5	LOS GATOS	101 S SANTA CRUZ AV	LOS GATOS	354 6666
47	F3	MILPITAS	450 S ABEL ST	MILPITAS	262 2322
60	E1	MISSION STATION	1050 KIELY BLVD	SANTA CLARA	243 7926
79	D4	MORGAN HILL	16600 S MONTEREY HWY	MORGAN HILL	779 2484
52	B2	MOUNTAIN VIEW	211 HOPE ST	MOUNTAIN VIEW	967 5721
76	A5	NEW ALMADEN	21300 ALMADEN RD	NEW ALMADEN	268 7730
44	A1	PALO ALTO	380 HAMILTON AV	PALO ALTO	323 1361
61	D5	PARKMOOR STATION	1545 PARKMOOR AV	SAN JOSE	294 0585
52	F3	PLAZA STN	141 S TAAFFE AV	SUNNYVALE	738 1150
67	B6	ROBERTSVILLE STATION	1175 BRANHAM LN	SAN JOSE	265 1014
62	A2	ST JAMES PARK	105 N 1ST ST	SAN JOSE	291 7511
81	C4	SAN MARTIN	200 E SAN MARTIN AV	SAN MARTIN	683 2252
61	B1	SANTA CLARA	1200 FRANKLIN MALL	SANTA CLARA	275 7631
65	B5	SARATOGA	19630 ALLENDALE AV	SARATOGA	867 3086
43	F3	STANFORD UNIV BRANCH	LASUEN	STANFORD UNIV	322 0059
62	B3	STATION A	149 E SAN ANTONIO ST	SAN JOSE	295 7847
61	F5	STATION B	1074 LINCOLN AV	SAN JOSE	293 5885
55	E6	STATION D	70 S JACKSON AV	SAN JOSE	251 5291
52	F2	SUNNYVALE	580 N MARY AV	SUNNYVALE	732 0121
64	F6	VILLAGE STATION	14376 SARATOGA AV	SARATOGA	867 3086
65	E1	WESTGATE STATION	4285 PAYNE AV	SAN JOSE	244 1500
66	E2	WILLOW GLEN STATION	1750 MERIDIAN AV	SAN JOSE	275 7722
		SCHOOLS - PRIVATE ELEMENTARY			
67	B3	ACHIEVER CHRISTIAN	800 IRONWOOD DR	SAN JOSE	264 6789
72	F3	APOSTLES LUTHERAN	5828 SANTA TERESA BLVD	SAN JOSE	225 0107
65	F3	CAMPBELL CHRISTIAN	1125 W CAMPBELL AV	CAMPBELL	374 7260
60	E3	CARDEN EL ENCANTO	615 HOBART TER	SANTA CLARA	244 5041
71	D3	CARDEN SCH OF ALMADEN	220 BELGATOS RD	LOS GATOS	356 9126

PAGE	GRID	NAME	ADDRESS	CITY	PHONE
67	B6	CHALLENGER SCHOOL	1325 BOURET DR	SAN JOSE	723 0111
71	C1	CHALLENGER SCHOOL	4455 UNION AV	SAN JOSE	559 3939
62	E4	CHRISTIAN COM ACADEMY	1523 MCLAUGHLIN AV	SAN JOSE	279 0846
72	D3	COUNTRY SCHOOL-ALMADEN	6835 TRINIDAD DR	SAN JOSE	997 0424
44	C2	ECOLE FRANCO	870 N CALIFORNIA AV	PALO ALTO	328 2338
62	C1	FIVE WOUNDS	1390 FIVE WOUNDS LN	SAN JOSE	293 0425
51	D6	FORD COUNTRY DAY SCHL	12335 STONEBROOK CT	LOS ALTOS HLS	948 4752
60	F5	HARKER ACADEMY	500 SARATOGA AV	SAN JOSE	249 2510
71	A4	HILLBROOK SCHOOL	16000 MARCHMONT DR	LOS GATOS	356 6116
67	D6	HOLY FAMILY	4848 PEARL AV	SAN JOSE	978 1355
44	D3	KEYS SCHOOL	2890 MIDDLEFIELD RD	PALO ALTO	328 1711
61	C2	KINDERWOOD CHILD DEV	270 WASHINGTON ST	SANTA CLARA	296 0606
63	B5	LIBERTY BAPTIST	2790 S KING RD	SAN JOSE	274 5613
51	F5	LOS ALTOS CHRISTIAN	625 MAGDALENA	LOS ALTOS	948 3738
71	E4	LOS GATOS CHRISTIAN	16845 HICKS RD	LOS GATOS	268 1502
48	C4	MILPITAS CHRISTIAN	1435 CLEAR LAKE AV	MILPITAS	262 2630
48	D4	MILPITAS CHRISTIAN	3435 BIRCHWOOD LN	SAN JOSE	945 6530
52	B5	MIRAMONTE SCHOOL	1175 ALTAMEAD DR	LOS ALTOS	967 2783
63	A3	MOST HOLY TRINITY	1940 CUNNINGHAM AV	SAN JOSE	259 1010
66	A3	OLD ORCHARD	400 CAMPBELL AV	CAMPBELL	378 5935
51	E5	PINEWOOD	327 FREMONT RD	LOS ALTOS	
51	F5	PINEWOOD LOWER CAMPUS	477 FREMONT AV	LOS ALTOS	962 9076
61	A6	PRIMARY PLUS	3500 AMBER DR	SAN JOSE	248 2464
60	D5	QUEEN OF APOSTLES	4950 MITTY WY	SAN JOSE	252 3659
48	B3	RAINBOW BRIDGE CENTER	1500 YOSEMITE DR	MILPITAS	945 9090
53	D5	RAINBOW MONTESSORI	3421 MONROE ST	SANTA CLARA	249 1606
52	E6	RESURRECTION ELEM	1395 HOLLENBECK AV	SUNNYVALE	245 4571
65	B5	SACRED HEART	13718 SARATOGA AV	SARATOGA	867 9241
65	B5	ST ANDREWS	13601 SARATOGA AV	SARATOGA	867 3493
79	D5	ST CATHERINE	17500 PEAK AV	MORGAN HILL	779 9950
66	F3	ST CHRISTOPHER	2278 BOOKSIN AV	SAN JOSE	269 4210
61	B1	ST CLARE	725 WASHINGTON ST	SANTA CLARA	246 6797
52	D3	ST CYPRIAN	195 LEOTA AV	SUNNYVALE	738 3444
44	B1	ST ELIZABETH SETON N	1095 CHANNING AV	PALO ALTO	326 9004
66	C6	ST FRANCES CABRINI	15325 WOODARD RD	SAN JOSE	377 6545
56	A4	ST JOHN VIANNEY	4601 HYLAND AV	SAN JOSE	258 7677
52	A3	ST JOSEPH	1120 MIRAMONTE AV	MOUNTAIN VIEW	967 1839
59	F4	ST JOSEPH OF CUPERTINO	10120 N DE ANZA BLVD	CUPERTINO	252 6441
60	F2	ST JUSTIN	2655 HOMESTEAD RD	SANTA CLARA	248 1094
53	D6	ST LAWRENCE	1971 ST LAWRENCE DR	SANTA CLARA	296 2260
61	E3	ST LEO THE GREAT	1051 W SAN FERNANDO	SAN JOSE	293 4846
66	B3	ST LUCY	76 E KENNEDY AV	CAMPBELL	378 7454
53	A4	ST MARTIN	597 CENTRAL AV	SUNNYVALE	736 5534
61	C4	ST MARTIN OF TOURS	300 O'CONNOR DR	SAN JOSE	287 3630
83	F1	ST MARY	7900 CHURCH ST	GILROY	842 2827
70	D4	ST MARY	30 LYNDON AV	LOS GATOS	354 3944
51	E5	ST NICHOLAS	12816 S EL MONTE AV	LOS ALTOS HLS	941 4056
62	B2	ST PATRICK	51 N 9TH ST	SAN JOSE	294 5761
59	B1	ST SIMON	1840 GRANT RD	LOS ALTOS	968 1572
72	F3	ST STEPHEN	500 SHAWNEE LN	SAN JOSE	227 1235
71	E2	ST TIMOTHY	5100 CAMDEN AV	SAN JOSE	265 0244
55	E1	ST VICTOR	3150 SIERRA RD	SAN JOSE	251 1740
51	E4	ST WILLIAM	401 ROSITA AV	LOS ALTOS	948 3086
66	D4	SAN JOSE CHRISTIAN	2350 LEIGH AV	SAN JOSE	371 7741
60	C6	SANTA CLARA VLY LUTHRN	5825 BOLLINGER RD	CUPERTINO	252 0250
52	A3	SOUTHBAY CHRISTIAN	1134 MIRAMONTE AV	MOUNTAIN VIEW	961 5781
59	D1	SOUTH PENINSULA HEBREW	1030 ASTORIA DR	SUNNYVALE	738 3060
79	D4	SOUTH VALLEY CHRISTIAN	145 WRIGHT AV	MORGAN HILL	779 8850
52	E4	SUNSHINE CHRISTIAN	445 S MARY AV	SUNNYVALE	736 3286
71	D3	VALLEY CHRISTIAN	220 KENSINGTON WY	LOS GATOS	559 4400
67	B4	VALLEY CHRISTIAN	1175 HILLSDALE AV	SAN JOSE	723 4060
66	A3	WEST VALLEY	95 DOT AV	CAMPBELL	378 4327
		SCHOOLS - PRIVATE MIDDLE			
53	D6	LAWRENCE ACADEMY	2000 LAWRENCE CT	SANTA CLARA	296 3013
72	D6	VALLEY CHRISTIAN JR HS	1150 RAJKOVICH WY	SAN JOSE	978 1400
		SCHOOLS - PRIVATE HIGH			
60	D5	ARCHBISHOP MITTY H S	5000 MITTY WY	SAN JOSE	252 6610
61	D2	BELLARMINE COLLEGE PRP	850 ELM ST	SAN JOSE	294 9224
44	A2	CASTILLEJA SCHOOL	1310 BRYANT ST	PALO ALTO	322 2131
62	E4	CHRISTIAN COM ACDMY HS	1523 MCLAUGHLIN AV	SAN JOSE	279 0846
72	E5	COUNTY SCHOOL-ALMADEN	6835 TRINIDAD DR	SAN JOSE	997 0424
53	D6	LAWRENCE ACADEMY	2000 LAWRENCE CT	SANTA CLARA	296 3013
63	B5	LIBERTY BAPTIST H S	2790 KING RD	SAN JOSE	274 5613
52	A1	MOUNTAIN VIEW ACADEMY	360 BAILEY AV	MOUNTAIN VIEW	967 2324
62	B3	NOTRE DAME H S	596 S 2ND ST	SAN JOSE	294 1113
51	B2	PINEWOOD PRIVATE	26800 FREMONT RD	LOS ALTOS HLS	941 1532
66	F3	PRESENTATION H S	2281 PLUMMER AV	SAN JOSE	264 1664
52	A4	ST FRANCIS H S	1885 MIRAMONTE AV	MOUNTAIN VIEW	968 1213
52	A3	SOUTH BAY CHRISTIAN	1134 MIRAMONTE AV	MOUNTAIN VIEW	961 5781
66	B3	VALLEY CHRISTIAN H S	I W CAMPBELL AV	CAMPBELL	374 9530
		SCHOOLS - PUBLIC ELEMENTARY			
44	A1	ADDISON	650 ADDISON AV	PALO ALTO	322 5935
72	D2	ALLEN	5845 ALLEN AV	SAN JOSE	998 6205
77	B1	ALMADEN	1295 DENTWOOD DR	SAN JOSE	998 6207
51	F3	ALMOND	550 ALMOND AV	LOS ALTOS	941 0470
71	B3	ALTA VISTA	200 BLOSSOM VALLEY DR	LOS GATOS	356 6146
72A	B2	ANDERSON	5800 CALPINE DR	SAN JOSE	225 6556
60	F6	ANDERSON, LEROY	4000 RHODA DR	SAN JOSE	243 6031
62	F2	ARBUCKLE	1970 CINDERELLA LN	SAN JOSE	259 2910
65	A4	ARGONAUT	SHADOW MOUNTAIN DR	SARATOGA	867 4773
71	F2	ATHENOUR	5200 DENT AV	SAN JOSE	265 8455
54	E5	BACHRODT	102 SONORA AV	SAN JOSE	998 6211
66	D4	BAGBY	1840 HARRIS AV	SAN JOSE	377 3882
65	D3	BAKER	4845 BUCKNALL RD	SAN JOSE	379 2101

1991 SANTA CLARA COUNTY POINTS OF INTEREST

PAGE	GRID	NAME	ADDRESS	CITY	PHONE
72A	E4	BALDWIN, JULIA	280 MARTINVALE LN	SAN JOSE	226 3370
53	A2	BISHOP	450 N SUNNYVALE AV	SUNNYVALE	736 4585
66	D1	BLACKFORD	1970 WILLOW ST	SAN JOSE	266 8771
71	A3	BLOSSOM HILL	16400 BLOSSOM HILL RD	LOS GATOS	356 3141
72A	B3	BLOSSOM VALLEY	420 ALLEGAN CIR	SAN JOSE	227 4260
65	A2	BLUE HILLS	12300 DESANKA AV	SARATOGA	257 9282
66	F3	BOOKSIN	1590 DRY CREEK RD	SAN JOSE	998 6213
53	E6	BOWERS	2755 BARKLEY AV	SANTA CLARA	985 0171
53	E5	BRACHER	2700 CHROMITE DR	SANTA CLARA	984 1682
53	D6	BRIARWOOD	1930 TOWNSEND AV	SANTA CLARA	554 6202
44	C6	BRIONES, JUANA	4100 ORME AV	PALO ALTO	856 0877
55	B1	BROOKTREE	1781 OLIVETREE DR	SAN JOSE	923 1910
83	E1	BROWNELL	7800 CARMEL ST	GILROY	842 3135
52	B3	BUBB	525 HANS AV	MOUNTAIN VIEW	965 9697
51	C3	BULLIS-PURISSIMA	25890 W FREMONT RD	LOS ALTOS HLS	941 3880
79	B1	BURNETT	85 TILTON AV	MORGAN HILL	779 5241
48	B1	BURNETT, WILLIAM	400 FANYON ST	MILPITAS	945 2431
63	D6	CADWALLADER	3799 CADWALLADER RD	SAN JOSE	270 4958
65	F5	CAPRI	850 CHAPMAN DR	CAMPBELL	379 5750
71	B2	CARLTON	2421 CARLTON AV	SAN JOSE	356 1141
67	D5	CARSON, RACHEL	4245 MEG DR	SAN JOSE	998 6287
63	A2	CASSELL	1300 TALLAHASSEE DR	SAN JOSE	259 2653
66	B1	CASTLEMONT	3040 E PAYNE AV	CAMPBELL	379 8775
52	A1	CASTRO, MARIANO	505 ESCUELA AV	MOUNTAIN VIEW	964 7555
63	D3	CEDAR GROVE	2702 SUGAR PLUM DR	SAN JOSE	270 4950
52	D5	CHERRY CHASE	1138 HEATHERSTONE WY	SUNNYVALE	736 1153
55	C1	CHERRYWOOD	2550 GREENGATE DR	SAN JOSE	923 1915
68	B4	CHRISTOPHER	565 COYOTE RD	SAN JOSE	227 8550
60	A3	COLLINS	10401 VISTA DR	CUPERTINO	252 6002
53	B1	COLUMBIA COMMUNITY	739 MORSE AV	SUNNYVALE	735 9500
65	D1	COUNTRY LANE	5140 COUNTRY LN	SAN JOSE	252 3444
52	E5	CUMBERLAND	824 CUMBERLAND AV	SUNNYVALE	736 8368
56	B4	CURETON	3720 E HILLS DR	SAN JOSE	258 5066
47	E2	CURTNER	275 REDWOOD AV	MILPITAS	945 2434
55	C6	DARLING, ANNE	333 N 33RD ST	SAN JOSE	998 6209
70	E3	DAVES AVENUE	17770 DAVES AV	LOS GATOS	395 6311
67	F6	DEL ROBLE	5345 AVD ALMENDROS	SAN JOSE	225 5675
60	D6	DE VARGAS	5050 MOORPARK AV	SAN JOSE	252 0303
60	B6	DILWORTH	1101 STRAYER DR	SAN JOSE	253 2850
62	F2	DORSA	1290 BAL HARBOR WY	SAN JOSE	259 2460
68	B1	DOVE HILL SCHOOL	1460 COLT WY	SAN JOSE	270 4964
44	C1	DUVENECK	705 ALESTER AV	PALO ALTO	322 5946
60	D6	EASTERBROOK	4660 EASTUS DR	SAN JOSE	253 3424
68	C6	EDENVALE	285 AZUCAR	SAN JOSE	227 7060
60	D3	EISENHOWER	277 RODONOVAN DR	SANTA CLARA	248 4313
44	C3	EL CARMELO	3024 BRYANT ST	PALO ALTO	856 0960
84	A2	ELIOT	470 7TH ST	GILROY	842 5618
53	A4	ELLIS	550 E OLIVE AV	SUNNYVALE	736 4936
83	E2	EL ROBLE	930 THIRD ST	GILROY	842 8234
55	C6	EMPIRE GARDENS	1060 E EMPIRE ST	SAN JOSE	998 6221
77	D1	ENCINAL	9530 N MONTEREY HWY	MORGAN HILL	779 5221
44	A4	ESCONDIDO	890 ESCONDIDO RD	STANFORD	856 1337
63	E6	EVERGREEN	3010 FOWLER RD	SAN JOSE	270 4966
44	D4	FAIRMEADOW	500 E MEADOW DR	PALO ALTO	856 0845
66	D5	FAMMATRE	2800 NEW JERSEY AV	SAN JOSE	377 5480
59	E4	FARIA	10155 BARBARA LN	CUPERTINO	252 0706
66	B6	FARNHAM	15711 WOODARD RD	SAN JOSE	377 3321
64	F5	FOOTHILL	13919 LYNDE AV	SARATOGA	867 4036
65	E4	FOREST HILL	4450 MCCOY AV	SAN JOSE	378 9533
62	E6	FRANKLIN	420 TULLY RD	SAN JOSE	286 2540
60	B5	FREMONT OLDER	19500 CL DE BARCELONA	CUPERTINO	252 3103
72	F2	FROST, EARL	530 GETTYSBURG DR	SAN JOSE	225 1881
59	E3	GARDEN GATE	10500 ANN ARBOR AV	CUPERTINO	252 5414
61	F4	GARDNER	502 ILLINOIS AV	SAN JOSE	998 6225
85	F3	GLEN VIEW	600 W 8TH ST	GILROY	842 8292
72A	A3	GLIDER	511 COZY DR	SAN JOSE	227 1505
62	F1	GOSS	2475 VAN WINKLE LN	SAN JOSE	258 8172
62	B1	GRANT	470 E JACKSON ST	SAN JOSE	998 6227
72	F6	GRAYSTONE	6982 SHEARWATER DR	SAN JOSE	998 6317
71	F4	GUADALUPE	6044 VERA CRUZ DR	SAN JOSE	268 1031
81	C3	GWINN	95 NORTH ST	SAN MARTIN	779 5219
67	B5	HACIENDA VALLEY VIEW	1290 KIMBERLY DR	SAN JOSE	998 6259
60	F2	HAMAN	865 LOS PADRES BLVD	SANTA CLARA	244 6893
68	A6	HAYES	5035 POSTON DR	SAN JOSE	227 0424
44	B1	HAYS, WALTER	1525 MIDDLEFIELD RD	PALO ALTO	322 5956
66	A4	HAZELWOOD	775 WALDO RD	CAMPBELL	378 1410
68	B3	HELLYER	725 HAZELWOOD AV	SAN JOSE	227 8333
61	E3	HESTER	1460 THE ALAMEDA	SAN JOSE	998 6235
67	F3	HILLSDALE	3200 WATER ST	SAN JOSE	227 7822
52	E6	HOLLENBECK	1185 HOLLENBECK RD	SUNNYVALE	739 4134
63	C4	HOLLY OAK	2995 ROSSMORE WY	SAN JOSE	274 2033
44	C5	HOOVER, HERBERT	800 BARRON AV	PALO ALTO	856 1377
62	F3	HUBBARD	1745 JUNE AV	SAN JOSE	251 1296
52	B4	HUFF	253 MARTENS AV	MOUNTAIN VIEW	
46	F6	HUGHES,KATHRYN	4949 CALLE DE ESCUELA	SANTA CLARA	988 2390
80	C3	JACKSON	2700 FOUNTAIN OAKS DR	MORGAN HILL	779 8301
83	F1	JORDAN	7743 HANNA ST	GILROY	842 5922
82	D6	KELLEY, ROD SCHOOL	8755 KERN AV	GILROY	847 1932
62	E4	KENNEDY, ROBERT F	1602 LUCRETIA RD	SAN JOSE	286 2530
73	B2	LAKESIDE	19621 BLACK RD	LOS GATOS	354 2372
53	C1	LAKEWOOD	750 LAKECHIME DR	SUNNYVALE	745 6156
52	C2	LANDELS, EDITH	115 DANA ST	MOUNTAIN VIEW	965 4675
48	C5	LANEVIEW	2095 WARMWOOD LN	SAN JOSE	923 1920
82	E6	LAS ANIMAS	8450 WREN AV	GILROY	842 6414
65	E2	LATIMER	4250 LATIMER AV	SAN JOSE	379 2412
68	E1	LAURELWOOD	4280 PARTRIDGE DR	SAN JOSE	270 4983
60	C2	LAURELWOOD	955 TEAL DR	SANTA CLARA	554 1390
73	D4	LEXINGTON	19700 SANTA CRUZ HWY	LOS GATOS	354 9340
71	F2	LIETZ	5300 CARTER AV	SAN JOSE	264 8314
59	D5	LINCOLN	21710 MCCLELLAN RD	CUPERTINO	252 4798
56	A3	LINDA VISTA	100 KIRK AV	SAN JOSE	258 4938
78H	B3	LOMA PRIETA	23845 SUMMIT RD	LOS GATOS	353 1106
71	E2	LONE HILL	4949 HARWOOD RD	SAN JOSE	269 1173
72	B4	LOS ALAMITOS	6130 SILBERMAN DR	SAN JOSE	998 6297
68	A3	LOS ARBOLES	455 LOS ARBOLES AV	SAN JOSE	227 0555
72A	F4	LOS PASEOS	121 AVENIDA GRANDE	SAN JOSE	578 8800
62	B3	LOWELL	625 S 7TH ST	SAN JOSE	998 6243
52	A5	LOYOLA	770 BERRY AV	LOS ALTOS	964 5165
61	D4	LUTHER BURBANK	4 WABASH AV	SAN JOSE	295 1813
56	A5	LYNDALE	13901 NORDYKE DR	SAN JOSE	251 4010
61	A5	LYNHAVEN	881 S CYPRESS AV	SAN JOSE	248 6386
80K	D3	MACHADO	15130 SYCAMORE AV	MORGAN HILL	779 8393
48	D5	MAJESTIC WAY	1855 MAJESTIC WY	SAN JOSE	923 1925
62	A1	MANN, HORACE	555 N 7TH ST	SAN JOSE	998 6237
65	D6	MARSHALL LANE	14114 MARILYN LN	SARATOGA	379 4311
56	B6	MARTEN	14271 STORY RD	SAN JOSE	258 1188
62	E1	MAYFAIR	2000 KAMMERER AV	SAN JOSE	258 5078
46	F3	MAYNE, GEORGE	TAYLOR & SCHOOL STS	ALVISO	262 3600
55	F3	MCCOLLAM	3311 LUCIAN AV	SAN JOSE	258 1006
62	D2	MCKINLEY	651 MACREDES AV	SAN JOSE	286 3520
63	A3	MEYER	1824 DAYTONA DR	SAN JOSE	258 8208
60	A6	MEYERHOLZ	6990 MELVIN DR	SAN JOSE	252 7450
62	E2	MILLER	1250 S KING RD	SAN JOSE	258 2214
63	D5	MILLBROOK	3200 MILLBROOK DR	SAN JOSE	270 6767
60	E2	MILLIKIN	2720 SONOMA PL	SANTA CLARA	554 6661
72A	B2	MINER	5629 LEAN AV	SAN JOSE	225 2144
54	B2	MONTAGUE	750 LAURIE AV	SANTA CLARA	988 3052
44	F5	MONTA LOMA	460 THOMPSON AV	MOUNTAIN VIEW	967 7879
59	B2	MONTCLAIRE	1160 ST JOSEPH AV	LOS ALTOS	736 0718
65	C6	MONTGOMERY, JOHN J	2010 DANIEL MALONEY DR	SAN JOSE	270 6718
79	E5	MORGAN HILL	17020 MONTEREY ST	MORGAN HILL	779 5246
56	B6	MT PLEASANT	14275 CANDLER AV	SAN JOSE	258 6451
65	B1	MUIR	6560 HANOVER DR	SAN JOSE	252 5265
48	B3	MURPHY, MARTIN	1500 YOSEMITE DR	MILPITAS	262 2223
59	F1	NIMITZ	545 E CHEYENNE DR	SUNNYVALE	736 2180
44	A5	NIXON, LUCILLE	1711 STANFORD AV	STANFORD	856 1622
55	F1	NOBLE	3466 GROSSMONT DR	SAN JOSE	923 1935
71	E3	NODDIN	1755 GILDA WY	SAN JOSE	356 2126
80	A4	NORDSTROM	1425 E DUNNE AV	MORGAN HILL	779 5278
48	B5	NORTHWOOD	2760 TRIMBLE RD	SAN JOSE	923 1940
63	D3	NORWOOD CREEK	3241 REMINGTON WY	SAN JOSE	270 6726
52	C6	OAK AVENUE	1501 OAK AV	LOS ALTOS	964 2187
72A	B2	OAK RIDGE	5920 BUFKIN DR	SAN JOSE	578 5900
44	D2	OHLONE	950 AMARILLO AV	PALO ALTO	856 1726
62	C2	OLINDER	890 E WILLIAM ST	SAN JOSE	998 6245
55	A4	ORCHARD	711 E GISH RD	SAN JOSE	998 2830
71	D1	OSTER	1855 LENCAR WY	SAN JOSE	266 8121
55	E4	PAINTER	500 ROUGH & READY DR	SAN JOSE	258 1458
44	E3	PALO VERDE	3450 LOUIS RD	PALO ALTO	856 1672
80K	E1	PARADISE VALLEY	1400 LA CROSSE DR	MORGAN HILL	779 8391
67	E5	PARKVIEW	350 BLUEFIELD DR	SAN JOSE	226 4655
65	F2	PAYNE	3750 GLEASON AV	SAN JOSE	241 1788
60	D1	POMEROY	1250 POMEROY AV	SANTA CLARA	554 0834
39	F6	POMEROY, MARSHALL	1505 ESCUELA PKWY	MILPITAS	945 2424
53	B5	PONDEROSA	804 PONDEROSA AV	SUNNYVALE	245 6009
48	B3	RANDALL	1300 EDSEL DR	MILPITAS	945 5587
72	E3	RANDOL	762 SUNSET GLEN DR	SAN JOSE	998 6380
67	A5	REED	1524 JACOB AV	SAN JOSE	998 6247
64	E1	REGNART	1170 YORKSHIRE DR	CUPERTINO	255 5250
63	B2	ROGERS, WILLIAM	2999 RIDGEMONT DR	SAN JOSE	258 3686
48	C3	ROSE	250 ROSWELL DR	MILPITAS	945 5580
66	A2	ROSEMARY	401 W HAMILTON AV	CAMPBELL	378 2261
82	E2	RUCKER	325 SANTA CLARA AV	GILROY	842 6471
48	D6	RUSKIN	1401 TURLOCK LN	SAN JOSE	923 1950
63	A1	RYAN	1241 MCGINNESS AV	SAN JOSE	258 4936
72	F4	SAKAMOTO	6280 SHADELANDS DR	SAN JOSE	227 3411
72A	D4	SAN ANSELMO	6670 SAN ANSELMO WY	SAN JOSE	578 2710
62	E1	SAN ANTONIO	1855 E SAN ANTONIO S	SAN JOSE	258 8582
63	C1	SANDERS, ROBERT	3411 ROCKY MOUNTAIN DR	SAN JOSE	258 7288
81	C4	SAN MARTIN	100 NORTH ST	SAN MARTIN	779 5220
51	D1	SANTA RITA	700 LOS ALTOS AV	LOS ALTOS	941 3288
72A	D3	SANTA TERESA	6200 ENCINAL DR	SAN JOSE	227 3303
62	E3	SANTEE	1313 AUDUBON DR	SAN JOSE	286 3807
84	E3	SAN YSIDRO	2220 PACHECO PASS	GILROY	842 0292
64	F6	SARATOGA	14592 OAK ST	SARATOGA	867 3476
66	E6	SARTORETTE	3850 WOODFORD DR	SAN JOSE	264 4380
67	B4	SCHALLENBERGER	1280 KOCH LN	SAN JOSE	998 6253
54	A6	SCOTT LANE	1925 SCOTT BLVD	SANTA CLARA	985 1050
68	A3	SEVEN TREES	3975 MIRA LOMA WY	SAN JOSE	227 6834
55	F4	SHIELDS	2851 GAY AV	SAN JOSE	258 4916
72	C5	SIMONDS	6515 GRAPEVINE WY	SAN JOSE	998 6251
48	C4	SINNOTT, JOHN	2025 YELLOWSTONE AV	MILPITAS	945 2441
52	D1	SLATER, KENNETH L	325 GLADYS AV	MOUNTAIN VIEW	964 7392
62	F4	SLONAKER	1601 CUNNINGHAM AV	SAN JOSE	259 1941
63	A4	SMITH	2025 CLARICE DR	SAN JOSE	270 6751
47	E3	SPANGLER	140 N ABBOTT AV	MILPITAS	945 5592
51	F4	SPRINGER	1120 ROSE AV	MOUNTAIN VIEW	964 3374
59	C3	STEVENS CREEK	10300 AINSWORTH DR	CUPERTINO	245 3312
68	C5	STIPE, SAMUEL E	5000 LYNG DR	SAN JOSE	227 7332
60	A2	STOCKLMEIR / ORTEGA	572 DUNHOLME WY	SUNNYVALE	732 3363
62	F6	STONEGATE	2605 GASSMANN DR	SAN JOSE	227 6411
55	E2	SUMMERDALE	1100 SUMMERDALE DR	SAN JOSE	923 1960
60	D3	SUTTER	3200 FORBES AV	SANTA CLARA	554 0690
72A	C4	TAYLOR, BERTHA	410 SAUTNER DR	SAN JOSE	226 0462
67	C5	TERRELL	3925 PEARL AV	SAN JOSE	998 6255
45	B6	THEUERKAUF	1625 SAN LUIS AV	MOUNTAIN VIEW	967 5593
55	F2	TOYON	995 BARD ST	SAN JOSE	923 1965
61	D3	TRACE	651 DANA AV	SAN JOSE	998 6257
63	D2	VALLE VISTA	2400 FLINT AV	SAN JOSE	238 3525
70	F4	VAN METER	16445 LOS GATOS BLVD	LOS GATOS	356 5131
55	C3	VINCI PARK	1311 VINCI PARK WY	SAN JOSE	923 1970

PAGE	GRID	NAME	ADDRESS	CITY	PHONE
79	D5	WALSH	353 W MAIN AV	MORGAN HILL	779 5211
62	B4	WASHINGTON	100 OAK ST	SAN JOSE	998 6261
39	F5	WELLER	345 BOULDER ST	MILPITAS	945 2428
59	D2	WEST VALLEY	1635 BELLEVILLE WY	SUNNYVALE	245 0148
61	A3	WESTWOOD	435 SARATOGA AV	SANTA CLARA	554 0308
63	A5	WHALEY	2655 ALVIN AV	SAN JOSE	270 6759
52	C1	WHISMAN	310 EASY ST	MOUNTAIN VIEW	967 5541
67	A1	WILLOW GLEN	1425 LINCOLN AV	SAN JOSE	998 6265
63	A6	WILDMILL SPRINGS	2880 AETNA WY	SAN JOSE	281 1861
47	F5	ZANKER, PEARL	1585 FALLEN LEAF DR	MILPITAS	945 2438

SCHOOLS - PUBLIC JUNIOR HIGH

PAGE	GRID	NAME	ADDRESS	CITY	PHONE
72A	D4	BERNAL INTERMEDIATE	6610 SAN IGNACIO DR	SAN JOSE	578 5731
52	B5	BLACH	1120 COVINGTON RD	LOS ALTOS	964 1196
63	C1	BOEGER	1944 FLINT AV	SAN JOSE	238 1440
72	E6	BRET HARTE MIDDLE	7050 BRET HARTE DR	SAN JOSE	998 6270
79	D4	BRITTON MIDDLE	80 W CENTRAL AV	MORGAN HILL	779 5200
61	B2	BUCHSER, EMIL	1111 BELLOMY ST	SANTA CLARA	984 2900
54	F6	BURNETT	850 N 2ND ST	SAN JOSE	998 6267
66	A3	CAMPBELL	295 W CHERRY LN	CAMPBELL	378 4955
72	B5	CASTILLERO MIDDLE	6384 LEYLAND PARK DR	SAN JOSE	998 6385
65	E2	CASTRO, ELVIRA MIDDLE	4600 STUDENT LN	SAN JOSE	379 3620
45	A5	CRITTENDEN	1701 ROCK ST	MOUNTAIN VIEW	967 7235
59	D2	CUPERTINO	1650 BERNARDO AV	SUNNYVALE	245 0303
71	F3	DARTMOUTH MIDDLE	5575 DARTMOUTH DR	SAN JOSE	264 1122
68	B5	DAVIS, CAROLINE INT	5035 EDENVIEW DR	SAN JOSE	227 0616
51	D1	EGAN	100 W PORTOLA AV	LOS ALTOS	941 6174
78H	B2	ENGLISH, CLARENCE MID	23800 SUMMIT RD	LOS GATOS	353 1123
62	E4	FAIR, J W	1702 MCLAUGHLIN AV	SAN JOSE	286 3505
63	A2	FISCHER, CLYDE L	1720 HOPKINS DR	SAN JOSE	258 6244
70	F3	FISHER	17000 ROBERTS RD	LOS GATOS	356 2141
56	B4	GEORGE, JOSEPH	277 MAHONEY DR	SAN JOSE	259 2402
52	A3	GRAHAM, ISAAC NEWTON	1175 CASTRO ST	MOUNTAIN VIEW	965 9292
72	F3	HERMAN, LEONARD INT	5955 BLOSSOM AV	SAN JOSE	226 1886
61	D3	HOOVER, HERBERT	1635 PARK AV	SAN JOSE	998 6274
60	B6	HYDE	19325 BOLLINGER RD	CUPERTINO	252 6290
59	D6	KENNEDY	821 BUBB RD	CUPERTINO	253 1525
63	B5	LEY VA GEORGE	1865 MONROVIA DR	SAN JOSE	270 4992
67	A2	MARKHAM, EDWIN MIDDLE	2105 COTTLE AV	SAN JOSE	998 6277
62	E1	MATHSON, LEE	2050 KAMMERER AV	SAN JOSE	251 3232
65	B1	MILLER	6151 RAINBOW DR	SAN JOSE	252 3755
61	B6	MONROE	1055 S MONROE ST	SAN JOSE	296 8808
48	C5	MORRILL MIDDLE	1970 MORRILL AV	SAN JOSE	923 1930
67	B6	MUIR, JOHN MIDDLE	1260 BRANHAM LN	SAN JOSE	998 6281
72A	F4	MURPHY, MARTIN MIDDLE	141 AVENIDA ESPANA	SAN JOSE	779 8351
63	B2	OCALA	2800 OCALA AV	SAN JOSE	923 2800
55	F4	PALA	149 N WHITE RD	SAN JOSE	258 4996
60	B1	PETERSON, MARIAN	1380 ROSALIA AV	SUNNYVALE	720 8540
55	E2	PIEDMONT MIDDLE	955 PIEDMONT RD	SAN JOSE	923 1945
66	D4	PRICE, IDA MIDDLE	2650 NEW JERSEY AV	SAN JOSE	377 2532
63	E4	QUIMBY OAK	3190 QUIMBY RD	SAN JOSE	270 6735
48	C4	RANCHO MILPITAS	1915 YELLOWSTONE AV	MILPITAS	945 5561
65	B5	REDWOOD	13925 FRUITVALE AV	SARATOGA	867 3042
65	C1	ROGERS MIDDLE	4835 DOYLE RD	SAN JOSE	253 7262
65	D5	ROLLING HILLS	1585 MORE AV	CAMPBELL	378 1461
55	E4	SHEPPARD	480 ROUGH & READY RD	SAN JOSE	258 4323
48	D6	SIERRAMONT MIDDLE	3155 KIMLEE DR	SAN JOSE	923 1955
83	F1	SOUTH VALLEY	385 I.O.O.F. AV	GILROY	847 2828
44	D4	STANFORD, JANE L MID	480 E MEADOW DR	PALO ALTO	856 1713
72	D2	STEINBECK MIDDLE	820 STEINBECK DR	SAN JOSE	998 6395
52	D5	SUNNYVALE	1080 MANGO AV	SUNNYVALE	736 7292
68	A2	SYLVANDALE	653 SYLVANDALE AV	SAN JOSE	227 1804
39	F6	RUSSELL, THOMAS MIDDLE	1500 ESCUELA PKWY	MILPITAS	945 2312
71	C2	UNION	2130 LS GATOS-ALMDN RD	SAN JOSE	371 0366

SCHOOLS - PUBLIC HIGH

PAGE	GRID	NAME	ADDRESS	CITY	PHONE
60	F5	BLACKFORD	3800 BLACKFORD AV	SAN JOSE	241 0330
71	F1	BRANHAM	1570 BRANHAM LN	SAN JOSE	265 8440
54	F6	BROADWAY	1050 N 5TH ST	SAN JOSE	998 6285
48	B2	CALAVERAS HILLS CONT	1331 E CALAVERAS BLVD	MILPITAS	945 2398
79	E4	CENTRAL	17960 MONTEREY ST	MORGAN HILL	779 5244
60	B5	CUPERTINO	10100 FINCH AV	CUPERTINO	735 6375
61	C6	DEL MAR	1224 DEL MAR AV	SAN JOSE	298 0260
55	F4	FOOTHILL CONTINUATION	230 PALA AV	SAN JOSE	259 4464
52	F6	FREMONT	1279 SUNNYVLE-SARATOGA	SUNNYVALE	735 6222
83	F3	GILROY	750 W 10TH ST	GILROY	847 2424
67	D6	GUNDERSON	620 GAUNDABERT LN	SAN JOSE	998 6340
51	C1	GUNN, HENRY M	780 ATASTRADERO RD	PALO ALTO	354 8200
67	F2	HILL, ANDREW	3200 SENTER RD	SAN JOSE	227 8800
59	E3	HOMESTEAD	21370 HOMESTEAD RD	CUPERTINO	735 6311
55	D4	INDEPENDENCE	1776 EDUCATIONAL PK DR	SAN JOSE	729 3911
71	D2	LEIGH	5210 LEIGH AV	SAN JOSE	377 4470
72	E5	LELAND	6677 CAMDEN AV	SAN JOSE	998 6290
55	F5	LICK, JAMES	57 N WHITE RD	SAN JOSE	729 3580
61	D4	LINCOLN	555 DANA AV	SAN JOSE	998 6300
79	F2	LIVE OAK	1505 E MAIN AV	MORGAN HILL	779 5210
51	E2	LOS ALTOS	201 ALMOND AV	LOS ALTOS	968 6571
70	E5	LOS GATOS	20 HIGH SCHOOL CT	LOS GATOS	354 2730
65	C1	LYNBROOK	1280 JOHNSON AV	SAN JOSE	735 6456
70	E3	MARK TWAIN CONT	17421 FARLEY RD W	LOS GATOS	354 1919
39	F6	MILPITAS	1285 ESCUELA PKWY	MILPITAS	945 5500
59	D5	MONTA VISTA	21840 MCCLELLAN RD	CUPERTINO	735 6157
52	C5	MOUNTAIN VIEW	3535 TRUMAN AV	MOUNTAIN VIEW	940 4600
83	F1	MT MADONNA CONT	7663 CHURCH ST	GILROY	842 4313
63	C1	MOUNT PLEASANT	1750 S WHITE RD	SAN JOSE	251 7820
72A	B1	OAK GROVE	285 BLOSSOM HILL RD	SAN JOSE	225 9332
63	A3	OVERFELT	1835 CUNNINGHAM AV	SAN JOSE	259 0540
44	A2	PALO ALTO	50 EMBARCADERO RD	PALO ALTO	329 3710
48	E6	PIEDMONT HILLS	1377 PIEDMONT RD	SAN JOSE	729 3950
72	B2	PIONEER	1290 BLOSSOM HILL RD	SAN JOSE	998 6310
65	C2	PROSPECT	18900 PROSPECT RD	SARATOGA	253 1662
62	C1	SAN JOSE	275 N 24TH ST	SAN JOSE	998 6320
60	E2	SANTA CLARA	3000 BENTON ST	SANTA CLARA	985 5900
72A	A3	SANTA TERESA	6150 SNELL AV	SAN JOSE	578 9100
64	F5	SARATOGA	20300 HERRIMAN AV	SARATOGA	867 3411
52	C5	SHORELINE CONTINUATION	1299 BRYANT AV	MOUNTAIN VIEW	940 4656
68	C1	SILVER CREEK	3434 SILVER CREEK RD	SAN JOSE	274 1700
55	D6	VALLEY CONTINUATION	1875 LAWRENCE RD	SANTA CLARA	983 2100
65	D5	WESTMONT	4805 WESTMONT AV	CAMPBELL	378 1500
53	D5	WILCOX	3250 MONROE ST	SANTA CLARA	554 6300
67	A2	WILLOW GLEN	2001 COTTLE AV	SAN JOSE	998 6330
62	E4	YERBA BUENA	1855 LUCRETIA AV	SAN JOSE	279 1500

SHOPPING CENTERS

PAGE	GRID	NAME	ADDRESS	CITY	PHONE
72	B1	ALMADEN FASHION PLAZA	49 ALMADEN FASHION PZ	SAN JOSE	264 3766
66	C6	CAMBRIAN PARK PLAZA	UNION & CAMDEN AVS	SAN JOSE	
55	E4	CAPITOL SQUARE	390 N CAPITOL AV	SAN JOSE	923 5535
52	D4	CHERRY CHASE	638 CHERRY CHASE CTR	SUNNYVALE	736 4158
59	F4	CUPERTINO CROSSROADS	STEVENS CK & DE ANZA	CUPERTINO	
63	B4	EASTRIDGE	1 EASTRIDGE CENTER	SAN JOSE	274 0360
65	D2	EL PASEO DE SARATOGA	CAMPBELL & SARATOGA	SAN JOSE	374 1822
72	C1	HILLVIEW PLAZA	WINFIELD & BLOSSOM HL	SAN JOSE	
59	F5	MCCLELLAN SQUARE	MCCLELLAN & DE ANZA	CUPERTINO	
61	A1	MERVYN'S PLAZA	SCOTT & EL CAMINO REAL	SANTA CLARA	
72	D1	OAKRIDGE MALL	925A BLOSSOM HILL RD	SAN JOSE	578 2910
66	C3	PRUNEYARD	1875 S BASCOM AV	CAMPBELL	371 0811
72	B1	PUEBLO PLAZA	BLOSSOM HILL & GALLUP	SAN JOSE	
44	E6	SAN ANTONIO	2550 EL CAMINO REAL W	MOUNTAIN VIEW	948 8004
43	E1	STANFORD	72 STANFORD SHOP CTR	PALO ALTO	328 0886
52	F4	SUNNYVALE TOWN CENTER	2502 TOWN CENTER LN	SUNNYVALE	245 3270
61	B4	TOWN & COUNTRY VILLAGE	2980 STEVENS CREEK BL	SAN JOSE	248 8000
60	B4	VALLCO FASHION PARK	10123 N WOLFE RD	CUPERTINO	255 5660
61	B4	VALLEY FAIR	2801 STEVENS CREEK BL	SAN JOSE	248 4450
65	D2	WESTGATE	1600 SARATOGA AV	SAN JOSE	379 9350

TRANSPORTATION

PAGE	GRID	NAME	ADDRESS	CITY	PHONE
61	F3	AMTRAK STATION	65 CAHILL ST	SAN JOSE	287 7462
44	F6	CALTRAIN	S RENGSTORFF&CRISANTO	MOUNTAIN VIEW	
52	B2	CALTRAIN	VIEW ST & EVELYN AV	MOUNTAIN VIEW	
43	F1	CALTRAIN	UNIVERSITY AV&ALMA ST	PALO ALTO	
44	B3	CALTRAIN	PARK BL&CALIFORNIA AV	PALO ALTO	
61	E2	CALTRAIN	STOCKTON AV & EMORY ST	SAN JOSE	
61	F3	CALTRAIN	CAHILL ST&SN FERNANDO	SAN JOSE	
54	C6	CALTRAIN	RAILROAD AV&FRANKLN ST	SANTA CLARA	
46	C6	CALTRAIN	LWRNCE EXP&LWRNCE STA	SUNNYVALE	
52	F3	CALTRAIN	EVELYN AV & S FRANCES	SUNNYVALE	
38	E5	PALO ALTO AIRPORT	1925 EMBARCADERO RD	PALO ALTO	856 7833
62	B2	PARK & RIDE	LATIMER & WINCHESTER	CAMPBELL	
39	E5	PARK & RIDE	SCOTT CREEK RD & I-80	FREMONT	
83	F1	PARK & RIDE	MONTEREY & HOWSON	GILROY	
84	A2	PARK & RIDE	10TH ST & CHESTNUT ST	GILROY	
70	E4	PARK & RIDE	SARATOGA & SANTA CRUZ	LOS GATOS	
47	E2	PARK & RIDE	WELLER & MAIN	MILPITAS	
79	B2	PARK & RIDE	TILTON & SANTA TERESA	MORGAN HILL	
79	D4	PARK & RIDE	MAIN & HALE	MORGAN HILL	
44	B4	PARK & RIDE	EL CM REAL & PAGE MILL	PALO ALTO	
48	B6	PARK & RIDE	CAPITOL & CROPLEY	SAN JOSE	
55	E1	PARK & RIDE	SIERRA & PIEDMONT	SAN JOSE	
55	E4	PARK & RIDE	CAPITOL & MCKEE	SAN JOSE	
55	E5	PARK & RIDE	MCKEE RD & JACKSON AV	SAN JOSE	
55	D5	PARK & RIDE	CAPITOL EXPWY & AV A	SAN JOSE	
59	F5	PARK & RIDE	BOLINGR/SRTGA/SUNYVLE	SAN JOSE	
60	D6	PARK & RIDE	MOORPARK & LAWRENCE	SAN JOSE	
61	D6	PARK & RIDE	FRUITDALE & SW EXPWY	SAN JOSE	
63	B3	PARK & RIDE	TULLY & CAPITOL	SAN JOSE	
65	D2	PARK & RIDE	HAMILTON & ATHERTON	SAN JOSE	
65	D5	PARK & RIDE	QUITO RD & WESTMONT AV	SAN JOSE	
71	E1	PARK & RIDE	BRANHAM & CAMDEN	SAN JOSE	
72	C5	PARK & RIDE	WINFIELD & COLEMAN	SAN JOSE	
72	D5	PARK & RIDE	CAMDEN & ALMADEN	SAN JOSE	
72A	A1	PARK & RIDE	SNELL & BLOSSOM	SAN JOSE	
72A	D3	PARK & RIDE	STA TERESA&SN IGNACIO	SAN JOSE	
60	C1	PARK & RIDE	EL CAMINO & LAWRENCE	SANTA CLARA	
81	C4	PARK & RIDE	SAN MARTIN & MONTEREY	STA CLARA CO	
65	B2	PARK & RIDE	PROSPECT & MILLER	SARATOGA	
63	B3	REID HILLVIEW AIRPORT	2500 CUNNINGHAM AV	SAN JOSE	299 3511
54	D5	SAN JOSE INTERNATIONAL	1661 AIRPORT BLVD	SAN JOSE	277 4000

WINERIES

PAGE	GRID	NAME	ADDRESS	CITY	PHONE
72	A3	ALMADEN VINEYARDS	1530 BLOSSOM HILL RD	SAN JOSE	269 1312
82C	F5	CASA DE FRUTA WINERY	6680 PACHECO PASS HWY	STA CLARA CO	842 9316
83	C1	CONROTTO WINERY	1690 HECKER PASS HWY	GILROY	842 3053
70	E5	DOMAINE M MARION	300 COLLEGE AV	LOS GATOS	395 7914
82H	D1	FORTINO WINERY	4525 HECKER PASS HWY	GILROY	842 3305
79	F3	GUGLIELMO WINERY	1480 E MAIN AV	STA CLARA CO	779 2145
82H	D1	HECKER PASS WINERY	4605 HECKER PASS HWY	GILROY	842 8755
61	E3	J LOHR WINERY	1000 LENZEN AV	SAN JOSE	288 5057
81H	E3	KIRIGIN CELLARS	11550 WATSONVILLE RD	STA CLARA CO	847 8827
82H	F1	LIVE OAKS WINERY	3875 HECKER PASS HWY	GILROY	842 2401
63	E5	MIRASSOU VINEYARDS	3000 ABORN RD	SAN JOSE	274 4000
80	B4	PEDRIZZETTI WINERY	1645 SAN PEDRO AV	MORGAN HILL	779 7389
91	B2	RAPAZZINI WINERY	4350 S MONTEREY HWY	GILROY	842 5649
81	C4	SAN MARTIN WINERY	13000 DEPOT AV	SAN MARTIN	683 2672
82H	E1	SUMMERHILL VINEYARDS	3920 HECKER PASS HWY	GILROY	842 3032
64	A2	SUNRISE WINERY	13100 MONTEBELLO RD	CUPERTINO	741 1310
82H	E1	THOMAS KRUSE WINERY	4390 HECKER PASS HWY	GILROY	842 7016

1991 SANTA CLARA COUNTY TRANSIT INFORMATION

Santa Clara County Transportation Agency, a convenient alternative, provides extensive bus and light rail service throughout the county.

Personal Trip Planning

Trip Planning assistance is available to you Monday through Friday, 5:30 a.m. - 10:00 p.m. and Saturday/Sunday 7:30 a.m. - 6:00 p.m. Please have pen, paper and the following information ready:

- departure point (nearest cross street)
- destination (nearest cross street)
- time you wish to travel

County Transit Information is (408) 287-4210.

Toll free from: Palo Alto .... (415) 965-3100
South County .... (408) 683-4151

Teleprinter for the hearing impaired: .... (408) 299-4848

Visit our Information Center located in downtown San Jose at 4 North Second Street or the Palo Alto Transit Center (CalTrain Station) at 95 University Avenue.

Fares

	Adult (18-64)	Youth (5-17)	*Senior/ Disabled
Regular	$ .75	$ .50	$ .10
Mid-day Service, Mon-Fri (9:30 a.m. - 2:30 p.m.)	.25	.25	.10
Express Service	1.00	1.00	1.00
Day Pass	1.50	.75	.20
Express Day Pass	2.00	2.00	2.00

*Certified disabled and seniors 65 and older.

Children under 5 years ride free with an accompanying fare paying passenger (maximum of 3 children).

County Transit drivers do not carry change. Please have exact change ready when boarding.

Guide dogs and signal dogs are the only pets allowed.

Monthly Flash Passes are convenient and economical. They are available for adults, youths, seniors and the disabled. Call County Transit for the locations where passes are sold.

Buses

There are 80 routes that serve Santa Clara County including extensions to the Menlo Park Train Depot (San Mateo County-SamTrans) and to the Fremont BART Station (Alameda County-BART/AC Transit). 50 routes are wheelchair accessible.

Express Bus Routes

County Transit operates 20 Express bus routes linking residential areas of the country with Silicon Valley Industrial centers. Major employers work with County Transit to develop and refine commuter services.

Park and Ride Facilities

31 Park and Ride lots are located in convenient areas throughout Santa Clara County to encourage ridesharing. Parking in the lots is free. Call SCCTA for a location near you.

All Park and Ride lots may be used as a convenient meeting point for car pool and vanpool passengers and most are served by Express bus routes. Many lots have special features such as passenger shelters, transit schedule signs and bicycle lockers.

Light Rail

Our newest addition, Light Rail Transit, currently extends from Alma St. through downtown San Jose (Civic Center) to the industrial centers along North First Street to Old Ironsides. In the future, Light Rail service will extend southward from Alma St. to South San Jose (Santa Teresa and Almaden areas).

Light Rail operates every 10-30 minutes from 6 a.m. until midnight, seven days a week.

The fare for Light Rail is the same as for a bus. All passes acceptable on buses are also acceptable on Light Rail.

South County Dial-A-Ride

Door-to-door Dial-A-Ride is available within six areas in Morgan Hill, San Martin and Gilroy. It is not available to those who live within one-quarter mile of a rapid transit route. For more information, call County Transit.

Bikes on Buses, Light Rail

Bikes are allowed on many bus lines. Call SCCTA for specific Information. Bikes are allowed on Light Rail vehicles seven days a week.

Historic Trolleys

Restored historic trolleys operate along the 1.5 mile downtown San Jose Transit Mall loop. The trolleys operate every 10 minutes from 11 a.m. until 6 p.m. seven days a week. Fares are 25 cents for youths (ages 5-17) and adults (ages 18-64) and 10 cents for seniors (aged 65 years and older) and certified disabled passengers.

Stadium Services

Santa Clara County Transportation Agency cooperates with San Jose State University in providing transportation from downtown San Jose to Spartan Stadium. During the football season, Sports Bus Service is available from convenient locations to and from Candlestick Park for all 49er home games.

CalTrain Information

For information regarding fares, tickets, schedules or train/bus connections or any questions and/or comments concerning CalTrain service, please call:

The Peninsula Commute Service

Hotline .... (415) 557-8661
Toll free (Voice or TDD) .... (415) 558-8661

Monday through Friday, 7 a.m. to 5 p.m.